THE OXFORD HANDBOOK OF

GENDER, WAR, AND THE WESTERN WORLD SINCE 1600

THE OXFORD HANDBOOK OF

GENDER, WAR, AND THE WESTERN WORLD SINCE 1600

Edited by

KAREN HAGEMANN,
STEFAN DUDINK,

and

SONYA O. ROSE

OXFORD
UNIVERSITY PRESS

Library of Congress Cataloging-in-Publication Data
Names: Hagemann, Karen, editor. | Dudink, Stefan, editor. | Rose, Sonya O.,
editor.
Title: The Oxford handbook of gender, war and the Western World since 1600
/ edited by Karen Hagemann, Stefan Dudink, and Sonya O. Rose.
Description: Oxford ; New York : Oxford University Press, [2020] | Series:
Oxford handbooks | Includes bibliographical references and index.
Identifiers: LCCN 2020021157 | ISBN 9780199948710 (hardback) |
ISBN 9780199948727 (ebook) | ISBN 9780197513125 (epub)
Subjects: LCSH: Women and war—History. | War—Sex differences. | War and
society—History.
Classification: LCC U21.75 .O94 2020 | DDC 355.02082/091821—dc23
LC record available at https://lccn.loc.gov/2020021157

CONTENTS

Preface ix

About the Companion Website xiii

List of Illustrations xv

Contributors xix

Introduction: Gender and the History of War—The Development
of the Research 1
KAREN HAGEMANN

PART I FROM THE THIRTY YEARS' WAR AND COLONIAL CONQUEST TO THE WARS OF REVOLUTION AND INDEPENDENCE

1. War and Gender: From the Thirty Years' War and Colonial
Conquest to the Wars of Revolution and Independence—
an Overview 37
STEFAN DUDINK AND KAREN HAGEMANN

2. Wars, States, and Gender in Early Modern European Warfare,
1600s–1780s 74
PETER H. WILSON

3. War, Culture, and Gender in Colonial and Revolutionary
North America 96
SERENA ZABIN

4. War, Gender, and Society in Late Colonial and Revolutionary
Spanish America 117
CATHERINE DAVIES

5. Gender, Slavery, War, and Violence in and beyond the Age
   of Revolutions   136
   ELIZABETH COLWILL

6. Society, Mass Warfare, and Gender in Europe during and after
   the Revolutionary and Napoleonic Wars   158
   ALAN FORREST

7. History and Memory of Army Women and Female Soldiers,
   1770s–1870s   176
   THOMAS CARDOZA AND KAREN HAGEMANN

8. Citizenship, Mass Mobilization, and Masculinity in
   a Transatlantic Perspective, 1770s–1870s   201
   STEFAN DUDINK

PART II WARS OF NATIONS AND EMPIRES

9. War and Gender: Nineteenth-Century Wars of Nations and
   Empires—an Overview   227
   STEFAN DUDINK, KAREN HAGEMANN, AND MISCHA HONECK

10. War Mobilization, Gender, and Military Culture in
    Nineteenth-Century Western Societies   268
    ROBERT A. NYE

11. Gender and the Wars of Nation-Building and Nation-Keeping
    in the Americas, 1830s–1870s   289
    AMY S. GREENBERG

12. Imperial Conquest, Violent Encounters, and Changing Gender
    Relations in Colonial Warfare, 1830s–1910s   309
    ANGELA WOOLLACOTT

13. The "White Man," Race, and Imperial War during the Long
    Nineteenth Century   328
    MARILYN LAKE

14. Changing Modes of Warfare and the Gendering of Military
    Medical Care, 1850s–1920s   347
    JEAN H. QUATAERT

PART III THE AGE OF THE WORLD WARS

15. War and Gender: The Age of the World Wars and Its Aftermath—an Overview   369

    KAREN HAGEMANN AND SONYA O. ROSE

16. Gendered War Mobilization, Culture, and Music in the Age of World Wars   410

    ANNEGRET FAUSER

17. Total Warfare, Gender, and the "Home Front" in Europe during the First and Second World Wars   432

    SUSAN R. GRAYZEL

18. Citizenship and Gender on the American and Canadian Home Fronts during the First and Second World Wars   451

    KIMBERLY JENSEN

19. History and Memory of Female Military Service in the Age of World Wars   470

    KAREN HAGEMANN

20. States, Military Masculinities, and Combat in the Age of World Wars   498

    THOMAS KÜHNE

21. Colonial Soldiers, Race, and Military Masculinities during and beyond World Wars I and II   519

    RICHARD SMITH

22. Sexuality, Sexual Violence, and the Military in the Age of the World Wars   539

    REGINA MÜHLHÄUSER

23. Gender, Peace, and the New Politics of Humanitarianism in the First Half of the Twentieth Century   561

    GLENDA SLUGA

24. Gender, Demobilization, and the Reordering of Societies after the First and Second World Wars   585

    KAREN HAGEMANN

25. Gendering the Memories of War and Holocaust in Europe
and the United States   611
FRANK BIESS

PART IV FROM THE GLOBAL COLD WAR TO THE CONFLICTS OF THE POST-COLD WAR ERA

26. War and Gender: From the Global Cold War to the Conflicts
of the Post–Cold War Era—an Overview   635
KAREN HAGEMANN AND SONYA O. ROSE

27. Gender, the Wars of Decolonization, and the Decline of Empires
after 1945   677
RAPHAËLLE BRANCHE

28. Post-1945 Western Militaries, Female Soldiers, and Gay and
Lesbian Rights   698
KAREN HAGEMANN AND D'ANN CAMPBELL

29. Conceptualizing Sexual Violence in Post–Cold War
Global Conflicts   727
DUBRAVKA ZARKOV

30. The United Nations, Gendered Human Rights, and Peacekeeping
since 1945   746
SANDRA WHITWORTH

31. Gender, Wars of Globalization, and Humanitarian Interventions
since the End of the Cold War   767
KRISTEN P. WILLIAMS

Index   789

PREFACE

War sells. This becomes obvious if one visits American and European bookstores. But most books intended for a broader readership remain remarkably conventional, despite all the changes in the historiography on military and war. One innovative approach that is still rare in books for a broader audience is the gender perspective on the past and present of military and war. This was the major reason why, after some hesitation, Karen Hagemann accepted the invitation by Nancy Toff of Oxford University Press to become the editor of an Oxford handbook on gender and war. Stefan Dudink (Radboud University Nijmegen) and Sonya O. Rose (University of Michigan at Ann Arbor) became her coeditors. We shared the aim of a handbook that explores the continuities and changes from the early modern period to the present within a global geographical scope and envisioned chapters that are thematic, comparative, and transnational.

The editors started to work on the project together in 2010, first developing the outline of the handbook and discussing it during a workshop with local experts at the Institute for the Arts & Humanities (IAH) at the University of North Carolina (UNC) at Chapel Hill. We agreed on a reference work jointly written by specialists in the history of military and war and experts in gender and women's studies covering the period from the Thirty Years' War to the Wars of Globalization that investigates how gender, understood as an amalgam of ideals and practices that give meaning to and socially differentiate male and female, contributed to the shaping of warfare and the military more generally and was at the same time transformed by them. Furthermore, we concurred that the regional focus would need to reflect the state of research on gender and war, which is best developed for eastern and western Europe, the Americas, and Australia, and the long-term processes of colonization and empire-building originating in early modern Europe and their aftermath in the Americas, Asia, Africa, and Australia. After Oxford University Press approved the outline and the intensively debated title, we invited possible authors from different disciplines who are experts in the field and were willing to explore broad, comparative, and transnational questions. The cooperation with our international team of twenty-eight authors from seven countries and three continents was simply superb. The editors would like to thank all authors for their collaboration, which allowed for the successful completion of the handbook.

Editors and authors met in February and September 2014 for two workshops and conferences at the IAH in Chapel Hill to present first results of our research to the public and discuss drafts of the papers, with colleagues from universities in North Carolina joining in as commentators. These two events were crucial for the further development of the project and would not have been possible without the financial support of several institutions. They include Duke University, the German Historical Institute in Washington, DC, the Triangle Institute for Security Studies in Durham, UNC Chapel Hill, the International Institute for Social Studies at the Erasmus University Rotterdam, and the Radboud University Nijmegen. Our special thanks go to the German Historical Institute and the several centers, departments, and institutions at UNC and Duke that generously sponsored the two events, including the UNC Center for European Studies, the UNC Department of History, the UNC IAH and the UNC College of Arts & Sciences, the Duke History Department, and the Duke Council for European Studies. We also would like to thank the undergraduate and graduate assistants who helped with the organization of the events.

In 2014, we decided to combine the Oxford handbook with a digital humanities project—*GWonline, the Bibliography, Filmography and Webography on Gender and War since 1600* (http://gwc.unc.edu/welcome)—which we launched at UNC Chapel Hill in April 2017. This digital humanities project collects and organizes secondary literature, women's autobiographies, films, and websites with online collections of primary sources to make these resources available to the broader public, in addition to providing a literature search by handbook chapters and recommendations for the teaching of central conflicts. The development of *GWonline* would not have been possible without the generous support of UNC ITS Research Computing. In addition, the UNC Chapel Hill Department of History, Center for European Studies, College of Arts & Sciences, Curriculum in Peace, War and Defense, IAH, and Libraries as well as the Triangle Institute for Security Studies supported the project. We want to thank them in addition to the excellent GWonline team, especially system specialist William Schulz from UNC ITS Research Computing, and the undergraduate and graduate students who worked for *GWonline*.

Two fellowships granted to Karen Hagemann in 2015 and 2016 helped the editors work together on editing the submitted chapters and writing the general introduction and the jointly composed introductory overview chapters for the four periods that structure the handbook. We met for one editors' workshop at the American Academy Berlin, where Karen Hagemann was the German Transatlantic Program Berlin Prize Fellow during spring 2015, and three editors' workshop at the Netherlands Institute for Advanced Study in Wassenaar, where she was a European Institutes for Advanced Study Senior Fellow during the academic year 2015–16. We would like to thank these two institutions for their generous support of the project and their hospitality. Radboud University Nijmegen generously helped with the funding of illustrations and the needed permissions. Last, but not least, it is a great pleasure to warmly thank our colleague, Dirk Bönker (Duke University) for his support of the work on the handbook, and Björn Hennings for the careful work on the index. We would like to express special gratitude to Derek Holmgren, our outstanding editorial assistant, who helped the editors with great attention to detail and many excellent suggestions in the process of editing, index preparation, and proofreading the different versions of the chapters and selected bibliographies. Many thanks!

Karen Hagemann
Stefan Dudink
Sonya O. Rose

ABOUT THE
COMPANION WEBSITE

Related to this handbook is the digital humanities project *GWonline, the Bibliography, Filmography and Webography on Gender and War since 1600*, which was initiated by Karen Hagemann and Stefan Dudink and developed under Karen Hagemann's directorship by a team of undergraduate and graduate students at the University of North Carolina at Chapel Hill with the aim of making research on the subject of gender and war more accessible for the public. *GWonline* collects and organizes titles of secondary literature, women's autobiographies, films and websites mainly with primary documents on the subject, in addition to providing a literature search by handbook chapter and recommendations for the teaching of central conflicts. Alongside full-text searching, the project enables users to explore *GWonline* through multiple entry points: author or director, publication or release date, collection, major wars, keywords, or Oxford handbook chapters. The literature search allows users to check via WorldCat whether articles, books, and other resources are available in their local libraries. Furthermore, users can download full lists of their searches as RTF files.

The not-for-profit project is a collaboration of UNC Chapel Hill's ITS Research Computing, the Department of History, the Curriculum in Peace, War and Defense, and the UNC Library and Information Technology. It would not have been possible without their support and all the work of the team of the undergraduate and graduate students. Readers of the handbook are encouraged to enrich their learning experience by consulting this resource. For more information, please go to the website: http://gwc.unc.edu/welcome

LIST OF ILLUSTRATIONS

0.1. *The German War*, oil painting by Pavel Nikolaevich Filonov
(1883–1941), [n.p.], 1914/15. © State Russian Museum, St. Petersburg.   2

1.1. *War Scene of the Thirty Years War*, oil painting by Sebastian Vrancx
(1573–1647), [n.p., n.d.]. 150619586: DEA/G. DAGLI ORTI/Getty Images.   38

1.2. *Napoleon on the Battlefield of Eylau, February 9, 1807*, oil painting by
Antoine-Jean Gros (1771–1835), [n.p.], 1808. Musée du Louvre, Paris.
Photo © RMN-Grand Palais (musée du Louvre)/Daniel Arnaudet.   39

1.3. *Soldiers Plundering a Farm during the Thirty Years War*, oil painting
by Sebastian Vrancx (1573–1647), [n.p.], 1620. Deutsches Historisches
Museum, Berlin/A. Psille.   58

1.4. *The Attack on the Prussian Camp at Hochkirch on 14 October 1758*,
oil painting by Hyacinth de La Pegna (1707–72), [n.p.], 1759/60.
Heeresgeschichtliches Museum, Vienna.   59

1.5. *English Barracks*, caricature by Thomas Rowlandson (1756–1827),
hand-colored etching and aquatint, [n.p.], 1788. Brown University
Library, Anne S. K. Brown Military Collection.   60

9.1. *Thanks to Grant*, front page of *Harper's Weekly. Journal of Civilization*,
February 6, 1864, wood engraving on newsprint by Thomas Nast
(1840–1902). The Museum of Fine Arts, Houston, TX.   228

9.2. *Völker Europas, wahrt eure heiligsten Güter* (Peoples of Europe, Guard
Your Holiest Assets), lithograph by Hermann Knackfuß (1848–1915),
based on a draft by the German emperor, Wilhelm II (1859–41),
[n.p.], 1895. Deutsches Historisches Museum, Berlin. /S. Ahlers.   229

9.3. *American Progress*, painting by John Gast (1842–96), [n.p.], 1872.
Library of Congress, Prints and Photographs Division, Washington,
DC, LC-DIG-ppmsca-09855.   246

9.4. *Florence Nightingale an Angel of Mercy, Scutari Hospital 1855*,
colored mezzotint by Charles Algernon Tomkins after a painting by
James E. Buttersworth (1817–94), London, 1855. © The Trustees of the
British Museum, London.   255

9.5.   *The White Man's Burden (Apologies to Rudyard Kipling)*, in *Judge*, April 1, 1899, cartoon by Victor Gillam (1858–1920). Ohio State University, Billy Ireland Cartoon Library & Museum.   257

15.1.   *At Neuve Chapelle. Your Friends Need You. Be a Man*, British war poster by the Parliamentary Recruiting Committee, designed by Frank Brangwyn (1867–1956), London, 1915. Library of Congress, Prints and Photographs Division, Washington DC, LC-USZC4-11190.   370

15.2.   *Hilf auch Du mit!* (You Help as Well!), German war poster by the Reich Propaganda Department of the National Socialist German Workers' Party, designed by Theo Matejko (1893–1946), Vienna, 1941. Hoover Institution Archives, Poster Collection, GE 1070.   371

15.3.   *Halt the Hun! Buy U.S. Government Bonds, Third Liberty Loan,* poster by the US Government, designed by Henry Raleigh (1880–1945), Chicago, [1918]. Library of Congress, Prints and Photographs Division, Washington DC, LC-USZC4-2792.   384

15.4.   *Frankreichs Schuld* (France's Guilt), front page of a special issue of the National Socialist magazine *Illustrierter Beobachter*, Munich, May 1940. Deutsches Historisches Museum, Berlin/I. Desnica.   385

15.5.   *I'm Proud of YOU FOLKS Too!*, American war poster by the US Navy's Industrial Incentive Division, designed by Jon Whitcomb (1906–88), [n.p.], 1944. Courtesy of the Historical Museum at Fort Missoula.   386

16.1.   *Women of Britain Say—"Go!,"* British war poster, published by the Imperial Maritime League, designed by E. V. Kealy, London, 1915. © Imperial War Museum, London (Art. IWM PST 2763).   414

16.2.   *Destroy This Mad Brute. Enlist. US Army*, American war poster, produced by the Committee on Public Information, designed by Harry R. Hopps (1869–1937), San Francisco, 1917. Library of Congress, Prints and Photographs Division, Washington DC, LC-DIG-ds-03216.   415

16.3.   Front page of *Pour les funérailles d'un soldat* (For the Funeral of a Soldier), a 1912 composition by Lili Boulanger (1893–1918), edition published by Editions Ricordi, Paris, 1919. Fondation Internationale Nadia et Lili Boulanger, Paris.   419

19.1.   *The Girl behind the Man behind the Gun*, British poster published by the Queen Mary's Army Auxiliary Corps during World War I, unknown artist, London, 1918. © Imperial War Museum, London (Art. IWM PST 13167).   475

19.2.   *Belgian Red Cross. Donations may be sent to the Hon. Treasurer, the Rht. Hon. the Lord Mayor of London, or to the President, Baron C. Goffinet,* poster by the British Red Cross, designed by Charles Buchel (1872–1950), London, 1915. Library of Congress, Prints and Photographs Division, Washington DC, LC-USZC4-11243.   478

19.3. *Hilf Siegen als Luftnachrichtenhelferin!* (Help to Win as an Air Force
Signal Corps Auxiliary), poster by the Reich Propaganda Department
of the National Socialist German Workers' Party for the Air Force,
unknown artist, c. 1942 [n.p., n.d.]. Hollandse Hoogte, Den Haag.   486

19.4. *WAAC—This Is My War Too!*, poster by the US Army Recruiting
Publicity Office, designed by Dan Smith, c. 1943 [n.d., n.p.]. © Victoria
and Albert Museum, London.   487

26.1. *16,000,000 Gefallene, 29,000,000 Krüppel, 36.000.000 Heimatlose.
Wofür? Internationaler Frauentag März 1946. Für Weltfrieden*
(16,000,000 Fallen Soldiers. 29,000,000 Cripples. 36,000,000
Homeless. FOR WHAT? International Women's Day March 1946.
For World Peace), poster by the Social Democratic Party of Austria,
designed by Victor Theodor Slama (1890–1973), Vienna, 1946. Hoover
Institution Archives, Poster Collection, GE 1553.   636

26.2. *They Depend on You! U.S. Army Nurse Corps*, poster by the Recruiting
Publicity Bureau of the US Army, unknown artist, [n.p., n.d.], 1953.
The University of North Carolina at Greensboro, University Libraries,
The Betty H. Carter Women Veterans Historical Project.   660

26.3. *GIRLS SAY YES to Boys Who Say NO. Proceeds from the Sale of This
Poster Go to the Draft Resistance*, photo by Jim Marshall, designed
by Larry Gates, [n.p.], 1968. Collection of the Oakland Museum of
California, All of Us or None Archive, Gift of the Rossman Family/
© Jim Marshall Photography LCC.   662

26.4. *Cambodge Vietnam Laos: Victoire*, poster printed on behalf of the
prime minister of the unified Vietnam, Phạm Văn Đồng (1906–2000),
unknown artists, [n.p.], 1976. 651331152: Marka/Getty Images.   664

26.5. *Women in Peacekeeping: The Power to Empower. International Day
of United Nations Peace Keeping. 29 May 2009*, poster by the United
Nations, 2009. UN Photo.   666

Contributors

Frank Biess is a professor of history at the University of California–San Diego. His main field of research is twentieth-century German history, with an emphasis on social and political history as well as the history of memory, gender, and, more recently, the history of emotions. His publications include *Homecomings: Returning POWs and the Legacies of Defeat* (2006); *Conflict, Continuity, and Catastrophe in Modern Germany*, edited with Hanna Schissler and Mark Roseman (2007); *Histories of the Aftermath: The Legacies of the Second World War in Europe*, edited with Robert Moeller (2010); *Science and Emotions after 1945: A Transatlantic Perspective*, edited with Daniel Gross (2014); and *German Angst? Fear and Democracy in the Federal Republic Germany* (2020).

Raphaëlle Branche is a professor of modern and contemporary history at Paris Nanterre University and at the Institut des sciences sociales du politique. Her research focuses on violence in colonial settings and more specifically in Algeria. Her books include *La torture et l'armée pendant la guerre d'Algérie, 1954–1962* (2001); *L'embuscade de Palestro, Algérie 1956* (2010); *Rape in Wartime*, edited with Fabrice Virgili et al. (2012); and *Combatants of Muslim Origin in European Armies in the Twentieth Century: Far from Jihad*, edited with Xavier Bougarel and Cloé Drieu (2017). Her most recent publication focuses on family memories of the Algerian War in France: *Qu'as-tu fait en Algérie, papa? Enquête sur un silence familial* (2020).

D'Ann Campbell is a professor of history at Culver Stockton College and previously held posts at the US Coast Guard Academy and the US Military Academy. For 2016–18, Campbell was the Distinguished Visiting Professor of Military History at the US Air Force Academy. Her research on women and the Second World War includes studies of US servicewomen during the war years and a comparative study of women in combat roles in four countries. Her publications include "Servicewomen of World War II," *Armed Forces and Society* 16, no. 2 (1990); and "Women in Combat: The World War II Experience in the United States, Great Britain, Germany, and the Soviet Union," *The Journal of Military History* 57, no. 2 (1993).

Thomas Cardoza is a professor of history and chair of the Department of Humanities of the Truckee Meadows Community College in Reno, Nevada. His research interests are in the fields of military history, childhood studies, women's history, and Napoleonic studies. His publications include *Intrepid Women: Cantinières and Vivandières of the French Army* (2010); *The American Experiment* (2015); *A Boy Soldier in Napoleon's*

Army: The Military Life of Jacques Chevillet (2017); and numerous articles on women and children in French history.

Elizabeth Colwill is an associate professor of American studies at the University of Hawai'i Mānoa. She specializes in the cultural histories of gender, slavery, and revolution in the Atlantic world, with a focus on the Francophone Caribbean. Her recent publications include "Freedwomen's Familial Politics: Marriage, War and Rites of Registry in Post-Emancipation Saint-Domingue," in *Gender, War, and Politics: Transatlantic Perspectives, 1750–1850*, edited by Karen Hagemann et al. (2010); "Gendering the June Days: Race, Masculinity, and Slave Emancipation in Saint Domingue," *Journal of Haitian Studies* 15, no. 1/2 (2009); and "Fêtes de l'hymen, fêtes de la liberté: Matrimony and Emancipation in Saint-Domingue, 1793," in *The World of the Haitian Revolution*, edited by David Patrick Geggus and Norman Fiering (2009).

Catherine Davies is a professor of Hispanic and Latin American studies and director of the Institute of Modern Languages Research, School of Advanced Study, University of London. She specializes in nineteenth- and twentieth-century Spanish/Spanish American literature and cultural history. Recent research has focused on gender studies and the independence wars in Spanish America. Her publications include *Latin American Women's Writing: Feminist Readings in Theory and Crisis*, edited with Anny Brooksbank Jones (1996); *A Place in the Sun? Women's Writing in Twentieth-Century Cuba* (1997); with Claire Brewster and Hilary Owen, *South American Independence: Gender, Politics, Text* (2006); and "Gendered Interpretations of Independence Poetry: Mexico and Peru 1820–1822," in *Power, Place and Representation: Contested Sites of Dependence and Independence in Latin America*, edited by Bill Richardson and Lorraine Kelly (2017).

Stefan Dudink teaches gender studies at Radboud University Nijmegen, the Netherlands. His main field of research is the history of gender and sexuality in modern Western political and military cultures, with a focus on the Netherlands. His publications include a monograph on Dutch, late nineteenth-century liberalism, *Deugdzaam Liberalisme: Sociaal-Liberalisme in Nederland, 1870–1901* (1997); and the volumes *Masculinities in Politics and War: Gendering Modern History*, edited with Karen Hagemann and John Tosh (2004); *Representing Masculinity: Male Citizenship in Modern Western Culture*, edited with Karen Hagemann and Anna Clark (2007); and "Low Countries Histories of Masculinity," a special issue of *BMGN—Low Countries Historical Review* 127, no. 1 (2012).

Annegret Fauser is the Cary C. Boshamer Distinguished Professor of Music and adjunct professor in women's and gender studies at the University of North Carolina. Her research focuses on music and culture of the nineteenth and twentieth centuries, in particular that of France and the United States. Her authored books include *Der Orchestergesang in Frankreich zwischen 1870 und 1920* (1994); *Musical Encounters at the 1889 Paris World's Fair* (2005); *Sounds of War: Music in the United States during World War II* (2013); *The Politics of Musical Identity: Selected Writings* (2015); and *Aaron*

Copland's "Appalachian Spring" (2017). In addition, she has published several edited books, most recently with Mark Everist, *Stage Music and Cultural Transfer: Paris, 1830–1914* (2009); and with Michael A. Figueroa, *Performing Commemoration: Musical Reenactment and the Politics of Trauma* (2020).

Alan Forrest is a professor of modern history at the University of York (Emeritus). He has published widely on modern French history, especially on the French Revolution and empire and on the history of war. Authored recent books include *The Legacy of the French Revolutionary Wars: The Nation-in-Arms in French Republican Memory* (2009); *Napoleon* (2011); *Waterloo* (2015); and *The Death of the French Atlantic: Trade, War, and Slavery in the Age of Revolution* (2020). Among the volumes he has published are *Soldiers, Citizens and Civilians: Experiences and Perceptions of the Revolutionary and Napoleonic Wars, 1790–1820*, edited with Karen Hagemann and Jane Rendall (2009); *War Memories: The Revolutionary and Napoleonic Wars in Modern European Culture*, edited with Étienne François and Karen Hagemann (2012); and *The Routledge Companion to the French Revolution in World History*, edited with Matthias Middell (2015).

Susan R. Grayzel is a professor of history at Utah State University. Her research focuses on twentieth-century British and European history with a special focus on the history of war and society, especially gender, women, and war. Her books include *Women's Identities at War: Gender, Motherhood, and Politics in Britain and France during the First World War* (1999); *Women and the First World War* (2002); *Gender, Labor, War and Empire: Essays on Modern Britain*, coedited with Philippa Levine (2009); *At Home and under Fire: Air Raids and Culture in Britain from the Great War to the Blitz* (2012); and *Gender and the Great War*, edited with Tammy M. Proctor (2017).

Amy S. Greenberg is the George Winfree Professor of History and Women's Studies at Penn State University. She is a historian of antebellum America with a particular interest in the relationship between the United States and the rest of the world in the decades before the Civil War. She has published widely on gender and/or the territorial expansionism of the nineteenth-century United States. Her books include *Manifest Manhood and the Antebellum American Empire* (2005); *Manifest Destiny and American Territorial Expansion: A Brief History with Documents* (2012); *A Wicked War: Polk, Clay, Lincoln, and the 1846 US Invasion of Mexico* (2012); and, most recently, *Lady First: The World of First Lady Sarah Polk* (2019).

Karen Hagemann is the James G. Kenan Distinguished Professor of History and an adjunct professor of the Curriculum in Peace, War, and Defense at the University of North Carolina at Chapel Hill. She has published widely in modern German, European, and transatlantic history and gender history. Her most recent monograph is *Revisiting Prussia's Wars against Napoleon: History, Culture and Memory* (2015; German, 2019). Her volumes include *Home/Front: The Military, War and Gender in Twentieth-Century Germany* (2002); *Masculinities in Politics and War: Gendering Modern History*, edited with Stefan Dudink and John Tosh (2004); *Gender, War, and Politics: Transatlantic Perspectives, 1775–1830*, edited with Gisela Mettele and Jane Rendall (2010); *Gender and* *the Long Postwar: The United States and the Two Germanys, 1945–1989*, edited with Sonya Michel (2014); and *Gendering Post-1945 German History: Entanglements*, edited with Donna Harsch and Friederike Brühöfener (2019).

Mischa Honeck is a professor of North American and British History at the University of Kassel. His main research interests are the histories of race, ethnicity, gender, youth, and childhood in the United States and the transatlantic world. His edited volumes include: *Germany and the Black Diaspora: Points of Contact, 1250–1914* edited with Martin Klimke and Anne Kuhlmann (2013); and *War and Childhood in the Era of the Two World Wars* edited with James Marten (2019). He is the author of *We Are the Revolutionists: German-Speaking Immigrants and American Abolitionists after 1848* (2011); and *Our Frontier Is the World: The Boy Scouts in the Age of American Ascendancy* (2018).

Kimberly Jensen is a professor of history and gender studies at Western Oregon University. Her research addresses questions of women, citizenship, and civil liberties in the United States in the period of the First World War and its aftermath, the history of women and medicine, and women's transnational activism. She is the author of *Mobilizing Minerva: American Women in the First World War* (2008); and *Oregon's Doctor to the World: Esther Pohl Lovejoy and a Life in Activism* (2012). With Erika K. Kuhlman, she coedited the anthology *Women and Transnational Activism in Historical Perspective* (2010). In addition, she recently published "Gender and Citizenship," in *Gender and the Great War*, edited by Tammy Proctor and Susan Grayzel (2017).

Thomas Kühne is the director of the Strassler Center for Holocaust and Genocide Studies at Clark University, where he holds the Strassler Chair in Holocaust History. His research focuses on Nazi perpetrators and bystanders, on military cultures, and more broadly on the construction of collective identity through mass violence. His recent books include *Belonging and Genocide: Hitler's Community, 1918–1945* (2010/2013); *The Holocaust and Local History*, edited with Tom Lawson (2011); *Globalizing Beauty: Body Aesthetics in the 20th Century*, edited with Hartmut Berghoff (2013); and *The Rise and Fall of Comradeship: Hitler's Soldiers, Male Bonding and Mass Violence in the Twentieth Century* (2017).

Marilyn Lake is Professorial Fellow in History at the University of Melbourne. She has published widely on gender, war, empire, nationalism, feminism, and race. Her publications include *Getting Equal: The History of Australian Feminism* (1999); *Connected Worlds: History in Transnational Perspective*, edited with Ann Curthoys (2005); *Gender and War: Australians at War in the Twentieth Century*, edited with Joy Damousi (2005); and most recently *Drawing the Global Color Line: White Men's Countries and the International Challenge of Racial Equality* (2008), coauthored with Henry Reynolds; *What's Wrong with Anzac? The Militarization of Australian History* (2010); and *Progressive New World: How Settler Colonialism and Transpacific Exchange Shaped American Reform* (2019).

Regina Mühlhäuser is a senior researcher at the Hamburg Foundation for the Advancement of Research and Culture and a Co-Coordinator of the International

Research Group 'Sexual Violence in Armed Conflict'. Her research focuses on violence, sexuality and gender in times of armed conflict, in particular during World War II in Europe and Asia. Her publications include *Krieg und Geschlecht: Sexuelle Gewalt im Krieg und Sex-Zwangsarbeit in NS-Konzentrationslagern*, edited with Insa Eschebach (2008); "Between 'Racial Awareness' and Fantasies of Potency: Nazi Sexual Politics in the Occupied Territories of the Soviet Union, 1942–1945," in *Brutality and Desire*, edited by Dagmar Herzog (2009); *In Plain Sight: Sexual Violence in Armed Conflict*, edited with Gaby Zipfel and Kirsten Campbell (2019); and *Sex and the Nazi Soldier: Violent, Commercial and Consensual Contacts during the War in the Soviet Union, 1941–1945* (2020).

Robert A. Nye is the Thomas Hart and Mary Jones Horning Professor of the Humanities and professor of history emeritus at Oregon State University. His main research interest is nineteenth- and twentieth-century European and French intellectual and cultural history. His several publications include the monographs *Crime, Madness, and Politics in Modern France: The Medical Concept of National Decline* (1984); *Masculinity and Male Codes of Honor in Modern France* (1993); and *Sexuality: An Oxford Reader* (1999). He coedited with Erika Milam the 2015 volume of *Osiris* titled *Scientific Masculinities* and has published several scholarly articles and chapters.

Jean H. Quataert is the State University of New York (SUNY) Distinguished Research Professor of History (Emerita) at Binghamton University, SUNY. She is a trained historian of German history. More recently, she has turned to new research agendas that include human rights and transnational and global history. Her books include *Staging Philanthropy: Patriotic Women and the National Imagination in Dynastic Germany, 1813–1916* (2001); *The Gendering of Human Rights in the International Systems of Law in the Twentieth Century* (2006); *Gendering Modern German History: Rewriting Historiographies*, edited with Karen Hagemann (2008); *Advocating Dignity: Human Rights Mobilizations in Global Politics* (2009); and most recently "A New Look at International Law: Gendering the Practices of Humanitarian Medicine in Europe's 'Small Wars,' 1879–1907," *Human Rights Quarterly* 40 (2018).

Sonya O. Rose is a professor emerita and former Natalie Zemon Davis Collegiate Professor of History, Sociology, and Women's Studies at the University of Michigan, Ann Arbor. Her main field of research is modern Britain, gender and labor history, the histories of national identity, empire and citizenship, and the history of sexuality. Her publications include *Limited Livelihoods: Gender and Class in Nineteenth-Century England* (1992); *Gender and Class in Modern Europe*, edited with Laura L. Frader (1996); *Gender, Citizenship and Subjectivities*, edited with Kathleen Canning (2002); *Which People's War? National Identity and Citizenship in Wartime Britain, 1939–1945* (2003); *At Home with the Empire*, edited with Catherine Hall (2006); and *What Is Gender History?* (2010).

Glenda Sluga is a professor of international history at the University of Sydney and, since the fall 2019, a professor of international history and capitalism at the European University Institute in Florence. She has published widely on the cultural history of international relations, internationalism, the history of European nationalisms, sovereignty, identity, immigration, and gender history. In 2006, she was appointed a member of the International Scientific Committee for the History of UNESCO. Her books include, with Barbara Caine, *Gendering European History: 1780–1920* (2000); *The Problem of Trieste and the Italo-Yugoslav Border* (2001); *The Nation, Psychology, and International Politics, 1870–1919* (2006); *Internationalism in the Age of Nationalism* (2013); *Women, Diplomacy and International Politics since 1500*, edited with Carolyn James (2016); and *Internationalisms: A Twentieth Century History*, edited with Patricia Clavin (2017).

Richard Smith is a senior lecturer in the Department of Media, Communications and Cultural Studies, Goldsmiths, University of London. He has written widely on the experience of West Indian troops in both world wars and the race and gender implications of military service in comparative context. His publications include the monograph *Jamaican Volunteers in the First World War: Race, Masculinity and the Development of National Consciousness* (2004); and several articles and book chapters, including, most recently, "The Multicultural First World War: Memories of the West Indian Contribution in Contemporary Britain," *Journal of European Studies* 45, no. 4, (2015); and "Loss and Longing: Emotional Responses to West Indian Soldiers during the First World War," in *The British Empire and The First World War*, edited by Ashley Jackson (2017).

Sandra Whitworth is a professor of political science and is also appointed to the graduate program in gender, feminism, and women's studies at York University in Toronto. She served for six years as home-base editor of the *International Feminist Journal of Politics*. Her publications include *Feminism and International Relations* (1994); *Men, Militarism and UN Peacekeeping: A Gendered Analysis* (2004); and *International Relations*, with Joshua Goldstein and Jon C. Pevehouse (2013). She has written various articles and book chapters on issues such as gender in Canadian foreign policy and human rights and was invited (with coauthor Dyan Mazurana) to produce the 2002 UN Secretary-General Study *Women, Peace and Security*.

Kristen P. Williams is a professor of political science at Clark University. Her research interests are in the field of international relations, focusing on nationalism, ethnic conflict, gender, and international relations theory. Her publications include *Despite Nationalist Conflicts: Theory and Practice of Maintaining World Peace* (2001); with Neal G. Jesse, *Identity and Institutions: Conflict Reduction in Divided Societies* (2005) and *Ethnic Conflict: A Systematic Approach to Cases of Conflict* (2011); and with Joyce P. Kaufman, *Women, the State, and War: A Comparative Perspective on Citizenship and Nationalism* (2007), *Women and War: Gender Identity and Activism in Times of Conflict* (2010), and *Women at War, Women Building Peace: Challenging Gender Norms* (2013). She is coeditor, with Steven E. Lobell and Neal G. Jesse, of *Beyond Great Powers and Hegemons: Why Secondary States Support, Follow, or Challenge* (2012), and with Joyce P. Kaufman, *Women, Gender Equality, and Post-Conflict Transformation: Lessons Learned, Implications for the Future* (2017).

Peter H. Wilson is the Chichele Professor of the History of War and a university academic fellow at All Souls College at the University of Oxford. His work examines the political, social, military, and cultural history of German-speaking central Europe across the sixteenth to early nineteenth centuries. He is currently principal investigator of a five-year research project on the "European Fiscal-Military System 1530–1870" funded by the European Research Council 2018–23. His many books include *Absolutism in Central Europe* (2000); *From Reich to Revolution: German History 1558–1806* (2004); as editor, *A Companion to Eighteenth-Century Europe* (2008); *Europe's Tragedy: A History of the Thirty Years War* (2009), which was the winner of the Distinguished Book Award of the Society for Military History; *The Thirty Years War: A Sourcebook* (2010); *The Holy Roman Empire: A Thousand Years of Europe's History* (2016); and *Lützen* (2018).

Angela Woollacott is the Manning Clark Professor of History at the Australian National University. Her research has been in the fields of gender and war, modern British and British Empire history, Australian history, whiteness, gender and modernity, settler colonialism, and transnational biography. Her monographs include *On Her Their Lives Depend: Munitions Workers in the Great War* (1994); *To Try Her Fortune in London: Australian Women, Colonialism and Modernity* (2001); *Gender and Empire* (2006); *Race and the Modern Exotic: Three "Australian" Women on Global Display* (2011); *Settler Society in the Australian Colonies: Self-Government and Imperial Culture* (2015); and *Don Dunstan: The Visionary Politician Who Changed Australia* (2019). Her most recent volumes include *Transnational Ties: Australian Lives in the World*, edited with Desley Deacon and Penny Russell (2008); and *Transnational Lives: Biographies of Global Modernity, 1700–present*, edited with Desley Deacon and Penny Russell (2010).

Serena Zabin is a professor of history and the director of American studies at Carleton College. Her work focuses on the American colonies as part of the eighteenth-century British Empire. Her first monograph is *Dangerous Economies: Status and Commerce in Imperial New York* (2009). She is also the author of *The New York Conspiracy Trials of 1741: Daniel Horsmanden's Journal of the Proceedings* (2004), a volume intended for the undergraduate classroom; and *The Boston Massacre: An Intimate History* (2020).

Dubravka Zarkov is an associate professor of gender, conflict, and development at the International Institute of Social Studies, Erasmus University Rotterdam. Her main fields of research are gender, sexuality, and ethnicity in the context of war and violence, as well as their media representations. She authored *The Body of War: Media, Ethnicity and Gender in the Break-up of Yugoslavia* (2007); and *Gender, Conflict, Development* (2008); and coedited with Cynthia Cockburn, *The Postwar Moment: Militaries, Masculinities and International Peacekeeping* (2002). Most recently, she published "From Women and War to Gender and Conflict? Feminist Trajectories," in *The Oxford Handbook of Gender and Conflict*, edited by Fionnuala Ní Aoláin et al. (2018).

INTRODUCTION

Gender and the History of War—
The Development of the Research

KAREN HAGEMANN

THE Russian avant-garde artist Pavel Nikolaevich Filonov painted *The German War* (Figure 0.1) in the first year of World War I. Finished shortly before his conscription into the Russian army, the painting reflects his approach to "analytical art," which he had developed in his 1912 essay, "Canon and Law." By dividing "the objects in his paintings into a myriad of atoms, placing them beside one another on the pictorial surface as though he was creating a mosaic picture of atomic structure, . . . he strove to unveil the underlying structure" of the "ever-changing material world."[1] Accordingly, in *The German War*, painted in restrained gray–brown, the forms break up into "splinters," reuniting in crystals and new variations. Depending on the viewer's perspective, the painting conveys different facets, but all point to the same underlying "structure," the core of war: the chaos of violence and destruction.

This painting not only visually encapsulates war at its core—violence, devastation, distress, disorder, and death—but also represents our multifaceted perspective on the theme of gender and war in this Oxford handbook. In seeking to replace the old "master narratives" of the conventional history of military and war, it is not enough merely to add the *theme* of women and gender and make it the *subject* of our study. A more interesting picture—often paradoxical and ambiguous—can be obtained by using *gender* as a *methodology*, as a *category of analysis*, for the study of military and war. As such, gender works in the interplay with other relational categories like *class*, *race*, *ethnicity*, or *sexuality*. Their specific meanings and their entanglement depend on the historical context and are thus constantly changing.

Such a multifaceted approach to gender history is not our invention. Gender historians have discussed it since the late 1980s. One important contribution to this debate was

FIGURE 0.1. *The German War*, oil painting by Pavel Nikolaevich Filonov (1883–1941), [n.p.], 1914/15.

the 1998 essay, "The Non-Unity of History as Historiographical Challenge," written by Karin Hausen for a volume on gender history and general history. In the essay, she emphasized how dubious it is, from the perspective of gender history, to accept the notion that "general history" and its "master narratives" are truly "general."[2] She shows that the reconceptualization of history as the history of (hu)mankind, which evolved during the Enlightenment and was reinforced by the professionalization of history writing as an academic discipline during the nineteenth century, deployed a novel hierarchy with fateful consequences: the general or "universal" in humanity was viewed as embodied by the male sex. The gender order challenged by new, revolutionary ideas of equal human rights was stabilized by references to "nature," based on perceived physiological differences between men and women, which positioned them in different cultural and social spheres. The "male sphere" of politics, the military, and war became the "public" and universal—and, as such, the only suitable subject of historiography—while the complementary "female sphere" of the family and the home was construed as "private," politically insignificant, and unworthy of serious academic study.[3] To dismantle this powerful construction, which informed Western historiography until the advent of women's and gender history in the 1970s, Hausen recommended the "non-unity of history" as a feminist program. She called for a critical discussion of the accomplishments and distortions of the fiction of the "unitary" program and suggested that the unity insinuated by historical master narratives should be replaced by the "multiplicity of history."[4]

We follow this approach in full awareness that analyzing, interpreting, and writing history still means telling stories and crafting narratives and that this implies making decisions about lenses and focal points. Our focus is on gender as both a subject of study and a methodology for the analysis of the history of military and war.[5] The handbook poses two central questions: First, how has gender been shaped by war and the military and simultaneously helped to shape them? And, second, how did the relation between war and the military on the one hand and gender on the other change over time and in different regions? These two questions are explored in thirty-one chapters by specialists in the history of military and war and experts in gender and women's studies, drawing from the disciplines of history, cultural studies, political science, and international relations. The collection proceeds chronologically through the history of warfare since the seventeenth century. Its content reflects the state of research on the history of gender and war. Therefore, the main geographical focus of the handbook in several chapters is on the best explored regions of eastern and western Europe, the Americas, and Australia. But it also systematically covers the long-term processes of colonization and empire-building originating in early modern Europe and their aftermath in the Americas, Asia, Africa, and Australia, which are more recent fields of research. The handbook thus allows for temporal comparison that explores continuities and changes over the longue durée, for regional comparisons, and for an assessment of transnational influences on the entangled relationships between and among gender and war. It thus suggests on the one hand a closer integration of the approaches of the history of military and war and gender history; and emphasizes on the other hand the necessity to "provincialize" the so-called *Western world* by treating it as a changing and contested construct and as a historical phenomenon transformed through colonial and imperial expansion, which created complex relations with long-lasting consequences.

The following overview discusses the development and state of research on gender and war; examines the key concepts of the volume, *gender, war, violence, and sexual violence*; and explains the aims, central questions, and theoretical approach of the handbook, its regional and temporal focus, and its organization.

Gendering the Past and Present of War—the Development of Scholarship

The study of the past and present of military and warfare is booming. Books on the subject fill shelves in bookstores and libraries. One format that has become especially popular in recent years is the voluminous handbook or compendium, which is generally perceived to represent the state of the art of a research field. Both readers and publishers seem to like it, because it is assumed to provide a summarizing overview, an "authoritative and up-to-date survey" of past and present research, and a "critical examination of the progress and direction of debates."[6] However, the predominantly male authors and editors of the handbooks and compendiums on the history of military and war published in the past decade do not seem to think that women's and gender studies have contributed much to the field. The absence of gender as a subject and methodology of the history of war in these mainstream publications is striking.[7] In most cases, they have at best one or two "additional" chapters on the subject of women; rarely do they include chapters that use gender as an analytical approach.[8]

Even in the early twenty-first century, most scholars and readers appear to conceive the subject of military and war as genuinely masculine. The maleness of the military and war seems so self-evident to most military historians as to require no critical scrutiny. This is hardly surprising in regard to traditional military historiography, which Dennis E. Showalter so aptly dubbed "drum and trumpet history."[9] In general, history of this kind is written from a conservative perspective, which is defined by an often uncritical identification with the state and the military. Its objects of study—wars, battles, weapon systems, generals, military organization, and military tactics—remain a male affair in a dual sense. Most researchers are still men and the scholarly focus is mainly on men, without addressing their gender at all. The maleness of the military is taken for granted and conceptualized as being universal.[10]

Such a dual maleness of military history applies, however, not only to the conventional drum and trumpet history but also to most of the so-called new military history that emerged in the 1970s and is informed by social history. Its focus became the relationship between military, war, and society. The framework of the new military history encompasses economic structures, military mentalities, and networks of relationships within the military, in addition to relations between the military and civilian society.[11] Nevertheless, the implicitly assumed and universalized maleness of the subject has usually remained unquestioned. Even the increasing integration of the history of everyday life and cultural history into military history since the early 1990s has changed little in this regard. Military historians have begun to pay attention to the previously neglected lifeworlds and experiences of ordinary men in the military and war, but these studies continue to accept the maleness of the subject as a quasi-natural given. The same may be said about many of the cultural histories of the military and war. Even in their analysis of military symbols, rituals, and festivities, of bellicose discourse and the culture of war, most of these studies still do not integrate gender as an analytical category.[12] The recent reinvention of a more conventional military history, with its focus on operations, combat, and the battlefield, compounds this lack of engagement.[13]

As a result, most works of military history have focused on male actors without addressing their gender, their culturally and socially constructed masculinity, or their relationships as men to other men, as well as to women. Research in the history of military and war has also long neglected women—whether as soldiers' wives, workers in war industries, military nurses, female soldiers, or volunteers for wartime welfare. In 1982, Geoffrey Best was still able to write in the introduction of his book *War and Society in Revolutionary Europe, 1770–1870*, without fear of criticism, "We need not concern ourselves with women, who had very little part in our story."[14] He also did not concern himself with a gender perspective to explore, for example, constructions of military masculinity of his male subjects. The authors and editors of many recent publications on the history of military and war, including handbooks and companions, still seem to hold a similar opinion. Even though in the early twenty-first century they do not explicitly deny that gender shapes military and warfare, and that it is shaped by them, they do so implicitly.

Research on Women, Gender, and War in Political and Social Sciences

The continuing omission of women and gender from the mainstream history of military and war, as defined by textbooks, handbooks, and companions, is remarkable.[15] It stands in stark contrast to the attention devoted to this subject in women's studies since the 1980s. Political and social scientists published the first pathbreaking books that shaped the feminist conceptualization of women/gender and war. Cynthia Enloe's 1983 *Does Khaki Become You? The Militarization of Women's Lives* and Jean Bethke Elshtain's 1987 *Women and War* became instant classics of feminist theory with their forthright criticism of the gender order of militarism, defined as the ideology that a country should maintain a strong military capability and be prepared to use it aggressively to defend or promote its national interests.[16] Enloe analyzed the expansion of military institutions in Western and Western-dominated societies and the extent to which women were drawn into them. She established that the military had produced an "archetypal gender-construct" with male combatants as the antithesis of female civilians. In this construct, military masculinity found its very justification in the protection of women and their femininity. The result, Enloe argued, was that the culture of war and militarism and its discourse impressed on men a sense of agency, power, and superiority over women. In her attempt to deconstruct this gender hierarchy and the model it is based on, she demonstrated the many ways in which women were and are involved in warfare and how increasingly difficult it is for modern military institutions to demarcate "separate spheres" for the men and women they employ.[17]

With a similar agenda, Elshtain examined how the dual myth of men as "just warriors" and women as "beautiful souls" has served since antiquity to create and secure men's identity as "warriors" and that of women as "peaceful noncombatants." She too demonstrated how this myth was undermined on the one hand by the reality of male and female behavior in the history of war, society, and culture and on the other hand by the "moral imperatives of a just war."[18] Both publications and other early works, such as Nancy Loring Goldman's 1982 volume, *Female Soldiers: Combatants or Noncombatants? Historical and Contemporary Perspectives,* spurred intensive discussion and more research on the role of women in military and war and, conversely, the importance of the military and war for the place of women in society.[19]

This research was furthered by four developments. First was the major role women played in international antinuclear and peace movements in North America, western Europe, and Japan, starting in the late 1940s and continuing through the 1980s. The approach of most female activists in these movements was based on traditional maternal feminism. They contended that women as mothers had a special interest in peace and thus fought for it more emphatically than did men.[20] Second, this widespread thinking, which conceptualized women as more peaceful than men, was undercut by the participation of female combatants in the Wars of Decolonization in Asia and Africa during the same period. Not only in the First and Second Indochina Wars (1946–54 and 1955–75), female guerrilla fighters played an important role in the liberation armies. Pictures of armed Vietnamese women prevalent in the Western media during the Vietnam War were also highlighted by the international protest movement against the American involvement in Indochina, which interpreted them as a sign that the liberation struggle enjoyed broad support in the population.[21]

A third contributing factor since the 1980s was the intensifying attempts, initially by the British and American and, later, by other Western militaries, to open their ranks to more women. These efforts were fostered by the move to professional armies (in the United Kingdom in 1961 and in the United States in 1973) that needed to actively recruit new soldiers. The policy of including more women in the military to resolve manpower problems challenged conventional ideas about the gender order, which envisioned the military as an all-male institution and women as maternal champions of peace. The increasing inclusion of women in the military was embraced and encouraged, especially in the United States, by liberal feminists active in the new women's movement that had gained more and more influence in Western societies since the late 1960s. They demanded the equal integration of women into the armed forces, because for them the military was the main institution that defined the hierarchical gender order. They believed that women would only become equal in society when they became equal in the military and gained access to combat positions.[22]

Fourth, the demand of the gay rights movement, emerging in the 1970s, for the equal integration of gays and lesbians into the military and the growing support for this demand in Western societies challenged dominant concepts of heterosexual military masculinity. Thus, the call for the equal integration of women, gays, and lesbians into the Western armed forces was met by fierce opposition in the military, politics, and society.[23] These four developments had a profound impact on scholarship on the subject of women, the military, and war in the political and social sciences and the study of international relations in the 1980s and 1990s and defined its themes.[24]

In the post–Cold War era, the wars fought at the doorstep of western Europe in the former Yugoslavia between 1991 and 2001 further stimulated research on women, gender, and war and led to the exploration of new subjects. The importance of rape and other forms of sexual violence in warfare became a major theme of scholarship. The initial focus was on the mass rape of women; later, researchers also addressed sexual violence against men.[25] Gender and genocide became another issue of growing significance. The wars in the former Yugoslavia, especially the Bosnian Conflict (1992–95) and the Kosovo War (1998–99), but also the Rwandan genocide (April–July 1994)—the mass killing of Tutsi and moderate Hutu by members of the Hutu-majority government, which was the culmination of the Rwandan Civil War (1990–94)[26]—demonstrated the gender- and often also age-selective nature of detention and mass killing. Both the Serbian military in Bosnia and Kosovo and the Hutu troops in Rwanda first killed noncombatant men of "battle age." Women and children were also slaughtered, but more often they became the targets of sexual violence.[27]

These and other armed conflicts and genocide in the post–Cold War era led to an increasing number of interventions by nongovernmental organizations, the United Nations (UN), and the North Atlantic Treaty Organization. These interventions took different forms, from humanitarian and peacekeeping missions to combative peace enforcement and counterinsurgency. This development, in turn, inspired research on old and new forms of humanitarianism and human rights and their gendered dimensions. Attention focused not only on the analysis of the gender-specific structure and policy of international humanitarian organizations or UN peacekeeping missions, but also on how humanitarian interventions affected men and women differently.[28]

Despite the growing attention to women in the military and war and, since the 1990s, the increasing number of publications that used the approach of gender, a comprehensive account on the interrelatedness of gender and war was still missing. This changed with the 2001 publication of *War and Gender: How Gender Shapes the War System and Vice Versa*, by international relations scholar Joshua S. Goldstein. He shifted attention from women to gender, which for him included "both men and women," and asserted that "the *connection* of war with gender" is "more stable, across cultures and through time, than either gender roles outside of war [or] the forms and frequency of war itself." In Goldstein's view, the selection of men as potential combatants (and of women for feminine war-support roles) has "helped shape the war system" since antiquity. He noted, "In turn, the pervasiveness of war in history has influenced gender profoundly."[29] With this central argument, his book had a lasting influence on subsequent research on gender and war in different disciplines, which increased further after the turn of the millennium.

Nevertheless, most work by male authors "on the nature, cause and consequences of war individually and collectively [still] omits gender analysis," observed political scientist Laura Sjoberg in her 2013 *Gendering Global Conflict: Toward a Feminist Theory of War*.[30] This book stirred much discussion, because Sjoberg contended that the omission of gender analysis from international relations studies "is a grave error." For her, "The meanings, causes, and consequences of war cannot be understood without reference to gender. Using gender as a category of analysis transforms the study of war. . . . The feminist tradition in IR [International Relations] has demonstrated that the theory and practice of war have been gendered throughout modern history and that gendered elements are important causal and constitutive factors." Like other feminist scholars in her field, she argued that the "gender 'neutrality'" of the discipline "masks gender subordination."[31]

The Study of War in Women's and Gender History

The feminist debates in political and social sciences and international relations over the conceptualization of women, gender, and war influenced women's and gender historians who had begun to explore the subject since the early 1980s. Initially, their focus was on Western countries such as Australia, Britain, Canada, France, Germany, and the United States during the age of the two world wars. Two themes stood at the center of this pioneering scholarship: the work of women in the war industries and the propaganda that attempted to mobilize them for war support.[32] In the late 1980s, research expanded to include new subjects, such as female war experiences on the home front, the gendered demobilization policies after the First and Second World Wars, and the legacy of both conflicts in postwar societies.[33] These themes reflect the fact that most women's and gender historians of the first two generations started their careers in social history and, since the late 1980s, were inspired by its intensified interest in the history of everyday life.[34]

Two developments in particular influenced subsequent research on the history of women, gender, and war. The first was the *poststructuralist turn*, which led many in the historical profession away from social history toward cultural studies and discourse analysis. Second, and related to the first, was the shift from women to gender as a subject of study.[35] As early as 1976, Natalie Zemon Davis called on her colleagues "to understand the significance of the sexes and of gender groups in historical terms."[36] Accordingly, during the 1980s, feminist historians reconceptualized their field. They moved away from an "additional approach" that focused on women as a subject of research and simply added their stories to the dominant master narratives. Instead, they used gender as an analytical category for their historical research. They studied gender images, gender relations, and the constructions of the gender order in an attempt to critically deconstruct and rewrite the master narratives. It is no wonder that historian Kathleen Canning, in 1994, looking back on this early scholarship, recognized the formative role of women's history and feminist theory in the epistemological debates that rocked the historical profession in the 1980s. Writing in *Signs*, an interdisciplinary journal in women's studies that was at the forefront of new thinking about historical knowledge, she made the case that women's history set the stage for the "reception of various strains of poststructuralism, including French feminism," in the historical profession more generally. Canning observed, "If not always hand-in-hand, feminist and post-structuralist critiques of historical 'master-narratives' interrogated, dissembled, and recast historical paradigms in light of new histories of women and gender and of race, ethnicity, and sexuality."[37]

Nevertheless, it took until the mid-1980s for a systematic poststructuralist conceptualization of gender as a theoretical and methodological approach for the rewriting of history to be formulated, when Joan W. Scott published her pathbreaking 1986 article, "Gender: A Useful Category of Historical Analysis," in the *American Historical Review*.[38] In short order, this became far beyond the American history profession, the most influential article in the field. Scott conceptualized gender as both "a constitutive element of social relationships based on perceived differences between the sexes" and "a primary way of signifying relationships of power." She emphasized that "changes in the organization of social relationships always correspond to changes in representations of power" and vice versa. Furthermore, she identified four constitutive and connected dimensions in which gender, entangled with other categories of difference such as class, race, ethnicity, or sexuality, is a crucial "element": cultural representation; normative concepts and structures like laws and legal regulations; social relations, institutions, and movements; and subjective and collective identities.[39] Although Scott's suggestions were not, as she emphasized twenty years later, "the origins of the gender concept, even among historians," her article "was a site where several lines of thought converged."[40] It presented in convincing clarity a poststructuralist approach to gender history and thus enabled a more systematic study of subjects like politics, military, and war from a gender perspective, challenging their habitual status in historical scholarship as "un-gendered" and "universal."[41]

Scott's poststructuralist conceptualization of gender became influential also in the developing field of a women's and gender history of military and war. Her article "Rewriting History" in the pioneering 1987 volume *Behind the Lines: Gender and the Two World Wars*, edited by Margaret R. Higonnet and others, was instrumental. Here, Scott urged researchers to focus not only on the transformations of the gender system "in the course of the extraordinary conditions generated by wartime," but also on political representations of gender in the context of war. These representations "may not have anything to do with real women or the relations between the sexes." However, they did play a large role in the "general" politics of war.[42] This suggested shift offered a solution to two important disputes that began in the field in the mid-1980s. The first focused on the impact of the world wars on the position of women in the economy, society, and politics, and the second concentrated on women as victims and perpetrators in authoritarian, male-dominated states and institutions.

In the first debate, some historians, such as Arthur Marwick, claimed that the First World War in particular was a catalyst of female liberation mainly because of three developments: the war resulted in an expansion of women's work opportunities into new areas of the labor force previously reserved for men; women gained the right to vote in several postwar countries; and the ideal of the independent "New Woman" became popular in the interwar period.[43] Other historians, such as Ute Daniel and Susan Grayzel, challenged this interpretation, pointing mainly to the persistence of hierarchies between the two sexes. They underscored the short-term character of many wartime changes and noted the economic, social, and cultural demobilization policies that attempted the reconstruction of the prewar gender order. Postwar gender discourse, they argued, still emphasized marriage and motherhood "as the national duty and source of feminine fulfillment." The notion of the New Woman was for the majority of interwar women, even those who were young and single, at best an ideal propagated by the media of the new mass culture, especially illustrated magazines and movies.[44] Starting in the late 1980s, this dichotomist interpretation was challenged by a series of studies that focused on women's everyday war and postwar experiences. These works indicated that the novel opportunities for economic and social independence generated by the First World War seem indeed to have fostered "new mobility and self-confidence" at least in some women, even when the hierarchical gender order as such did not change.[45]

Scott's suggestion to focus on both representations of gender and the changing gender system during wartime offered a conceptual resolution to the dispute. The combination of both perspectives helped to reconcile the "paradoxical progress and regress that has characterized women's status and representation during the two world wars," as Margaret and Patrice L.-R. Higonnet argued in their essay "The Double Helix," in the volume *Behind the Lines*. The Higonnets introduced the metaphor of the double helix to characterize the paradox that "women may be allowed to move 'forward' in terms of employment or social policy" when the home front is mobilized, "yet the battlefront—preeminently a male domain—takes economic and cultural priority. Therefore, while women's objective situation does change, relationships of domination and subordination [are] retained through discourses that systematically designate unequal gender relations." In this way, they sought to overcome a binary construction of continuity versus changes.[46] The metaphor of the double helix has been highly influential: it is still widely used for the conceptualization of this paradox, which can be observed in various regional and historical contexts before, during, and after the era of the world wars.

The second dispute that occupied scholars of women and gender in the 1980s and beyond was stirred by research on the role of women in the Third Reich and their involvement in the Holocaust and the Second World War. The core question of this so-called *Historikerinnenstreit* (female historians' quarrel) was whether German women had become "perpetrators" in the "men's state" of the Third Reich or whether they mostly had been "victims" in the gender hierarchy of National Socialism. The debate emerged fully after the 1987 publication of *Mothers in the Fatherland: Women, the Family and Nazi Politics* by the American historian Claudia Koonz. She insisted that German women had not been outcasts of the Third Reich but that they had shared responsibility for its crimes. Ordinary women could be victims of Nazi misogyny, but they could also benefit from it and sometimes become facilitators of racial persecution.[47] German historian Gisela Bock reviewed the book quite critically in the prominent German history journal *Geschichte und Gesellschaft*. Bock emphasized the misogynist power hierarchy in the Nazi system, citing as one key example the sterilization policy of the Nazi state that affected mainly German women selected because of their supposed social or racial "inferiority."[48] On the Anglo-American side, most feminist historians supported Koonz's position, but in West Germany several feminist scholars of the first generation, still committed to a stark *Opfer–Täter* (victim–perpetrator) binary, perceived ordinary women as victims of Nazism.[49]

The debate, which continued into the 1990s, led a younger generation of women and gender historians on both sides of the Atlantic to develop an approach emphasizing the wide spectrum of female behavior in the Third Reich: from "German women in the Nazi killing fields,"[50] like female guards in concentration camps; health and welfare workers and policewomen inside Germany and in the occupied territories, who enforced the racial policy of the Nazis; and Wehrmacht auxiliaries, who supported the genocidal warfare; to ordinary citizens who acted as informers and bystanders. They also analyzed the spectrum of behavior of women who were victims of the Holocaust, who helped the victims of political or racial persecution, who protested Nazi policy, or who actively supported the resistance. In their analyses, they emphasized the challenging life-and-death decisions women often had to make.[51] This new research focused on the room to maneuver that women, like men, had in Nazi Germany and the regions occupied by its military. It demonstrated that a poststructural analysis can help to overcome binary constructions, to understand ambiguities and paradoxes, and to analyze the subtle gradations in power across class, race, ethnic, age, and gender lines.[52] The theoretical and methodological insights of the *Historikerinnenstreit* were therefore important far beyond the study of the Third Reich and the Holocaust. They also informed the research on armed conflict, occupation, collaboration, and genocide in other regions and periods[53]; on women in other fascist regimes like Italy[54]; on women in the Spanish Civil War[55]; and on women who served as nurses, female auxiliaries, soldiers, and partisans in the allied militaries of the First and Second World Wars.[56]

In a contemporary context that instigated an increasing interest in the subject of women, gender, and war in the 1980s and 1990s, the poststructuralist turn was crucial because it allowed a new, more complex understanding of this subject and furthermore enabled historians to explore new themes. One of these themes was men, masculinity, the military, and war. Only a small number of innovative scholars had studied constructions of military masculinity before this turn; two of the most influential were Klaus Theweleit and George L. Mosse. In 1977, Theweleit published his seminal book *Männerphantasien* (*Male Fantasies*), which was translated into English in 1987. In this study, he explored the protofascist mentality of *Freikorps* soldiers after the First World War and their bodily experiences.[57] In 1990, Mosse, building on his earlier studies on nationalism, war, and sexuality, published *Fallen Soldiers: Reshaping the Memory of the World Wars*. This book provided a profound analysis of the masculine "myth of the war experience"—a vision of war that masks its horror, consecrates its memory, and ultimately justifies its purpose. Beginning with the Napoleonic Wars (1803–15), Mosse traced the origins of this myth and its symbols and examined the role of war volunteers and their ideals of masculinity in creating and perpetuating it.[58]

Mosse's books have inspired historical studies of masculinity, military, and war since the early 1990s, many of them influenced by poststructuralist thinking, and belonged to the first in the field of the history of masculinity.[59] Most of these studies are situated squarely within the field of gender history and have sought to apply its concepts and methods. By employing the perspective of the history of masculinity, historians have shown how politics and war have become the seemingly natural homelands of masculinity.[60] They emphasize the multiplicity of notions of masculinity that compete with and challenge the "hegemonic masculinity" in a specific historical context and period and explore their intersectionality with other constructions of differences—not only class, race, and ethnicity, but crucially also sexuality, age/generational affiliation and familial status.[61] Furthermore, they reveal that military and war, particularly in Western cultures, were often based on a heteronormative notion of martial masculinity that excludes "Others," such as homosexual, "non-White," or "non-Christian" men. More recent studies that explore male subjectivity emphasize the flexibility and fluidity of male experiences in wartime.[62] One theme of special importance for historians who work on masculinity, military, and war is the linkage between different forms of military mobilization, including universal conscription, citizenship rights, and constructions of masculinity. This link became a central argument in the exclusion of women from political representation since the American and French Revolutions (1775–83 and 1789–99). Only men who took up arms to protect family, home, and country when the nation was in danger or needed to be liberated were perceived as "real men" and earned the right to be(come) citizens.[63] The work by historians of masculinity on military and war thus exhibits in an especially striking way the importance of gender history, not only for our understanding of armed forces and conflicts, but also for the very structure of Western politics and society.

This makes it all the more surprising that most work by gender historians on military and war published since the 1990s still focuses mainly on women.[64] What has changed in the subsequent decades is the extension of the explored regions and periods, as well as themes, questions, and approaches. These changes were influenced both by events of the day and by the general development of historiography. The post–Cold War conflicts, in particular the wars in former Yugoslavia and the Rwandan genocide, sparked greater interest in the theme of mass violence, especially sexual violence, in warfare and genocide in historical scholarship, too.[65] Gender historians began to investigate old and new forms of humanitarianism and armed conflict as well.[66] Still understudied, however, is the post-1945 history of international peace activism and peace movements with their highly gendered ideology and political practice.[67]

The development of the field of the history of gender and war was further fostered by the paradigmatic move of the general historiography from regional and national history to comparative studies and transnational[68] and global history.[69] This shift stimulated scholarship on gender and war in the history of regions outside western and central Europe, North America, and Australia. Since the 1990s, the number of publications on gender and war in southern Europe has grown remarkably.[70] Research on the subject in eastern European and Russian history has also expanded significantly, stimulated by the opening of the archives in former communist countries.[71] Moreover, the fall of the Berlin Wall and the collapse of communism gave a boost to the investigation of the post-1945 gender history of the Global Cold War and, with it, the short- and long-term effects of the Second World War on the gender order. Postwar gender history became more diverse and comparative.[72]

In the 1990s, gender historians began to study the theme of gender and war in other regions of the globe, especially Latin America, Africa, and Asia. This trend was stimulated by a more general move to colonial and postcolonial studies. Since the late 1970s, scholars in this field have tried to create awareness of the interactive nature of relations between colonial and imperial powers and the colonized. They have emphasized the significance of cultures outside Europe for the self-perception of the so-called Western European civilization. Conceptually based in the field of cultural studies, such approaches highlight social diversity and interrogate power relations.[73] Concomitantly, new importance was attached to issues of nation-building, the formation of identity with reference to colonialists and colonized, wars of colonization, imperial warfare, and the struggles for decolonization. Since the millennium, scholarship by gender historians on colonial and imperial wars increasingly covers all regions of European expansion, after long having centered on the British Empire, the by-far largest empire in the nineteenth and twentieth centuries.[74] Key themes were the gendered policies of colonization, the related gendered practices of violence in South America by the Portuguese and Spanish and in North America by the British and French, and the role of men and women in the anticolonial struggle in the Americas[75]; the constructions of masculinity and femininity in the context of the frontier wars on the Australian and North American continents; the aftermath of these wars for the gender order of settler societies[76]; the connection between colonialism, gender, warfare, and the slave trade[77]; and nineteenth- and twentieth-century colonial and imperial conflicts and their gender order in the Americas, Asia, and Africa.[78] More recently, attention has turned to the gender dimensions of the Wars of Decolonization in the Middle East, Africa, and Asia, which reached their peak after 1945, and the anti-imperial and revolutionary struggle in Latin America, which intensified during the 1960s. A central theme of this scholarship is the gender-specific participation in these conflicts and its legacy for postwar gender relations.[79] But we need much more research on gender, military, and warfare in Africa, Asia, and Latin America. The state of research is still quite unbalanced and covers eastern and western Europe, North America, and Australia far better than other parts of the world.

Another important influence on the scholarship on gender and war since the 1990s was the move from political and social to cultural history.[80] The gendered culture of military and war and the gendering of war memories became new topics of research. Gender historians started to explore gendered representations of military and war in popular culture, literature, art, and music, as well as the gendering of military symbols, rituals, and festivals. Moreover, the gendered construction of individual and collective war memories and gendered practices of war commemoration became subjects of study.[81] In this scholarship, the concept of *identity*, understood as a highly gendered construction of the qualities, beliefs, and expressions that define a person, group, institution, nation, or state, became a key theoretical element. War memories proved crucial for the creation of collective identities of armies, nations, and states. For this reason, war memories are vitally important and at the same time contested in postwar societies; the gendering of these memories is a central part of social reordering.[82]

The widening of the temporal scope was another important change in the historiography of gender, war, and the military since the 1990s. An increasing number of publications explored the early modern period and the long nineteenth century.[83] Recent years have also seen the first studies on women and war in antiquity and the Middle Ages, but both periods still need much more research.[84] One of the first subjects of the scholarship on the early modern period were "amazons" and cross-dressed women in the armed forces who appropriated the right to bear arms and to fight often disguised as men. These women created controversy in their own time and stirred the interest of gender historians because they challenged the gender order in a fundamental way and revealed the fluidity of gender constructions.[85] Historians of women and gender, furthermore, explored the lives of female camp followers—soldier's concubines and wives, sutlers, and prostitutes—in early modern armies and the situation of women who served officially as uniformed sutlers and laundry women or supplied such services in a less organized manner for nineteenth-century armies.[86] Moreover, the medical services that soldiers' and officers' wives, nuns, volunteers in patriotic women's associations, and trained nurses provided in different and changing ways for the military during armed conflicts became a subject of research, as did the professionalization of this service since the second half of the nineteenth century.[87] Scholarship also examined women's patriotic support for the nineteenth-century Wars of Nation-Building and the short- and long-term aftermath of their efforts.[88]

In general, however, there is still a dearth of publications on women, gender, and warfare prior to the twentieth century.[89] Even the gender dimension of the Thirty Years' War (1618–48)[90] and the Seven Years' War (1856–63),[91] two of the most important early modern conflicts, and the mid-nineteenth-century European Wars of Unification, which led to the foundation of the Italian nation-state in 1861 and the German one in 1871,[92] or the mid-nineteenth century conflicts in Latin America, like the devastating Paraguayan War, also known as the War of the Triple Alliance (1864–70), are vastly understudied. Eras of war that have been better explored by gender historians include the period of the transatlantic Wars of Revolutions and Independence (1770s to 1820s)[93]—and here in particular the American Revolutionary War (1775–83),[94] the Napoleonic Wars,[95] and the Spanish American Wars of Independence (1808–30)[96]—the Crimean War (1853–56),[97] and the American Civil War (1861–65).[98]

Despite all the research gaps that still exist, it is difficult to overlook the substantial contribution of women's and gender historians to the history of military and warfare. They both changed and raised a challenge to the historiography of the subject and contributed to its development a burgeoning field of research that gained growing recognition outside the circles of military history experts. The wide variety of methods and questions with which gender scholars are currently studying the military and war is remarkable, making it all the more troubling how little this is recognized by many historians and other experts of military and war, who continue to ignore research by gender scholars and often judge their work without really knowing it. Even today, mainstream studies can claim in an authoritative habitus to offer *the* history of military and/or war without systematically including the gender dimension. This finding reflects a continuing "gender blindness."

CONCEPTUALIZING GENDER, WAR, AND VIOLENCE

The development of the study of gender, the military, and war informs the approach and content of this handbook and our understanding of its key concepts: *gender, war*, and *violence*. It demonstrates that reflecting on the gender of the military and war can only be fruitful and yield new insights if we conceptualize *gender* as an analytical concept. As such, gender is, in the words of Joan W. Scott, "above all an invitation to think critically about how the meanings of sexed bodies are produced, deployed, and changed."[99] This demands that we abandon the notion still common among military historians that gender is something natural that can be taken for granted, as well as the widespread equation of gender with women. Research on the history of the military and war requires an understanding of gender as knowledge about sexual differences produced by culture and society—a knowledge that is always relative and produced in complex ways in specific historical discursive contexts. This knowledge refers not just to ideas, cultural representations, and practices, but also to economic, social, and political structures and institutions, laws and regulations, social movements, everyday behavior, and collective and individual identity formation. In short, it refers to everything that helps to shape political, economic, and social relationships. Gender operates in intersectionality with other "categories of difference," such as class, race, ethnicity, age, sexuality, age/generational affiliation, and familial status in a manner that orders the world asymmetrically and hierarchically, inseparable from its political, economic, and social organization.[100]

In contrast to many works by feminist scholars that focus on women, the military, and war, this handbook emphatically takes gender to refer to both women and men, along with the related constructions of femininity and masculinity, which are in turn entangled with other constructions of differences. In doing so, it avoids the implicit assumption guiding much of the existing literature that only women's relation to the military and war requires explanation—a way of thinking that regards men's place in the military and war as somehow self-evident and not worthy of exploration. Drawing on gender studies and the history of masculinity and war, the handbook approaches the relations of women *and* men as well as femininity *and* masculinity to the military and war as the variable outcomes of multiple historical processes and therefore in need of historical explanation.

The development of the scholarship since the 1980s demonstrates that this shift from women to gender is most fruitful for the history of military and war, which is of special interest to gender historians given the power of war to both radically destroy and force-fully impose order. From the perspective of the study of gender, this makes the military and war fascinating objects of research, because they exhibit the variability and contin-gency of specific regimes of gender and their discourses as well as their stability and longevity over time. More than four decades of research on the history of gender, the military, and war have brought to light the many ways in which armed conflict produced challenges to as well as confirmations of gender orders. At the same time, this research has highlighted how, conversely, gender helped shape the military and war in their his-torically specific forms.

Nonetheless, there is plenty of room for further advances. Studies of the history of gender and war tend to analyze changing constructions of gender in depth while treat-ing the military dimension of the subject in relatively general terms. The present hand-book aims for greater historical specificity by making full use of insights offered by the scholarship on both the history of military and war and the history of women and gen-der. Such an approach that emphasizes the historical specificity not only of gender but also of the military and war calls for a critical evaluation of the contested definitions of *war* and *violence*. From the perspective of gender history, every schematic conceptual-ization of these terms is problematic. Despite certain continuities, the form and content of war and violence are in constant flux, requiring us to historicize and contextualize them as deliberately as we do the concept of gender.

For a historical analysis that spans four centuries, we cannot rely on an understanding of war that is tailored for a specific period. Thus, the old and today canonical definition of war offered by the Prussian general and military theorist Carl von Clausewitz in his classic text *On War*, published in 1832, does not work for our project.[101] Clausewitz introduced a definition of war that reflected his experience of warfare in the era of the French Revolutionary and Napoleonic Wars (1792–1815). Accordingly, he defined war as "a clash of wills," "an act of force to compel our enemy to do our will," and "the con-tinuation of policy [*sic*] by other means." For him, war was the means to achieve a polit-ical goal that could not be analyzed in isolation from its purpose.[102] Therefore, he differentiated between "the nature of war" in general, which he thought had an essen-tial continuity, and the "character of individual wars," which could vary. In the brief history of warfare in *On War*, Clausewitz privileged "political change in explaining changes in war's character" over new military technologies. This clearly reflects devel-opments in his own lifetime. In the era of transatlantic revolutions, the decisive changes lay less in new weaponry than in the mobilization of "the resources of the state through its identification with the nation." The "people in arms," mobilized by patriotic-national ideas, fought against each other in "absolute wars" that aimed for the complete defeat of the enemy. Clausewitz's emphasis on politics, policy, and the nation-state was well suited for understanding the interstate conflicts among Western states in the nine-teenth and twentieth centuries. However, it is less helpful when applied to wars during the Middle Ages and the early modern period, the Wars of Empire and the Wars of Decolonization in the modern era, or the current Wars of Globalization.[103]

For a historical approach, which on the one hand aims to explore gender and the changing character of warfare over four centuries and in different regions of the globe beyond the so-called Western world, and on the other hand is interested in the gendered relations between war, the military, society, and culture, we need a more open understanding of war based on the changing historical practice of warfare. The definition should allow us to discern not only continuities and changes, but also the broad variety of intrastate and interstate, symmetrical and asymmetrical, small and large armed conflicts far beyond Europe and North America. A useful approach for such an understanding is offered by historian Hew Strachan and international relations scholar Sybille Scheipers in their 2011 volume *The Changing Character of War*. We suggest focusing on four of the five dimensions that define war for them: "First, war involves the use of force, although there can be states of war in which active hostilities are suspended, and some would argue that the threat of the use of war (as in the Cold War) constitutes war." But, in essence, combat in different forms is what defines war. "Second, war rests on contention. If one party attacks another, the other must respond for war to occur, or else what will follow will be murder, massacre, or occupation. This reaction means that possibly the most important feature of war is reciprocity." Third, "war assumes a degree of intensity and duration to the fighting: scale matters, and skirmishes and border clashes are not necessarily war." Fourth, "war is fought for some aim beyond fighting itself."[104] Strachan and Scheipers emphasize, in addition, that "those who fight do not do so in a private capacity," but we find this problematic, because several past and present armed conflicts were started because of motives like greed and the hunger for power and were and are organized as private enterprises.

Our understanding of war focuses on the mutual use of force to kill and injure people and to destroy military, economic, social, and cultural resources. The form and content of war depend on the specific historical context, which includes politics, economy, society, and culture. They are all affected by and in turn affect warfare. Such a conceptualization of the term *war*, which we use interchangeably with *armed conflict*, as historically specific and relational still leaves several questions open, especially from a gender perspective: When do wars start? When do they end? What is their short- and long-term aftermath? When does a postwar period end? Who counts as a party to war? Who or what is the object of the study of war?[105] In this handbook we try to give answers to these and other related questions with a focus on specific themes, periods, and regions. All the authors were asked to write a chapter on a theme pivotal for the study of gender, the military, and war and apply a regionally or temporally comparative or transnational approach. In accordance with our understanding of history writing, we emphasize the "non-unity of history" and avoid sweeping generalizations.

A comprehension of war that focuses on the use of force to kill, injure, and destroy must conceptualize the term *violence*, which is, like war, a highly contested concept. Violence can take many forms and possesses different characteristics, resulting in a broad range of definitions in different disciplines, some quite expansive and others very restrictive. The former tend to conceptualize violence in terms of a violation of rights and the latter as an intentional act of excessive or destructive force.[106] For the historical analysis of gender and war, a restrictive definition, which limits violence to an intentional physical attack by force, seems most useful.[107] When violence is conceptualized in this way as a "continuum in war"—a systematic part of each "war system"[108]—it too has to be historicized and contextualized. Only then can we identify and understand the widely varying, specific forms of violence and the different perceptions they engender. Our understanding follows legal scholar Willem de Haan, who calls violence "a multi-faceted, socially constructed and highly ambivalent phenomenon": "It is multifaceted because there are many forms of violence; it is socially constructed because who and what is considered as violent varies according to socio-cultural and historical conditions; and it is highly ambivalent in the ways it is socially sanctioned, legitimized and institutionalized, as well as culturally transmitted and experienced. Depending on context and perspective, violent actions may either be condemned and considered immoral, illegal and disruptive or admired and perceived as moral, legal and functional."[109]

Like war, violence is a highly gendered practice, which in the context of armed conflict encompasses two dimensions: the power to injure and the vulnerability to injury. Since antiquity, the former has been connoted as male and the latter as female.[110] One important aspect of the power to injure in war is *sexual violence*, which includes rape, sexual mutilation, sexualized torture, sexual humiliation, forced prostitution, sexual slavery, and forced pregnancies or abortions. Even though its victims are commonly imagined as female, they also can be male and of any age. And as the sexual assault of Iraqi detainees in the Abu Ghraib prison by female US soldiers during the Iraq War (2003–11) reminded the shocked public in 2003, women can be sexual perpetrators too.[111] Recent scholarship conceptualizes sexual violence as an inherent part of war violence, but emphasizes its varying pattern across conflicts, armed groups, and small units.[112] Rape was and is not necessarily "a weapon of war" or a "war strategy"; this depends on the specific historic context. The frequency of the rape of civilians, for example, has differed dramatically over time, as recent comparative work by political scientist Elisabeth Jean Wood has reminded us. She therefore suggested conceptualizing sexual violence in war, including rape, as a "practice," rather than as a "weapon" or "strategy."[113] Researchers in different disciplines also discussed the connections between genocide, femicide, and mass rape in war, which all aim in different ways for the "genocidal destruction" of a group. But their scholarship showed that here, too, a very careful analysis of individual conflicts is necessary. The fact that sexual violence occurs during a genocide does not make it automatically genocidal.[114] The purpose of war rape, for example, was often more to demonstrate and exercise power against the vanquished, to exact revenge, to weaken the opponent's morale, and/or to challenge the male, martial, or national honor of the enemy.[115] Only through a cautious historicization and contextualization of the three key concepts, gender, war, and violence, can the ways they interact and intersect be understood adequately.

WRITING A GENDER HISTORY OF WAR—THE HANDBOOK'S APPROACH

The handbook's approach is defined by its two central questions and our understanding of the three key concepts of gender, war, and violence. The state of research on gender and war frames its temporal and regional scope as well as its content, determining the possibilities and limits of our project. One major aim of the handbook is to take a long view on the continuities and changes in the history of gender and war. Because of the small number of studies on the ancient and medieval periods, we decided to start in the early modern era with the Thirty Years' War and its long-term aftermath, because it was one of the longest and most destructive conflicts in European history.[116] The handbook ends in the post–Cold War era with its global conflicts. Its chapters are organized chronologically in four parts. The first part starts with the Thirty Years' War and early colonial conquests and ends with the Wars of Revolution and Independence, covering the period from the 1600s to the 1820s. The second part explores the nineteenth century Wars of Nations and Empires starting in the 1830s and ending in the 1910s. The third part examines the Age of the World Wars between the 1910s and the 1940s. And the fourth part, starting in the 1940s, includes the Global Cold War, the Wars of Decolonization, and the Wars of Globalization in the post–Cold War Era that started in the early 1990s. It ends in the second decade of the twenty-first century. Because of the state of research, the first half of the twentieth century receives more treatment than any other period.

The boundaries between these four chronological parts are fluid and vary depending on the themes and regions covered. Long-term developments and links between periods are addressed throughout. Several thematic chapters thus cross the boundaries of the four time periods, which we employ mainly as starting points for explorations of transformations in gender and modes of warfare over time. This helps us to bring into view variable and changing ways of organizing and waging war, with an emphasis on their mutually constitutive relations with gender. With our approach, we do not intend to present the military and war as prime motors of historical change. We do, however, believe that a chronological structure of the handbook provides a good starting point for an exploration of continuities and changes in the relation of the military, war, and gender.

As the overview of the development of scholarship on gender and war reveals, most of the existing work consists of detailed and contextualized case studies with a relatively limited temporal and spatial scope. In emphasizing the many mutually constitutive relations between gender and war, this handbook draws on the wealth of available studies, which for a long time focused primarily on eastern and western Europe, North America, and Australia. Only later and mainly in the context of colonial history was the subject of gender and war studied for Africa, Asia, and Latin America. The handbook tries to take the existing body of work in a new direction by integrating it into a framework that covers a longer time span and a wider geographical terrain than is usually the case. In doing so, we put particular emphasis on transnational relations and comparisons between different regions and periods, features that in today's literature are still rare.

While the temporal scope of the handbook is limited to the periods referred to as early modern and modern, our narratives do not assume a given, singular nature of "modernity" or its inevitable and unidirectional rise. Quite the contrary, we question these assumptions from the perspective of a gender history of war. We ask, for instance, what happens when gender is integrated into histories of war and state formation, with their conventional assumption of clear-cut boundaries between state and society, military, and civilian spheres. A focus on gender shows that these presumably firm boundaries partly rested on their symbolic association with notions of dichotomous gender differences and that these associations served to mask the persistent instability of such boundaries.

In a similar way, the handbook engages with recent developments in colonial, postcolonial, and global history to move beyond the nation-state and "the West" as the seemingly self-evident frameworks for the writing of history. For this reason, we chose the title "Oxford Handbook on Gender, War, *and* the Western World." We neither wanted to claim to be writing *the* "Oxford Handbook on Gender and War" nor that on "Gender and War *in* the Western World." The former title has an authoritative ring that would not reflect our approach to gender history, while the latter would connect gender and war too emphatically with the Western world. By using "*and*" in the title, we attempt to signal our effort to "provincialize" Europe and the Americas by approaching their histories as particular histories among others.[117] The so-called Western world is treated in the handbook both as a changing and contested construct and as a historically contingent phenomenon shaped by and transformed through colonial and imperial expansion that created a nexus of complex relations with long-lasting consequences in which the so-called Western world was embedded. Even the nineteenth- and twentieth-century history of gender and war in Europe and North America can therefore not be understood without the long-term processes of colonization and empire-building originating in sixteenth-century Europe and their aftermath in the Americas, Africa, Asia, and Australia.[118] For the study of nation- and empire-building as well colonial and imperial expansion insights drawn from the history of gender and war serve valuable heuristic functions. They demand a critical rethinking of prevailing assumptions about the nature of the nation-state and its putative rise to dominance in the nineteenth and twentieth centuries, as well as the connections between nation-state building, colonial expansion and the creation of empires. A focus on gender is a useful tool for illuminating and thinking about the coexistence of sovereignty and subjugation, of nation-state and empire, in the modern world. It shows that we cannot and should not study empires and nation-states independently of each other.

We also do not see warfare in the Western world as a universal model or believe in the idea of larger, allegedly coherent civilizational ways of war. We do not follow, for example, Geoffrey Parker, who has posited a "Western way of war" and emphasized its superiority over other types of warfare. According to Parker, this supposed Western way of war had been characterized by five elements, which in turn explain its success: technological superiority and the adoption of new technology; superior discipline and training; a long tradition of aggressive, combat-oriented military theory; the ability to innovate and adapt to new challenges; and the creation of a political economy and state structure to sustain the superior mobilization of military resources.[119]

To realize the handbook's innovative and challenging agenda, we decided early on to avoid chapters that focus on specific regions or countries. Instead, we identified five historical processes that provide a framework for the analysis of regional and temporal developments: first, changes in the form and technology of warfare and of specific types of war (such as mercenary wars, national wars, colonial and imperial wars, frontier warfare, total wars, wars of decolonization); second, state formation and nation-building; third, colonialism and imperialism; fourth, national liberation and anticolonialism; and fifth, the promulgation of war and violence and the attempts to control and prevent them (such as state control, peace movements, international agreements, institutions, and laws). The gendered analysis of these five historical processes sets the stage for the study of the ways in which gender and war have mutually shaped each other. In addition, we identified six themes that are central for the history of gender and war in the four centuries covered. These themes include gendered representations of the military and war; gendered war mobilization and war support by society; gendered experiences on the battlefronts and the so-called home fronts; gender, war, and (sexual) violence; gender, military service, and citizenship; and gendered demobilization, postwar societies, and war memories.

The organization of the handbook reflects its major aim, a longue-durée perspective on the history of gender and war that explores continuity and changes. Each of the four parts opens with a longer chapter that discusses characteristics and conceptualizations of the history of warfare during the period, provides a broad overview of the developments, reflects on them from the perspective of gender, and examines central themes of the research on gender and war. Each part continues with five to ten essays with varying thematic, geographical, and temporal scopes. As a supplement to the select bibliographies provided for each chapter, a much more extensive bibliography for each chapter and much more material can be found on the website of *GWonline, the Bibliography, Filmography, and Webography on Gender and War since 1600*, a digital humanities project related to this handbook, based at the University of North Carolina at Chapel Hill.[120] We hope that, taken together, the handbook and the digital humanities project will not only make the extensive research in the field of gender and war available to a broad audience beyond experts in women's and gender studies, but also pose a decided challenge to the conventional historiography on military and war, with its continuing gender blindness.

NOTES

1. Josephine Karg, "The Role of Russian Symbolist Painting for Modernity: Mikhail Vrubel's Reduced Forms," in *The Symbolic Roots of Modern Art*, ed. Michelle Facos and Thor J. Mednick (Farnham: Ashgate, 2015), 47–59, 54. On Pavel Filonov, see John E. Bowlt, "Pavel Filonov: His Painting and His Theory," *Russian Review* 34, no. 3 (1975): 282–92.

2. Karin Hausen, "Die Nicht-Einheit der Geschichte als historiographische Herausforderung: Zur historischen Relevanz und Anstößigkeit der Geschlechtergeschichte," in *Geschlechtergeschichte und Allgemeine Geschichte: Herausforderungen und Perspektiven*, ed. Hans Medick and Anne-Charlott Trepp (Göttingen: Wallstein Verlag, 1998), 17–55.

3. Bonnie G. Smith, *The Gender of History: Men, Women and Historical Practice* (Cambridge, MA: Harvard University Press, 1998); Angelika Epple, *Empfindsame Geschichtsschreibung: Eine Geschlechtergeschichte der Historiographie zwischen Aufklärung und Historismus* (Cologne: Böhlau, 2003); Angelika Epple and Angelika Schaser, eds., *Gendering Historiography: Beyond National Canons* (Frankfurt am Main: Campus, 2009); and Falko Schnicke, *Die männliche Disziplin: Zur Vergeschlechtlichung der deutschen Geschichtswissenschaft, 1780–1900* (Göttingen: Wallstein, 2015).

4. Hausen, "Die Nicht-Einheit," 25–26 and 36–37.

5. Lynn Hunt, "The Challenge of Gender: Deconstruction of Categories and Reconstruction of Narratives in Gender History," in Medick and Trepp, *Geschlechtergeschichte*, 57–98.

6. For a description of guiding principles for Oxford handbooks, see the introductory comment at https://global.oup.com/academic/content/series/o/oxford-handbooks-ohbk/?cc=nl&lang=en&, accessed May 26, 2017.

7. See, for example, Julian Lindley-French and Yves Boyer, eds., *The Oxford Handbook of War* (Oxford: Oxford University Press, 2012). They aim "to bring together many different and differing perspectives and experiences to consider war" and do not have even *one* chapter on gender. See Julian Lindley-French and Yves Boyer, "Introduction," in Lindley-French and Boyer, *The Oxford Handbook of War*, 1–6. Also lacking any inclusion of women/gender are Geoffrey Parker, ed., *Cambridge History of Warfare* (Cambridge: Cambridge University Press, 2005); and Melvyn P. Leffler and Odd Arne Westad, eds., *The Cambridge History of the Cold War*, 3 vols. (Cambridge: Cambridge University Press, 2010).

8. One or, at best, two chapters that consider women/gender are included in John Horne, ed., *Companion to World War I* (Chichester, UK: Wiley–Blackwell, 2010); Roger Chickering et al., eds., *The Cambridge History of War and the Modern World* (Cambridge: Cambridge University Press, 2012); Thomas W. Zeiler and Daniel M. DuBois, eds., *A Companion to World War II* (Chichester, UK: Wiley–Blackwell, 2013); John Ferris and Evan Mawdsley, eds., *The Cambridge History of the Second World War*, vol. 1, *Fighting the War* (Cambridge: Cambridge University Press, 2015); Richard J. B. Bosworth and Joseph A. Maiolo, eds., *The Cambridge History of the Second World War*, vol. 2, *Politics and Ideology* (Cambridge: Cambridge University Press, 2015); Michael Geyer and Adam Tooze, eds., *The Cambridge History of the Second World War*, vol. 3, *Total War: Economy, Society and Culture* (Cambridge: Cambridge University Press, 2015); Richard H. Immerman and Petra Goedde, eds., *The Oxford Handbook of the Cold War* (Oxford: Oxford University Press, 2012); and Dan Stone, ed., *The Oxford Handbook of Postwar European History* (Oxford: Oxford University Press, 2012). Only *The Cambridge History of the First World War*, ed. Jay Winter, 3 vols. (Cambridge: Cambridge University Press, 2014) does a better job by including in its third volume on civil society several chapters that integrate or focus on gender/women. Even better in this respect is *1914–1918-Online: International Encyclopedia of the First World War*, ed. Oliver Janz et al., accessed May 21, 2017, http://www.1914-1918-online.net/.

9. Dennis E. Showalter, "A Modest Plea for Drums and Trumpets," *Military Affairs* 39, no. 2 (1975): 71–74; and Showalter, "History, Military," in *The Reader's Companion to Military*

History, ed. Robert Cowley and Geoffrey Parker (Boston: Houghton Mifflin, 1996), 204–07.

10. See Torbjörn L. Knutsen, "Old, Unhappy, Far-off Things: The New Military History of Europe," *Journal of Peace Research* 24, no. 1 (1987): 87–98; Michael S. Neiberg, "War and Society," in *Palgrave Advances in Modern Military History*, ed. Matthew Hughes and William James Philpott (New York: Palgrave Macmillan, 2006), 41–60; and Joanna Burke, "New Military History," in Hughes and Philpott, *Palgrave Advances*, 258–79.

11. See Thomas Kühne and Benjamin Ziemann, eds., *Was ist Militärgeschichte?* (Paderborn: Schöningh, 2000); Hughes and Philpott, *Palgrave Advances*; and Stephen Morillo, *What Is Military History?*, 2nd ed. (Cambridge, MA: Polity Press, 2013).

12. See Morillo, *What Is Military*, 96–102; Anne Lipp, "Diskurs und Praxis: Militärgeschichte als Kulturgeschichte," in Kühne and Ziemann, *Was ist Militärgeschichte*, 211–28; and Wayne E. Lee, "Mind and Matter: Cultural Analysis in American Military History: A Look at the State of the Field," *Journal of American History* 93, no. 4 (2007): 1116–42.

13. See Dennis E. Showalter, "Militärgeschichte als Operationsgeschichte: Deutsche und amerikanische Paradigmen," in Kühne and Ziemann, *Was ist Militärgeschichte*, 115–26; and Robert M. Citino, "Review Essay: Military Histories Old and New: A Reintroduction," *American Historical Review*, 112, no. 4 (2007): 1070–90.

14. Geoffrey Best, *War and Society in Revolutionary Europe, 1770–1870* (London: Fontana, 1982), 18.

15. On this widely used yet analytically imprecise notion of the "mainstream," see Karen Hagemann and Jean H. Quataert, "Gendering Modern German History: Comparing Historiographies and Academic Cultures in Germany and the United States through the Lens of Gender," in *Gendering Modern German History: Themes, Debates, Revisions*, ed. Hagemann and Quataert (New York: Berghahn Books, 2007), 1–39.

16. Cynthia Enloe, *Does Khaki Become You? The Militarization of Women's Lives* (Boston: South End Press, 1983); Enloe, *Bananas, Beaches and Bases: Making Feminist Sense of International Politics* (London: Pandora, 1989); Enloe, *Maneuvers: The International Politics of Militarizing Women's Lives* (Berkeley: University of California Press, 2000); Jean Bethke Elshtain, *Women and War* (New York: Basic Books, 1987); and Elshtain and Sheila Tobias, eds., *Women, Militarism and War: Essays in History, Politics, and Social Theory* (Savage, MD: Rowman & Littlefield, 1990).

17. Enloe, *Does Khaki*, esp. 207–20.

18. Elshtain, *Women and War*.

19. Nancy Loring Goldman, ed., *Female Soldiers: Combatants or Noncombatants? Historical and Contemporary Perspectives* (Westport, CT: Greenwood Press, 1982); Klaus Latzel et al., eds., *Soldatinnen: Gewalt und Geschlecht im Krieg vom Mittelalter bis Heute* (Paderborn: Schöningh, 2011); and Barton C. Hacker and Margaret Vining, eds., *A Companion to Women's Military History* (Leiden: Brill, 2012).

20. See, for example, April Carter, *Peace Movements: International Protest and World Politics since 1945* (London: Longman, 1992); and Cynthia Cockburn, *Antimilitarism: Political and Gender Dynamics of Peace Movements* (New York: Palgrave Macmillan, 2012).

21. See Sandra C. Taylor, *Vietnamese Women at War: Fighting for Ho Chi Minh and the Revolution* (Lawrence: University Press of Kansas, 1999); and the chapter by Raphaëlle Branche on "Gender, the Wars of Decolonization, and the Decline of Empires after 1945" in this handbook.

22. For the research, see the chapter by Karen Hagemann and D'Ann Campbell on "Post-1945 Western Militaries, Female Soldiers, and Gay and Lesbian Rights" in this handbook.

23. One study by a well-known military historian that pointedly articulated the danger of this "threat" is Martin van Creveld, *Men, Women and War* (London: Cassell, 2001).

24. See Hagemann and Campbell, "Post-1945 Western Militaries" in this handbook.

25. One of the first book publications on this fraught subject was Alexandra Stiglmayer, ed., *Mass Rape: The War against Women in Bosnia-Herzegovina* (Lincoln: University of Nebraska Press, 1994). See also the chapter by Dubravka Zarkov on "Conceptualizing Sexual Violence in Post–Cold War Global Conflicts" in this handbook.

26. On the Rwandan genocide, see Georgina Holmes, *Women and War in Rwanda: Gender, Media and the Representation of Genocide* (London: I. B. Tauris, 2014).

27. An early article was Roger W. Smith, "Women and Genocide: Notes on an Unwritten History," *Holocaust and Genocide Studies* 8, no. 3 (1994): 315–34. More generally, see Adam Jones, ed., *Gendercide and Genocide* (Nashville, TN: Vanderbilt University Press, 2004); Elisa von Joeden-Forgey, "Gender and Genocide," in *The Oxford Handbook of Genocide Studies*, ed. Donald Bloxham and A. Dirk Moses (Oxford: Oxford University Press, 2015), 61–80; and Amy E. Randall, *Genocide and Gender in the Twentieth Century: A Comparative Survey* (London: Bloomsbury Academic, 2015); on gender, see Adam Jones, *Genocide: A Comprehensive Introduction* (London: Routledge, 2015), 464–98.

28. See Brendan Simms and D. J. B. Trim, *Humanitarian Intervention: A History* (Cambridge: Cambridge University Press, 2011). From a gender perspective, see Cynthia Cockburn and Dubravka Zarkov, eds., *The Postwar Moment: Militaries, Masculinities and International Peacekeeping* (London: Lawrence & Wishart, 2002); and Sandra Whitworth, *Men, Militarism and UN Peacekeeping: A Gendered Analysis* (Boulder, CO: Lynne Rienner, 2004). For the research, see also the chapters by Sandra Whitworth on "The United Nations, Gendered Human Rights, and Peacekeeping since 1945," and Kristen P. Williams on "Gender, Wars of Globalization, and Humanitarian Interventions since the End of the Cold War" in this handbook.

29. Joshua S. Goldstein, *War and Gender: How Gender Shapes the War System and Vice Versa* (Cambridge: Cambridge University Press, 2001), 9.

30. Laura Sjoberg, *Gendering Global Conflict: Toward a Feminist Theory of War* (New York: Columbia University Press, 2013), 3. See also Sjoberg, "Introduction to Security Studies: Feminist Contributions," *Security Studies* 18, no. 2 (2009): 183–213. Important publications include Laura J. Shepherd, *Gender, Violence and Security: Discourse as Practice* (London: Zed Books, 2008); Laura Sjoberg and Sandra Via, eds., *Gender, War and Militarism: Feminist Perspectives* (Westport, CT: Praeger Security, 2010); Joyce P. Kaufman and Kristen P. Williams, *Women and War: Gender Identity and Activism in Times of Conflict* (Sterling, VA: Kumarian Press, 2010); and Kaufman and Williams, *Women at War, Women Building Peace: Challenging Gender Norm* (Boulder, CO: Lynne Rienner, 2013); J. Ann Tickner, *A Feminist Voyage through International Relations* (Oxford: Oxford University Press, 2014); Tickner and Laura Sjoberg, *Feminism and International Relations: Conversations about the Past, Present, and Future* (London: Routledge, 2011); Nicole Detraz, *International Security and Gender* (Cambridge, MA: Polity, 2012); and Laura Sjoberg, *Gender, War, and Conflict* (Cambridge, MA: Polity, 2014).

31. Sjoberg, *Gendering Global Conflict*, 2–3; for the discussion, see Sara Meger et al., "Review Symposium: Gender and Politics. A Discussion of Laura Sjoberg's Gendering Global Conflict: Toward a Feminist Theory of War," *Perspectives on Politics* 12, no. 1 (2014): 168–79. On the recent development of the debate on political and social science, see also Fionnuala

Ní Aoláin et al., eds., *The Oxford Handbook of Gender and Conflict* (Oxford: Oxford University Press, 2017), especially the chapter by Dubravka Zarkov, "From Women and War to Gender and Conflict?: Feminist Trajectories," 17–24; as well as Simona Sharoni et al., eds., *Handbook on Gender and War* (Celtenham: Edward Elgar, 2016).

32. Monographs from the 1970s were Arthur Marwick, *Women at War, 1914–1918* (London: Croom Helm, 1977); Dörte Winkler, *Frauenarbeit im "Dritten Reich"* (Hamburg: Hoffmann und Campe, 1977); and Leila J. Rupp, *Mobilizing Women for War: German and American Propaganda, 1939–1945* (Princeton, NJ: Princeton University Press, 1978). Monographs from the 1980s include Maurine Weiner Greenwald, *Women, War and Work: The Impact of World War I on Women Workers in the United States* (Westport, CT: Greenwood Press, 1980); Gail Braybon, *Women Workers in the First World War: The British Experience* (London: Croom Helm, 1981); Maureen Honey, *Creating Rosie the Riveter: Class, Gender, and Propaganda during World War II* (Amherst: University of Massachusetts Press, 1984); Ruth Roach Pierson, *They're Still Women after All: The Second World War and Canadian Womanhood* (Toronto: McClelland & Stewart, 1986); Serna Berger Gluck, *Rosie the Riveter Revisited: Women, the War, and Social Change* (Boston: Plume, 1987); and Ute Daniel, *Arbeiterfrauen in der Kriegsgesellschaft: Beruf, Familie und Politik im Ersten Weltkrieg* (Göttingen: Vandenhoeck & Ruprecht, 1989), English translation, *The War from Within: German Working-Class Women in the First World War* (Oxford: Berg, 1997).

33. Influential studies of the late 1980s and early 1990s were Elaine Tyler May, *Homeward Bound: American Families in the Cold War Era* (New York: Basic Books, 1988); Robert Moeller, *Protecting Motherhood: Women and the Family in the Politics of Postwar Germany* (Berkeley: University of California Press, 1993); Susanne Rouette, *Sozialpolitik als Geschlechterpolitik: Die Regulierung der Frauenarbeit nach dem Ersten Weltkrieg* (Frankfurt am Main: Campus, 1993); Susan Kent, *Making Peace: The Reconstruction of Gender in Interwar Britain* (Princeton, NJ: Princeton University Press, 1993); Mary Louise Roberts, *Civilization without Sexes: Reconstructing Gender in Postwar France, 1917–1927* (Chicago: University of Chicago Press, 1994); Angela Woollacott, *On Her Their Lives Depend: Munitions Workers in the Great War* (Berkeley: University of California Press, 1994); Birthe Kundrus, *Kriegerfrauen: Familienpolitik und Geschlechtsverhältnisse im Ersten und Zweiten Weltkrieg* (Hamburg: Christians, 1995); and Laura Lee Downs, *Manufacturing Inequality: Gender Division in the French and British Metalworking Industries, 1914–1939* (Ithaca, NY: Cornell University Press, 1995).

34. Dorothee Wierling, "The History of Everyday Life and Gender Relations: On Historical and Historiographical Relationships," in *The History of Everyday Life: Reconstructing Historical Experiences and Ways of Life*, ed. Alf Lüdtke (Princeton, NJ: Princeton University Press, 1995), 149–68.

35. For an introduction, see Catherine Belsey, *Poststructuralism: A Very Short Introduction* (Oxford: Oxford University Press, 2002); Simon Gunn, *History and Cultural Theory* (Harlow: Pearson Longman, 2006); and Alessandro Arcangeli, *Cultural History: A Concise Introduction* (London: Routledge, 2012).

36. Natalie Zemon Davis, "Women's History in Transition: The European Case," *Feminist Studies* 3, no. 3/4 (1976): 83–103, 90.

37. Kathleen Canning, "Feminist History after the Linguistic Turn: Historicizing Discourse and Experience," *Signs* 19, no. 2 (1994): 368–404, 370–71.

38. Joan W. Scott, "Gender: A Useful Category of Historical Analysis," *American Historical Review* 98, no. 4 (1986): 1053–75; and Scott, *Gender and the Politics of History* (New York: Columbia University Press, 1999).

39. Scott, "Gender," 1067–69.

40. Joan W. Scott, "Unanswered Questions," in "AHR Forum: Revisiting 'Gender: A Useful Category of Historical Analysis,'" *American Historical Review* 113, no. 5 (2008): 1422–1429, 1423.

41. For the international development of the historiography on women and gender, see Karen Offen et al., eds., *Writing Women's History: International Perspectives* (Bloomington: Indiana University Press, 1991); Johanna Gehmacher, *Frauen- und Geschlechtergeschichte: Positionen, Perspektiven* (Innsbruck: Studien-Verlag, 2003); Kathleen Canning, *Gender History in Practice: Historical Perspectives on Bodies, Class, and Citizenship* (Ithaca, NY: Cornell University Press, 2006); Hagemann and Quataert, *Gendering Modern German History*; "AHR Forum: Revisiting 'Gender: A Useful Category of Historical Analysis,'" *American Historical Review* 113, no. 5 (2008): 1344–430; Alexandra Shepard and Garthine Walker, eds., *Gender and Change: Agency, Chronology and Periodisation* (Oxford: Wiley–Blackwell, 2009); Laura Lee Downs, *Writing Gender History* (London: Bloomsbury Academic, 2010); Sonya O. Rose, *What Is Gender History?* (Cambridge, MA: Polity Press, 2010); and Renata Ago et al., eds., *Genre, femmes, histoire en Europe: France, Italie, Espagne, Autriche* (Nanterre: Presses universitaires de Paris Ouest, 2014).

42. Joan W. Scott, "Rewriting History," in *Behind the Lines: Gender and the Two World Wars*, ed. Margaret R. Higonnet et al. (New Haven, CT: Yale University Press, 1987), 21–30, 26.

43. Esp. Marwick, *Women*.

44. For example, Susan R. Grayzel, "Women and Men," in Horne, *Companion to World War I*, 263–78, 274; also Daniel, *War*.

45. Françoise Thébaud, "The Great War and the Triumph of Sexual Division," in *A History of Women in the West*, vol. 5, *Toward a Cultural Identity in the Twentieth Century*, ed. Françoise Thébaud (Cambridge, MA: Harvard University Press, 1994), 21–75, 23. For example, Braybon, *Women Workers*; and later Penny Summerfield, *Reconstructing Women's Wartime Lives: Discourse and Subjectivity in Oral Histories of the Second World War* (Manchester: Manchester University Press, 1998).

46. Margaret R. Higonnet and Patrice L.-R. Higonnet, "The Double Helix," in Higonnet, *Behind the Lines*, 31–50; the quote is from the introduction to the volume, p. 6.

47. Claudia Koonz, *Mothers in the Fatherland: Women, the Family and Nazi Politics* (New York: St. Martin's Press, 1988).

48. Gisela Bock, "Die Frauen und der Nationalsozialismus," *Geschichte und Gesellschaft* 15, no. 4 (1989): 563–79.

49. On the *Historikerinnenstreit*, see Atina Grossmann, "Feminist Debates about Women and National Socialism," *Gender & History* 3, no. 3 (1991): 350–58; Adelheid von Saldern, "Victims or Perpetrators? Controversies about the Role of Women in the Nazi State," in *Nazism and German Society 1933–1945*, ed. David Crew (London: Routledge, 1994), 141–66; Carola Sachse, "Frauenforschung zum Nationalsozialismus," *Mittelweg 36*, no. 6 (1997): 24–42; and Claudia Koonz, "A Tributary and a Mainstream: Gender, Public Memory, and the Historiography of Nazi Germany," in Hagemann and Quataert, *Gendering Modern German*, 147–67.

50. Wendy Lower, *Hitler's Furies: German Women in the Nazi Killing Fields* (Boston: Houghton Mifflin, 2013).

51. For the development of the research, see Judith Tydor Baumel-Schwartz, *Double Jeopardy: Gender and the Holocaust* (Portland, OR: Vallentine Mitchell, 1998); Insa Eschebach et al., eds., *Gedächtnis und Geschlecht: Deutungsmuster in Darstellungen des Nationalsozialistischen Genozids* (Frankfurt am Main: Campus, 2002); Gisela Bock, ed., *Genozid und Geschlecht:*

Jüdische Frauen im Nationalsozialistischen Lagersystem (Frankfurt am Main: Campus, 2005); Lisa Pine, "Gender and Holocaust Victims: A Reappraisal," *Journal of Jewish Identities* 1, no. 2 (2008): 121–41; Myrna Goldenberg and Amy H. Shapiro, eds., *Different Horrors, Same Hell: Gender and the Holocaust* (Seattle: University of Washington Press, 2013); Sonja M. Hedgepeth and Rochelle G. Saidel, eds., *Sexual Violence against Jewish Women during the Holocaust* (Hanover, NH: University Press of New England, 2010); and Andrea Petö et al., eds., *Women and the Holocaust: New Perspectives and Challenges* (Warsaw: Instytut Badań Literackich PAN, 2015).

52. See Kirsten Heinsohn et al., eds. *Zwischen Karriere und Verfolgung: Handlungsräume von Frauen im nationalsozialistischen Deutschland* (Frankfurt am Main: Campus 1997); Sybille Steinbacher, ed., *Volksgenossinnen: Frauen in der NS-Volksgemeinschaft* (Göttingen: Wallstein, 2007); Johanna Gehmacher and Gabriella Hauch, eds., *Frauen- und Geschlechtergeschichte des Nationalsozialismus: Fragestellungen, Perspektiven, neue Forschungen* (Innsbruck: Studienverlag, 2007); and Koonz, "A Tributary."

53. Christopher R. Browning et al., eds., *Holocaust Scholarship: Personal Trajectories and Professional Interpretations* (Basingstoke: Palgrave Macmillan, 2015).

54. Victoria De Grazia, *How Fascism Ruled Women: Italy, 1922–1945* (Berkeley: University of California Press, 1993).

55. Mary Nash, *Defying Male Civilization: Women in the Spanish Civil War* (Denver, CO: Arden Press, 1995).

56. See, for this literature, the chapters by Jean H. Quataert, "Changing Modes of Warfare and the Gendering of Military Medical Care, 1850s–1920s," and Karen Hagemann, "History and Memory of Female Military Service in the Age of World Wars," in this handbook.

57. Klaus Theweleit, *Männerphantasien* (Frankfurt am Main: Verlag Roter Stern, 1977), English translation, *Male Fantasies* (Minneapolis: University of Minnesota Press, 1987).

58. George L. Mosse, *Fallen Soldiers: Reshaping the Memory of the World Wars* (New York: Oxford University Press, 1990); Mosse, *The Nationalization of the Masses: Political Symbolism and Mass Movements in Germany from the Napoleonic Wars through the Third Reich* (New York: H. Fertig, 1975); and Mosse, *Nationalism and Sexuality: Respectability and Abnormal Sexuality in Modern Europe* (New York: H. Fertig, 1985).

59. Early studies are Michael C. Adams, *The Great Adventure: Male Desire and the Coming of World War I* (Bloomington: Indiana University Press, 1990); Graham Dawson, *Soldier Heroes: British Adventures, Empire and the Imagining of Masculinities* (London: Routledge, 1994); and Joanna Bourke, *Dismembering the Male: Men's Bodies, Britain and the Great War* (Chicago: University of Chicago Press, 1996).

60. See Karen Hagemann, "'We Need Not Concern Ourselves . . .' Militärgeschichte—Geschlechtergeschichte—Männergeschichte: Anmerkungen zur Forschung," *Traverse. Zeitschrift für Geschichte. Revue D'Histoire* 31, no. 1 (1998): 75–94; Stefan Dudink et al., eds., *Masculinities in Politics and War: Gendering Modern History* (Manchester: Manchester University Press, 2004); and Robert A. Nye, "Western Masculinities in War and Peace," *American Historical Review* 112, no. 2 (2007): 417–38. See also the chapters by Stefan Dudink on "Citizenship, Mass Mobilization, and Masculinity in a Transatlantic Perspective, 1770s–1870s," Robert A. Nye on "War Mobilization, Gender, and Military Culture in Nineteenth-Century Western Societies," Marilyn Lake on "The 'White Man,' Race, and Imperial War during the Long Nineteenth Century," Thomas Kühne on "States, Military Masculinities, and Combat in the Age of World Wars," and Richard Smith on "Colonial Soldiers, Race, and Military Masculinities during and beyond World Wars I and II" in this handbook.

61. For the contested concept of hegemonic masculinity, see R. W. Connell, *Masculinities* (Berkeley: University of California Press, 1995); Connell and James W. Messerschmidt, "Hegemonic Masculinity: Rethinking the Concept," *Gender and Society* 19, no. 6 (2005): 829–59; and John Tosh, "Hegemonic, Masculinity and the History of Gender," in Dudink et al., *Masculinities*, 41–60.

62. Exemplary studies are Thomas Kühne, *Kameradschaft: Die Soldaten des Nationalsozialistischen Krieges und das 20. Jahrhundert* (Göttingen: Vandenhoeck & Ruprecht, 2006), English translation: *The Rise and Fall of Comradeship: Hitler's Soldiers, Male Bonding and Mass Violence in the Twentieth Century* (Cambridge: Cambridge University Press, 2017); Michael Roper, *The Secret Battle: Emotional Survival in the Great War* (Manchester: Manchester University Press, 2009); and Jason Crouthamel, *An Intimate History of the Front: Masculinity, Sexuality, and German Soldiers in the First World War* (New York: Palgrave Macmillan, 2014).

63. For the research, see Dudink, "Citizenship, Mass Mobilization" in this handbook; and Dudink and Karen Hagemann, "Masculinity in Politics and War in the Age of Democratic Revolutions, 1750–1850," in Dudink et al., *Masculinities*, 3–21.

64. The following anthologies represent the development of research since the 1990s: Miriam Cooke and Angela Woollacott, eds., *Gendering War Talk* (Princeton, NJ: Princeton University Press, 1993); Joy Damousi and Marilyn Lake, eds., *Gender and War: Australians at War in the Twentieth Century* (Cambridge: Cambridge University Press, 1995); Billie Melman, ed., *Borderlines: Genders and Identities in War and Peace, 1870–1930* (New York: Routledge, 1997); Karen Hagemann and Stephanie Schüler-Springorum, eds., *Home/Front: The Military, War, and Gender in Twentieth-Century Germany* (Oxford: Berg, 2002); Nicole Ann Dombrowski, ed., *Women and War in the Twentieth Century: Enlisted with or without Consent* (New York: Routledge, 2004); Ana Carden-Coyne, ed., *Gender and Conflict since 1914: Historical and Interdisciplinary Perspectives* (New York: Palgrave, 2012); and Christa Hämmerle et al., eds., *Gender and the First World War* (Basingstoke: Palgrave, Macmillan, 2014); and David J. Ulbrich and Bobby A. Wintermute, *Race and Gender in Modern Western Warfare* (Berlin: de Gruyter, 2018). See also the literature in the chapters by Susan R. Grayzel on "Total Warfare, Gender, and the 'Home Front' in Europe during the First and Second World Wars," Kimberly Jensen on "Citizenship and Gender on the American and Canadian Home Fronts during the First and Second World Wars," and Karen Hagemann on "Gender, Demobilization, and the Reordering of Societies after the First and Second World Wars" in this handbook.

65. See Dagmar Herzog, ed., *Brutality and Desire: War and Sexuality in Europe's Twentieth Century* (Basingstoke: Palgrave Macmillan, 2009); Elizabeth D. Heineman, ed., *Sexual Violence in Conflict Zones: From the Ancient World to the Era of Human Rights* (Philadelphia: University of Pennsylvania Press, 2011); and Raphaëlle Branche and Fabrice Virgili, eds., *Rape in Wartime* (Basingstoke: Palgrave Macmillan, 2012). See also the chapters by Regina Mühlhäuser on "Sexuality, Sexual Violence, and the Military in the Age of the World Wars," and Zarkov, "Conceptualizing Sexual Violence" in this handbook.

66. See Michael Barnett, *Empire of Humanity: A History of Humanitarianism* (Ithaca, NY: Cornell University Press, 2011); Glenda Sluga, *Internationalism in the Age of Nationalism* (Philadelphia: University of Pennsylvania Press, 2013); and Karen Garner, *Shaping a Global Women's Agenda: Women's NGOs and Global Governance, 1925–1985* (Manchester: Manchester University Press, 2010). For the research, see the chapters by Jean H. Quataert on "Changing Modes of Warfare," and Glenda Sluga on "Gender, Peace, and the New Politics of Humanitarianism in the First Half of the Twentieth Century" in this handbook.

67. Interesting studies are Catherine Foster, *Women for All Seasons: The Story of the Women's International League for Peace and Freedom* (Athens, GA: University of Georgia Press, 1989); Heloise Brown, *"The Truest Form of Patriotism": Pacifist Feminism in Britain, 1870–1902* (Manchester: Manchester University Press, 2003); Jennifer A. Davy et al., eds., *Frieden—Gewalt—Geschlecht: Friedens- und Konfliktforschung als Geschlechterforschung* (Essen: Klartext, 2005); Annika Wilmers, *Pazifismus in der internationalen Frauenbewegung (1914–1920): Handlungsspielräume, politische Konzeptionen und gesellschaftliche Auseinandersetzungen* (Essen: Klartext, 2008); David S. Patterson, *The Search for Negotiated Peace: Women's Activism and Citizen Diplomacy in World War I* (New York: Routledge, 2008); and Cynthia Cockburn, *Anti-Militarism: Political and Gender Dynamics of Peace Movements* (Basingstoke: Palgrave Macmillan, 2012).

68. See as an introduction Deborah Cohen and Maura O'Connor, eds., *Comparison and History: Europe in Cross-National Perspective* (New York: Routledge, 2004); and Heinz-Gerhard Haupt and Jürgen Kocka, eds., *Comparative and Transnational History: Central European Approaches and New Perspectives* (New York: Berghahn Books, 2009).

69. Introductions are Sebastian S. Conrad, *What Is Global History?* (Princeton, NJ: Princeton University Press, 2016); and Pierre-Yves Saunier, *Transnational History* (Basingstoke: Palgrave Macmillan, 2013).

70. See, for example, Jane Slaughter, *Women and the Italian Resistance, 1943–1945* (Denver, CO: Arden Press, 1997); Janet Hart, *New Voices in the Nation: Women and the Greek Resistance, 1941–1964* (Ithaca, NY: Cornell University Press, 1996); Magaret Poulos, *Arms and the Woman: Just Warriors and Greek Feminist Identity* (New York: Columbia University Press, 2009); David Boyd Haycock, *I Am Spain: The Spanish Civil War and the Men and Women Who Went to Fight Fascism* (Brecon: Old Street, 2012); and Jelena Batinić, *Women and Yugoslav Partisans: A History of World War II Resistance* (New York: Cambridge University Press, 2015).

71. See Maria Bucur and Nancy M. Wingfield, eds., *Gender and War in Twentieth-Century Eastern Europe* (Bloomington: Indiana University Press, 2006); and Maren Röger and Ruth Leiserowitz, eds., *Women and Men at War: A Gender Perspective on World War II and Its Aftermath in Central and Eastern Europe* (Osnabrück: Fibre Verlag, 2012). Important studies include Laurie Stoff, *They Fought for the Motherland: Russia's Women Soldiers in World War I and the Revolution* (Lawrence: University Press of Kansas, 2006); Stoff, *Russia's Sisters of Mercy and the Great War: More Than Binding Men's Wounds* (Lawrence: University Press of Kansas, 2015); Maria Bucur, *Heroes and Victims: Remembering War in Twentieth-Century Romania* (Bloomington: Indiana University Press, 2009); Anna Krylova, *Soviet Women in Combat: A History of Violence on the Eastern Front* (Cambridge: Cambridge University Press, 2010); Karen Petrone, *The Great War in Russian Memory* (Bloomington: Indiana University Press, 2011); Roger D. Markwick and Euridice Charon Cardona, *Soviet Women on the Frontline in the Second World War* (Basingstoke: Palgrave Macmillan, 2012); and Maren Röger, *Kriegsbeziehungen: Intimität, Gewalt und Prostitution im besetzten Polen 1939 bis 1945* (Frankfurt am Main: S. Fischer, 2015).

72. For the current state of research, see Claire Duchen and Irene Bandhauer-Schöffmann, eds., *When the War Was Over: Women, War, and Peace in Europe, 1940–1956* (London: Leicester University Press, 2000); Hagemann and Schüler-Springorum, *Home/Front*, 297–358; Joanna Regulska and Bonnie G. Smith, eds., *Women and Gender in Postwar Europe: From Cold War to European Union* (London: Routledge, 2012); Karen Hagemann and Sonya Michel, eds., *Gender and the Long Postwar: The United States and the Two Germanys, 1945–1989* (Baltimore: Johns Hopkins University Press, 2014); Francisca de

Haan, ed., "Gendering the Cold War in the Region: An Email Conversation between Malgorzata (Gosia) Fidelis, Renata Jambresic Kirin, Jill Massino and Libora Oates-Indruchova," *aspasia* 8 (2014): 162–90; and Helen Laville, "Gender and Women's Rights in the Cold War," in Immerman and Goedde, *The Oxford Handbook of the Cold War*, 523–39.

73. Birthe Kundrus, "Blind Spots: Empire, Colonies, and Ethnic Identities in Modern German History," in Hagemann and Quataert, *Gendering*, 86–87. For an introduction to postcolonial history, see Catherine Hall, ed., *Cultures of Empire: Colonizers in Britain and the Empire in the Nineteenth and Twentieth Centuries: A Reader* (New York: Routledge, 2000); and Frederick Cooper, *Colonialism in Question: Theory, Knowledge, History* (Berkeley: University of California Press, 2005).

74. See Jane Burbank and Frederick Cooper, *Empires in World History: Power and the Politics of Difference* (Princeton, NJ: Princeton University Press, 2010); with a gender perspective, Philippa Levine, ed., *Gender and Empire* (Oxford: Oxford University Press, 2004); and Angela Woollacott, *Gender and Empire* (New York: Palgrave Macmillan, 2006).

75. See, for the research, the chapters by Serena Zabin on "War, Culture, and Gender in Colonial and Revolutionary North America," and Catherine Davies on "War, Gender, and Society in Late Colonial and Revolutionary Spanish America" in this handbook.

76. See, for the research, the chapters by Angela Woollacott, "Imperial Conquest, Violent Encounters, and Changing Gender Relations in Colonial Warfare, 1830s–1910s," and Lake, "The 'White Man'" in this handbook.

77. See, for the research, the chapter by Elizabeth Colwill on "Gender, Slavery, War, and Violence in and beyond the Age of Revolution" in this handbook.

78. See, for the research, the chapters by Woollacott, "Imperial Conquest," Amy S. Greenberg, "Gender and the Wars of Nation-Building and Nation-Keeping in the Americas, 1830s–1870s," Lake, "The 'White Man,'" and Smith, "Colonial Soldiers," in this handbook.

79. See, for the research, the chapter by Branche, "Gender, the Wars of Decolonization," in this handbook. On the role of gender in the revolutionary conflicts in Latin America, see, for example, Rosario Montoya, *Gendered Scenarios of Revolution: Making New Men and New Women in Nicaragua, 1975–2000* (Tucson: University of Arizona Press, 2012); Jocelyn Viterna, *Women in War: The Micro-Processes of Mobilization in El Salvador* (New York: Oxford University Press, 2014); and Tine Destrooper, *Come Hell or High Water: Feminism and the Legacy of Armed Conflict in Central America* (Leiden: Brill, 2015).

80. For an introduction, see Peter Burke, *What Is Cultural History?* (Cambridge, MA: Polity Press, 2004); and Arcangeli, *Cultural History*.

81. For this research, see the chapters by Nye on "War Mobilization, Gender, and Military Culture," Annegret Fauser on "Gendered War Mobilization, Culture, and Music in the Age of World Wars," and Frank Biess on "Gendering the Memories of War and Holocaust in Europe and the United States" in this handbook.

82. For the debate on gender and memory, see Selma Leydesdorff et al., eds., *Gender and Memory* (New York: Oxford University Press, 1996); and Sylvia Paletschek and Sylvia Schraut, eds., *The Gender of Memory: Cultures of Remembrance in Nineteenth- and Twentieth-Century Europe* (Frankfurt am Main: Campus, 2008).

83. See Karen Hagemann, "Militär, Krieg und Geschlechterverhältnisse: Untersuchungen, Überlegungen und Fragen zur Militärgeschichte der Frühen Neuzeit," in *Klio in Uniform: Probleme und Perspektiven einer modernen Militärgeschichte der Frühen Neuzeit*, ed. Ralf

Pröve (Cologne: Böhlau, 1997), 35–88; Hagemann and Pröve, eds., *Landsknechte, Soldatenfrauen und Nationalkrieger: Militär, Krieg und Geschlechterordnung im historischen Wandel* (Frankfurt am Main: Campus, 1998); John A. Lynn, *Women, Armies and Warfare in Early Modern Europe* (Cambridge: Cambridge University Press, 2008); and the chapter by Peter H. Wilson on "Wars, States, and Gender in Early Modern European Warfare, 1600s–1780s" in this handbook.

84. See, for example, Jacqueline Fabre-Serris and Alison Keith, eds., *Women and War in Antiquity* (Baltimore: Johns Hopkins University Press, 2015); Jorit Warner, "Keep the Women out of the Camps: Women and Military Institutions in the Classical World," in Hacker and Vining, *A Companion*, 17–60; and, as an example for the many studies on Joan of Arc, Marina Warner, *Joan of Arc: The Image of Female Heroism* (Berkeley: University of California Press, 2000).

85. See Dianne Dugaw, *Warrior Women and Popular Balladry, 1650–1850* (Cambridge: Cambridge University Press, 1989); Julie Wheelwright, *Amazons and Military Maids: Women Who Dressed as Men in the Pursuit of Life, Liberty and Happiness* (London: Pandora, 1989); Sarah Colvin and Helen Watanabe-O'Kelly, eds., *Women and Death: Warlike Women in the German Literary and Cultural Imagination since 1500* (Rochester, NY: Camden House, 2009); Rudolf Dekker and Lotte C. van de Pol, *The Tradition of Female Transvestism in Early Modern Europe* (New York: St. Martin's Press, 1989); Elisabeth Krimmer, *In the Company of Men: Cross-Dressed Women around 1800* (Detroit, MI: Wayne State University Press, 2004); and Helen Watanabe-O'Kelly, *Beauty or Beast? The Woman Warrior in the German Imagination from the Renaissance to the Present* (Oxford: Oxford University Press, 2010).

86. See, for example, Beate Engelen, *Soldatenfrauen in Preußen: Eine Strukturanalyse der Garnisonsgesellschaft im späten 17. und 18. Jahrhundert* (Münster: LIT, 2005); Holly A. Mayer, *Belonging to the Army: Camp Followers and Community during the American Revolution* (Columbia: University of South Carolina Press, 1996); Thomas Cardoza, *Intrepid Women: Cantinières and Vivandières of the French Army* (Bloomington: Indiana University Press, 2010); and Jennine Hurl-Eamon, *Marriage and the British Army in the Long Eighteenth Century: "The Girl I Left behind Me"* (Oxford: Oxford University Press, 2014). An overview is provided in the chapter by Thomas Cardoza and Karen Hagemann on "History and Memory of Army Women and Female Soldiers, 1770s–1870s" in this handbook.

87. See, for example, Anne Summers, *Angels and Citizens: British Women as Military Nurses, 1854–1914* (London: Routledge, 1988); Judith Ann Giesberg, *Civil War Sisterhood: The U.S. Sanitary Commission and Women's Politics in Transition* (Boston: Northeastern University Press, 2000); Jean H. Quataert, *Staging Philanthropy: Patriotic Women and the National Imagination in Dynastic Germany, 1813–1916* (Ann Arbor: University of Michigan Press, 2001); and Anne Powell, *Women in the War Zone: Hospital Service in the First World War* (Stroud: Sutton, 2008). For an overview of the research, see Barton C. Hacker, "Reformers, Nurses and Ladies in Uniform: The Changing Status of Military Women (c. 1815–1914)," in Hacker and Vining, *Companion*, 93–136.

88. See Karen Hagemann, "Frauen, Nation und Krieg: Die Bedeutung der antinapoleonischen Kriege für die Geschlechterordnung—Geschichte, Nachwirkung und Erinnerung," in *1813 im europäischen Kontext*, ed. Birgit Aschmann and Thomas Stamm-Kuhlmann (Stuttgart: Steiner, 2015), 217–40; and Quataert, *Staging Philanthropy*.

89. See Philip T. Hoffman, *Why Did Europe Conquer the World?* (Princeton, NJ: Princeton University Press, 2015), 22.

90. Exceptions are Mary Elizabeth Ailes, *Courage and Grief: Women and Sweden's Thirty Years' War* (Lincoln, NE : University of Nebraska Press, 2018); and the respective chapters in Hagemann and Pröve, *Landsknechte*; and Lynn, *Women, Armies and Warfare*. See also the chapter by Wilson, "Wars, States, and Gender" in this handbook.

91. See the chapter by Zabin, "War, Culture, and Gender" in this handbook, which focuses on the French and Indian War (1754–63) and the American Revolutionary War (1775–83).

92. Exceptions are Lucy Riall, *Garibaldi: Invention of a Hero* (New Haven, CT: Yale University Press, 2007); and the respective chapters in Hagemann and Pröve, *Landsknechte*.

93. For the research, see Karen Hagemann et al., eds., *Gender, War, and Politics: Transatlantic Comparisons, 1775–1830* (New York: Palgrave Macmillan, 2010).

94. See Mary Beth Norton, *Liberty's Daughters: The Revolutionary Experience of American Women, 1750–1800* (Boston: Little, Brown, 1980); Norton, *Founding Mothers & Fathers: Gendered Power and the Forming of American Society* (New York: Alfred A. Knopf, 1996); Mayer, *Belonging*; Carol Berkin, *Revolutionary Mothers: Women in the Struggle for America's Independence* (New York: Alfred A. Knopf, 2005); and the chapter by Zabin, "War, Culture, and Gender" in this handbook.

95. For the research, see Karen Hagemann et al., eds., "Gender, War and the Nation in the Period of the Revolutionary and Napoleonic Wars—European Perspectives," special issue, *European History Quarterly* 37, no. 4 (2007); and the chapter by Alan Forrest on "Society, Mass Warfare, and Gender in Europe during and after the Revolutionary and Napoleonic Wars" in this handbook.

96. For the research, see Catherine Davies et al., *South American Independence: Gender, Politics, Text* (Liverpool: Liverpool University Press, 2006); and the chapter by Davies, "War, Gender, and Society" in this handbook.

97. See Helen Rappaport, *No Place for Ladies: The Untold Story of Women in the Crimean War* (London: Aurum, 2007). There are numerous works on Florence Nightingale; a recent publication is Judith Lissauer Cromwell, *Florence Nightingale, Feminist* (Jefferson, NC: McFarland & Company, 2013).

98. The first influential publications were Catherine Clinton and Nina Silber, eds., *Divided Houses: Gender and the Civil War* (New York: Oxford University Press, 1992); Clinton, *Tara Revisited: Women, War & the Plantation Legend* (New York: Abbeville Press, 1995); and Elizabeth D. Leonard, *All the Daring of the Soldier: Women of the Civil War Armies* (New York: W. W. Norton, 1999). See also the chapter by Greenberg, "Gender and the Wars of Nation-Building" in this handbook.

99. Scott, "Unanswered Questions," 1423.

100. For our approach to gender history, see especially Scott, "Gender as a Useful Category"; "AHR Forum: 'Revisiting 'Gender'"; and Rose, *What Is Gender History?*

101. Carl von Clausewitz, *On War*, trans. Michael Howard and Peter Paret (Oxford: Oxford University Press, 2007).

102. Ibid., 13 and 28–29.

103. Hew Strachan and Sybille Scheipers, "Introduction: The Changing Character of War," in *The Changing Character of War*, ed. Strachan and Scheipers (Oxford: Oxford University Press, 2011), 1–24, 11.

104. Strachan and Scheipers, "Introduction," 6–7.

105. Sjoberg, *Gender, War*, 10–11. For her definition of the concept of war, see Sjoberg, "Theories of War," in Aoláin et al., *The Oxford Handbook of Gender and Conflict*, 3-16.

106. See Vittorio Bufacchi, "Two Concepts of Violence," *Political Studies Review* 3, no. 2 (2005): 193–204.

107. See Benjamin Ziemann, *Gewalt im Ersten Weltkrieg: Töten—Überleben—Verweigern* (Essen: Klartext, 2013), 9–13.

108. Cynthia Cockburn, "Gender Relations as Causal in Militarization and War: A Feminist Standpoint," in *Making Gender, Making War: Violence, Military and Peacekeeping Practices*, ed. Annica Kronsell and Erika Svedberg (New York: Routledge, 2012), 26–28.

109. Willem de Haan, "Violence as an Essentially Contested Concept," in *Violence in Europe: Historical and Contemporary Perspectives*, ed. Sophie Body-Gendrot and Pieter Spierenburg (New York: Springer, 2008), 28–29.

110. Klaus Latzel et al., "Soldatinnen in der Geschichte: Weibliche Verletzungsmacht als Herausforderung," in Latzel et al., *Soldatinnen*, 11–49.

111. Elizabeth D. Heineman, "Introduction: The History of Sexual Violence in Conflict Zones," in Heineman, *Sexual Violence*, 2. For the scholarly debate on sexual violence and war, see also the chapter by Zarkov, "Conceptualizing Sexual Violence" in this handbook.

112. Elisabeth Jean Wood, "Armed Groups and Sexual Violence: When Is Wartime Rape Rare?" *Politics & Society* 37, no. 1 (2009): 132; and Wood, "Sexual Violence during War: Toward an Understanding of Variation," in *Order, Conflict and Violence*, ed. Stathis N. Kalyvas et al. (Cambridge: Cambridge University Press, 2008), 321–51.

113. Wood, "Armed Groups," 132; and Wood, "Conflict-Related Sexual Violence and the Policy Implications of Recent Research," *International Review of the Red Cross* 96, no. 894 (2014): 457–78.

114. See for example, Lisa Sharlach, "Rape as Genocide: Bangladesh, the Former Yugoslavia, and Rwanda," *New Political Science* 22, no. 1 (2000): 89–102; Sherrie L. Russell-Brown, "Rape as an Act of Genocide," *Berkeley Law Scholarship Repository* 21, no. 2 (2003): 350–74; Matthias Bjørnlund, "'A Fate Worse Than Dying': Sexual Violence during the Armenian Genocide," in Herzog, *Brutality and Desire*, 16–58; and more generally Carol Rittner and John Roth, eds., *Rape: Weapon of War and Genocide*, ed. (St. Paul, MN: Paragon House, 2012).

115. Claudia Card, "Rape as a Weapon of War," *Hypatia* 11, no. 4 (1996): 5–18.

116. Dieter Langewiesche, "Eskalierte die Kriegsgewalt im Laufe der Geschichte?" in *Moderne Zeiten? Revolution und Gewalt im 20. Jahrhundert*, ed. Jörg Baberowski (Göttingen: Vandenhoeck & Ruprecht, 2006), 12–36.

117. Dipesh Chakrabarty, *Provincializing Europe: Postcolonial Thought and Historical Difference*, rev. ed. (Princeton, NJ: Princeton University Press, 2007), esp. 3–23.

118. Ibid.; see Michael Geyer, "The Subject(s) of Europe," in *Conflicting Memories: Europeanizing Contemporary History*, ed. Konrad H. Jarausch and Thomas Lindenberger (New York: Berghahn Books, 2007), 254–80.

119. Geoffrey Parker, "The Western Way of War," in *The Cambridge Illustrated History of Warfare: The Triumph of the West*, ed. Geoffrey Parker (Cambridge: Cambridge University Press, 1995), 2–9; for the debate see Stefan Dudink und Karen Hagemann, "War and Gender: From the Thirty Years' War and Colonial Conquest to the Wars of Revolution and Independence—an Overview" in this handbook; and Lawrence Sondhaus, *Strategic Culture and Ways of War* (London: Routledge, 2006).

120. This website with more than 8,600 entries collects and organizes secondary literature, women's autobiographies, films, and informative websites to make them accessible to the public. The project, directed by Karen Hagemann, is the joint work of a team of graduate and undergraduate students of the University of North Carolina (UNC) at Chapel Hill, Department of History, UNC IT Research, and the UNC Libraries. For more, please visit http://gwc.unc.edu/welcome.

SELECT BIBLIOGRAPHY

"AHR Forum: Revisiting 'Gender: A Useful Category of Historical Analysis.'" *American Historical Review* 113, no. 5 (2008): 1344–430.

Aoláin, Fionnuala Ní, Naomi Cahn, Dina Francesca Haynes, and Nahla Valji, eds. *The Oxford Handbook of Gender and Conflict*. Oxford: Oxford University Press, 2017.

Burbank, Jane, and Frederick Cooper. *Empires in World History: Power and the Politics of Difference*. Princeton, NJ: Princeton University Press, 2010.

Chakrabarty, Dipesh. *Provincializing Europe: Postcolonial Thought and Historical Difference*. Rev. ed. Princeton, NJ: Princeton University Press, 2008.

Chickering, Roger, Dennis Showalter, and Hans van de Ven, eds. *The Cambridge History of War*. Vol. 4, *War and the Modern World, 1850–2005*. Cambridge: Cambridge University Press, 2012.

Cohn, Carol, ed. *Women and Wars*. Cambridge, MA: Polity Press, 2013.

Connell, R. W. *Masculinities*. Berkeley: University of California Press, 1995.

Dudink, Stefan, Karen Hagemann, and John Tosh, eds. *Masculinities in Politics and War: Gendering Modern History*. Manchester: Manchester University Press, 2004.

Enloe, Cynthia. *Globalization and Militarism: Feminists Make the Link*. Lanham, MD: Rowman & Littlefield, 2007.

Enloe, Cynthia. *Maneuvers: The International Politics of Militarizing Women's Lives*. Berkeley: University of California Press, 2000.

Goldstein, Joshua S. *War and Gender: How Gender Shapes the War System and Vice Versa*. Cambridge: Cambridge University Press, 2001.

Heineman, Elizabeth D., ed. *Sexual Violence in Conflict Zones: From the Ancient World to the Era of Human Rights*. Philadelphia: University of Pennsylvania Press, 2011.

Higonnet, Margaret Randolph, Jane Jensen, Sonya Michel, and Margaret Collins Weitz, eds. *Behind the Lines: Gender and the Two World Wars*. New Haven, CT: Yale University Press, 1987.

Kaufman, Joyce P., and Kristen P. Williams. *Women and War: Gender Identity and Activism in Times of Conflict*. Sterling, VA: Kumarian Press, 2010.

Morillo, Stephen, and Michael F. Pavkovic. *What Is Military History?* Cambridge, MA: Polity Press, 2013.

Parker, Geoffrey, ed. *The Cambridge History of Warfare*. New York: Cambridge University Press, 2005.

Scott, Joan W. "Gender: A Useful Category of Historical Analysis." *American Historical Review* 98, no. 4 (1986): 1053–75.

Sharoni, Simona, et al. eds. *Handbook on Gender and War*. Celtenham: Edward Elgar, 2016.

Shepard, Alexandra, and Garthine Walker, eds. *Gender and Change: Agency, Chronology and Periodisation*. Oxford: Wiley–Blackwell, 2009.

Sjoberg, Laura. *Gendering Global Conflict: Toward a Feminist Theory of War*. New York: Columbia University Press, 2013.

Strachan, Hew, and Sibylle Scheipers, eds. *The Changing Character of War*. Oxford: Oxford University Press, 2011.

Ulbrich, David J., and Bobby A. Wintermute. *Race and Gender in Modern Western Warfare*. Berlin: de Gruyter, 2018.

PART I

FROM THE THIRTY YEARS' WAR AND COLONIAL CONQUEST TO THE WARS OF REVOLUTION AND INDEPENDENCE

CHAPTER 1

....

WAR AND GENDER

*From the Thirty Years' War and Colonial
Conquest to the Wars of Revolution and
Independence—an Overview*

....

STEFAN DUDINK AND KAREN HAGEMANN

THE Flemish painter Sebastian Vrancx lived in an early modern world in which war was the order of the day. Born five years into the Eighty Years' War (1568–1648) between the Netherlands and Spain, he died a year before it ended, by which time it already had been entwined for three decades with the Europe-wide Thirty Years' War (1618–48). Vrancx's oeuvre contains many war scenes, including paintings depicting confrontations between soldiers and locals during the plundering of villages or attacks on travelers.[1] Their appeal derived partly from the gendered trope of civilian suffering. The recurrent presence of women among the victims of violent soldiers likely contributed to the mixture of horror, fascination, and empathy these images evoked. At first glance, the undated *War Scene of the Thirty Years War* (Figure 1.1) seems to be one of these paintings. Some interpretations describe the eye-catching group of women at its center as civilians fleeing before the enemy, projecting gendered ideas about modern warfare onto the painting.[2] Rather than civilian victims of war, the women in this painting were, in fact, camp followers: the men, women, and children who formed the large trains that followed the aggregated contract armies of the Thirty Years' War on campaign and constituted a regular feature of early modern warfare. The jugs, baskets, and other luggage some of the women carry are the household goods of soldier couples or tools of the trade of sutlers who supply food and drink to soldiers. The chicken dangling from the waist of one woman is an iconographic sign of the foraging and pillaging done by female camp followers, through which they contributed to the maintenance of the campaign community.[3]

FIGURE 1.1 *War Scene of the Thirty Years War*, oil painting by Sebastian Vrancx (1573–1647) showing a large army train with camp followers, [n.p., n.d.].

(150619586: DEA/G. DAGLI ORTI/Getty Images)

Vrancx's painting opens a window onto a world of European warfare lasting from the fifteenth to the seventeenth century in which campaign communities included large numbers of male and female noncombatants. These camp followers occupied a central place in aggregated contract armies because they contributed to their maintenance and logistics. After the mid-seventeenth century, this world of warfare gradually gave way. A new world emerged in which war was increasingly fought by state commission armies, military and civilian spheres slowly became more separate, and women and other noncombatants were pushed to the margins of and, from the late eighteenth century on, out of military life. Between the 1770s and the 1830s, with the emergence of mass warfare based on volunteer units, militias, and universal conscription, armed forces transformed into all-male institutions—although never entirely. The military still needed women for washing, cooking, sewing, serving, and nursing, but its leadership attempted to severely curtail their numbers and to regulate their presence in different ways.[4]

This transformation of the military into an all-male institution was mirrored in eighteenth- and nineteenth-century visual representations of war in which far fewer women were present than before. They created an image of military and warfare as masculinized arenas. Most depictions of revolutionary and national mass warfare

FIGURE 1.2 *Napoleon on the Battlefield of Eylau, February 9, 1807*, oil painting by Antoine-Jean Gros (1771–1835), depicting Napoleon I visiting the battlefield in eastern Prussia the day after the French army's bloody victory over the Russians and Prussians, [n.p.], 1808.

(Musée du Louvre, Paris. Photo © RMN-Grand Palais (musée du Louvre)/Daniel Arnaudet)

portrayed men fighting as protectors of family, home, and nation. Antoine-Jean Gros's *Napoleon on the Battlefield at Eylau, February 9, 1807* (1808) (Figure 1.2) does this, too, but also addresses dying in war. The large painting was a propaganda piece intended to glorify an indecisive battle with thirty thousand French casualties.[5] It depicts Napoleon Bonaparte visiting the battlefield of Eylau in eastern Prussia the day after France's bloody victory over the Prussian and Russian troops. The emperor on his white horse in the center of the painting, surrounded by his commanders and doctors, inspects the battlefield. He is dressed demurely, and his pose conveys compassion and a Christ-like power to heal and resurrect. He is the victor, but because of his moral qualities in victory, he is absolved from responsibility for the suffering he has inflicted on the enemy—a fact the wounded survivors are aware of, looking up at him in astonishment at his magnanimity. The role of the military hero is delegated to Marshal Joachim Murat, who enters the scene in a magnificent uniform from the right, saber in hand, atop a rearing brown horse. Through this painting, Gros celebrated Napoleon as a compassionate emperor. He depicted Napoleon's victory without denying the horrors of war, which are represented by the casualties in the foreground consisting almost exclusively of enemy soldiers.[6]

The complex political message of the painting, which Napoleon approved, is expressed by contrasting divergent masculinities—splendid heroism and abject suffering, total subordination, and a superiority so total it can afford magnanimous compassion—within the male universe of national mass warfare. The complete absence of civilians in the painting is also noteworthy. The legitimacy of the Napoleonic regime depended on its ability to control and appease the civilian population in its own state and in occupied and allied territories. But because of the growing scope of warfare, the regime had to demand ever more recruits and greater financial and material support. The painting addressed the growing discontent among the civilian population. It attempted to restore trust in Napoleon as a good and compassionate leader of victorious armed forces, which deserved the much-needed support of the civilian population.

The paintings by Vrancx and Gros encapsulate the significant changes in the entangled histories of war and gender from the Thirty Years' War to the revolutionary and Napoleonic Wars. The following introduces key concepts used to write these histories, such as *military revolution*, *limited war*, and *total war*, presents an overview of major developments, examines them against the background of the wider history of warfare in the early modern period, and discusses the state of research and central themes in the history of war and gender in this period.

CONCEPTUALIZING EARLY MODERN WARFARE

To explain the dismantling of the campaign community of the aggregated contract army and the decreasing number of women who followed the state commission armies on campaigns after 1650, women's and gender historians turned to the concept of a *military revolution*.[7] This notion, introduced by Michael Roberts in 1955, appealed to both military historians and the broader historical profession because it linked transformations in the tactics of warfare between 1560 and 1660 to state formation and other wider social and political developments.[8] Roberts used the term to refer to the changes in tactics that were part of the military reforms of Prince Maurice of Orange, Stadtholder of all the provinces of the Dutch Republic except for Friesland from 1585 until his death in 1625, and Gustavus Adolphus, king of Sweden from 1611 to 1632. Battle, Roberts argued, had in the course of the sixteenth century increasingly tended toward deadlock. The massive, slow-moving squares of pikemen surrounded by musketeers that dominated European battlefields were powerful defensive units, but not suited for maneuvering and unlikely to gain the upper hand in confrontations with formations of similar strength.[9] As a result, "war eternalized itself."[10] The new tactics, revolving around smaller, shallower units, which were deployed in linear formations, allowed for an intensification of firepower and greater mobility, which, in turn, increased the possibilities for tactical maneuvering. They changed the nature of war and inaugurated, according to Roberts, a revolution that "stands like a great divide separating mediaeval society from the modern world."[11]

The new tactics required investments in growing numbers of soldiers and their subjection to intensive drill. The widened scope of warfare also increased the size of armies. Roberts contended that these developments together led to "an increase in the authority of the state," because only states, as opposed to the owners of private armies, were capable of supplying the resources demanded by the new mode and scale of warfare.[12] States strove to make their military monopolies absolute. They rid themselves of irregular and private troops, establishing instead permanent armies and navies run by centralized administrations. Troops, Roberts argued, were now recruited by the state. The government provided them with standardized weaponry and took over the responsibility for supply with arsenals. As the scale of war and the size of armies and states grew, means to finance them had to be found. New and sophisticated structures of credit provided states with the required finances, as did increased power for the central state in matters of taxation.[13]

Roberts's text deeply influenced the scholarship on states and militaries in the early modern period. Women's and gender historians also took up his argumentation in the 1980s. They explained the diminishing place of women in early modern armies as a result of the rise of state commission armies. States increasingly attempted to reduce the number of camp followers and to bring those noncombatants deemed indispensable for supply firmly under military control.[14]

Problematizing the "Military Revolution"

By the time women's and gender historians took up the notion of a military revolution, a profound revision and critique of the idea had begun to emerge.[15] Although supportive of the general thesis of an early modern military revolution, Geoffrey Parker revised major elements of it. He challenged the idea that the changes in battle tactics and a shift to the offensive exemplified by Swedish warfare were the driving forces behind the military revolution. Instead, Parker pointed to changes in siege warfare dating back to the fifteenth century. He argued that improvements in artillery had made the medieval high, thin walls of fortresses and fortified cities vulnerable. In response, a new style of building fortifications emerged during the second half of the fifteenth century, which became known as the *trace italienne*. The fortifications now had low, thick walls with protruding, angled bastions that enabled the defenders' flanking fire to cover the surrounding terrain, making it hard for besiegers to approach. As these new fortifications arose in many parts of Europe after 1500, the advantage switched to the defensive. Sieges became costly and lengthy: extended and complex siege lines needed to be dug, built, manned, and defended for long periods of time. There, Parker argued, lay one of the origins of the growth of army size and everything that followed from it in terms of state control over armies and the process of state formation.[16]

Jeremy Black also criticized Roberts's depiction of the relation between military change and state formation. He claimed that the crucial developments in weaponry and tactics that shaped European warfare in the long run happened between 1660 and 1760, with intensive innovation taking place around 1700. Black pointed to the development of the ring bayonet, which led to the disappearance of the pike. From the 1690s on, more and more infantry soldiers were armed with the same, increasingly standardized weapon: a musket fitted with a bayonet. The muskets were improved after the replacement of the matchlock with the more reliable flintlock, which allowed for more rapid fire. Linear formations and longer, thinner lines of soldiers with the new muskets increased firepower—as well as casualty rates. Simultaneously, army size started to grow, which continued into the nineteenth century.[17] Black presented these changes as more radical than the reforms between 1560 and 1660. Crucially, he argued they were the effect, rather than the cause, of advances in state formation. Reversing the relationship Roberts had suggested, Black wrote that the "more stable domestic circumstances," especially the reconciliation of crown and elites, in most states after 1660 had made it possible for changes in weaponry and tactics, which resulted in larger and stronger armies, to occur.[18]

David Parrott also challenged the concept of a military revolution, but by questioning the powerful, sometimes near-teleological narrative of the rise of the modern, Western state that underlies it. He disputed the idea that the state, and the state alone, was capable of realizing, organizing, and financing the increase in the scale of warfare presumed to be at the heart of this revolution. Instead, he noted the continued importance of private military enterprise and of social elites in providing and organizing the manpower and resources for war. This argument necessitated a reevaluation of the place of mercenary warfare in the history of early modern Europe.[19] The picture of inevitable conflict of interest between rulers and mercenaries was replaced by an interpretation of mercenary warfare as potentially beneficial to both these parties. After 1600, mercenaries developed into military enterprisers who offered to raise, equip, and supply troops and made available to a ruler their ability to raise funds. They did not ask for up-front payment, but were instead willing to wait for a return on their investment after the troops had gone to war. Military enterprisers raised large numbers of troops, sometimes entire armies, and relied on a network of subcontractors that provided money, men, and goods.[20]

Parrott argued that this practice served the interests of rulers, military enterprisers, and elites. For rulers, it solved the problem of financing war and persuading elites to share its financial burdens. Military enterprisers raised capital that states with limited credit reliability could not access. For elites, investment in mercenary warfare offered the prospect of returns in a context of war that rendered other investments unprofitable. These revenues came from the war taxes ("contributions") enterprisers were entitled to impose on the populations of occupied territories. This made all three groups interested in military victory. Defeat diminished the chances of obtaining territory from which contributions could be extracted; victory and the destruction of enemy forces considerably increased them.[21] Parrott held that there was no simple, straightforward relationship between an increased scale and scope of warfare and advances in state formation in early modern Europe. Like other aspects of politics in this period, to build or reform armies was not an act of will of a sovereign state or ruler, but required negotiations and compromises between the ruler and sociopolitical elites.[22]

From this interpretation, Parrott came to a conclusion that runs counter to the central assumption of the military-revolution thesis about a symbiosis of military and state power that is presumed to have been central not just to the history of war and warfare in the early modern period, but also to the history of Western modernity more generally. He argued that mutually reinforcing dynamics between an expansion of the scale and scope of warfare and the growing power of the state can be found only in the two centuries between approximately 1750 and 1950. In these two centuries, "war and the state appear to be tightly interlocked." Before and after these years, however, it was "an anomaly" for a military to be recruited and administered exclusively by the state. In these periods, the dominant pattern of the organization of warfare was shaped by "varying forms of public–private partnership," not the fully state-controlled military.[23]

The extensive criticisms of the military-revolution thesis have raised doubts about the value of the concept that has nevertheless proven to be remarkably resilient. Peter H. Wilson argued that women's and gender historians have contributed to giving "a new lease of life" to the contested chronology associated with the military-revolution thesis. He pointed to important continuities in the organization of early modern armies and warfare after 1650—and extended this argument to the women married to soldiers. Since the second half of seventeenth century they remained in increasing numbers in the standing armies' garrisons during conflicts; they less and less followed the troops as camp followers during campaigns.[24] Analyses such as those by Parrott and Wilson suggest that an adequate understanding of war, and of gender and war, in the early modern period is helped by a critical rethinking of the conceptual framework of the military revolution and the supposedly clear-cut opposition between state and society on which it rests.

A critical rethinking is also underway in another branch of historiography influenced by the military revolution thesis: the history of European expansion and colonialism. This is true in particular of Geoffrey Parker's thesis that the military innovations produced in this revolution were central to the success of early European colonial ventures: "The key to the Westerners' success in creating the first truly global empires between 1500 and 1750 depended upon precisely those improvements in the ability to wage war which have between termed 'the military revolution.'" Central to these improvements were, according to Parker, the coordinated musket firing produced by elaborate drill, *trace italienne*–style artillery fortifications, and the broadside sailing ship. These new technologies and methods, he argued, were at the heart of Western military superiority and the colonial empires that rested on it.[25]

Parker's narrative, which joined the military revolution with the rise of the West, resonated with many historians, but was also criticized as Eurocentric by historians studying the military histories of the Russian and Ottoman Empires. Their research undermined both the notion of a specific or even unique "Western way of war," of which the military revolution presumably formed a prominent part, and the idea that during most of the early modern period the West held a significant technological and military advantage over the rest of the world.[26] In what was perhaps the most radical revision of a Eurocentric concept of a military revolution, military historians of Asia began to interpret the military revolution as a long-term, Eurasia-wide phenomenon that started in fourteenth-century China and continued its life in a dynamics of transfer between Asia and Europe.[27] Their studies suggested that both the notion that the military revolution was a specifically Western phenomenon and the idea that Western military superiority necessarily followed from it need critical rethinking—as does the unambiguous opposition between Western and non-Western (military) histories that underlies them.[28]

From Limited Wars to Total Warfare?

The central place of the military-revolution paradigm in discussions of early modern warfare came with a relative paucity of conceptual work on the eighteenth century. Developments in that era were often presented as continuations of processes that had their origins in the (late) seventeenth century, leaving little room for reflection on the specific nature of eighteenth-century warfare.[29] *Limited wars* were one form of warfare considered to have been specific to that era. As wars from the late seventeenth century on became increasingly costly and once again threatened to become indecisive, rulers looked for ways to limit the expense of war while increasing its military and political efficacy. War of maneuver seemed to offer these benefits. It did not concentrate on massive battles and the opponent's annihilation, but rather on skillful threats to the supply and communication lines and the flank and rear of the enemy's troops in the hope of obstructing their advance, forcing them into territory where they would be cut off from supplies, or leading them into retreat. With its practice of carefully considered exertion of pressure on one's opponent, war of maneuver resembled diplomacy and was a way of preparing for negotiations.[30] In line with the ideological justifications of absolutism as the political form best suited to bring and safeguard peace, limited warfare held an important place in eighteenth-century strategic thinking.[31]

Echoing these deliberations, military historians long referred to eighteenth-century conflicts as *cabinet wars*, or *guerres en dentelle* ("wars in lace")—designations with gendered undertones. In this tradition, as Ciro Paoletti argued, limited warfare appeared as "a genteel minuet. Generals in powdered wigs and elegant clothes ponderously maneuvered their only slightly less finely attired soldiers in a slow graceful military dance, which only by chance might include a battle."[32] The suggestion of aristocratic effeminacy points to the origin of this characterization: the writings of military theorists of the period of the Wars of Revolution and Independence (1770s–1820s), who contrasted the new "people's wars" with the ancien régime "wars of princes." Later generations of military historians continued this line of interpretation.[33] Since the late 1990s, historians have begun to move beyond it. In their interpretation, large-scale battles and lengthy, exhausting sieges were standard elements of the operational repertoire of eighteenth-century warfare, which was no less bloody, violent, or ferocious than that of earlier times.[34]

Nevertheless, the questionable interpretation of eighteenth-century warfare as "limited" reappears in current analyses of conflicts in the era of the Wars of Revolution and

Independence. As Roger Chickering points out, two "master narratives" organized the history of warfare in this transitional era.[35] In the first of these—the military-revolution framework—especially the French Revolutionary and Napoleonic Wars (1792–1815) appear as a continuation of earlier processes that led to an increase in the scale and intensity of war. Perceived as such, there is not much that is specific to these wars; they are a point on a line that, in Michael Roberts's words, leads from the 1660s straight "to the abyss of the twentieth century."[36]

Much more specificity is attributed to the French Revolutionary and Napoleonic Wars in the second narrative, which equates the modernity of modern warfare with it becoming total. From this perspective, these wars inaugurated the era of *total war* and thus mark a crucial caesura in the history of warfare. In this narrative, the conflicts between 1792 and 1815 either foreshadowed total war, which then came into its own during the two world wars of the twentieth century, or already were fully fledged total wars themselves. In either case, the wars are depicted as having characteristics that fundamentally distinguish them from the supposedly limited warfare of an earlier age, the most important of which are armies of an unparalleled size based on mass recruitment (of volunteers, militias, and conscripts) mobilized by patriotic-national propaganda; an unequaled breadth of their operational scope; unprecedented levels of social and economic mobilization to support the mass warfare; the emergence of the new war aim of complete destruction of the enemy; and, as part of it, a tendency toward the erosion of the distinction between soldiers and civilians.[37]

In their insightful and influential interpretations of the French Revolutionary and Napoleonic Wars as total wars, Jean-Yves Guiomar and David A. Bell highlighted the political aspects of total war. For Guiomar, politically defined war aims were a crucial feature of total war in this period. These aims were both "vast and vague": ambitions to extend the influence of the revolution beyond the borders of France and to liberate other subject peoples. War aims of such a political nature, Guiomar argued, produced wars that could not be stopped by those who started them.[38] Bell, too, located the specificity of total war in its political nature. What marked the wars of 1792 to 1815, in Bell's view, was "a political dynamic that drove the participants relentlessly toward a condition of total engagement and the abandonment of restraints."[39] This political dynamic was fueled by an Enlightenment revaluation of war and the military as redemptive and regenerating forces capable of saving societies in danger of succumbing to the stagnation and decay produced by extended periods of peace and excessive civilization. This Enlightenment legacy resounded in the language of revolutionary-war enthusiasts, who proclaimed its power to regenerate the nation and argued that the war France should engage in could only be apocalyptic, since it was to be waged in the service of worldwide liberation and, ultimately, peace.[40]

Critics of the notion of total war, such as Wilson, argued that "like all other absolute concepts, the entire idea [of total war] is fundamentally flawed because totality can never be reached."[41] In addition, according to Chickering, the notion of total war, when grafted onto a narrative of modernization, obtains a questionable teleological character, resulting in a history of war in which total war gradually but necessarily asserts itself in accordance with its own inner logic.[42] Nevertheless, he claimed that total war captures a salient aspect of the history of war since the late eighteenth century: a "dramatic broadening of the purview of armed conflict." From Chickering's perspective, the challenge to historians, therefore, is to use the concept while liberating it from the constraints that inhere in the dominant narratives of total war.

The emphasis on a political dynamic that drove war toward a condition of "total engagement," as Bell termed it, is also useful for understanding the gender dimensions of the French Revolutionary and Napoleonic Wars ignored by most historians of the subject. Gender historians emphasize the highly gendered nature of patriotic-national propaganda, which was used to mobilize soldiers and civilians for war support. They also demonstrate that the forms of war support required in people's wars were themselves gendered. One early example of the gender order of national war is the *levée en masse* (mass levy) of August 1793 in Revolutionary France, which demanded that older and married men support the war effort with arms and encouragement; that young men of military age become soldiers; and that women ensure that these warriors were equipped with tents and uniforms and also care for sick and wounded soldiers.[43] In addition, the emergence of the new war aim of a crushing and complete defeat of the enemy meant that in contested and occupied regions, civilians were increasingly targeted, not only by military violence, but also by weapons such as the blockade of trade to wreck the opposition's economy.[44]

MAJOR CONFLICTS AND CHANGING WARFARE

In early modern Europe, war seemed natural to rulers, who took conflict for granted and put little trust in the usefulness of nonviolent means, such as diplomacy, to achieve their aims.[45] Europe's great powers were at war more often than not during the seventeenth and eighteenth centuries.[46] Some studies tend to reflect, rather than historically analyze, this ineluctability of war in the early modern period. In these works, war appears as a necessary component of an international system that was shaped over a longer period of time by relatively unchanging, structural rivalries, in which states, to varying degrees of rationality, pursued their interests.[47] This approach rests on the assumption that states, as the actors operating in this field of forces, were already in place and fully formed. That is a problematic premise given that in this period, state *formation* significantly contributed to the widespread presence of war.

This insight is central to Johannes Burkhardt's work on early modern "densification of war" (*Kriegsverdichtung*), which he explained as resulting from the tensions produced by incomplete processes of state-building.[48] A "special degree of bellicosity" marked these processes because they produced wars that were not fought between fully developed states, but conflicts over the question regarding what construct of the state was to emerge as dominant. Central to these conflicts was an opposition between universal and pluralist concepts of state-building. Based on the notion of a single Christendom, the concept of a *monarchia universalis* (universal monarchy) implied the political unity of Europe under one ruler or dynasty. In sharp contrast to the hierarchical nature of these ideals of a universal empire or monarchy, the pluralist concept revolved around relations of equality between political units that recognized each other's sovereignty. In addition, processes of early modern state-building generated wars because states-in-the-making tried to repair their weaknesses in ways that led to war. They relied on monarchic-dynastic leadership to provide them with political stability and legitimacy. With dynasticism, however, came the whims of individual rulers and succession crises, both of which were conducive to war. Weak early modern states looked for cohesion in religion ("confessionalization") and availed themselves of the economic support that commercial capitalist economies could offer. Religious wars and wars over trade and colonies often ensued.

The Thirty Years' War, 1618–48

For Burkhardt, the conflict that sparked the Thirty Years' War was a case of bottom-up state formation against Habsburg universalism.[49] By rejecting a new Habsburg king in 1617, the predominantly Protestant Estates of Bohemia defied the universalist claims of their Catholic Habsburg rulers and embarked on a course toward sovereignty. The 1618 decision to offer the throne to Calvinist Frederick V, Elector Palatine—and his decision to accept—triggered a war that ended the attempt to build an independent state. This war became infamous for its scope and levels of destruction. The entwinement of the Bohemian–Habsburg conflict with another war of bottom-up state formation, between the Netherlands and the Spanish Habsburgs, widened the conflict and resulted in a Spanish–Austrian alliance that outlasted the war. Above all, however, conflicting forms of state-building, fueled by processes of confessionalization and the international alliances they came with, set aflame the Holy Roman Empire.

The competitive nature of the European state system in the era of the Thirty Years' War, as well as the fact that this conflict was increasingly fought in several theaters simultaneously, played an important part in the spectacular increase of army size in this period. The case of France most clearly exemplifies this development. Around 1600, the paper strength of the French army during times of peace did not much exceed 10,000 and during war this could rise to 55,000.[50] Effective strength was certainly lower, but it is difficult to determine with precision. After France entered the Thirty Years' War, these figures went up considerably. One official projection for 1636 arrived at more than 200,000—a figure modern historians argue must be reduced to 100,000 for a reliable estimate of the number of troops in the field, but even then, the increase is substantial. In 1650, effective strength stood at 125,000.[51]

Burkhardt's interpretation of the Peace of Westphalia, which in 1648 brought the war to an end, reflected his assumption that the state is the dominant political form of modernity. He saw the peace as creating a pluralist European system of states, in which no power could "claim the universal legacy of Europe, occupy a clearly superior or dominant position, or even organize Europe into a single state." After 1648, he concluded, the legitimate model for the political organization of Europe was the "coexistence of equal states of moderate proportions" that recognized each other as equal sovereigns.[52] Others argued that the signatories to the treaty pursued imperial ambitions, in Europe or overseas, or were subjected to such ambitions long after 1648. From that perspective, the Peace of Westphalia represents a moment in a longer history of the modern state and empire.[53] Persistent universalist ambitions are visible in a further increase of the size of armies, which is again most clearly indicated by the French armed forces. At the height of the Dutch Wars (1672–78), effective strength reached 250,000, and during the war of the League of Augsburg (1688–97) it rose to 340,000. The absolute figures for smaller powers in the same period are lower, but their troop counts, too, grew by a factor of two or three. States whose power waned saw their army size decline. Spanish effective strength, for instance, fell from 100,000 in 1650 to 50,000 in 1710.[54]

Before 1650, these growing numbers of soldiers were recruited through various methods that reflected the nature of the early modern state and the limits to its abilities. Involuntary methods included conscription, which was introduced in a developed form only in Sweden, and the much more widely established practice of impressment of criminals and others thought to be dangerous or useless to society. Since these undesirables made for bad soldiers, states and commanders were careful to limit the number of them in their forces. Recruitment into militias relied on compulsion as well as a citizen's sense of obligation. Badly equipped and trained, and to be deployed only locally, militiamen, too, were of limited military use. Given the preference for volunteers and their availability in overcrowded labor markets, most efforts went into recruiting them. This was done either by a commissioned officer who offered drink and a bounty or through contractors who raised troops. The contractors could be compensated for initial costs, or they speculated on future profits from systems of contributions, and so they paid out of pocket for wages, equipment, and supplies well into a campaign. The latter system reached massive proportions during the Thirty Years' War.[55]

The Wars of the 1660s to the 1780s

After 1648, wars of state formation continued to occur. Burkhardt saw them as "relapses" to older dynamics or the effects of "unresolved issues" stemming from these dynamics.[56] In numerous wars in the second half of the seventeenth and early eighteenth centuries, universalist aspirations, or the echoes thereof, played a part in belligerents' motivations. The expansionist aspects of the wars of Louis XIV, who ruled France from 1643 until his death in 1715, reflected the continuing French ambitions to replace the Habsburgs as Europe's leading power. Habsburg Austria faced Ottoman universalist designs of an Islamic nature, which it managed to withstand during the Siege of Vienna (1683), after which it reversed the military balance of power. From the Long War of 1683–99, an indecisive land war between the Habsburg and the Ottoman Empires, the former embarked on an expansionist course itself, at the cost of the Ottomans. Sweden failed to undermine the Habsburg Empire during the Thirty Years' War, but did establish the Swedish Empire in the Baltic. In the Great Nordic War (1700–21), the Swedes encountered Russian universalist territorial ambitions, pursued by a leader, Peter the Great, who ruled the Tsardom of Russia and later the Russian Empire from 1682 until his death in 1725. His aspirations were underlined by his taking on the title of Russian emperor in 1721.

Universalist ambitions emerged in the War of the Spanish Succession (1701–14) in which France vied for the Spanish Crown and for domination over the Austrian Habsburgs.[57] This war also demonstrates the importance of dynasticism. When Charles II, king of Spain since 1665, died childless in 1700, competing claims to the vacant throne were bound to clash. Louis XIV accepted the will, which offered the entire Spanish Empire to his grandson, rather than to an Austrian Habsburg relative, knowing this would bring war. Soon Louis faced an Austrian, British, Dutch, and Prussian coalition determined to check France's power on the continent and overseas. Britain made its growing military power felt with successful campaigns on the continent and an affirmation of its status of major naval power. France, after initial successes, saw its opponents gain the upper hand.

The War of the Spanish Succession demonstrates the growing entwinement of European and colonial war. As the European colonial presence expanded, war over preeminence in Europe extended to war over colonial possessions. The prize that Spain represented was its Central and South American empire. Conquered and settled since the late fifteenth century, the Spanish American colonies formed the largest stretch of overseas territory governed by European rulers. In 1700 it was bigger than both the Portuguese colonies in South America and the British and French settlements to the north. In 1701–14, war overseas was located mostly in North America. In Queen Anne's War (1702–13), French, Spanish, and British troops and their Indigenous allies and proxies fought in a series of conflicts from Spanish Florida, the English province of Carolina, New England, Acadia, and Canada to Newfoundland. In South America, the French attacked Portuguese Brazil, invading Rio de Janeiro (1710–11) after earlier attacks on Portuguese outposts in Africa.

France narrowly escaped defeat in Europe. The Spanish throne went to Louis XIV's grandson, but on the condition that the French and Spanish monarchies were never to be united. Spain made territorial concessions and for thirty years lost to Britain the *asiento*, the right to supply the Spanish colonies with enslaved Africans. Britain benefited most from the war, both as a European and as an imperial power. Its imperialism partly derived from claims to preeminence within Europe and was not different from Spanish or French overseas expansion, which primarily served continental ambitions. Gradually, however, Britain would leave behind continental universalism, and its basis in a notion of a unified Christendom, to turn into an imperial power with wider—global—ambitions, different from its early modern ancestor.

Universalism and dynasticism were also important factors in the War of the Austrian Succession of 1740–48.[58] In the absence of a male heir and given the preclusion of women, Charles VI, Holy Roman Emperor from 1711 to 1740, had made European powers agree to his decision to leave the Habsburg hereditary possessions to his daughter, Maria Theresa, who ruled as archduchess of Austria and queen of Hungary and Croatia from 1740 to 1780 and was Holy Roman Empress from 1745 to 1765. After the death of her father in 1740, several powers broke their promise, in some cases citing supposedly stronger claims to Habsburg lands. Among them was Prussia, whose role in this conflict and the subsequent Seven Years' War (1756–63) was that of a newcomer to the European state system, trying to force its way in by means of war. In 1740, King Frederick II, who reigned in Prussia from 1740 to 1786, sent his army into the rich province of Silesia. As other powers made their own bids for territorial expansion, a wider European war ensued. Britain sided with Austria, while France allied with the Prussians, aiming to weaken its long-term enemy, Austria. The colonial rivalry between these two states again led to the conflict's expansion beyond the European continent. In North America, the British and French fought in Britain's northern provinces (1744–48); in Asia they battled on land and on sea for control over trading posts on India's eastern coast (1746–48).

Much as in the War of Austrian Succession, the later Seven Years' War was driven by colonial Franco-British competition and continental Austro-Prussian rivalry, though these respective alliances had reversed from the earlier war.[59] Knowing the Austrian desire to regain Silesia, Frederick II decided on a preemptive strike and attacked Austria's ally Saxony in August 1756, putting in motion the European machinery of alliance-making. Prussia had only one major ally, Britain, and faced a coalition of Austria, France, Spain, Russia, and Sweden. Only because this coalition was internally divided did the Prussian state survive and hold on to Silesia.

The British–French part of the conflict in Europe started with French victories at sea in 1756 and British fears of a French invasion, but by 1759 Britain had firmly established its naval dominance in European waters. In North America, a string of British victories forced France to give up almost all its possessions, the bulk of which Britain obtained. The colonial conflict was also fought in the Caribbean, along the coast of West Africa, and in India, where the East India Company, supported by the British government, weakened France's presence on the Indian east coast, laying the foundations for the company's control of Bengal and Bihar and, eventually, for Britain's empire in India.

Britain emerged from the Seven Years' War with a national debt that had doubled. Attempts to make its American colonies share this financial burden sparked a revolt that became the American Revolutionary War (1775–83), also called the War of Independence.[60] In the face of British threats to resort to force, the Second Continental Congress of 1775 decided to organize a regular Continental army that managed to withstand the British and their hired German troops. The conflict entered its decisive phase when this war, too, spread to a wide geographical scope. The decisions by France (1778) and Spain (1779) to enter the war put added pressure on the British. These decisions also brought the war to the Gulf of Mexico, the Caribbean, Central America, the

Mediterranean, and India. The prospect of an imperial war across the globe made Britain give in. With the Treaty of Paris (1783), the rebellious thirteen colonies obtained their independence.

As competition intensified in central and eastern Europe in the course of the eighteenth century, further increases in army size followed. From the early years of the War of the Spanish Succession in 1702–5 to the height of the War of the Austrian Succession in 1745, Austria's effective strength doubled from 100,000 to 200,000 soldiers. In the same period, Prussia's effective strength more than tripled: from 40,600 to 135,000 men under arms. Russia surpassed all European states with an effective strength that increased from 200,000 during the early years of the Great Northern War in 1702–5 to 344,000 in the first three years of the Seven Years' War.[61] Absolute numbers on average peaked in the two decades after 1750, but because of overall population growth in the eighteenth century, army size as a percentage of the entire population decreased throughout the century. In France, for instance, it fell from 2.0 percent in 1700 to 0.69 percent in 1789; in Russia it dropped from 1.25 percent in 1700 to 0.83 percent in 1796. Only in the exceptional case of Prussia did this figure increase, from 1.71 percent in the early eighteenth century to 3.4 percent in 1786.[62] As a rule of thumb, historians have held that 1 percent of the population is the maximum for sustainable recruitment in this period.[63] In the course of the eighteenth century, army size tended to regress toward that figure. The long period of war that started in the last decade of the century, however, upset the balance again.

These increases were linked to changes in warfare and mobilization. After 1650, involuntary recruitment became more important in states' policies. More convicted criminals and other outcasts than before were drafted. The militia also became a key recruitment mechanism. States forced more men to serve in the militia and used it to supply regular forces with soldiers. Some states—Prussia (1733) and Austria (1770) in particular—introduced canton systems of conscription. Contracting was transformed into a business of states as troops, many of them forced to serve, were rented out by foreign rulers. Nobles in some ways also took over from contractors when they put their capital in the service of monarchs in the context of a system of purchased commissions that required officers to recruit their units. Although the steady increase in army size after 1650 made states turn to involuntary recruitment more often, volunteers continued to make up the majority of soldiers, and economic conditions continued to ensure their supply until the French Revolutionary Wars (1792–1802).

The shifts in modes of recruitment after 1650 reflected European rulers' ambitions to establish permanent armies under their direct control, organized and paid for by state-supervised administrative and fiscal systems. Preferably domestically recruited, such armies were to be run by professionalized officers who constituted a permanent structure of command and enforced higher standards of discipline. The rise of the state commission army, also called the standing army, is often presented as a profound caesura in early modern military history, but, as discussed before, entirely state-organized and state-financed armies were beyond the reach of ancien régime states. The services of private financiers and merchants, as well as cooperation of social and economic elites, remained crucial for the making of large, permanent armies. The massive standing armies were not kept afoot by the state alone.[64]

As armies grew, and in particular as infantry soldiers became proportionally more numerous, they were increasingly composed of commoners.[65] The common soldiers in early modern armies were not the stereotypical "scum of the earth," as contemporaries and historians often saw them, but formed a neat representation of the laboring classes of their times: peasants and semiskilled artisans in the seventeenth century, joined by manual laborers and men from skilled trades such as tailoring and shoemaking in the eighteenth century.[66] In contrast, the social composition of the officer class became more homogenous. In the armies raised by contractors, men without an aristocratic background could join the ranks of officers. From the late seventeenth century onward, officers' posts fell under a nearly complete aristocratic monopoly. The number of non-noble and foreign officers dropped, and in the course of the eighteenth century, a professionalized aristocratic officer class played the leading role in European armed forces.[67]

In eighteenth-century armies dominated by infantry, cavalry became gradually less important, but it could still play a vital role in battle. The proportion of pikes to guns in infantry units began to decrease during the sixteenth century and continued to do so in the seventeenth. With the introduction of the socket bayonet after 1680, pikemen disappeared from the battlefield altogether. Tactics revolving around intense firepower and bayonet attacks required elaborate drill and came with an increased emphasis on discipline. Since the late seventeenth century, infantry was supported on the battlefield and in sieges by an artillery of improved quality and accuracy.[68] Next to massive—and numerous, more limited—sieges and battles, *small war* was a crucial element of early modern warfare. Raids by light cavalry and the pillaging of villages and towns were planned parts of wider operations, which, although they brought little glory, were often employed on a massive scale.[69]

The Wars of the 1780s to the 1830s

Burkhardt's argument about Europe's long and violent road toward a state system based on the mutual recognition of sovereignty is in some respects compatible with Paul W. Schroeder's influential analysis of the French Revolutionary and Napoleonic Wars. Schroeder saw these wars as constituting a turning point in European international politics after which an eighteenth-century competitive balance of power gave way to nineteenth-century notions of concert and political equilibrium. Through the wars from 1792 to 1815, Europe's leaders arrived at the insight that relations between "coordinate ... rather than superordinate and subordinate" states did not necessarily imply war, but "could be restrained by consensus and bounded by law."[70] As a result, Schroeder claimed, the frequency and violence of wars declined dramatically in the nineteenth century.[71] The Vienna settlement of 1815 did bring Europe an unprecedentedly long period of peace, as Schroeder wrote. However, the picture of Europe's nineteenth century as one of relative peace rests on ignoring or declaring marginal to the central story the wars on Europe's own periphery and tucking away Wars of Empires in favor of a metropolitan perspective.[72] Approaching Europe and its colonies and empires as interconnected historical spaces results in a different picture. It brings into view the more than two decades of war in Latin America that were tied to the French Revolutionary and Napoleonic Wars, as well as the fact that after 1815 the coordinate states of Europe engaged in a violent subjection of large parts of the non-Western world on a wider scale than before, which also caused repeated anticolonial uprisings and war.

One of the first major and successful anticolonial struggles was the American War of Independence fought with militiamen and conscripts against the British ancien régime army. The American revolutionaries inspired their French counterparts, who also tried to mobilize with patriotic-national propaganda for a mass army based on volunteers and conscripts. The 1789 Revolution in France established a new political regime, but this soon took up familiar ambitions for French hegemony in Europe.[73] Starting in April 1792, France was, once again, at war with a wide European coalition of monarchies including Austria, Britain, Prussia, and Russia. Early victories over Prussian and Austrian troops formed the starting point for the expansion of territory and influence in the Austrian Netherlands (1792–93), the United Dutch Provinces (1794–95), the German territories on the western banks of the Rhine (1797), Italy (1797), and Switzerland (1798). The French Revolutionary Wars ended in 1802. General Napoleon Bonaparte, however, who came into power as first consul of France with the coup of 18 Brumaire in 1799 and crowned himself emperor in 1804, continued revolutionary imperial politics with non-stop warfare until his final defeat in 1815. The loss of the Franco-Spanish fleet at Trafalgar (1805) thwarted French ambitions to invade Britain. On the European continent, however, the years 1805–7 were a period of continuous victory for Napoleon's armies.

Inevitably, the French Revolutionary and Napoleonic Wars, too, were fought outside Europe. France's Egyptian and Syrian campaign (1798–1801) was undertaken to further French commercial interests and to harm those of Britain, but the scheme faltered as British troops made Napoleon withdraw. During the Haitian Revolution (1791–1804), French, British, and Spanish armies and those of the formerly enslaved fought a war to control the most lucrative of France's colonies. Napoleon's attempts in 1802–3 to recon-quer the island and reintroduce slavery failed, and the new Republic of Haiti declared its independence in December 1804. Elsewhere in the Caribbean, successive British attempts between 1804 and 1810 to drive out competing colonial powers cost France almost all its remaining possessions in the area.

In Europe, Napoleon's string of victories was broken after his invasion of Spain in 1808. Guerrilla warfare by the Spanish and the supporting force of British and Portuguese troops drove the French out of Spain by late 1813. Napoleon's invasion of Russia in June 1812 ended disastrously seven months later. Russia, Prussia, Austria, and Britain now formed the core of a new coalition that overwhelmed Napoleon's troops at the Battle of Leipzig (October 1813). By March 1814, the Austrians and Prussians approached Paris, forcing Napoleon's abdication on April 6, 1814. Within a year he was back, having escaped exile on the island of Elba off the Italian coast. The final defeat awaited him at Waterloo (June 1815), which ended twenty-three years of near-continuous war.

In 1815, the Napoleonic Wars were over in Europe, but they had started wars of inde-pendence across the Atlantic Ocean that continued for another fifteen years.[74] The

French invasion of Portugal and Spain in 1807–8 had weakened the hold of those countries' imperial governments over their colonies. A wish for greater autonomy on the part of colonial elites and more widely felt desires for independence led to political, and eventually military, conflicts that intensified following the restoration of the imperial regimes in Lisbon and Madrid after 1815. The Spanish American Wars of Independence (1808–30) led to the making of a string of independent states and as good as ended the Spanish and Portuguese colonial presence in Latin America. From Paraguay in 1811 to Mexico in 1830, new states emerged out of wars that often turned into civil wars. Because many of these struggles remained unsettled after independence, violent conflict became endemic, with the military often functioning as the mainstay of weakly developed states.

One major change in warfare in the period of the Wars of Revolution and Independence was the further increase of the size of armies, especially on the European continent. Again, France led the way. The 1793 *levée en masse* created a massive army of over 600,000 troops.[75] Throughout the revolutionary and Napoleonic period, France managed to keep afoot armies that were much larger than their ancien régime predecessors, forcing its adversaries into a similar expansion. Universal conscription was introduced by France during the revolutionary wars; Austria and Prussia followed during the Napoleonic Wars with militia systems that supplemented the professional army and tried to mobilize volunteers. But many states continued to rely on ancien régime modes of recruitment and nevertheless were able to increase the size of their armies too. As a result of this development, Austria had forces numbering close to 600,000 in 1809.[76] In August 1813, the Prussian army had 281,000 men under arms.[77] In that year, Austria, Prussia, Russia, and their allies had 570,000 troops at their disposal for battle against Napoleon. The French-led coalition could bring 410,000 men into the field.[78] This development resulted in battles of unprecedented size. Over 565,000 soldiers were involved in the Battle of Leipzig in October 1813, which became the largest and most lethal battle in history until World War I. In comparison, the largest battle of the Thirty Years' War, the first Battle of Breitenfeld (September 1631) saw 77,000 troops clash, and at Malplaquet (September 1709) during the War of the Spanish Succession, 170,000 men fought.[79] To be sure, these three battles were exceptional in their time; most battles were smaller, but in general armies and battles became larger between 1600 and the early nineteenth century. This development had far-reaching consequences for the relation between war, military, and gender.

WAR, THE MILITARY, AND GENDER

In 1981, Barton C. Hacker demonstrated in his pathbreaking article "Women and Military Institutions in Early Modern Europe: A Reconnaissance" that "women were a normal part of European armies at least from the fourteenth until well into the nineteenth century." He emphasized that his focus on this period did not mean that "women were absent from earlier European or from Western armies; they followed classical armies and medieval armies as well."[80] Hacker was the first to argue that early modern armed forces "could not have functioned as well, perhaps could not have functioned at all, without the service of women."[81] His article inspired some interest in the study of women and early modern warfare, but in 1996 Peter H. Wilson still could accurately write that historians had barely scratched the surface.[82]

Only very slowly since the mid-1990s have scholars of military and war of the early modern period integrated a gender perspective into their research. Compared to the gender history of military and war of the nineteenth and especially the twentieth century, research on the previous eras is still astonishingly underdeveloped. Some monographs on the role of soldiers' women in eighteenth-century armies such as the British and Prussian exist,[83] but we still have no monographs that explore major conflicts like the Thirty Years' War or the Seven Years' War from a gender perspective.[84] The gender dimension of seventeenth- and eighteenth-century colonial conquest and warfare in different regions of the globe also needs much more examination. To date, colonial New England is the best researched region.[85] Better studied from a gender perspective are the American Revolution, the French Revolutionary and Napoleonic Wars, the Haitian Revolution, and the Spanish American Wars of Independence.[86]

Overviews that cover the entangled development of war, military, and gender from the sixteenth to the early nineteenth century are rare and focus on Europe. One of the first attempts to bring together military, women's, and gender historians for such a project was a conference in Berlin in 1997 that resulted in a German-language volume on military, war, and the gender order in a historical perspective published one year later.[87] John A. Lynn's 2008 monograph, *Women, Armies and Warfare in Early Modern Europe*, was the first English-language survey on the theme of women, armies, and warfare in early modern Europe.[88] In a current overview of the research on gender and war in European history for the period of 1600 to the 1780s, Peter H. Wilson advocates a closer integration of the approaches from military history and women's and gender history and argues that this would allow historians to better understand the impact of gender on war, as well as its place in war and military institutions. He demonstrates this by showing how gender featured in the regulatory framework consolidated by later seventeenth-century states to curb warfare's costs and excesses and by exploring the place of gender in command, combat, and logistical support. His general thesis is that change across this period remained a matter of degree rather than absolutes, with the characterization of male and female roles and spaces in the military and war broadly similar to those prior to 1650, but marked by greater regulation and permanence.[89] Alan Forrest and others suggested a similar argument for the period of the Revolutionary and Napoleonic Wars in Europe.[90]

Current studies on the eighteenth- and early nineteenth-century Americas likewise emphasize gradual change and continuities over the disruption of upheavals, riots, and revolutions. Serena Zabin, in her examination of war, culture, and gender from the early colonial conflicts and the Seven Years' War to the American Revolutionary War and the War of 1812, and Catherine Davies, in her exploration of the impact of warfare and militarization on the social and gender order in the Spanish Atlantic Empire in the transformative period from the 1780s to the 1830s that includes early anticolonial uprisings and the Spanish American Wars of Independence, both emphasize how ideas about the gender order shaped society, warfare, and military culture. They stress the previously underexplored gender dimension of the warfare of the Indigenous nations in the Americas against their White American, British, French, and Spanish colonizers. In this warfare, which was often organized around structures of kinship, women played an important role.[91]

Female Soldiers, Camp Followers, and Other Army Women

The research on women in early modern militaries and warfare began with studies on cross-dressed female soldiers, who were already a subject of fascination for contemporaries because they turned the dominant ideas of the gender order upside down by challenging the male right to bear arms and kill on behalf of the state or another higher power, like the churches. These female soldiers, often labelled "amazons," not only attracted considerable attention in the contemporary public, but also inspired poets, novelists, and historians to write about them. However, these popular-history narratives reveal little about the real experiences of military service of female soldiers or other army women. Instead, they inform us about the dominant ideas of the gender order of war. Research by women and gender historians, literary studies scholars, and art historians on the subject of cross-dressed female soldiers first appeared in the 1980s. Most authors were especially interested in the contemporary perception, cultural representations, and collective recollection of these women.[92]

In the 1980s, the scholarship by feminist historians on female camp followers and army women in the early modern period also took off. The already-mentioned 1981 article by Hacker was the first publication from a feminist perspective on this subject. His research contended, and later studies on Europe and the Americas confirmed, that women were in one way or another part of all early modern military communities. The experience of the women in the trains of the armies on campaign did not vary much during the seventeenth and eighteenth centuries. A more dramatic change emerged only in the period of the Wars of Revolution and Independence, which affected mainly three related dimensions: first, the number of women following the armies in their trains, which was further reduced and controlled when different forms of volunteering and universal conscription permitted mass warfare; second, the importance of camp followers and army women for the logistic of the troops on campaign, which dramatically decreased because of a reorganization and professionalization of armies; and third, their position in the military, which became more regulated. State and army leaders had tried to reduce the number of married soldiers since the second half of the seventeenth century, but only now they were able to do so successfully because of military reforms that accompanied the introduction of universal conscription in armies like the French and Prussian. The main tasks of women in the military, however, stayed the same: washing, sewing, cooking, and nursing for soldiers and officers and providing female company. In general, it was mainly women from the working classes who joined the army as cross-dressed female soldiers, camp followers, and officially recognized auxiliaries. Most of them were driven by social and economic pressures. As members of the campaign community, they endured the same hardships and dangers as the soldiers did.[93]

In the Indigenous armies of Spanish South America and North America that fought against the White colonizers, women were involved in different roles, often including combat. In the Tupac Amaru and Catarista rebellions (1780–83) in the Peruvian Andes (today Peru and Bolivia), called in Indigenous history the "Great Rebellions," for example, between 6,000 and 20,000 armed men *and* women rose up against the Spanish colonial authorities in an attempt to revive an Incan state and were brutally defeated. The male *and* female rebel leaders were captured, executed, or deported. Overall, the estimated death toll of all ethnicities, but mainly Indigenous people, was 100,000 because the Spanish implemented a harsh retaliation regime against both combatants and noncombatants.[94]

Visual Gendered Representations of the Military and War

One of the ways by which contemporaries learned about the gender order in the military was from visual representations like the fascinating sixteenth- and seventeenth-century etchings and woodcuts that show lansquenets (*Landsknechte*) and female camp followers of the aggregated contract armies.[95] Contemporary artists produced these prints for wealthy burghers, who were fascinated by the enigmatic "Otherness" of military life. The prints reassured them in their bourgeois civility. One of these sixteenth-century artists was Daniel Hopfer, who lived in the southern German town of Augsburg and is widely believed to have been the first to use etching in printmaking, which allowed the production of several prints for the market.[96] Interestingly, Hopfer's depictions of soldier couples who worked together for their subsistence and shared a bed, married or not, were not morally judgmental. They show strong women who endure war with their partners. His images reflected one dimension of the reality of the gender relations in the aggregated contract armies, similar to the picture in Sebastian Vrancx's *War Scene of the Thirty Years War* (Figure 1.1) discussed at the start of this chapter: the importance of women as camp followers for early modern armies.[97] Another dimension is the violence in the relations between soldiers and civilians in general and women in particular, much like Vrancx's oeuvre shows in its scenes of soldiers plundering villages and attacking travelers. One example is his oil painting, *Soldiers Plundering a Farm during the Thirty Years' War*, from 1620 (Figure 1.3), which emphasizes the mercilessness of the soldiers' attack: they steal from, rape, and kill helpless civilians.

Neither Vrancx's paintings of the Thirty Years' War nor later visual representations of the warfare of state commission armies in the eighteenth century have yet been sufficiently studied from a gender perspective, even though there is much to learn from them about the gendered perception of warfare by educated contemporaries. The paintings by Hyacinth de La Pegna that document battles of the Seven Years' War, for example, could be a rich resource for such analysis. The French painter created several

FIGURE 1.3 *Soldiers Plundering a Farm during the Thirty Years War*, oil painting by Sebastian Vrancx (1573–1647), [n.p.], 1620.

(Deutsches Historisches Museum, Berlin/A. Psille)

artworks commissioned by the Austrian court. In 1755, Empress Maria Theresia appointed him *peintre extraordinaire* (extraordinary painter), which came with an apanage and regular commissions. One example is the oil painting *The Attack at Hochkirch on 17 October 1758* from 1759/60 (Figure 1.4). It shows the nighttime Austrian attack on the large Prussian camp, which ended with an Austrian victory and the well-ordered retreat of the Prussian army. The battle marked a turning point in the history of the conflict: Austria finally seized the offensive initiative. The painting indicates the dimensions of the battle and the formation of the fighting in lines with muskets and bayonets, but it also hints at the role of women in warfare. In the left corner of the foreground it shows three women, one with a child, whom the Austrian soldiers surprise in their tents at the periphery of the Prussian camp. Their male companions, dressed like officers, have already been killed. Without male protection, the women can only beg for mercy. These helpless women represent the female vulnerability to injury in war. With vulnerable women at its margins, the painting confirms the contemporary belief, shared by governments and military leadership, that warfare is a "man's business," where women should have no place.[98]

In the second half of the eighteenth century, the message from visual representations of women in the military seems to have been increasingly that soldiers' wives should stay in the garrison, serve the men, and ensure their well-being. One example is the

FIGURE 1.4 *The Attack on the Prussian Camp at Hochkirch on 14 October 1758*, oil painting by Hyacinth de La Pegna (1707–72), depicting Prussian and Austrian soldiers fighting in close combat in the battle at Hochkirch during the Seven Years' War, [n.p.], 1759/60.

(Heeresgeschichtliches Museum, Vienna)

work of the English artists Thomas Rowlandson. In his 1788 caricature *English Barracks* (Figure 1.5), he shows the simplicity and domestic bliss of virile English soldiers and their orderly wives in the garrison—a picture that, as we know from research by Jennine Hurl-Eamon, had little to do with the reality of garrison life.[99] But it reassured the men of the English middle and upper classes, the potential buyers of the caricature, that everything was in order in the British military, including gender relations. In the complementary caricature *French Barracks* from 1791, Rowlandson satirizes the effeminacy and foppishness of the French soldiers and officers, the squalidness of their womankind, and the untidiness of their joint garrison life, reassuring the public in a situation of heightened tensions between Britain and France—one year before the start of the French Revolutionary Wars—that the English had little to fear from the French revolutionary army.[100]

The gendered visual representations of military and war from the French Revolutionary and Napoleonic Wars are more studied than eighteenth-century art from both sides of the Atlantic. French art became propagandistic, intended to idealize first the revolution and later Napoleon and his empire. Neoclassicism was the predominant artistic style in France toward the end of the eighteenth century, influenced by a rediscovery of the art of the ancient world. Artists invoked the ancient classical world in service of contemporary ideas

FIGURE 1.5 *English Barracks*, caricature by Thomas Rowlandson (1756–1827), showing the barracks life of English soldiers with their wenches, wives, and children, hand-colored etching and aquatint, [n.p.], 1788.

(Brown University Library, Anne S. K. Brown Military Collection)

or events. Especially in paintings of Napoleonic France, the works often revolved around the military and a glorification of Napoleon's campaigns. Battle paintings were increasingly produced for public buildings and became larger than ever before. One major subject was the contesting images of military masculinity, their frictions, and change. The already-discussed painting by Antoine-Jean Gros, *Napoleon on the Battlefield at Eylau, February 9, 1807*, from 1808 (Figure 1.2), is one example. Several artists produced battle paintings and heroic art with national heroes at their center, like Gros, Jacques-Louis David, Jean-Auguste-Dominique Ingres, or Anne-Louis Girodet.[101] At the same time, a growing market for satirical, often subversive, visual commentary on current affairs, including warfare, developed. Its artists, like Rowlandson, intensively used gender stereotypes for their caricatures, which became an important political medium especially, but not only, in the countries that fought against Napoleon, such as Britain, Austria, Prussia, and Russia.[102]

War Mobilization, Masculinity, and Citizenship

Constructions of military masculinity became a theme of research by gender historians in the 1990s, and one central period of their studies was the transitional era from the eighteenth to the nineteenth century, first with a focus on Europe. The research by gender historians is based on and closely related to the research by military historians on the changing forms of military mobilization.[103] Two of the major questions were how the leaders of states and militaries were able to mobilize men for the growing armies and what role concepts of masculinity and citizenship played here. The focus of this research is the interrelationship between the emergence of new ways of mass mobilization of volunteers, militias, and conscripts; the development of new ideas of gender as a universal, natural binary opposition; and the rise of the notion of men as universal male political subjects since the Age of the Wars of Revolution and Independence. The introduction of universal male citizenship with the French Revolution and the derivation of first volunteering and later universal male conscription as a male duty based on this right had a long-lasting aftermath that also affected other countries because it created a nexus between masculinity, military duties, and citizenship rights. This nexus, often considered by contemporaries to be effective in military terms but politically dangerous, was introduced and transformed in other historical contexts, for example, by France's opponents Austria and Prussia in 1809 and 1813. Where it was rejected, like in Britain, it nevertheless made its presence felt in what became a conscious refusal of the model of the modern citizen-soldier army in favor of other, perhaps less effective but politically more reliable, modes of mobilization. Always controversial and never fully implemented, even in contexts where it was supposedly fully endorsed, the model of universal conscription and, with it, the citizen-soldier loomed large in the background of all nineteenth-century debates over military reform and political citizenship.[104] In a century in which the rising women's movement increasingly called for civil and political equality of women, the nexus between masculinity, military duties, and citizenship was also an argument against equal political citizenship for women.[105]

Society, Gender, and the Costs of War

Mass warfare on the unprecedented scale of the Age of the Wars of Revolution and Independence was possible only because the civilian population—men and women alike—was mobilized through patriotic-national propaganda, which presented the period's conflicts as a "holy war," "people's war," "war of national defense," or a "struggle for the liberation of the nation." Civilians had to support the war not only politically, but also financially and practically. The *levée en masse* of 1793 set out an inspiring example even for France's enemies. Whereas French women were to become "republican mothers" who supported the revolutionary struggle with war work, charity, and nursing, women in the ancien régime states that fought against France had to support the conflict in a similar way as "patriotic mothers." The "national emergency situation" of a people's war everywhere opened opportunities for women, especially from the middle and noble classes, in arenas of public life that had previously been closed to them. They were allowed—it was said—to expand their "motherly duties" beyond their families because the "nation was in danger."[106]

Alan Forrest and others argued that during the French Revolutionary and Napoleonic Wars the mobilization of society indeed played an important role for the financial, material, and practical support of warfare. The population was asked to donate money and material goods for the equipment of volunteers and militiamen; contribute to war charity for war invalids, soldiers' wives, war widows, and orphans; and help with medical care for sick and wounded soldiers.[107] At the same time, civilians, including women and children, more systematically than before became targets of economic warfare. This was the case especially with Napoleon's economic blockade, the Continental System (1806–14), which brought into effect a large-scale embargo against British trade and affected the economies and societies of most countries on the European continent that France forced to comply with it.[108] The research on the economic and social aftermath of the Napoleonic Wars in different regions and for different social groups started only recently.[109]

Similar to earlier conflicts, civilians also became victims of sometimes-atrocious war violence.[110] Scorched-earth operations were part of established strategy in early modern Europe. In earlier conflicts, two operations in particular placed civilians at risk: sieges and the search for plunder during the sacking that followed capitulation. During the Napoleonic Wars, the sheer size of armies and the number of the troops massed for battles affected civilians more widely. Soldiers on both sides lived off the land, destroyed villages and towns with their shelling, and devastated gardens and fields. The campaigns uprooted large numbers of civilian refugees and brought deadly epidemics to the regions the troops marched through and fought over.[111] More research is needed on the everyday history of early modern conflicts and campaigns from a gender perspective to determine the dimensions and forms of violence against civilians. This will help answer the question of whether the Napoleonic Wars were indeed the first conflicts on the European continent in which civilians were deliberately targeted as part of a strategy to destroy the enemy's capacity and will to fight. The existing research indicates that this was a strategy in European warfare before the Revolutionary and Napoleonic Wars. Civilians were also regularly targeted in earlier colonial warfare.

In general, the costs of war in terms of soldiers and civilians' deaths, let alone in terms of damage to infrastructure and economy, are difficult to establish. The quantification of the costs of early modern war in human life is challenging. Most soldiers died after battle. They died of wounds incurred during battle, but also of diseases and epidemics. These affected civilians, too—but not only during war.[112] In light of such problems, historical work on the lethality of war is often based on data that allow for comparison at the cost of simplification. Concentrating exclusively on interstate wars involving or between European great powers and using only numbers on "battle-connected deaths"—that is, deaths of soldiers during and as a result of battle—Jack S. Levy related these statistics to the size of the European population as a way of establishing the changing "intensity" of war since 1500. Levy concluded that although the frequency of war dropped between 1500 and the late twentieth century, the intensity increased considerably at an average of 0.46 percent annually, doubling every 150 years. The seventeenth century combined a very high frequency of war with a relatively low intensity; during the eighteenth century the frequency was lower than in the other four centuries, but intensity rose.[113] This tells us something about the development of war's lethality in the early modern period, but the picture remains limited. The number of soldiers' deaths on campaigns as a result of disease and exposure is not included, and neither is the number of deaths of civilians or of liminal groups such as camp followers. Civil wars and wars between small states are not represented, and Levy's work also excludes wars between states and nonstate entities or colonial wars in which limited numbers of Western troops were capable of doing great damage to Indigenous societies.[114]

Although no reliable calculations of long-term developments exist, the available sources have given rise to a narrative of paradox about the impact of early modern war on the lives of civilians. On the one hand, in the wake of the politicoreligious wars of the sixteenth century, there emerged after 1648 an increased awareness of the need to protect civilians against the violence and destruction of war. Attempts were made to bring war and soldiers under control, although civil war and colonial war remained outside these attempts at regulation. Underlying these developments was an increased differentiation between combatants and noncombatants, of soldiers and civilians, both as cultural categories and in social practices. The way armies and warfare developed tended, on the other hand, to do ever greater damage to civilians' lives. The growing size of armies and of the attendant scope of war increased the toll on civilians, if only because the expansion of armies led them to operate in developed, relatively densely populated areas where they could easily obtain food and forage.[115] The increasing differentiation between soldiers and civilians, but also the progressive blurring of this boundary, were the result of the same set of military transformations that had enabled the expansion of war's scope. The standing army, with its large numbers of soldiers who were permanently under arms, had helped create legal and social differences between soldiers and civilians; it also made possible, however, wars in which this difference had little meaning.

Furthermore, several conflicts seldom have been recognized as wars and thus do not feature in the research by military historians. As Elizabeth Colwill argues, the transatlantic slave trade is one such example. It can be thought of as being predicated on and itself constituting "an ongoing state of war"[116]—a state of war the lethality of which is hard to account for in models that build on more limited notions of war. She contends that a definition of war restricted to conventional battles orchestrated by monarchs or nation-states elides slavery as a primary form of state-sponsored violence at the heart of Europe's colonial wars until the nineteenth century. This form of warfare involved the forcible conversion of persons to chattel through the legal and military arms of the state—a conversion secured through the subjection of sexual, productive, and reproductive labor and the erasure of genealogies and family ties. In this sense, slavery could be seen as a protracted state of war. Armed conflict fueled the slave trade, slave revolts blended into "official" wars, and enslaved people sometimes spoke of slavery as a state of war.

Sexual Violence

There is one important form of cruelty that is not included in most narratives of early modern warfare: sexual violence. In 2011, Elizabeth D. Heineman published one of the first volumes that explored the subject also for the pre-twentieth-century period under the title *Sexual Violence in Conflict Zones*.[117] For her, sexual violence "includes (but is not limited to) rape, sexual mutilation, sexual humiliation, forced prostitution, and forced pregnancy. Victims can be male and female."[118] The term *conflict zones* describes "situations of mass armed conflicts, or 'lethal intergroup violence,' whether or not there has been a formal declaration of war, and whether or not state actors play a leading role in the conflict."[119] This approach is especially useful for the analysis of sexual violence in early modern warfare in Europe and its colonies, because it includes a broad variety of forms of sexual violence and of conflicts and emphasizes the often-blurred borders between war and peace. As the volume by Heineman demonstrated, sexual violence was as much a part of early modern warfare as it was part of later conflicts, but it played out in distinct ways in different types of conflict.

Antonia I. Castañeda therefore argued that in colonial warfare, "sexual violence functioned as an institutionalized mechanism for ensuring subordination and compliance. It was one instrument of sociopolitical terrorism and control—first of women and then of the group under conquest."[120] She showed that during the Spanish conquest of Alta California in the second half of the eighteenth century, soldiers regularly raped Amerindian women. This sexual violence against the racial Other "became a punishable offense only when it was the source of military or political problems."[121] Similarly, Angela Woollacott emphasizes the important role of sexual violence, including forced prostitution and sexual slavery, in the colonial expansion of Britain and France and their attempts to suppress Indigenous resistance during the nineteenth century.[122]

In the context of the American Revolution, sexual violence played a different role, as the work by Sharon Block on rape and sexual power in early America has shown. She claimed "that sexual power is contingent upon other forms of power. While early American men regularly used the power of their social location as masters, fathers, or powerful authority figures to coerce sex, military personnel relied on their status as warriors to coerce sex."[123] Block asserted that this led to an increase of sexual violence, mainly by British soldiers, who perceived the rebelling American population as the occupied enemy Other during the American Revolutionary War. For them, rape, like plundering, was part of the spoils of war. The revolutionary press, in turn, reported regularly about the sexual assaults by the enemy and seized on them as an indication of the "illegitimacy of British rule, because legitimate patriarchs, whether as individuals or as fathers of the nation, did not rape. Stories of rape confirmed American determination for rebellion, rhetorically creating a collective body of male resisters to British imperial rule," who had to protect American girls and women.[124]

Gendered War Memories

Traumatic war experiences formed not only the individual recollection of conflicts, but also collective memory, which was and is gendered. But for the early modern period, despite the memory-history boom of the past decades, only a small number of studies from a gender perspective exists. The focus of these works is furthermore on the collective memories of the Age of the Wars of Revolution and Independence.[125] This research shows that gender was one of the most important interpretive patterns that structured the process of memory production. Women were often the "subjects of memory" because they transmitted more differentiated, complex, and often ambiguous communicative memories; but at the same time they were the "objects of oblivion" in the production of the lasting cultural memory dominated by men.[126] In this gendered process of memory production, women's memories tended to disappear from the public recollection, not because they did not exist, but because they were regarded as insignificant. This is especially true of nineteenth-century national cultures of memory, which—based on the constructed division between the "public" and the "private sphere"—associated men with "public memory" and women with "private memory." This distinction subsequently framed female memories as less important and excluded them from the national memory culture. As a result, women's support and involvement in the conflicts of the period of the Wars of Revolution and Independence tended to be forgotten in national memories. The collective recollection concentrated on the male war heroes.[127]

CONCLUSION

Concepts such as military revolution or total war, which are often used to capture the nature of the development of war in the early modern period and the Age of the Wars of Revolution and Independence, suggest radical ruptures and dramatic changes. Changes in weaponry, tactics, and strategy certainly occurred in this era. One area of change that is of particular importance is that of the spectacular increase in the scope of war and in the size of armies and battles, because these changes were profoundly shaped by and affected notions and practices of gender. But radical change existed alongside deep continuities, which recent research has begun to emphasize and which are important for the period's gender history. The insight, for instance, that the state continued to rely much longer than often assumed on the resources of sociopolitical elites and private enterprisers in its attempts to create permanent, standing armies points to a long continuity in the organization of warfare. This continuity extends to and is reflected in the field of gender and gender relations. Despite attempts at exclusion and control, and efforts to reduce their number, the presence of women in standing armies, their garrisons, and campaigns continued into the nineteenth century. Such continuities help put in perspective the modernity of nineteenth- and twentieth-century war. More research, however, is needed on the early modern gender history of military and war before we can draw more definite conclusions about ways in which gender and war after 1800 were shaped by early modern patterns and developments.

NOTES

1. For this subgenre and examples of Vrancx's paintings on this theme, see Michel P. van Maarseveen et al., *Beelden van een strijd: Oorlog en kunst vóór de Vrede van Munster 1621–1648* (Zwolle: Waanders, 1998), 133–47, 148–63, 315, 316, 320, 323, and 324.
2. As, for instance, on the Getty Images website, accessed May 12, 2017, http://www.gettyimages. ca/detail/illustration/population-fleeing-before-enemy-by-sebastian-vrancx-stock-graphic/153415207.
3. John A. Lynn, *Women, Armies, and Warfare in Early Modern Europe* (Cambridge: Cambridge University Press, 2008), 219.
4. See the chapter by Thomas Cardoza and Karen Hagemann on "History and Memory of Army Women and Female Soldiers, 1770s–1870s" in this handbook.
5. Marc Gerstein, "'Le Regard Consolateur Du Grand Homme': Le Concours Pour La Bataille D'Eylau," in *Dominique-Vivant Denon: L'Oeil De Napoléon*, ed. Pierre Rosenberg (Paris: Editions de la Réunion des musées nationaux, 1999), 321–39.
6. See David O'Brien, "Propaganda and the Republic of the Arts in Antoine-Jean Gros's *Napoléon Visiting the Battlefield of Eylau the Morning after the Battle*," *French Historical Studies* 26, no. 2 (2003): 281–314.
7. Barton C. Hacker, "Women and Military Institutions in Early Modern Europe: A Reconnaissance," *Signs* 6, no. 4 (1981): 643–71; Lynn, *Women*, 225–26; Mary Elizabeth Ailes, "Camp Followers, Sutlers, and Soldiers' Wives: Women in Early Modern Armies (c. 1450–c. 1650)," in *A Companion to Women's Military History*, ed. Barton C. Hacker and Margaret Vining (Leiden: Brill, 2012), 61–91; and John A. Lynn, "Essential Women, Necessary Wives, and Exemplary Soldiers: The Military Reality and Cultural Representation of Women's Military Participation (1600–1815)," in Hacker and Vining, *A Companion to Women's Military History*, 93–136.
8. Michael Roberts, "The Military Revolution, 1560–1660," in *Essays in Swedish History* (London: Weidenfeld & Nicolson, 1967), 195–225.
9. Ibid., 196; and Michael Roberts, "Gustav Adolf and the Art of War," in *Essays*, 56–81.
10. Roberts, "Gustav Adolf," 60.
11. Roberts, "Military Revolution," 195.
12. Ibid., 204.
13. Ibid., 205–8.
14. See Lynn, "Essential Women."
15. Clifford J. Rogers, ed., *The Military Revolution Debate: Readings on the Military Transformation of Early Modern Europe* (Boulder, CO: Westview Press, 1995).
16. Geoffrey Parker, "The 'Military Revolution,' 1560–1660—a Myth?," *Journal of Modern History* 48, no. 2 (1976): 195–214.
17. Jeremy Black, *A Military Revolution? Military Change and European Society 1550–1800* (Houndmills, Basingstoke: Macmillan, 1991), 20–22 and 28–30.
18. Ibid., 67–77.
19. Michael Howard, *War in European History* (Oxford: Oxford University Press, 1976), 37. For a critical analysis, see David Parrott, *The Business of War: Military Enterprise and*

Military Revolution in Early Modern Europe (Cambridge: Cambridge University Press, 2012), 4–8.

20. David Parrott, "From Military Enterprise to Standing Armies: War, State and Society in Western Europe, 1600–1700," in *European Warfare, 1350–1750*, ed. Frank Tallett and D. J. B. Trim (Cambridge: Cambridge University Press, 2010), 74–95.

21. Ibid., 77–85.

22. Ibid., 77.

23. David Parrott, "Had a Distinct Template for a 'Western Way of War' Been Established before 1800?," in *The Changing Character of War*, ed. Hew Strachan and Sibylle Scheipers (Oxford: Oxford University Press, 2011), 48–63, 56.

24. See Peter H. Wilson, "German Women and War, 1500–1800," *War in History* 3, no. 2 (1996): 127–60; and the chapter by Peter H. Wilson on "Wars, States, and Gender in Early Modern European Warfare, 1600s–1780s" in this handbook.

25. Geoffrey Parker, *The Military Revolution: Military Innovation and the Rise of the West, 1500–1800* (Cambridge: Cambridge University Press, 1988), 4.

26. Michael C. Paul, "The Military Revolution in Russia, 1550–1682," *Journal of Military History* 68, no. 1 (2004): 9–45; and Gábor Ágoston, "Firearms and Military Adaptation: The Ottomans and the European Military Revolution," *Journal of World History* 25, no. 1 (2014): 85–124.

27. Laichen Sun, "Military Technology Transfers from Ming China and the Emergence of Northern Mainland Southeast Asia (c. 1390–1527)," *Journal of Southeast Asian Studies* 34, no. 3 (2003): 495–517; and Tonio Andrade, "An Accelerating Divergence? The Revisionist Model of World History and the Question of Eurasian Military Parity: Data from East Asia," *Canadian Journal of Sociology/Cahiers canadiens de sociologie* 36, no. 2 (2011): 185–208.

28. See Frank Jacob and Gilmar Visoni-Alonzo, *The Military Revolution in Early Modern Europe: A Revision* (Basingstoke: Palgrave Macmilan, 2016).

29. See Jeremy Black, *Warfare in the Eighteenth Century* (London: Cassell, 1999); Peter H. Wilson, "Warfare in the Old Regime 1648–1789," in *European Warfare, 1453–1815*, ed. Jeremy Black (Basingstoke: Macmillan, 1999), 69–95; Ciro Paoletti, "War, 1688–1812," in *A Companion to Eighteenth-Century Europe*, ed. Peter H. Wilson (Malden, MA: Blackwell, 2009), 464–78; and David Parrott, "Armed Forces," in *The Oxford Handbook of the Ancien Régime*, ed. William Doyle (Oxford: Oxford University Press, 2012), 59–74.

30. Parrott, "Armed Forces," 71.

31. Wilson, "Warfare," 88–89.

32. Paoletti, "War, 1688–1812," 464.

33. Winfried Mönch, "'Rokokostrategen': Ihr Negativer Nachruhm in der Militärgeschichts-schreibung des 20. Jahrhunderts: Das Beispiel von Reinhard Höhn und das Problem des 'Moralischen' Faktors," *Aufklärung* 11, no. 2 (1999): 75–97.

34. Paoletti, "War, 1688–1812," 468; and Parrott, "Armed Forces," 72.

35. Roger Chickering, "Introduction: A Tale of Two Tales; Grand Narratives of War in the Age of Revolution," in *War in an Age of Revolutions, 1775–1815*, ed. Roger Chickering and Stig Förster (Cambridge: Cambridge University Press, 2010), 1–17.

36. Roberts, "Military Revolution," 218.

37. See Roger Chickering, "Total War: The Use and Abuse of a Concept," in *Anticipating Total War: The German and American Experiences, 1871–1914*, ed. Manfred F. Boemeke et al. (Cambridge: Cambridge University Press, 1999), 13–28. Also see the discussion of the concept of total war in the chapter by Karen Hagemann and Sonya O. Rose on "War and Gender: The Age of the World Wars and Its Aftermath—an Overview" in this handbook.

38. Jean-Yves Guiomar, *L'Invention de la guerre totale, XVIIIᵉ-XXᵉ siècle* (Paris: Le Félin Kiron, 2004), 19–20.

39. David A. Bell, *The First Total War: Napoleon's Europe and the Birth of Modern Warfare* (London: Bloomsbury, 2007), 8.

40. Ibid., 79–83 and 113–19; and Bell, "The Birth of Militarism in the Age of Democratic Revolutions," in *War, Demobilization and Memory: The Legacy of War in the Era of Atlantic Revolutions*, ed. Alan Forrest et al. (Basingstoke: Palgrave Macmillan, 2016), 30–47.

41. Peter H. Wilson, "Was the Thirty Years War a 'Total War'?," in *Civilians and War in Europe, 1618–1815*, ed. Erica Charters et al. (Liverpool: Liverpool University Press, 2012), 21–35, 23.

42. Chickering, "Total War," 15, 20, and 23.

43. See Harriet B. Applewhite and Darline Gay Levy, "Women and Militant Citizenship in Revolutionary Paris," in *Rebel Daughters: Women and the French Revolution*, ed. Sara E. Melzer and Leslie W. Kabine (New York: Oxford University Press, 1992.), 79–101.

44. See Chickering, "Total War," 13–28.

45. Jeremy Black, "Introduction," in Black, *European Warfare*, 1–22.

46. Johannes Burkhardt, *Der Dreißigjährige Krieg* (Frankfurt am Main: Suhrkamp, 1992), 9–12.

47. See Nicola M. Sutherland, "The Origins of the Thirty Years War and the Structure of European Politics," *English Historical Review* 107, no. 424 (1992): 587–625; and Brendan Simms, *Europe: The Struggle for Supremacy, from 1453 to the Present* (New York: Basic Books, 2013).

48. For the following, see Burkhardt, *Dreißigjährige Krieg*; Burkhardt, "Die Friedlosigkeit der Frühen Neuzeit: Grundlegung einer Theorie der Bellizität Europas," *Zeitschrift für Historische Forschung* 24, no. 4 (1997): 509–74; Burkhardt, "The Thirty Years' War," in *A Companion to the Reformation World*, ed. R. Pho-chia Hsia (Oxford: Blackwell, 2004), 272–90; and Burkhardt, "Wars of States or Wars of State-Formation?," in *War, the State and International Law in Seventeenth Century Europe*, ed. Olaf Asbach and Peter Schröder (Farnham: Routledge, 2016), 17–34.

49. See Burkhardt, *Dreißigjährige Krieg*; Geoffrey Parker, ed. *The Thirty Years' War* (London: Routledge, 1997); Peter H. Wilson, *The Thirty Years War: Europe's Tragedy* (Cambridge, MA: Harvard University Press, 2009); and Hans Medick, *Der Dreissigjährigen Krieg: Zeugnisse vom Leben mit Gewalt* (Göttingen: Wallstein, 2018).

50. John A. Lynn, "The Pattern of Army Growth, 1445–1945," in *Tools of War: Instruments, Ideas, and Institutions of Warfare, 1445–1871*, ed. Lynn (Urbana: University of Illinois Press, 1990), 1–27, 2–3.

51. Ibid., 3.

52. Burkhardt, "Thirty Years' War," 285.

53. See, for instance, Jane Burbank and Frederick Cooper, *Empires in World History: Power and the Politics of Difference* (Princeton, NJ: Princeton University Press, 2010), 182–83.

54. Wilson, "Warfare," 80.

55. Geoff Mortimer, "War by Contract, Credit and Contribution: The Thirty Years War," in *Early Modern Military History, 1450–1815*, ed. Geoff Mortimer (Basingstoke: Palgrave Macmillan, 2004), 101–17.

56. Burkhardt, "Wars of States," 26.

57. John A. Lynn, *The Wars of Louis XIV, 1667–1714* (London: Longman, 1999).

58. Matthew S. Anderson, *The War of the Austrian Succession, 1740–1748* (London: Longman, 1995); and Reed Browning, *The War of the Austrian Succession* (New York: St. Martin's, 1993).

59. On the Seven Years' War, see Fred Anderson, *Crucible of War: The Seven Years' War and the Fate of Empire in British North America* (New York: Alfred A. Knopf, 2000);

Mark H. Danley and Patrick J. Speelman, eds., *The Seven Years' War: Global Views* (Boston: Brill, 2012); and Marian Füssel, *Der Preis des Ruhms: Eine Weltgeschichte des Siebenjährigen Krieges* (München: Beck, 2019).

60. See Jeremy Black, *The War for America: The Fight for Independence, 1775–1783.* 2d edn. (Burton-on-Trent: Wrens Park, 1998); Stephen Conway, *A Short History of the American Revolutionary War* (London: I. B. Tauris, 2013); and John E. Ferling, *Whirlwind: The American Revolution and the War That Won It* (New York: Bloomsbury Press, 2015).

61. Jürgen Luh, *Kriegskunst in Europa 1650–1800* (Cologne: Böhlau, 2004), 17.

62. Bernhard R. Kroener, "'Das Schwungrad an der Staatsmaschine'? Die Bedeutung der bewaffneten Macht in der europäischen Geschichte der Frühen Neuzeit," in *Krieg und Frieden: Militär und Gesellschaft in der Frühen Neuzeit,* ed. Bernhard R. Kroener and Ralf Pröve (Paderborn: Schöningh, 1996), 1–23, 7.

63. Frank Tallett, "Soldiers in Western Europe, c. 1500–1790," in *Fighting for a Living: A Comparative History of Military Labour, 1500–2000,* ed. Erik-Jan Zürcher (Amsterdam: Amsterdam University Press, 2013), 135–67, 145.

64. Ibid., 160–61; and Parrott, "Armed Forces," 67–68.

65. Laurent Henninger, "Military Revolutions and Military History," in *Palgrave Advances in Modern Military History,* ed. Matthew Hughes and William J. Philpott (Basingstoke: Palgrave Macmillan, 2006), 8–22.

66. David Parrott, "Military," in *Europe 1450 to 1789: Encyclopedia of the Early Modern World,* ed. Jonathan Dewald (New York: Charles Scribner's Sons, 2004), 117–38; and Peter Way, "'The Scum of Every Country, the Refuse of Mankind': Recruiting the British Army in the Eighteenth Century," in Zürcher, *Fighting,* 291–329.

67. Wilson, "Warfare," 76; and Wilson, "New Approaches under the Old Regime," in Mortimer, *Early Modern Military History,* ed. Mortimer, 135–54.

68. See Clifford J. Rogers, "Tactics and the Face of Battle," in Tallett and Trim, *European Warfare,* 203–35; and Carol B. Stevens, "Warfare on Land," in *The Oxford Handbook of Early Modern European History, 1350–1750,* ed. Hamish Scott (Oxford: Oxford University Press, 2015), 561–90.

69. Simon Pepper, "Aspects of Operational Art: Communications, Cannon and Small War," in Tallett and Trim, *European Warfare,* 81–201.

70. Paul W. Schroeder, *The Transformation of European Politics, 1763–1848* (Oxford: Clarendon Press, 1994), 803.

71. Ibid., v.

72. See the chapter by Stefan Dudink, Karen Hagemann, and Mischa Honeck on "War and Gender: Nineteenth-Century Wars of Nations and Empires—an Overview" in this handbook.

73. Geoffrey Best, *War and Society in Revolutionary Europe, 1770–1870* (London: Fontana, 1982); David Gates, *The Napoleonic Wars, 1803–1815* (London: Pimlico, 2003); and Charles Esdaile, *Napoleon's Wars: An International History 1803–1815* (London: Allen Lane, 2007).

74. See John Charles Chasteen, *Americanos: Latin America's Struggle for Independence* (Oxford: Oxford University Press, 2008).

75. Alan Forrest, "*La patrie en danger*: The French Revolution and the First *Levée en masse*," in *The People in Arms: Military Myth and National Mobilization since the French Revolution,* ed. Daniel Moran and Arthur Waldron (Cambridge: Cambridge University Press, 2003), 8–32, 12.

76. Gunther E. Rothenberg, *Napoleon's Great Adversaries: The Archduke Charles and the Austrian Army, 1792–1814* (London: B. T. Batsford, 1982), 126.

77. Karen Hagemann, *Revisiting Prussia's Wars against Napoleon: History, Culture and Memory* (Cambridge: Cambridge University Press, 2015), 62.

78. Gunther E. Rothenberg, *The Napoleonic Wars* (London: Cassell, 2001), 176–84.

79. Micheal Clodfelter, *Warfare and Armed Conflicts: A Statistical Reference to Casualty and Other Figures, 1500–2000*, 2nd ed. (Jefferson, NC: McFarland, 2002), 38, 76, and 186.

80. Hacker, "Women," 643.

81. Ibid., 644.

82. See Wilson, "German Women and War."

83. Recent studies are Beate Engelen, *Soldatenfrauen in Preußen: Eine Strukturanalyse der Garnisonsgesellschaft im späten 17. und im 18. Jahrhundert* (Münster: LIT, 2005); and Jennine Hurl-Eamon, *Marriage and the British Army in the Long Eighteenth Century: "The Girl I Left behind Me"* (Oxford: Oxford University Press, 2014).

84. An exception for the Thirty Years' War with a focus on Sweden is, Mary Elizabeth Ailes, *Courage and Grief: Women and Sweden's Thirty Years' War* (Lincoln, NE: University of Nebraska Press, 2018).

85. See Ann M. Little, *Abraham in Arms: War and Gender in Colonial New England* (Philadelphia: University of Pennsylvania Press, 2007); and Holly A. Mayer, *Belonging to the Army: Camp Followers and Community during the American Revolution* (Columbia: University of South Carolina Press, 1996).

86. See Karen Hagemann et al., eds., *Gender, War, and Politics: Transatlantic Perspectives, 1775–1830* (Basingstoke: Palgrave Macmillan, 2010); and Hagemann et al., eds., "Gender, War and the Nation in the Period of the Revolutionary and Napoleonic Wars—European Perspectives," special issue, *European History Quarterly* 37, no. 4 (2007); as well as the literature in the chapters by Serena Zabin on "War, Culture, and Gender in Colonial and Revolutionary North America," Catherine Davies on "War, Gender, and Society in Late Colonial and Revolutionary Spanish America," and Alan Forrest on "Society, Mass Warfare, and Gender in Europe during and after the Revolutionary and Napoleonic Wars" in this handbook.

87. Karen Hagemann and Ralf Pröve, eds., *Landsknechte, Soldatenfrauen und Nationalkrieger: Militär, Krieg und Geschlechterordnung im historischen Wandel* (Frankfurt am Main: Campus, 1998); and Hagemann, "Militär, Krieg und Geschlechterverhältnisse: Untersuchungen, Überlegungen und Fragen zur Militärgeschichte der Frühen Neuzeit," in *Klio in Uniform: Probleme und Perspektiven einer modernen Militärgeschichte der Frühen Neuzeit*, ed. Ralf Pröve (Cologne: Böhlau, 1997), 35–88.

88. Lynn, *Women*; and Lynn, "Essential Women."

89. See Wilson, "Wars, States, and Gender" in this handbook.

90. See Hagemann, "Gender, War and the Nation"; and Forrest, "Society, Mass Warfare" in this handbook.

91. See Zabin, "War, Culture, and Gender," and Davies, "War, Gender, and Society" in this handbook; and also Wayne E. Lee, ed., *Empires and Indigenes: Intercultural Alliance, Imperial Expansion, and Warfare in the Early Modern World* (New York: New York University Press, 2011).

92. See Cardoza and Hagemann, "History and Memory" in this handbook.

93. Ibid.

94. See Davies, "War, Gender, and Society" in this handbook.

95. Matthias Rogg, *Landsknechte und Reisläufer: Bilder Vom Soldaten—Ein Stand in der Kunst des 16. Jahrhunderts* (Paderborn: Schöningh, 2002); Rogg, "'Wol auff mit mir, du schoenes weyb': Anmerkungen zur Konstruktion von Männlichkeit im Soldatenbild des

16. Jahrhunderts," in Hagemann and Pröve, *Landsknechte*, 51–73; and Christiane Andersson, "Von 'Metzen' und 'Dirnen': Frauenbilder in Kriegsdarstellungen der Frühen Neuzeit," in Hagemann and Pröve, *Landsknechte*, 117–98.

96. One well-known example is the etching *Soldier and Female Companion*, by Daniel Hopfer (1470–1536), 1525–30; it can be viewed at http://www.britishmuseum.org/research/collection_online/collection_object_details/collection_image_gallery.aspx?assetId=1325 237001&objectId=1446311&partId=1.

97. Rogg, "Wol auff," 56–65.

98. Marian Füssel, "Die Kultur der Niederlage. Wahrnehmung und Repräsentation einer Schlacht des Siebenjährigen Krieges am Beispiel von Hochkirch 1758," in *Der Siebenjährige Krieg (1756–1763): Ein europäischer Weltkrieg im Zeitalter der Aufklärung*, ed. Sven Externbrink (Berlin: De Gruyter, 2011), 261–73.

99. Hurl-Eamon, "*The Girl.*"

100. *French Barracks*, carticature by Thomas Rowlandson (1791), it can be viewed at The Met, http://www.metmuseum.org/art/collection/search/392857.

101. See, for instance, David O'Brien, "Another lieu de mémoire? Napoleonic Painting, the Museum, and French Memory," in *War Memories: The Revolutionary and Napoleonic Wars in Modern European Culture*, ed. Alan Forrest et al. (Basingstoke: Palgrave Macmillan, 2012), 291–316; and O'Brien, *After the Revolution: Antoine-Jean Gros, Painting and Propaganda under Napoleon* (University Park: Pennsylvania State University Press, 2006).

102. See Ian Haywood, *Romanticism and Caricature* (Cambridge: Cambridge University Press, 2013); and Forrest et al., *War Memories*, 245–91.

103. See the chapter by Stefan Dudink on "Citizenship, Mass Mobilization, and Masculinity in a Transatlantic Perspective, 1770s–1870s" in this handbook.

104. Stefan Dudink et al., eds., *Representing Masculinity: Citizenship in Modern Western Culture* (Basingstoke: Palgrave Macmillan, 2008); and Dudink et al., eds., *Masculinities in Politics and War: Gendering Modern History* (Manchester: Manchester University Press, 2004), 3–40.

105. Hagemann et al., *Gender, War, and Politics*, esp. 93–126.

106. See ibid., 227–306.

107. See Alan Forrest et al., "Introduction: Nations in Arms—People at War," in *Soldiers, Citizens and Civilians: Experiences and Perceptions of the Revolutionary and Napoleonic Wars, 1790–1820*, ed. Forrest et al. (Basingstoke: Palgrave Macmillan, 2009), 1–23; and Forrest, "Society, Mass Warfare" in this handbook.

108. Katherine Aaslestad and Johan Joor, eds., *Revisiting Napoleon's Continental System: Local, Regional, and European Experiences*(Basingstoke: Palgrave Macmillan, 2014).

109. Alan Forrest et al., *War, Demobilization*, 203–70; and Jennifer Heuer et al., eds., "Ending War: Revisiting the Aftermath of the Napoleonic Wars," special issue, *Journal of Military History* 80, no. 1 (2016).

110. Philip G. Dwyer, "'It Still Makes Me Shudder': Memories of Massacres and Atrocities during the Revolutionary and Napoleonic Wars," *War in History* 16, no. 4 (2005): 381–405; Dennis Showalter, "Matrices: Soldiers and Civilians in Early Modern Europe, 1648–1789," in *Daily Lives of Civilians in Wartime Europe, 1618–1900*, ed. Linda S. Frey and Marsha L. Frey (Westport CT: Greenwood Press, 2007), 59–91; and Medick, *Der Dreissigjährige Krieg*.

111. Gavin Daly, "Plunder on the Peninsular: British Soldiers and Local Civilians during the Peninsular War, 1808–1813," in Charters et al., *Civilians and War*, 209–40;

Leighton S. James, "Invasion and Occupation: Civilian–Military Relations in Central Europe during the Revolutionary and Napoleonic Wars," in Charters et al., *Civilians and War*, 225–40; and Karen Hagemann, "'Unimaginable Horror and Misery': The Battle of Leipzig in October 1813 in Civilian Experience and Perception," in Forrest et al., *Soldiers, Citizens*, 157–80.

112. Wilson, *Thirty Years War*, 786–95.

113. Jack S. Levy, *War in the Modern Great Power System: 1495–1975* (Lexington: University Press of Kentucky, 1983), 128–29 and 139–40. Building on Levy, Charles Tilly came to similar conclusions in *Coercion, Capital, and European States, A.D. 990–1990* (Cambridge, MA: Blackwell, 1990), 72–74.

114. Jack S. Levy et al., "Continuity and Change in the Evolution of Warfare," in *War in a Changing World*, ed. Zeev Maoz and Azar Gat (Ann Arbor: University of Michigan Press, 2001), 15–48.

115. Linda S. Frey and Marsha L. Frey, "Introduction," in Frey and Frey, *Daily Lives*, 1–22; and Forrest et al., "Introduction."

116. See the chapter by Elizabeth Colwill on "Gender, Slavery, War, and Violence in and beyond the Age of Revolutions" in this handbook.

117. Elizabeth D. Heineman, ed., *Sexual Violence in Conflict Zones: From the Ancient World to the Era of Human Rights* (Philadelphia: University of Pennsylvania Press, 2011).

118. Ibid., 2.

119. Ibid.

120. Antonia I. Castañeda, "Sexual Violence in the Politics of Conquest: Amerindian Women and the Spanish Conquest of Alto California," in Heineman, *Sexual Violence*, 39–55, 55.

121. Ibid., 54.

122. See the chapter by Angela Woollacott on "Imperial Conquest, Violent Encounters, and Changing Gender Relations in Colonial Warfare, 1830s–1910s" in this handbook.

123. Sharon Block, "Rape in the American Revolution: Process, Reaction and Public Re-Creation," in Heineman, *Sexual Violence*, 25–38.

124. Ibid., 35; and Sharon Block, *Rape and Sexual Power in Early America* (Chapel Hill: University of North Carolina Press, 2006).

125. Hagemann, *Revisiting*; Hagemann, "Reconstructing 'Front' and 'Home': Gendered Experiences and Memories of the German Wars against Napoleon—a Case Study," *War in History* 16, no. 1 (2009): 25–50; as well as some of the chapters in Forrest et al., *War Memories*, esp. 154–92; and Hagemann et al., *Gender, War and Politics*, esp. 307–60.

126. Aleida Assmann, "Geschlecht und kulturelles Gedächtnis," *Freiburger FrauenStudien* 19 (2006): 29–46.

127. Hagemann, "Reconstructing"; see also Davies, "War, Gender, and Society," and Zabin, "War, Culture, and Gender" in this handbook.

SELECT BIBLIOGRAPHY

Anderson, Fred. *Crucible of War: The Seven Years' War and the Fate of Empire in British North America*. New York: Alfred A. Knopf, 2000.

Bell, David A. *The First Total War: Napoleon's Europe and the Birth of Warfare as We Know It*. Boston: Houghton Mifflin, 2007.

Block, Sharon. *Rape and Sexual Power in Early America*. Chapel Hill: University of North Carolina Press, 2006.

Burbank, Jane, and Frederick Cooper. "Empire, Nation and Citizenship in the Revolutionary Age." In *Empires in World History: Power and the Politics of Difference*, 219–50. Princeton, NJ: Princeton University Press, 2010.

Charters, Erica, Eve Rosenhaft, and Hannah Smith, eds. *Civilians and War in Europe, 1618–1815*. Liverpool: Liverpool University Press, 2012.

Chasteen, John Charles. *Americanos: Latin America's Struggle for Independence*. Oxford: Oxford University Press, 2008.

Chickering, Roger, and Stig Förster, eds. *War in an Age of Revolution, 1775–1815*. Cambridge: Cambridge University Press, 2010.

Ferling, John E. *Whirlwind: The American Revolution and the War That Won It*. New York: Bloomsbury Press, 2015.

Forrest, Alan, Karen Hagemann, and Jane Rendall, eds. *Soldiers, Citizens and Civilians: Experiences and Perceptions of the Revolutionary and Napoleonic Wars, 1790–1820*. Basingstoke: Palgrave Macmillan, 2009.

Frey, Linda S., and Marsha L. Frey, eds. *Daily Lives of Civilians in Wartime Europe, 1618–1900*. Westport, CT: Greenwood Press, 2007.

Füssel, Marian. *Der Preis des Ruhms: Eine Weltgeschichte des Siebenjährigen Krieges*. München: Beck, 2019.

Hacker, Barton C. "Women and Military Institutions in Early Modern Europe: A Reconnaissance." *Signs* 6, no. 4 (1981): 643–71.

Hagemann, Karen, and Ralf Pröve, eds. *Landsknechte, Soldatenfrauen und Nationalkrieger: Militär, Krieg und Geschlechterordnung im historischen Wandel*. Frankfurt am Main: Campus, 1998.

Hagemann, Karen, Jane Rendall, and Gisela Mettele, eds. *Gender, War, and Politics: Transatlantic Comparisons, 1775–1830*. New York: Palgrave Macmillan, 2010.

Little, Ann M. *Abraham in Arms: War and Gender in Colonial New England*. Philadelphia: University of Pennsylvania Press, 2007.

Lynn, John A. "Essential Women, Necessary Wives, and Exemplary Soldiers: The Military Reality and Cultural Representation of Women's Military Participation (1600–1815)." In *A Companion to Women's Military History*, edited by Barton C. Hacker and Margaret Vining, 93–136. Leiden: Brill, 2012.

Lynn, John A. *Women, Armies, and Warfare in Early Modern Europe*. Cambridge: Cambridge University Press, 2008.

McFarlane, Anthony. *War and Independence in Spanish America*. New York: Routledge, 2014.

Medick, Hans. *Der Dreissigjährigen Krieg: Zeugnisse vom Leben mit Gewalt*. Göttingen: Wallstein, 2018.

Moran, Daniel, and Arthur Waldron, eds. *The People in Arms: Military Myth and National Mobilization since the French Revolution*. Cambridge: Cambridge University Press, 2003.

Parker, Geoffrey, ed. *The Cambridge History of Warfare*. New York: Cambridge University Press, 2005.

Parrott, David. "Had a Distinct Template for a 'Western Way of War' Been Established before 1800?" In *The Changing Character of War*, edited by Hew Strachan and Sibylle Scheipers, 48–63. Oxford: Oxford University Press, 2011.

Rogers, Clifford J., ed. *The Military Revolution Debate: Readings on the Military Transformation of Early Modern Europe*. Boulder, CO: Westview Press, 1995.

Wilson, Peter H. *Europe's Tragedy: A New History of the Thirty Years War*. London: Penguin, 2009.

Wilson, Peter H. "German Women and War, 1500–1800." *War in History* 3, no. 2 (1996): 127–60.

CHAPTER 2

WARS, STATES, AND GENDER IN EARLY MODERN EUROPEAN WARFARE, 1600s–1780s

PETER H. WILSON

THE transformations of the military and warfare in Europe between the early seventeenth and the late eighteenth centuries were quite dramatic and affected societies in many ways, as much as changes in the economy, technology, the political system, and society in these two hundred years shaped the armed forces and the conduct of war. Across the period, these changes in preparing, conducting, and controlling war in Europe were largely gradual and related to broader social, economic, and cultural factors as much as to innovations in military thinking and technology. One factor was a transformation in the thinking about gender. If we want to understand the impact of the changes in the military and warfare on the gender order and vice versa, we need a closer integration of approaches from military and gender history so that we can decipher the impact of gender on war, as well as its place in war and military institutions. The following survey is informed by this approach. It studies changes in the European military and warfare between the 1600s and 1780s from the perspective of gender history. In the center of the exploration stand three themes: first, the importance of gender in the regulatory framework consolidated by later seventeenth-century states to curb warfare's costs and excesses; second, the place of gender in command, combat, and logistical support; and third, military institutions as elements within a corporate social and gender order.

GENDER AND WAR IN EARLY MODERN EUROPEAN HISTORY

Three main approaches have characterized writing on early modern European warfare. A concentration on "war and society" has dominated scholarship since the 1980s, with some claiming this has produced a "new military history."[1] More recently, the focus has moved away from more conventional social and economic questions about military personnel and has broadened to include more cultural aspects and investigations of experience and perception.[2] Meanwhile, political history has continued to examine the relationship of war and state/institution-building.[3] Throughout, "conventional" military history has traditionally remained concerned with military organizations and the conduct of war, but has shifted recently toward a more cultural approach, notably in the current attempt to define "characters" or "ways" of war.[4]

Questions relating to gender have largely been confined to the first approach and, until recently, usually were limited to discussions of male–female relations as a dimension of wider "military–civil" interaction. Gender issues usually feature only in the second approach as objects of state regulation, such as the development of martial law and its distinctions between (primarily male) combatants and (often female) civilians. Finally, gender aspects rarely feature in the third approach, beyond the treatment of women and other civilians as "victims" of violence. I argue that we must combine all three approaches, not only to gain a more satisfactory understanding of warfare, but also especially to (re)integrate gender with military history for early modern Europe.

Social historians have stressed the corporate character of early modern European society, especially in France, Italy, and Spain, and central Europe, though less so for Britain. Europe was commercializing, but remained predominantly agrarian, a basic fact that risks being obscured by the current preoccupation with "Atlantic history" and global connections.[5] Corporate status was expressed as *liberties*, or local and specific rights and identities, not as abstract, universal *Liberty*. The household headed by a married couple was the cornerstone of this social (and economic and political) order, even though a significant proportion of the population was poorly integrated or marginalized. Regardless of confession, the post-Reformation churches promoted marriage as the foundation of a stable order. Marriage was simultaneously encouraged as an ideal and limited through age and material preconditions to reduce opportunities for the poor to (legitimately) reproduce. Marriage was thus associated with autonomy and respectability, conferring a higher level of access to legal rights and protection than was available to those who were unmarried. Householders were often enfranchised in their local community, meaning that they could vote in village or municipal assemblies centuries ahead of their participation in national elections. While such political enfranchisement was generally restricted to the husband, the wife also enjoyed status and rights relating to what were (largely) considered complementary, if different, tasks.[6]

States were comparatively weak, especially compared to those after 1800, and, like the social order, politics remained primarily local. Even relatively small states, like the Dutch Republic, were composite patchworks of communities and provinces with their own identities, laws, and interests. Central power derived some autonomy as the (generally) acknowledged arbiter in this order, brokering deals between local and provincial elites and their clients and opponents. However, even the most would-be "absolute" monarch could achieve little without at least the tacit compliance of local power holders, including householders at the micro level.[7]

Varying degrees of centralization had been achieved by the late eighteenth century through concentrating sovereign powers in a single internally and internationally recognized "national" government. This process was primarily responsible for the two types of wars plaguing early modern Europe. Civil wars determined the form and reach of central authority, while interstate conflict delineated the geographic extent of each government's jurisdiction and its status within what remained, essentially, a hierarchical international order. Beginning at the close of the Middle Ages, these developments had reached roughly their halfway point by 1650. The era of civil wars was drawing to a close as elites accepted the monopolization of indivisible sovereign powers by a central government. It was obvious this process could not be reversed and that previously autonomous provinces and communities had to accept higher levels of integration within a common political order. Domestic politics increasingly shifted from contesting monopoly formation to disputes over social distribution of its benefits and burdens and the uses to which these more potent powers should be put. In most countries these matters remained restricted to informal bargaining, for example, through clientele politics at a royal court, with only narrow fiscal issues open for discussion in formal parliaments or assemblies. Formal politics were more broadly based in Britain, the Dutch Republic, and Sweden, though informal channels remained important in these countries too. The real significance of the revolutionary era after 1789 was in providing compelling arguments to strengthen centralization by dismantling corporate liberties, while (to a lesser extent) opening formal influence over sovereign powers to a broader elite by creating or extending enfranchisement in national representative institutions.

Interstate wars continued after 1650, helping to cement the definition of *war* as an instrument of state policy. The system was mutually reinforcing and self-defining, since sovereignty acquired full meaning only if recognized by existing sovereigns. This aspect was largely completed at the peace settlements ending the War of Spanish Succession (1701–14). For example, Prussia was accepted as a sovereign kingdom and permitted to participate in the negotiations, whereas other notables, such as the Duke of Lorraine, were heard politely but excluded from the real talks. Broad agreement on sovereignty thus firmly identified states as the sole "proper authorities" entitled to wage war within the prevailing theories of "just war."[8] These theories also guided official attitudes to the purpose of war (to restore peace by overturning perceived injustice) and its proper conduct. Religion remained a potent factor in international relations after the 1648 Peace of Westphalia that ended the Thirty Years' War (1618–48), one of the longest and most destructive conflicts in European history, a conflict over the hegemony in the Holy

Roman Empire and at the same time a religious war.[9] The sectarian differences, however, did not inhibit the dissemination of common conventions to curb violence and limit its impact, particularly on civilians who now emerged more clearly as an internationally recognized group. This inhibited the "qualitative escalation" characterizing European colonial conquest and warfare elsewhere in the world, where Europeans (and those of European origin) and their Indigenous opponents often retaliated in kind to what they regarded as "inhumane" violence, thereby successively widening the boundaries of the "acceptable" in warfare in Europe.[10]

These trends feature prominently in the widespread characterization of warfare between 1648 and 1789 as "limited" in contrast to the preceding "age of religious wars" and the subsequent conflicts of the era of the French Revolutionary and Napoleonic Wars (1792–1815). This historiographical convention has led some to trivialize "old regime" warfare as a genteel "pursuit of kings" waged by small armies of disinterested mercenaries. Even more serious studies persist in emphasizing a fundamental shift around 1650, as "contract armies" were supposedly replaced by "state-commission armies." The former are generally regarded as a transitional state, used by monarchs who, as yet, lacked sufficiently developed administrations to maintain large forces directly. Renewed institutional development after 1648 (what used to be called *absolutism*) strengthened European states, allowing them to replace supposedly "independent" military contractors with forces paid directly from taxation and under officers commissioned by central authority.[11] In fact, state–contractor relations were rarely purely mercenary, while elements of entrepreneurship persisted well beyond 1650.[12]

The debate is directly pertinent to gender and warfare, because the conventional chronology has been given a new lease of life by John A. Lynn's 2008 book *Women, Armies, and Warfare in Early Modern Europe*, the first general survey of the subject.[13] In his interpretation, contract armies formed large, mobile "campaign communities" composed to a considerable extent by women who were essential to the "pillage economy" on which such forces allegedly depended. By contrast, state-commissioned forces were permanent "standing armies," living in fixed "garrison communities."[14] Troops no longer moved aimlessly in search of food, but were supplied in their garrisons during peacetime and then marched out on campaign in war accompanied by much smaller numbers of "necessary women" providing limited support (cleaning, mending, cooking, nursing) while male civilian contractors supplied food and fodder. It was this transition that enabled European governments to "limit" war. Women were eventually excluded altogether by the professionalization of the support services and the emergence of new, mass-conscript armies.

This interpretation has important implications. Military and political arguments outweigh social or cultural factors in explaining the changing place of gender in European warfare. In short, changes in warfare, notably the desire for greater mobility, led to the exclusion of women as "unnecessary baggage."[15] This paradigm overestimates the presence of women with armies prior to 1650 and underestimates their place thereafter.[16]

Both the standard chronology and the pillage economy argument perpetuate the "mercenary myth" that soldiers changed fundamentally in their origins and motivations, either with the rise of standing armies or later in the revolutionary era. Already prior to 1650, the vast majority of soldiers were subjects of their paymasters and were bound by multiple loyalties, identities, and motives, not simply economic ones. There is no real evidence that they cared less about the causes they fought for than other soldiers prior to the 1790s (and in many cases well beyond that). The real point is not that early modern soldiers were especially enthusiastic; rather, later ones were often motivated by more mundane reasons than desired by nationalists and idealists.[17]

Pre-1650 governments did not give commanders free rein to plunder, since this would compromise monarchs' claims to be fighting a legitimate war by proper means (an important element of monarchical cultural capital). The main exception was when destruction was used as a deliberate strategic weapon, something that continued well after 1650.[18] Plundering is wasteful, haphazard, and ill-suited to the long-term maintenance of large armies. Contract armies were also never entirely mobile, but always disbursed some units to hold important towns and other places. Some of these garrisons were maintained continually for several years—a practice that would have been impossible if they relied solely on plunder. However, governments did experience serious difficulties trying to collect and disburse resources centrally, so they largely gave up paying soldiers directly. Instead, they developed the "contributions system" whereby commanders were permitted to draw supplies and money directly from local communities using existing local institutional structures and networks. The fact that this system was open to abuse and failed to provide all that was needed explains much of the disorder and destruction characterizing struggles like the Thirty Years' War.[19]

Rather than sustaining armies, pillaging was important in enabling women to accompany them. It was part of a wider "economy of makeshifts" empowering individuals to survive in a precarious environment, but not fundamental to sustaining the army as a whole. The arguments Lynn advanced to explain why people joined the campaign community work better for men than for women. Though regulated to a degree, the campaign community indeed displayed a libertine lifestyle that may have attracted men to enlist. However, women's roles were essentially defined by the common division of labor between the sexes in the economy and society outside the army: cleaning, cooking, mending, nursing, and food procurement. Moreover, their status and their reputation suffered by association with soldiers who were generally despised by settled society. Their presence was merely tolerated, not encouraged by the authorities who were already advancing the kind of efficiency arguments employed to rationalize women's exclusion from military institutions around 1800.

The campaign community was scarcely a pleasant environment. Its main attraction was in providing a form of community to those who were already marginalized or disadvantaged by settled social organization or for those from communities seriously disrupted by war. Joining the army allowed both men and women without property to form a joint household based on a clear division of labor, even when their relation was not legally sanctioned as a marriage. Such a relationship offered some protection and material security. In their own way, they tried to live the ideal of a household headed by man and his wife, who in a complementary way worked together for the family income, which was gaining increasing influence, especially in the middle classes, since the post-Reformation era.[20] This explains the presence of numerous male noncombatants also accompanying late sixteenth- and early seventeenth-century armies. While women were singled out in contemporary criticism, male grooms, lackeys, and numerous adolescent servants formed a significant proportion of the "camp followers." For example, the Spanish garrison in Münster in 1598 had 787 boys and male servants, compared to only 111 women, while records of Swedish and German units in the Thirty Years' War indicate an average ratio of 1 male to 1 female camp follower.[21] This suggests we should question the extent of the shift from a fairly transient, mobile, and female-dominated campaign community to a more stable, male-dominated garrison community after 1650, especially as women continued to be present in both garrisons and on campaign into the nineteenth century.

THE POST-1650 REGULATORY FRAMEWORK

There was no peace dividend after the wars of the first half of the seventeenth century, because European rulers used the argument of "necessity" to convert wartime contributions into permanent military taxes, now under central supervision. These taxes paid for what became permanent armies, especially as a new cycle of prolonged conflict convulsed much of Europe between 1672 and 1721. Command and control were centralized, while representative assemblies, city councils, and aristocratic grandees largely lost the right to maintain their own forces, except in Poland-Lithuania. Contractual elements persisted through, for example, officer commissions remaining open to purchase in Britain, France, Austria, and elsewhere. Crucially, while individual officers retained a significant personal economic investment in their units, the state "owned" the regulatory framework dictating the legal and institutional structures of armies and navies.[22]

The basic outlines of this regulatory framework were set around 1520, when soldiers increasingly became subject to "Articles of War" and other legally binding guidelines devised by state officials, rather than themselves. Regulations became more comprehensive and standardized between about 1570 and 1620, and though the rules were revised and expanded further during the wars after 1672, very few new features were added. Rather than innovative forms of supervision, the real difference in the period after the Thirty Years' War, starting in the mid-seventeenth century, was that rules became more tightly enforced thanks to the establishment of permanent subunits within armies, like regiments, companies, and other institutionalized military formations. Since the late fifteenth or early sixteenth century, most large monarchies had effectively maintained permanent armies, but few outside Spain had grouped their soldiers in units that endured beyond individual conflicts. The standing armies created from the 1660s and 1670s were composed of units that enjoyed far higher levels of institutional stability than their predecessors. Individual units were now much less likely to be disbanded or amalgamated at the end of each conflict. Instead, they were reduced by discharging a significant proportion of the common soldiers, while retaining the officers, the noncommissioned officers, and those men considered fittest and most reliable as a cadre that could be expanded with new recruits or conscripts in case of a new war.[23]

These permanent formations assisted enforcement of Articles of War through closer supervision, greater institutional continuity, and administrative routine, including institutional memory fostered through oral tradition and (by the mid-eighteenth century) written regimental histories. The consolidation of an institutional culture around the permanent formations and their identities helped promote military professionalism, as did a clearer career structure, at least for officers. Finally, supervision was assisted by an expanded and more effective network of local officials who, for example, checked the passes of soldiers on furlough and assisted officers in selecting recruits, especially through the limited forms of conscription adopted by poorer monarchies, such as Prussia, Denmark, and Sweden.[24]

Regulation of soldiers' marriages was one of the few genuine innovations after 1650 and was a direct consequence of the greater permanence among personnel and military formations. Though morality remained a significant underlying factor, relentless fiscal logic largely dictated policy in this area. European states drew lessons from sixteenth- and early seventeenth-century conflicts, resolving to master indiscipline by ensuring they honored their promises to pay and feed soldiers. The desire to maintain large armies necessitated reducing per capita costs. Minor adjustments were made between about 1670 and 1714, but thereafter hardly any governments increased soldiers' pay before the 1790s, despite prices doubling or even quadrupling across that period. Soldiers were expected to remain single because their wages and rations were barely adequate to maintain themselves.[25]

While institutionally specific to the military, efforts to restrict soldiers' marriages were part of wider strategies limiting plebeian unions to those considered sufficiently mature and economically independent to form a stable household. Though frequently used as cheap labor on state projects, soldiers were not generally expected to contribute economically to society; therefore, their drain on the public purse was to be kept to a minimum. The Brandenburg-Prussian army offers a fairly typical example. From 1665, soldiers had to notify their company commander if they intended to marry. Their officer's permission was required from 1682 in a conscious effort to limit the number of married men to an official quota per company. Similar measures were introduced in Britain in 1685.[26]

Enforcement depended on the inclination of individual regimental commanders or, as in the case of the Piedmontese army, the ability of soldiers to find civilian clergy willing to marry them, regardless of regulations.[27] Between 40 and 60 percent of the bishopric of Münster's soldiers were married in the 1720s and 1730s, when the official quota stood at 25 percent.[28] Like much early modern legislation, official tolerance of infractions resulted from passive resistance and popular pressure. Soldiers and women clearly desired the social status and opportunities associated with marriage. Soldiers frequently deserted if permission was denied. In the highly competitive military market of the German-speaking lands, recruiters often enticed trained soldiers to desert to their service by allowing them to marry.[29] Despite broadly similar regulatory policies, actual practice thus varied considerably across Europe. Britain was exceptional in restricting marriage to only 6 to 10 percent of personnel, whereas the proportion in France was probably around 15 percent.[30] Piedmont was roughly in the middle, with about a quarter of its soldiers legally married, while German rates were among the highest, at around 30 percent. Prussia relaxed its earlier restrictions in a deliberate effort to reduce desertion by anchoring its personnel to local society. Around half of Prussian ordinary soldiers were married after 1763.[31]

Marriage policy affected recruitment and, hence, the broader social impact of military preparedness in a clear example of gender intersecting with other concerns to influence military institutions and practice. This was most pronounced in those countries where standing armies most resembled peacetime cadres: the German lands, Scandinavia, and the Italian states. Peacetime forces, especially after 1714, contained a far higher proportion of older, often married personnel than wartime formations. Mobilization would see superannuated or infirm personnel discharged and replaced by larger numbers of younger, single men. States employing limited conscription, like Russia and the Scandinavian and German lands, all targeted the younger sons of large families, taking older, married men only as a last resort.[32] The desire to preserve the tax base was the main reason for exempting householders. Conversely, demobilization could see married men singled out, as in France in 1715, as the authorities sought to reduce any chance they might have to pay for soldiers' wives.[33] Marriage policy played less of a role in Britain, France, the Dutch Republic, and, to some extent, also Spain, because military recruitment in all these countries was affected more by competition between army and navy over manpower, while all were sufficiently rich to recruit foreigners when necessary.

GENDER AND MILITARY ROLES

Most historians investigate male and female participation in warfare separately, for example, by trying to categorize the roles played by men and women in military institutions.[34] This method can be useful for some questions, but an investigation structured by aspects of military activity yields different insights into the interrelationship between gender and war. Command was doubly male, reflecting the patriarchal structure of authority and war as a masculine activity. States permitting female rule allowed women to assume overall direction of war and military policy, but not to command in the field in what remained an age of warrior kings, such as Charles XII, king of Sweden from 1697 to 1718; Peter the Great, Russian tsar from 1682 to 1725; Frederick the Great, king of Prussia from 1740 to 1786; and the British monarch George II, in power from 1727 to 1760, who was the last to lead his troops in battle. Even relatively unmilitary kings accompanied their armies on campaign, including Louis XV of France, on the throne from 1715 to 1774, who was present at the Battle of Fontenoy (May 1745).

By contrast, both contemporary and subsequent historical writings view female military authority through a gendered lens. A good example is Maria Theresa, the female ruler of the Habsburg dominions, reigning from 1740 to 1780, who deliberately played up her status as a young wife and mother at an assembly of Hungarian nobles in 1741 to rally their support at the start of the War of Austrian Succession (1740–48). While noting her keen interest in her army, contemporaries and later commentators invariably stressed her "maternal" concern for ordinary soldiers' welfare and her indulgence toward incompetent generals, including her brother-in-law, Prince Charles Alexander of Lorraine.[35]

Officially, regular forces were exclusively male and the battlefield and exercise ground were purely masculine spaces. Post-1650 land warfare was characterized by a division into grand operations of large, concentrated forces intended to bring the enemy to battle or to capture major towns. Combat might involve anything upward of 100,000 men crammed into a few square kilometers fighting in densely packed formations intended to maximize the deadly effect of short-range black powder firearms or close-order weaponry like swords, pikes, and bayonets. Men were killed or maimed by opponents they could usually see, if they were not shrouded in dense clouds of smoke or dust. Actions were almost invariably fought in daylight and were over within a few hours once the forces deployed.

Accompanying such grand-scale operations was what contemporaries described as *little war*, waged by smaller units of "light troops" who would be classed variously as *special forces* or *irregulars* today. They ranged far beyond the main army, operating ahead as scouts or foragers or to screen major movements, including covering retreats. Little war was characterized by small-scale skirmishes, often fought in looser formations and requiring cunning on the part of junior officers, who employed ruses to deceive or ambush opponents. As such, it was considered a subordinate, less honorable aspect of war than major operations. While some men could rise to prominence as little-war commanders, few acquired the prestige or fame accorded to those winning major battles: if Johann Nicolaus von Luckner, a German officer in French service who rose to become a marshal of France in 1791, is remembered at all today, it is as the dedicatee of the "War Song of the Army of the Rhine" in 1792, now known as the "Marseillaise," rather than for his military exploits as a hussar officer. Most commanders of light troops yearned to be recognized as peers of regular officers.[36]

Women were far more likely to be involved in little war or sieges than in major battles, since commanders preferred to avoid fighting major engagements in built-up areas. Little war frequently involved raids on enemy supply dumps and the attack and defense of farms, villages, and other small, usually unfortified settlements. Aristocratic women had commanded the defense of manor houses and other small positions prior to 1650, usually because they had been left in charge by male relatives who were away serving with the larger field armies. Such positions were no longer considered important military targets by the later seventeenth century, and defenders often withdrew or capitulated in return for "free passage" if confronted by an enemy in sufficient strength. Women still participated in the defense of larger places, especially laboring to improve or repair defenses, as well as simply being caught up in fighting during bombardment or, worse, if the defending commander refused to surrender and the attackers tried to take the town by assault. Involvement was considered a matter of necessity and was not regarded as especially remarkable, given that women performed a wide range of hard manual labor in the civilian economy.[37]

While scarcely genteel, siege warfare was governed by conventions intended to minimize civilian casualties and reduce the risks to both attackers and defenders, especially at the point of surrender. Smaller towns were now more likely to be considered "open" and therefore not military targets. Defense of more strategic locations generally focused on prepared positions defended by regular troops. Prior to 1650, civilians and especially female inhabitants were likely to be expelled as "useless mouths" by garrison commanders keen to conserve food stocks. The trope of comparing a besieged town to an assault on maidenly virtue was already well established before 1650 and continued throughout the period under review, not least because most commentators on war were well versed in classical literature, which was also replete with such comparisons.[38]

Some women fought disguised as men.[39] Their numbers were always very few: around 60 have been identified in the British army and navy between 1660 and 1832, with another 119 Dutch cross-dressers between 1550 and 1840, most of whom were soldiers or sailors.[40] While in absolute terms these numbers fall far short of the 400 women known to have served during the American Civil War (1861–65), there is little evidence to conclude that transvestitism increased across the first half of the nineteenth century. The forces mobilized in North America between 1861 and 1865 were significantly larger than those in Europe between 1650 and 1789, suggesting the proportion of cross-dressers probably remained roughly constant. These cases have attracted a disproportionate amount of scholarly and popular attention, much of it explicitly celebratory, presenting historical examples as role models for contemporary agendas.[41] Most research has concentrated on the literary and dramatic presentation of such women, as well as the real or fictional autobiographies of the most famous examples. Of 300 plays premiering in London between 1660 and 1700, 90 featured women dressing as men, many of them as soldiers, while similar stories featured in at least 120 English ballads in the two centuries after 1650.[42] Such evidence is far easier to identify and access than the criminal and administrative records that occasionally reveal less prominent cases. Another problem has been anachronistic assumptions about "sexual orientation," a concept unknown in early modernity.

It is also often difficult to determine whether these were genuine cases of *gender passing*, defined as "where a member of one designated biological sex takes on attributes of the other for the purposes of being *successfully* mistaken for a member of the assumed sex."[43] Accounts of elite women posing as soldiers generally suggest that passing was not intended, such as in the case of Henriette von Pfalzburg, who accompanied the army of her brother, Charles IV, the Duke of Lorraine, dressed as a man in 1635, on one occasion firing a cannon.[44] It has been suggested that contemporaries were often aware of these women's true gender, at least once they had been unmasked, and that such knowledge was a way of shaming men into performing their "proper" roles as warriors.[45] This certainly appears plausible with Hannah Snell, who had a successful stage career performing arms drill in theaters after leaving the British army in 1751.[46] Some female personnel received official recognition in the form of pensions. One of the most successful was Mary Lacy, who served as a marine and then a master shipwright at the Portsmouth naval dockyard before being pensioned in 1771 and becoming a prominent local house builder.[47] Other, lesser known female soldiers were celebrated locally, such as Anna Sophia Dettloffin, who was (perhaps inevitably) dubbed the "Pomeranian Amazon" when her service in the Prussian army became known after the Seven Years' War (1756–63).[48]

However, discovery could prove embarrassing for male comrades who felt duped. Generally, any behavior outside narrow parameters met with considerable popular hostility. One Piedmontese soldier consorting with young boys in cafes and the barracks was shunned by his comrades, who initially used the opportunity for blackmail before denouncing him to the authorities.[49] Female cross-dressers were often regarded as freaks: Aal the Dragoon was even stuffed and displayed in an anatomical museum in Rotterdam after her death in 1710.[50] Catharina Margaretha Linck was executed after four years of service as a soldier married to another woman in 1721, having been denounced by her mother-in-law.[51] These cases suggest we might need to reappraise the prevailing scholarly assumption that gender definitions remained fluid prior to the 1770s and, consequently, early modern gender roles were performative with a person's gender being assumed on the basis of their clothing and behavior.[52] Virtually all contemporary cross-dressers' accounts stressed their fear of discovery, suggesting that the ideas about gender differences were already quite solid, based mainly on Christian theology, but not yet "anthropologized" and thus universalized as in the nineteenth century.[53]

War was still regarded as the ultimate test of manliness, but martial glory was socially constructed and constricted. Prevailing ideals drew heavily on classical models and Christianity, combining physical prowess with moral virtue. The political need to legitimate war required the army to be a moral, as well as efficient, instrument. This dovetailed with the general disciplining agenda of early modern European states, which expected subjects to be pious, obedient, thrifty, and morally upright. The ethos of the noble warrior was reserved for officers, especially senior, aristocratic ones. This provided social and ideological compensation for the greater subordination of officers to state authority after 1650. Assertive free will was replaced by self-restraint, corporate loyalty, and gentlemanly moderation, though with some variation across Europe. Subordination was manifest in the requirement by the early eighteenth century that officers wear uniforms, thus appearing like ordinary soldiers as the state's liveried servants. French and British officers still embraced a life of conspicuous consumption and regarded their Prussian counterparts as staid and serious.[54] Officers were expected to lead by example and disdain danger. Formal training remained secondary to an aristocratic ethos that transcended military–civil boundaries. A sense of innate superiority, knowledge of horsemanship, and practice in hunting continued to be regarded as essential attributes for command in most European armies until well into the nineteenth century.[55]

Warrior manliness was not celebrated by all men, however. The professionalization of the military civilized the rest of the male population, restricting martial prowess and values to an occupational group. This opened more space for an intellectual critique of war, especially through civilian advocacy of the nobility of learning and alternative ideals of heroism, such as overcoming personal dangers and misfortune with quiet fortitude.[56] However, the close association between nobility and bearing arms encouraged the male urban elite to collect fine weapons and serve as officers in civic guards, long after such formations ceased to have a real military function. The fashion for wearing swords spread to public officials, intellectuals, and students, the latter being notorious for dueling in Germany. Status outweighed any association between weapons carrying and political rights, something that has been given undue prominence in discussions of this aspect from a gender perspective, with the literature drawing overwhelmingly on Anglo-American examples that were exceptional relative to most of Europe.[57] In fact, the exclusion of women from civic enfranchisement was a consequence not merely of disbarment from civic militias, but also of their secondary status within the community. Male Jews faced similar restrictions in early modern Germany, for instance.[58] Advocates of militia service in mid-eighteenth-century Britain did disarm their opponents by presenting them as effeminate for refusing a patriotic duty, yet the British militia was always championed as a politically desirable alternative to a permanent professional army.[59] Continental militias were subordinate auxiliaries of regular militaries and were frequently used to draft the rural poor directly into professional units in wartime. Recruits were expected to meet certain physical requirements, such as possession of good teeth to bite the paper cartridges as part of the process of loading muskets, as well as being of sufficient height to handle long-barreled firearms. Cultural factors played a part, too, since especially tall recruits were preferred for elite units for their imposing appearance.

Military-technical language rationalized the construct of the soldier as "healthy and strong men," but this did not prevent women passing themselves off as men. More challenging than the appearance as men was the emulation of men's behavior. A key element in cross-dressers' fear of discovery was thus the need to be "one of the lads" by sharing in the lusty sexual and drinking culture generally characterizing professional military units. This aspect of male camaraderie was heightened by the official restrictions on marriage, but could be also found in civilian groups, such as journeymen and merchant sailors, who also endured enforced celibacy for long periods.[60] The high incidence of illegitimate births in garrison towns, as well as evidence of mass, even systematic, rape during the War of Austrian Succession and Seven Years' War suggests this was a very real part of masculine military culture.[61] Nonetheless, the widespread desire of soldiers to marry indicates limits to womanizing bachelorhood. The joint household of a working couple—married or not—offered the best chances for long-lasting economic survival both inside and outside the army for men and women from lower social strata.[62]

Drill was intended to form unruly men into obedient soldiers and to "correct" perceived physical and behavioral deficiencies ranging from bad posture to loose morals. Discipline was expected to be internalized, with soldiers subsuming their identity and autonomy within their unit. This was essential to sustain the "culture of forbearance" required if men were to endure harrowing battlefield conditions, often being powerless to retaliate against long-range enemy fire.[63] There was little opportunity or expectation for individual heroism, especially as the socially prestigious aspects of martial tasks remained the preserve of officers.

The social distinctions embedded in the military hierarchy made armies to patriarchal institutions for soldiers as well as wives. Officers and monarchs referred to soldiers as "children," assuming (as we have seen) parental responsibility over their marriage choices and supervising numerous aspects of their daily lives. Paternalism was expressed also in the expectation that soldiers would not grow—they were not expected to show initiative or to gain the skills or experience associated with promotion beyond noncommissioned officers. While officers and civilian commentators generally wanted soldiers to be pious, thrifty, and obedient, they generally also expected them to behave badly. To an extent, a culture of "license" prevailed, with officers regarding some infractions of official norms as acceptable means of preserving morale and fighting ability. Others simply despaired, believing soldiers (and by extension the poor generally) incapable of high moral standards. Similar problems were to bedevil later efforts to use military service as the "school of the nation."[64]

The maintenance of permanent armies in peacetime and the emphasis on regular drill made military spectacle a more common element in daily life during the eighteenth century. In addition to projecting state power, reviews and parades placed men on show to both the male and the female gaze. While it may be true that "women validate masculinity by watching," early modern soldiers "were arguably the most powerless dressers in their society."[65] Every aspect of soldiers' appearance was tightly regulated by the mid-eighteenth century, down to powdered hair, pigtails, and false moustaches. While public appearance in uniform could bring status and attract female admiration, it could also lead to ridicule as "feminized" compared to more sober male bourgeois attire that became more and more fashionable starting during the Enlightenment.[66]

Women remained important in noncombatant support despite official efforts to restrict their presence after 1650. The British army had female nurses as part of its permanent establishment from the 1680s. They were supposed to be Protestants of good character and were responsible for bringing water to the wounded, hygiene, and evicting "idle or loose women" from hospitals. Around 20 to 60 female nurses were employed in the army's central hospitals during the 1690s and 1700s, handling between 350 and 1,900 patients at any one time. Officers still believed that male nurses were more suitable for the rigors of campaigning, though by mid-century all nurses appear to have been women.[67]

A limited number of soldiers' wives were permitted to accompany their husbands on campaign as "necessary women" in ratios varying from 1 to every 10 to 20 men. Britain found it easier to enforce official quotas during the eighteenth century, since most of its major campaigns required expeditionary forces to board transport ships, where access could be controlled. Necessary women received rations and sometimes pay in return for performing a wide range of "female" chores, such as washing, foraging, cooking, and medical care. A few were employed on a permanent basis, even in garrisons. At the end of the eighteenth century, the French army allowed 7 to 10 laundresses for every infantry regiment, while especially privileged women were licensed as sutlers to sell food and drink on campaign to supplement official rations.[68] Most noncombatant logistical personnel were male, however, and have generally been neglected by scholars. The Swedish army invading Russia in 1709 comprised 24,300 soldiers, 300 artillery transport personnel, 1,100 administrators, and 4,000 grooms, laborers, draymen, stable lads, and boys compared to 1,700 wives, children, and serving girls.[69]

In contrast to France and Britain, both of which expected civilian poor relief to care for soldiers' wives in wartime and widowhood, German governments assumed responsibility in the 1670s by providing free accommodation and modest support payments to official wives while their husbands served in the field. Württemberg maintained 949 women when it sent 11,000 troops to help Austria in the Seven Years' War.[70] Beginning in the 1690s, it became widespread to pay three "death months" to officers' widows. Regular pensions to officers' widows were fairly common after 1714 and were later extended to the widows and orphans of some ordinary soldiers. These measures reflected broader corporate and state paternalism. Payments were made according to the widow's husband's military rank, not her personal need. Similar arrangements had existed for clergy in the German lands since the sixteenth century and were developed also for civilian public officials in the eighteenth century.[71]

GENDER AND THE MILITARY AS CORPORATE SOCIETY

Most soldiers lived among civilians, either lodged in inns, in Britain's case, or billeted on households that were compensated through tax deductions.[72] During the eighteenth century, barracks remained small, concentrated in fortresses or capital cities for elite units. Cavalry in particular were accommodated in villages or small towns providing access to fodder for their horses. Married soldiers lived with their wives, regardless of whether they were in barracks or billets.

Among civilians, soldiers and their families were legally distinct in most continental states. France placed all soldiers' wives under martial law after 1706, for instance. Distinctions could extend to separate rules governing inheritance, as in Saxony.[73] This could bring disadvantages. Because soldiers did not pay local taxes, city councils did not regard them as their responsibility and denied them poor relief. This proved a major factor in the development of the state welfare measures previously described and, likewise, the differences between Britain and the continent.[74] However, even British regiments remained fairly tight-knit communities internally stratified by the formal military hierarchy. Wives whose husbands were promoted were given different laundry duties, for instance.[75]

Starting in the mid-eighteenth century, the military corporate identity embracing both male and female members was challenged by advocates of a new relationship between army and society. This provided political and military arguments supplementing those from science and philosophy that were already promoting the concept of different social "gender roles" for men and women based on the newly discovered physical differences between the sexes that led to the assumption of different "gender characters."[76] Whereas previous discussions equated good soldiers with ideal subjects, now they were intended to become ideal citizens with a more active political stake in society. These arguments grew louder after 1792 with the rapid extension of state power, which abolished corporate and local liberties in the name of both liberty and efficiency. All men were now, at least theoretically, supposed to serve their nation as soldiers. Biological expressions of the nation as virile allowed men to reconcile subservience to the draft with manliness. Heroism was simultaneously democratized, exemplified by the institution of medals for ordinary soldiers as well as officers, in place of the earlier cash payments to the former.

Soldiering, now, became a rite of male passage in most European countries, restricted with the return of peace in 1815 to around three years, rather than being a potentially lifelong occupation as it could have been prior to 1792. Barracks become exclusively male spaces. The departure of armies on campaign was already an occasion for emotional parting, but now separation became a structural element, especially as conscripts were selected from young, single men (like their early modern counterparts). Dispensing temporarily with female companionship in order to serve the nation assumed a prominent place in ideals of manliness. Similarly, women were now largely spared the rigors of campaigning and were expected to remain in the tranquil domestic sphere their brave menfolk were defending.[77]

CONCLUSION

Change remained a matter of degree rather than absolutes in the period between the Thirty Years' War in the first half of the seventeenth century and the French Revolutionary Wars at the end of the eighteenth century. The characterization of male and female roles and spaces remained similar to that prior to 1650, but was marked by greater regulation and permanence. Broader attitudes to gender generally proved more significant for the relation between gender, military, and war than changes in warfare or military institutions, with the latter usually reinforcing the former. Male soldiers' roles were affected by paternalism embedded in the military hierarchy and reinforced by the evolution of military practice, which placed a premium on a "culture of forbearance." Male–female relations centered on the institution of marriage as a socially desirable and officially regulated ideal. Armies contained elements of both the garrison and the campaign community, with women having a place in both. Male and female roles were affected by social as well as gender distinctions. Broader social values were important throughout, with, for instance, strong parallels between the ideal soldier and the ideal subject. There was considerable variation within the general pattern across Europe, with conditions in Britain often being different from those on the continent. Finally, the social, political, and military aspects must be combined to achieve a better understanding of the relationship of war and gender.

NOTES

1. Peter H. Wilson, "British and American Perspectives on Early Modern Warfare," *Militär und Gesellschaft in der Frühen Neuzeit* 5, no. 2 (2001): 108–18.
2. For example, Lorraine White, "The Experience of Spain's Early Modern Soldiers: Combat, Welfare and Violence," *War in History* 9, no. 1 (2002): 1–38; and Yuval Noah Harari, *The Ultimate Experience: Battlefield Revelations and the Making of Modern War Culture, 1450–2000* (Basingstoke: Palgrave Macmillan, 2008).
3. Important examples include Charles Tilly, *Coercion, Capital and European States*, AD *990–1992* (Oxford: Wiley–Blackwell, 1992); and Thomas Ertman, *Birth of the Leviathan: Building States and Regimes in Medieval and Early Modern Europe* (Cambridge: Cambridge University Press, 1997).
4. David Parrott, "Had a Distinct Template for a 'Western Way of War' Been Established before 1800?," in *The Changing Character of War*, ed. Hew Strachan and Sybille Scheipers (Oxford: Oxford University Press, 2011), 48–63.
5. Jorge Cañizares-Esguerra and Benjamin Breen, "Hybrid Atlantics: Future Directions for the History of the Atlantic World," *History Compass* 11, no. 8 (2013): 597–609; and "Forum: Beyond the Atlantic," special issue, *William and Mary Quarterly* 63, no. 4 (2006). On the history of the Holy Roman Empire at the heart of Europe in this period, see Peter H. Wilson, *The Holy Roman Empire, 1495–1806* (Basingstoke: Palgrave Macmillan, 2011).
6. Good introductions to the extensive literature on these topics include Joel F. Harrington, *Reordering Marriage and Society in Reformation Germany* (Cambridge: Cambridge University Press, 1995); Heide Wunder, *He Is the Sun, She Is the Moon: Women in Early Modern Germany* (Cambridge, MA: Harvard University Press, 1998); and Peter Blickle, *Das alte Europa vom Hochmittelalter bis zur Moderne* (Munich: Beck, 2008).
7. Again, the literature on these topics is vast. Particularly insightful contributions include Wayne te Brake, *Shaping History: Ordinary People in European Politics, 1500–1700* (Berkeley: University of California Press, 1998); Daniel H. Nexon, *The Struggle for Power in Early Modern Europe: Religious Conflict, Dynastic Empires and International Change* (Princeton, NJ: Princeton University Press, 2009); John H. Elliott, "A Europe of Composite Monarchies," *Past and Present* 137, no. 1 (1992): 48–71; and Johannes Burkhardt, "Die Friedlosigkeit der Frühen Neuzeit: Grundlegung einer Theorie der Bellizität Europas," *Zeitschrift für Historische Forschung* 24 (1997): 509–74.
8. James Turner Johnson, *Ideology, Reason and the Limitation of War: Religious and Secular Concepts, 1200–1740* (Princeton, NJ: Princeton University Press, 1975).
9. The broad thrust of current research is to relativize the Peace of Westphalia (1648) as the birth of a secular international order: David Onnekink, ed., *War and Religion after Westphalia, 1648–1713* (Farnham: Ashgate, 2009).
10. Wayne E. Lee, *Barbarians and Brothers: Anglo-American Warfare, 1500–1865* (Oxford: Oxford University Press, 2011), esp. 4. For an example of conventions, see Peter H. Wilson, "Prisoners in Early Modern European Warfare," in *Prisoners in War*, ed. Sybille Scheipers (Oxford: Oxford University Press, 2010), 39–56.

11. For a measured discussion of these changes, see David Parrott, *The Business of War: Military Enterprise and Military Revolution in Early Modern Europe* (Cambridge: Cambridge University Press, 2012).

12. Jeff Fynn-Paul, ed., *War, Entrepreneurs, and the State in Europe and the Mediterranean, 1300–1800* (Leiden: Brill, 2014).

13. John A. Lynn, *Women, Armies, and Warfare in Early Modern Europe* (Cambridge: Cambridge University Press, 2008). Earlier, see Barton Hacker, "Women and Military Institutions in Early Modern Europe: A Reconnaissance, " *Signs* 6, no. 4 (1981): 643–71.

14. The latter term was first coined by Beate Engelen in *Soldatenfrauen in Preußen: Eine Strukturanalyse der Garnisonsgesellschaft im späten 17. und im 18. Jahrhundert* (Münster: LIT, 2005).

15. This line of argument has been developing since the pioneering study by Hacker, "Women and Military Institutions."

16. For a similar study, see Karen Hagemann and Ralf Pröve, eds., *Landsknechte, Soldatenfrauen und Nationalkrieger: Militär, Krieg und Geschlechterordnung im historischen Wandel* (Frankfurt am Main: Campus, 1998).

17. Stefan Kroll, *Soldaten im 18. Jahrhundert zwischen Friedensalltag und Kriegserfahrung: Lebenswelten und Kultur in der kursächsischen Armee 1728–1796* (Paderborn: Schöningh, 2006), 365–79.

18. Ronald Thomas Ferguson, "Blood and Fire: Contribution Policy of the French Armies in Germany (1668–1715)" (PhD diss., University of Minnesota, 1970).

19. Peter H. Wilson, *Europe's Tragedy: The Thirty Years War* (London: Allen Lane, 2009), esp. 399–409; and Wilson, "Strategy and the Conduct of War," in *Ashgate Research Companion to the Thirty Years' War*, ed. Olaf Asbach and Peter Schröder (Farnham: Ashgate, 2014), 269–81.

20. See Karen Hagemann, "Militär, Krieg und Geschlechterverhältnisse: Untersuchungen, Überlegungen und Fragen zur Militärgeschichte der Frühen Neuzeit," in *Klio in Uniform: Probleme und Perspektiven einer modernen Militärgeschichte der Frühen Neuzeit*, ed. Ralf Pröve (Cologne: Böhlau, 1997), 35–88; and Bernhard R. Kroener, "'. . . und ist der Jammer nit zu beschreiben': Geschlechterbeziehungen und Überlebensstrategien in der Lagergesellschaft des Dreißigjährigen Krieges," in Hagemann and Pröve, *Landsknechte*, 279–97.

21. Hermann Terhalle, "Der Achtzigjährigen Krieg zwischen dem König von Spanien und den Niederlanden in seinen Auswirkungen auf das Westmünsterland an Beispielen," in *1568–1648: zu den Auswirkungen des Achtzigjährigen Krieges auf die östlichen Niederlande und das Westmünsterland*, ed. T. Timothy Sodmann (Vreden: Landeskundliches Institut Westmünsterland, 2002), 171–229, 178; and Peter Engerisser, *Von Kronach nach Nördlingen: der Dreißigjährige Krieg in Franken, Schwaben und der Oberpfalz 1631–1635* (Weissenstadt: Späthling, 2004), 514. See, generally, Mary Elizabeth Ailes, "Camp Followers, Sutlers, and Soldiers' Wives: Women in Early Modern Armies (c. 1450–1650)," in *A Companion to Women's Military History*, ed. Barton C. Hacker and Margaret S. Vining (Leiden: Brill, 2012), 61–92; and Ailes, *Courage and Grief: Women and Sweden's Thirty Years War* (Lincoln: University of Nebraska Press, 2018).

22. For officers' economic stake in regimental management, see Alan J. Guy, *Oeconomy and Discipline: Officership and Administration in the British Army, 1714–1763* (Manchester: Manchester University Press, 1985). The second volume of Fritz Redlich's classic study provides a wealth of detail on this for the period 1650–1800, but suffers from an overly materialist interpretation: *The German Military Enterpriser and His Workforce: A Study in Economic and Social History*, 2 vols. (Wiesbaden: Steiner, 1964–65).

23. John A. Lynn, *Giant of the Grand Siècle: The French Army, 1610–1715* (Cambridge: Cambridge University Press, 1997); and Olaf van Nimwegen, *The Dutch Army and the Military Revolutions, 1588–1688* (Woodbridge: Boydell, 2010); Peter H. Wilson, *War, State and Society in Württemberg, 1677–1793* (Cambridge: Cambridge University Press, 1995); and Wilson, *German Armies: War and German Politics, 1648–1806* (London: University College of London Press, 1991).

24. For these, see Peter H. Wilson, "Social Militarization in Eighteenth Century Germany," *German History* 18, no. 1 (2000): 1–39; and Michael Busch, *Absolutismus und Heeresreform: Schwedens Militär am Ende des 17. Jahrhunderts* (Bochum: Winkler, 2000).

25. Redlich, *German Military Enterpriser*, 2:235–57.

26. Engelen, *Soldatenfrauen*, 41–68; Jennine Hurl-Eamon, *Marriage and the British Army in the Long Eighteenth Century* (Oxford: Oxford University Press, 2014), 28–42; and Hagemann, "Militär, Krieg und Geschlechterverhältnisse."

27. Sabrina Loriga, "Soldaten in Piemont im 18. Jahrhundert," *L'Homme* 3, no. 1 (1992): 64–87.

28. Jutta Nowosadtko, *Stehendes Heer im Ständestaat: Das Zusammenleben von Militär- und Zivilbevölkerung im Fürstbistum Münster 1650–1803* (Paderborn: Schöningh, 2011), 250.

29. Further discussion of these aspects in Peter H. Wilson, "German Women and War 1500–1800," *War in History* 3, no. 2 (1996): 127–60; and Wilson, "The Politics of Military Recruitment in Eighteenth-Century Germany," *English Historical Review* 117, no. 472 (2002): 536–68.

30. Hurl-Eamon, *Marriage*, 26, 29, 33; and Andre Corvisier, *L'Armée française de la fin du xviie siècle au ministère de Choiseul*, 2 vols. (Paris: Presses universitaires, 1964), 2:757–63.

31. Wilson, "German Women," 144.

32. See examples in John L. H. Keep, *Soldiers of the Tsar: Army and Society in Russia, 1462–1874* (Oxford: Oxford University Press, 1985), 148–49; and Peter K. Taylor, *Indentured to Liberty: Peasant Life and the Hessian Military State, 1688–1815* (Ithaca, NY: Cornell University Press, 1994). For Russia, see also Carol B. Stevens, "Women and War in Early Modern Russia," in Hacker and Vining, *Companion*, 387–408.

33. Isser Woloch, "War-Widows' Pensions: Social Policy in Revolutionary and Napoleonic France," *Societas* 6, no. 4 (1976): 235–54.

34. For example, Linda Grant De Pauw, *Battle Cries and Lullabies: Women in War from Prehistory to the Present* (Norman: University of Oklahoma Press, 2000), 7–25.

35. Christopher Duffy, *The Army of Maria Theresa: The Armed Forces of Imperial Austria, 1740–1780* (Doncaster: Terence Wise, 1990), 18–20, 29, and 34.

36. Theodor Horstmann, *Generallieutenant Johann Nicolaus von Luckner und seine Husaren im Siebenjährigen Kriege*, ed. Michael Hochedlinger (Osnabrück: Biblio, 1997); and Martin Rink, *Vom "Partheygänger" zum Partisanen: Die Konzeption des kleinen Kriegs in Preußen 1740–1813* (Frankfurt am Main: Lang, 1999).

37. Lynn, *Women*, 202–8; and Brian Sandberg, " 'Generous Amazons Came to the Breach': Besieged Women, Agency and Subjectivity in the French Wars of Religion," *Gender & History* 16, no. 3 (2004): 654–88.

38. Christopher Duffy, *Fire and Stone: The Science of Fortress Warfare, 1660–1860* (London: Greenhill Books, 1996); and Duffy, *Siege Warfare*, 2 vols. (London: Routledge, 1979–1985), esp. 1:249–57; Lynn, *Women*, 202–8; and Sandberg, "Generous Amazons."

39. See also the chapter by Thomas Cardoza and Karen Hagemann on "History and Memory of Army Women and Female Soldiers, 1770s–1870s" in this handbook.

40. Fraser Easton, "Gender's Two Bodies: Women Warriors, Female Husbands and Plebeian Life," *Past and Present* 180, no. 1 (2003): 131–74; and Rudolf M. Dekker and Lotte van de

Pol, *The Tradition of Female Transvestism in Early Modern Europe* (Basingstoke: Macmillan, 1989). See also Lynn, *Women*, 164–202. For women at sea, see Suzanne J. Stark, *Female Tars: Women aboard Ship in the Age of Sail* (London: Pimlico, 1998); and David Cordingly, *Heroines and Harlots: Women at Sea in the Great Age of Sail* (London: Macmillan, 2002).

41. Julie Wheelwright, *Amazons and Military Maids: Women Who Dressed as Men in Pursuit of Life, Liberty and Happiness* (London: Pandora, 1989); and Elizabeth Ewing, *Women in Uniform through the Centuries* (London: B. T. Batsford, 1975), 28–36.

42. Wheelwright, *Amazons*, 7; and Diane Dugaw, *Warrior Women and Popular Balladry, 1650–1850* (Cambridge: Cambridge University Press, 1989).

43. Chris Mounsey, "Introduction," in *Presenting Gender: Changing Sex in Early Modern Culture*, ed. Chris Mounsey (Lewisburg, PA: Bucknell University Press, 2001), 15. See also De Pauw, *Battle Cries*, 23–24.

44. Helmut Lahrkamp, *Jan van Werth: Sein Leben nach archivalischen Quellenzeugnissen* (Cologne: Verlag der Löwe, 1962), 45.

45. See Scarlet Bowen, "The Real Soul of a Man in Her Breast: Popular Oppression and British Nationalism in Memoirs of Female Soldiers, 1740–1750," *Eighteenth-Century Life* 28, no. 3 (2004): 20–45.

46. Matthew Stephens, *Hannah Snell: The Secret Life of a Female Marine, 1723–1792* (London: Ship Street Press, 1999); and *The Female Soldier or, The Surprising Life and Adventures of Hannah Snell* (1750; repr. Los Angeles: William Andrews Clark Memorial Library, 1989).

47. Peter Guillery, "The Further Adventures of Mary Lacy: 'Seaman,' Shipwright, Builder," *History Workshop Journal* 49, no. 1 (2000): 212–19. Her autobiography has been edited by Margarette Lincoln, *The History of the Female Shipwright* (London: National Maritime Museum, 2008).

48. Marian Füssel, "Frauen in der Schlacht? Weibliche Soldaten im 17. und 18 Jahrhundert," in *Soldatinnen: Gewalt und Geschlecht im Krieg vom Mittelalter bis heute*, ed. Klaus Latzel et al. (Paderborn; Schöningh, 2011), 159–78, 169–70.

49. Loriga, "Soldaten," 81–82.

50. Dekker and van de Pol, *Female Transvestism*, 73; see 86–87 for popular hostility.

51. Angela Steidele, *In Männerkleider: Das verwegene Leben der Catharina Margaretha Linck alias Anastasius Rosenstengel* (Vienna: Böhlau, 2004); and Brigitte Eriksson, "A Lesbian Execution in Germany, 1721: The Trial Records," *Journal of Homosexuality* 6, no. 1–2 (1980/81): 27–40.

52. As argued by Laura Gowing, *Common Bodies: Women, Touch and Power in Seventeenth-Century England* (New Haven, CT: Yale University Press, 2003), 20.

53. See Karen Hagemann and Jane Rendall, "Gender, War, and Politics: Transatlantic Perspectives on the Wars of Revolution and Liberation, 1775–1830," in *Gender, War, and Politics: Transatlantic Perspectives, 1775–1830*, ed. Karen Hagemann et al. (Basingstoke: Palgrave Macmillan, 2010), 1–40.

54. Keith Thomas, *The Ends of Life: Roads to Fulfilment in Early Modern England* (Oxford: Oxford University Press, 2009), 58–65; and Christopher Duffy, *The Army of Frederick the Great* (Chicago: Emperor's Press, 1996), 64.

55. As exemplified in one British officer's struggle for recognition, David Buttery, *Messenger of Death: Captain Nolan and the Charge of the Light Brigade* (Barnsley: Pen & Sword Military, 2008).

56. Michael Kaiser, "Ist er vom Adel? Ja. Id satis videtur: Adelige Standesqualität und militärische Leistung als Karrierefaktoren des Dreißigjährigen Krieges," in *Geburt oder*

Leistung?: Elitenbildung im deutsch-britischen Vergleich, ed. Franz Bosbach et al. (Munich: Saur, 2003), 3–90; and Thomas, *Ends of Life*, 66–74.

57. Jean Bethke Elshtain, *Women and War* (New York: Basic Books, 1987); and R. Claire Snyder, *Citizen-Soldiers and Manly Warriors: Military Service and Gender in the Civic Republican Tradition* (New York: Rowman & Littlefield, 1999).

58. B. Ann Tlusty, *The Martial Ethic in Early Modern Germany: Civic Duty and the Right to Bear Arms* (Basingstoke: Palgrave Macmillan, 2011).

59. Matthew McCormack, "The New Militia: War, Politics and Gender in 1750s Britain," *Gender & History* 19, no. 3 (2007): 483–500.

60. Merry E. Wiesner, "*Wandervogels* and Women: Journeymen's Concepts of Masculinity in Early Modern Germany," *Journal of Social History* 24, no. 4 (1991): 767–82; and Isaac Land, *War, Nationalism and the British Sailor, 1750–1850* (Basingstoke: Palgrave Macmillan, 2009), 29–55.

61. Kroll, *Soldaten*, 405–12.

62. See Jutta Nowosadtko, "Soldatenpartnerschaften: Stehendes Heer und weibliche Bevölkerung im 18. Jahrhundert," in Hagemann and Pröve, *Landsknechte*, 297–321.

63. John A. Lynn, *Battle: A History of Combat and Culture* (Boulder, CO: Westview Press, 2003), 128–29.

64. There are strong parallels between early modern European conditions and those noted by Stephen Neufeld, *The Blood Contingent: The Military and the Making of Modern Mexico, 1876–1911* (Albuquerque: University of New Mexico Press, 2017).

65. Quotations from Leo Braudy, *From Chivalry to Terrorism: War and the Changing Nature of Masculinity* (New York: Alfred A. Knopf, 2003), 110; and Hurl-Eamon, *Marriage*, 90.

66. See Sabina Brändli, *"Der herrlich biedere Mann": Vom Siegeszug des bürgerlichen Herrenanzuges im 19. Jahrhundert* (Zurich: Chronos, 1998).

67. Eric Gruber von Arni, *Hospital Care and the British Standing Army, 1660–1714* (Aldershot: Ashgate, 2006); and Paul E. Kopperman, "Medical Services in the British Army, 1742–1783," *Journal of the History of Medicine and Allied Sciences* 34, no. 4 (1979): 428–55.

68. Thomas Cardoza, *Intrepid Women: Cantinières and Vivandières of the French Army* (Bloomington: Indiana University Press, 2010), 12–58.

69. Peter Englund, *The Battle of Poltava: Birth of the Russian Empire* (London: Gollancz, 1992), 56–57.

70. "Payments during the 1760–1 Campaign," A32 Bd. 4 fol. 314–61, Hauptstaatsarchiv, Stuttgart; see also Engelen, *Soldatenfrauen*, 457–584.

71. Bernd Wunder, "Pfarrwitwenkassen und Beamtenwitwen-Anstalten vom 16.–19. Jahrhundert: Die Entstehung der staatlichen Hinterbliebenversorgung in Deutschland," *Zeitschrift für Historische Forschung* 12, no. 4 (1985): 429–98; Wunder, "Die Institutionalisierung der Invaliden-, Alters- und Hinterbliebenenversorgung der Staatsbediensteten in Österreich 1740–1790," *Mitteilungen des Instituts für Österreichische Geschichtsforschung* 92 (1984): 341–406; and Engelen, *Soldatenfrauen*, 502–53.

72. Billeting was illegal in Britain after 1679, condemned as an element of political tyranny contrary to political liberties: James Douet, *British Barracks, 1660–1914: Their Architecture and Role in Society* (London: Stationary Office, 1998).

73. Walther Thensius, *Die Anfänge des stehenden Heerwesens in Kursachsen unter Johann Georg III. und Johann Georg IV* (Leipzig: Quelle & Meyer, 1912), 125.

74. Markus Meumann, "Soldatenfamilien und unehelicher Kinder: Ein soziales Problem im Gefolge der stehenden Heeren," in *Krieg und Frieden: Militär und Gesellschaft in der*

Frühen Neuzeit, ed. Bernard R. Kroener and Ralf Pröve (Paderborn: Schöningh, 1996), 219–36.

75. Hurl-Eamon, *Marriage*, 133.

76. See Karen Hagemann, *Revisiting Prussia's Wars against Napoleon: History, Culture, and Memory* (Cambridge: Cambridge University Press, 2015), 107–13; and Cissie Fairchilds, *Women in Early Modern Europe, 1500–1700* (Harlow: Longman, 2007).

77. For more, see the chapter by Stefan Dudink on "Citizenship, Mass Mobilization, and Masculinity in a Transatlantic Perspective, 1770s–1870s" in this handbook.

SELECT BIBLIOGRAPHY

Ailes, Mary Elizabeth. *Courage and Grief: Women and Sweden's Thirty Years War*. Lincoln: University of Nebraska Press, 2018.

Dekker, Rudolf M., and Lotte van de Pol. *The Tradition of Female Transvestism in Early Modern Europe*. Basingstoke: Macmillan, 1989.

Dugaw, Dianne. *Warrior Women and Popular Balladry, 1650–1850*. Cambridge: Cambridge University Press, 1989.

Engelen, Beate. *Soldatenfrauen in Preußen: Eine Strukturanalyse der Garnisonsgesellschaft im späten 17. und 18. Jahrhundert*. Münster: Lit Verlag, 2005.

Füssel, Marian. "Frauen in der Schlacht? Weibliche Soldaten im 17. und 18. Jahrhundert zwischen Dissimulation und Sensation." In *Soldatinnen. Gewalt und Geschlecht im Krieg vom Mittelalter bis heute*, edited by Klaus Latzel, Franka Maubach, and Silke Satjukow, 159–78. Paderborn: Schöningh, 2011.

Hacker, Barton C. "Women and Military Institutions in Early Modern Europe: A Reconnaissance." *Signs* 6, no. 4 (1981): 643–71.

Hagemann, Karen. "Militär, Krieg und Geschlechterverhältnisse: Untersuchungen, Überlegungen und Fragen zur Militärgeschichte der Frühen Neuzeit." In *Klio in Uniform: Probleme und Perspektiven einer modernen Militärgeschichte der Frühen Neuzeit*, edited by Ralf Pröve, 35–88. Cologne: Böhlau, 1997.

Hagemann, Karen, and Ralf Pröve, eds. *Landsknechte, Soldatenfrauen und Nationalkrieger. Militär: Krieg und Geschlechterordnung im historischen Wandel*. Frankfurt am Main: Campus, 1998.

Hurl-Eamon, Jennine. *Marriage and the British Army in the Long Eighteenth Century: "The Girl I Left behind Me."* Oxford: Oxford University Press, 2014.

Keep, John L. H. *Soldiers of the Tsar: Army and Society in Russia, 1462–1874*. Oxford: Oxford University Press, 1985.

Lee, Wayne E. *Barbarians and Brothers: Anglo-American Warfare, 1500–1865*. Oxford: Oxford University Press, 2011.

Loriga, Sabina. "Soldaten in Piemont im 18. Jahrhundert." *L'Homme* 3, no. 1 (1992): 64–87.

Lynn, John A. *Giant of the Grand Siècle: The French Army, 1610–1715*. Cambridge: Cambridge University Press, 1997.

Lynn, John A. *Women, Armies, and Warfare in Early Modern Europe*. Cambridge: Cambridge University Press, 2008.

Nowosadtko, Jutta. *Stehendes Heer im Ständestaat: Das Zusammenleben von Militär- und Zivilbevölkerung im Fürstbistum Münster 1650–1803*. Paderborn: Schöningh, 2011.

Parrott, David. *The Business of War: Military Enterprise and Military Revolution in Early Modern Europe*. Cambridge: Cambridge University Press, 2012.

Stevens, Carol B. "Women and War in Early Modern Russia," in *A Companion to Women's Military History*, ed. Barton C. Hacker and Margaret S. Vining, 387–408. Leiden: Brill, 2012.

Tlusty, B. Ann. *The Martial Ethic in Early Modern Germany: Civic Duty and the Right of Arms*. Basingstoke: Palgrave Macmillan, 2011.

Wilson, Peter H. *German Armies: War and German Politics, 1648–1806*. London: University College of London Press, 1991.

Wilson, Peter H. "German Women and War, 1500–1800." *War in History* 3, no. 2 (1996): 127–60. Reprinted in *Warfare in Europe, 1650–1792*, edited by Jeremy Black, 45–78. Ashgate: Aldershot, 2005.

Wilson, Peter H. *The Thirty Years War: Europe's Tragedy*. Cambridge, MA: Belknap Press of Harvard University Press, 2009.

CHAPTER 3

....

WAR, CULTURE, AND GENDER IN COLONIAL AND REVOLUTIONARY NORTH AMERICA

....

SERENA ZABIN

WARFARE in seventeenth- and eighteenth-century America, from the conflicts between colonizing Europeans and Indigenous people to the Seven Years' War (1756–63), the American Revolutionary War (1775–83), and the War of 1812, fought between the United States and Great Britain until 1815, has only recently come to be considered in gendered terms. In the past few years, scattered questions of honor and masculinity have informed studies about military culture.[1] With few exceptions, scholars have considered women objects of violence rather than vital participants in war and military culture. Similarly, the study of men has focused on them primarily as officers or warriors, but only rarely as rank-and-file soldiers and almost never as gendered beings.[2] This research tends to assume a close association of heroic manliness and risking one's life in battle, which stretches transhistorically across centuries and even cultures.

In fact, however, ideas of masculinity, femininity, and even warfare are specific to time and place. Changes in war and warfare in seventeenth- and eighteenth-century America were not limited to the battlefield. Instead, developments in military goals, personnel, and state support had unexpected consequences for the relationships between men and women as well as concepts of gender in these contexts and beyond. In the period of early colonial wars between the 1600s and 1750s, the new world of warfare created by these conflicts between European and Indigenous nations produced both new practices and new goals to these wars. As a result, assumptions about gender, especially about the place of women in both peace and war in these conflicts, shifted in both colonial and Native cultures.

In the 1750s and 1760s, the early colonial wars between small communities of settlers and individual Native American nations widened into an enormous imperial conflict between Europeans with pan-Native alliances, which became known as the Seven Years' War. For the first time, the British and the French both sent professional armies to fight in North America in what the British also labeled the French and Indian War (1754–63). The arrival of these British and French regiments reshaped military cultures and desta-bilized old gender practices and ideologies on all sides. In these professional armies, the place of women in war shifted from the diplomats and pawns they had been in earlier conflicts to essential support personnel. At the same time, ideals of military masculinity turned away from the battlefield and toward a larger vision of the imperial state. The unanticipated consequence of keeping a large part of Britain's professional army in North America during the peace that followed the Seven Years' War turned out to become the American Revolution.

The American Revolution and its War of Independence, culminating from 1775 to 1783, can be conceptualized as an early anticolonial conflict, stretching as it did from city to country, from White farms to Native American fields, and from rebellion to nation-building. Its pervasiveness had a particularly marked impact on gender orders in the building of the new nation. Women's contributions to the American war effort, which men both desired and feared, were quickly forgotten in a reinvigorated patriarchal ideal of the newly founded United States. This ideal contributed also to the War of 1812 and completed the domestication of femininity in American military projects.

The following will explore the changing interrelationship among gender, war, the mil-itary, and political culture to demonstrate the social and cultural outcomes of military conflicts in America between 1600 and the early nineteenth century. Two themes stand in the center: on the one hand, the contested and changing constructions of military masculinity of Native Americans, British and French White settlers, and the British and French armies that were brought to North America especially in the context of the Seven Years' War; and on the other hand, women's different and changing involvement in war-fare, which is related to the contested and changing representations of femininity in the different war societies.

COLONIAL WARS, 1600S–1750S

European settlers in North America encountered a world of warfare very different from the one to which they were accustomed. Early modern European armies expected that men would lead in both diplomacy and tactics.[3] Women played supporting roles that were essential to the army's ability to function, but they had no power, prestige, or impact. In contrast, Native warfare across sixteenth- and seventeenth-century North America depended on a very different division of gendered labor. Because Native war-fare tended to be oriented toward the goal of capturing prisoners rather than winning territory or economic gain in the sixteenth and seventeenth centuries, the place of pris-oners is a key component to understanding war as waged by Native Americans. From the southwestern to northeastern corners of the American continent, captive women (and men) became pawns, slaves, and sometimes family in new regions and new cultures. At the same time, women belonging to victorious villages or Native nations had an immense amount of power to determine the fate of captives. Because killing was itself only a limited component of Native warfare, we must expand our sense of Native warfare to include the impact that women had on diplomacy and hostage taking.[4]

Since familial, matrilineal relationships so predominantly shaped Native politics, including Native warfare, women at all ends of the spectrum of power played essential roles, although the actual act of warfare was almost entirely limited to men. Women were both engines and pawns in Native wars. Senior women were "peace chiefs" and diplomats in most, if not all, Native nations. Their participation in war councils was a central part of their political power, and, as a result, such women had a central role in the beginnings, endings, and even intensity of warfare. These women rose to their positions of authority in large part through their kin connections to warriors and diplomats.[5]

Little is known about these female councils, in part because European observers rarely recorded their comments. Europeans' lack of interest in women's councils reflects their own ideas about the gender order in which women played no part in negotiations about war, peace, and politics. One female Quaker minister recalled attending a peace conference in 1755 in which a Native women's council was present. She reminisced, "Several of their women sat in this conference, who, for fixed solidity, appeared to me like Roman matrons. They scarcely moved, much less spoke, during the time it was held; and there was a dignity in the behavior and countenance of one of them, that I cannot forget."[6] Nonetheless, women were able to make their wishes known. Before 1675, for example, Iroquois women were instrumental in urging warriors to undertake "mourning wars" in order to find captives to compensate for family members killed by war or disease. Most important, women had the power to determine the fates of both male and female prisoners taken in war. Gunlög Maria Fur points out that Native politics were not all-male spaces, but instead required both men and women to establish the political preconditions necessary for peace. The Delaware warriors sometimes in council referred to each other as "sister," not as a derogatory term, but one that indicated that they would consider peacemaking as well as war-making in their council decision.[7]

Further north, women also often chose which prisoners would be adopted, which would be killed, and, sometimes, which would be used as slaves who could be exchanged with other nations. Early in the eighteenth century, French nobleman Baron de Lahontan explained in his report on his voyages to North America in 1683–84 that Iroquois women had the power of life or death over prisoners:

> If the Woman or Girl has a mind to save the Prisoners which often happens she takes him by the hand and after conducting him into the Hut cuts his Bonds and orders him Cloaths Arms Victuals and Tobacco. This favour usually accompanied with these words: *I have given thee life, I have knock'd off thy chain, pluck up a good heart, serve well, be not ill minded and thou shalt have whereupon to thee for the loss of thy Country and thy Relations.* Sometimes the Iroquois Women adopt the Slaves that are presented to 'em and then they are look'd upon as Members of the Nation.[8] (emphasis in the original)

Women thus transformed the war aims of taking prisoners into a political and cultural process of incorporating strangers into the nation.

But women were not always powerful actors in these wars. As unwilling captives in Native wars, White, Black, and Native women all had enormous social and political meanings for Native warriors. Although throughout the seventeenth and eighteenth centuries Native warriors took European men, women, and children captive, they tended to focus on children and younger women, who were more likely to assimilate into their captives' families. Male prisoners, by contrast, were more likely to be ritually killed than assimilated. Unlike Europeans, Native Americans rarely, if ever, included battlefield rape as an element of warfare. Much more commonly, women were taken as captives and adopted into new households, a process that likely involved sexual coercion if not outright violence. Such adoption practices ran counter to European ideas of warfare, in which women had no role except as supporting personnel. Enemy women, in the view of the French, English, and Spanish militaries, might be raped, assaulted, or starved, but never integrated into the victor's community. Native Americans from the Southeast to the Great Lakes, by contrast, organized their war practices to take women as prisoners. Warfare for seventeenth-century Algonquians was predicated on the act of taking prisoners, rather than for commercial or territorial gain. Native American nations both valued women as a spoil of war and sometimes imagined them as sufficiently culturally mutable to become family.[9]

Capturing and integrating strangers could be a violent and gendered process for Native warriors. Illinois warriors near the Great Lakes occasionally carved war clubs that commemorated both their kills and their prisoners, leaving the clubs, one early eighteenth-century English memorialist claimed, "for his own glory . . . in places where he has been on some expedition in order that his enemies may know who killed their people and of what nation he was."[10] For these warriors, the capturing of prisoners was closely tied to their sense of masculine glory. Not so for European warriors. Even those Europeans who initially imagined race as mutable or who might even have encouraged intermarriage between European men and Native women never imagined such intermarriage as a war aim. For the French or the Spanish, and very occasionally the English, intermarriage might be a way of avoiding war, perhaps, or of cementing alliances among royalty, but never an inspiration for war itself. As European soldiers saw it, if women were in any way caught up in war, they were auxiliaries, not objects.[11]

Sustained military and economic contact between Europeans and Native Americans had an impact on the place of women in colonial warfare. In southeastern North America, African women captured in war by Native American tribes became less likely to be incorporated into families. Instead, their potential place in Native societies slowly contracted until their only possible status was as a slave. This shift was in part a result of the extension of the practice of slavery by Whites in the Southeast and the Southwest. Early in the nineteenth century, for example, both the Chickasaw and the Comanche redefined captives from prisoners who could be executed or exchanged for political purposes to slaves whose value lay in their labor. This shift from prisoner of war to enslaved worker made female captives particularly attractive for both sexual and domestic labor. It also helped both nations hold on to their political power in the face of European encroachments.[12]

Colonial governments also became factors in Native warfare. When Native warriors seized French or English women, colonial governments were often willing to pay appreciable sums for their return.[13] Susannah Johnson from Charlestown, New Hampshire, was nine months pregnant when she and her family were captured by Abanaki in August 1754, just after the beginning of the French and Indian War. In 1796, nearly forty years after her release and return to her hometown in 1758, she recorded and published her own story. In her recollections she wrote that when she gave birth on the trail, her captor immediately recognized his potential earnings: "He clapped his hands with joy, crying 'two monies for me, two monies for me.'"[14]

Warfare with Europeans over the seventeenth and eighteenth centuries changed some of these gendered expectations of war for many Native American nations, especially in European-settled areas along the eastern seaboard. As warfare with Europeans intensified and as European diplomats increasingly dealt only with Native men, notions of kinship as a way of organizing and controlling diplomacy and war fell away, decreasing women's power over war aims and decisions. Yet, overall, the seizing of women—even as they became pawns or potential moneymaking objects of redemption by European governments—persisted. Europeans often reacted with horror at the targeting of women for capture in Native warfare, but they also shared with Natives an understanding that masculinity was closely tied to prowess in warfare. Nowhere in North America, scholars have remarked, was it a compliment to call a warrior a "woman." All cultures shared an ideology of masculinity that was tied to combat itself. Warfare in colonial America was predicated on this mutual definition of battle-tested manliness. Up and down the eastern seaboard, men agreed that to refuse to fight was to be "like a woman."[15]

Thus, the place of women in warfare continued to be a major dividing line between Native and European ways of war throughout the eighteenth century, even as both cultures gained considerably more practice in fighting each other. In the single arena of warrior conduct and particularly issues of masculine honor, however, Europeans and Native Americans seemed to share a definition of gender ideologies. Colonial wars both reinforced martial ideals of masculinity and called into question the place of women in cross-cultural warfare.

WARS FOR EMPIRE, 1750S–1760S

The expanded presence of European armies in North America that began with the Seven Years' War introduced new forms of military culture to the continent. The Seven Years' War was fought for nine years in the North American theater between 1754 and 1763 and for seven in the European theater between 1756 and 1763. The conflict involved most of the great powers of the era and affected Europe, North America, Central America, the West African coast, India, and the Philippines. In North America, France and Great

Britain were the primary combatants. For these struggles over the colonies of British America and New France, the French were far more successful in gaining the support of Native American allies. They also began the war with more advantages. Although the population in the British colonies was twice that of New France (1.5 million British to 700,000 French), France's population was three times larger than Britain's and its army was ten times the size. Nonetheless, after France's initial victories in the first few years, the tide turned against them in 1758. One reason was that the French government sent far fewer troops to North America than the British. The former fought with c. 10,000 regulars, the latter with c. 42,000 regulars. In addition, both heavily depended on militia (infantry and marines) and provincial troops, and the French also on the support of the Native nations. In the end Great Britain was the winner of this conflict in the "New World," gaining the bulk of New France in North America, Spanish Florida, and some individual Caribbean islands in the West Indies.[16]

The Seven Years' War was the first time that European armies had met on North American soil. Although both had occasionally used ports in North America as garrisons for regiments before they were redeployed elsewhere earlier in the eighteenth century, the stationing of armies intended to fight rather than refuel was unprecedented. The presences of these armies introduced two new forms of European military culture to North America that had enormous implications for both military and civilian gender orders: the attitudes these armies produced about both the honor of White male officers and the work of White female camp followers laid the groundwork for the war itself and its future political implications.

The battles of the Seven Years' War completely changed the balance of power in North America between European nations: France ceded all its claims to North American colonies east of the Mississippi River, except New Orleans. Initially, the war itself did not do much to expand White claims to Native land. But the military culture that these two armies engendered laid the groundwork for the expansion of first European, then American, state power throughout North America.[17] The cult of honor practiced by European officers and the hard work performed by women who accompanied the armies seem entirely unconnected to each other, separated by a deep gulf of White social status between officers and privates. Yet, surprisingly, they worked together through the institution of a state-sponsored army to shape state-sponsored power in North America. In the second half of the eighteenth century, the expansion of European state power over increasing stretches of the North American continent depended on particular gender practices throughout the French, British, Native, and, eventually, American armies.

White men living in the colonies before 1755 were very rarely full-time soldiers. They were more likely to belong to informally constituted militias that gathered in response to a specific call for action. When they did join the French or British armies, they did so less as professional soldiers and more as patriotic citizen-soldiers who fought on a temporary basis to protect their own homes. Professional soldiers at the private rank, by contrast, had indefinite enlistment periods (often for life, or for as long as the men were physically able to fight) and were deployed anywhere the state demanded. Thus, the goals of colonial soldiers were often less about proving their valor and more about earning enough money to sustain their households. Bounties for enlistment were an essential tool for persuading British colonists to join an expeditionary force. These bounties were sometimes in cash at the time of enlistment. Even more attractive, however, was the promise of land for family farms after the war. This land, however, would first have to be wrested from Native control. The ability of an ex-soldier to earn enough money or property to fulfill an eighteenth-century vision of masculinity that was a married head of household was often dependent on imperial wars. Similarly, French Canadian marines saw their role as defenders of the French Crown's commercial interests. Their own economic futures were tied to those of the French Empire that they were defending.[18]

Before the Seven Years' War, English colonial militias and French Canadian marines were only loosely hierarchical, and their officer corps were fluid and rarely consisted of aristocrats. This less formal command structure offered privates the possibility to rise in the military hierarchy. One example is the British mobilization for King George's War (1744–48), named for George II, king of Great Britain from 1727 to 1763, and part of the War of Austrian Succession (1740–48). In North America, British, French, and Native American combatants mainly fought in the British provinces of New York, Massachusetts Bay, New Hampshire, and Nova Scotia.[19] When the acting governor of New York, George Clarke attempted to raise troops to send to this war in 1740, he offered commissions to men based on their ability to fill their companies with volunteers rather than on their social status. He later explained his policy. He wrote that he had found "almost all who declared their willingness to go, did it personally if such and such were to command them, for they were unwilling to inlist [sic] with anyone whom they did not know."[20] These colonial soldiers were not prepared to defer to anyone with a commission; they insisted on having a say in the command structure.[21]

The arrival of regular French and British troops in the context of the Seven Years' War changed all that, injecting claims of honorable (and dishonorable) masculinity to the officer class while discounting ordinary troops' concerns about compensation and autonomy. Aristocratic values of gentility informed officer behavior, as these men imported enormous supplies of food, clothing, and furniture to ensure that they could live in the style they considered appropriate, even on the battlefield. Despite the sumptuary laws that Louis XV, king of France from 1715 to 1774, issued in March 1756, French officers like General Louis-Joseph de Montcalm, the commander of the French forces in North America during the Seven Years' War, requested thousands of livres' worth of luxuries and food from France. Foodstuffs like olives, capers, and semolina flour ("I omit the vermichelly and the macaroni," Montcalm wrote to his mother) were intended to demonstrate the superiority of French regular officers—both their palates and their status—over Canadian militia officers and Native American warriors.[22]

Montcalm and his British counterparts began the Seven Years' War determined to behave like aristocrats. They would heroically and proudly lead men into battle, where they would bravely stand up to attack by other Europeans, or so they hoped. But French officers were forced to shift these definitions of honorable conduct as a result of the Seven Years' War. When fortune turned against the French, its army officers came to believe that they had to redefine the meaning of honor. As they began to lose battles and ground after 1758, officers started to claim that it was loyalty to the French Crown that made them honorable officers, rather than success in battle—an enormous shift from earlier Canadian masculine identities. One historian has recently argued that it was this conflict over these changing visions of honorable martial culture that led France to give up New France to Britain at the end of the Seven Years' War. Similarly, Jeffery Amherst, the commander in chief of the British forces in North America, claimed that his victory over the French was a result not of courage, but of careful competence.[23]

British officers also began to redefine manhood as a result of imperial state-building throughout the Seven Years' War. As British army officers struggled to make sense of warfare in the North American wilderness rather than in the European or West Indian theaters to which they were accustomed, they began to put as much emphasis on the process as the outcome of any military engagement. Sir William Johnson, who commanded Iroquois and colonial militia forces during the Seven Years' War and was appointed British superintendent of Indian Affairs for the northern colonies by the king in 1756, penned "Some Hints for a Commanding Officer" in 1755. Here, he reminded his newly minted provincial officers, "Let nothing ruffle your Temper[;] be always cool happen what will." He also noted, following the standards of his French foes, "A General officer must keep a good Table."[24]

As they gained experience fighting in America, regular officers feared that combat in the wilderness might diminish their honor. Contrasting their own definition of "behavior befitting an officer and a gentleman" against their Native and French foes, as well as their colonial allies, British officers decried the "skulking" way of woodland warfare. To such men, these modes of "savage" warfare looked a great deal like the very acts of cowardice or effeminacy that might inspire a duel or a court martial among British officers. In driving the French out of North America and beating back Native American attacks, British officers boasted that their military success was a result of their "firmness, prudence and intrepidity," rather than tactical choices. The expansion of the British Empire, in their words, depended more on an officer's character than on his prowess.[25]

Indeed, even those British officials like Sir William Johnson who were deeply sympathetic to and understanding of Native ways of war preferred the masculinity of European officer honor, even of foes, to the undoubted martial accomplishments of his Native warriors. Already a decade earlier during King George's War, Johnson had written with greater admiration of a well-dressed French officer than of his own successful Native warriors. Describing a 1747 battle that pitted Mohawks and New Yorkers against the French, he told Governor George Clinton, in office from 1743 to 1753, "One of the French Officers[,] the Indians say[,] was a young Man dressed in blue with a broad Gold lace who fought with undaunted courage till he was grievously wounded and then he called out for quarters in the Indian language but perceiving his wounds were mortal they [British-allied Mohawks] dispatched him[;] this is esteemed the galantest Action performed by the Indians since the commencement of the present War." Meanwhile, the Mohawks, angered by an injury to their chief, had "inraged, fought more like Devils than Men."[26] The young French officer with the gold lace fought unsuccessfully but with honor; the unmanned (and undressed) Mohawks were gallants only by virtue of their mercy killing of an injured man.

By the late 1760s, the role of the British army in North America had shifted. France's army was gone from Canada, and after 1766, military conflicts with Native Americans were sporadic and small in scale. To control their new empire, the British left a large contingent of soldiers as a peacekeeping force in North America. Their role was to guard against French colonists and French-allied Native Americans who might not have transferred their loyalties to Great Britain. The British government also hoped to use the troops to support customs officials and tax collectors. Their goal was to create a stronger and more centralized British administration, not to fight wars.

This force was the largest peacetime army Great Britain had ever maintained. And so, as much as officers wished to define their masculinity largely through their battlefield experience, those in North America had few opportunities to do so. As a sort of pension plan for officers, George III decided to cut the number of privates by nearly 40 percent, but to leave most of the officers in their rank. The result was that most officers, especially in the years between the Seven Years' War and the American Revolution, were far more likely to see garrison duty than heroic engagements. In the British Isles as well as in its colonies, the British Crown tended to use its regiments as customs enforcers or riot police during peacetime. Not surprisingly, officers hated being sent on riot duty, because it had no opportunities for glory but many possibilities for failure. Secretary of War Viscount Barrington admitted to Secretary of State Viscount Weymouth in 1768 that it was "a most Odious Service which nothing but Necessity can justify."[27]

Peacetime armies thus were forced to redefine a British soldier's sense of manliness. As the British colonel William Eyre wrote sadly on learning that he had to stay in America after the Peace of Paris had concluded the war in 1763, "Such it Seems is my Destiny, so I shall Endeavour to be Satisfied with My Lot; it's what we Are Subject to as Soldiers, it's our Duty to Obey."[28] Obedience and deference were now necessary elements of even a colonel's sense of self. Far from leading a charge into battle, from which one might earn glory or heroic death, army officers in peacetime had to reimagine the qualities of an honorable military man. Competent administration rather than bravery had become the standard by which officers' honor would be measured once the fighting was over.

During wartime, military masculinity was not just defined in relation to other men. Soldiers also derived gendered meaning from their relationships with army women. Early modern armies consisted of both men and women. European women rarely participated in either peace talks or battles. Instead, they provided material, social, and logistical support. The work that women did in the army ranged from explicit to hidden and from paid to reviled. Correspondingly, their presence in British fighting forces was both regular and contested.[29] Working for the army was one of the few ways that a woman married to a private soldier could accompany her husband. The British army determined by the middle of the eighteenth century that it would allow for six women to travel with each company, or roughly sixty women per regiment. The army needed a few women, primarily as laundresses and nurses, and was willing to pay for them with both wages and rations. Officers from the regular army envisioned working women as part of a necessary labor force. Privates saw them as part of their families; many fiercely resented any attempts to leave them behind. Their commanding officers were sometimes sympathetic. Although officers frequently denigrated these women as "prostitutes," lazy, and likely carriers of venereal disease, they also colluded with privates in supporting with travel and rations many more women than the approved number.[30]

Because many officers treated all women who traveled with the army as morally objectionable (regardless of their marital or sexual status), some subsumed all of women's work under the umbrella of sexual labor. The American officers who served alongside the British regulars in the 1740s and 1750s felt even more strongly than many of their British counterparts that the army should be an all-male space in order to protect themselves and their men from immoral influences. As Native and provincial forces gathered to prepare for an attack on Crown Point in 1755, colonial officers argued that only soldiers should live in the camp. Sir William Johnson, then commander of the regular and Iroquois troops, did not agree. He distinguished between prostitutes, whom he claimed to be happy to remove, and women who did essential labor. As he wrote to the Connecticut commander at the end of July 1755, "As to bad Women following or being harbored in our Camp I shall discountenance it to the utmost of my Power. As to Men's Wives while they behave Decently they are suffered in all Camps & thought necessary to Wash & mend."[31] Provincial officers were not convinced and three weeks later voted to send all the women of the camp to Albany.

In both the British and the American armies, women's presence did not necessarily contribute to their improved status. While men's participation in the army, even when coerced, could garner them patriotic approbation, women's mere presence in a military camp was fraught with suspicion. Many men assumed that women in military camps had to be vicious in their morals or at least sexually depraved.[32] Captain Samuel Jenks, for example, an officer in the Massachusetts Provincial Forces in 1760, scornfully wrote of the quarrel between one of his soldiers and his mistress, "On their passage they fell into disputes At length he struck her which inraged hir so that after several fits & efforts jumpt over board This coolt her courage for her sweetheart held her under water untill she was amost expiring They then took her in stript off her cloaths & drest anew & so the fray ended I wish it were the fate of all these sort of ladys that follow the army."[33] Jenks mentioned women approvingly only when they were absent; he regularly spent his evenings drinking toasts "to wives and sweethearts." On a cold, rainy day, he and his fellow officers spent the day in front of the fire, feet wrapped in blankets, "disputing of matters in love & matrimony & other diversion to pass away such tedious weather."[34]

At the same time, however, Jenks regularly recorded his struggles with the camp washerwomen to find his laundry. "Lost 2 of my best shirts to day by a washer woman," he noted in disgust.[35] Provincial and regular soldiers alike realized that military success depended on the labor of women. If a comparison against enemies' ways of war helped define military masculinity, a sharp sexual division of labor made clear military men's dependence on women's work. The peacetime army permitted an even larger number of families than the standard restrictions of 60 women per regiment. When the British ministry sent reinforcements to the permanent garrison in Halifax in 1750, the regiment that came from Ireland consisted of 290 privates, 130 women, and 50 children.[36] The military work of defense that the garrison was intended to do clearly would require the work of women to complete it. As the British state attempted to expand its power over both Native and French Canadians, it turned to women of the army to help them hold the line. British forts at the edges of the empire depended on the family structures and domestic labor that army women performed to create stable British communities.[37]

FROM THE AMERICAN REVOLUTION TO THE WAR OF 1812

As the British government tried to consolidate its control of its newly expanded possessions in North America, it used both administrators and troops to draw the colonies more closely into the centralized British Empire. The government could use the peacetime army to patrol interactions between Native Americans and the British settlers and soldiers as well as to crack down on the smuggling that cut into the empire's customs revenues. But the British Parliament had hoped to cut military expenditures once the Seven Years' War had ended. To pay the costs of maintaining this army in North America, the British government looked to the American colonies for tax revenues.

Colonists objected to the new taxes on principle, insisting that their rights as proud members of the British Empire had been trammeled by a series of taxes to which they had not agreed. In the first ten years of the protests over taxes, few colonists or administrators considered revolution. But imperial officials met each colonial protest with an increasingly hard line that ratcheted up the tension between colonies and government. Finally, matters came to a head after the Tea Act of 1773. Radical colonists insisted that no tea would enter colonial ports, and in Boston men dumped the taxed tea into the harbor. The British government punished Boston by closing the port, suspending the government charter, taking control of the courts, and putting Massachusetts under military rule. By the spring of 1775, British soldiers and New England militia had entered into the Battle of Lexington and Concord in April, and the Battle of Bunker Hill in June of that year.

The American Revolutionary War, 1775–83

Even more than the Seven Years' War, the American Revolutionary War, as both a military event and a catalyst for producing a nation, had the power to thoroughly reshape gender orders, sometimes radically and sometimes quite regressively. In the context of a revolutionary war, gender conflicts from enlistment to fashion were refracted through the lens of the military contest. Even once the war was over, its memory shaped gender relationships in the new nation.

When the British Tenth Regiment of Foot marched into the towns of Lexington and Concord west of Boston on April 19, 1775, they did not find a formal army waiting for them. Instead, members of the town's militias defended their local stores of ammunition. Other towns sent militias in support, and when the British troops retreated to Boston, militias surrounded the city and blocked them in. When General George Washington, the commander of the Continental army, arrived in Massachusetts in July soon after the Battle of Bunker Hill on June 17, 1775, he saw more than twenty thousand militiamen from towns throughout New England encamped outside Boston.[38] Washington found that this enormous encampment looked a lot like an army, especially in terms of the women who had come to support troops both personally and materially. Frustrated with the lack of hierarchy he perceived among both the soldiers and the women, he demanded the creation of a regular army on the British model.

The Continental army and the town-based militias eventually developed into separate entities with different roles. Even more important, they held different appeals for men and for some women.[39] In both the northern and the southern states, officers had a hard time finding men willing to sign up for the Continental army. Longer enlistments—from one to three years, and occasionally for "the duration"—did not appeal to men who were heads of households or farms. Because they would not be able to take care of their crops and thus support the wives and children whose dependence was essential to their role as heads of households, such men avoided service in the Continental army. In particular, aspiring married men who could not afford sufficient enslaved labor to take care of their property preferred to sign up for militia service.[40] Militias thus became an institution for propertied White men whose masculinity depended on their ability to support and control their families.

Poorer, younger, unmarried men, often without property, had fewer options and were more likely to see advantages in joining the Continental army. As states found it increasingly difficult to fulfill their enlistment quotas, men could negotiate for better enlistment bonuses. Congress also offered elite men incentives to join the army, primarily through status as officers and the promise of a significant pension after the war ended.[41] The army that Congress created looked much like the British army that many of its officers had known.[42] It not only encouraged marked distinctions between officers and privates, but also depended heavily on women to do the labor of nursing, washing, and cleaning. Because there was no mechanism for sending home soldiers' pay, women who depended on their husbands for subsistence remained with them as the army marched.[43]

Indeed, when George Washington attempted to drive women away from the military camps around Boston after the Battle of Bunker Hill in July 1775, he soon found that he could not maintain an army without women. His soldiers refused to wash clothes, insisting that it was women's work only, and he soon found his troops decimated by disease.[44] Enslaved men and women also found possibilities in the war. Although Washington initially balked at the idea of any African Americans in the army, his desperate need for soldiers eventually convinced him to allow both free African American men and some slaves to join the Continental army. In 1777, some states promised freedom to enslaved men who enlisted. While free Black women probably worked for the army like their

White counterparts, Congress made no provision for enslaved women to gain their freedom through service to the newly formed nation.

Both enslaved men and women found far more support from the British army. Most famously, in 1775, the governor of Virginia, John Murray, Fourth Earl of Dunmore, promised freedom to any man willing to bear arms for the British. Accompanying the eight hundred men who flocked to Dunmore were at least the same number of women and children.[45] Other British commanders soon followed Murray's lead, promising freedom to both women and men who joined the army.[46] White women's participation in the war was at least as contested as that of enslaved men. Just as Europeans and Natives had shared a language of gendered insult in the seventeenth and early eighteenth centuries, the new Continental army drew on slurs of effeminacy and unmanliness to distinguish itself from its enemies. Unlike in earlier wars, however, when political elites shunned the idea of White women participating in war, this time American Whigs both desired and rejected White women's participation. As a result, despite the occasional opportunities that the war offered these women, the political and cultural aftereffects of the military conflict produced a new gender order.

Conflicts over fashion had simmered in revolutionary America even before war was declared. The nonimportation and nonconsumption movements of the late 1760s and early 1770s held up homespun and simplicity as patriotic fashion, a sartorial mode that few White Americans embraced happily. When the battles of Lexington and Concord, the first military engagements of the American Revolutionary War in April 1775, released colonials' military rage and spurred the creation of the Continental army, men discovered that they could once again wear fashionable clothes legitimately, so long as they were in the military mode. Although there was a fine line between foppishness and appropriate fashion, American men paid close attention to their appearance in uniform. Hairstyles in particular became a flashpoint for gender conflict. Men—officers and occasionally privates—wished to powder their hair "à la Macaroni." When Captain John Laurens wrote home to his father, the president of the Continental Congress, for hair powder in 1778, the elder Laurens was unable to secure any for him. "My hairdresser recommends to you to substitute flour," he advised his son earnestly. It was better for a representative of the Continental army to flour his head than appear unfashionable. For men, soldiers' fashion could be both patriotic and appealing to the opposite sex.[47]

Women found, however, that their attempts at fashion could brand them as traitors. Four months after Laurens sought his fashion advice, Congress vented its anger against loyalist collaborators in Philadelphia by a street demonstration in which "some Gentlemen purchased the most Extravagant high head dress that could be got and Dressed an old Negro Wench with it." Using an elderly, enslaved woman to mock the claims to fashion and status that it was supposed to confer on women, Congress made clear that only military men could be the arbiters of fashion.[48] In fact, even flouring one's head could not unman a Continental soldier in the same way that powder could taint a British soldier with effeminacy. Comparing the British soldier unfavorably with an American, the poet Philip Freneau wrote, "No fop in arms, no feather on his head / No glittering toys the manly warrior had."[49] Appearance had become central to Americans' sense of martial masculinity.

Like the military mode of fashion, men in uniform wielded symbolic as well as physical violence during the American Revolutionary War. Stories about rape in particular had surprisingly little to say about women, but communicated a great deal about gendered power. Accounts of violence against women by soldiers might become political, rather than personal, morality tales about the violence of the British Empire against its colonies. Conversely, similar stories were circulated, often by and to loyalist women, about the violations of their bodily integrity practiced by rebels. Even when these stories characterized women as victims of military masculinity, their retelling by women was itself an act of resistance. In this way, women found a place for feminine participation in the war.[50]

Other aspects of the American Revolutionary War showed women and men acting in concert rather than against each other. Unlike in earlier eighteenth-century colonial wars, women's military participation was now celebrated and occasionally remunerated by the White Americans. Most famously, a cross-dressing soldier, Deborah Sampson, was one of a handful of women who received a military pension when the war ended. As an acknowledgment of the contributions of at least some military washerwomen, the US Congress granted pensions to a few camp followers, including to an army wife named Sarah Osborne.[51]

In the first years of the war, Washington did his best not to use the militia. He concentrated his attention on turning the Continental army into a professional force. Particularly after the harsh winter of 1777–78 that the army spent at Valley Forge, the army became a more coherent unit and was one of the first truly national institutions. Americans needed the army to create the nation, but once the war was over, the army receded in the national imagination, often to the distress of its veterans.[52] It was the "citizen-soldiers" of the militia, not the professionalized soldiers of the Continental army, who were celebrated in the new United States.[53] This emphasis on "minutemen" not only erased the contributions of army veterans, but also hid the work that the women who had supported the army had done to create the new nation. Instead, the militiamen who had stayed close to home to protect women and children became the heroes. Their desire to maintain patriarchal households became part of the mythology of the new United States.

Thus, despite these indications of appreciation for military contributions that the United States offered to a few women, the official memories of women's participation in the American Revolution were partial and limited. They were restricted primarily to two roles: keeping alive the memory of martyred men and performing the symbolic cultural work of bereft widows.[54] The restriction of White women's opportunities for inclusion in the memory of the Revolutionary War was intensified by the backlash against their political participation in the creation of the new nation. Rather than taking a place as rights- (and arms-) bearing citizens, White women were restricted to a position as wives and mothers whose job was to mold men into citizens.[55]

The Political Aftermath of the American Revolutionary War

Some women did find, for a time, that the American Revolutionary War had created political possibilities for them. After radicals in some states insisted that all veterans be enfranchised, the traditional bond between property and suffrage began to fray. In New Jersey from 1776 to 1807, unmarried adult women, both White and Black, were allowed to cast ballots. Moreover, although suffrage in New Jersey was supposed to be limited to independent women of means, observers sometimes took women's right to vote in that state to mean that *all* adult women could vote. In 1797, Abigail Adams, the wife of President John Adams, in office from 1797 to 1801, imagined that she could have voted if Massachusetts had been as "liberal" as New Jersey. Although the New Jersey legislature eventually convinced itself that it had never been the intent of the framers of the state constitution to allow women to vote, it was hard to put the genie back in the bottle again. White women continued to influence politics through writing, salons, and celebrations. Nonetheless, men like John Adams continued to insist that women were "unfit for Practice and Experience, in the great Business of Life, and the hardy Enterprises of War, as well as the arduous Cares of State."[56]

Even those women living outside the political boundaries of the United States found their political power increasingly circumscribed by the new nation. Male settlers swarming into Kentucky, Tennessee, and other parts of the eighteenth-century West used a traditional ideal of patriarchal households to claim government support for military action against Native Americans. They used this same language of vulnerable women in need of protection to compel the new federal government to grant White men political rights in the United States. These rights in the new states were predicated on the exclusion of White women, enslaved people, and Native Americans from the body politic. As the British army had done after the Seven Years' War, American settlers used White families in general—and White women in particular—to claim state power over Native land. Settlers and their government supporters framed the next round of wars against Native Americans as the conflict between civilized White families and Native Americans who targeted vulnerable White women. As one historian has noted, "The nation's territorial destiny became a triumph of the domestic order over the wild and savage frontier."[57]

When adapting to a continent with only two White powers left, Britain controlling the territory of Canada and the United States increasingly attempting to control the vast rest of the North American continent still owned by Native nations, Native Americans in the Southeast found the United States undermining warrior culture, the traditional site of Native masculinity. As a result, both Creek and Cherokee women found their own political power diminished, particularly their powers to control property and make war.[58] The story of Milly Francis neatly reveals the ways that long-standing gendered divisions in Creek military culture were upended by the imperial project of the new United States. During the first Seminole War of 1818, the Red Stick Creeks took a Georgia militiaman captive. In a ritual remarkably similar to the one by which Pocahontas was said to have spared the life of John Smith, Milly Francis saved the life of the settler Duncan McKrimmon from death in order to have him adopted into Creek culture. But only a month later, American military forces rescued McKrimmon and executed Francis's father, a Creek prophet. McKrimmon turned the tables on Francis by offering to marry her if she was willing to leave Creek country and live with him in "the settled parts of Georgia." She declined his proposal. Just as the imposition of colonial values on the Creeks after the American Revolution devalued warrior culture and attempted to push Creek men into the traditionally female realm of husbandry, the same imperial forces pushed Native women out of their traditional roles as arbiters of peace and prisoners.[59]

The complete domestication of femininity in American military projects became evident in the War of 1812.[60] In this final military conflict against the British, the United States appealed to family values and especially the willingness of women to populate the nation. Rejecting Thomas Malthus's moral condemnation of population expansion, Americans argued that their future greatness was entirely predicated on their ability to have children, or, more precisely, for American women to have children. The War of 1812 was sold in American popular culture as a necessary conflict to allow unfettered American reproduction. White Americans' ability to hold on to their "empire for liberty" against the British and their Native allies would require the expansion of the nation's population. Marital and martial ardor went hand in hand. As a result, White women's military and national contributions in this war were to be purely reproductive. In the end, however, this reproductive labor counted more than men's military contributions. Although the War of 1812 was militarily inconclusive, Americans claimed victory simply by having children.[61]

CONCLUSION

The War of 1812 solidified a long move for military men away from a culture of battlefield masculinity and toward that of bourgeois *pater familias*. Where once a warrior's honor might have been tied to the number of female prisoners he captured or the bravery with which he faced death, changes in both the practices and the goals of war over the previous two hundred years had reshaped ideals of masculinity itself. As White Americans continued to fight Native Americans for control over North America using state and local militias, the United States increasingly framed these wars as battles for family homesteads. White men's identification as fathers and husbands animated their military ardor.[62] The women they imagined themselves to be protecting were given little formal role in these militias, even as they continued to support barricaded forts and homesteads. Meanwhile, Cherokee women persisted in trying to use their traditional power as diplomats to contain the conflicts between settlers and Native Americans. Even in those contexts, however, they repositioned themselves as wives and mothers, not political figures. As the history of Native American removal shows, however, they did not succeed.[63]

NOTES

1. In addition to those cited below, see John A. Ruddiman, *Becoming Men of Some Consequence: Youth and Military Service in the Revolutionary War* (Charlottesville: University of Virginia Press, 2014); Christian Ayne Crouch, *Nobility Lost: French and Canadian Martial Cultures, Indians, and the End of New France* (Ithaca, NY: Cornell University Press, 2014); Kathleen Wilson, "Rethinking the Colonial State: Family, Gender, and Governmentality in Eighteenth-Century British Frontiers," *The American Historical Review* 116, no. 5 (2011): 1294–322; Benjamin Irvin, *Clothed in Robes of Sovereignty: The Continental Congress and the People out of Doors* (New York: Oxford University Press, 2011); John Phillips Resch and Walter Sargent, eds., *War and Society in the American Revolution: Mobilization and Home Fronts* (DeKalb: Northern Illinois University Press, 2007); and Ann M. Little, *Abraham in Arms: War and Gender in Colonial New England* (Philadelphia: Pennsylvania State University Press, 2007).

2. The most essential work on Native women as participants in war culture can be found in Juliana Barr, *Peace Came in the Form of a Woman: Indians and Spaniards in the Texas Borderlands* (Chapel Hill: University of North Carolina Press, 2007); Pekka Hämäläinen, *The Comanche Empire* (New Haven, CT: Yale University Press, 2009); Gunlög Maria Fur, *A Nation of Women: Gender and Colonial Encounters among the Delaware Indians* (Philadelphia: University of Pennsylvania Press, 2009); and Wayne E. Lee, "Peace Chiefs and Blood Revenge: Patterns of Restraint in Native American Warfare, 1500–1800," *Journal of Military History* 71, no. 3 (2007): 701–41.

3. See also the chapter by Peter H. Wilson on "Wars, States, and Gender in Early Modern European Warfare, 1600s–1780s" in this handbook.

4. Jon Parmenter, "After the Mourning Wars: The Iroquois as Allies in Colonial North American Campaigns, 1676–1760," *William and Mary Quarterly* 64, no. 1 (2007): 39–76; Daniel K. Richter, "War and Culture: The Iroquois Experience," *William and Mary Quarterly* 40, no. 4 (1983): 528–59; and Christina Snyder, *Slavery in Indian Country: The Changing Face of Captivity in Early America* (Cambridge, MA: Harvard University Press, 2010).

5. Barr, *Peace Came*; Lee, "Peace Chiefs"; and Theda Perdue, *Cherokee Women: Gender and Culture Change, 1700–1835* (Lincoln: University of Nebraska Press, 1998).

6. Cited in Kari Elizabeth Rose Thompson, "Inconsistent Friends: Philadelphia Quakers and the Development of Native American Missions in the Long Eighteenth Century" (PhD diss., University of Iowa, 2013), 53.

7. Fur, *Nation of Women*, 160–98.

8. Louis Armand de Lom d'Arce baron de Lahontan and Victor Hugo Paltsits, *New Voyages to North-America*, 2 vols. (Chicago: A. C. McClurg, 1905), 2:506.

9. James Brooks, *Captives & Cousins: Slavery, Kinship, and Community in the Southwest Borderlands* (Chapel Hill: University of North Carolina Press, 2002); Michelle LeMaster, *Brothers Born of One Mother: British–Native American Relations in the Colonial Southeast* (Charlottesville: University of Virginia Press, 2012); and Brett Rushforth, *Bonds of Alliance: Indigenous and Atlantic Slaveries in New France* (Chapel Hill: University of North Carolina Press, 2012).

10. Cited in Rushforth, *Bonds of Alliance*, 57.

11. For intermarriage, see David Hackett Fischer, *Champlain's Dream* (New York: Simon & Schuster, 2008); for general European attitudes toward women and warfare, see Barton C. Hacker, "Women and Military Institutions in Early Modern Europe: A

Reconnaissance," *Signs* 6, no. 4 (1981): 643–71; and John A. Lynn, *Women, Armies, and Warfare in Early Modern Europe* (Cambridge: Cambridge University Press, 2008); as well as Wilson, "Wars, States, and Gender."

12. Hämäläinen, *Comanche Empire*, 252; and Snyder, *Slavery*.

13. Parmenter, "After the Mourning," 39–76; and Snyder, *Slavery*.

14. Susanna Johnson, *A Narrative of the Captivity of Mrs. Johnson Containing an Account of Her Sufferings, during Four Years with the Indians and French* (Walpole, NH: David Carlisle, 1796), 39.

15. Tyler Boulware, "'We Are Men': Native American and Euroamerican Projections of Masculinity during the Seven Years' War," in *New Men: Manliness in Early America*, ed. Thomas A. Foster (New York: New York University Press, 2011), 51–70; Lee, "Peace Chiefs"; and Little, *Abraham in Arms*, 13.

16. Fred Anderson, *Crucible of War: The Seven Years' War and the Fate of Empire in British North America, 1754–1766* (New York: Alfred A. Knopf, 2000); and Crouch, *Nobility Lost*.

17. Anderson, *Crucible of War*, 505.

18. Crouch, *Nobility Lost*.

19. S. E. D. Shortt, "Conflict and Identity in Massachusetts: The Louisbourg Expedition of 1745," *Social History/Histoire Sociale* 5, no. 10 (1972): 165–85; John W. Shy, *Toward Lexington: The Role of the British Army in the Coming of the American Revolution* (Princeton, NJ: Princeton University Press, 1965), 3–44.

20. Edmund Bailey O'Callaghan et al., *Documents Relative to the Colonial History of the State of New-York: Procured in Holland, England, and France, 1837–1908* (Albany, NY: Weed, Parsons, 1853), 4:167.

21. Fred Anderson, *A People's Army: Massachusetts Soldiers and Society in the Seyen Years' War* (Chapel Hill: University of North Carolina Press, 1984).

22. Quoted in Crouch, *Nobility Lost*, 109.

23. Crouch, *Nobility Lost*; and Anderson, *Crucible of War*, 409.

24. Sir William Johnson, *The Papers of Sir William Johnson* (Albany: University of the State of New York, 1921–1965), 1:539–40.

25. Boulware, "We Are Men"; and Arthur N. Gilbert, "Law and Honour among Eighteenth-Century British Army Officers," *The Historical Journal* 19, no. 1 (1976): 75–87. Quotation from Gage to Halifax, October 12, 1764, in Clarence Edwin Carter, ed., *The Correspondence of General Thomas Gage with the Secretaries of State, 1763–1773* (Hamden, CT: Archon Books, 1969), 1:40.

26. "Extract of a Letter from Colonel Johnson to Governor Clinton, 24 April, 1747," in O'Callaghan et al., *Documents*, 6:343.

27. Viscount Barrington to Weymouth, April 18, 1768, WO 4/83, 316–17, cited in E. P. Thompson, "The Moral Economy of the English Crowd in the Eighteenth Century," *Past & Present*, 50, no. 1 (1971): 76–136, 121.

28. Stanley McCrory Pargellis, ed. *Military Affairs in North America, 1748–1765: Selected Documents from the Cumberland Papers in Windsor Castle* (New York: D. Appleton–Century, 1936), 461.

29. See Wilson, "Wars, States, and Gender."

30. Paul E. Kopperman, "The British High Command and Soldiers' Wives in America, 1755–1783," *Journal of the Society for Army Historical Research* 60, no. 241 (1982): 14–34; Holly A. Mayer, *Belonging to the Army: Camp Followers and Community during the American Revolution* (Columbia: University of South Carolina Press, 1996); Judith L. Van

Buskirk, *Generous Enemies: Patriots and Loyalists in Revolutionary New York* (Philadelphia: University of Pennsylvania Press, 2002); and Kathleen Wilson, *The Island Race: Englishness, Empire and Gender in the Eighteenth Century* (London: Routledge, 2003).

31. Johnson to Phineas Lyman, Albany, July 27, 1755, in Johnson, *Papers*, 1:783.

32. Caroline Cox, *A Proper Sense of Honor: Service and Sacrifice in George Washington's Army* (Chapel Hill: University of North Carolina Press, 2004).

33. Samuel Jenks, "Journal of Captain Samuel Jenks," in *Proceedings of the Massachusetts Historical Society*, vol. 5 (1889–1890), 352–91, 364.

34. Ibid., 383.

35. Ibid., 367.

36. Stanley McCrory Pargellis, *Lord Loudoun in North America* (New Haven, CT: Yale University Press, 1933), 31.

37. Holly A. Mayer, "From Forts to Families: Following the Army into Western Pennsylvania, 1758–1766," *The Pennsylvania Magazine of History and Biography* 130, no. 1 (2006): 5–43.

38. Nathaniel Philbrick, *Bunker Hill: A City, a Siege, a Revolution* (New York: Viking, 2013).

39. Stephen Conway, "The British Army, 'Military Europe,' and the American War of Independence," *William and Mary Quarterly* 67, no. 1 (2010): 69–100.

40. Michael A. McDonnell, "Class War? Class Struggles during the American Revolution in Virginia," *William and Mary Quarterly*, Third Series, 63, no. 2 (2006): 305–44.

41. Caroline Cox, "The Continental Army," in *The Oxford Handbook of the American Revolution*, ed. Edward G. Gray and Jane Kamensky (Oxford: Oxford University Press, 2013), 161–76.

42. Conway, "The British Army."

43. Jennine Hurl-Eamon, *Marriage and the British Army in the Long Eighteenth Century: "The Girl I Left behind Me"* (Oxford: Oxford University Press, 2014), 50–51.

44. Kathleen M. Brown, *Foul Bodies: Cleanliness in Early America* (New Haven, CT: Yale University Press, 2009).

45. Woody Holton, *Forced Founders: Indians, Debtors, Slaves, and the Making of the American Revolution in Virginia* (Chapel Hill: University of North Carolina Press, 1999), 156.

46. Maya Jasanoff, *Liberty's Exiles: American Loyalists in the Revolutionary World* (New York: Alfred A. Knopf, 2011), 49.

47. Kate Haulman, *The Politics of Fashion in Eighteenth-Century America* (Chapel Hill: University of North Carolina Press, 2011).

48. Kate Haulman, "A Short History of the High Roll," *Common-Place* 2, no. 1 (2001), accessed September 4, 2016, http://www.common-place.org/vol-02/no-01/lessons/.

49. Quoted in Haulman, *Politics of Fashion*, 163.

50. Sharon Block, "Rape without Women: Print Culture and Politicization of Rape, 1765–1815," *Journal of American History* 89, no. 3 (2002): 849–68; Sarah M. S. Pearsall, *Atlantic Families: Lives and Letters in the Later Eighteenth Century* (Oxford: Oxford University Press, 2010); and Pearsall, "Women in the American Revolutionary War," in Gray and Kamensky, *Oxford Handbook of the American Revolution*, 273–90.

51. Pearsall, "Women"; and Alfred F. Young, *Masquerade: The Life and Times of Deborah Sampson, Continental Soldier* (New York: Alfred A. Knopf, 2004). See also the chapter by Thomas Cardoza and Karen Hagemann on "History and Memory of Army Women and Female Soldiers, 1770s–1870s" in this handbook.

52. James Kirby Martin, ed., *Ordinary Courage: The Revolutionary War Adventures of Joseph Plumb Martin* (Chichester, UK: Wiley–Blackwell, 2013).

53. Cox, *per Sense*, 237.

54. Sarah J. Purcell, *Sealed with Blood: War, Sacrifice, and Memory in Revolutionary America* (Philadelphia: University of Pennsylvania Press, 2002).

55. Rosemarie Zagarri, *Revolutionary Backlash: Women and Politics in the Early American Republic* (Philadelphia: University of Pennsylvania Press, 2007).

56. Jan Ellen Lewis, "Rethinking Women's Suffrage in New Jersey, 1776–1807," *Rutgers Law Review* 63, no. 3 (2011): 1017–36.

57. Honor Sachs, *Home Rule: Households, Manhood, and National Expansion on the Eighteenth-Century Kentucky Frontier* (New Haven, CT: Yale University Press, 2015), 147.

58. Carol Berkin, *Revolutionary Mothers: Women in the Struggle for America's Independence* (New York: Alfred A. Knopf, 2005); Perdue, *Cherokee Women*; Purcell, *Sealed with Blood*; and Zagarri, *Revolutionary Backlash*.

59. Eliga H. Gould, *Among the Powers of the Earth: The American Revolution and the Making of a New World Empire* (Cambridge, MA: Harvard University Press, 2012), 178–79; and Claudio Saunt, *A New Order of Things: Property, Power, and the Transformation of the Creek Indians, 1733–1816* (Cambridge: Cambridge University Press, 1999).

60. Alan Taylor, *The Civil War of 1812: American Citizens, British Subjects, Irish Rebels, & Indian Allies* (New York: Alfred A. Knopf, 2010).

61. Nicole Eustace, *1812: War and the Passions of Patriotism* (Philadelphia: University of Pennsylvania Press, 2012).

62. Anne Farrar Hyde, *Empires, Nations, and Families: A History of the North American West, 1800–1860* (Lincoln: University of Nebraska Press, 2011); and Adam Jortner, *The Gods of Prophetstown: The Battle of Tippecanoe and the Holy War for the American Frontier* (Oxford: Oxford University Press, 2011).

63. Perdue, *Cherokee Women*.

SELECT BIBLIOGRAPHY

Anderson, Fred. *Crucible of War: The Seven Years' War and the Fate of Empire in British North America, 1754–1766*. New York: Alfred A. Knopf, 2000.

Barr, Juliana. *Peace Came in the Form of a Woman: Indians and Spaniards in the Texas Borderlands*. Chapel Hill: University of North Carolina Press, 2007.

Berkin, Carol. *Revolutionary Mothers: Women in the Struggle for America's Independence*. New York: Alfred A. Knopf, 2005.

Block, Sharon. "Rape without Women: Print Culture and Politicization of Rape, 1765–1815." *Journal of American History* 89, no. 3 (2002): 849–68.

Brooks, James. *Captives & Cousins: Slavery, Kinship, and Community in the Southwest Borderlands*. Chapel Hill: University of North Carolina Press, 2002.

Brumwell, Stephen. *Redcoats: The British Soldier and War in the Americas, 1755–1763*. Cambridge: Cambridge University Press, 2002.

Conway, Stephen. "The British Army, 'Military Europe,' and the American War of Independence." *William and Mary Quarterly* 67, no. 1 (2010): 69–100.

Crouch, Christian Ayne. *Nobility Lost: French and Canadian Martial Cultures, Indians, and the End of New France*. Ithaca, NY: Cornell University Press, 2014.

Eustace, Nicole. *1812: War and the Passions of Patriotism*. Philadelphia: University of Pennsylvania Press, 2012.

Foster, Thomas A., ed. *New Men: Manliness in Early America*. New York: New York University Press, 2011.

Fur, Gunlög Maria. *A Nation of Women: Gender and Colonial Encounters among the Delaware Indians*. Philadelphia: University of Pennsylvania Press, 2009.

Hagemann, Karen, Gisela Mettele, and Jane Rendall, eds. *Gender, War and Politics: Transatlantic Perspectives, 1775–1830*. Basingstoke: Palgrave Macmillan, 2010.

Lee, Wayne E. "Peace Chiefs and Blood Revenge: Patterns of Restraint in Native American Warfare, 1500–1800." *Journal of Military History* 71, no. 3 (2007): 701–41.

LeMaster, Michelle. *Brothers Born of One Mother: British–Native American Relations in the Colonial Southeast*. Charlottesville: University of Virginia Press, 2012.

Little, Ann M. *Abraham in Arms: War and Gender in Colonial New England*. Philadelphia: University of Pennsylvania Press, 2007.

MacLeitch, Gail D. *Imperial Entanglements: Iroquois Change and Persistence on the Frontiers of Empire*. Philadelphia: University of Pennsylvania Press, 2011.

Mayer, Holly A. *Belonging to the Army: Camp Followers and Community during the American Revolution*. Columbia: University of South Carolina Press, 1996.

Perdue, Theda. *Cherokee Women: Gender and Culture Change, 1700–1835*. Lincoln: University of Nebraska Press, 1998.

Resch, John Phillips, and Walter Sargent, eds. *War and Society in the American Revolution: Mobilization and Home Fronts*. DeKalb: Northern Illinois University Press, 2007.

Wilson, Kathleen. "Rethinking the Colonial State: Family, Gender, and Governmentality in Eighteenth-Century British Frontiers." *American Historical Review* 116, no. 5 (2011): 1294–322.

CHAPTER 4

WAR, GENDER, AND SOCIETY IN LATE COLONIAL AND REVOLUTIONARY SPANISH AMERICA

CATHERINE DAVIES

MILITARY conflicts and wars reconfigured Spanish South America in the transformative period from the 1780s to the 1830s, beginning with the Indigenous anticolonial uprisings and, later, the Spanish American Wars of Independence. Warfare and the militarization resulting from it had a massive impact on the social and gender order in the Spanish Atlantic Empire in this period. Two of the largest anticolonial Amerindian uprisings in the history of Latin America, the Tupac Amaru and Catarista Rebellions (1780–83) in the Peruvian Andes (today's Peru and Bolivia) and the Rebellion of the Comuneros (1781) in New Granada (today's Colombia), as well as the subsequent Spanish American Wars of Independence (1808–30), had a particularly far-reaching aftermath.[1] The chapter first discusses the historiography on gender and late colonial and revolutionary Spanish America, followed by an exploration of two central themes: the changing character of warfare in Spanish America in the period of the 1780s to the 1830s and the multiple gender dimensions of the anticolonial rebellions of the 1780s and the later wars of independence, including the different forms of participation of women.

Gender and the Historiography on Late Colonial and Revolutionary Spanish America

For a gendered analysis of the effects of the military conflicts and wars that shaped Spanish America during these fifty years, an understanding of *gender* as a set of historically specific ideas and practices that give meaning to and socially differentiate male and female is particularly pertinent. Gender works in interdependence and interrelatedness with the constructions of other differences, such as *class, race, ethnicity,* and *sexuality*.[2] Such an approach allows us to explore whether the military and war contributed to a virilization and militarization of the dominant ideas of masculinity in Spanish America during this period. It also enables us to examine specifically the role of women in the rebellions and wars of the time and to test the thesis of security scholar Carol Cohn, that every person who enters the world of warfare "must adopt the masculine position in order to be successful."[3]

Major themes studied in the huge and growing historiography on the Spanish American Wars of Independence in the early nineteenth century are military strategies and operations, the soldier heroes, the political institutions, and the political decisions of the governing classes.[4] Until the postmillennium period, however, mainstream historiography did not consider gender, unlike race and ethnicity, an important category of analysis.[5] In most scholarship on the wars of independence, considerations of gender are conspicuously absent. An example is the otherwise excellent overview by Jeremy Adelman published in *The Oxford Handbook of Latin American History* in 2010.[6] Most studies that focus on the military and war in Spanish America in this period refer almost exclusively to men, without gender considerations. This might be seen to confirm the contentious argument that masculinity is militarized in war and militarism masculinizes society, presented by sociologist Joshua Goldstein in his seminal 2001 study *War and Gender: How Gender Shapes the War System and Vice Versa*.[7] Juan Luis Ossa Santa Cruz, for example, in his 2014 monograph *Armies, Politics and Revolution: Chile, 1808–1826*, argued that during the wars of independence in Chile, the public and political sphere became increasingly militarized, with military officers making decisions that were both military and political; the military thus became the privileged "masters of their country and . . . more powerful than other elite members."[8] Yet, Ossa Santa Cruz's interesting study might have profited from further exploring the importance of gender relations. All the military officers were indeed men, but women were the glue that held the elite families of colonial society together, as Ossa Santa Cruz also pointed out: "Family connections were the most powerful weapon the revolutionaries had." Accordingly, several leading colonial judges put their political ideas on hold to protect their revolutionary in-laws.[9] The use of gender as a relational category would make these findings stronger and more plausible, as demonstrated by the 2009 study of Rodolfo Terragno, in which he examined the private life of military hero General José de San Martín to understand his relationships with women, his decision-making and emotions, and his personality.[10]

Research that used gender as an analytical category for the study of the history of colonial and revolutionary Spanish America started in the 1990s and tends to focus on topics such as war on the home front,[11] politics, the nation and citizenship,[12] marriage and the family, sexuality, and emotional regimes.[13] Earlier works centered on the history of women, an approach that continues to be strong in the field of Latin American history.[14] Since the 1980s, several publications have examined the role of women in the history of colonial Spanish America from the fifteenth to the early nineteenth centuries.[15]

This scholarship, which at times merely added women to common "master narratives" without questioning how they were constructed, was preceded by works published in the first decades of the twentieth century on women who were deemed "national heroines." Such studies emphasized the contributions patriotic women made to the independence cause. For obvious reasons, they focused on women who had actively supported independence and whose names were later recorded for posterity in nationalist historiography to commemorate the centenary, celebrated in 1910, or other related anniversaries.[16] One of the most important of these books, by José D. Monsalve, was republished by the Colombian Academy of History in 2010, the year of the bicentenary, in a beautifully illustrated edition with a new title, *Heroínas de la Independencia*.[17] Over time, however, some of the early accounts have been shown to have been inaccurate and exaggerated.

The bicentenary of 2010 prompted a resurgence of interest in women's history that has led to an unprecedented explosion of scholarship on women's involvement in the conflicts of late colonial and revolutionary Spanish America. This is evidence of a concerted effort across the Americas to recover the female subject in the anticolonial and independence process and to challenge the conventional historical representation of women. This new scholarship aims for a demystification of "patriotic heroines" and a deconstruction of the highly gendered accounts of the Spanish American Wars of Independence that were created for nationalist political purposes. In addition, the very concept of *heroine* (as exclusively White, Catholic, educated, and usually high status) has been challenged.[18] In these studies, usually by women and gender historians, everyday life, family relations, women's networks and sociability, and women's class and family interests in wartime stand at the center. The lens of gender is also employed to study familial and social relationships. The emphasis is on women's agency in the domestic and public spheres, especially women operating in influential families, which is where most of the documentation is to be found.[19] This focus on the history of women has resulted in a much fuller understanding of gender relations in Spanish America throughout this period.

One important area of current research is the biographies of important women such as Manuela Sáenz, the partner and companion of revolutionary hero Simón Bolívar, and María Antonia Bolívar, Bolívar's eldest sister, who staunchly opposed his campaign.[20] Many more women deserve to be the subjects of scholarly biographies. One example is Manuela Sanz de Santamaría de González Manrique.[21] She was born in 1740 in Bogotá, the daughter of Francisco Sanz de Santamaría and Petronila Prieto y Ricaurte, who had both participated in the Comunero Rebellion. Married to Francisco Tadeo González Manrique, son of the president of the High Court (*Audiencia*), she played an important role on behalf of the insurgents in the extensive networks of the most wealthy and powerful patrician families.[22] She was well educated; translated texts from Latin, French, and Italian; and assisted her husband in his profession, natural history. The couple was acquainted with the well-known Prussian geographer, naturalist, and explorer Alexander von Humboldt.

The increasing body of research on women and gender in colonial and revolutionary Spanish America points to a highly gendered political culture, with clearly defined "spheres," particularly for the middle- and upper-class men and women of the Creole elite. But it also demonstrates how in wartime discursively constructed gender lines were constantly challenged and women's space of action extended outside domestic life and the private sphere. To counter the perceived danger of "gender fluidity" for society and the state, the "feminine" was often associated with "weakness," an undermining threat to the authority of the *pater familias*.[23] Men who challenged the established gender order might be represented as "effeminate." Like women who were perceived as "masculine" or "virile," they could be ridiculed in public. However, as Lisa Vollendorf and Grady C. Wray emphasize, the significance of local context strongly cautions against any universally applied concept of femininity, patriarchy, or hegemonic masculinity in Spanish American colonial society.[24]

MILITARY AND WARFARE IN COLONIAL AND REVOLUTIONARY SPANISH AMERICA

The Spanish Atlantic Empire, which had reached the peak of its power in the sixteenth and seventeenth centuries, comprised dominions governed by the Spanish Crown in the Americas extending almost five million square miles. In the 1780s, the territories were divided administratively into the Viceroyalty of New Spain (most of today's United States through Mexico to Panama), the Viceroyalty of New Granada (including Caracas, Quito, Bogotá, and Guayaquil), the Viceroyalty of Peru (with Lima, the most important city in the Spanish Americas), the Viceroyalty of La Plata (including Buenos Aires), and the Kingdom of Chile. The Bourbon reforms during the eighteenth century, a set of economic, fiscal, and political legislation promulgated by the Spanish Crown under various kings of the House of Bourbon, led to a tightening of the monarch's control (including the expulsion of the Jesuits in 1767) and caused discontent among the Creole elites and Indigenous peoples, as evidenced in the rebellions of the 1780s.[25]

The Spanish dominions in the Americas were relatively stable and prosperous throughout the eighteenth century, with the major exceptions of the Indigenous uprisings in Peru, Upper Peru, and New Granada in the 1780s, as well as several British naval incursions on Spanish American ports, such as the invasions of the

River Plate in 1806 and 1807. The uprisings of broad swathes of Indigenous peoples, *mestizos*, and Creoles, largely against the Bourbon fiscal reforms, in Peru (the Great Rebellion of Tupac Amaru II in 1780–82) and in New Granada (the Rebellion of the Comuneros, 1781) were unprecedented, massive, and extremely violent.

In 1779, Spanish King Charles III, ruling from 1759 to 1788, raised sales taxes (known as the *alcabala*) on goods produced and sold in the colonies, partly to fund Spain's participation in the American Revolutionary War. José Gabriel Condorcanqui Noguera, with claims to the Inca lineage and known as Tupac Amaru II, and his wife, Micaela Bastidas Puyucahua, called for an uprising against the colonial tax collectors. They led an unsuccessful assault near Cuzco in southeastern Peru, assisted by their extended family networks. In this "Great Rebellion," between 6,000 and 20,000 armed men and women rose up against the colonial authorities in an attempt to revive an Incan state. Tupac Amaru II and his wife were captured and brutally executed along with their immediate family and other leaders, including several prominent women. Nevertheless, the rebellion extended south to the Lake Titicaca region with its urban center, La Paz. It was now led by a lowly Indian, Julian Apaza, called Tupac Katari; his wife Bartolina Sisa; and Tupac Amaru's cousin, Diego Cristobal. La Paz was besieged for six months, during which 10,000 people died. The rebel leaders, including several women, were captured, executed, or deported in 1782 and 1783. Overall, the estimated death toll (of all ethnicities, but mainly Indigenous) was 100,000.[26]

The 1781 Comunero Rebellion in the Viceroyalty of New Granada against the Spanish authorities also demanded an end to the fiscal measures introduced by Charles III and a return to administration that ensured the good of the "community." In this uprising, some 20,000 poorly armed men and women of diverse backgrounds and ethnicities were involved, led primarily by José Antonio Galán.[27] This initially successful revolt was in the end defeated by the Spanish authorities, but its influence led to similar uprisings with the same outcome as far north as Mérida and Timotes, now in Venezuela.[28]

These early uprisings against fiscal reforms and colonial rule did not produce a general anticolonial uprising in Spanish America. The British invasions of the River Plate in 1806 and 1807, an unsuccessful attempt to seize control of the Spanish territories located around the Platine Basin in South America (today part of Argentina and Uruguay), did not lead immediately to an uprising against Spain either, but they set an important precedent for the mass mobilization and militarization of local people independent of official governmental control.[29] The British aimed to preempt Napoleonic expansion into the Americas resulting from the Napoleonic Wars (1803–15) in Europe, at which time Spain was a reluctant ally of France.[30]

During the British invasion of Buenos Aires in 1806, the city council, established without viceregal authority, armed and recruited on a hitherto unprecedented scale some 8,200 men of all classes between the ages of fourteen and fifty (from a total population of about 41,000). In two months, seventeen volunteer military corps were formed, including one corps of slaves (some of whom were subsequently freed) and two of Native Americans (including those from the Pampas), in addition to the five corps of veterans. Urban militias had never before been raised in this way in the Spanish dominions. Class and race differences were broken down between men who were now armed, united in a common purpose, and grouped into military units according to race, caste, Spanish regional identity, or type of military force. Women were excluded from the mobilization. Nevertheless, they too played a major part in the popular resistance, including in armed combat. The impact on the colonial order, including race and gender hierarchies, was notable, with repercussions extending well into the independence period.[31] The ensuing Argentine War of Independence (initially fought against Napoleonic Spain) dated from 1810 to 1818.

Until Napoleon's invasion of the Spanish Peninsula in 1808, the usurpation of the Spanish throne by Bonaparte's brother Joseph, and the resulting power vacuum, revolution and independence from Spain were not seriously considered in Spanish America. At this time, the population of the Americas numbered around 13.5 million. Ethnically diverse and racially mixed, it was divided into hierarchies according to genealogy, wealth, and race, with particular terms to denote differences: the *castas* referred to all "mixed-race" peoples; *pardo* (mulatto, or dark skinned), *zambo* (of mixed African and Indigenous ancestry), and *mestizo* (Indigenous and White). Just under half of the population were Indigenous Native Americans, a third mestizo or mulatto Creoles, and a fifth White. The white (or passing as white) Creoles were the dominant elite, usually second- or third-generation Spanish (often Basque and Catalan) and other European settlers, and more recent incomers attached to Spanish colonial government, justice, and administration. The White elite was urban based. At the end of the eighteenth century, women were in the majority in almost all the cities. For example, 65 percent of the population in Quito in 1797, and 51 percent of the population in Colombia in 1825 were women. They dominated in all the non-White groups.[32]

The large-scale and local military conflicts of the Spanish American Wars of Independence began in 1810, after independence was declared from Napoleonic Spain in Buenos Aires and Chile. The fighting intensified after 1814, when Ferdinand VII of Spain, who was twice king of Spain (in 1808 and again from 1814 to his death in 1833), was restored to the throne and sent Spanish troops led by General Pablo Morillo, a veteran of the Peninsular War (1808–14) against the French occupation of the Iberian Peninsula, to "reconquer" the Americas. Despite a brief period of reconciliation in the early 1820s, when a liberal military coup in Spain reestablished the liberal Spanish Constitution of 1812 during the *Trienio Liberal* (1820–23), fighting began again in 1823. The last major battle was at Ayacucho in December 1824. Great Britain recognized the independence of Mexico, Argentina, and Gran Colombia in 1825. Ultimately, the conflict in Spanish America, as in Spain, was a hemispheric civil war within the Spanish monarchy between autocracy on the one hand and new forms of more representative government on the other.[33] As Anthony McFarlane concludes in his 2014 study *War and Independence in Spanish America*, these were "long and exhausting wars of attrition [that] gradually wore down Spain's political will and military resources," but once started, "Spanish America's wars took on a life of their own."[34]

The kinds of warfare experienced in Spanish America during the 1810s and 1820s fall into the broad categories outlined by Robert L. Scheina in the first volume of his 2003 *Latin America's Wars*: first, wars of independence against the monarchs of Europe and their colonial and imperial wars; followed by the age of the *caudillo*, mainly in the postindependence period; and finally wars of conquest against Native Americans.[35] The Spanish American Wars of Independence were fundamentally civil wars between royalist sympathizers (who preferred the authority of the Spanish Crown and colonial government to that of local republican elites) and patriots, revolutionaries, rebels, or insurgents (who fought for local, regional, or continental political control and reform). The royalists were aided by expeditionary forces sent from Spain after 1815, the largest consisting of 10,500 soldiers. The revolutionaries were assisted after 1815 by veterans of the Napoleonic army (mainly French), by British weapons,[36] and, after 1819, by the British Legions, which comprised British and Irish volunteers and mercenaries, numbering 7,000 men.[37]

The warfare and violence included all kinds of armed conflict: small skirmishes and large battles, sieges and blockades of cities and towns, naval warfare, and guerrilla warfare. The causes of war were similarly varied, ranging from the ideology of independence, reform, and revolution to race wars, boundary wars, *caudillo* wars (factional struggles between strongmen), and, after the defeat of the royalists, wars of centralism versus federalism, which continued throughout the century. Not all areas were affected in the same way or at the same time. The greatest destruction was in Venezuela and New Granada and Mexico. Armies traveled vast distances on foot, including crossing the Andes and the desert plains. Scheina describes this type of conflict as wars fought by "fleas" (very small armies) on the "back of an elephant" (a large land mass).[38] As for tactics, the weapons used most were lances, knives, and small firearms; on the plains the cavalry was dominant, because Native Americans were often skilled on horseback, and the Indigenous troops were hardy and resilient with the capability of walking long distances at high altitude.

The forces opposing independence were the relatively small regular troops of the Spanish imperial army stationed in the Americas, the larger local militia in the main centers of government and the ports, and the expeditionary armies brought over from Spain after the Peninsular War. Neither side possessed a large regular army. The imperial forces in Peru from 1787 consisted of 1,680 regular troops of veterans, with small detachments in Lima, Cuzco, and Tarma, supplemented by a militia, about a third of which were properly trained. The Creole officers were local landowners, miners, and merchants with part-time commissions whose officer status gave them social prestige and exemption from civil jurisdiction.[39] During the wars of independence, the Creole officers of the imperial army and the militia could fight on either side, and they sometimes switched allegiance mid-battle. The Numancia battalion of 650 men, the best of the royalist forces, changed sides in 1820 and joined San Martín's patriot army, persuaded, it is said, by women and priests. The vast majority of the fighting men on both sides were levees (including slaves, free Blacks, and Indigenous) recruited forcefully from local populations, often under penalty of death. The Indigenous peoples tended to support the king, and the freed slaves and slaves supported whichever side gave them their freedom first or offered more opportunities. The *mulattos*, or *pardos*; *mestizos*; and the plainsmen, or *llaneros*, could similarly take either side. These wars were often "feudal" wars, with a *caudillo*, or "toughest of the tough," leading his peasants and commanding their loyalty on the basis of his personal bravery and martial skills.[40] Unlike the Napoleonic Wars in Europe, there were few major battles, the largest being the Battle of Boyacá (August 1819), in today's Bolivia, where 3,200 revolutionaries, including 1,200 raw recruits, fought against 3,000 royalists led by General José María Barreiro, and the Battle of Carabobo (June 1821), at which 5,000 royalists commanded by General Miguel La Torre fought 6,300 revolutionaries led by Bolívar.[41]

The widespread warfare in Spanish America in the first decades of the nineteenth century was disastrous for society and the economy. According to Michael Clodfelter, the population of Venezuela dropped by 100,000 in the fifteen-year period between 1810 and 1825. Scheina estimates that about a quarter of Venezuela's one million inhabitants were killed; and Robert Harvey believes that more than a quarter of a million were killed in the struggle for Gran Colombia's independence.[42] These figures may be compared to the estimated 300,000 Spanish who died in the Peninsular War.[43] The majority of those killed were men. The 1824 census in La Paz reported "excessively low" numbers of men between the ages of fifteen and twenty-five and uncommonly high numbers of single women of marriageable age. The vast majority of Spanish America's 13 to 14 million people, at least 50 percent of whom were women, suffered violence at some time in the first three decades of the nineteenth century.[44] The ongoing social disruption, violence, and warfare in Spanish South America in the early 1780s and between the 1810s and 1830s had a far-reaching impact on the colonial social and gender order.

GENDERING THE FIRST ANTICOLONIAL REBELLIONS OF THE 1780S

The large anticolonial rebellions against Spanish rule in the 1780s were shaped by a very different military culture from that of the wars of independence only thirty years later. In the Great Rebellion of 1780–81 in the Cuzco region of Peru, women played a much more prominent role as leaders and combatants than in later wars. Five years in the planning, this partially messianic movement was the largest rebellion in Spanish colonial history and Spain's greatest military challenge in the Americas since the sixteenth century. As stated, the death toll was around 100,000.[45] The rebellion, initially against the colonial tax collectors, not the Crown, was led by Quechua-speaking Micaela Bastidas and her husband, José Gabriel Condorcanqui Noguera, called Tupac Amaru II, whose ten-year legal claim as rightful heir to the Inca throne was in process. The rebellion also involved the couple's three sons, aged nineteen, eighteen, and ten. After a six-month rampage through the highlands, during which the leaders lost control of their thousands of followers, Bastidas and Tupac Amaru were captured, adjudicated, and brutally executed. In total, forty leaders were tried, including four women, and nine were executed, including two of Bastidas and Tupac Amaru's sons. The appalling manner of the men's and women's executions was intended to set an example and to divest the victims of any recognition of status or respect. The rebellion extended to La Paz, besieged in

1781, and continued in the south under the leadership of the Aymara-speaking Kataristas and Tupac Amaru's relatives until 1783.[46]

The Great Rebellion fully involved both sexes. Based on traditional Andean dualism and gender parallelism (a world divided into two interdependent gender spheres) and strong Inca kinship ties, women's and men's roles were complementary. In Inca society, women were important in everyday life. Marriage was a unity of two equals so that both sexes contributed in "complementary but commensurate" ways to the household.[47] Particularly powerful were the female heads of family, *caciques* (chiefs) or *curacas* (intermediaries between the commoners and the colonial authorities), who acquired high status through marriage or birth. Spanish law gave the Inca elite (men and women) the status of European nobility, exemption from head-tax demands, the authority to raise forced-labor drafts (for example, for the Potosí mines), and landownership. The female *curacas* could enter into business transactions and sign contracts, and many claimed private ownership, because of their descent, of communal lands.[48] Kinship ties, reciprocal obligations, and common lands ensured lifelong loyalty from extended family networks (cousins, aunts, nieces, in-laws) belonging to the territorially based community, or *ayllu*. Men and women could raise mass support and take major strategic and tactical decisions. Two women were particularly powerful in the Great Rebellion: the *curaca* Tomasa Tito Condemayta, provincial chief of Acomayo and Cuzco and head of a brigade of women soldiers, and Micaela Bastidas, who proved to be a talented military commander. Bastidas was not Indigenous, but an illegitimate *mestiza* of mixed Spanish and possibly *pardo* (Black) descent and, like all her kin, a devout Catholic. Tupac Amaru, a *curaca*, was respected and considered both a mestizo and an Indian; after the uprising, he was referred to by the colonial authorities as "the Indian, José."[49] Ethnic identities in the region at the time were porous. Indigenous peoples (Quechua and later Aymara), *mulattos*, *mestizos*, white Creoles, and Spanish, including the clergy, were involved on both sides.[50]

The partnership of Micaela Bastidas and Tupac Amaru II worked well, as indicated by their extensive correspondence and the trial proceedings; she dealt with the logistics at base camp at Tungasuca, and he fought on the front line.[51] Together, they devised a strategy: she advised her husband continually, feeding him information on the enemy's movements and berating his delays and vacillations. Witnesses testified that she was to be feared more than her husband. In his 2014 study of the rebellion, Charles Walker refers throughout to "the couple," and one of his objectives is to place Bastidas "in the limelight . . . More than accompanying or backing her husband she led the rebellion alongside him."[52] She was an active partner in the marriage as a merchant muleteer and she collected debts, hired field hands, and oversaw the finances. In warfare, she was an exceptionally able leader: she "excelled at paying the troops, managing supplies, keeping discipline, posting sentinels, watching for spies."[53] Her correspondence shows she was liaising daily with women of the colonial elite. In her trial, several nuns were interviewed and attested to coercion by Bastidas and the *cacica* Tomasa.[54]

Both Micaela Bastidas and Tupac Amaru II claimed status, privilege, and authority on the basis of royal birth and, for Bastidas, legitimate Catholic marriage into the Inca nobility. Tupac Amaru demonstrated his high status by his bearing, manners, and appearance. Contemporaries described him as cultured, haughty, and brave in battle; he wore expensive clothes and gold, and his hair was long. A trial witness characterized him as "elegantly dressed: black velvet coat and knee breeches, a ruffled shirt, a vest, linen, silk stockings, gold buckles, shoes, a Spanish beaver hat."[55] Tall, strong, handsome, intelligent, courteous, and almost White, he exemplified Inca regal masculinity.[56] Bastidas represented the complementary strong femininity to Tupac Amaru's Inca virile masculinity. Most of the time she remained at base camp during the fighting, but she took part when necessary and was reputedly more violent, cruel, and unforgiving than the menfolk. The participation of women in this "vicious bloodbath" in which no prisoners were taken was perceived by the Spanish colonial troops with disgust.[57] After the killing of 576 Creoles in the Church of Sangarará, Bastidas and Tupac Amaru were excommunicated by the Catholic bishop of Cuzco, which for Walker was the greatest blow to the legitimacy of their campaign.[58] To fight this enemy, civilian men of the colonial elite joined military ranks; the priests and even the bishop of Cuzco abandoned their robes and mounted horses to fight the rebels. The deacon dressed in military uniform to lead his army of priests.[59]

The Katarista rebellion in 1782–83 was even more violent, targeting mainly white and *mestizo* Creoles. Again, many Indigenous women were involved. The most prominent was Tupac Katari's wife, Bartolina Sisa, and his sister, Gregoria Apaza. Following defeat, in October 1783, 78 prisoners, including 35 women and 17 children, were forcibly marched in chains across the high mountains from La Paz to Lima to be transported in what has become known as the infamous Caravan of Death. On the outside wall of the Pantheon of Illustrious Heroes in Lima there is a statue of Micaela Bastidas, and inside the Pantheon is a plaque on which is listed the names of the numerous women and children who died of thirst, starvation, hypothermia, and brutality on the forty-day march to Lima. In sum, high-status Indigenous and mestizo women played a full part in the mass rebellions of the 1780s as strategists, tacticians, and combatants, and all women were fully involved in the fighting. Alongside the men, they paid the price of defeat. These were largely race wars targeting white Creoles in Peru, the seat of colonial power. In the wars of independence, which extended across the whole of Spanish America, the Creole elites fought among themselves so that men and women of all classes and ethnicities experienced warfare and were involved on both sides.

WOMEN AND MEN IN THE
WARS OF INDEPENDENCE

Just thirty years after the defeat of the Indigenous rebellions in the Andes, the colonial authorities once more faced a political crisis, this time originating in Europe. Military insurgency and civil disobedience escalated across the region, resulting in the Spanish American Wars of Independence. Again, women of all *castas* and classes were fully involved on both sides. Research by women's historians has revealed the full extent to which plebeian women, known by different names across the subcontinent (*rabonas, juanas, cholas, soldaderas, guarichas*), were active on a massive scale in front-line fighting, accompanying the troops and ministering to their needs. These women, predominantly belonging to the *castas*, were the family members or loved ones of the farmers, herders, and ordinary men who constituted the rank and file of the troops.[60]

Women were not only present as camp followers, but also participated in battles and skirmishes and even became military officers on the patriots' side. Especially in guerrilla or irregular warfare, women formed and led women's battalions. One of the two most prominent women military leaders was the mestiza Lieutenant Colonel Juana de Azurduy, wife of Manuel Ascensio Padilla, who with her husband led an army of some 6,000 in Upper Peru, today's Bolivia. The airport in Sucre, Bolivia, is named after her, and she was posthumously elevated to the rank of general in the Argentine army in 2009.[61] She led her own battalion of women named *Los Leales*, the Loyals, who fought in sixteen conflicts. The other was Francisca de Zubiaga y Bernales, known as "La Mariscala," who was the wife of Marshal Agustín Gamarra, twice president of Peru. Zubiaga was a formidable woman, a skilled swordswoman and shot, bore three children, and died at the age of thirty-one. There are engravings and paintings of these national heroines, and their feats and salons were described in the chronicles of the time. Attempts to prove the veracity of these accounts and to find accurate biographical details in the archives have been arduous, in the case of Azurduy, and largely unsuccessful for Zubiaga.[62]

More commonly, however, women (elite and nonelite) fought together as groups in defensive or offensive operations to protect or recover their estates, property, towns, or communities. In the context of war and patriotic mobilization, dressing up in military uniform became fashionable for both men and women. Manuela Sáenz, Bolívar's lover and companion, who was married to the English doctor James Thorne, served as Bolívar's secretary and was later promoted to colonel in the Hussars. She liked to parade before the soldiers in her bright-red jacket. Sáenz was an accomplished horsewoman and saved Bolívar from attempts on his life on at least two occasions. After Bolívar's death in 1830, she was forced into exile and moved to Paita in Northern Peru. Her service was forgotten and she died in poverty during a diphtheria epidemic in 1856. A statue is dedicated to her in Quito, and in 2010 she was given a full state burial in Venezuela.[63]

In the rearguard or on the home front, women who supported the patriot campaign played a crucial role, too. They bankrolled the insurgent military campaigns by donating jewels and precious metals and by fundraising. They prepared food, equipment, uniforms, and munitions, thus functioning as army ordinance and logistics corps. They cared for wounded soldiers and converted their homes into hospitals, thus serving as medical corps. They printed and distributed revolutionary pamphlets on a continent with few printing presses and little paper, and they delivered public speeches against the royalist military authorities, as if employed by a ministry of propaganda. Like resistance guerrillas, they hid refugees and disrupted the enemy's plans. Like military intelligence, they worked as spies passing information on the movement of royalist troops to insurgents.

These arrangements were informal but no less vital to the patriots' success and no less worthy of serious consideration.[64]

Patriot women's contributions to the struggle for liberation were presented to the public as an indicator of broad support for the cause. In patriotic propaganda and later in the collective memories of the wars, these women were stylized as martyrs and heroines, thus contributing to the commemoration of independence. During the wars, it was vital to mobilize not only men for the military but also all society for war support. Patriot women's contributions, in particular the sacrifice of mothers who helped raise troops by sending their sons to war, reinforced the idea that the whole nation supported the struggle for liberation. General José de San Martín, who liberated the south of the continent (Argentina, Chile, and Peru), was one of the keenest to recognize women's contributions. In 1822, he created the Order of the Sun, a medal of freemasonry inspiration, which was awarded to 145 women (Dames of the Order of the Sun) of suitable credentials.[65] Although this fact is discussed in mainstream historiography, the extent of the gender implications has not been fully appreciated. San Martín was sufficiently astute to realize the power of women in the family and the home. He knew that if he could persuade the governing elites (half of whom were women) to join him, he need not engage in fighting other than with the garrisons held by the royalist soldiers. In this he was largely successful, especially in Peru.

Because of the length of the conflicts, the escalating violence, and the often-changing front lines, support for either side was not without risk for civilians, both women and men. Women who supported the rebels were often punished with financial penalties, exile, reclusion in convents, house arrest, imprisonment, physical abuse, public exhibition, rape, and execution. Women who seduced soldiers and persuaded them to desert or change sides and women who cross-dressed faced the death penalty, though women of the elite were treated more leniently by the authorities than women from the popular sectors.[66] Historian Evelyn Cherpak reports that 48 female patriots were executed and 119 were arrested or exiled in the wars in Colombia alone. Spanish General Pablo Morillo exiled over 140 women from Bogotá, and the colonial authorities in New Granada executed more than 50 women.[67] Victims of this persecution included the seamstress Policarpa Salavarrieta, who was found guilty of spying and executed in Bogotá in front of 3,000 soldiers in 1817, and the Neogranadine María Antonia Santos Plata, who had organized and led the rebel guerrillas in the province of El Socorro against the Spanish expeditionary forces during the Reconquest of New Granada. She was found guilty of high treason and executed in 1819. Ten days after Santos's execution, independence was proclaimed in Boyacá (Colombia), and she was officially proclaimed a martyr to the cause. Today, a small statue of Policarpa Salavarrieta stands in the Plaza de los Andes, Bogotá.[68]

In short, women operating in a militarized world had to assume characteristics attributed to men (leadership, courage, audacity) to survive and to be valued. They could be punished as men, and they could be praised (by friend) or ridiculed (by foe) for their virility. In the absence of men, women also had to assume administrative and financial roles and represent themselves when drawing up contracts. This was not new; widows and unmarried women had done this previously, but it was now more widespread, acceptable, and necessary. Women used their husband's loyalty to one side or another to successfully sue for divorce, separation, or property ownership. Thus, women (commoners and elite) were showcased in the public arena, for good or for bad, and hailed alongside men as respected martyrs and heroes or denigrated as rabble or treacherous enemies. They assumed a public, political, and military profile, thus challenging the traditional gender order.

In general, the Spanish American Wars of Independence contributed to a militarization not only of masculinity but also of political culture in general. This directly affected women's claims for political rights during postconflict recovery. Arguably, only in politically stable democracies in which individual rights are acknowledged and in which compromise leads to consensus can women gain recognition as political subjects.[69] In unstable societies, order is necessarily imposed by force, usually by the military, and therefore usually by armed men. In new state formations, the power of "strong" men may be institutionalized and will subject all nonmen (women and children) and all noncompliant, unarmed men who are in weaker positions (because of health, physique, sexuality, age, class, race, or religion). In other words, chaos leads to the imposition of order on society, which often results in the abuse of male authority and domination; hegemonic masculinity becomes synonymous with strength, violence, and control. Strong men subject the populace (including all women) in the name of order to allegedly protect that same populace.

CONCLUSION

Since 2010, revisionist historians have questioned previous assumptions about the independence and preindependence conflicts in Spanish America and have reassessed the significance of everyday life, civil society, social class, race, ethnicity, and gender. During the decades of revolution and constitutional transformation, all issues pertaining to government (political rights, nationality, and citizenship) were opened to debate. Women, as a social group, contributed to the patriot cause and to the making of civil society, yet they were largely excluded from the public sphere thereafter on grounds of gender.[70]

In postindependence Spanish America, republicanism replaced absolutism. Absolutism had denied political rights to almost all individual men and women, but the new republican constitutions, which abolished slavery and ended legal discrimination against Indigenous and mixed-race men, denied political rights to women only, elite and commoners alike. Discourses of individual rights equated individuality with masculinity: "Women were excluded as a social sector because ultimately gender (rather than class or caste) was the criterion for political exclusion. Indeed, it was on this basis that the *res publica* was made possible, in that its functioning was made possible by the separation of the public world and private life; only the public was political and it was the business of men."[71] If the wars of independence were revolutionary for men irrespective of class and race (a topic still hotly debated in the scholarship), they were not so for women, even though women were as much affected by the wars as men and were crucial to the success of the independence struggle.

But some change did come about during and after the wars; hierarchies were challenged and social interrelations reconfigured to an extent, particularly in the cities. The political crisis and social fragmentation created a chink in the armor of the patriarchal *pater familias*. Secularization and the state's assumption of the welfare and educational responsibilities of the Catholic Church provided a route for women to enter state machinery as caregivers and educators. What was needed, above all, was a public discourse that challenged dominant gender categories, gave new meanings to conceptions of the feminine and masculine, and recognized women as historical and political subjects in their own right. This would take time, but the second generation of women, the daughters of the heroes of independence, took up the challenge in the 1840s and, with a liberated press, began to write and publish as never before. Women writers thus contributed to public culture by representing women as rational individuals, patriots, and citizens of the state. Primary textual sources, written by men and women, such as memoirs, firsthand accounts, published official reports, the periodical press, educational treatises, opinion pieces, narrative fiction, and poetry, are important for tracing these conceptual shifts in the gender order.[72] They provide rich resources for detecting the often-subtle indications of changing gender relations in societies affected by warfare and its aftermath.

Investigation into women's experiences in the wars is currently popular not only in Spanish American academic circles, but also more generally, as evidenced in the many bestselling historical novels and films featuring women protagonists set in the Spanish American Wars of Independence.[73] More research, however, is needed on the experiences of ordinary people, both men and women, and how their lives were affected by warfare, disease, displacement, famine, natural disasters, conscription, loss of life and property, family breakdown, criminality, physical abuse, and so on. Gender considerations are still lacking in mainstream historiography, especially work on the diverse array of masculinities in operation in this period of conflict. More than anything else, there must be archival research to distinguish, where possible, fact from fiction and to understand not only the elites but also the vast majority of the gendered population.

NOTES

1. See Robert L. Scheina, *Latin America's Wars*, vol. 1, *The Age of the Caudillo, 1791–1899*, and vol. 2, *The Age of the Professional Soldier* (Washington, DC: Potomac Books, 2003). This chapter does not cover Spanish North America or New Spain (part of today's United States, Mexico, and Central America).

2. See Stefan Dudink et al., eds., *Masculinities in Politics and War: Gendering Modern History* (Manchester: Manchester University Press, 2004); and Dudink et al., eds., *Representing Masculinity: Citizenship in Modern Western Culture* (Basingstoke: Palgrave Macmillan, 2008). For intersecting social identities, see Leslie McCall, "The Complexity of Intersectionality," *Signs* 30, no. 3 (2005): 1771–800.

3. Carol Cohn, "Wars, Wimps, and Women: Talking Gender and Thinking War," in *Gendering War Talk*, ed. Miriam Cooke and Angela Woollacott (Princeton, NJ: Princeton University Press, 1993), 227–46, 238.

4. Timothy E. Anna, *Spain and the Loss of America* (Lincoln: University of Nebraska Press, 1983); Christon I. Archer, ed., *The Wars of Independence in Spanish America* (Wilmington, DE: Scholarly Resources, 2000); Matthew Brown, *Adventuring through Spanish Colonies: Simón Bolívar, Foreign Mercenaries and the Birth of New Nations* (Liverpool: Liverpool University Press, 2006); John C. Chasteen, *Americanos: Latin America's Struggle for Independence* (Oxford: Oxford University Press, 2008); Jaime E. Rodriguez Ordóñez, *The Independence of Spanish America* (Cambridge: Cambridge University Press, 2008); and Anthony McFarlane, *War and Independence in Spanish America* (New York: Routledge, 2014).

5. Nancy Priscilla Naro, ed., *Blacks, Coloureds and National Identity in Nineteenth-Century Latin America* (London: Institute of Latin American Studies, 2003); Rebecca Earle, *The Return of the Native: Indians and Myth-Making in Spanish America, 1810–1930* (Durham, NC: Duke University Press, 2007); and Peter Blanchard, *Under the Flags of Freedom: Slave Soldiers and the Wars of Independence in South America* (Pittsburgh, PA: University of Pittsburgh Press, 2008).

6. Jeremy Adelman, "Independence in Latin America," in *The Oxford Handbook of Latin America History*, ed. José M. Moya (Oxford: Oxford University Press, 2010), 153–80. Two separate essays in *The Oxford Handbook of Latin America History* refer to gender and sexuality, Asunción Lavrin, "Sexuality in Colonial Spanish America," 132–52; and Donna J. Guy, "Gender and Sexuality in Latin America," 375–81, but neither refers to the wars of independence at any length.

7. Joshua S. Goldstein, *War and Gender: How Gender Shapes the War System and Vice Versa* (Cambridge: Cambridge University Press, 2001), 251–331.

8. Juan Luis Ossa Santa Cruz, *Armies, Politics and Revolution: Chile, 1808–1826* (Liverpool: Liverpool University Press, 2014), 14.

9. Ibid., 67.

10. Rodolfo Terragno, *Diario íntimo de San Martín* (Buenos Aires: Sudamericana, 2009); and Terragno, *Josefa: Biografía de María Josefa Morales de los Ríos, la amiga secreta de San Martín* (Buenos Aires: Sudamericana, 2015).

11. Sherry Johnson, "Maintaining the Home Front: Widows, Wives and War in Late Eighteenth-Century Cuba," in *Gender, War and Politics: Transatlantic Perspectives, 1775–1830*, ed. Karen Hagemann et al. (Basingstoke: Palgrave Macmillan, 2010), 206–24.

12. Sarah Chambers, *From Subjects to Citizens: Honor, Gender and Politics in Arequipa, Peru, 1780–1854* (University Park: Pennsylvania State University Press, 1999); and Catherine Davies et al., *South American Independence: Gender, Politics, Text* (Liverpool: Liverpool University Press, 2006).

13. Guiomar Dueñas Vargas, *Del amor y otras pasiones: Elites, política y familia en Bogotá 1778–1870* (Bogota: Universidad Nacional de Colombia, 2014); Ann Twinam, *Public Lives, Private Secrets: Gender, Honor, Sexuality and Illegitimacy in Colonial Hispanic America* (Stanford, CA: Stanford University Press, 1999); and Jeffrey M. Shumway, *The Case of the Ugly Suitor and Other Histories of Love, Gender and Nation in Buenos Aires, 1776–1870* (Lincoln: University of Nebraska Press, 2005). On the history of sexuality, see also Lavrin, "Sexuality."

14. See Evelyn Cherpak, "The Participation of Women in the Independence of Gran Colombia, 1780–1830," in *Latin American Women: Historical Perspectives*, ed. Asunción Lavrin (Westport, CT: Greenwood Press, 1978), 219–34; and Guy, "Gender and Sexuality."

15. See, for more literature, Susan Migden Socolow, *The Women of Colonial Latin America* (Cambridge: Cambridge University Press, 2000); and Lisa Vollendorf and Grady C. Wray, "Gender in the Atlantic World: Women's Writing in Iberia and Latin America," in *Theorising the Ibero-Atlantic*, ed. Harald E. Braun and Lisa Vollendorf (Leiden: Brill, 2013), 99–116.

16. Valuable early studies include Adolfo Carranza, *Patricias Argentinas* (Buenos Aires: Sociedad Patricias Argentinas, 1910); José Macedonio Urquidi, *Bolivianas ilustres* (La Paz: Escuela Tipográfica, 1918); Elvira García y García, *La mujer peruana a través de los siglos* (Lima: Imprenta Americana, 1924); and, above all, José Dolores Monsalve, *Mujeres de la independencia* (Bogota: Imprenta Nacional, 1926).

17. José Dolores Monsalve, *Heroínas de la independencia*, 2nd ed. (Bogota: Academia Colombiana de Historia, 2010).

18. Mirla Alcibíades, *Mujeres e independencia: Venezuela 1810–1821* (Caracas: Casa Nacional de las Letras Andrés Bello, 2013), 270–72.

19. One of the most significant publications is Sara Beatriz Guardia, ed., *Las mujeres en la independencia de América Latina* (Lima: Centro de Estudios la Mujer en la Historia de América Latina, 2010), which was sponsored by UNESCO.

20. See Pamela S. Murray, *For Glory and Bolivar: The Remarkable Life of Manuela Sáenz, 1797–1856* (Austin: University of Texas Press, 2008); and Inés Quintero, *La criolla principal: María Antonia Bolívar, la hermana del Libertador* (Bogota: Editorial Aguilar, 2008).

21. See Monsalve, *Heroínas*, 21–24; Cherpak, "Participation of Women," 220; and Socolow, *Women*, 170–71. The date of death of Manuela Sanz de Santamaría de González Manrique is unknown.

22. For a study of the governing elites and their marriage alliances, including the Sanz de Santamaría clan, see Victor M. Uribe-Uran, *Honorable Lives: Lawyers, Family, and Politics in Colombia, 1780–1850* (Pittsburgh, PA: University of Pittsburgh Press, 2000). Even family histories often do not include birth and death dates for women. See José María Restrepo Sáez and Raimundo Rivas, *Genealogías de Santa Fe* (Bogota: Librería Colombiana, 1928); and José Joaquín París de la Roche, *Los Parises: Una familia de próceres* (Bogota: Imprenta de Juan Casis, 1919).

23. Davies, *South American Independence*, 33–55.

24. Vollendorf and Wray, "Gender," 115–16.

25. See Charles F. Walker, *The Tupac Amaru Rebellion* (Cambridge, MA: Harvard University Press, 2014); and John Leddy Phelan, *The People and the King: The Comunero Revolution in Colombia, 1781* (Madison: University of Wisconsin Press, 1978).

26. Walker, *Tupac Amaru Rebellion*, 277.

27. Phelan, *The People*.

28. Carlos E. Muñoz Oraá, *Los comuneros de Venezuela: una rebelión popular de pre-independencia* (Merida: Universidad de los Andes, 1971).

29. Malyn Newitt, ed. *War, Revolution and Society in the Rio de la Plata, 1808–1810: Thomas Kinder's Narrative of a Journey to Madeira, Montevideo and Buenos Aires* (Oxford: Signal Books, 2010), 10–13.

30. See William Burke, *Additional Reasons for our Immediately Emancipating Spanish America Deduced from the New and Extraordinary Circumstances of the Present Crisis* (London: J. Ridgway, 1808).

31. Ben Hughes, *The British Invasion of the River Plate, 1806–1807: How the Redcoats Were Humbled and a Nation Was Born* (Barnsley: Pen & Sword, 2013), 34, 73, 88, 211.

32. Socolow, *Women*, 112–13. Aida Martínez Carreño, "Mujeres y familia en el siglo XIX 1819–1899," in *Las mujeres en la historia de Colombia*, vol. 2, *Mujeres y sociedad*, ed. Magdala

Velásquez Toro (Barcelona: Norma/Presidencia de la República de Colombia, 1995), 292–321.

33. Rodriguez, *Independence*.

34. McFarlane, *War and Independence*, 409–10.

35. See Scheina, *Latin America's Wars*, 1:1–84, 235–70, 365–74.

36. Rafe Blaufarb, "Arms for Revolutions: Military Demobilization after the Napoleonic Wars and Latin American Independence," in *War, Demobilization and Memory: The Legacy of War in the Era of Atlantic Revolutions*, ed. Alan Forrest et al. (Basingstoke: Palgrave Macmillan, 2016), 100–18.

37. Brown, *Adventuring*, 40–41.

38. Scheina, *Latin America's Wars*, 1:427.

39. John Fisher, *Bourbon Peru, 1750–1824* (Liverpool: Liverpool University Press, 2003), 36.

40. Scheina, *Latin America's Wars*, 1:426.

41. Ibid., 35, 36.

42. Michael Clodfelter, *Warfare and Armed Conflicts: A Statistical Reference to Casualty and Other Figures, 1618–1991* (Jefferson, NC: McFarland, 1991), 348–49; Robert Harvey, *Liberators: Latin America's Struggle for Independence, 1810–1830* (Woodstock, NY: Overlook Books, 2000), 192; and Scheina, *Latin America's Wars*, 1:40. See also Matthew White, "Statistics of Wars, Oppressions and Atrocities of the Nineteenth Century (the 1800s)," 2011, accessed August 1, 2015, http://www.necrometrics.com.

43. Boris Urlanis, *Wars and Population* (Moscow: Progress Publishers, 1971), 182; Josep Fontana, *Historia de España*, vol. 6, *La época del liberalismo* (Barcelona: Marcial Pons, 2007) quotes Ronald Fraser's estimates of 215,000 to 375,000 casualties resulting from combat, violence, hunger, and disruption, 79.

44. Alberto Crespo, *La vida cotidiana en La Paz durante la Guerra de la independencia 1800–1825* (La Paz: Editorial de la Universidad de San Andrés, 1975), 51–52.

45. Walker, *Tupac Amaru Rebellion*, 6. For sources, see Ward Stavig and Ella Schmidt, eds. and trans., *The Tupac Amaru and Catarista Rebellions: An Anthology of Sources* (Indianapolis: Hackett, 2008). There are numerous studies of the Great Rebellion, but few in English.

46. Fisher, *Bourbon Peru*, 45. Stavig and Schmidt, *Tupac Amaru and Catarista Rebellions*, 215–43.

47. Irene Silverblatt, *Moon, Sun and Witches: Gender Ideologies and Class in Inca and Colonial Peru* (Princeton, NJ: Princeton University Press, 1987), 8.

48. Ibid., 113, 115, 124.

49. Pedro de Angelis, ed., *Documentos relativos a la historia antigua y moderna de las provincias del Rio de la Plata*, vol. 5, *Documentos para la historia de la sublevación de José Gabriel de Tupac Amaru, Cacique de la Provincia de Tinta en el Perú* (Buenos Aires: Imprenta del estado, 1836), 30.

50. Walker, *Tupac Amaru Rebellion*, 61–64. See also Leon G. Campbell, "Ideology and Factionalism during the Great Rebellion, 1780–1782," in *Resistance, Rebellion and Consciousness in the Andean Peasant World, 18th to 20th Centuries*, ed. Steve J. Stern (Madison: University of Wisconsin Press, 1987), 110–39.

51. Luis Durand Flórez, ed., *Colección documental del Bicentenario de la Revolución Emancipadora de Tupac Amaru*, vol. 4, *Los procesos a Tupac Amaru y sus compañeros, II* (Lima: Comisión Nacional del Bicentenario de la Rebelión Emancipadora de Túpac Amaru, 1980–82), 8–90.

52. Walker, *Tupac Amaru Rebellion*, 8, 9.

53. Ibid., 21.

54. Durand Flórez, *Los procesos*, 4:8–90. For Bastidas's letters to the nuns, see Durand Flórez, *Colección*, vol. 1, *Documentos varios del Archivo de Indias*, 323–24, 369, 523.
55. Durand Flórez, *Colección*, vol. 5, *Los procesos a Tupac Amaru y sus compañeros, III*, 11.
56. Walker, *Tupac Amaru Rebellion*, 20, 64.
57. Ibid., 12.
58. Ibid., 9.
59. Flórez, *Los procesos*, 5:24.
60. See Guardia, *Las mujeres*. Biographical details and references to archival and bibliographical sources may be accessed on a dedicated map-based digital resource, "Gendering Latin American Independence," accessed March 23, 2020, https://www.nottingham.ac.uk/genderlatam.
61. The airport is named after Azurduy, but the city is named after the independence hero Antonio José de Sucre.
62. Berta Wexler, *Las heroínas altoperuanas como expresión de un colectivo 1809–1825: Juana de Azurduy y las mujeres en la revolución altoperuana* (Villa Constitución: Universidad Nacional de Rosario, 2013); and Mary G. Berg, "Ficciones de la historia: Zubiaga de Gamarra," in Guardia, *Las mujeres*, 413–20.
63. Will Grant, "Venezuela Honours Simon Bolivar's Lover Manuela Saenz," *BBC News*, July 5, 2010, http://www.bbc.co.uk/news/10504821.
64. See Guardia, *Las mujeres*.
65. John Lynch, *San Martín: Argentine Soldier, American Hero* (New Haven, CT: Yale University Press 2009), 148; and Davies et al., *South American Independence*, 147–48.
66. Lucía Provencio Garrigós, "Perspectivas analíticas y temáticas de los estudios sobre las mujeres en las independencias latinoamericanas," *Tiempos de América* 17 (2010): 59–84.
67. Cherpak, "Participation of Women," 224.
68. See "Estatua de policarpa salavarrieta," accessed September 9, 2017, http://www.historvius.com/estatua-de-policarpa-salavarrieta-1708/.
69. Davies et al., *South American Independence*, 14–23, 268–70.
70. Sara Beatriz Guardia, "Presentación," in Guardia, *Las mujeres*, 11–14.
71. Davies et al., *South American Independence*, 4.
72. Joyce Contreras Villalobos, *Mercedes Marín del Solar (1804–1866): Obras reunida* (Santiago: Dirección de Bibliotecas, Archivos y Museos, 2015); Josefa Acevedo de Gómez, *A Treatise on Domestic Economy, for the Use of Mothers and Housewives*, introduction Catherine Davies (Nottingham: Critical, Cultural and Communications Press, 2007); and Ana María Agudelo Ochoa, *Devenir escritora: Nacimiento y formación de las narradoras colombianas en el siglo XIX (1840–1870)* (Lima: Centro de Estudios Literarios Antonio Cornejo Polar, 2015).
73. Examples include Ana María Cabrera, *Macacha Güemes* (Buenos Aires: Emecé, 2011); Florencia Canale, *Pasión y traición: Los amores secretos de Remedios de Escalada de San Martín* (Buenos Aires: Planeta, 2011); and Flor Romero, *Yo, La Pola* (Bogota: Intermedio, 2010).

SELECT BIBLIOGRAPHY

Alcibíades, Mirla. *Mujeres e independencia: Venezuela 1810–1821*. Caracas: Casa Nacional de las Letras Andrés Bello, 2013.
Blanchard, Peter. *Under the Flags of Freedom: Slave Soldiers and the Wars of Independence in South America*. Pittsburgh, PA: University of Pittsburgh Press, 2008.

Blaufarb, Rafe. "Arms for Revolutions: Military Demobilization after the Napoleonic Wars and Latin American Independence." In *War, Demobilization and Memory: The Legacy of War in the Era of Atlantic Revolutions*, edited by Alan Forrest, Karen Hagemann, and Michael Rowe, 100–18. Basingstoke: Palgrave Macmillan, 2015.

Chambers, Sarah. *From Subjects to Citizens: Honor, Gender, and Politics in Arequipa, Peru, 1780–1854*. University Park: Pennsylvania State University Press, 1999.

Chasteen, John Charles. *Americanos: Latin America's Struggle for Independence*. Oxford: Oxford University Press, 2008.

Cherpak, Evelyn. "The Participation of Women in the Independence of Gran Colombia 1780–1830." In *Latin American Women: Historical Perspectives*, edited by Asunción Lavrin, 219–34. Westport, CT: Greenwood Press, 1978.

Davies, Catherine. "The Gender Order of Postwar Politics: Comparing Spanish South America and Spain, 1810s–1850s." In *War, Demobilization and Memory: The Legacy of War in the Era of Atlantic Revolutions*, edited by Alan Forrest, Karen Hagemann, and Michael Rowe, 182–202. Basingstoke: Palgrave Macmillan, 2015.

Davies, Catherine, Claire Brewster, and Hilary Owen. *South American Independence: Gender, Politics, Text*. Liverpool: Liverpool University Press, 2006.

Dueñas Vargas, Guiomar. *Del amor y otras pasiones: Elites, política y familia en Bogotá, 1778–1870*. Bogota: Universidad Nacional de Colombia, 2014.

Guardia, Sara Beatriz, ed. *Las mujeres en la independencia de América Latina*. Lima: Centro de Estudios la Mujer en la Historia de América, 2010.

Lynch, John. *San Martín: Argentine Soldier, American Hero*. New Haven, CT: Yale University Press, 2009.

Moya, José M., ed. *The Oxford Handbook of Latin America History*. Oxford: Oxford University Press, 2010.

Murray, Pamela S. *For Glory and Bolivar: The Remarkable Life of Manuela Saenz*. Austin: University of Texas Press, 2008.

Naro, Nancy Priscilla, ed. *Blacks, Coloureds and National Identity in Nineteenth-Century Latin America*. London: Institute of Latin American Studies, 2003.

Phelan, John Leddy. *The People and the King: The Comunero Revolution in Colombia, 1781*. Madison: University of Wisconsin Press, 1978.

Scheina, Robert L. *The Age of the Caudillo*. Vol. 1, *Latin America's Wars*. Washington, DC: Brassey's, 2003.

Silverblatt, Irene. *Moon, Sun and Witches: Gender Ideologies and Class in Inca and Colonial Peru*. Princeton, NJ: Princeton University Press, 1987.

Socolow, Susan Migden. *The Women of Colonial Latin America*. Cambridge: Cambridge University Press, 2000.

Twinam, Ann. *Public Lives, Private Secrets: Gender, Honor, Sexuality and Illegitimacy in Colonial Hispanic America*. Stanford, CA: Stanford University Press, 1999.

Walker, Charles F. *The Tupac Amaru Rebellion*. Cambridge, MA: Harvard University Press, 2014.

CHAPTER 5

GENDER, SLAVERY, WAR, AND VIOLENCE IN AND BEYOND THE AGE OF REVOLUTIONS

ELIZABETH COLWILL

HISTORIANS often define wars within clear temporal boundaries marked by an onset of hostilities between armies sponsored by sovereign states and concluded with peace treaties, however ephemeral. The history of the transatlantic slave trade, by contrast, presents a chronology of war of *longue durée*: one that begins with European expansion and continues through the uneven abolition of the trade and, arguably, through emancipation itself. In contrast to episodic wars christened with proper names—like the Seven Years' War (1756–63), the American Revolutionary War (1775–83), the Spanish American Wars of Independence (1809–30)—the transatlantic slave trade was predicated on a protracted state of war. The institution of slavery in the Americas did not end with the British Slave Trade Act (1807), nor with the Slavery Abolition Act (1833) that emancipated slaves in the British Empire, nor with the wave of similar government regulations elsewhere, including fourteen Northern states by the mid nineteenth century. It endured in the Southern states of the US until 1865 and other regions even further into the nineteenth century. Rooted in the forcible subjection of the productive, reproductive, and sexual labor of the enslaved, the slave order was secured by the violence of masters, militias, and the power of the state. In that sense, slavery itself constituted an ongoing state of war.[1]

Even if we limit the parameters for war to discrete periods of open conflict between groups of armed combatants, the history of slavery suggests chronologies of war—including slave revolts and emancipatory struggles—that spill beyond the temporal boundaries of war as traditionally understood. Neither slave revolts nor slave emancipation can be contained within the timeline of the Age of Revolutions (1770s–1840s). In fact, as Laurent Dubois described, "the paradox of the Age of Revolution is that it both weakened and strengthened slavery," overturning some slave regimes and reviving others.[2] Slavery thus prompts a reimagining of the scope, chronology, and parameters of war, while the entangled histories and troubled legacies of slave emancipation and revolution disrupt classic narratives of this age.

If the study of slavery troubles the scholarly terrain of war, so too does the analytic of gender. Forged in the crucible of conflict, slave regimes in the Americas were gendered from their inception. A gender analytic forces us to revise dominant narratives of both slavery and war, because the Wars of Revolution and Independence in the eighteenth and nineteenth centuries gave rise to gendered struggles over emancipation and gendered practices of citizenship and statecraft. War turned slaves into soldiers, devastated families, and triggered new diasporas. Gendered violence was endemic to conventionally defined warfare. Yet a focus on gender requires that we also consider "war by other means," from the coerced reproductive and sexual labor of slavery to the gendered and racialized forms of political and economic dispossession that characterized postemancipation societies.

The past decades have seen exponential growth in the scholarship on gender and slavery in the Americas, much of which is partitioned along the lines of empire, language, and discipline.[3] Pathbreaking research has exposed gender as an idiom of power in negotiations among Indigenous populations and Europeans and highlighted the intertwined legacies of Indigenous and African slavery in etching the boundaries of race, gender, empire, and citizenship.[4] Scholars of Atlantic slavery and the African diaspora have shed new light on enslaved women's diverse experiences of labor, reproduction, and sexual and family life.[5] Others have turned their attention to the ways in which the language and rituals of revolution and emancipation were gendered, along with how marginalized groups practiced citizenship. Since the histories of slavery and emancipation are interwoven with colonial wars, slave revolts, and revolutions, war provides the context for many discrete studies of women in slave societies. Only since the 1990s have scholars adopted both war and gender as the analytic frame for studies of slavery and emancipation.[6] Colin Dayan's *Haiti, History and the Gods*, published in 1995, was among the pathbreaking contributions that drew attention to the racialized and gendered violence that pervaded colonial warfare in a slave society.[7] Subsequent comparative studies of gender and emancipation, as well as scholars of diaspora, have explored terrain beyond the boundaries of a single empire or nation-state.[8] On the whole, we have become far more aware, in Jennifer Morgan's words, of how "the transatlantic slave trade produced and mobilized gendered articulations of power," including complex racialized hierarchies, structures of violence, and forms of resistance.[9]

This is not to suggest that we collapse all forms of conflict under a single rubric or propose a new typology of warfare. But an exclusive focus on episodic empire-based wars may obfuscate more continuous or subterranean forms of warfare over laws, bodies, and psyches through which the struggle to control land and labor unfolded. There are continuities between "official" state-sponsored wars fought by enlisted men and forms of gendered violence at the heart of enslavement. Violence—racialized, sexual, and reproductive violence—was endemic to the institution of slavery.[10] Armed conflict fueled regional and transatlantic slave trades, slave revolts blended into "official" wars, and enslaved people themselves sometimes spoke of slavery as a state of war.[11]

The study of slavery through the lens of gender alters our understanding of war, and the study of war through a gendered lens illuminates practices of statecraft and processes of slave emancipation. At the heart of the following analysis are therefore competing claims to sovereignty and citizenship in the wars of revolution and emancipation of the late eighteenth and nineteenth centuries. Although the period of the American Revolutionary War, the Haitian Revolution (1791–1804), and the Spanish American Wars of Independence forms a primary locus of conflict, it is necessary to move beyond their temporal and geographic boundaries and explore instead—consistent with a more expansive concept of war—the gendered violence of settler colonialism and the slave trade, as well as the intertwined nature of war and emancipation.

WAR, REPRODUCTION, AND THE TRANSATLANTIC SLAVE TRADE

The transatlantic slave trade, which forcibly transported some 12.5 million slaves over nearly four centuries, fueled warfare along Atlantic coasts as it transformed social and political relationships within and among African, European, and Indigenous states and peoples.[12] Drawing into its net both state and nonstate actors, the trade extended and transformed an extensive internal African commerce in slaves in both Muslim and non-Muslim regions and built on existing hierarchies of servile labor, organized on "the basis of families, communal work parties, marriage contracts and other arrangements."[13] Slavery became an important source of revenue for the centralizing states along the Bight of Benin and the Gold Coast, its victims harvested from local raids, piracy, European coastal depredations, and interstate conflict.[14] The transatlantic slave trade thus assumed as its modus operandi both commercial cooperation and a state of war.

The enslavement of Indigenous people was intimately entwined with the politics of war, trade, and alliance that were part and parcel of settler colonialism and the emergent transatlantic slave trade. As Brett Rushforth reminds us, "slavery took many forms in the early modern Americas, and this variety persisted in both Indigenous and colonial settings long after the African slave trade overshadowed other slaving cultures."[15] Colonization by the early modern European states was inseparable from the decimation of Indigenous populations and the expansion of an Atlantic market tied to the slave trade.[16] In the Americas, the Spanish and Portuguese initially relied on local systems of taxation and tribute, backed by force of arms, to procure Indigenous labor—efforts in which African auxiliaries, slave and free, were enlisted from the outset.[17] The tenuous foothold of the Spanish and Portuguese in the first century of contact with the Americas provided opportunities for male auxiliaries of African descent to gain their freedom by fighting in colonial forces. Those opportunities gradually eroded with the catastrophic decline in local populations.[18] Women of African descent—servants, slaves, and personal dependents of Spanish masters—figured among the first unarmed auxiliaries, their numbers soon dwarfed by laborers imported en masse from Africa to work in mines and on plantations.[19] By the end of the seventeenth century, the British and Dutch vied for commercial ascendancy along what had once been Portuguese outposts on the Gold Coast of Africa, while local chiefs jockeyed for control over persons, territory, and goods. There, as elsewhere along the coast and its hinterlands, the adoption of European weaponry by the late seventeenth century extended the scale and geographical scope of warfare, producing dependents, captives, and refugees who fueled the transatlantic trade in slaves.[20]

The dramatic increase in demand for African slaves as plantation laborers took a devastating demographic toll, to the point that, in John Thornton's words, "in the late eighteenth century much of Africa reached demographic exhaustion."[21] Africans died in wars between states, during capture, on forced marches toward African coasts, in barracoons, with "bloody flux" on shipboard, and in chains. Estimates vary, but as many as one-third of those captured died before transportation to the Americas—a statistic that lends credence to the interpretation of slavery as a state of war.[22] Indeed, Gad Heuman and Trevor Burnard have concluded that "death was the single most important feature of the slave experience in the Americas."[23]

By the mid-eighteenth century, four continents were closely knit in a skein of commerce and war and linked by the transatlantic slave trade, which was gendered from its inception. As Stephanie Smallwood explains, women and girls claimed as captives in wars in Africa would profit the victors either as assimilated household laborers and wives or as commodities sold into regional and, increasingly, transatlantic markets. In many regions, the demand for slaves to serve domestically expanded alongside the demand for slaves for export. Females were considered desirable within African markets to expand the reproductive and productive capacities of the household.[24] Men, women, and children swept into the transatlantic trade together suffered the dehumanizing process of commodification, but sellers, buyers, and middlemen considered carefully the specific gender balance of their human cargo to accommodate the labor requirements of particular markets. Although eunuchs, followed by women and girls, brought the highest prices in the internal African trade, market dynamics determined gender ratios; over time, in the words of Davis Eltis, "Europeans brought more females to the Americas and Africans sold more males into the transatlantic trade than either buyers or sellers would have preferred."[25] The value ascribed to reproductive and sexual as well as productive labor of enslaved women at the point of sale varied by region and period, but resulted on average in a higher proportion of men to women on Middle Passage. Nonetheless, the significance of enslaved women's labor is incontestable: 36 percent of all Africans transported to the Americas prior to 1820 were female, and 80 percent of the five million women who crossed the Atlantic prior to 1820 were African.[26]

While in the early colonial period enslaved women of African descent might labor alongside Indigenous and White indentured servants, by the eighteenth century racialized ideologies of gender and sexuality subjected enslaved women to distinct forms of servitude.[27] The slippery status of colonial slavery on the frontier had offered Atlantic Creoles some maneuvering room and the enslaved some prospect of freedom through self-purchase, but options eroded with the spread of plantation societies. By the mid-eighteenth century, enslaved women worked in cities, on farmsteads, and increasingly on rice, indigo, tobacco, and sugar plantations in Brazil, the Caribbean, and the plantation South. The proportion of women to men employed in fieldwork rose further after the abolition of the slave trade in 1807.[28] While the right to marry, testify at court, become literate, or possess property varied by region, religion, and imperial regime,[29] nowhere did womanhood provide immunity for the enslaved from menial, reproductive, or sexual labor.

The violence at the heart of slavery involved the subjection of productive, reproductive, and sexual capabilities to the will of the master. The forms of reproductive control varied dramatically according to region and epoch. Sugar planters in eighteenth-century Barbados chose to trade their slaves' reproductive capacities for cheap new slave imports, sacrificing reproduction for the pursuit of profit. A century later, nineteenth-century British legislators sought to ameliorate conditions of enslavement to bolster live births in their Caribbean colonies. Entanglements of love, sex, and power in liaisons between enslaved women and their masters notwithstanding, reproduction throughout the Americas remained a contested aspect of every slave regime, sexual access a master's sovereign right, and rape a weapon of war.[30]

"Expectations regarding gender and reproduction," Morgan has argued, "were central to racial ideologies, the organization of labor and the nature of slave community and resistance." Women's responsibilities for reproduction spilled beyond childbearing to the forms of cultural reproduction that lay at the heart of creolization. In the Black Atlantic, a site of hybrid and shifting diasporic identities, women animated practices of cultural survival and transformation. Yet against this creative force, the market continued to claim bodies and birth slaves. By the eighteenth century, plantation societies had rooted the slave or free status of a child in the mother's womb, converted to a vessel of "hereditary racialized slavery."[31] This act, which embedded the violence of the slave regime in women's very flesh, laid bare the gendered foundations of slave regimes throughout the Americas.

ARMED SLAVE REVOLTS

The slave trade relied on acts of intimate and state-sponsored violence that provoked, in response, both armed and everyday forms of resistance. Slave revolts aboard ship plagued captains of slave ships from the earliest days of the trade. In fact, scholars now estimate that revolts occurred on one of every ten voyages.[32] Young men may have presented the greatest threat, but women were involved as well, as the example of a revolt on the slave ship *Amitié* on May 4, 1787, indicates.[33]

Like the *Amitié* revolt, most shipboard rebellions ended in defeat. In one celebrated exception to that rule, forty-nine men who had together suffered the brutal Middle Passage mutinied when they were reshipped from Havana on the *Amistad*. Once recaptured, their bid for freedom generated a series of legal cases that reached the US Supreme Court in 1841. Marcus Rediker has highlighted the ways in which masculinity, age, cultural heritage, and military training shaped their opportunity for success. At least two-thirds of the enslaved men aboard ship were trained warriors and wielded authority in their communities of origin.[34] Thornton also makes a strong case for the martial influence of African cultures under slavery and the transatlantic "military" sources of the slave revolts, particularly in Saint-Domingue, where sugar plantations were populated, in part, by Africans captured during the Kongo civil wars (1665–1709).[35]

Men, both African and Creole, dominated leadership and the rank and file in many rebellions, but the archives do provide glimpses of women in combat in slave rebellions and the First and Second Maroon Wars (1731 and 1795–96)—conflicts between the Jamaican Maroons (Africans who escaped from slavery and formed independent settlements) and the colonial British authorities—that besieged plantation societies in the eighteenth and nineteenth centuries.[36] After decades of intermittent battles with forces often composed of White and Creole planters, Indigenous soldiers, and slaves impressed into military service, the Maroons forced their enemies to sign formal treaties that recognized their independence. Even in the early twenty-first century, female insurgents remain powerful symbols of resistance in Jamaica, Guadeloupe, and Cuba. The relative fluidity of women's roles in the context of slave rebellions and Maroon wars contrasts with strict gender prescription—though not always practice—during early colonial wars waged by European states well before the rise of professionalizing armies.[37]

Despite important research on women of African descent, both slave and free, we have only a fragmentary record of women in armed combat in slave rebellions. A gender analytic, however, does more than seek women insurgents to enrich the historical record; it suggests questions that dislodge armed rebellion as the apogee of resistance. Scholars who work within intersectional frameworks have been at the forefront of a generation of research that highlights the panoply of factors—including the destruction of families and sexual violence—that fueled revolt. Sensitive to the diverse pathways and gendered expressions of resistance, they have emphasized the fluid boundaries between overt rebellion and more subtle forms of resistance through which women sought to limit reproduction, assert religious authority, challenge the law, or resist the spatial confines of the plantation.[38] Aisha Finch has argued that a focus on armed rebellion— whether it celebrates male leaders, the insurgent masses, or the occasional woman rebel—privileges a model of armed insurrection that highlights the aggressive masculine subject as the foundation of "black oppositional cultures." She has drawn attention instead to the discursive masculinization of particular (violent) acts, whatever the sex of the actor, and has highlighted the "circuits of knowledge" through which women shaped the possibilities of insurgency during the Cuban resistance in the 1840s.[39]

Public hangings and tortures, restrictions on vodou, limitations on travel, regulations of marriage, and surveillance of births all suggest that masters recognized that they held their power through force and that women, as well as men, constituted a threat.[40] Fears of uprisings and rumors of poisoning were rampant, particularly in slave societies of the Caribbean and Latin America in which enslaved people outnumbered free individuals.[41] Most slave revolts were limited in scope and brutally suppressed. Nonetheless, armed rebellions occurred with increasing frequency from the late eighteenth through the nineteenth centuries—a history that extends the timeline of "revolutionary wars" while it challenges the idea of revolt as an exclusively masculine enterprise. Slave revolts were more likely in plantation economies that relied on large units of production, in regions with large Black majorities, and in contexts of severe scarcity. The presence of antislavery politics in some cases fueled revolts.[42] Violent rebellions had conflicting goals, ranging from the 1835 Malê Revolt in Salvador, Bahia, in which African men re-created a military force to overthrow the government, to "ameliorative" uprisings in the British Caribbean to force masters to grant customary rights.[43] Wars of empire could provide both impetus and opportunity, as in the 1760 rebellion in Jamaica in the context of the Seven Years' War. The Haitian Revolution and the American Civil War (1861–65) provide powerful evidence that internal conflicts among elites and revolts by the enslaved could together provide a driving force in war and revolution.[44]

ARMED SLAVES IN REGULAR ARMIES

Despite these legacies of resistance, slaveholding classes throughout the Americas armed male slaves in defense of their own interests.[45] As Christopher Leslie Brown has demonstrated, in virtually every slave society from Africa to the Americas, political elites recruited slaves when their power was threatened.[46] In the forms of military slavery dominant in Africa and the Middle East, boys acquired from the local population were trained as professional warriors, who obtained a corporate identity as a masculine military elite. In the Americas, by contrast, "elites enlisted slaves less to acquire loyal subjects than to address shortages of manpower."[47] Enslaved men captured fugitives and fought against Maroons, Indigenous populations, slave insurgents, or other European empires.[48] Whether in the service of change or the status quo, as Brown explains, elites deployed enslaved men as soldiers in the Americas to amass power. In this sense, arming slaves should be seen as "an instrument of statecraft."[49]

By the second half of the eighteenth century, conflicts such as the Seven Years' War had swept into battle slaves, free people of mixed descent, and Indigenous inhabitants and provoked an ongoing search for military manpower.[50] Free men of mixed race had long served in slave-hunting forces and in militias at home and abroad, proudly wielding their military service as the foundation of claims to rights.[51] Despite the antipathy felt by the planter classes to arming their own slaves, slaves were requisitioned by warring states, engaged as bodyguards by masters, and eventually commandeered into republican and royalist regiments from Argentina to North America. Military slaves were widely used in the campaigns against Indigenous peoples from the early days of contact through battles in Spanish Florida and the Caribbean during the revolutionary era.[52] To the extent that soldiering presented an opportunity for status and mobility in an era of relatively permeable boundaries between slave and free, it provided an exclusively masculine pathway to a group identity, and, at times, to freedom.

The institution of slavery provided the foundation of Atlantic empires riven by war. Yet these very wars, whether inspired by European states' quest for empire or elites' desire for independence, held the potential to become freedom fights for slaves-turned-soldiers, as demonstrated by the emergence of the citizen-soldier in Spanish Florida, among British Loyalists in revolutionary North America, in eighteenth-century Saint-Domingue, and in the Spanish American Wars of Independence.[53] The military roles played by men of African and mixed descent had precedents in earlier Wars of Empire, such as the Seven Years' War. Empires' claims to territorial sovereignty and masters' claims to sovereign power over their human property provoked competing claims to self-sovereignty on the part of the enslaved, now with arms in hand.

That said, the relationship between war, revolution, and emancipation was complex. While war alone was never a sufficient condition for slave emancipation, the Age of Revolutions saw the abolition of the slave trade in Britain and the United States, as well as a wave of emancipations in the Americas. On the one hand, "wars were as bad for the slave-trading business as revolution," David Eltis has claimed, citing a 30 to 50 percent decline in the volume of slaves traded during the Seven Years' War and the American Revolutionary War and episodically in the period of the Haitian Revolution and the Napoleonic Wars (1803–15).[54] On the other hand, those temporary interruptions, like the British abolition of the slave trade, provided no permanent brake on the importation of enslaved people. Demand burgeoned in the last decades of the eighteenth century, with enslaved Africans arriving in the Americas between 1776 and 1830 at an average of 80,000 per year.[55] Slavery, even when severed in revolutionary outbreaks such as the Haitian Revolution, reemerged, hydra-like, in Cuba and Brazil.

The Napoleonic Wars changed the power dynamics between victorious Britain and defeated France and sounded the death knell of the Spanish Empire, but they did not signify the end of either colonialism or slavery. In Brazil and the United States, wars of independence preceded emancipation by more than a half century. In the British Caribbean, where emancipation unfolded in stages, gradual "amelioration" and "apprenticeships" followed the abolition of the slave trade, while in Martinique and Guadeloupe, emancipation awaited a second French Revolution in 1848. In Cuba, emancipation (1886) followed decades of armed conflict among Creole elites, metropolitan forces, and the enslaved.[56] Everywhere, war or the threat of insurrection underlay the concession of freedom to the demands of the enslaved. And everywhere, gender influenced the process of emancipation and the nature of the peace.

WAR, DIASPORA, AND EMANCIPATION

The wars and revolutions that swept four continents from the mid-eighteenth through the nineteenth centuries gave birth not only to new nations and ideologies, but also to gendered diasporas and labor systems. As Lisa Lowe has pointed out, the conjunction of the British abolition of the slave trade and the government's decision to import Chinese coolies to Trinidad as plantation laborers was no accident. In the ensuing decades, tens of thousands of east and south Asian indentured men and women, imported to the Americas to supplement African, Indigenous, and Creole labor, would find themselves classified and categorized within an evolving nexus of racialized sexual hierarchies.[57]

Wars against empire throughout the Americas took on the character of colonial wars, as colonists marked privileges and borders against internal enemies, whether Indigenous, free Black, or slave. In this light, the great revolutions of this epoch (American, French, Haitian, and Spanish American) appear less as a set of distinct—or purely liberating— phenomena than as an explosive brew of interests, allegiances, and possibilities. Chasing clues across continents, historians of the Black Atlantic have moved beyond generalizations about "Black masses" to follow the traces of Atlantic Creoles and Black loyalists, missionaries, and Maroons. Archival sources read against the grain allow glimpses of not only the movements of soldiers and armies but also the internal displacements they occasioned. War displaced hundreds of thousands, each new battle propelling a fresh wave of refugees into exile. War fractured families and fashioned new forms of kinship; at times, war ruptured the shackles of the enslaved. The history of slavery through the optic of gender allows us to reconceive war within the social networks, racial hierarchies, and structures of intimacy that linked diverse individuals in an ongoing diaspora.[58]

War and revolution provided pathways to freedom through manumission, marronage, and—for men—military service.[59] In the Francophone Caribbean and Spanish America, soldiers freed their wives through marriage. The Spanish American Wars of Independence opened opportunities for escape, eroded owners' authority, and strengthened the bargaining power of enslaved men and women.[60] Women used their military connections to advocate for their families and take their cases to court. In Spanish America, women who accompanied family members as camp followers demanded freedom as repayment for their labor.[61] Black soldiers hoarded military wages to purchase their wives' freedom.[62] Women were manumitted throughout the Americas at higher rates than were men, and rates of manumission increased during the revolutions.[63] Both women and men initiated petitions for freedom on behalf of family members and dependents.[64]

The meanings of revolution depended on social location. The free Black merchant in New Orleans, the Creole *ménagère* (mixed-race mistress) in Saint-Domingue, and the African cane cutter with two children would each have developed her own calculus of risks and strategies for survival. But in every case, war transformed women's lives. Enslaved women acted as insurgents, spies, and fugitives; army cooks and nurses; provisioners of troops; and objects of exchange. Thousands voluntarily left their masters to follow family members into insurrectionary forces. Others found themselves refugees against their will as homes became battlegrounds, and plantations, along with their families' provisioning plots, were torched. War also reinforced the gendered divide between military and plantation labor. From Saint-Domingue to Spanish America and later the Confederacy, women remained on plantations by the thousands during wartime, sustaining families and cultivating crops. Women served on many fronts, performing the labor that sustained warfare.[65]

War also inflicted on the enslaved population experiences of rupture and trauma distinct in fundamental ways from the wartime suffering of their masters. In the wake of the slave revolution in Saint-Domingue, colonists emigrated, selling some members of enslaved families and bearing others—frequently women or children—across the seas in their flight. One-third of the runaways during the American Revolution were women—an increase in the numbers of women escapees replicated elsewhere in the revolutionary era.[66] Freedwomen bore free children only to mourn their re-enslavement when the warfront shifted or when, as in Guadeloupe in 1802, imperial armies suppressed insurrectionary forces and restored the slave regime at the cost of some 10,000 lives.[67] Devastating mortality rates altered the ratio of women to men and, in some regions, led to a decline in births among people of African descent. On all sides of the conflict, rape served as a tool of war.[68] The world of revolution was a shockingly insecure world for the enslaved, especially for enslaved women, sidelined from insurgent armies as insurrectionary forces were disciplined into professionalized armies. In its violent invasions, dislocations, and work of destruction, war continued the pattern of slave trade itself.

But the story of revolution was far more than a story of ruptured genealogies. A diasporic lens requires us to attend not only to war's work of destruction but also to the cultural crossings and invented identities produced by migratory trajectories. The circuitous pathways of people of African descent against the backdrop of revolution illustrate the agency of individuals who found in the collision of empires the opportunity to leverage their own freedom. In that world, Francisco Menéndez, brought to America as a young Mandinga slave in the early 1700s, could reinvent himself as a free Spanish subject and militia leader in Spanish Florida. "Rosalie of the Poulard nation" crossed boundaries of ocean and empire in her efforts to preserve family and freedom during the era of the Haitian Revolution. While soldiering provided geographic and social mobility for individual men, revolution also provided opportunities for families to claim their freedom.[69]

Fictive and blood kin served as patrons, dependents, allies, and sometimes political pawns in times of war. Notarial records provide rich evidence of the importance of marital alliances, godparenting, and rites of baptism across racial lines in relationships and political communities forged in diaspora. Jane Landers and David Geggus have followed the pathway of Georges Biassou, the insurgent general of Saint-Domingue who fought for the Spanish Crown but was defeated by Toussaint Louverture. Exiled to Cuba, Biassou exerted considerable influence as patron and "titular head of an ever-expanding family" that linked the "former Black Auxiliaries of Carlos IV with members of the free black community in St. Augustine, many of whom were former fugitives from the United States and had experienced the American Revolution."[70]

Formal peace treaties between European nations initiated new diasporic trajectories, often with tragic outcomes. Consider the 100,000 soldiers, families, and strangers in the North American colonies who abandoned their homes to cast their lot with the British in response to the promise of freedom. Under threat of re-enslavement by American Patriots, some 50,000 fled to postwar misery on the harsh Nova Scotia coast after 1783, when the British reneged on their promise of one hundred acres per family. Some 1,000 of these refugees were later recruited as settlers for the colony of Freetown, Sierra Leone, as part of a Christian abolitionist, colonial venture. Promised twenty acres for every man, ten for every wife, and five for each child, the freedpeople were again betrayed. Many died from starvation and disease in their first years in Freetown.[71]

GENDER, WAR, AND STATECRAFT: THE EXAMPLE OF SAINT-DOMINGUE

"Slavery was not a sideshow [in America]," according to James Oliver Horton: "it was the main event."[72] For enslaved peoples in the era of revolutionary wars, emancipation was the main event. The Caribbean theater of war functioned as a microcosm of conflict rooted in the violence of the triangular trade; the rivalries of British, French, Dutch, and Spanish imperial regimes; and a diaspora of displaced peoples and revolutionary ideals. There, as elsewhere, competing claims to liberty unfolded hand in hand with war. The case of revolutionary Saint-Domingue provides a striking example of how gender determined pathways to emancipation and influenced practices of statecraft in the context of war.

In Saint-Domingue, formal emancipation by the French National Convention in February 1794 followed the massive slave revolution of August 1791. Yet even here, emancipation proceeded unevenly, propelled by the unpredictable course of international war and internal social and political fissures. Although 1791 marked a definitive rupture between slavery and freedom for some, for others, including Black and mixed-race leaders, slavery long remained on the bargaining table. The mission of French republican commissioners, on their arrival in 1792, included both the suppression of the slave revolution and the enforcement of racial equality among free men. But the French declaration of war in Europe in April 1792 fundamentally altered the nature of warfare in the Caribbean theater. By the summer of 1793, as European soldiers died by the thousands of yellow fever and the British and Spanish competed to recruit Black insurgents from French territory, the commissioners found themselves increasingly isolated from all except their allies among the *gens de couleur* (free men of color). Faced with the defection or emigration of most White colonists, a desperate shortage of military manpower, and a direct challenge to their own authority by republican General François Galbaud du Fort, they turned to the Black majority.[73]

In June 1793, in a decision propelled both by political commitment and by military necessity, the French commissioner Léger-Félicité Sonthonax issued a proclamation that conferred freedom and citizenship on all Black insurgents who agreed to fight for the French Republic. Significantly, this bid for the loyalty of the Black insurgents had a broader reach: it promised to ameliorate the slave regime and made special provisions for the improved treatment of women, including "more consideration and respect for pregnant and nursing women."[74] Some weeks later, in July 1793, the French commissioner offered freedom to women in the North Province who married free men. Military service thus provided a pathway to emancipation for men, and marriage did so for women: a process that invested freedmen—particularly soldiers—with the authority to bestow freedom on their wives and children. In August 1793, Sonthonax's historic decree of general emancipation transformed the terrain of war and the nature of the French Republic as all slaves in the North Province, male and female, were named citizens of the French Republic. In February 1794, at the height of the Terror, the French Convention extended universal emancipation throughout the French Empire, but a gendered logic of citizenship and a gendered narrative of freedom endured.[75]

The case of Saint-Domingue also sheds new light on war, gender, and state formation. By the summer of 1794, General Louverture had abandoned the Spanish and cast his lot with the French Republic. He rose steadily to power between 1795 and 1798, recruiting a massive army from the ranks of freedmen, who expelled the Spanish and the British and then defeated Louverture's mixed-race opponents in southern Saint-Domingue in the War of the Knives (1799–1800).[76] In those years, Louverture's performance of martial masculinity was essential to the delicate balancing act through which he sought to perform subjection to French colonial rule and revive the plantation economy, yet wield power sufficient to prevent the restoration of slavery. In sum, even prior to the declaration of Haitian independence that he did not live to witness, Louverture balanced complex problems of political allegiance as he engaged in a practice of state-building—even nation-building—within the French Empire.

Revolutionary proclamations, letters, and government decrees from this period document how Louverture negotiated between colonial loyalty and political autonomy through the elaboration of gendered notions of citizenship. His promotion of marriage, Christianity, and militarism was not just a discursive strategy; it also served as the foundation of citizenship, social order, and morality—a path to economic vitality and political legitimacy. Louverture rented plantation land to high-ranking military men and imposed through force of arms a system of conscripted labor rooted in a gendered division of labor. He paired this with a social and matrimonial program designed to ensure public order and economic progress.[77] For Louverture, the family thus conscripted in the service of the state was central to the art of statecraft. If nation-building requires a kind of cultural coalescence, rendered invisible even as it occurs, the elaboration of gendered cultural and labor practices works to naturalize the state itself. The gendered political culture of the postemancipation state in Saint-Domingue served to bridge the competing claims of empire and nation. Indeed, Louverture's survival depended on preserving that balance.

Freedom itself, ever tenuous, was fought and won a second time in Saint-Domingue in a brutal war of shifting alliances that pitted Napoleon's armies and naval fleet against troops, refugees, and civilians divided by class, color, and origin. In December 1801, a massive French fleet under General Charles Leclerc prepared to sail to overturn Black rule and restore the plantation system.[78] The war of conquest that followed amounted to a war of extermination.[79] The victory of the insurgents and declaration of Haitian independence in January 1804 illuminate the sacralization of the citizen-soldier in the forging of the new nation. As Mimi Sheller has argued, the conflation of Haitian citizenship with martial masculinity had profound consequences postindependence for the gender division of labor, the distribution of land grants, women's legal status, and the militarization of society.[80]

Awash in a sea of slaver empires, Haiti preserved its independence and freedmen preserved the title of citizen. But in most newly independent states from the United States to Latin American republics, neither independence nor republican revolution proved an immediate guarantor of liberty. Anticolonial struggles, liberalism, and the rhetoric of natural rights were fully compatible with the elaboration of new racial justifications for slavery and the legal subjection of women of all races. While the slave trade was abolished through Central and South America by 1830—Brazil excepted—full emancipation through most of South, though not Central, America would await the second half of the nineteenth century. In Brazil, Cuba, and Puerto Rico, sugar exports and slavery expanded after the Haitian Revolution in a haunting reminder of the contradictions of liberty. Nonetheless, the wave of revolutions that swept the Atlantic had a profound effect on the fate of slavery in Spanish America. Here, as elsewhere, "warfare was the catalyst for revolutionary ideas and practices"[81] and "broke the back of colonial slavery."[82]

CONCLUSION

Theorists of the "Western way of war" have linked the emergence of modern methods of warfare to democratic citizenship and constitutional government.[83] Yet the intimate connections between the expansion of "modern" warring empires, the transatlantic slave trade, and slave economies in the Americas suggest a far more contradictory legacy. A definition of *war* limited to defined fields of battle orchestrated by monarchs or nation-states elides a primary form of state-sponsored violence that lay at the heart of European Wars of Empire—slavery itself. Slavery spawned a panoply of armed conflicts: African inter- and intrastate wars, wars of expansion, wars between empires, slave uprisings, shipboard revolts, civil wars, revolutions, and wars of independence. Conventional definitions of war also elide the interlinkages between intimate domains and the violence of states. Slavery involved, by definition, the forcible conversion of persons to chattel through the legal and military arms of the state—a conversion secured through the subjection of sexual, productive, and reproductive labor; the violence of shackles and the auction block; and the legal erasure of genealogy and family ties. The study of slavery and gender raises the question posed by theorist Judith Butler: How might particular "frames of war" exclude from our line of vision whole categories of destruction?[84]

The intersecting histories of slavery and gender suggest the need to extend our reach beyond the boundaries of wars and revolutions with proper names to attend to the continuities between official wars and forms of gendered violence that defined the institution of slavery and the process of emancipation. Those acts of violence proved more subtle and pervasive than traditional definitions of state-based war allow. Furthermore, it is necessary to denaturalize revolutionary scripts that equated war with martial manhood and represented emancipation as universal freedom. Consider the case of the "free womb laws" that granted freedom to newborns, but not their mothers, while protracting children's servitude, often until they reached the age of majority.[85] Just as colonial slavery marked the legal condition of a child—free or unfree—in the mother's womb, this "gradual" path to freedom was rooted, paradoxically, in the wombs of mothers who did not yet own their own persons. As Camillia Cowling has demonstrated, in Cuba and Brazil mothers used the contradictions within the free womb laws to gain access to their children and to argue for their own freedom at court. In this sense, free womb laws represented "war by other means."[86]

If the history of slavery from the perspective of gender suggests that we rethink the meanings of war, it also requires that we rethink the nature of peace. War provided the motor of colonial expansion, displacement, and diaspora; it also opened the liberatory promise of revolution and slave emancipation. But as continued encroachments on Indigenous lands would prove, formal treaties brought no end to contests over power and freedom. From the British Caribbean and Spanish America to the former Confederate States of America and finally Brazil, new regimes of "free labor" based on indenture and debt peonage would displace slavery, the racial "difference" of African, Creole, and Asian laborers marked within evolving gendered taxonomies of virtue and vice.[87] "Degrees of unfreedom," in the words of Lisa Lowe, "unevenly distributed across the globe" would characterize "peace" in the wake of emancipation.[88] Taking an unfamiliar path by reconceiving conventional frames of war and peace may allow us to follow the traces of people who were themselves on the threshold of the unknown.

NOTES

1. The preamble of John Brown's 1858 abolitionist constitution reads: "slavery, throughout its entire existence in the United States, is none other than a most barbarous, unprovoked and unjustifiable war of one portion of its citizens upon another portion—the only conditions of which are perpetual imprisonment and hopeless servitude or absolute extermination—in utter disregard and violation of those eternal and self-evident truths set forth in our Declaration of Independence." Quoted in W. E. B. Du Bois, *John Brown*, ed. John David Smith (London: M. E. Sharpe, 1997), 131. Nineteenth-century abolitionists from John Brown to William Lloyd Garrison described slavery as a state of war, as did John Locke in his *Second Treatise of Government* (chap. IV, sec. 24, 1690). I am grateful to Stephanie McCurry for this insight and the reference.
2. Laurent Dubois, "Slavery in the Age of Revolution," in *The Routledge History of Slavery*, ed. Gad Heuman and Trevor Burnard (London: Routledge, 2011), 267–80; and David Eltis,

"Revolution, War, Empire: Gendering the Transatlantic Slave Trade, 1776–1830," in *Gender, War and Politics: Transatlantic Perspectives, 1775–1830,* ed. Karen Hagemann et al. (Basingstoke: Palgrave Macmillan, 2010), 41–57.

3. Kirsten E. Wood, "Gender and Slavery," in *The Oxford Handbook of Slavery in the Americas,* ed. Robert L. Paquette and Mark M. Smith (Oxford: Oxford University Press, 2010), 513–34.

4. See Juliana Barr, *Peace Came in the Form of a Woman: Indians and Spaniards in the Texas Borderlands* (Chapel Hill: University of North Carolina Press, 2007); Kirsten Fischer, *Suspect Relations: Sex, Race, and Resistance in Colonial North Carolina* (Ithaca, NY: Cornell University Press, 2001); Barbara Krauthamer, *Black Slaves, Indian Masters: Slavery, Emancipation, and Citizenship in the Native American South* (Chapel Hill: University of North Carolina Press, 2013); Tiya Miles, *Ties That Bind: The Story of an Afro-Cherokee Family in Slavery and Freedom* (Berkeley: University of California Press, 2005); Miles, *The Dawn of Detroit: A Chronicle of Slavery and Freedom in the City of the Straits* (New York: New Press, 2017); Margaret Ellen Newell, *Brethren by Nature: New England Indians, Colonists, and the Origins of American Slavery* (Ithaca, NY: Cornell University Press, 2015); and Wendy Warren, *New England Bound: Slavery and Colonization in Early America* (New York: W. W. Norton, 2016).

5. See Hilary Beckles, *Centering Woman: Gender Discourses in Caribbean Slave Society* (Kingston: Ian Randle, 1999); Barbara Bush, *Slave Women in Caribbean Society, 1650–1838* (Bloomington: Indiana University Press, 1990); Marisa J. Fuentes, *Dispossessed Lives: Enslaved Women, Violence, and the Archive* (Philadelphia: University of Pennsylvania, 2016); David Barry Gaspar and Darlene Clark Hine, eds., *Beyond Bondage: Free Women of Color in the Americas* (Urbana: University of Illinois Press, 2004); Bernard Moitt, *Women and Slavery in the French Antilles, 1635–1848* (Bloomington: Indiana University Press, 2001); Marietta Morrissey, *Slave Women in the New World: Gender Stratification in the Caribbean* (Lawrence: University Press of Kansas, 1989); Verene Shepherd et al., eds., *Engendering History: Caribbean Women in Historical Perspective* (New York: St. Martin's Press, 1995); and Amy Dru Stanley, *From Bondage to Contract: Wage Labor and the Market in the Age of Slave Emancipation* (Cambridge: Cambridge University Press, 1998).

6. John D. Garrigus, "'To Establish a Community of Property': Marriage and Race before and during the Haitian Revolution," *Journal of the History of the Family* 12, no. 2 (2007): 142–52; Elizabeth Colwill, "'Fêtes de l'hymen, fêtes de la liberté': Marriage, Manhood and Emancipation in Saint-Domingue, 1793," in *The World of the Haitian Revolution,* ed. David Patrick Geggus and Norman Fiering (Indianapolis: University of Indiana Press, 2009), 125–55; Colwill, "Freedwomen's Familial Politics: Marriage, War and Rites of Registry in Post-Emancipation Saint-Domingue," in Hagemann et al., *Gender, War,* 71–89; Laurent Dubois, "Gendered Freedom: Citoyennes and War in the Revolutionary French Caribbean," in ibid., 58–70; Pamela Scully and Diana Paton, eds., *Gender and Slave Emancipation in the Atlantic World* (Durham, NC: Duke University Press, 2005); Melanie J. Newton, *The Children of Africa in the Colonies: Free People of Color in Barbados in the Age of Emancipation* (Baton Rouge: Louisiana State University Press, 2008); Rebecca Hartkopf Schloss, *Sweet Liberty: The Final Days of Slavery in Martinique* (Philadelphia: University of Pennsylvania Press, 2009); Mimi Sheller, *Citizenship from Below: Erotic Agency and Caribbean Freedom* (Durham, NC: Duke University Press, 2012); Aisha K. Finch, *Rethinking Slave Rebellion in Cuba: La Escalera and the Insurgencies of 1841–1844* (Chapel Hill: University of North Carolina Press, 2015); Camillia Cowling, *Conceiving Freedom: Women of Color, Gender, and the Abolition of Slavery in Havana and Rio de Janeiro* (Chapel Hill: University of North

Carolina Press, 2013); Natasha Lightfoot, *Troubling Freedom: Antigua and the Aftermath of British Emancipation* (Durham, NC: Duke University Press, 2015); Stephanie McCurry, *Confederate Reckoning: Power and Politics in the Civil War South* (Cambridge, MA: Harvard University Press, 2010); and McCurry, *Women's War: Fighting and Surviving the American Civil War* (Cambridge, MA: Harvard University Press, 2019).

7. Colin (Joan) Dayan, *Haiti, History, and the Gods* (Berkeley: University of California Press, 1995). On the sexualization of race, see Doris Garraway, *The Libertine Colony: Creolization in the Early French Caribbean* (Durham, NC: Duke University Press, 2005); and John D. Garrigus, "Redrawing the Color Line: Gender and the Social Construction of Race in Pre-Revolutionary Haiti," *Journal of Caribbean History* 30, nos. 1 & 2 (1996): 28–50. On North America, see Jill Lepore, *New York Burning: Liberty, Slavery, and Conspiracy in Eighteenth-Century Manhattan* (New York: Random House, 2005); and Lepore, *The Name of War: King Philip's War and the Origins of American Identity* (New York: Alfred A. Knopf, 1998).

8. See Saidiya Hartman, *Lose Your Mother: A Journey along the Atlantic Slave Route* (New York: Farrar, Straus and Giroux, 2007); Jennifer Morgan, *Laboring Women: Gender and Reproduction in New World Slavery* (Philadelphia: University of Pennsylvania Press, 2004); Sheller, *Citizenship from Below*; Lisa Lowe, *The Intimacies of Four Continents* (Durham, NC: Duke University Press, 2015); Rebecca J. Scott and Jean M. Hébrard, *Freedom Papers: An Atlantic Odyssey in the Age of Emancipation* (Cambridge, MA: Harvard University Press, 2012); and Lorelle Semley, *To Be Free and French: Citizenship in France's Atlantic Empire* (Cambridge: Cambridge University Press, 2017).

9. Morgan, *Laboring Women*, 138; and Marisa J. Fuentes, *Dispossessed Lives: Enslaved Women, Violence, and the Archive* (Philadelphia: University of Pennsylvania, 2016).

10. Garraway, *The Libertine Colony*, 22–23; Daina Ramey Berry and Leslie M. Harris, eds., *Sexuality and Slavery: Reclaiming Intimate Histories in the Americas* (Athens, GA: University of Georgia Press, 2018); and Trevor Burnard, *Mastery, Tyranny, and Desire: Thomas Thistlewood and His Slaves in the Anglo-Jamaican World* (Chapel Hill: University of North Carolina Press, 2004).

11. See Ada Ferrer, *Freedom's Mirror: Cuba and Haiti in the Age of Revolution* (New York: Cambridge University Press, 2014), 234; and Steven Hahn, "Forging Freedom," in Heuman and Burnard, *Routledge History*, 289–313.

12. Trevor Burnard, "The Atlantic Slave Trade," in Heuman and Burnard, *Routledge History*, 80–98.

13. Paul E. Lovejoy, "Slavery in Africa," in Heuman and Burnard, *Routledge History*, 35–51, 42; and John K. Thornton, *Africa and Africans in the Making of the Atlantic World, 1400–1800*, 2nd ed. (Cambridge: Cambridge University Press, 1998), 109.

14. Thornton, *Africa and Africans*, 117; and Stephanie E. Smallwood, *Saltwater Slavery: A Middle Passage from Africa to American Diaspora* (Cambridge, MA: Harvard University Press, 2007), 33–64.

15. The scope of this essay does not permit the attention to the interplay between Indigenous and African slaveries that the subject deserves. A rich literature has illuminated the spectrum of captivity, servitude, and slavery practiced in Indigenous and settler societies, as well as the relationship between war and the colonial enslavement of an estimated two to four million Indigenous people. In addition to the citations in note 3, see Brett Rushforth, *Bonds of Alliance: Indigenous and Atlantic Slaveries in New France* (Chapel Hill: University of North Carolina Press, 2012), 8; Cristina Snyder, *Slavery in Indian Country: The Changing*

Face of Captivity in Early America (Cambridge, MA: Harvard University Press, 2010); and James F. Brooks, *Captives & Cousins: Slavery, Kinship, and Community in the Southwest Borderlands* (Chapel Hill: University of North Carolina Press, 2002).

16. Robin Blackburn, *The American Crucible: Slavery, Emancipation and Human Rights* (London: Verso, 2011).

17. Matthew Restall, "Black Conquistadors: Armed Africans in Early Spanish America," in "The African Experience in Early Spanish America," ed. Matthew Restall and Jane Landers, special issue, *The Americas* 57, no. 2 (2000): 171–205; Jane Landers, "Transforming Bondsmen into Vassals: Arming Slaves in Colonial Spanish America," in *Arming Slaves: From Classical Times to the Modern Age*, ed. Christopher Leslie Brown and Philip D. Morgan (New Haven, CT: Yale University Press, 2006), 120–45; and Peter M. Voelz, *Slave and Soldier: The Military Impact of Blacks in the Colonial Americas* (New York: Garland, 1993).

18. Thornton, *Africa and Africans*, 41.

19. Restall, "Black Conquistadors," 173–75.

20. See Smallwood, *Saltwater Slavery*, 20–29, 77–79, 117.

21. Thornton, *Africa and Africans*, 117.

22. Vincent Brown, *The Reaper's Garden: Death and Power in the World of Atlantic Slavery* (Cambridge, MA: Harvard University Press, 2008), 33; Sowande' Mustakeem, *Slavery at Sea: Terror, Sex, and Sickness in the Middle Passage* (Urbana: University of Illinois Press, 2016); and Marcus Rediker, *The Slave Ship: A Human History* (New York: Penguin Books, 2007).

23. Gad Heuman and Trevor Burnard, "Introduction," in Heuman and Burnard, *Routledge History*, 1–18, 5. Compare, however, Brown's important analysis of "mortuary politics," *Reaper's Garden*; Vincent Brown, "Social Death and Political Life in the Study of Slavery," *American Historical Review* 114, no. 5 (2009): 1231–49; and Daina Ramey Berry, *The Price for Their Pound of Flesh: The Value of the Enslaved, from Womb to Grave, in the Building of a Nation* (Boston: Beacon Press, 2017). See also Terri L. Snyder, *The Power to Die: Slavery and Suicide in British North America* (New York: New York University Press, 2015).

24. Smallwood, *Saltwater Slavery*, 27.

25. Lovejoy, "Slavery in Africa," 40; quote in David Eltis, "Revolution, War, Empire," 46; and Smallwood, *Saltwater Slavery*, 83–84.

26. Eltis, "Revolution, War, Empire," 42, 46.

27. Morgan, *Laboring Women*; Warren, *New England Bound*; Fischer, *Suspect Relations*; and Ira Berlin, *Many Thousands Gone: The First Two Centuries of Slavery in North America* (Cambridge, MA: Harvard University Press, 1998).

28. Eltis, "Revolution, War, Empire," 46.

29. Ben Vinson and Herbert S. Klein, *African Slavery in Latin America and the Caribbean*, 2nd ed. (New York: Oxford University Press, 2007); and Peter Blanchard, *Under the Flags of Freedom: Slave Soldiers and the Wars of Independence in Spanish South America* (Pittsburgh, PA: University of Pittsburgh Press, 2008).

30. Garraway, *The Libertine Colony*; and Burnard, *Mastery*. On violence committed by plantation mistresses, see Thavolia Glymph, *Out of the House of Bondage: The Transformation of the Plantation Household* (New York: Cambridge University Press, 2008); and Stephanie E. Jones-Rogers, *They Were Her Property: White Women as Slave Owners in the American South* (New Haven, CT: Yale University Press, 2019).

31. Morgan, *Laboring Women*, 138; and Barbara Bush, "Hard Labor: Women, Childbirth, and Resistance in Caribbean Slave Societies," in *More Than Chattel: Black Women and Slavery in the Americas*, ed. David Barry Gaspar and Darlene Clark Hine (Bloomington: Indiana

University Press, 1996), 193–217. On abolitionism and control of reproduction, see Sasha Turner, *Contested Bodies: Pregnancy, Childrearing, and Slavery in Jamaica* (Philadelphia: University of Pennsylvania Press, 2017). See also Marie Jenkins Schwartz, *Birthing a Slave: Motherhood and Medicine in the Antebellum South* (Cambridge, MA: Harvard University Press, 2006).

32. James Sidbury, "Resistance to Slavery," in Heuman and Burnard, *Routledge History*, 204–20, 214; and David Richardson, "Shipboard Revolts: African Authority, and the Atlantic Slave Trade," in "New Perspectives on the Transatlantic Slave Trade," ed. David Eltis and Philip Morgan, special issue, *William and Mary Quarterly* 58, no. 1 (2001): 69–92.

33. See Scott and Hébrard, *Freedom Papers*,18.

34. Marcus Rediker, "The African Origins of the Amistad Rebellion, 1839," *International Review of Social History* 58, no. 21 (2013): 15–34; and Rediker, *The Amistad Rebellion: An Atlantic Odyssey of Slavery and Freedom* (New York: Penguin Books, 2013).

35. John K. Thornton, " 'I Am the Subject of the King of Congo': African Political Ideology and the Haitian Revolution," *Journal of World History* 4, no. 2 (1993): 181–214.

36. See Philippe Girard, "*Rebelles* with a Cause: Women in the Haitian War of Independence, 1802–04," *Gender & History* 21, no. 1 (2009): 60–85; Girard, "French Atrocities during the Haitian War of Independence," *Journal of Genocide Research* 15, no. 2 (2013): 133–49; Richard Price, *Alabi's World* (Baltimore: Johns Hopkins University Press, 1990); Sidbury, "Resistance to Slavery"; Alvin O. Thompson, *Flight to Freedom: African Runaways and Maroons in the Americas* (Kingston: University of the West Indies Press, 2006); and Jane Landers, "Maroon Women in Colonial Spanish America: Case Studies in the Circum-Caribbean from the Sixteenth through the Eighteenth Centuries," in Gaspar and Hine, *Beyond Bondage*, 3–18.

37. Jenny Sharpe, *Ghosts of Slavery: A Literary Archaeology of Black Women's Lives* (Minneapolis: University of Minnesota Press, 2003); Dubois, "Gendered Freedom"; Gad Heuman, ed., *Out of the House of Bondage: Runaways, Resistance and Marronage in Africa and the New World* (London: Frank Cass, 1986); Kamau Brathwaite, "Nanny, Palmares, and the Caribbean Maroon Connexion," in *Maroon Heritage: Archaeological Ethnographic and Historical Perspectives*, ed. Kofi E. Agorsah (Kingston: Canoe Press, 1994), 119–38; Bush, *Women and Slavery*, 125–50; Sylviane A. Diouf, *Slavery's Exiles: The Story of the American Maroons* (New York: New York University Press, 2014); and Michael Craton, *Testing the Chains: Resistance to Slavery in the British West Indies* (Ithaca, NY: Cornell University Press, 1982).

38. See, among others, Barbara Bush, *Slave Women*; Bush, " 'The Family Tree Is Not Cut': Women and Cultural Resistance in Slave Family Life in the British Caribbean," in *In Resistance: Studies in African, Caribbean, and Afro-American History*, ed. Gary Y. Okihiro (Amherst: University of Massachusetts Press, 1986), 117–132; and Stephanie Camp, *Closer to Freedom: Enslaved Women and Everyday Resistance in the Plantation South* (Chapel Hill: University of North Carolina Press, 2004). See also Jane G. Landers and Barry M. Robinson, eds., *Slaves, Subjects, and Subversives: Blacks in Colonial Latin America* (Albuquerque: University of New Mexico Press, 2006); Laurent Dubois, *A Colony of Citizens: Revolution and Slave Emancipation in the French Caribbean, 1787–1804* (Chapel Hill: University of North Carolina Press, 2004); and Matt Childs, *The Aponte Rebellion in Cuba and the Struggle against Slavery* (Chapel Hill: University of North Carolina Press, 2006).

39. Aisha Finch, " 'What Looks Like a Revolution': Enslaved Women and the Gendered Terrain of Slave Insurgencies in Cuba, 1843–1844," *Journal of Women's History* 26, no. 1 (2014): 112–34, esp. 113, 120; and Finch, *Rethinking Slave Rebellion*.

40. Camp, *Closer to Freedom.*
41. Gad Heuman, "Slave Rebellions," in Heuman and Burnard, *Routledge History*, 220–33.
42. Ibid., 222.
43. See ibid., 220–33; and Finch, "What Looks Like," 112–34.
44. On the US Civil War, see McCurry, *Confederate Reckoning*; and McCurry, *Women's War.*
45. Brown and Morgan, *Arming Slaves.*
46. Brown, "The Arming of Slaves in Comparative Perspective," in ibid., 330–53, 331.
47. Ibid., 337.
48. David Geggus, "The Arming of Slaves in the Haitian Revolution," in Brown and Morgan, *Arming Slaves*, 210.
49. Brown, "Arming Slaves in Comparative," 333.
50. Kathleen DuVal, *Independence Lost: Lives on the Edge of the American Revolution* (New York: Random House, 2015); and Jane G. Landers, *Atlantic Creoles in the Age of Revolution* (Cambridge, MA: Harvard University Press, 2010).
51. John Garrigus, *Before Haiti: Race and Citizenship in French Saint-Domingue* (New York: Palgrave Macmillan, 2006); and Voelz, *Slave and Soldier.*
52. Landers, "Transforming Bondsmen," 120–45.
53. David Geggus, *Haitian Revolutionary Studies* (Bloomington: Indiana University Press, 2002); Jane G. Landers, *Atlantic Creoles*; Peter Blanchard, "The Slave Soldiers of Spanish South America: From Independence to Abolition," in Brown and Morgan, *Arming Slaves*, 255–73; and Seth Miesel, " 'The Fruit of Freedom': Slaves and Citizens in Early Republican Argentina," in Landers and Robinson, *Slaves, Subjects*, 273–306. On Saint-Domingue, see Geggus, "The Haitian Revolution"; and Laurent Dubois, "Citizen Soldiers: Emancipation and Military Service in the Revolutionary French Caribbean," in Brown and Morgan, *Arming Slaves*, 233–54.
54. Eltis, "Revolution, War, Empire," 48.
55. Ibid., 41–45.
56. George Reid Andrews, *Afro-Latin America, 1800–2000* (Oxford: Oxford University Press, 2004), 75; and Rebecca Scott, *Slave Emancipation in Cuba: The Transition to Free Labor, 1860–1899* (Pittsburgh, PA: University of Pittsburgh Press, 2000).
57. Lisa Lowe, "The Intimacies of Four Continents," in *Haunted by Empire: Geographies of Intimacy in North America*, ed. Ann Laura Stoler (Durham, NC: Duke University Press, 2006), 191–212.
58. Rashauna Johnson, *Slavery's Metropolis: Unfree Labor in New Orleans during the Age of Revolutions* (Cambridge: Cambridge University Press, 2016); DuVal, *Independence Lost*, 13–14, 43; Miles, *Ties That Bind*; Semley, *To Be Free and French*; Lowe, *Intimacies*; Landers, *Atlantic Creoles*; and Scott and Hébrard, *Freedom Papers.*
59. See, among others, Peter Blanchard, "The Slave Soldiers," 268; Cassandra Pybus, *Epic Journeys of Freedom: Runaway Slaves of the American Revolution and Their Global Quest for Liberty* (Boston: Beacon Press, 2006), 200; and Michael Zeuske, "Two Stories of Gender and Slave Emancipation in Cienfuegos and Santa Clara, Central Cuba: A Microhistorical Approach to the Atlantic World," in *Gender and Emancipation in the Atlantic World*, ed. Pamela Scully and Diana Paton (Durham, NC: Duke University Press, 2005), 181–98.
60. Andrews, *Afro-Latin America*, 57; and Blanchard, *Under the Flags*, 141–59.
61. Blanchard, "Slave Soldiers," 268.
62. Blanchard, *Under the Flags*, 157, 152.

63. Geggus, "Slave and Free," 265.

64. Discussed in Dubois, "Gendered Freedom," 66–67; original document translated by Dubois in Laurent Dubois and John D. Garrigus, eds., *Slave Revolution in the Caribbean: A Brief History with Documents, 1789–1804* (New York: Bedford, 2006), 136–38.

65. McCurry, *Confederate Reckoning*; and Landers, "Transforming Bondsmen," 127.

66. Gary Nash, *The Forgotten Fifth: African Americans in the Age of Revolution* (Cambridge, MA: Harvard University Press, 2006).

67. Dubois, *Colony of Citizens*.

68. For Saint-Domingue, see Jeremy D. Popkin, *You Are All Free: The Haitian Revolution and the Abolition of Slavery* (Cambridge: Cambridge University Press, 2010).

69. Landers, *Atlantic Creoles*, 15–54; Scott and Hébrard, *Freedom Papers*; and Lisa A. Lindsay and John Wood Sweet, eds., *Biography and the Black Atlantic* (Philadelphia: University of Pennsylvania Press, 2013).

70. Geggus, *Haitian Revolutionary Studies*; quotation in Landers, *Atlantic Creoles*, 89.

71. Pybus, *Epic Journeys*; Simon Schama and Caryl Phillips, *Rough Crossings: The Slaves, the British, and the American Revolution* (New York: Ecco, 2005); and Polasky, *Revolutions without Borders*, 75, 83–85, 99–106.

72. In Brian Brunius and David McCarthy, *Slavery and the Making of America*, directed by William R. Grant, aired February 9, 2005 (New York: Ambrose, 2005), DVD.

73. Carolyn E. Fick, *The Making of Haiti: The Saint Domingue Revolution from Below* (Knoxville: University of Tennessee Press, 1990); and Popkin, *You Are All Free*.

74. Proclamation, June 21, 1793, Polverel, Sonthonax, Dxxv9/90, doc. 12, Archives Nationales.

75. Elizabeth Colwill, "Gendering the June Days: Race, Masculinity, and Slave Emancipation in Saint Domingue," *Journal of Haitian Studies* 15, no. 1–2 (2009): 103–24; Colwill, "Fêtes de l'hymen"; and Sue Peabody, "Négresse, Mulâtresse, Citoyenne: Gender and Emancipation in the French Caribbean, 1650–1848," in Scully and Paton, *Gender and Slave*, 56–78.

76. Laurent Dubois, *Avengers of the New World: The Story of the Haitian Revolution* (Cambridge, MA: Harvard University Press, 2004).

77. Sheller, *Citizenship from Below*; Colwill, "Freedwomen's Familial Politics," 71–89; and Semley, *To Be Free and French*, 24–68.

78. Girard, "Rebelles"; and Girard, "French Atrocities."

79. See Leonora Sansay, *Secret History; or, The Horrors of St. Domingo*, ed. Michael J. Drexler (Peterborough, Ont.: Broadview, 2007).

80. Sheller, *Citizenship from Below*. See also Fick, "The Haitian Revolution," 394–414; and John Garrigus, "Race, Gender, and Virtue in Haiti's Failed Foundational Fiction: 'La mulâtre comme il y a peu de blanches' (1803)," in *The Color of Liberty: Histories of Race in France*, ed. Sue Peabody and Tyler Stovall (Durham, NC: Duke University Press, 2003), 73–94.

81. Catherine Davies et al., *South American Independence: Gender, Politics, Text* (Liverpool: Liverpool University Press, 2011), 11.

82. Andrews, *Afro-Latin America*, 55.

83. See Victor Davis Hanson, *The Western Way of War: Infantry Battle in Classical Greece* (New York: Alfred A. Knopf, 1989); and Geoffrey Parker, "Introduction: The Western Way of War," in *The Cambridge History of Warfare*, ed. Geoffrey Parker (Cambridge: Cambridge University Press, 2005), 1–11.

84. Judith Butler, *Frames of War: When Is Life Grievable?* (New York: Verso, 2009).

85. Blanchard, *Under the Flags*. In Spanish America, free womb laws were the "contested outcome of independence wars directed (in large part) by masters but won (in large part) by slaves" (Andrews, *Afro-Latin America*, 64). See Rebecca J. Scott, "Gradual Abolition and the Dynamics of Slave Emancipation in Cuba, 1868–86," *The Hispanic American Historical Review* 63, no. 3 (1983): 449–77.
86. Cowling, *Conceiving Freedom*, 9.
87. Lowe, "The Intimacies," 204. See also Moon-Ho Jung, *Coolies and Cane: Race, Labor, and Sugar in the Age of Emancipation* (Baltimore: Johns Hopkins University Press, 2006).
88. Quoted by Ann Laura Stoler, "Intimidations of Empire: Predicaments of the Tactile and Unseen," in Ann Laura Stoler, *Haunted by Empire*, 1–22, 11.

SELECT BIBLIOGRAPHY

Berry, Daina Ramey. *The Price for Their Pound of Flesh: The Value of the Enslaved, from Womb to Grave, in the Building of a Nation*. Boston: Beacon Press, 2017.

Berry, Daina Ramey, and Leslie M. Harris, eds. *Sexuality and Slavery: Reclaiming Intimate Histories in the Americas*. Athens, GA: University of Georgia Press, 2018.

Blackburn, Robin. *The American Crucible: Slavery, Emancipation and Human Rights*. London: Verso, 2011.

Brown, Christopher Leslie, and Philip D. Morgan, eds. *Arming Slaves: From Classical Times to the Modern Age*. New Haven, CT: Yale University Press, 2006.

Brown, Vincent. *The Reaper's Garden: Death and Power in the World of Atlantic Slavery*. Cambridge, MA: Harvard University Press, 2008.

Bush, Barbara. *Slave Women in Caribbean Society: 1650–1838*. Bloomington: Indiana University Press, 1990.

Campbell, Gwyn, Suzanne Miers, and Joseph C. Miller, eds. *Women and Slavery*. Vol. 2, *The Modern Atlantic*. Athens, OH: Ohio University Press, 2007.

Davis, David Brion. *The Problem of Slavery in the Age of Revolution: 1770–1823*. Ithaca, New York: Cornell University Press, 1975, 1999.

Dayan, Colin. *Haiti, History, and the Gods*. Berkeley: University of California Press, 1998.

Dubois, Laurent. *A Colony of Citizens: Revolution and Slave Emancipation in the French Caribbean, 1787–1804*. Chapel Hill: University of North Carolina Press, 2004.

DuVal, Kathleen. *Independence Lost: Lives on the Edge of the American Revolution*. New York: Random House, 2015.

Finch, Aisha K. *Rethinking Slave Rebellion in Cuba: La Escalera and the Insurgencies of 1841–1844*. Chapel Hill: University of North Carolina Press, 2015.

Geggus, David Patrick. *Haitian Revolutionary Studies*. Bloomington: Indiana University Press, 2002.

Hartman, Saidiya. *Lose Your Mother: A Journey along the Atlantic Slave Route*. New York: Farrar, Straus, and Giroux, 2007.

Heuman, Gad, and Trevor Burnard, eds. *The Routledge History of Slavery*. London: Routledge, 2011.

Miles, Tiya. *The Dawn of Detroit: A Chronicle of Slavery and Freedom in the City of the Straits*. New York: New Press, 2017.

Miles, Tiya. *Ties That Bind: The Story of an Afro-Cherokee Family in Slavery and Freedom*. Berkeley: University of California Press, 2005.

Morgan, Jennifer L. *Laboring Women: Gender and Reproduction in New World Slavery*. Philadelphia: University of Pennsylvania Press, 2004.

Mustakeem, Sowande' M. *Slavery at Sea: Terror, Sex, and Sickness in the Middle Passage*. Urbana: University of Illinois Press, 2016.

Paton, Diana. *No Bond but the Law: Punishment, Race, and Gender in Jamaican State Formation*. Durham, NC: Duke University Press, 2004.

Scott, Rebecca J., and Jean M. Hébrard. *Freedom Papers: An Atlantic Odyssey in the Age of Emancipation*. Cambridge, MA: Harvard University Press, 2012.

Scully, Pamela, and Diana Paton, eds. *Gender and Slave Emancipation in the Atlantic World*. Durham, NC: Duke University Press, 2005.

Smallwood, Stephanie E. *Saltwater Slavery: A Middle Passage from Africa to American Diaspora*. Cambridge, MA: Harvard University Press, 2008.

CHAPTER 6

....

SOCIETY, MASS WARFARE, AND GENDER IN EUROPE DURING AND AFTER THE REVOLUTIONARY AND NAPOLEONIC WARS

....

ALAN FORREST

REVOLUTIONARY ideologies alone cannot explain the social effects of the French Revolutionary and Napoleonic Wars (1792–1815) or the changes in gender relations that resulted from them. They played their part, especially during the later 1790s, when France was extending its imperium across much of the continent and sought to impose its political values on the lands it conquered. But just as important was the sheer scale of warfare in these years. Mass armies were raised by all the belligerent states. Extensive financial and material support was demanded in the form of taxes and tributes, requisitions, and quartering; and civilians were called on to provide clothing, armaments, and medical care for the troops.[1] Some historians, most notably David Bell and Jean-Yves Guiomar, have argued that these wars should be thought of as the first instances in history of *total war*—war that affected all classes of society, regardless of their ethnicity, gender, or race, and that massively mobilized economic and cultural resources.[2] The term total war has been contested, not least by historians of twentieth-century warfare, but there is no doubting the ferocity with which these wars were fought or the overarching ambition of the powers engaged in them.[3] Militaries deliberately targeted civilians, most notably by the use of economic blockades like the Continental System (1806–14), imposed by Napoleon in response to a naval blockade of the French coast enacted by the British government.[4] They produced their share of massacres and atrocities.[5] And they had lasting effects for societies, economies, cultures, and politics that bear comparison with the world wars of the twentieth century.[6]

The French Revolutionary and Napoleonic Wars had great impact on the social and gender order of Europe, but research has focused principally on armies and campaigns, states and nations, and there has been little attempt to use gender as a discrete analytical category. This has changed since the late 1980s, when women's and gender historians started to work on the period, focusing first on the French Revolution (1789–99)[7] and later on the Napoleonic Empire (1804–14/15) and the French Revolutionary and Napoleonic Wars.[8] As a consequence, there is now a substantial body of work that not only regards "gender" as an important subject in its own right, but also uses it as a methodology that explains the importance of constructions of femininity and masculinity, both in the political discourse of the time and for war mobilization and demobilization.[9] But some argue that there is still a "perception gap" and that much mainstream scholarship on these wars ignores the work of women's and gender history. Three themes are central to this analysis: first, the major changes in warfare in Europe during this period and the costs they imposed on society; second, the interactions between soldiers and the civilian population; and third, the ways in which women were affected by and contributed to the war effort.

New Mass Warfare and the Social Costs of War

As the conflict spread inexorably across the continent, from Portugal in the west to Russia in the east, few remained unaffected by its impact. Three European powers—France, Austria, and Great Britain—were at war virtually continuously from the formation of the First Coalition in 1792 until Napoleon's defeat at Waterloo in June 1815.[10] Across Europe, millions of men were called on to fight, whether by conscription, by impressment, or though the enrollment of volunteers, as the armies of all the belligerent states grew to an unprecedented size. The "nation in arms" that France instituted and others copied did not involve everyone directly in the fighting (that remained largely the prerogative of young, able-bodied men). But it went far to define male experience in these years and to identify the capacity to endure military violence as a basic characteristic of masculinity.[11] In some families, this endurance was not limited to a single generation: men whose fathers volunteered in 1792 to defend French territory against attack would themselves be in uniform in 1814 as France once more faced an Allied invasion. For so many men, this was a war without end, a war that determined their chances of marriage, of fathering children, and of survival into old age.[12]

Women were not conscripted in any of the belligerent nations, but virtually all the armies of the era seem to have boasted a few "heroic virgins," women who dressed as men and fought courageously alongside their male comrades. The legend of these women was used in war propaganda to shame men into battle and in postwar memory to demonstrate the breadth of patriotic war support in the population; those female soldiers who died in battle and posed no threat to the postwar gender order found an honorable place in nineteenth-century nationalist histories.[13] The small number of French revolutionary "amazons," who made no secret of their sex and demanded the right to bear arms as women and, with it, equal citizenship for women, were perceived negatively by the public, even by male revolutionaries, because they challenged the dominant ideas about the gender order.[14]

In every country, war marked out separate spheres for men and women—but not only between men and women. Just as important were the distinctions it forged between combatants and noncombatants, soldiers and civilians, the young and the old, as it increasingly prioritized the needs of the armies in the competition for scarce resources. Large numbers of women, children, and the elderly were left to cope as best they could, with little or no welfare provision to which they could turn. The wars affected whole communities, changing established assumptions about work and leisure and leaving death and destruction in their wake. They would leave deep scars—economic, social, demographic, and emotional—that took decades, if not generations, to heal. Governments called on their people to provide the resources necessary for waging war on this scale. Taxes rose, requisitions were ordered, art treasures were seized, and local economies suffered twenty years of dislocation as coasts were blockaded, industry turned to war production, and agriculture was called on to feed the mass armies that now crisscrossed the continent.

Not all young men could be mobilized. No army—not even the French in 1813 after the calamitous losses suffered in Russia during the previous winter—required or wanted the services of every young man. Generals needed soldiers who knew something of their trade, who could handle weapons and sustain the line under fire; the last thing they wanted was an uninitiated mass of youngsters who would crumble at the first hint of danger. Conscripts had to be trained, armed, and equipped, which required the services of noncombatants; leatherworkers, gunsmiths, saddlers, and seamstresses all had a vital part to play, with the consequence that, though the whole population was not required for the actual fighting, it was mobilized for war support. No country, even in wartime, can afford to leave its fields untilled or its factories unmanned. In the Napoleonic era, though the phrase was never used, wars were fought on the home front as well as in the regiments. And on that home front, men and women assumed different roles, depending on their proximity to the armies and the moving front lines, their social status and skills, their specific location (in towns, villages, or the countryside), and the dominant ideas of the gender order in their specific culture. Especially in the lower social strata, women's work complemented that of men in the daily struggle for survival. In the majority of households, men and women, married or not, shared the work of a family economy.[15]

Meanwhile, on campaign, the armies themselves needed civilian workers and military auxiliaries: sutlers to sell food and drink to soldiers; doctors, surgeons, and nurses for ambulances and infirmaries; carters to transport military supplies; gunsmiths to carry out repairs on damaged muskets; seamstresses to mend uniforms; and cobblers to produce thousands of army boots. Civilians, especially those whose homes were close to war fronts, were called on to increase their production targets to supply the armies, both their own and those of the invader. Women for the most part remained at home, as the armies traveled longer distances across the continent. But the armies were never a wholly masculine space. Indeed, the French army continued to call on the services of women as *cantinières* (sutlers) right through to the eve of the First World War, while the British army at Waterloo may have been accompanied by as many as 33,000 women, many of them army wives.[16] European armies had since time immemorial been accompanied by swarms of camp followers: women—and sometimes their young children—who accompanied their husbands and boyfriends, sold food and drink to the troops, and found employment as laundresses for the army. Others made a living from prostitution, selling sexual favors to the men. Armies had tended to treat them with tolerance in an age when there was no provision for military brothels of the kind that would be familiar in twentieth-century wars.[17]

With the increasing size of armies from the 1790s, however, attempts to reduce the number of women and children who followed the armies became ever more strict.[18] Camp followers came with a cost, though only the Prussians refused to allow women in the army altogether after the dramatic defeats at Jena and Auerstedt in 1806, where the large numbers of camp followers had made an orderly retreat impossible. Back at home, Prussia's women were expected to contribute to the war effort in a multiplicity of ways. In the absence of male labor following the introduction of conscription in 1813, many had to assume the hard, manual jobs on the farm that their husbands or brothers would customarily have carried out. One way or another, the wars affected their lives and challenged traditional gender roles.[19]

War did not spare civilians its physical ravages. Towns were besieged, villages and cottages torched, farms looted, and livestock driven away as rival armies marched across their neighbors' territory, often pillaging as they went. In German central Europe, the passage of Napoleon's Grande Armée on its way to Russia in 1812 resulted in the seizure of up to 90 percent of horses and cattle, depriving many of their means of making a livelihood and leaving local agriculture bereft of the draught animals on which it depended. Routes to markets were disrupted, roads and bridges cut, and public buildings requisitioned for the use of the military. The result was an economic hecatomb because everything was sacrificed to the needs of the army. As for crops and flour stocks, the military took what it needed—Napoleon's army lived off the lands it marched through—and desperate soldiers often stole or pillaged what the army did not requisition legally. The French were not alone in this. Where armies passed, the countryside was often left scarred and stripped bare of the resources local peasants needed to keep themselves alive through the following winter.[20] But, it should be stressed, such despoliation was not without precedent. The wars of the seventeenth and eighteenth centuries had prepared Europe for destruction of this kind.[21] More than a century after the Thirty Years' War (1618–48), people still shuddered at the memory of Swedish depredations across southern Germany.

Soldiers carried diseases, too, which did not spare the communities they passed through, and after great battles neighboring cities were transformed into giant military hospitals to cope with the wounded and dying. In Saxony in 1812–13, diseases brought by soldiers killed as many as 10 percent of local people and a far higher proportion of Leipzig's doctors and nurses.[22] And as foreign territories were invaded and occupied, new levels of violence were unleashed on the local population. In some areas, large numbers were displaced from their homes, as happened in Hamburg in December 1813, when some 20,000 poor who were unable to feed themselves—around a fifth of the population—were forced by Napoleon's army to leave the city.[23] As refugees, they had to load their possessions onto carts and seek safety elsewhere, to relatives, to the open countryside, to other cities. Townspeople could so easily become pawns in the fighting, as when the British bombarded Copenhagen in 1807 or when the Russians torched Moscow in 1812, imposing a terrible price on the citizenry. Major battles were occasionally fought in and around cities, reducing their suburbs and surrounding villages to piles of rubble; Leipzig in 1813 is the most famous example.[24]

Civilians were the victims of economic warfare, too. With the imposition of the British blockade and Napoleon's Continental System, civilians were deliberately targeted as states used the economy as a weapon of war. Indeed, the Continental System became Napoleon's principal weapon against Britain after the Battle of Trafalgar in October 1805 had removed any possibility of a successful attack from the sea. His purpose was deterrence: if civilians suffered economically, if traders' profits fell and companies went bankrupt, and if Britain was deprived of its markets for colonial goods, the Commons would soon tire of war and sue for peace.[25] Civilians here were seen as legitimate collateral damage. Had the Continental System been fully implemented, much of Russia and the Baltic would have been condemned to penury.[26]

ENCOUNTERS OF SOLDIERS AND CIVILIANS

Whereas for the strategists of war the civilian population might be commodified and treated as an unclassified, ungendered whole, for the soldiers who passed through villages or laid siege to towns and cities, the people they encountered were real human beings, often suffering terrible deprivations and apprehensive of the threats that the arrival of armed men posed for their communities. Troops spread fear in civilian communities, especially where, as in Spain, that fear was fueled by rumor and by eyewitness accounts of what had happened elsewhere. The aftermath of a battle was often bloody, with troops keen to avenge themselves on the people they held responsible for their suffering and for the deaths of their colleagues. It was a more or less accepted practice, indeed, that when a town had held out against a besieging army, its fall was followed by a period of looting and destruction, in which anyone offering resistance to the victorious army might be cut down on the spot. In such reprisal attacks, men and women could expect to be treated differently, though, in one way or another, all were made to suffer. Men—especially men of military age or those caught bearing weapons—could expect little mercy. They risked death at the hands of an enemy who had often few resources for holding prisoners and who feared that they might take up arms against them in a future conflict. Some women shared their fate, and atrocities against civilians were noted on both sides.[27]

More commonly, women were treated as trophies of war and were used by the victorious troops for their sexual pleasure. Rape was not uncommon, though it was rarely recorded. The women of the towns the soldiers passed through were treated as fair game, especially when, following the raising of a siege, an army was let loose on the community for twenty-four to forty-eight hours.[28] But we still know very little about sexual violence in warfare in this period. Autobiographical accounts indicate that some of the soldiers were clearly upset by what they experienced; there is evidence of distaste, even moral outrage, at the actions of the enemy and, on occasion, their own troops.[29] Although military law in most armies forbade rape and officers could impose severe penalties on those convicted, there was little consistency. In a war fought by mass armies and manned by young conscripts, the imposition of a tight moral code was hard to achieve.

In many parts of Europe, French victory led to occupation and long-term exploitation, a fate shared by some larger powers, most notably by Prussia after its devastating defeat in the Battle of Jena and Auerstedt (October 1806).[30] Lasting occupation and exploitation, however, also provided a breeding ground for resistance, protest, and insurrection, with the consequence that states showed little tolerance of dissent, often responding with immediate and disproportionate reprisals against civilians. In many parts of the Napoleonic Empire, officials and gendarmes could seem terribly heavy handed in their dealing with political protestors, leaving local people with a sense of outrage and hurt. In Spain, brutality was legion, and it would be immortalized, though not always accurately, by the Spanish artist Francisco Goya in his series of etchings, *The Disasters of War*, created between 1810 and 1820.[31]

Extreme violence was not restricted to the Iberian Peninsula, nor was it the sole preserve of soldiers. In Hamburg and in other cities in northern Germany, including the former Prussian territories of the Kingdom of Westphalia, in the winter of 1813, conscripts resisted incorporation into Napoleon's army and ordinary people, including many women, took to the streets in anti-French riots. In the violence that followed, crowds destroyed palisades and attacked customs posts, threw French officials into canals, and tore down French flags and imperial eagles. But the brutality of the army's response only made matters worse, creating a welling up of anti-French sentiment.[32] In other occupied regions of the Napoleonic Empire, too, the French faced increased resistance the longer war and occupation lasted, such as opposition to the conscription of more and more young men; to rising taxes, tributes, and tolls; and to the costs of quartering, equipping, and feeding the large armies in the face of economic decline.[33]

Relations between an occupying army and the civil population were seldom easy—and they were all the more fractured when preexisting tensions and a sense of cultural or political superiority by the French was present. Nowhere was this truer than in southern Spain, where French troops were accosted by peasants bearing primitive weapons and taking guidance from their priests in a sort of holy war against the invader. Similarly, in southern Italy, the French army encountered resistance from civilians they perceived as "barbaric." In the Calabrian town of Lauria, for example, Marshal André Masséna was faced with house-to-house fighting and heavy losses and ordered that the town be torched and its inhabitants slaughtered as they fled in April 1806. More than 700—some 10 percent of the population—were killed in the fighting. Another 341 were taken prisoner to be shot or hanged in the days that followed.[34]

This, according to Philip Dwyer, was a massacre symptomatic of many that occurred when the army was exhausted by prolonged guerrilla fighting and in which the French described priests as "holding bibles in one hand and weapons in the other." Dwyer admits that the attack may have been carried out for purely military purposes, as the standard tactics of a counterinsurgency campaign. But he makes two important points. First, in this, as in many other cases, the commanders who ordered the killing "dressed it in the rhetoric of an enlightened army fighting the forces of ignorance and superstition." And second, there was nothing exceptional, nothing even unusual, about these tactics. It happened wherever the French army encountered armed resistance from civilians or where guerrilla fighters took refuge among them. "It is safe to say," he concludes, "that there was not a region or country invaded by the French in which massacres did not occur. In Belgium, in Germany, in Switzerland, Holland, Italy, Spain and Russia whole towns were razed and their inhabitants massacred."[35] And though in the imperial armies such repression was systemic, there were reported massacres across Europe when armies were let loose on civilian populations. Killing, rape, and indiscipline were not a French monopoly. The British in the Iberian Peninsula committed atrocities of their own, as did Prussian troops in 1814, in a belated act of vengeance for what they had suffered at Jena and Auerstedt. Moreover, the Cossacks were feared in central and western Europe as much by opposing armies as by civilian populations—to the extent that their very name could be used to excuse military failures.[36]

How can we explain this level of violence? It is undeniable that large armies traveled far across the European continent, and, removed from the morally constraining influences of home, they may indeed have been tempted to commit crimes against civilians, especially sexual assaults on women. But does the explanation go deeper? Michael J. Hughes suggests that there was something more, that "the aggressive militaristic character of Napoleonic France was reinforced through the inculcation of a concept of masculinity that required the soldiers of the Consulate and Empire to demonstrate their manhood through displays of their martial and sexual prowess."[37] The two were closely linked in all European armies, tied in, too, with a very masculine notion of honor whereby the young men in a community became soldiers to fight the enemy and protect their own women and children from attack. Even those armies that, for reasons of good discipline, sought to exclude women to reinforce their separate identity knew that this goal was unattainable; hence, their aim became more modest: to incorporate women into regimental life without damaging military efficiency.[38] It was never an easy balance to strike. The fantasy of bright uniforms, with all their associations of heroism, was, in Scott Hughes Myerly's words, "especially appealing to those who wanted to bolster their self-esteem and sexual appeal."[39] The swagger of military parades, where soldiers made a show of martial masculinity before an admiring audience of women and girls, had always had sexual connotations. And the songs that the armies sang, whether marching songs when on duty or drinking songs in their leisure hours, made no secret of their sexual desires. But the aggressively heterosexual tone of many of the songs in the Napoleonic armies suggests something more: a willingness to motivate soldiers by offering them sexual trophies as a reward for their efforts.[40]

There was a sense, too, in many armies of the period that other cultures were inferior, less heroic, less masculine than their own, which made taking their women in war less morally reprehensible. Stereotypes were rife—Prussians considering Poles and Russians less civilized than themselves, northern Europeans showing scant regard for the peasant communities of the Mediterranean, the French scorning the rural poverty they encountered in Spain.[41] Some of the worst atrocities were committed when troops were faced by communities they barely understood and that had customs and approaches to fighting that filled them with terror: Cossack horsemen, for instance, in the east or slave rebellions in the Caribbean. Again, there could be a strong element of vengeance for the high losses they themselves had suffered at rebel hands or a sense that they had to make examples of those who had abused and massacred their own soldiers.

The expedition sent out by Napoleon in 1802 to recapture Saint-Domingue and reimpose slavery in the colony soon found itself with a terrible reputation for mass slaughter, if not wholesale genocide. Clearly, the orders did not come from Paris, and a great deal of responsibility for the excessive levels of retribution must lie with local field commanders, men sickened by the torture suffered by their soldiers and by the indiscriminate massacre of White planters on the island. General Charles Leclerc, commander of the French forces sent to Haiti, ordered that captured guerrillas and runaway slaves should be shot or hanged, extreme measures he justified by reference to the violence of the context in which he was operating. But though he might talk of the need for "a war of extermination," there was no attempt to slaughter the entire Black population or to conduct the ethnic cleansing of the island. Contemporary observers were content to comment that these were isolated massacres, a normal byproduct of war.

But Leclerc was replaced in 1802 by General Donatien de Rochambeau, who went much further. In the months that followed, he made clear that he wanted to speed up the cycle of death. Those convicted were to be drowned in batches, rather as they had been in the Loire under the Terror; and he added new tortures of his own or reinvented cruel forms of execution that had been abandoned for decades. These included burning at the stake, an occasional crucifixion, or the particularly horrid fate that the Spaniards had inflicted on Natives during their conquest of Hispaniola and the British had visited on Maroons in Jamaica: "the use of dogs to flush out rebels from the woods during military operations, but also to devour rebels in makeshift arenas."[42] In the colonial sphere there were few, if any, limits to the suffering that Europeans felt justified to incite.

WOMEN AND WAR

While on campaign, armies were a largely male preserve, with camps and barracks becoming an increasingly segregated space. Generals preferred to maintain control over their men, to prevent them from fraternizing in the wider community, in the hope that isolation in a martial and masculine environment would encourage the spread of military values. War was a test of masculinity in which civilians had little part to play. As we have seen, women were rarely directly engaged in the fighting of the official armies: the number who cross-dressed, hid their sex, or simply accompanied their husbands to the battlefield to take part in armed combat was never as great as the symbolic importance of the few might suggest.[43] In the whole of the French army, historians have discovered not more than fifty to a hundred. In Prussia, not more than twenty are known.[44] Most were discovered only because of injuries or death. The majority came from the lower classes, like the soldiers, and they joined the ranks for a variety of motives: patriotism, a desire for adventure, the hope of being able to stay with male relatives, or the lack of other prospects or of protection from the evils of war.[45]

Like other civilians, women were poorly protected from the violence of war. To join or support the army was a strategy of safekeeping, especially in guerrilla warfare, where women could become more involved. In the northern Italian valleys and later in southern Italy, Spain, and Russia, they took an active military role, harboring guerrilla fighters, bandits, smugglers, and others engaged in small wars against invading armies. As in all wars, they ran the risk of reprisals and degradation at the hands of the enemy, while those who associated with guerrilla fighters or regular soldiers risked forging a reputation for sexual immorality and loose living. Many women were caught up in operations over which they had no control—but that was not always the case, as whole communities might join in the battle against the invading army. In Andalusia and in western Russia, civilians—many of them peasants, including women—earned the hatred of invading troops by the acts of cruelty they perpetrated against them and by their refusal to hand over men whom the military condemned as terrorists. In Spain there are repeated accusations by the French of torture, of the killing and stripping of prisoners, of mutilation, and of sexual humiliation by village women.[46] Soldiers, it was claimed, were seized, stripped naked, and used as sexual trophies; some were subjected to the most gruesome tortures, having their genitals mutilated before being buried alive in the sand to die slowly in the Mediterranean heat, their bodies exposed and humiliated in front of the village community.

These stories are rarely proved, and some were surely exaggerated as they passed from mouth to mouth or camp to camp or were repeated in soldiers' letters back home, taking bloodcurdling images of the enemy back to friends and family. The same images recur, often expressed in identical words, as soldiers repeated what they had observed or, more likely, heard from others. Some of the stories were undoubtedly fabricated, and the outrages against the soldiers' bodies exaggerated, as part of a well-established and highly gendered medium of war propaganda. Yet it hardly matters whether they were true; they were believed, they spread anger and panic, and they passed into military folklore. Women caused a particular frisson of horror when they joined in collective acts of sexual degradation on the bodies of prisoners. Women's violence was deemed to be "unnatural"—as later it would be in the Paris Commune (1871), which unleashed a stream of vituperation against the unbridled fury of the *pétroleuses* (the women accused of burning much of Paris)[47]—and constituted a terrifying inversion of the laws of nature, especially where it was used to inflict sexual humiliation on the male body. In the aftermath of 1871, the language of dehumanization would be clear: writer after writer talked of furies, viragos, and jackals as they systematically condemned a violence they characterized as that of a lesser species. So in the Napoleonic Wars violent women were variously depicted as unnatural, bestial, and subhuman. Whether in the civil war in the Vendée (1793–99) or later in the Peninsular War (1808–14), their actions were routinely used to justify the extreme levels of violence and repression that ensued after a rebellion was put down.

It is too easy to portray these women, and civilians more generally, as the passive victims of war, reduced to powerlessness by their lack of armed force in a world where physical strength and armed might prevailed. This stereotyped perception overlooks the active part that civilians, and especially women, played in war support in this period—a part that encouraged them to show great personal initiative. Women made contributions to the war effort in many ways. In most parts of Europe, they helped to supply the military; they were called on to make donations, to sew uniforms, to provide nursing support for the sick and wounded. In some regions they did even more. They supported the patriotic cause with their publications and helped to organize ceremonies and rituals such as flag consecrations, thanksgiving and victory celebrations, and peace and homecoming festivals.[48] They also founded patriotic associations that helped to equip the militias and volunteers and later took care of the victims of war—wounded and sick soldiers, widows and orphans, impoverished soldiers' wives, exiles and refugees, prisoners of war, and penniless returning veterans.[49]

All these forms of female war support, mostly provided by women from the middle and upper classes who did not have to work for a living, were badly needed by states and armies that were ill prepared for war on this scale. Medical care and charity for war victims were seriously deficient. The motives of the female volunteers were quite mixed and complex, as can be seen from their autobiographical accounts. They shared the patriotism of their menfolk; they wanted to help suffering war victims out of a sense of Christian compassion; they worried about their conscripted fathers, husbands, and brothers and hoped that other women elsewhere would help them in a similar way. These activities opened up possibilities for greater social participation and social interaction, but the women rarely perceived them as an act of "liberation." They linked no political demands to these forms of war support, which marked them as very different from those who served in the French Revolution or, a century later, in the First World War.[50]

The medical services that women provided as nuns, nurses, or housewives demanded particular strength and willingness to sacrifice. Not only did they provide supplies and nurse troops in field hospitals and the many improvised hospitals in towns and cities close to war fronts, but also they took wounded soldiers and officers into their own homes—whether voluntarily or mandated by their municipality—offering them food and drink and caring for them at great risk to their own safety and that of their families, since soldiers spread deadly epidemics.[51] These acts of charity were not restricted to men on their own side, either. British, French, and German soldiers on campaign occasionally tell of the unexpected acts of kindness they had received from complete strangers, usually women, at moments when their lives were in danger. Even more occasionally, they stayed on to marry them, incidentally creating an interesting diplomatic problem for the authorities once the war was over. Such cases were exceptional, but they were one element, and a not insignificant one, in spreading humanity across frontiers and creating international understanding in the postwar world. In the process, their personal worlds had been expanded to include unimaginable experiences and familiarity with foreign languages and customs.[52]

In most parts of Europe, war charity and military medical care were, as in the past, mainly provided by nuns and sisters of the churches, female camp followers, and individual women in cities, towns, and villages close to battlefields. In German central Europe, however, these forms of war support became organized in new ways during the so-called Wars of Liberation of 1813–14 and 1815. As many as six hundred patriotic women's associations were founded, mainly in 1813/14, to support the struggle against Napoleonic France, more than two-thirds of them in Prussia alone. Here, as elsewhere, the appeal to set up these women's associations came from above. In March 1813, one day after the introduction of universal wartime conscription by the Prussian King, twelve Hohenzollern princesses called on the women of the "Prussian nation" to support the "liberation of their fatherland." They were asked to found patriotic women's associations with the aim, first, to collect money for the equipment of the volunteers and the new militia (Landwehr) and secondly to organize the care for sick and wounded soldiers and other victims of the war. They equated this voluntary female service with the volunteering of men for war. By lending their names and their moral authority to the cause, the Hohenzollern princesses had enabled women in this situation of "national emergency" to become active outside the private sphere. Again, it was middle- and upper-class women who responded in large numbers to this call. But when the war ended and the "national emergency" was over, the authorities and the press requested that female activities in the public sphere end too and that the women's associations be closed. Now women were needed again at home to welcome the returning veterans and heal the wounds of war in the "bosom of the family." Only 10 percent of the patriotic women's associations continued after 1815.[53] Nevertheless, they had established a "distinct cultural world" that would be a model for later patriotic women's associations, especially during the German Wars of Unification (1864–71).[54]

While such women's associations were largely confined to German central Europe, in other parts of the continent, especially in England, women are also to be found championing patriotic or moral causes during the French Revolutionary and Napoleonic Wars and speaking openly on political issues throughout the war years. Here, they involved themselves in public life in various guises, joining support groups for the troops in the field and acting as intellectual leaders in their own right, supporting moral causes from radical politics to antislavery. Some were openly feminist, adding their voices to the call to widen the suffrage made by the English writer Mary Wollstonecraft in her 1792 publication, *A Vindication of the Rights of Woman*.[55] But it was in the movement against the slave trade that Englishwomen from across the social spectrum threw themselves most assiduously into the political debates of the day. Early women activists among the English abolitionists, like Elizabeth Heyrick, were some of the movement's most radical members. They sometimes even advocated the immediate abolition of slavery in Britain's colonies at a time when the leader of the abolitionist movement, William Wilberforce, still believed that it should concentrate on bringing an end to the slave trade.[56] And, although women were excluded from holding office in the Society for Effecting the Abolition of the Slave Trade, about 10 percent of the financial supporters of the organization were women, while in some areas, notably in and around Manchester, they made up over a quarter of its subscribers. A number of these women were prominent in the Society of Friends (Quakers), and it is perhaps significant that they, like their male counterparts, were generally attracted into public life because of their religious faith. These women used the various political and cultural genres open to them, such as writing poems and stories on the iniquities of slavery. They ranged widely in social backgrounds, from the Whig aristocrat Georgiana, Duchess of Devonshire, to writers like Mary Birkett Card and Amelia Opie. Such women may not have had the vote, but they were politically engaged and felt deeply about what was, in England at least, one of the salient public issues of their day.[57]

The concentration of patriotic and reforming women's activities in northern Europe during the war years invites comment and calls for some explanation. It would appear that these activities were not spread evenly across the map and that women were notably more vocal, and more prepared to step into public roles, in some countries than in others. Why? The state of women's education may have been one factor, since it was unevenly spread across Europe, and many of those women who did engage in political or patriotic movements were noticeably well educated. Northern Europe had higher levels of literacy and was a more urbanized space, and these initiatives were more often urban than rural. Germany west of the River Elbe had the highest literacy rate in Europe in the early nineteenth century.[58] Religion may have played a part here, too, to the extent that the Protestant Church attached greater importance to literacy as the tool through which the individual could read the Word of God. But we must be careful not to be too determinist, since the north–south divide was anything but clear. The literacy rate was very high in the Catholic south of Germany as well. In France, southern cities such as Aix, Toulouse, and Bordeaux were centers of the eighteenth-century Enlightenment. In addition, Britain and France had a long tradition of political radicalism and humanism and seemed more prepared to offer moral leadership on public issues like constitutionalism or the campaign against slavery.[59]

CONCLUSION

Once peace was signed and the armies were finally disbanded, the problems for civilians, and for women in particular, were not over. The years following mass demobilization were marked by instability and social unrest in many parts of Europe, as returning soldiers found only poverty and unemployment. Women were usually the ones who had to heal the wounds of war by caring for wounded and disabled husbands who often faced long years of sickness, misery, and depression resulting from their war experiences. In the war commemorations that followed, moreover, civilian contributions to the war effort were largely forgotten as postwar societies gloried in the masculine values of their warriors and mythologized their part in creating new national identities. During the long years of war, patriotic rhetoric had become militarized across much of Europe, and the values of valor and sacrifice had become inscribed on the escutcheons of nations.[60]

But it was not only women whose war service was forgotten in the postwar years. Not all men had fought (indeed, the figure rarely exceeded around 10 percent of the male population). The war support that had been given by male civilians, those who had not been asked to fight, whether because of their age, their state of health, or their family situation or because they worked in a sector that was deemed essential to the war effort, was also largely neglected in the collective memory of the wars that focused on military heroes and their sacrifice. Such men had no war tales to tell, no moments of heroism to look back on. In an era when military sacrifice was so passionately valued, their lives could seem strangely shallow, and it could be difficult to sublimate a lingering shame, a pervasive sense of guilt and worthlessness. Theirs were not the stories that the nineteenth-century world wanted to hear or the memoirs they would rush to read. Whereas in wartime they had been valued for the roles they could perform to assist the armies, with the return of peace they risked being marginalized anew.[61]

NOTES

1. See, for example, Alan Forrest et al., eds., *War, Demobilization and Memory: The Legacy of War in the Era of Atlantic Revolutions* (Basingstoke: Palgrave Macmillan, 2016), especially the introduction; Forrest et al., *Soldiers, Citizens and Civilians: Experiences and Perceptions of the French Wars, 1790–1820* (Basingstoke: Palgrave Macmillan, 2009); Roger Chickering and Stig Förster, eds., *War in an Age of Revolution, 1775–1815* (Cambridge: Cambridge University Press, 2010); and Karen Hagemann and Katherine Aaslestad, eds., "Collaboration, Resistance, and Reform: Experiences and Historiographies of the Napoleonic Wars in Central Europe," special issue, *Central European History* 39, no. 4 (2006).

2. David Bell, *The First Total War: Napoleon's Europe and the Birth of Warfare as We Know It* (Boston: Houghton Mifflin, 2007); and Jean-Yves Guiomar, *L'invention de la guerre totale, 18ᵉ–20ᵉ siècle* (Paris: Editions du Felin, 2004).

3. See also the introduction to Chickering and Förster, *War.*

4. Katherine B. Aaslestad and Johan Joor, eds., *Revisiting Napoleon's Continental System: Local, Regional and European Experiences* (Basingstoke: Palgrave Macmillan, 2014).

5. Philip G. Dwyer and Lyndall Ryan, "Massacre in the Old and New Worlds, c. 1780–1820," *Journal of Genocide Research* 15, no. 2 (2013): 111–15.

6. See Forrest et al., *War, Demobilization*.

7. Works include Joan B. Landes, *Women and the Public Sphere in the Age of the French Revolution* (Ithaca, NY: Cornell University Press, 1988); Sara E. Melzer and Leslie W. Rabine, eds., *Rebel Daughters: Women and the French Revolution* (Oxford: Oxford University Press, 1992); Dominique Godineau, *The Women of Paris and Their French Revolution* (Berkeley: University of California Press, 1998); Jennifer N. Heuer, *The Family and the Nation: Gender and Citizenship in Revolutionary France, 1789–1830* (Ithaca, NY: Cornell University Press, 2005); and June K. Burton, *Napoleon and the Woman Question: Discourses of the Other Sex in French Education, Medicine, and Medical Law, 1799–1815* (Lubbock: Texas Tech University Press, 2007).

8. On the state of research, see Karen Hagemann et al., eds., *Gender, War, and Politics: Transatlantic Perspectives, 1775–1830* (Basingstoke: Palgrave Macmillan, 2010); Hagemann et al., eds., "Gender, War and the Nation in the Period of the Revolutionary and Napoleonic Wars—European Perspectives," special issue, *European History Quarterly* 37, no. 4 (2007); Waltraud Maierhofer et al., eds., *Women against Napoleon: Historical and Fictional Responses to His Rise and Legacy* (Frankfurt am Main: Campus, 2007); and Charles Esdaile, *Women in the Peninsular War* (Norman: University of Oklahoma Press, 2014).

9. With a focus on masculinity, see Karen Hagemann, *"Männlicher Muth und Teutsche Ehre": Nation, Militär und Geschlecht zur Zeit der Antinapoleonischen Kriege Preußens* (Paderborn: Schöningh, 2002); Stefan Dudink et al., eds., *Masculinities in Politics and War: Gendering Modern History* (Manchester: Manchester University Press, 2004), 22–136; Hagemann et al., *Gender, War, and Politics*, 93–168; and Hagemann, "The Military and Masculinity: Gendering the History of the French Wars, 1792–1815," in Chickering and Förster, *War*, 331–52. See also the chapter by Stefan Dudink on "Citizenship, Mass Mobilization, and Masculinity in a Transatlantic Perspective, 1770s–1870s" in this handbook.

10. On Waterloo, see Jeremy Black, *The Battle of Waterloo* (New York: Random House, 2010); and Alan Forrest, *Waterloo* (Oxford: Oxford University Press, 2015).

11. Christopher E. Forth, *Masculinity in the Modern West: Gender, Civilization and the Body* (Basingstoke: Palgrave Macmillan, 2008), 114.

12. See, for more, Alan Forrest, *Napoleon's Men: The Soldiers of the Revolution and Empire* (London: Hambledon, 2002); and Forrest, *Conscripts and Deserters: The Army and French Society during the Revolution and Empire* (New York: Oxford University Press, 1989).

13. See Karen Hagemann, "'Heroic Virgins' and 'Bellicose Amazons': Armed Women, the Gender Order, and the German Public during and after the Anti-Napoleonic Wars," in Hagemann et al., "Gender, War," special issue, *European History Quarterly* 37, no. 4 (2007): 507–27.

14. See Darline Levy and Harriet B. Applewhite, "Women and Militant Citizenship in Revolutionary Paris," in Melzer and Rabine, *Rebel Daughters*, 79–101.

15. See Heide Wunder, *He Is the Sun, She Is the Moon: Women in Early Modern Germany* (Cambridge, MA: Harvard University Press, 1998); and the chapter by Peter H. Wilson on "Wars, States, and Gender in Early Modern European Warfare, 1600s–1780s" in this handbook.

16. Catriona Kennedy, "From the Ballroom to the Battlefield," in Forrest et al., *Soldiers, Citizens*, 137–56.

17. Thomas Cardoza, *Intrepid Women: Cantinières and Vivandières of the French Army* (Bloomington: University of Indiana Press, 2010), 215–21.

18. See Karen Hagemann, "Militär, Krieg und Geschlechterverhältnisse: Untersuchungen, Überlegungen und Fragen zur Militärgeschichte der Frühen Neuzeit," in *Klio in Uniform: Probleme und Perspektiven einer modernen Militärgeschichte der Frühen Neuzeit*, ed. Ralf Pröve (Cologne: Böhlau, 1997), 35–88.

19. See, for example, Karen Hagemann, *Revisiting Prussia's Wars against Napoleon: History, Culture and Memory* (Cambridge: Cambridge University Press, 2015), 194–207; and Catriona Kennedy, *Narratives of the Revolutionary and Napoleonic Wars: Military and Civilian* (Basingstoke: Palgrave Macmillan, 2013).

20. See, for instance, the account of the Moscow campaign in Jacques-Olivier Boudon, *Napoléon et la campagne de Russie, 1812* (Paris: Armand Colin, 2012).

21. John Childs, *Armies and Warfare in Europe, 1648–1789* (Manchester: Manchester University Press, 1982), 144.

22. Karen Hagemann, "'Unimaginable Horror and Misery': The Battle of Leipzig in October 1813 in Civilian Experience and Perception," in Forrest et al., *Soldiers, Citizens*, 157–78.

23. See Karen Hagemann, "Reconstructing 'Front' and 'Home': Gendered Experiences and Memories of the German Wars against Napoleon—a Case Study," *War in History* 16, no. 1 (2009): 25–50; and Katherine B. Aaslestad, "Postwar Cities: The Cost of the Wars of 1813–1815 on Society in Hamburg und Leipzig," in Forrest et al., *War, Demobilization*, 220–37.

24. See Hagemann, "Unimaginable Horror."

25. François Crouzet, "Wars, Blockade and Economic Change in Europe, 1792–1815," *Journal of Economic History* 24, no. 4 (1964): 567–88.

26. Anita Čerpinska, "Riga Export Trade at the Time of the Continental Blockade, 1807–1812," in Aaslestad and Joor, *Revisiting*, 241–58.

27. Graphic accounts of atrocities are to be found in Charles Esdaile, *Peninsular Eyewitnesses: The Experience of War in Spain and Portugal, 1808–1813* (Barnsley: Pen & Sword Military, 2008), esp. 1–82.

28. Stephen Conway, "British Soldiers at Home: The Civilian Experience in Wartime," in *Civilians and War in Europe, 1618–1815*, ed. Erica Charters et al. (Liverpool: Liverpool University Press, 2012), 129–46.

29. Alan Forrest, "La guerre de l'Ouest vue par les soldats républicains," in *La guerre civile: entre histoire et mémoire*, ed. Jean-Clément Martin (Nantes: Ouest éditions, 1995), 91–99.

30. See Hagemann, *Revisiting*, 33–46; and Hagemann, "'Desperation to the Utmost': The Defeat of 1806 and the French Occupation in Prussian Experience and Perception," in *The Bee and the Eagle: Napoleonic France and the End of the Holy Roman Empire*, ed. Alan Forrest and Peter H. Wilson (Basingstoke: Palgrave Macmillan, 2008), 191–214.

31. See Francisco de Goya, *The Disasters of War* (London: Phaidon, 1937).

32. Katherine Aaslestad, *Place and Politics: Local Identity, Civic Culture and German Nationalism in North Germany during the Revolutionary Era* (Leiden: Brill, 2005), 266–71.

33. See Charles J. Esdaile, ed., *Popular Resistance in the French Wars: Patriots, Partisans and Land Pirates* (Basingstoke: Palgrave Macmillan, 2005); and Michael Rowe, ed., *Collaboration and Resistance in Napoleonic Europe: State Formation in an Age of Upheaval, c.1800–1815* (Basingstoke: Palgrave Macmillan, 2003).

34. David A. Bell, *Napoleon: A Concise Biography* (Oxford: Oxford University Press, 2015), 71–72.

35. Philip G. Dwyer, "Violence and the Revolutionary and Napoleonic Wars: Massacre, Conquest and the Imperial Enterprise," *Journal of Genocide Research* 15, no. 2 (2013): 117–31, 124.

36. Dominic Lieven, *Russia against Napoleon: The Battle for Europe, 1807 to 1814* (London: Allen Lane, 2009), 4–5 and 297–99.

37. Michael J. Hughes, *Forging Napoleon's Grande Armée: Motivation, Military Culture and Masculinity in the French Army, 1800–1808* (New York: New York University Press, 2012), 15.

38. David French, *Military Identities: The Regimental System, the British Army and the British People, c. 1870–2000* (Oxford: Oxford University Press, 2005), 128.

39. Scott Hughes Myerly, *British Military Spectacle from the Napoleonic Wars through the Crimea* (Cambridge, MA: Harvard University Press, 1996), 58.

40. Hughes, *Forging*, 130.

41. See in this context Larry Wolff, *Inventing Eastern Europe: The Map of Civilization on the Mind of the Enlightenment* (Stanford, CA: Stanford University Press, 1994), 4.

42. Philippe Girard, "French Atrocities during the Haitian War of Independence," *Journal of Genocide Research* 15, no. 2 (2013): 133–49, 142–43.

43. See the chapter by Thomas Cardoza and Karen Hagemann on "History and Memory of Army Women and Female Soldiers, 1770s–1870s" in this handbook.

44. Dominique Godineau, "De la guerrière à la citoyenne: Porter les armes pendant l'Ancien Régime et la Révolution Française," *Clio* 20 (2004): 43–69; and Hagemann, "Heroic Virgins."

45. David Hopkin, "The World Turned Upside Down: Female Soldiers in the French Army of the Revolutionary and Napoleonic Wars," in Forrest et al., *Soldiers, Citizens*, 77–98.

46. Jean-Marc Lafon, *L'Andalousie et Napoléon: contre-insurrection, collaboration et résistances dans le Midi de l'Espagne (1808–1812)* (Paris: Nouveau Monde Editions, 2007), 104; and Charles J. Esdaile, *Fighting Napoleon: Guerrillas, Bandits and Adventurers in Spain, 1808–1814* (New Haven, CT: Yale University Press, 2004).

47. Gay L. Gullickson, *Unruly Women of Paris: Images of the Commune* (Ithaca, NY: Cornell University Press, 1996), 4.

48. Karen Hagemann, "Celebrating War and Nation: Gender, Patriotism and Festival Culture during and after the Prussian Wars of Liberation," in Hagemann et al., *Gender, War*, 284–304.

49. See Rita Huber-Sperl, "Organized Women and the Strong State: The Beginnings of Female Associational Activity in Germany, 1810–1840," *Journal of Women's History* 13, no. 4 (2002): 81–105; and Karen Hagemann, "Female Patriots: Women, War and the Nation in the Period of the Prussian-German Anti-Napoleonic Wars," *Gender & History* 16, no. 2 (2004): 396–424.

50. See Hagemann, "Female Patriots."

51. See Hagemann, "Unimaginable Horror."

52. Bernhard Struck, "Conquered Territories and Entangled Histories: The Perception of Franco-German and German–Polish Borderlands in German Travelogues, 1792–1820," in *War Memories: The Revolutionary and Napoleonic Wars in Modern European Culture*, ed. Alan Forrest et al. (Basingstoke: Palgrave Macmillan, 2012), 95–113.

53. Hagemann, "Female Patriots"; and Dirk Reder, *Frauenbewegung und Nation: Patriotische Frauenvereine in Deutschland im frühen 19. Jahrhundert (1813–1830)* (Cologne: SH-Verlag, 1998).

54. Jean H. Quataert, *Staging Philanthropy: Patriotic Women and the National Imagination in Dynastic Germany, 1813–1916* (Ann Arbor: University of Michigan Press, 2001), 90.

55. Gary Kelly, *Revolutionary Feminism: The Mind and Career of Mary Wollstonecraft* (Basingstoke: Palgrave, 1996).

56. Elizabeth Heyrick, *Immediate, Not Gradual Abolition; or, An Inquiry into the Shortest, Safest and Most Effectual Means of Getting Rid of West Indian Slavery* (London: Hatchard, 1824).

57. See, for example, Cora Kaplan and John Oldfield, eds., *Imagining Transatlantic Slavery* (Basingstoke: Palgrave Macmillan, 2010); and James Walvin, *The Quakers: Money and Morals* (London: Murray, 1998).

58. François Furet and Jacques Ozouf, *Reading and Writing: Literacy in France from Calvin to Jules Ferry* (Cambridge: Cambridge University Press, 1982), 16–19; and Hagemann, *Revisiting*, 83–86.

59. See, for instance, Robert D. Cornwall and William Gibson, eds., *Religion, Politics and Dissent, 1660–1832* (Farnham: Ashgate, 2010).

60. Hagemann, "Reconstructing"; and Hagemann, *Revisiting*, 249–397.

61. Philip Dwyer, "War Stories: French Veteran Narratives and the 'Experience of War' in the Nineteenth Century," *European History Quarterly* 41, no. 4 (2011): 561–85.

Select Bibliography

Aaslestad, Katherine B., and Karen Hagemann, eds. "Collaboration, Resistance and Reform: Experiences and Historiographies of the Napoleonic Wars in Central Europe." Special issue, *Central European History* 39, no. 4 (2006).

Aaslestad, Katherine B., and Johan Joor, eds. *Revisiting Napoleon's Continental System: Local, Regional and European Experiences.* Basingstoke: Palgrave Macmillan, 2014.

Cardoza, Thomas. *Intrepid Women: Cantinières and Vivandières of the French Army.* Bloomington: Indiana University Press, 2010.

Charters, Erica, Eve Rosenhaft, and Hannah Smith, eds. *Civilians and War in Europe, 1618–1815.* Liverpool: Liverpool University Press, 2012.

Chickering, Roger, and Stig Förster, eds. *War in an Age of Revolution, 1775–1815.* Cambridge: Cambridge University Press, 2010.

Dwyer, Philip G., and Lyndall Ryan, eds. *Theatres of Violence: Massacre, Mass Killing and Atrocity throughout History.* New York: Berghahn Books, 2012.

Esdaile, Charles. *Women and the Peninsular War.* Norman: University of Oklahoma Press, 2014.

Forrest, Alan. *Napoleon's Men: The Soldiers of the Revolution and Empire.* London: Hambledon, 2002.

Forrest, Alan, Etienne François, and Karen Hagemann, eds. *War Memories: The Revolutionary and Napoleonic Wars in Modern European Culture.* Basingstoke: Palgrave Macmillan, 2012.

Forrest, Alan, Karen Hagemann, and Jane Rendall, eds. *Soldiers, Citizens and Civilians: Experiences and Perceptions of the Revolutionary and Napoleonic Wars, 1790–1820.* Basingstoke: Palgrave Macmillan, 2009.

Forrest, Alan, Karen Hagemann, and Michael Rowe, eds. *War, Demobilization and Memory: The Legacy of War in the Era of Atlantic Revolutions.* Basingstoke: Palgrave Macmillan, 2016.

Hagemann, Karen. *Revisiting Prussia's Wars against Napoleon: History, Culture, and Memory.* Cambridge: Cambridge University Press, 2015.

Hagemann, Karen, Katherine Aaslestad, and Judith Miller, eds. "Gender, War and the Nation in the Period of the Revolutionary and Napoleonic Wars—European Perspectives." Special issue, *European History Quarterly* 37, no. 4 (2007).

Hagemann, Karen, Gisela Mettele, and Jane Rendall, eds. *Gender, War, and Politics: Transatlantic Perspectives, 1775–1830.* Basingstoke: Palgrave Macmillan, 2010.

Heuer, Jennifer. *The Family and the Nation: Gender and Citizenship in Revolutionary France, 1789–1830.* Ithaca, NY: Cornell University Press, 2005.

Hippler, Thomas. *Citizens, Soldiers and National Armies: Military Service in France and Germany, 1789–1830.* London: Routledge, 2008.

Hughes, Michael J. *Forging Napoleon's Grande Armée: Motivation, Military Culture and Masculinity in the French Army, 1800–1808.* New York: New York University Press, 2012.

Lieven, Dominic. *Russia against Napoleon: The Battle for Europe, 1807 to 1814.* London: Allen Lane, 2009.

Maierhofer, Waltraud, Gertrud M. Roesch, and Caroline Blend, eds. *Women against Napoleon: Historical and Fictional Responses to His Rise and Legacy.* Frankfurt am Main: Campus, 2007.

Rowe, Michael, ed. *Collaboration and Resistance in Napoleonic Europe: State Formation in an Age of Upheaval, 1800–1815.* Basingstoke: Palgrave Macmillan, 2003.

CHAPTER 7

....

HISTORY AND MEMORY OF ARMY WOMEN AND FEMALE SOLDIERS, 1770s–1870s

....

THOMAS CARDOZA AND KAREN HAGEMANN

CROSS-DRESSED female soldiers in eighteenth- and nineteenth-century armies continue to be a subject of fascination. These women, who turned the dominant ideas of the gender order upside down, already attracted considerable attention in the contemporary public and inspired poets, novelists, and historians to write about them.[1] But female soldiers constituted only a small portion of all women in armed forces on campaign. Other, much larger and often-forgotten groups were the female camp followers who accompanied the armed forces, the women who officially served as army auxiliaries, especially as sutlers and laundry women, and the nurses who helped sick and wounded soldiers.[2] Their integration in the military differed from country to country and changed as a result of transformations in military systems and, consequently, the nature of warfare: from eighteenth-century European and colonial conflicts with state commission armies to mid- and late nineteenth-century national and imperial wars with professionalized and industrialized armed forces that were increasingly based on universal conscription.

As a result of these transformations, fewer women served in the military in different capacities, officially and unofficially, during the nineteenth century than at any other point from the seventeenth through the twenty-first centuries. "Women's participation with armies in the field" already had started to change "dramatically since the second half of the seventeenth century," historian John A. Lynn observed. Before then, women (together with children and male servants, including "boys") accompanied the troops of the aggregated contract armies on campaign in large numbers. These camp followers were "essential to the character of armies and to the logistic system that kept them in the field" because they were part of a military economy that was based on pillaging and plundering. After 1650, soldiers' wives in the train of the developing state commission armies were less and less important to the logistics of war, but they were still integral for the survival of the soldier couple and the well-being of soldiers and officers in the units, who needed their washing, sewing, cooking, and nursing as much as the female company.[3]

Other historians, such as Peter H. Wilson, caution against overrating the importance of the women in the early modern train for the reproduction of the troops. He emphasizes that neither governments nor military leaderships ever considered and treated them as part of the regular logistical systems; rather, they always perceived them as a major problem and burden. According to Wilson, the work of the female camp followers was mainly important for the subsistence of the women and their partners. This, he argues, was one major reason why the attempts of sovereigns and military leaders to limit marriage by soldiers, and thereby reduce the number of camp followers, more or less failed during the eighteenth century.[4] For Wilson, the increasing attempts to limit marriages by soldiers were a result not only of the military rationale that with the growing size of the troops a large train became less expedient, but also of social and economic motives. He argues that governments wanted to reduce the train because of the conflicts between military and society caused by their troops' pillaging and plundering, which therefore were increasingly declared illegal. In addition, they attempted to reduce the number of married soldiers, because pay in the lower ranks was so meager that a soldier could not feed a family. Authorities worried that soldiers' wives resorted to prostitution and theft for survival, and they wanted to prevent any further increase of the clientele receiving poor relief.[5] Despite all governmental and military attempts, however, the percentage of married soldiers seems to have increased in many militaries since the end of the seventeenth century. And where these attempts reached their aim, the result was an unintended increase of unmarried soldier couples and illegitimate children, which led to a further deterioration of the livelihood of army women and increasing costs for poor relief.[6]

The situation changed in the Age of the Wars of Revolution and Independence (1770s–1820s), when the size of the armed forces dramatically increased further because they relied now on recruitment through different forms of mass mobilization (volunteers, militias, conscription) to supplement professional soldiers. To ease the logistic burdens posed by larger armies that lived off the land, military leaderships did ever more to reduce the number of camp followers and army women. Subsequently, the number of women in the armed forces decreased further and they became subject to greater regulation. In the course of the nineteenth century, militaries in Europe and the Americas became, more than ever before, all-male institutions.[7]

In the following exploration of the history and memory of army women, nurses and cross-dressed female soldiers in the eighteenth and nineteenth centuries, the focus is first on the transformative period of the Age of the Wars of Revolution and Independence, especially the American Revolutionary War (1775–83) and the French Revolutionary and the Napoleonic Wars (1792–1815), and afterward on subsequent developments until the second half of the nineteenth century, with a focus first on

European conflicts and then the American Civil War (1861–65) as the first modern, industrialized conflict.

WOMEN IN THE ARMIES OF THE AGE OF THE WARS OF REVOLUTION AND INDEPENDENCE

Parallel to the changes in military systems and the conduct of warfare during the Age of the Wars of Revolution and Independence, the dominant ideas about the gender order of war changed too. Since antiquity, the "power to injure" in war was associated with men.[8] This attribution, however, became cemented in the context of continuing warfare during the American and French Revolutionary Wars and the Napoleonic Wars. In the pervasive patriotic-national propaganda of the era, the new mass warfare—the so-called people's war—based on volunteer units, militias, or universal conscription essentially assigned all men the duty to defend family, home, and country during wartime.[9] At the same time, a new link between military service and political rights developed in the contemporary discourse, which gained increasing influence since the French Revolution (1789–99). In the complementary image, women were constructed as "vulnerable to injury" and in need of male protection. The primary social tasks accorded to them were caring and nurturing. The new demands that national mass wars placed on both men and women rested on changes in ideas about the gender order introduced in the second half of the eighteenth century. Traditional Christian and corporatist legitimations of gender difference, which came under attack during the Enlightenment, were replaced by an "anthropological" mode of explanation. Gender differences were now regarded as rooted in men's and women's different "physiology" and "nature." This proposition assigned men and women tasks in the state, military, economy, and society that were defined as natural, complementary, and universal. What is important for our subject is that the changes in the military system and the thinking about the gender order that developed during the late eighteenth and early nineteenth century, especially in the West, were entangled and reinforced each other. They became a model for all nations striving to become a nation-state. In this way, the military became more than ever before a "gender-defining" institution.[10]

At the very heart of the gender line that differentiated men from women in the imagined gender order of the new nineteenth-century nation-states stood military service and with it the male right—and, in wartime, the duty—to kill. This association between men and the "power to injure" informed even the peacetime gender order, because all men either had already been or could potentially become soldiers who would protect family, home, and country. Women were asked in the "national emergency situation" of war to fulfill their complementary "patriotic duties," mainly war charity and nursing. This gender order of national war was demanded for the first time in revolutionary France during the *levée en masse* (mass levy) of August 1793: young men of military age were to become soldiers, and old men were to support the war effort with material and ideas. Women, by contrast, were to ensure that the warriors were equipped with tents and uniforms, to care for sick and wounded soldiers, and to bolster the men's fighting resolve. The model gained influence over the long nineteenth century; it informed not only the policies of states and militaries regarding women in the armed forces but also the public representation, perception, and remembrance of these women.[11]

Women in the American Revolutionary War

The different avenues for female participation in the American Revolutionary War still conformed to conventional women's roles in eighteenth-century warfare. Historians estimate that tens of thousands of women joined the military in various capacities during this conflict: as camp followers, "women of the army," nurses, female soldiers disguised as men, and women serving as irregular fighters affiliated with the local militias. Statistics for the American Revolutionary War are unreliable, but certainly the armed forces fighting in this conflict were still small compared to the size of Napoleon's Grande Armée thirty years later. The Continental army, including the various militias, fluctuated in size over the course of the war and averaged some 40,000 men, compared to the 48,000 men of the British army, which was supported on the North American continent by thousands of colonial loyalists, German mercenaries, and Native American allies.

In the eight years of the war, the Continental army under the command of General George Washington reached a total enlistment of some 376,700 soldiers, including 145,000 militiamen.[12] The number and percentage of women in the military was comparatively small. Linda Grant de Pauw estimated that over the course of the conflict "20,000 individual women served as women of the army" or camp followers and "a much smaller number, a few hundred perhaps, fought in uniform with the Continental line." Most of the female camp followers were not officially recognized, meaning that they were not legally subject to military discipline, were not listed on muster roles with officially assigned military functions, and did not draw pay or rations.[13] The British army had fewer women camp followers, because it more strictly regulated the stream of women who joined the troops on their journey across the Atlantic. The British military gave them an officially recognized position as "wives on the strength" of the regiment who were allowed to travel with the troops and were entitled to half rations. In the 1780s, their median number was 14 per 100 men in an infantry regiment.[14] But during the campaign on the American continent, more women joined the units of the British army as unofficial camp followers.[15]

The numbers of women furthermore differed in both armies, between units, and they changed over time. Long-serving regiments usually had more women than did new units, because their number seems to have increased during conflicts; one reason was the growing enlistment of men.[16] Soon after the conflict had started, the leadership of the Continental army realized that large groups of camp-following women posed a hurdle for the conduct of warfare, but they also knew that they would lose men if they tried to reduce their number. The soldiers wanted their families close by, cared for, and protected. This created a dilemma, because the army leaders could not afford to lose soldiers, but also could not feed the increasing number of impoverished civilians who fled to the camps for safety and food. They could barely provision the troops. Washington and his generals therefore aimed for a compromise: reducing the number of dependents traveling with the army rather than banning them altogether. On August 4, 1777, two years after the conflict had started, Washington wrote in a general order, "The multitudes of women in particular, especially those who are pregnant, or have children, are a clog upon every movement. The Commander in Chief earnestly recommends it to the officers commanding brigades and corps, to use every reasonable method in their power, to get rid of all such as are not absolutely necessary; and the admission of and continuance of any, who shall, or may have come to the army since its arrival in Pennsylvania, is positively forbidden."[17] But the attempts to reduce the number of camp followers failed.

In general, the female military experience in the American Revolutionary War, on both sides, was like that in eighteenth-century European wars and colonial conquest, because the military system and form of warfare were alike (not even frontier and guerrilla warfare were new), and the social background of the women who followed the drums was comparable as well. These women mainly came from the working classes and saw no alternative. They were driven by social and economic hardship. Faced with unemployment and the destruction of war, they joined the army as a common last resort that promised relative "security," especially if they accompanied their fiancé or husband.[18] As members of the campaign community, female camp followers and army women endured the same conditions as the soldiers did. They joined them on long, exhausting marches with heavy baggage and bivouacked with them in the open air or slept with them in tents or improvised huts. They dug trenches and secured fortifications, even under fire, and in these and many other situations they shared the dangers of war with the men—attacks, encirclements, sieges, hasty retreats—and endured the same miseries—starvation, injury, and illness—in addition to pregnancy and childbirth.[19]

Unofficial female camp followers and officially recognized army women took on the same tasks in both armies. They cooked, did laundry, and cleaned, whether for ordinary soldiers or as officers' servants. Others earned a living as sutlers who peddled wares legally and illegally, inside or outside the military camp boundaries. Most licensed sutlers were men, but they usually partnered with their wives in this enterprise. In general, both armies expected that all women serving the military accept military authority and obey their respective Articles of War, especially when they were provisioned.[20]

In addition, women served as nurses. Especially the Continental army preferred female nurses to male ones, not only because nursing the sick has traditionally been a female responsibility, but also because every woman nursing meant one more man freed for fighting in the line. A nurse could hope to receive regular pay and retain her job throughout the war. A July 1775 resolution by the Second Continental Congress that met with interruptions at different places from May 1775 to March 1781, allowed one nurse for every ten patients in Continental hospitals and promised a salary of two dollars per month. In 1776, the Congress raised nurses' pay to four dollars per month and doubled it again to eight dollars per month in 1777. Despite all efforts to increase the number of female nurses for the army, there remained a shortage throughout the war, because the work was dirty and dangerous. In the military hospitals the personnel were exposed to deadly diseases such as smallpox and camp fevers.[21]

Only a small number of women were actively involved in combat. Among them were the water carriers for artillery units. Water was needed for swabbing out the barrel of a cannon after firing, before it could be reloaded, to slake sparks, and to remove unexploded powder. Because of the continuous shortage of manpower, women were used for this essential task.[22] One such example is the heroine Molly Pitcher, who was loved and remembered by the nineteenth- and twentieth-century American public. She is said to have followed her husband, an artilleryman, to war and became involved in the Battle of Monmouth in June 1778, when the Continental army attacked the rear of the British army in New Jersey. At first, according to the narrative, she attended to the revolutionaries by giving them water, but when her husband was injured and carried from the battlefield, she took his place at the cannon. She continued to "swab and load" it the rest of the day, using her husband's ramrod.[23] Today we know that Molly Pitcher was a construct, a composite heroine, merged from several stories of real army women. What characterized her myth and made her figure acceptable for the patriotic public and suitable for the national memory is that she was presented as a caring wife who only dared to replace her husband in a situation of military emergency. Her role in combat and her bravery were constructed as brief, contingent, and spontaneous.[24]

It was much harder to find public recognition and support for the small number of women who joined the ranks of the Continental army disguised as men; they even struggled to get pension payments. The story of Deborah Sampson Gannett, born in Plympton, Massachusetts, in 1760 offers an illustrative example. Her father, who was in the navy, died early, and she had to serve in several households. Later, she became a schoolteacher. In 1782, in the seventh year of the American Revolutionary War, she enlisted, dressed as a man, in the Continental army. She was twenty-two when she joined the army and had served seventeen months under the name of Robert Shurtliff when she was wounded, discovered as a woman, and honorably discharged at West Point, New York, shortly before the war ended in 1783. Two years later, she married a farmer from Sharon, Massachusetts, and the impoverished couple had three children. Their poverty was one reason why Sampson petitioned the Massachusetts state legislature for back pay in 1792; the army had withheld her pay because she was a woman. Her petition passed through the state's senate, was approved, and was signed by the governor. Sampson won notoriety when journalist Herman Mann published a biography in 1797 that presented her as an exceptional woman driven by extraordinary patriotism.[25] This relative fame proved important in later years when Samson earned some income through paid lectures, though her financial situation deteriorated. In 1804, she therefore petitioned for a military pension, which was denied until 1816, when her petition came before the US Congress and was approved. The stories of Molly Pitcher and Deborah

Sampson helped to shape the long-term collective recollection of female soldiers in the American Revolutionary War.

Women in the French Revolutionary and Napoleonic Wars

Although the Seven Years' War (1756–63) had already been a global conflict, the French Revolutionary and Napoleonic Wars were the first modern wars affecting not only all of Europe, but extending far beyond its shores. Contemporaries experienced an unprecedented extent of military and civilian mobilization for war.[26] The wars lasted more than twenty years and were primarily conducted as national wars with mass armies legitimized by patriotic-national propaganda. The number of soldiers mobilized surpassed anything previously seen. More than two million Frenchmen, 7 percent of the male population, served between 1792 and 1813, mobilized as volunteers or conscripts. Another million were conscripts from allied and annexed regions. France's enemies on the European continent likewise had to mobilize volunteers, create militias, and introduce different forms of conscription, at least for wartime, to be able to increase the size of their armed forces and fight France.[27] We do not know how many women joined the troops of the French Revolutionary and Napoleonic Wars as camp followers, officially recognized army women, and cross-dressed female soldiers, but we know with certainty that all military leaderships attempted to severely reduce the number of camp followers. They disbanded large baggage trains and tried to exclude female camp followers from the new mass armies.[28]

In the French revolutionary army, women served in three capacities: as *femmes soldats* (female soldiers), *blanchisseuses* (laundresses), and *vivandières* (sutlers). The revolutionary leadership adamantly opposed *femmes soldats*. It blamed the women in its armed forces for the unsuccessful conduct of its troops in the first year of the French Revolutionary Wars (1792–1802). To reduce their number, the National Convention, established in September 1792, passed a law in April 1793 to ban all "useless women" from the army, including all *femmes soldats*, while allowing only a limited number of *blanchisseuses* and *vivandières*.[29] This law was also a response to the Jacobin women organized in the Société des citoyennes républicaines révolutionnaires (Society of Revolutionary Republican Women) who, since the outbreak of war, claimed the right to bear arms and to defend their country in order to become citizens with equal political rights. The women's request, exceptional in its time, challenged the social and political order of the young revolutionary republic. Jacobin revolutionaries and moderate Girondins alike responded first through ridicule. In October 1793, the Jacobin-controlled National Convention went a step further and banned not only the Society of Revolutionary Republican Women, like all other female political associations, but also the participation of women in public political debates and even their wearing of the national cockade, the symbol of the revolution. They justified this decision with the supposedly natural roles of men and women in society, politics, and the military.[30]

Politically active women and women who wanted to bear arms were perceived as threats to the aspired national gender order of war envisioned with the *levée en masse* of August 1793.[31]

The revolutionaries in the French War Ministry profoundly mistrusted all women in the army, but were not able to do completely without their service. They therefore tried to do everything to regulate and limit the number of *blanchisseuses* and *vivandières* still in service. The law from April 1793 permitted no more than 4 *blanchisseuses* per battalion or 12 per demibrigade. With 198 demibrigades in 1793, this would amount to a total of 2,376 *blanchisseuses* in the infantry alone. Their actual number, however, was much higher, as indicated by the steady stream of regulations over the next decade that tried to reduce them. The regulation of *vivandières* was more open for interpretation. The French ancien régime army had allowed 8 per regiment. After 1793 the number was smaller, but they continued their service because soldiers and officers needed them. During the French Revolutionary Wars, more and more licenses included both positions, *blanchisseuses* and *vivandières*, resulting in the breakdown of the distinction between the two groups. At any given time during the wars, their estimated number stood at around 5,000. Since the early nineteenth century the term *cantinière* (canteen-keeper) was used for the officially approved female general-purpose auxiliaries in the French army. An important improvement of the position of female *vivandières* and later *cantinières* was that as of April 1793 they were officially allowed to own their own licenses, so they became independent businesswomen and no longer needed a husband who officially owned their property. Nevertheless, they usually were married to secure protection by their husbands' units. Under the Napoleonic Empire (1804–1814/15), the French military continued this practice. With the size of the Grande Armée, the number of officially approved female auxiliaries grew. They joined the troops on all their campaigns across Europe and shared their fate.[32]

The major opponent of the French in this era, the British, also tried to reduce the number of camp-following women, but they did not create a position similar to the officially patented French female auxiliaries until the First World War. The United Kingdom continued to regulate the number of women joining the troops with the number of wives on the strength. Their average number was reduced between 1790 and 1795 from 14 to 7.5 per 100 men per infantry regiment, but the difference between regiments carried on. The prestigious guard regiments had greater ease in obtaining permission to marry than their counterparts in the regiments of the line.[33]

In later years, during the Napoleonic Wars and afterward, the percentage of ordinary soldiers in the British military to whom the right to marriage was granted remained small, on average 6 per 100 men, but as high as 10 in exceptional cases, such as the guard regiments.[34] This, nevertheless, led to large numbers of women on the British campaigns of the era. Charles J. Esdaile estimated, for example, that 1,600 officially recognized army women accompanied the 40,000 British men sent to the Iberian Peninsula in 1808. These women, who usually earned their living during campaign by doing laundry, sewing, cooking, and other businesses, shared the miseries and dangers of war with the soldiers, much like the unknown number of Portuguese and Spanish women who unofficially followed the troops in large numbers; they usually became unmarried companions of soldiers during the campaign on the Iberian Peninsula.[35]

In the Prussian military, the number of camp-following women was steeply reduced in the context of the military reforms that the monarchy started after the devastating defeat by the Napoleonic army at the Battle of Jena and Auerstedt in October 1806. One discussed cause of the disaster was that the Prussian army still had relied on a large baggage train, which had clogged the roads, leading to a chaotic retreat and the army's dissolution. In July and November 1809, two government decrees completely expelled women and children from the military. Furthermore, the new Articles of War from August 1808 established the regulation that no soldier could marry without the approval of his company commander. If he nonetheless wedded, he was to be punished with three months of fortress confinement, and his marriage was to be annulled. In addition, regiments were to be moved regularly from one province of the monarchy to another to prevent soldiers from settling down, "civilizing," and losing their "martial spirit."[36] However, we know nothing about the implementation of these regulations and the everyday history of women related to soldiers, married or not, in this period. In the many war memoirs of Prussian volunteers, staff sergeants, officers, and generals published in the decades after the victory over Napoleon, we find remarkably little on army women in the units, which they had commanded or belonged to during the "Wars of Liberation" (1813–15). This indicates either that there were indeed not many army women or that the men chose to omit them from the narratives they constructed for posterity.[37]

What was remembered were the activities of the nearly 600 patriotic women's associations founded during the wars of 1813–15 in German-speaking Central Europe, including the Habsburg monarchy; more than 400 of them were active in Prussia alone. An "Appeal to the Women in the Prussian State" by the Hohenzollern princesses published in March 1813 started this movement. It called upon girls and women of all ranks to found "Women's Associations for the Good of the Fatherland" throughout Prussia and support the war by collecting money and goods for needy "defenders of the fatherland." But soon the activities broadened as the war went on, encompassing all areas of wartime nursing care and relief for the victims of war. It was mainly women of the nobility and upper middle classes who followed this appeal, because they had the time and the financial resources. Ordinary women had to work for a living. With their voluntary support of military nursing, these associations responded to the failure of the military medical care provided by the different war powers fighting in Central and Western Europe in 1813–15. Only 10 percent of these associations continued their work in the postwar era, when the "national emergency" situation ended and women were relegated to home and family again, but their work became an inspiration and model for later generations of middle- and upper-class women in the second half of the nineteenth century.[38]

Crossed-Dressed Female Soldiers

The research on women who, disguised as men, joined the armies of the French Revolutionary and Napoleonic Wars is far more developed than that on ordinary army women, even though their numbers were much smaller. Historians have identified twenty-two Dutch women who served in different armies in this period, eighty women who joined the French army (fifty of them in 1792/93), and twenty-two women who fought in the Prussian army of the Anti-Napoleonic Wars (1806–15).[39] We will never know exactly how many women joined military ranks during the French Revolutionary and Napoleonic Wars disguised as men, but most likely there were more than historians have discovered. It seems that many succeeded in hiding their identity, at least for some time. In the everyday of war, dressing and acting like a man and carrying a gun made a soldier. This comment of a French commander on an "artilleryman" in his unit is typical: "She so well hid her sex that during the month she lived in the middle of my men, no one suspected her, and after the fact, each of us was astonished at his stupidity."[40] Cross-dressed female soldiers passed the preinduction physical exam because military surgeons rarely made recruits take off their clothes. Most often, they seem to have been discovered when they were undressed because of injury, illness, or death.

As a result, almost all the authenticated cases came to light, and to historians' attention, because their disguise as men failed and officials recorded their discovery. Only a few women served openly, for example, during the brief period in 1792/93 when the French army permitted it. Therefore, we cannot preclude that more women served in disguise, and even more moved about the theaters of war dressed as men (simply because this was safer) without actively serving as soldiers. In this context, historical scholarship has addressed the question whether the number of crossed-dressed female soldiers was increasing in the Age of the Wars of Revolution and Independence. No definitive answer is possible, but it is likely that mobilization for a revolutionary uprising, national struggle for liberation, or civil war made it easier for women to volunteer for military service disguised as men. The pressing demand for soldiers led to superficial medical examinations. Men of all ages and statures were accepted. As armies and their recruiting processes, including the medical examination, became more professional during the nineteenth century, it became much more complicated for disguised women to join the military.[41]

Historians also debate the motives of female soldiers in this period. They ask to what extent patriotism, nationalism, or revolutionary verve might have been a motive, though evidence is rare. To the best of our knowledge, most of the usually young and single women who joined the armies as cross-dressed soldiers had motives similar to those of camp followers or officially recognized auxiliaries. They were driven by their economic, social, and personal circumstances. One common thread running through the biographies of most of these women was their desire to escape an unstable home, whether they were orphans, victims of cruel stepparents, or simply subject to abuse and parental control. Some joined military life while living far from home, family, and support networks, because it seemed to offer the only way of making a living. Yet others were children of retired soldiers, meaning that they were, in fact, returning to a life they had known from birth or went with a brother, husband, or lover, but even in these cases there were usually other reasons as well.[42]

Contemporaries were fascinated by cross-dressed female soldiers and labeled them "amazons" or "heroic virgins." They learned about them in the press, in poems, and in novels. In the public they were traditionally presented in an ambiguous way: usually as deviant women who transgressed the gender boundaries because they were more adventurous or passionate than was good for the fairer sex. Following a man into war was a common trope. In general, they stood, like army women of all kinds, under the suspicion of immoral behavior or, worse, being "whores." Demonstration of superior morality and virginity was necessary to dispel this suspicion. Only in specific circumstances, particularly in situations of national emergency, were they also presented as extraordinarily patriotic.[43]

We know so little about these women because they rarely published autobiographical accounts. Most of them were not able to read and write. The few published memoirs were mainly written to earn money and necessarily with the market in mind, so they tended to be adventurous folklore with exotic stories, or they attempted to serve the patriotic-nationalist cause. These texts reveal little about the real female experiences of military service. Instead, they inform us about the dominant ideas of the national gender order of war and the women's strategies for public self-representation.[44]

These issues are exemplified by three of the first and most popular autobiographical accounts written by women who participated in the French Revolutionary and Napoleonic Wars. Their memoirs were published in the first half of the nineteenth century and republished later in edited versions. The texts were part of a very small number of war memoirs written by women. Men who had served in the military composed the vast majority of the thousands of autobiographical accounts published in nineteenth-century Europe. Their texts left a long-lasting imprint on the collective memory of the French Revolutionary and Napoleonic Wars and contributed to the erasure of the female participation from the recollection of these conflicts.[45]

One of the first memoirs was published by Regula Engel in 1821. Born in Zurich in 1769, Engel was the daughter of a Swiss mercenary, and at the age of seventeen, she ran away from her family to marry Florian Engel, a sergeant-major from Bünden who served in a Swiss unit of the French army and rose to the rank of colonel. Between 1792 and 1815, she followed her husband despite an increasing number of children (twenty-one, of whom five survived) in every campaign of the French army while wearing a uniform. She experienced the fire of battles, wounding, and captivity (in 1809 by the Austrians). During the Battle of Waterloo in June 1815, her husband and two sons died, and she was found, severely injured, in an officer's uniform.[46] Claudia Ulrich demonstrated that Engel's adventurous story, which she published with the hope of an income, is a mix of fantasy and reality, but its readers seem to have liked it exactly for this reason; it sold well, was republished in 1825 under the title *Swiss Amazon* and was followed by a second part in 1828. But it did not help Engel, who had published the first edition herself, to make a living. As widow of a Swiss officer of the dissolved Napoleonic army, she could not hope for a pension and was impoverished.[47]

Equally exotic was the memoir by Nadezhda Durova, first published in Russia in 1836, where it became a sensation, much like Engel's memoir had been in the German-speaking lands of Europe.[48] Durova, the daughter of a Russian major, was born in an army camp at Kiev in 1783, and her father placed her in the care of his soldiers. After he had retired from service, she continued to demonstrate an ardent love for everything military, including weapons. Supposedly, she married in 1801 and gave birth to a son in 1803. Four years later, at the age of twenty-four, she disguised herself as a young man and deserted her son and husband, enlisting under the name Alexander Sokolov in a Polish Uhlan (light cavalry) regiment. Despite the discovery of her sex by her superiors, she was allowed to stay in the army and became a decorated soldier in the Russian cavalry during the Napoleonic Wars. Durova fought in several battles, including Smolensk and Borodino during Napoleon's Russian campaign from June to December 1812. When she retired from the army in 1816, she was highly decorated and held the rank of *stabs-rotmistr*, the equivalent of a captain.[49]

A third, similar memoir was published in France in 1842 by Marie-Thérèse Figueur, better known by her nom de guerre, "Madame Sans-Gêne." In contrast to most female soldiers of the time, she did not disguise her sex when she enlisted in 1793, serving for twenty-two years under her own name in the French revolutionary army and the Grande Armée. Figueur was born in 1774 in Talmay, near Dijon, the daughter of a miller and merchant. She was orphaned at nine years and was entrusted to a maternal uncle, a sous-lieutenant in an infantry regiment that fought in the counterrevolutionary Federalist uprising in 1793, which Figueur supported too. Captured by the forces of the revolutionary government and now nineteen years old, she was induced to enlist as a cavalry trooper in the Légion des Allobroges. She first experienced battle at the siege of Toulon from September to December 1793, where she was injured for the first time. Many more battles followed during her service in the French army, which only ended with the defeat of Napoleon in 1815. Her memoirs are, on the whole, more accurate in the details of her service than the two earlier publications, but she was also not entirely truthful in her writing.[50]

All three female war memoirs and their different, later editions provide valuable insights into what nineteenth-century society *expected* military women to be.[51] Written with the hope of appealing to a mass audience, the accounts were carefully excised and sanitized. Their authors, who had deviated from the dominant model of the wartime national gender order and challenged the male prerogative to bear arms and fight, were forced to tell their stories in a way that adhered to the prevailing ideas about gender roles, so accordingly, they presented themselves as exceptions to the rule. This strategy worked. The three memoirs became public successes and had a long-lasting impact on the public perception and collective memory of female soldiers.[52] Thus, the few cross-dressed female soldiers were surely not crucial for the functioning of the military or the outcome of the conflicts, but they had an enormous symbolic importance for the conveyance of the gender order of war.

The three memoirs indicate that army women and female soldiers only found public acceptance if they did not too unduly challenge gender norms. Two rhetorical strategies seem to have been available for this purpose in the contemporary discourse: emphasizing the "exceptional character" of the woman and her adventures or presenting her as a "maiden" or "virgin," irrespective of the reality. Examples of the former approach are the memoirs by Engel and Figueur, while Durova's account belongs to the latter. Her rewriting is especially telling. Durova, who had abandoned her husband and child to join the army, excised from her memoirs six years of her life to hide that fact, and she blatantly lied about the circumstances leading up to her enlistment, claiming she ran away from her father's house as a girl.[53] Even the title, *The Cavalry Maiden*, was a lie to conceal aspects of her life that would outrage the reading public: she claimed she was a virgin, played down her involvement in combat, and concealed her commanding rank. She asserted that she had never shed any blood and had only saved lives, because such was the behavior expected by the public.[54] We know that Durova's unit engaged in several battles and that she was indeed in command, but she went out of her way to gloss over actual combat. In place of the fighting, she emphasized her domestic role in her unit.[55] Even in recounting her discharge from the army, Durova stuck to the conventional narrative of female submission to paternal will: at the end of a home leave, her father asked her to return to his household. In only a few lines, she said farewell to "past happiness, glory, danger, uproar, glitter and a life of ebullient activity," since her father wanted it that way.[56] The narrative in Durova's memoirs stood in sharp contrast to her appearance and behavior after the discharge from the army: she insisted on a cropped haircut and wearing male attire and her cross of Saint George. She lived the life of a man in the Russian countryside until her death. There were thus two Nadezhda Durovas: the literary construct of a patriotic, virtuous maiden and dutiful daughter and the real-life woman who left her family for a life of adventure and then retired to the life of a man in a remote provincial town. The former appealed to public tastes and gender norms; the latter clearly did not.

The real experience of the era's female soldiers is difficult to reconstruct from their autobiographical accounts and the rare, other sources we find in libraries and archives. Clearly, female soldiers' experiences varied a great deal. Some served openly, like Marie-Thérèse Figueur, who for a time even became a national hero. Some faced early exposure and expulsion, while others served for years cross-dressed as men, often enlisting multiple times. Francina Gunningh Broese, for example, who was born in the small Dutch town of Kampen in 1783, enlisted as Frans Gunningh Sloet three times between 1806 and 1814. She joined a Dutch unit that served Napoleon, but deserted without ever being discovered. Then she signed on with the Prussian army and was discovered only after being wounded in battle. After being mustered out of the Prussian forces, she enlisted again with the Dutch in 1813 and fought until the peace in 1814. This time, she was discharged without being discovered, only being unmasked after the war in December of 1814 when she tried to marry a young woman.[57] Her story, like Nadezhda Durova's service from 1806 to 1816, shows that long-term masquerade was possible.

In most cases of female soldiers who became known, civil and military authorities as well as public opinion demanded not only that they had remained chaste and virtuous during their service, but also that they readapted to the gender norms after their discharge and became proper women again. Sloet clearly did not adhere to that expectation; she even tried to marry another woman while still masquerading as a man and thus faced arrest. Most female soldiers' treatment after their discharge depended more on upholding gender norms than on anything else.

One known example of successful adaption is Friederike Krüger, who fought in the Prussian army against Napoleon in the so-called Wars of Liberation of 1813–15. She, too, came from poverty. The daughter of peasants from Mecklenburg, she worked as a seamstress until she disguised herself as a man and enlisted at the age of twenty-four. In the spring of 1813, she joined the Kolberg regiment of the newly introduced *Landwehr* (militia) under the name of August Lübeck. She was quickly discovered as a woman, but her superiors allowed her to remain because she had distinguished herself in battle. During her service she reached the rank of a noncommissioned officer. When she was discharged from the Prussian army after the war in 1815, she had been decorated with the Iron Cross and the Russian Order of Saint George. She retired with a royal pension, married a corporal in the first year after the war, and settled down to be a wife and mother. Thus, she took up the expected female roles. Newspapers of the time reported her story, but in postwar society she was quickly forgotten, and her grave does not mention her military service except obliquely, noting that she had received two military medals, which adorned the monument, and that the gravestone was paid for by the king. Aside from these hints, she died in 1848 simply as the wife of the local tax collector.[58]

Most female soldiers who survived did not find a place in public war memories. If a woman was not known through published memoirs or popular biography, dying a "hero's death" on the battlefield was the other path to remembrance. One example of the latter is Eleanore Prochaska. She was the daughter of a Prussian noncommissioned officer from Potsdam, an orphan, and, later, an impoverished domestic servant, fitting the typical profile of a military woman of her era. In March 1813, immediately after the declaration of war against France by King Frederick William III of Prussia, the twenty-eight-year-old woman enrolled under the name of August Renz in the legendary voluntary unit of the Lützow Free Corps. Frederick William III had authorized the corps in February 1813 to enlist primarily young men "from abroad" (that is, the other German states) who could arm and clothe themselves. In August 1813, the Lützow Free Corps had grown to a size of 3,600 men and some women, including Prochaska. Until her death in October 1813, she fought with the Lützowers for the "liberation of the Prussian and German fatherland." She was discovered to be a woman only after her mortal injury.

She quickly became a national hero as the "Joan of Arc of Potsdam." The press reported about her and several poems praised her. She was immortalized in two dramas, one with music by Ludwig van Beethoven, both of which recommended her fighting spirit and courage as a "model" for men and boys. Her example was meant to shame German soldiers into fighting in the Wars of Liberation against Napoleonic France: a heroic virgin who chose death in battle rather than dishonor was what the German patriots needed for their war propaganda. Prochaska received an extravagant military funeral and, far from fading into obscurity, decades later, two monuments were erected at her places of death and birth. She was able to become a female national hero only because she died. Death prevented her from becoming a threat to the gender order of the postwar society. During the long nineteenth century, she became the only cross-dressed soldier in the German lands for whom two monuments were erected.[59]

The history of army women and female soldiers in the forces of the Wars of Revolution and Independence between the 1770s and the 1820s is fraught with disagreement and doubt, yet such women were more common than the conventional military historiography suggests. Research by women's and gender historians since the 1980s indicates that thousands of girls and women joined the ranks of the military as female soldiers, camp followers, or, as in the French army, in the newly created official function as *blanchisseuses* and *vivandières* in the various conflicts of the transatlantic world during this era. They met with various reactions, from dismissal and hostility to respect and recognition, the latter mainly in declared situations of "national emergency" during revolutionary conflicts and wars of liberation.

WOMEN IN EUROPEAN CONFLICTS OF THE NINETEENTH-CENTURY

Several historians have argued that the era of camp-following army women and cross-dressed female soldiers ended after the Napoleonic Wars, and there is some truth to this. Most European powers pursued a massive demobilization of their armies after these wars. A period of relative peace started on the European continent after 1815. Over the course of the nineteenth century, the increasing professionalization of European armies limited opportunities for women to join the ranks as disguised female soldiers. Army leaderships of all major powers tried to further reduce and regulate the number of women who officially or unofficially served as auxiliaries.

But peace is a relative concept; several smaller conflicts continued on the European continent until the Italian (1848–70)[60] and German (1864–71)[61] Wars of Unification. We know that women fought, for example, in the Greek War of Independence (1821–32)[62] and the Carlist Wars in Spain (1833–76).[63] They were also involved in the various smaller uprisings and revolutions across Europe. Women took part in street fighting in Paris and other French cities during the July Revolution of 1830 and again in the European Revolution of 1848–49. In central Europe, the uprisings and their repression in this revolution also saw women on the barricades in Berlin, Frankfurt am Main, Vienna, Budapest, and other cities. Democratic and socialist women, furthermore, supported their menfolk, who fought in the civil wars of the revolution against state militaries, by providing food and drink, casting bullets, and nursing the wounded.[64]

Thousands of anarchist and socialist women fought in the spring of 1871 to defend the Paris Commune, a revolutionary government controlled by radical socialists and anarchists that ruled Paris from 18 March to 28 May 1871, against the conservative government of the French Third Republic and its armed forces. They took up arms, helped to build barricades, and cared for wounded fighters. The revolutionary working-class women, denounced by conservatives as *pétroleuses* and accused of deliberately setting fire to buildings in Paris, worked and lived under such desperate conditions that they felt they had nothing to lose. Like their male comrades they were mercilessly killed or imprisoned under miserable circumstances by the regular French army during "*La semaine sanglante*" (The Bloody Week) of May 21–28, 1871. After its victory over the *communards*, the French army officially recorded the capture of 43,522 prisoners, of these 1,054 were women, and 615 were young people under the age of sixteen. At least 6,000 to 7,000 *communards* died.[65]

Women also played a role in the wars fought at the borders of Europe or abroad. The Crimean War (1853–56) involved the Russian, British, French, and Ottoman Empires, all of which used women as official or unofficial auxiliaries and nurses.[66] In addition, the global imperial powers, especially Britain and France, fought several colonial wars in Africa and Asia.[67] All these conflicts created demand for soldiers, as did conflicts across the Atlantic, like the US–Mexican War (1846–48), the French intervention in Mexico (1861–67), and the American Civil War.[68] And with the demand for soldiers, the demand for the logistic work of the day-to-day support of armies increased. Thus, the European and American militaries still needed women who served as official or unofficial auxiliaries and nurses in wartime.

The forms and functions of the employment of these women did not change much compared to the period of the Napoleonic Wars. Laws enshrined the position of official army women, the high commands grudgingly accepted their necessity, and the soldiers appreciated their support. Compared to the British wives on the strength, the position of the French *cantinières* was more regulated and less imperiled. As a sign of their status, in the 1830s *cantinières* in some units began to fashion military uniforms for themselves, a practice that subsequently spread throughout the army. In addition to official army women, most armies continued to pick up considerable numbers of foreign women while on campaign. These unofficial camp followers faced a range of military responses to their presence, from willing complicity by the men and the commander of a unit, who usually profited from their service, to arrest and corporal punishment by the military authorities who attempted to uphold military laws and discipline. Often, the borders between authorized and unauthorized women in the armies were fluid. In the reality of war, women aligned to a soldier continued to try to join the forces because they saw no alternative for their survival. The purpose of all army women was to supplement the armies' deplorable logistics systems by acting as laundresses and alternative providers of food and drink. On campaign, the latter continued to include pillaging and plundering. If they themselves did not plunder, *cantinières* or *vivandières* bought pillaged goods from soldiers and others, which they then resold at a profit.[69]

The experiences of army women were as varied as the conflicts in which they participated. But in general they continued to share all the miseries and dangers of travel, march, camp, and battle with their units, including the risk of being exposed to or becoming involved in combat. The public response to them changed and depended on the political environment. For example, during the Second Empire (1852–70), the French *cantinière* achieved a popular, if romanticized, status as an icon of the French military. Napoleon III doubled their numbers in 1854, and they served in special uniforms alongside their units in every campaign, notably in the Crimean War, the Second Italian War of Independence (1859), the French intervention in Mexico, the colonization of Cochinchina (1858–62), and the Franco-Prussian War (1870–71). To protect the women's reputation, a French law set standards for their moral and orderly behavior.

But the Third Republic started a process of slow decline, beginning with a reduction of the permitted number of *cantinières* in 1875 and culminating in 1890 with a ban on wearing uniforms. *Cantinières* were instead required to wear a simple, gray civilian dress with an arm patch. They were no longer allowed to join their regiments on campaign or maneuvers. This effectively ended the role of *cantinières* and led in 1905 to their elimination by the Ministry of War, which replaced them with male *cantiniers* with the requirement that they be retired veterans.[70]

In the British public, from the beginning, the reputation of the wives on the strength was less positive. They faced suspicion of their morality and virtue and often were perceived as whores. It did not help that the British army expected an officer to refuse the request of a soldier to marry until he had conducted a strict inquiry into the woman's morals. The position of a wife on the strength was finally eliminated by 1900.[71] In the decade before the First World War, the British and French militaries, like their Prussian and German counterparts decades before, became officially all-male institutions. Technological innovations, such as steam laundries, railroads, and canned rations, allowed military organizations to replace the services these women provided at the same time that growing civilian feminist and women's suffrage movements threatened men's sense of control and superiority.

The more women lost their place as auxiliaries in the European armies during the nineteenth century, the more they gained an increasingly recognized position in military medical care. The number of patriotic-minded female middle- and upper-class volunteers who underwent professional training for future wartime nursing increased steadily since the Crimean War. The work of Florence Nightingale, the celebrated British social reformer and founder of professional wartime nursing, was a model here. She had gained renown beyond Britain for her organisation of nursing during the Crimean War. After the war, she began training female volunteers for wartime nursing, financed by private sponsors. This development was furthered by the first Geneva Convention "for the Amelioration of the Condition of the Wounded in Armies in the Field," signed by twelve European states, which led to the founding of the International Committee of the Red Cross in 1876 and several national Red Cross organizations.[72] In an increasing number of states middle-and upper-class women prepared themselves for and became active in this war service on a voluntary or professional basis. Again, patriotic women's associations were founded to organize this form of female war support.[73] One early example or organized female military nursing is the American Civil War.

ARMY WOMEN AND FEMALE SOLDIERS IN THE AMERICAN CIVIL WAR

As the largest conflict of its time and the first industrialized war, the American Civil War is the best researched with respect to the role of women in mid-nineteenth-century warfare.[74] When the Union and Confederate forces faced each other between 1861 and 1865, massive changes in the organization of the military and new technologies had together transformed the face of warfare. The North and South both raised volunteer and conscription armies that fought mostly in the South and reached sizes that were unprecedented on the North American continent. Over the four years of the conflict, some 2.2 million men in total served in the Union army; its peak strength was 698,000 men. The Confederate army was approximately 750,000 to 1 million men strong, and its peak strength was 360,000 soldiers. With deaths of some 620,000 to 750,000 soldiers in total, the toll was higher than the number of American military deaths in World Wars I and II combined. One major reason for this was that the American Civil War was the first industrialized conflict: railroads and steamboats were used for transportation, and techniques of mass production were utilized for the manufacturing of weapons and equipment. The deadliest of the new weapons were rapid-fire arms and modern rifles.[75]

Armies of that size needed the support of women. Thousands of them participated in the conflict on both sides in three different capacities: as so-called daughters (or mothers) of the regiment, sutlers, and battlefield and field-hospital nurses. The daughters or mothers of the regiment were all-purpose helpers who had joined their parents or husband in the field. Different from sutlers who sold supplies and tended to the sick and wounded, the regimental daughters and mothers did everything from laundry, sewing, and cooking to nursing. By far, most women served as nurses. An estimated 3,200 women held paid positions as army nurses in the North and the South. They were badly needed because the military medical system was ill-prepared for the large number of injured and sick soldiers.[76] Dorothea Dix, an experienced prewar hospital reformer, was appointed superintendent of army nurses by the Union army and became well known. The fifty-nine-year-old tried to reorganize the nursing system and set guidelines for nurse candidates because she wanted to protect the reputation of the women nurse corps and to prevent the exploitation of individual nurses by doctors and patients. The guidelines required that volunteers had to be aged thirty-five to fifty and plain-looking; they were instructed to wear simple black or brown dresses and no jewelry or cosmetics.[77]

In addition, women joined the two armies as soldiers. Estimates of their numbers vary greatly from the confirmed 250 to at least 1,000 or more.[78] How many cross-dressed women joined the ranks we will never know, because most of them served until discharge without discovery. One of these cases was Jennie Hodgers, who was born in Clogherhead, Ireland, in 1843 and immigrated to the United States with her parents. At the age of nineteen, she assumed the name Albert D. J. Cashier and joined the 95th Illinois Infantry in September 1862. Her discovery did not come until 1915, and the subsequent pension investigation proves revealing: men in her own unit did not know that she was a woman until they were told by government investigators.[79] The regiment fought in at least forty battles. Hodgers managed to live out her entire adult life as Albert Cashier until finally discovered in old age by a doctor. After her death in 1915, her martial identity nevertheless persisted. She was buried in uniform, and the tombstone was inscribed "Albert D. J. Cashier, Co. G, 95 Ill. Inf." A fellow veteran, Lon P. Dawson, documented her life after her death in a biography titled *Known as Albert D. J. Cashier: The Jennie Hodgers Story*.[80] The exigencies of a civil war in which two armies desperately needed recruits, and therefore often forwent the medical examination of volunteers, seem to have encouraged and enabled women to join the ranks undiscovered. Similar to army women, most female soldiers did not win any recognition after the war and were not included in the collective memory of the American nation.[81]

CONCLUSION

The collective memory of army women and female soldiers offers a complex and ambivalent picture. Most women who followed the drums in eighteenth- and nineteenth-century Europe and North America as army women, nurses, and cross-dressed female soldiers stayed in the dark of history. Only some of them reached the pantheon of national memory, especially the ones who stepped out of their usual role as army women in an exceptional moment and became involved in combat in a supportive role or as an emergency replacement of fallen soldiers, such as in the example of the composite hero Molly Pitcher.[82] Military historians and the public long ignored the many functions of female camp followers and officially licensed auxiliaries for the maintenance of the campaign community in conflicts of the era. It was not until the 1980s that women's and gender historians interested in the history of military and war discovered them. In the early twenty-first century their numbers and their importance are still contested in the scholarship, even for the better researched cases of the American, British, and French militaries. Although precise statistics remain elusive, historians agree that far more women were in involved in eighteenth- and nineteenth-century warfare than was long assumed.

The small number of female soldiers who cross-dressed as men received far more public attention. Most of these women, especially when they were not discovered, remained in obscurity. The ones who were unmasked often garnered a brief note or two in the contemporary press as a sensation, an extraordinary—and morally suspicious— anomaly that confirmed the existing ideas about the gender order. If they survived, with some exceptions, they were forced by society, the military, and the political administration to redress as a woman and assume the culturally expected female duties of marriage and forming a family.

Only some of the surviving female soldiers made it into national collective memory. On the one hand are the few women from the period of the Age of the Wars of Revolution and Independence who wrote memoirs. Their texts created attention and informed the stereotypes about female soldiers, fueling a feedback loop in which they had to play to readers' expectations to be successful on the market. On the other hand, women who died on the battlefield sometimes had the chance to be remembered, because death rendered them safe to society—they could not threaten the gender order. They nevertheless needed to fit (or were made to fit) the public image of the patriotic virgin who rose above the limitations of her sex as a result of her exceptional passion to defend or liberate the nation. In this way, they could be stylized, through their bravery and their willingness to sacrifice, as models for male soldiers. In the later, nationalist public historiography of the nineteenth century, through their supposed virtuous love for the nation these women became role models for girls, but they simultaneously functioned as cautionary tales warning them not to transgress the boundaries of their sex.

NOTES

1. The most important studies are Dianne Mary Dugaw, *Warrior Women and Popular Balladry, 1650–1850* (Cambridge: Cambridge University Press, 1989); Julie Wheelwright, *Amazons and Military Maids: Women Who Dressed as Men in the Pursuit of Life, Liberty and Happiness* (London: Pandora, 1989), 132–66; Rudolf Dekker and Lotte C. van de Pol, *The Tradition of Female Transvestism in Early Modern Europe* (New York: St. Martin's Press, 1989); Sylvie Steinberg, *La confusion des sexes: le travestissement de la Renaissance à la Révolution* (Paris: Fayard, 2001); Elisabeth Krimmer, *In the Company of Men: Cross-Dressed Women around 1800* (Detroit, MI: Wayne State University Press, 2004); and Helen Watanabe-O'Kelly, *Beauty or Beast? The Woman Warrior in the German Imagination from the Renaissance to the Present* (New York: Oxford University Press, 2010).

2. See Peter H. Wilson, "German Women and War, 1500–1800," *War in History* 3, no. 2 (1996): 127–60; John A. Lynn, *Women, Armies, and Warfare in Early Modern Europe* (Cambridge: Cambridge University Press, 2008); Lynn, "Essential Women, Necessary Wives, and Exemplary Soldiers: The Military Reality and Cultural Representations of Women's Military Participation," in *A Companion to Women's Military History*, ed. Barton C. Hacker and Margaret Vining (Leiden: Brill, 2012), 93–136; Barton C. Hacker, "Reformers, Nurses, and Ladies in Uniform: The Changing Status of Military Women (c. 1815–c. 1914)," in Hacker and Vining, *A Companion to Women's Military History*, 137–88; and Klaus Latzel et al., eds., *Soldatinnen: Gewalt und Geschlecht im Krieg vom Mittelalter bis Heute* (Paderborn: Schöningh, 2011).

3. Lynn, "Essential Women," 93. See also Barton C. Hacker, "Women and Military Institutions in Early Modern Europe: A Reconnaissance," *Signs* 6, no. 4 (1981): 643–71; and Hacker, "Where Have All the Women Gone? The Pre-Twentieth Century Sexual Division of Labor in Armies," *Minerva* 3, no. 1 (1985): 107–48.

4. See Wilson, "German Women," 122–24; as well as the chapter by Wilson on "Wars, States, and Gender in Early Modern European Warfare, 1600s–1780s" in this handbook; and Karen Hagemann, "Venus und Mars: Reflexionen zu einer Geschlechtergeschichte von Militär und Krieg," in *Landsknechte, Soldatenfraue und Nationalkrieger: Militär, Krieg und Geschlechterordnung im Historischen Wandel*, ed. Karen Hagemann and Ralf Pröve (Frankfurt am Main: Campus, 1998), 13–50.

5. See Hagemann, "Venus und Mars," 19–20; Lynn, "Essential Women," and *Women*, 78–89; exemplary studies are Beate Engelen, *Soldatenfrauen in Preußen: Eine Strukturanalyse der Garnisonsgesellschaft im späten 17. und im 18. Jahrhundert* (Münster: LIT, 2005), 41–203; and Jennine Hurl-Eamon, *Marriage and the British Army in the Long Eighteenth Century: "The Girl I Left behind Me"* (Oxford: Oxford University Press, 2014), 28–88.

6. Karen Hagemann, "Militär, Krieg und Geschlechterverhältnisse: Untersuchungen, Überlegungen und Fragen zur Militärgeschichte der Frühen Neuzeit," in *Klio in Uniform: Probleme und Perspektiven einer modernen Militärgeschichte der Frühen Neuzeit*, ed. Ralf Pröve (Cologne: Böhlau, 1997), 35–88.

7. See the chapter by Alan Forrest on "Society, Mass Warfare, and Gender in Europe during and after the Revolutionary and Napoleonic Wars" in this handbook.

8. Klaus Latzel et al., "Soldatinnen in der Geschichte: Weibliche Verletzungsmacht als Herausforderung," in Latzel et al., *Soldatinnen*, 11–49.

9. See the chapter by Stefan Dudink on "Citizenship, Mass Mobilization, and Masculinity in a Transatlantic Perspective, 1770s–1870s" in this handbook; as well as Karen Hagemann, "The Military and Masculinity: Gendering the History of the French Wars, 1792–1815," in *War in an Age of Revolution, 1775–1815*, ed. Roger Chickering and Stig Förster (Cambridge: Cambridge University Press, 2010), 331–52.

10. See, for more, Karen Hagemann et al., eds., *Gender, War and Politics: Transatlantic Perspectives, 1775–1830* (Basingstoke: Palgrave Macmillan, 2010).

11. See Harriet B. Applewhite and Darline G. Levy, "Women and Militant Citizenship in Revolutionary Paris," in *Rebel Daughters: Women and the French Revolution*, ed. Sara E. Melzer and Leslie W. Kabine (New York: Oxford University Press, 1992), 79–101.

12. Michael Clodfelter, *Warfare and Armed Conflicts: A Statistical Encyclopedia of Casualty and Other Figures, 1494–2007*, 2nd ed. (Jefferson, NC: McFarland, 2002), 146.

13. Linda Grant De Pauw, "Women in Combat: The Revolutionary War Experience," *Armed Forces & Society* 7, no. 2 (1981): 209–26.

14. Ibid.

15. Hurl-Eamon, *Marriage*, 22–23.

16. Holly Mayer, "Bearing Arms, Bearing Burdens: Women Warriors, Camp Followers and Home-Front Heroines of the American Revolution," in Hagemann et al., *Gender, War and Politics*, 169–87; and Mayer, *Belonging to the Army: Camp Followers and Community during the American Revolution* (Columbia: University of South Carolina Press, 1996).

17. "General Order, 4. August 1777," in *The Papers of George Washington, Revolutionary War Series*, vol. 10, 11 June 1777–18 August 1777, ed. Frank E. Grizzard, Jr. (Charlottesville: University Press of Virginia, 2000), 496–97.

18. Mayer, "Bearing Arms," 173–76; and Karen Hagemann, "'Heroic Virgins' and 'Bellicose Amazons': Armed Women, the Gender Order, and the German Public during and after the Anti-Napoleonic Wars," *European History Quarterly* 37, no. 4 (2007): 507–527.

19. Lynn, "Essential Women," 119–20; and Hacker, "Reformers, Nurses."

20. Mayer, "Bearing Arms," 178–79.

21. Ibid.; see also Grant De Pauw, "Women in Combat," 213–14.

22. Grant De Pauw, "Women in Combat," 214–17.

23. Anne Rockwell, *They Called Her Molly Pitcher* (New York: Alfred A. Knopf, 2002).

24. Emily Lewis Butterfield, "'Lie There My Darling, While I Avenge Ye!': Anecdotes, Collective Memory, and the Legend of Molly Pitcher," in *Remembering the Revolution: Memory, History, and Nation Making from Independence to the Civil War*, ed. Michael A. McDonnell et al. (Amherst: University of Massachusetts Press, 2013), 198–216.

25. See the reprint, Herman Mann, *The Female Review: Life of Deborah Sampson, the Female Soldier in the War of the Revolution* (Tarrytown, NY: W. Abbatt, 1916); for more on Sampson, see Judith Hiltner, "'She Bled in Secret': Deborah Sampson, Herman Mann and "The Female Review'," *Early American Literature* 34, no. 2 (1999): 190–220; and Alfred Fabian Young, *Masquerade: The Life and Times of Deborah Sampson, Continental Soldier* (New York: Alfred A. Knopf, 2004).

26. See the chapter by Forrest on "Society, Mass Warfare" in this handbook.

27. Hagemann, "The Military," 335–36.

28. See Karen Hagemann, *"Mannlicher Muth und Teutsche Ehre". Nation, Militär und Geschlecht zur Zeit der Antinapoleonischen Kriege Preußens* (Paderborn: Schöningh, 2002), 81–83; Thomas Cardoza, *Intrepid Women, Cantinières and Vivandières of the French Army* (Bloomington, Indiana University Press, 2010), 59–102; and Hurl-Eamon, *Marriage*, 1–88.

29. Cardoza, *Intrepid Women*, 49–50.

30. See Applewhite and Levy, "Women."

31. Hagemann et al., *Gender, War and Politics*.

32. Thomas Cardoza, "'Habits Appropriate to Her Sex': The Female Military Experience in France during the Age of Revolutions," in Hagemann et al., *Gender, War and Politics*, 188–205; and Cardoza, *Intrepid Women*, 47 and 30–102.

33. Hurl-Eamon, *Marriage*, 13–21; and Myna Trustram, *Women of the Regiment: Marriage and the Victorian Army*, (Cambridge: Cambridge University Press, 1984) 31.

34. Trustram, *Women*, 30–31.

35. Charles Esdaile, *Women in the Peninsular War* (Norman: University of Oklahoma Press, 2014), 74.

36. Hagemann, *Mannlicher Muth*, 81–83.

37. Karen Hagemann, *Revisiting Prussia's Wars against Napoleon: History, Culture, and Memory* (Cambridge: Cambridge University Press, 2015), 301–34.

38. See Jean H. Quataert, *Staging Philanthropy: Patriotic Women and the National Imagination in Dynastic Germany, 1813–1916* (Ann Arbor: University of Michigan Press, 2001), 21–5; and Karen Hagemann, "Female Patriots: Women, War and the Nation in the Period of the Prussian-German Anti-Napoleonic Wars," *Gender & History* 16, no. 3 (2004): 396–424 .

39. Dekker and van de Pol, *The Tradition*; Dominique Godineau, "De la guerrière à la citoyenne: porter les armes pendant l'ancien régime et la révolution française," *Clio* no. 20 (2004): 43–69; and Hagemann, "Heroic Virgins," 508.

40. Anthony Dedem de Gelder, *Général hollandais sous le premier empire: Mémoires du général Bon de Dedem de Gelder, 1774–1825* (Paris: E. Plon Nouritt, 1900), 280–81.

41. Hagemann, "Heroic Virgins," 510–12.

42. David Hopkin, "The World Turned Upside Down: Female Soldiers in the French Armies of the Revolutionary and Napoleonic Wars," in *Soldiers, Citizens and Civilians: Experiences and Perceptions of the French Wars, 1790–1820*, ed. Alan Forrest et al. (Basingstoke: Palgrave Macmillan, 2009), 77–95.

43. See Dugaw, *Warrior Women*; Wheelwright, *Amazons*; and Krimmer, *In the Company*.

44. Hagemann, *Revisiting*, 301–34.

45. See Philip G. Dwyer, "Public Remembering, Private Reminiscing: French Military Memoirs and the Revolutionary and Napoleonic Wars," *French Historical Studies* 33, no. 2 (2010): 231–58.

46. [Regula Engel], *Lebensbeschreibung der Wittwe des Obrist Florian Engel von Langwies [...]. Von ihr selbst beschrieben* (Zurich: self-pub., 1821).

47. See Claudia Ulbrich, "Deutungen von Krieg in den Lebenserinnerungen der Regula Engel," in *Krieg und Umbruch um 1800: Das französisch dominierte Mitteleuropa auf dem Weg in eine neue Zeit*, ed. Ute Planert (Paderborn: Schöningh, 2008), 297–314; and Stephanie M. Hilger, "Autobiographical Selves: The Lebensbeschreibung of Regula Engel (1761–1853), the 'Swiss Amazon,'" *Women in German Yearbook* 25 (2009): 127–48.

48. Nadezhda Durova, *Kavelerist-devitsa. Proisshestvie v Rossii* (1836), English translation: *The Cavalry Maiden: Journals of a Russian Officer in the Napoleonic Wars*, trans. Mary Fleming Zirin (Bloomington: Indiana University Press, 1989).

49. Durova, *The Cavalry Maiden.*
50. Marie-Thérèse Figueur, *Les campagnes de Mlle Thérèse Figueur, aujourd'hui Madame Veuve Sutter, ex-dragon aux 15ᵉ et 9ᵉ regimens de 1793 à 1815* (Paris: Dauvin et Fontaine, 1842). Her service record in the French archives verifies these appendices: Service historique de la défense, 1Yi, "Figueur."
51. David M. Hopkin, "Female Soldiers and the Battle of the Sexes in Nineteenth-Century France: The Mobilization of a Folk Motif," *History Workshop Journal* 56, no. 1 (2003): 78–104.
52. Ulbrich, "Deutungen."
53. Durova, *The Cavalry Maiden*, 15.
54. Ibid., 141.
55. Ibid., 133, 173.
56. Ibid., 224–25.
57. Dekker and van de Pol, *Tradition*, 62.
58. Hagemann, "Heroic Virgins," 516–18.
59. Ibid., 515–16.
60. See the chapters by Benedetta Gennaro, "One in a Mille: Countess Martini della Torre," 13–34; Giovanna Summerfield, "Peppa la Cannoniera: Citizenship in Action," 35–50; and Susan Amatangelo, "'Sono briganta, io, non donna di brigante': The Female Brigand's Search for Identity," 52–72, in *Italian Women at War: Sisters in Arms from the Unification to the Twentieth Century*, ed. Susan Amatangelo et al. (Madison, WI: Fairleigh Dickinson University Press, 2016).
61. See Jean H. Quataert, "German Patriotic Women's Work in War and Peace Time, 1864–90," in *On the Road to Total War: The American Civil War and the German Wars of Unification, 1861–1871*, ed. Stig Förster and Jörg Nagler (Cambridge: Cambridge University Press, 1997), 449–77.
62. David Brewer, *The Flame of Freedom: The Greek War of Independence, 1821–1833* (London: John Murray, 2001).
63. See Catherine Davies, "The Gender Order of Postwar Politics: Comparing Spanish South America and Spain, 1810s–1850s," in *War, Demobilization and Memory: The Legacy of War in the Era of Atlantic Revolutions*, ed. Alan Forrest et al. (Basingstoke: Palgrave Macmillan, 2016), 182–202.
64. Gabriella Hauch, "Women's Space in the Men's Revolution of 1848," in *Europe in 1848: Revolution and Reform*, ed. Dieter Dowe et al. (New York: Berghahn Books, 2001), 639–82.
65. Carolyn Jeanne Eichner, *Surmounting the Barricades: Women in the Paris Commune* (Bloomington: Indiana University Press, 2004); and Gay L. Gullickson, *Unruly Women of Paris: Images of the Commune* (Ithaca, NY: Cornell University Press, 1996).
66. Helen Rappaport, *No Place for Ladies: The Untold Story of Women in the Crimean War* (London: Aurum, 2007).
67. See the chapter by Angela Woollacott on "Imperial Conquest, Violent Encounters, and Changing Gender Relations in Colonial Warfare, 1830s–1910s" in this handbook.
68. See the chapter by Amy S. Greenberg on "Gender and the Wars of Nation-Building and Nation-Keeping in the Americas, 1830s–1870s" in this handbook.
69. See also, for the following, Hacker, "Reformers"; Cardoza, *Intrepid Women*, 127–214; and Trustram, *Women*, 10–115.
70. Cardoza, *Intrepid Women*, 127–214; and Gil Mihaely, "L'effacement ou la cantinière ou la virilisation de l'armée française au XIXᵉ siècle," *Revue d'histoire du XIXe siècle* no. 30 (2005): 21–43.

71. Trustram, *Women*, 10–115.
72. Hacker, "Reformers."
73. See Quataert, *Staging Philanthropy*, 177–216; for the development of military nursing see the chapter by Jean H. Quataert "Changing Modes of Warfare and the Gendering of Military Medical Care, 1850s–1920s" in this handbook; and the section "Gender, Early Humanitarianism, and Peace Activism" in the chapter by Stefan Dudink, Karen Hagemann, and Mischa Honeck on "War and Gender: Nineteenth-Century Wars of Nations and Empires—an Overview in this handbook."
74. See Elizabeth D. Leonard, *All the Daring of the Soldier: Women of the Civil War Armies* (New York: W. W. Norton, 1999); DeAnne Blanton, *They Fought Like Demons: Women Soldiers in the Civil War* (New York: Vintage, 2002); Richard H. Hall, *Women on the Civil War Battlefront* (Lawrence: University Press of Kansas, 2006); Jane E. Schultz, *Women at the Front: Hospital Workers in Civil War America* (Chapel Hill: University of North Carolina Press, 2004); and Greenberg, "Gender and the Wars of Nation-Building."
75. Clodfelter, *Warfare*, 304–6.
76. Mary Elizabeth Massey, *Bonnet Brigades* (New York: Alfred A. Knopf, 1966), citations refer to the reprint edition, *Women in the Civil War* (Lincoln: University of Nebraska Press, 1994), xviii; and Hall, *Women*, 12–24.
77. Pamela D. Toler, *Heroines of Mercy Street: The Real Nurses of the Civil War* (New York: Little, Brown, 2016), esp. 9–31; and Schultz, *Women*.
78. Hall, *Women*, 11; and Blanton, *They Fought*, 6–7.
79. J. Himes, "Deposition in the Case of Albert Cashier," 1915, repr. in DeAnne Blanton, "Women Soldiers of the Civil War," *Prologue Magazine* 25, no. 1 (1993): 27–33.
80. See Lynda Durrant, *My Last Skirt: The Story of Jennie Hodgers, Union Soldier* (New York: Clarion Books, 2006).
81. Blanton, *They Fought*, 163–204; and Alice Fahs and Joan Waugh, eds., *The Memory of the Civil War in American Culture* (Chapel Hill: University of North Carolina Press, 2004).
82. Another example is Agustina Zaragoza, whom John Lawrence Tone discusses in "A Dangerous Amazon: Agustina Zaragoza and the Spanish Revolutionary War, 1808–1814," *European History Quarterly* 37, no. 4 (2007): 548–61.

SELECT BIBLIOGRAPHY

Blanton, DeAnne. *They Fought Like Demons: Women Soldiers in the American Civil War.* Baton Rouge: Louisiana State University Press, 2002.

Cardoza, Thomas. *Intrepid Women: Cantinières and Vivandières of the French Army.* Bloomington: Indiana University Press, 2010.

Dekker, Rudolf, and Lotte C. van de Pol. *The Tradition of Female Transvestism in Early Modern Europe.* New York: St. Martin's, 1989.

Dugaw, Dianne Mary. *Warrior Women and Popular Balladry, 1650–1850.* Cambridge: Cambridge University Press, 1989.

Eichner, Carolyn Jeanne. *Surmounting the Barricades: Women in the Paris Commune.* Bloomington: Indiana University Press, 2004.

Esdaile, Charles J. *Women and the Peninsular War.* Norman: University of Oklahoma Press, 2014.

Hacker, Barton C. "Reformers, Nurses, and Ladies in Uniform: The Changing Status of Military Women (c. 1815–c. 1914)." In *A Companion to Women's Military History*, edited by Barton C. Hacker and Margaret Vining, 137–88. Leiden: Brill, 2012.

Hagemann, Karen. "'Heroic Virgins' and 'Bellicose Amazons': Armed Women, the Gender Order, and the German Public during and after the Anti-Napoleonic Wars." *European History Quarterly* 37, no. 4 (2007): 507–27.

Hauch, Gabriella. "Women's Space in the Men's Revolution of 1848." In *Europe in 1848: Revolution and Reform*, edited by Dieter Dowe, Heinz-Gerhard Haupt, and Jonathan Sperber, 639–82. New York: Berghahn Books, 2001.

Hopkin, David. "The World Turned Upside Down: Female Soldiers in the French Armies of the Revolutionary and Napoleonic Wars." In *Soldiers, Citizens and Civilians: Experiences and Perceptions of the French Wars, 1790–1820*, edited by Alan Forrest, Karen Hagemann, and Jane Rendall, 77–98. Basingstoke: Palgrave Macmillan, 2009.

Hurl-Eamon, Jennine. *Marriage and the British Army in the Long Eighteenth Century: "The Girl I Left behind Me."* Oxford: Oxford University Press, 2014.

Latzel, Klaus, Franka Maubach, and Silke Satjukow, eds. *Soldatinnen: Gewalt und Geschlecht im Krieg vom Mittelalter bis Heute.* Paderborn: Schöningh, 2011.

Lynn, John A. "Essential Women, Necessary Wives, and Exemplary Soldiers: The Military Reality and Cultural Representations of Women's Military Participation." In *A Companion to Women's Military History*, edited by Barton C. Hacker and Margaret Vining, 93–136. Leiden: Brill, 2012.

Lynn, John A. *Women, Armies, and Warfare in Early Modern Europe.* Cambridge: Cambridge University Press, 2008.

Mayer, Holly A. *Belonging to the Army: Camp Followers and Community during the American Revolution.* Columbia: University of South Carolina Press, 1996.

Rappaport, Helen. *No Place for Ladies: The Untold Story of Women in the Crimean War.* London: Aurum, 2007.

Trustram, Myna. *Women of the Regiment: Marriage and the Victorian Army.* Cambridge: Cambridge University Press, 1984.

Watanabe-O'Kelly Helen. *Beauty or Beast? The Woman Warrior in the German Imagination from the Renaissance to the Present.* Oxford: Oxford University Press, 2010.

Wheelwright, Julie. *Amazons and Military Maids: Women Who Dressed as Men in the Pursuit of Life, Liberty and Happiness.* London: Pandora, 1989.

Wilson, Peter H. "German Women and War, 1500–1800." *War in History* 3, no. 2 (1996): 127–60.

CITIZENSHIP, MASS MOBILIZATION, AND MASCULINITY IN A TRANSATLANTIC PERSPECTIVE, 1770s–1870s

STEFAN DUDINK

THE French Revolutionary and Napoleonic Wars (1792–1815) inaugurated the mass warfare that was to become central to the history of war in the modern period. An analysis of the ways these wars affected, and were shaped by, notions and practices of masculinity requires understanding their specific nature. The wars of the revolutionary and Napoleonic era cannot be separated from the radical political changes and social transformations in this period. This entwinement has contributed to an interpretation of these conflicts as constituting an equally radical break in the history of war and warfare. Most clearly, this is the case in analyses of these wars as the first *total wars* that locate their specificity in an underlying new political dynamic that called for a society's total engagement in war and an unprecedented leaving behind of restraints.[1] Accounts of the French Revolutionary and Napoleonic Wars that focus more narrowly on tactics and strategy, however, have also traditionally stressed that they represent a break with previous modes of warfare. In these interpretations, increased mobility on and away from the battlefield, a proclivity among commanders for seeking out and entering pitched battle, and a redefinition of the aim of battle—complete destruction of enemy forces rather than obtaining an advantageous change in the strategic balance of power—were identified as the core elements of a new way of waging war that was to define warfare in modern times.[2]

Historians have criticized such views for the assumption that the French Revolutionary and Napoleonic Wars necessarily reflect the revolutionary rupture out of which they emerged and as being too close to the interpretations of these wars by contemporary participants and observers who tried to make sense of twenty-three years of violence and sociopolitical turmoil.[3] Questioning the supposedly different nature of these wars, Michael Broers, for instance, contends that these wars were not "harbingers of the new," but were instead the last great wars fought without modern technology and on the basis of early modern tactics.[4] Stressing continuity and, in some instances—such as troops living off the land, the shock delivered by heavy cavalry—the "retrograde" nature of revolutionary and Napoleonic warfare, Broers discerns profound change only in one aspect of these wars: "Their scale and what was entailed in managing it."[5] To be sure, meaningful military transformation might have taken place only in terms of scale, but this is not a minor detail of these wars. Both in absolute numbers and relative to population size, they represent a quantitative leap in the development of the size of armies and battles.[6] This kind of mass mobilization required the development of a state machinery that combined sophisticated bureaucratic techniques of registration with the use of blunt force in imposing its recruitment policies. It also came with elaborate ideological justifications and exhortations, which often were part of a wider emerging discourse of the nation.[7]

The practices and ideologies of mass mobilization and those of masculinity in the Age of Revolutions (1770s–1840s) were mutually constitutive. The integration, mostly forced, of hundreds of thousands of men into the state's military apparatus was often presented as a glorious coming together of nation, state, and military after a long period of separation that had been harmful to them all. This reunion then appeared as animated by qualities that invariably were associated with masculinity: virtue, valor, courage, heroism, love of fatherland, self-sacrifice. In many cases, but not always, the renewed conjoining of nation, state, and military was institutionally expressed in a male duty to serve, coupled with a male right to political citizenship. The (re)articulations of notions of state, military, nation, masculinity, and citizenship in the processes of mass mobilization in the decades before, during, and in the aftermath of the French Revolutionary and Napoleonic Wars offer rich opportunities to historicize gender and its relations to war in this period. In the following, the ways mass mobilization and masculinity shaped each other will be explored by first giving an overview of the systems of recruitment used for mass mobilization and the social identities that formed the basis for the selection of recruits and, second, by analyzing the rhetoric of masculinity deployed in processes of mass mobilization and in the gendered politics of citizenship that mass mobilization spawned.

RECRUITING MEN

European military theorists of the era of the French Revolutionary and Napoleonic Wars were greatly inspired by the American Revolutionary War (1775–83) as an example of a victorious citizen army. For the American revolutionaries, the establishment of both national independence and a democratic republic depended on the outcome of the war with Britain. They started the war with militias of volunteers that, according to the revolutionary rhetoric, performed their duties as citizens by becoming soldiers. The local amateur militias were important in securing victory for the revolutionaries, in particular when the war became one of guerrilla skirmishes, as it did in the South, but they could not win the war. One of the first decisions of the Second Continental Congress of 1775 was therefore to create the Continental army, initially intended to be an army of volunteers, given the public resistance against any standing army that was perceived as the mainspring of tyranny and corruption.

As the war continued, however, the congress was forced to assent to short-term conscription. Nevertheless, the republican rhetoric of the virtuous citizen-soldier retained its prominence in encouraging Americans to take up arms and justify the war, even though the ranks of the army troops also included enslaved persons and British deserters—men who were not even eligible for militia membership. In total, the Continental army reached an enlistment of some 376,700 soldiers, including 145,000 militiamen.[8] Demonstrating the power of revolutionary ideology for war mobilization, the victory over Britain inspired military reformers on the other side of the Atlantic.[9]

Late eighteenth-century states such as Britain could also field substantial armies at times of war using different systems of recruitment.[10] In Britain, as in France, the larger part of regular armies consisted of men recruited voluntarily—to varying degrees—by officers the state had commissioned to raise troops. In the course of the eighteenth century, both the British and the French states had increased their control over this decentralized system of enlistment by commissioned officers. Foreign soldiers, hired either individually or as units, contributed to the numbers of men serving in several armies. Systems of conscription were in place in other states. One example is Russia, which ruthlessly conscripted its peasants in large numbers and, until 1793, for life. In the Prussian (1733) and Austrian (1770) cantonal systems, the draftees also predominantly came from the rural poor. In the case of Prussia, exemptions granted to entire regions, cities, and numerous occupations and professions left only poor men and peasants from East Elbia liable to serve.[11] During peacetime they were required to serve with their regiments for a limited period each year, after which they returned to their families and occupations. France and Britain had no system of conscription, but recruitment for the militia at times approximated the selective practices of conscription found elsewhere. And although the militia was intended for self-defense and required active service only during times of war, in France during the eighteenth century it was progressively incorporated into the regular army.[12]

Systems of recruitment continued to differ after the start of the French Revolutionary Wars in 1792, but these differences have sometimes been overshadowed by the importance attributed to the system of universal conscription introduced in revolutionary France. Such an emphasis on French developments is not entirely unjustified. The institution of universal male conscription during the French Revolution (1789–99) did spawn a dynamic of diffusion throughout Europe in which the national conscript army was more or less willingly introduced, or forcefully imposed, elsewhere. Where it was rejected, the national conscript army still made its presence felt in a conscious refusal of a model of military recruitment that was deemed politically dangerous because of its associations with democratic citizenship.

This dynamic of diffusion should not blind us, however, to the fact that a great number of the troops that fought during the 1792–1815 period had been mobilized on the basis of ancien régime systems of recruitment. Gender historians have also paid considerable attention to French universal conscription, and this, too, is understandable. After all, as André Rauch notes, universal conscription changed the masculine condition.[13] The conscription of all men *as* men not only homogenized men's experiences during a part of their lives, but also contributed to the making of the social identity of "man" as one that transcended identity categories such as class and religion. In other systems of recruitment, however, these identities retained their importance—and to a certain extent this was the case in French modes of universal conscription as well.

In France, a revolutionary enthusiasm to take up arms initially was expressed only in volunteering for the National Guard, the revolutionary militia that had been set up in 1789 to support the new National Assembly and ensure domestic security.[14] In December 1789, the National Assembly rejected a proposal to introduce universal conscription that it deemed to be incompatible with citizens' liberty. It decreed that recruitment for the regular army was to proceed on a voluntary basis only.[15] Faced with the threat of imminent war in early 1791, the assembly continued to adhere to the voluntary principle when it issued a decree calling for volunteers to offer themselves to serve. The more than 100,000 troops responding to the call seemed to confirm that the revolutionary leadership was correct in relying on volunteers. In addition to a widely shared mood of revolutionary enthusiasm, the wider social basis of the volunteer units compared to those of the regular army appeared to justify the idea that the nation born of the revolution would defend itself.[16]

The optimism faded, however, when a renewed call for volunteers failed in the context of grim political and military outlooks for French revolutionaries in the war they had started in April 1792 to fight against the "enemies of the revolution," led by the ancien régime powers of Austria, Britain, and Prussia. The government was forced to resort to measures that, although couched in ideologically expedient terms of voluntarism, relied on the state's power of coercion. The first *levée des 300,000* of February 1793 produced only half its goal of new recruits, because of shortcomings of the administrative machinery, resistance from the targeted population, and insufficient state power to overcome it.[17] Benefitting from a bureaucratic apparatus that had begun to strengthen its hold over French society, the *levée en masse* (mass levy) of August 1793 proved more successful. Furthermore, the *levée en masse* better lived up to the ideological premises on which it rested than had its predecessor. By not allowing replacement—that is, paying a substitute to take one's place as a soldier—it more fully respected the ideal of equality and, as a result, provoked less resistance.[18] The massive army of over 600,000 troops that the *levée* helped create enabled revolutionary France to win victories through the rest of the decade. And because it did not set a limited period of service, men recruited in 1793, if they survived, would still be fighting in Napoleon's campaigns of the next century.[19]

Before the century was over, however, fresh troops were needed, leading the government to introduce conscription through the Loi Jourdan of September 1798, a law named after French General Jean-Baptiste Jourdan. It stipulated the registration of all men aged between twenty and twenty-five as potential conscripts. The need for troops to regenerate or expand the army determined the number of men who would be required to serve. Although no substitution was allowed initially, two years after the law's introduction it became possible again to escape service via this route.[20] This draconian conscription law met with resistance and attempts at evasion that the state gradually managed to overcome. Special military-police forces played no small part in enforcing the law, which turned conscription into a routine procedure and formed the legislative basis for recruitment throughout the Napoleonic period.[21]

As Thomas Hippler contends, we do well to think of the introduction of general conscription in France in 1793 and 1798 and in Prussia in 1813/14 as "a single transnational process"—an argument than can also be extended to Austria's 1809 legislation to establish a *Landwehr* (militia).[22] It was the encounter with the might of Napoleon's Grande Armée with conscripts from France and the occupied and allied territories of the Napoleonic Empire (1804–14/15) that set Austria and Prussia on a course of reform in which Prussia in particular imported central elements of revolutionary France's military innovations—albeit to its own political ends. Devastating defeat against the French at the Battle of Jena and Auerstedt in October 1806 shook the Prussian state and military to their core. Its army nearly destroyed, Prussia faced occupation followed by a peace settlement that came with the loss of half of its territory and crippling reparation payments. In this context, critics of the old Prussian army, whose voices had gone unheard before 1806, found themselves in a position to shape what Karen Hagemann calls an "agenda of reform and revenge."[23] This agenda, all items of which had been discussed by military thinkers before 1806, included an army reorganization amounting to a near total break with ancien régime ideas and practices.

Among the first things to go, in 1807, was the practice of recruiting foreigners who had previously made up half to two-thirds of Prussia's army. The abolishment of corporal punishment followed in 1808, accompanied by decrees that allowed commoners to become officers and established merit as the basis of promotion. This was supposed to pave the way for the centerpiece of the reforms: the mutual rapprochement of military and civil society through universal conscription. The most contested of the reformers' projects, conscription took the longest to be introduced. The French had imposed strict limitations on the size of the Prussian army and had ruled out the introduction of a system of universal conscription, and there was moreover considerable resistance against it among Prussian military and political elites. It was only in the context of the announcement of an alliance with Russia on February 20, 1813—the strategic precondition for a victory over Napoleon—that the king essentially introduced wartime conscription through a March 1813 edict that created Prussia's own *Landwehr*.[24] The Prussian army in the coalition that defeated Napoleon totaled 281,000 men in August 1813—more than 10 percent of the male population. Of the total number of troops, volunteers accounted for 8 percent and militiamen of the *Landwehr* for 46 percent; the rest belonged to the standing army (*Linienarmee*). The willingness to sacrifice themselves for the liberation of the fatherland associated with these volunteer troops would long hold center stage in the commemoration of the Prussian wars against Napoleon.[25]

Prussia carried over universal conscription into peacetime with the Military Service Law of September 1814. Under this law, every twenty-year-old man was to serve for three years in the standing army, followed by a further two years in the reserves. After this, fourteen more years of service in the *Landwehr* were required, albeit under a mild regime of annual one-month exercises and shooting on Sundays. Intended to be active only in times of war, organized relatively independent of the line army, and commanded by its own corps of (middle-class) officers, the *Landwehr* was the object of various ideological projections. It was supposed to keep alive the spirit of self-sacrifice of 1813 and to form a bridge between military and society, which, together with the abolishment of exemptions and substitutions, provided legitimacy to the entire project of universal conscription. It was also a crucial part of a system that at comparatively low costs turned large numbers of young men into soldiers. With the *Linienarmee* annually taking in only a portion of recruits for their three years of service (around 40,000), the overall size of the army was modest (usually around 130,000 men), which kept costs down. But given the relatively short time these men served before being replaced by new cohorts of young men, there was a high total output of trained soldiers whose ability to fight would be kept intact in the reserves and *Landwehr*.[26] In 1826, more than 5 percent of the male population served in the *Linienarmee* and *Landwehr* together. Partly because of this efficiency, the Prussian system of universal conscription, which was exceptional and quite radical at the time of its introduction, eventually became the model for Europe.[27]

The other main adversaries of France, unlike Prussia, predominantly relied on established models of recruitment that proved to be equally capable of mobilizing huge numbers of troops. The exception was Austria, which contributed the largest number of troops to the allied forces during the so-called Wars of Liberation of 1813–15.[28] It could do this by steadily adjusting its cantonal system of conscription and by eventually introducing a *Landwehr* in 1808/9. As in the old Prussian model, conscription until then had been highly selective because of the many exemptions it allowed and it also compensated for its demands on conscripts' lives and labor power with a system of furloughs. After 1796, defeats against France led to a gradual abolishment of various exemptions and a consequent widening of the social basis of conscription. Recruitment in the non-German lands of the empire remained selective, however, as fear of the political effects of arming potentially unruly peoples continued to shape Austria's recruitment policies. In addition, Austria introduced elements of universal conscription with the establishment in 1808/9 of a *Landwehr* that was recruited from all men between eighteen and forty-five years old and would eventually deliver about 25 percent of the total troops. In August 1813, Austria contributed 300,000 men of the 800,000 troops of the sixth coalition against Napoleon massed in central Europe.[29]

Russia did not need to make drastic changes to its recruiting system to create a massive army on the scale of the reformed Austrian and Prussian armies. It also did not rely on hiring foreign troops. The Russian army consisted exclusively of conscripted men. Its system of recruitment, the core of which had been in place since the early 1700s, ensured that Russia could field an enormous army. This conscription scheme divided the peasant population into blocks of 500 men, from which 1 was recruited per year—a number that could be raised in times of war. Initially, the men were drafted into the army for life, but in 1793 the term of service was reduced to twenty-five years. This system of recruitment that emerged out of a society with an enormous peasant population, that was still organized in hereditary orders and with institutions such as serfdom, gave the poor Russian Empire the largest army of Europe in the 1750s.[30] For it to expand even further in times of emergency—as during the Napoleonic Wars (1803–15)—all that was needed were levies of more than 1 man per recruitment unit or the issuing of exceptional levies. In 1812, an initial levy of 2 men per recruitment block was followed by two more levies, which each drafted 8 men per 500 "souls" into the tsar's military. It enabled Russia in June 1812 to mobilize no fewer than 800,000 men for its struggle against the invasion of the *grande armée* of 685,000 men under Napoleon's command, which proved costly for both sides since nearly half of all soldiers died during this five-month campaign that ended in Russian victory.[31]

Britain did not introduce conscription for its army until the First World War and seemingly relied on traditional forms of recruitment. Underneath a veneer of continuity, however, changes took place that allowed for a massive expansion of British manpower: a small army of 40,000 men in 1792 grew to some 250,000 soldiers by 1813.[32] In addition to raising the number of men willing to enlist voluntarily in the regular professional army, Britain relied on the transfer of large numbers of men from the militia to regular army regiments. Through bounties and by ballot, 110,000 men (were) transferred from the militia to the regular army in the course of the Napoleonic Wars.[33] The introduction of conscription in the French style was rejected, but the number of men recruited between 1807 and 1813 approached the number conscription would have yielded.[34] The Royal Navy, too, continued to rely on volunteers, supplemented with substantial numbers of men recruited through sometimes violent practices of impressment.[35] While nearly 30,000 men served in the navy in 1793, by 1812 the number had risen to almost to 145,000, of which about one-fifth had been pressed.[36]

As the examples of the major powers indicate, diverse systems of recruitment were in place in Europe during the French Revolutionary and Napoleonic Wars. The differences between these systems, however, were relative in view of their shared capacity to raise huge numbers of troops. In terms of their effect on the masculine condition, a similar picture of relative difference appears. The men who fought in these wars were never recruited only as men, either in traditional practices of recruitment or in revolutionary systems. In the former, various social identities, in addition to gender, determined who served or was made to serve. Most prominent among these identities were class and its associated categories, such as occupation, and—equally entwined—religious, regional, and national identities. The importance of these social identities was reduced when states widened the social basis of recruitment. Under Austria's 1808 *Landwehr* law, for instance, educated men from the middle and noble classes were enlisted for the first time, and in Britain recruitment of Irish Catholics was helped by the removal of many of the Catholic civic disabilities in the early 1790s.[37] Nevertheless, in systems of recruitment based on ancien régime models, differences between men continued to be more important than their shared manhood in determining who served.

Differences between men, however, were not only of importance in ancien régime recruitment practices. Revolutionary universal conscription, too, differentiated among men. The famous decree of the *levée en masse* of August 1793 explicitly mobilized only young and unmarried men for military service. They were to occupy the ideologically and politically most prized position of citizen-soldiers who "shall go to battle."[38] A system of recruitment in which gender appeared to be the central organizing principle was crucially inflected by age and marital status.[39] Dorit Geva situates the decree at the beginning of a tradition in French conscription law—one that lived on deep into the nineteenth century—of granting exemptions and the possibility of substitution to fathers, married men, and, in some cases, brothers, brothers-in-law, sons, and grandsons, whose familial status and duties were seen as overriding their duty to serve.[40] Pointing to the origins of this tradition in early French conscription legislation, she asserts that "the Revolutionary and then Napoleonic state distinguished between men based on their household authority, and did not treat all men as equal, abstract, and universal."[41]

THE RHETORIC OF MASCULINITY

A rhetoric of masculinity was most prominent in the context of projects of recruitment and mobilization that widened the social basis of military mobilization, either through the introduction of new systems or through the adjustment of existing ones.[42] One of the first modern wars during which such a rhetoric was extensively used was the Seven Years' War (1756–63) that involved every European great power of the time and spanned five continents, affecting Europe, the Americas, West Africa, India, and the Philippines. Early Anglophone observers of that war presented British victory in its North American theater as almost preordained. In their view, this outcome had been as good as inevitable given Britain's superior manliness and French effeminacy.[43] In the early years of the war, however, with defeats in North America and the Mediterranean, British public opinion identified the decay of the country's manly virtues as the root cause of their suddenly precarious military situation. Amid other signs of moral corruption, a general state of effeminacy was pointed to as the greatest danger to Britain's independence.[44]

This critique of British manners and morals that emerged during the Seven Years' War was based on a much older discourse, reaching back into the Renaissance and Classical antiquity, about effeminacy and its part in the downfall of political communities. Its eighteenth-century version presented effeminacy as the product of commerce and luxury that posed a threat to almost all civilized societies. British, Dutch, and Prussian critics often depicted France as the country that originated such effeminacy.

Yet, in the end, no civilized or commercial country escaped this offensive label. It was, as Christopher Forth and Bertrand Taithe write, "hurled back and forth across the Western world during the 1700s" and used by social and political commentators to criticize the male elites of their own societies in particular.[45]

In times of war these critics associated effeminacy with a loss of manly valor, underlying which was a debilitating separation of citizen and soldier. In British discourse, their moral and physical weakness made citizens—always imagined as having been originally, in better times, citizen-soldiers—turn away from military duties. Effeminate citizens left the protection of their countries to professional standing armies and foreign mercenaries, whose worth as soldiers was limited, but were bound to be used as instruments of oppression by rulers with tyrannical inclinations. The conclusion was inevitable: citizens needed to become manly soldiers again if they valued their independence and liberty.[46] In Britain, critics praised the militia as the institution that, once revitalized, would reunite citizen and soldier, military and nation, and halt the country's moral and military decay. Both British society and military were expected to be reinvigorated by the rejoining of citizens and soldiers in the militia. A revitalized spirit of manly virtue would spread from the militia to society at large and undo its moral corruption. The military was believed to regain its strength because, unlike professional soldiers and foreign mercenaries, citizen-soldiers were assumed to be motivated by patriotism and the desire to protect their community.[47]

In the end, France lost the Seven Years' War, and the humiliation of this defeat inspired a period of national self-scrutiny similar to that in Britain. French analyses of the dire military situation were, like those in Britain, shaped by a narrative of decay resulting from commerce and luxury. And in France, too, critics presented the reunion of citizen and soldier as a remedy for a general state of moral weakness that had brought the country to the brink of collapse. In France, the institution assumed to be able to best embody this reunion was a citizen army. In this French discourse, the Greeks and Romans of Classical antiquity exemplified the military and moral benefits of the union of citizen and soldier—which also provided examples of the fall of empires resulting from diminished virtue, the relevance of which to the French situation was hard to miss.[48]

In French diagnoses of moral and military decay, couched in references to the history of antiquity, effeminacy was a central trope. In a 1763 publication, philosophe Gabriel Bonnot (Abbé) de Mably praised the classical unity of citizen and soldier and warned that if men's employment is purely civil, it will necessarily lead to an effeminization of morals and manners, which in turn is bound to undermine the military capacity of the state.[49] In 1772, Jacques-Antoine-Hippolyte, Comte de Guibert, a noble officer at the Ministry of War who had fought in the Seven Years' War, published his *Essai général de tactique*. A success with the French Enlightened reading public, the *Essai* advocated a new, fierce kind of warfare that could be fought only by a citizen army. The Greek and Roman entwinement of political and military institutions provided the exemplum to be followed, held up provocatively to a state he accused of indifference to both martial education for its youth and its state of effeminacy.[50] Joseph Marie Servan de Gerbey had also fought in the Seven Years' War and was a major in the French army when he published *Le Soldat Citoyen* (1780), which contained a radical argument for obligatory military service for all male citizens aged eighteen to forty. Rome once more featured as the telling example of manly valor and love for "la patrie," as well as the demise of these virtues as a result of commerce and luxury. According to Servan de Gerbey, "With their souls corrupted and their arms weakened, one feared these effeminate citizens were to find themselves in very painful circumstances."[51]

The American Revolutionary War provided the French with a contemporary example of the manly valor of a citizen army. According to Julia Osman, in French public opinion the war was perceived through a lens polished by the classical narrative: "Papers constructed an image of the American army and militia that eerily matched the image of ancient warfare so prevalent in reform literature."[52] Readers learned about American men who had trained as soldiers from their childhood, were farmers or artisans *and* soldiers, fought fiercely in a "natural" style of warfare, fought to the last man, and were motivated by a deep love for their country.[53] Conveniently ignoring the many ways in which the American forces did not live up to the standards of a citizen army, such accounts provided a screen onto which Frenchmen could project their fantasies about the existence of virtuous classical warfare in the present and their desires for reforming their own military and society.[54] French participation in the war encouraged the development of such feelings. For one poet, French participation offered a morality tale that nearly wrote the Americans out of their own war for independence: not only was it France's war, but also it was a war that heralded "the end of an effeminate century."[55]

The French revolutionaries of 1789 appropriated the honor of establishing a citizen army and ending the curse of effeminacy for themselves, even though the ruthless conscription on which the armies of the revolution eventually relied undermined any claims that their soldiers fought out of love for the fatherland alone. The rhetoric of reuniting citizen and soldier, nation and military, persisted throughout the revolutionary and Napoleonic period and into the nineteenth century. The rewards of this reunion always were presented as the overcoming of a state of effeminacy and the remasculinization of military and society. The persistence of this rhetoric was partly the result of the early modern notion of masculinity it revolved around. The notion of masculinity as a precarious quality that could all too easily be lost and degenerate into a state of effeminacy might on the surface not appear as a powerful rhetorical tool. The very precariousness of masculinity, however, made for effective rhetoric. The fact that the permanent and secure possession of masculinity could never be assumed, but always had to be guarded or regained, called for permanent vigilance and constant action.[56] Accounts of the way a people fell into a state of effeminacy also offered more rhetorical opportunities than suspected. Effeminacy was usually linked to long-term socioeconomic and cultural transformations—the rise of civilization, commerce, and luxury—which also affected the military and the state. The pervasive nature of a state of effeminacy made it hard to see how to begin to reverse it. Clearly, more was required than an individual act of will or collective moral reform. But how could institutions, such as the military or the state, that had also fallen victim to the dangers of effeminacy inject the nation with a virtuous masculinity they did not themselves possess? The vagueness about where to start projects of remasculinization turned out to be a valuable rhetorical asset. It allowed different political and military regimes and movements to come up with the answer that best suited their interests and ideological preferences. Effeminacy could be used rhetorically to justify different systems of recruitment and mass mobilization in the service of various political projects: democratic revolution, autocratic empire, the making of a nation and nation-state.

During the French Revolution, the answer to the question of how to overcome male effeminacy was found in the revolutionary fractures out of which a new society and a new "regenerated man" were believed to have been born. A "new man," regenerated morally, intellectually, and physically, was believed to be the product of the deep rupture of the revolution. His manly virtue was expected to lead his nation into a glorious future.[57] As Alan Forrest contends, the language of regeneration was also used in relation to the military and war: "The apparent willingness of all classes and conditions to defend the common cause, was integral to this image of regeneration."[58] In propaganda, the volunteers who took up arms during the early years of the revolutionary wars appeared as embodiments of the spontaneous rebirth of French manhood. This image would be endlessly exploited: Once the new republic began to oblige its young men to serve, they were still referred to as volunteers, and the various *levées* were invariably presented as spontaneous popular uprisings.[59] In the French colony of Saint-Domingue in 1793, the republican commissioners, in an attempt to maintain control over the island, emancipated insurgent slaves who were prepared to fight for the Republic. By doing so, they claimed, the Republic had turned slaves into new men, "hommes nouveaux": free citizen-soldiers.[60]

With the introduction of ever more coercive regimes of conscription, however, the French authorities increasingly presented military service as the precondition for, rather than the result of, collective and individual regeneration. Attempts after 1812 by the Napoleonic regime to force the sons of the Italian upper classes into military service, for instance, built on the idea that only a strong government and military service could undo the effeminacy and regenerate the martial spirit of young men from Italian leading families.[61] French officials were of the opinion, as Michael Broers writes, that Italian men had lost the warlike inclinations of their ancestors. In their view, Catholicism, weak government, and overbearing mothers "had led to the effective emasculation of the Italian male."[62] Their manly virtue could be restored, not through a spontaneous process of revolutionary regeneration, but by hard-handed French policies of coercion and militarization.

Later in the century, during the Risorgimento (1848–71), the period of struggle for Italian unification, Italian nationalists used the vocabulary of effeminacy, manliness, and regeneration once again in their calls to arms. The manliness they appealed to in their rallying cries for a popular uprising through which an Italian nation was supposed to unite and establish its state could not be the product of revolution, since they aimed to start one, and it could not be instilled by the military either, since they hoped to create an army.[63] This could only be a manliness of autogeneration, of men who refound manly virtue by and in themselves. The carefully styled exceptional heroism of the Italian republican patriot and general Giuseppe Garibaldi was intended to inspire such a process of self-transformation. The depiction of Garibaldi's soldier masculinity, not coincidentally the product of exile, consisted, in Lucy Riall's view, of a mixture of militant Jacobinism and romantic sensibilities. There was much of the classical citizen-soldier in this image, such as the emphasis on the fact that Garibaldi, unlike a mercenary or professional soldier, fought only out of devotion to the cause and refused all rewards for his victories.[64] As a tool of mobilization, the image of Garibaldi as "a soldier, a military hero who shows the way forward to the glorious day when Italy will rise again to a new life," was highly successful.[65] An estimated 100,000 men volunteered to fight in the First War of Italian Independence (1848–49) alone.[66]

In this rhetoric, masculinity appeared fragile, and the question of how it could best be preserved did not receive an unequivocal answer. Paradoxically, this was not a weakness, but a part of this rhetoric's effectiveness. In a similar way, the fact that masculinity was not a unitary category at first sight appears as a rhetorical weakness, but actually reinforced calls for mass mobilization. Differences between men could thwart recruitment policies, as in the case of exemptions granted on the basis of social position or familial status and duties. Such differences could also, however, help widen the social reach of projects of mass recruitment and mobilization. In her meticulous reading of speeches, poems, pamphlets, and other texts encouraging Prussian and German men to take up arms against Napoleon in the periods of the Anti-Napoleonic Wars (1806–15), Karen Hagemann demonstrates how the diversity of masculinities present in these calls to arms helped achieve a mass mobilization that was unprecedented in its breadth.[67]

Bound together by an overarching motif of manly "death for the fatherland," these texts contained divergent models of patriotic masculinity, designed to mobilize different groups of men. Next to a "man at arms"—a patriotic-minded soldier in the standing army, expected to possess a moderate degree of autonomy and flexibility in battle—the main category was that of the "citizen as national warrior," who, previously exempt from service, dutifully went to war in defense of home and fatherland. The latter category came in three age- and class-specific variants. The variant of the "Christian militiaman" primarily targeted men of the rural and urban lower classes. It stressed religious duty, loyalty to the king, and, above all, men's duties as rescuers and protectors of home, wives and daughters, mothers and sisters. Whereas the Christian militiaman was assumed to fight out of attachment to the territorial state, the "citizen in uniform" was presumed to go to war in the service of German national unity. Aimed mainly at educated middle-class men, this variant stressed their autonomy, expressed in their taking up arms of their own accord, and hinted at links between the duty to serve and the obtaining of political rights. The variant of the "young war hero" suggested a generational conflict between sedate middle- and upper-class fathers and their energetic and virile sons, who volunteered to go to war. These youngsters were depicted as animated by a sensibility that shaped both their intense ties to other young men and women and their no less profound love for their fatherland. Such deeply felt attachments were supposed to make them fearless when it came to dying a sacrificial death for the fatherland. Because these diverse presentations of masculinity could encourage various groups of men, they played a crucial role in the ideological mobilization of Prussian men for war. Combined with strict Prussian policies concerning exemptions and substitution, this ideological element legitimized and enabled a Prussian mobilization that, in fact, during the "Wars of Liberation" came closer to recruiting all men than French conscription during the revolution or under Napoleon ever did.[68]

THE GENDERED POLITICS OF CITIZENSHIP

The mass mobilization in the era of the Wars of Revolution and Independence came with a politics of citizenship. The duty to serve and the rights of citizenship were linked—but not always, and the meanings of citizenship could differ profoundly. Citizenship, defined through its ties with military service, was gendered. It was a right of men and was associated with notions of masculinity. But it was never a right of all men, and the meanings of masculinity involved could be remarkably diverse. The call on French men in the wake of the Seven Years' War to become citizen-soldiers again, for instance, had very little to do with a notion of citizenship as a set of political rights. In the aftermath of this war, citizenship referred to patriotism, and the manly quality it implied was that of a willingness to make sacrifices for the fatherland, not the autonomy and capacity for judgment that political citizenship required of men.[69]

During the French Revolution, citizenship did get defined in terms of political rights. Unprecedented large numbers of men were granted political and civil rights following the Declaration of the Rights of Man and Citizen in August 1789. Significantly, the institutionalization of a duty to serve followed the granting of political rights.[70] Only after 1792, with the country at war, did the notion that citizenship also involved duties, specifically in the form of a duty to defend the community in time of war, enter the discourse. With the French Constitution of June 1793, the balance between rights and duties shifted. The military obligations of the citizen toward the state increased, as his political rights were circumscribed and granted to fewer and fewer men.[71]

In revolutionary France, the equation of political rights with military duties existed for only a short-lived moment. Duty soon superseded rights and its universal application to all men never became a reality. Nevertheless, it helped justify the exclusion of women from political citizenship and, in addition to defining political citizenship as male, increasingly associated it with aggressive virility.[72] Despite its very limited realization, the equation of universal *male* political rights and military duties formed a powerful ideological category during the revolution, as well as beyond the revolution and the French borders.

In post-1806 Prussian debates over army reform and the introduction of universal conscription, all parties were deeply aware of its ties to political rights. Most Prussian reformers aimed for a constitutional Prussian monarchy in a German federation and rejected the radical republicanism of the "Jacobins" that they saw as connected to French universal conscription. Their aim was to enjoy its military advantages without its political risks. Nevertheless, the introduction of universal conscription was accompanied by references to future extensions of civil and political rights, signaling an awareness on the part of the Prussian political elites that military duty and political rights could no longer be entirely separated.[73] British authorities too, during the era of the French Revolutionary and Napoleonic Wars, were concerned about the political consequences of the mobilization of men from various classes, political backgrounds, regions, and religious denominations. They feared that arming so many men who did not belong to the formal political nation would result in calls for the extension of suffrage or worse.[74] They were right: arguments for political rights after 1815 were couched in terms of patriotism and its rewards, a language the nation was taught during the wars and that would eventually help bring about the 1832 Reform Act, which changed the electoral system in the United Kingdom and extended the parliamentary franchise.[75] After the Napoleonic Wars, most European states not only reduced the size of their armies in the process of postwar military demobilization. They also returned to politically proven, less politically dangerous forms of recruitment, relying on professional soldiers and a limited number of conscripts whose long-term service made them semiprofessionals and part of a military community that was safely separated from civil society.[76]

Considered a danger by post-Napoleonic states, the ideological potential and appeal of the equation of citizenship and military service was nurtured by those who opposed Restoration politics—despite the deep unpopularity of peacetime military service among the men who were made to serve. Prussia's early liberal and German-nationalist patriots who had hoped conscription would come with political rights kept the idea alive after 1815. An association in which the idea continued its existence were the student fraternities (*Burschenschaften*) where the future elite was trained in a complex set of political values and practices: resistance against the authoritarian monarchic state, internal structures of a partially democratic nature, a cult of the Anti-Napoleonic Wars, and the duel as the means of proving one's masculinity. During the European Revolution of 1848–49, of the more than 800 members of the short-lived Frankfurt Parliament, the first freely elected parliament for all of Germany, around 150 had a background in the fraternities and belonged mostly to the liberal and democratic factions.[77]

The Frankfurt Constitution of March 1849, introduced by the new parliament, asserted the right of all German men to carry arms to protect themselves and their fatherland. In claiming this right, they articulated a vision of a new democratic political order in which all arms-carrying men were equals—and from which women were excluded.[78] When the German monarchs and princes refused to recognize the Frankfurt Constitution and mobilized their armed forces against the Frankfurt Parliament, the revolutionaries took up arms to force the implementation of the constitution. They did not stand a chance against the regular armies they faced. Nevertheless, radical liberals, democrats, and socialists in exile continued to sing the praise of a citizen army. They joined a long historical line of military and political thinkers when they identified Swiss militia forces in particular as an exemplary citizen army. In contrast to the standing armies of authoritarian states, according to them, the Swiss militia did justice to the right of male citizens to rule and defend themselves, while it also brought the full fighting potential of all male members of a free and manly nation into the military.[79] In the late 1850s, liberal nationalists were convinced that the manly valor of a people's militia would make it both invincible and a protector of constitutional liberty. They tried to turn gymnastics associations into armed organizations that would provide protomilitary training.[80]

The ideological power of the nexus of military duty and citizenship rights also persisted because for excluded groups of men, military service proved to be an effective claims-making practice. For Jewish men in particular, serving in the military offered a way of demonstrating their worth to the state in the hope that service would be rewarded with rights. Masculinity often played a part in Jewish men's attempts to show their worth. The integration of Jewish men into European militaries did not begin, however, in a context of voluntary service and claims to the extension of rights. Austrian Jews did not declare themselves willing and fit to serve, but found themselves declared as such, when in 1788 existing conscription legislation was extended to cover the Jews. As a part of his wider policies to make Jews and other marginal groups useful to the state, Emperor Joseph II, sole ruler of the Austrian Habsburg domains from 1780 to 1790, proclaimed that "the Jew as a man and as a fellow citizen [Mitbürger] will perform the same service that everyone is obligated to do."[81] Initially drafted only in small numbers and their service restricted to the transport corps, more than 35,000 Jewish men would eventually fight in the Austrian army during the Napoleonic Wars.[82]

In France, the gentile philosophe Henri Jean-Baptiste (Abbé) Grégoire in 1788 published an influential essay on Jewish emancipation, framed in terms of the need to regenerate a people that, forced to live off commerce and moneylending, had become degenerate and effeminate.[83] If they were to take up occupations that instilled civic qualities and became artisans or farmers, Jews would be able return to the state of virtue they had known in ancient Palestine. This would even make them suited to become soldiers, since a kernel of manly heroic valor was still present in them.[84] During the French Revolution, Jewish men who claimed equal rights sometimes argued that obtaining these rights would help their "regeneration." They also, however, pointed to their service in the revolutionary National Guard as evidence of the fact that they were already willing and able "to shed their blood for the glory of the nation and the support of liberty."[85] After French Jews were granted the rights of citizenship in September 1791, they volunteered for the National Guard and professional army in great numbers, as a sign of their emancipation and out of a desire to belong to the body politic. Under Napoleon, they experienced what it meant to be citizens whose duties exceeded their rights. Dissatisfied with their presumed lack of willingness to defend their country, Napoleon made military service obligatory for all Jewish men, without the possibility of replacement other Frenchmen were granted.[86]

In Prussia during the "Wars of Liberation," Jewish men had been welcomed as volunteers and militia men. In the Restoration era, however, the formal links between military service and civil rights were severed by the Prussian state. Nevertheless, enough of the assumption that military service and emancipation were connected survived for Jewish leaders in 1842 to protest government plans to exempt all Jewish men from the draft and only offer them optional entry into the army. Fearing this once again would lead to exclusion and harm their prospects for full emancipation, especially the prospect of access to positions in public service, the Jewish leadership insisted that Jews be drafted. The issue of masculinity played an important role in their protest. The example of hundreds of volunteering Jewish men who had displayed manly valor during the wars of 1813–15 had not sufficed to dispel the belief that Jews were innately cowards. Military service was a crucial means for Jewish men to demonstrate their courage and manliness; being excluded from it as unfit, they feared, would leave them stuck with the stigma of cowardice and effeminacy.[87] In 1845, the government opted for universal, compulsory military service for Jews, but it did not grant them full equality in military matters. Jewish officers were to be eligible only for field promotions, not commissions.[88]

Military service did not always imply a connection, however frail or contested, to civil rights. Russia's 1827 decision to conscript Jews in the western provinces of the empire just made them equal to Russian peasants, subjected to a harsh regime of twenty-five years of service. No rewards in terms of civil rights awaited them, and emancipation only came with the breakdown of the tsarist regime in 1917.[89] In other countries, emancipation was a reality or imaginable, but nevertheless came at the price of becoming subject to the state's military. Why did Jewish men, desiring emancipation, choose this path as volunteers, community leaders, and willing conscripts? Derek Penslar suggests that subjection to the state's military was at the same time a form of empowerment. In an analysis that is suggestive of the way military service conferred a sense of masculinity on Jewish soldiers, he writes that serving in the military offered Jews who wanted emancipation the opportunity "to exercise the coercive power that inhered in the state. Military power would flow through them as neural impulses flow through human limbs.... Emancipation... was a form of liberation that could be attained and experienced only through the subordination of the self to the demands of the state."[90]

African American soldiers serving in the Union army during the American Civil War (1861–65) seem to have experienced a similar form of empowerment derived from being endowed with the right to exercise violence. African American men had lobbied intensively for the right to take up arms against the South. Joining the war offered them the chance to contribute to the end of slavery and, by proving their martial equality to White men, gave them a claim to equal political citizenship. In 1862, the US Congress allowed the recruitment of freedman, more than 180,000 of whom would join the Northern forces.[91] Fighting in the war was particularly dangerous for African Americans. Death or slavery awaited them after capture, and Confederate troops meted out the cruelest forms of torture and humiliation to Black soldiers. Despite these dangers, Black men served in large numbers. Drew Gilpin Faust points to the desire for vengeance and retribution that African American men could satisfy by taking up arms. The war, she contends, gave Black men the opportunity "to become the agent rather than the victim of violence," a process in which this agency obtained a political meaning.[92] For Frederick Douglass, an abolitionist and one of the leaders of the northern Black community, violence was effective, as well as instructive and liberating. His own fight with a White overseer, he wrote, had allowed him to reclaim his "manly independence."[93] As Faust argues, this also held true for Black soldiers. For them, "killing was the instrument of liberation; it was an act of personal empowerment and the vehicle of racial emancipation. To kill and to be, as soldiers, permitted to kill was ironically to claim a human right."[94]

The meanings of citizenship and the strength of its ties to military service differed from place to place and changed over time. After 1860, both the United States and Europe entered a period in which, once again, army size increased and the ability to recruit huge numbers of soldiers became an important factor in shaping states' chances in the international military arena. Several states adopted variations of the Prussian model of universal conscription, with its steady output of high numbers of reliable reserves.[95] With universal conscription came a new round in the politics of citizenship, preserved and nurtured since the revolutionary era by oppositional politicians, intellectuals, and groups of marginalized men. In a context of a universal male duty to serve, equal rights for equal sacrifices began to sound like an inescapable logic. Claims to citizenship, as a result, were increasingly articulated as demands for universal male suffrage.

Derek Penslar writes that "prior to the emancipation of women at the very end of the nineteenth century and continuing into the twentieth, emancipation of any specific social group was conceptually linked with military service, even in countries that did not regularly have a draft, such as the United States or the United Kingdom."[96] The long persistence and wide dispersion of the ties between military service and citizenship were the result of the great debt states incurred to their male population through policies of mass recruitment and mobilization. The claims to civil and political rights made by men who reminded the state of these debts were hard to refute. Their power derived from the fact that, unlike other qualifications for male political citizenship such as independence or productivity, military service could be construed as services rendered and sacrifices made for the state, rather than for society, and therefore called for recognition by the state. In addition, the men who made these claims could not be accused of being unfit for citizenship; their very willingness to sacrifice all for their countries demonstrated their fitness.

Such claims, however, did not work always or for everyone. After the Civil War, full civil and political rights for African American men in the United States were still several wars away. The dominance in British politics of independence grounded in property ownership as requisite for political rights, as well as stringent residency requirements, excluded soldiers from citizenship until 1918, despite the considerable broadening of the male franchise in the course of the nineteenth century.[97] In some contexts, appeals to military service were not central to debates over citizenship for men. In imperial postcolonial societies, like Australia or New Zealand, a capacity for self-government was at the heart of qualifications for male citizenship. Initially conceptualized as a deeply masculine quality, self-government nevertheless allowed for the early extension of the suffrage to women in these countries, which preceded the institution of universal male military service. This extension, however, must be understood in the context of the simultaneous exclusion of all non-Whites from the vote, that is, as part of a process in which self-government became a less gendered and more racialized category.[98] Where the nexus of military service and political citizenship held a central position in debates over extension of the franchise, it formed an obstacle on the road toward political rights for women. Faced with this deeply gendered political category, feminists developed arguments about women's specific, nonmilitary contributions to society and state—an ideological move that simultaneously reaffirmed and undermined the power of the nexus of military duty and male political citizenship.

CONCLUSION

The mass recruitment and mobilization that emerged in the Age of Revolutions never targeted men exclusively as men. Both in revolutionary and in reformed ancien régime systems of recruitment, other social identities, such as class, age, familial status, and religion, determined which men served. And yet these wars and their practices and ideologies of recruitment played an important part in giving two entwined ideas great ideological power: the notions that all men (should) serve and that in return for performing their military duties, all men deserve the rights of political citizenship. Drawing on the idea of reward for sacrifice, oppositional politicians, intellectuals, and groups of marginalized men kept alive the equation of military service with political citizenship throughout the nineteenth century—and in the process tied the nexus of service and citizenship more tightly to masculinity.

The fact that not all men serve and fight has often done little to undermine the claim that all men are intrinsically or potentially soldiers and are therefore deserving of rights, whereas all women are not. There is more to learn on why this is so. Studying the ways societies have dealt with men whose status as noncombatants threatened to expose this contradiction may be a promising way to address the issue. The investigation of the development of systems of recruitment will benefit from a further development of comparative and transnational work. Analyses of the role of notions and practices of masculinity in these systems do not yet exist for many countries. Comparative and transnational work on the importance of various ways of arguing for male citizenship, such as through a capacity for self-government, will help to further put in perspective the categorical equation of military duty with political rights, which for a long time has been believed to have been central not just to the French Revolution, but also to most of the wider world.

NOTES

1. David A. Bell, *The First Total War: Napoleon's Europe and the Birth of Modern Warfare* (London: Bloomsbury, 2007), 8; and Jean-Yves Guiomar, *L'Invention de la guerre totale, XVIIIᵉ-XXᵉ siècle* (Paris: Le Félin Kiron, 2004), 19–20. For a discussion of the concept

"total war" see also the chapter by Karen Hagemann and Sonya O. Rose "War and Gender: The Age of the World Wars and Its Aftermath—an Overview" in this handbook.

2. Michael Howard, *War in European History* (Oxford: Oxford University Press, 1976), 75–93; Geoffrey Best, *War and Society in Revolutionary Europe, 1770–1870* (London: Fontana, 1982), 63–188; and MacGregor Knox, "Mass Politics and Nationalism as Military Revolutions: The French Revolution and After," in *The Dynamics of Military Revolution, 1300–2050*, ed. MacGregor Knox and Williamson Murray (Cambridge: Cambridge University Press, 2001), 57–73.

3. Ute Planert, "Innovation or Evolution? The French Wars in Military History," in *War in an Age of Revolution, 1775–1815*, ed. Roger Chickering and Stig Förster (Cambridge: Cambridge University Press, 2010), 69–84.

4. Michael Broers, "Changes in War: The French Revolutionary and Napoleonic Wars," in *The Changing Character of War*, ed. Hew Strachan and Sibylle Scheipers (Oxford: Oxford University Press, 2011), 64–78, 64.

5. Ibid., 69; T. C. W. Blanning, *The French Revolutionary Wars, 1787–1802* (New York: Edward Arnold, 1996); and Roger Chickering, "Introduction: A Tale of Two Tales: Grand Narratives of War in the Age of Revolution," in Chickering and Förster, *War in an Age*, 1–17.

6. See the chapter by Stefan Dudink and Karen Hagemann on "War and Gender: From the Thirty Years' War and Colonial Conquest to the Wars of Revolution and Independence—an Overview" in this handbook.

7. See Annie Crépin, "The Army of the Republic: New Warfare and a New Army," in *Republics at War, 1776–1840: Revolutions, Conflicts and Geopolitics in Europe and the Atlantic World*, ed. Pierre Serna et al. (Basingstoke: Palgrave Macmillan, 2013), 131–47.

8. Michael Clodfelter, *Warfare and Armed Conflicts: A Statistical Encyclopedia of Casualty and Other Figures, 1494–2007*, 2nd ed. (Jefferson, NC: McFarland, 2002), 146.

9. See Stefan Dudink and Karen Hagemann, "Masculinity in Politics and War in the Age of Democratic Revolutions, 1750–1850," in *Masculinities in Politics and War: Gendering Modern History*, ed. Stefan Dudink et al. (Manchester: Manchester University Press, 2004), 3–21.; for more, see Stephen Conway, *A Short History of the American Revolutionary War* (London: I. B. Tauris, 2013).

10. See Dudink and Hagemann, "War and Gender."

11. Dierk Walter, "Meeting the French Challenge: Conscription in Prussia, 1807–1815," in *Conscription in the Napoleonic Era: A Revolution in Military Affairs?*, ed. Donald Stoker et al. (London: Routledge, 2009), 24–45.

12. John Childs, *Armies and Warfare in Europe 1648–1789* (New York: Holmes & Meier, 1982), 45–56; Jeremy Black, *European Warfare, 1660–1815* (London: UCL Press, 1994), 218–24; M. S. Anderson, *War and Society in Europe of the Old Regime 1618–1789* (Stroud: Sutton, 1998), 111–28; and Frank Tallett, "Soldiers in Western Europe, c. 1500–1790," in *Fighting for a Living: A Comparative History of Military Labour, 1500–2000*, ed. Erik-Jan Zürcher (Amsterdam: Amsterdam University Press, 2014), 135–67.

13. André Rauch, *Crise de l'identité masculine, 1789–1914* (Paris: Hachette, 2000), 48.

14. Thomas Hippler, "Volunteers of the French Revolutionary Wars: Myths and Interpretations," in *War Volunteering in Modern Times: From the French Revolution to the Second World War*, ed. Christine G. Krüger and Sonja Levsen (Basingstoke: Palgrave Macmillan, 2010), 23–39.

15. Annie Crépin, *Défendre la France: Les Français, la guerre et le service militaire, de la guerre de sept ans à Verdun* (Rennes: Presses Universitaires de Rennes, 2005), 71–89.

16. Jean-Paul Bertaud, *La Révolution armée: Les soldats-citoyens et la Révolution française* (Paris: Editions Robert Laffont, 1979), 68–69; and Alan Forrest, *Soldiers of the French Revolution* (Durham, NC: Duke University Press, 1990), 60–64.

17. Alan Forrest, *Conscripts and Deserters: The Army and French Society during the Revolution and Empire* (New York: Oxford University Press, 1989), 68–75.

18. Alan Forrest, "*La patrie en danger*: The French Revolution and the First *Levée en masse*," in *The People in Arms: Military Myth and National Mobilization since the French Revolution*, ed. Daniel Moran and Arthur Waldron (Cambridge: Cambridge University Press, 2003), 8–32.

19. Ibid., 12, 30.

20. Forrest, *Soldiers*, 82–88.

21. Forrest, *Conscripts*, 187–218; and Isser Woloch, *The New Regime: Transformations of the French Civic Order, 1789–1820s* (New York: W. W. Norton, 1994), 411–26.

22. Thomas Hippler, *Citizens, Soldiers and National Armies: Military Service in France and Germany, 1789–1830* (London: Routledge, 2008), 8; for Austria, see Arthur Mark Boerke, "Conscription in the Habsburg Empire to 1815," in Stoker et al., *Conscription*, 66–83; and Karen Hagemann, "'Be Proud and Firm, Citizens of Austria!' Patriotism and Masculinity in Texts of the 'Political Romantics' Written during Austria's Anti-Napoleonic Wars," *German Studies Review* 29, no. 1 (2006): 41–62.

23. Karen Hagemann, "*Mannlicher Muth und Teutsche Ehre*": Nation, Militär und Geschlecht zur Zeit der Antinapoleonischen Kriege Preußens (Paderborn: Schöningh, 2002), 75–77; and Hagemann, *Revisiting Prussia's Wars against Napoleon: History, Culture and Memory* (Cambridge: Cambridge University Press, 2015), 38 and 52–57.

24. Hagemann, *Mannlicher Muth*, 73–104; Ute Frevert, *A Nation in Barracks: Modern Germany, Military Conscription and Civil Society* (Oxford: Berg, 2004), 10–30; and Walter, "Meeting," 27–35.

25. Hagemann, *Revisiting*, 62; for the contested memories, see parts III–V of the book.

26. Hagemann, *Mannlicher Muth*, 84–91; Frevert, *Nation in Barracks*, 47–50; and Walter, "Meeting," 39–41.

27. Dierk Walter, *Preußische Heeresreformen 1807–1870: Militärische Innovation und der Mythos der "Roonschen Reform"* (Paderborn: Schöningh, 2003), 88–103.

28. Hagemann, *Revisiting*, 64.

29. Boerke, "Conscription," 76–80.

30. William C. Fuller, "The Imperial Army," in *The Cambridge History of Russia*, ed. Dominic Lieven (Cambridge: Cambridge University Press, 2006), 3:530–53.

31. Alexander Mikaberidze, "Conscription in Russia in the Late Eighteenth and Early Nineteenth Centuries: 'For Faith, Tsar and Motherland,'" in Stoker et al., *Conscription*, 46–65, 47.

32. Kevin Linch, *Britain and Wellington's Army: Recruitment, Society and Tradition, 1807–1815* (Basingstoke: Palgrave Macmillan, 2011), 50.

33. Roger Knight, *Britain against Napoleon: The Organization of Victory* (London: Penguin Books, 2014), 439.

34. Linch, *Wellington's Army*, 150.

35. Kevin McCranie, "The Recruitment of Seamen for the British Navy, 1793–1815: 'Why Don't You Raise More Men?,'" in Stoker et al., *Conscription*, 84–101.

36. Anthony Page, *Britain and the Seventy Years War, 1744–1815: Enlightenment, Revolution and Empire* (London: Palgrave Macmillan, 2015), 109.

37. Hagemann, "Be Proud," 43; and Page, *Britain*, 117.

38. Quoted in Alan Forrest, "Conscription as Ideology: Revolutionary France and the Nation in Arms," in "The Comparative Study of Conscription in the Armed Forces," ed. Lars Mjøset and Stephen Van Holde, special issue, *Comparative Social Research* 20, no. 2 (2002): 95–115, 103.

39. Annette F. Timm and Joshua A. Sanborn, *Gender, Sex and the Shaping of Modern Europe: A History from the French Revolution to the Present Day* (London: Bloomsbury, 2016), 48–50.

40. Dorit Geva, "Where the State Feared to Tread: Conscription and Local Patriarchalism in Modern France," *The Annals of the American Academy of Political and Social Science* 636 (2011): 111–28.

41. Dorit Geva, *Conscription, Family, and the Modern State: A Comparative Study of France and the United States* (Cambridge: Cambridge University Press, 2013), 29.

42. See Anna Clark, "The Rhetoric of Masculine Citizenship: Concepts and Representations in Modern Western Political Culture," in *Representing Masculinity: Male Citizenship in Modern Western Culture*, ed. Stefan Dudink et al. (Basingstoke: Palgrave Macmillan, 2007), 3–22.

43. Ann M. Little, *Abraham in Arms: War and Gender in Colonial New England* (Philadelphia: University of Pennsylvania Press, 2007), 205.

44. Matthew McCormack, *Embodying the Militia in Georgian England* (Oxford: Oxford University Press, 2015), 14–19.

45. Christopher E. Forth and Bertrand Taithe, "Introduction: French Manhood in the Modern World," in *French Masculinities: History, Culture and Politics*, ed. Christopher E. Forth and Bertrand Taithe (Basingstoke: Palgrave Macmillan, 2007), 1–14, 6–7.

46. McCormack, *Embodying*, 19–27.

47. Ibid.

48. Julia Osman, *Citizen Soldiers and the Key to the Bastille* (Basingstoke: Palgrave Macmillan, 2015), 55–79.

49. Gabriel de Mably, *Entretiens de Phocion sur le Rapport de la Morale avec la Politique: Traduits du Grec de Nicoclès, avec des Remarques* (Amsterdam: 1763), 233–34.

50. Jacques-Antoine-Hippolyte Guibert, *Essai Général de Tactique* (London: Chez les Libraires Associés, 1772), c.

51. Joseph Servan de Gerbey, *Le Soldat Citoyen, ou Vues Patriotiques sur la Manière la Plus Avantageuse de Pouvoir à la Défense du Royaume* (Paris: 1780), 49–50.

52. Osman, *Citizen Soldiers*, 82.

53. Ibid., 83–86.

54. Dudink and Hagemann, "Masculinity in Politics," 8; and Osman, *Citizen Soldiers*, 96.

55. Quoted in Osman, *Citizen Soldiers*, 101.

56. Stefan Dudink, "Masculinity, Effeminacy, Time: Conceptual Change in the Dutch Age of Democratic Revolutions," in Dudink et al., *Masculinities*, 90.

57. Antoine de Baecque, *The Body Politic: Corporeal Metaphor in Revolutionary France*, trans. Charlotte Mandell (Stanford, CA: Stanford University Press, 1993), 137–46.

58. Forrest, "La patrie," 23. On the "ideological polyvalence" of volunteering during the French Revolution, see Hippler, "Volunteers," 24.

59. Forrest, "La patrie," 26.

60. Quoted in Elizabeth Colwill, "Freedwomen's Familial Politics: Marriage, War and Rites of Registry in Post-Emancipation Saint-Domingue," in *Gender, War and Politics: Transatlantic*

Perspectives, 1775–1830, ed. Karen Hagemann et al. (Basingstoke: Palgrave Macmillan, 2010), 71–89, 72.

61. Michael Broers, "Noble Romans and Regenerated Citizens: The Morality of Conscription in Napoleonic Italy, 1800–1814," *War in History* 8, no. 3 (2001): 249–70.

62. Ibid., 254, 257.

63. Lucy Riall, "Men at War: Masculinity and Military Ideals in the Risorgimento," in *The Risorgimento Revisited: Nationalism and Culture in Nineteenth-Century Italy*, ed. Silvana Patriarca and Lucy Riall (Basingstoke: Palgrave Macmillan, 2012), 152–70.

64. Lucy Riall, *Garibaldi: Invention of a Hero* (New Haven, CT: Yale University Press, 2007), 45–58.

65. Ibid., 56.

66. Riall, "Men at War," 157.

67. See Karen Hagemann, "Of 'Manly Valor' and 'German Honor': Nation, War and Masculinity in the Age of the Prussian Uprising against Napoleon," *Central European History* 30, no. 2 (1997): 187–220; and Hagemann, *Revisiting*, 130–70.

68. Hagemann, *Mannlicher Muth*, 309–50; and Hagemann, *Revisiting*, 145–54.

69. Osman, *Citizen Soldiers*, 73–74.

70. Dudink and Hagemann, "Masculinity in Politics," 12.

71. Alan Forrest, "Citizenship and Military Service," in *The French Revolution and the Meaning of Citizenship*, ed. Renée Waldinger et al. (Westport, CT: Greenwood Press, 1993), 153–65.

72. Joan B. Landes, "Republican Citizenship and Heterosocial Desire: Concepts of Masculinity in Revolutionary France," in Dudink et al., *Masculinities*, 96–115.

73. Hagemann, *Mannlicher Muth*, 75–92; and Hagemann, *Revisiting*, 47–72.

74. Page, *Seventy Years War*, 123.

75. Linda Colley, *Britons: Forging the Nation, 1707–1837* (New Haven, CT: Yale University Press, 1992), 318–19 and 334–50.

76. Best, *War and Society*, 191–256.

77. Christian Jansen, "Einleitung: Die Militarisierung der Bürgerlichen Gesellschaft im 19. Jahrhundert," in *Der Bürger als Soldat: Die Militarisierung Europäischer Gesellschaften im langen 19. Jahrhundert—Ein Internationaler Vergleich*, ed. Christian Jansen (Essen: Klartext, 2004), 9–23.

78. Frevert, *Nation in Barracks*, 117–99; and Gabriella Hauch, "Did Women Have a Revolution? Gender Battles in the European Revolution of 1848/49," in *1848: A European Revolution? International Ideas and National Memories of 1848*, ed. Axel Körner (New York: St. Martin's, 2000), 64–81.

79. Rudolf Jaun, "'Das Einzige Wahre und Ächte Volksheer': Die Schweizerische Miliz und die Helvetische Projektion Deutscher Radikal-Liberaler und Demokraten 1830–1870," in Jansen, *Der Bürger*, 68–82.

80. Frank Lorenz Müller, "The Spectre of a People in Arms: The Prussian Government and the Militarisation of German Nationalism, 1859–1864," *English Historical Review* CXXII, no. 495 (2007): 82–104.

81. Michael Silber, "From Tolerated Aliens to Citizen-Soldiers: Jewish Military Service in the Era of Joseph II," in *Constructing Nationalities in East Central Europe*, ed. Pieter M. Judson and Marsha L. Rozenblit (New York: Berghahn Books, 2005), 19–36, 25.

82. Derek J. Penslar, *Jews and the Military: A History* (Princeton, NJ: Princeton University Press, 2013), 42.

83. H. Grégoire, *Essai sur la régénération physique, morale et politique des juifs* (Paris: Stock, 1988), 58–60, first published in 1788.

84. Ronald Schechter, *Obstinate Hebrews: Representations of Jews in France, 1715–1815* (Berkeley: University of California Press, 2003), 90–92.

85. Ibid., 172–73.

86. Penslar, *Jews*, 51, 54.

87. Frevert, *Nation in Barracks*, 65–69.

88. Penslar, *Jews*, 55.

89. Yohanan Petrovsky-Shtern, *Jews in the Russian Army, 1827–1917: Drafted into Modernity* (Cambridge: Cambridge University Press, 2009), 2, 16.

90. Penslar, *Jews*, 81.

91. Jim Cullen, "'I's a Man Now': Gender and African-American Men," in *Divided Houses: Gender and the Civil War*, ed. Catherine Clinton and Nina Silber (New York: Oxford University Press, 1992), 76–91; and the chapter by Amy S. Greenberg on "Gender and the Wars of Nation-Building and Nation-Keeping in the Americas, 1830s–1870s" in this handbook.

92. Drew Gilpin Faust, *This Republic of Suffering: Death and the American Civil War* (New York: Alfred A. Knopf, 2012), 55.

93. Quoted in ibid., 52.

94. Ibid., 55.

95. Walter, *Heeresreformen*, 110.

96. Penslar, *Jews*, 9.

97. Sonya O. Rose, "Fit to Fight but Not to Vote? Masculinity and Citizenship in Britain, 1832–1918," in Dudink et al., *Representing Masculinity*, 131–50.

98. Marilyn Lake, "The Gendered and Racialised Self Who Claimed the Right to Self-Government," *Journal of Colonialism and Colonial History* 13, no. 1 (2012), https://muse.jhu.edu/article/475173; and Angela Woollacott, *Settler Society in the Australian Colonies: Self-Government and Imperial Culture* (Oxford: Oxford University Press, 2015), 98–151.

SELECT BIBLIOGRAPHY

Bell, David A. *The First Total War: Napoleon's Europe and the Birth of Modern Warfare*. Boston: Houghton Mifflin, 2007.

Broers, Michael. "Changes in War: The French Revolutionary and Napoleonic Wars." In *The Changing Character of War*, edited by Hew Strachan and Sibylle Scheipers, 64–78. Oxford: Oxford University Press, 2011.

Dudink, Stefan, Karen Hagemann, and Anna Clark, eds. *Representing Masculinity: Male Citizenship in Modern Western Culture*. Basingstoke: Palgrave Macmillan, 2008.

Dudink, Stefan, Karen Hagemann, and John Tosh, eds. *Masculinities in Politics and War: Gendering Modern History*. Manchester: Manchester University Press, 2004.

Forrest, Alan. *Soldiers of the French Revolution*. Durham, NC: Duke University Press, 1990.

Forth, Christopher E., and Bertrand Taithe, eds. *French Masculinities: History, Culture and Politics*. Basingstoke: Palgrave Macmillan, 2007.

Frevert, Ute. *A Nation in Barracks: Modern Germany, Military Conscription and Civil Society*. Oxford: Berg, 2004.

Geva, Dorit. *Conscription, Family, and the Modern State: A Comparative Study of France and the United States.* Cambridge: Cambridge University Press, 2013.

Guiomar, Jean-Yves. *L'Invention de la guerre totale, XVIIIe–XXe siècle.* Paris: Le Félin Kiron, 2004.

Hagemann, Karen. *Revisiting Prussia's Wars against Napoleon: History, Culture and Memory.* Cambridge: Cambridge University Press, 2015.

Hagemann, Karen, Gisela Mettele, and Jane Rendall, eds. *Gender, War, and Politics: Transatlantic Perspectives, 1775–1830.* Basingstoke: Palgrave Macmillan, 2010.

Hippler, Thomas. *Citizens, Soldiers and National Armies: Military Service in France and Germany 1789–1830.* London: Routledge, 2008.

Krüger, Christine G., and Sonja Levsen, eds. *War Volunteering in Modern Times: From the French Revolution to the Second World War.* Basingstoke: Palgrave Macmillan, 2010.

McCormack, Matthew. *Embodying the Militia in Georgian England.* Oxford: Oxford University Press, 2015.

Moran, Daniel, and Arthur Waldron, eds. *The People in Arms: Military Myth and National Mobilization since the French Revolution.* Cambridge: Cambridge University Press, 2003.

Osman, Julia. *Citizen Soldiers and the Key to the Bastille.* Basingstoke: Palgrave Macmillan, 2015.

Penslar, Derek J. *Jews and the Military: A History.* Princeton, NJ: Princeton University Press, 2013.

Riall, Lucy. "Men at War: Masculinity and Military Ideals in the Risorgimento." In *The Risorgimento Revisited: Nationalism and Culture in Nineteenth-Century Italy*, edited by Lucy Riall and Silvana Patriarca, 152–70. Basingstoke: Palgrave Macmillan, 2013.

Stoker, Donald, Frederick C. Schneid, and Harold D. Blanton, eds. *Conscription in the Napoleonic Era: A Revolution in Military Affairs?* London: Routledge, 2009.

Zürcher, Erik-Jan, ed. *Fighting for a Living: A Comparative History of Military Labour, 1500–2000.* Amsterdam: Amsterdam University Press, 2014.

PART II

WARS OF
NATIONS AND
EMPIRES

CHAPTER 9

....

WAR AND GENDER

Nineteenth-Century Wars of Nations and Empires—an Overview

....

STEFAN DUDINK, KAREN HAGEMANN, AND MISCHA HONECK

In February 1864, *Harper's Weekly: Journal of Civilization* printed on its front page the wood engraving *Thanks to Grant* showing Lady Liberty (known as Columbia at the time) pinning a medal on General Ulysses S. Grant's uniform jacket. Grant was known to the readers of *Harper's Weekly* as the new commanding general of the Union army. By the time of the image's publication, the American Civil War (1861–65) had lasted almost three years and had generated far greater casualties than either side had anticipated, but was beginning to turn in favor of the Union. (See Figure 9.1.) *Harper's Weekly*, like other public voices of the Union, attributed this change in fortune to Grant. The print displays a grateful nation, represented by the Union flags and Columbia, who honors the hero with a victor's wreath. The illustration clearly served a propagandistic purpose, which was to bolster the fighting spirits of the war-weary Union. At a deeper level, however, the print exemplifies the gendered figurations of nationhood, soldiering, and citizenship that started to circulate on both sides of the Atlantic in the late eighteenth century and undergirded the wars waged in the Western world from the post-Napoleonic period to the First World War.[1] In expressing her gratitude to Grant, Columbia reinforces the masculinity of both the general and the military as the chief institution devoted to defending the nation, rendered here and elsewhere as a female body that was at once desirable and vulnerable. The idea that protecting the nation was tantamount to protecting the weaker sex not only masculinized war itself, but also advanced a gendered logic in which military service and claims to citizenship were closely intertwined.

This logic was shared by political elites in most Western nations during the nineteenth century.[2] Nations, as imagined communities, are partly called into existence through cultural representations (texts, images, and symbols), which help to limit and legitimize people's access to the resources of the nation-state. They are based, despite all the rhetoric of national unity, on constructed differences of gender, class, and often race

FIGURE 9.1 *Thanks to Grant,* front page of *Harper's Weekly. Journal of Civilization,* February 6, 1864, showing Columbia pinning a medal on General Ulysses S. Grant's uniform jacket for a Union victory during the American Civil War, wood engraving on newsprint by Thomas Nast (1840–1902).

(The Museum of Fine Arts, Houston, TX)

and ethnicity. According to Anne McClintock, "The representation of male *national power* depends" on the prior construction of these differences. Excluded "from direct action as national citizens, women are subsumed symbolically into the national body politic as its boundary and metaphoric limit."[3] They became the symbolic bearers of a nation. Accordingly, most nations are represented by an allegorical female figure like Columbia. Depending on the specific historical context, the meaning of these allegorical female representations could differ.[4] Such representations could embody not only female grace in need of male protection, as in the case of the first image, but also the will of the whole nation to fight. One example is an 1895 lithograph by German painter Hermann Knackfuß, based on a draft by the German emperor, Wilhelm II (see Figure 9.2). The lithograph, titled *Peoples of Europe, Guard Your Holiest Assets*, was a present from the German emperor for Tsar Nicholas II of Russia, symbolizing the German request to keep at bay the perceived imminent danger of a Chinese onslaught. It shows the archangel Michael, the patron of Germany, embodying a muscular and valorous Christian masculinity, urging the nations of Europe, represented by the allegorical female embodiments of Britain, France, Germany, Italy, Austria-Hungary, and Russia, to fight the "Yellow Peril." The archangel points to the flowering European landscape,

FIGURE 9.2 *Völker Europas, wahrt eure heiligsten Güter* (Peoples of Europe, Guard Your Holiest Assets), lithograph by Hermann Knackfuß, based on a draft by the German emperor, Wilhelm II, representing the German request to control the perceived imminent danger of a Chinese onslaught, [n.p.], 1895.

(© Deutsches Historisches Museum/S. Ahlers.)

threatened by a powerful wall of fire from the East (indicated by the Buddha in its center). Germania, with drawn sword, supported by Russia with her arm around Germania's shoulder, and the French Marianne, who is standing next to Germania with spear in hand, are ready to fight. The other European nations follow, but only reluctantly.[5]

The Yellow Peril was also the theme of many other contemporary publications and cartoons of the time in Western countries. Fusing the categories of race and gender, this trope reflected a basic tenet of late nineteenth-century imperialism: that the survival of Euro-American civilization depended on the supremacy of White men and their ability to subjugate the world's other races. The imperialist fear of Eastern resistance against Western imperialism was further stimulated by the so-called Boxer Rebellion (1899–1901), a War of Empire in China defined by the armed uprising against the presence of the major imperial powers, America, Austria, Britain, France, Germany, Italy, Japan, and Russia, competing over influence in China, followed by brutal wars of "pacification" jointly fought by armed forces of these powers. Many of the visualizations of the Yellow Peril imagined the Boxer Rebellion in terms of a conflict between Christian civilization and Asian barbarism.

These two images are part of the visual archive pertaining to two distinct yet related moments in the history of Europe, North America, and beyond in the nineteenth century. The first was the period of European and US Wars of Nation-Building at mid-century, which marked the restructuring of states, empires, and warfare in an age of industrialization, nationalization, and globalization. The second moment was the period of heightened imperial war and global violence at the close of the century, which encompassed the formation of a global world of empires in the era of the so-called new imperialism and the consolidation of worldwide networks of capital, commerce, communication, knowledge, and armed force and other forms of violence.

The two images highlight the nexus of gender and war in the nineteenth century. They illuminate the pivotal importance of languages of gender in ideological mobilizations for war, both national and imperial, and its ideological work in representing nations, empire, and warfare in general. The projection of an idealized gender order lent meaning to and naturalized pursuits of war and empire while projecting a distinct counterpoint to the actual disruptions and crises of gender orders that accompanied the waging of war. Gender intersected with other categories of difference, such as class and race, to define political, legal, and military subject positions at a time when invocations of "the people" and "nations" had moved to the center of politics and war.

The following examines the intertwined histories of gender and war from the end of the transatlantic period of the Wars of Revolution and Independence (1770s–1820s) to the outbreak of the First World War in 1914. First it discusses the question of how to conceptualize nineteenth-century war and warfare and to define key concepts like *total war*, *imperialism*, and *militarism* that historians have used to make sense of the presence of war and military pursuits during this time. Then it gives an overview of the major Wars of Nations and Empires waged from the 1830s to the early 1910s that tries to do justice to both the often porous and fluid boundaries between national, colonial, and imperial armed conflicts and the changes in warfare and military organization in an age of industrialized and nationalized warfare. Finally, it explores how to gender such an analysis of nineteenth-century warfare and the attempts to control it.

CONCEPTUALIZING NINETEENTH-CENTURY WAR AND WARFARE

Periodization matters for the understanding of war and warfare in the nineteenth century. Although temporal scopes do not determine interpretations, they can favor specific understandings of the past over others. The selection of historical events and transformations that comes with the choice of a temporal frame gives greater credibility to some ways of seeing and conceptualizing the past. In histories of war and warfare, the frame of a "long" nineteenth century that runs from the 1770s to the 1910s is probably the most common periodization of this century. The period begins with the Wars of Revolution and Independence, which included the American Revolutionary War (1775–83), the French Revolutionary Wars (1792–1802), the Napoleonic Wars (1803–15), and continues in the Americas with the Spanish American Wars of Independence (1808–30). It ends with the First World War (1914–18). The conflicts of immense scope and destructiveness at the beginning and end of the long nineteenth century readily invite an interpretation of the century in light of these wars. This interpretation, in view of the unprecedented scope and destructiveness of World War I, often described as the first "modern total war," is then likely to focus on the emergence of a war of this magnitude out of seeds planted in the Age of the Wars of Revolution and Independence at its beginning. An interpretation of the nineteenth century as the era of the gestation of total war does not necessarily follow from the 1770s–1910s timeframe, but it does derive some of its credibility from it.

An alternative periodization conceptualizes the nineteenth century as a relatively short era from the 1830s to the 1910s. This approach signals an ambition not to interpret this period's Wars of Nations and Empires exclusively or predominantly in light of the massive conflicts at its beginning and end or to focus on the trajectory between them. This timeframe helps to lessen the grip of a narrative of total war on interpretations of war and warfare in the nineteenth century. Thus, it favors understandings of this period that equally require critical analysis, especially of the contested notion of the nineteenth century as a peaceful time. This periodization gains credibility from its disconnection from the years of intense violence that mark its beginning and end in the framework of a long nineteenth century. It emphasizes the importance of war and warfare in the period from the 1840s to the 1870s and conceptualizes the century in a spatial framework that goes beyond Europe and North America by including the frontier warfare in North America, Australia, and New Zealand as well as the many colonial and imperial wars fought by European powers, especially on the Asian and African continents.

A Century on the Path to Total War?

While one of the purposes of using the notion of a short nineteenth century is to create some distance from narratives of total war, the concept of total war is still useful for grasping vital aspects of the development of war since the late eighteenth century, in particular the widening of the scope of armed conflict and the importance of the development of a gender order of national war that started in the period of the Age of the Wars of Revolution and Independence, which will be discussed later. But narratives of the rise of total war during the long nineteenth century tend to elide varieties of military experience that do not fit the pattern of development it presumes.[6] They also are prone to centering on a modernization of war and warfare that originates in the late eighteenth- and early nineteenth-century revolutionary wars, which is propelled forward by the twin forces of the nationalization and democratization of war. Ute Frevert described the first of these forces as the process in which war became the expression of international enmity and was increasingly thought of as the activity through which a nation defined and asserted itself—an idea that became the ultimate justification for going to war. She conceptualized the democratization of war as the quantitative expansion of the group conducting war, to the point where it potentially included the entire population. Combined with innovations in military technology and tactics, war's nationalization and democratization dramatically expanded its scope, resulting in 1914 in a war that was both "absolute and total."[7]

Analyses such as these capture important aspects of the history of nineteenth-century conflicts. At the same time, however, they obscure characteristics of war and warfare in that period that represent continuities with earlier practices, breaks with the process of modernization, or returns to earlier modes of waging war. Nineteenth-century European armies were not only involved in symmetrical warfare between states driven by international enmity. Their work was also internal and performed in the service of securing the power of state. It ranged from policing urban unrest and rural uprisings to quelling revolutions and low-intensity warfare in unruly regions—tasks that could also be undertaken externally in territories of allies.[8]

Colonial wars, too, were generally not fought between nation-states and tend to fall outside the purview of histories of total war. Nineteenth-century armies did not always resemble the national mass army based on generalized conscription that exemplifies the democratization of war. In the half century after 1815, most European states preferred to rely on smaller (semi)professional armies with long terms of service that guaranteed their safe separation from civilian society.[9] Several features of some of the major wars of the century did not point forward to modern total war, but backward to a pre-Napoleonic past. In terms of causes, aims, and various aspects of its tactics and technology, the Crimean War (1853–56), for instance, was a "cabinet war."[10] In narratives of the rise of modern total war, these nonmodern aspects are downplayed or superseded in the analysis by characteristics of the war that seem to point forward to total war.[11] That is the fate of many aspects of war in the nineteenth century that do not fit the narrative of total war, in particular when they belong to the history of war before the 1860s.

No counternarrative or narrative that integrates the nonmodern aspects of nineteenth-century war into a new, more inclusive, overall conceptualization has emerged yet. The starting point for such a conceptualization might lie in the increasing awareness that the military modernity of total war spawned during the long nineteenth century was relatively short lived. Similar to warfare in the post-1945 world, nineteenth-century warfare was characterized by its *limited* nature, at least compared with the Age of the World Wars.[12] This makes it hard to fit it into a linear history of total war.[13] The insight that total war was only one passing outcome of the history of war in the nineteenth century may open up a view of war in that century that does justice to its varieties.

A Peaceful Century?

In the narrative of total war, the nineteenth century appears as the road that leads from one period of destructive war to an even worse one. The Eurocentric interpretation of the century as peaceful, by contrast, cuts it off from the years of intense violence that bracket it.[14] In Paul W. Schroeder's view of Europe's nineteenth century as "pacific" and "more peaceful than any predecessor in European history," this separation is the result of the insight that European statesmen reached in the wake of the French Revolutionary and Napoleonic Wars: "Taught slowly and painfully by repeated defeats and disaster, [they] finally and suddenly succeeded in learning how to conduct international politics differently and better."[15] Abandoning the eighteenth-century international politics of a competitive and conflict-laden balance of power, they accepted a set of restraints that offered the guarantee that unavoidable rivalry and competition would not destroy them. The result was a century in which wars were few and limited: There were no wars involving all or most of the great powers between 1815 and 1914, and there were no wars between any great powers in the periods 1815–1854 and 1871–1914. Although five wars between great powers were fought in the 1854–1871 period, these were, Schroeder argued, of "limited" duration, scope, and severity.[16]

To determine and compare the more or less bellicose or violent nature of different eras is a complex matter.[17] Definitions of seemingly self-evident categories tend, to varying degrees, to shape the outcomes of such comparisons, beginning with the most crucial category of all: war. The customary concentration on wars between great powers excludes the internal warfare, referred to in the previous section, as well as wars involving middle and small powers, some of which were of considerable significance. A string of wars in the Balkans starting in the middle of the century, for instance, ended in the Balkan Wars of 1912–13 that marked the point after which these peripheral wars became central to the outbreak of the conflict that shattered the "peaceful" century.[18]

The Wars of Empire also do not figure in accounts of a peaceful European nineteenth century. Their number and destructiveness necessitate an amending of these accounts. This might seem a criticism that misses the mark. Notions of a peaceful nineteenth century usually refer to a narrowly defined Europe; criticizing these notions by calling for a wider geographical scope looks like an attempt to win the argument by changing the subject. The point, however, is that by 1815 the subject itself had already changed profoundly. Toward the end of what has been called "the first age of global imperialism" between 1760 and 1830, Europe and its empires undoubtedly constituted an interconnected space, which requires us to discuss questions of the peacefulness of the century in that wider context.[19] Jürgen Osterhammel's interpretation of the success of the Congress of Vienna (1814–15), which stood at the end of the period of the Napoleonic Wars with the defeat of France, echoes this point. One of the reasons that the mechanisms to control conflict agreed on during the congress worked, Osterhammel contended, was because it was decided that they applied to a narrowly defined Europe alone, insulating Congress Europe from conflicts on its periphery and in the wider world.[20] This "conscious deglobalization of international politics" demonstrates, paradoxically, how much European statesmen were aware of the fact that wars were fought in an interconnected European/non-European space and were shaped by its dynamics—and that peace depended on the success of an attempt to divide it.

Michael Geyer and Charles Bright took the argument one step further by challenging the Eurocentric historiography that has projected Europe's presumed nineteenth-century peacefulness onto the world. Moving beyond an exclusive focus on great-power and interstate wars, they came to the conclusion that from a global perspective the period between 1840 and 1880 was marked by a multiplication and intensification of violent conflicts. They point out that of the six deadliest conflicts in this period, only three involved European great powers (the Crimean War, the Franco-Prussian War of 1870–71, and the Russo-Turkish War of 1877–78), one was fought between small powers (the War of the Triple Alliance against Paraguay of 1864–70), and two—the deadliest of the six—were civil wars (the Taiping Wars in China of 1850–64 and the American Civil War). They add to this the observation that most warfare in this period was of a decentered and low-intensity nature, but capable of enormous destruction. The result is a perspective on warfare beyond great-power and interstate war that reveals a long period of worldwide, endemic violence at the heart of the nineteenth century.[21]

Mid-Century Transformations

Drawing on a similar interpretation of the middle of the nineteenth century as a period of "military cataclysms," some historians have contended that these years form the turning point in the history of war at which "modern war" emerges.[22] In the words of Hans van de Ven, the middle of the century constituted a "hinge in time," with profound changes in the areas of armaments, tactics, military organization, and the relationship between states and their militaries.[23] In addition to discussions of the place of these changes in the long-term history of war, scholars have tried to capture these transformations' nature in conceptual terms, turning, in several instances, to the framework of military revolutions.

From the middle decades of the century on, breech-loading rifles increased the infantry's accuracy and firepower, and rifled, breech-loading steel canons did the same for the artillery. Steam-propelled, ironclad warships offered the navies that could afford them greater speed and maneuverability and, in combination with large-caliber and revolving gun turrets, an impressive ability to project power. Advances in transportation and communication—the railroad, the steamship, the telegraph—made it possible to deploy forces faster, over longer distances, and in a centrally coordinated manner. In terms of tactics, improved infantry equipment appeared to give the advantage to the defender. As Prussian operational doctrine demonstrated, however, this advantage could also be integrated in an overall approach of a more offensive nature, in which fast mobilization and subsequent invasion of enemy territory were followed by the staking out of defensive positions, awaiting and immobilizing an enemy moving at a slower pace, and then, finally, attacking him from the side or the rear.[24] Concerning recruitment, a system based on general, relatively short-term conscription and the formation of large, well-trained reserve forces appealed to more and more governments, given its ability to increase the number of troops in a relatively affordable and efficient way.

Several of these transformations were successfully introduced or taken up by Prussia. John A. Lynn refers to the mid-nineteenth-century Prussian army as a "paradigm army," that is, an army that defines the core characteristics of a specific stage in military evolution and serves as the model for its age.[25] Others have tried to capture the nature of these changes in the conceptual language of military revolutions, building on Michael Roberts's 1955 argument that changes in tactics of late sixteenth-century warfare stood at the beginning of a wide-ranging set of transformations of not only war, but also fundamental aspects of state and society.[26] On the basis of a differentiation between true military revolutions that come with "systematic changes in politics and society" and revolutions in military affairs that might implement radically new approaches of war in military organizations (but do not bring about fundamental sociopolitical transformations), the Prussian case has been designated as a revolution in military affairs.[27] This revolution has been further categorized as part of a wider military revolution that appeared in the context of the industrial revolution.[28]

Familiar criticism of the conceptual language of military revolution applies in this case, too. Some scholars ask how much insight is gained by using the metaphor *revolution*, which connotes profound and sudden change, for conceptualizing processes of transformation that happened over long periods. This criticism also applies to the notion of military revolutions as "additive" in their effects. MacGregor Knox and Williamson Murray used the term to describe the "*industrial* military revolution" of the nineteenth century as a development building on a *military* revolution they associate with the French Revolution and the power of mass armies mobilized by patriotic-national propaganda it unleashed.[29] At the same time, the notion of a military revolution does capture a crucial aspect of the mid-century transformations. In its original formulation by Roberts, the idea of a military revolution pointed to a direct symbiosis between military innovations and processes of state formation. The existence of this relation has turned out to be questionable for the early modern context. Between 1750 and 1950, however, it adequately describes how transformations of war and of the state reinforced each other.[30] The wider scale and higher technological and logistical complexity of mid-nineteenth-century warfare demanded ever more of the state's capacity to sustain and coordinate war. In the states that rose to the occasion, war became a major element of practices of state formation.

The Nineteenth Century's New Imperialism

Mid-nineteenth-century warfare also highlighted the growing differences in military capability between the Western and non-Western world.[31] As a result of the "second military revolution," the technological gap between Western armies and their colonial adversaries widened considerably.[32] This played a part in ending the period of imperial retreat ongoing since 1815 for several European countries—with the major exception of the steadily expanding British Empire.[33] In the last decades of the century, this reinvigorated process of expansion culminated in a "new imperialism," marked by a feverish competition for acquiring overseas territories, driven and supported by military, commercial, and civil lobbies in the metropole. A new round of technological innovation accompanied the new imperialism, most notoriously in the form of the machine gun and the steam-powered gunboat. In one line of interpretation, "Europe's great powers owed their colonial conquests to these military–technological advances," which allowed small forces to annex vast territories.[34] The assumption, however, that military modernity, technological innovation, and imperial conquest are intrinsically linked has been fundamentally questioned.

Bruce Vandervort claimed that although technology was central to the imperial conquests made by European and European American armies, "it was hardly the decisive factor."[35] The nineteenth-century expansion of the British Empire was well under way before the mid-century military transformation set in. Britain brought the whole of the Indian subcontinent under its control before 1850; it furthermore defeated China and appropriated Hong Kong in the First Opium War of 1839–42. After 1850, the new technology found its way to colonial battlefields at a slower pace than is often assumed. Technological innovations such as the machine gun were often less central to imperial conquest than a later mythology has suggested. Decidedly nonmodern weaponry was sometimes resorted to, for instance, around 1900 in the final stages of the Dutch struggle to establish colonial rule over the periphery of the East Indies archipelago, during which the Dutch relied on the naked saber.[36]

Small Western forces were capable of annexing and controlling vast territories, not primarily because of their superior technology, but because of their ability to divide and conquer Indigenous peoples. The recruitment of soldiers from the Indigenous peoples was both the result of this policy and its expression. Armies composed of the colonized were crucial to the British in India and Africa, the Dutch in the East Indies, and the French in North Africa and Indochina. The US Army recruited Native Americans as combatants and scouts during the American–Indian Wars fought west of the Mississippi River (1811–1924). Not modern military technology, Vandervort asserted, but Indigenous troops were crucial to Western success in frontier and imperial war.[37] These troops were rarely treated on an equal footing with the White soldiers with whom they fought. This is hardly surprising given that colonial and imperial warfare intensified at a time when "scientific" racism was becoming one of the prime handmaidens to empire. Theories of racial difference, at times moderated by religious beliefs, had already accompanied earlier colonial enterprises, but the development of quasi-scientific methods of measuring the supposed inferiority of non-White peoples played into the hands of Europeans and North Americans who were eager to maintain their global dominance as older systems of slavery and indentured servitude were gradually disappearing.[38] For the most part, recruiting colonized men had little to do with improving their status and everything to do with creating loyal subjects who would accept their subordinate position within the White empires they served.[39]

Together with the large number of Indigenous people who were used as porters to carry supplies in areas of Asia and Africa without roads and railroads, the significant presence of colonial troops sometimes made imperial warfare reminiscent of warfare in the early modern period. Women and children were present among the press-ganged carriers, and they also accompanied Indigenous soldiers who insisted that their wives and children join them on campaigns. As a result, the number of noncombatants regularly exceeded that of soldiers, similar to early modern campaign communities.[40] In a manner reminiscent of the army wives of the early modern period, "the wives of the *Tirailleurs sénégalais* in France's West African army carried gear, made camp, cooked meals, and mended clothes."[41] Imperial warfare was the product of the rise of mid-nineteenth-century modern war only to a limited extent.

Militarization and Militarism

In terms of their impact on society, the transformations during the mid-century inaugurated processes of militarization in several Western societies—as well as among some of its adversaries. Large and powerful militaries occupied an increasingly prominent place in societies in which the ambition to develop military force was embraced by ever-wider social groups and emphatically articulated in various cultural realms. The appearance of the concept of *militarism* in the 1860s signaled an awareness of these developments among contemporaries.[42] Emerging initially among German-speaking critics of Prussian policies, it soon traveled to France, where it was taken up by opponents of Louis-Napoléon Bonaparte, known as Napoleon III, who was elected president of France in 1848, made himself emperor in 1852 after a coup d'état, and based his power on the military. The French defeat in the Franco-Prussian War led to his downfall in 1870. From the France of Napoleon III, the term went on to pervade political language throughout Europe and in the United States and gradually became an analytical concept used by historians and social scientists, but often maintained its critical-polemical edge. The concept has generally been used to refer to an imbalance between things military and civil, be it an overrepresentation of soldiers in political institutions, a too-large capacity of the military to appropriate society's resources for its own purposes, or an overly dominant presence of military values in civilian society and culture. As an effect of two world wars, the imbalance that militarism points to has often come to be associated with excess, irrationalism, and antimodernism, in particular among the nations held responsible for the outbreak of these wars.

In an analysis that refuses a schematic association of militarism with the presumed irrationalism of some nations, Roger Chickering proposed a synthetic approach. Militarism, he posited, should be understood as a set of "cultural transformations that began after 1850 . . . to redefine the relationship between armed forces and society."[43] In societies in which compulsory education and universal military service trained young men in military virtues, militarism amounted to an erasure of the line between male citizen and soldier. It encouraged citizens "to think and behave like soldiers, to embrace violent international antagonism as a natural or positive feature of human affairs."[44] The most ardent advocates of military values propagated a "bellicist" ideology of national revitalization and the realization of historical progress through war.[45] More moderate military values were disseminated in a routinized fashion by schools, media, and other agents of civic socialization. The resulting "consonance" between armed forces and civic cultures enabled late nineteenth- and early twentieth-century Western societies to mobilize the enormous armed forces that became the norm in this period.[46]

Chickering did not limit his analysis of militarism to Prussia/Germany or attribute a specific paradigmatic status to this case, as has long been a historiographic commonplace. He pointed to the presence of differing militarisms throughout Europe, in the United States, and in Japan, but also called attention to the limits of its dispersion. Despite attempts to emulate European military practices and institutions by countries hoping to resist Western imperialism through a process of "self-strengthening," militarism established itself in few places outside Europe.[47] Its establishment, in Europe and elsewhere, was always the product of processes of transfer that produced commonalities between different militarist formations that, at the same time, were marked by specific national circumstances. Contemporary observers of late nineteenth-century militarism, as Dirk Bönker emphasized, were aware of these commonalities and of the underlying mutual entanglements between militarist societies.[48] In the current use of the concept by historians, this awareness has resurfaced. The study of militarism is no longer about pathological exceptions, but concentrates on widely shared features of nineteenth-century societies produced in a transnational dynamic.

WARS AND WARFARE IN THE "SHORT NINETEENTH CENTURY"

The nineteenth century saw major innovations and transformations in warfare, changes that manifested themselves in large conflicts, in which the rise of new nationalist and imperialist ideologies and changing practices of war-making influenced each other. The short nineteenth century was defined by Wars of Nation-Building, like the Wars of Unification of Germany and Italy, and Wars of Nation-Keeping, like the American Civil War, as well as (post)colonial wars, Wars of Empires, and frontier wars everywhere around the globe.

Wars of Nation-Building, Wars of Nation-Keeping, and (Post)colonial Conflicts

One of the main catalysts for war in the nineteenth-century Western world was nationalism. Inspired by the American Revolution (1765–83) and the French Revolution (1789–99) and hardened in the era of the French Revolutionary and Napoleonic Wars and the Spanish American Wars of Independence, the belief that a people bound together by descent, language, and history had a right to sovereign statehood ripened into a dominant political force after 1815. Explanations about the origins and contours of nationalism vary, but most historians agree that ideologies of national self-determination articulated on both sides of the Atlantic were contingent and contested but nonetheless powerful cultural and social constructs. Regardless of whether one follows Eric Hobsbawm's formula of "the invention of tradition" or takes up the definition of the nation as an "imagined community" by his colleague, Benedict Anderson, there exists a broad scholarly consensus that nationalism imposed, rather than extracted, the imperative of cultural homogeneity on very diverse population groups.[49] Such processes were bound to be violent, especially when the demands of competing nationalisms meshed with the dynamics of state formation and the growing "territorialization" of state power—the efforts of nation- and empire-states to derive maximum benefit from utilizing the human and material resources within their borders.[50]

The post-Napoleonic Wars of Nation-Building in Europe and North America, the heyday of which lasted from 1848 to 1871, accelerated many of these dynamics. Although the gendered correlation between patriotism and citizenship predated the 1830s, expressing itself most visibly in the virtuous male citizen-soldier of the Wars of Revolution and Independence of the 1770s to the 1820s, it was during the Wars of Nation-Building of the nineteenth century that this correlation came into full bloom.[51] These wars differed in duration, scope, and intensity, but most of the wars fought on behalf of the tenets of national independence and popular self-rule either fit into the category of interstate wars or took on the form of revolutionary civil wars. What these wars had in common, according to Andreas Wimmer, was that they reflected a long-term "shift from empire, dynasticism, and theocracy to national principles of legitimizing political power" that gained momentum with new waves of social, ethnic, and racial conflict.[52]

In Europe, the first major international conflict that could not be contained by the balance-of-power system devised at the Congress of Vienna was the Crimean War. Popular nationalist sentiments surfaced frequently in this war, even as the warring factions consisted of traditional empires—Russia on one side and Great Britain, France, and the Ottoman Empire on the other. The resolve of Great Britain and France to halt Russian expansionism at the expense of the Ottomans and defend their own interests in the region took a heavy toll on the armies involved. In total, 880,000 Russian and Greek soldiers fought against 975,850 British, French, Sardinian, and Turkish soldiers. With 700,000, 400,000, and 300,000 soldiers, respectively, the Russian, French, and Ottoman Empires sent the biggest armies into battle. Until the Treaty of Paris (1856) settled territorial disputes, the Russians suffered more than 450,000 casualties, many a result of disease or exposure to harsh weather conditions, while the French, British, and Ottomans lost 162,000 soldiers combined.[53]

What made the Crimean War significant beyond these figures was the heightened role of the press in shaping distinctly national public spheres. Technological advances made it possible for reports from the front to reach audiences in England and France at a faster pace. The electric telegraph, which was developed around mid-century, not only facilitated communication among the commanders in the field but also allowed journalists to rapidly share and disseminate their war reports. Early war photographers, such as Roger Fenton, made haunting images of battlefields and surviving soldiers and generated with them a more realistic public picture of warfare. Photojournalists and newspapermen played an ever more crucial role in whipping up patriotism, but critical reports, such as those that flew from the pen of the Irish war correspondent William Howard Russell, writing for the British newspaper *The Times*, also galvanized citizens around movements opposed to their governments' conduct.[54]

The forces of mechanization and medialization left an even greater imprint on the Wars of German Unification, which encompassed the Second Schleswig War (1864), the Austro-Prussian War (1866), and the Franco-Prussian War. Advanced weaponry, in particular the Dreyse needle gun and superior artillery, as well as the effective use of railroads, gave the Prussian and later German armies a decisive edge over their opponents. The Franco-Prussian War amounted to the largest nineteenth-century land war on the European continent between 1815 and 1914. Of the more than 2 million men mobilized for battle (1.2 million German and 910,000 French soldiers), approximately 116,000 German and over 700,000 French combatants were killed, wounded, or captured in a short conflict that led to the creation of the German Empire. During the siege of Paris, on January 18, 1871, Prussian King Friedrich Wilhelm IV was proclaimed Wilhelm I, Emperor of Germany, in the Palace of Versailles. The same day, the new German constitution came into effect, creating a unified German nation-state under Prussian leadership that excluded its rival, Austria.[55] War propaganda on both sides fanned the flames of nationalism, transforming a contest of militarized aristocratic elites into a "people's war" that fused assumptions of cultural superiority with a quasi-religious sense of national destiny.[56] Impassioned depictions of France as the national "archenemy," which harkened back to the propaganda of the period of the Anti-Napoleonic Wars of 1806–15, assuaged differences of class, region, and religion. Conversely, the atrocities committed by German soldiers against civilians during the Franco–Prussian War allowed the French to read the German invasion as a metaphorical rape of "Mother" France.[57] The demand for unconditional surrender reflected a nascent culture of total warfare, in which armed conflict was presented in irreconcilably antagonistic terms and excessive violence was justified as necessary to ensure national survival.[58]

This desire to inflict absolute defeat on the enemy was in part rooted in the mid-century revolutionary conflagrations that swept the Atlantic world. Armed struggle punctuated the European Revolution of 1848–49 with its civil wars, which aimed to topple hereditary systems of privilege and to democratize the relationship between rulers and ruled within sovereign nation-states. Divisions between bourgeois liberals and democratic and socialist radicals weakened the insurrectionary movements in France, the German states, Austria, Hungary, and Italy during the revolution. Most of the popular uprisings also failed because the revolutionary militias proved no match for the regular armies loyal to the old order.[59] Still, the violent intranational and intraimperial clashes between different political factions that had climaxed in urban barricade fighting and small-scale civil wars had a series of implications for how future revolutions and wars were to be fought. With the European counterrevolution dissolving civic militias that had revived the notion of an armed male citizenry, the liberal ideal of the voluntary citizen-soldier gave way to its antirevolutionary counterpart, the citizen-conscript, after states like Prussia went on to reform their conscription regimes based on the idea of universal male service.[60] Both Prussia's battlefield successes and the increased prospect of a great-power war congealed a preference for large standing armies through various systems of conscription across Europe, which made the likelihood of facing armed conflict a shared experience for much of the continent's young male population. Concurrently, the events of 1848–49 militarized revolutionary politics. The new dictum for radical democrats in Europe and North America, to which many "Forty-Eighters" immigrated in the early 1850s because of their persecution in the postrevolutionary restoration, was that political and social transformation could not precede war, but had to be achieved through war that required professionally trained and politically principled soldiers.[61]

Two overlapping wars fought to achieve national unification or, respectively, preserve national unity, the Second Italian War of Independence (1859) and the American Civil War, revealed the extent to which revolutionary pathos had become associated with a militarized nationalism. Giuseppe Garibaldi, the celebrated leader of the Italian Risorgimento movement, which fought for independence and unification since 1815, came to epitomize this fusion with particular clarity. A fervid "Garibaldi cult," facilitated by the mass production of books, portraits, songs, and fashion items, captured the public imagination as "patriots" on the Italian Peninsula were fighting for their independence.[62] Cutting across political and geographical lines, identification with the Risorgimento spread as far as North America, where northern unionists and southern secessionists locked in deadly strife claimed Garibaldi as one of their own. Garibaldi's fame also shone brightly in South America, where Italian nationalists had lived in exile from 1836 to 1848 and participated in some of the local post-Bolivarian wars of independence. Chief among them was the Uruguayan Civil War (1839–51), during which Garibaldi gained valuable experience in guerrilla warfare as the leader of a small force of Italian expatriates—techniques that he later used in Europe.[63]

Most nineteenth-century nation-states were born in wars.[64] Italy, too, gained its independence in three armed struggles against the Austrian Empire in 1848–49, 1859, and 1866. It became a kingdom on February 18, 1861, but secured its territory and gained Venice during the Third Italian War of Independence (1866), which was related to the Austro-Prussian War. The length and scale of these conflicts was distinctly smaller than that of the German Wars of Unification. In this conflict in total 600,000 Austrians and Germans under Austrian leadership fought against 500,000 Prussians and Germans as well as 300,000 Italians under Prussian leadership. During three months of fighting, more than 71,000 Austrians and 37,000 Germans and Italians were killed or fatally wounded.[65] The Battle of Solferino, fought in Lombardy in June 1859 during the Second Italian War of Independence, was nevertheless the largest battle and bloodiest confrontation since the Battle of Leipzig of October 1813. An estimated 130,000 Austrian troops and a combined total of 140,000 French and allied Piedmontese troops fought in this battle. The suffering of the approximately 40,000 sick and wounded soldiers left on the theater of war without any sufficient medical care shocked the European public.[66]

In many ways, the competing visions of national expansion that exploded in the American Civil War—one founded in the slaveholding plantation economy of the South, the other promoted by the agrarian and industrial elites of the North—echoed the divisions within Europe's nation-building projects. Unionists painted their Southern opponents as the offspring of the landed aristocracies of the Old World, whereas Confederates argued that slavery provided stability in a transatlantic world thrown into turmoil by the rivalries of class and race. In recent years, historians have moved beyond domestic frames of analysis to show how combatants on both sides made sense of the American Civil War by embedding the conflict in a wider international context.[67] As US President Abraham Lincoln, in office from 1861 to 1865, was universalizing the significance of the war by asking "whether any nation" conceived on the principles of liberty and equality "can long endure," many Northerners began to embrace the destruction of the slaveholding oligarchy as a prerequisite of national unity.[68] The idea that the nation-state would reach its final form through the clash of opposing models of government not only facilitated the revolutionary act of emancipating 4 million African American slaves but also escalated the violence directed at noncombatants. Vicious battles with staggering death tolls were accompanied by scorched-earth policies in the latter stages of the war in which invading Union armies laid waste to the Southern plantation economy, leaving a trail of women and children without food and shelter. In total, 2 million men had fought in the Union army (with 698,000 at its peak) and up to 1 million in the Confederate army (with 360,000 at its peak). The war destroyed much of the infrastructure of the American South. It still ranks as the bloodiest conflict in US history. When the last Confederate forces surrendered in April 1865, hundreds of thousands had died. The estimated numbers vary from at least 620,000 to 750,000 soldiers and, in addition, 50,000 civilians.[69]

In Latin America, the War of the Triple Alliance, which was fought by Paraguay against Brazil, Uruguay, and Argentina over territorial disputes in its border regions, was comparable in magnitude to the American Civil War in lives lost. After six years of bloodshed, some 430,000 people had perished. Most historians of Latin America hold that the war killed about two-thirds of Paraguay's male population, turning the country into a demographic wasteland that recovered only slowly after taking on a numerically superior enemy alliance. The victors paid dearly as well, with the Empire of Brazil registering approximately 50,000 fallen soldiers and as many dead civilians.[70] While the outcome of the War of the Triple Alliance strengthened Brazil's position as the leading power in South America, it also set in motion decisive political transformations in that nation, including the abolition of slavery in 1888 and the formation of the First Brazilian Republic one year later.

These staggering figures have led some historians to underline the capacity of the emerging culture of industrialized warfare to inflict destruction on soldiers and civilian populations to a degree that was previously unimaginable. Napoleonic infantry tactics, such as approaching the enemy in close columns and forming firing lines or garish cavalry charges, proved disastrous once the introduction of long-range, rapid-fire rifles and shrapnel-showering cannons gave solidly entrenched defenders the upper hand. Military leaders on many sides struggled to reconcile old notions of battlefield heroism, which tended to valorize hand-to-hand combat, with the newly innovated weaponry produced in iron and steel manufacturing, along with advancements in transportation (steamships and railroads), that made armies more mobile and more lethal. This "bubbly froth" on the surface of traditional societies, as Bruce Porter described the impact of industrialization, altered both the conduct of war and its perception.[71]

What remains a matter of debate is the question of just how destructive and vicious the nineteenth-century Wars of Nations were, especially when compared to armed conflict in the centuries before and after. Mark Neely, for example, offered a contrarian view by pointing to certain restraints that prevented Civil War–era Americans, and by extension their European contemporaries, from descending into all-out violence, chief among them fellow feelings of Whiteness and religion.[72] There is little doubt that improved sanitation, rising vaccination rates, and the development of safer anesthetic procedures played their part in keeping greater numbers of wounded soldiers alive. Still, it is possible to contend that the question of how reckless approaches to war were could sometimes depend less on the firepower available to warring parties than on specific contexts where gendered and racialized forms of Othering and potentially genocidal ideologies of race and colonialism made annihilatory practices more likely.

Nationalism's push toward ethnic homogenization is often seen as inimical to empire, and it was the nationalist wars of the early twentieth century that spelled doom for the Austrian, Russian, and Ottoman Empires. In the nineteenth century, however, nationalism and empire were not quite as opposed as they may seem. Many of the key actors in the wars outlined in this section were empire-states that proved themselves capable of co-opting the affective power of nationalism for imperial ends. The legacies of the big intrastate and interstate wars thus often merged seamlessly with the more localized forms of conflict that characterized colonial warfare.

Wars of Empires and Frontier Wars

Looking at nineteenth-century processes of nation-making from the vantage point of war, it becomes evident that nationalist narratives did not constitute their own context but gained traction in a world dominated by imperial power structures. Many of the same Western societies that reinvented themselves as "nations" in that period betrayed marked affinities for settler colonialism, economic expansionism, and scientific racism—the three pillars of the Euro-American project of colonizing the world that peaked around 1900. Though couched in the language of "civilization," imperialism generated unrestrained forms of warfare, resulting in streams of blood and tears on the continents that became the objects of White colonial greed.

Africa, in particular, became the focus of European desires for conquest and control in the second half of the nineteenth century. The "Scramble for Africa" between 1881 and 1914, during which technologically superior European powers partitioned the continent in pursuit of raw materials to feed their growing industrial economies, was steeped in violence. In the 1870s, Europeans possessed not more than 10 percent of Africa; on the eve of World War I, White empires controlled 90 percent of the continent. Strategic rivalries among the Europeans intensified once Germany and Italy made their colonial ambitions known. In part to avoid war between the colonizers, the Berlin Conference (1884–85) established a framework for legitimizing current and future claims of European powers in Africa. This included confirming the Congo Free State, a territory more than seventy times the size of Belgium, as essentially the property of the Belgian King Leopold II, who reigned from 1865 to 1909. The harsh, inhuman conditions under which local workers collected natural rubber for export became the subject of an international scandal. During Leopold's rule in the Congo from 1885 to 1908, the Indigenous population shrank dramatically, with several historians estimating that beatings, mutilations, sleep deprivation, diseases, or severe exhaustion killed as many as 8 million Africans.[73]

Resistance against the efforts of the colonizers to expropriate their land and press Indigenous men and women into oppressive, slave-like labor regimes sparked a series of bloody insurrections. For British Africa alone, historians have counted up to forty conflicts between 1869 and 1902, which they classified as small colonial wars or punitive expeditions.[74] The Second Boer War (1899–1902) exceeded both frames, pitting the British Empire against the South African descendants of Dutch settlers, the Boers. Some 347,000 British regulars and up to 150,000 colonial forces fought against 88,000 Boers whose struggle for independence cost more than 70,000 lives, among them an estimated 25,000 women and children.[75] Retaliatory actions against Indigenous populations, including torture and rape, were a common means of imperial subjugation. In the case of the Herero and Nama Revolts in German South West Africa (1904–8), such actions culminated in a genocide when German colonial troops sent entire families to die of thirst and starvation in the desert. The total number of deaths is estimated between 24,000 and 100,000 Herero and 10,000 Nama.[76]

White colonizers routinely justified the atrocities they committed in Africa and elsewhere with the racist trope that they were fighting against "savages" who stood outside European notions of "civilized" warfare. Prisoners were rarely taken, and wounded enemies were left to die on the battlefield. Moreover, in colonial frontier societies where the boundaries between war and everyday violence were fluid, imperial rule depended heavily on military policing carried out by White administrators in concert with Indigenous auxiliaries, such as the Senegalese and Algerian *tirailleurs* in French Africa, the askari in German East Africa, or the sepoys and Sikhs in British India.[77] However, relying on the loyalty of Native fighters whom Whites identified as descending from "martial races" could also backfire. Take the example of the Indian Rebellion (1857–58), also known as the Indian Mutiny, which started as an upheaval of sepoy soldiers in the British colonial army that sparked a series of insurrections in central and northern India. Though quashed within one year, the insurrections deepened racist prejudices and fomented fears of future uprisings.[78] Imperial anxieties about the indefensibility of global color lines led to instances of pan-imperial military cooperation. Most prominent among those was the international force that put an end to the Boxer Rebellion, during which both sides engaged in indiscriminate killings, robbery, rape, and torture. This uprising at the end of Qing dynasty was initiated by the Militia United in Righteousness (Yihetuan), known in English as the "Boxers," since many of their members had been practitioners of the martial arts. The Yihetuan were motivated by nationalist sentiments as well as opposition to Western colonialism and the Christian missionary activities associated with it.[79]

The connections between domestic Wars of Nation-Building and imperial frontier wars are glaringly evident in the case of the United States. First coined in the 1840s and popularized by images such as John Gast's 1872 painting *American Progress* (see Figure 9.3), the national myth of *Manifest Destiny*, which propagated the belief that White Americans had a Christian mission to settle and civilize an entire continent, obscured the fact that westward expansion rested on the decimation of Native American peoples.[80] The painting shows White settlers moving west guided and protected by the "spirit of the frontier," a goddess-like allegorical figure dressed in a white Roman toga (alerting to the tradition of republicanism), which brings the light of civilization to the American West, supported by new technologies like the railway and the telegraph, driving Native Americans and bison into the dark of the periphery. The painting became popular in the United States as a print and represented, as well as masked, the aggressive ideology of the North American frontier wars.

Not all violent dislocations conducted by White settlers and officials were triggered by wars. For example, in the Trail of Tears (1838)—a wave of forced removals of 16,500 Cherokees, Seminoles, Chickasaws, and Choctaws, an estimated 4,000 of whom died—the US government used intimidation and threats to push these groups out of their homelands in the Southeast.[81] In other places, Native American tribes resorted to armed resistance. The most prolonged confrontations, which often involved a series of

FIGURE 9.3 *American Progress*, painting by John Gast (1842–96), propagating the belief that White Americans had a Christian mission to settle and civilize an entire continent, [n.p.], 1872.
(Library of Congress, Prints and Photographs Division, Washington, DC, LC-DIG-ppmsca-09855)

armed conflicts between the US Army and various Indian nations, included the Apache Wars (1849–86) and the raids and counterraids that occurred on Native American lands on the Great Plains. It was there, during the Great Sioux War of 1876, that Native warriors defeated a cavalry regiment at the Battle of the Little Bighorn (June 1876) in Montana. Eventually, however, the Plains Indians were forced to surrender, and the Wounded Knee Massacre (December 1890), which refers to the killing of up to 300 Native Americans by US soldiers in southwestern South Dakota, effectively ended fighting in that region.[82]

Settler colonialism reared its ugly head in other regions of the world as well. For example, no serious historian of the British Empire in the early twenty-first century disputes the devastating impact that the arrival of White colonizers had on the Indigenous populations of Australia, New Zealand, and Canada. All three societies, which Marilyn Lake fittingly termed "settler nation-states,"[83] crafted collective self-images of their countries as hospitable to immigrants while concealing the legacies of conquest, violence, and dispossession that eradicated Native inhabitants whom the intruders deemed too "primitive" or "uncivilized." In light of the ruthless frontier campaigns, such as the intermittent killings committed by White Australians and their Native auxiliaries in Queensland between 1831 and 1918, during which more than an estimated 50,000 Aboriginal men, women, and children lost their lives, Dirk Moses and Henry Reynolds labeled British colonial rule in Australia and New Zealand "genocidal."[84]

The US–Mexican War (1846–48) constituted a frontier war of a different sort as it meshed efforts of national consolidation with expansionistic ambitions. There are good reasons for subsuming this conflict under the rubric of imperial frontier war rather than a European-style War of Nation-Building: Americans racialized their enemies, viewed Texas and California as lands for White settlement, and disregarded the interests of Indigenous peoples.[85] Militarily, the war was a one-sided affair. After a string of victories, mostly the result of superior weaponry, US troops entered Mexico City in September 1847 and forced the Mexicans to relinquish ownership of a large territory comprising California and much of today's southwestern United States. For the duration of the conflict, the United States dispatched roughly 100,000 regular soldiers and militias against 82,000 Mexicans and lost some 14,000 men, most through disease. The number of Mexican casualties, military and civilian, is harder to ascertain, but most estimates range from 15,000 to 40,000 deaths.[86]

After defeating Spain in the Spanish–American War (1898), which led to the American acquisition of Cuba, Guam, and Puerto Rico, the United States transitioned from continental to oceanic empire when it annexed Hawaii (1898) and then the Philippines (1899–1902). Some historians have interpreted the racialized warfare practiced by US troops in the Philippine–American War, in which Filipino nationalists fought to establish an independent government, as a continuation of the violence perpetrated by White settlers against Native Americans. Yet, in trying to defeat the insurgents, US soldiers also employed more modern methods of terrorizing the enemy, in particular the "water-cure"—a variant of waterboarding—and the use of concentration camps to round up local civilians and prisoners.[87] Concentration camps were a technique of imperial warfare that was hardly unique to the Americans; they had already been used in varying degrees by their Spanish predecessors and by the British in their fight against the Boers. More generally, their very existence has animated historiographical debates over the extent to which military strategies born in colonial settings of exposing civilians to certain death by hunger and incarceration foreshadowed the genocidal qualities of the total wars of the twentieth century.[88]

There is little disagreement among scholars that colonial wars were notoriously brutal and punctuated with exterminationist rhetoric and tactics. At the same time, policies of total disregard of human life that defined later genocides were usually circumscribed by a series of influences intrinsic to the age of high imperialism. Most significantly, empires that counted among their possessions colonies of exploitation relied on Indigenous labor to generate revenue. Another moderating factor was Christian missionaries who saw in Native populations souls to convert, not bodies to destroy. Nevertheless, the dichotomy of "civilization" and "savagery" that informed the period's colonial frontier wars left a deep imprint on Western ways of war in furnishing a sense of boundless possibilities as to how to fight enemies that were Othered and dehumanized.

GENDER, EARLY HUMANITARIANISM, AND PEACE ACTIVISM

If post-Napoleonic societies in Europe and the Americas continued to gravitate toward war, there were also citizens who offered a vision of the international system in which people openly despised war or sought to tame it with humanitarianism and peace activism. While scholars from a variety of disciplinary backgrounds tend to view humanitarianism (understood as compassion in times of war) as a timeless global phenomenon, the desire to save the lives of soldiers and reduce the suffering of the victims of war acquired a mounting urgency in the nineteenth century and was from the beginning a highly gendered and gendering activity.[89] This desire for humanitarian help in wartime could be driven by practical considerations, such as professionalizing and improving the medical care provided to soldiers, but it could also extend to grand schemes to institutionalize normative efforts for the advancement of peacemaking and human rights.[90]

Female initiative was instrumental in promoting humanitarian policies on and beyond the battlefield. The British reformer Florence Nightingale, an advocate of professional nursing, is closely associated with the origins of organized humanitarian action. During the Crimean War, Nightingale and her coworkers laid the foundation for the modern nursing profession by exposing the unhygienic conditions in the British army and working to ensure sufficient medical supplies for the wounded. Complementing Nightingale's vision of alleviating wartime agony were the ideas developed by the Swiss entrepreneur and social reformer Henry Dunant, whose tour of the battlefield at Solferino in 1859, during the Second Italian War of Independence, marked the beginning of the establishment of volunteer relief associations that would lead to the founding of the International Committee of the Red Cross in 1863 and the first Geneva Convention for the Amelioration of the Condition of the Wounded in Armies in the Field, signed in 1864 by thirteen European states. The ten articles of this treaty have been expanded over the centuries to comprise sixty-four articles in the early twenty-first century that protect soldiers who are out of battle as a result of sickness or injury, as well as medical and religious personnel and civilians in the zone of battle.[91]

In Germany, Princess Louise of Prussia, from 1854 to 1907 the grand duchess of Baden, responded to the failing military medical system during the Second Italian War of Independence by initiating the patriotic women's association of Baden in 1859, which became the model in the next decade for several other women's associations all over Germany that helped in military medical care and collaborated with the German Red Cross founded in 1864.[92] In the United States, Clara Barton, the founder of the American Red Cross in 1881, followed these models. She worked as a hospital nurse during the American Civil War and later aided soldiers and civilians stricken by war on both sides of the Atlantic.[93] Scholars often cite these pioneers' attempts to set up binding international norms regarding the treatment of combatants and noncombatants, regardless of their status as friend or enemy, as proof of the rising significance of organized transnational networks.

Next to transnational humanitarianism, peace, in the words of Sandi E. Cooper, increasingly became a "citizen's mission" during the short nineteenth century, "a subject of private conferences, of specialized periodicals, of national and international societies, of university and school curricula, and of challenges to parliamentary candidates."[94] In the developing peace activism, women and men worked together, but usually in highly gendered ways.[95] Antiwar sentiments had deep roots in individual religious sects formed in the upheavals of the Protestant Reformation, such as the Quakers. By the nineteenth century, however, theories of nonviolence undergirded multiple strands of social reform.[96] Garrisonians, who advocated the direct emancipation of slaves without compensation to their owners, and other religiously inspired abolitionist groups attached their crusade to end slavery to a form of pacifism that renounced all use of force and physical violence.[97] Peace movements also overlapped nationally as well as transnationally with the struggle for women's rights. Many female activists legitimized their public roles with references to a "maternal feminism" based on the assumption of "natural differences between the sexes" that envisioned women as "spiritual mothers" and innate advocates of peace.[98] Arbitration, which encompassed a series of initiatives to peacefully settle international conflicts, became a rallying cry for male and female peace activists on both sides of the Atlantic. One well-known advocate of arbitration and disarmament was the Austrian Bohemian pacifist and novelist Bertha von Suttner, author of the pacifist bestseller, *Die Waffen nieder!* (Lay Down Your Arms!), first published in 1889, with thirty-seven editions and translations into twelve languages. In 1905, she became the first woman to be solely awarded the Nobel Peace Prize.[99]

From the beginning, nineteenth-century humanitarianism and pacifism coexisted uneasily with nationalist demands to defend and protect one's own country and to prioritize care for those who had taken up arms for this purpose. This tension also played out in the spaces of cross-border cooperation carved out by the era's manifold peace movements. Cosmopolitan sensibilities occupied center stage at a series of peace congresses held in major European cities, most notably in London, Paris, and Frankfurt, in the 1840s and 1850s. The resolutions passed at these conventions, which were attended by delegates from Europe and North America, reflected an idealistic approach to international relations, although the proceedings were hampered by differences of gender, class, religion, and political temperament. Radical pacifists who pledged to renounce all wars and abstain from military service clashed with conservative reformers who focused on arbitration and disarmament.[100]

Competing allegiances to global peace and national security surfaced also during the international peace conferences in the Dutch city of The Hague in 1899 and 1907, although the results achieved at these meetings were quite remarkable. Notions of "civilized warfare," first formulated by the German American legal scholar Franz Lieber during the American Civil War, were expanded and internationalized during these conferences with conventions that introduced rules to spare the lives of wounded and surrendering soldiers and discouraged violence against unarmed civilians. Furthermore, the delegates of the 1899 conference, many of whom were women, succeeded in establishing the Permanent Court of Arbitration, which called on rival powers to settle their disputes through mediation.[101]

Despite their idealistic tone, the calls for peace that rang out at these conferences rarely fused with revolutionary demands to upend existing power structures. Most of the middle- and upper-class men and women engaged in the period's antiwar movements did not imagine peace as a utopian scheme for the world to unite, and their promotion of greater international amity remained preoccupied with ensuring the stability and prosperity of the Western world. The inequalities of race and empire were thrown into sharp relief at the 1899 Hague conference, where the Euro-American delegates claimed to act in the interest of "civilization." Many of the nations represented at the conference were also colonial powers that made sure that the same protective measures introduced to tame warfare did not apply to the subjugation of "savages." Colonized peoples were neither invited to attend the Hague conferences nor were they signatories to the convention. Unable to fully transcend the dichotomy of civilization and barbarism, transnational humanitarian networks before World War I more often than not functioned as a corollary to racism and imperialism, not as their antithesis.[102]

Gendering Wars of Nations and Empires

The conceptualization of the nineteenth century as a *short century*, starting with the 1830s and ending with the 1910s, is helpful if we want to understand the specific character of this period defined by Wars of Nations and Empires from the perspective of the history of the military. The perspective of women's and gender history, however, leads to a different conceptualization; for this approach, the concept of a *long nineteenth century* that includes the period of the Wars of Revolution and Independence from the 1770s to the 1830s makes much more sense. We cannot understand the development until the Age of the World Wars without taking into account the transformations during this early period, during which, parallel to the changes in military systems and the conduct of warfare, characterized by a "nationalization" of wars, the dominant ideas about the gender order of war and peace changed too, as several women's and gender historians have noted.[103] The research on the period of the Wars of Revolution and Independence therefore must be the starting point for any exploration of gender and national, colonial, and imperial warfare during the nineteenth century.[104] This different periodization of the nineteenth century from the perspective of the history of military and war and gender history is one example for the "nonunity" and "multiplicity of history" that characterize our approach to the study of gender and war.[105]

The Legacy of the Wars of Revolution and Independence

Most women and gender historians who work on the Wars of Revolution and Independence agree that it was in this era that the basic outlines of the modern notion of a gender order of war and peace were developed in the patriotic-national discourse to legitimate the new form of mass warfare with armed forces based on volunteers, militias, conscripts, and professional soldiers. These men of all social strata fought, according to the discourse, in "peoples wars," "national wars," "wars of revolution," or "wars of liberation," which had to be supported by all civilians at home, including women, in a variety of ways: with money, material, work, charity, and care. The new national, mass wars could only be fought successfully if the civilian population was mobilized as well. Without their voluntary and forced support, maintaining large armed forces was not possible for states and militaries. In the center of the patriotic-national propaganda and culture that was developed and needed for war mobilization stood a complementary and, at its core, hierarchical image of male and female tasks in warfare. Men as citizens and soldiers had to protect family, home, and country when the nation was in danger or needed to be liberated from an internal or external enemy. They had the duty and right to fight—the "power to injure"—on behalf of and controlled by the state or in the name of a higher power, like the imagined nation or the revolutionary people. Connected to this duty and right was their political citizenship in the nation-state, either existing or yet to be created. Depending on the historical circumstances, men were called up either as citizens to fight and protect their rights, like in revolutionary and Napoleonic France, or as "subjects" who were promised more political rights if they followed the call to fight, like in several monarchical states that fought against France. The specific formation of the nexus changed, but the core idea—political rights in exchange for military duties—stayed the same.[106]

Women were constructed in this image as daughters, sisters, housewives, and mothers in need of male protection, because as a sex they were "vulnerable to injury." Only in times of "national emergency" were they allowed, even requested in the public dis-course, to expand their "womanly and motherly duties" beyond home and family to support the national war efforts by collecting money and goods, organizing war charity, and helping in military medical care. At the same time, they were excluded by the joint powers of discourse, laws, and culture from the male-defined businesses of military, war, and politics. Their exclusion was based on the enlightened assumption that gender differences were rooted in men's and women's different "physiology" and "nature," which led to the conclusion that men and women universally had different "gender characters" and thus different but complementary tasks in the state, military, economy, society, and family.[107]

To be sure, this idea of a gender order, which stressed "separate spheres" for men and women, circulated among transatlantic elites in the late eighteenth and early nineteenth centuries and became more and more dominant. However, it was not shared by all in the middle and upper classes, nor did it necessarily affect the lives or the culture of the men and women who formed the majority of the urban and rural populations, let alone enslaved and free African-born, Creole, or Indigenous peoples in the Americas. Recent scholarship suggests that despite the powerful attempts to create a dominant model of the gender order in war and peace, there were no universal concepts of masculinity and femininity, either in the era of the Wars of Revolution and Independence or in the following century.[108] In the words of Katherine Aaslestad and Judith Miller, gender relations "were profoundly shaped by local conflicts and norms, and the models themselves moved rapidly across boundaries only to be reconfigured in their new contexts.... If gender lines appeared to harden during the war[s] [of the age of revolutions], that development emerged from the instability of a new gender axis where manhood was not a given, and instead had to be performed, repeated and naturalized."[109] Such an approach to gender history makes it necessary to view gender not simply as a concept or ideal order formed by discourse or produced through legislation or economic and social structures, though prescription, law, and material relations all had powerful effects. Gender also must be understood through the practices of men and women in daily life, in peace and war, and the individual and collective identities they constructed. And here we need far more research on the long nineteenth century.[110]

An important part of these often-contested practices was the "battles of the sexes." Already during the French Revolution, some Jacobin women challenged the exclusion of women from war and consequently from politics by questioning the new model of the national gender order of war that the revolutionaries propagated. For the male revolutionaries, this exceptional request threatened to turn the social and political order of the young republic upside down. They responded with a legislation that systematically excluded women from all forms of political and military participation, justifying it with the supposedly natural roles of men and women as mother and housewives.[111] This did not, however, prevent a small number of French women from dressing as men and joining the revolutionary army to fight for their country.[112]

The struggle of female radicals for more political equality continued in the civil wars and revolutionary upheavals of the short nineteenth century. Two examples are the civil wars of the European Revolution of 1848–49 and the short-lived Paris Commune in the spring of 1871. But unfortunately, the research by women's and gender historians on both events, especially the European Revolution, is still underdeveloped.[113] Historians in general rarely consider the role of women in these struggles. Women started their independent democratic women's associations during both events and developed with them their own forms of female activism. Their associations collected money for weapons and munitions, organized the medical care for the revolutionary fighters, helped them to flee or migrate, and took care of their families. Many helped to build barricades and produce bullets; some joined the armed struggle of the revolutionaries.[114]

In the second half of the nineteenth century, the struggle for equal political rights was also taken up by the rising women's movement, which not only fought, divided by class and race, for equal civil rights in family and marriage and equal access to education and paid work, but also demanded more political rights for women. The moderate middle- and upper-class women's associations demanded equal franchise with men (which meant the extension of the existing class- and race-based voting system); the more radical groups of left-liberal and socialist women called for universal suffrage for all men and women independent of class and race. The suffrage movement reached its peak in the last decade before World War I.[115] In this struggle, women's movement activists increasingly used the old nexus of military service and political citizenship rights for their own purpose by equating their voluntary patriotic war service with the men's fighting to insist on equal political rights. During World War I, this argument was even used by liberal and socialist women's leaders, who had supported pacifism before the start of the conflict, to legitimate their support of the war efforts of their nation.[116]

Gender images and relations were in these multiple ways at the core of the political, economic, and social order in times of war and peace, because they helped to create a notion of a "natural basis" of this order with hierarchies that seemed to be "innate." The nation at war—like in peacetime—was imagined as a "valorous family of the people" in which men and women, old and young, rich and poor had their "organic" place. Gender hierarchically organized the imagined community of the nation in the interplay with other constructions of difference, especially class, race, and ethnicity in a seemingly "natural" and thus universal way. It also helped to organize states and empires in a similar manner by informing laws, norms, institutions, policies, and movements.[117]

In both nation-states and empires, White middle and upper-class men stood at the top together with White women of their own social strata as their subordinated complement. Below them in society and culture stood, externally, all "barbarian and savage others." Internally, subordinated groups included the men and women of the working class, non-Christians, and racial Others like enslaved and free African-born, Creole, or Indigenous peoples. Such thinking unfolded its effects far into the twentieth century and affected not only Europe and North America, but also all the territories their states had occupied and colonized. It was contested, to be sure, but seems to have succeeded in becoming the dominant ideal of nations and empires in the West by constant reinvention and cultural reinforcement. For the latter, the construction of the collective memories of the period of the Wars of Revolution and Independence played an important role. For many European and American countries, the wars of the Age of Revolutions led to the birth of "their nation"—at least in the imagination of the supporters of nationalist movements.[118]

Gender, War, and Nation

An important function of the gender order of war was to mobilize the needed support for the growing armed forces in wartime. Men had to be marshaled for the military and civilians for the backing of war at home. Thus, a "home front" existed long before the term was invented by war propaganda during World War I.[119] The work of Stefan Dudink and others showed the close interrelationship between the emergence of new ways of mass mobilization—volunteers, militias, and universal conscription—and the rise of notions of gender as a universal, natural binary opposition and of the notion of men as universal male political subjects since the Age of Revolutions. The introduction of male citizenship during the French Revolution and the derivation of universal male conscription as a duty based on this right had a lasting impact that affected other countries as well, because it created the nexus between male military duties and citizenship rights. This nexus, often considered by contemporaries to be effective in military terms but politically dangerous, was introduced and transformed in other contexts too. Where it was rejected, it nevertheless made its presence felt in what became a conscious refusal of the model of the modern citizen-soldier army in favor of other, perhaps less effective but politically more reliable modes of mobilization. Always controversial and never fully implemented, even in contexts where it was supposedly fully endorsed, the model of universal conscription loomed large in the background of all nineteenth-century debates over military reform and political citizenship.[120]

In the practice of revolutionary, national, and imperial armed forces, the political nexus between military service and political citizenship rights played out quite differently depending on specific historical contexts with dissimilar political and military traditions. Furthermore, even in the same armed forces it had divergent meanings for soldiers from different social backgrounds, racial or ethnical identities, and rank. On the American continent, similar to Europe, the decades in the mid-nineteenth century were marked by intensive warfare in the name of nationalism. The two most important conflicts for the formation of gender and race relations in nineteenth-century North America were the US–Mexican War and the American Civil War. War and martial masculinity were often mutually reinforcing during wartime, while more restrained practices of manhood gained precedence after war's end.[121]

Wartime practices of womanhood were shaped by the demands of warfare during the US–Mexican War and the Civil War, leading—like in other countries and conflicts—in many cases to short-term increases in female autonomy and authority. Women of all classes, races, and ethnicities needed to replace the fighting men, not only at home and in their families, but also on their estates, farms, or businesses.[122] If they were not forced to work for their own living or had to support their family, they were encouraged by the war propaganda to volunteer outside their home for war charity or medical care. Female professional and voluntary nurses were very much in demand during the American Civil War and the Wars of Independence and Unification in Europe. As armies began to grow in the late eighteenth century, the military medical system had to expand too and needed more external support. The founding of national Red Cross organizations beginning in the 1860s and the increasing professional training of middle- and upper-class women as nurses were ways to address these issues.[123]

In the imagination of nations and their war cultures, women who, like Florence Nightingale and Clara Barton, volunteered in wartime to help wounded and sick soldiers as nurses became the complement to the heroic soldier who sacrificed his life at the altar of the fatherland. In poems, paintings, and prints from the second half of the nineteenth and the first half of the twentieth century, nurses who served in war were portrayed as "angels of mercy." One early example is a colored mezzotint after a painting by the British artist James E. Buttersworth from the Crimean War, which is titled *Florence Nightingale an Angel of Mercy, Scutari Hospital 1855* (see Figure 9.4). The text reads, "When all the Medical Officers have retired for the night, and silence and darkness have settled down upon those miles of prostate sick, she may be observed alone with a little lamp in her hand making her solitary rounds." Many later representations of similar scenes portrayed Nightingale less realistically and more angel-like, dressed in white as in, for instance, the 1891 painting *The Lady with the Lamp* by the English artist Henrietta Rae, which became very popular as a lithograph reproduction.[124]

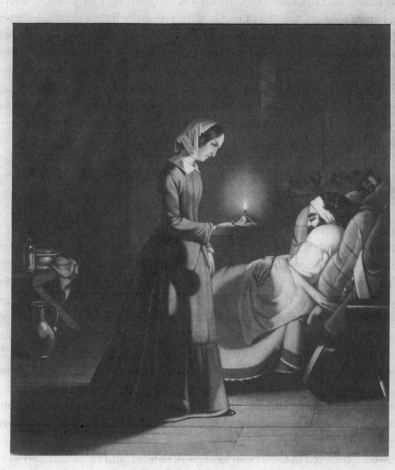

AN ANGEL OF MERCY.

"When all the Medical Officers have retired for the night, and silence and darkness have settled down upon those miles of prostrate sick, she may be observed alone, with a little lamp in her hand, making her solitary rounds"

FIGURE 9.4 *Florence Nightingale an Angel of Mercy, Scutari Hospital 1855*, colored mezzotint by Charles Algernon Tomkins after a painting by James E. Buttersworth (1817–94), portraying Nightingale, "the lady with the lamp," as a field-hospital nurse during the Crimean War, London, 1855.

Unlike the middle- and upper-class women who supported war through charity, voluntary medical care, or professional nursing, the lower-class women who assisted in military medical care for money or joined the armies as camp followers, auxiliaries, and cross-dressed female soldiers rarely found any recognition, either during wartime or in the national memory of wars. The recollection of the war experiences of these women was suppressed in collective memory. Especially the war support of camp followers and officially recognized auxiliaries was quickly and long-lastingly forgotten. The few cross-dressed female soldiers, too, fell into obscurity, especially if they survived the wars. Yet by the latter half of the nineteenth century, some of these female soldiers were rediscovered in nationalist narratives, and their public image became more positive. Their portrayal, however, was one-dimensional: They were girls and women who rose above the limitations of their sex to defend a "nation in danger." They served as examples of extraordinary female patriotism, and, as such, their actions stayed out of reach for ordinary women, who should limit themselves to "appropriate" female forms of patriotism like war charity and war nursing.[125]

Gender, War, and Empire

The nineteenth century was characterized by the rapid expansion of, first, the British and, later, the French and other empires and fierce interimperial rivalries, in particular over Africa, which became the focus of European desires for conquest and control in the 1880s. The warfare that characterized colonial/imperial expansion was often diffuse and chaotic. It included the struggle against Indigenous resistance sparked by imperial invasions, gradual conquests of colonial territories, and the suppression of uprisings. The contact zones of aggressively expanding colonialism were structured by violence, in places ranging from the British settler colonies of Canada, Australia, and New Zealand to Crown colonies of various European empires, including British India, the Dutch East Indies, and French Indochina. The intersections of gender and militarized violence on the frontiers deeply shaped the daily life of colonial societies. One important dimension of these violent encounters was sexual violence, which needs to be explored further by future research.[126]

White men believed in their right to exploit, control, and rule—not only in the colonies, where they exercised absolute power over the male and female bodies of the Indigenous peoples. The transnational emergence of the gendered and racialized figure of the "White man" became formative in the constitutive relations of colonial conquest and imperial rule across the nineteenth and into the twentieth century. As the self-styled bearer of a "civilizing mission" to Indigenous peoples, the White man became a perpetrator of violence and atrocity when imperial rule and colonial settlement encountered continuing resistance and guerrilla warfare. In the process, the older ideal of the "moral manliness" of the citizen soldier, who only fought for the defense of his own nation, gave way to a more modern notion of masculinity characterized by toughness, aggression, and a capacity to use firearms to "pacify the Natives." This ideal of manliness was justified by the "civilizing mission" of the White men.[127]

One public representation of this new ideal of masculinity is the hymn to US imperialism, "The White Man's Burden," by the British novelist and poet Rudyard Kipling.[128] In the poem, Kipling urged the United States to take up the "burden of empire," as had Britain and other European nations. The publication of the poem in the *McClure's Magazine* in

"THE WHITE MAN'S BURDEN."

FIGURE 9.5 *The White Man's Burden (Apologies to Rudyard Kipling)*, cartoon in the American satirical magazine *Judge*, April 1, 1899, by Victor Gillam (1858–1920), criticizing the rhetoric the United States used to legitimate the Philippine–American War.

(Ohio State University, Billy Ireland Cartoon Library & Museum)

February 1899 coincided with the beginning of the Philippine–American War and the US Senate's ratification of the treaty that placed Puerto Rico, Guam, Cuba, and the Philippines under American control. The US government justified its imperial policy as a "moral necessity": Its duty was to develop and modernize the conquered lands to help carry the "foreign barbarians" to "civilization." This racialized rhetoric of the "White Man's Burden" became a euphemism for imperialism, and many anti-imperialists couched their opposition by using this phrase. One example is the cartoon *The White Man's Burden* by Victor Gillam in the American satirical magazine *Judge* from April 1, 1899 (see Figure 9.5).[129] The cartoon showed Britain and the United States carrying the "savages" from Africa and Asia on their backs upward toward "civilization," overcoming "oppressions," "superstition," "ignorance," "brutality," "slavery," and so on.

CONCLUSION

Research on gender, war, and peace in the nineteenth century indicates the importance of this century for the development of modern warfare, humanitarianism, and the peace movement. From the perspective of the history of military and warfare, a conceptualization of the nineteenth century as the short period between the 1830s to the 1910s makes sense, because it signals the ambition not to interpret this period's Wars of Nations and Empires exclusively or predominantly in the light of the massive conflicts at the beginning and end of the century and the trajectory between them. Instead, it emphasizes the specific character and interconnectedness of the Wars of Nations and Empires in this century, along with its importance for the development of organized humanitarianism and peace activism, which was highly gendered from its beginning. But from the perspective of women's and gender history, the conceptualization as a long nineteenth century seems more meaningful. After all, it was in the period of the Wars of Revolution and Independence, lasting from the 1770s to the 1830s, that, parallel to the changes in the military systems and the conduct of warfare characterized by a "nationalization" of wars, the dominant ideas about gender, war, and peace changed too and the basic outlines of the modern notion of a national gender order of war and peace were developed in the patriotic-national discourse. These developments influenced the thinking about war and peace far into the twentieth century.

Interestingly, however, despite the obvious importance of the nineteenth century—defined in whatever way—for the history of gender, military, and warfare, the gender research on this period is still very underdeveloped compared to work on the twentieth century. So far, the focus of the research is mainly on the transatlantic Wars of Revolution and Independence at the beginning and the US–Mexican War and American Civil War in the middle of the nineteenth century. The gender dimensions of colonial and imperial warfare in the nineteenth century only became a subject of research in the past decade. From a gender perspective, least explored are the mid-century European conflicts, starting with the civil wars of the European Revolution of 1848–49 and continuing with the Italian Wars of Independence and the German Wars of Unification.[130] Only the Crimean War is an exception.[131]

This state of research leaves many subjects unexplored. They include such important themes as the limits of the ideal of military manhood and the ways it was challenged by alternative or competing models of masculinity, represented, for example, by male peace activists, draft dodgers, or deserters. We also know still very little about the diversity of male experiences of military service and warfare formed by the interplay of class, race, ethnicity, and military rank during the Wars of Nations and Empires of the century. Furthermore, the mobilization of civil society—especially women of different social, racial, and ethnic backgrounds for war; their specific war experiences in different conflicts; and the gendered memories of these wars—needs much more research, as does the whole issue of sexual violence in nineteenth-century warfare.

NOTES

1. See the chapter by Stefan Dudink on "Citizenship, Mass Mobilization, and Masculinity in a Transatlantic Perspective, 1770s–1870s" in this handbook.
2. See Stefan Dudink and Karen Hagemann, "Masculinity in Politics and War in the Age of Democratic Revolutions, 1750–1850," in *Masculinities in Politics and War: Gendering*

Modern History, ed. Dudink et al. (Manchester: Manchester University Press, 2004), 3–22.

3. Anne McClintock, *Imperial Leather: Race, Gender, and Sexuality in the Colonial Conquest* (New York: Routledge, 1995), 353–54.

4. See Silke Wenk, "Gendered Representations of the Nation's Past and Future," in *Gendered Nations: Nationalism and Gender Order in the Long Nineteenth Century*, ed. Ida Blom et al. (Oxford: Berg, 2000), 63–77.

5. See Asmut Brückmann, *Die europäische Expansion: Kolonialismus und Imperialismus 1492–1918* (Stuttgart: Klett, 1999), 79; and Philipp Gassert, "'Völker Europas, wahret Eure Heiligsten Güter': Die Alte Welt und die Japanische Herausforderung," in *Der Russisch-Japanische Krieg, 1904/05: Anbruch einer neuen Zeit?*, ed. Maik Hendrik Sprotte and Wolfgang Seifert (Wiesbaden: Harrasowitz Verlag, 2007), 277–94.

6. Roger Chickering, "Total War: The Use and Abuse of a Concept," in *Anticipating Total War: The German and American Experiences, 1871–1914*, ed. Manfred F. Boemeke et al. (Cambridge: Cambridge University Press, 1999), 13–28.

7. Ute Frevert, "War," in *A Companion to Nineteenth-Century Europe 1789–1914*, ed. Stefan Berger (Malden, MA: Blackwell, 2006), 417–31, 420–21, and 430.

8. Jeremy Black, "Introduction," in *European Warfare, 1815–2000*, ed. Black (Basingstoke: Palgrave Macmillan, 2002), 1–26; and Dennis Showalter, "Europe's Way of War, 1815–64," in Black, *European Warfare*, 27–50.

9. Showalter, "Europe's Way," 32–35.

10. For a discussion of this term, see the chapter by Stefan Dudink and Karen Hagemann on "War and Gender: From the Thirty Years' War and Colonial Conquest to the Wars of Revolution and Independence—an Overview" in this handbook.

11. Hans van de Ven, "A Hinge in Time: The Wars of the Mid Nineteenth Century," in *The Cambridge History of War*, vol. 4, *War and the Modern World*, ed. Roger Chickering et al. (Cambridge: Cambridge University Press, 2012), 16–44.

12. For a discussion of this term, see the chapter by Karen Hagemann and Sonya O. Rose on "War and Gender: From the Global Cold War to the Conflicts of the Post–Cold War Era—an Overview" in this handbook.

13. Chickering, "Total War," 21.

14. Paul W. Schroeder, "International Politics, Peace and War, 1815–1914," in *The Nineteenth Century: Europe 1789–1914*, ed. T. C. W. Blanning (Oxford: Oxford University Press, 2000), 158–209.

15. Paul W. Schroeder, *The Transformation of European Politics 1763–1848* (Oxford: Oxford University Press, 1994), vi–vii.

16. Schroeder, "International Politics," 209 and 158.

17. See the chapter by Dudink and Hagemann, "War and Gender" in this handbook.

18. Dominik Geppert et al., eds., *The Wars before the Great War: Conflict and International Politics before the Outbreak of the First World War* (Cambridge: Cambridge University Press, 2015).

19. For the notion of "the first age of global imperialism," see Christopher Alan Bayly, *The Birth of the Modern World, 1780–1914* (Oxford: Oxford University Press, 2004), 110.

20. Jürgen Osterhammel, *The Transformation of the World: A Global History of the Nineteenth Century* (Princeton, NJ: Princeton University Press, 2014), 473.

21. Michael Geyer and Charles Bright, "Global Violence and Nationalizing Wars in Eurasia and America: The Geopolitics of War in the Mid-Nineteenth Century," *Comparative Studies in Society and History* 38, no. 4 (1996): 619–57.

22. This is the assumption that, for instance, guides the periodization of the *Cambridge History of War*. See Hans van de Ven, "Introduction to Volume IV," in Chickering, *Cambridge History*, 1–5, 1.

23. Van de Ven, "A Hinge," 18.

24. Dennis Showalter, *The Wars of German Unification* (London: Hodder Arnold, 2004), 246–47.

25. John A. Lynn, "The Evolution of Army Style in the Modern West, 800–2000," *The International History Review* 18, no. 3 (1996): 505–45, 510 and 521–23.

26. Michael Roberts, "The Military Revolution, 1560–1660," in *Essays in Swedish History* (London: Weidenfeld & Nicolson, 1967), 195–225. For a discussion of the concept and its changing understanding, see the chapter by Dudink and Hagemann, "War and Gender" in this handbook.

27. On military revolutions and revolutions in military affairs, see Williamson Murray and MacGregor Knox, "Thinking about Revolutions in Warfare," in *The Dynamics of Military Revolution, 1300–2050*, ed. Knox and Murray (Cambridge: Cambridge University Press, 2001), 6–14. On Prussia, see Dennis E. Showalter, "The Prusso-German RMA [revolution in military affairs], 1840–1871," in Knox and Murray, *The Dynamics*, 92–113; and Geoffrey Wawro, *Warfare and Society in Europe, 1792–1914* (London: Routledge, 2000). Wawro uses the term interchangeably with "military revolution." In another publication, he alternates "military revolution" and "military–technological revolution," which is a subcategory of "revolution in military affairs"; Wawro, "War, Technology, and Industrial Change, 1850–1914," in Chickering, *Cambridge History*, 45–68.

28. Murry and Knox, "Thinking," 13.

29. Ibid., 6–7.

30. David Parrott, "Had a Distinct Template for a 'Western Way of War' Been Established before 1800?," in *The Changing Character of War*, ed. Hew Strachan and Sibylle Scheipers (Oxford: Oxford University Press, 2011), 48–63.

31. Van de Ven, "A Hinge," 18–19.

32. Bruce Vandervort, "War and Imperial Expansion," in Chickering, *Cambridge History*, 69–93, 74.

33. A. G. Hopkins, "Overseas Expansion, Imperialism, and Empire, 1815–1914," in Blanning, *Nineteenth Century*, 210–40.

34. Wawro, *Warfare and Society*, 135–36.

35. Vandervort, "War and Imperial," 77.

36. Ibid., 81, 77–78; and Vandervort, "Colonial Wars, 1815–1960," in Black, *European Warfare*, 147–71.

37. Vandervort, "War and Imperial Expansion," 85–90; and Vandervort, "Colonial Wars," 158–60. On the usage of colonial soldiers in the Age of World Wars, see the chapter by Richard Smith on "Colonial Soldiers, Race, and Military Masculinities during and beyond World Wars I and II" in this handbook.

38. On scientific racism and empire, see Frank Dikötter, "The Racialization of the Globe: Historical Perspectives," in *Racism in the Modern World: Historical Perspectives on Cultural Transfer and Adaptation*, ed. Manfred Berg and Simon Wendt (New York: Berghahn Books, 2011), 20–40.

39. See also the chapters by Angela Woollacott on "Imperial Conquest, Violent Encounters, and Changing Gender Relations in Colonial Warfare, 1830s–1910s," and Smith, "Colonial Soldiers" in this handbook.

40. Vandervort, "War and Imperial," 79–80; and Vandervort, "War in the Non-European World," in *Palgrave Advances in Modern Military History*, ed. Matthew Hughes and William J. Philpott (Basingstoke: Palgrave Macmillan, 2006), 195–213. See also the chapters by Peter H. Wilson on "Wars, States, and Gender in Early Modern European Warfare, 1600s–1780s," and Thomas Cardoza and Karen Hagemann on "History and Memory of Army Women and Female Soldiers, 1770s–1870s" in this handbook.

41. Vandervort, "War and Imperial," 91–92.

42. Werner Conze et al., "Militarismus," in *Geschichtliche Grundbegriffe: Historisches Lexicon zur politisch-sozialen Sprache in Deutschland*, ed. Otto Brunner et al. (Stuttgart: Klett-Cotta, 1978), 4:1–47.

43. Roger Chickering, "War, Society and Culture, 1850–1914: The Rise of Militarism," in Chickering, *Cambridge History*, 119–41.

44. Ibid., 125.

45. Ibid., 131–32. On the concept of bellicism, see Jörn Leonhard, *Bellizismus und Nation: Kriegsdeutung und Nationsbestimmung in Europa und den Vereinigten Staaten 1750–1914* (Munich: R. Oldenbourg Verlag, 2008), esp. 3–44.

46. Ibid., 141. See also the chapters by Dudink, "Citizenship, Mass Mobilization," and Robert A. Nye on "War Mobilization, Gender, and Military Culture in Nineteenth-Century Western Societies" in this handbook.

47. Chickering, "War, Society," 134–35.

48. Dirk Bönker, *Militarism in a Global Age: Naval Ambitions in Germany and the United States before World War I* (Ithaca, NY: Cornell University Press, 2012), 7.

49. Eric Hobsbawm and Terence Ranger, eds., *The Invention of Tradition* (Cambridge: Cambridge University Press, 1983); and Benedict Anderson, *Imagined Communities: Reflections on the Origins and Spread of Nationalism* (London: Verso, 1991). For a recent overview of the history of nationalism, see Lloyd S. Kramer, *Nationalism in Europe and America: Politics, Cultures, and Identities since 1775* (Chapel Hill: University of North Carolina Press, 2011).

50. On territorialization, see Charles S. Maier, "Consigning the Twentieth Century to History: Alternative Narratives for the Modern Era," *American Historical Review* 105, no. 3 (2000): 807–31.

51. See the chapters by Alan Forrest, "Society, Mass Warfare, and Gender in Europe during and after the Revolutionary and Napoleonic Wars," and Dudink, "Citizenship, Mass Mobilization" in this handbook.

52. Andreas Wimmer, *Waves of War: Nationalism, State Formation, and Ethnic Exclusion in the Modern World* (New York: Cambridge University Press, 2013), 4.

53. Micheal Clodfelter, *Warfare and Armed Conflicts: A Statistical Reference to Casualty and Other Figures, 1500–2000*, 2nd ed. (Jefferson, NC: MacFarland, 2001), 203.

54. See, for example, Stephanie Markovits, *The Crimean War in the British Imagination* (Cambridge: Cambridge University Press, 2009); and Orlando Figes, *The Crimean War: A History* (New York: Metropolitan Books, 2011), 303–24.

55. Clodfelter, *Warfare and Armed*, 207–11. See also Mark Hewitson, *The People's Wars: Histories of Violence in the German Lands, 1820–1888* (New York: Oxford University Press, 2017), 412–13.

56. On the concept of people's war, see Stig Förster, "Facing 'People's War': Moltke the Elder and Germany's Military Options after 1871," *Journal of Strategic Studies* 10, no. 2 (1987): 209–30; and Förster and Jörg Nagler, eds., *On the Road to Total War: The American Civil*

War and the German Wars of Unification, 1861–1871 (New York: Cambridge University Press, 1997), 4–11.

57. Kramer, *Nationalism*, 115. See also Michael Jeismann, *Das Vaterland der Feinde: Studien zum Nationalen Feindbegriff und Selbstverständnis in Deutschland und Frankreich 1792–1918* (Stuttgart: Klett-Cotta, 1992).

58. See Förster and Nagler, *On the Road*, 11–15. For a discussion of the concept, see Hagemann and Rose, "War and Gender."

59. See Dieter Dowe et al., eds., *Europe in 1848: Revolution and Reform* (New York: Berghahn Books, 2001); and Jonathan Sperber, *The European Revolutions, 1848–1851*, 2nd ed. (New York: Cambridge University Press, 2005).

60. See Dierk Walter, *Preussische Heeresreformen, 1807–1870: Militärische Innovation und der Mythos der "Roonschen Reform"* (Paderborn: Schöningh, 2003); also Dudink, "Citizenship, Mass Mobilization" in this handbook.

61. See Dudink and Hagemann, "Masculinity in Politics and War," 15–18; and Andrew Zimmerman, "From the Rhine to the Mississippi: Property, Democracy, and Socialism in the American Civil War," *Journal of the Civil War Era* 5, no. 1 (2015): 3–37.

62. Lucy Riall, *Garibaldi: Invention of a Hero* (New Haven, CT: Yale University Press, 2007).

63. Ibid., 39–41.

64. See the overview by Dieter Langewiesche, *Der gewaltsame Lehrer: Europas Kriege in der Moderne* (Munich: Beck, 2019), 261–336.

65. Clodfelter, *Warfare and Armed*, 205–7.

66. For the Italian Wars of Independence see Lucy Riall, *The Italian Risorgimento: State, Society, and National Unification* (London: Routledge, 1994).

67. See Andrew M. Fleche, *The Revolution of 1861: The American Civil War in the Age of Nationalist Conflict* (Chapel Hill: University of North Carolina Press, 2012); and Jörg Nagler et al., eds., *The Transnational Significance of the American Civil War* (New York: Palgrave Macmillan, 2016).

68. Abraham Lincoln, "The Gettysburg Address," in *The Collected Works of Abraham Lincoln*, ed. Roy P. Basler (New Brunswick, NJ: Rutgers University Press, 1952), 7:23.

69. Clodfelter, *Warfare and Armed*, 304–6. For good syntheses of the American Civil War, see James M. McPherson, *Battle Cry of Freedom: The Civil War Era* (New York: Oxford University Press, 2003); and John Keegan, *The American Civil War* (London: Vintage, 2009). On scorched-earth campaigns in the American Civil War, such as General William T. Sherman's "March to the Sea," see James M. McPherson, "From Limited War to Total War in America," in Förster and Nageler, *On the Road*, 295–310.

70. Gabriele Esposito, *Armies of the War of the Triple Alliance, 1864–70: Paraguay, Brazil, Uruguay and Argentina* (Oxford: Osprey, 2015), 3.

71. Bruce Porter, *War and the Rise of the State: The Military Foundations of Modern Politics* (New York: Free Press, 1994), 151.

72. Mark E. Neely Jr., *The Civil War and the Limits of Destruction* (Cambridge, MA: Harvard University Press, 2007).

73. See, for example, Adam Hochschild, *King Leopold's Ghost: A Story of Greed, Terror, and Heroism in Colonial Africa* (New York: Houghton Mifflin, 1998), 3.

74. Osterhammel, *The Transformation*, 488.

75. See, for example, Gregory Fremont-Barnes, *The Boer War, 1899–1902* (Oxford: Osprey, 2003); John Gooch, ed., *The Boer War: Direction, Experience, and Image* (London:

Routledge, 2013); and Helen Bradford, "Regendering Afrikanerdom: The 1899–1902 Anglo-Boer War," in Blom et al., *Gendered Nations*, 207–29.

76. Dominik J. Schaller, "From Conquest to Genocide: Colonial Rule in German Southwest Africa and German East Africa," in *Empire, Colony, Genocide: Conquest, Occupation, and Subaltern Resistance in World History*, ed. A. Dirk Moses (New York: Berghahn Books, 2008), 296–324; and Joachim Zeller and Jürgen Zimmerer, eds., *Genocide in German South-West Africa: The Colonial War (1904–1908) in Namibia and Its Aftermath* (Monmouth: Merlin Press, 2008).

77. See also Smith, "Colonial Soldiers" in this handbook.

78. Jill C. Bender, *The 1857 Indian Uprising and the British Empire* (New York: Cambridge University Press, 2016), 1–26.

79. See David J. Silbey, *The Boxer Rebellion and the Great Game in China* (New York: Hill & Wang, 2012); and Diana Preston, *A Brief History of the Boxer Rebellion: China's War on Foreigners, 1900* (London: Robinson, 2002).

80. On the roots of the *Manifest Destiny* phrase, see Reginald Horsman, *Race and Manifest Destiny: The Origins of American Racial Anglo-Saxonism* (Cambridge, MA: Harvard University Press, 1981), 219–20.

81. See Theda Perdue and Michael D. Green, *The Cherokee Nation and the Trail of Tears* (New York: Viking, 2007); also Mary Stockwell, *The Other Trail of Tears: The Removal of the Ohio Indians* (Yardley, PA: Westholme, 2014).

82. See Peter Cozzens, *The Earth Is Weeping: The Epic Story of the Indian Wars for the American West* (New York: Alfred A. Knopf, 2016); and Jason Hook and Martin Pegler, *To Live and Die in the West: The American Indian Wars, 1860–90* (New York: Routledge, 2013).

83. See the chapter by Marilyn Lake on "The 'White Man,' Race, and Imperial War during the Long Nineteenth Century" in this handbook.

84. A. Dirk Moses, "An Antipodean Genocide? The Origins of the Genocidal Moment in the Colonization of Australia," *Journal of Genocide Research* 2, no. 1 (2000): 89–106; and Henry Reynolds, *An Indelible Stain? The Question of Genocide in Australia's History* (Ringwood: Viking, 2001).

85. See the chapter by Amy S. Greenberg, "Gender and the Wars of Nation-Building and Nation-Keeping in the Americas, 1830s–1870s" in this handbook as well as her monograph, *A Wicked War: Polk, Clay, Lincoln, and the Invasion of Mexico* (New York: Alfred A. Knopf, 2012).

86. Spencer C. Tucker, ed., *The Encyclopedia of the Mexican–American War: A Political, Social, and Military History* (Santa Barbara, CA: ABC-CLIO, 2013), 126.

87. Paul A. Kramer, "Race-Making and Colonial Violence in the U.S. Empire: The Philippine–American War as Race War," *Diplomatic History* 30, no. 2 (2006): 169–219, 201–2; and Jonathan Hyslop, "The Invention of the Concentration Camp: Cuba, Southern Africa, and the Philippines, 1896–1907," *South African Historical Journal* 63, no. 2 (2011): 251–76.

88. See, in particular, Isabel V. Hull, *Absolute Destruction: Military Culture and the Practices of War in Imperial Germany* (Ithaca, NY: Cornell University Press, 2005); and Jürgen Zimmerer, "Colonialism and the Holocaust: Towards an Archeology of Genocide," in *Genocide and Settler Society: Frontier Violence and Stolen Indigenous Children in Australian History*, ed. A. Dirk Moses (New York: Berghahn Books, 2004), 49–76.

89. See Nye, "War Mobilization, Gender" and the chapter by Jean H. Quataert on "Changing Modes of Warfare and the Gendering of Military Medical Care, 1850s–1920s" in this handbook.

90. See Michael N. Barnett, *Empire of Humanity: A History of Humanitarianism* (Ithaca, NY: Cornell University Press, 2011), esp. 19–96.

91. See David P. Forsythe, *The Humanitarians: The International Committee of the Red Cross* (Cambridge: Cambridge University Press, 2005), esp. 13–50; and Quataert, "Changing Modes" in this handbook.

92. See Jean H. Quataert, *Staging Philanthropy: Patriotic Women and the National Imagination in Dynastic Germany, 1813–1916* (Ann Arbor: University of Michigan Press, 2001), 54–89.

93. David H. Burton, *Clara Barton: In the Service of Humanity* (Westport, CT: Greenwood Press, 1995); and Julia Irwin, *Making the World Safe: The American Red Cross and a Nation's Humanitarian Awakening* (New York: Oxford University Press, 2013).

94. Sandi E. Cooper, *Patriotic Pacifism: Waging War on War in Europe, 1815–1914* (New York: Oxford University Press, 1991), 5.

95. See the chapter by Glenda Sluga on "Gender, Peace and the New Politics of Humanitarianism in the First Half of the Twentieth Century" in this handbook.

96. David Cortright, *Peace: A History of Movements and Ideas* (Cambridge: Cambridge University Press, 2008), esp. 23–44.

97. See Enrico Dal Lago, *William Lloyd Garrison and Giuseppe Mazzini: Abolition, Democracy, and Radical Reform* (Baton Rouge: Louisiana State University Press, 2013).

98. See Kathryn Kish Sklar and James Brewer Stewart, eds., *Women's Rights and Transatlantic Antislavery in the Era of Emancipation* (New Haven, CT: Yale University Press, 2007); Heloise Brown, *"The Truest Form of Patriotism": Pacifist Feminism in Britain, 1870–1902* (New York: Palgrave, 2003); and Bonnie S. Anderson, *Joyous Greetings: The First International Women's Movement* (New York: Oxford University Press, 2000).

99. See Arthur Eyffinger, *"The Stars of Eternal Truth and Right": Bertha von Suttner's Campaigning for Peace, Social Justice and Womanhood* (Oisterwijk: Wolf Legal, 2013).

100. See Nye, "War Mobilization, Gender" in this handbook.

101. See Shabtai Rosenne, *The Hague Peace Conferences of 1899 and 1907 and International Arbitration: Reports and Documents* (The Hague: Kluwer Law International, 2001); Peter Maguire, *Law and War: International Law and American History* (New York: Columbia University Press, 2010), 39–42.

102. See Maartje Abbenhuis et al., eds., *War, Peace and International Order? The Legacies of the Hague Conferences of 1899 and 1907* (London: Routledge, 2017).

103. See Karen Hagemann et al., eds., *Gender, War and Politics: Transatlantic Perspectives, 1775–1830* (Basingstoke: Palgrave Macmillan, 2010); and Katherine Aaslestad, Karen Hagemann, and Judith A. Miller, eds., "Gender, War and the Nation in the Period of the Revolutionary and Napoleonic Wars—European Perspectives," special issue, *European History Quarterly* 37, no. 4 (2007).

104. See the chapters by Catherine Davies, "War, Gender, and Society in Late Colonial and Revolutionary Spanish America," Serena Zabin, "War, Culture, and Gender in Colonial and Revolutionary North America," Forrest, "Society, Mass Warfare" Cardoza and Hagemann, "History and Memory" and Dudink, "Citizenship, Mass Mobilization" in this handbook.

105. For more, see the discussion in "Introduction: Gender and the History of War—The Development of the Research" by Karen Hagemann in this handbook.

106. See Dudink and Hagemann, "Masculinity in Politics"; and Dudink, "Citizenship, Mass Mobilization" in this handbook.

107. For more, see Karen Hagemann et al., "Introduction: Gender, War and Politics: Transatlantic Perspectives on the Wars of Revolution and Liberation, 1775–1830," in Hagemann et al., *Gender, War and Politics*, 1–40.

108. Ibid., 3–4.

109. Katherine B. Aaslestad and Judith A. Miller, "Gender, War and Politics: The Wars of Revolution and Liberation—Transatlantic Comparisons, 1775–1820," *Bulletin of the German Historical Institute* 41 (2007): 128–36, 136.

110. Hagemann et al., "Introduction: Gender, War," 3–4.

111. See Darline Gay Levy and Harriet B. Applewhite, "Women and Militant Citizenship in Revolutionary Paris," in *Rebel Daughters: Women and the French Revolution*, ed. Sara E. Melzer and Leslie W. Rabine (Oxford: Oxford University Press, 1991), 70–101.

112. See Cardoza and Hagemann, "History and Memory" in this handbook.

113. See Gabriella Hauch, "Women's Space in the Men's Revolution of 1848," in Dowe et al., *Europe in 1848*, 639–82; Gay L. Gullickson, *Unruly Women of Paris: Images of the Commune* (Ithaca, NY: Cornell University Press, 1996); and Carolyn Jeanne Eichner, *Surmounting the Barricades: Women in the Paris Commune* (Bloomington: Indiana University Press, 2004).

114. Hauch, "Women's Space."

115. See Martin Pugh, *The March of the Women: A Revisionist Analysis of the Campaign for Women's Suffrage, 1866–1914* (Oxford: New York: Oxford University Press, 2000); Blanca Rodriguez-Ruiz and Ruth Rubio-Marin, eds., *The Struggle for Female Suffrage in Europe: Voting to Become Citizens* (Leiden: Brill, 2012); and Nancy Isenberg, *Sex and Citizenship in Antebellum America* (Chapel Hill: University of North Carolina Press, 1998).

116. See Angela K. Smith, *Suffrage Discourse in Britain during the First World War* (London: Routledge, 2016).

117. See Hagemann et al., "Introduction: Gender, War," 1–40; and Blom et al., eds., *Gendered Nations*.

118. See Nye, "War Mobilization, Gender" in this handbook.

119. On the history of the term *home front*, see Hagemann and Rose, "War and Gender" in this handbook.

120. For the literature, see Dudink, "Citizenship, Mass Mobilization" in this handbook.

121. Greenberg, "Gender and the Wars of Nation-Building" in this handbook; and Greenberg, *A Wicked War*; Catherine Clinton and Nina Silber, eds., *Battle Scars: Gender and Sexuality in the American Civil War* (Oxford: Oxford University Press, 2006); Clinton and Silber, *Divided Houses: Gender and the Civil War* (Oxford: Oxford University Press, 1992); and LeeAnn Whites, *Gender Matters: Civil War, Reconstruction, and the Making of the New South* (New York: Palgrave Macmillan, 2005).

122. See Greenberg, "Gender and the Wars of Nation-Building" in this handbook; and LeeAnn Whites and Alecia P. Long, eds., *Occupied Women: Gender, Military Occupation, and the American Civil War* (Baton Rouge: Louisiana State University Press, 2009).

123. See more in Cardoza and Hagemann, "History and Memory," and Quataert, "Changing Modes" in this handbook.

124. On Nightingale, see Mark Bostridge, *Florence Nightingale: The Woman and Her Legend* (London: Viking, 2008).

125. See Cardoza and Hagemann, "History and Memory" in this handbook.

126. See Woollacott, "Imperial Conquest" in this handbook; Adele Perry, *On the Edge of Empire: Gender, Race, and the Making of British Columbia, 1849–1871* (Toronto: University

of Toronto Press, 2001); Angela Woolacott, *Gender and Empire* (Basingstoke: Palgrave Macmillan, 2006); Philippa Levine, ed., *Gender and Empire* (Oxford and New York: Oxford University Press, 2007), esp. the chapter by Catherine Hall, "Of Gender and Empire: Reflections on the Nineteenth Century"; and Angela Woollacott, *Settler Society in the Australian Colonies: Self-Government and Imperial Culture* (Oxford: Oxford University Press, 2015).

127. See Lake, "The 'White Man'" in this handbook; Lake and Henry Reynolds, *Drawing the Global Colour Line: White Men's Countries and the International Challenge of Racial Equality* (Cambridge: Cambridge University Press, 2008); and Heather Streets, *Martial Races: The Military, Race and Masculinity in British Imperial Culture, 1857–1914* (Manchester: Manchester University Press, 2004).

128. Rudyard Kipling, "The White Man's Burden: The United States & The Philippine Islands, 1899," in *Rudyard Kipling's Verse: Definitive Edition* (New York: Doubleday, 1929).

129. On the war, see David J. Silbey, *A War of Frontier and Empire: The Philippine-American War, 1899–1902* (New York: Hill & Wang, 2007); and Kristin Hoganson, *Fighting for American Manhood: How Gender Politics Provoked the Spanish–American and Philippine–American Wars* (New Haven, CT: Yale University Press, 2000).

130. See Susan Amatangelo, ed., *Italian Women at War: Sisters in Arms from the Unification to the Twentieth Century* (Madison: Rowman & Littlefield, 2016), 13–72; Quataert, *Staging Philanthropy*, 54–216; and, with very little inclusion of the gender dimension, Alexander Seyferth, *Die Heimatfront 1870/71: Wirtschaft und Gesellschaft im deutsch-französischen Krieg* (Paderborn: Schöningh, 2007).

131. Helen Rappaport, *No Place for Ladies: The Untold Story of Women in the Crimean War* (London: Aurum, 2007).

SELECT BIBLIOGRAPHY

Bayly, Christopher Alan. *The Birth of the Modern World, 1780–1914*. Oxford: Blackwell, 2004.

Blom, Ida, Hagemann, Karen, and Catherine Hall, eds. *Gendered Nations: Nationalisms and Gender Order in the Long Nineteenth Century*. Oxford: Berg, 2000.

Chickering, Roger, Dennis Showalter, and Hans van de Ven, eds. *The Cambridge History of War*. Vol. 4, *War and the Modern World*. Cambridge: Cambridge University Press, 2012.

Clinton, Catherine, and Nina Silber, eds. *Divided Houses: Gender and the Civil War*. Oxford: Oxford University Press, 1992.

Cooper, Sandi E. *Patriotic Pacifism: Waging War on War in Europe, 1815–1914*. New York: Oxford University Press, 1991.

Dowe, Dieter, Heinz-Gerhard Haupt, Dieter Langewiesche, and Jonathan Sperber, eds. *Europe in 1848: Revolution and Reform*. New York: Berghahn Books, 2001.

Dudink, Stefan, Karen Hagemann, and John Tosh, eds. *Masculinities in Politics and War: Gendering Modern History*. Manchester: Manchester University Press, 2004.

Eichner, Carolyn Jeanne. *Surmounting the Barricades: Women in the Paris Commune*. Bloomington: Indiana University Press, 2004.

Greenberg, Amy S. *Manifest Manhood and the Antebellum American Empire*. Cambridge: Cambridge University Press, 2005.

Greenberg, Amy S. *A Wicked War: Polk, Clay, Lincoln, and the Invasion of Mexico*. New York: Alfred A. Knopf, 2012.

Hoganson, Kristin. *Fighting for American Manhood: How Gender Politics Provoked the Spanish-American and Philippine-American Wars*. New Haven, CT: Yale University Press, 2000.

Kramer, Lloyd S. *Nationalism in Europe and America: Politics, Cultures, and Identities since 1775*. Chapel Hill: University of North Carolina Press, 2011.

Langewiesche, Dieter. *Der gewaltsame Lehrer: Europas Kriege in der Moderne*. Munich: Beck, 2019.

Levine, Philippa, ed. *Gender and Empire*. Oxford and New York: Oxford University Press 2007.

Osterhammel, Jürgen. *The Transformation of the World: A Global History of the Nineteenth Century*. Princeton, NJ: Princeton University Press, 2014.

Quataert, Jean H. *Staging Philanthropy: Patriotic Women in the National Imagination in Dynastic Germany, 1813-1916*. Ann Arbor: University of Michigan Press, 2001.

Riall, Lucy. *Garibaldi: Invention of a Hero*. New Haven, CT: Yale University Press, 2008.

Streets, Heather. *Martial Races: The Military, Race and Masculinity in British Imperial Culture, 1857-1914*. Manchester: Manchester University Press, 2004.

Wawro, Geoffrey. *Warfare and Society in Europe, 1792-1914*. London: Routledge, 2000.

Whites, LeeAnn. *Gender Matters: Civil War, Reconstruction, and the Making of the New South*. New York: Palgrave Macmillan, 2005.

Woollacott, Angela. *Gender and Empire*. Basingstoke: Palgrave Macmillan, 2006.

Woollacott, Angela. *Settler Society in the Australian Colonies: Self-Government and Imperial Culture*. Oxford: Oxford University Press, 2015.

CHAPTER 10

....

WAR MOBILIZATION, GENDER, AND MILITARY CULTURE IN NINETEENTH-CENTURY WESTERN SOCIETIES

....

ROBERT A. NYE

THE British jurist Edward Creasy began his 1851 classic *The Fifteen Decisive Battles of the World from Marathon to Waterloo* by proclaiming, "It is an honorable characteristic of the Spirit of this Age that projects of violence and warfare are regarded among civilized states with steadily increasing aversion." He ended his book with the observation that "we see no captive standards of our European neighbors brought to our shrines." Instead, "we see the banners of every civilized nation waving over the arena of our competition with each other in the arts that minister to our race's support and happiness."[1] Creasy invoked here the key ideas that governed war and peace in the West until at least 1914, if not longer: the integrative power of free trade, the distinguishing concept of race, the ideal of civilization, and the principle of honor, which he equates with diminished warfare and violence. Two generations after the "French Wars"—the French Revolutionary and Napoleonic Wars (1792–1815)—that convulsed Europe, contemporaries could imagine the transformation of martial conflict into a peaceful world of free trade and national cultural development.

Gender was an important organizing principle for the mobilization of peoples for war and nation in Western societies, mainly in Europe and the United States, during the nineteenth century. Military and civilian cultures became more intimately conjoined and societies more progressively militarized. Despite the militarization and nationalization of military and political cultures, the balance between peace and bellicosity remained in a state of fragile equilibrium until the summer of 1914, sustaining an optimistic vision of further integration while simultaneously mobilizing the ideas and sentiments that overwhelmed it.

Nineteenth-century nationalism and internationalism were indissolubly linked through the concept of state sovereignty, which the new field of international law acknowledged as its own cornerstone. But internationalism, as Glenda Sluga has shown, "was also imagined through the same language of race and civilizational difference that gave twentieth-century nationalism its unflattering timbre."[2] In this worldview, putative racial differences, aptitude for civilization, concepts of individual and national honor, and prevailing gender ideals could serve as signifiers on behalf of either warfare or peace, as fighting causes or reasons for caution. The internationalists of the era were unable to tame the militarization of Western cultures and prevent the outbreak of war in 1914 because the values and ideals they embraced so closely resembled those of the militarists and nationalists they hoped to restrain.

The role of gender in creating this conundrum was decisive. The differences between men and women were often contrasted as dramatically as those of race and civilization, and they were positioned within civilizational and racial hierarchies by virtue of the same popular evolutionary perspective that explained the supposed capacities and incapacities of Whites and Blacks, civilized and savage.[3] In this discourse, civilizations, as opposed to primitive cultures, featured a more starkly gendered division of social and economic labor, contrasting male and female dress styles and differential spheres of rights and duties. They conferred on women particular moral and spiritual qualities said to be lacking in less civilized races.[4] These distinctions were respected for the most part throughout the nineteenth century, but, paradoxically, the increasing mobilization of civilians in preparation for war narrowed the gender gap in ways both real and symbolic, with the effect of eventually exposing noncombatants to dangers never before imagined.

Women had been a part of the machinery of war since early modern times as camp followers, officer's wives, food provisioners, and prostitutes.[5] Beginning with the Napoleonic Wars (1803–15), women and women's work were incorporated into wartime activities in newly organized forms and in segregated spaces beyond the battlefield.[6] Though they were denied full political and legal citizenship, throughout the nineteenth century women participated in organizations and activities that readied their nation for war. Most men were also politically disenfranchised through much of the century, but their path to universal manhood suffrage was expedited by the spread of schemes of national conscription that made men's moral claim on full citizenship irresistible.[7]

The Napoleonic Wars had awakened powerful feelings of attachment to the military accomplishments of peoples and nations, which were preserved in the form of histories, songs, symbols, and monuments.[8] In the course of the nineteenth century, the bonds between the military, civilians, and the nation were cultivated and intensified and at the same time became more and more gendered. A male-dominated military culture increasingly extended its influence beyond the armed forces.[9] By the end of the nineteenth century, the major nation-states of Europe and North America possessed the legal, social, and bureaucratic structures for waging war on a large scale and had developed an array of cultural and symbolic tools for commanding the allegiance of their citizens that could overcome class, sectarian, and regional resistance to mobilization for war. But after the German Wars of Unification (1864–71) and despite the growth of rival alliances, armaments, and new military technologies, a war between the great powers was by no means inevitable, nor was popular assent to war guaranteed. It would take unforeseen events to upset the equilibrium that had been established within the family of civilized nations.

The key to understanding the disruption of this delicate balance lies in an analysis of the concept of *military culture*, and in recent years historians have provided two useful definitions. The first definition considers military culture as a particular self-contained form of institutional culture featuring threefold relationships: among members, between members and nonmembers, and between members and the state. The emphasis is on difference and on the codes and ethos that structured an exclusive military society.[10] The second definition focuses on the place of military culture in the larger society, "whereby that culture consisted of a web of meanings, reference points, norms and social customs pertaining to everyday life," in other words, on the "impact and meaning of military symbols, ideals and behavior in society as a whole."[11] The nineteenth-century evolution of militarism, itself a new term invented at mid-century, depended on the interplay between these two kinds of military culture.[12]

The gendered ironies of this interplay are striking. As modern conscription flooded the ranks with more civilians, military culture became more segregated and more pointedly masculine. As women sought to mobilize auxiliary support for soldiers, they found themselves confined to roles similar to those they filled at home, though their images were sometimes deployed in ways that stretched these conventions to the limit. However, rather than infusing military culture with civilian ideals, civil society was penetrated by the values and ideals of military culture in a variety of ways. Women's ostensible confinement to private life did not shield them from these military influences; indeed, their contributions to national readiness and their own conceivable path to full citizenship were predicated on their embrace of traditional gender roles. In addition, men and boys gradually adopted some of the values and practices once exclusive to military culture and kept them alive in organizational life and sport.

In the following, three themes stand at the center: the legacy of the Napoleonic Wars for European military culture and its development in the age of national and imperial wars; the interplay between the introduction of universal conscription and the militarization of civil society and popular culture; and their relations to gendered war support and commemoration.

THE LEGACY OF THE NAPOLEONIC WARS

Memories of military glory in the era of the Napoleonic Wars were kept alive during the nineteenth century in official and informal ways. Military heroes such as British field marshal Arthur Wellesley, First Duke of Wellington, Prussian field marshal Gebhard

Leberecht von Blücher, and Russian field marshal Mikhail Kutuzov were celebrated in statues and monuments; after a decent hiatus, Napoleon's ashes were brought back from St. Helena in 1840, paraded through Paris to military marches, and buried in the Invalides.[13] Participation in such spectacles became commonplace on the part of the professional armies of the era, which were dependent on the "allure of display" to attract recruits who were "the better sort of man": taller, healthier, or easily regimented. Garrison towns were particularly familiar with the colorful uniforms, bands, and the erect posture and drill precision of troops on parade.[14] In France, even before Napoleon's official rehabilitation since the 1830s, political and war memorials amalgamated revolutionary with Napoleonic symbols: the eagle, the *cocarde* and phrygian bonnet, the laurel crown, and the *coq gaulois*.[15]

Napoleonic military legends were also transmitted outside official venues. Bonaparte's veterans returned to their villages to a modest celebrity, well traveled and more literate than the locals and eager to tell their tales of heroism and sacrifice.[16] They represented military masculinity and the ideal of national service in otherwise remote regions; their exploits and fraternal bonds were portrayed in memoirs, in millions of popular *images d'épinal* (brightly colored prints), and in stories by French novelists such as Marie-Henri Beyle known as Stendhal, Honoré de Balzac, Victor Hugo, Guy de Maupassant, and Émile Zola.[17] According to Gérard de Puymège, the stereotypical Napoleonic veteran, Nicolas Chauvin, was invented to serve as a military everyman in popular culture, featured in plays, poems, broadsides, and engravings as "the perfect cultural model" of the ideal soldier: patriotic, tractable, and conformist.[18] As in France, other European powers involved in the Napoleonic Wars produced a wave of autobiographies, war memoirs, and novels that remembered the "time of the French."[19] The boom of the historical novel in nineteenth-century literature was partly a reflection of the public interest in this "heroic" period. German authors Ludwig Rellstab, Luise Mühlbach, and Theodor Fontane; the British writers Jane Austen, Charlotte Brontë, and William Makepeace Thackeray; and the Russian novelist Leo Tolstoy were translated and read in other parts of the continent and the British Isles. In addition to poetry, popular biographies and histories carried on the memories of the wars. Historical novels increasingly addressed female readers, so women and the home front played a much more crucial role in historical novels than in war memoirs, which were written and published by men primarily for male readers.[20]

In addition, the soldiers who fought in the Napoleonic Wars participated in a penumbra of honor previously associated with noble status. Bonaparte encouraged this democratic expansion of honor in military culture by creating the Legion of Honor in 1802 to tie meritorious military service to *La Patrie* (the fatherland) and to himself, remarking at the time that French soldiers "have but one sentiment: honor, it is therefore necessary to encourage this sentiment; they need distinction."[21] In the French army, the "sentiment" of bravery under fire was the principal quality that merited this recognition. Similarly, with universal conscription in March 1813, Prussia introduced not only the Iron Cross, the first medal that could be given to *every* honorable soldier for military bravery, but also a whole set of rituals and military ceremonies that recognized the heroic service of professional soldiers, militiamen, and volunteers, and honored the "death for the fatherland" of fallen "heroes." The French Legion of Honor and the Prussian Iron Cross created lasting traditions.[22] In peacetime armies of the first half of the nineteenth century, the practice of awarding medals and honors became increasingly common, as did the incentive offered to every man to earn promotion, acquire a more brilliant uniform, and thus attain a greater measure of honor within the culture of military life.[23] As we shall see, principles of honor also influenced codes of military conduct in nineteenth-century armies respecting the treatment of civilians; soldiers internalized the notion that they fought to defend the honor of women, region, regiment, and fatherland.[24]

MILITARY CULTURE IN THE AGE OF NATIONAL AND IMPERIAL WARS

The Wars of Nation-Building and Nation-Keeping and the imperial wars fought in the second half of the nineteenth century opened a new era in the conduct and meaning of warfare and the militarization of culture. The Crimean War (1853–56) was a "cabinet" war undertaken for annexation and adjustments in the balance of power, but the American Civil War (1861–65) and the later stages of the Italian Wars of Unification (1848–70) and the German Wars of Unification were driven by a nationalist ideology, which profoundly strengthened the bonds between civilians and the state.[25] These wars for nation and empire created, in the words of John Horne, a "new ideological geography of nationhood" and, thus, "a new vocabulary of national integrity."[26]

Nationalist "geographies" were based in part on cultural myths grounded in historical memory. Italian unification coincided with a literary and artistic Risorgimento, which had been imbued with the unified concept of nation, language, and culture for a generation and more.[27] The German victories of 1866–71 spawned a "myth of national rebirth" drawing on a foundational narrative of an ancient nation that had endured centuries of foreign occupation until the victory over Napoleonic France in 1815 provided a temporary redemption.[28] In France, the Republican call to arms by statesman Léon Gambetta during the siege of Paris in 1870 had the effect of rekindling the memory of the revolutionary *levée en masse*, the powerful ideal of the nation in arms that blended region, dialect, and class in one fighting force.[29]

These nationalist wars, fought against national enemies, continued to erode the line between enemy soldiers and civilians that had already been an indicator of the "first total wars," the Napoleonic Wars, with their massive armies and battles of heretofore unknown size.[30] The Prussian military reforms of 1859 adopted strategic plans aimed at the complete destruction of enemy forces and degradation of the civilian will to resist, though these measures were first applied by Union forces against the Confederacy in the last stages of the American Civil War.[31] The aims and practices of warfare were additionally influenced by the great powers' experience of colonial conquests after 1870, nudging the evolution of warfare in the same direction.[32]

The changing practices of warfare were intensively reported in the press. Technological changes in newspaper production, growing national literature markets, and rising literacy rates initiated a new mass press by the middle of the nineteenth century.[33] The Crimean War was the first European war to be widely covered. Morse code and underwater cable shortened communication times and made press coverage of the war feasible and lucrative, inspiring the *Times* of London to send four correspondents to the Crimea. Journalists sent lurid dispatches home about blundering leadership and suffering soldiers, which was aimed at engaging readers in a style that evoked the sentimental novels of the day.[34] These accounts prompted an outpouring of sympathy and a flood of relief funds. Among other consequences, this support enabled Florence Nightingale to train and transport nurses to the front, providing the British public with unprecedented images of brave and steadfast femininity.[35] Similar women's volunteer efforts arose in Germany during its Wars of Unification and on both sides of the American Civil War. The press reported widely on the women who shared in the sacrifice of the soldiers, which encouraged female readers to form closer bonds of civic attachment to their respective nation-states.[36]

It took little time for governments and generals to realize both the advantages and the dangers to military objectives and morale inherent in a mass press. In many countries on the European continent, censorship of the press had a long tradition; but now, even in Britain, with its much more liberal laws, uncensored reporting ended with the Crimean War.[37] However, the majority of newspapers and periodicals did not require official encouragement to sanctify the national cause and demonize its foes in wartime or to contrast their own "civilized" behavior with the "barbarism" of the enemy. Civilian casualties and guerrilla warfare in the American Civil War and the Franco-Prussian War of 1870–71 spurred the press to levels of hatred and racial caricature that circulated in journalistic and literary publications until 1914.[38] Neutral Britain had a benign attitude toward Prussia and the other German states during the Franco-Prussian War, but the siege of Paris and fierce repression of the French irregular military, the *francs-tireurs*, inspired some British artists to caricature Prussian king and German emperor Wilhelm I as a brutal enemy of civilization, trampling a prostrate, female France under the hooves of his horse.[39]

Jacob Vogel has written persuasively of the "folkloric militarism" that drove the love for all things military after the mid-century wars. This cultural militarism had a long tradition, which reached back to the period of the Napoleonic Wars. Already, contemporaries of this era, such as the Prussian military reformer Carl von Clausewitz, had argued for the self-constituting influence of wars on collective identity and of the ennobling and virilizing example of military sacrifice.[40] Sixty years later, states did not need to take a guiding hand in the militarization of civil society too—indeed, they were often suspicious of it—because popular sentiment usually took the lead.[41] Official, government-sponsored propaganda existed, though it was unevenly developed in different states and less common in comparison to the twentieth century, but press barons, writers, and other opinion makers were pleased to accommodate influential politicians who wished their policies to be publicly represented.[42] In general, war propaganda was increasingly deployed as governments mobilized mass armies to fight national wars. Coercion alone would not suffice in the era of universal conscription, and propaganda was needed to bind soldiers and the men and women of civil society to the national cause.[43]

UNIVERSAL CONSCRIPTION AND THE MILITARIZATION OF CIVIL SOCIETY

Of the great powers, only Great Britain and the United States failed to implement some form of conscription after 1870. France had taken the lead in 1798. Prussia introduced universal conscription in 1813 for wartime and in 1814 for peacetime. Yet between 1815 and the 1850s, most European states did not adhere to a system of general, "modern" conscription, preferring other forms of military organization, while Prussia used a system of highly selective conscription. In the 1860s, Prussia shifted to a system of general conscription, which then became the hegemonic model of military organization in the German Empire and later in Europe (despite continuing variations and exceptions). This development occurred at the same time as the professionalization of the military.[44] Professional officers met the challenge of perpetually training raw recruits by isolating them from civilian life in barracks, strictly enforcing internal rules and respect for military hierarchy, and engaging in endless drills and war exercises. None of this was so different from preconscription armies; the bonding mechanisms of drill, the inculcation of military bearing, and teaching of unquestioned obedience had historically produced efficient fighting men.[45] The difference was that the experience of military service now became an integral part of the life cycle of most young men, raising them to manhood and familiarizing them with the joys and miseries of an exclusive masculine sociability.

Military training became a rite of passage in the general sense of separating men from their civilian habits and in the specific sense of sexual initiation. In rural France, village lads escorted the new recruit to the nearest brothel to be able to proclaim him "good for girls" and "fit for service."[46] In peacetime, mass-conscription armies generally drafted young and unmarried men, which made military service one crucial dividing line between youth and mature adulthood for eligible males. The shared experience of military service connected young men of different regional, ethnic, and social backgrounds.[47] They were taught the elementary hygiene, sewing, and washing skills they needed to sustain themselves, incorporating this sense of independence into their fledgling manhood.[48] The British regimental system, which until 1916 was based on locally recruited men instead of conscription, shortened service in 1870 from twenty-one to twelve years. This brought it more into alignment with the goals of continental conscription systems of training men for life in "a military rather than a warlike spirit" and for later marriage and citizenship.[49] The conjunction of training in arms, service to the nation, and demonstration of their fitness to marry encouraged men to also see their coming of age as the defining moment of their full citizenship.

Following their service in the reserves, many men joined veteran's organizations, where they could continue their military idyll. Thousands of local groups had been formed in European countries by the 1880s. In the German Empire alone, "warrior" and veteran societies had three million members in 1913. These groups had begun everywhere as mutual aid societies for veterans who had fallen on hard times in the decades after the Napoleonic Wars, but they soon became important venues for male sociability and for recreations featuring shooting competitions. Veterans invested in dress uniforms and sidearms in order to march on special occasions such as the king or emperor's birthday or a national and imperial jubilee; thus decked out, they were often accorded places of honor in local festivities.[50]

Men who had experienced the "non-risk rite of passage" of peacetime training had notably romanticized views on the masculine virtues of military life, an outlook shared by many noncombatant literary men reflecting on the lessons of the most savage nineteenth-century wars.[51] Thomas Rohrkrämer has remarked that after 1890, German reservists who had seen no combat were incorporated into veterans' organizations, where their sense of being still unproven led them to adopt aggressive and militaristic opinions and behavior.[52] Other historians have observed that veterans who had suffered the horrors of war believed that young men would not grow into manhood without experiencing military conflict. As David W. Blight has written of one American Civil War veteran, his nostalgia for the soldier life made him "a candidate for the cycles of selective memory that would both plague and inspire Civil War veterans."[53]

The other imperishable memories gleaned from wartime experience were negative stereotypes of the hated foe. The earnest atmosphere of national reconciliation in a reunited America, which included apparently friendly battle reunions like those held by Gettysburg veterans in 1913 and 1938, concealed unresolved sentiments of rage.[54] After the Napoleonic and the Franco-Prussian Wars, nationalist propaganda on both sides depicted the French and German "Other" as the "eternal enemy," images that were still being used during World Wars I and II.[55] Individual and collective war memories, the commemoration of the war dead, and images of the enemy all became crucial parts of national and military culture after the wars.

Gendered War Support
and Commemoration

Memorials to honor the dead had the power to keep negative sentiments about the enemy alive, but they also performed integrative functions. Women were indispensable to commemoration as organizers and volunteers and as symbols of national unity.

Contemporary ideas about the gender order regarded men as different in their respective ways (class, occupation, capacity), but women's traditional generative and maternal images encouraged their representation as unifying symbols (Britannia, Germania, Marianne, Lady Liberty) and as redeemers of men fallen in battle. The Niederwald memorial that kept watch on the Rhine, inaugurated in 1883, was part "valkyrie, mother, virgin and lorelei," qualities echoed in French images of Marianne throughout the Third Republic.[56] Michael Dorsch has studied the myriad statues executed in France after the Franco-Prussian War representing fallen or wounded soldiers surmounted by colossal images of strong, masculine women comforting the defeated "while offering a hopeful vision of the vengeance and retribution yet to come."[57]

Postwar commemoration was driven by not only state direction, but also volunteer activities of veteran organizations and other patriotic associations. Patriotic women's associations, supported mainly by middle- and upper-class women, were founded during the German Wars of Unification in most German states and continued their work until World War I. These associations trained nurses, provided medical care for soldiers, organized philanthropic work for war victims, and coordinated war commemorations.[58] Similarly, French women were instrumental in raising money for tombs and staging commemorations to the dead after the Franco-Prussian War. What began as memorial ceremonies to mourn the dead near the 1870 Lorraine battlefield of Mars-la-Tour became an annual all-day event with 20,000 visitors, a museum, and patriotic speeches. Speakers on these occasions did not dwell on the causes or blame for these deaths, but increasingly sought to provide meaning and lessons in sacrifice and patriotism to the living, not least that female war support was essential.[59] Like in Britain and Germany, elsewhere in Europe more middle- and upper-class women trained for the gendered work of organizing and staffing Red Cross and nursing services in the decades before Word War I.[60]

In mid-Victorian Britain, battle surgeons and the medical officers who fought epidemics at home emphasized their heroic sacrifices in treating the sick and wounded and carefully distinguished their masculine work from the maternal and caring work of Florence Nightingale and her nurses. Several surgeons earned Victoria Crosses in the Crimean conflict, but the new martial image of medicine was tempered by the emergence of a rhetoric of medical humanitarianism articulated in the Geneva Convention of 1864, which protected medical personnel and wounded soldiers on the battlefield. The result was a synthesis of the heroic and the caring aspects of medicine that united doctors and nurses in a common national cause.[61] The national mission of battlefield medicine was further underlined in every European nation in 1906, when a new Geneva Convention ended the neutrality of Red Cross medical services and put them under the command of each nation's military.[62]

This is one example of new forms of merged identities that developed in the context of gendered war commemoration. Other historians have pointed to the multiple layers of overlapping "national, regional and class allegiances," challenging the notion that patriotic feeling is a unitary concept or emotion.[63] More examples can be found in newly united Germany, where festivals and commemorative practices in the different states continued to mourn or celebrate local martyrs and heroes, but in a way that nested the local *Heimat* within the greater community of the German nation, harmonizing social action and symbolic representation.[64] When local and national identities were in conflict in war commemoration, unifying symbols or celebrations emerged to transcend them. The birthday of Emperor Wilhelm I and *Sedantag*, commemorating victory in the Battle of Sedan (September 1870), played this role in the German Empire; in the Habsburg Empire the birthdays and jubilees of Emperor Franz Joseph I, honoring him as "first soldier of the monarchy," served a similar function.[65]

However, virtually everywhere after mid-century, it was the army and military images that served as the symbols of national unity and "schools for the nation": in recently united nations with distinct class and regional divisions, multinational empires like Austria-Hungary, or old nations like France, where religious and political differences ran deep. In places where political and linguistic identities were particularly complicated, gender symbolism could have an outsized influence in commanding loyalties. In Alsace-Lorraine, French, German, Alsatian, and confessional identities neutralized one another, which allowed popular representations of women in regional costumes to become the symbols of the ravished "lost" provinces for Francophile Alsatians and French *revanchistes* in the *métropole*.[66]

MILITARIZING POPULAR CULTURE

The soldier's image improved markedly in the second half of the nineteenth century with its increasing number of conscription armies, partly on account of their briefer service and reintegration into civilian life, but also because popular and high culture alike found incentives to celebrate them. Governments, painting academies, and musical establishments promoted new "national" art forms, commissioned patriotic opera and dance, and insisted on performing the music of native composers on important occasions, but the vast growth of military music and themes was overwhelmingly a response to popular demand.[67]

The opportunities for public military display increased dramatically after mid-century. A proliferation of royal birthdays, jubilees, centennials, empire days, and public military exercises provided occasions for parades, brass bands, and full military dress in garrison towns and capitols. The "band revolution" of the early nineteenth century, based in large part on cheaper, simplified brass instruments, permitted even small towns to field marching bands and invest in colorful uniforms modeled on military dress. Civilian and military band competitions in large public venues were common throughout Europe and North America.[68] The variety and ostentation of military uniforms reached a high point in the second half of the nineteenth century. Military painters like Édouard Detaille and Jean-Louis Ernest Meissonier in France, Elizabeth Butler in Britain, and Anton von Werner in Germany recaptured uniforms of the past and present in their popular and much-reproduced work. Everything military became quite popular in the public, beyond middle- and upper-class circles. Many were familiar with the distinctive costumes of regimental units and enjoyed military parades or music.[69]

There is consensus among historians that military spectacles and the publicity of imperial conquest raised the status of soldiers and military values and helped erase public memories of the drunken, disorderly "lifer" of yesteryear.[70] Soldiers appeared regularly on stage in popular music hall revues and dramas to represent patriotic or imperial themes.[71] In Germany, over eight hundred plays about the army were performed in theaters between 1870 and 1914, all admiring thanks to censorship.[72] The 1893 song "Private Tommy Atkins," which began with the line "Tommy dear, we'll back you 'gainst the world," was the biggest London music hall hit before 1914.[73]

The European mass press lionized the "heroes" of empire in story and graphic displays.[74] Colonial explorations and military campaigns were closely followed, and popular writers invented a new genre of adventure stories for men and boys that celebrated suffering, dedication, and the military virtues. When women appeared in this type of literature, they were vulnerable and often sexually threatened.[75] The volunteers who organized national celebrations and philanthropies, journalists, writers, artists, musicians, and the custodians of popular entertainment knew a popular cause when they saw one.

National Bodies, Civilization, and Civic Heroism

The cultural discourse that articulated and synthesized the various elements of civic militarism most successfully at the end of the nineteenth century was a language of national health that equated the fitness of the nation with the fitness of its citizens, and, especially, with the fitness of the soldiers who must defend it. Manpower was still the basis of military power, and by this measure the French had fallen behind other European states. The gender and sexual elements in this rhetoric applied to every nation. The French worried about birth rates, the British about the "deterioration" of the urban masses, the Italians about degeneration, the Germans about weakening heterosexual desire, and the Americans about commercialism and the closing of the frontier to manly exploration.[76]

The shared concerns in this brew were women's reproductive fitness and the fighting qualities of men, matters sometimes subsumed into a language of race and gender.[77] A man's sacrifice was to serve bravely; a woman's sacrifice could be to raise relief funds, nurse in a future conflict, or pay the "blood tax" of pregnancy and childbirth. European feminists commonly based the appeal for full citizenship rights precisely on these grounds.[78] The cultivation of sport and physical fitness in the schools in the 1870s was a public initiative, but the private sporting movement drew inspiration from many of the biomedical concerns that drove educators.[79] The "games revolution" may have originated as a form of rational recreation to distract wayward youth, but it soon developed a military agenda that was even more directly expressed through the spread of boy brigades and scouting in Europe and North America.

The ultimate influence of military values on civilian culture took the form of the new category of civic heroism. Civic heroes could contribute to the fatherland philanthropically, as volunteers to national causes, or in the more direct sense of risking life and limb to rescue or protect the vulnerable. Public and private institutions bestowed medals and honors to reward bravery or generosity in elaborate ceremonies that resembled their military counterparts.[80] Women were eligible for these awards as well and were praised in the same language of sacrifice to the nation as male recipients. In France, it became common in such moments to evoke the supreme example of Joan of Arc or the suffering but resolute women of the lost provinces.

Despite worries about fitness and the debilitating effects of "civilization,"[81] Western nations at the end of the nineteenth century regarded themselves as civilizing and Christianizing forces in a barbaric world. A central component of this self-image was the conviction that European warfare was, as Carl von Clausewitz had written in his classic study On War, first published in German in 1832, "far less cruel and destructive than wars between savages" because the Western powers followed rules of engagement in which war was a "duel on a larger scale," aimed at ending an opponent's resistance with superior fighting force.[82] In practice, the chief constraint on uninhibited violence was the honor code that gentlemen, soldiers, and states observed to settle their differences. The duel of honor, which still flourished everywhere in continental Europe, was highly regulated by mid-century. Its protocols required antiquated weaponry, closely administered combat, and preliminary negotiations between seconds.[83] Decades after the first efforts to regulate military conflicts in Paris (1856), St. Petersburg (1868), and Brussels (1874), twenty-six nations gathered at The Hague in 1899 at the initiative of Tsar Nicholas II of Russia, where they followed the model of dueling protocols in their discussions of armaments limitations, the rules of war, and international arbitration.[84]

The results of the peace conferences at The Hague (1899, 1907) were far from discouraging in the eyes of international peace organizers, a large proportion of whom were women.[85] "Asphyxiating" or poisonous gases were banned, as were "dum-dum" (exploding) bullets and the random release of bombs from airborne balloons. Protections against undefended towns and harbors were extended to noncombatants under the codifications of the laws and customs of war, and the dueling conventions that prescribed fairness in combat influenced the rules drafted to protect disabled, disarmed, or surrendering soldiers. Finally, the Permanent Court of Arbitration was established in 1899 that was specifically based on the duel.[86] In the event of a dispute, rival powers were encouraged to choose two arbitrators from a permanent list at the court who would then negotiate in the presence of an "umpire" (surarbitre) with the ability to break tie votes. Contemporary opinion leaders were optimistic that this alliance of peace-loving women and honorable men might be the savior of Western civilization.

A close examination of the transcripts of the Hague conferences reveals the contradictory features of this optimism. The twenty-six sovereign states represented in 1899 drew a decisive line between themselves and the "barbarous" or "savage" peoples outside the orbit of Western nations. A French delegate, Léon Bourgeois, emphasized that the "purpose of civilization" is to rise "above the struggle for existence among men." In a parallel register, the British delegate John Ardagh argued against the ban of dum-dum bullets (being used by British imperial soldiers) by saying, "In civilized war a soldier penetrated by a small projectile is wounded, [and] withdraws to the ambulance.... It is very different with a savage. Even though pierced two or three times, he does not cease to march forward."[87] As we have seen, codes of masculine honor guided the work of the conference, leading the Dutch delegate to pronounce that in matters of adherence to weapons limitations, "there is no better watchman than the nation's honor. Let us believe it!" But participants also acknowledged an "honor" problem and agreed that arbitration proceedings must exclude disputes arising from "vital interests or national honor."[88]

Two conundrums appear in the language of the Hague proceedings: the civilized/uncivilized binary and the "honor problem." The latter problem arose from the modern conflation of individual and national honor, in which national status was embedded in the assessments of matters of resolve, strength, and integrity that governed individual sensitivity to matters of personal honor. This development is not surprising in light of the nineteenth-century democratization of a rhetoric of honor that was personified in national symbols and leaders and deeply felt by soldiers and citizens alike.[89] In nations increasingly mobilized to fight future wars, this masculine sentiment had an irresistible appeal.

By 1914, Western nations had been engaged for over fifty years in colonial wars of conquest in Africa, Asia, and the Pacific against "savage" peoples in which the rules of war that governed conflict between "civilized" states had no jurisdiction. The distinction between enemy soldiers and civilians dissolved in combat against "uncivilized" races and the Clausewitzian duels of civilized warfare could become campaigns of racial extermination; the fact that colonial domains were also sites of missionary activity meant that Christian selfhood was also engaged in the struggle against a heathen Other.[90] In the atmosphere of international tension that marked the decades before 1914, the ubiquitous language of civilizational hierarchy was invidiously employed by Western nations against one another for shortcomings large and small and blossomed poisonously after the war began.[91] The proud accomplishments of honor and civilization celebrated by the family of civilized nations did not provide a sufficiently stable foundation on which to build a peaceful international order.

Shortly after the beginning of the war, Austrian founder of psychoanalysis Sigmund Freud wrote, "Our disillusionment on account of the uncivilized behavior of our fellow-citizens of the world during the war were unjustified. They were based on an illusion to which we had given way. In reality our fellow citizens have not sunk so low as we feared, because they had never risen so high as we believed."[92]

Conclusion

During the nineteenth century, men and women in Western nation-states were gradually organized in gendered social formations that could be quickly mobilized to fight wars on a large scale. Young men served time in mass conscription armies that initiated them into adult society and taught them the masculine virtues of courage and personal honor. Middle- and upper-class women served in nursing and philanthropic organizations that schooled them in devotion and how to care for the sick and wounded. Both men and women in these gendered zones acquired the habit of thinking about their service as a sacrifice to the greater national cause.

At the same time, all citizens were exposed to a growing militarization of civil society, in which themes of patriotism and past military accomplishments circulated in the forms of art, music, sporting, and veteran's organizations; organized military spectacles; and government propaganda. Journalists and writers found that accounts of military and civic heroism attracted swarms of newly literate readers and were far more popular than stories about the numerous prewar pacifist organizations or the intermittent efforts of governments to regularize the laws of war or limit the growth of arms. The long era of metropolitan peace following 1871, with its absence of great-power war (except the Russo-Japanese War, 1904–5), was not ended by a rising tide of bellicosity, but when war began again on the European continent in 1914, it was immediately clear that the military cultures of the great powers, which had prospered for well over half a century, had been successful in their work.

Notes

1. Edward Creasy, *The Fifteen Decisive Battles of the World from Marathon to Waterloo* (New York: Thomas Y. Crowell, n.d.), ix, 446–47.
2. Glenda Sluga, *Internationalism in the Age of Nationalism* (Philadelphia: University of Pennsylvania Press, 2013), 3.
3. Cynthia Eagle Russett, *Sexual Science and the Victorian Construction of Womanhood* (Cambridge, MA: Harvard University Press, 1989).
4. Ann Towns, "The Status of Women as a Standard of 'Civilization,'" *European Journal of International Relations* 15, no. 4 (2009): 681–706.
5. See the chapters by Peter H. Wilson on "Wars, States, and Gender in Early Modern European Warfare, 1600s–1780s," and Catherine Davies on "War, Gender, and Society in Late Colonial and Revolutionary Spanish America" in this handbook.
6. See the chapters by Alan Forrest on "Society, Mass Warfare, and Gender in Europe during and after the Revolutionary and Napoleonic Wars," and Thomas Cardoza and Karen Hagemann on "History and Memory of Army Women and Female Soldiers, 1770s–1870s" in this handbook; on France, also see Cardoza, *Intrepid Women: Cantinières and Vivandières of the French Army* (Bloomington: Indiana University Press, 2010).
7. See the chapter by Stefan Dudink on "Citizenship, Mass Mobilization, and Masculinity in a Transatlantic Perspective, 1770s–1870s" in this handbook.

8. Joan B. Landes, "Republican Citizenship and Heterosexual Desire: Concepts of Masculinity in Revolutionary France," in *Masculinities in Politics and War: Gendering Modern History*, ed. Stefan Dudink et al. (Manchester: Manchester University Press, 2004), 96–115; and Karen Hagemann, "German Heroes: The Cult of the Death for the Fatherland in Nineteenth-Century Germany," in Dudink et al., *Masculinities*, 116–36.

9. Stefan Dudink and Karen Hagemann, "Masculinity in Politics and War in the Age of Democratic Revolutions, 1750–1850," in Dudink et al., *Masculinities*, 3–21; and John Horne, "Masculinity in Politics and War in the Age of Nation-States and World Wars, 1850–1950," in Dudink et al., *Masculinities*, 22–40.

10. Peter H. Wilson, "Defining Military Culture," *Journal of Military History* 72, no. 1 (2008): 11–41.

11. Laurence Cole, *Military Culture and Popular Patriotism in Late Imperial Austria* (Oxford: Oxford University Press, 2014), 3, 15.

12. Also Isabel V. Hull, *Absolute Destruction: Military Culture and the Practices of War in Imperial Germany* (Ithaca, NY: Cornell University Press, 2005). For a discussion of the concept of *militarism*, see the chapter by Stefan Dudink, Karen Hagemann, and Mischa Honeck on "War and Gender: Nineteenth-Century Wars of Nations and Empires—an Overview" in this handbook.

13. Alan Forrest et al., eds., *War Memories: The Revolutionary and Napoleonic Wars in Modern European Culture* (Basingstoke: Palgrave Macmillan, 2012).

14. Scott Hughes Myerly, *British Military Spectacle from the Napoleonic Wars through the Crimea* (Cambridge, MA: Harvard University Press, 1996), 53–64; and Jakob Vogel, *Nationen im Gleichschritt: Der Kult der "Nation in Waffen" in Deutschland und Frankreich* (Göttingen: Vandenhoeck & Ruprecht, 1997).

15. Catharine Savage Brosman, *Visions of War in France: Fiction, Art, Ideology* (Baton Rouge: Louisiana State University Press, 1999), 30–35; and Sudhir Hazareesingh, "Napoleonic Memory in Nineteenth-Century France: The Making of a Liberal Legend," *MLN* 120, no. 4, French Issue (2005): 747–73.

16. David M. Hopkin, *Soldier and Peasant in French Popular Culture, 1766–1870* (Suffolk, UK: Boydell Press, 2002), 54–55, 220–21, 269–75.

17. Brian Joseph Martin, *Napoleonic Friendship: Military Fraternity, Intimacy, and Sexuality in Nineteenth-Century France* (Durham: University of New Hampshire Press, 2010).

18. Gérard de Puymège, "The Good Soldier Chauvin," in *Realms of Memory: The Construction of the French Past*, vol. 2, *Traditions*, ed. Pierre Nora and Lawrence D. Kritzman (New York: Columbia University Press, 1997), 332–60; see also Ouriel Reshef, *Guerres, mythes et caricatures: au Berceau d'une mentalité française* (Paris: Presses de la Fondation des sciences politiques, 1984).

19. Karen Hagemann, *Revisiting Prussia's Wars against Napoleon: History, Culture, Memory* (Cambridge: Cambridge University Press, 2015), 249–396; Forrest et al., *War Memories*; and Philip G. Dwyer, "Public Remembering, Private Reminiscing: French Military Memoirs and the Revolutionary and Napoleonic Wars," *French Historical Studies* 33, no. 2 (2010): 231–58.

20. See Hagemann, *Revisiting*, 37–396, 395–96; Lars Peters, *Romances of War: Die Erinnerung an die Revolutions- und Napoleonischen Kriege in Grossbritannien und Irland 1815-1945* (Paderborn: Schöningh, 2012); and Ruth Leiserowitz, *Heldenhafte Zeiten: Die polnischen Erinnerungen an die Revolutions- und Napoleonischen Kriege 1815-1945* (Paderborn: Ferdinand Schöningh, 2017).

21. Quoted in Joseph Clarke, "Valour Knows neither Age nor Sex: The Recueil des Actions Héroïques and the Representation of Courage in Revolutionary France," *War in History* 20, no. 1 (2013): 50–75, 75; and Michael J. Hughes, "Making Frenchmen into Warriors: Martial Masculinity in Napoleonic France," in *French Masculinities: History, Culture and Politics*, ed. Christopher J. Forth and Bertrand Taithe (Basingstoke: Palgrave Macmillan, 2007), 31–63.

22. Karen Hagemann, "National Symbols and the Politics of Memory: The Prussian Iron Cross of 1813, Its Cultural Context and Its Aftermath," in Forrest et al., *War Memories*, 215–44.

23. Myerly, *British Military Spectacle*, 87, 92–94.

24. Wilson, "Defining Military Culture," 34–35; Ute Frevert, "Honor, Gender, and Power: The Politics of Satisfaction in Pre-War Europe," in *An Improbable War: The Outbreak of World War I and European Political Culture before 1914*, ed. Holger Afflerbach and David Stevenson (New York: Berghahn Books, 2007), 233–55; Michael Fellman, "At the Nihilist Edge: Reflections on Guerilla Warfare during the American Civil War," in *The Road to Total War: The American Civil War and the German Wars of Unification*, ed. Stig Förster and Jörg Nagel (Cambridge: Cambridge University Press, 1997), 519–40; and Joshua Sanborn, *Drafting the Russian Nation: Military Conscription, Total War and Mass Politics, 1905–1925* (Dekalb: Northern Illinois University Press, 2011), 144–46.

25. See the chapter by Amy S. Greenberg on "Gender and the Wars of Nation-Building and Nation-Keeping in the Americas, 1830s–1870s" in this handbook.

26. John Horne, "Defeat and Memory in Modern History," in *Defeat and Memory: Cultural Histories of Military Defeat in the Modern Era*, ed. Jenny Macleod (Basingstoke: Palgrave Macmillan, 2008), 11–29, 17.

27. Sylvana Patriarca and Lucy Riall, eds., *The Risorgimento Revisited: Nationalism and Culture in Nineteenth-Century Italy* (Basingstoke: Palgrave Macmillan, 2012).

28. Christian Koller, "Defeat and Foreign Rule as a Narrative of National Rebirth: The German Memory of the Napoleonic Period in the Nineteenth and Early Twentieth Centuries," in Macleod, *Defeat and Memory*, 30–45.

29. Alan Forrest, *The Legacy of the French Revolutionary Wars: The Nation-in-Arms in French Republican Memory* (Cambridge: Cambridge University Press, 2009), 2–4, 181–82.

30. David A. Bell, *The First Total War: Napoleon's Europe and the Birth of Warfare as We Know It* (New York: Houghton Mifflin, 2007); see Forrest, " Society, Mass Warfare, and Gender" in this handbook.

31. Manfred Messerschmidt, "The Prussian Army from Reform to War," 263–82; and Herman M. Hattaway, "The Civil War Armies: Creation, Mobilization and Development," in *On the Road to Total War: The American Civil War and the German Wars of Unification*, ed. Stig Förster and Jörg Nagler (Cambridge: Cambridge University Press, 1997), 173–98.

32. Hull, *Absolute Destruction*.

33. Martyn Lyons, *A History of Reading and Writing in the Western World* (Basingstoke: Palgrave Macmillan, 2010).

34. Stefanie Markovits, *The Crimean War in the British Imagination* (Cambridge: Cambridge University Press, 2009), 23–24, 46–54.

35. Mary Poovey, *Uneven Developments: The Ideological Work of Gender in Mid-Victorian England* (Chicago: University of Chicago Press, 1989). See also the chapter by Jean H. Quataert on "Changing Modes of Warfare and the Gendering of Military Medical Care, 1850s–1920s" in this handbook.

36. Jean H. Quataert, "German Patriotic Women's Work in War and Peacetime, 1864–90," in Förster and Nagel, *On the Road*, 449–78; Drew Gilpin Faust, *Mothers of Invention: Women of the Slaveholding South in the American Civil War* (Chapel Hill: University of North Carolina Press, 1996), 17, 81–93; and Nina Silber, *Daughters of the Union: Northern Women Fight the Civil War* (Cambridge, MA: Harvard University Press, 2005), 10–12.

37. Peter Young and Peter Jesser, *The Media and the Military: From the Crimea to Desert Strike* (New York: St. Martin's Press, 1997), 21–28; and, more generally, Lyons, *A History.*

38. Michael E. Nolan, *The Inverted Mirror: Mythologizing the Enemy in France and Germany, 1898–1914* (Oxford: Berghahn Books, 2005); Stéphane Audoin-Rouzeau, "French Public Opinion in 1870–71 and the Emergence of Total War," in Förster and Nagel, *On the Road*, 393–411; and Phillip S. Paludan, "The Better Angels of Our Nature: Lincoln, Propaganda and Public Opinion in the North during the Civil War," in Förster and Nagel, *On the Road*, 357–76.

39. Richard Scully, *British Images of Germany: Admiration, Antagonism, Ambivalence, 1860–1914* (Basingstoke: Palgrave Macmillan, 2012), 180–81.

40. Hagemann, *Revisiting*, 130–54.

41. Jakob Vogel, "Military, Folklore, *Eigensinn*: Folkloric Militarism in Germany and France, 1871–1914," *Central European History* 33, no. 4 (2000): 487–504; and Vogel, *Nationen.*

42. Gary S. Messinger, *British Propaganda and the State in the First World War* (Manchester: Manchester University Press, 1992), 11; and Mark Hampton, "The 'Objectivity' Ideal and Its Limitations in 20th-Century British Journalism," *Journalism Studies* 9, no. 4 (2008): 477–93.

43. See Forrest, "Society, Mass Warfare, and Gender" in this handbook.

44. Roland G. Foerster, ed., *Die Wehrpflicht: Entstehung, Erscheinungsformen und politisch-militärische Wirkung* (Munich: Oldenbourg, 1994).

45. Myerly, *British Military Spectacle.*

46. Anne-Marie Sohn, *"Sois un Homme!" La Construction de la Masculinité au XIXe Siècle* (Paris: Seuil, 2009), 205–17.

47. Laurence Cole, "Military Veterans and Popular Patriotism in Imperial Austria, 1870–1914," in *The Limits of Loyalty: Imperial Symbolism, Popular Allegiances, and State Patriotism in the Late Hapsburg Monarchy*, ed. Laurence Cole and Daniel Unowsky (Oxford: Berghahn Books, 2007), 36–61.

48. Ute Frevert, *A Nation in Barracks: Modern German Military Conscription and Civil Society* (Oxford: Berg, 2007), 70–75.

49. Cunningham Robertson, Commander of 28th Foot Regiment, quoted in David French, *Military Identities: The Regimental System, the British Army and the British People c. 1870–2000* (Oxford: Oxford University Press, 2005), 26–27.

50. Frevert, *A Nation*; Thomas Rohkrämer, *"Der Militarismus der Kleinen Leute": Die Kriegervereine im Deutsche Kaiserreich, 1871–1914* (Munich: Oldenbourg, 1990); and Cole, "Military Veterans," 36–61.

51. Jeremy Black, *Warfare in the Western World, 1882–1975* (Bloomington: Indiana University Press, 2001), 26; also John Stauffer, "Embattled Manhood and New England Writers," in *Battle Scars: Gender and Sexuality in the American Civil War*, ed. Catherine Clinton and Nina Silber (New York: Oxford University Press, 2006), 120–39.

52. Thomas Rohrkrämer, "Heroes and Would-Be Heroes: Veterans' and Reservists' Associations in Imperial Germany," in *Anticipating Total War: The German and American Experiences*, ed. Manfred E. Boemeke et al. (Cambridge: Cambridge University Press, 1999), 189–216.

53. David W. Blight, "No Desperate Hero: Manhood and Freedom in a Union Soldier's Experience," in *Divided Houses: Gender and the Civil War*, ed. Catherine Clinton and Nina Silber (New York: Oxford University Press, 1992), 55–75, 63; and Reid Mitchell, "Soldiering, Manhood, and Coming of Age: A Northern Volunteer," in Clinton and Silber, *Divided Houses*, 43–54.

54. Caroline E. Janney, *Remembering the Civil War: Reunion and the Limits of Reconciliation* (Chapel Hill: University of North Caroline Press, 2013).

55. Michael Jeismann, *Das Vaterland der Feinde: Studien zum nationalen Feindbegriff und Selbstverständnis in Deutschland und Frankreich 1792–1918* (Stuttgart: Klett-Cotta, 1992).

56. Patricia Mazon, "Germania Triumphant: The Niederwald National Monument and the Liberal Moment in Imperial Germany," *German History* 18, no. 2 (2000): 162–92, 171; Maurice Agulhon, *Marianne au combat: l'imagerie et la symbolique républicaines de 1789 à 1880* (Paris: Flammarion, 1979); and Charlotte Tacke, *Denkmal im sozialen Raum: Nationale Symbole in Deutschland und Frankreich im 19. Jahrhundert* (Göttingen: Vandenhoeck & Ruprecht, 1995).

57. Michael Dorsch, *French Sculpture following the Franco-Prussian War, 1870–80: Realist Allegories and the Commemoration of Defeat* (Farnham: Ashgate 1988), 97.

58. Jean H. Quataert, *Staging Philanthropy: Patriotic Women in the National Imagination in Dynastic Germany, 1813–1916* (Ann Arbor: University of Michigan Press, 2001); and Quataert, "German Patriotic," 449–77.

59. Rachel Chrastil, *Organizing for War: France, 1870–1914* (Baton Rouge: Louisiana State University Press, 2010), 85–89.

60. Bertrand Taithe, *Defeated Flesh: Medicine, Welfare, and Warfare in the Making of Modern France* (Lanham, MD: Rowman & Littlefield, 1999).

61. Michael Brown, "'Like a Devoted Army': Medicine, Heroic Masculinity and the Literary Paradigm in Victorian Britain," *Journal of British Studies* 49, no. 3 (2010): 592–622.

62. Maartje Abbenhuis, *An Age of Neutrals: Great Power Politics, 1815–1914* (Cambridge: Cambridge University Press, 2014), 165.

63. Richard J. Evans, "Afterword," in Cole and Unowsky, *The Limits*, 223–32, 224.

64. Alon Confino, *The Nation as a Local Metaphor: Württemberg, Imperial Germany and National Memory, 1871–1918* (Chapel Hill: University of North Carolina Press, 1997), 11. See also Celia Applegate, *A Nation of Provincials: The German Idea of Heimat* (Berkeley: University of California Press, 1990).

65. Vogel, *Nationen*; Erwin Fink, "Symbolic Representations of the Nation: Baden, Bavaria, and Saxony, c.1860–80," in *Different Paths to the Nation: Regional and National Identities in Central Europe and Italy, 1830–70*, ed. Laurence Cole (Basingstoke: Palgrave Macmillan, 2007), 200–219; and Daniel L. Unowsky, *The Pomp and Politics of Patriotism: Imperial Celebration in Habsburg Austria, 1848–1916* (West Lafayette, IN: Purdue University Press, 2005).

66. Detmar Klein, "Becoming Alsatian: Anti-German and Pro-French Cultural Propaganda in Alsace, 1898–1914," in *French Music, Culture, and National Identity*, ed. Barbara L. Kelley (Rochester, NY: Rochester University Press, 2008), 215–33; and Elizabeth Vlossak, *Marianne or Germania? Nationalizing Women in Alsace, 1870–1946* (Oxford: Oxford University Press, 2010), 37–43, 191–94.

67. Jeffrey Richards, *Imperialism and Music: Britain, 1876–1953* (Manchester: Manchester University Press, 2001), 124; and Benjamin Curtis, *Music Makes the Nation: Nationalist Composers and Nation-Building in Nineteenth Century Europe* (Amherst, NY: Cambria Press, 2008).

68. Trevor Herbert and Helen Barlow, *Music and the British Military in the Long Nineteenth Century* (Oxford: Oxford University Press, 2013), 1–21, 163–75.

69. Alison Mathews David, "Decorated Man: Fashioning the French Soldier, 1852–1914," *Fashion Theory* 7, no. 1 (2003): 3–38; Thomas Abler, *Hinterland Warriors: European Empires and Exotic Uniforms* (Oxford: Berg, 1999); John Springhall, "'Up Guards and at Them': British Imperialism and Popular Art, 1880–1914," in *Imperialism and Popular Culture*, ed. John M. MacKenzie (Manchester: Manchester University Press, 1986), 49–72; Paul Usherwood and Jenny Spencer-Smith, *Lady Butler, Battle Artist, 1846–1933* (Gloucester: Alan Sutton, 1987); Brosman, *Visions of War in France*, 57–59; French, *Military Identities*, 50–55; and Frevert, *A Nation*, 212.

70. Herbert and Barlow, *Music*, 177–83; W. S. Hamer, *The British Army: Civil–Military Relations, 1885–1905* (Oxford: Clarendon Press, 1970), 215–17; Frevert, *A Nation*, 149–55; and John Peck, *War, the Army, and Victorian Literature* (London: Palgrave Macmillan, 1998).

71. Penny Summerfield, "Patriotism and Empire: Music Hall Entertainment, 1870–1914," in MacKenzie, *Imperialism*, 17–48; Richards, *Imperialism*, 194–269; and Dave Russell, *Popular Music in England, 1840–1914: A Social History* (Montreal: McGill–Queens University Press, 1987).

72. Robert Justin Goldstein, *The Frightful Stage: Political Censorship of the Theater in Nineteenth-Century Europe* (New York: Berghahn Books, 2009), 50.

73. Richards, *Imperialism*, 262–69.

74. Edward Berenson, *Heroes of Empire: Five Charismatic Men and the Conquest of Africa* (Berkeley: University of California Press, 2011); and John M. MacKenzie, ed., *European Empires and the People: Popular Responses to Imperialism in France, Britain, The Netherlands, Belgium, Germany and Italy* (Manchester: Manchester University Press, 2011).

75. Paula M. Krebs, *Gender, Race, and the Writing of Empire: Public Discourse and the Boer War* (Cambridge: Cambridge University Press, 1999), 49–62; and Graham Dawson, *Soldier Heroes: British Adventure, Empire and the Imagining of Masculinities* (London: Routledge, 1999).

76. On these topics, see Robert A. Nye, *Crime, Madness and Politics in Modern France: The Medical Concept of National Decline* (Princeton, NJ: Princeton University Press, 1984); Daniel Pick, *Faces of Degeneration: A European Disorder, c.1848–1918* (Cambridge: Cambridge University Press, 1989); and Amy Kaplan, "Romancing the Empire: The Embodiment of American Masculinity in the Popular Historical Novel of the 1890s," *American Literary History* 2, no. 4 (1990): 659–90.

77. Paul Crook, *Darwinism, War and History: The Debate over the Biology of War from the "Origin of Species" to the First World War* (Cambridge: Cambridge University Press, 1994), 80.

78. Chrastil, *Organizing for War*; Margaret A. Darrow, *French Women and the First World War: War Stories of the Home Front* (New York: Berg, 2000), 30–33; and Quataert, *Staging*.

79. See Richard Holt et al., eds., *European Heroes: Myth, Identity, Sport* (London: Frank Cass, 1996); Pierre Arnaud, *Le Militaire, L'écolier, le gymnaste: naissance de l'éducation physique en France (1869–1889)* (Lyon: Presses universitaires de Lyon, 1991); J. A. Mangan, ed., *Tribal Identities: Nationalism, Europe, Sport* (London: Frank Cass, 1996); and Michael Kruger, "Body Culture and Nation-Building: The History of Gymnastics in Germany in the Period of Its Foundation as a Nation-State," *International Journal of the History of Sport* 13, no. 3 (1996): 409–17.

80. Venita Datta, *Heroes and Legends of Fin-de-Siècle France: Gender, Politics, and National Identity* (Cambridge: Cambridge University Press, 2011); and John Price, *Everyday Heroism: Victorian Construction of the Heroic Civilian* (London: Bloomsbury Academic, 2013).

81. Christopher Forth, *Masculinity in the Modern West: Gender, Civilization and the Body* (Basingstoke: Palgrave Macmillan, 2010).

82. Michael Howard and Peter Paret, eds. and trans., *Carl Von Clausewitz on War* (Princeton, NJ: Princeton University Press, 1984), 75–76.

83. Robert A. Nye, *Masculinity and Male Codes of Honor in Modern France* (New York: Oxford University Press, 1993), 172–215.

84. See also Quataert, "Changing Modes" in this handbook.

85. Sandi E. Cooper, "Pacifism in France, 1889–1914: International Peace as a Human Right," *French Historical Studies* 17, no. 2 (1991): 359–86; and Roger Chickering, *Imperial Germany and a World without War: The Peace Movement and German Society, 1892–1914* (Princeton, NJ: Princeton University Press, 1976).

86. Arthur Eyffinger, *The 1899 Hague Peace Conference: "The Parliament of Man, the Federation of the World"* (The Hague: Kluwer Law International, 1999), 370–71; and Shabtai Rosenne, ed., *The Hague Peace Conferences of 1899 and 1907 and International Arbitration: Reports and Documents* (The Hague: Asser Press, 2001), 136–37.

87. Effinger, *The 1899 Hague*, 247, 227.

88. Rosenne, *Hague Peace Conferences*, 46; and Effinger, *The 1899 Hague*, 370–71.

89. Paul Robinson, *Military Honour and the Conduct of War: From Ancient Greece to Iraq* (New York: Routledge, 2006), 167–70; and Geoffrey Best, *Honor among Men and Nations: Transformation of an Idea* (Toronto: University of Toronto Press, 1982).

90. Gangolf Hübinger, "Religion and War in Imperial Germany," in Boemeke et al., *Anticipating Total War*, 125–36; see also Susan A. Brewer, *Why America Fights: Patriotism and War Propaganda from the Philippines to Iraq* (Oxford: Oxford University Press, 2009), 4–45.

91. Kevin Cramer, "A World of Enemies: New Perspectives on German Military Culture and the Origins of the First World War," *Central European History* 39, no. 2 (2006): 270–98; Niall Ferguson, "Prisoner Taking and Prisoner Killing: The Dynamics of Defeat, Surrender, and Barbarity in the Age of Total War," in *The Barbarization of Warfare*, ed. George Kassameris (New York: New York University Press, 2006), 126–58; and Joanna Bourke, "Barbarization vs. Civilization in Time of War," in Kassameris, *Barbarization of Warfare*, 19–38.

92. Sigmund Freud, *Civilization, War and Death: Selections from Three Works by Sigmund Freud*, ed. John Rickman (London: Hogarth Press, 1939), 11.

SELECT BIBLIOGRAPHY

Boemeke, Manfred E., Roger Chickering, and Stig Förster, eds. *Anticipating Total War: The German and American Experiences, 1871–1914*. Cambridge: Cambridge University Press, 1999.

Chrastil, Rachel. *Organizing for War: France, 1870–1914*. Baton Rouge: Louisiana State University Press, 2010.

Cole, Laurence. *Military Culture and Popular Patriotism in Late Imperial Austria*. Oxford: Oxford University Press, 2014.

Dudink, Stefan, Karen Hagemann, and John Tosh, eds. *Masculinities in Politics and War: Gendering Modern History*. Manchester: Manchester University Press, 2004.

Forrest, Alan, Étienne François, and Karen Hagemann, eds. *War Memories: The Revolutionary and Napoleonic Wars in Modern European Culture*. Basingstoke: Palgrave Macmillan, 2012.

Förster, Stig, and Jörg Nagel, eds. *On the Road to Total War: The American Civil War and the German Wars of Unification*. Cambridge: Cambridge University Press, 1997.

Frevert, Ute. *A Nation in Barracks: Modern German Military Conscription and Civil Society*. Oxford: Berg, 2004.

Hagemann, Karen. *Revisiting Prussia's Wars against Napoleon: History, Culture, and Memory*. Cambridge: Cambridge University Press, 2015.

Hull, Isabel V. *Absolute Destruction: Military Culture and the Practices of War in Imperial Germany*. Ithaca, NY: Cornell University Press, 2005.

Janney, Caroline E. *Remembering the Civil War: Reunion and the Limits of Reconciliation*. Chapel Hill: University of North Carolina Press, 2013.

Kassameris, George. *The Barbarization of Warfare*. New York: New York University Press, 2006.

MacKenzie, John M., ed. *Imperialism and Popular Culture*. Manchester: Manchester University Press, 1986.

Macleod, Jenny, ed. *Defeat and Memory: Cultural Histories of Military Defeat in the Modern Era*. Basingstoke: Palgrave MacMillan, 2008.

Markovits, Stephanie. *The Crimean War in the British Imagination*. Cambridge: Cambridge University Press, 2009.

Myerly, Scott Hughes. *British Military Spectacle from the Napoleonic Wars through the Crimea*. Cambridge, MA: Harvard University Press, 1996.

Nye, Robert A. *Masculinity and Male Codes of Honor in Modern France*. Oxford: Oxford University Press, 1993.

Patriarca, Sylvana, and Lucy Riall, eds. *The Risorgimento Revisited: Nationalism and Culture in Nineteenth-Century Italy*. Basingstoke: Palgrave Macmillan, 2012.

Sanborn, Joshua. *Drafting the Russian Nation: Military Conscription, Total War, and Mass Politics, 1905–1925*. Dekalb: Northern Illinois Press, 2011.

Savage Brosman, Catharine. *Visions of War in France: Fiction, Art, Ideology*. Baton Rouge: Louisiana State University Press, 1999.

Vogel, Jakob. *Nationen im Gleichschritt: Der Kult der "Nation in Waffen" in Deutschland und Frankreich*. Gottingen: Vandenhoeck & Ruprecht, 1997.

....

CHAPTER 11

GENDER AND THE WARS OF NATION-BUILDING AND NATION-KEEPING IN THE AMERICAS, 1830s–1870s

....

AMY S. GREENBERG

THE middle decades of the nineteenth century in the Americas were marked by dramatic warfare in the name of nationalism. In the period following the Spanish American Wars of Independence (1808–30), the three most important conflicts were the US–Mexican War (1846–48), the American Civil War (1861–65), and the War of the Triple Alliance, also known as the Paraguayan War, between Paraguay and an alliance of Brazil, Argentina, and Uruguay (1864–70).[1] From the 1830s through the 1870s, there was almost always a war being fought somewhere in the Western Hemisphere, but the most important conflicts had two things in common: the outcome had significant determining effects on the sovereignty or dominion over at least one of the nations involved, and both participants and observers interpreted the causes, progress, and outcomes of these encounters as crucial to manhood, womanhood, and gender relations.

These assumptions were not entirely fanciful. War and a martial vision of masculinity that grounded a man's worth in his ability to dominate others were often (but not always) mutually reinforcing: military encounters upheld violence as a positive attribute in men, while violent men promoted war as a means to an end. During ongoing conflicts, nationalism was grounded in sacrifice, and citizenship was intimately linked to military service.[2] In the course of protracted conflicts, that link was rarely questioned, but in the aftermath of many of the most devastating conflicts, such as the independence movements in Latin America and the American Civil War, martial expressions of manhood were pathologized as unproductive and devalued in favor of more restrained practices of manhood that looked to work and family as the measurement of a man's worth.[3]

But warfare did not affect masculinity alone. The demands of war also shaped practices of womanhood, in many cases leading to increased female autonomy and authority during wartime. This autonomy rarely lasted long. Even women who actively served in the military did not benefit from the general understanding that citizenship was grounded in military sacrifice. From their sacrifice, they might gain financial benefit for example by a pension, but never citizenship. More likely was that some privileged women of these new nations, or newly sanctified nations, gained new levels of authority, within the homes and society at large, as "Republican Mothers." At the same time, their subservience was ensured by a widespread division between public and private that granted authority and the right to privacy to male heads of households within their domains.[4]

In virtually all Wars of Nation-Building and Nation-Keeping in the Americas, the individual virtue of both men and women was understood to have national importance. Virtue for women was almost always equated with chastity, and most postwar nations saw an increase in social policing of female sexuality. In the aftermath of war, male virtue was largely understood to consist of working hard and providing for and protecting their dependents (including wives). This virtue was understood to be the bedrock of citizenship. As a result, while elite women emerged from wars with new levels of social respect, poor women or women unable or unwilling to conform to moral standards found their actions newly scrutinized, condemned, and often criminalized.[5]

Investigations of this topic in Central and South America are relatively limited. The main theme in most of the research has been the extent to which women were able to exploit the turmoil of war to undermine patriarchy and increase social, political, and economic opportunities.[6] Good individual studies have been written on the effects of the wars of independence from Spain on the rights of women, particularly in Peru, Gran Colombia, and Ecuador.[7] But some key conflicts of the mid-century period, including the bloodiest interstate conflict in South American history, the Paraguayan War, which killed an estimated 400,000 soldiers and civilians, have received limited attention from gender scholars, particularly scholars of masculinity.[8]

By contrast, the importance of women's work to the American Civil War has been celebrated since the war first came to a close, and the juxtaposition of the centennial of the war with the civil rights movement in 1965 resulted in a renaissance of studies of Northern women's benevolent work that offered optimistic assessments of women's power to change both history and their own condition through determined effort.[9] Although the general public is captivated by the presence of female soldiers and spies in the Union and Confederate armies, scholars are more likely to focus on the displacement of both African American and White women and families by war and the centrality of the home front in both the North and the South (including resistance by women) to the ultimate outcome of the war.[10] A second major theme has been the agency of freedwomen in the transition from slavery, successfully putting to rest any notion that it was President Abraham Lincoln, in office from 1861 to 1865, who "freed the slaves."[11]

Studies of the impact of the Civil War on American masculinities are of more recent vintage, but the subject has received sustained historical interest since 1982, when Bertram Wyatt-Brown posited that Northern and Southern White men held different conceptions of honor, which prevented compromise on the eve of the Civil War.[12] In recent decades, scholars have considered not only the extent to which ideals of manhood provoked the American Civil War and motivated men in battle, but also whether masculine ideals were transformed by the experience of war. The relationship of race to masculinity is another important theme in the literature, particularly the extent to which both slaveholding and being a part of a slaveholding culture shaped the masculinities of White Southerners, as well as the relationship of war to masculinity for Black men.[13]

The US–Mexican War has received only a fraction of the historical attention accorded the American Civil War, but scholars of Mexico and the United States have argued that the war was provoked by ideals of manhood and contributed to the transformation of masculine ideals in both countries. Literary scholars have noted the importance of gendered tropes in the literature of the US–Mexican War in the United States, and scholars of Mexico have investigated the important role played by Mexican women, both as *soldaderas* and on the home front.[14] Although wars with Native Americans were nearly constant in the middle decades of the nineteenth century in the United States and also on the northern frontier in Mexico, thus far, only the Second Seminole War with the United States (1835–42) has been a subject of close gender analysis. Laurel Clark Shire's argument that images of Indian atrocities against White women lent national support to the fight against the Seminole and empowered settler colonialism in Native lands is likely applicable to other frontier conflicts in the nineteenth-century United States.[15]

The following will examine the gendered implications of nation-building or *people's wars*—understood as constitutive of the nation—in the Americas between the aftermath of Latin American independence movements in the 1830s and the later Paraguayan War during the 1860s, through the US–Mexican War of the 1840s and the US Civil War of the 1860s.[16] Three major themes will be explored: first, the impact of warfare on families, households, and states in the postwar nations of South and Central America; second, the rise of the citizen-soldier during the US–Mexican War; and third, the gendered language of nation and war and the roles of women and men in the actual conflict during the American Civil War.

FAMILY, HOUSEHOLD, AND STATE IN THE NEWLY INDEPENDENT NATIONS OF SOUTH AND CENTRAL AMERICA

Many of the new Latin American nation-states founded in the context of the Spanish American Wars of Independence, including Bolivia (1809–25), Argentina (1810–18), Chile (1810–26), Mexico (1810–21), Venezuela (1810–23), Uruguay (1811), Peru (1811–24), Gran Colombia (1815–20), and Ecuador (1820–22), spent the 1830s wrestling with the social and economic fallout from these wars of liberation. In keeping with the pattern of liberal revolutions in the Atlantic world, these wars reinforced upper-class male authority by linking citizenship rights to military participation. This was true in cases, such as Gran Colombia, where there was not a high rate of female participation in those wars, as well as in Mexico, where high levels of female support for independence and direct military engagement won women temporary respect and acclaim without changing their employment opportunities or other material conditions. In all cases, the men who emerged as leaders in their new nations—for instance, Francisco de Paula Santander, the president of the Republic of Gran Colombia from 1819 to 1826 and of the Republic of New Granada from 1832 to 1837—grounded their authority in large part over their control of their households.[17]

One example can be seen in newly independent Venezuela, which in the 1830s was marked by a lengthy struggle for power between two groups of men with distinctly different gendered practices and ideals, as Arlene Díaz has shown in her 2004 book *Female Citizens, Patriarchs, and the Law in Venezuela, 1786–1904*. The first were military leaders, such as Simón Bolívar, who insisted that Venezuela should be led by those who *"derramaron su sangre"* (spilled their blood) in the creation of the nation.[18] The second were oligarchs like Francisco de Paula Santander, who supported liberalism and claimed their rights to power based on their extensive landownership and education. The oligarchs linked the military with a continuation of the costly and deadly independence movement of the past two decades. They further condemned the military as "barbarous" aristocratic parasites unworthy of leading a nation into modernization.[19] These two models of manhood were figuratively at war with one another from at least 1830 through the 1860s. By the 1870s, bourgeois masculine values (hard work, sobriety, and education) had won out over military ideas of honor for a large segment of the population.[20]

Both masculine ideologies shared the conviction that the household was a sacred space controlled by a male patriarch that the law had little right to invade. At the same time in newly national Venezuela, motherhood gained traction as a social function valuable to the state, gaining some accused women legal pardon and leniency during a period when criminals of both sexes were being tried and punished with increasing frequency. "Virtuous" women were entitled to an extra degree of respect and credit, not only because the home was a sacred space where a husband's power was to be respected, but also because these women would bring up the next generation of citizens. Hence, war and the desire to distance independent Venezuela from the legacy of Spanish cruelty offered some accused female Venezuelans extra protection under the law while also adding new value to the ideal of domesticity.[21]

The discourse on republican honor in postwar Peru, too, was explicitly masculine, as Sarah Chambers has demonstrated in her pathbreaking 1999 study, *Subjects to Citizens: Honor, Gender, and Politics in Arequipa, Peru*. She describes Arequipa as a representative provincial Latin American city in Peru without major racial conflict. Here, honor was distinctly defined as masculine: "Because republican authorities needed men as workers, soldiers and political partisans, they were willing to reinforce patriarchal privileges in the private sphere in exchange for more respectable male conduct in public."[22] Women's speech was marginalized because republican political theory defined public opinion as the result of "rational" debate among male citizens, as opposed to the female gossip prevalent in the crowded neighborhoods and small towns of colonial Latin America.[23]

In Peru, men made claims to citizenship based on their military service, but the wartime shortage of agricultural labor led authorities to praise hard work as a crucial contribution to the state. A good work ethic therefore became a key component of respectability in Peruvian society. Plebeians who rejected other aspects of bourgeois morality, like temperance, took pride in their status as productive citizens. Honor for women remained grounded in chastity, but it also gave rise to a philosophy of "republican womanhood" in which women were embraced for nurturing republican virtue in their families. As one pupil at a female seminar in 1833 put it, "The fair sex ... will be the compass that guides the domestic ship along the path of honor."[24]

In the new nations of postwar Latin America, only some women were able to win the respect of men because of their active support of the struggle for independence. Women had participated in these wars in a wide variety of ways. Nevertheless, there were only two primary ways that women's military service was understood in public postwar memory: as heroic soldiers or camp followers. Some Latin American women were able to win men's respect through battlefield heroics. By seemingly rejecting their femininity and embracing a masculine role, they were capable of temporarily subverting the gender order.[25] This was not the case in the United States, as will be discussed later, or in all Latin American nations. Indeed, military service usually dishonored women in Peru, for example, since the assumption was that their morals would be corrupted by exposure to war and soldiers. The women who had actively supported the struggle for liberation with their fighting challenged the dominant gender order in postwar societies.[26] Therefore, with very few exceptions, military women were equated with the camp followers, those women who accompanied the armies, often at great danger to themselves, and performed the traditional services expected from women, including cooking, cleaning, nursing, and sex.[27]

Different from the many women who had actively supported the American Wars of Nation-Building, men who had fought in these wars and who had previously been politically marginalized because of their class or ethnicity gained new citizenship rights as a result of military service.[28] At best, women could hope to secure compensation for their service. For example, in a few cases in Peru in 1839, female spies were compensated for their military activities. Rather than call for political inclusion, as some radical women in revolutionary France did in the early 1790s,[29] women in Peru chose to manipulate the language of domesticity so that elite women could demand a right to education and recognition of their social value as mothers and arbiters of morality. In Venezuela, claims of motherhood led to clemency from criminal behavior, but this was a singular case.

Elsewhere in the Americas, poor women saw an increased level of policing of their morality after wars, along with a general rise in criminal prosecution. The experience of Antioquia, Colombia, was not dramatically different from that of Peru. Citizenship here was also grounded in the protection of the "traditional" family, and women who were not sexually virtuous were arrested as vagrants. Across the Americas, "good masculinity entailed public virtue; good femininity, private morality."[30] A somewhat different gender regime emerged in Chihuahua, in northern Mexico. In a region subject to repeated raids by Apache warriors over a period of decades, it is not surprising that the residents welcomed a standard of masculine honor grounded in military struggle against the Apache. Manhood, properly understood, was highly martial. It encompassed productive labor, but highlighted the defense of virtuous "White" (non-Apache) women against the "barbaric" marauders.[31]

No discussion of war in Latin America would be complete without a consideration of the Paraguayan War that started in October 1864 and ended in March 1870. This conflict between Paraguay and the alliance of Argentina, the Empire of Brazil, and Uruguay was the deadliest and bloodiest interstate war over territorial disputes in Latin America's history. It ended in total defeat for Paraguay, which by the war's end was completely devastated and had suffered catastrophic losses to its population; historians estimate the range from 21,000 to 200,000 dead. Argentine and Brazilian troops occupied Paraguay until 1876. It took decades for Paraguay to recover from the economic and social destruction and demographic losses. The war helped the Brazilian Empire to reach its peak of political and military influence, becoming the great power of South America.[32]

While scholars have yet to fully consider the implications on the War of the Triple Alliance, or Paraguayan War, on manhood, the six-year war killed perhaps 70 percent of Paraguay's male population (estimates on this point vary widely), leaving the country "a land of women, widows, invalids and orphans," with a gender ratio of three women to every one man. Paraguayan women were an active presence in the army as both camp followers and soldiers in a drawn-out guerrilla resistance, and they were also crucial to the war effort as farmers and producers.[33] After six years of almost incomprehensible suffering, including widespread death by famine and rape and murder at the hands of an occupying Brazilian army, Paraguay's women were left to rebuild the country's economy as best they could. They farmed, traded, and worked as street vendors. Nevertheless, upward of a third of all Paraguayan households had already been headed by women before the war, in large part as a result of illegitimacy and male labor patterns. As such, postwar conditions, although "indescribably bad" in many cases, did not dramatically change women's work in Paraguay. Nor did the war result in an improvement of women's status. While some women hoped for a more liberal postwar constitution that would ensure their civil rights, there was no push for suffrage or formal political rights, in part, scholars argue, because Paraguay had no prewar democratic tradition. As elsewhere in Latin America, the end of war brought a hardening of moral values. Postwar newspapers upheld motherhood as the ideal model for women, and the few surviving men embraced patriarchy. In the end, war brought little change to gender roles in Paraguay.[34]

Manhood and the Citizen-Soldier during the US–Mexican War

The war between the United States and Mexico started in April 1846 and ended in February 1848 with the Treaty of Guadalupe Hidalgo, which forced Mexico to cede the territories of Alta California and Santa Fe de Nuevo México to the United States in exchange for $15 million. The victorious United States thus gained half of the young Mexican Republic's territory. The roots of war lay in the conviction of a large proportion of White US citizens that Mexicans were racially inferior and no more entitled to their land than the Indian tribes of North America. Hostilities officially commenced after US President James K. Polk, in office from 1845 to 1849, sent an army of 4,000 men deep into territory claimed by Mexico in April 1846, in the wake of the 1845 US annexation of Texas, which Mexico still considered Mexican territory since the government did not recognize the treaty signed by Mexican General Antonio López de Santa Anna after the Texas Revolution (1835–36) a decade earlier. The Mexican president Mariano Paredes y Arrillaga, in office only 1845–46, responded by declaring the country in a state of defensive war because of hostilities "begun by the United States of America." After Mexican troops killed fourteen Americans on territory they considered their own, President Polk informed the US Congress that "American blood had been spilled on American soil," and he asked for 50,000 volunteers and $10 million to "prosecute the existing war."[35]

In the United States, enthusiasm for the war was initially high, with war fervor fanned by passionate editorials in inexpensive urban "penny" newspapers. Essayist and journalist Walt Whitman, then editor of the Brooklyn newspaper *Daily Eagle*, declared, for example, that Mexico "must be thoroughly chastised." America's White men overwhelmingly agreed. Thousands of men hoping to volunteer were turned away when they found the new volunteer regiments already full. The 59,000 volunteers who ultimately fought alongside 27,000 members of the regular US Army left for Mexico with every expectation that their war service would be short and dramatic, with ample opportunity to distinguish themselves through masculine heroics. Many of them also expected to find romance in Mexico, a vision encouraged by dime novels and story papers that visualized the war as an "international race romance." Although the citizens of the United States felt little in common with the citizens of Mexico, an examination of the war reveals a number of similarities in the relationship between gender and war in both countries.[36] The US–Mexican War had the highest mortality rate of any American war, excepting the Civil War. Some 12,500 US soldiers perished, most from disease. The Mexican army was similar in overall numbers of troops to that of the United States, with 19,000 well-trained permanent troops and between 15,000 and 40,000 additional men conscripted or drawn from militia units. At least 25,000 Mexicans, including many civilians, died.[37]

In Mexico and the United States, much of the hard fighting was done by conscripts and regulars who failed to conform to masculine ideals of responsibility and citizenship. Enlisted men in the regular US Army were viewed with contempt by a nation that venerated independence and held a deep suspicion of standing armies. Soldiers were also subject to harsh physical punishment. As a result, army enlistment was the employment of last resort in the United States. The fact that 40 percent of enlisted men were recently arrived immigrants from Europe, many not yet naturalized, further damaged the army's social standing. Poor immigrants were demonized as lazy, profligate, and cowardly. Many native-born Americans questioned their ability to gain manly independence. Catholics were particularly demonized as effeminate and irrational. In short, immigrants appeared to threaten the masculine ideal of the soldier-citizen. In point of fact, many of these recent immigrants were puzzled by the idea of Manifest Destiny—the belief that settlement across the North American continent was a duty and destiny for the United States—and were less than fully committed to the war against Mexico. The US–Mexican War had the highest desertion rate of any US war, and many of those deserters were recent immigrants.[38]

Mexicans hardly thought better of their army conscripts. As in other parts of the Americas, to have honor, to be an *hombre de bien*, was viewed as essentially incompatible with service in the regular army. As Peter Beattie has noted about the nineteenth-century Brazilian army, "In some ways, the barracks were a male equivalent of the bordello; both attempted to distance 'dangerous' male and female 'loners' from 'honorable' family households."[39] The state directives in Mexico for assembling an army offered heavily gendered critiques of the masculinity of the future soldiers. Along with "criminals," men forced into the army were to be drawn from the population of "those that frequent taverns or bordellos, loafers, professional gamblers, men living with women they are not married to, married men who mistreat their wives, men who do not fulfill family obligations, incorrigible sons."[40] Married men, particularly fathers with children, were to be exempted. Conscription was itself a means to enforce gender norms, with recruits largely drawn from the ranks of those who had failed to fulfill their expected roles as "male providers."[41]

As Peter Guardino has shown, both countries ignored the contributions of the regular or conscripted soldiers while publicly celebrating the manhood of the more elite units (volunteers in the United States and the National Guard in Mexico) that did relatively little hard fighting. These men refused to be subjected to corporal punishment. They were praised as the model of citizen-soldiers who sacrificed for the good of the nation. Indeed, volunteering to fight against Mexico was grounds for a future political career in the United States, a nation that, while fearing a standing army, has also drawn the bulk of its political leaders from the ranks of citizen-soldiers since the time of the American Revolutionary War (1775–83), most notably the first US president (from 1789 to 1797) and former commander in chief of the Continental army, George Washington.[42]

Tens of thousands of American men volunteered for war in 1846/47, intent on demonstrating masculine bravery in hand-to-hand combat. Mexicans were fighting to protect their homes and families. But American volunteers, inspired to a large degree by racism, envisioned Mexico as a land of cowardly men and beautiful, easily seduced women. Yet war proved profoundly disappointing to most of these volunteers. Opportunities for organized combat were rare, and women were less welcoming of their advances than they hoped. Men were far more likely to die from disease in unsanitary camps than in battle. And with the exception of the highly celebrated Battle of Buena Vista (February 1847), there was little hand-to-hand combat. Instead, battles were tests of artillery, and US military dominance from start to finish was in large part attributable to vastly superior American artillery.[43] Volunteers engaged in depredations against civilians, including plunder, rape, and murder, which shocked their commanding officers. Ironically, enlisted soldiers, although demeaned as unmanly, were far less likely to turn on the innocent than the unregulated volunteers. When word of these atrocities made it back to the United States, citizens worried that the virtue of their young men was being destroyed by service in Mexico, that they would become unfit to return to proper society. This gender critique became a key component of the antiwar movement.[44]

While few American women participated in the war in Mexico, some openly protested the war in newspaper editorials, and many more petitioned the US Congress to bring the war to a close.[45] Mexican women, by contrast, played a major role in supporting the armies, in this as in other nineteenth-century conflicts. As camp followers and auxiliaries on the front, they were largely responsible for cooking, laundry work, caring for the sick and wounded, and, in many cases, actively fighting. The figure of the female soldier took on outsized importance to both Mexicans and Americans. For Mexico, the heroic female soldier represented the extent of the nation's rejection of invasion, while figures like the "Maid of Monterrey," serving water to injured soldiers of all uniforms on the battlefield, helped humanize the invasion of a neighboring republic for US soldiers.[46] Cross-dressed female Mexican soldiers who fell in love with American volunteers were a common narrative device in cheap US dime novels published during the war. These international romances, which almost always resulted in marriages, helped convince American readers that the annexation of Mexican territory was natural and welcome to the seemingly effeminate Mexican nation as to the manly United States.[47] These tropes would be repeated in the 1850s, as American filibusters, or private armies, invaded Latin America and the Caribbean intent on annexing new lands to the United States. Visions of martial manhood and willing women not only drove men to invade countries with which the United States was at peace, but also led many more back home to support their illegal actions as the proper use of power by a "potent" young nation like the United States.[48]

Nation, Home, and Gender in the American Civil War

The mid-nineteenth century's deadliest war of nationalism was the American Civil War, which resulted in the deaths of between 660,000 and 850,000 Americans, or at least 2.5 percent of the overall US population. Roughly 2.1 million Northerners and 880,000 Southerners fought in the war. Nearly a quarter of the North's soldiers were immigrants, and the vast majority on both sides volunteered for the war. Best estimates are that 6 percent of Northern soldiers were conscripted and perhaps 12 percent of the South's soldiers.[49] When seven Southern states of the thirty-four US states seceded in January 1861, they did so out of profoundly conservative motives. The citizens of the South hoped to keep their "traditional" way of life intact, complete with slavery, plantation agriculture, and patriarchal households where men of all classes held greater levels of authority over wives and children than in Northern states. Indeed, one reason why nonslaveholding Whites supported secession just as vigorously as did slaveholders was because they understood their own households as analogous to plantations, realms where their authority was absolute. Gender was just one aspect of American life transformed by this conflict.[50]

The Northerners and Southerners who volunteered to fight were both convinced that their opponents were less manly than themselves, and most were intent on winning honor through hand-to-hand combat. Without question, men believed that service in the war would prove their manhood. For no group was this more true than for African Americans, who lobbied the Union government tirelessly during the first two years of the war for the right to bear arms against the enemy.[51] They were not only motivated by the desire to destroy slavery, but also recognized that battle offered a singular opportunity to prove their equality. "Let the black man get upon his person the brass letters 'U.S.,'" Frederick Douglass, the African American abolitionist and social reformer and a tireless promoter of Black enlistment wrote, "and there is no power on earth which can deny that he has earned the right to citizenship in the United States."[52] Given the importance of military service for the construction of masculinity and citizenship rights, it is perhaps not surprising that there was widespread resistance to arming Black men. But in 1862, the US Congress repealed a 1792 law barring Black men from the military and passed a confiscation act enabling President Abraham Lincoln to employ freedmen to fight the South. The Confederacy threatened to execute any Black soldier they captured, so risks for Black soldiers were particularly high; nonetheless, roughly 180,000 African Americans served in the Union army during the war.[53]

While many White soldiers gained a new level of respect for their Black colleagues, racism was not ameliorated in the North as a result of Black soldiering. In 1863, working-class New Yorkers rioted in response to laws drafting men into military service. The mostly Irish rioters resented that wealthy men could buy exemption from service, while Black men were excluded because they were not citizens. This left the poor to fight. Many immigrants had only recently left Europe, and rather than look to war to prove their manhood, they saw freed slaves as potential competition for jobs. Rioters turned against Black residents of the city in what quickly escalated into the worst race war in the country's history. At least 120 civilians were killed, including 11 Black men who were lynched during the rioting.[54]

The Draft Riots make it clear that not all Northern men saw war as a crucial test of manhood. But most soldiers, both Black and White, emerged from the war with a new-found conviction about their masculine virtues. This does not mean that war remotely conformed to their expectations. As in the US–Mexican War, the reality of warfare with heavy artillery and the increasing usage of the Union Gatling gun, an early rapid-fire machine gun, made a mockery of their early dreams of bravery proven through hand-to-hand combat. Most soldiers found conflict profoundly alienating, and a new ideal of courage emerged over the course of the war, one grounded in the ability to survive, rather than the nerve to face a combatant without flinching.[55]

Women were hardly passive bystanders to the US Civil War. Over four hundred women disguised themselves as men and fought for either the North or the South. A few women gained notoriety as spies, and many others did this work without discovery.[56] But far more significant was the work done by women from both sides, sewing uniforms and supplying troops. Some 200,000 Northern women volunteered in relief agencies that sent food, medicine, and clothing to the front. Southern women produced the majority of clothing worn by Confederate soldiers. This work fell within the bounds of prewar ideals of feminine labor, but as the war drew on, White women on both sides were forced to reconsider their own expectations about women's work and proper female behavior. Northern White women found new economic opportunities during the war, as the absence of male workers opened up over 100,000 jobs, including in federal bureaus that hired women as clerks. Women flocked to work as nurses and teachers when men left for the front, and these were jobs that they as a sex retained as "women's work" after war's end.[57]

For Southern White women, the experience was far more dramatic. At the start of the war, both Southern White men and women shared a belief that women should be kept insulated from the war. Yet, with war all around them, that was clearly impossible. While rape of White women was limited, Black women were frequent rape victims. With men away, White women took on virtually all the jobs previously reserved for men, including overseeing slaves and running businesses, as well as processing and marketing crops. Absent soldiers came to realize that economic success at home was in the hands of their wives, sisters, and daughters. As they relinquished control over work previously deemed unsuitable for the female sex, they undermined the conservative ideology that led to war in the first place.[58]

Southern women also became politically active. Not only were elite White women the key creators of the ideology of Confederate nationalism, but also ordinary White women were increasingly likely to contact government officials as the war went on, demanding their assistance in coping with the absence of their male relatives and the material hardships of war. Confederate mobilization forged for White Southern women "a radically changed and far more direct relationship to the state."[59] Women were also an integral part of the war of occupation. They were active, responsive, and the critical bottom rail in the war of occupation within the larger Civil War. In New Orleans, for example, Southern women continued to protest the occupation of New Orleans after Major General Benjamin Butler of the Union army famously attempted to stifle dissent by comparing protesting women to prostitutes. In most cases, however, Southern White women did not long for or even welcome this expanded sphere of influence, which they had to fill out because of the requirements of war. As Stephanie McCurry writes in her 2010 study, *Confederate Reckoning: Power and Politics in the Civil War South*, "It was not so much that White women emerged incisively out of the recesses of the household into public life during the war as that the state came barging in their front door, catapulting them into a relationship they had never sought but could hardly refuse."[60] Indeed, this development can be observed elsewhere during wars based on mass armies for which states mobilized with universal conscription, such as in Europe already during the French Revolutionary and Napoleonic Wars (1792–1815).[61]

Among the many adjustments both sides needed to make after the US Civil War were ones of gender. White husbands and wives hoped to recreate the prewar patriarchal gender order. This desire was shared by many of the newly freed African American men and women, who reunited with lost partners, legally married, and thus were folded into "civilized" society along state-sanctioned lines. The ideal of these households was one of middle-class domesticity, with a husband firmly in the public sphere earning money and the wife at home governing the household.[62] While most White women willingly surrendered their paid employment and returned to the home, the very limited financial opportunities for freedmen in the South meant that most Black women had no such option. Regardless of their wishes, they had to continue to work outside the home.

Wartime military service led some Black men to expect increased respect by Whites, as well as the prerogative of maintaining a patriarchal household, but racism limited the fulfillment of both those desires. Black veterans in the North gained little credit among Whites as a result of their service, while in the South Black veterans found themselves singled out by White men who believed their status was threatened by the freedom of a group once clearly beneath them. Southern White men and women were unwilling to extend their definition of manhood to Black men or women, and because military service was so closely aligned with citizenship, Black veterans were singled out for abuse. Whether legally married or not, Black women in the South continued to be subject to widespread abuse by White men.[63]

As husbands and wives renegotiated their postwar expectations and responsibilities for one another, so too did women renegotiate their relationships to the state. The federal government was the nation's largest employer of Northern women during the war. After the war, some of these women approached President Lincoln in letters. One was a resident of Macon County, Illinois, who wrote in September 1861, "Haven't we sent our Father; our Brothers, Our dear Husbands to support you?" If women "lent their support to the government," she reasoned, "did it not then mean that the government must be accountable to its women?" "We did look forward to a speedy termination of the war . . . but now what can we expect?"[64] The fact that women petitioned the state for pensions for their husbands and families reveals that in the North, as in the South, war led White women into the public sphere.

The key issue of sectional reconciliation had a gendered component as well. In the spring of 1867, widespread famine was predicted across the Southern landscape devastated by war. But Northern resentment against the active role that Southern women played during secession and war was so fierce that it fostered opposition against any help. The former Union general Benjamin Butler suggested as a Republican congressman after the war that the South's White women "who stood by and viewed without compassion the miseries endured by our noble soldiers" deserved to "experience a little starvation, themselves."[65] But the Congress decided differently; it passed a famine relief bill during the spring of 1867. Judith Giesberg argues that this resolution was a necessary step in reconciliation. By reinventing the federal government as a "paternal provider," Congress was able to bring Southern women into a relationship of dependency to the state. In its refusal to exact vengeance against Southern White women, the US Congress helped renormalize gender relations under the mantle of a new paternalism, which helped the Northern public forget the extent to which Southern women were active war participants.[66]

Yet unlike in the US–Mexican War of the 1840s, the experiences of the American Civil War were difficult for society to forget. The latter war also brought long-term changes to gender norms and gender relations in the United States. As in South America, the end of war brought with it a hardening of moral standards, particularly regarding female sexuality. Exposure to pornography and prostitution during the war led veteran and US Postal Inspector Anthony Comstock on a moral crusade that ultimately resulted in an 1873 federal ban on all "obscene literature," including educational texts about human reproduction and birth control.[67]

Confederate efforts to maintain patriarchy were only relatively more successful than their efforts to maintain slavery. Despite the fact that most women willingly returned to positions of subservience in their households after the war, women in both the North and the South emerged from this lengthy conflict with new skills and an appreciation of their capabilities. Although most Southern White women voluntarily embraced subservience, this did little to offset the feeling of inadequacy among White men faced with newly enfranchised freedmen.[68] Nevertheless, the South's reigning ideology of martial manhood was not banished: violent oppression became a fact of life for the South's African American freedmen and freedwomen, who, particularly after the political "redemption" of the South by the Democratic Party in the 1877, were terrorized, beaten, and murdered by paramilitary groups including the Ku Klux Klan. Southern White men supported violence against the Black population at the same time that they consented to reunification with their "brothers" in the North.[69]

But with the victory of North over South, more restrained ideals of manhood, grounded in success in business and family, took on new salience and power nationally. Ironically, many Northern veterans struggled to live up to Gilded Age standards of manhood. They believed their military sacrifice entitled them to respect and honor, but found themselves held in contempt by a nation that no longer considered martial achievement a standard of masculine virtue. Martial practices never completely disappeared from the North, but they would not be fully embraced by American society again until the wars of the late 1890s.[70]

CONCLUSION

Participants in the Wars of Nation-Building and Nation-Keeping in North, Central, and South America during the middle decades of the nineteenth century understood their conflicts in explicitly gendered terms. Men conceptualized war as an opportunity to prove the masculine virtue of both themselves and their nations. Whether women participated in these conflicts as combatants or camp followers, on the home front or as supportive observers, warfare opened up new opportunities. In the short term, many of these changes appeared to undermine patriarchy. But with a few important exceptions, such as Northern women who ended the Civil War with a reputation as competent nurses and teachers, those opportunities were of limited duration, and patriarchy was reestablished soon after the return of peace.

Despite insights provided by several decades of scholarship into the relationship between gender and war in the Americas in the mid-nineteenth century, there is still a great deal to learn. Transnational studies, like Peter Guardino's examination of manhood during the US–Mexican War, offer opportunities to evaluate how gender norms travel during and between wars.[71] As of yet, we know very little about the role of gender in America's nearly ceaseless frontier wars with Native Americans. It would be particularly worthwhile to consider how the gender dynamics of the American Civil War related to the wars on Native Americans during the 1860s and 1870s. To some extent, these wars were continuous with the Civil War; that is, they were part of the Civil War. In Colorado and New Mexico, for example, Colonel John Chivington led Union soldiers against Confederates and Native Americans, including the infamous 1864 massacre of some 150 Cheyenne and Arapaho noncombatants (mostly women, children, and elderly) at Sand Creek.[72]

Furthermore, much of the literature about the role of women in war, particularly in Latin America, is still engaged in recapturing heroic stories, rather than documenting the full scope of behavior, including disreputable activities like prostitution and participation in the underground economy.[73] Finally, it is worth asking how the manhood of those who stayed home from war differed from that of combatants. Deeper investigation into these questions holds the promise of uncovering new insights into gender and warfare in the Americas.

NOTES

1. Some of the best general histories of the US–Mexican War include Peter Guardino, *The Dead March: A History of the Mexican-American War* (Cambridge, MA: Harvard University Press, 2017); Amy S. Greenberg, *A Wicked War: Polk, Clay, Lincoln and the 1846 U.S. Invasion of Mexico* (New York: Alfred A. Knopf, 2012); Josefina Zoraida Vázquez, *México al tiempo de su guerra con Estados Unidos, 1846–1848* (Mexico City: Fondo de Cultura Económica, 1997); John S. D. Eisenhower, *So Far from God: The U.S. War with*

Mexico, 1846–1848 (Norman: University of Oklahoma Press, 2000); and Ernesto Chávez, *The U.S. War with Mexico: A Brief History with Documents* (Boston: St. Martin's Press, 2008).

The literature on the US Civil War is among the vastest in America history; more than sixty thousand books have been published on the topic. For an excellent recent introduction to major themes of the war, see Aaron Sheehan-Dean, ed., *A Companion to the U.S. Civil War*, 2 vols. (Chichester, UK: Wiley–Blackwell, 2014); and Hugh Tulloch, ed., *The Routledge Companion to the American Civil War Era* (London: Routledge 2006). Key treatments include James M. McPherson, *Battle Cry of Freedom: The Civil War Era* (New York: Oxford University Press, 1988); Philip Paluden, *A People's Contest: The Union and the Civil War, 1861–1865* (New York: Harper & Row, 1998); Allen C. Guelzo, *Fateful Lightning: A New History of the Civil War and Reconstruction* (New York: Oxford University Press, 2012); and Jean Baker et al., *The Civil War and Reconstruction* (New York: W. W. Norton, 2000).

2. This pattern is evident in both North and South American wars during this period. See, for example, Peter Guardino, "Gender, Soldiering, and Citizenship in the Mexican–American War of 1846–1848," *American Historical Review* 119, no. 1 (2014): 23–46; Amy S. Greenberg, *Manifest Manhood and the Antebellum American Empire* (Cambridge: Cambridge University Press, 2005); Catherine Davies et al., eds., *South American Independence: Gender, Politics, Text* (Liverpool: Liverpool University Press, 2006), 21–23; Sarah Chambers, *From Subjects to Citizens: Honor, Gender, and Politics in Arequipa, Peru* (University Park: Pennsylvania State University Press, 1999); Brian Craig Miller, "Manhood," in Sheehan-Dean, *Companion*, 2:795–810; and Ana María Alonso, *Thread of Blood: Colonialism, Revolution, and Gender on Mexico's Northern Frontier* (Tucson: University of Arizona Press, 1995).

3. Gerald F. Linderman, *Embattled Courage: The Experience of Combat in the American Civil War* (New York: Free Press, 1987); 240–65; Davies, *South American Independence*, 269; Chambers, *Subjects to Citizens*, 247–54; Greenberg, *Manifest Manhood*, 274–76.

4. Quote in Arlene Díaz, *Female Citizens, Patriarchs, and the Law in Venezuela, 1786–1904* (Lincoln: University of Nebraska Press, 2004), 212. See also Drew Gilpin Faust, *Mothers of Invention: Women in the Slaveholding South in the American Civil War* (Chapel Hill: University of North Carolina Press, 1996), 244–53; Davies, *South American Independence*, 17–18, 268–70; and Karen Racine, "Latin American Independence," *Oxford Bibliographies*, November 21, 2012, accessed May 10, 2016, http://www.oxfordbibliographies.com/view/document/obo-9780199766581/obo-9780199766581-0011.xml.

5. Evelyn Cherpak, "The Participation of Women in the Independence Movement in Gran Colombia, 1780–1830," in *Latin American Women: Historical Perspectives*, ed. Asunción Lavrin (Westport, CT: Greenwood Press, 1978): 219–34; and Nicola Beisel, *Imperiled Innocents: Anthony Comstock and Family Reproduction in Victorian America* (Princeton, NJ: Princeton University Press, 1997), 37.

6. See Racine, "Latin American Independence"; Claire Brewster, "Women and the Spanish–American Wars of Independence: An Overview," in "Latin America: History, War, and Independence," ed. Catherine Davies, special issue, *Feminist Review* 79 (2005): 20–35.

7. Important studies of women in postrevolutionary Latin America include Davies, *South American Independence*; Chambers, *Subjects to Citizens*; Cherpak, "Independence Movement"; Díaz, *Female Citizens*, 120; Deborah E. Kanter, *Hijos del Pueblo: Gender, Family, and Community in Rural Mexico, 1730–1850* (Austin: University of Texas, 2008);

Sonia Salazar Garcés and Alexandra Sevilla Naranjo, *Mujeres de la revolución de Quito* (Quito, Ecuador: Fondo de Salvamento del Patrimonio Cultural, 2009).

8. The role of manhood in the Paraguayan War has yet to be explored. On women in the Paraguayan War, see Olinda Massare de Kostianovsky, *La mujer paraguaya: su participación en la Guerra Grande* (Asunción: Escuela Técnica Salesiana, 1970); Barbara J. Ganson, "Following Their Children into Battle: Women at War in Paraguay, 1864–1870," *The Americas* 46, no. 3 (1990): 335–71; Barbara Potthast, "Protagonists, Victims, and Heroes: Paraguayan Women during the 'Great War,'" in *I Die with My Country: Perspectives on the Paraguayan War, 1864–1870*, ed. Hendrik Kraay and Thomas Whigham (Lincoln: University of Nebraska Press, 2004), 44–66. The latter two sources argue that traditional gender roles did not fundamentally change in Paraguay, although the war killed the majority of the country's men.

9. See Judith Giesberg, "Women," in Sheehan-Dean, *Companion*, 2:779–94. An earlier but still strong treatment is Drew Gilpin Faust, "'Ours as Well as That of Men': Women and Gender in the Civil War," in *Writing the Civil War: The Quest to Understand*, ed. James McPherson and William Cooper Jr. (Columbia: University of South Carolina Press, 1998), 228–40. The earliest extended celebration of women's work in the war is Frank Moore, *Women of the War: Their Heroism and Self-Sacrifice* (Hartford, CT: S. S. Scranton, 1866). A key example of celebratory centennial history is Mary Elizabeth Massey, *Bonnet Brigades* (New York: Alfred A. Knopf, 1966).

10. Key recent works on women in the American Civil War include Judith Giesberg, *Army at Home: Women and the Civil War on the Northern Home Front* (Chapel Hill: University of North Carolina Press, 2009); LeeAnn Whites and Alecia P. Long, eds., *Occupied Women: Gender, Military Occupation, and the American Civil War* (Baton Rouge: Louisiana State University Press, 2009); Stephanie McCurry, *Confederate Reckoning: Power and Politics in the Civil War South* (Cambridge, MA: Harvard University Press, 2010); and Faust, *Mothers of Invention*.

11. Karen Abbott, *Liar, Temptress, Soldier, Spy: Four Women Undercover in the Civil War* (New York: Harper & Row, 2014). Elizabeth D. Leonard, *All the Daring of the Soldier: Women of the Civil War Armies* (New York: W. W. Norton, 1999) offers a far more reliable account of female soldiering. Important studies of the home front include Amy Murrell Taylor, *Embattled Freedom: Journeys Through the Civil War's Slave Refugee Camps* (Chapel Hill: University of North Carolina Press, 2018); Lesley Schwalm, *A Hard Fight for We: Women's Transition from Slavery to Freedom in South Carolina* (Urbana: University of Illinois Press, 1997); Thavolia Glymph, *Out of the House of Bondage: The Transformation of the Plantation Household* (Cambridge: Cambridge University Press, 2008); and Kate Masur, *An Example for All the Land: Emancipation and the Struggle over Equality in Washington, D.C.* (Chapel Hill: University of North Carolina Press, 2010). Important early works on the experience of African American women in the transition from slavery to freedom include Deborah Gray White, *Ar'n't I a Woman? Female Slaves in the Plantation South* (New York: W. W. Norton, 1985); and Jacqueline Jones, *Labor of Love, Labor of Sorrow: Black Women, Work, and the Family, from Slavery to the Present* (New York: Basic Books, 1985).

12. Bertram Wyatt-Brown, *Southern Honor: Ethics and Behavior in the Old South* (New York: Oxford University Press, 1982); and Miller, "Manhood," 795–810.

13. Key works on masculinity in the Civil War include Linderman, *Embattled Courage*; James McPherson, *For Cause and Comrades: Why Men Fought in the Civil War* (New York:

Oxford University Press, 1997); Lorien Foote, *The Gentlemen and the Roughs: Manhood, Honor, and Violence in the Union Army* (New York: New York University Press, 2010); Nina Silber, *Gender and the Sectional Conflict* (Chapel Hill: University of North Carolina Press, 2008); LeeAnn Whites, *The Civil War as a Crisis of Gender: Augusta, Georgia, 1860–1890* (Athens, GA: University of Georgia Press, 1995); Reid Mitchell, *The Vacant Chair: The Northern Soldier Leaves Home* (New York: Oxford University Press, 1993); and Craig Thompson Friend and Lorri Glover, eds. *Southern Manhood: Perspectives on Masculinity in the Old South* (Athens, GA: University of Georgia Press, 2004). On race and masculinity, see Stephanie McCurry, *Masters of Small Worlds: Yeoman Households, Gender Relations and the Political Culture of the Antebellum South Carolina Low Country* (Oxford: Oxford University Press, 1995); and Jim Cullen, " 'I's a Man Now': Gender and African American Men," in *Divided Houses: Gender and the Civil War*, ed. Catherine Clinton and Nina Silber (New York: Oxford University Press, 1992), 76–91.

14. Key works on the gender history of the US–Mexican War include Guardino, "Gender, Soldiering"; and Greenberg, *Manifest Manhood*; and Shelley Streeby, *American Sensations: Class, Empire, and the Production of Popular Culture* (Berkeley: University of California Press, 2002). On Mexico's female soldiers, see Elizabeth Salas, *Soldaderas in the Mexican Military: Myth and History* (Austin: University of Texas Press, 1990).

15. On the Second Seminole War, see Laurel Clark Shire, "Turning Sufferers into Settlers: Gender, Welfare, and National Expansion in Frontier Florida," *Journal of the Early Republic* 33, no. 3 (2013): 489–521; and Clark, "The Rights of a Florida Wife: Slavery, U.S. Expansion and Married Women's Property Law," *Journal of Women's History* 22, no. 4 (2010): 39–63. Gender and war with Indigenous people on Mexico's northern frontier is covered in Alonso, *Thread of Blood*.

16. Stig Förster and Jörg Nagler, "Introduction," in *On the Road to Total War: The American Civil War and the German Wars of Unification*, ed. Stig Förster and Jörg Nagler (London: Cambridge University Press, 1997), 4–15.

17. Cherpak, "Independence Movement," 219–34; Davies, *South American Independence*, 268–70. See also the chapter by Catherine Davies on "War, Gender, and Society in Late Colonial and Revolutionary Spanish America" in this handbook.

18. Díaz, *Female Citizens*, 120.

19. Matthew Brown, *Adventuring through Spanish Colonies: Simón Bolívar, Foreign Mercenaries and the Birth of New Nations* (Liverpool: Liverpool University Press, 2006).

20. Díaz, *Female Citizens*, 174.

21. Ibid., 168–70, 211–12.

22. Chambers, *Subjects to Citizens*, 5.

23. Ibid.

24. Ibid., 201–2.

25. Cherpak, "Independence Movement," 219–22.

26. See the chapter by Thomas Cardoza and Karen Hagemann on "History and Memory of Army Women and Female Soldiers, 1770s–1870s" in this handbook.

27. Chambers, *Subjects to Citizens*, 208; Racine "Latin American Independence." See also Ganson, "Following Their Children," 356–58, 365.

28. See the chapter by Stefan Dudink on "Citizenship, Mass Mobilization, and Masculinity in a Transatlantic Perspective, 1770s–1870s" in this handbook; as well as Dudink et al., eds., *Masculinities in Politics and War: Gendering Modern History* (Manchester: Manchester University Press, 2004), 3–40; Dudink et al., eds., *Representing Masculinity: Citizenship in*

Modern Western Culture (Basingstoke: Palgrave Macmillan, 2008), 25–150; and Karen Hagemann et al., eds., *Gender, War, and Politics: Transatlantic Perspectives, 1775–1830* (Basingstoke: Palgrave Macmillan, 2010), 93–126.

29. See Dominique Godineau, *The Women of Paris and Their French Revolution* (Berkeley: University of California Press, 1998).

30. Quoted in Davies, *South American Independence*, 269; Chambers, *Subjects to Citizens*, 253.

31. Alonso, *Thread of Blood*.

32. An overview of the conflict provide, Chris Leuchars, *To the Bitter End: Paraguay and the War of the Triple Alliance* (Westport, CT: Greenwood Press, 2002); and Thomas Whigham, *The Paraguayan War* (Lincoln: University of Nebraska Press, 2002).

33. Quoted in Ganson, "Following Their Children," 368; and Potthast, "Protagonists," 44–60.

34. Potthast, "Protagonists," 56; and Ganson, "Following Their Children," 368–71.

35. Clary, *Eagles and Empire*, 98–100; and Amy S. Greenberg, *Manifest Destiny and American Territorial Expansion: A Brief History with Documents* (Boston: St. Martin's Press, 2012), 23–26.

36. "War with Mexico," Brooklyn *Daily Eagle*, May 11, 1846; Greenberg, *A Wicked War*, 96, 130; and Streeby, *American Sensations*, 81–101.

37. Greenberg, *A Wicked War*, 268.

38. Edward M. Coffman, *The Old Army: A Portrait of the American Army in Peacetime, 1784–1898* (New York: Oxford University Press, 1986), 119–20; Paul Foos, *A Short, Offhand Killing Affair: Soldiers and Social Conflict during the Mexican-American War* (Chapel Hill: University of North Carolina Press, 2002), 22–23, 32–33; and Greenberg, *A Wicked War*, 130.

39. Peter Beattie, *The Tribute of Blood: Army, Honor, Race and Nation in Brazil, 1864–1945* (Durham, NC: Duke University Press, 2001), 9.

40. Quoted in José Antonio Serrano Ortega, *El contingente de sangre: Los gobiernos estatales y departamentales y los métodos de reclutamiento del ejército permanente mexicano, 1824–1844,* (Mexico City: Instituto Nacional de Antropología e Historia, 1993), 79–80; and Guardino, "Gender, Soldiering," 32.

41. Guardino, "Gender, Soldiering," 27.

42. Ibid.; and Greenberg, *A Wicked War*, 269. On the longer history of presidents and the military, see Alexander DeConde, *Presidential Machismo: Executive Authority, Military Intervention, and Foreign Relations* (Boston: Northeastern University Press, 2000).

43. Greenberg, *A Wicked War*, 114–61.

44. Ibid., 131–35, 232–37.

45. Nancy Isenberg, *Sex and Citizenship in Antebellum America* (Chapel Hill: University of North Carolina Press, 1998), 103–54; and Greenberg, *A Wicked War*, 198–99.

46. Florencia E. Mallon, *Peasant and Nation: The Making of Postcolonial Mexico and Peru* (Berkeley: University of California Press, 1995), 76–77, 472; Salas, *Soldaderas*, 28–35; Isenberg, *Sex and Citizenship*, 141; and Robert W. Johannsen, *To the Halls of the Montezumas: The Mexican War in the American Imagination* (New York: Oxford, 1985), 137–38.

47. Streeby, *American Sensations*, 102–38.

48. Greenberg, *Manifest Manhood*; and Streeby, *American Sensations*.

49. Thomas Leonard Livermore, *Numbers and Losses in the Civil War in America, 1861–1865* (Boston: Houghton, Mifflin, 1901), 1–2, 35; McPherson, *Battle Cry*, 606; and Andre M. Fleche, "African-American Soldiering," in Sheehan-Dean, *Companion*, 1:297–98.

50. McCurry, *Masters*.

51. Cullen, "I's a Man," 78–79.
52. Ibid., 81.
53. Fleche, "African-American Soldiering," 297–315.
54. Iver Bernstein, *The New York City Draft Riots: Their Significance for American Society and Politics in the Age of the Civil War* (Oxford: Oxford University Press, 1990).
55. Linderman, *Embattled Courage*.
56. See Cardoza and Hagemann, "History and Memory" in this handbook.
57. William J. Barney, *The Oxford Encyclopedia of the Civil War* (Oxford: Oxford University Press, 2011), 347–50.
58. Faust, *Mothers of Invention*.
59. McCurry, *Confederate Reckoning*, 88.
60. Ibid., 156; Whites and Long, *Occupied Women*.
61. See Hagemann, *Gender, War and Politics*, esp. 1–40.
62. Katherine M. Franke, "Becoming a Citizen: Reconstruction Era Regulation of African American Marriages," *Yale Journal of Law and the Humanities* 11, no. 2 (1999): 251–310.
63. Cullen, "I's a Man," 76–91; and Catherine Clinton, "Reconstructing Freewomen," in Clinton and Silber, *Divided Houses*, 306–19.
64. Nina Silber, *Daughters of the Union: Northern Women Fight the Civil War* (Cambridge, MA: Harvard University Press, 2005), 133.
65. Quoted in Judith Giesberg, "Epilogue," in Whites and Long, *Occupied Women*, 185.
66. Giesberg, "Epilogue," 186.
67. Beisel, *Imperiled Innocents*, 37.
68. Faust, *Mothers of Invention*, 244–52.
69. David W. Blight, *Race and Reunion: The Civil War in American Memory* (Cambridge, MA: Harvard University Press, 2001), 11, 108–14.
70. Greenberg, *Manifest Manhood*, 275; Foote, *Gentlemen*, 177–78; and Nina Silber, *The Romance of Reunion: Northerners and the South, 1865–1900* (Chapel Hill: University of North Carolina Press, 1993).
71. Guardino, *The Dead March*.
72. The best work on this topic thus far is Shire, "Turning Sufferers"; and Clark, "Rights of a Florida Wife." On the 1860s wars against Native Americans, see Ari Kelman, *A Misplaced Massacre: Struggling over the Memory of Sand Creek* (Cambridge, MA: Harvard University Press, 2013), 3–43; and Susan Lee Johnson, *Roaring Camp: The Social World of the California Gold Rush* (New York: W. W. Norton, 2000).
73. See, for example, Salazar Garcés and Sevilla Naranjo, *Mujeres*.

SELECT BIBLIOGRAPHY

Alonso, Ana María. *Thread of Blood: Colonialism, Revolution, and Gender on Mexico's Northern Frontier.* Tucson: University of Arizona Press, 1995.

Beattie, Peter M. *The Tribute of Blood: Army, Honor, Race and Nation in Brazil, 1864–1945.* Durham, NC: Duke University Press, 2001.

Blanton, DeAnne, and Lauren M. Cook. *They Fought Like Demons: Women Soldiers in the American Civil War.* Baton Rouge: Louisiana State University Press, 2002.

Chambers, Sarah C. *Subjects to Citizens: Honor, Gender, and Politics in Arequipa, Peru, 1780–1854.* University Park: Pennsylvania State University Press, 1999.

Clinton, Catherine, and Nina Silber, eds. *Battle Scars: Gender and Sexuality in the American Civil War*. Oxford: Oxford University Press, 2006.

Davies, Catherine, Claire Brewster, and Hilary Owen, eds. *South American Independence: Gender, Politics, Text*. Liverpool: Liverpool University Press, 2006.

Faust, Drew Gilpin. *Mothers of Invention: Women of the Slaveholding South in the American Civil War*. Chapel Hill: University of North Carolina Press, 1996.

Foos, Paul. *A Short, Offhand Killing Affair: Soldiers and Social Conflict during the Mexican-American War*. Chapel Hill: University of North Carolina Press, 2002.

Foote, Lorien. *The Gentlemen and the Roughs: Violence, Honor, and Manhood in the Union Army*. New York: New York University Press, 2010.

Greenberg, Amy S. *Manifest Manhood and the Antebellum American Empire*. Cambridge: Cambridge University Press, 2005.

Greenberg, Amy S. *A Wicked War: Polk, Clay, Lincoln and the 1846 U.S. Invasion of Mexico*. New York: Alfred A. Knopf, 2012.

Guardino, Peter. "Gender, Soldiering, and Citizenship in the Mexican–American War of 1846-1848." *American Historical Review* 119, no. 1 (2014): 23–46.

Guardino, Peter. *The Dead March: A History of the Mexican-American War*. Cambridge, MA: Harvard University Press, 2017.

Harper, Judith E. *Women during the Civil War: An Encyclopedia*. London: Routledge, 2004.

Hugh Tulloch, ed. *The Routledge Companion to the American Civil War Era*. London: Routledge, 2006.

Mallon, Florencia E. *Peasant and Nation: The Making of Postcolonial Mexico and Peru*. Berkeley: University of California Press, 1995.

McCurry, Stephanie. *Confederate Reckoning: Power and Politics in the Civil War South*. Cambridge, MA: Harvard University Press, 2010.

McPherson, James M. *Battle Cry of Freedom: The Civil War Era*. New York: Oxford University Press, 1988.

Silber, Nina. *Gender and the Sectional Conflict*. Chapel Hill: University of North Carolina Press, 2008.

Taylor, Amy Murrell. *Embattled Freedom: Journeys Through the Civil War's Slave Refugee Camps*. Chapel Hill: University of North Carolina Press, 2018.

Vázquez, Josefina Zoraida. *México al tiempo de su guerra con Estados Unidos, 1846–1848*. Mexico City: Fondo de Cultura Económica, 1997.

Whites, LeeAnn. *Gender Matters: Civil War, Reconstruction, and the Making of the New South*. New York: Palgrave Macmillan, 2005.

CHAPTER 12

....

IMPERIAL CONQUEST, VIOLENT ENCOUNTERS, AND CHANGING GENDER RELATIONS IN COLONIAL WARFARE, 1830s–1910s

....

ANGELA WOOLLACOTT

FROM the 1830s to the 1910s, the contact zones of aggressively expanding colonialism were structured by violence in places ranging from the British settler colonies of Canada, Australia, and New Zealand to Crown colonies of various European empires, including British India, the Netherlands East Indies, and French Indochina. Because these colonies were carved out by warfare and conquest, European rule typically depended on the continued threat of violent suppression in the face of insurrections and uprisings that were common to colonial societies. The visible presence of troops, their continual availability to colonial regimes, and the widespread deployment of Indigenous men as soldiers and police all sustained the rule of colonizers. Colonial warfare was diffuse and chaotic in nature in both imperial expansion and the Indigenous resistance which was inevitably sparked by imperial invasions and gradual conquests of colonial territories.

European colonialism emerged in the late fifteenth century when European navigators began to explore and then claim other parts of the globe for their monarchs. In the early modern period, Spain, Portugal, and the Netherlands were the leading imperial powers, followed by Britain and France. By 1800, Europeans occupied or controlled one-third of the globe's land surface, and by 1870, this proportion had leapt to two-thirds. In 1913, the combined holdings of Britain, France, Germany, Italy, Belgium, the Netherlands, Denmark, Spain, and Portugal accounted for over 84 percent of the world. Britain alone ruled over a quarter of the earth's surface and a third of the world's population.[1] The period from approximately 1875 to 1914 is often called the *Age of Imperialism* or the *Age of Empire* because these decades witnessed the acceleration of the deliberate, competitive carving up of remaining territories between the imperial powers in their rush to maximize their own wealth and status vis-à-vis their competitors. Germany, Japan, and the United States joined the imperial race around the globe of the old Western empires like Britain, France, the Netherlands and Belgium, Portugal, and Spain and the Habsburg and Ottoman Empires.[2]

Between 1880 and 1914, most of the world outside Europe and the Americas (that is, Asia, Africa, and Oceania) was partitioned into territories under the formal rule or informal dominion of one or another of these imperial powers. There were no independent states left in the Pacific—it was completely divided between the British, French, Germans, Dutch, Americans, and Japanese. Between 1876 and 1915, about one-quarter of the globe's land surface was distributed or redistributed as colonies among a handful of states. Britain increased its territories by some 4 million square miles, France by around 3.5 million, Germany more than 1 million, and Belgium and Italy just under 1 million each. The United States acquired about 100,000 square miles, mostly from Spain through the Spanish–American War (1898), and Japan took about the same amount from China, Russia, and Korea.[3]

By the 1830s, then, European imperialism was deeply entrenched and already controlled much of the globe. The period between the 1830s and the 1910s is significant for the rapid expansion of the British and French Empires in particular and fierce interimperial rivalries, as well as the late rise of non-European empires. Nineteenth-century European empires shared common features, such as the crucial role of navies, the opening of trade beyond monopoly companies, the work of missionaries, and the spread of settler colonialism. But they differed also, including in the timing of the emancipation of slaves; the use and ending of convict transportation; labor, carceral, and administrative systems; and the rights and political representation of Indigenous people and colonials. Perhaps the empires' strongest connection was their mutual rivalry, which spurred their aggressive expansionism and resort to force.[4] Once the Napoleonic Wars (1803–15) had ended and internal European conflicts after the Congress of Vienna in 1814–15 were in hiatus, the spread of empires included vast migrations of people looking for a new life in the colonies. Many of these migrants came from Europe. Settler colonialism spread across extensive territories in Africa, Australasia, Canada, and the western United States. From the 1840s onward, a series of gold rushes spurred migrations around the Pacific Rim, including California, Australia, New Zealand, and regions of South America. Surges of new European settlers contributed to destabilization and resistance in colonies. At the same time, the colonies of direct rule, such as French Indochina and British India, relied on militarism and threat of violence and, indeed, also fought rebellions and anticolonial wars.[5]

Warfare was integral to imperial expansion, and historically contingent notions of gender were intertwined with it. From the late fifteenth century, European expeditions of exploration, merchant fleets, and naval forces all contributed to the territorial conquests and spread of Western empires. As recent scholarship on both the Atlantic and the Pacific worlds has delineated, relations onboard vessels in this expanding maritime world were structured by axes of naval authority as well as class and racial hierarchies, which also shaped changing relations of masculinity.[6] These relations between ranks of men were mediated by physical violence, including punishment by the lash. The high tide of European imperialism was linked to the ascendancy of Western industrialization, including mechanization, large-scale engineering projects, steamships, and railways. On land, imperial armies often relied on the support of Indigenous laborers for the engineering projects that supported their occupation, such as the construction of roads, bridges, telegraph lines, and railways. Colonized men (as well as in some instances male convicts) performed the menial and arduous labor for such projects, with European men, themselves divided by class, supervising and ordering them in hierarchical ranks of racialized manhood.

Changing relations of masculinity also included the diverse forms of male homosexuality under colonialism, including between colonizing men and interracial relations between colonizer and colonized. Some historians have seen European colonies as offering an "easy range of sexual opportunities," including homosexual relations available to colonizing men.[7] While travel also created opportunities of privacy for lesbian women, we know little about lesbian relations in the colonies other than among convicts.[8] For men, however, colonialism fostered expeditions, trading bases, and outposts where homosociality and homoeroticism flourished, and the military forces on which colonial rule depended spawned homosexual encounters. Historical research on male colonial homosexuality has shown its enormous variety: from exploitative relations for colonizers' gratification to those based on sentimentality, repression, or fantasy. It complicates our understanding of the war-related mission of the British imperialist T. E. Lawrence to free the Arabs from Ottoman rule, for example, to learn of his 1910s love affair with a young Arab man named Selim Ahmed or Dahoum.[9] Encampments of European armies stationed in colonies led to prostitution and concubinage among poor colonized boys, such as the *i diavoletti*, or "little devils," in the early twentieth-century Italian colony in Eritrea, who rented themselves out in ongoing relationships with Italian soldiers.[10]

Imperial armies recruited Indigenous soldiers through force and various other forms of inducement. European commanding officers and their European troops assumed superiority over Indigenous units, and Indigenous soldiers adapted traditional fighting skills and notions of manhood to new styles of warfare. Heroic manliness was associated with imperial conquest, since for both colonizers and Indigenous people manhood was measured at least in part by fighting skills and preparedness for violence. Indigenous men were employed as troops and police in colonies, occupying the lowest ranks and often compelled to carry out the most extreme violence of suppression.[11] Racial hierarchies within armed forces shaped military strategies as well as daily lives in and beyond army cantonments, including for the wives, partners, and children of soldiers, and for women and children forced into prostitution or concubinage. Women provided support services such as cooking and laundry for armies, both stationary and on the move. In troop towns, around camps, and in naval ports, prostitution was a staple means of earning money for women who lacked other choices. At the same time, rape was a common weapon of conquering forces and sometimes even their goal.

In recent decades, work in the fields of women's and gender history and the "new imperial history" has contributed to our understanding of the contingent historical relationship between gender and warfare in globally scattered contact zones. Among other insights, recent historical scholarship has called into question conceptual divisions between colonies of exploitation and direct rule, on the one hand, and settler colonies on the other. We are learning to see dynamics common to colonialism in various settings, including the ways in which warfare in settler colonies such as New Zealand and Australia should be recognized as such, even when the frontier armies were not composed of regular troops in Western-style uniform. James Belich, for example, has argued that the Maori, through their fortifications, military engineering, and battle tactics in the Waikato War (1863–64) on the North Island, presented such a formidable foe to the British that they subsequently drew lessons from them.[12] Elizabeth Vibert has suggested that fur traders and other early colonizing European men in North America were impressed by the hunting skills of Native American men, to the point that those skills became part of their benchmarks for masculine hunting and fighting prowess.[13]

War, militarism, and the threat of force shaped gender relations under colonialism.[14] In encounters between invading imperial armies and Indigenous defending forces around the world, some women became warriors. There were abundant instances of women joining the fray as soldiers or actively supporting troops in ways that challenged norms of femininity (though this would become much more widespread in the twentieth century, both in Western armed forces and in anticolonial liberation struggles).[15] In various colonies, female warriors' roles in colonial resistance led to subsequent mythologies of powerful women, including the rani (queen) of Jhansi, who fought the British during the Indian Rebellion (1857–58) and after whom a regiment of female soldiers would be named in World War II. The Rani of Jhansi Regiment was formed in 1943 as part of the Indian National Army to fight against the British for India's freedom.[16] In the province of Aceh in northern Sumatra, the anti-Dutch resistance warrior Cut Nyak Dhien gained prominence during the turn-of-the-twentieth-century struggles to preserve Aceh's autonomy. Despite the traditionally masculine gendering of the warrior in local Islamic culture, she later became an Indonesian national hero.[17]

The study of gender, warfare, and colonialism between the 1830s and the 1910s has thus traversed much ground and raised myriad questions. In the following, four themes will stand in the center: gendered violence and imperial conquest as manifested in the stories of rape and sexual assault found in captivity narratives; the representation of interracial sexual assault during the Indian Rebellion and in instances of settler frontier warfare; militarized prostitution associated with standing imperial armies, as well as militarized concubinage; and the relations between Western civilization, imperial conquest, and White masculinities.[18] These themes allow insight into the nexus between colonial warfare and gender systems in sites ranging from India to the Netherlands Indies and from Canada to Australia and New Zealand and thus a representative range of the contact zones of nineteenth- and early twentieth-century European colonialism.

GENDERED VIOLENCE AND IMPERIAL CONQUEST

European settler colonialism established itself in the sixteenth and seventeenth centuries, but it rapidly increased in scale from the late eighteenth century onward, surging in particular in the 1820s. The industrial revolution that began in Britain in the late eighteenth century and extended to various European countries and later the United States, the European population explosion, and the development of railways and later steamships all contributed to the spread of settlers westward in North America and across parts of the Southern Hemisphere. James Belich contends that in the century following the 1820s, there was a "settler revolution" in which massive flows of migrants spread the Anglophone world across the globe. Central to this were the approximately twelve million British migrants who moved to colonies in North America, Australia, New Zealand, and southern Africa. But the settler revolution also included the massive movement westward across the United States, especially between 1850 and 1920 when some ten million native-born Americans moved west.[19]

Despite imperial casuistry about colonial lands being "unoccupied" by Indigenous peoples, settler colonialism necessitated their removal in violent frontier encounters. Frontier warfare was widespread and often prolonged in the North American west, Africa, Australia, and New Zealand. Sexual conquest was a tool of colonial conquest, naturalized and unacknowledged as the violence it was. In settler colonies, rape and bartering for sexual services shaped daily life for Indigenous women and undermined traditional gender relations for the colonized. In the 1860s, for example, White male violence against First Nations women in British Columbia was justified through racialized assumptions of women's sexual immorality. Adele Perry notes that White male travelers in frontier British Columbia saw First Nations women as just part of their travel adventures. As the Canadian R. H. Alexander wrote in the journal of his 1862 overland trip from Canada to British Columbia, "We went through the bush after some Indian girls and had some great fun."[20] Sexual assault of Indigenous women fed into First Nations' resentment and resistance of White colonization.

Warfare—often consisting of killings followed by reprisals—occurred all over the Australian frontier, albeit at different times and in many locations. On the island of Tasmania, from its first convict settlement in Hobart in 1804, it was a grim story for the Indigenous people. Because the land in Tasmania was perceived as fertile and desirable, and because the scale of the island made it feasible, the settlers essentially rounded up or killed most of the Aboriginal people. Eventually known as the "Black War," this episode is thought to have ended by 1832.[21] In Victoria, the 1830s and 1840s saw the worst of the violence. In the northern reaches of New South Wales in what would in 1859 become the separate colony of Queensland, violent resistance by Aboriginal people and harsh, unequal reprisals by settlers occurred from the 1840s. It was common practice to force Aboriginal people from their lands or into a relationship of dependence on settlers.

In late nineteenth- and early twentieth-century Queensland, Aboriginal women were believed to constitute a majority of prostitutes beyond metropolitan Brisbane.[22] Blaming Aboriginal women's lack of morality and Aboriginal men's abuse of their women for women's prostitution served to obscure Aboriginal destitution, White sexual abuse of Aboriginal women, and the history of pervasive sexual assault stemming from the early period of frontier warfare. In the mid-nineteenth century, as the first British settlers took land by force, rape of Aboriginal women was widespread. Aboriginal resentment of such abuse was one trigger for the recurrent attacks and reprisals, the cycle of often-deadly skirmishes that constituted frontier warfare.[23]

Fears of interracial rape and miscegenation structured conceptions of White woman-hood, circulated globally, and justified instances of land grabbing in settler colonies as well as harsh repression of Indigenous men in many places. In western Canada in 1887, for example, allegations of Blackfoot sexual assaults on settler women bolstered calls for government limits on Indigenous peoples' freedom of movement.[24] In 1830s–40s Australia, sensational narratives of White women being taken captive by Indigenous men for lascivious purposes gained widespread currency, and they had the specific local effects of justifying repression of Aboriginal people. The first and probably most popular of these captivity narratives was sparked by the 1836 shipwreck of the *Stirling Castle* off the coast of southern Queensland on what is now Fraser Island. Captain James Fraser and other survivors eventually made it ashore, where they were taken in by the Ngulungbara, Badtjala, and Dulingbara groups. The captain died, but his wife, Eliza Fraser, survived. Several of the other survivors made it to another island, where they were able to contact British authorities.

A rescue party was sent, including a convict who had previously escaped from prison, lived on the island for six years, and learned a local language. Eliza Fraser's rescue involved an overnight trip during which the convict rescuer may have raped her, but there was no evidence of rape by an Indigenous man. Fraser was delivered to Moreton Bay, thence to Sydney, and finally returned to England, where she sold melodramatic accounts of her experiences to the press. Fraser's story took on a life of its own, circulating globally, including being given local settings such as North America, replete with tepees and Native Americans; the sensational version distorted actual events and featured innuendos of violent sexual assault of a White woman by Indigenous men.[25]

Thus, by 1840, when the White Woman of Gippsland narrative emerged from what is now a northeastern area in the state of Victoria, newspaper audiences were well primed. On December 28, 1840, Scottish settler Angus McMillan published in the *Sydney Herald* a report of an expedition he had recently undertaken to find a route from the Gippsland interior to the coast, a coastline that had been the site of several shipwrecks. He and his party startled a camp of Kurnai people who ran off, leaving behind various European goods. McMillan's detailed inventory of the abandoned objects included bloodstained clothing, a lock of a European woman's hair, and the body of a two-year-old White boy. McMillan's account concluded by noting that as the group ran off, one of the women constantly looked behind her while men brandishing spears drove them away. He concluded that she was a White woman captive, and thus was born the myth of the White Woman of Gippsland. No evidential basis for the White Woman has ever been discovered, despite three official search parties and a private expedition in the 1840s, discussion in the New South Wales Legislative Assembly, local and international newspaper reports, and, beginning in the 1870s, versions of the myth in fiction and poetry. These fabricated tales often rendered the White Woman as a sexual captive.[26]

As Kate Darian-Smith and Julie Carr have contended, the timing of the myth is key to understanding its ideological dimensions. Starting in 1839, British settlers invaded Gippsland to open it up as grazing country, and McMillan's account was central to this process of conquest by presenting frontier violence in the guise of rescuing the imagined woman captive. The bloodiness of the ensuing violence is inscribed in local place names, such as Butcher's Creek and Slaughterhouse Gully, and by 1847, it was clear that the Europeans had won. The myth of a sexually violated White woman was a weapon of war, which deployed contemporary notions of men's "honor" and role as protectors and served to justify land grabbing and the massacre of Kurnai people.[27] These sensationalized stories dramatized White women's supposed sexual vulnerability and Aboriginal men's imagined rapaciousness to mask the violence of settlers' dispossession of Indigenous people.

INTERRACIAL SEXUAL ASSAULT, THE INDIAN "MUTINY," AND FRONTIER WARFARE

In the seventeenth and eighteenth centuries, the British Empire depended on British trading interests in scattered locations around the world and the British colonies in the Americas. India was key: the expanding British presence in India had begun with mercantile interests in the seventeenth century, and Indian trade was lucrative while the British bases there were strategically located for further ventures into Asia and the Pacific. But Britain's position became complicated by the growing political and military involvements of the East India Company, which had a British royal charter for a monopoly on Indian trade. By the 1760s, the British simultaneously asserted their dominance over the Mughal rulers and the French East India Company with its colonies along the eastern coast of India, including Pondicherry. The Seven Years' War (1756–63) between the British and the French was fought in India in addition to the Americas, West Africa, the Philippines, and Europe, a result of the global rivalry between these two dominant European powers. The outcome was the extension of British interests in India, primarily in Bengal, though the French presence continued.[28]

By 1763, the British East India Company held important interests under lease or concession on the mainland of India and elsewhere, administered by so-called presidencies and supported by military force. Many of the soldiers in the British military forces were sepoys, Indians who served in the British military for money. In 1805, there were around 155,000 of them. No sepoy could rise through the ranks to attain commissioned status. Because the East India Company's army was such a large employer, this racial barrier was significant.[29]

Most of India had been brought under British control by the 1830s. The governor general lived in Bengal and ruled with the assistance of an executive council that excluded Indians. Bombay and Madras had their own governors, who were also British appointees. Nevertheless, the East India Company faced lingering problems of inefficiency and corruption. When its charter was due for renewal by the British government in 1833, the East India Company's control was considerably reduced. Importantly, it lost its monopoly over trade.[30]

Then, in a complete shock to the British, a major rebellion erupted in India's north in 1857—the events that became known as the "Indian Mutiny," a name now rejected in favor of either the Rebellion or the War of 1857–58 because *mutiny* implies disloyalty to legitimate rulers. The rebellion began when Indian soldiers at Meerut near Delhi revolted, killing their officers and all the other Britons they could find. They set fire to their cantonment and then marched on Delhi to proclaim the Mughal ruler the head of Hindustan (or India). When word of this revolt spread, similar uprisings against the British erupted in other parts of northern India.[31] While its roots were in Indian resentment of British presence and rule, the rebellion was largely sparked by the way that the British were running their army. The East India Company had organized its army, then consisting of about 250,000 men, mostly Indians, without any regard to Indian religious differences or cultural practices. These problems in the army were the specific causes of unrest, but the uprising was fueled by a deep resentment of British power and economic and political control in India—in short, antipathy toward British imperialism that spread well beyond the army.[32] It took two years of hard fighting for the British to completely quash the uprising and its ensuing rebellions.[33]

During and after the Indian Rebellion, a dominant British narrative emerged in which the rape and torture of Englishwomen was a key rhetorical device. These stories came to undergird violent, repressive measures by the Raj, the colonial rule of the British Empire in India between 1858 and 1947, both at the time and in subsequent decades. We know from the work of scholars such as Jenny Sharpe and Nancy Paxton that while British men, women, and children were indeed killed, there is little evidence of Indian men raping English women. Subsequent official investigations found no evidence of systematic rape or torture, even in the notorious massacre at Kanpur during the rebellion in 1857.[34] Much of the "news" reported from India at the time relied on impassioned, hearsay accounts. Between 1857 and 1947, more than eighty novels were written in English about the events of the rebellion. These stories commonly enacted in their plots the concept of "a fate worse than death," as proper English heroines chose death rather than fall sexual victim to an Indian man.[35] These mutiny rape stories, so popular in Britain, not only broadcast colonial gendered and racial tropes, but also entrenched definitions of femininity that cast women as needing male protection and as under the threat of sexual assault, helping to police metropolitan moves toward women's social autonomy.

When one of the worst massacres of White settlers by Aborigines occurred in southern Queensland in October 1857, settlers unsurprisingly drew parallels with the ongoing Indian uprising. On October 27, 1857, a large group of Aborigines attacked the Hornet Bank station homestead of the Fraser family on the Dawson River in south-central Queensland, killed all but one of the men, raped the mother and two of her daughters, and then killed the women and children. In sum, eleven Whites, among them several of the Fraser family's employees, were killed. According to Gordon Reid's research on the events, including the multiple and protracted reprisal killings, "at least 150 Aborigines died; the total may have been 300."[36] Settlers justified their brutal reprisals by drawing connections between the actions of the Aboriginal people in the Dawson River area and the sepoys in India.

For some time, the Jiman (Yee-man) and other Aboriginal people in the region had been under pressure from the settlers encroaching on their lands and taking them as pastoral properties. There had been widespread rape, assault, and abuse of Aboriginal women and numerous instances of unprovoked violence by the White settlers. Yet, the settlers cast the attack on Hornet Bank station as murderous and treacherous, in similar terms to those used about the sepoys. While the Queensland press was divided in their responses to the killing of the Frasers, with at least one paper calling for fairness toward the Aborigines, the *Moreton Bay Free Press* commented, "Little did we imagine that when reading the horrible indecencies inflicted upon, and the subsequent butchery of, one-hundred-and-seventy-nine women and children at Cawnpore, that a tragedy of similar nature was being enacted at our very doors."[37]

For settlers in Queensland, the primary reason for their protracted vigilante violence was to establish their hold over the land. They told colonial officials that the recent and sparse nature of settlement meant that they were vulnerable to Aboriginal attack, and they further complained about the inadequate and inefficient Native Police forces. They believed, with some reason, that if they had not acted in reprisal, comparable subsequent attacks would have been made on other stations. Racial reasoning, too, was invoked to justify the disproportionate killing of Aborigines. Gender and sexuality were part of the mix, with the rape of the Fraser females considered a horrific part of the attacks and linked to the greatly exaggerated stories of the sexual assault of British women emanating from India.[38]

Colonial panics sparked by lurid fears of interracial sexual assault erupted in various sites. As scholars of colonialism have pointed out, fears of the sexual assault of White women by colonized men often peaked during real or perceived crises of control.[39] In some instances in the early twentieth century, such as in Southern Rhodesia and New Guinea, these panics were not during wars.[40] But they had links to panics sparked during colonial wars such as in 1850s India and Queensland. The continuing circulation in imperial and Western culture of such gendered and racialized fears was a lasting legacy of these wars.

MILITARIZED PROSTITUTION

In some militarized colonial societies, official and semiofficial forms of organized prostitution developed to service imperial troops. In the increasingly hegemonic nineteenth-century British Empire, military expenditure shifted to the army instead of the navy, reflecting imperial demands for territorial colonial rule over naval warfare. As Britain gradually expanded its geographical and political control in India, colonial society became thoroughly militarized. In the wake of the Indian Rebellion in 1857–58, the British government assumed control of the East India Company's army and increased the ratio of White to Indigenous soldiers, such that by the 1860s, there were 65,000 British troops to 140,000 sepoys.[41]

Indian and British troops were kept apart in separate units. Both had British officers, but the officers of the British troops considered themselves superior to the officers of the Indian troops. The British held exclusive control over the artillery, so that in the event of another uprising they could use the weapons to overpower any rebels. Indian regiments were recruited only from Indian peoples considered loyal to Britain—thus, Bengalis and Marathas, for example, were excluded, while Sikhs, Gurkhas, and Rajputs were put in the front ranks. Heather Streets has demonstrated the ways in which British military officials actively constructed what became the popular idea of "martial races," the notion that some "races" were inherently warlike, strong, and manly. This long-lived conception idealized Scottish Highlanders, Punjabi Sikhs, and Nepalese Gurkhas as masculine races that produced the best soldiers and were targeted for military recruiting. Military officials consciously cultivated the connections between the three groups, in an ideology that equated loyalty, valor, and martial qualities with manliness.[42] At the same time, different Indian groups were dispersed across the army's Indian regiments to prevent any unified identity that could lead to insurrection.

As Philippa Levine has argued, the spread of the army under the British Raj profoundly shaped India's landscape and its economy. British colonial reach expanded within the Indian subcontinent, causing the proliferation of cantonments housing troops and, along with them, the nearby bazaars. The cantonments and their bazaars became newly organized social and trading spaces. The militarization of colonial India led to the growth of prostitution to service the expanding army. Ironically, given their despised social status in British India, it was poor women suspected of prostitution who had the most contact with the imperial medical bureaucracy run by the Sanitary Department beginning in 1864.[43] Specialized in treating venereal diseases, lock hospitals to forcibly confine and treat Indigenous women were first established in India during the late eighteenth century and proliferated with the expansion of contagious diseases ordinances in the mid-nineteenth century. While women were controlled, blamed, and punished in the campaigns against venereal disease, infection rates of British troops in India ran as high as nearly 40 percent of hospital admissions in 1859 and over 50 percent in 1895.[44]

Prostitutes in India were racially diverse, including some Japanese, Mauritian, and Burmese women and even a few Europeans,[45] but the fact that they were predominantly Indigenous meant that militarized and paid sex was a pervasive cross-racial relationship under British colonial rule. Thus, while actual warfare in colonial India was limited to sporadic wars of conquest or the suppression of rebellion particularly in 1857–58, British rule depended on the visible presence of troops and, in turn, on the commodification of women's sexual services. Relationships between armies and camp-following women were far from new.[46] The expanding and medicalized relationship between prostitutes and the military in late nineteenth-century British India, however, was a signal development in what Cynthia Enloe has pointed to as the transnational investment of government authority in military prostitution, protecting the male customers while also sustaining their masculinity.[47]

MILITARIZED CONCUBINAGE

Colonized men, other than soldiers and police (such as the Native Police in the Australian colonies), were commonly infantilized or subordinated through being compelled into menial and laboring jobs. At the same time, colonized women and children (sometimes including boys) were pushed by the disruption of their traditional livelihoods and circumstance into prostitution and concubinage. The sex ratio imbalance among colonizers, with relatively few settler or colonizing women, especially in colonialism's early stages, shaped gender relations across axes of race and power. Racialized conceptions of colonized women centered on sexual services for colonizing men and the domestic labor of unsanctioned marriages and unequal household partnerships. In some colonies, such as the Italian colonies in North Africa and the Dutch East Indies, systems of concubinage shaped societies with clearly defined racial hierarchies.[48]

The thousands of islands that constitute Indonesia occupy a maritime crossroad between the Indian Ocean, the Pacific Ocean, and the South China Sea. Over the centuries, they have been influenced by seafaring peoples such as Indians, Chinese, Arabs, and Europeans, especially the Portuguese and the Dutch. Navigators from the Netherlands first encountered this vast archipelago at the end of the sixteenth century, when the Dutch sought to wrest the valuable spice trade from the Portuguese. In 1602, the Dutch East India Company (the Dutch name was Vereenigde Oostindische Compagnie) was formed and allowed by the Dutch government to have considerable autonomy in its colonizing of the Indonesian islands—including waging war to advance its mercantile interests. Most of the local peoples had lived as subsistence farmers in villages and towns for centuries, with rice production particularly intensive in central and eastern Java. Older Hindu-based traditions were overlaid with Islam, which had arrived in the fifteenth century. Like the British East India Company's encroachment in India, the Dutch East India Company intervened in local wars and thus extended its control, especially over Java. By the late eighteenth century, the Dutch were at war with the British over access to the region. In 1799, with the Dutch East India Company reduced by war and floundering, the Dutch government took direct control of these valuable colonies.[49]

Concubinage evolved early in the Netherlands Indies, beginning in the seventeenth century. From 1830 on, the Royal Netherlands East Indies Army, administered by the minister of the colonies, continued this tradition, such that army barracks housed the wives and children of Native soldiers, as well as separate quarters for the European soldiers that included segregated areas for those living with concubines. Interracial concubinage was recognized in the colonial civil code and practiced by senior officers in addition to ordinary soldiers. The racial logic that underlay the tolerance of concubinage was enshrined in the prohibition against returning to the Netherlands with a Native wife. By the late nineteenth century, attitudes began to change. Religious disapproval of interracial concubinage became strong enough to cause a decline in the practice. Even so, in 1911, 23 percent of European soldiers had concubines.[50]

For Indigenous women, life as a concubine had its perils. When Dutch soldiers returned to the Netherlands, they left behind both their concubines and their children, who then lacked a living, support for their children, and somewhere to live.[51] For Indigenous women, concubinage increasingly was essentially a form of prostitution, albeit with one long-term customer. A major consequence of concubinage was *métissage* and the creation of the Indo-European community. Like prostitution, concubinage was a militarized institutionalization of Indigenous women's subordination under European colonialism. Yet, especially in some more remote colonial locations with high sex ratio imbalances, women's sexual and domestic services could be in considerable demand. Some European men developed affection for their concubines, despite their servile status, complicating colonial social and racial hierarchies. *Métissage* contributed to that racial and moral blurring, through both mixed-race offspring and the Indo-European women who themselves became concubines. As in other European colonies, mixed-race people in the Netherlands Indies were shunned, allowed limited opportunities, and socially segregated. Thus, although the East Indies Army had no monopoly on the practice that also occurred on plantations, the concubinage it supported had far-reaching consequences for gender and racial relations.[52]

Europeans also practiced concubinage in other colonies in Southeast Asia, including French Indochina and British Burma. In the nineteenth and early twentieth centuries, Indigenous women's status in Burma and Indochina was affected by wars of conquest and militarily enforced colonial rule, partly because of prostitution and concubinage. Prior to British colonization, Burmese women had conducted much of the internal trade and had run businesses, including textile manufacturing. Under militarily enforced colonial rule following the wars of the 1820s, 1850s, and 1885 in lower and then upper Burma, foreign men took over commerce: British men ran the larger businesses, while Indian and Chinese men took over smaller trading. Women lost jobs and livelihoods, and they faced new gender restrictions because of the introduction of missionary-led ideas about women belonging in the domestic sphere. As landholding and mortgage systems became colonized as well, women who lost their land and could not pay debts were often pushed into undesirable marriages, prostitution, or concubinage.[53] We have a vivid portrayal of the harrowingly unequal relationship between a British man and his Burmese concubine in the 1934 novel *Burmese Days* by the British writer George Orwell, based on his experiences in the colonial police service in Burma during the 1920s. Yet Ma Khin Mar Mar Kyi points out that, according to Burmese custom, Orwell's character and his concubine were in fact legally married through his payment of a bride price in front of her parents.[54]

As with much else about colonialism, changes in gender relations related to colonial wars and their aftermath were complex and negotiated. The New Zealand Wars were fought episodically from the 1840s to the 1870s, in the north of the North Island as well as the Taranaki and Waikato areas.[55] In the latter region, from 1864 to 1866, Maori women participated as combatants in the war against the British forces and settlers, including some who were taken prisoner and some who were killed.[56] However, recent scholarship on interracial relations in nineteenth-century New Zealand has pointed toward Maori women's agency in forging relationships that offered them both economic and emotional benefits.

The sealing and whaling trades were early forms of European economic imperialism, soon followed by the land-grabbing pastoralism and agriculture, which sparked the intense, if regionally limited, New Zealand Wars. Angela Wanhalla has shown that in the early nineteenth-century North Island, where whalers spent less time on shore, there was a sex trade closer to prostitution. On the South Island, in contrast, the practices of European men who engaged in sealing and whaling led to more stable and productive unions that Wanhalla likens to those that emerged in fur-trading areas of Canada. In southern New Zealand, these interracial unions were sometimes just for the sealing or whaling season, but they also included short- and long-term marriages. In the settlement of Maitapapa in the Otago region, from the 1830s on, interracial marriages became so dominant as to produce a majority mixed-descent population later in the century.[57] On the North Island, Maori women's sexual and economic negotiations preceded warfare while being integral to the evolving and ultimately explosive relations of colonialism. On the South Island, the relative absence of warfare may have been connected with the higher occurrence of interracial marriage.

WESTERN CIVILIZATION, IMPERIAL CONQUEST, AND WHITE MASCULINITIES

Despite changes over time and differences between colonies, warfare and the sustained use of violent suppression shaped gender ideologies and gendered relations of power in war itself; militarized colonial regimes; and violent frontier daily life for both European colonizers and the colonized. Christian evangelizing that accompanied colonial conquest imposed bourgeois European notions of gendered respectability. But ideologies of civility and Western civilization could hardly mask colonizers' behavior that relied fundamentally on male violence or the threat of violence. In Africa, for example, imperial conquest was linked to the creation of imperial and religious heroes—all White men, of course—such as the Welsh journalist and explorer Henry Morton Stanley in the Congo occupied by the troops of Belgian King Leopold from the late 1870s and the conflict between British general Charles Gordon and the Mahdi of Omdurman in 1880s Sudan, a revolt later fought by British field marshal Herbert Kitchener in the 1890s.[58]

In the decades on either side of the turn of the twentieth century, the European imperial powers rushed to take colonial territories in expeditions and wars marked by extreme, asymmetrical violence. European manly heroism was a little harder to envisage when the Gatling and other early machine guns were deployed against Indigenous warriors armed with traditional weapons. Such unequal contests were therefore reported in obfuscating ways. Other gendered depredations of imperial expansion, such as the sexual abuse of Indigenous women during explorers' expeditions, typically went unreported.[59]

Heroic masculinity became so fused with ideas of imperial conquest and rule that it routinely served to obscure colonial violence. There is evidence that, at least in some instances, violent masculinity became associated with quotidian colonial administration, such as the case of Carl Hahn, the Native Commissioner of Ovamboland in South African–controlled South West Africa from 1915. Patricia Hayes has shown how the German-descended but English-identified Hahn was considered an enlightened administrator in his "indirect rule" of the Ovambo. He further gained a reputation for his seeming attempts to preserve traditional culture and his ethnographic knowledge. Yet "Cocky" Hahn was brutal in his administration, a fact that came to light in the official investigation of a complaint against him in 1923. Not only was Hahn notorious for the floggings practiced in his district, but also he was known to beat Indigenous men and to kick them when he grew tired of beating. In one allegation by another White official, Hahn reportedly came up behind an Ovambo woman servant kneeling to polish the veranda of his residence and made a running kick directly to her genitals.[60] It is hard to imagine a more graphic instance of the gendering of colonial subordination and violence. As in the militarization of prostitution and concubinage in colonial regimes ranging from British India to the Netherlands Indies, women's sexual service, quotidian labor, and gendered subordination were tied together inextricably.

CONCLUSION

The "new imperial history" has helped to demonstrate the gendering effects of war and violence as constitutive of colonialism across a range of settings. This scholarship has opened up questions about the gendered dimensions of violent territorial conquest and sustained colonial rule. But much research still needs to be done, such as comparative studies across and between the colonies of the British, French, Dutch, Belgian, German,

Italian, and Portuguese imperial powers and also with the imperial expansion of other Western powers, such as the United States in the Caribbean and the Philippines in the late nineteenth and early twentieth centuries. The colonial rule of non-Western powers, such as the Ottomans, Russia, and Japan, remains fertile ground for study and comparison as well. There is reason to think that the gendered causes and consequences of militarism and their imbrication with colonialism transcended imperial boundaries, yet the cultural, social, and economic specificities show sufficient variations to warrant further investigation.

The structures of military cantonments and the regulations governing sexual relations between standing imperial armies and the local people over whom they ruled have been studied in only some instances. We still have much to learn about how Indigenous women and men accommodated invading troops in both the first instance and the longer term, as well as the social and cultural ramifications of *métissage* and economic interdependence. We must continue to grapple with the gendered impulses that drove militarist imperialism from its metropolitan roots, but perhaps even more, we must understand the gendered effects of imperial wars and violent colonialism both in metropoles and in and between colonies.

Finally, an important subject for further research is the experience of colonial warfare from the perspectives of Indigenous and colonized peoples. For reasons common to historical research on subordinated groups, the voices of colonized people are harder to hear because archives typically consist of the records of military victors and imperial rulers. Scholarship in recent decades has sought to imagine, and to some extent to document, the experiences of Indigenous people, but more work is necessary. Ideally, research would include local languages and, perhaps by necessity, oral testimony handed down through generations. We need to know more about how the violence of imperial expansion undercut traditional gender relations; affected Indigenous women and men differentially; resulted in gendered forms of exploitation and dependence; and led to new gender expectations among both colonizers and colonized. Although most studies of colonialism have focused on the colonizers, we do not yet fully understand the gendered effects of frontier warfare on them. Research could also further explore the vectors through which the intersections of gender and violence on colonial frontiers had transnational effects and the embodied and representational ways in which they moved from colony to colony, empire to empire, and colony to metropole.

NOTES

1. Statistics are from Alice L. Conklin and Ian C. Fletcher, *European Imperialism, 1830–1930: Climax and Contradictions* (Boston: Houghton Mifflin, 1998), 1.
2. Eric J. Hobsbawm, *The Age of Empire, 1875–1914* (New York: Vintage Books, 1989); Daniel R. Headrick, *The Tentacles of Progress: Technology Transfer in the Age of Imperialism, 1850–1940* (New York: Oxford University Press, 1988); and Mark I. Choate, "New Dynamics and New Imperial Powers, 1876–1905," in *The Routledge History of Western Empires*, ed. Robert Aldrich and Kirsten McKenzie (London: Routledge, 2014), esp. chap. 8, 118–34.

3. On this epoch of imperialism, see Conklin and Fletcher, *European Imperialism*; Hobsbawm, *Age of Empire*; and Jane Burbank and Frederick Cooper, *Empires in World History: Power and the Politics of Difference* (Princeton, NJ: Princeton University Press, 2010).

4. On the nineteenth-century empires, see Burbank and Cooper, *Empires*, 287–330.

5. James Belich, *Replenishing the Earth: The Settler Revolution and the Rise of the Anglo-World 1783–1939* (Oxford: Oxford University Press, 2009); Choate, "New Dynamics"; and Tony Ballantyne, "The Theory and Practice of Empire Building: Edward Gibbon Wakefield and 'Systematic Colonisation,'" in Aldrich and McKenzie, *Routledge History*, 89–101.

6. For example, Kathleen Wilson, *The Island Race: Englishness, Empire and Gender in the Eighteenth Century* (London: Routledge, 2003).

7. Ronald Hyam, *Empire and Sexuality: The British Experience* (Manchester: Manchester University Press, 1990), 1. For a more thoughtful analysis, see Christopher Lane, *The Ruling Passion: British Colonial Allegory and the Paradox of Homosexual Desire* (Durham, NC: Duke University Press, 1995).

8. On lesbianism among convicts in the Australian colonies, see Joy Damousi, *Depraved and Disorderly: Female Convicts, Sexuality and Gender in Colonial Australia* (Cambridge: Cambridge University Press, 1997); and on imperial travel and lesbianism, see Angela Woollacott, "White Colonialism and Sexual Modernity: Australian Women in the Early Twentieth Century Metropolis," in *Gender, Sexuality and Colonial Modernities*, ed. Antoinette Burton (London: Routledge, 1999), 49–63.

9. Robert Aldrich, *Colonialism and Homosexuality* (London: Routledge, 2003), esp. 71–79.

10. Daniela Baratieri, "Italy's Sexual El Dorado in Africa," in *Imperial Expectations and Realities: El Dorados, Utopias and Dystopias*, ed. Adrekos Varnava (Manchester: Manchester University Press, 2015), 166–90, 178–81.

11. On colonized men serving as troops, see Heather Streets, *Martial Races: The Military, Race and Masculinity in British Imperial Culture, 1857–1914* (Manchester: Manchester University Press, 2010); Jonathan Richards, *The Secret War: A True History of Queensland's Native Police* (St. Lucia: University of Queensland Press, 2008); and Moshe Gershovich, *French Military Rule in Morocco: Colonialism and Its Consequences* (Portland, OR: F. Cass, 2000).

12. James Belich, *The New Zealand Wars and the Victorian Interpretation of Racial Conflict* (Auckland, New Zealand: Auckland University Press, 1986).

13. Elizabeth Vibert, "Real Men Hunt Buffalo: Masculinity, Race and Class in British Fur Traders' Narratives," in *Cultures of Empire: Colonizers in Britain and the Empire in the Nineteenth and Twentieth Centuries: A Reader*, ed. Catherine Hall (New York: Routledge, 2000), 281–97.

14. Militarism, which I define as officially inculcated support for military values and systems, has been historically contingent. For a discussion of the meanings of militarism, see the chapter by Stefan Dudink, Karen Hagemann, and Mischa Honeck, "War and Gender: Nineteenth-Century Wars of Nations and Empires—an Overview" in this handbook.

15. Angela Woollacott, *Gender and Empire* (Basingstoke: Palgrave Macmillan, 2006), 104–21.

16. Rozina Visram, *Women in India and Pakistan: The Struggle for Independence from British Rule* (Cambridge: Cambridge University Press, 1992), 46–47.

17. Anthony Reid, *An Indonesian Frontier: Acehnese and Other Histories of Sumatra* (Singapore: Singapore University Press, 2005), 336.

18. See the chapter by Marilyn Lake on "The 'White Man,' Race, and Imperial War during the Long Nineteenth Century" in this handbook.

19. Belich, *Replenishing the Earth*, 58, 65.

20. Adele Perry, *On the Edge of Empire: Gender, Race, and the Making of British Columbia, 1849–1871* (Toronto: University of Toronto Press, 2001), 61–62.

21. Lyndall Ryan, *Tasmanian Aborigines: A History since 1803* (Sydney: Allen & Unwin, 2012).

22. Philippa Levine, *Prostitution, Race and Politics: Policing Venereal Disease in the British Empire* (New York: Routledge, 2003), 235–36.

23. On the nature of frontier warfare in Australia, see Henry Reynolds, *The Other Side of the Frontier: Aboriginal Resistance to the European Invasion of Australia* (Ringwood: Penguin Books, 1982); and on the dynamics of the early period of frontier warfare, see Inga Clendinnen, *True Stories: History, Politics, Aboriginality* (Sydney: ABC Books, 1999).

24. Sarah Carter, *The Importance of Being Monogamous: Marriage and Nation Building in Western Canada to 1915* (Edmonton: University of Alberta Press, 2008), 159.

25. Kay Schaffer, *In the Wake of First Contact: The Eliza Fraser Stories* (Cambridge: Cambridge University Press, 1995); Ian J. McNiven et al., eds., *Constructions of Colonialism: Perspectives on Eliza Fraser's Shipwreck* (London: Leicester University Press, 1998); and Kay Schaffer and D'Arcy Randall, "Transglobal Translations: The Eliza Fraser and Rachel Plummer Captivity Narratives," in *Colonial and Postcolonial Incarceration*, ed. Graeme Harper (London: Continuum, 2001), 105–23.

26. Kate Darian-Smith, "Marking Capture: White Women Captives in Australia," in *Citizenship, Women and Social Justice: International Historical Perspectives*, ed. Joy Damousi and Katherine Ellinghaus (Melbourne, Australia: History Department, University of Melbourne, 1999), 71–78; and Julie Carr, *The Captive White Woman of Gippsland: In Pursuit of the Legend* (Carlton South, Vic.: Melbourne University Press, 2001).

27. Darian-Smith, "Marking Capture"; and Carr, *Captive White Woman*.

28. On Britain in India, see Philippa Levine, *The British Empire: Sunrise to Sunset*, 2nd ed. (London: Routledge, 2013), esp. 61–81.

29. Burbank and Cooper, *Empires*, 308.

30. Barbara D. Metcalf and Thomas R. Metcalf, *A Concise History of Modern India*, 3rd ed. (Cambridge: Cambridge University Press, 2012), 56–91.

31. Ibid., 92–122.

32. One source of resentment was the 1856 annexation of the state of Oudh.

33. Many peasants rebelled in support of the sepoys, and in the cities of Delhi and Lucknow support for the uprising included offensive fighting and devastation.

34. Jenny Sharpe, *Allegories of Empire: The Figure of Woman in the Colonial Text* (Minneapolis: University of Minnesota Press, 1993), 64.

35. Nancy L. Paxton, *Writing under the Raj: Gender, Race, and Rape in the British Colonial Imagination, 1830–1947* (New Brunswick, NJ: Rutgers University Press, 1999), 111.

36. Gordon Reid, *A Nest of Hornets: The Massacre of the Fraser Family at Hornet Bank Station, Central Queensland, 1857, and Related Events* (Melbourne, Australia: Oxford University Press, 1982), ix.

37. *Moreton Bay Free Press*, November 18, 1857, quoted in ibid., 74.

38. Reid, *A Nest of Hornets*, 75, 94; and Jessie Mitchell, "'Great Difficulty in Knowing Where the Frontier Ceases': Violence, Governance, and the Spectre of India in Early Queensland," *Journal of Australian Colonial History* 15 (2013): 43–62.

39. For example, Ann Laura Stoler, "Making Empire Respectable: The Politics of Race and Sexual Morality in Twentieth-Century Colonial Cultures," in *Dangerous Liaisons: Gender,*

Nation, and Postcolonial Perspectives, ed. Anne McClintock et al. (Minneapolis: University of Minnesota Press, 1997), 344–73.

40. For example, Jock McCulloch, *Black Peril, White Virtue: Sexual Crime in Southern Rhodesia, 1902–1935* (Bloomington: Indiana University Press, 2000); and Amirah Inglis, *Not a White Woman Safe: Sexual Anxiety and Politics in Port Moresby, 1920–1934* (Canberra: Australian National University Press, 1974).

41. Levine, *Prostitution*, 32.

42. Streets, *Martial Races*.

43. Levine, *Prostitution*, 33–34.

44. Ibid., 44, 270.

45. Ibid., 205.

46. See the chapters by Peter H. Wilson on "Wars, States, and Gender in Early Modern European Warfare, 1600s–1780s," and Thomas Cardoza and Karen Hagemann on "History and Memory of Army Women and Female Soldiers, 1770s–1870s" in this handbook.

47. Cynthia Enloe, *The Morning After: Sexual Politics at the End of the Cold War* (Berkeley: University of California Press, 1993), 145.

48. On the *madama* system in the Italian colonies, see Baratieri, "Italy's Sexual El Dorado," 174–76; and on concubinage in the Dutch East Indies, see Ann Laura Stoler, *Carnal Knowledge and Imperial Power: Race and the Intimate in Colonial Rule* (Berkeley: University of California Press, 2002).

49. See Robert Cribb, ed., *The Late Colonial State in Indonesia: Political and Economic Foundations of the Netherlands Indies, 1880–1942* (Leiden: KILTV Press, 1994); Frances Gouda, *Dutch Culture Overseas: Colonial Practice in the Netherlands Indies, 1900–1942* (Amsterdam: Amsterdam University Press, 1995); and Susie Protschky, "Environment and Visual Culture in the Tropics: The Netherlands Indies, c. 1830–1949," in Aldrich and McKenzie, *Routledge History*, 382–95.

50. Hanneke Ming, "Barracks-Concubinage in the Indies, 1887–1920," *Indonesia* 35 (1983): 65–95, 71.

51. Ibid., 72.

52. Stoler, *Carnal Knowledge*, 50–51.

53. Ma Khin Mar Mar Kyi, "In Pursuit of Power: Politic, Patriarchy, Poverty and Gender Relations in New Order Myanmar/Burma" (PhD diss., Australian National University, 2012), 69–71.

54. George Orwell, *Burmese Days* (San Diego, CA: Harvest Books, 1934); and Kyi, "In Pursuit of Power," 75.

55. Angela Wanhalla, *In/Visible Sight: The Mixed-Descent Families of Southern New Zealand* (Wellington, New Zealand: Bridget Williams Books, 2009), 5–11.

56. Judith Binney, *Encircled Lands: Te Urewera, 1820–1921* (Wellington, New Zealand: Bridget Williams Books, 2009), 71–72, 97.

57. Wanhalla, *In/Visible Sight*.

58. Janice Boddy, *Civilizing Women: British Crusades in Colonial Sudan* (Princeton, NJ: Princeton University Press, 2007), 16–24.

59. On the stunning violence and devastation caused by some supposedly heroic "explorers'" expeditions, see Felix Driver, *Geography Militant: Cultures of Exploration and Empire* (Oxford: Blackwell, 2001).

60. Patricia Hayes, "'Cocky' Hahn and the 'Black Venus': The Making of a Native Commissioner in South West Africa, 1915–46," *Gender & History* 8, no. 3 (1996): 364–92.

SELECT BIBLIOGRAPHY

Aldrich, Robert. *Colonialism and Homosexuality*. London: Routledge, 2003.

Aldrich, Robert, and Kirsten McKenzie, eds. *The Routledge History of Western Empires*. London: Routledge, 2014.

Belich, James. *Replenishing the Earth: The Settler Revolution and the Rise of the Anglo-World 1783–1939*. Oxford: Oxford University Press, 2009.

Burbank, Jane, and Frederick Cooper. *Empires in World History: Power and the Politics of Difference*. Princeton, NJ: Princeton University Press, 2010.

Clancy-Smith, Julia, and Frances Gouda, eds. *Domesticating the Empire: Race, Gender, and Family Life in French and Dutch Colonialism*. Charlottesville: University Press of Virginia, 1998.

Conklin, Alice L., and Ian Christian Fletcher, eds. *European Imperialism, 1830–1930: Climax and Contradictions*. Boston: Houghton Mifflin, 1998.

Conrad, Sebastian. *German Colonialism: A Short History*. Cambridge: Cambridge University Press, 2012.

Cooper, Nicola. *France in Indochina: Colonial Encounters*. Oxford: Berg, 2001.

Erickson, Lesley. *Westward Bound: Sex, Violence, the Law and the Making of a Settler Society*. Vancouver: University of British Columbia Press, 2011.

Headrick, Daniel R. *The Tentacles of Progress: Technology Transfer in the Age of Imperialism, 1850–1940*. New York: Oxford University Press, 1988.

Hobsbawm, Eric J. *The Age of Empire, 1875–1914*. New York: Vintage, 1989.

Levine, Philippa. *The British Empire: Sunrise to Sunset*. 2nd ed. London: Routledge, 2013.

Levine, Philippa. *Prostitution, Race and Politics: Policing Venereal Disease in the British Empire*. London: Routledge, 2003.

Metcalf, Barbara D., and Thomas R. Metcalf. *A Concise History of Modern India*. 3rd ed. Cambridge: Cambridge University Press, 2012.

Nettelbeck, Amanda, Louis A. Knafla, Russell Charles Smandych, and Robert Foster. *Fragile Settlements: Aboriginal Peoples, Law, and Resistance in South-West Australia and Prairie Canada*. Vancouver: University of British Columbia Press, 2016.

Perry, Adele. *On the Edge of Empire: Gender, Race, and the Making of British Columbia, 1849–1871*. Toronto: University of Toronto Press, 2001.

Reynolds, Henry. *The Other Side of the Frontier: Aboriginal Resistance to the European Invasion of Australia*. Ringwood: Penguin Books, 1982.

Stoler, Ann Laura. *Carnal Knowledge and Imperial Power: Race and the Intimate in Colonial Rule*. Berkeley: University of California Press, 2002.

Streets, Heather. *Martial Races: The Military, Race and Masculinity in British Imperial Culture, 1857–1914*. Manchester: Manchester University Press, 2004.

Woollacott, Angela. *Gender and Empire*. Basingstoke: Palgrave Macmillan, 2006.

CHAPTER 13

THE "WHITE MAN," RACE, AND IMPERIAL WAR DURING THE LONG NINETEENTH CENTURY

MARILYN LAKE

IN 1910, speaking to a conference in London on the subject of "Nationalities and Subject Races," the widely traveled Dutch socialist politician Henri van Kol launched a strong attack on the past actions of imperial powers that, in his view, brought the professed "superiority of the white man" and his claims to "civilization" into serious doubt. In his paper, "The General Condition of the Coloured Races under the White Man's Rule," van Kol elaborated on "the ferocity of the white man" and the atrocities committed under imperial rule around the world.[1] He asked whether the White man had, in his indiscriminate violence, forfeited his right to rule.

The "White man"—whether understood as the bearer of civilization or the perpetrator of colonial atrocities—was a global figure whose subjective identity was produced in the relations of imperial rule.[2] In processes of conquest and colonization, men of distinct European nationalities—whether American, British, French, Dutch, or German—were transformed and merged into a new kind of transnational figure who came to be feared by the colonized and lauded by the colonizers as the "White man." He based his right to rule on claims to superiority, but many questioned that conceit. "What is whiteness," asked African American writer W. E. B. Du Bois in 1910, "that one should so desire it?" Surveying the past century, he came to realize that "whiteness is the ownership of the earth forever and ever. Amen."[3] But the White man would not, in fact, prove quite so omnipotent.

To consider constructions of manhood in the historical framework of imperial warfare and colonial rule is to recognize that in the long nineteenth century, manhood, like womanhood, was a racialized and gendered condition. While White privilege was built on the bloodshed of conquest, the condition of the White man constituted through imperial rule was complex: defined by power even as he was haunted by his vulnerability;

beset by fear even as he asserted his mastery; seemingly omnipotent, yet fundamentally frangible. In frontier wars, White men were as likely to forfeit their manhood as to prove it. The ferocity of the White man, as observed by Henri van Kol, was one outcome of these acute and deadly tensions.

Non-White women and men were routinely denied the status of womanhood and manhood. Variously cast as savages and primitives ruled by their instincts and passions, colonized peoples were understood to be lesser beings.[4] Indigenous women were routinely raped and abused.[5] In the Australian colonies, the "marauding white man" became a target of feminist critique, shaping reforms that focused on securing better protection, the sanctity of the person, and economic independence for Aboriginal women.[6] In the eyes of Mary Bennett, a British imperial reformer and advocate of Aboriginal rights, White men's rapacity disqualified them from governing the Natives. "Not mean white men," she wrote in 1932 in the *Australian Board of Missions Review*, "but in fact all white men in frontier culture."[7] Angered at the conditions she found on the Western Australian frontier, she elaborated, "We are apt to think...that only a bad white man could molest a native woman, but this is not so. Wherever there is a white man's camp there is need for protection for these girls. It is the average ordinary white man who is to blame for this trouble."[8] In the view of maternal feminists across the British Empire, who believed that women as spiritual mothers had a distinctive role to play in society and in politics, the depredations of White men created a special imperial burden and responsibility for White women.[9]

Indigenous men might redeem their manhood in the eyes of British imperialists through demonstrations of martial prowess. When imperial armies and expeditionary forces brought different imperial "races" to fight together as soldiers, as, for example, in response to the Indian Rebellion (1857–58), or in the Sudan (1885), or to fight the Boxer Rebellion (1899–1901) in China, some ethnic/religious groupings—notably Scottish Highlanders, Indian Sikhs, and Nepali Gurkhas—earned a reputation as "martial races."[10] Even if they were thought to lack the capacity for self-government, these men might be hailed as superior fighters and exemplars of masculine heroism. It was their perceived loyalty to empire, however, as much as their bravery in battle or capacity for self-sacrifice, that rewarded these groups with their special status as honorary White men. In his book on *The New Zealand Wars* during the 1860s, Jamie Belich highlighted British recognition of "Maori military prowess."[11] At the Battle of Te Ranga, on June 21, 1864, often seen as bringing the war between British troops and rebel Maori fighters to an end, the Maori were defeated by the British, but valorized as noble, principled, and brave fighters. Successful insurgents were not usually credited with manly courage or patriotism.

More often, Indigenous peoples were deemed treacherous, cowardly, and savage. Thus did Sir George Arthur, who served as the British governor of the colony of Van Diemen's Land (later named Tasmania) between 1824 and 1836, pronounce, "Acts of violence on the part of natives are generally to be regarded, not as retaliating for any wrongs which they conceived themselves collectively or individually to have endured, but as proceeding from a wanton and savage spirit inherent in them, and impelling them to mischief and cruelty."[12]

Those sympathetic to Indigenous resistance at the time and since have preferred to cast acts of violence and retaliation as a form of "guerrilla warfare" deserving recognition as honorable combat.[13] In his recent account of *The Forgotten War* for control of the Australian continent, Henry Reynolds characterizes Aboriginal resistance to British occupation as a species of "guerrilla warfare,"[14] but such "guerrilla" tactics, as Paul Kramer points out in his study of the Filipino resistance to American occupation during and after the Philippine–American War (1899–1902), did not qualify in the eyes of White men as "civilized warfare."[15] Scattered organization, a lack of apparent hierarchy, "loosely disciplined troops little distinguishable from savages," "a reliance on rural supplies little distinguishable from looting," and "forms of concealment and deception that violated Euro-American standards of masculine honour in combat" all confirmed to European commentators that local warriors were neither manly nor honorable.[16]

The changing meanings and experiences of manhood were shaped by historical context and imperial, class, gender, and race relations. In the nineteenth century, "manliness"—an ideal code of character and conduct—was, as Gail Bederman argues with respect to the United States, understood in terms of the related concepts of civilization and Whiteness: the ideal White man embodied "civilized manliness."[17] Civilized White men claimed to be the "most manly ever evolved—firm of character; self-controlled; protectors of women and children."[18] "By invoking the discourse on civilization," Bederman contends, "many Americans found a powerfully effective way to link male dominance to white supremacy." By the late nineteenth century, however, the concept of *masculinity*—a new, more virile, construct emphasizing physical manhood—began to challenge the older ideal of moral manliness.[19]

The following explores constructions of White masculinity in the context of imperial warfare and colonial rule during the long nineteenth century, drawing especially from research on the histories of British, Dutch, and French imperialism in Asia and Africa and studies of settler colonialism in Australia, Canada, New Zealand, and North America. It thus brings together and extends disparate histories of empire, colonial rule, masculinity, and race with a focus on settler societies. It argues that a key shift occurred during the long nineteenth century from an ideal of manhood characterized by moral manliness to a masculinity defined in terms of virility and aggression in response to the increasing resistance to imperial conquest on colonial frontiers across the globe. Physical prowess and ruthlessness began to be more highly valued in men alongside bush skills, horsemanship, and a capacity to deal with "the realities of the frontier," including Indigenous resistance to the occupation of country.[20]

IMPERIAL WARFARE AND CHANGING MASCULINITIES

The key context for the changing understanding of masculinity over the course of the long nineteenth century was the experience of imperial warfare and colonial rule in the wider world. The new imperial masculinity embodied at the beginning of the twentieth century by colonists, frontiersmen, bushmen, and adventurers was exemplified in the United States in the "Rough Rider" Theodore Roosevelt, US president from 1901 to 1909, who had led American troops into Cuba during the Spanish–American War of 1898. Across European empires, the power of colonizers and frontiersmen in the old and new colonies in Asia and Africa began to depend on their preparedness to kill, rather than the manly capacity for self-restraint.[21] Even in Canada, where patriots liked to claim that their colonizing ventures were more peaceable than in the United States, understandings of manhood became increasingly associated with out-of-doors virility. Furthermore, research has shown that with the rise of imperial sentiment in late nineteenth-century Canada, gun culture became increasingly popular among boys and graphic depictions of manhood became more muscular.[22]

Guns were ubiquitous on the African, American, and Australian frontiers.[23] "Armed conflict" between Europeans and Africans "was a frequent feature of the early years of colonization" during the so-called Scramble for Africa, the invasion, occupation, colonization, and annexation of African territory by European powers between 1881 and 1914, as Dane Kennedy pointed out.[24] The same can be said of the colonization of the Australian continent by the British, which had begun in the late eighteenth century. "The Natives needed to be brought into subjection," wrote Niel Black, a pioneer pastoralist and politician in the Port Philip District of New South Wales, in his travel journal in 1839. Once "tamed by means of a few doses of lead," they could be managed by "threats till they become civilized, but they, like all savages, are treacherous and not much to be trusted."[25] Recent research on the Australian colony of Queensland—where the Native Mounted Police were employed to put down Aboriginal resistance—has uncovered the extreme brutality entailed in the expansion of settlement. Increasingly, White authorities demanded new kinds of men to deal with "Aboriginal trouble." "The commandant of the native police force," said one legislator, "must be a man who was not afraid of the saddle—must in fact be a thorough bushman."[26] Soft, urban types from the colonial metropolis of Sydney were thought to lack the qualities required to meet these new challenges. One pastoralist told a select committee that Sydney men had "no idea of the bush, and do not know how to manage blacks." Another agreed: "I think one good man on a station would be worth more than all [who] could be sent from Sydney—a good bushman I mean."[27]

The Queensland frontier in the late nineteenth century was the bloodiest in colonial Australia, with many thousands of Aborigines slaughtered in a deadly series of "punitive raids," "reprisals," and "dispersals."[28] Colonial violence was also a crucial underpinning of the Queensland sugar industry established in the same decades. The expansion of the sugar industry was only made possible, as Tracey Banivanua-Mar has argued, by an imperial labor trade that robbed Pacific islands of a high proportion of their men. The violence that occurred on Pacific beaches and Queensland plantations was intimately connected to the "concurrent pioneering violence of Australian settler colonialism."[29]

The fate of Australian Aborigines was also on Henri van Kol's mind when he addressed the conference on "Nationalities and Subject Races" in London in 1910. "A big volume would be needed," he told his audience, to "describe all the injustices and the monstrous deeds of the so-called civilised nations against the coloured races":

> The 'death-holes' on the Philippines; the disappearing natives of Australia; the Red Indians destroyed in the United States; the decimation of the Hereres by the Germans; the barbarism of French officers in the Soudan and Madagascar, are as many new evidences. And—I must acknowledge it with deep shame for my own country—also the massacre in Sumatra of the Atchinese by Holland. Nearly forty years this free and independent people—about 500,000 men, women and children, in number—has struggled with a heroism, scarcely paralleled in history, against our modern and murderous weapons.[30]

With this record of barbarity and ferocity, van Kol suggested, the White man's rule must surely be brought to an end. All truly civilized people must welcome the dawning of a new age in which "violence and oppression of the colored races will make place for the liberty and rights of men of all colours."[31]

Van Kol had worked in the Dutch East Indies as an engineer on irrigation works for the colonial government in Java. Back in the Netherlands in the 1880s, he was a founder of the Dutch Social Democratic Party and was elected to Parliament in 1897. He became an increasingly vocal critic of Dutch imperialism and in particular the Aceh/Atjeh Wars in the Dutch East Indies (1873–1914). The Aceh was a Sultanate located at the northern end of Sumatra, where the Dutch faced over four decades of fierce resistance against their colonial rule. Despite his criticism, van Kol still justified the Dutch presence on Sumatra's neighboring island of Java with reference to White investment in the colony's infrastructure, the development of industry, education, healthcare, modernization, and abolition of forced labor. Van Kol himself owned a coffee plantation in East Java and used some of the profits to finance the Dutch labor movement. The White man's investment in colonialism was of many kinds and served a diverse range of interests.

By 1910, when van Kol addressed the London conference, it was widely recognized that colonial rule entailed the destruction and dispossession of Native peoples and subject races and the violent suppression of local resistance. The 1845 Dahra massacre by the French in Algeria, the Indian Rebellion of 1857–58, the uprising in 1865 at Morant Bay in Jamaica, and the Maori Wars of the same decade—the latter three uprisings against British rule—became the stuff of legend. In Canada, the suppression of an uprising by the Métis and an associated rebellion by First Nations Cree and Assiniboine in 1885 saw the federal government's final assertion of control over Indigenous communities in the west. The execution of the legendary Métis leader of the rebellion Louis Riel and eight Indian men was intended to convey an object lesson, with Prime Minister Sir John A. Macdonald observing that "the execution of the Indians ... ought to convince the Red man that the White man governs."[32] The legacy of the suppression of the rebellion, however, has proved rather more complex. Today, statues in Manitoba honor Louis Riel as a Canadian hero.[33]

IMPERIALISTS AS BEARERS OF CIVILIZATION

Despite the widespread violence, including genocidal episodes, that accompanied European imperial expansion, officials and settlers reassured themselves that empire was a moral project and that, as its agents, they were bringing the light of civilization to backward savages. Given the power of this self-innocenting conceit, colonial rule necessarily rested on disavowal and denial of the massacres, murderous rampages, and "abominable atrocities" enacted in the name of civilization.[34] Authorities and settlers routinely employed discursive strategies of euphemism and evasion, excuse and exoneration, outright censorship, or simply silence. Although Aborigines were "slaughtered in great numbers," reported Australian pastoralist Niel Black in his journal in 1839, there was "never a word said about it."[35]

Violent repression in French colonies was also "minimized" in contemporary, metropolitan French perception and continues to be evaded in much historiography. "While there is wide-ranging evidence from diverse sources indicating that imperial conquest was brutal," as Bertrand Taithe has written of the Voulet-Chanoine Mission in French Soudan—a military expedition sent out from Senegal in 1898 to conquer the Chad Basin and unify all French territories in West Africa—"the reality of its violence was always minimized or censored in the French media and in much subsequent historiography."[36] Across colonial frontiers, "pacification" was deemed necessary to bring the benefits of "civilization" to the Natives and to secure White men's rule. The "power of the sword" was necessary, it was said, to bring "the rule of peace." White men's justifications for appropriating and colonizing other peoples' countries rarely lay in boasts of superior force or a greater capacity for violence. Although Theodore Roosevelt was a notable exception in his 1886 book *The Winning of the West*, most imperialists emphasized their elevated role as bearers of the "civilizing mission" or *mission civilisatrice*.[37]

Writing of the French republic, Robert Nye has suggested that it was men's assumed capacity for self-abnegation, their self-mastery, their very disinterestedness, and their impassiveness that were said to make men fit for citizenship.[38] Women, assumed to be ruled by their passions and impulses, were excluded from republican citizenship and, by extension, the government of empire. But it was not just the French who embodied the civilized virtues. Men from a range of imperial powers—Americans, Belgians, British, French, Dutch, and Germans—routinely invoked their supposedly innate honor, courage, restraint, reason, and superior intellect to justify their role in imperial conquest and colonial government. They did so as White men charged, so they thought, to rule over and protect all dependent peoples—women as well as the peoples of "Coloured races."[39]

British and French men competed in their claims to be the most civilized rulers of Native peoples, to qualify as White men par excellence. In the French Empire of the Third Republic (1870–1940), according to Alice Conklin, the *civilizing mission* was elevated to official imperial doctrine. France, after all, understood *civilisation* as a quintessentially French achievement. The Third Republic claimed a particular obligation to civilize and colonize Africa, even at the expense of "spilled blood." In 1883, French journalist Gabriel Charmes wrote in the *Revue des Deux Mondes*, "If France were able to establish itself permanently in North Africa, to penetrate to central Africa, to make its influence felt in the entire Sahara and to win the [Western] Sudan, if in these immense regions where only fanaticism and brigandage reign today, it were to bring—even at the price of spilled blood—peace, commerce, tolerance, who could say this was a poor use of force?...Having taught millions of men civilization and freedom would fill it with the pride that makes great peoples."[40] British imperialists argued, on the other hand, that empire was a natural part of Britishness, a moral project to which the British nation had been specially assigned by providence. Sir Charles P. Lucas, a colonial official and theorist of empire, argued that of all European nations, Britain was best qualified to do the work of empire. First, it had the longest experience in managing "subject races." Second, the men who ruled the empire were upright, honest, and well rewarded. Third, they were possessed of British "character" defined by "a sense of justice and love of fair play" fostered in "the great English public schools."[41] Moreover, with their Anglo-Saxon gift for self-government, it was the British who were best qualified to assume the "white man's burden" in bringing ordered liberty and the rule of law to subject races.[42]

In the work of empire, conquering and governing were clearly represented as gendered activities. White men could supposedly "retain by justice that which [they] had won by the sword" and had both "the desire and capacity to govern."[43] According to Alice L. Conklin, "French imperial ideology consistently identified civilization with one principle more than any other: mastery."[44] White men were expected to exercise mastery over nature and wilderness, over their bodies and passions, and over themselves and others. They were to exercise discipline and control. Too often in practice, however, they found themselves desperately out of control, mired in violence, perpetrators of sexual assault, given to everyday abuses of power. In his account of the making of empire in southern Africa, when the Xhosa fought nine wars of resistance between 1779 and 1879, first against the Dutch and then the British, Richard Price points to the role of daily acts of violence, as well as routine humiliations, in securing imperial rule.[45]

In the French colony of Vietnam, violence also underpinned the civilizing project. Following naval interventions in the 1840s, armed conquest continued through the 1860s and 1870s, during which time France carved for itself a huge colony. French Indochina, established in 1887, included Annam, Tonkin, Cochinchina (which together form today's Vietnam), and the Kingdom of Cambodia. Hanoi became the capital. Here, the civilizing power of the French was incorporated into its urban forms and put on display. With its stately, tree-lined streets, imposing municipal buildings, Catholic cathedral, and imitation nineteenth-century opera house, Hanoi assumed the air and status of an imperial capital. It was built to convey the idea, as Michael G. Vann has suggested, "that the French intervention was a crusade for civilization," demonstrating the orderliness and permanence of colonial rule. But the façade of civilization also served to disguise inherent instabilities arising from the colonial situation. The city was born in violence and built on violence: "Racialized violence saturated every aspect of life in colonial Hanoi." According to Vann, violence in the forms of both mundane punishments and the repression of revolt was so omnipresent that it became a central feature of White identity. It dehumanized the indigenes as well as the colonizers who presumed to rule over them.[46]

THE RIGHT TO RULE

The privileged status of White manhood was forged in the racialized contexts of colonialism, but those contexts—and political relations—differed and changed over time.[47] In British settler societies, White colonists occupied a complex position as both colonizers and colonized. The successors of the British in their appropriation of Indigenous lands, colonials were also subject to British rule and the enormity of British condescension. To ameliorate their sense of inferiority as colonials, they insisted on their difference from other colonial subjects by asserting a right to self-government that inhered in their Whiteness.[48]

In many of his writings, such as his 1897 *Impressions of South Africa*, British liberal statesman James Bryce emphasized the distinction between Britain's two kinds of colonies. There were "those which have received the gift of self-government and those which are governed from home through executive officials placed over [them]." The latter were "tropical colonies" with "a predominantly coloured population."[49] But he also acknowledged that South Africa presented an anomaly: "While democratic as regards one of the races, [it] cannot be safely made democratic as regards the other."[50] Bryce stressed that some way out of this contradiction would need to be found. In South Africa for several decades, the violence of apartheid provided the White man's solution. Thus did the rulers of a "black man's country" seek to represent it as a "white man's country."

In 1906, Australian liberal leader Alfred Deakin, taking a cue from Australian-born New Zealand Prime Minister Richard Seddon, reiterated the significance of Bryce's distinction between two different kinds of British colonies: "Though united in the whole, the Empire is, nevertheless, divided broadly into two parts, one occupied wholly or mainly by a white ruling race, the other principally occupied by coloured races who are ruled. Australia and New Zealand are determined to keep their place in the first class.... The ambition of the Australasian States is to keep within the Empire a place parallel and equal to that of the Mother Country."[51] Australia was governed by a "white ruling race" and sought recognition as "equal" in status to the Mother Country. In its imperial ambitions in the Pacific, the new commonwealth looked to emulate the United States, the great Anglo-Saxon republic over the ocean, which in its own imperial turn in the 1890s had occupied Hawaii (1893), Cuba (1898), and the Philippines (1899–1902). Like Americans and the British, Australians were confident in their capacity as Anglo-Saxons to rule over others.[52] If necessary, the right to rule would be established through the use of force.

Because White men ruled and non-Whites were subject to the power of the ruling race, Indigenous men were emasculated. Mrinalini Sinha has shown the ways in which, in late nineteenth-century India, "English masculinity" and "Bengali effeminacy" were constituted in terms of each other in the relations of imperial rule. Nineteenth-century British historian Thomas Babington Macaulay had characterized Bengali "effeminacy" as rendering the Native unfit for self-government: "Whatever the Bengali does he does languidly. His favourite pursuits are sedentary. He shrinks from bodily exertion; and though voluble in dispute, and singularly pertinacious in the war of chicane he seldom engages in personal conflict, and scarcely ever enlists as a soldier. There never perhaps existed a people so thoroughly fitted by habit for a foreign yoke."[53] The effeminate Bengali—feeble, delicate, and languid in physical attributes—was also said to be lacking in moral manliness. "During many ages he has been trampled on by men of bolder and more hardy breeds. Courage, independence, veracity are qualities to which his constitution and his situation are equally unfavourable."[54]

By the end of the nineteenth century, White men across the empire had presumed to monopolize the status of manhood itself. "Not-white" men—Africans, African Americans, Australian Aborigines, Asiatics, Pacific Islanders, and Indian subjects of the British Empire—were thus systematically robbed of their manhood. While van Kol elaborated on the "ferocity of the white man" at the conference on "Nationalities and Subject Races" in London, speakers from various "subject nationalities" detailed the impact of imperial rule on their diminished sense of self. In a paper on "The Present Condition of India," Indian nationalist Lajpat Rai charged that "the present system of arbitrary rule in India" was "sapping our manhood." British authorities could not tolerate "a spirit of manliness" in the people's demands that took the place of the expected "unquestioned obedience, unbounded forbearance, and undisturbed quietude." British imperial rule was "polluting the very foundations of our manhood."[55] Similarly, at the Universal Races Congress in London in 1911, W. E. B. Du Bois defined the experience of racial subordination in the United States in gendered terms as a kind of emasculation. The challenge of racial equality was "whether at last the Negro will gain full recognition as a man, or be utterly crushed by prejudice and superior numbers." That was "the present Negro problem of America."[56] Or, as Aboriginal man Ted Breckenridge told the New South Wales police, "You rob me of the rights of a man. You rob me of my freedom."[57]

During the nineteenth century, constructions of White manhood were shaped not only by relations of imperial rule, but also by the advent of democracy—and manhood suffrage—in North America and Australasia in the 1850s. Liberal democracy enshrined the idea that modern political status inhered not in Old World ideas of estate or property or hereditary privilege, but in the condition of manhood itself, an idea expressed in the ideals of manhood suffrage, self-government, and self-sovereignty. Because it was believed that only White men were capable of self-government and self-sovereignty, the advent of democracy worked paradoxically to exacerbate the divide between men of different races—between "White men" and "Asiatics" and "Whites" and "Natives"—as well as between men and women. As Alan Atkinson has argued in *The Europeans in Australia*, in this context of ascendant democracy, the docile, subservient, languid figure of the Chinaman was considered an "antitype of masculine virtue even worse than hereditary privilege."[58]

As the British-born Australian historian and journalist Charles H. Pearson contended in his 1893 work of postcolonial prophecy *National Life and Character: A Forecast*, for

White men to be governed by non-White men meant that "their pride of place" would be "humiliated."[59] It was this unbearable prospect that provoked White men in the southern United States to embark on their terrible campaigns of violence and intimidation following radical Reconstruction. Lynchings peaked in 1892, during Australia's decade of federal constitution-making, when the architects of the new Commonwealth of Australia determined that the new nation-state must be racially homogeneous—citing the American "history lesson" that democratic equality demanded racial exclusion. Thus was the new federal government granted power to expel Pacific Islanders, brought to work on sugar plantations in Queensland in the nineteenth century, as well as to exclude "Asiatics" from immigration. In 1895, Charles Powers—a liberal member of the Queensland Legislative Assembly, an advocate of women's suffrage, and future member of the High Court of Australia—was confident of the answer when he asked the colonial Parliament, "Is there a single member who would give votes to aborigines, Japanese, Chinese, Hindus, negroes and South Sea Islanders? I do not think so."

In the British colonies of settlement, the imperialist became a democrat and the democrat an imperialist. In the self-governing colonies of the New World, as in the republics of France and the United States, the right to and capacity for self-government and the government of others was theorized as a gendered and racialized capacity. As supposedly self-disciplined, disinterested, upright, rational persons, White men considered themselves naturally—and if Anglo-Saxons historically—suited to govern themselves and others. Theodore Roosevelt was perhaps unusual among the political leaders of settler societies in his praise of White men's capacity for violence. "The winning of the west," he wrote, "was the great epic feat in the history of our race."[60] The true test of the frontiersman's virility was his willingness to engage in savage warfare.

HONORABLE WARFARE AND NARRATIVES OF NATION AND EMPIRE

According to Roosevelt in his multivolume history of frontier warfare *The Winning of the West*, the bloody defeat of Native Americans was the crucible in which the supremacy of the White race and the American nation was forged. Roosevelt also welcomed war with Spain as an opportunity to test the nation's manhood and thus its national character.[61] Richard Slotkin has argued that nation-building forged though imperial warfare was the basis of a founding American myth, with the slaughter of Native Americans celebrated in numerous cultural forms such as Wild West shows, stage melodramas, novels, and Westerns.[62] More recent work has cast the dispossession and destruction of Native Americans as genocide.[63]

Earlier settler-colonial narratives of nation, including in the United States, tended to cast Indigenous peoples as doomed by evolution to disappear, as in the trope of the "Vanishing Indian" or in the "scientific" idea of "dying races" unfit to withstand the forces of progress and modernity, a popular conceit to relieve colonizers of responsibility for frontier slaughter.[64] Canadian nation-builders favored narratives of partnership with Native Americans as exemplified in the fur trade, eloquently expressed in the idea of *métissage*. New Zealanders point to the symbolic importance of the Treaty of Waitangi of 1840 as a founding expression of partnership between Maori and Pakeha. The historiographies and national literature of British settler societies celebrated manly "pioneers" (and "women pioneers," too), who peaceably subdued the wilderness to build homes, farms, and communities where none had been before.

For frontier warfare to assume a legitimate, manly, and honorable place in White men's nation- or empire-building narratives, it had to be framed by a persuasive and preferably heroic narrative. In late nineteenth-century Britain, as Heather Streets and Graham Dawson have reminded us, "tales of army adventures abounded, reflecting an increasingly jingoistic, militaristic and imperially minded popular culture."[65] In colonial contexts, however, a tendency to violence was equally associated with weakness, impulsiveness, and a lack of discipline, signaling a loss of self-control and a relapse into barbarism. Ferocity was thought to be akin to savagery. The deep anxiety that troubled brutalized settlers was that their "civilization" was a mere veneer. The violence of imperial conquest and settler colonialism continually raised the question of who was civilized and who was savage: "Threaded through the triumphant narrative of settlement ran, *sotto voce*, an alternative saga of white men lost to the Christian and liberal humanitarian principles that should have guided their behavior."[66]

In discussions of White men's responsibility for the death and destruction of Aboriginal people in settler colonies, tensions were evident between older discourses on civilization as a moral project and newer conceptions of the necessity of force and the inevitability of spilled blood. Warfare had to be imagined as honorable—waged against a worthy enemy in a just cause according to recognized rules—for it to be seen as compatible with manliness and honor. The campaign of Van Diemen's land governor Sir George Arthur to drive the Aborigines into captivity in the 1820s and 1830s was, according to Henry Reynolds, "by far the largest military operation within Australia in the nineteenth century," yet Arthur continually regretted the resulting violence as "lawless," lamentable, and "cruel."[67] British colonists in Australia were, after all, as even some contemporaries acknowledged, "intruders" and "aggressors" on Indigenous peoples' lands.

By the end of the nineteenth century, many White men of conscience were, like Henri van Kol, ashamed of the extent of the violence against Indigenous peoples and subject races and worried about its implications. In many colonies, observers feared they were complicit in and witness to an "impending catastrophe."[68] Settler wars of extermination were rarely a source of manly pride for colonists, but instead were conducive to shameful silence. Later generations have named the colonizing process "genocidal."[69] Surveying new work in imperial history, Stephen Howe has concluded, "For British North America and for Australasia, the case for numerous genocidal episodes—by even restricted definitions, since large-scale deliberate killing was repeatedly involved—seems to me very strong."[70] New research continues to confirm van Kol's assessment that during the nineteenth century, settlers and republican American citizens had ruled over extensive killing fields. In a recent review of the "American Genocide Debate," Benjamin Madley has argued, "The near-annihilation of North America's indigenous peoples remains a formative event in US history."[71]

In African and Asian colonies where White men always constituted a besieged minority, they were finally defeated, and most departed following decolonization. Their imperial pasts were shed and expelled from national historiographies back home. In the British settler colonies of North America and Australasia—the exemplary "White men's countries"—colonists came to stay and multiply. Their intention was to fully occupy and transform the lands that once belonged to Indigenous peoples. New work on the history of empire in the past several years has insisted we recognize "settler colonialism" as a distinctive formation that, to quote leading theorist Patrick Wolfe, was characterized by "a logic of elimination," with the White man allocated a leading role not as civilizing agent of empire, but as perpetrator of genocide.[72]

In his 2010 book *Settler Colonialism* and the journal he founded, called *Settler Colonial Studies*, Australian theorist Lorenzo Veracini elaborated the case for understanding settler colonialism as a new kind of global formation, characterized by the following four features: a triangular relationship in which settlers set themselves against both the imperial center and the Indigenous peoples; the disavowal of Indigenous presence; the difference from other forms of colonialism; and the impossibility of true decolonization. The fundamental characteristic of settler colonialism is that it is peculiarly destructive of Indigenous societies.[73] The settler colonialism model has been criticized on several grounds, not least for its seeming assumption that Indigenous societies did actually disappear. In fact, their survival against the odds and subsequent contribution to the new societies—and the expeditionary forces dispatched overseas to defend them—has been ironically a key means by which Indigenous peoples have integrated into new martial narratives of nation in Australia, Canada, and New Zealand in recent years.

Empires were extended and colonial settlement established through violent wars of possession and dispossession, the questionable morality and legality of which necessarily entailed processes of denial and disavowal. The settler nation-states of Australia, Canada, New Zealand, and the United States were founded in colonial conquest, through treaties, violence, or cooperation or a mixture of all these methods (there were different ways to legitimate dispossession). Yet, the conquest and defeat of Indigenous peoples never became central to celebratory national narratives of masculine heroism. The extent of violence in settler societies was repressed in subsequent nation-building narratives that in many cases banished Indigenous peoples from historical texts altogether. Popular and academic scholars put forth alternative narratives of nation-building, whether focused on pioneering settlement or democratic innovation or, in the case of the United States, revolution. In the cases of Australia, Canada, and New Zealand, however, a symbolic deficit persisted. For White men, military warfare remained the ultimate test of manhood and nationhood.

In popular imperial culture, a willingness to fight for empire was increasingly equated with ideal masculinity, with news reporting that celebrated the feats of soldiers fighting on imperial frontiers. Though the White dominions of the British Empire achieved nationhood in political negotiations, many still believed that true nationhood could only be proven in war, just as war provided the supreme test of manhood. Imperial officials were keen to promote this message when they were charged with enlisting recruits for expeditionary forces to fight in the Boer (South African) War (1899–1902), in the Boxer Rebellion in China, and in Europe in 1914.

Thus, the government and the press began to argue that the conditions of life in settler colonies provided excellent training for participation in imperial defense. Colonists' preparedness to fight alongside the Mother Country in the Boer War proved that they were exemplary White men. It was "at last recognized," wrote John F. Owen in the *Fortnightly Review* in 1900, "that though Colonial, they are real soldiers, as fit for fighting, as brave and ready to shed blood for the Empire they are proud of, as those of the Mother Country: and more than that, it is seen that for some purposes of War, the conditions of their ordinary life prepare them better that those existing in Britain itself."[74]

From the imperial point of view, the Boer War offered colonials a chance to demonstrate their manhood, but this proved to be a mere rehearsal for the Great War in Europe in 1914. At the landing of the Australian Imperial Force at Gallipoli in April 1915, the official British reporter Ellis Ashmead-Bartlett was full of praise for the performance of the colonial troops: "In less than a quarter of an hour the Turks were out of their second position, either bayoneted or fleeing.... But then the Australians, whose blood was up, instead of entrenching, rushed northwards and eastwards, searching for fresh enemies to bayonet.... These raw colonial troops in these desperate hours proved worthy to fight side by side with the heroes of Mons, the Aisne, Ypres and Neuve Chapelle."[75] The influential Australian correspondent Charles Bean transformed the military defeat of Allied forces at Gallipoli into ultimate triumph by reporting that the men's achievement lay in "the mettle of the men themselves. To be the sort of man who would give way when his mates were trusting to his firmness... to live the rest of his life haunted by the knowledge that he had set his hand to a soldier's task and had lacked the grit to carry it through— that was the prospect which these men could not face. Life was very dear, but life was not worth living unless they could be true to their idea of Australian manhood."[76] Postwar nationalist mythologizing resounded the theme that World War I saw a triumph of settler colonial manhood. In the context of empire, military valor was defined in terms of imperial loyalty. Nation-building followed suit in commemorating the formative feats of military manhood.

CONCLUSION

Since the early 2000s in the former settler colonies of Australia, Canada, and New Zealand, there has been a resurgence of war commemoration in the service of narratives proclaiming the birth of a nation.[77] Military action in the service of empire—focused on Gallipoli in the cases of Australia and New Zealand and on the Battle of Vimy Ridge (April 1917) in the case of Canada—has paradoxically been deemed crucial to nation-building even as the imperial wars of dispossession were repressed or displaced. A war fought in support of empire has been transformed in national myth-making as a crucible for independent nationhood. "Those who embrace a new secular religion of militarism," wrote Ian Mackay and James Swift of current commemorative efforts in Canada, "color the Great War fought for Empire as the Birth of the Nation."[78]

For White colonial settlers, this was an honorable war fought according to the rules of civilized warfare, whereas frontier wars were best forgotten. The bravery of Indigenous warriors who fought against the invading colonizers in defense of their lands in Australasia and North America is rarely commemorated in national monuments or war museums, though Indigenous communities themselves commemorate their resistance. Rather, the centenary of World War I has led to new attention being given to the military prowess of the Indigenous recruits who fought alongside White men in proving their national and imperial loyalty. The excessive investment (symbolic and financial) of the British White Dominions in the Great War as foundational to their national identity is, arguably, a compensatory project, making good their "failure" to achieve nationhood in a war of independence. In the classic formulation of the Prussian historian and militarist Heinrich von Treitschke, "Only in war does a nation become a nation."[79] At the same time, militarist foundational myths in all three settler states serve as a postcolonial strategy of national integration, bringing Indigenous and settler men into the same masculine, military national tradition.[80] By conscripting the Great War to serve as a shared creation myth and highlighting the participation of Indigenous soldiers in that war, these nations founded at the end of the nineteenth and beginning of the twentieth centuries as White men's countries have sought to redeem their reputations from the foundational frontier violence and colonial dispossession.

It is fruitful to bring what are usually separate historiographies on imperialism and colonialism and gender and race relations into conversation to chart the ways in which the figure of the "White man" was constructed in the contexts of imperial warfare and colonial rule. Over time, this figure shifted from incorporation of moral ideals of manliness toward newer understandings of masculinity that celebrated physical strength, virility, and readiness to engage in brutal, violent behaviors in the face of Indigenous resistance to imperial conquest and colonial rule. The racialized and transnational figure of the White man emerged historically in contexts in which Europeans confronted various "Others," including Aborigines, Africans, Asiatics, Native Americans, and Pacific Islanders, peoples over whom White men asserted their authority and right to rule.

Despite representing himself as the bearer of civilization, the White man engaged in acts of "barbarity" that threatened his very sense of self. Disavowal and dissimulation were thus essential to the colonizing process. Decolonization saw the White man depart from most of Africa and Asia, but in settler colonial countries he was there to stay—and those democracies would be extended from the turn of the century to include White women as self-governing subjects who sought to claim their own role as "pioneers." White women were complicit in the colonizing violence that accompanied dispossession in settler societies.

More research is needed on different colonies to establish the ways in which British, French, and Dutch colonizers, for example, became White men in the eyes of the colonized, which also shaped their sense of self, as evident in the opening testimony of Henri van Kol. Clearly, not all actual White men embodied the ideal of the upright White man or engaged in the brutal violent behaviors associated with White men on imperial frontiers. It was, nevertheless, a powerful representation invoked both to justify and to critique the imperial and colonial projects. More work is needed to ascertain how men on the ground engaged with this representation or challenged it, including in ways that ultimately undermined its pervasive power.

NOTES

1. *Nationalities and Subject Races: Report of Conference Held in Caxton Hall, Westminster, June 28-30, 1910* (London: PS King & Son, 1911), 107.
2. Marilyn Lake, "On Being a White Man, Australia, circa 1900," in *Cultural History in Australia*, ed. Hsu-Ming Teo and Richard White (Sydney: University of North South Wales Press, 2003), 98–112.
3. W. E. B. Du Bois, "The Souls of White Folk," *Independent*, August 18, 1910, 339.
4. See, for example, depictions of the Maori: Brendan Hokowhitu, "Tackling Maori Masculinity: A Colonial Genealogy of Savagery and Sport," *The Contemporary Pacific* 16, no. 2 (2004): 259–84.
5. See the chapter by Angela Woollacott on "Imperial Conquest, Violent Encounters, and Changing Gender Relations in Colonial Warfare, 1830s–1910s" in this handbook.
6. Marilyn Lake, "Frontier Feminism and the Marauding White Man," in *Gender and Imperialism*, ed. Clare Midgeley (Manchester: Manchester University Press, 1998), 123–36; Lake, "Frontier Feminism and the Marauding White Man," in *Empire, Nation, Colony*, ed. Napur Chauduri and Ruth Pierson (Bloomington: Indiana University Press, 1998), 94–105; and Fiona Paisley, *Loving Protection? Australian Feminism and Aboriginal Women's Rights, 1919-1939* (Melbourne, Australia: Melbourne University Press, 2000).
7. Mary Bennett to *Australian Board of Missions Review*, April 15, 1932; see further Marilyn Lake, "Colonised and Colonising: The White Australian Feminist Subject," *Women's History Review* 2, no. 3 (1993): 377–86; and Alison Holland, *Just Relations: The Story of Mary Bennett's Crusade for Aboriginal Rights* (Perth: UWA Publishing, 2015).
8. Mary Bennett to *Daily News*, December 13, 1933.
9. Antoinette Burton, "The Feminist Quest for Identity: British Imperial Suffragism and Global Sisterhood 1900–1915," *Journal of Women's History* 3, no. 2 (1991): 46–81; and Burton, *Burdens of History: British Feminists, Indian Women and Imperial Culture, 1865-1915* (Chapel Hill: University of North Carolina Press, 1994). On maternal feminism, see Gisela Bock and Pat Thane, eds., *Maternity and Gender Politics: Women and the Rise of the European Welfare States, 1880s-1950s* (London: Routledge, 1991); Seth Koven and Sonya Michel, eds., *Mothers of a New World: Maternalist Politics and the Origins of Welfare States* (New York: Routledge, 1993); Linda Gordon, "Putting Children First: Women, Maternalism, and Welfare in the Early Twentieth Century," in *U.S. History as Women's History: New Feminist Essays*, ed. Linda K. Kerber et al. (Chapel Hill: University of North Carolina Press, 1995), 63–86; and Judith Smart, "Modernity and Mother-Heartedness: Spirituality and Religious Meaning in Australian Women's Suffrage and Citizenship Movements, 1890s–1920s," in *Women's Suffrage in the British Empire: Citizenship, Nation and Race*, ed. Ian Christopher Fletcher et al. (London: Routledge, 2000), 51–67.

10. Heather Streets, *Martial Races: The Military, Race and Masculinity in British Imperial Culture* (Manchester: Manchester University Press, 2004), 156–89. On the Maori as a martial race, see Francheska Walker, "'Descendants of a Warrior Race': The Maori Contingent, New Zealand Pioneer Battalion, and Martial Race Myth, 1914–19," *War and Society* 31, no. 1 (2012): 1–21.

11. James Belich, *The New Zealand Wars and the Victorian Interpretation of Racial Conflict* (Auckland: Auckland University Press, 1986); and Walker, "Descendants," 1–21.

12. Sir George Arthur, quoted in Henry Reynolds, *The Forgotten War* (Sydney: NewSouth Publishing, 2013), 102.

13. Jonathon Richards, "Frontier Warfare in Australia," in *Before the Anzac Dawn: A Military History of Australia to 1915*, ed. Craig Stockings and John Connor (Sydney: NewSouth Publishing, 2013), 21–38.

14. Reynolds, *Forgotten War*.

15. Paul A. Kramer, *The Blood of Government: Race, Empire, the United States, and the Philippines* (Chapel Hill: University of North Carolina Press, 2006).

16. Ibid., 132; and Reynolds, *Forgotten War*.

17. Gail Bederman, *Manliness and Civilization: A Cultural History of Gender and Race in the United States, 1880–1917* (Chicago: University of Chicago Press, 1995), 23–31 and 71.

18. Ibid., 25.

19. Ibid., 18–23.

20. Angela Woollacott, "Frontier Violence and Settler Manhood," *History Australia* 6, no. 1 (2009): 1–15; Woollacott, "Manly Authority, Employing Non-White Labour, and Frontier Violence 1830s–1860s," *Journal of Australian Colonial History* 15 (2013): 23–42; and Jessie Mitchell, "'Great Difficulty in Knowing Where the Frontier Ceases': Violence, Governance and the Spectre of India in Early Queensland," *Journal of Australian Colonial History* 15 (2013): 43–62.

21. See, for example, Lesley Erickson, *Westward Bound: Sex, Violence, the Law and the Making of Settler Society* (Vancouver: UBC Press, 2011), 26.

22. R. Blake Brown, "'Every Boy Ought to Learn to Shoot and Obey Orders': Guns, Boys, and the Law in English Canada from the Late Nineteenth Century to the Great War," *Canadian Historical Review* 93, no. 2 (2002): 196–226.

23. Andrew Kilsby, "The Rifle Clubs," in Stockings and Connor, *Before the Anzac*, 148–73; Richard Slotkin, *Gunfighter Nation: The Myth of the Frontier in Twentieth-Century America* (Norman: University of Oklahoma Press, 1998): and Brown, "Every Boy."

24. Dane Kennedy, *Islands of White: Settler Society and Culture in Kenya and Southern Rhodesia, 1890–1938* (Durham, NC: Duke University Press, 1987), 129.

25. Maggie MacKellar, *Strangers in a Foreign Land: The Journal of Niel Black and Other Voices from the Western District* (Carlton, Vic.: Miegunyah Press, 2008), 119. Quoted in Penny Russell, *Savage or Civilised? Manners in Colonial Australia* (Sydney: University of New South Wales Press, 2010). See also Woollacott, "Frontier Violence."

26. Kellar, *Strangers*, 119; Russell, *Savage or Civilised*, 55.

27. Mitchell, "Great Difficulty," 51.

28. Henry Reynolds, *An Indelible Stain? The Question of Genocide in Australia's History* (Ringwood: Viking Books, 2001), 112–18 and 130–33; and Henry Reynolds, *Why Weren't We Told? A Personal Search for the Truth about Our History* (Ringwood: Viking Books, 1999), 104–9. See also Angela Woollacott, *Settler Society in the Australian Colonies: Self-Government and Imperial Culture* (New York: Oxford University Press, 2015).

29. Tracey Banivanua-Mar, *Violence and Colonial Dialogue: The Australian-Pacific Indentured Labor Trade* (Honolulu: University of Hawaii Press, 2007), 7.

30. Mitchell, "Great Difficulty," 109.

31. Ibid., 110.

32. Erickson, *Westward Bound*, 21.

33. Jennifer Reid, *Louis Riel and the Creation of Modern Canada: Mythic Discourse and the Postcolonial State* (Albuquerque: University of New Mexico Press, 2008). For Riel's international and imperial significance, see Geoff Reid and Todd Webb, "'The Catholic Mahdi of the North West': Louis Riel and the Metis Resistance in Transatlantic and Imperial Context," *Canadian Historical Review* 93, no. 2 (2012): 171–95.

34. On abominable atrocities in Algeria, see William Gallois, "Dahra and the History of Violence in Early Colonial Algeria," in *The French Colonial Mind*, vol. 2, *Violence, Military Encounters and Colonialism*, ed. Martin Thomas (Lincoln: University of Nebraska Press, 2011), 2–35.

35. Russell, *Savage or Civilised*, 93; Lisa Ford, *Settler Sovereignty: Jurisdiction and Indigenous People in America and Australia, 1788-1836* (Cambridge, MA: Harvard University Press, 2010); and in another imperial context, Elizabeth Kolski, *Colonial Justice in British India: White Violence and the Rule of Law* (Cambridge: Cambridge University Press, 2009).

36. Bertrand Taithe, "Losing Their Mind and Their Nation? Mimicry, Scandal, and Colonial Violence in the Voulet-Chanoine Affair," in Thomas, *French Colonial Mind*, 2: 26–52, 34–35.

37. Alice L. Conklin, *A Mission to Civilize: The Republican Idea of Empire in France and West Africa, 1895-1930* (Stanford, CA: Stanford University Press, 1997), 11–37.

38. Robert Nye, *Masculinity and Male Codes of Honor in Modern France* (New York: Oxford University Press, 1993), 304.

39. Marilyn Lake, "The Gendered and Racialised Self Who Claimed the Right to Self-Government," *Journal of Colonialism and Colonial History* 13, no. 1 (2012), https://muse.jhu.edu/article/475173.

40. Gabriel Charmes in *Revue des Deux Mondes*, quoted in ibid., 13.

41. Peter J. Cain, "Character, 'Ordered Liberty' and the Mission to Civilise: British Moral Justification of Empire, 1870–1914," *Journal of Imperial and Commonwealth History* 40, no. 4 (2012): 557–78, 560.

42. Ibid., 563.

43. Ibid., 562.

44. Conklin, *Mission*, 5.

45. Richard Price, *Making Empire: Colonial Encounters and the Creation of Imperial Rule in Nineteenth-Century Africa* (Cambridge: Cambridge University Press, 2008), 197–98.

46. Michael G. Vann, "Fear and Loathing in French Hanoi: Colonial White Images and Imaginings of 'Native' Violence," in Thomas, *French Colonial Mind*, 2: 52–77, 52–53.

47. Marilyn Lake and Henry Reynolds, *Drawing the Global Colour Line: White Men's Countries and the International Challenge of Racial Equality* (Cambridge: Cambridge University Press, 2008).

48. Lake, "Gendered and Racialised."

49. James Bryce, *Impressions of South Africa*, quoted in Lake and Reynolds, *Drawing*, 71.

50. Ibid. On comparable cases in Kenya and Rhodesia, see Kennedy, *Islands of White*.

51. Quoted in Lake, "Gendered and Racialised," 17.

52. Kramer, *Blood of Government*.

53. Quoted in Mrinalini Sinha, *Colonial Masculinity: The "Manly Englishman" and the "Effeminate Bengali" in the Late Nineteenth Century* (Manchester: Manchester University Press, 1995), 15.

54. Ibid.

55. Lala Rajpat Rai, "The Present Condition of India," in *Nationalities and Subject Races*, 21–28.

56. Quoted in Lake and Reynolds, *Drawing*, 257.

57. Quoted in Marilyn Lake, *Faith: Faith Bandler, Gentle Activist* (Sydney: Allen & Unwin, 2002), 74.

58. Alan Atkinson, *The Europeans in Australia: A History* (Melbourne, Australia: Oxford University Press, 1997–2004), 2:316.

59. Charles Henry Pearson, *National Life and Character: A Forecast* (London: Macmillan, 1893).

60. Theodore Roosevelt, "Manhood and Statehood," in Lake and Reynolds, *Drawing*, 100.

61. Bederman, *Manliness*, 170–92.

62. Slotkin, *Gunfighter Nation*, 36–62.

63. Benjamin Madley, "Reexamining the American Genocide Debate: Meaning, Historiography, and New Methods," *American Historical Review* 120, no. 1 (2015): 98–139.

64. See, for example, Pearson, *National Life*; Tom Holm, *The Great Confusion in Indian Affairs: Native Americans and Whites in the Progressive Era* (Austin: University of Texas Press, 2005); and Russell McGregor, *Imagined Destinies: Aboriginal Australians and the Doomed Race Theory, 1880–1939* (Melbourne, Australia: Melbourne University Press, 1997).

65. Graham Dawson, *Soldier Heroes: British Adventure, Empire and the Imagining of Masculinities* (London: Routledge, 1994).

66. Russell, *Savage or Civilised*, 45.

67. Reynolds, *Why Weren't We*, 60, 69.

68. Ibid., 71, 73.

69. Reynolds, *Indelible Stain*; A. Dirk Moses, "An Antipodean Genocide? The Origins of the Genocidal Moment in the Colonization of Australia," *Journal of Genocide Research* 2, no. 1 (2000): 89–107; and Moses, ed., *Empire, Colony, Genocide: Conquest, Occupation, and Subaltern Resistance in World History* (New York: Berghahn Books, 2008).

70. Stephen Howe, "British Worlds, Settler Worlds, World Systems, and Killing Fields," *Journal of Imperial and Commonwealth History* 40, no. 4 (2012): 704.

71. Madley, "Reexamining."

72. See Patrick Wolfe, *Settler Colonialism and the Transformation of Anthropology: The Politics and Poetics of an Ethnographic Event* (London: Cassell, 1999); and Wolfe, "Settler Colonialism and the Elimination of the Native," *Journal of Genocide Research* 8, no. 4 (2006): 387–409.

73. Lorenzo Veracini, *Settler Colonialism: A Theoretical Overview* (Basingstoke: Palgrave Macmillan, 2010). See also the journal he founded in 2011, *Settler Colonial Studies*.

74. John F. Owen, "The Military Forces of Our Colonies," *Fortnightly Review* 73 (1900): 477–93, 477.

75. Marilyn Lake et al., *What's Wrong with Anzac? The Militarisation of Australian History* (Sydney: University of New South Wales Press, 2010).

76. Ibid., 2.

77. Chris Pugsley, *The ANZAC Experience: New Zealand, Australia and Empire in the First World War* (Auckland, New Zealand: Reed, 2004).

78. Ian McKay and Jamie Swift, *Warrior Nation: Rebranding Canada in an Age of Anxiety* (Toronto: Between the Lines, 2011), 72.

79. Henry Reynolds, "Are Nations Really Made in War?," quoted in Lake et al., *What's Wrong*, 35.

80. Marilyn Lake, "Monuments of Manhood and Colonial Dependence: The Cult of Anzac as Compensation," in *Memory, Monuments and Museums: The Past in the Present*, ed. Marilyn Lake (Melbourne, Australia: Melbourne University Press, 2006), 43–57.

Select Bibliography

Bederman, Gail. *Manliness and Civilization: A Cultural History of Gender and Race in the United States, 1880–1917*. Chicago: University of Chicago Press, 1995.

Belich, James. *The New Zealand Wars and the Victorian Interpretation of Racial Conflict*. Auckland, New Zealand: Auckland University Press, 1986.

Conklin, Alice L. *A Mission to Civilize: The Republican Idea of Empire in France and West Africa, 1895–1930*. Stanford, CA: Stanford University Press, 1997.

Erickson, Lesley. *Westward Bound: Sex, Violence, the Law and the Making of Settler Society*. Vancouver: University of British Columbia Press, 2011.

Hall, Catherine. *Civilizing Subjects: Metropole and Colony in the English Imagination, 1830–1867*. Chicago: University of Chicago Press, 2002.

Kennedy, Dane. *Islands of White: Settler Society and Culture in Kenya and Southern Rhodesia, 1890–1938*. Durham, NC: Duke University Press, 1987.

Kolski, Elizabeth. *Colonial Justice in British India: White Violence and the Rule of Law*. Cambridge: Cambridge University Press, 2010.

Kramer, Paul A. *The Blood of Government: Race, Empire, the United States and the Philippines*. Chapel Hill: University of North Carolina Press, 2006.

Lake, Marilyn, and Henry Reynolds. *Drawing the Global Color Line: White Men's Countries and the International Challenge of Racial Equality*. Cambridge: Cambridge University Press, 2008.

Mackay, Ian, and Jamie Swift. *Warrior Nation: Rebranding Canada in an Age of Anxiety*. Toronto: Between the Lines, 2011.

Moses, A. Dirk, ed. *Empire, Colony, Genocide: Conquest, Occupation, and Subaltern Resistance in World History*. New York: Berghahn Books, 2008.

Price, Richard. *Making Empire: Colonial Encounters and the Creation of Imperial Rule in Nineteenth-Century Africa*. Cambridge: Cambridge University Press, 2008.

Pugsley, Chris. *The ANZAC Experience: New Zealand, Australia and Empire in the First World War Reed*. Auckland, New Zealand: Reed, 2004.

Reynolds, Henry. *An Indelible Stain? The Question of Genocide in Australia's History*. Ringwood: Viking Books, 2001.

Russell, Penny. *Savage or Civilized? Manners in Colonial Australia*. Sydney: University of New South Wales Press, 2010.

Slotkin, Richard. *Gunfighter Nation: The Myth of the Frontier in Twentieth Century America*. New York: Atheneum, 1992.

Streets, Heather. *Martial Races: The Military, Race and Masculinity in British Imperial Culture, 1857–1914*. Manchester: Manchester University Press, 2004.

Thomas, Martin, ed. *The French Colonial Mind*. Vol. 2, *Violence, Military Encounters and Colonialism*. Lincoln: University of Nebraska Press, 2011.

Veracini, Lorenzo. *Settler Colonialism: A Theoretical Overview*. Basingstoke: Palgrave Macmillan, 2010.

Woollacott, Angela. *Settler Society in the Australian Colonies: Self-Government and Imperial Culture*. Oxford: Oxford University Press, 2015.

CHAPTER 14

....

CHANGING MODES OF
WARFARE AND THE
GENDERING OF MILITARY
MEDICAL CARE,
1850s–1920s

....

JEAN H. QUATAERT

BETWEEN the 1850s and the 1920s, patterns of humanitarian services operating at the nexus of war, law, and medicine changed dramatically. This period opened with the earliest societal efforts to promote international cooperation in reorganizing state military medical services and ended with the creation of permanent international public health initiatives under the League of Nations after World War I. While contingent and uneven, this widening embrace of humanitarian work was fostered by law, notably the Geneva Convention, one of the earliest formulations and, still, in the early twenty-first century, the cornerstone of international humanitarian law (the laws of war). Codifying the convention in 1864 initiated developments that placed international law at the foundation of the growing integration of international society and its many permanent institutions. Designed at first to ensure impartial medical care to all wounded soldiers on the battlefield, irrespective of their status as friend or foe, treaty revisions in 1906 expanded protections to include the rights of prisoners of war. The medical agenda gradually embraced de facto attention to civilian sickness and suffering in wartime as well.

Prior to the First World War, forty-five states and empires had acceded to the Geneva Convention, giving the legal regime a remarkably global scope. Ratifying the law, in effect, brought a dynamic reform agenda into national life because the law required medical provisioning for the soldiers and sailors. The agreement also presumed the creation of national volunteer relief societies, known as Red Cross and, after 1878, Red Crescent Societies, to supplement the work of each official military medical corps in wartime and help with natural disasters in peacetime. By 1914, thirty-eight member states had fully organized national Red Cross or Red Crescent Societies. They, too, were found all over the globe. Most of the societies sponsored mobile medical field hospitals and units, with close ties to the philanthropic communities of their host countries. Their members raised money and materials and sent medical personnel and equipment to, or operated in, wars' battlefields, even if their own country did not participate in the particular armed conflict. War was an ever-present reality in the lives of Red Cross and Red Crescent medical staff and their avid domestic supporters.[1]

Between the 1850s and the 1920s, new patterns of humanitarianism with a gendered military medical service at its center developed, which responded to changing modes of warfare. These new patterns of humanitarianism stood in a complex relationship to both law and society. As codified in new law, they demanded impartial and nonpartisan medical care for wounded and sick soldiers in wartime. In return, the law protected medical staff on the battlefield by placing its work *hors de combat* (outside the fight). It declared these medical actions to be humanitarian—selfless, neutral, and removed from politics. Humanitarian notions, however, also were rooted in shifting gender norms in society. Hailed in their earliest formulations as a shared vision—a "noble cause," a "humane" venture "dear to every lover of humanity"—they animated well-placed military officers, doctors, reformers, politicians, and men and women philanthropists in civil societies. Blending science and morality, this vision underpinned an evolving "sanitary science" for the armies in the field designed to "ameliorate suffering."[2] The notion had its own concrete manifestations and served to interlink an increasingly dense medical network of organizations, publications, symbols, and actions in global society. The materiality of the ideal in institutional form and medical practices makes humanitarianism a rich and rewarding focus of historical investigation. With its immediate attention on the suffering wounded soldier, it drew on sentiments of care, empathy, and selfless actions that were typically coded female. But the processes of (re)gendering battlefield service were complex and contentious.

Exploring the gender dynamics in a study of war, law, and medicine necessarily draws together several distinct historiographies. It requires an incorporation into the analysis of perspectives opened by the field of global history, with its interest in transnational and international networks forging structural and cross-border interconnections.[3] Of particular interest is the work of the International Committee of the Red Cross, which Madeleine Herren has called the "best known manifestation of internationalism" in the nineteenth century. Its daily operations on the front lines as well as the home front were tied to the changing nature and intensity of warfare.[4] Arrogating itself power, the International Committee of the Red Cross assumed responsibility for overseeing the wartime protections safeguarded by the Geneva Conventions and coordinated the transnational relief movement it spawned.

As an international movement, the Red Cross imposed a set of common goals, legally inviolable signs (the cross, although modified by the Ottoman Empire's adoption of the crescent in 1877), and humanitarian language on each national branch organization. These commonalities constitute what Christopher Bayly calls "global uniformities," products of the increasing cross-border ties that were working to construct the global community.[5] But national comparison also reveals differences in the interplay of domestic and transnational civic activist and professional pressures that gendered wartime services. The evolution of military medical services in Britain and the United States as well as Germany and Japan, for example, followed alternative paths to the similar end of gendering through dynastic and republican authorities in addition to "Western" models of modernization. Furthermore, different motives sustained the work of the medical staff in these countries. Comparison also sheds light on the contradictions in the law's restricted *legal* definition of war as solely armed conflict between sovereign states and humanitarian battlefield service operating also in what contemporaries called *small wars*—the many colonial wars between the self-proclaimed imperial forces of civilization and so-called uncivilized peoples. In these small wars and civil wars, for that matter, Geneva Convention reciprocal protections did not apply.[6]

Most central for the study of this new field of global history is a gender analysis. So far, this field, as Merry Wiesner-Hanks notes, largely neglects the gendered implications of the historical forces creating global interconnections.[7] Dynamic processes of *gendering* professional military medical services took place around the globe after 1850, combining global patterns with local and lived experiences and meanings. A focus on gender links shifting societal gender norms to the evolving practices of humanitarian care on the battlefield. It shows an emerging gender order that simultaneously reinforced and challenged gender norms—but not necessarily social norms. Volunteer Red Cross leadership and service remained largely the preserve of educated and privileged social groups with extensive ties to each state's ruling political and military elites. Methodologically, this approach incorporates into a history of military medical provisioning the ongoing structural changes in societies, notably widening medical training for men and, increasingly, women; the emergence of professional organizations, such as gender-specific international lawyers' or nurses' associations; and feminist and women's movements, with their transnational connections.

Uneasily combining humanitarian understandings of selfless action with a sense of patriotic duty to the nation in wartime, battlefield service opened new opportunities for medically trained men and women. Most doctors in the service were commissioned medical officers or former officers in the case of the Red Cross. Other men were conscripted or volunteer soldiers recruited as nurses and also orderlies, transport workers, and stretcher bearers. Despite the ongoing and, appreciably, self-evident gendering of professional medicine, incorporating women, even as nurses, became the disruptive and troubling element in many national settings. There was nothing automatic about gendered battlefield service, as the following will demonstrate in an exploration of the themes discussed here.

THE WARS OF NATIONS IN THE 1850S AND 1860S AND NEW HUMANITARIAN VISIONS

By the mid-1850s, a discourse of humanitarianism had returned to global society, tied squarely to war's human costs. In earlier decades, humanitarian sentiments had animated the transatlantic anti–slave trade and abolition movements, which harnessed the

Enlightenment concept of common humanity for their causes.[8] But now, a growing number of philanthropic individuals, educated people, and high state and military officials became concerned with the plight of wounded soldiers on the battlefield. Deeming warfare a tragic but ever-present reality, they focused on "humanizing" war by mitigating its excesses. Turning attention to soldiers' sufferings, seen as the common human fate of all combatants whatever their state membership, religion, or ethnicity, they proclaimed a global obligation to action. Narrowing what was understood as human suffering worthy of international concern—omitting, for example, contemporary victims of famines in newly subjugated colonial lands or poverty and social injustice at home—this understanding shaped a set of humanitarian practices that became integral to and constitutive of the newly emerging international legal order.[9]

While not absent from the global scene, war had been relatively scarce on the European continent after the French Revolutionary and Napoleonic Wars (1792–1815); instead the major European powers fought elsewhere for colonial conquests.[10] With the spread of nationalist territorial demands and identification with minority, often Christian, communities in the Ottoman Empire, wars returned to Europe as the standard extensions of political and territorial contests: with the Crimean War (1853–56), the Italian Wars of Independence (1848–70) and German Wars of Unification (1864–71).[11] The North American continent also experienced bloody wars during this time: the US–Mexican War (1846–48) and the American Civil War (1861–65).[12] All these conflicts were followed avidly across the Atlantic by the reading public through the new linkages of telegraph communications and wartime journalism.[13] But it was in Europe that practical efforts first emerged as an urgent reform agenda to tackle the armies' failures to provide adequate medical care for their wounded and sick soldiers. The global system after 1850, with its ever-greater technological and economic modes of integration, was a decidedly European-dominated one.

The nature of warfare had changed dramatically since the seventeenth and eighteenth centuries, when old regimes fought wars with mercenary and conscript armies of relatively small size (compared to the armies of the Napoleonic Wars) and military nursing was mainly provided by officers and soldiers' wives and other camp followers.[14] With the mobilization of mass armies, which were based on universal conscription in an increasing number of states, first France, Austria, and Prussia, military medical care had to change too. After the 1860s, universal conscription became the rule, though not exclusively, on the European continent—Britain did not introduce it until 1916. Commanders believed that it would be easier to replace soldiers with universal conscription than to invest manpower in their care and transport. As a result, similar to the time of the Napoleonic Wars, mid-century military medical care was still haphazard, poorly provisioned, and often entrusted to untrained soldiers or even local civilians pressed into service.

Yet, this was a new era of people's wars in two fundamental ways. First, the French Revolution had linked male participation in the state to active heroic duty and sacrifice. The male citizen-soldier defending the republic or, as loyal subject, the dynastic family and collective nation, became a defining trope of identity for the formation of nation and imperial states. Either by law or by expectation, masculine duty meant the defense of the state.[15] But a soldier was someone's husband, father, or brother. The new context helps explain mounting public interest in the suffering soldier.[16] Government leaders and military authorities found they had to pay more and more attention to public opinion in wartime, a second meaning of the term *people's wars*. The term captures the intrusion of the public into matters of war and peace and, thus, foreign affairs, stirred increasingly by the spread of literacy, a nascent mass press, and the widening of horizons beyond national frontiers.[17] A letter about the nursing work of Florence Nightingale in the Crimea written to the British War Office as early as 1854 reflects the new imperative of reform, even though Britain had no universal male conscription: "The health and comfort of the troops are judged now by a very different standard from which prevailed in former occasions."[18] Convergence of these complex sentiments and values helped establish new international organizations and codify international law.

INSTITUTIONALIZING BATTLEFIELD SERVICE BY LAWS AND ORGANIZATIONS

Innovations in wartime medical care were tied partly to the intersection of the graphic ideas and broad societal receptivity of two iconic European figures at the center of the gendered face of battlefield service, although in ways largely unanticipated by either. One was Florence Nightingale, who, reflecting on her wartime experiences in the Crimea, issued a broad program for bringing nurses into military hospitals in Britain in 1858. For decades thereafter from her sickbed in London, she directed the professionalization of female nurses for reorganized civilian hospital work and inspired the Nightingale Training School model of study, practice, and discipline, which spread far and wide in global societies, reaching the United States in 1873, Japan in the later 1880s, and China by the early 1920s.[19] Yet, her main passion of integrating fully trained and disciplined female nurses into field-hospital work faced significant obstacles resulting from the persistent hostility of many of Britain's male military medical officers and the War Office.

As a reformer, Nightingale was a vocal opponent of voluntary philanthropy. She declared it "most important" that her reform mission "be free, once and forever, from the injurious, untrue, and derogatory appendage of public patronage."[20] Medical care of soldiers and sailors was the sole obligation of the sovereign state, she held. She hoped for the inclusion of trained female nurses in this professionalized and state-controlled service. In practice, in Britain, the forerunner of the British Red Cross Society, the National Aid Society, which relied on patronage and voluntary contributions to fund medical relief work, proved more receptive to women's war work than the War Office.[21] The pattern held true for many national branches of the international Red Cross movement in its formative decades.

The second iconic figure was Henry Dunant, a Swiss businessman responsible in good measure for founding the International Committee of the Red Cross. His travels brought him to Solferino in Northern Italy in June 1859. In this major battle of the Second Italian War of Independence (1859), the French army under Napoleon III and the Sardinian army under Victor Emmanuel II totaling 140,000 men fought against Austrian troops numbering 130,000 men under Emperor Franz Joseph I.[22] What Dunant saw on the battlefield haunted him: 30,000 wounded soldiers from both belligerent camps dying after the battle because of inadequate medical attention. Returning to Geneva, he wrote a scathing account entitled *A Memory of Solferino*, which he self-published in 1862 as an "open letter to world leaders and opinion makers" and sent to Europe's dynastic courts, prominent military leaders, doctors, writers, and philanthropists. The book became an instant success, translated quickly into seven European languages. With its searing details of horror and misery, it effectively evoked humanitarian sentiments, creating immediate, visceral connections between distant readers and his symbol of suffering humanity, the soldier's mutilated body. Time and again, he reminded readers of the families' pain in the soldiers' suffering.[23] Humanitarian sensibilities expressed by the antislavery campaigns had rarely envisioned the slave as a human being with rights; Dunant, in contrast, tied his vision to a legal regime, which his movement helped create.

The keys to Dunant's success were two innovations for the age. The first was his proposal for *permanent* voluntary relief associations formed and trained in peacetime and designed to supplement the states' military medical corps in wartime. Second, he recognized the need for *permanent* treaty law that remained open for states to accede to, even if they had not attended the original drafting conference. In the new calculations of people's wars, his appeal found consistent support among high government and military authorities. It led to a diplomatic conference called by the neutral Swiss government in Geneva in 1864, where state representatives drafted the convention. Dunant had recognized the need for states to declare a universal sign of inviolability (the cross and later, de facto, the crescent), setting up a legal zone of safety for medical work amid the violence of war. This conference set the stage for subsequent civil society and governmental intersections that brought matters of law, war, and peace to the forefront of societal debates.[24]

In its origins, Dunant's vision was a masculine project, one in which, as Geoffrey Best writes boldly, the "manhood of the 'civilized countries' was in a strikingly real sense attending to its own interests." A deep gender ambivalence, however, ran through Dunant's influential memoir. When he described the ad hoc responses of local inhabitants to soldiers' needs at Solferino, he wrote self-evidently about women's valuable medical and social services; when he prescribed the personnel for his envisioned national associations, he virtually excluded what he called "weak and ignorant" women. In its own ironic twist, Dunant's project found ardent support among contemporary women—female dynasts in the courts of Europe and privileged ladies in women's patriotic associations, which had been working to aid veterans of the French Revolutionary and Napoleonic Wars as well as the poor and destitute in urban societies.[25] Typically under dynastic patronage, most of these organizations on the continent became subsumed under Red Cross leadership, assuring the movement a considerable (female) membership extending deep into society, although increasingly brought under military regulations.

Complementing Nightingale's inspirations, the societies early on also established scientific nurse training for war work.[26]

Unsettled was the role of the volunteer Red Cross societies at the heart of Dunant's vision. In 1864, military leaders in Geneva had balked at recognizing a place for volunteers on the battlefield and excluded them from the legal safeguards. But the founding of national wartime relief societies continued apace, aided by the simultaneous evolution of the small, all-male philanthropic group in Geneva that first had pushed Dunant's vision. Declaring itself the International (Central) Committee in 1875, the exclusive Swiss body effectively coordinated the founding and running of national societies and offered guidance in interpreting the law. Over time, the wartime medical services of the branch societies became indispensable to states' overall defense agendas. Revision of the Geneva Convention in 1906 formally brought the volunteer battlefield personnel under legal protections. Through its central organ, the *International Bulletin* sent around the globe, the many national publications, and reports of its activities in the local presses, the movement spread the word about the "great work of humanity" (*grande oeuvre d'humanité*) at the heart of its proclaimed nonpartisan humanitarian mission.[27]

GENDER AND THE PROFESSIONALIZATION OF MILITARY MEDICAL PROVISIONING

Army medical staff and Red Cross volunteers were caught up in military and technological changes that increased the need for their services and secured their expanding role in newly codified international law. After relative stasis for nearly a century, in the 1860s the use of newly emerging inventions and technologies, such as breech-loading rifles and artillery, machine guns, expanding bullets, and metal hulled steamships, began to influence the machinery of war, leading to deadlier, more varied, and more precise weaponry. The pace of change accelerated relentlessly, and in his comprehensive history of the laws of war, Best listed them as including "quick firers, smokeless powder, melanite, mines, torpedoes, submarines, gas, aerial bombs." Coupled with mounting imperialist and nationalist rivalries, Europe's military leaders feared sudden technological advantage by enemy states, which reinforced the earlier effort at collective norm setting in Geneva. The global system was being fashioned by forces compelling war as well as by movements, practices, and institutions designed to tame its excesses—or, ideally, ban war altogether.[28]

Independently, similar concerns were being voiced from many sides of civil society by newly professionalized international lawyers, Red Cross personnel in the field witnessing the shortcomings in existing law, peace movements burgeoning throughout the Atlantic world, and activists in transnational women's movements, many of whom linked women's enfranchisement to a more peaceful international order.[29] These diverse and at times contradictory interests nonetheless coalesced in the calling of two diplomatic conferences at The Hague in the Netherlands in 1899 and 1907. Here, international lawyers, diplomats, and military officials wrote new treaty law to limit the states' means and methods of waging war and instituted permanent mechanisms favoring arbitration over armed conflict to settle disputes between sovereign states; they created the Permanent Court of Arbitration. The growing, internationally minded public eagerly followed news of the negotiations; it was public expectations, after all, that gave the conferences their enduring, if somewhat misleading, name, the Peace Conferences.[30]

But the humanitarian project at the heart of Red Cross activism was not pacifist, however much it relied on international law and an engaged public, some of which, to be sure, fell into the pacifist camp. One telling illustration makes the point. In 1911, Mabel T. Boardman, leader of the American Red Cross from 1905 to 1919, contacted Andrew Carnegie, industrialist turned philanthropist and active peace advocate who, one year earlier, had founded the Carnegie Endowment for International Peace. She wanted him to contribute to an initiative she called a "peace activity," a new permanent fund for international relief in peacetime. His secretary refused, explaining Carnegie's assessment of Red Cross work: "Mr. Carnegie is primarily interested in peace and arbitration as a means of affecting it. He takes little interest in the Red Cross believing it pre-supposes war, and wants to abolish war, to pull it up by the roots if possible rather than to mitigate its severities. He regarded the [proposed new fund] as a connection with war. He does not see it as something separate and distinct from the other work of the Red Cross and until he [does] he will not open his purse strings."[31] Medical personnel under Geneva Conventions protections operated in a complex social field where humanitarian understandings remained fluid and open, attracting a wide range of adherents with many different motives.

The gendering of military medical services reflected the same pulls of civil society involvement, state and military self-interest, and geopolitical contingencies as those underwriting new humanitarian law. A few examples drawn from Britain, the United States, Germany, and Japan show shared patterns of development as well as crucial differences in the complex global environment. In each case, change occurred in two phases: the first of experimentation and the second of centralization and professionalization, consolidating a medically integrated gender hierarchy of service under state imprimatur. The shift took place, furthermore, because of perceived shortcomings in battlefield services in what became formative wars. Imperial Germany took the first steps at reorganizing its military and civilian medical hierarchy after the bruising experiences of French guerrilla campaigns prolonging the Franco-Prussian War (1870–71), the last War of Nations in mid-nineteenth-century Europe.[32] In 1878, authorities issued the first of several revised mobilization orders for the realm that drew the female and male Red Cross components into contingency planning for future war.[33]

In Britain and the United States, Wars of Empire proved causative: the South African War (1899–1902) between two *European* peoples, as one British officer tellingly called his country's conflict with the Boers, the Spanish–American War (1898), and the Philippine–American War (1899–1902). The institutional change placed the volunteer medical corps under the equivalent war departments. In the United States, the step required a coup that removed Clara Barton—a pioneering nurse, founder of the American Red Cross in 1882, and its popular leader, as the organization's president—and by 1905 created, in the words of a contemporary observer explaining the events to the International Committee, "virtually a government Annex in place of the civilian management."[34] In Britain, a similar outcome, too, was effected in 1905, although the change had been resisted for several years by leaders of the old National Aid Society, who feared becoming a "war department committee masquerading as the British Red Cross."[35] In both cases, regulatory change strengthened state control and professionalization of the organization on the one hand and the low place of female nurses in the military medical hierarchy on the other.

Japan had its own path, reflecting the extensive modernization project of the Meiji reformers after 1868. It shows, nonetheless, striking parallels as well as the transnational exchanges that were characteristic of Red Cross developments more widely. Determined to model government and military institutions on European best practices, the new Japanese leaders sent delegations to study European institutions, including a group that met with the International Committee in Geneva. After ratifying the Geneva Convention in 1886, the government formalized a Red Cross Society in a top-down initiative closely modeled on German institutions. The training of its army physicians mandated they take internships in European hospitals; most Japanese doctors studied in Germany or Britain. There, they experienced the indispensable role of professional nursing, among other innovations. The Sino-Japanese War of 1894–95 proved decisive, strengthening a nursing branch under the close supervision of aristocratic ladies that initially drew on war widows and other financially strapped respectable women. As part of their military reforms, the Japanese instituted the first professional women's nursing corps in Asia; by 1904, the country boasted the largest national branch in the international movement.[36] But influence went in other directions, too. When the British government reorganized the country's territorial defenses in 1909, it used Japanese precedents for its Voluntary Aid Defense system.[37]

These patterns capture only the timing and larger structural changes accompanying a few states' adherence to the Geneva Conventions. They say nothing about the social context for gender change or how the military and volunteer medical staff in the field understood their work. As a comparative gender issue, these questions are poorly examined in the national historiographies and open a rewarding arena for future research. The following brief examination of the ways "efficient" (the contemporary code for trained female nurses) women entered British and US medical corps is drawn partly from archival sources. The sources also show the shifting place of men in the military medical hierarchy. In both countries, incorporating women reflected autonomous civil society initiatives in marked contrast, for example, to Japan. There, training women for war work was solely a government initiative, while Imperial Germany represents an intermediary case with nursing training organized in religiously inspired motherhouses tied to the Red Cross and dynastic patronage.

In Britain, the cause of the integration of women into war work found its major protagonist in the leadership of the new British National Society for Aid to the Sick and

Wounded in War (NAS), created in 1870 at the start of the Franco-Prussian War to aid wounded soldiers of both belligerent camps. With the NAS the British Red Cross was officially founded. A few of its key members had attended the Geneva Conferences. It was then that the British organization instituted agents in the field to coordinate medical work and procurement (an innovation subsequently adopted by other countries), using only men—army surgeons contracted for the job or socially well-positioned amateurs with innate administrative skills such as the British humanitarian worker and businessman Vincent Kennett-Barrington. Coordination among the medical staff and with military authorities remained haphazard at first, with admittedly "much blundering."[38]

In 1870, the society had 899 auxiliary committees and 400 staff, but only one of its mobile ambulance units utilized female nurses: the Roman Catholic Mother and Sisters of All Saints, known popularly as the "ladies ambulance."[39] Nursing was still part of male orderlies' diverse tasks. It was in the deadly colonial wars in Africa in the late 1870s and 1880s, which set new precedents lasting decades, that the NAS for the first time began to aid its own soldiers, introducing potential rivalry with the Army Medical Corps jealous of its prerogatives and standing with the public. Treading a delicate line, NAS leaders publicized their intentions at the start of the Anglo–Zulu War in 1879. They praised the government for its "ample and complete" supply of surgeons and materials, which left the society "only a small scope of expenditures on luxuries, tobacco, newspapers etc. and the engagement of some nursing sisters."[40] The statement was too modest, because the NAS coordinated a private initiative underwritten by an Evangelical Protestant Deaconesses' Institution and Training Hospital in London founded by a German former doctor who modeled it on the influential nursing institute of the Evangelical *Diakonie* Kaiserswerth in the German Rhineland. Florence Nightingale once had considered joining the German order too. The hospital sent a small corps of trained nurses to southern Africa; the favorable press back home appreciably shamed the government into supplying its own nursing sisters who had been training at Netley, a village on the south coast of Hampshire and the location of the Royal Army Victorian Hospital.

With this precedent in mind, NAS leaders petitioned the government to fund privately the training of a small nursing order at Netley, which it supported from 1881 to 1885. In April 1885, the government issued the first of its regulations creating an army nursing corps, which incorporated the small Red Cross unit into its ranks. With a preference for war widows, officers' daughters, and well-born women, the nursing sisters were strictly subordinated to the male army medical officers and hospital surgeons; supervised in turn by a lady matron, they ran the wards day and night and performed most nursing tasks formerly done by the orderlies. In the emerging medical hierarchy, orderlies were subordinated to nurses, which produced all manner of friction for decades; in addition, the sisters instructed men in the Royal Army Medical Corps who had been chosen to train as nurses. This medical hierarchy was tested, tweaked, and expanded in the ongoing colonial wars but retained these major characteristics for decades. In these small wars, furthermore, medical work did not embrace reciprocal humanitarian principles, even if it was carried out under the Red Cross. Neither the army nor the volunteers, or so the evidence seems to indicate, aided to any significant degree the wounded enemy Native insurgents. The medical staff cared exclusively for its own troops.

Only after military victory ended the war did the British Red Cross evoke the nonpartisan humanitarian principle of reciprocal care. In a telling notice published shortly after the September 1898 massacre at Omdurman during the Mahdist or Sudan War (1881–99), where at least 11,000 Dervish insurgents were killed and more than double that number were wounded, NAS leader General Lord Robert Loyd-Lindsey Wantage wrote that he had placed at the disposal of the imperial governor "as the best means of showing in a practical form the Society's sympathy with all sufferers from wounds or sickness in the recent operations in Sudan, irrespective of nationality, 300£ pounds to be applied to the Egyptian soldiers and a sum of 200£ pounds for the purchase and immediate dispatch to Omdurman of articles urgently needed for the Dervish wounded who are being treated by the Egyptian medical staff."[41] The Red Cross placed its humanitarian sentiments in the service of the consolidation of new imperial rule.

Private initiatives across the seas also secured for US women nurses a formal place in battlefield service. At the founding of the American Red Cross in 1882, Clara Barton had negotiated a separate agreement with the International Committee known as the "American amendment," claiming distance from the "scenes of European battlefields" and all manner of warfare. The clause equated relief measures for large-scale disasters with war preparation and war work, which was the legal rationale behind the formation of national societies globally. Between 1882 and 1898, the American branch had no formal ties with the military; it demonstrated its practical value though highly publicized and acclaimed organized relief ventures for victims of the Michigan forest fire in 1871 and the Johnstown flood in 1889, for example.

During these same years, many new hospitals were established, including Bellevue in New York City, a highly respected medical school training women and men nurses in the Nightingale method. With the outbreak of the Spanish–American War in 1898, the Red Cross offered its services to the military, including its trained nurses. Insistent negotiations with the US War Department's Surgeon General George Miller Sternberg secured its operatives a formal role: at base hospitals on the mainland and on the hospital ships ferrying the wounded home for care and subsequently also in the small war in the Philippines but not, as Sternberg explained, "to accompany soldiers in the field or to camps of instruction."[42] Authorities used "enlisted men" of the Hospital Corps to care for the sick in field hospitals during active operations. These privates, he continued in an interesting formulation, constituted the "Red Cross organization of the regular military service, the non-combatants in accordance with the terms of the Geneva Convention, many medical students and even graduates in medicine."

Yet, war's necessities drew more women into service, facilitated by "Auxiliary 3" of the Red Cross for the Maintenance of Trained Nurses, a virtually all-woman committee of well-positioned ladies under Elizabeth Mills-Reid, the wife of New York Tribune editor Whitelaw Reid. Auxiliary 3, the only female organization among the diverse auxiliaries established by the Red Cross to coordinate a civilian war effort, in tandem with the Medical Department, helped secure a permanent nursing corps within the regular army in 1901. In the interim, brokered by the auxiliary, women nurses were sent to Cuba to deal with an immediate threat of yellow fever; similar outbreaks of contagious diseases expanded the numbers of female nurses at the base hospitals. An informal sex division of labor emerged in nursing: Male nurses worked the hospital ships, also doing heavy cleaning, and nursed the Spanish prisoners of war. Female nurses remained in charge of the wards but also oversaw the "proper feeding" of sick patients.[43]

Diverse motives drew women into Red Cross service, as seen in nurses' letters and memoirs and also biographies. Something as individual as personal commitment defies easy generalization, however. Sentiments of American nurses in 1899 included "love of the work," a commitment to "relieving suffering" and pride in the care of ordinary soldiers whose lives "won't be sung." They also reflected a fierce loyalty to the hospital unit and, by extension, to the Red Cross organization; this same devotion to the group and to deeply forged friendships remained characteristic in the service throughout World War I. Some nurses were strongly patriotic, projecting their notion of duty to the nation, while others took pride in the demonstration of *women's* capabilities. As Marjorie Henschall, nurse superintendent in the Philippines, wrote to Elizabeth Mills-Reid, also referencing the constant tensions with some male medical officers in the field, "it has been hard fought but...worth it not only for our reputation as nurses but as *women.*" Given the contemporaneous activism of women's movements in civilian society, this view could translate into feminist politics—for the "advancement of our sex," as another nurse expressed it.[44]

Gender integration of battlefield services spread slowly around the globe in a pace of change that reflected distinct cultural and political contexts. Numerous exceptions to this mixed-sex practice existed, however, adding a rich texture to battlefield service. In the Balkan Wars (1912–13), for example, the British War Office authorized the Red Cross to send an all-male mobile hospital unit to Bulgaria; through local Red Crescent initiatives, Muslims from Britain's Indian colony deployed a medical division for Ottoman troops that also used exclusively male nurses. Yet, in the same war, the British feminist Mabel St. Clair Stobart, through her army and Red Cross connections, raised, trained, and commanded the first all-woman unit (the Women's Convoy Corps) of doctors, nurses, truck drivers, and cooks sent to Bulgaria to demonstrate women's capacities for national defense beyond existing Red Cross feminine prototypes of hospital nursing and volunteer first-aid training. Stobart's mission captured a brand of "rough and ready" practical feminism that set important precedents for World War I.[45]

Medical Humanitarianism in World War I and Postwar Developments

The unexpected length and human cost of World War I for all belligerent nations enormously taxed and expanded battlefield services, the main outlines of which had been set in the prewar periods. From the viewpoint of battlefield services, two observations offer a distinct contribution to the vibrant debates about the war and postwar developments. The first is the legally ambiguous slippage between war work and civilian relief occasioned by a spiraling spread of contagious diseases that threatened soldiers and civilians alike starting in 1915. The second involves the bourgeois feminist response to the outbreak of war: suspension of the suffrage campaign in the name of national unity and determination to "do one's bit" for national defense. In this political calculus, showcasing women's valuable contributions to the war effort was expected to translate into full enfranchisement after the war. "The more women we could get to help, the greater the gain for the women's movement," wrote the Scottish medical doctor and suffragist Elsie Inglis to Millicent Fawcett, the leader of the National Union of Women's Suffrage Societies (NUWSS), in October 1914.[46]

Prodded by medically trained women doctors committed to women's rights, the NUWSS, Britain's largest women's association, agreed to sponsor and fund all-women volunteer mobile hospital units for *front-line* service. Known as the Scottish Women's Hospitals under the able supervision of Elsie Inglis, they recruited an all-female medical staff and women mechanics and ambulance drivers, pushing Stobart's model further. These units were a defining feature of the First World War, reflecting the particular confluence of moderate feminist mobilizations and international Red Cross networks. As one former volunteer commented in May 1941 comparing her experience with the practice of nursing during the Second World War, they now "are working more alongside the men I think than as a feminist thing by itself." Heralded and followed avidly by the contemporary press, the Scottish Women's Hospitals prototype stretched prevailing gender assumptions about women's war work, although its impact on political developments is more difficult to calculate.[47]

Shortly after the outbreak of war, Inglis offered her Scottish Women's Hospitals model to the War Office. Officials refused to authorize these unusual formations, so she put them at the disposal of the International Red Cross. Funded by societal subscriptions, they went out under its authority, to France first, then to the eastern front—notably Serbia, Russia, and Romania—and later to Corsica, where a hospital unit accompanied around 60,000 Serbian soldiers and countless civilian refugees fleeing to safety. Here, they not only aided the troops until many returned to battle, but also instituted extensive hygienic training in maternal and infant care for Serbian women, which was deemed essential to rebuilding the future nation. Inglis originally had deployed her hospitals to Serbia in 1915 to help contain a dangerous epidemic of typhus, demonstrating the necessity of attending to the civil population equally affected by diseases silently spreading back and forth from the front to the home front. Among other programs, they staffed strategically positioned ad hoc stations for inoculations and other medical necessities.[48]

This wartime attention to civilian medical needs was at odds with a formal reading of the Geneva Conventions. There had been earlier slippage related to authorized relief during natural disasters. The American amendment mentioned earlier, which equated war work and disaster relief, is the case in point, but in the Russo–Turkish War (1877–78), the Red Crescent, for example, sought permission from the International Committee of the Red Cross to aid sick Bulgarian refugees fleeing en masse into Istanbul.[49] But as late as 1914, even the American Red Cross officially restricted support of noncombatants according to the law. By 1916, however, Red Cross leaders active in the European theaters accepted that battlefield war services necessitated two closely intertwined components: war work and civilian work.[50]

The growing coordination of the latter field might seem to lead inevitably to the proclaimed "peace program" after the war, when humanitarian relief services turned from soldiers' needs to those of women and children, seen as humanity's newer victims of war's ravages, epidemics, and poor societal understandings of public health. Under the new League of Nations founded in January 1920 as a result of the Paris Peace Conference (1919–20), this commitment established an international public health agenda centering in good measure on the public health nurse.[51] The structural change was not inevitable; it was the outcome of deep, bitter negotiations around the meaning of humanitarian service, which after the war was again up for grabs. Making public health an international commitment reflected the new international balance of power in the victor's peace.

Elevating the role of the public health nurse also might seem an international acknowledgment of the wartime accomplishments of nursing in particular. And in some respects, this interpretation is valid. However, the institutions for coordinated public health excluded nurses in leadership and policy-making positions for a decade. Even more significant, immediate postwar commemoration and subsequent memory smothered nurses in a set of homogenizing humanitarian assumptions of female self-sacrifice and quiet duty. Drawing on long-standing stereotypes of the profession, to be sure, these sentiments transformed the challenging job into traditional women's work. Lost were the wide range of tasks women did amid the dangers of war, as exemplified by the exploits of the staff of the Scottish Women's Hospitals. Their courageous record receded from memory, only to be brought out as patriotic tropes by a nation calling again on women to do their bit in World War II.

CONCLUSION

A gender analysis of intersecting global and local patterns in the evolution of humanitarian wartime services inspired by international law is fruitful. But the questions raised here should be explored beyond Britain, the United States, Germany, and Japan, to include Latin America, with its regional traditions of international law and extensive nation-state developments, and other regions around the globe. In addition, more empirical research is needed to examine the ways the medical staff understood its service. How did former military officers and soldiers who also served in Red Cross capacities in their careers make the transition from presumed martial masculinity to impartial humanitarian service? How did they understand themselves as men? Were there particular brands of Red Cross masculinity—complementing shifting valences of femininity? Finally, how did women's battlefield service intersect with commitments to political change? Even in the First World War, there was no automatic bartering of service for suffrage. Intriguing evidence from the life stories of some Scottish Women's Hospitals mechanics and truck drivers unschooled in Geneva values (although they did their non-partisan duty to aid German and Austrian prisoners of war) shows a strong pull of nationalist and, later, anticommunist sentiments that translated into conservative imperial interwar politics.[52] Placing these personal narratives into the changing global structures still remains to be done.

NOTES

1. Jean H. Quataert, "War-Making and the Restraint of Law: The Formative Years, 1864–1914," in *The Cambridge History of War: War and the Modern World, 1850–2005*, ed. Roger Chickering et al. (Cambridge: Cambridge University Press, 2012), 142–62.

2. These quotes reflect contemporary usage of the term humanitarian in its connection to warfare. See, for example, W. B. Bowles from the US Sanitary Commission in Paris to Henri Dunant, May 14, 1864, AF 5, 4, Archive of the International Committee of the Red Cross (hereafter cited as AICRC); and Charles Burgess to the Geneva Central Committee, London, July 30, 1870, AF 8, 1863–1886, 2/69, AICRC. For recent scholarship, see Michael Barnett, *Empire of Humanity: A History of Humanitarianism* (Ithaca, NY: Cornell University Press, 2011), who sets the campaign to address the soldiers' plight in a wider context of humanitarian actions; and Bruno Cabanes, *The Great War and the Origins of Humanitarianism, 1918–1924* (Cambridge: Cambridge University Press, 2014). Cabanes sees transnational humanitarian interventions as a product of the First World War, thereby missing this earlier history.

3. Examples of this new history are Akira Iriye, *Global Community: The Role of International Organizations in the Making of the Contemporary World* (Berkeley: University of California Press, 2002); and David Northrup, "Globalization and the Great Convergence: Rethinking World History in the Long Term," *Journal of World History* 16, no. 3 (2005): 249–67.

4. Madeleine Herren, *Internationale Organisationen seit 1865: Eine Globalgeschichte der internationalen Ordnung* (Darmstadt: Wissenschaftliche Buchgesellschaft, 2009), 23.

5. Christopher A. Bayly, *The Birth of the Modern World, 1780–1914: Global Connections and Comparisons* (Malden, MA: Blackwell, 2004), 1.

6. In contemporary usage, the term referred to rebellions, armed conflicts, and military struggles that were fought between the regularly trained and disciplined European (and American) soldiers, including their colonial allies, and unconventional or "seemingly" irregular forces. For its main theoretician, see C. E. Callwell, *Small Wars: Their Principles and Practice* (1906; repr., Lincoln: University of Nebraska Press, 1996).

7. Merry E. Wiesner-Hanks, "World History and the History of Women, Gender and Sexuality," *Journal of World History* 18, no. 1 (2007): 53–67.

8. Lynn Festa, "Humanity without Feathers," *Humanity: An International Journal of Human Rights, Humanitarianism, and Development* 1, no. 1 (2010): 3–27.

9. Mike Davis, *Late Victorian Holocausts: El Niño Famines and the Making of the Third World* (London: Verso, 2001).

10. See the chapters by Alan Forrest on "Society, Mass Warfare, and Gender in Europe during and after the Revolutionary and Napoleonic Wars," and Stefan Dudink, Karen Hagemann,

and Mischa Honeck "War and Gender: Nineteenth-Century Wars of Nations and Empires—an Overview" in this handbook.

11. Dennis Showalter, *The Wars of German Unification* (London: Bloomsbury Academic, 2004); and Trevor Royale, *Crimea: The Great Crimean War, 1854–1856* (New York: St. Martin's Press, 2000). For British perspectives on changing medical wartime services, see Neil Cantilie, *A History of the Army Medical Department*, vol. 2 (Edinburgh: Churchill Livingstone, 1974). For comparative purposes, see Stig Förster and Jörg Nagler, eds., *On the Road to Total War: The American Civil War and the German Wars of Unification, 1861–1871* (Cambridge: Cambridge University Press, 1997).

12. See the chapter by Amy S. Greenberg on "Gender and the Wars of Nation-Building and Nation-Keeping in the Americas, 1830s–1870s" in this handbook.

13. See the chapter by Robert A. Nye on "War Mobilization, Gender, and Military Culture in Nineteenth-Century Western Societies" in this handbook.

14. See the chapter by Peter H. Wilson on "Wars, States, and Gender in Early Modern European Warfare, 1600s–1780s" in this handbook.

15. See the chapter by Stefan Dudink on "Citizenship, Mass Mobilization, and Masculinity in a Transatlantic Perspective, 1770s–1870s" in this handbook. Also see Stefan Dudink et al., eds., *Masculinities in Politics and War: Gendering Modern History* (Manchester: Manchester University Press, 2004), 3–40.

16. For patterns established already in the Napoleonic Wars, see Karen Hagemann, "Female Patriots: Women, War and the Nation in the Period of the Prussian–German Anti-Napoleonic Wars," *Gender & History* 16, no. 3 (2004): 397–424.

17. See Nye, "War Mobilization" in this handbook.

18. The examples are from Great Britain, but they are duplicated in other national contexts. See Sue M. Goldie, ed., *"I Have Done My Duty." Florence Nightingale in the Crimean War, 1854–56* (Iowa City: University of Iowa Press, 1987), 8; and Redmond McLaughlin, *The Royal Army Medical Corps* (London: Leo Cooper, 1972), 1–2. People's wars also captured the change in tactics, with popular armed resistance using guerrilla warfare.

19. Celia Davies, "Professionalizing Strategies as Time- and Culture-Bound: American and British Nursing circa 1893," in *Nursing History: New Perspectives, New Possibilities*, ed. Ellen Condliffe Lagemann (New York: Teachers College, 1983), 47–63; Aya Takahashi, *The Development of the Japanese Nursing Profession: Adopting and Adapting Western Influences* (London: Routledge, 2004), 37–53, has a chapter entitled "'Nightingale-ism' in Japan"; see also Sonya Grypma, *Healing Henan: Canadian Nurses at the North China Mission, 1888–1947* (Vancouver: University of British Columbia Press, 2008).

20. Florence Nightingale, *Subsidiary Notes as to the Introduction of Female Nursing into Military Hospitals in Peace and in War, Presented by Request to the Secretary of State for War* (London: Harrison and Sons, 1858), 3–8.

21. See Roy Wake, *The Nightingale Training School, 1860–1996* (London: Haggerston Press, 1998). Wake also provides details on the circulation of the Nightingale training strategy in global society.

22. See Arnold Blumberg, *A Carefully Planned Accident: The Italian War of 1859* (Cranbury, NJ: Associated University Presses, 1990).

23. J. Henry Dunant, *Memory of Solferino* (Washington, DC: American National Red Cross, 1939), 40, 42, 51–52, 56, for graphic references to the suffering soldier (quote on p. 40).

24. Jean H. Quataert, "International Law and the Laws of War, 1864–1914," in *1914–1918 Online: International Encyclopedia of the First World War*, 1–20, http://www.1914-1918-online.net.

For studies on subsequent law-making conferences, see A. Pearce Higgins, *The Hague Peace Conferences and Other International Conferences Concerning the Laws and Usages of War: Texts of Conventions with Commentaries* (Cambridge: Cambridge University Press, 1909) for the law; and Arthur Eyffinger, *The 1899 Hague Peace Conference: "The Parliament of Man, the Federation of the World"* (The Hague: Kluwer Law International, 1999) for their social history.

25. See Forrest, "Society, Mass Warfare, and Gender" in this handbook; and Hagemann, "Female Patriots."

26. Geoffrey Best, *Humanity in Warfare: The Modern History of the International Law of Armed Conflict London* (London: Weidenfeld & Nicolson, 1980), 147; Dunant, *Memory*, 74, 89–90; and Jean H. Quataert, *Staging Philanthropy: Patriotic Women and the National Imagination in Dynastic Germany, 1813–1916* (Ann Arbor: University of Michigan Press, 2001), 39–49, 67–74.

27. Ernst von Holleben (1815–1908), the new Prussian Central Committee chairman, to Geneva, 1872, AF 13, 2/494 (F), AICRC. The phrase also shows up in various permutations, notably D. Pechedjimaldji, the Ottoman Red Crescent leader, to the International Committee affirming their common work, November 12, 1876, AF, 19, 2/30 (T) Constantinople, AICRC, and *Bulletin International des Sociétés de Secours aux militaires blessés*, 13, no. 51 (Geneva: B. Soullier, 1882), 163.

28. Best, *Humanity in Warfare*, 159. See also the chapter by Glenda Sluga on "Gender, Peace, and the New Politics of Humanitarianism in the First Half of the Twentieth Century" in this handbook.

29. Herren, *Internationale Organisationen*, 34–37, 47–49; Jean H. Quataert, *The Gendering of Human Rights in the International Systems of Law in the Twentieth Century* (Washington, DC: American Historical Association, 2006), 5–12; Margarethe Leonore Selenka, ed., *The International Demonstration of Women for the Peace-Conference of May 15, 1899* (Munich: August Schapp, 1900); and Ralph Uhlig, *Die Interparlamentarische Union, 1899–1914: Friedenssicherungsbemühungen im Zeitalter des Imperialismus* (Stuttgart: Franz Steiner, 1988).

30. The Hague lawmaking, at its root, was an empirical project drawing on existing law, notably the much emulated Leiber Code for military conduct issued during the American Civil War (1863), contemporary legal compendia collected by international lawyers, and studied state practice. For the diverse sources, see Thomas Barclay, *International Law and Practice, with Appendices* (London: Sweet & Maxwell, 1917); and Adam Roberts and Richard Guelff, eds., *Documents on the Laws of War* (Oxford: Clarendon Press, 1982).

31. RC 200 Records of the American National Red Cross 1881–1916, March 6, 1911, April 10, 1911, box 29, no. 219, "Other Specific Funds," NARA.

32. Stig Förster and Jörg Nagler, "Introduction," in Förster and Nagler, *Road to Total War*, 4–11; and Robert Thomas, "The Wars against Paris," in ibid., 541–564.

33. Quataert, *Staging Philanthropy*, 74–89; and the retrospective assessment of the Ministry of War, *Sanitäts-Bericht über die Deutsche Heere im Kriege gegen Frankreich 1870/71*, vol. 1, *Administrativer Theil: Sanitätsdienst bei den Deutschen Heeren* (Berlin: Ernst Siegfried Mittler und Sohn, 1884), v–vii, which details the first steps in the reorganization of the German medical and volunteer services in light of the experiences of the Franco-German War.

34. John Hitz, March 24, 1905, 5/2/433, AICRC. See also Stella Bingham, *Ministering Angels* (London: Osprey, 1979).

35. Buckingham Palace, July 11, 1905, D/Wan/16/1/22, British Red Cross Archives (hereafter cited as BRCA).

36. Nagao Ariga, *The Red Cross Society of Japan: Its Organization and Activity in Time of Peace and War* (St. Louis: Sam L. F. Myerson, 1904).

37. Bingham, *Ministering Angels*, 11–16; also Takahashi, *Japanese Nursing Profession*, 96–102.

38. Florence Nightingale, marked private and confidential, June 16, 1885 (The Egyptian campaign), D/Wan/8/2/1, BRCA, one of a series of letters referencing noted shortcomings in provisioning and coordination. Also, Peter Morris, ed., *First Aid to the Battlefront: Life and Letters of Sir Vincent Kennett-Barrington* (Phoenix Mill, Stroud, Gloucestershire: Alan Sutton, 1992), 40, captures the sense of displacement by the professionalization of volunteer service. In his own words, "I am rather too much of a free hand, too much inclined to my hobby of having a very elastic organisation untrammelled by red tape, in fact like the Boers—so that I could move rapidly, fill up gaps."

39. National Aid Society, *Report of the Operation of the British National Society for Aid and the Sick and Wounded in War during the Franco-German War, 1870–1871* (London: Harrison and Sons, 1871), "Expenditures from July 20 to March 31, 1871" for the active staff. Also, Philip Frank to Loyd Lindsay, January 17, 1871, D/Wan/1/2/204, BRCA, letter describing the commendation Dr. Frank received after the war for his services and noting the common understanding that women's work at the time was solely for the duration of the war.

40. Major Young, the Red Cross agent in the field during the Zulu war, to the patron of the NAS ladies' committee, June 12, 1879, D/W/4/1/8, BRCA. Also, Brian Best and Katie Stossel, *Sister Janet: Nurse and Heroine of the Anglo-Zulu War* (Barnsley: Pen & Sword Military, 2006).

41. Cutting from the *Nursing Record and Hospital World*, October 22, 1898, Sudan Expedition 1898, D/Wan/3/5, BRCA.

42. Surgeon General Sternberg to Whitelaw Reid, July 19, 1898, Records of the American Red Cross, 1881–1916, 900, 32, RG 200, NARA, establishing the precedent.

43. Spanish–American War, Aux. 3, Nurses, cataloging their work, RG 200, 900, 3, NARA.

44. Reports by Margarie Henshall and Lida G. Starr, RG 200, 900, 18, NARA; and Anita Newcomb-McGee to Mrs. Shrady, June 30, 1899, and Beatrice Van Homrich to Mrs. Reid, February 16, 1899, 900, 3, NARA, among others in the collection.

45. Zuhal Ozaydin, "The Indian Muslims Red Crescent Society's Aid to the Ottoman State during the Balkan War in 1912," *Journal of the International Society for the History of Islamic Medicine* 2, no. 4 (2003): 12–18; and Mabel Annie St Clair Stobart, *War and Women: From Experience in the Balkans and Elsewhere* (London: G. Bell & Sons, 1913), 4, 14.

46. Elsie Inglis to Millicent Fawcett, October 1914, GB/106/2/SWH/A 17/1 (old catalogue), Fawcett Library (which became the Women's Library), London, letter marked private.

47. There is an extensive but narrowly framed historiography on the Scottish Women's Hospitals. Among others, see Leah Leneman, *In the Service of Life: The Story of Elsie Inglis and the Scottish Women's Hospitals* (Edinburgh: Mercat Press, 1994). The quote is from Dr. Honor Bone writing Vera Holme after hearing her reflections on BBC, May 25, 1941, 7JVH/2/4/07, Women's Library (WL), London.

48. Elsie Inglis, Individual Staff Biographies, C/5/2/7, WL, detailing her decision to go to Serbia.

49. Dr. Péchedimaldji to the Central Committee, September 12, 1877, 19, 2/73 T Constantinople, AICRC, marked "very confidential."

50. The massive outbreak of contagious diseases encouraged the shift to civilian care. Among other sources, see Medical Relief Units "Memorandum," August 25, 1916, RG 200, box 41, 591.4, NARA, which consolidated the shift. Also, Monica Krippner, *The Quality of Mercy: Women at War, Serbia, 1915–18* (Newton Abbot: David & Charles, 1980), 34–35.

51. For the debates about its establishment, see "Establishment of an International Health Organization," R 811–1, 1919, League of Nations Archive; and for a historical assessment, see Paul Weindling, ed., *International Health Organisations and Movements, 1918–1939* (Cambridge: Cambridge University Press, 1995).

52. Greg Grandin, "The Liberal Tradition in the Americas: Rights, Sovereignty and the Origins of Liberal Multilateralism," *American Historical Review* 117, no. 1 (2012): 68–91. Papers of Elsie Edith Bowerman, 7ELB, WL, whose career reflects a wide spectrum of feminism, including interwar ties to Flora Drummond and the right-wing Women's Guild of Empire.

SELECT BIBLIOGRAPHY

Ariga, Nagao. *The Red Cross Society of Japan: Its Organization and Activity in Time of Peace and War*. St. Louis: Samuel F. Myerson, 1904.

Barnett, Michael. *Empire of Humanity: A History of Humanitarianism*. Ithaca, NY: Cornell University Press, 2011.

Bayly, C. A. *The Birth of the Modern World: Global Connections and Comparisons, 1780–1914*. Malden, MA: Blackwell, 2004.

Best, Geoffrey. *Humanity in Warfare: The Modern History of the International Law of Armed Conflict*. London: Weidenfeld & Nicolson, 1980.

Bloxham, Donald, and Robert Gerwarth, eds. *Political Violence in Twentieth Century Europe*. Cambridge: Cambridge University Press, 2011.

Bourke, Joanna. *Dismembering the Male: Men's Bodies, Britain, and the Great War*. Chicago: University of Chicago Press, 1996.

Cabanes, Bruno. *The Great War and the Origins of Humanitarianism, 1918–1924*. Cambridge: Cambridge University Press, 2014.

Canning, Kathleen. *Gender History in Practice: Historical Perspectives on Bodies, Class, and Citizenship*. Ithaca, NY: Cornell University Press, 2006.

Charlesworth, Hilary, and Christine Chinkin. *The Boundaries of International Law: A Feminist Analysis*. Manchester: Manchester University Press, 2000.

Dülffer, Jost, and Robert Frank, eds. *Peace, War and Gender from Antiquity to the Present: Cross Cultural Perspectives*. Essen: Klartext Verlag, 2009.

Herren, Madeleine. *Internationale Organisationen seit 1865: Eine Globalgeschichte der internationalen Ordnung*. Darmstadt: Wissenschaftliche Buchgesellschaft, 2009.

Hutchinson, John F. *Champions of Charity: War and the Rise of the Red Cross*. Boulder, CO: Westview Press, 1996.

Iriye, Akira. *Global Community: The Role of International Organizations in the Making of the Contemporary World*. Berkeley: University of California Press, 2002.

Irwin, Julia F. *Making the World Safe: The American Red Cross and a Nation's Humanitarian Awakening*. Oxford: Oxford University Press, 2013.

Jones, Heather. *Violence against Prisoners of War in the First World War: Britain, France and Germany, 1914–1920*. Cambridge: Cambridge University Press, 2011.

Quataert, Jean H. *Staging Philanthropy: Patriotic Women and the National Imagination in Dynastic Germany, 1813–1916*. Ann Arbor: Michigan University Press, 2001.

Summers, Anne. *Angels and Citizens: British Women as Military Nurses, 1854–1914*. London: Routledge, 2002.

Takahashi, Aya. *The Development of the Japanese Nursing Profession: Adopting and Adapting Western Influences*. London, Routledge, 2005.

Wake, Roy. *The Nightingale Training School, 1860–1996*. London: Haggerston Press, 1998.

Weindling, Paul, ed. *International Health Organisations and Movements, 1918–1939*. Cambridge: Cambridge University Press, 1995.

PART III

THE AGE OF THE WORLD WARS

CHAPTER 15

....

WAR AND GENDER

The Age of the World Wars and Its Aftermath—an Overview

....

KAREN HAGEMANN AND SONYA O. ROSE

THE recruitment poster *At Neuve Chapelle* appeared across World War I Britain in the wake of the devastating battle in northern France in March 1915 (Figure 15.1). It portrays a soldier on his knees calling out, "Your friends need you. Be a man." To the soldier's side, an apparent casualty of the battle lies on the ground; next to him, another service-man stands tall and looks toward the horizon with field glasses. In the background, a soldier holds up his arms in utter despair. The poster underscores what was then taken for granted—combat as a male preserve—and emphasizes that, as responsible men, sol-diers take control of the events, including bonding together as "comrades" to help one another. At first glance, it is astonishing that a poster meant to recruit volunteers for war did not hide the death and suffering of combat. Indeed, until the implementation of the Military Service Act in January 1916, British armed forces, unlike their allies and ene-mies, depended on a volunteer army. Yet the portrayal owed much to the fact that by early 1915, the massive number of fallen soldiers and the need for replacements could not be denied. Their death was instead glorified as a heroic "sacrifice for the motherland."[1]

The poster illustrates the deployment of gendered imagery in war propaganda, which not only targeted soldiers at the battlefront, but also attempted to mobilize civilians—men and women, old and young—for war support at the *home front*, a term that was invented in the war propaganda of World War I (1914–18). The message was that only through the close coaction of both battlefront and home front could the conflict be suc-cessfully won.[2] Usually war propaganda imagined the home front as feminine and the battlefront as masculine. One illustration of this complementary image is a German poster with the headline *You Help As Well!* (*Hilf auch Du mit!*), from 1941 (Figure 15.2). It shows the portrait of a Wehrmacht soldier that looms above a group of three women of different ages—a female factory worker, a Red Cross nurse, and an agricultural laborer—suggesting that these women as "helpers" had to support the soldiers' war effort by all

FIGURE 15.1 *At Neuve Chapelle. Your Friends Need You. Be a Man*, British war poster by the Parliamentary Recruiting Committee, aiming for the mobilization of volunteers during World War I, designed by Frank Brangwyn (1867–1956), London, 1915.

(Library of Congress, Prints and Photographs Division, Washington DC, LC-USZC4-11190)

FIGURE 15.2 *Hilf auch Du mit!* (You Help as Well!), German war poster by the Reich Propaganda Department of the National Socialist German Workers' Party, attempting to mobilize women for the needed war support during World War II, designed by Theo Matejko (1893–1946), Vienna, 1941.

(Hoover Institution Archives, Poster Collection, GE 1070)

possible means. At the same time, this poster clearly reinforces the gendered hierarchy in the relation between battlefront and home front that not only Nazi Germany imagined. The former was envisioned as solely male and superior (literally above the women in the image) and the latter as primarily female and subordinated. Strikingly similar posters can be found in the archives of most other belligerent powers for both world wars.

Other important avenues of war propaganda were leaflets and articles in newspapers and illustrated magazines, music and other arts, and mass media such as photography, radio, and film. War propaganda was crucial for war mobilization since antiquity, but in the age of industrialized mass warfare it became ever more important, because now the war support of whole societies and their economies became necessary.[3] The images deployed in war propaganda are fascinating representations of the gender order in an age of highly industrialized mass warfare, when the home front became more essential and civilians consequently became a target of warfare. Civilians were the victims of economic blockades, forced labor, bombing of towns and cities, execution in prisons and camps, mass killing, genocide, and sexual violence, including mass rape and forced prostitution. During World War II (1939–1945) and the Holocaust, which cannot be separated, this led to higher casualty rates of civilians than of soldiers. The blurring of the borders between home front and battlefront is one reason that military historians termed the period of the two world wars the age of "total" warfare.[4] A history of war in this period must emphasize the fluidity not only of the so-called home front and battlefront, but also of the periodization of the two world wars and their short- and long-term aftermaths, as well as the interconnectedness of the First and Second World Wars with the many smaller conflicts of the time, including imperial conquests and anticolonial struggles. We therefore use the comprehensive term *Age of the World Wars* for this period.

The following overview of the history of warfare and society in the Age of the World Wars emphasizes this fluidity. It first discusses the concept of *total war* and its usefulness for a gendered history of the highly industrialized warfare in this period. Then it examines some of the general trends in the development of warfare. The last section explores the research on some of the major themes of a gender history of military of war of the period and discusses the extent to which war in the first half of the twentieth century was a "gendering activity," one "that ritually marks the gender of all members of society."[5]

Conceptualizing Highly Industrialized Warfare

Most historians agree that the two world wars were highly industrialized, global, mass conflicts. More contested is the conceptualization of the two world wars as *total wars*. One reason is that this term was born in a particular historical context—in the interwar period as military strategists in different countries reflected back on the "Great War" and ruminated about what might happen in the war to come.[6] During the Second World

War, the term became infamous because of its use in the war propaganda of Nazi Germany. After 1945, military historians used the concept of total war mainly to describe warfare in the Age of the World Wars, because they believed that four ideal-typical elements of warfare interacted and reinforced each other in this period: the "totality" of war aims, methods, mobilization, and control.[7]

Since the 1990s, there has been an intensive discussion about the concept of total war. Roger Chickering, among other critics of the concept, argued that it structures the principle narrative framework of nineteenth- and twentieth-century military history in a teleological way: "This narrative traces the titanic expansion of warfare during the last two centuries, the growth not only of scope and duration of military operation but also the systematic blurring of lines between soldiers and civilians, between war and society." It imposes "coherence on the vast particularities of the past." He therefore asked if it "has not encouraged a misunderstanding of both the character of warfare in the nineteenth century" and the forces that culminated in the First and Second World Wars.[8]

This is a valid criticism, which led Chickering and Stig Förster to suggest a use of the concept of total war independent of its specific historical context as an "'ideal type,' a model that features a number of salient characteristics, elements, or ingredients," but "can never be fully realized."[9] With this suggestion, they hoped to provide an analytical category that allows historians to explore what characterized warfare in the nineteenth and twentieth centuries and what marked its similarities, differences, and changes. For Chickering, the following five dimensions ideal-typically define a total war: First, the theaters of war extend simultaneously into large areas of the world. Second, war is conducted with mass armies made up of passionate, ideologically motivated citizens in uniform. Third, the "mobilization for war no longer stops at the borders of civilian life," because "all members of the belligerent states" participate more or less in the mighty efforts necessary to conduct a war successfully. Fourth, "all members of the belligerent states are now the legitimate targets of military action." And fifth, the "war aims are accordingly directed towards the extermination of the enemy."[10] In his view, the concurrence of all five factors differentiates the First and Second World Wars from earlier conflicts, even though the individual factors had not been equally developed in both wars and by all belligerents. Furthermore, he emphasized that to use this concept as an ideal type is not to assume that warfare became truly "total" in reality. Ambivalence, frictions, ruptures, and contradictions marked actual practices of states, militaries, economies, and societies.

For a gender history of the Age of the World Wars, this understanding of total war as an ideal-typical analytical category is useful because it draws attention to the blurring of the constructed borders between home front and battlefront.[11] This erosion was especially pronounced in the two world wars, but as historians like Peter H. Wilson emphasized, it had begun long before the twentieth and even the nineteenth century. In the early modern period, the population had to pay for wars through taxes and other material support and was a target of warfare.[12] While not on the scale of nineteenth- and twentieth-century conflicts, early modern wars still caused considerable destruction, and few people were able to escape their effects entirely. Atrocities are nothing peculiar to the world wars either.[13] For these reasons, some historians use the term total war for the analysis of earlier mass conflicts,[14] but this utilization is highly contested, not least because it has "proved impossible to rid the concept of an implicit comparison between the era of its own origins and the era to which it is applied for analysis."[15] We therefore limit the use of the ideal-typical concept of total war to the Age of the World Wars and the following Wars of Decolonization and emphasize that many of the features of twentieth-century mass warfare existed also in conflicts before and after the First and Second World Wars.[16]

New in the era of the world wars were foremost the levels of industrialization and mass mobilization, along with the employment of massive resources of the state, economy, and society for the single purpose of warfare. These developments resulted in an unprecedented scale and extent of warfare. Highly industrialized mass warfare, based on the use of science and technology, allowed a dramatic increase in the number of soldiers, a further spatial extension of warfare, and a shift to material-intensive fighting, which resulted in the enormity of the number casualties. To be sure, the industrialization of warfare had already started with the mid-nineteenth-century American Civil War (1861–65), the Italian Wars of Independence (1848–70) and German Wars of Unification (1864–71). Some of the means of the industrialized warfare of the first half of the twentieth century—trains to transport troops and new communications technology—had already been deployed in earlier conflicts. Machine guns were first used in the US Civil War and were subsequently improved in the Franco-Prussian War (1870–71). In 1911, the Italian military was the first to employ air warfare when it seized Ottoman-dominated North African territory in today's Libya.[17]

The key difference between these earlier conflicts and the two world wars was the scale of industrialized mass warfare with new communication and military technologies and weaponry. Already during the First World War, belligerents directed ever more industrial production to the output of weapons, munitions, and other supplies for their armies. As a result of mass-scale industrialization and technological improvements, including increased power and range, artillery barrages claimed nearly half of all fallen soldiers. The mass use of explosives—shells, grenades, and mines—left landscapes completely devastated at war's end. Air warfare, too, became an important feature of the First World War. The public focused on the aerial battles of fighter planes, but military aviation was also crucial for targeting and observing artillery fire. Air power was soon directed against civilians as well: German zeppelins and other aircraft conducted bombing raids on Britain beginning in 1915. These raids resulted in some casualties, but the main effect was to instill terror in the civilian population. In response, the Allies engaged in urban bombing, and when the war ended, their air forces were prepared to wage a major campaign against German cities. The dominating British navy with its warships, including submarines, attempted to stop all trade to central Europe between 1914 and 1919, and in return, German submarines were a menace to merchant shipping and to oceanliners. Both economic blockades were intended to starve the enemy into submission. On land, the tank, first used by the British at the Battle of the Somme in September 1916, was constantly improved. One of the most fearsome new weapons of the First World War was poison gas, which ranged from disabling chemicals, such as tear gas and mustard gas, to lethal agents including phosgene and chlorine. Germany used poison gas first, but later Britain and France did as well. The use of poison gas was outlawed by international convention in 1925, although Italy used it again in the Second Italo–Ethiopian War (1935–36). Militaries went into World War II expecting the use of chemical bombs, which the Imperial Japanese army indeed employed, for example, in the Battle of Changde (1943) against Chinese troops.[18]

World War II saw further advancements of military technology. Weapons were made much more mobile through the extensive use of tanks and portable machine guns. Air warfare and the use of bombers to target civilians and destroy cities became a predominant method of combat, producing the highest civilian casualty rate in history and culminating in the use of nuclear bombs at the war's end. In addition, strategic bombing took on a new, mass quality, turning interwar fantasy and limited technology into an operational and material reality. Combat at sea, too, was transformed by the new centrality of naval aviation. Aircraft carriers supported the air war, and submarines were made more sophisticated, leading to new forms of detection and defense. As a result of the advancements of military technology, mechanized warfare became central to land warfare; the American and British armies were fully mechanized by the end of World War II.[19]

This development of warfare had the effect of an increasing need for civilian war support on the so-called home front and made civilians, including women and children, an ever more important target of warfare. The extensive war support of a belligerent's own population at the home front was, however, not enough. During the First World War, but on a much larger scale during the Second, governments exploited prisoners of war and the civilian population of occupied territories for forced labor. Such radical erasure of the distinctions between battlefront and home front and, with it, the gender lines was *the* central characteristic of the First, but especially the Second World War.

IMPERIAL, NATIONAL, AND CIVIL CONFLICTS IN THE AGE OF WORLD WARS

The First and Second World Wars and the Holocaust still dominate in European and North American collective memory. Because of their extent and their aftermath, these two wars overshadow other, smaller conflicts in this period: imperial and national wars, civil and revolutionary wars, anticolonial struggles and genocides—many of them related to the two world wars. The inclusion of these many conflicts in the historiography results in a more fluid periodization of the two world wars with shifting borders between "peace" and "war."[20]

Thirty-eight countries were involved in the First World War, which officially began on July 28, 1914, and lasted until November 11, 1918. The conflict was preceded by the Balkan Wars (1912–13) and continued with mass violence in central and eastern Europe, where the Russian Civil War (1917–22) proved the most destructive among other simultaneous conflicts.[21] The leading Central Powers of Germany, Austria-Hungary, and Bulgaria (1915–18) were supported by the Ottoman Empire. The chief Allied powers, Britain and its Commonwealth (including Australia, New Zealand, and Canada), France, and Russia (1914–17)—known as the Triple Entente—were aided from the beginning by Japan and joined by Italy in 1915 and the United States in 1917. Colonial troops from both the British and the French Empires participated on the battlefields as combatants and laborers. The British even deployed their Chinese Labour Corps to support troops at the western front.[22] Only some countries in Europe, such as Denmark, the Netherlands, Norway, Spain, Sweden, and Switzerland, remained neutral.

Historians estimate that a total of more than 71 million mobilized soldiers (roughly 60 million from Europe) fought in this conflict, with battlefields spanning a territory of 4 million square kilometers in Europe, Africa, the Middle East, Asia, and the South Pacific. Some 9.4 million soldiers died, and 21 million were wounded. More than 950,000 civilians were killed in the conflicts themselves; in addition, an estimated 6 million people died of disease and famine during and after the war.[23] Because of its magnitude, contemporaries called the First World War the "Great War." In relation to the population, this war was nevertheless "proportionally not much more lethal" than earlier mass-scale conflicts.[24] The essential differences were, as discussed, the highly industrialized character of World War I, which demanded and allowed a much greater extent of mobilization of soldiers and civilians for war, the increased destructive power of modern weapons, and the organizing power of the state.[25]

The Second World War became even larger: seventy-two countries were involved; the conflict covered a territory of 22 million square kilometers. From a Eurocentric perspective, the invasion of Poland by Nazi Germany on September 1, 1939, is typically understood as the war's beginning and the official German surrender on May 8, 1945, as its end. In the Asian theater, however, the Second World War had already begun earlier with the occupation of China by Japan on July 7, 1937, and it came to an end later on September 2, 1945. Similar to the First World War, several conflicts preceded the Second World War: the Japanese invasion of Manchuria (1931–32), the Italian invasion of Ethiopia (1935–36), and the Spanish Civil War (1936–39). After 1945, conflicts continued. Most notable were the Greek Civil War (1946–49) and the anticolonial liberation struggles, first primarily in Asia. During World War II, the Allied powers under the leadership of Britain and its Commonwealth, France, the Soviet Union (1941–45), and the United States (1941–45) fought against the Axis powers of Nazi Germany, Fascist Italy (1940–43), Imperial Japan (1940–45), and their allies. Historians calculate that in total, the belligerents mobilized 80 to 110 million soldiers. The numbers of casualties are still in question, but estimates suggest 70 to 85 million war-related deaths, including 25.5 million soldiers; 29 to 30.5 million civilians killed by military activity, war crimes, and genocide; and 19 to 28 million civilians who perished as a result of famine and disease.[26] During the conflict, more civilians than soldiers died; about 55 percent of the fatalities were civilians, whereas in World War I civilians accounted for about 10 percent of fatalities.

The Soviet Union suffered the highest casualty rates, with 8.6 million military and 16.9 million civilian fatalities.[27] World War II became the deadliest conflict in history.

The First World War and Its Aftermath

Long before the outbreak of the First World War, there were visible harbingers of the danger of a future conflict. One was the arms race on land and at sea that characterized geopolitics in Europe and elsewhere in the decades before the war. Armaments production further accelerated in the last years prior to 1914; between 1908 and 1913, military spending in Europe increased in total by 50 percent.[28] The system of political and military alliances meant to maintain a peaceful power balance de facto heightened the danger of a conflict. So, too, did the growth of nationalism and ethnic strife within a system of competing European imperial states struggling for world dominance and the increasing influence of a culture of militarism. Through belligerent rhetoric, nationalist, imperialist, and militarist ideologies fostered mental readiness for war in each of the large powers.[29] Pointing to the portents of the conflict is not to say that World War I was inevitable. The earlier wars in the Balkans in 1912–13 did not escalate into a continental conflict,[30] and the proponents of war faced opposition even in the last weeks before the conflict began, mainly from parts of the labor movement, the liberal women's movement, and pacifists. Most of these prewar opponents, however, supported the "defense" of their "own" countries after the war had started.[31]

In the end, the July Crisis that followed the assassination of Franz Ferdinand, heir to the throne of Austria-Hungary, in Sarajevo on June 28, 1914, triggered war. Fighting began with the Austro-Hungarian declaration of war on the Kingdom of Serbia on July 28, 1914. Following escalation through Russian, French, and then German general mobilizations, the conflict expanded with the German declarations of war on Russia and France, respectively, on August 1 and 3, 1914, and its invasion of Belgium and northern France on August 4, 1914. Combat spread eastward into Russian-dominated Poland and the "borderlands" of the Russian Empire, including Galicia and Lithuania. The armies of the various empires, along with Italy, from 1915 a member of the Allied powers, fought battles in southern and southeast Europe and confronted the Ottomans in Turkey. The African continent became a zone of combat very early in the war as British and French imperial troops attacked the German colonies of Togoland and Cameroon. Throughout the war, battles raged across the African continent, including in east and southwest Africa, the latter involving troops from South Africa. Portuguese East Africa, a target of the German war effort, was also a site of conflict. In East Africa, the fighting continued briefly after the war in Europe had officially ended. Battles were waged in areas of the Middle East that had been under Ottoman control, including Mesopotamia, Persia, the Sinai, and Palestine. Meanwhile, in Asia in August 1914, Japan conquered Germany's settlement in Tsingtao, China. Japan also took German-colonized Pacific islands. New Zealand and Australia likewise occupied Samoa, New Guinea, and the Solomon Islands, all previously under German control. In the course of this global expansion of the conflict, war at sea played an increasingly important role.[32]

The final Allied push toward the German border began in October 1918. With the advance of the British, French, and American armies, the alliance of the Central Powers began to collapse. Turkey signed an armistice at the end of October, and Austria-Hungary followed on November 3. The German agreement to the armistice of November 11 was made possible by the revolution of sailors, soldiers, and workers that forced Emperor Wilhelm II, in power since 1888, to abdicate and led to the founding of the Weimar Republic. The Treaty of Versailles, signed on June 28, 1919, officially ended the state of war between Germany and the Allied powers. Germany had to "accept the responsibility . . . for causing all the loss and damage" (Article 231). The treaty forced the new German republic to disarm, make substantial territorial concessions, and pay extensive reparations to the Entente powers. Austria and Hungary had to sign similar peace treaties too. The United States, under Democratic President Woodrow Wilson, was among the signatories of the Treaty of Versailles, but the Republican Party majority in the US Senate refused to ratify the treaty, in large measure because of their objections to US participation in the League of Nations, which was founded on January 10, 1920, in accordance with the treaty. As a result, the United States signed individual peace treaties with Germany, Austria, and Hungary in 1921.[33]

The aftermath of the First World War changed the global political landscape. The Austro-Hungarian, German, Ottoman, and Russian Empires crumbled, borders were redrawn, several new countries were created, and others regained their independence. The British and French Empires expanded after the war, because the territories of the German and Ottoman Empires were distributed to the Allied powers as League of Nations mandates. Britain gained control of Palestine, Transjordan, Iraq, Tanganyika, and parts of Cameroon and Togo, while its dominions acquired mandates of their own, such as the Union of South Africa, which gained South West Africa (today Namibia). France procured mandates over the former territories of the Ottoman Empire that make up what are now Syria and Lebanon, as well as most of the former German colonies of Togo and Cameroon.[34]

War and violence continued in several countries after World War I officially had ended. In the wake of the Bolshevik Revolution in October 1917, class conflicts were becoming ever more violent, and the Russian example inspired rebellions and revolutionary upheaval in not only central European states like Austria, Germany, and Hungary, but also other parts of the globe. In Finland, Russia, and many other countries of eastern Europe, civil war started in 1917/18 and continued for varying lengths of time. The bloodiest was the Russian Civil War (1917–22/23); some historians estimate 7 to 12 million casualties, mostly civilians, during this conflict.[35] In Italy, violent conflicts persisted and in October 1922 led to Benito Mussolini's National Fascist Party taking power. Everywhere, militant nationalism was gaining more influence; ethnic hostilities and antisemitism flared. As the empires of Britain and France expanded, they violently suppressed uprisings, especially in Iraq and Egypt under British control. Ethnic conflict continued to plague the Aegean region in western Turkey after the dissolution of the

Ottoman Empire, ending in an internationally organized compulsory transfer of minority populations. The "Convention Concerning the Exchange of Greek and Turkish Populations" from January 1923, led to the forced transfer of 1.6 million people who were made refugees and de jure denaturalized from their homelands. This forcible population exchange separated ethno/religious groups, leading to ethnic homogenization in both Greece and Turkey, a process that started with the Armenian genocide (1915–17) carried out by the Young Turks.[36] Paramilitarism featured in all these conflicts because of the absence of state authority in some cases and in other areas as an adjunct to state-organized warfare or in opposition to state forces.[37]

The outcome of the First World War fostered the rise of the United States to world-power status, but the country quickly turned to isolationism.[38] President Wilson had championed a more peaceful world order and thus supported the establishment of the League of Nations with the aim of preventing wars and solving or ameliorating international disputes. But the country never joined the league because of Republican opposition.[39] Subsequently, the league was doomed to failure, despite widespread support by the postwar pacifist movement, the labor movement, and the newly elected democratic and labor governments in countries like Austria and Germany, Britain, Finland, France, and Sweden.[40]

The Second World War and Beyond

The Second World War started in Asia, where Japan pursued an imperialist policy of expansion after the First World War, beginning with the invasion of Manchuria in 1931 and continuing in the Second Sino-Japanese War from 1937 to 1945.[41] One early indicator of the brutality of Japanese warfare was the "Rape of Nanking," the mass murder of up to a quarter of a million residents of the Chinese capital between December 1937 and January 1938.[42] On September 27, 1940, Japan signed the Tripartite Pact with Germany and Italy, entering the military alliance of the Axis powers. As a response, the United States and Britain tried to curb Japanese aggression through their support for China and the imposition of economic sanctions on Japan.

Driven by the ambition to displace the United States as the dominant power in the Pacific and secure its trade zone, Japan attacked the US fleet at Pearl Harbor in Hawaii on December 7, 1941. In response, the United States immediately declared war on Japan. Following the attack on Pearl Harbor, the Japanese launched offensives against Allied forces in Southeast Asia, with simultaneous attacks on Hong Kong, British Malaya, and the Philippines. Through its aggressive strategy, Japan achieved a series of military successes in 1942. It conquered Guam and Wake Island, the Philippines, the Dutch East Indies, Hong Kong, Malaya, Singapore, and Burma. Only Thailand remained officially neutral. But the tide started to turn in the summer of 1942, and the joined forces of the United States and the British Commonwealth slowly gained naval and air supremacy in the Pacific. Despite its defeat in the Philippines and elsewhere and the threat of the conquest of its empire in China by the Soviet Union, which indeed occupied Manchuria on

August 9, 1945, only the use of nuclear bombs against the Japanese cities Hiroshima and Nagasaki by the United States on August 6 and 9, 1945, respectively, finally forced Imperial Japan to officially surrender on September 2.[43]

Europe and the Atlantic became the second main theater of World War II. The Nazi government, in power since January 30, 1933, had systematically prepared for war. The first steps in the Nazis' expansionist policy were the annexation of Austria (*Anschluss*) on March 12, 1938, and the seizure of the Sudetenland, the Czechoslovakian border regions inhabited primarily by German speakers, in October 1938, which was made possible by the Munich Agreement between Britain and France, Germany, and Italy on September 30, 1938. On March 15, 1939, the occupation of Czechoslovakia followed, which led to the creation of the German Protectorate of Bohemia and Moravia.[44] Five months later, World War II officially began in Europe, when Nazi Germany invaded Poland on September 1, 1939, and Britain and France declared war in response shortly after.[45]

As a consequence of the Nazi–Soviet Pact of August 23, 1939, the Red Army invaded eastern Poland in mid-September and annexed the area to the Union of Soviet Socialist Republics (USSR). The Nazis' move into Poland was central to their goal of acquiring *Lebensraum*: ethnic Germans were to replace ethnic Poles and Jews on Polish lands annexed to Germany. The Red Army occupied the Baltic countries in June 1940. Meanwhile, the Wehrmacht attacked and occupied the neutral countries of northern and western Europe (Denmark, Norway, the Netherlands, Belgium, and Luxembourg) in May 1940. In the same month, Germany invaded France, forcing the evacuation of British forces. Fascist Italy then declared war on Britain and France. France signed an armistice that allowed the southern part of the country to be nominally governed by an authoritarian puppet regime based in Vichy (1940–44), while the remainder, including Paris, fell under direct German occupation.[46]

In April 1941, Germany attacked and occupied Yugoslavia and Greece, and in June 1941, its forces invaded the Soviet Union, beginning what was to be a war of both annihilation and attrition. In 1942, the Nazis and their Axis power allies—expanded to include Bulgaria, Finland, Hungary, and Romania—occupied all of Europe with the exception of Britain, areas of the Soviet Union, and the neutral countries Ireland, Portugal, Spain, Sweden, and Switzerland.[47] Although the Nazi regime had perpetrated mass killings since the outbreak of war and invasion of Poland—including the executions of disabled Germans under the "euthanasia" program codenamed T4 as well as massacres of Polish elites and Jews—the scope and pace of the killing of Jews increased greatly as part of the invasion of the Soviet Union. Following mass-shooting massacres of Jews in the Soviet Union, the first extermination camps began operation in December 1941.[48]

The tide of the war in the European theater reversed only slowly in 1942/43. After Hitler had declared war on the United States on December 11, 1941, it became involved in the European war theater, too. They joined the Allies in bombing campaigns that caused massive destruction and civilian casualties in Germany. After the Soviet victories in the Battles of Moscow (October 1941 to January 1942) and Stalingrad (August 1942 to February 1943), the Allied invasion of Italy in September 1943, and the invasion of Normandy by Allied troops in June 1944, the Wehrmacht had to retreat. Its last major offensive took place in the winter of 1944–45, when US forces prevailed in the Ardennes in France and Belgium. The final battles in Europe took place in late April and early May 1945 with Berlin at the center, followed by Germany's unconditional surrender on May 8, 1945.[49]

The leaders of the three main Allied powers, the United Kingdom, the United States, and the USSR, redrew the borders of Europe and Asia during the 1945 conferences at Yalta (February 4–11) and Potsdam (July 7–August 2), which led to new struggles after the official end of the war.[50] In Europe, the Greek Civil War between the army of the conservative Greek government, which was supported by Britain and the United States, and the communist-controlled Democratic Army of Greece, backed by the governments of its neighbors Yugoslavia, Albania, and Bulgaria, continued until October 1949 and ended with the defeat of the Democratic Army of Greece.[51] This conflict led the US government under President Harry S. Truman to announce the Truman Doctrine on March 12, 1947, which became the foundation of American foreign policy during the Cold War (1946–91). It established that the United States would provide political, military, and economic assistance to all democratic nations under threat from external or internal authoritarian forces. One major aim of the Truman Doctrine was to "contain" communist influence globally. The conflict between the two new superpowers—the Soviet Union and the United States—cast a shadow over the globe and divided Europe into two blocs until the end of the Cold War marked by the dissolution of the Soviet Union in 1991.[52]

The rise of anticolonial movements in Africa and Asia led to ever more armed conflicts, the Wars of Decolonization from the 1940s to the 1970s. Two days after Japan's surrender, Indonesia, which had been occupied by the Japanese, declared independence from the Netherlands. After defeat in battle, the Dutch officially transferred sovereignty in December 1949. The First Indochina War (1946–54) saw France unsuccessfully attempt to restore colonial rule.[53] The Philippines also declared its independence from the United States immediately after the end of the war. On October 24, 1945, it became a founding member of the United Nations (UN), the new international organization meant to prevent war and solve international problems.[54] Similar to the First World War, the Second World War had a long-lasting aftermath.[55]

GENDERING THE HISTORY OF
THE TWO WORLD WARS

More visible than in earlier conflicts, women participated in the First and Second World Wars, not only at the so-called home front, in war industries, and through war welfare, but increasingly also close to the front lines as military doctors and nurses, auxiliaries, soldiers, and partisans. Old and new media showed women in the many different roles of war support requested by governments and their administrations, militaries, and nongovernmental actors, such as women's associations. Along with the popular propaganda medium of posters, advertisements and photographs in illustrated magazines presented images of the necessary female war support. This call itself was nothing novel, but the extent of its necessity was new in the industrialized total warfare of the Age of World Wars—and so, accordingly, were its scope and visibility. The propaganda also addressed men primarily as soldiers, but the demand for male war support through military service had a long tradition in war propaganda.

The visibility of the female war participation was one reason that the research by feminist historians in the 1970s and 1980s focused on the exploration of this subject. In the early twenty-first century, the period of the two world wars is the best-researched era in women's and gender histories of military and war. With the expansion of women's history to gender history in the 1980s, the study of masculinity, military, and violence in the Age of World Wars slowly became a subject of research too. It allowed a new understanding of the contested discourses on military masculinity and the many competing practices and experiences of men in wartime.

Two major historiographical debates during the 1980s and 1990s were of particular importance for the research on the Age of the World Wars. In the first dispute, historians argued over the question of whether the First World War was a catalyst of women's liberation. In the second, they quarreled over the role of German women in the Third Reich and their involvement in the Holocaust and the Second World War.[56] Both debates led to a more nuanced understanding of how gender functions in wartime. The result of the first debate is that present-day scholarship emphasizes the paradox that although "women's objective situation" did change during the war, "relationships of domination and subordination" were "retained through discourses," representations, and collective memories "that systematically designate unequal gender relations."[57] In this way, historical research overcame the binary construction of continuity versus changes in the analysis of the gender order and gender relations in war societies and their aftermath.

The second debate led to an approach explaining that women could be both victims and perpetrators. It allowed the exploration of the broad spectrum of female behavior in the Third Reich, the Second World War, and the Holocaust, ranging from perpetrators to bystanders to victims. The latter group includes women persecuted because of their race, religion, political conviction, or protest and resistance against the Nazi regime. This approach influenced the research on gender and war through its emphasis on the broad variety of female and male war participation, its recognition of ambiguities in human behavior, and, most important, its dismantling of the conceptualization of men as perpetrators and women as victims per se.

Gender Images, War Propaganda, and Postwar Memories

The mobilization for war through highly gendered propaganda during the world wars was an early subject of research by women's and gender historians.[58] Gendered images characterized the propaganda used for war mobilization as well as the cultural representations of war in a variety of ways. They were meant to boost the fighting spirit by stirring collective feelings like patriotism, racism, and desire for revenge; to mobilize men and women for gender-specific forms of war support; and to organize the collective postwar memories along gender lines.[59]

The "Othering" and demonization of the enemy and the call for "revenge" have been common features of war propaganda since antiquity, but reached a new quality in the Age of World Wars. One early instance from World War I is the widespread Allied rhetoric of the "Rape of Belgium" by Germany in 1914.[60] It referred to the German mistreatment of civilians during the invasion and subsequent occupation of neutral Belgium at the beginning of the conflict and was used in Britain to build popular support for the war and, in the United States, to promote the American intervention in the European war. The poster *Halt the Hun!*, published by the US Government in 1917/18 with the aim to mobilize support for the "Third Liberty Loan," shows an American soldier stopping a German "Hun" from laying hands on a frightened mother with a small child in her lap (see Figure 15.3). The German soldier has blood on his hands. This motif and the poster background of a burning landscape clearly allude to the Rape of Belgium.

Fed by escalating racism, the gendered Othering of the enemy was even more virulent during World War II. American propaganda presented Japanese soldiers as evil, sneaky "Japs" who abused White women.[61] Nazi propaganda tried to denigrate the Allies by claiming that they were controlled by the "Jewish world conspiracy." One illustration of this racialized masculinity is a poster from 1941–42 with the title, *Behind the Enemy Powers: The Jew*. It shows a stereotyped Jewish capitalist behind the curtain of the flags of the United Kingdom, the United States, and the Soviet Union.[62] The Nazis also tried to discredit the Allies by denouncing their use of non-White soldiers. Striking is a 1940 placard, titled *France's Guilt*, which was a reprint of the cover of the illustrated Nazi magazine *Illustrierter Beobachter*. In its center stands the racist depiction of a large French African soldier holding his rifle. He holds the French banner brocaded with the French republican motto, "*Liberté—Egalité—Fraternité.*" A caricatured Algerian soldier, White French officer, and top-hatted Jew stand behind him amid a landscape in ruins (Figure 15.4). Britain, in turn, promoted the joint struggle of male soldiers of all races to bolster the sense of a united imperial front, as the widely distributed 1941 recruitment poster *The British Commonwealth of Nations: Together* demonstrates.[63]

Gendered representations were also utilized to motivate young men to volunteer and to boost the fighting spirit of soldiers by showing inspiring examples of heroic manliness, as the British poster from 1915 discussed in the introduction of this chapter indicates (Figure 15.1). While the ideal of a heroic military masculinity was widespread and dominated by the themes of virility and combat readiness, the visual style varied over time, and national differences emerged as well. One well-researched example is World War II Britain, for which Sonya O. Rose identified "a temperate masculinity" as the hegemonic ideal, which combined elements of the "interwar construction of 'anti-heroic' masculinity" with those "long associated with the soldier-hero—traits most clearly exemplified by combat soldiers." The counterimage was the aggressive "hyper-masculinity" of the Nazi propaganda, which, like Soviet propaganda, featured the

FIGURE 15.3 *Halt the Hun! Buy U.S. Government Bonds, Third Liberty Loan,* poster by the US Government referring to the "Rape of Belgium," the mistreatment of civilians during the invasion and subsequent occupation of neutral Belgium in the fall of 1914, designed by Henry Raleigh (1880–1945), Chicago, [1918].

(Library of Congress, Prints and Photographs Division, Washington DC, LC-USZC4-2792)

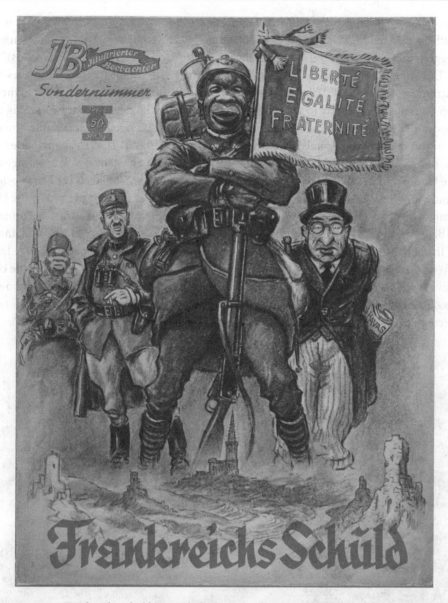

FIGURE 15.4 *Frankreichs Schuld* (France's Guilt), racist cartoon on the front page of a special issue of the National Socialist magazine *Illustrierter Beobachter*, published during the German invasion of France in May 1940, reminding German readers of the French use of colonial soldiers from North Africa during World War I, Munich, 1940.

(Deutsches Historisches Museum, Berlin/I. Desnica)

"steely" front-line soldier.[64] Furthermore, research identified a "modernization" in the iconography of male war heroes that reflected the industrialization of warfare and the importance of new technology. Bomber pilots became new war heroes, especially during the Second World War, as seen in a 1945 poster from the US Army Air Forces titled *O'er the Ramparts We Watch*. It features a good-looking, young air force pilot in a leather jacket holding a bomb. He rises out of the clouds, but the composition of the image suggests that he is an integral part of his flight squadron (on which his success depends).[65]

The omnipresent imagery of military masculinity was complemented by images of patriotic women, who did "their bit" to "help" men win the war, as mothers who sent their sons and husband bravely to war; as thrifty housewives who dealt with the rationing of food and fuel; as workers in the war economy, where they replaced the conscripted men; as nurses in military hospitals; and, especially during World War II, even as auxiliaries in the military who freed soldiers to fight at the front lines. The constant appeal to women at the home front was to help the soldiers at the battlefront. One example is the Nazi poster from 1941 discussed in the introduction (Figure 15.2); another is a 1943 placard by the US Employment Service titled *Do the Job HE Left Behind*, which shows an attractive woman in blue overalls working in a technical job in the metal industry.[66] The men who remained at the home front because their skilled work was needed in the war economy were less often portrayed on war posters. One rare example is a placard produced in 1944 by the US Navy's Industrial Incentive Division, captioned *I Am Proud of YOU FOLKS Too!* It shows a sailor shaking hands with two industrial workers, an older man and a woman, in the attempt to remind those at home that their war effort was important, too (Figure 15.5).

FIGURE 15.5 *I'm Proud of YOU FOLKS Too!*, American war poster by the US Navy's Industrial Incentive Division, published during World War II to maintain civilian morale and motivate male and female factory workers to take an active, enthusiastic stake in the war effort, designed by Jon Whitcomb (1906–88), [n.p.], 1944.

(Courtesy of the Historical Museum at Fort Missoula)

Contrary to the reality, war propaganda in the Age of World Wars often depicted a gender order that emphasized the role of men as protectors of family, home, and country. Only the "emergency situation" of war opened the spaces for women at the home front to do everything necessary to support the soldiers and to free men for the battlefront, including work and service in areas previously reserved for men. Propaganda, especially in the new medium of film, promised (depending on the political agenda of the war power) either a return to the prewar gender order based on the male breadwinner–female homemaker family or a new order of society based on social and gender equality. While war propaganda usually represented women and men as both contrasting and complementary, the practices of war and specific war experiences constantly challenged this ideal of a binary gender order.[67]

The cultural construction of the recollection of the war years addressed these challenges to the gender order and society by propagating the return to "normalcy." Gender images in postwar movies—but also in novels and illustrated magazines, on war monuments, and in commemoration ceremonies—shaped the selective collective memories of the wars. Victorious nations especially remembered their soldiers as war heroes. Women's war nursing and war charity were recalled as complementary patriotic service, as was the sacrifice of war widows in their capacities as both mothers and wives. But female forms of war support and war experiences that had crossed the gender lines tended to be forgotten in collective memories after the world wars because they challenged the political, cultural, and social attempts to "normalize" the gender order and, with it, the social order of postwar societies. This does not mean, however, that individual men and women were willing or able to forget.[68]

Gendered War Support and Experiences at the Home Front

Civilian war support and war experiences at the multiple home fronts are well researched for the world wars.[69] Because of the scale and scope of the two conflicts, wartime service of some kind was expected of most adult men and women, although class, race, nationality, age, marital status, and the number of children determined whether these expectations were to be met voluntarily or through legal requirements. Both the form of the requested war support and the war experiences of civilians depended on the specific time and place and changed over the course of a conflict. It also made an important difference if the fighting took place on home territory, close by, or far away; if the home territory was free or occupied; if economic blockade or air war reached the civilians; and if warfare and occupation were combined with mass killings and genocide.

One of the best-researched subjects of war support at the home front is women's work in the war economy. Women became a crucial part of the labor reserve during World War I. They replaced conscripted men in war industries, trade, transportation, services, and administration. At first glance, the percentage of women employed in full-time work rose dramatically during the war. In 1918, it reached 36 percent in Germany, 38 percent in Britain, 41 percent in France, and 42 percent in Russia.[70] However, the real growth of the share of working women was much less dramatic than these percentages suggest. In most war economies, the rise reflected the general trend of an increase in full-day female employment in industry, commerce, and administration, which had already begun before the turn of the century. Furthermore, most women hired during the war were to be employed in their new positions "for the duration of the war only."[71]

A similar trend can be observed for the Second World War. The percentage of women in the war industries rose, but the extent depended on the level of industrialization and the degree of women's involvement in full-day, prewar employment. The higher the employment rate of women before the war, the lower its increase during the war, because the labor reserve, especially of single women, was already exhausted. For this reason, the proportion of married women in full-time work saw the greatest increase. The Soviet Union was exceptional in that the proportion of women among all employed persons increased from 40 to 60 percent between 1940 and 1944, which was a consequence of massive mobilization for the army and the extraordinarily high casualty rate.[72]

Men's work at the home front is far less researched. We know much more about the men who joined the armed forces and their war experiences than about those who stayed home in reserved occupations.[73] The few existing studies indicate that depending on the level of national mobilization for the military, the number was quite high. In World War II Britain, for example, at the peak of armed forces employment in 1944, 5 million men between the ages of nineteen and fifty-one served in the military, but 10 million men of fighting age stayed at the home front. Half of them worked in reserved occupations, which included farming, industrial work, healthcare, administration, and the Merchant Navy.[74] Unless the men were visibly elderly, contemporaries suspected these civilian men of shirking and perceived them as "unmanly," even when they were needed in their jobs or were unable to serve. They became emasculated in the public imagination.[75] This was one reason why the male members of the British Home Guard, the defense organization of the British army, tried by all means to retain the Home Guard as an all-male preserve. They wanted to emphasize their "manliness" through their membership. Between 1940 and 1944, the Home Guard encompassed 1.5 million local male volunteers otherwise ineligible for military service. Women did not gain full membership until the end of 1944.[76]

Another reason that men jealously guarded home defense was its increasing importance in the Age of World Wars. During World War I, the possibilities of air warfare were seriously tested for the first time, but the extent was still small. "Post-war bombing surveys in 1919 concluded," according to Richard Overy, "that the destructive power of bombing was meager with the existing technology, but asserted that the raids had exerted a 'tremendous moral effect.'"[77] During World War II, technological developments made air warfare an important part of war strategy. With the global extension of the conflicts and the front-line use of air power, all the embattled territories became targets of bombing, but military planners preferred to target densely populated urbanized and industrialized regions with the aim of destroying war industries and crushing popular moral. Air warfare resulted in devastation and death. Overy estimated that during the war the Allied air forces alone dropped almost two million tons of bombs on European targets. Millions of houses were destroyed. Hundreds of thousands of civilians were killed; the highest numbers were in the Soviet Union with more than 500,000 and Germany with 400,000 dead civilians as a result of bomb attacks.[78] However, neither the attacks on eastern European cities starting in 1939 by the German air force and its "Blitz" of Britain in 1940–41 nor the increasingly intensive bombing of German cities by the Allies between 1942 and 1945 achieved the goal of breaking popular morale.[79]

Not until the first decade of the new millennium did scholarship begin to explore the gendered experiences of the air war, which had unsettled the gender lines in the embattled regions for two reasons: women were systematically targeted as part of the civilian population and, at the same time, increasingly mobilized for the aerial and home defense.[80] Especially the latter could lead to conflicts and tensions, as evidenced by the controversy that surrounded women's service in the British Home Guard.[81] In other countries, women faced less resistance. In Nazi Germany, 620,000 (3 percent) of the nearly 22 million who joined the Reich Air Defense Organization (*Reichsluftschutzbund*) in 1942–43 were women.[82] The Soviet Union mobilized more than 100,000 women for the civil air defense, in addition to 300,000 women who served in combat and home-front antiaircraft formations between 1941 and 1945.[83] In view of this development, recent studies argue that air warfare greatly contributed to the militarization of women during World War II.[84]

Gendered Experiences of Economic Warfare and Occupation

One important recent area of research is the gendered experience of economic warfare and occupation by civilians.[85] Blockades were an important strategy of warfare long before the twentieth century, but during the world wars they targeted not only the enemy's war economy but also its civilian population on a new scale. During World War I, the blockade of Germany and its allies by Britain and the other Allied and Associated Powers caused such dramatic shortages of food, fuel, and fertilizer that it led to starvation and disease on a mass scale. Because women were primarily responsible for feeding their families, they struggled most. In Austria and Germany, growing hunger and the lack of sufficient state support combined with war weariness caused hunger riots and street protests by women, which further destabilized the war-torn societies. Similarly in Russia, subsistence rioting by women and workers fueled the revolutionary situation between 1915 and 1917.[86]

To prevent such upheaval during World War II, the Nazi regime attempted by all means to protect the German home front from such shortages. This policy drove the merciless economic exploitation of all occupied territories, from which the Nazis appropriated not only foodstuffs, fuel, raw materials, and goods of industrial production, but also labor.[87] Although the exploitation of occupied territories was not new to warfare, what distinguished the Nazi policy was its racist and imperialist agenda, the quest for *Lebensraum* in the east. In its *Generalplan Ost* (General Plan East), the Nazi government planned to colonize central and eastern Europe, which entailed the systematic enslavement, expulsion, and mass killing of most Slavic peoples deemed by the Nazis "racially inferior." *Generalplan Ost* went hand in hand with the Holocaust. In the territories of the occupied USSR, this policy caused the deaths of an estimated one-fifth of the prewar population. The Nazi occupation regimes in northern and western Europe, where the population was perceived as "racially equal," were less brutal, but worsened during the war because of the urgency of the needs of the bombarded German homeland and the retreating Wehrmacht. This led to an increase of the resistance against the occupation.[88]

During both world wars, the economic exploitation of the occupied territories and their defeated armies also included the use of forced labor by prisoners of war (POWs) and civilians—men and women alike—to relieve the pressure on the workforce at the home front. Already during World War I, mobile warfare, made possible by new technologies, led to a much higher number and percentage of captured soldiers than in earlier conflicts, especially at the eastern front. Germany, Austria-Hungary, and Russia took an estimated number of 8 to 9 million POWs. Most of them were used as forced laborers. Of the 1.6 million POWs captured by Germany, 90 percent were forced to work in agriculture and industry. Because of the comparatively static nature of warfare at the western front, fewer soldiers were taken prisoner there. Britain captured only 130,000 German POWs, and Germany took 170,000 British POWs.[89]

During World War II, the number of exploited forced laborers increased dramatically. Especially the Third Reich and the Japanese Empire compelled labor from millions of POWs and large numbers of male and female civilians in the occupied territories to keep the wartime economy going. Nazi Germany abducted approximately 12 million people from almost twenty European countries between 1939 and 1945; about two-thirds of them came from eastern Europe. In 1944, of the 10 million foreign forced laborers, 6.5 million were civilians, 2.2 million were POWs, and 1.3 million were camp inmates. They accounted for nearly one-quarter of Germany's entire workforce. One-third of the civilian forced laborers in Nazi Germany were women, mostly from Poland and the Soviet Union. More than 50 percent of these Polish and Soviet female laborers were younger than twenty-four.[90] The Japanese Empire exploited more than 10 million Chinese civilians (men and women), 1.3 million Koreans, and nearly 140,000 Allied POWs. In total 4 percent of the Japanese work force during World War II were slave laborers.[91] One notorious example was the construction of the Burma–Siam Railway in which 100,000 Burmese and Malay Indian laborers perished, as did an estimated 60,000 Allied POWs.[92]

We need more studies on the gendered dimension of such policies of economic exploitation and forced labor, which went hand in hand with internment, mass resettlement, and sexual violence.[93] One important subject in this context is forced prostitution, which reached a shocking extent during World War II. Recent scholarship estimates the total number of women forced into prostitution by Imperial Japan, euphemistically called "comfort women," at 360,000 to 400,000 in 2,000 brothels. Of these women, at least 140,000 to 160,000 were Korean. The rest came from other Asian countries, most from China, but some also from the European colonial powers in Asia, like Britain and the Netherlands.[94] The Wehrmacht had an estimated five hundred brothels in 1942. Up to 34,140 European women were forced to serve as prostitutes during the German occupation.[95] As these examples demonstrate, occupation regimes could become extremely destructive and murderous. This was not only in the cases of Nazi Germany and Imperial Japan, but also in the imperial response to anticolonial rebellion after the First and Second World Wars.[96]

War Service, Gender, and Citizenship

Men bore the brunt of the military service, but far from all men served in the armed forces, and the percentage of men who volunteered or were enlisted to fight differed greatly by country and between conflicts. During the First World War, an estimated 50 percent of the British men aged between fifteen and forty in 1911 served, while in France, 79 percent of all men between fifteen and forty in 1911 were conscripted. In Imperial Germany, 81 percent of eligible men entered military service. In the United States, which only joined the war in 1917, the percentage was far lower.[97] During the Second World War, the percentage of mobilized men again differed greatly. The number was especially high in Nazi Germany and the Soviet Union, respectively, with 17.3 million and 34.4 million men in service.[98]

The military and, at its core, combat were represented and perceived as a male domain. The armed forces remained the main institution for the construction of masculinity well into the post-1945 period.[99] Military service made men into soldiers and, vice versa, soldiers into men. Training to be a soldier meant learning not only to use weaponry, but also how to be disciplined, follow orders, and be subordinate to officers. Conscripts, moreover, needed to adopt the attitude of superiority and an aggressive stance toward the enemy.[100] This, however, did not mean that men's everyday experience of war reflected the martial ideal. New research shows instead the diversity and the fluidity of ideas of military masculinity in daily life.[101]

Furthermore, the conceptualization of soldiers in Western armies changed from the First to the Second World War. Thomas Kühne was one of the first who demonstrated that traditional concepts of exclusive and heroic masculinity gave way to inclusive, protean masculinities, thereby facilitating the integration of soldiers with different personalities and social backgrounds into the cohesive face-to-face combat group that proved crucial for the fighting morale of modern armies. While men within these homosocial groups could perform a broad range of seemingly contradictory, manly and femininely coded emotions and practices, these groups still relied on the exclusion of women and men perceived as "Others."[102]

We know much more about the men who joined the armed forces and their war experiences than about their male Others, who included conscientious objectors and deserters[103] and, depending on the historical context, Jewish, African American, or colonial soldiers and foreign volunteers. Colonial soldiers formed an especially large, but nevertheless long-forgotten group. Millions of them served Belgium, Britain, France, the Netherlands, Portugal, and Spain in several conflicts during the Age of World Wars.

Imperial loyalty and the hope of postwar political patronage often motivated colonial troops to imperial military service. As a result, their service contributed to masculine visions of independent nationhood and citizenship following the world wars.[104] Men from occupied or foreign territories volunteered or were forced to fight as well. Examples include the International Brigades of the Spanish Civil War, in which 32,000 to 35,000 volunteers from different countries fought for the Second Spanish Republic,[105] the partisan and resistance movements in the territories occupied by Nazi Germany, and the *Ostlegionen* (Eastern Legions) of the German Wehrmacht, which consisted of non-Russian personnel from occupied eastern European countries, many of them former POWs.[106] For all these groups we need more research that focuses on the specific military masculinity of these groups of men in arms.

Women, too, served the military in increasing numbers during the First and Second World Wars. They were also constructed as Others of the soldiers, but as needed complementary Others, whose main function was to support the servicemen and set them free for the battlefront. Most popular in public perception became the quickly growing group of women who served as nurses and doctors in military hospitals or tried to heal the wounds of war through welfare and international humanitarian work. Their service, which was a result of the gendering and professionalization of military medical care and welfare since the late nineteenth century, stayed in the traditional framework of a gender order, which envisioned women as caring and nurturing.[107] The majority of women who served the military were professional nurses and voluntary nurses aids, often under the supervision of the Red Cross.

One aspect in which the use of women in military medical care differed in both world wars and between countries was the location of their deployment: only at home, in the rear, or also on the battlefield. During the First World War, the Scottish Women's Hospital with female medical personnel (including doctors) who attended to soldiers on or near the battlefront in Serbia and France was still an exception. During the Second World War, many more women—a growing portion of whom were female doctors— provided military medical care near the front lines. The largest contingent of women doctors, some 80,000, worked in the Red Army. In addition, 200,000 women were engaged as combat medics. The Russian Red Cross furthermore trained a total of 500,000 women as paramedics for local air defenses and 300,000 as auxiliary nurses and paramedics for all regions of the Soviet Union.[108] Historians have begun to analyze this form of female war service, but much more research is needed. This is also the case for war welfare and international humanitarian work during and after the wars in this period, about which we still know relatively little.[109]

The quickly expanding number of women who joined the militaries as auxiliaries, soldiers, and partisans during World War I, but especially in World War II, were perceived with more skepticism by the public, because their service seemed to challenge the boundaries of the wartime gender order, in which men served at the battlefront and women at the home front. Thus, the extent of this form of female military service was well hidden by governments. The proportion of women in the Western Allied armed forces is estimated for the United States at 2 percent and for the United Kingdom at up to 9 percent; in comparison, women constituted 5 percent of the German Wehrmacht, and up to 3 percent of the personnel of the Red Army. In total, an estimated 520,000 women, of whom at least 120,000 fought on the front lines served in the military of the USSR. In addition, hundreds of thousands of women joined the partisan armies fighting against Nazi occupation all over Europe, in which the percentage of women varied greatly, but could reach up to 15 or 20 percent.[110]

Ideas about gender differences shaped the composition of the military in both wars. It was mainly the armies' growing manpower needs—freeing soldiers for duty at the front instead of service in administration, communications, and logistics at home and in the rear—that opened the traditionally male-coded space of the military for women. The more women were needed and integrated in the military, the more it was necessary for politicians and military leaders to draw, at least for the public, clear gender lines in the armed forces. Participation in combat became, in their rhetoric, a male prerogative. The only exceptions were Russia in World War I and the USSR in World War II. In practice, however, even this gender line became blurred in most war powers through technological advances, especially in aerial defense.[111]

The different forms of war service led to demands for political, social, and civil citizenship rights by previously excluded groups in the nations and empires involved in the world wars. Among these groups were women, workers, African Americans, colonial subjects, and discriminated ethnic minorities. To legitimate their demands, they often used the traditional patriotic or revolutionary rhetoric of the duty to protect the fatherland and the right to be or to become a citizen, which in turn spurred debates about citizenship.[112] Indeed, the term *citizenship* had various meanings: it could signify a political status assigned to individuals by states, a relation of belonging to specific communities, or a set of social practices that defined the relationships between peoples and states and among peoples within communities. Gender, class, race, ethnicity, and age were important markers used to assign different citizenship rights and, in return, demand different obligations from citizens.[113]

Political citizenship was one core issue of struggle in the first half of the twentieth century. Workers and women attained universal suffrage in several countries after the First World War, including in Austria, Britain, Czechoslovakia, Germany, Hungary, Ireland, Poland, the Netherlands, Russia, Spain, Sweden, and the United States. But in the United Kingdom, the 1918 Representation of the People Act granted suffrage to women only over the age of thirty, because unlike the young men who had fought at the battlefront, young women were not perceived as trustworthy, despite their own war service at the home front. It took another ten years for all British women over the age of twenty-one to finally get the vote on equal terms with men.[114]

Contemporaries believed that women obtained suffrage as a recognition of their long struggle in the prewar era and as a reward for their patriotic war services, but historical research indicates that two postwar developments were more important in many countries: the political revolutions in Russia, Germany, and Austria and the creation of new nation-states with democratic constitutions like Czechoslovakia, Hungary, and Poland. The second wave of countries that granted women equal suffrage after World War II, including Bulgaria, China, France, Italy, Israel, India, and Japan, confirms the importance of political changes in postwar societies for granting women the right to vote.[115]

The participation of colonial soldiers in the two world wars furthered the aspirations among colonial elites and nascent revolutionaries for home rule and self-governance. These educated elites were aware of the strong association between male war service and political citizenship that had existed in Western thinking since the late eighteenth century.[116] Accordingly, the French government passed a law in 1916 that granted full citizenship to all *originaires*, the residents of the "Four Communes" (*quatre communes*) in Senegal (Gorée, Dakar, Rufisque, and Saint-Louis), which were the four oldest colonial towns in French West Africa, to recognize their contributions to the war effort on the western front.[117] In India and other colonies, a movement for self-governance (similar to dominion status) grew both during and especially after the First World War.[118] In Canada and the United States, the war experience reinforced the demands by African American men and women for equal civil, social, and political citizenship. Underprivileged ethnic minorities like Italians and Irish, too, claimed expanded citizenship as a reward for their wartime service. At the same time, suspicion of and prejudice against immigrants from the enemy countries grew during the First World War; they became so strong during the Second World War that some ethnic groups in the Allied countries were deprived of all citizenship rights, such as the 120,000 Japanese-origin citizens interned by the United States and the 320,000 German- and Austrian-origin residents, including Jews, interned by the United Kingdom.[119]

In Nazi Germany and Fascist Italy, the idea of the "community of the people" under a charismatic leader replaced the liberal rhetoric of citizenship. Basic democratic political rights were abolished for men and women, and civil and social rights were only granted to racially and socially "worthy" subjects. The peoples in territories occupied by the Axis powers were deprived of the rights of citizenship as well; they were expected to serve the occupiers, if they were not slated for destruction.[120] Both states were at first glance "men's states" in which only men had access to political decision-making in the state's administrations and the Nazi and Fascist movements, which led to the perception of women as "victims" of Nazism and Fascism in the early research by women's historians. But since the late 1980s an increasing number of studies has demonstrated that both movements designed for "worthy" women, who supported their political agenda, an important complementary space in the envisioned "community of the people" as current and future mothers of the nation and the family. This included their involvement in the persecution system of both states. One of women's crucial tasks was, next to the education of children and youths, the care for the health and reproduction of "the people." Especially in Nazi Germany this led to the involvement of hundreds of thousands of women, who were working voluntarily or professionally in health and youth care as well as welfare, in the policy of a social and racial "cleansing" of the population of "unworthy" members including criminals, "social deviants," the mentally and physically disabled, gays and lesbians, Sinti and Roma, and Jews. This policy extended during the Second World War to the occupied territories in the East, the envisioned new *Lebensraum* of the German people, which first had to "be emptied" from its former Jewish and Slavic inhabitants.[121]

Gender, Genocide, and Sexual Violence

War and mass violence were inextricably linked in the Age of World Wars. Beyond violence in battle, a broad range of violent acts accompanied both world wars, including mass killings, genocide, and sexual violence. The interdisciplinary scholarship on the subject has extensively discussed the definition of *genocide* and differentiated it from *mass killings*. Alan Kramer suggested, for example, that mass killings are "distinguished from genocide by reciprocity," because both sides in a war might perpetrate mass killings, whereas the victims of genocide are usually completely defenseless; their killing is ethnically and racially motivated and aims at their extermination.[122]

This still leaves open the question of how to define genocide. In the 2010 *Oxford Handbook of Genocide Studies*, Donald Bloxham and A. Dirk Moses proposed radically historicizing the concept and avoiding the use of the Holocaust as the ideal type because of its "uniqueness." As such, they criticized not only historians' inattention, at least until the 1990s, to the long-term history of genocides since antiquity, but also their overlooking of smaller genocides in the context of colonial warfare, Wars of Decolonization, and civil wars during the nineteenth and especially twentieth centuries.[123] For similar reasons, Bloxham and Moses rejected as too narrow the definition of genocide in the 1948 UN "Convention on the Prevention and Punishment of the Crime of Genocide," which was largely based on the experience of the Holocaust. The UN Convention defines genocide as any of the following acts "committed with intent to destroy, in whole or in part, a national, ethnical, racial or religious group, as such: (a) killing members of the group; (b) causing serious bodily or mental harm to members of the group; (c) deliberately inflicting on the group conditions of life calculated to bring about its physical destruction in whole or in part; (d) imposing measures intended to prevent births within the group; (e) forcibly transferring children of the group to another group."[124] Bloxham and Moses contended that the UN definition led to a situation in which acts that did not result in death have not been taken seriously in estimating the toll of victims. Its result was, furthermore, as Helen Fein asserted, that especially gendered forms of violence, including sexual violence, were long ignored.[125] Fein and other gender scholars in the field, like Elisa von Joeden-Forgey, insisted "that a consideration of gender is crucial to the understanding of the crime of genocide, because genocide is an historical process that is, at its core, about group reproduction. The perpetrators must either annul reproduction within the group or appropriate the progeny in order to destroy the group in the long run. While the perpetrators' ultimate aim is the material destruction of the target group, the means used to achieve this end tend to target men and women according to their perceived and actual positions within the reproductive process."[126] Such an approach allows historians to identify the multiple roles that gender and sexuality play in the practice of genocide and, crucially, to understand the different functions of sexual violence in genocide and warfare.[127]

Even though most scholars in the early twenty-first century agree that genocide has a long history far beyond the Holocaust, many historians insist, as does Eric D. Weitz, that genocides in the twentieth century were distinct because they were a product of "modernity's defining feature, the combined forces of new technologies of warfare, new administrative techniques that made populations the choice objects of state policies and that categorized people along strict lines of nation and state." Moreover, the two largest twentieth-century genocides, the Armenian genocide and the Holocaust, were inextricably linked with total warfare.[128]

The first documented genocide of the twentieth century was that of the Herero and Nama by Imperial Germany (1904–8) in response to the tribes' rebellion against German colonial rule in South West Africa. The first phase of this genocide was characterized by widespread death from starvation and dehydration, because the retreating Herero were prevented by German forces from leaving the Namib Desert. Once defeated, thousands of Hereros and Namas were imprisoned in concentration camps, where the majority died of diseases, abuse, and exhaustion. Already during this genocide, the murder was gendered: the men were systematically killed or interned in concentration camps, and the women and children were driven into the desert, where many died. Historians estimate the number of deaths between 65,000 and 85,000 Herero and 10,000 Nama.[129]

The dimensions of the Armenian genocide perpetrated by the Young Turks in the destabilized Ottoman Empire between 1915 and 1917 were much larger. Governed by the ruling nationalist party, the Committee for Union and Progress, the Turkish regime adopted a pan-Turkic ideology to justify the elimination of non-Turkic peoples. Estimates of the number of Armenian victims range between 800,000 and 1.5 million. More recent scholarship on the Armenian genocide points to "distinct gendered aspects" of this ethnically motivated mass killing. Like the earlier genocide of the Herero and Nama, men were executed, especially if they were of military age. Women, children, the elderly, and the infirm were deported in death marches to concentration camps in the Syrian desert, exposing women to sexual abuse that included rape, sexual slavery, and forced marriage accompanied by compulsory conversion to Islam.[130] The Young Turks also targeted the Assyrian (1914–18) and the Pontian Greek (1914–22) Christian minorities. Approximately 150,000 to 300,000 of the former and 350,000 of the latter were killed.[131]

Similar to the Armenian genocide, which was made possible by the First World War, the Second World War provided the necessary conditions for the Holocaust. As the research of the past decades has shown, the Wehrmacht willingly fulfilled its role as an agent of murder on a massive scale for the Nazi state.[132] Increasingly, this research also has included the gender dimension, even though the relevance of gender for the study of the Holocaust has long been contested.[133] According to Lisa Pine, a major argument was "that a differentiation of the victims by gender detracts from the fact that all Jews—men, women and children—were equally destined for murder by the Nazi regime."[134] In the early 1980s, feminist scholars began to challenge this position. They investigated the lives of women in the Holocaust and explored how gender affected Jewish experiences under Nazi domination.[135] Today, a gendered approach is a "mainstream part of the history of the Holocaust."[136] Nevertheless, most of the scholarship by feminist historians still focuseed on women. Research on men and masculinity in the context of the Holocaust remains scarce.[137]

Still contested is the definition of the *Holocaust*. Some scholars only use this term for the systematic, bureaucratic, state-sponsored persecution and murder of 6 million Jews by the Nazi regime and its collaborators. Others include all groups persecuted by the Nazis, including victims of the "euthanasia" program, Sinti and Roma, homosexuals, Jehovah's Witnesses, political prisoners, and Soviet POWs, which brings the total death toll to 11 million.[138] For most Holocaust victims, gender differences were important in two ways: on the one hand, Nazi assumptions about gender informed the practices of persecution; on the other hand, an individual's sex shaped the specific Holocaust experience. One example for the first is the imprisonment of girls and women for gender-specific reasons like alleged prostitution, illegal abortion, and illegal sexual relations with foreign POWs.[139] Another is the persecution of gay men, whom the Nazis perceived as far more dangerous than lesbians. An estimated number of 50,000 homosexual men were imprisoned during the Third Reich; between 5,000 and 15,000 ended up in concentration camps.[140]

Several recent studies examined how an individual's sex, along with other factors like age, shaped the experience of the Nazi-perpetrated genocide. Jewish men were often the first to be imprisoned and hunted down. Especially in the early stages of the Holocaust, men were more likely to be killed. Women and children remained in the ghettos or were killed later.[141] Mainly the young—both men and women—joined underground resistance movements in the more than one hundred ghettos in the east between 1941 and 1943. Armed Jewish resistance also developed outside the ghettos and even in camps. Here too, more often younger Jews had the strength to go underground and join resistance or partisan movements.[142] Later, in the camp system, however, men had a better chance to survive, because skilled labor was increasingly needed by the Nazi regime. Some men were thus spared, while women, including expectant mothers and children, were executed immediately after their arrival in the death camps. As a result, on average, only one-third of the survivors of the extermination camps were women.[143]

Sexual violence was an important part of the gendered experience of the Holocaust, even though it took scholars until the 1990s to recognize that.[144] The broad spectrum of sexual violence in the context of war and genocide includes rape, sexual mutilation, sexualized torture, sexual humiliation, forced prostitution, sexual slavery, and forced pregnancies. The experience of brutality, destruction, and death during war clearly lowered the threshold at which sexual violence occurred. At the same time, mass mobilization and unprecedented mobility presented new opportunities for soldiers and civilians to engage in consensual amorous encounters and instrumental and commercial sex. Often the boundaries between consensual and forced, nonviolent and violent sexuality were fluid.[145] Two of the most extreme forms of sexual violence are forced prostitution and mass rape during and after the Second World War.[146]

CONCLUSION

Beginning in the 1980s, women's and gender historians questioned the perception of many contemporaries and generations of historians that the two world wars lastingly changed the place of women in the economy, society, and politics. They argued that most changes were limited to wartime and, furthermore, were presented merely as an exceptional necessity in the "emergency situation" of war. Simultaneously, war propaganda promoted, especially in the West, men's and women's traditional family roles and the idea that both should return to "normalcy" after war. Gendered demobilization policies in most Western postwar societies stipulated that women vacate their wartime workplaces to allow the male veterans to return to their prewar jobs, reintegrating into the workforce and thereby into civilian life. Men were supposed to become again the main breadwinners of their families. Women were asked to go back to their primary tasks in the household and family. They were expected to heal the physical and mental wounds of the returning veterans in the family. But even though postwar demobilization policies tried to guarantee that the overall gender order was only marginally transformed by the two world wars, that did not mean that the day-to-day gender relations returned to the prewar reality after the conflicts ended. Furthermore, the Western ideal of the Cold War gender order was contradicted and fractured by the development in the communist societies in the East that promoted "women's emancipation" by means of labor force participation, and by the Wars of Decolonization. The postwar anticolonial struggles, which continued until the 1980s, not only required the mobilization of men for combat once more through highly militarized, virile images of masculinity, as during the world wars, but women too once again became involved in these conflicts in different functions, including fighting.[147]

NOTES

1. Nicoletta F. Gullace, *"The Blood of Our Sons": Men, Women, and the Renegotiation of British Citizenship during the Great War* (Basingstoke: Palgrave Macmillan, 2002), 99–116.
2. On the invention of the term home front, see Pierre Purseigle, "Home Fronts: The Mobilization of Resources for Total War," in *The Cambridge History of War*, ed. Roger Chickering et al. (Cambridge: Cambridge University Press, 2012), 257–84; and Susan Grayzel, "Men and Women at Home," in *The Cambridge History of the First World War*, ed. Jay Winter (Cambridge: Cambridge University Press, 2014), 3:96–120.
3. See David Welch, *Propaganda, Power and Persuasion: From World War I to Wikileaks* (London: I. B. Tauris, 2014).
4. Karen Hagemann, "Introduction Home/Front: The Military, Violence and Gender in the Age of the World Wars," in *Home/Front: The Military, War and Gender in Twentieth-Century Germany*, ed. Hagemann and Stefanie Schüler-Springorum (Oxford: Berg, 2002), 1–42.
5. Margaret R. Higonnet et al., eds., *Behind the Lines: Gender and the Two World Wars* (New Haven, CT: Yale University Press, 1987), 4.

6. Stig Förster, ed., *An der Schwelle zum Totalen Krieg: Die militärische Debatte über den Krieg der Zukunft 1919–1939* (Paderborn: Schöningh, 2002); and Roger Chickering and Förster, eds., *Shadows of Total War: Europe, East Asia, and the United States, 1919–1939* (Cambridge: Cambridge University Press, 2003), esp. 151–254.

7. Stig Förster and Myrian Gessler, "The Ultimate Horror: Reflections on Total War and Genocide," in *A World at Total War: Global Conflicts and the Politics of Destruction, 1937–1945*, ed. Roger Chickering et al. (Cambridge: Cambridge University Press, 2005), 53–68; and Hew Strachan, "On Total War and Modern War," *The International History Review* 22, no. 2 (2000): 341–70.

8. Summary in Roger Chickering, "World War I and the Theory of Total War: Reflections on the British and German Cases, 1914–1915," in *Great War, Total War: Combat and Mobilization on the Western Front, 1914–1918*, ed. Chickering and Stig Förster (Cambridge: Cambridge University Press, 2000), 35–56.

9. Roger Chickering and Stig Förster, "Are We There Yet? World War II and the Theory of Total War," in Chickering et al. *A World*, 1–18, 2.

10. Roger Chickering, "Militärgeschichte als Totalgeschichte im Zeitalter des totalen Krieges," in *Was ist Militärgeschichte?*, ed. Benjamin Ziemann and Thomas Kühne (Paderborn: Schöningh, 2000), 301–12, 306; also Chickering, "Total War: The Use and Abuse of a Concept," in *Anticipating Total War: The German and American Experiences, 1871–1914*, ed. Manfred F. Boemeke et al. (Cambridge: Cambridge University Press, 1999), 13–28.

11. Chickering and Förster, "Are We There," 2.

12. Peter H. Wilson, "Was the Thirty Years War a 'Total War'?," in *Civilians and War in Europe, 1618–1815*, ed. Erica Charters et al. (Liverpool: Liverpool University Press, 2012), 21–35.

13. Philip Dwyer and Lyndall Ryan, eds., *Theatres of Violence: Massacre, Mass Killing and Atrocity throughout History* (New York: Berghahn Books, 2012); and Dirk Moses, ed., *Empire, Colony, Genocide: Conquest, Occupation, and Subaltern Resistance in World History* (New York: Berghahn Books, 2008).

14. David A. Bell, *The First Total War: Napoleon's Europe and the Birth of Warfare as We Know It* (Boston: Houghton Mifflin, 2007), esp. 1–20; Stig Förster and Jörg Nagler, eds., *On the Road to Total War: The American Civil War and the German Wars of Unification, 1861–1871* (Cambridge: Cambridge University Press, 1997); and the chapter by Stefan Dudink and Karen Hagemann on "War and Gender: From the Thirty Years' War and Colonial Conquest to the Wars of Revolution and Independence—an Overview" in this handbook.

15. Wilson, "Was the Thirty Years War," 22.

16. For the conceptualization of the Wars of Decolonization after 1945 as total wars see the chapter by the Raphaëlle Branche on "Gender, the Wars of Decolonization, and the Decline of Empires after 1945" in this handbook.

17. See also in the following, Jeremy M. Black, *War and Technology* (Bloomington: Indiana University Press, 2013), 101–227; Martin van Creveld, "Technology and War I: To 1945," in *The Oxford History of Modern War*, ed. Charles Townshend (Oxford: Oxford University Press, 2005), 201–23, esp. 214–23; and Gerhard L. Weinberg, *A World at Arms: A Global History of World War II*, 2nd ed. (Cambridge: Cambridge University Press, 2005), 536–81.

18. See Creveld, "Technology and War," 214–23.

19. Ibid.

20. See also in the following, Jeremy Black, *The Age of Total War, 1860–1945* (Westport, CT: Praeger, 2006); Michael S. Neiberg, *Fighting the Great War: A Global History* (Cambridge, MA: Harvard University Press, 2009); Weinberg, *World at Arms*; and Jane Burbank and

Frederick Cooper, "War and Revolution in a World of Empires: 1914 to 1945," in *Empires in World History: Power and the Politics of Difference*, ed. Jane Burbank and Frederick Cooper (Princeton, NJ: Princeton University Press, 2010), 369–412.

21. Hew Strachan, "The First World War as a Global War," *First World War Studies* 1, no. 1 (2010): 3–14.

22. Guoqi Xu, *Strangers on the Western Front: Chinese Workers in the Great War* (Cambridge, MA: Harvard University Press, 2011).

23. We are fully aware of the methodological problems inherent to war statistics; we thus only use them to indicate trends. For World War I, we use Jay Winter, "Demography," in *A Companion to World War I*, ed. John Horne (Chichester: Wiley–Blackwell, 2010), 248–62, 249; and, in addition, Michael Clodfelter, *Warfare and Armed Conflicts: A Statistical Reference to Casualty and Other Figures, 1500–2000* (Jefferson, NC: McFarland, 2002), 484–592, esp. 479–83.

24. Wilson, "Was the Thirty," 26; and David Gates, *The Napoleonic Wars, 1803–1815* (London: Arnold, 1997), 272.

25. Alan Kramer, *Dynamics of Destruction: Culture and Mass Killing in the First World War* (Oxford: Oxford University Press, 2007), 2.

26. Clodfelter, *Warfare*, 484–592, esp. 581–92.

27. Estimates from "Fatalities," *Second World War*, accessed February 15, 2017, http://www. Secondworldwar.co.uk/index.php/fatalities. See also Clodfelter, *Warfare*, 495–517; and Chris Bellamy, *Absolute War: Soviet Russia in the Second World War* (New York: Alfred A. Knopf, 2007).

28. David Fromkin, *Europe's Last Summer: Who Started the Great War in 1914?* (New York: Alfred A. Knopf, 2004), 94; Dominik Geppert et al., eds., *Conflict and International Politics before the Outbreak of the First World War* (Cambridge: Cambridge University Press, 2015); and Dirk Bönker, *Militarism in a Global Age: Naval Ambitions in Germany and the United States before World War I* (Ithaca, NY: Cornell University Press, 2012). On the causes of World War I, see also Christopher Clark, *The Sleepwalkers: How Europe Went to War in 1914* (London: Penguin Books, 2013).

29. See the chapter by Stefan Dudink, Karen Hagemann, and Mischa Honeck on "War and Gender: Nineteenth-Century Wars of Nations and Empires—an Overview" in this handbook.

30. See Richard C. Hall, *The Balkan Wars, 1912–1913: Prelude to the First World War* (London: Routledge, 2000); and Geppert, *Conflict*.

31. See the chapters by Robert A. Nye on "War Mobilization, Gender, and Military Culture in Nineteenth-Century Western Societies," and by Glenda Sluga on "Gender, Peace, and the New Politics of Humanitarianism in the First Half of the Twentieth Century" in this handbook.

32. See Neiberg, *Fighting*; on specific regions, see Peter Gatrell, *Russia's First World War: A Social and Economic History* (Harlow: Pearson-Longman, 2005); Anne Samson, *World War I in Africa: The Forgotten Conflict among the European Powers* (London: I. B. Tauris, 2012); Frederick R. Dickinson, *World War I and the Triumph of a New Japan, 1919–1930* (Cambridge: Cambridge University Press, 2013); and Hans-Lukas Kieser et al., eds., *World War I and the End of the Ottoman World: From the Balkan Wars to the Armenian Genocide* (London: I. B. Tauris, 2015).

33. Margaret MacMillan, *Peacemakers: The Paris Conference of 1919 and Its Attempt to End War* (London: J. Murray, 2001); and Alan Sharp, *Consequences of Peace: The Versailles Settlement—Aftermath and Legacy* (London: Haus, 2010).

34. See Robert W. D. Boyce, *The Great Interwar Crisis and the Collapse of Globalization* (Basingstoke: Palgrave Macmillan, 2009); and Susan Pedersen, *The Guardians: The League of Nations and the Crisis of Empire* (Oxford: Oxford University Press, 2015), esp. 17–106.

35. Evan Mawdsley, *The Russian Civil War* (New York: Pegasus Books, 2007), 287.

36. Tammy M. Proctor, *Civilians in a World at War, 1914–1918* (New York: New York University Press, 2010), 239–66.

37. Robert Gerwarth and John Horne, eds., *War in Peace: Paramilitary Violence in Europe after the Great War* (Oxford: Oxford University Press, 2012).

38. John A. Thompson, *A Sense of Power: The Roots of America's Global Role* (Ithaca, NY: Cornell University Press, 2015), esp. 93–150.

39. Pedersen, *Guardians*; and Bruno Cabanes, *The Great War and the Origins of Humanitarianism, 1918–1924* (Cambridge: Cambridge University Press, 2014).

40. David Cortright, *Peace: A History of Movements and Ideas* (Cambridge: Cambridge University Press, 2008), esp. 45–108; and Geoff Eley, *Forging Democracy: The History of the Left in Europe, 1850–2000* (Oxford: Oxford University Press, 2002), esp. 139–261.

41. See S. C. M. Paine, *The Wars for Asia, 1911–1949* (New York: Cambridge University Press, 2012).

42. Ibid., 109–222.

43. Ibid.; and Weinberg, *World at Arms*, 842–93.

44. Weinberg, *World at Arms*, 6–48; Bruce G. Strang, ed., *Collision of Empires: Italy's Invasion of Ethiopia and Its International Impact* (Farnham: Ashgate, 2013); and Stanley G. Payne, *The Spanish Civil War* (Cambridge: Cambridge University Press, 2012).

45. See also Weinberg, *World at Arms*.

46. Ibid., 48–186.

47. Ibid.

48. See Omer Bartov, ed., *The Holocaust: Origins, Implementation, Aftermath* (New York: Routledge, 2015).

49. Weinberg, *World at Arms*, 910–20.

50. Michael S. Neiberg, *Potsdam: The End of World War II and the Remaking of Europe* (New York: Basic Books, 2015).

51. André Gerolymatos, *Red Acropolis, Black Terror: The Greek Civil War and the Origins of Soviet–American Rivalry, 1943–1949* (New York: Basic Books, 2004).

52. Denise M. Bostdorff, *Proclaiming the Truman Doctrine: The Cold War Call to Arms* (College Station: Texas A&M University Press, 2008).

53. Christopher A. Bayly and Tim Harper, *Forgotten Wars: The End of Britain's Asian Empire* (London: Allen Lane, 2007); and Christopher E. Goscha and Christian F. Ostermann, eds., *Connecting Histories: Decolonization and the Cold War in Southeast Asia, 1945–1962* (Stanford, CA: Stanford University Press, 2009).

54. Stanley Meisler, *United Nations: A History* (New York: Grove Press, 2011).

55. Tony Judt, *Postwar: A History of Europe since 1945* (London: Pimlico, 2007), 1–10.

56. For the literature, see Karen Hagemann, "Introduction: Gender and the History of War—The Development of the Research" in this handbook.

57. Margaret R. Higonnet and Patrice L.-R. Higonnet, "The Double Helix," in Higonnet et al., *Behind the Lines*, 31–50; the quote is from the introduction of the volume, 1–19, 6.

58. Early examples are Leila J. Rupp, *Mobilizing Women for War: German and American Propaganda, 1939–1945* (Princeton, NJ: Princeton University Press, 1978); and Maureen Honey, *Creating Rosie the Riveter: Class, Gender, and Propaganda during World War II* (Amherst: University of Massachusetts Press, 1984).

59. See the chapter by Annegret Fauser on "Gendered War Mobilization, Culture, and Music in the Age of World Wars" in this handbook; as well as Robert L. Nelson, *German Soldier Newspapers of the First World War* (Cambridge: Cambridge University Press, 2011); Celia Malone Kingsbury, *For Home and Country: World War I Propaganda on the Home Front* (Lincoln: University of Nebraska Press, 2010); and Susan A. Brewer, *Why America Fights: Patriotism and War Propaganda from the Philippines to Iraq* (Oxford: Oxford University Press, 2009), 46–140.

60. British poster, *Remember Belgium. Enlist Today*, London, Parliamentary Recruiting Committee, [1915], accessed March 10, 2017, http://www.loc.gov/pictures/resource/cph.3g10881/. For the history of the invasion, see Larry Zuckerman, *The Rape of Belgium: The Untold Story of World War I* (New York: New York University Press, 2004).

61. See Robert Heide and John Gilman, *Home Front America: Popular Culture of the World War II Era* (San Francisco: Chronicle Books, 1995), 33–34.

62. German poster, *Behind the Enemy Powers: The Jew*, artist unknown, ca. 1942, United States Holocaust Memorial Museum, accessed March 10, 2017, https://www.ushmm.org/information/press/press-kits/traveling-exhibitions/state-of-deception/behind-the-enemy-powers-the-jew.

63. British recruitment poster, *The British Commonwealth of Nations: Together*, artist unknown, 1941, Imperial War Museum, London, accessed March 10, 2017, http://www.iwm.org.uk/collections/item/object/17043.

64. Sonya O. Rose, *Which People's War? National Identity and Citizenship in Britain, 1939–1945* (Oxford: Oxford University Press, 2003), 152–53.

65. US Air Force poster, *O'er the Ramparts We Watch*, artist Jes Wilhelm Schlaikjer, 1945, University of Northern Texas Digital Library, accessed March 10, 2017, http://digital.library.unt.edu/ark:/67531/metadc218/. On the new masculine ideal of the aviator, see Peter Fritzsche, *A Nation of Fliers: German Aviation and the Popular Imagination* (Cambridge, MA: Harvard University Press, 1992); and Martin Francis, *The Flyer: British Culture and the Royal Air Force, 1939–1945* (Oxford: Oxford University Press, 2008).

66. Poster by the US Employment Service, *Do the Job He Left Behind*, designed by Robert George Harris, 1943, Hagley Museum, Wilmington, accessed March 9, 2017, http://digital.hagley.org/islandora/object/islandora:2339077.

67. See the chapter by Karen Hagemann on "Gender, Demobilization, and the Reordering of Societies after the First and Second World Wars" in this handbook; and Jochen Hellerbeck, "Battles for Morale: An Entangled History of Total War in Europe, 1939–1945," in *Cambridge History of the Second World War*, ed. Michael Geyer and Adam Tooze (Cambridge: Cambridge University Press, 2015), 3:329–62.

68. See the chapters by Frank Biess on "Gendering the Memories of War and Holocaust in Europe and the United States," and Karen Hagemann on "History and Memory of Female Military Service in the Age of World Wars" in this handbook.

69. See the chapters by Susan R. Grayzel on "Total Warfare, Gender, and the 'Home Front' in Europe during the First and Second World Wars," and by Kimberly Jensen on "Citizenship and Gender on the American and Canadian Home Fronts during the First and Second World Wars" in this handbook; as well as Susan R. Grayzel and Tammy M. Proctor, eds., *Gender and the Great War* (Oxford: Oxford University Press, 2017).

70. Antoine Prost, "Workers," in Winter, *Cambridge History of the First World War*, 2:325–57, 332–41; and Laura Lee Downs, "War Work," in Winter, *Cambridge History of the First World War*, 3:72–95.

71. See Hagemann, "Gender, Demobilization" in this handbook.
72. See Geoffrey Cocks, "Hors de combat: Mobilization and Immobilization in Total War," in Geyer and Tooze, *Cambridge History of the Second World War*, 3:363–84, 375–77; Rüdiger Hachtmann, "The War of the Cities: Industrial Labouring Forces," in Geyer and Tooze, *Cambridge History of the Second World War*, 3:298–328, 306–11; and Hellerbeck, "Battles for Morale."
73. See Laura Ugolini, *Civvies: Middle-Class Men on the English Home Front, 1914–18* (Manchester: Manchester University Press, 2013); and Linsey Robb, *Men at Work: The Working Man in British Culture, 1939–1945* (Basingstoke: Palgrave Macmillan, 2015).
74. Robb, *Men at Work*, 2.
75. See Maureen Healy, *Vienna and the Fall of the Habsburg Empire: Total War and Everyday Life in World War I* (Cambridge: Cambridge University Press, 2004), 268–73; and Gullace, *The Blood*, 73–116.
76. See Penny Summerfield and Corinna Peniston-Bird, *Contesting Home Defence: Men, Women and the Home Guard in the Second World War* (Manchester: Manchester University Press, 2007), esp. 206–39.
77. Richard Overy, "Air Warfare," in Townshend, *The Oxford History*, 262–79, 266.
78. Ibid., 275.
79. Ibid.
80. See Susan R. Grayzel, *At Home and Under Fire: Air Raids and Culture in Britain from the Great War to the Blitz* (Cambridge: Cambridge University Press, 2012); Summerfield and Peniston-Bird, *Contesting*; and Nicole Kramer, *Volksgenossinnen an der Heimatfront: Mobilisierung, Verhalten, Erinnerung* (Göttingen: Vandenhoeck & Ruprecht, 2011).
81. Summerfield and Peniston-Bird, *Contesting*, 91.
82. Kramer, *Volksgenossinnen*, 116.
83. Roger D. Markwick and Euridice Charon Cardona, *Soviet Women on the Frontline in the Second World War* (Basingstoke: Palgrave Macmillan, 2012), 156; and Anna Krylova, *Soviet Women in Combat: A History of Violence on the Eastern Front* (Cambridge: Cambridge University Press, 2010), 3.
84. See Grayzel, *At Home*; and Summerfield and Peniston-Bird, *Contesting*.
85. See Grayzel, "Total Warfare."
86. Healy, *Vienna*; Belinda Davis, *Home Fires Burning: Food, Politics and Everyday Life in World War I Berlin* (Chapel Hill: University of North Carolina Press, 2000); and Barbara Engel, "Not by Bread Alone: Subsistence Rioting in Russia during World War I," *Journal of Modern History* 69, no. 4 (1997): 696–721.
87. Nicholas Stargardt, "Wartime Occupation by Germany: Food and Sex," in *Cambridge History of the Second World War*, ed. Richard Bosworth and Joseph Maiolo (Cambridge: Cambridge University Press, 2015), 2:385–441; and Paul H. Kratoska and Ken'ichi Goto, "Japanese Occupation of Southeast Asia, 1941–1945," in Bosworth and Maiolo, *Cambridge History of the Second World War*, 2:508–32.
88. Stargardt, "Wartime Occupation"; and Timothy Snyder, *Bloodlands: Europe between Hitler and Stalin* (New York: Basic Books, 2010).
89. Heather Jones, "Prisoners of War," in Winter, *Cambridge History of the First World War*, 2:266–92; and Iris Rachamimov, "Military Captivity in the Two World Wars: Legal Framework and Camp Regimes," in Chickering, *Cambridge History of War*, 4:214–35. On the use of civilians for forced labor during World War I, see Proctor, *Civilians*, 40–75; on the much smaller number of POWs at the western front, see Brian K. Feltman, *The Stigma*

of Surrender: German Prisoners, British Captors, and Manhood in the Great War and Beyond (Chapel Hill: University of North Carolina Press, 2014); and John Lewis-Stempel, *The War behind the Wire: The Life, Death and Glory of British Prisoners of War, 1914–18* (London: Weidenfeld & Nicolson, 2014).

90. Mark Spoerer, and Jochen Fleischhacker, "Forced Laborers in Nazi Germany: Categories, Numbers, and Survivors." *The Journal of Interdisciplinary History* 33, no. 2 (2002): 169–204.

91. Bob Moore, "Prisoners of War," in *The Cambridge History of the Second World War*, ed. John Ferris and Evan Mawdsley (Cambridge: Cambridge University Press, 2015), 1:664–89; and Richard Rice, "Japanese Labor in World War II," *International Labor and Working-Class History*, no. 38 (1990): 29–45.

92. Peter Duus, "Introduction: Japan's Wartime Empire—Problems and Issues," in *The Japanese Wartime Empire, 1930–1945*, ed. Duus et al. (Princeton, NJ: Princeton University Press, 1996), xi–xlvii , xxxviii; Kratoska and Goto, "Japanese Occupation," 553–57; and Kevin Blackburn and Karl Hack, "Japanese-Occupied Asia from 1941 to 1945: One Occupier, Many Captivities and Memories," in *Forgotten Captives in Japanese Occupied Asia*, ed. Kevin Blackburn and Karl Hack (New York: Routledge, 2008): 1–20, 5–6.

93. See Proctor, *Civilians*, 113–52 and 203–38; Nicole Dombrowski Risser, *France under Fire: German Invasion, Civilian Flight and Family Survival during World War II* (Cambridge: Cambridge University Press, 2012); and Elizabeth Harvey, *Women and the Nazi East: Agents and Witnesses of Germanization* (New Haven, CT: Yale University Press, 2003).

94. Caroline Norma, *The Japanese Comfort Women and Sexual Slavery during the China and Pacific Wars* (London: Bloomsbury Academic, 2016), 3; and Bernice Archer, "Internee Voices: Women and Children's Experience of Being Japanese Captives," in Blackburn and Hack, *Forgotten Captives*, 224–42.

95. Nanda Herbermann, *The Blessed Abyss: Inmate #6582 in Ravensbrück Concentration Camp for Women*, ed. Hester Baer and Elizabeth R. Baer (Detroit, MI: Wayne State University Press, 2000), 33; see also Christa Paul, *Zwangsprostitution: Staatlich errichtete Bordelle im Nationalsozialismus* (Berlin: Edition Hentrich, 1994); Insa Meinen, *Wehrmacht und Prostitution im besetzten Frankreich* (Bremen: Edition Temmen, 2002); Robert Sommer, *Das KZ-Bordell: Sexuelle Zwangsarbeit in nationalsozialistischen Konzentrationslagern* (Paderborn: Schöningh, 2009); and Regina Mühlhäuser, *Eroberungen: Sexuelle Gewalttaten und intime Beziehungen deutscher Soldaten in der Sowjetunion 1941–1945* (Hamburg: Hamburger Edition, 2012), English translation: *Sex and the Nazi Soldier: Violent, Commercial and Consensual Contacts during the War in the Soviet Union, 1941–1945* (Edinburgh: Edinburgh University Press 2020).

96. See Mark Mazower, *Hitler's Empire: Nazi Rule in Occupied Europe* (London: Allen Lane, 2008); Ian Rutledge, *Enemy on the Euphrates: The British Occupation of Iraq and the Great Arab Revolt, 1914–1921* (London: Saqi Books, 2014); and Branche, "Gender, the Wars of Decolonization" in this handbook.

97. Mark Roseman, "War and the People: The Social Impact of Total War," in Townshend, *Oxford History of Modern War*, ed. Townshend, 280–302; and Odile Roynette, "The Military at Home," *1914–1918 Online*, accessed December 26, 2016, http://encyclopedia.1914-1918-online.net/article/the_military_at_home, 3.

98. Rüdiger Overmans, *Deutsche militärische Verluste im Zweiten Weltkrieg* (Munich: Oldenbourg, 2004), 215; and Catherine Merridale, *Ivan's War: Life and Death in the Red Army, 1939–1945* (New York: Metropolitan Books, 2006), 23–49.

99. See the chapter by Karen Hagemann and D'Ann Campbell on "Post-1945 Western Militaries, Female Soldiers, and Gay and Lesbian Rights" in this handbook.

100. Ute Frevert, *A Nation in Barracks: Modern Germany, Military Conscription and Civil Society* (Oxford: Berg, 2004), 247–58; and Yonson Ahn, "'Taming Soldiers': The Gender Politics of Japanese Soldiers in Total War," in *Gender Politics and Mass Dictatorship: Global Perspectives*, ed. Jie-Hyun Lim and Karen Petrone (Basingstoke: Palgrave Macmillan, 2010), 213–34.

101. Jason Crouthamel, *An Intimate History of the Front: Masculinity, Sexuality and German Soldiers in the First World War* (Basingstoke: Palgrave Macmillan, 2014); and Michael Roper, *The Secret Battle: Emotional Survival in the Great War* (Manchester: Manchester University Press, 2009).

102. See Thomas Kühne, *The Rise and Fall of Comradeship: Hitler's Soldiers, Male Bonding and Mass Violence in the Twentieth Century* (Cambridge: Cambridge University Press, 2017); and the chapter by Kühne on "States, Military Masculinities, and Combat in the Age of World Wars" in this handbook.

103. See Lois S. Bibbings, *Telling Tales about Men: Conceptions of Conscientious Objectors to Military Service during the First World War* (Manchester: Manchester University Press, 2009); Charles Glass, *The Deserters: A Hidden History of World War II* (New York: Penguin Press, 2013); and Maria Fritsche, "Proving One's Manliness: Masculine Self-perceptions of Austrian Deserters in the Second World War," *Gender & History* 24, no. 1 (2012): 35–55.

104. See the chapter by Richard Smith on "Colonial Soldiers, Race, and Military Masculinities during and beyond World Wars I and II" in this handbook.

105. See R. Dan Richardson, *Comintern Army: The International Brigades and the Spanish Civil War* (Lexington: University of Kentucky Press, 1982).

106. Joachim Hoffmann, *Die Ostlegionen 1941–1943: Turkotataren, Kaukasier und Wolgafinnen im deutschen Heer* (Freiburg/Breisgau: Rombach, 1976); and Antonio J. Munoz, ed., *The East Came West: Muslim, Hindu, and Buddhist Volunteers in the German Armed Forces, 1941–1945* (Bayside, NY: Axis Europa Books, 2002).

107. See the chapter by Jean H. Quataert on "Changing Modes of Warfare and the Gendering of Military Medical Care, 1850s–1920s" in this handbook; more generally, see David P. Forsythe, *The Humanitarians: The International Committee of the Red Cross* (Cambridge: Cambridge University Press, 2005); and Anne Powell, *Women in the War Zone: Hospital Service in the First World War* (Gloucestershire: History Press, 2009).

108. Markwick and Cardona, *Soviet Women*, 56–83; more generally, Penny Starns, *Nurses at War: Women on the Frontline, 1939–45* (Stroud: Sutton, 2000); and Evelyn M. Mohahan and Rosemary Neidel-Greenlee, *And If I Perish: Frontline U.S. Army Nurses in World War II* (New York: Alfred A. Knopf, 2003).

109. See Sluga, "Gender, Peace" in this handbook.

110. See Hagemann, "History and Memory" in this handbook.

111. For a comparison, see Beate Fieseler et al., "Gendering Combat: Military Women's Status in Britain, the United States, and the Soviet Union during the Second World War," *Women's Studies International Forum* 47 (2014): 115–26.

112. See, for the tradition of this debate, the chapter by Stefan Dudink on "Citizenship, Mass Mobilization, and Masculinity in a Transatlantic Perspective, 1770s–1870s" in this handbook.

113. See Jensen, "Citizenship" in this handbook.

114. Gullace, *The Blood*, 167–194.

115. Caroline Daley and Melanie Nolan, eds., *Suffrage and Beyond: International Feminist Perspectives* (New York: New York University Press, 1994).

116. See Dudink, "Citizenship" in this handbook.

117. Larissa Kopytoff, "French Citizens and Muslim Law: The Tensions of Citizenship in Early Twentieth Century," in *The Meanings of Citizenship*, ed. Richard Marbach and Marc W. Kruman (Detroit; MI: Wayne State University Press, 2015), 320–38.

118. Nirja Gopal Jayal, *Citizenship and Its Discontents: An Indian History* (Cambridge: Harvard University Press, 2013), 136–63.

119. Richard Reeves, *Infamy: The Shocking Story of the Japanese American Internment in World War II* (New York: Henry Holt, 2015); and Richard Dove, ed., *"Totally Un-English"? Britain's Internment of "Enemy Aliens" in Two World Wars* (Amsterdam: Rodopi, 2005).

120. See Diemut Majer, *"Non-Germans" under the Third Reich: The Nazi Judicial and Administrative System in Germany and Occupied Eastern Europe with Special Regard to Occupied Poland, 1939–1945* (Baltimore: Johns Hopkins University Press, 2003).

121. There is a plethora of research on this subject, a good overview of the scholarship is provided in the chapter by Claudia A. Koonz, "A Tributary and a Mainstream: Gender, Public Memory, and Historiography of Nazi Germany," in *Gendering Modern German History: Rewriting Historiography*, ed. Karen Hagemann and Jean H. Quataert (New York: Berghahn Books, 2007), 147–68; for Nazi Germany, see Wendy Lower, *Hitler's Furies: German Women in the Nazi Killing Fields* (Boston: Houghton Mifflin Harcourt, 2013); for Italy, see Victoria De Grazia, *How Fascism Ruled Women: Italy, 1922–1945* (Berkeley: University of California Press, 1992), esp. 234–71.

122. Kramer, *Dynamic*, 2; and Norman M. Naimark, *Fires of Hatred: Ethnic Cleansing in Twentieth-Century Europe* (Cambridge, MA: Harvard University Press, 2001).

123. Donald Bloxham and A. Dirk Moses, "Introduction: Changing Themes in the Study of Genocide," in *The Oxford Handbook of Genocide Studies*, ed. Bloxham and Moses (Oxford: Oxford University Press, 2010), 1–17.

124. Cited in Helen Fein, "Genocide and Gender: The Use of Women and Group Destiny," *Journal of Genocide Research* 1, no. 1 (1999): 43–63, 44.

125. Ibid., 43–45.

126. Elisa von Joeden-Forgey, "Gender and Genocide," in Bloxham and Moses, *Oxford Handbook of Genocide Studies*, 61–80, 62; also Fein, "Genocide and Gender," 43.

127. The most recent anthologies are Adam Jones, ed., *Gendercide and Genocide* (Nashville, TN: Vanderbilt University Press, 2004); Amy E. Randall, ed., *Genocide and Gender in the Twentieth Century: A Comparative Survey* (London: Bloomsbury Academic, 2015); and JoAnn DiGeorgio-Lutz and Donna Gosbee, eds., *Women and Genocide: Gendered Experience of Violence, Survival, and Resistance* (Toronto: Women's Press, 2017).

128. Eric Weitz, "The Modernity of Genocides: War, Race, and Revolution in the Twentieth Century," in *The Specter of Genocide: Mass Murder in Historical Perspective*, ed. Robert Gellately and Ben Kiernan (Cambridge: Cambridge University Press, 2003), 53–74.

129. See Dominik J. Schaller, "Genocide in German Southwest Africa and German East Africa," in Mosese, *Empire, Colony, Genocide*, 296–324; and Jürgen Zimmerer and Joachim Zeller, eds., *Genocide in German South-West Africa: The Colonial War (1904–1908) in Namibia and Its Aftermath* (Monmouth, Wales: Merlin Press, 2008).

130. Matthias Bjørnlund, "'A Fate Worse Than Dying': Sexual Violence during the Armenian Genocide," in *Brutality and Desire: War and Sexuality in Europe's Twentieth Century*, ed. Dagmar Herzog (Basingstoke: Palgrave Macmillan, 2011), 16–58 See also Katherine Derderian, "Common Fate, Different Experience: Gender-Specific Aspects of the Armenian Genocide, 1915–1917," *Holocaust and Genocide Studies* 19, no. 1 (2005): 1–25 More generally, Taner Akçam, *The Young Turks' Crime against Humanity: The Armenian Genocide and Ethnic Cleansing in the Ottoman Empire* (Princeton, NJ: Princeton University Press, 2012).

131. Adam Jones, *Genocide: A Comprehensive Introduction* (London: Routledge, 2006), 161, 163; and Hannibal Travis, "The Assyrian Genocide: A Tale of Oblivion and Denial," in *Forgotten Genocides: Oblivion, Denial, and Memory*, ed. René Lemarchand (Philadelphia: University of Pennsylvania Press, 2011), 123–36.

132. See Waitman W. Beorn, *Marching into Darkness: The Wehrmacht and the Holocaust in Belarus* (Cambridge, MA: Harvard University Press, 2014); Wolfram Wette, *The Wehrmacht: History, Myth, Reality* (Cambridge, MA.: Harvard University Press, 2006); and Hannes Heer and Klaus Naumann, eds., *War of Extermination: The German Military in World War II, 1941–1944* (New York: Berghahn Books, 2000).

133. For the development and state of research, see Delia Ofer and Leonore J. Weitzman, eds., *Women in the Holocaust* (New Haven, CT: Yale University Press, 1998); Koonz, "A Tributary and a Mainstream," 147–68; Lisa Pine, "Gender and Holocaust Victims: A Reappraisal," *Journal of Jewish Identities* 1, no. 2 (2008): 121–41; and Myrna Goldenberg and Amy H. Shapiro, eds., *Different Horrors, Same Hell: Gender and the Holocaust* (Seattle: University of Washington Press, 2013), esp. Doris L. Bergen, "What Do Studies of Women, Gender, and Sexuality Contribute to the Understanding of the Holocaust," in ibid., 16–36.

134. Pine, "Gender and Holocaust," 122–23.

135. An early publication was Carol Rittner and John K. Roth, eds., *Different Voices: Women and the Holocaust* (New York: Paragon House, 1993).

136. Pine, "Gender and Holocaust," 122–23; and Christopher R. Browning et al., eds., *Holocaust Scholarship: Personal Trajectories and Professional Interpretations* (Basingstoke: Palgrave Macmillan, 2015).

137. See Stephen R. Haynes, "Ordinary Masculinity: Gender Analysis and Holocaust Scholarship," *Journal of Men's Studies* 10, no. 2 (2002): 143–63; recent exceptions are Maddy Carey, *Jewish Masculinity in the Holocaust: Between Destruction and Construction* (London: Bloomsbury, 2017), and some of the articles in the special issue "Masculinity and the Third Reich," ed. Thomas Kühne, *Central European History* 51, no. 3 (September 2018).

138. See Donald L. Niewyk and Francis R. Nicosia, *The Columbia Guide to the Holocaust* (New York: Columbia University Press, 2000), 45–52.

139. Jane Caplan, "Gender and the Concentration Camps," in *Concentration Camps in Nazi Germany: New Histories*, ed. Caplan and Nikolaus Wachsmann (London: Routledge, 2010), 82–107; and Myrna Goldenberg, "Sex-Based Violence and the Politics and Ethics of Survival," in Goldenberg and Shapiro, *Different Horrors*, 99–128.

140. "Nazi Persecution of Homosexuals," United States Holocaust Memorial Museum, accessed March 15, 2017, https://www.ushmm.org/information/exhibitions/online-exhibitions/special-focus/nazi-persecution-of-homosexuals; see also Günter Grau, *Hidden Holocaust? Gay and Lesbian Persecution in Germany, 1933–45* (Chicago: Fitzroy Dearborn, 1995).

141. See, most recently, Anika Walke, *Pioneers and Partisans: An Oral History of Nazi Genocide in Belorussia* (New York: Oxford University Press, 2015); and Walke, "Jewish Youth in the Minsk Ghetto: How Age and Gender Mattered," *Kritika* 15, no. 3 (2014): 535–62.

142. Doreen Rappaport, *Beyond Courage: The Untold Story of Jewish Resistance during the Holocaust* (Somerville, MA: Candlewick Press, 2012).

143. Raul Hilberg, *Perpetrators, Victims, Bystanders: The Jewish Catastrophe, 1933–1945* (New York: Harper Collins, 1992), 130.

144. The most recent studies on sexual violence in the context of the Holocaust are Insa Eschebach and Regina Mühlhäuser, eds., *Krieg und Geschlecht: Sexuelle Gewalt im Krieg und Sex-Zwangsarbeit in NS-Konzentrationslagern* (Berlin: Metropol, 2008); Sonja M. Hedgepeth and Rochelle G. Saidel, eds., *Sexual Violence against Jewish Women during the Holocaust* (Waltham, MA: Brandeis University Press, 2010); Anna Hájková, ed. "Sexuality, Holocaust, Stigma," special issue, *German History* 38, no. 3 (2020); and Mühlhäuser, *Sex and the Nazi Soldier*.

145. See the chapter by Regina Mühlhäuser on "Sexuality, Sexual Violence, and the Military in the Age of the World Wars" in this handbook.

146. See Norman M. Naimark, *The Russians in Germany: A History of the Soviet Zone of Occupation, 1945–1949* (Cambridge, MA: Belknap Press, 1995); Mary Louise Roberts, *What Soldiers Do: Sex and the American GI in World War II France* (Chicago: University of Chicago Press, 2013); Miriam Gebhardt, *Crimes Unspoken: The Rape of German Women at the End of the Second World War* (Cambridge, MA: Polity Press, 2015); and Caroline Norma, *The Japanese Comfort Women and Sexual Slavery during the China and Pacific Wars* (London: Bloomsbury Academic, 2016).

147. See Hagemann, "Gender, Demobilization," and Branche, "Gender, the Wars of Decolonization" in this handbook.

SELECT BIBLIOGRAPHY

Black, Jeremy. *The Age of Total War, 1860–1945*. Westport, CT: Praeger, 2006.

Bloxham, Donald, and A. Dirk Moses, eds. *Oxford Handbook of Genocide Studies*. Oxford: Oxford University Press, 2010.

Branche, Raphaëlle, and Fabrice Vigili, eds. *Rape in Wartime*. Basingstoke: Palgrave Macmillan, 2012.

Browning, Christopher R., Susannah Heschel, Michael R. Marrus, and Milton Shain, eds. *Holocaust Scholarship: Personal Trajectories and Professional Interpretations*. Basingstoke: Palgrave Macmillan, 2015.

Burbank, Jane, and Frederick Cooper. "War and Revolution in a World of Empires: 1914 to 1945." In *Empires in World History: Power and the Politics of Difference*, edited by Jane Burbank and Frederick Cooper, 369–412. Princeton, NJ: Princeton University Press, 2010.

Bucur, Maria, and Nancy M. Wingfield, eds. *Gender and War in Twentieth-Century Eastern Europe*. Bloomington: Indiana University Press, 2006.

Chickering, Roger, Dennis Showalter, and Hans van de Ven, eds. *The Cambridge History of War*. Vol. 4. *War and the Modern World, 181–410*. Cambridge: Cambridge University Press, 2012.

Clark, Christopher. *The Sleepwalkers: How Europe Went to War in 1914*. London: Penguin Books, 2013.

Ferris, John, Richard Bosworth, Joseph Maiolo, Michael Geyer, and Adam Tooze, eds. *The Cambridge History of the Second World War*. 3 vols. Cambridge: Cambridge University Press, 2015.

Goldenberg, Myrna, and Amy H. Shapiro, eds. *Different Horrors, Same Hell: Gender and the Holocaust*. Seattle: University of Washington Press, 2013.

Grayzel, Susan R. *Women and the First World War*. Harlow: Longman, 2002.

Grayzel, Susan R., and Tammy M. Proctor, eds. *Gender and the Great War*. New York: Oxford University Press, 2017.

Hacker, Barton C., and Margaret Vining, eds. *A Companion to Women's Military History*. Leiden: Brill, 2012.

Hagemann, Karen, and Stefanie Schüler-Springorum, eds. *Home/Front: The Military, War and Gender in Twentieth-Century Germany*. Oxford: Berg, 2002.

Herzog, Dagmar, ed. *Brutality and Desire: War and Sexuality in Europe's Twentieth Century*. Basingstoke: Palgrave Macmillan, 2011.

Higonnet, Margaret Randolph, Jane Jensen, Sonya Michel, and Margaret Collins Weitz, eds. *Behind the Lines: Gender and the Two World Wars*. New Haven, CT: Yale University Press, 1987.

Neiberg, Michael S. *Fighting the Great War: A Global History*. Cambridge, MA: Harvard University Press, 2009.

Randall, Amy E., ed. *Genocide and Gender in the Twentieth Century: A Comparative Survey*. London: Bloomsbury Academic, 2015.

Sluga, Glenda. *Internationalism in the Age of Nationalism*. Philadelphia: University of Pennsylvania Press, 2013.

Weinberg, Gerhard L. *A World at Arms: A Global History of World War II*. 2nd ed. Cambridge: Cambridge University Press, 2005.

Winter, Jay, ed. *The Cambridge History of the First World War*. 3 vols. Cambridge: Cambridge University Press, 2014.

CHAPTER 16

....

GENDERED WAR MOBILIZATION, CULTURE, AND MUSIC IN THE AGE OF WORLD WARS

....

ANNEGRET FAUSER

IN 1946, the American composer Marc Blitzstein published *A Musician's War Diary*, recalling his wartime work first for the Army Eighth Air Force and then for the Office of War Information, the propaganda agency of the United States. He finished his reminiscences showcasing the powers of propaganda through the example of a French film version (1944) of the opera *Carmen* (1875) by French composer Georges Bizet, starring the actors Viviane Romance and Jean Marais. In Blitzstein's telling, the film's music reveals the insidious emasculation of French culture through the powers of German indoctrination:

> The film is neither good nor bad. [Viviane] Romance, a really top-form slut type, now plays Carmen, the real slut, as though she were a milliner. It is the music track that interests me; all out of Bizet's *Carmen*, so abjectly obedient that the arranger has accompanied certain sequences with simple oom-pahs from the "Toreador" song, four bars repeated again and again. I am impressed. At least this musician knows he's no Bizet and doesn't tamper with or imitate the original. That is up until the climax; suddenly, out of nowhere, the music breaks into the big love-death motif from Wagner's *Tristan und Isolde*—then back to Bizet again for the finish! . . . Obviously, the thing is a sickening demonstration of a sop to the Nazi Ministry of Propaganda which they expected to be their public. The Allies just got in too soon.[1]

At first glance, Blitzstein's story about inserting a few measures of music by the German composer Richard Wagner into a French film score might seem like a trifle in the context of so destructive a global conflict as World War II (1939–45). Yet from his somewhat self-righteous American perspective, Blitzstein put his finger smartly on the perils and power of propaganda in waging cultural war. The point of this cautionary tale is, in effect, its very triviality because it made visible the potential long-term effects of propaganda on a nation's image. For Blitzstein and many other propaganda warriors, culture presented the soul of a nation. In the case of *Carmen*, the film submitted a work commonly viewed as quintessentially French—whatever that might mean to whomever—to German expressive and artistic dominion. Bizet's music was reduced to band-like "oompahs" on the one hand, while on the other, it was effaced by Wagnerian pomposity that had a no less trivializing effect than turning a "real slut," if an irresistibly French one, into a *gemütlich* (homey) bourgeois "milliner." The Nazis might approve, but too late; the Allies would save the day. And as a result, the Free French would need to recover their cultural as much as political identity as they emerged from occupation.[2]

This story vividly demonstrates the centrality of art for propaganda. Consequently, the scholarship exploring the role of art in the context of war mobilization during the age of world wars is vast. Cultural historians, historians of art and music, as well as film and media scholars all engaged with the subject in recent decades. They examined the continuing role of words, spread through leaflets, brochures, the press, sermons, poetry, and novels.[3] Visual arts—especially paintings, prints, and posters—were identified as vital media in modern propaganda.[4] This includes the increasing prominence of photography, which became more and more popular given the changes in technology that allowed for the reprinting of photos in magazines and later also newspapers. While the Crimean War (1853–56) and the American Civil War (1861–65) were important stepping stones for this development, World War I (1914–18) came to serve as a watershed moment in the use of photography, because now individual soldiers, too, owned cameras and deployed them to chronicle their experiences at the front.[5] During the interwar years, radio and film joined the gramophone as rapidly developing and widely distributed mass media, the influence of which reached a peak during World War II.[6] With the acoustic turn in recent scholarship, publications focused also on the role of music (and sound) in the context of propaganda and war mobilization.[7] Furthermore, since the 1980s, research on propaganda also includes *gender* as an analytical lens.[8]

Gender, culture, and music were thoroughly entangled in war propaganda in the Age of World Wars. New media technologies, and with them music and the other audiovisual arts, served as tools for propaganda, as means of commemoration, and as escapist entertainment. Art was instrumentalized in propaganda efforts, and gender intersected with musical composition and performance in both wars. Music's semantic slipperiness made it a fascinating tool for transnational reinterpretation as notions of gender shifted in the interwar years. Music intersected with technologies such as radio and film to construct gender roles considered appropriate by governments in the 1930s and during World War II, especially in the hands of the state apparatus.

Based on these conceptual deliberations, five themes stand at the center of the following contribution: first, the general role of art for war propaganda in the service of mobilization and morale building; second, the intersection of music, as one form of war propaganda, with gender during World War I; third, the issues of commemoration, reconciliation, and musical identity politics in the interwar years; fourth, music, gender, and technological innovation in the changing media landscape of the 1930s; and finally, the interconnections of music, war, and gender in World War II.

ART AND PROPAGANDA

World War II was, in a sense, the endpoint of transnational developments that had tested and pushed the boundaries of concerted propaganda efforts in the service of twentieth-century warfare and that would quickly be adapted still further to the shifting demands of the Cold War and its aftermath. This modern form of propaganda had its roots in nineteenth-century mass culture; yet given the rise of new media technologies after 1900, culture entered the battlefield in increasingly powerful ways. Such propaganda made use of art in an intentionally structural and targeted manner, whether at the behest of governments across the political spectrum—from democratic to fascist—or by way of cultural institutions, from Hollywood studios to the Berlin Philharmonic Orchestra, or of individual artists acting as national champions.[9]

Propaganda, as David Welch points out, is a slippery term; nevertheless, it generally carries an emphasis on the deliberate management of information for the purpose of persuasion.[10] Propaganda is also predicated on simplifying the complexities of international entanglements to focus the message, often through the sharpening of dichotomies and the evocation of stereotypes. Finally, propaganda is never value neutral: good and bad are moral taxonomies with a legacy rooted in the older forms of propaganda that emerged from Counter-Reformation Rome and that cast a long shadow over the concept's secular history.[11] In wartime propaganda, such dichotomies tend to focus on a good Self and a different, usually bad, Other. In this constellation of signifiers, it is no surprise, then, that on the one hand wartime propaganda had a particular interest in using dichotomous, stereotypical notions of gender for purposes of persuasion and, on the other hand, that gender politics became a target of home-front propaganda efforts. The cultural work of wartime propaganda thus drew on existing gender constructions in attacking the enemy while at the same time using the conflict to focus on reconfiguring gender at home for the purposes both of conflict and of any ensuing peace. But when art and culture enter the mix, the Blitzstein example reveals another layer to the work of propaganda: art is used as the medium to carry the message; yet, art itself becomes a target for propaganda not least, though not only, in terms of gender. Masculinized art—especially a nation's own art—is posited as one that can contribute to a healthy and strong nation in both war and peace; feminized art, by contrast, will weaken it unless it can somehow be contained within properly gendered, and usually domestic, functions.[12]

A particularly striking example for such gendering, also from World War II, comes from the German side of propaganda warfare, in the radio broadcasts of "Mr. O.K." and "Dr. Anders." The man behind the pseudonyms, Max Otto Koischwitz, had taught in the German departments of Columbia University and Hunter College in the 1930s before returning in late 1939 to Berlin, where he became a leading propaganda warrior at the German State Radio. From spring 1940, his programs about literature, music, drama, philosophy, and politics were broadcast in English and directed to German American listeners and American students and scholars of German studies in the United States to win their support for National Socialist ideas.[13] In a program in June 1941, Koischwitz addressed art as a signifier for a nation's strength—or lack thereof—when he spoke about Martha Graham, the influential American modern dancer and choreographer, contrasting the masculinity of German culture with the effeminacy of America as symbolized by the dancer herself: "Strange as it may seem, whenever I think of America, of specifically American art, I cannot help thinking of your art, Martha Graham. Is it perhaps because the United States depends far more on women than on men? The American boy is dominated by his mother; the American husband by his wife and the American father by his daughter. If one thinks of specifically German art, one would never think of a woman."[14]

Koischwitz thus related a masculinized form of artistic production to a nation's political and social structure and the way in which both actual and idealized men and women were cast therein: should women have a progressive role, as in the United States, then both the society as such and any art it engendered, so the argument ran, would be feminized to a debilitating degree.

Such gendering could also be used internally. Already in World War I, military recruitment posters drew on gendered stereotypes on both sides of the Atlantic, as numerous examples show. For instance, the British recruitment poster by E. V. Kealy titled *Women of Britain Say—"Go!"* (Figure 16.1), from 1915, shows a group of two women, a white housewife and a younger, colored woman—perhaps a nanny from the reaches of the British Empire—with a child gazing out a window, as uniformed men march off to war in the background. It aims at both women—who must stoically endure all wartime sacrifice—and at the men told why they should fight. An American recruitment poster by Harry R. Hopps titled *Destroy This Mad Brute. Enlist. US Army* (Figure 16.2), from 1918, by contrast, turns to mythology. In an adaptation of the rape of Europa to suit the geography of the United States, the artist replaced Jove with a King Kong–type gorilla about to step on American shores, wearing a German steel helmet with the engraving "Militarism" and carrying a big club with the inscription "*Kultur*" (culture). The brutish Germanic monster reveals the underbelly of an out-of-control militaristic masculinity that turns even "culture" into a bloodstained club, whereas the damsel in distress plays on every trope of white, helpless femininity.

Numerous other recruitment posters drew on similar notions of masculine militarism versus feminized fragility even if the female body—whether Britannia, Columbia, Germania, or Marianne—then needed to assume Amazonian garb to go on the attack. The complexities were clear also in those images that recruited women to munitions factories which emphasized traditional feminine virtues, a particularly important and pervasive form of gender containment in societies leery of women's professional activities and the so-called New Woman, for all that—as cultural analyst Pearl James points out—such posters also "reflect more radical possibilities for female subjectivity" by

FIGURE 16.1 *Women of Britain Say—"Go!,"* war poster, published by the Imperial Maritime League with the aim to ensure Britain's women's support for the voluntary enlistment of their fiancés and husbands during World War I, designed by E. V. Kealy, London, 1915.

(© Imperial War Museum, London (Art. IWM PST 2763))

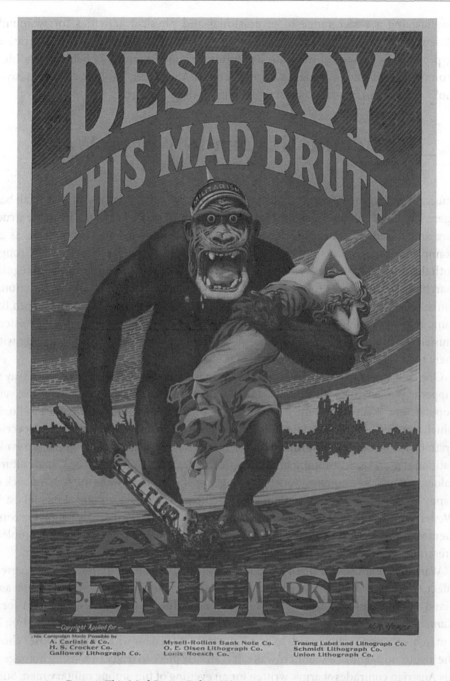

FIGURE 16.2 *Destroy This Mad Brute. Enlist. US Army*, American war poster, produced by the Committee on Public Information during World War I with the aim to mobilize public war support, designed by Harry R. Hopps (1869–1937), San Francisco, 1917.

(Library of Congress, Prints and Photographs Division, Washington DC, LC-DIG-ds-03216) emphasizing a wider range of professional and physical activities for women.[15] Masculinities, too, were stereotyped in those years: whether drawing on noble, agrarian, or proletarian images of masculinity, action-oriented manliness became the ideal promoted across the belligerent nations even if, as the poster "Women of Britain Say— 'Go!'" (Figure 16.1) reveals, it must remain under the female gaze.

MUSIC AND GENDER IN WORLD WAR I

Music, as well as the visual arts, was involved in fighting the First World War in all belligerent nations. In music, gender comes into play on a number of levels, from the structure and sound of a musical work to its function. A military march can serve as an example for the construction of gender in and through music. It relates to war through both the musical material—from its brass, wind, and percussion timbres to the regular marching meter and the foursquare, clear-cut harmonic language—and its functional connection with the public masculinity of military parades and action. Thus, both the sonic markers of the march and the genre itself are gendered masculine in Western music.[16] Such signifiers can then be deployed in other musical contexts, carrying with them their gendered connotations, whether masculine or feminine.

One could easily contrast, for example, the march-like character of "It's a Long Way to Tipperary," a favorite with British soldiers written by Jack Judge in 1912, with the very popular 1914 "Keep the Home Fires Burning" by the Welsh composer Ivor Novello, in which a slower, more ballad-like manner and stepwise melody fit well with the text's celebration of women's domestic function back home. But musical signifiers could also evoke nations at war—most prominently through their national anthems—or other cultural values, not least by a compositional play on genre: if invoking a waltz might hark back to happy and joyful memories, symphonic structures could evoke culture at its highest in Western musical thought of the time. Finally, music is also particularly suited for commemoration, given that the shared act of listening in concert transcended one problem presented by the visual arts through their reliance on individualized contemplation.[17]

Wartime composers of that period knew how to draw on these sonic tropes to great effect. Composer Arnold Schoenberg, for example, wrote a march for string quartet and piano in 1916 with the title *Die eiserne Brigade* (The Iron Brigade), intended for a *Kameradschaftsabend* (social evening) with fellow officers. Yet—as is the convention in a march—the trio section needs to bring musical contrast for which the composer chose the joyous nostalgia of a Viennese waltz. It is an easy piece to read as a rousing homage to his Austrian comrades at arms, written for an evening of fun among military men. Such military-march tropes were ubiquitous in popular music as well, on both sides of the Atlantic. One famous American example is the legendary war song from 1917, "Over There," by the Broadway entertainer and composer George M. Cohan. Its chorus imitates military fanfares in the melody with a text that promises that "the Yanks are coming" with "the drums rum-tumming ev'rywhere."[18] Both Schoenberg and Cohan wrote pieces that served the traditional wartime function where music is used to project a forceful and militaristic masculinity of camaraderie and adventure. Theirs are works in a long tradition of belligerent music drawing on both martial and popular idioms, with roots that include such sixteenth-century potboilers as *La Guerre* by the French Renaissance composer Clément Janequin celebrating the French victory at the Battle of Marignano in September 1515.[19]

Where music in the twentieth century effected a qualitative shift in the context of war, however, was in its transnational use for both propaganda and commemoration. This form of music, too, has its roots in earlier times, especially the commemorative cults of the French Revolution where such a work as the *Marche lugubre* (Mournful March)— written by the French composer François-Joseph Gossec in 1790 commemorating the citizens who had died in the so-called Nancy affair (the crushing of a military mutiny in France in the same year)—fixed a musical idiom that had its echoes across European soundscape. One reflection can be found in the famous funeral march of the 1804 Symphony no. 3 in E-flat Major (the *Eroica*) by German composer Ludwig van Beethoven.[20]

In World War I, however, such commemorative tropes were put to use in works that glorified sacrifice for the sake of the nation and ennobled nationalist ideologies in a transnational horizon. Here the gendered binaries, the juxtaposition of masculine and feminine, embodied within nineteenth-century musical rhetoric lay at the heart of both a problem and its solution. Commemoration involves honoring the fallen (a masculine task) as well as mourning them (by long cross-cultural tradition, a feminine one) on behalf of a nation that must still assert its masculinity even as it seeks to regain a postwar balance of gendered values. In 1915–17, the British composer Edward Elgar wrestled with the apparent contradictions (though they are not) in his setting of three poems by the English poet Laurence Binyon as a symphonic cantata for soprano (or tenor), chorus, and orchestra under the title *The Spirit of England*. Dedicated "to the memory of our glorious men," the work culminated with a setting of Binyon's perhaps most famous poem, "For the Fallen."[21] The work is about England, her heroism, and her sacrifice, as well as the construction of community in a commemorative piece of art. The composition conjured community through musical means: The combination of a single solo voice with chorus and orchestra that Elgar deployed in *The Spirit of England* is well established as a symbolic representation of the individualized voice of a mourning community, in turn stepping out of, and blending in with, the communal musical expression.

Elgar's work—like numerous others on both sides of the conflict—drew in its musical texture, genre, and form on a gendered hierarchy of musical signifiers that also carried national overtones. Elgar brings together in "For the Fallen" a vocal fugue reminiscent of George Frideric Handel (though born in Germany, a resolutely "British" composer) with a soaring melody, carried by the soprano soloist, all over a symphonic orchestral texture. Thus, his music combines the "masculine" (erudite fugue; complex symphony) and the "feminine" (the soprano melody) to merge commemoration and lament, although the latter must inevitably give way to a stronger (read, patriarchal) national chorus.[22] That chorus also serves another function, however: the war was not yet won when Elgar's work was first performed in Birmingham in October 1917. But the fact that many of these masculine gestures are drawn from a European musical tradition that belonged firmly to the "enemy" (Germany) did not—nay, could not—worry Elgar given this tradition's presumed universality within the pantheon of "great" music. The great British war poets could more easily invoke an elegiac pastoralism, but music, precisely because of its perceived feminization, needed to be of sterner stuff.

COMMEMORATION, RECONCILIATION, AND MUSICAL IDENTITY POLITICS IN THE INTERWAR YEARS

Elgar's *The Spirit of England*, long broadcast annually by the BBC for Armistice Day, also served the purpose of commemoration after the war ended—as did numerous other works across the globe.[23] Not all these pieces emerged from particular wartime or immediate postwar circumstances, nor were they necessarily commemorative in their original intent. Elgar's "Nimrod" from his *Variations on an Original Theme for Orchestra (Enigma)* from 1899 is an intriguing case in point—with its tempo slowed down significantly as a result—as, for a later period, is American composer Samuel Barber's *Adagio for Strings* (1938). Rather, appropriate works were chosen from the across the canon of Western music, including the "universal" Beethoven, who could easily be adopted for mourning (the funeral march from the *Eroica*) or for victory (his Symphony no. 9 in D Minor at the official German celebration of the fall of the Berlin Wall, marking the end of the Cold War). One more recent musical work that was adapted for commemoration after World War I was *Pour les funérailles d'un soldat* (1913), written for mixed choir, baritone solo, and orchestra by Lili Boulanger, on a poem by Alfred de Musset. Its 1919 edition presents on the cover a dead soldier, vulnerable, naked save for his sword, with arms spread as if crucified, on a background of the French tricolored flag (Figure 16.3).[24]

Commemoration in the face of the "accumulated presence of death" of World War I challenged traditional artistic responses in terms of sculpture and other monumental arts.[25] Rather than heroic soldier monuments, postwar commemorative art often drew on signifiers of Christian sacrifice, with mothers and other women cast as mourning figures. The cover art on Boulanger's piece corresponded to a musical work that imagined the interstitial moment between the digging of the grave, with the community of mourners waiting, and the arrival of the priest for the funeral service of a soldier. Over and over, the orchestra evokes the famous sequence, "Dies irae, dies illa," from the Requiem Mass, a musical signifier that would have been heard all too often in the services for the dead in France and other Catholic countries, but that had also found its place in the concert halls of Europe and America in such famous works as French composer Camille Saint-Saëns's *Danse macabre* (1874) or Austrian composer Gustav Mahler's Symphony no. 2 (1895). Yet at the same time, Boulanger's score drew on

FIGURE 16.3 Front page of *Pour les funérailles d'un soldat* (For the Funeral of a Soldier), a 1912 composition by Lili Boulanger (1893–1918), edition published by Editions Ricordi, Paris, 1919.

(Fondation Internationale Nadia et Lili Boulanger, Paris)

hypermasculine sonic signifiers with drums and march rhythms when referring to war as the source of heroic death.[26]

Whether through newly composed works or the reconfiguration of older ones, musical commemoration of the war became an important aspect of interwar public ritual to which, in particular, the new technology of the radio contributed, with the same work broadcast on the same date each year, be it Elgar's *Spirit of England* on Armistice Day (November 11) or the martial *Marseillaise* on La fête nationale (July 14). But commemoration during the interwar years also turned to other important historical moments as markers of political and cultural identity. In 1927, music and politics came together in high public, and publicized, fashion given the centenary of Beethoven's death and the tenth anniversary of the Russian October Revolution. In the Soviet Union, the Narkompros (Commissariat for Enlightenment) embraced Beethoven as a revolutionary educator and "universal symbol of revolutionary heroism and freedom."[27] A rousing performance by *Persimfans*—a conductorless orchestra created as an alternative to the authoritarian structure of the traditional symphony orchestra—of Beethoven's Ninth Symphony in March was celebrated as the crowning and communal evocation of Beethoven, the revolutionary hero. The adaptation of Beethoven in a manner tailored for the specific situation in the Soviet Union was part and parcel of what Katerina Clark has called "the great appropriation."[28] How central especially the Ninth Symphony was to configuring a masculine, empowered music for the new Soviet state can be seen in Russian composer Dmitri Shostakovich's Symphony no. 2 (*To October*) (1927), which modeled the trajectory of the Ninth Symphony in condensed form. It culminated in a revolutionary chorus setting a text by Russian poet Alexander Bezymensky in an ideal finale that merged the glorification of Lenin and the October Revolution of 1917 with the Beethovenian heroic style in a virile display of cultural power. Only later, with Shostakovich's Symphony no. 5 (1937), would the implications of that style be rendered more complex, both on its home turf and in terms of its reception in the West—reflecting the changed political culture in the Stalinist Soviet Union.[29]

In the immediate postwar period, culture was mobilized not only for commemoration, however, but also for reconciliation through artistic enterprises that tried to translate into the cultural realm such political initiatives as the League of Nations. The PEN club, an international association of "Poets, Essayists and Novelists," was established in 1921 in London; in music, the International Society for Contemporary Music became a major force from its establishment in Salzburg in 1923. The society was conceived as a neutral and deliberately apolitical space of postwar encounters, with annual festivals of new music from across the Western world.[30]

These and other attempts to fashion an internationalist artistic field offered a creative opening where gender constructions became much more fluid. The wartime feminine/masculine binary started to be weakened in fashion, film, and stage, whether in the major European capitals (for example, Paris and Berlin emerged as feminized spaces for cultural production) or in the United States. Instead, richer and more varied representations of gender found their way into the arts, one that celebrated androgyny and imagined gender bending, as in the streamlined bodies of flappers or the homogenizing uniforms of the Soviet Blue Blouse theater collective (Sinyaya Bluza). The Blue Blouses served as the model for the international agitprop of the later 1920s and 1930s with its living newspapers, acrobatic acts, and political sketches. Their emphasis on modernity, urbanity, and athleticism in which female and male bodies were often undistinguished offered a countermodel to the more traditional gender roles that, only a few years later and with war once more on the horizon, would be reimposed both on the political left, by the tenets of socialist realism, and, of course, on the fascist right.[31]

GENDER, MUSIC, AND TECHNOLOGY

A fascinating early example that mediates these issues into sleek propaganda through the technology of sound film is Leni Riefenstahl's *Triumph of the Will* (1935), one of the best-known indoctrination products of the Third Reich, which had garnered very strong responses from Allied filmmakers who—while rejecting its propagandistic overtones—admired its filmic quality. The soundtrack was provided by Herbert Windt, a student of the Austrian composer Franz Schreker. His play on march tropes—whether belligerent or funerary—together with motifs from Wagner's *Meistersinger von Nürnberg* (1868) and popular Nazi songs, were blended into a score that gave a grounded quality to the images and message of the film. The masculinity of the Nazi leadership—especially Hitler—is constructed as both traditional and modern, especially in the opening sequence of the film when the airplane in which Hitler arrives is set against old Nuremberg. How influential Riefenstahl's vision of modern masculinity became can be seen a decade later in the documentary *Memphis Belle* (1944) for the US War Department by German-born American film director William Wyler, where similar tropes are woven together with a rather different kind of music, the modernist score by Gail Kubik. What these propaganda films share is the visual configuration of masculinity as domination, whether through technology or rhetoric. The music, however, constructs masculinity differently: a traditional idiom in Riefenstahl's film and a modernist one in the American one.[32]

Both film and radio were seen as effective means of propaganda by the governments of fascist Italy and Nazi Germany. Indeed, in Italy, the new technology was masculinized by what was considered its intrinsic power of persuasion, as Enrico Marchesi, the new president of Mussolini's Unione radiofonica italiana, emphasized in a 1926 celebratory address: "With this powerful and attractive instrument of cultural propaganda inside Italy and also one to promulgate Italianità abroad, we want to double all our strength to be useful for our country."[33] And so it did. Across all countries, radio programs carefully targeted audiences at home and abroad to convey the cultural superiority of the nation state and its political apparatus. Because of the acousmatic quality of the radio, the performance of gender—so strongly configured in Western culture as a visual one—was dependent on particularly clear sonic signifiers, whether in music or in speech. Indeed, women played an important role in the soundscape of radio, for instance, in the so-called women's radio of the Weimar Republic and Third Reich that emphasized domestic rather than professional achievement for its audiences.[34] Other countries, too, had women contribute to radio in a range of activities, from singer and actress to host and writer, though the transgression of normative gender roles was clearly frowned on. Indeed, when in 1934 the poet Silvia Guerrico, a popular radio host in Buenos Aires, broadcast an "amorous sermon" to a male Hollywood icon, critics called for "her banishment from the airwaves."[35] The performance of appropriate heteronormative gender roles both by women and by men translated seamlessly into state-sponsored radio propaganda by World War II.

In the meantime, popular songs, opera, symphonic music, jazz, church hymns, and military marches all found their way on the air, as did educational programs and celebrations of cultural productions at home and abroad. With the help of magazines and newspapers dedicated to recordings, radio stations began to reconfigure existing musical taxonomies to fit the new, acousmatic media. Divorced from its visual source, sound posed new epistemological and political challenges in terms of social control. Music's most dangerous quality was easily located in the grain of the sexualized voice and accompanying music: thus, in republican China, popular, supposedly "sexually obscene" songs were cast in a 1936 article as "prostitution in disguise, whose only talent is for poisoning society."[36] The gendered implication of this criticism is made even more explicit in the binary established between "soft music," the "fragrant and fleshy appeals" of which would render Chinese culture effeminate, and the leftist revolutionary hymns that embodied the very "hardness of real swords and real guns!"[37] Precisely the same arguments occurred in fascist Italy, where martial hymns served a better purpose than what the pro-Mussolini writer Adriano Lualdi called the "decadent travesty" and "spiritual nostalgias" of "gez" (the Italianized spelling of jazz), which were cast as clearly detrimental to the artistic and physical health of the nation.[38]

Jazz and other popular styles became contested ground, not just because of gender but also in terms of race. The modernist opera, *Jonny spielt auf* (Jonny plays up) (1926), by Ernst Krenek, an Austrian composer of Czech origin, plays with gender in the construction of race in fascinating ways because, at first glance, the work seems to masculinize jazz and the African American character of Jonny, in contrast to the somewhat feminized European composer, Max, who contemplates suicide for lack of inspiration. Yet as Max reconquers new music (and gets the girl), both jazz and the black jazz musician become relegated to the increasingly feminized role of muse and helpmate in the creation of a masculine modernist music.

These tropes were also part of the American movie *The Jazz Singer* (1927), directed by Alan Crosland, a film about a Jewish cantor's son enamored with jazz, credited as the first sound film released in Hollywood. The film's narrative closely associates the vaudeville performance of Al Jolson in blackface with his training in, and practice of, Eastern European Jewish cantillation. The final scene cuts directly from Jolson's "Kol Nidre" in the synagogue to his crooning, in blackface, of "Mammy" in the Winter Garden Theater. This juxtaposition challenges, in effect, the singer's masculinity as an unmarked white one by inflecting it through the ethnic identity politics of 1920s America. It stands in contrast to the Anglo-Saxon heroine, Mary Dale, who is shown as a plucky, all-American girl leading the way to a more normative performance of race and gender.[39] Here and elsewhere, femininity and masculinity are, indeed, inflected by the racialized context of their performance. This issue becomes even more acute when oppressed and minority population groups turn to performance of gender as a means of claiming cultural capital in as deeply racist a society as the interwar United States. It is perhaps not unexpected that the influential thinkers of the Harlem Renaissance, from W. E. B. Du Bois to Langston Hughes, promoted and performed genteel and traditional gender roles, especially during a period when in dominant white societies a transnationally oriented set of artists and thinkers configured the performance of gender roles more fluidly, whether in pseudoproletarian agitprop theater or in Berlin cabarets.[40]

That music might strengthen or undermine masculinity and the health of the state was a familiar trope in Western music, founded on the writings of ancient philosophers (Plato most prominently). For such a trope to work on a transnational scale, however, music needed to be conceived as a universal human expression, another Western concept, the global impact of which was aided by the use of new media in the service of imperialism and colonialism, on the one hand, and educational initiatives and literature on the other. Writers considered music "the greatest spiritual force known to mankind" and, therefore, much was at stake when nations drew on music to serve identity politics.[41] In the Soviet Union in 1931, for instance, composer Viktor Belïy eagerly identified musical markers that contravened Stalin's infamous slogan that Soviet music needed to be "national in form, proletarian in content." He came up with "the interval of the augmented second"—beloved in luscious exoticisms of late nineteenth-century music—as the representation of "an effeminate Orient, ridden with rickets."[42] Yet the trick lay not only in weeding out that which was effeminate, but also in what was barbaric and uncultured. Belïy's "Orient" is "ridden with rickets" because of its gendered and racial alterity—the two become merged—and therefore wholly uncivilized. The question was how to resist the barbarians at the door.

Two films, one produced in Mussolini's Italy and the other in Stalin's Soviet Union, show the spectrum of visual and sonic Othering while staying surprisingly homogeneous insofar as the representation of a disciplined masculinized Self is concerned. In *Scipione l'Africano* (Scipio Africanus: The Defeat of Hannibal) (1937) by Italian film director Carmine Gallone, the fascist "New Man," in the guise of a muscular Scipio, triumphs over Hannibal in the Battle of Zama.[43] Here, winning Africa for Rome in the Second Punic War was but a thinly disguised parallel for Mussolini's colonialist expansion, underlined by the fact that Mussolini made soldiers available to serve as extras in the climactic battle scene.

Another historic battle—this time in the thirteenth century—marks the culmination of Sergei Eisenstein's film *Alexander Nevsky* (1938), with music by composer Sergei Prokofiev. The Soviet film director Eisenstein negotiates the gender tropes in more nuanced ways. The German invaders—barbarians all—are oddly feminized in swirling capes and with a monk whose reedy organ playing veers on the androgynous. The Russians, however, are shown as overcoming any obstacle by soldiering up—old men, young women, and even children—for the sake of Mother Russia. But even at her most fierce in the Battle on the Ice, the maid Vasilia never loses feminine decorum, and in the end, she is restored into traditional gender roles by being betrothed to Buslai, a war hero from Novgorod. If the fascist battle in *Scipione l'Africano* was one of belligerent virility overcoming a wild mêlée of elephants and unregulated fighters from Africa, the Soviet version was one that threw an army of high-minded civilians under the leadership of a great military genius against a barbaric horde whose very unheroic reliance on material superiority (their suits of armor) could be turned against them in a gruesome—but incongruously comical—death of drowning. Indeed, Prokofiev's cartoonish scoring of the shot counts among the strokes of compositional genius within the genre.[44]

Music, War, and Gender in World War II

The Second World War was the crucible in which these various constellations of gender, war, culture, and music that had developed during and since World War I solidified for the purpose of cultural warfare by Allied and Axis powers alike. Propagandists had to forge a very careful path: a culture too feminized was perceived as weak; a culture too androgynous was seen as sterile; a culture too masculine, however, was in danger of appearing as brutish as the monster in the 1917 American propaganda poster. Yet for propaganda to work, it needed to rely on stereotypes and legible signifiers which—in terms of gender—meant a deployment of traditional tropes. What is fascinating about the uses of gender in propaganda is not whether gender was stereotyped—it was—but how each of the belligerent nations drew on contrasting notions of masculine and feminine in presenting their culture not only to serve the conflict itself but also in preparation of postwar social orders deemed worth fighting for.

As in World War I, music fulfilled a number of functions, from the belligerent call to arms to commemoration. Music to rally the population, however, was not so easy to come by, as American authorities, for instance, started to realize when they searched for an appropriate, unifying war song for the troops. The 1942 number by American songwriter Frank Loesser, "Praise the Lord and Pass the Ammunition," with its church-hymn allusions, was not martial enough to serve this function; other compositions, such as Oscar Hammerstein II and Kurt Weill's catchy "Hello There, Buddy on the Night Shift," were too much in the vein of Broadway entertainment. In the end, and perhaps not surprisingly, two songs from World War I served as the soundtrack of the Second World War: Cohan's "Over There" returned as music for marching into war—even if, following Pearl Harbor, that war was no longer quite "over there"—and Irving Berlin's "God Bless America" (1918) arrived on the scene in 1938 in the muscular rendition by American singer Kate Smith, which emphasized the song's martial quality. It served as a kind of unofficial national anthem since that belated first performance on CBS radio twenty years after Berlin had composed it.[45] With their four-square melodies over march rhythms and references to military fanfares in the accompaniment, both Cohan's and Berlin's songs fulfilled their martial mandate, but did so in no less significantly tempered forms. The verse of "Over There" tells sweethearts "not to pine" and mothers to be "proud," while "God Bless America" invokes the Manifest Destiny of a blessed nation "from the mountains, to the prairies, to the oceans, white with foam."

Sweethearts and mothers were fully represented by the women's voices that dominated the Allied airwaves, whether as the energetic embodiment of the nation such as Kate Smith's, the more wife-like by British singer Vera Lynn reminding soldiers that she would "be seeing you," or the girl-next-door Andrews Sisters (often in military uniform, no less) telling their boyfriends not to sit under the apple tree "with anyone else but me."[46] This is not to say that male entertainers stopped performing (or disappeared into the armed forces), but their sonic presence was more problematic, given that masculinity needed to be more closely controlled, either by way of slapstick humor, like the British-born American comedian and singer Bob Hope, or through heroic calls to action. This was a more difficult act to perform, especially for a singer, though it was easier for such famous American bandleaders as Artie Shaw or Glenn Miller, who took their jazz ensembles and entered military service.

Film, gramophone, and radio created a soundscape that was turned inward—with music aimed to bolster civic and military morale—as well as outward to serve as propaganda to win the hearts and minds of both enemies and allies alike. Whether "Tokyo Rose," the generic name given by Allied troops in the South Pacific to what they believed were multiple English-speaking female broadcasters of Japanese propaganda addressing US soldiers, or the "American Margaret," which played a similar role in the American propaganda addressing German soldiers, music contributed to the endeavor to seduce enemy armies away from duty. The idea was to soften soldiers' resolve by evoking visceral emotional responses to music, bypassing rational thought—or, putting it differently, to emasculate enemy warriors by choosing the "soft" music that ideologues from China to Germany had started to fear when media allowed for its widespread use.

Indeed, in terms of artistic propaganda, World War II provided a global laboratory with immediate feedback loops for such institutions as the American Office of Strategic Services, the British Ministry of Information, and the German Reich Ministry of Public Enlightenment and Propaganda. Besides sapping morale through the play on nostalgia, propaganda efforts also worked on creating division within an enemy nation. One of the more fascinating such initiatives was Japan's "Negro Propaganda Operations," whose shortwave emissions emphasized the brutality of white America against African Americans—using language similar to US depictions of Nazi Germans—and contrasted American racism with a portrayal of Japan as a civilized, disciplined, and enabling environment created by and for its nonwhite citizens. The head of this unit, Yasuichi Hikida, used African American prisoners of war with musical and acting talent to populate the broadcasts. Though the actual effects on US internal politics were, in the end, negligible, they did engender some echo in the African American community and reframed some of the American discussion about race, masculinity, and dignity.[47]

But propaganda used music in numerous other ways, too, filling the airwaves with carefully screened entertainment and nationalist cultural celebration. There are many reasons why music in and from World War II is among the best-known repertoire of the twentieth century, but this technologically mediated form of distribution to the point of saturation is one of them. When the Soviet Union had on its hands Dmitri Shostakovich's Symphony no. 7 (*Leningrad*), it used the work in a model fashion for propaganda, broad-casting performances and sending the work abroad in a widely publicized cloak-and-dagger operation that transported the microfilmed score out on a bomber, via Tehran. Its reception in Allied nations, especially the United States, became a triumph of Soviet artistic greatness, the work's composer celebrated as much as a war hero as the symphony was cast as a piece of musical heroism.[48] Among American works, Aaron Copland's *Fanfare for the Common Man* (1942), *Lincoln Portrait* (1942), *Rodeo* (1942), and *Appalachian Spring* (1944) count among the most enduring works of the repertoire, and the British William Walton's *Spitfire Prelude and Fugue* (1942) was one of his greatest successes. In the case of Nazi Germany, Carl Orff's *Carmina Burana* (1937) quickly moved from a concert work with some questionably modernist tendencies—so it was viewed at the time of its premiere—to a well-received staged wartime entertainment in 1941. Its famous monumental chorus "O Fortuna" reclaimed the masculine might of German music without the slightest element of irony, and—like Wagner's *Ride of the Valkyries*—it has since become a noisy concert favorite whose problematic ancestry is mostly silenced.

CONCLUSION

No other war was so completely defined by its sound world, musical and otherwise. World War II was the first in which the entire spectrum of the audiovisual was instru-mentalized for both internal and external communication as guns, airplanes, and sirens rained over nations the world over. Furthermore, given the iconic nature of numerous artifacts, whether such successful American movies as *Casablanca* (1942) and *White Christmas* (1945) or gramophone recordings by German American actress and singer Marlene Dietrich, these acoustic remnants have shaped modern perception of this period so that the voices of the historic actors and their music are inextricably bound up in the construction of this past.[49]

With the acoustic turn of historical research, these sound worlds have been moved to the forefront of scholarship to be explored for their cultural meanings.[50] What makes music so attractive in this context is both its multivalent signification—one that could be appropriated by historical players for their unique context—and its construction as an emotionally effective human expression, one often configured as universal and there-fore transnationally operative.[51] Given that music intersects with the construction of gender in numerous ways, both in the performance of gender in the act of music making and in the compositions themselves, music offers an intriguing window on the work of gender in war (and peace). That music does not come to reverberation without a specific context of creation and reception is an epistemological truism. This interplay between the sound object and its historical contexts, however, offers an access point that is unique in historiography because of music's performative presence, not only in historical discourse but also in contemporary performance.[52]

NOTES

1. Marc Blitzstein, "A Musician's War Diary," *New Masses*, August 13, 1946, 3–6, and August 20, 1946, 6–9.
2. On music in occupied France, see Myriam Chimènes and Yannick Simon, eds., *La Musique à Paris sous l'Occupation* (Paris: Cité de la Musique/Fayard, 2013).
3. See the chapter by Robert A. Nye on "War Mobilization, Gender, and Military Culture in Nineteenth-Century Western Societies" in this handbook; and, more generally, Philip M. Taylor, *Munitions of the Mind: A History of Propaganda from the Ancient World to the Present Day*, 3rd ed. (Manchester: Manchester University Press, 2003).
4. For example, Aviel Roshwald and Richard Stites, eds., *European Culture in the Great War: The Arts, Entertainment, and Propaganda, 1914–1918* (Cambridge: Cambridge University Press, 1999); Pearl James, ed., *Picture This: World War I Posters and Visual Culture* (Lincoln: University of Nebraska Press, 2009); and Christopher Murray, *Champions of the Oppressed? Superhero Comics, Popular Culture, and Propaganda in America during World War II* (Cresskill, NJ: Hampton Press, 2011).
5. For example, Anton Holzer and Ullrich Keller, eds., *Der Weltkrieg der Bilder: Fotoreportage und Kriegspropaganda in der illustrierten Presse 1914–1918* (Marburg: Jonas, 2013).
6. See, in general, on different media, Mark Connelly and David Welch, eds., *War and the Media: Reportage and Propaganda, 1900–2003* (London: I. B. Tauris, 2005); on the radio, Gerd Horten, *Radio Goes to War: The Cultural Politics of Propaganda during World War II* (Berkeley: University of California Press, 2003); on film, Leslie Midkiff DeBauche, *Reel Patriotism: The Movies and World War I* (Madison: University of Wisconsin Press, 1997); Clayton R. Koppes and Gregory D. Black, *Hollywood Goes to War: How Politics, Profits, and Propaganda Shaped World War II Movies* (Berkeley: University of California Press, 1987); James Chapman, *The British at War: Cinema, State, and Propaganda, 1939–1945* (London: I. B. Tauris, 1998); Thomas Doherty, *Projections of War: Hollywood, American Culture, and World War II* (New York: Columbia University Press, 1993); Jo Fox, *Film Propaganda in Britain and Nazi Germany: World War II Cinema* (Oxford: Berg, 2007); Michael Hammond and Michael Williams, eds., *British Silent Cinema and the Great War* (Basingstoke: Palgrave Macmillan, 2011); and John Morris, *Culture and Propaganda in World War II: Music, Film, and the Battle for National Identity* (London: I. B. Taurus, 2014).
7. Christina L. Baade, *Victory through Harmony: The BBC and Popular Music in World War II* (New York: Oxford University Press: 2012); Sarah Zalfen and Sven Oliver Müller, eds., *Besatzungsmacht Musik: Zur Musik- und Emotionsgeschichte im Zeitalter der Weltkriege (1914–1949)* (Bielefeld: Transcript Verlag, 2012); and Annegret Fauser, *Sounds of War: Music in the United States during World War II* (Oxford: Oxford University Press, 2013).
8. Leila J. Rupp, *Mobilizing Women for War: German and American Propaganda, 1939–1945* (Princeton, NJ: Princeton University Press, 1978); Maureen Honey, *Creating Rosie the Riveter: Class, Gender, and Propaganda during World War II* (Amherst: University of

Massachusetts Press, 1984); Celia Malone Kingsbury, *For Home and Country: World War I Propaganda on the Home Front* (Lincoln: University of Nebraska Press, 2010); Robert L. Nelson, *German Soldier Newspapers of the First World War* (Cambridge: Cambridge University Press, 2011); Christina Baade, "Between the Lines: 'Lili Marlene,' Sexuality, and the Desert War," in *Music, Politics, and Violence*, ed. Susan Fast and Kip Pegley (Middletown, CT: Wesleyan University Press, 2012), 83–103; and Rudolf Jaworski, *Mütter—Liebchen— Heroinen: Propagandapostkarten aus dem Ersten Weltkrieg* (Cologne: Böhlau, 2015).

9. Massimiliano Sala, ed., *Music and Propaganda in the Short Twentieth Century* (Turnhout: Brepols, 2014); and Philippe Poirrier, ed., *La Grande Guerre: une histoire culturelle* (Dijon: Editions universitaires de Dijon, 2015).

10. David Welch, *Propaganda: Power and Persuasion: From World War I to Wikileaks* (London: I. B. Tauris, 2014), 2.

11. Alexander J. Fisher, *Music, Piety, and Propaganda: The Soundscapes of Counter-Reformation Bavaria* (New York: Oxford University Press, 2014); and Jonathan Auerbach and Russ Castronovo, "Introduction: Thirteen Propositions about Propaganda," in *The Oxford Handbook of Propaganda Studies*, ed. Jonathan Auerbach and Russ Castronovo (New York: Oxford University Press, 2013), 1–16.

12. See Annegret Fauser, "Gendering the Nations: The Ideologies of French Discourse on Music (1870–1914)," in *Musical Constructions of Nationalism: Essays on the History and Ideology of European Musical Culture, 1800–1945*, ed. Michael Murphy and Harry White (Cork: Cork University Press, 2001), 72–103.

13. On Koischwitz, see John Carver Edwards, *Berlin Calling: American Broadcasters in the Service of the Third Reich* (New York: Praeger, 1991), 57–98; and Horst J. P. Bergmeier and Rainer E. Lotz, *Hitler's Airwaves: The Inside Story of Nazi Radio Broadcasting and Propaganda Swing* (New Haven, CT: Yale University Press, 1997), 55–59.

14. NBC Shortwave Monitoring Service, "Transcript of Talk Addressed to Martha Graham by the German Radio. Speaker Is Dr. Otto Koishwitz," June 15, 1941, box 318, Martha Graham Collection, Library of Congress, Division of Performing Arts, partially cited in Mark Franko, *Martha Graham in Love and War: The Life in the Work* (New York: Oxford University Press, 2012), 67.

15. See Pearl James, "Images of Femininity in American World War I Posters," in James, *Picture This*, ed. James, 273–311, 274; and Meg Albrink, "Humanitarians and He-Men: Recruitment Posters and the Masculine Ideal," in ibid., 312–39. For a discussion of brutish masculinity assigned to the German military, see Nicoletta F. Gullace, "Barbaric Anti-Modernism: Representations of the 'Hun' in Britain, North America, Australia, and Beyond," in ibid., 61–78.

16. See Susan McClary, *Feminine Endings: Music, Gender, and Sexuality* (Minneapolis: University of Minnesota Press, 1991); and Marcia J. Citron, *Gender and the Musical Canon* (Cambridge: Cambridge University Press, 1993).

17. For the nineteenth century, see, for example, Alexander Rehding, *Music and Monumentality: Commemoration and Wonderment in Nineteenth-Century Germany* (Oxford: Oxford University Press, 2009); on the appropriation of Beethoven for various purposes of commemoration, see Esteban Buch, *Beethoven's Ninth: A Political History* (Chicago: University of Chicago Press, 2003).

18. For an easily accessible reproduction of the score, see the Petrucci Music Library, accessed November 1, 2015, http://imslp.org/wiki/Over_There_%28Cohan,_George_Michael%29.

19. See Kate van Orden, *Music, Discipline, and Arms in Early Modern France* (Chicago: University of Chicago Press, 2005), 20–29.

20. See Raymond Monelle, *The Musical Topic: Hunt, Military and Pastoral* (Bloomington: Indiana University Press, 2006), 128–29; and Alexander Rehding, *Music and Monumentality*. See also Hermann Danuser, *Weltanschauungsmusik* (Schliengen: Edition Argus, 2009), 254–323.

21. Edward Elgar, *The Spirit of England: Three Poems by Laurence Binyon, Set to Music for Tenor or Soprano, Chorus, and Orchestra* (London: Novello, 1917). The complete dedication reads, "My portion of this work, I dedicate to the memory of our glorious men, with a special thought for the WORCESTERS."

22. See Glenn Watkins, *Proof through the Night: Music and the Great War* (Berkeley: University of California Press, 2003); Florence Doé de Maindreville and Stéphan Etcharry, eds., *La Grande Guerre en musique: vie et création musicales en France pendant la Première Guerre mondiale* (Brussels: PIE Peter Lang, 2014); and John Roger Paas, ed., *America Sings of War: American Sheet Music from World War I* (Wiesbaden: Harrassowitz Verlag, 2014).

23. See Rachel Cowgill, "Canonizing Remembrance: Music for Armistice Day at the BBC, 1922–7," *First World War Studies* 2, no. 1 (2011): 75–107.

24. For a discussion of *Pour les funérailles d'un soldat* in the framework of "patriotic symbolism," see Rachel Moore, *Performing Propaganda: Musical Life and Culture in Paris during the First World War* (Woodbridge: Boydell, 2018), 104.

25. Stefan Goebel, *The Great War and Medieval Memory: War, Remembrance and Medievalism in Britain and Germany, 1914–1940* (Cambridge: Cambridge University Press, 2007), 3; and Fauser, *Sounds of War*, 227–34.

26. Lili Boulanger, *Pour les funérailles d'un soldat* (Paris: Editions Ricordi, 1919).

27. Amy Nelson, *Music for the Revolution: Musicians and Power in Early Soviet Russia* (University Park: Pennsylvania State University Press, 2004), 189.

28. Katerina Clark, *Moscow, the Fourth Rome: Stalinism, Cosmopolitanism, and the Evolution of Soviet Culture, 1931–1941* (Cambridge, MA: Harvard University Press, 2011), 8; and Pauline Fairclough, *Classics for the Masses: Shaping Soviet Musical Identity under Lenin and Stalin* (New Haven, CT: Yale University Press, 2016).

29. Joseph Eugene Darby, "Shostakovich's Second, Third, and Fourth Symphonies: Problems of Context, Analysis, and Interpretation" (PhD diss., City University of New York, 1999).

30. On the International Society for Contemporary Music, see Anton Haefeli, *Die Internationale Gesellschaft für Neue Musik (IGNM): Ihre Geschichte von 1922 bis zur Gegenwart* (Zurich: Atlantis Musikbuch Verlag, 1982). See also Annegret Fauser, "The Scholar behind the Medal: Edward J. Dent (1876–1957) and the Politics of Music History," *Journal of the Royal Musical Association* 139, no. 2 (2014): 235–60.

31. See František Deák, "'Blue Blouse' (1923–1928)," *The Drama Review: TDR* 17, no. 1 (1973): 35–46.

32. Alfred W. Cochran, "The Documentary Film Scores of Gail Kubik," in *Film Music: Critical Approaches*, ed. Kevin J. Donnelly (New York: Continuum, 2001), 117–28; and Stefan Strötgen, "'I Compose the Party Rally...': The Role of Music in Leni Riefenstahl's *Triumph of the Will*," *Music and Politics* 2, no. 1 (2008): 1–13.

33. Cited in Mauro Fosco Bertola, *Die List der Vergangenheit: Musikwissenschaft, Rundfunk und Deutschlandbezug in Italien, 1890–1945* (Vienna: Böhlau Verlag, 2014), 249.

34. Kate Lacey, *Feminine Frequencies: Gender, German Radio, and the Public Sphere* (Ann Arbor: University of Michigan Press, 1996).

35. Christine Ehrick, *Radio and the Gendered Soundscape: Women and Broadcasting in Argentina and Uruguay, 1930–1950* (New York: Cambridge University Press, 2015), 1.

36. He Lutin (1936), cited in Andrew F. Jones, *Yellow Music: Media Culture and Colonial Modernity in the Chinese Jazz Age* (Durham, NC: Duke University Press, 2001), 116.

37. Nie Er, "A Brief Essay on Chinese Musical Drama" (1937), cited in ibid., 116–17.

38. Adriano Lualdi (1927), cited in Roberto Illiano and Massimiliano Sala, "Italian Music and Racial Discourses during the Fascist Period," in *Western Music and Race*, ed. Julie Brown (Cambridge: Cambridge University Press, 2007), 182–200, 198.

39. Andrea Most, *Making Americans: Jews and the Broadway Musical* (Cambridge, MA: Harvard University Press, 2004).

40. See, for example, Jeffrey O. G. Ogbar, ed., *The Harlem Renaissance Revisited: Politics, Arts, and Letters* (Baltimore: John Hopkins University Press, 2010); and Anna Pochmara, *The Making of the New Negro: Black Authorship, Masculinity, and Sexuality in the Harlem Renaissance* (Amsterdam: Amsterdam University Press, 2011).

41. Edward J. Dent, "The Universal Aspect of Musical History," in *Studien zur Musikgeschichte: Festschrift für Guido Adler zum 75. Geburtstag* (Vienna: Universal Edition, 1930), 11.

42. Viktor Belïy (1931), cited in Marina Frolova-Walker, *Russian Music and Nationalism from Glinka to Stalin* (New Haven, CT: Yale University Press, 2007), 310–11.

43. John Champagne, *Aesthetic Modernism and Masculinity in Fascist Italy* (London: Routledge, 2013).

44. On Prokofiev's score for *Alexander Nevsky*, see Kevin M. Bartig, *Composing for the Red Screen: Prokofiev and Soviet Film* (New York: Oxford University Press, 2013), 74–100.

45. See Sheryl Kaskovitz, *God Bless America: The Surprising History of an Iconic Song* (New York: Oxford University Press, 2013).

46. "I'll Be Seeing You" (1938 with lyrics by Irving Kahal and music by Sammy Fain) was one of Vera Lynn's signature numbers during World War II; the Andrews Sisters regularly performed and recorded the 1939 song, "Don't Sit under the Apple Tree (With Anyone Else but Me)," with lyrics by Lew Brown and Charles Tobias and music by Sam H. Stept.

47. Sato Masaharu and Barak Kushner, "'Negro Propaganda Operations': Japan's Short-Wave Radio Broadcasts for World War II Black Americans," *Historical Journal of Film, Radio and Television* 19, no. 1 (1999): 5–26.

48. Christopher Gibbs, "'The Phenomenon of the Seventh': A Documentary Essay on Shostakovich's 'War' Symphony," in *Shostakovich and His World*, ed. Laurel E. Fay (Princeton, NJ: Princeton University Press, 2004), 59–113.

49. Annegret Fauser, "Cultural Musicology: New Perspectives on World War II," *Zeithistorische Forschungen/Studies in Contemporary History* 8 (2011): 282–86.

50. See Jessica C. E. Gienow-Hecht, "Sonic History, or Why Music Matters in International History," in *Music and International History in the Twentieth Century*, ed. Jessica C. E. Gienow-Hecht (New York: Berghahn Books, 2015), 1–30.

51. In recent years, emotions—like music—have become a topic of historical inquiry. See Ute Frevert, "Was haben Gefühle in der Geschichte zu suchen," *Geschichte und Gesellschaft: Zeitschrift für historische Sozialwissenschaft* 35 (2009): 183–208.

52. Vanessa Agnew and Jonathan Lamb, eds., *Settler and Creole Reenactment* (Basingstoke: Palgrave Macmillan, 2009).

Select Bibliography

Auerbach, Jonathan, and Russ Castronovo, eds. *The Oxford Handbook of Propaganda Studies.* Oxford: Oxford University Press, 2013.

Baade, Christina L. *Victory through Harmony: The BBC and Popular Music in World War II.* New York: Oxford University Press: 2012.

Champagne, John. *Aesthetic Modernism and Masculinity in Fascist Italy*. London: Routledge, 2013.

Chapman, James. *The British at War: Cinema, State, and Propaganda, 1939–1945*. London: I. B. Tauris, 1998.

Clark, Katerina. *Moscow, the Fourth Rome: Stalinism, Cosmopolitanism, and the Evolution of Soviet Culture, 1931–1941*. Cambridge, MA: Harvard University Press, 2011.

Connelly, Mark, and David Welch, eds., *War and the Media: Reportage and Propaganda, 1900–2003*. London: I. B. Tauris, 2005.

Fauser, Annegret. *Sounds of War: Music in the United States during World War II*. Oxford: Oxford University Press, 2013.

Fox, Jo. *Film Propaganda in Britain and Nazi Germany: World War II Cinema*. Oxford: Berg, 2007.

Gienow-Hecht, Jessica C. E., ed. *Music and International History in the Twentieth Century*. New York: Berghahn Books, 2015.

Honey, Maureen. *Creating Rosie the Riveter: Class, Gender, and Propaganda during World War II*. Amherst: University of Massachusetts Press, 1984.

Horten, Gerd. *Radio Goes to War: The Cultural Politics of Propaganda during World War II*. Berkeley: University of California Press, 2003.

James, Pearl, ed. *Picture This: World War I Posters and Visual Culture*. Lincoln: University of Nebraska Press, 2009.

Kingsbury, Celia Malone. *For Home and Country: World War I Propaganda on the Home Front*. Lincoln: University of Nebraska Press, 2010.

Lacey, Kate. *Feminine Frequencies: Gender, German Radio, and the Public Sphere*. Ann Arbor: University of Michigan Press, 1996.

Moore. Rachel. *Performing Propaganda: Musical Life and Culture in Paris during the First World War*. Woodbridge: Boydell, 2018.

Morris, John. *Culture and Propaganda in World War II: Music, Film, and the Battle for National Identity*. London: I. B. Taurus, 2014.

Roshwald, Aviel, and Richard Stites, eds. *European Culture in the Great War: The Arts, Entertainment, and Propaganda, 1914–1918*. Cambridge: Cambridge University Press, 1999.

Rupp, Leila J. *Mobilizing Women for War: German and American Propaganda, 1939–1945*. Princeton, NJ: Princeton University Press, 1978.

Sala, Massimiliano, ed. *Music and Propaganda in the Short Twentieth Century*. Turnhout: Brepols, 2014.

Taylor, Philip M. *Munitions of the Mind: A History of Propaganda from the Ancient World to the Present Day*, 3rd ed. Manchester: Manchester University Press, 2003.

Welch, David. *Propaganda, Power and Persuasion: From World War I to Wikileaks*. London: I. B. Tauris, 2014.

CHAPTER 17

....

TOTAL WARFARE, GENDER, AND THE "HOME FRONT" IN EUROPE DURING THE FIRST AND SECOND WORLD WARS

....

SUSAN R. GRAYZEL

THE idea of the home as a front became increasingly incorporated into the waging of modern warfare in the Age of World Wars, which many historians describe as the age of "total warfare."[1] With the industrialization of warfare, civilians—women and men—"at home" were increasingly called into service in war industries, the agrarian production of food, war charity, and other forms of material support, including civil defense. At the same time, civilians ever more became targets of warfare: the focus of war propaganda, economic blockades, occupation, and violence in all forms. In the era of total warfare, this expanded to include threats of physical and sexual violence against individuals and groups, looting and destruction as a result of air war, and even genocide. The morale and what was often deemed "character" of both women and men, across a range of geographic, economic, and demographic divides, therefore came to figure extensively in the calculations of war-making modern states as the total wars of the twentieth century unfolded.[2]

Thus, when we discount the contributions and experiences of civilians, including women and children, to war making at home, we miss a vital part of the history of warfare. It is important to ask how and why states and leaders made use of the "home front" during the Age of World Wars and what happened at home in the main European participant states in both world wars: Austria-Hungary, Britain, France, Germany, Italy, and Russia/the Soviet Union. Answering these questions requires taking in a broad geographic scope, because many of these states were colonial empires. We must examine how civilians, especially women, mobilized to work in the war industries and for war charities, as well as how, when, where, and why civilians became major targets of economic warfare, destructive occupation policies, genocide, and attacks utilizing modern technology such as air power. Furthermore, it is necessary to take seriously the varying responses to the intrusion of the war-making state into the everyday lives of their inhabitants, including dissent and overt resistance, especially when civil wars then arose.[3]

Central themes of a gendered study of the two world wars as totals wars must be, on the one hand, the blurring of the borders between feminized home lands and masculinized battle zones, civilians and combatants, and, on the other hand, the heightening levels of violence aimed at noncombatants. Both had far-reaching consequences for gender identities and relations. Across European societies, the state had to negotiate and renegotiate relationships with its civilian population, especially women, who became instrumental in replacing the men absorbed into the mass mobilization for military service and playing a critical role in wartime economies. At the same time, traditional notions of sexuality and gender roles endured, as evident in the assumption that women remained vital to the maintenance of households and family life even under the conditions of total war. At their core, the processes by which domestic life in Europe became militarized during the First and Second World Wars were a cultural transformation.

By elevating the experiences of those at home to the status of a "front," the invented twentieth-century term *home front* signaled both the demonstrated importance of those at home to a successful war effort and the continued sense that those in such zones remained somehow "apart" from some more authentic realm of battle. "Home front" was fundamentally an ambiguous term. Furthermore, its potency was diminished, even at the moment of its origins during World War I (1914–18), as new modes of warfare penetrated the borders between civilians and combatants, so-called home front and front line. The term functioned as a form of propaganda, an assertion that the "home" might remain separate from the full impact of war. By the end of World War II (1939–45), the rubble of major European cities and the piles of civilian corpses belied the sense that meaningful distinctions about who participated in conflict could be made based on gender or geography.

In the following, four themes will be explored: first, the "home front" during World War I; second, the aftermath of this conflict and its influence on ideas about war and gender in interwar Europe; third, the participation of domestic spaces during World War II; and fourth, the legacy of the world wars at, and for, the home.

WAR AT HOME DURING WORLD WAR I

Le Feu (*Under Fire*) published 1916 by the French novelist Henri Barbusse, one of the most celebrated accounts of the First World War, begins with a sweeping panorama of the western front. As the narrative eye descends into the trenches, Barbusse describes men emerging from the muck and excrement of these shelters as barely discernable human figures. For decades after the end of the war, this remained the enduring image of World War I. Transcending ideas about masculinity or femininity, suffering over-whelmed everything, reducing humans to animals scrabbling for survival and on a scale that dwarfed distinctions even among combatants.[4]

Since the first appearance of Barbusse's text in serial form in 1916 and in widespread translations from the French by 1918, this dominant image of anguished, hapless men at arms enduring unspeakable deprivations and horrors has dominated the historiography of the war. For the most part, the contribution of gender history has tended to be supple-mentary; where men are concerned, it has focused on understanding the masculinity of soldiers.[5] There remains very little scholarship for both wars on civilian men generally and on the issues of masculinity in conjunction with those men deemed too old or young to fight, with the notable exception of those who refused to participate.[6] Britain serves as an important case study because it lacked a conscripted army until 1916, and the "White Feather" campaign illustrates the unease with which contemporaries viewed men who seemed to violate dominant gender norms. Thus, as part of efforts to shore up recruiting, some women in Britain handed out white feathers, an emblem of cowardice to "slackers" not in uniform. Other British propaganda also encouraged women to shun men who refused to put on a uniform and fight for their honor and safety: if a man could not be trusted to fight for Britain, he should not be trusted as a sweetheart.

However, this use of private sexuality to foster a militarized ideal man led also to savage critiques of the women who gave out the feathers as "immodest," or worse. As Nicoletta Gullace has shown, the white feather campaign was a quasi-official effort at sexually shaming men at home into joining the armed forces and fulfilling expectations about masculinity in wartime. Yet, what might be excusable early in the war became increasingly horrifying as the casualty lists mounted, so that the postwar memory of the white feather campaign features ignorant women giving these emblems to wounded men and being rightfully humiliated for their mistakes. War took place symbolically on the domestic front in this scenario, where men out of uniform at home raised a trou-bling spectacle, but women stepping beyond the bounds of helpmeet and nurturer became equally problematic.[7]

This example demonstrates the importance of gender for mobilizing both fronts—battle and domestic. In contemporary accounts, however, women have figured overwhelm-ingly in relationship to men at arms. Narratives of women's war experiences, dating from the war years themselves, have emphasized their sharing the dangers and priva-tions faced by men (under occupation and in proximity to battle zones), their efforts to try to substitute for men (in spaces from factories to pulpits), and/or their tending to men (as nurses and other medical personnel, as members of a variety of voluntary orga-nizations devoted to the care of military men, and as family members, especially wives and mothers). Occasionally, and especially as versions of the war as senseless slaughter came to shape its history, accounts celebrated the women who resisted the war and its militarism, highlighting the women who demanded an end to the conflict and worked to ensure that no such catastrophic event succeeded it.[8]

A variety of circumstances shaped the experiences of women, like other civilians, during World War I. One important factor was that this total war was a "war without limits," which led in the interpretation of some scholars to a "brutalization" of culture, of society, and of war making itself. One often-cited example of this brutalization is the "Rape of Belgium," a term used in propaganda as a shorthand for the treatment of civilian lives and spaces during the German invasion and occupation of neutral Belgium. Approximately 6,500 Belgian and French civilians were killed in the context of the invasion, and many more had their homes destroyed.[9] Other examples of brutalization can be found in the mowing down by machine guns of wave after wave of hapless men trying to cross no man's land; the asphyxiating clouds of poison gas that burned soldiers' lungs and skin; the drowning of voyagers from submarine attacks on nonmilitary ships; the genocidal murder of Armenians; the burning of schoolchildren in London in a direct hit from an air raid; and the starvation of children and the elderly in Austria-Hungary, Germany, and the Ottoman Empire because of the Allies' economic blockade.

A second important factor facing all war powers was the need to mobilize unprecedented numbers of men into armies and civilians into the war effort for this first instance of industrialized mass warfare. To sustain mass mobilization, war propaganda using the emerging mass media became more crucial than ever before. The role of propaganda cannot be disassociated from the study of gender during this war because state bureaucracies and censors sought to manage information circuits, restricting what could be said or seen or sung or set forth in any medium about the conflict.[10] Take, for example, the mobilization of civilian populations, especially women, into war work. A central feature of the historiography on gender and the war remains the economic role played by women in making up for labor shortages caused by the absence of men in crucial areas.[11] As Laura Lee Downs has shown, "war work" could encompass nearly everything that the state required to support its military endeavors. For women, it could include the expected domestic tasks of running households, although over time this could eventually encompass doing "the housekeeping of the army" as women took on noncombatant military roles to free men for the firing line.[12]

Geography was another factor that influenced war experiences at home to a great extent, in particular the ways in which women experienced shifts in their responsibilities for household and family survival in their roles as mothers, sisters, and daughters. In occupied zones such as Belgium, Northern France, and the area controlled by Germany in the east known as *Ober Ost*, feeding families required many women to engage in fraught negotiations with enemy men.[13] Those living in the urban areas of the Central Powers in Austria-Hungary and Germany faced serious deprivations, yet their complaints were met with a state response that blamed the enemy and its immoral blockade for the lack of food. Despite efforts to shift blame away from their own governments, anger increasingly mounted as malnutrition, hunger, and disease pervaded homes.[14] In territories where fighting occurred, civilians had to leave their destroyed houses and farms and became war refugees. At the western front, in Alsace-Lorraine, Belgium, and northeastern France, three million people lost their homes in the context of the German invasion. Later, another half million had to flee to the unoccupied territories of France.[15]

Even in the rural countryside outside the combat zone, wartime disrupted daily life. Writing to her soldier husband from her French village in the summer of 1915, Marie Pireaud spoke of the toll that shortages of labor and animals were taking on the harvest, wondering, "How many will there be who will not have enough to live?"[16]

For some, the dominant experiences of the war at home were deprivation, occupation, and violence, but for others, opportunity loomed larger than suffering. An increasing number of women crossed the seemingly fixed barriers of the prewar gender order, taking on a range of occupations previously reserved for men. Working-class women left domestic service to become metal workers, transport personnel, or army auxiliaries. Some even became female soldiers, but only active combatants in revolutionary Russia during the brief period of Menshevik rule in the summer of 1917. Middle-class women increasingly became white-collar workers, taking on new positions in administrations and offices, or joining public service in new officially sanctioned capacities as welfare supervisors or female police. They expanded the ranks of professional nurses and doctors and staffed the military medical system.[17] Images of women crossing the gender lines in the "national emergency" of war were on display in the media everywhere and shaped an understanding of the war as a "catalyst of women's emancipation," despite a much more complex reality.

The widespread entry of women into the world of waged work offers a key example of the often-paradoxical realities of wartime. Despite the perception of contemporaries and some later historians, the percentage of wage-earning women did not increase as dramatically as was commonly assumed. Instead, there were shifts in the sectors of the labor market in which women worked. Many women used the opportunities provided by the war to improve their position in the labor market and to move from agrarian and domestic labor to factory work. In the industrial sector, they transferred from feminized trades, such as clothing and textile factories, to those producing armaments. Educated women with professional training entered new segments of the workforce, like state welfare.[18] Such developments gave women increased wages and independence and were therefore perceived as a threat to the prewar gender order. Thus, as Deborah Thom has demonstrated, the British photographic record, for instance, was deliberately skewed to display as women war workers the young and the extraordinary. In addition, some publicly came to question the "decency and morality" of young and single female workers.[19]

Debates about women's war work during the conflict reflected the state's growing role in arranging domestic affairs and the ways in which women's participation remained particularly fungible. In Austria, as Christa Hämmerle has explained, when women took on the tasks of running the railways and the trams of Vienna, they could "metaphorically stand for the continual evaluation that the development of women's work during the war was sensational; thus, it was often overestimated." Yet, as she further points out, revisions of the Law on War Services (*Kriegsleistungsgesetz*) in March 1917 effectively put women in the armaments industry under strict control, unable to change jobs at will and subject to the continued onerous conditions of such work, including devolving real wages, long hours, and a substantial risk of injury.[20] Other wartime states, notably Germany and Britain, actively debated the compulsion of female war work.

The decisions not to develop such legislation had much less to do with labor and economic need than they did with cultural values, among them the fear of what compelling female labor might signal to the larger public.[21]

The actions of the German military in occupied France became a notorious example of the state using compulsory labor. Here, the requisitioning of workers involved both men and women, but Germany's enemies emphasized what was inflicted on women. A 1916 pamphlet hastily assembled by the French government (and just as quickly translated into English), entitled *The Deportation of Women and Girls from Lille*, began with an appeal from Bishop Alexis-Armand Charost that characterized the removal in the following terms: "To dismember the family, by tearing youths and girls from their homes, is not war; it is for us torture and the worst of tortures—unlimited moral torture."[22] Organized labor camps were not unique to northern France and Belgium; Germany also created them in its occupied territories of the east, and they existed in overseas European colonies. In all places where unwilling civilians were forced to perform mainly agricultural labor for their nation's enemies, the local populations characterized the coercion of such labor as immoral.[23] The expansion of such practices offers another example of the new role of the state, in this case that of an enemy polity, in waging total war.

The economic warfare exemplified by the Entente naval blockade of the Central Powers, which restricted the supply of fertilizer and food, among other products, further demonstrates that putting the protected category of "women and children" at risk could be a calculated war policy. The resulting inability of Austria-Hungary and Germany to meet the basic needs of their civilian populations led to a widespread extension of state powers in rationing food and fuel and an unprecedented suffering of civilians, particularly women who ended up in many calculations as the most malnourished. One result in these states was increased resistance to war itself. What began as food riots of youth and women developed into protests about war economics and strikes for higher salaries and turned into activities that denounced the monarchical state and called for peace—at least in the larger cities. As a result, as Belinda Davis has shown for Berlin, police reports became increasingly anxious about the seething unrest of the women queuing for food in the winter of 1917/18. Similar discontent can be found in Austria-Hungary.[24]

One component that may have intensified these protests had to do with anger that the official initiatives to preempt such discontent failed. At the war's start, such measures included extending state support to the dependents of those serving in the military in nearly every participant state. With varying provisions, means tested in some nations and not in others, payment to soldiers' families was meant to recognize the extra burden that the absence of the male breadwinner might place on his household.[25] Despite concerted efforts, the distribution of resources to soldiers' dependents did not always reflect proposals. So many men joined up in the early months of the conflict in Britain that a system based in part on volunteer labor could not keep up and ensure that military families did not suffer materially.[26] By the middle of the conflict, the rationing of food and fuel was meant to ensure their equitable distribution, but perceptions that this was markedly not so could frustrate good intentions. The anger of female dependents expecting support and the means to ensure the survival of their families that did not come can be seen in the radicalization of *soldatki* (soldiers' wives) in wartime Russia. This discontent in conjunction with protesting women workers in Petrograd helped ignite the Russian Revolution of February 1917.[27]

It was not just women protesting the war for economic reasons that troubled the status quo. Prewar feminism's resistance to military solutions to international problems, especially its evocation of the idea of a feminine moral force, in contrast to a masculine physical force, as an international feminist value, influenced key constituencies on the Left. A determined minority of feminists split with their national organizations over support for patriotic war efforts. Instead, they continued to express vocal opposition to war itself, almost from the moment of its outbreak. Thus, while some women participated in the violence of total war and the revolutions accompanying it, we must acknowledge the explicit and vocal rejection of violence as a means of resolving international conflict by other women.[28] Nor were women the only ones to reject war. Motivated by socialism, Marxism, or certain versions of Christianity, some men also refused to participate militarily in the conflict. Most visibly, with the introduction of conscription in Britain in 1916, a new identity became available to men who refused to fight: that of conscientious objector.[29]

The further extension of the state into civilian life during wartime and the often-mixed responses to it are also visible in two other related areas. The first was the response of states to aerial attacks. The absence of prewar preparation led to an improvised and only belatedly official response to such damage inflicted on those at home. When air raids first reached Paris in August and September 1914, there were no mechanisms to safeguard the civilian population. Perhaps unsurprisingly, what emerged publicly was less criticism of the French government for being unable to protect a civilian population than a wholesale condemnation of "German barbarism" as a reflection of deviant masculinity. This rhetoric did not change much over the course of the war as the range of areas attacked by air power and the scale of damage increased. Public voices continued to feminize the victims of these raids, in part to question the masculinity of those "knights of the air" who, from the safety of the clouds, killed infants in cradles.

It took some time before the state began to actively address the issue of how to manage this form of war making by creating warning signals and finding shelters. In the case of France, by the spring of 1918, this meant requisitioning cellars in private buildings in the heart of Paris for use as public shelters. Across the channel, the British government did not issue audible public warnings until the summer of 1917, in part because of concerns that such warnings would cause panic among the civilian population. By the war's end, a preliminary consensus that the state was now in the business of managing both civilian safety and civilian morale had emerged, with roles for all members of society in the war to come. Still, the feminization of air power's victims remained.[30]

The second expansion of state practice concerns the regulation of sexual commerce and attempts to control venereal disease. Such policies had several prewar precedents, notably in colonial settings, but they gained new focus under wartime circumstances. Here, the critical example is Britain rather than other states, such as France, that continued to promote official brothels and licensed prostitutes (in some cases, alongside the distribution of prophylactics). While a statement in every British soldier's pay packet contained a message from Field Marshal Herbert Kitchener warning him against "wine and women," the government also returned to the controversial practices of the Contagious Diseases Acts of 1864, which criminalized women who infected men with venereal diseases. Although a vociferous campaign had thwarted attempts to impose this legislation in England in the 1860s, the measures continued in the empire, and, in the climate of the First World War, such efforts returned, culminating in the passage of Defence of the Realm Regulation 40D from 1918, which made transmitting venereal disease to a member of His Majesty's Forces (or those of His Majesty's Allies) subject to criminal prosecution.[31] This took the threat of women's bodies to men at war to its logical end.

The regulation of women in order to protect men, especially those in the military, belies the complicated issue of sex work during the war. The spread of venereal disease was markedly on the rise among civilian as well as military populations. French doctors, for example, reported that from August 1914 to December 1915, rates of syphilis rose by almost 50 percent in comparison to prewar statistics. The role of military men in this upward trend can only be inferred from the fact that rates increased more near garrison towns and railway stations.[32] While state concern focused for the most part on venereal disease, the nature of sexual encounters between military men and civilian women, and that between civilian men and women, during the war absorbed media attention. In occupied zones, such as Belgium, northern France, or Serbia, some women became victims of sexual assault and others engaged in relationships in which they traded sex for material support.

Whatever their agency in these contacts, the behavior of women perceived to be fraternizing with the enemy was labeled prostitution, seen not only as a sign of their individual depravity but also as a collective betrayal of the nation.[33] Potential (and real) relationships between non-White colonial troops and French or British women were observed with particular anxiety. That this concern extended to the policing of White women nursing colonial troops shows how much mistrust of women's sexuality as an internal threat to national order reflected state concern with maintaining gender, race, and class hierarchies.[34] All these developments taken together demonstrate that we only can understand the First World War as a modern total war if we systematically use gender as one category of our analysis. It remains a vital marker of the blurring and crossing of the border between civilians and combatants, which became even more visible during World War II.

GENDERING THE AFTERMATH OF THE FIRST WORLD WAR AND THE WARS TO COME

Changes at home during the First World War had important implications for the wars that followed. It would be impossible to understand fully how European societies experienced the onslaught of another even more devastating conflict twenty years later without considering its legacy for key aspects of domestic life. Two of the most important of these changes help us to understand better the differences and similarities between the First and Second World Wars. First and foremost, there was widespread recognition by all states that the means of waging war had changed. As a result, preparation for a future war meant planning for a war potentially incorporating all populations and all spaces. Second, given the demographic losses incurred during the First World War, postwar states insisted on the continued need for women to embrace motherhood and domesticity in order to rebuild the nation. A variety of governments committed resources in new ways to support family allowances and to counter efforts to secure access to birth control. Both developments suggest the altered calculations required for waging war.

The arrival of air power and fears of a future war that would involve aircraft spraying chemical arms on densely populated European cities reshaped postwar debates. Government war planners, other constituent bodies of postwar nations, international advocates for disarmament, journalists, writers, and scientists imagined the next war as one of devastation involving aircraft and chemical weapons. For many interwar activists, especially some feminists, gender still lay at the core of new politics.[35] For instance, recognition of the altered circumstances of modern war contributed to the actions taken by some of the key organizations representing the international feminist community, such as the Women's International League for Peace and Freedom, founded in 1915 in The Hague during the International Women's Peace Congress. The activists of this organization highlighted the acute dangers that war now posed potentially to all women. During a meeting in Zurich in 1919, the league pledged itself to disarmament, asserting, "Women only benefit in a world based on justice not force."[36] An expanded postwar feminist notion of justice led to lobbying the League of Nations to take action both on aerial disarmament and on state support for domestic life in the form of motherhood or family allowances.[37]

At the same time, postwar governments began to prepare everyone at home to confront new modes of warfare. Despite international efforts to curtail their use, this could include the testing of both chemical weapons and defenses against them in imperial settings, as evidence from Britain reveals. Plans for civil defense and for the mobilization of all civilians, especially women, also began early in the interwar period. France passed its first legislation on what it called *défense passive* in 1922, and Britain began to create what would become Air Raids Precautions in 1924. It was not until the summer of 1935 that the British government issued its first public statement, which set the tone for the war preparations that followed. It categorically stated that there was "no guarantee of immunity" for anyone, regardless of gender, age, or geography, although the protection of colonial spaces was even more fraught.[38]

With the use of chemical weapons by Fascist Italy during the Second Italo-Ethiopian War (1935–36) and the return of aerial attacks against civilian targets to European soil during the Spanish Civil War (1936–39), such plans and the consequent debates over the expansion of state power over domestic life (including the evacuation of children, the blackout, and civil defense in the home) took on new urgency. Those reporting on Italy's devastating use of poison gas in 1935 and 1936 were clear on the implications: the use of these weapons against defenseless "women and children" made the European men wielding them despicable savages.[39] The acceleration of the decision to provide antigas protection for civilians in the aftermath of Ethiopia—from the 1937 marketing of the *Volksgasmaske* (people's gas mask) in Germany to the testing of baby antigas helmets on poor children in London in 1938—revealed widespread recognition of the new geographies of modern war.[40]

This was further compounded by the devastating air raids that accompanied the Spanish Civil War. The infamous April 1937 attack on Guernica caused an international uproar, as papers such as *L'Humanité* put photos of dead women ("mothers without doubt") on their front pages.[41] In *The Daily Mirror* in March 1938, the British feminist Charlotte Haldane addressed mothers like herself, asking them, "Have you ever thought of planning to protect a baby's life against the chief horror of modern warfare, death from the skies?" Haldane added that air power alone in its newest guise could prove just as terrifying as potential poison gas bombs: "The lesson of Spain proves that there is a far more horrible and dangerous method of murdering women and innocent children in large towns."[42] The entire process of interwar preparations for the next war raised questions about heroism, civic duty, and associated links to notions of masculinity and femininity.

Such changed expectations of what war would now entail took place against an altered postwar political, social, and cultural landscape. Across Europe, women struggled to navigate their formal entry into politics in the countries where they had acquired the vote after the war, which included Russia (1917); Germany, Hungary, and Poland (1918); Austria (1919); Czechoslovakia (1920); and Britain (1918/28).[43] In these key states, men and women had to negotiate their roles in emerging political regimes and ideologies with differing ideas about gender. This ranged from the emphasis on strength as the New Soviet Woman under the New Economic Policy in the Soviet Union in the 1920s and more complicated ideas about female comrades under Stalin to the renewed emphasis on extreme patriarchal gender norms in Nazi Germany and Fascist Italy (here combined with extended possibilities for girls and women to become active in their own party organizations). An anxiety about motherhood, women's increasing attempts to gain control over their bodies via access to birth control and legal abortion, and surplus women coexisted in the interwar period with the image of the emancipated "*Neue Frau*" (New Woman), "flapper," or "*Garçonne*" and the popularization of and, in some senses, new visibility given to male and female homosexuality. All this suggests that the interwar period was a time of tense renegotiating of the meanings of masculinity and femininity in states preparing for and/or experiencing violence and conflict. This context must inform our understanding of World War II.[44]

GENDER AND THE RETURN OF TOTAL WAR

The Second World War more than fulfilled the predictions of interwar European states, especially the recognition that civilians would be active participants in, and targets of, war. This can be seen in a variety of concrete factors that shaped the roles of those at home during this war. One was the emergence of civil defense, which redefined how both the state and its civilians should respond to the rise of air power. This, in turn, called for the mass mobilization of the entire population, regardless of gender or age, in ways that played out in a variety of forms in very different state systems.

Popular mobilization for the Second World War again had to contend with prescriptive ideas about gender, including ideals that saw soldiering as purely masculine and maintaining the domestic sphere as a feminine task. In Fascist Italy and Nazi Germany, despite a prewar rhetoric that depicted a wartime gender order in which the male battle-front was protecting the "female" home front, women were mobilized for war support in similar ways. The longer the conflict lasted, as in the Soviet Union, the more it encouraged an ideology of female comradeship and socialist emancipations. The Soviet and Nazi states both used women in the military: the Third Reich as auxiliaries (*Wehrmachtshelferinnen*) and the Soviet Union, among others, as female soldiers.[45]

Britain tried to do both: preserve a notion of a feminine home front while also fully mobilizing certain categories of women. The British government decided to conscript the labor of "mobile women"—a group that included first, in 1941, single women aged twenty to thirty and, by 1943, women from nineteen to thirty and fully excluded all mothers of children under fourteen years old. Gradually, previously exempt housewives were called into part-time war work, and by 1944, women up to age fifty were meant to register to determine if they should work outside the home for the war effort.[46] The Nazi government pursued a comparable policy, but at least in the early war years the pressure was less intense, because of the higher female prewar labor-force participation rate in Germany and the brutal, widespread, and increasing exploitation of prisoners of war and forced laborers.[47] Across Europe, the extension of women into waged work grew far beyond what had been seen in the First World War.

As was the case during World War I, states also increasingly intervened in all aspects of daily life. What one could wear, what one could eat, and where one could live or go were restricted by wartime state policies, which continually reminded civilians of their front-line status. This intervention reached a new and extremely brutal dimension in the occupied territories. Between September 1939 and December 1941, when first much of continental Europe and later large parts of the Western Soviet Union fell under the control of Nazi Germany, its occupation regime determined many of the war experiences of these civilian populations. The hardships associated with living under enemy control intensified during the Second World War as the Nazi regime was motivated by a racist agenda that targeted whole populations or sections of them as "racially unfit," overwhelmingly Jews, but also Slavs and Sinti and Roma, a process that relied on notions about the "inheritability of tainted blood." The range of abuse, persecution and mass murder committed under these auspices culminated in the Holocaust. Attacks on populations because of their sexuality or gender expression played a long underestimated role in these efforts as homosexuals were among the categories of people deemed unfit by the Nazis. Moreover, as in the First World War, sexual violence, including mass rape and forced prostitution, accompanied invading and occupying forces.[48]

Despite repression and violence, there were powerful efforts to resist occupying regimes. France offers one of the most well-studied examples of this, being a state that was, in 1940 through 1942, divided into zones of occupation (by both Italy and Germany) and the Vichy regime and, from 1942 to 1944, fully under foreign control. Like many places in occupied Europe, mobilization at home could take a decidedly subversive element as both women and men joined the resistance. While the myth of *La France résistante* exaggerated the extent to which the population challenged state authority, the resistance movement in France, as elsewhere, created opportunities for women and men to participate in defeating the enemy by doing everything from sustaining underground and alternative modes of communicating information to blowing up railway lines. In some instances, women used assumptions about their femininity to mislead occupying forces that did not see them as able to engage in active resistance; others did not. At the war's end, women accused of "horizontal collaboration"—sleeping with the enemy—were subject to the public shaming of the *tondues*. Their hair was publicly shaved and they were paraded, sometimes stripped of their clothes, through the streets.[49]

State encroachment into intimate life via the regulation of sexual behavior also continued as a legacy of the First World War. In Britain, concern about the "Good Time Girl" and the dangers of promiscuity as a means of spreading venereal disease continued. As Sonya O. Rose has pointed out, the policing of civilian women in their interactions with men at arms was exacerbated when it came to so-called interracial sex, for instance with African American troops on British soil.[50] Despite efforts at regulation, commercial as well as coercive sex of every variety flourished anywhere troops were gathered, from Hawaii to Paris to Bombay to Cairo.[51]

Given the expansion of state regulations—from home to workplace to market to street—it is not surprising that many such policies were predicated on gender expectations. The very nature of consumption changed under state control, but the assumption that women had the main responsibility to ensure that their families were fed and clothed did not. In the face of strict controls, black markets sprang up, which allowed working-class British mothers, for instance, to sell clothing rations to the more well off to obtain more food.[52] States trained their citizens in civil defense; they expected their populations, no matter the gender, to exhibit stoicism under bombing.[53] Across Europe, destroyed homes, livelihoods, and lives provided ample evidence that war had become one without limit.

CONCLUSION

Every study of the developments during the Age of World Wars must conceptualize this period along a continuum. Both wars ushered in new ways of mobilizing and recognizing the labor of noncombatants. The necessity of creating a civil defense regime across Europe reflects the fact that while air power changed what war at home could entail, serious attempts to curtail aerial bombardment after the First World War failed. Yet efforts to restrict one of the most dreaded weapons of that war succeeded: poison gas was not used on the battlefront or indiscriminately against civilian populations, as had been the case in World War I and the Second Italo-Ethiopian War. Efforts to curtail the use of nonconventional weapons continued, with some success, in the nuclear age, although not without a set of government measures across Europe to extend civil defense into defense against nuclear war. The state did not disavow a strategy of preparing civilians to face war at home.

That there could be limits imposed on war emerged in the postwar war crimes trials and some of the unfinished business of the Second World War. In Europe, prosecutors left out sexual violence as one of the charges leveled at postwar tribunals, although this was included in charges at separate trials against the Japanese government. Despite widespread and largely unpunished sexual abuse, it would be decades before rape entered into international law as a war crime.

The ongoing militarization of society was a key legacy of the world wars. On the one hand, we find an understandable desire across Europe to focus on domestic rebuilding and not on continuing to invest in preparations for war (civil defense notwithstanding). The rise of post-1945 welfare states across Western Europe, with their implicit pronatalism, and the provision of state-sponsored education, health, and housing in Eastern Europe show a willingness to invest in welfare in addition to weaponry. Yet, it would be hard to call states that continued to resist decolonization, often violently, and whose numbers included the Soviet Union, France, and Britain joining the "nuclear club" as engaging in demilitarization.[54]

A level of state intervention in daily, domestic life that the world wars made thinkable was another concrete legacy of these conflicts. We can thus find widespread continuity of state policy on civil defense from the interwar to the Cold War. The focus might have shifted from aerochemical war to nuclear war, but the practices maintained the need for civilian awareness and preparation, regardless of age, gender, or geography. Moreover, there is much we still do not know about the legacy of the violence of these wars. One such area is the very underresearched history of postwar domestic violence and of effects on a generation raised in extreme wartime violence.[55]

Most of the cultural work that transformed the roles of men and women during wartime began in the First World War. Thus, the crucial break with the past, in terms of mobilization and accepting a wider civilian role in war, came with that war, not later conflicts. Both men and women found themselves involved in war and living in societies that accepted a new level of state intervention in their daily lives as a result of the state's altered expectations of where war took place and whom it affected.

NOTES

1. For a discussion of the invention of the term *home front*, see Susan R. Grayzel, *Women's Identities at War: Gender, Motherhood, and Politics in Britain and France during the First World War* (Chapel Hill: University of North Carolina Press, 1999). See also how "front" is discussed as a new concept by John Horne, "Le Front," in *Vu du Front: Représenter La Grande Guerre* (Paris: Somogy Editions, 2014), 17–28; and for the gender dimensions, see

Krisztina Robert, "Constructions of 'Home,' 'Front,' and Women's Military Employment in First-World-War Britain: A Spatial Interpretation," *History and Theory* 52, no. 3 (2013): 319–43. The contested concept of *total war* is discussed in the chapter by Karen Hagemann and Sonya O. Rose on "War and Gender: The Age of the World Wars and Its Aftermath— an Overview" in this handbook.

2. For an introduction, see Margaret R. Higonnet et al., eds., *Behind the Lines: Gender and the Two World Wars* (New Haven, CT: Yale University Press, 1987); Susan R. Grayzel, *Women and the First World War* (Houndmills: Longman, 2002); Susan R. Grayzel and Tammy M. Proctor, eds., *Gender and the Great War* (Oxford: Oxford University Press, 2017); Karen Hagemann and Stefanie Schüler-Springorum, eds., *Home/Front: The Military, War, and Gender in Twentieth-Century Germany* (Oxford: Berg, 2002); Alison S. Fell and Ingrid Sharp, eds., *The Women's Movement in Wartime: International Perspectives, 1914–19* (Basingstoke: Palgrave Macmillan, 2007); Maren Röger and Ruth Leiserowitz, eds., *Women and Men at War: A Gender Perspective on World War II and Its Aftermath in Central and Eastern Europe* (Osnabrück: Fibre, 2012); Christa Hämmerle et al., eds., *Gender and the First World War* (Basingstoke: Palgrave Macmillan, 2014); and Maggie Andrews and Janis Lomas, eds., *The Home Front in Britain: Images, Myths and Forgotten Experiences since 1914* (Basingstoke: Palgrave Macmillan, 2014).

3. Internal conflict emerged in Ireland, Germany, and Russia, for instance, after the First World War, and women had key roles in these as they did in the Greek Civil War that arose from the Second World War. See the chapters by Karen Hagemann on "History and Memory of Female Military Service in the Age of World Wars," Regina Mühlhäuser on "Sexuality, Sexual Violence, and the Military in the Age of the World Wars," and Kimberly Jensen on "Citizenship and Gender on the American and Canadian Home Fronts during the First and Second World Wars" in this handbook. For a discussion of dissent during the First World War, see Erika Kuhlman, "Gender and Resistance," in Grayzel and Proctor, *Gender and the Great War*, 27–45.

4. See Henri Barbusse, *Le Feu* (Paris: E. Flammarion, 1917); and Susan R. Grayzel, "Teaching *Le Feu/Under Fire* by Henri Barbusse," *Film and Fiction for French Historians Online Bulletin*, February 2014, accessed September 11, 2015, http://h-france.net/fffh/classics/teaching-le-feuunder-fire-by-henri-barbusse/. On the battlefield experience, see Leonard V. Smith, *The Embattled Self: French Soldiers' Testimony of the Great War* (Ithaca, NY: Cornell University Press, 2007).

5. For more on masculinity, see the chapter by Thomas Kühne on "States, Military Masculinities, and Combat in the Age of World Wars" in this handbook.

6. For some recent work on male civilians, see Laura Ugolini, *Civvies: Middle-Class Men on the English Home Front, 1914–18* (Manchester: Manchester University Press, 2013). See also Tammy Proctor, *Civilians in a World at War, 1914–1918* (New York: New York University Press, 2010). For literature on male war resistance, including conscientious objectors, see Martin Ceadel, *Pacifism in Britain, 1914–1945: The Defining of a Faith* (Oxford: Oxford University Press, 1980); Thomas C. Kennedy, *The Hound of Conscience: A History of the No-Conscription Fellowship* (Fayetteville: University of Arkansas Press, 1981); Peter Brock, *Against the Draft: Essays on Conscientious Objection from the Radical Reformation to the Second World War* (Toronto: University of Toronto Press, 2006); and Lois S. Bibbings, *Telling Tales about Men: Conceptions of Conscientious Objectors to Military Service during the First World War* (Manchester: Manchester University Press, 2010).

7. Nicoletta F. Gullace, "White Feathers and Wounded Men: Female Patriotism and the Memory of the Great War," *Journal of British Studies* 36, no. 2 (1997): 178–206.

8. In addition to the works already cited in note 2, see emblematic eyewitness accounts such as Vera Brittain, *Testament of Youth: An Autobiographical Study of the Years 1900–1925* (London: Victor Gollancz, 1933); wartime examples like Léon Abensour, *Les Vaillantes: Héroines, Martyres et Remplaçantes* (Paris: Librairie Chapelot, 1917); Louis Barthou, *L'Effort de la Femme Française* (Paris: Bloud et Gay, 1917); Charlotte Payne, *Women after the War and Now* (London: Unwin, 1915); Annie S. Swan, *The Woman's Part* (London: Hodder & Stoughton, 1916); and Rudolf Voemel, *Deutsche Frauen, deutsche Treue! Ein Wort des Trostes an unsere deutschen Frauen und Jungfrauen* (Verlag des Westdeutschen Jünglingsbundes, 1914).

9. See John N. Horne and Alan Kramer, *German Atrocities, 1914: A History of Denial* (New Haven, CT: Yale University Press, 2001); Alan Kramer, *Dynamic of Destruction: Culture and Mass Killing in the First World War* (Oxford: Oxford University Press, 2007), esp. 6–30; and Ruth Harris, "The 'Child of the Barbarian': Rape, Race, and Nationalism in France during the First World War," *Past & Present*, no. 141 (1993): 170–206.

10. See the chapter by Annegret Fauser on "Gendered War Mobilization, Culture, and Music in the Age of World Wars" in this handbook.

11. Important studies on female war work during World War I are Gail Braybon, *Women Workers in the First World War* (London: Croom Helm, 1981); Ute Daniel, *The War from Within: German Working-Class Women in the First World War* (Oxford: Berg, 1997); Angela Woollacott, *On Her Their Lives Depend: Munitions Workers in the Great War* (Berkeley: University of California Press, 1994); Deborah Thom, *Nice Girls and Rude Girls: Women Workers in World War I* (London: I. B. Tauris, 1998); and Margaret H. Darrow, *French Women and the First World War: War Stories from the Home Front* (Oxford: Berg, 2000), 169–228.

12. See Laura Lee Downs, "War Work," in *The Cambridge History of the First World War*, vol. 3, *Civil Society*, ed. Jay Winter (Cambridge: Cambridge University Press, 2014), 72–95.

13. See Sophie De Schaepdrijver, "Populations under Occupation," in Winter, *The Cambridge History*, 3:242–56; Vejas Liulevicius, *War Land on the Eastern Front: Culture, National Identity and German Occupation in World War I* (Cambridge: Cambridge University Press, 2000); and Proctor, *Civilians*.

14. See Belinda Davis, *Home Fires Burning: Food, Politics, and Everyday Life in World War I Berlin* (Chapel Hill: University of North Carolina Press, 2000); and Maureen Healy, *Vienna and the Fall of the Habsburg Empire: Total War and Everyday Life in World War I* (Cambridge: Cambridge University Press, 2004).

15. Kramer, *Dynamic*, 6–30.

16. Quoted in Martha Hanna, *Your Death Would Be Mine: Paul and Marie Pireaud in the Great War* (Cambridge, MA: Harvard University Press, 2006), 53.

17. On the mobilization of women for the military, see Hagemann, "History and Memory" in this handbook. On humanitarian war work and war medicine, see the chapter by Jean H. Quataert on "Changing Modes of Warfare and the Gendering of Military Medical Care, 1850s–1920s" in this handbook.

18. See Downs, "War Work"; and Grayzel, *Women*.

19. Deborah Thom, "Making Spectaculars: Museums and How We Remember Gender in Wartime," in *Evidence, History and the Great War*, ed. Gail Braybon (New York: Berghahn Books, 2003), 48–66.

20. Christa Hämmerle, "Gendered Narratives of the First World War: The Example of the Former Austria," in *Narrating War: Early Modern and Contemporary Perspectives*, ed. Marco Mondini and Massimo Rospocher (Berlin: Duncker & Humblot, 2013), 173–87.

21. See Daniel, *War from Within*; Thom, *Nice Girls*; and Thom, "Gender and Work," in Grazel and Proctor, *Gender and the Great War*, 46–66.

22. Ministère des Affaires Etrangères, *The Deportation of Women and Girls from Lille* (London: Hodder & Stoughton, 1916), 16.

23. See the summation of these experiences and their historiography in Annette Becker, "Captive Civilians," in Winter, *The Cambridge History*, 2:257–82; also De Schaepdrijver, "Populations under Occupation."

24. See Davis, *Home Fires Burning*; Daniel, *War from Within*; Healy, *Vienna*; and Alexander Watson, *Ring of Steel: Germany and Austria-Hungary in World War I; The People's War* (New York: Basic Books, 2014). Austria-Hungary also saw various minority groups within the multiethnic state use the failings of the government as a way to assert nationalist agendas. See, for example, Claire Morelon, "The Urban–Rural Antagonism in Prague during the First World War in a Comparative Perspective," in *Frontwechsel: Österreich-Ungarns "Großer Krieg" im Vergleich*, ed. Wolfram Dornik et al. (Vienna: Böhlau, 2014), 325–44; and Tara Zahra, " 'Each Nation Only Cares for Its Own': Empire, Nation and Child Welfare Activism in the Bohemian Lands, 1900–1918," *The American Historical Review* 111, no. 5 (2006) 1378–402.

25. See Grayzel, *Women*, 9–28.

26. See Annmarie Hughes and Jeff Meek, "State Regulation, Family Breakdown, and Lone Motherhood: The Hidden Costs of World War I in Scotland," *Journal of Family History* 39, no. 4 (2014): 364–87.

27. Jane McDermid and Anna Hillyar, *Midwives of the Revolution: Female Bolsheviks and Women Workers in 1917* (London: University College of London Press, 1999).

28. See David S. Patterson, *The Search for Negotiated Peace: Women's Activism and Citizen Diplomacy in World War I* (New York: Routledge, 2008); Marie Sandell, *The Rise of Women's International Activism: Identity and Sisterhood between the World Wars* (London: I. B. Tauris, 2015); and Mona Siegel, *Peace on Our Terms: The Global Battle for Women's Rights after the First World War* (New York: Columbia University Press, 2020).

29. Kennedy, *Hound of Conscience*; and Bibbings, *Telling Tales*.

30. For this and the above paragraph, see Susan R. Grayzel, "The Souls of Soldiers: Civilians under Fire in First World War France," *Journal of Modern History* 76, no. 3 (2006): 588–622; and Grayzel, *At Home and under Fire: Air Raids and Culture in Britain from the Great War to the Blitz* (New York: Cambridge University Press, 2012), 76–78, for a discussion of the decision regarding air raid warnings.

31. See the discussion of the policing of wartime sexuality in Grayzel, *Women*; the classic work on the Contagious Diseases Acts is Judith Walkowitz, *Prostitution and Victorian Society: Women, Class, and the State* (Cambridge: Cambridge University Press, 1982); and the discussion of the imperial dimensions in Philippa Levine, *Prostitution, Race and Politics: Policing Venereal Disease in the British Empire* (London: Routledge, 2003).

32. Michelle K. Rhoades, "Renegotiating French Masculinity: Medicine and Venereal Disease during the Great War," *French Historical Studies* 29, no. 2 (2006): 293–327.

33. See Jovana Knezevic, "Prostitutes as a Threat to National Honor in Habsburg-Occupied Serbia during the Great War," *Journal of the History of Sexuality* 20, no. 2 (2011): 312–35.

34. Annabelle Melzer, "Spectacles and Sexualities: The 'Mise-en-Scène' of the 'Tirailleur Sénégalais' on the Western Front, 1914–1920," in *Borderlines: Gender and Identities in War and Peace, 1870–1930*, ed. Billie Melman (New York: Routledge, 1998), 213–44; Richard S. Fogarty, *Race & War in France: Colonial Subjects in the French Army, 1914–1918* (Baltimore: John Hopkins University Press, 2008), 202; Joe Lunn, *Memoirs of the Maelstrom: A*

Senegalese Oral History of the First World War (Portsmouth, NH: Heinemann, 1999); Alison S. Fell, "Nursing the Other: The Representation of Colonial Troops in French and British First World War Nursing Memoirs," in *Race, Empire and First World War Writing*, ed. Santanu Das (Cambridge: Cambridge University Press, 2011), 158–75; and Philippa Levine, "Battle Colors: Race, Sex and Colonial Soldiery in World War I," *Journal of Women's History* 9, no. 4 (1998): 104–30.

35. Siegel, *Peace on Our Terms*; Joyce Blackwell, *No Peace without Freedom: Race and the Women's International League for Peace and Freedom, 1915–75* (Carbondale: Southern Illinois University Press, 2004); see also the chapter by Glenda Sluga on "Gender, Peace, and the New Politics of Humanitarianism in the First Half of the Twentieth Century" in this handbook.

36. Jane Addams, "Presidential Address," in *Report of the International Congress of Women: Zurich, May 12 to 17, 1919* (Geneva: Women's International League for Peace and Freedom, 1919), 1. See also Catia Cecilia Confortini, *Intelligent Compassion: The Women's International League for Peace and Freedom and Feminist Peace* (New York: Oxford University Press, 2012).

37. Addams, "Presidential Address," 69, 85. See also Sluga, "Gender, Peace" in this handbook.

38. Grayzel, *At Home*, 201–15.

39. See Sir Hesketh Bell, Letter to Editor, "White and Black in Africa," *Times*, March 30, 1936.

40. For development of antigas protection in Britain, see Grayzel, *At Home*, 224–50; for more on the *Volksgasmaske*, see reports on international efforts in *Défense Passive*, 9N 299, Service Historique de la Défense (France).

41. "Mille Bombes Incendiares," *L'Humanité*, April 28, 1937.

42. Charlotte Haldane, "This Shocking Photo," *Daily Mirror*, March 8, 1938.

43. See Fell and Sharp, *Women's Movement*; Birgitta Bader-Zaar, "Women's Suffrage and War: World War I and Political Reform in a Comparative Perspective," in *Suffrage, Gender and Citizenship: International Perspectives on Parliamentary Reforms*, ed. Irma Sulkunen et al. (Newcastle: Cambridge Scholars Press, 2009), 193–218; Blanca Rodriguez-Ruiz and Ruth Rubio-Marin, eds., *The Struggle for Female Suffrage in Europe: Voting to Become Citizens* (Leiden: Brill, 2012); and Jad Adams, *Women and the Vote: A World History* (Oxford: Oxford University Press, 2014). For war service and citizenship in North America, see Jensen, "Citizenship and Gender" in this handbook.

44. See Claudia Koonz, *Mothers in the Fatherland: Women, the Family and Nazi Politics* (New York: St. Martin's, 1988); Victoria de Grazia, *How Fascism Ruled Women: Italy, 1922–1945* (Berkeley: University of California Press, 1993); Jill Stephenson, *Women in Nazi Germany* (London: Routledge, 2001); and Kevin Passmore, ed., *Women, Gender and Fascism in Europe, 1919–1945* (New Brunswick, NJ: Rutgers University Press, 2003). For an analysis of the tensions surrounding women's alleged postwar liberation, see Mary Louise Roberts, *Civilization without Sexes: Reconstructing Gender in Postwar France, 1917–1927* (Chicago: University of Chicago Press, 1994); and for a nuanced discussion of wartime and postwar sexual identity, see Laura Doan, *Disturbing Practices: History, Sexuality and Women's Experience of Modern War* (Chicago: University of Chicago Press, 2014).

45. Reina Pennington, *Wings, Women, and War: Soviet Airwomen in World War II Combat* (Lawrence: University of Kansas Press, 2002); Svetlana Alexievich, *The Unwomanly Face of War: An Oral History of Women in World War II* (New York: Random House, 2017); and the chapter by Hagemann, "History and Memory" in this handbook.

46. For earliest studies of this, see Gail Braybon and Penny Summerfield, *Out of the Cage: Women's Experiences in the Two World Wars* (London: Pandora, 1987), 155–68; Summerfield,

Reconstructing Women's Wartime Lives: Discourse and Subjectivity in Oral Histories of the Second World War (Manchester: Manchester University Press, 1998); Maggie Andrews, *Women and Evacuation in the Second World War: Femininity, Domesticity, and Motherhood* (London: Bloomsbury, 2019); and James Hinton, *Women, Social Leadership and the Second World War* (Oxford: Oxford University Press, 2002). For more direct military service, see Lucy Noakes, *Women in the British Army: War and the Gentle Sex, 1907–1948* (London: Routledge, 2006).

47. See Karen Hagemann, "Mobilizing Women for War: The History, Historiography, and Memory of German Women's War Service in the Two World Wars," *Journal of Military History* 75, no. 4 (2011): 1055–94.

48. Philippe Burrin, *France under the Germans: Collaboration and Compromise* (New York: New Press, 1996); Regina Mühlhäuser, *Sex and the Nazi Soldier: Violent, Commercial and Consensual Contacts during the War in the Soviet Union, 1941-1945* (Edinburgh: Edinburgh University Press, 2020); and Mary Louise Roberts, *What Soldiers Do: Sex and the American GI in World War II France* (Chicago, IL: University of Chicago Press, 2013); see also the chapter by Mühlhäuser, "Sexuality, Sexual Violence" in this handbook.

49. Margaret Collins Weitz, *Sisters in the Resistance: How Women Fought to Free France, 1940–1945* (New York: Wiley, 1998); for a firsthand account, see Lucie Aubrac, *Outwitting the Gestapo* (Lincoln: University of Nebraska Press, 1994); and on the tondues, see Fabrice Virgili, *Shorn Women: Gender and Punishment in Liberation France* (Oxford: Berg, 2002).

50. Sonya O. Rose, *Which People's War? National Identity and Citizenship in Britain, 1939–1945* (Oxford: Oxford University Press, 2003); and Rose, "Girls and GIs: Race, Sex, and Diplomacy in Second World War Britain," *The International History Review* 19, no. 1 (1997): 146–60.

51. See Mühlhäuser, "Sexuality, Sexual Violence" in this handbook; Beth Bailey and David Farber, *The First Strange Place: The Alchemy of Race and Sex in World War II Hawaii* (Baltimore: Johns Hopkins University Press, 1994); and John Costello, *Love, Sex and War, 1939–1945* (London: William Collins, 1985).

52. Mark Roodhouse, *Black Market Britain, 1939–1955* (Oxford: Oxford University Press, 2013), 47–48.

53. Richard Overy, *The Bombers and the Bombed: Allied Air War over Europe, 1940–1945* (New York: Penguin Books, 2014).

54. See also the chapter by Karen Hagemann on "Gender, Demobilization, and the Reordering of Societies after the First and Second World Wars" in this handbook.

55. There is some work on this, but mainly on psychology rather than broader implications for society. See Michal Shapira, *The War Inside: Psychoanalysis, Total War, and the Making of the Democratic Self in Postwar Britain* (Cambridge: Cambridge University Press, 2013).

Select Bibliography

Andrews, Maggie, and Janis Lomas, eds. *The Home Front in Britain: Images, Myths and Forgotten Experiences since 1914.* Basingstoke: Palgrave Macmillan, 2014.

Bucur, Maria, and Nancy M. Wingfield, eds. *Gender and War in Twentieth-Century Eastern Europe.* Bloomington: Indiana University Press, 2006.

Daniel, Ute. *The War from Within: German Working-Class Women in the First World War.* Oxford: Berg, 1997.

Darrow, Margaret H. *French Women and the First World War: War Stories from the Homefront.* Oxford: Berg, 2000.

Davis, Belinda J. *Home Fires Burning: Food, Politics, and Everyday Life in World War I Berlin.* Chapel Hill: University of North Carolina Press, 2000.

De Grazia, Victoria. *How Fascism Ruled Women: Italy, 1922–1945.* Berkeley: University of California Press, 1993.

Downs, Laura Lee. *Manufacturing Inequality: Gender Division in the French and British Metalworking Industries, 1914–1939.* Ithaca, NY: Cornell University Press, 1995.

Grayzel, Susan R. *At Home and under Fire: Air Raids and Culture in Britain from the Great War to the Blitz.* Cambridge: Cambridge University Press, 2012.

Grayzel, Susan R. *Women and the First World War.* London: Longman, 2002.

Grayzel, Susan R. *Women's Identities at War: Gender, Motherhood, and Politics in Britain and France during the First World War.* Chapel Hill: University of North Carolina Press, 1999.

Grayzel, Susan R., and Tammy M. Proctor, eds. *Gender and the Great War.* New York: Oxford University Press, 2017.

Hagemann, Karen, and Stefanie Schüler-Springorum, eds. *Home/Front: The Military, War, and Gender in Twentieth-Century Germany.* Oxford: Berg, 2002.

Hämmerle, Christa, Oswald Überegger, and Birgitta Bader-Zaar, eds. *Gender and the First World War.* Basingstoke: Palgrave Macmillan, 2014.

Healy, Maureen. *Vienna and the Fall of the Habsburg Empire: Total War and Everyday Life in World War I.* Cambridge: Cambridge University Press, 2004.

Higonnet, Margaret Randolph, Jane Jenson, Sonya Michel, and Margaret Collins Weitz, eds. *Behind the Lines: Gender and the Two World Wars.* New Haven, CT: Yale University Press, 1987.

Passmore, Kevin, ed. *Women, Gender and Fascism in Europe, 1919–1945.* New Brunswick, NJ: Rutgers University Press, 2003.

Pedersen, Susan. *Family, Dependence and the Origins of the Welfare State: Britain and France, 1914–1945.* Cambridge: Cambridge University Press, 1993.

Pollard, Miranda. *Reign of Virtue: Mobilizing Gender in Vichy France.* Chicago: University of Chicago Press, 1998.

Proctor, Tammy M. *Civilians in a World at War 1914–1918.* New York: New York University Press, 2010.

Röger, Maren, and Ruth Leiserowitz, eds. *Women and Men at War: A Gender Perspective on World War II and Its Aftermath in Central and Eastern Europe.* Osnabrück: Fibre, 2012.

Rose, Sonya O. *Which People's War? National Identity and Citizenship in Wartime Britain, 1939–1945.* Oxford: Oxford University Press, 2003.

Siegel, Mona L. *Peace on Our Terms: The Global Battle for Women's Rights after the First World War.* New York: Columbia University Press, 2020.

Woollacott, Angela. *On Her Their Lives Depend: Munitions Workers in the Great War.* Berkeley: University of California Press, 1994.

CHAPTER 18

CITIZENSHIP AND GENDER ON THE AMERICAN AND CANADIAN HOME FRONTS DURING THE FIRST AND SECOND WORLD WARS

KIMBERLY JENSEN

ON August 4, 1914, when Britain entered the First World War by declaring war on Germany, Canada was automatically brought into the conflict. As a British dominion, it had to follow foreign policy decisions of the British Parliament, but its government had the liberty to decide the level of involvement. The same happened again when the Second World War started. On September 1, 1939, Nazi Germany attacked Poland, two days later Britain and France declared war on Germany, nine days later Canada. In both world wars, the United States joined the struggle quite late compared to its European allies, which bore the brunt of both wars on the Continent. In World War I, the United States declared war on the German Empire on April 6, 1917, and in World War II the United States was pushed into the conflict by the Japanese attack on Pearl Harbor on December 7, 1941, and Nazi Chancellor Adolf Hitler's declaration of war against the United States on December 11, 1941. Following the Japanese declaration of war on the British Empire on December 8, 1941, and the attacks on Malaya, Singapore, and Hong Kong, Britain and its Dominions too declared war on Imperial Japan on December 8, 1941, which had started the Second World War in Asia with its occupation of parts of China already in July 1937.[1]

The extensive scholarship on both world wars in Canada and the United States has included since the 1980s an increasing number of studies on women, gender, and war.

First, the focus was on the subject of *women*, but historians have since incorporated *gender* as an analytical category in addition to and intersecting with the categories of *class, race, ethnicity, sexuality*, and *citizenship*. Many of these new studies look at the so-called home front.[2] They show that diverse groups of Americans and Canadians experienced a profound paradox in the war years and their aftermaths. In the age of industrialized *total war*, states needed their labor, support, and sacrifice more than ever before, and because of this, wartime brought new opportunities for a more complete citizenship for those who supported the "nation at war." This was especially true for members of groups who had experienced discrimination based on gender, race, class, ethnicity, and sexuality. As a result, new groups of Americans and Canadians claimed these opportunities.[3]

But wartime also brought imperatives for loyalty and national order that resulted in severe restrictions on civil liberties and citizenship in the name of national security during and after these conflicts. In the First World War, both nations designed programs and propaganda to define citizenship in the narrow confines of "100 percent Americanism" and "Canadian nationalism" at the expense of diversity and dissent. This call was connected with suspicion of those who did not follow such prescriptions and the insistence on traditional notions of the gender roles. The man was supposed to be the breadwinner and his wife a stay-at-home mother. Violence against those deemed disloyal "enemies" and large-scale "Red Scares" were part of the home-front experiences of both conflicts in Canada and the United States during and after both wars. The apparatus of the surveillance state over citizens and noncitizens expanded dramatically during both conflicts. Opponents of these wars faced powerful consequences as nation-states reestablished gendered prescriptions for loyalty, proper behavior, and wartime choices.[4]

The following will explore gendered concepts of citizenship and civil liberties discussed and pursued on the home fronts of Canada and the United States in the Age of the World Wars and study the consequences of those concepts for the lives of diverse Canadians and Americans. Individuals and groups acted to redefine and reshape official and legal definitions of citizenship. But both states responded often harshly and attempted to re-enforce the existing relations of power and the realities of race, ethnicity, economic class, and gender by limiting the privileges and obligations of their citizens.

CITIZENSHIP, CIVIL LIBERTIES, AND GENDER

Citizenship in the imperialist, expansionist, industrializing nations of Canada and the United States during the First and Second World Wars was both a profoundly gendered status and a fluid, contested category of identity. As Ruth Lister noted in her 2003 classic *Citizenship: Feminist Perspectives*, citizenship in this period (and in our own) was more than "a set of legal rules governing the relationship between the individual and the state" delineated from the top down. Rather, citizenship was a constantly shifting "set of social relationships" defining complex interactions among individuals, communities, and the state and also between individuals.[5] In 1950, T. H. Marshall emphasized in his pathbreaking *Citizenship and Social Class* that citizenship has three different but related dimensions: civic, political, and social.[6]

Other scholars have since added the category of economic citizenship. In the latter category, as Alice Kessler-Harris noted, women's civic relations to the state and to state services and systems have often related directly to their "family positions," while men's economic and civic identities have been formed "by virtue of their paid employment." Race, ethnicity, class, and gender identity also mediated the possibilities for full economic citizenship for all people. During the two world wars in Canada and the United States, women and men on home fronts expanded their claims to economic citizenship through paid employment, increasing opportunities to earn higher wages and to gain access to new fields of work. But they met resistance and definitions of this new work as temporary, "for the duration" of the conflict, and linked to patriotic, episodic opportunity during the wartime emergency only.[7] Thus, citizenship is a relational process comprising "rights and responsibilities, belonging and participation" of individuals in communities and nations.[8] In addition, the specific and gendered qualities of every citizen were related to social and cultural categories of respectability and behavior, marital status, and "moral character." The notion of a "respectable" citizen was developed in the public debate against the construction of the "anti-citizen" as a homosexual, or "slacker," an opponent of war, or "alien."[9]

During the two world wars, the rights of citizens to "basic liberties" or "fundamental freedoms" expressed in the US Constitution and Bill of Rights and the Canadian Constitution implied the possession of a group of civil liberties, among them rights to freedom of speech, religion, and the press. For some people, this included an evolving set of claims to individual liberty and safety, as well as what the 1948 United Nations Universal Declaration of Human Rights Article 3 terms individual "security of person."[10] As Christopher Capozzola has noted, some Americans created a new coalition based on "the concept of civil liberties, using rights as a weapon of defense" during the First World War. Individuals rejected the notion of citizenship as made up of coercive obligations and "imagined the citizen first and foremost as an individual and as a bearer of rights."[11] In this view, civil liberties existed as a protection against state-based coercion and violence. Yet, during the conflicts many government officials and citizens in these nations acted on the belief that individual civil liberties should be curtailed to promote national security. Each side, then, argued that they were promoting safety or security of person. The contests that developed as a result were vital test cases for the liberties of citizens in both nations in the twentieth century.

FEMALE WAR SUPPORT AND CONSTRUCTIONS OF WOMEN'S CITIZENSHIP

During the First and Second World Wars, ideas about and rules defining civic roles for residents of Canada and the United States were linked to the traditional Western notion of men's obligation of military service to defend the state as a foundation for citizenship rights. Military service opened the door to other civic rights and privileges, including voting, officeholding, and a military pension, an early form of state welfare.[12] Not all men had equal access to the military because imperialism and racism limited their rights to service and citizenship. As Linda Kerber has demonstrated, Canada and the United States—like most other modern states—did not conscript or call women as a group to regular military service (outside the medical department), and so they were "outside the boundaries of reciprocity and entitlement" that traditionally conferred the rights of citizenship.[13] The links between citizenship and military service were also based on a deep cultural view that cast men as the protectors and women as the protected in families, communities, and the nation, views that scripted propaganda and policy in both conflicts.[14]

During each war, the home-front labor of women and men for munitions and other war supplies, conservation of resources, and civilian funding of the war by purchasing bonds and making charitable contributions was essential for an Allied victory. Policymakers and propagandists therefore defined home-front wage work and volunteerism for the war as the equivalent to military service. This had several consequences for citizenship. One was to militarize women's home-front work by equating it to military service and citizenship for the period of the conflict. As Cynthia Enloe noted, "militarization is the step-by-step process by which something becomes *controlled by, dependent on or derives its value from* the military as an institution or militaristic criteria," such as supporting a national war effort.[15] Expanding opportunities for higher wages and occupational mobility were limited to the period of wartime and did not constitute a revolution in the workplace.

The Struggle for Equal Citizenship during World War I

Women working on the First World War home front in Canada engaged in new wage work, including in the munitions, street-railway, farming, and banking sectors, increasing the female participation in the work force from 1911 to 1921 by some 34 percent.[16] Kori Street consulted oral histories of women wage workers during the conflict and found that middle-class women most often viewed their work as part of a patriotic act of citizenship, while working-class women viewed theirs as pursuing a better economic opportunity. Canadian women pushed many boundaries, but at war's end, Street observed, "Women who were focused on careers and wages were considered to be 'bad girls' "; women who engaged in war work without requesting higher wages or complaining "would be rewarded by marriage." The partial "fluidity" in women's wartime work "did not result in a lasting challenge to, or transformation of, gender ideology . . . Canadian women were not perceived as dangerous enough to warrant the backlash experienced elsewhere."[17]

Maureen Greenwald found similar patterns for US women's wage work, which increased their numbers to some one million during the war years. In addition, women broke barriers into new job categories such as railroads and munitions. World

War I also brought more women in the United States into organized labor; stenographers, railroad workers, and telephone and telegraph operators went on strike for improved wages and working conditions. Women worked within industries to build a more complete economic citizenship. The US Women's Bureau reported that twelve plants had hired African American women as supervisors "because their black employees had demanded it of them."[18]

Moreover, many hundreds of thousands of Canadian and US women engaged in voluntary work on the home front as part of a massive attempt to support the war effort and to link women's participation with patriotic citizenship during the First World War. In Newfoundland, for example, members of the Canadian Women's Patriotic Association translated knitting for the troops to calls for the vote for women at the conclusion of the conflict. Female students at the University of Toronto pledged, as they joined the League of Patriotic Service of Women Students, to "serve the state" and "learn the meaning and responsibility of my citizenship."[19] Some 20,000 women, including students and women employed in cities, joined the US Woman's Land Army of America to replace men on farms, and for their work they received the same wages as men.[20] Across both nations, women engaged in significant volunteer work with the Red Cross, the Young Women's Christian Association, and the Salvation Army.[21]

The war provided an opportunity for women of color and members of ethnic communities to claim a more complete citizenship through wartime service for the state. African American women worked to support Black troops and their families and established local branches of the Emergency Circle of Negro War Relief. In Los Angeles, California, women who were members of racial and ethnic minorities in the city made their claims on patriotic citizenship in ethnically segregated auxiliaries of the Red Cross, including Japanese American and Jewish women. At Brownson House in Los Angeles, a settlement house under Catholic auspices, Mexican American women organized for Red Cross service. African American women worked within the Harriet Tubman and the Phyllis Wheatley Red Cross auxiliaries.[22] Indigenous women of Southern Ontario, Canada, established the Six Nations Women's Patriotic League to channel their own work to support men from their communities in the war effort. As Allison Norman concluded, league members expanded on organizing and campaigning skills developed in wartime to increase involvement in social reform at the conclusion of the conflict.[23]

In Canada and the United States during the First World War, women nurses and physicians sought home-front and military service as a way to enlarge their civic credentials but also as a way to expand their economic citizenship and professionalism. On the home front, these trained women served with the American and Canadian Red Cross and other voluntary organizations, such as the Young Women's Christian Association. Canadian women physicians numbered just under two hundred in the years before the war, and US women reached some 6,000 during the war years.[24] Nurses and physicians used their wartime experience to increase their membership in medical societies and advocated greater professional equality with men in the postwar world.

Women active in the women's movements of both countries struggled for equal citizenship rights long before the war had started. In many American states and in some

Canadian provinces, women had achieved the right to vote before the First World War. During the war, feminists in both nations used their war support to claim a wider female citizenship. They indeed experienced both enhanced opportunities and rewards. Many contemporaries (and later historians) credited women's support of wartime goals with the achievement of national women's suffrage in Canada in 1918 and in the United States in 1920.

But some activist women at the time saw the war as a violation of social justice causes in which they were engaged. Many Montreal suffragists, for example, opposed Canada's Wartime Elections Act of September 1917 that gave voting privileges to women with husbands and sons in the military because they saw it as linking female citizenship to militarism.[25] Members of the militant US National Woman's Party, formed in 1913, protested at the White House and demanded female suffrage. They were jailed. Their critique—the United States was fighting "for democracy" in Europe but denied equal rights to half of the nation—was not well received by the government.[26] Other women, including those who were involved in the peace movement, challenged their nation-states with the view that war had no place in modern society, that women suffered the violent consequences of war and should organize as citizens to oppose it. Women involved in the Socialist Party and organized labor most often viewed war as an aid to capitalist profits and imperialism that would prevent people from experiencing the benefits of citizenship.[27]

Practices of Citizenship during World War II

During the Second World War, women continued to create a link between their home-front war support and citizenship. Because they won the right to vote after World War I, women and their supporters could focus their efforts on equal economic and social citizenship, which would strengthen their ability to practice equal political citizenship. Canadian and US women workers in the war industries—White and African American women as well as Latina—who were needed during wartime and thus presented in war propaganda as "Rosie the Riveter" adapted to the links between home-front wage work and patriotic citizenship. As with World War I, policymakers and industrialists cast the contributions of these women workers as being "for the duration of the war" only and did not invest in infrastructure such as child-care facilities that would have expanded women's economic citizenship in a more permanent way at conflict's end. The Kaiser Shipyards in Portland, Oregon, and Vancouver, Washington, was the exception to this rule. Jeffrey Keshan described Canadian women workers' Second World War experience in wartime wage work as "two steps forward and one step back," and Ruth Pierson noted that Canadian women were "still women after all" and, similar to the situation in World War I, did not experience lasting gains in the workplace. These Canadian scholars, along with Amy Kesselman for the US experience, have shown that women workers faced gender-based discrimination and violence on the job as they made their claims for inclusion as patriotic citizens who did an equal job and asked for equal pay. African

American women endured segregation, poorer pay, and fewer child-care options in the shipyards while they sought a more equitable citizenship by their wartime work.[28]

Yet there were some tangible gains. As Elizabeth Escobedo argued, there was such a demand for aircraft production in Los Angeles from 1939 to peak production in 1943 that companies with wartime contracts sought out Mexicanas, African American women, Filipinas, and a small number of Chinese American women to enable them to keep up production. Los Angeles employers had women of color work side by side with White women, contributing, according to Escobedo, "to some measure of cross-cultural understanding and a breakdown of traditional racial boundaries." Women of color went from domestic service, food processing, and garment-making jobs to other light industry for higher wages, although employers discriminated among White women and women of color regarding types of jobs and wage rates. The production line offered access to the limited, but still important, Fair Employment Practice Committee, which was created in 1941 by the US government to implement Executive Order 8802 by President Franklin D. Roosevelt that banned discriminatory employment practices by federal agencies and all unions and companies engaged in war-related work. Mexicanas who worked in wartime aircraft production and who reflected on their contributions after the war "described their relationship with the United States with possessive pronouns," speaking of "our obligation to our country" and wanting to help "my country." This demonstrated that they "felt a sense of ownership and connection" to the nation, a civic belonging despite their historically outsider status.[29]

Many women wished to maintain the gains they had made in securing economic citizenship during the Second World War in the Canadian and US economy. But in the context of the economic demobilization policy after 1945—similar to the postwar period after the First World War—women were the first fired, and propaganda emphasized traditional roles of motherhood and homemaking; the baby boom that followed the Second World War in both nations was a tangible result of this process.[30] Amy Kesselman's research using oral history interviews suggested that women in the US shipyards handed down the gains they had experienced in wage work and citizenship to their daughters and were a foundation for the women's movement of the 1960s and beyond.[31]

Citizenship and Men's War Service

Another consequence of the linking of home-front work to military service and citizenship was to politicize and militarize men's home front-labor in both the First and the Second World Wars. Policymakers in Canada and the United States defined masculinity as the willingness to serve as a "citizen-soldier" to protect women and home, and for men on the home front, this meant working in essential industries or agriculture. Canada, like Britain, in World War I first used volunteer enlisted soldiers, but with the high numbers of fallen soldiers and volunteers, this was soon insufficient. Canada introduced conscription for the first time with the Military Service Act of August 1917; it followed Britain, which had introduced similar legislation in January 1916. Any exceptions from the Military Service Act were removed in April 1918, up to which time mainly men from eighteen to forty-one years old were liable to be called up for service. In the United States, too, conscription was introduced in World War I. The Selective Service Act of May 1917 required all males aged twenty-one to thirty to register for military service. In August 1918, the original age was extended to eighteen to forty-five. Conscription ended in all three countries in 1919.

After the start of World War II, Britain introduced the National Service Armed Forces Act, which conscripted all men eighteen to forty-one years old. Canada followed and in April 1941 introduced universal conscription. The United States passed the Selective Training and Service Act in September 1940, which required all men between the ages of twenty-one and thirty-five to register with local draft boards. When the United States entered the war, all men between eighteen and forty-five were made subject to military service, and all men aged eighteen to sixty-five were required to register.[32] These conscription laws meant that large numbers of men were *not* involved in fighting at the battlefront, but remained on the home front.

This same construction of masculinity also reflected the social and racial differences in male mobilization for war in these industrializing nations. Conscription in Canada and the United States privileged White, propertied men for deferments during both conflicts, exacerbating racial, ethnic, and class divisions in masculine citizenship achieved by service to the state. In the First World War, constructions of masculinity clearly focused on men as breadwinners. Legislators and administrators reached into wartime home fronts with what became known as "work-or-fight" laws, which benefitted male elites. In rural Southern states, as Jeanette Keith has shown, prominent White men maintained their agricultural work force by influencing draft boards to defer the draft status of African American men who worked for them, and they also demanded deferments for their own sons. This placed the draft burden on poor White men, who saw the conflict as a "rich man's war and a poor man's fight" and who resisted by avoiding the draft. But if men refused military service or did not want to work for the low wages then current, it would lead to crises on both home and war fronts. Legislators thus justified the work-or-fight laws that controlled poor laborers' choices. By May 1918, work or fight was also part of the federal Selective Service Act that controlled conscription. These statutes required men of draft age to be "regularly engaged in some useful employment" or face conscription. Leaders most often targeted African American men and men of other ethnic minority communities. In Georgia, for example, African American men could be punished if they did not carry employment cards with them at all times; those who agitated for better wages received threats of jail or army induction. Whites even used these laws to compel African American women in Southern states to engage in domestic service.[33]

The Canadian government encouraged privileged White men on the home front during World War I to "fight or pay" into a patriotic fund to benefit fighting men's wives, mothers, and children, enabling them to serve as surrogate protectors. Wages in the Canadian Expeditionary Force were too low for most soldiers to continue to support families at home, and the directors of the Canadian Patriotic Fund sought donations for soldiers' families rather than agitating for or legislating higher wages. They targeted men who were not in the military but who still needed to demonstrate their masculinity by being protectors and providers of women on the home front. Prince Arthur, Duke of Connaught, the governor general of Canada and president of the Canadian Patriotic Fund, sent an open letter to Canadians in August 1914 noting the "hardship in many families owing to the absence of the breadwinner" in military service. Contributions to the Canadian Patriotic Fund would "also afford to those who cannot go the opportunity of doing their duty to Canada and the Empire." Posters told home-front men, "When some men are giving their lives—what will you give?"[34] The Canadian Patriotic Fund also gave the Canadian state control over who received benefits according to ideas of "worthy" citizenship and habits of frugality and under which women would be punished for misconduct.[35]

In the United States, the administration of President Woodrow Wilson set up five separate "liberty bond" drives to help finance the war. These drives enabled the support of the Allies with loans and served as a means to finance the US war economy with a total of some $22 million. The administration used a massive propaganda campaign that featured civilians at the backs of larger-than-life soldiers saving European women and children through their liberty loan donations. Secretary of the Treasury William Gibbs McAdoo concluded, "We capitalized [monetized] the profound impulse called patriotism."[36]

Following the worldwide depression of the 1930s, masculinity and citizenship merged in the idea of being a wartime provider and breadwinner who was loyal to the nation's war aims in the Second World War. The Canadian government supported this notion by allowing men to claim up to six months of postponement from military service for "essential farm work" and by subsidizing provincial recruitment and placement of men in agriculture.[37] United States policymakers created a program that broke the link between wartime work and citizenship for Mexican "guest workers" with the Bracero program, which was designed to address agricultural labor shortages but withhold the promise of citizenship for men who worked the fields during the war. Contracts that supposedly secured health care, fair wages, and decent living and working conditions often disintegrated. Some healthcare workers refused to treat men enrolled in the program. "They came with their civil rights protected by contract," Erasmo Gamboa noted, "but those rights were quickly and consistently denied."[38]

But they were not the only men who, according to public discourse and government policy, had no right to citizenship. Conscientious objectors during both world wars, those who avoided the draft and radicals and opponents of the wars, were denied their manhood and thus the right to be "citizens" of the imagined community of the nation— even though they kept their legal citizenship rights in the nation-state. They were labeled "slackers," ineligible for the manly badge of citizenship through wartime service, and they were often disparaged as homosexual. As Margot Canaday demonstrated, this happened when the US government defined "sexual perversion . . . as inversely related to one's desirability for citizenship."[39]

The Limits of Gendered Wartime Citizenship

During both world wars, concepts of citizenship and civil liberties in Canada and the United States related specifically to contemporary definitions and practices of masculinity, femininity, and queer sexuality. Women's citizenship status was linked to models of approved femininity. Across both conflicts, policymakers and propagandists insisted that women could best serve their nation-states as active "patriotic mothers" who raised their children to support and defend the nation in time of war and encouraged their sons to fight for the war effort.[40] Shortly after World War I, in the United States the American Gold Star Mothers, Inc., was formed to provide support for mothers who had lost loved ones during the war. Families of servicemen had the custom of hanging a banner with a single gold star, known as a Service Flag, in the window of their homes, giving this organization its name. Gold Star Mothers and Gold Star Widows were acknowledged and honored because their sons and husbands had died in wartime service. They became one symbol of this definition of feminine citizenship. As Erika Kuhlman has shown, the US government even sponsored Gold Star pilgrimages to France "to reinvigorate nationalist sentiment and re-celebrate" the Allied victory, coopting women's suffering and sacrifice for particular civic definitions of the role of women citizens.[41]

Women who challenged this construction of patriotic femininity in public or even dared to criticize US wartime policies were harassed, charged, and jailed for their stance. In the First World War, as Kathleen Kennedy has demonstrated, they were required to forfeit their citizenship because they challenged the very notion of patriotic motherhood. One example is the Russian American Emma Goldman, a well-known anarchist and political activist who wrote and spoke against conscription. She was sentenced in 1917 to two years of imprisonment for conspiring to "induce persons not to register" for the newly instated draft. After her release from prison, she was arrested—along with hundreds of others—and deported to her native Russia.[42] Another example is Marie Equi, an early female physician, social reformer, and advocate for birth control. She was sent to San Quentin prison in 1918 for speaking out against the war as unfair to soldiers and workers. Her persecution was heightened because of her overt political "radicalism" and her lesbian identity.[43] Kate Richards O'Hare, a member of the American Socialist Party and war opponent, challenged patriotic motherhood directly. She accused the US government of exploiting women by asking them to consent to sending their sons, brothers, and husbands to death. Federal authorities arrested her for violating the Espionage Act of 1917, which criminalized interference with recruitment and enlistment of military personnel.[44] By refusing to adopt the civic qualities of patriotic motherhood, women who opposed the war became "scurrilous citizens" instead.[45] Women also lost their civil liberties when incarcerated, without due process, for venereal disease, which was a measure seen as a wartime "necessity" to protect troops.[46] Similar stories and fates of women opposing war can be found for the Second World War too.[47]

Women who claimed the right to bear arms and support the war actively were also seen as not "fitting in" in Canada and the United States during both wars. If they wanted to be armed to defend the state—and in the case of an occupation also to defend themselves from intimate violence—they were castigated as dangerous, mannish outsiders with no claim to citizenship and safety. Popular magazines and the press portrayed the female soldier as a dangerous, violent lesbian or a reckless heterosexual whose out-of-bounds sexuality, if not curbed, would foil all the efforts of the Allies to win the war.[48]

Likewise, women workers in First World War Canada who labored in "men's industries" and wore "men's clothes" "regularly faced hostility and censure," because they were challenging traditional female roles and crossing gender boundaries, especially if they were so bold as to demand pay equivalent to that of men. Many Canadians saw in them "monstrous" visions of lesbianism or out-of-bounds, unrestrained heterosexuality.[49] Similar experiences affected lesbians during World War II.[50] Deviant sexual behavior was a threat to the dominant gender order, especially in wartime. Yet the mobility of wartime offered the chance for gay men and lesbians to leave families and communities for work and a social life in urban centers that promoted the growth of gay and lesbian subcultures. Wartime "created a setting in which to experience same-sex love, affection and sexuality, and to participate in the group life of gay men and women."[51] They were pursuing their own idea of equal "citizenship."

These examples show that the gendered concepts of citizenship across Canada and the US home fronts in the First and Second World Wars were double-edged swords. By supporting the war effort, linking all actions on the home front to the stated goals of national war fronts, individuals could affirm or expand their claims for a more complete citizenship. Canadians and Americans of color, women, and immigrants who conformed to masculine and feminine ideals of civic status could find some rewards and some progress on the path to citizenship. But those who did not conform faced the denial of their citizenship rights or the possibility of civic status and equality. Disloyalty, pacifism, and opposition to the war, conscientious objection or desertion, socialism or feminism, and the presentation of a homosexual, transgender, or queer identity were all against the proper "qualities of a citizen" necessary for achievement of that civic status.[52]

Across the two conflicts, Canada and the United States honed the "top-down" concept of national citizenship by contrasting it with a sharpened definition of "aliens" as "anti-citizens" and inscribing alienage into law and custom in new ways. In the First World War, both governments established registration and surveillance for enemy aliens and incarcerated others.[53] Their actions drew on the state's growing surveillance apparatus and created new imperatives for citizenship status and new rules for naturalized citizenship. Noncitizen men residing in the United States who had their "first papers" for naturalization but who did not register for the draft were denied the possibility of naturalization after the First World War.[54] By 1918, the Wilson administration decided that all German women residing in the United States would also have to register as enemy aliens. This affected not only women who had been born in Germany. Federal legislation in effect from 1907 to 1922 required women married to noncitizen men to forfeit their US citizenship and take on the nationality of their husbands. This meant that women born in the United States and married to male German citizens also had to register and be surveilled in the United States. In Oregon, almost one-quarter of the 1,484 women who had to register were US-born women. A significant number of these US-born "enemy alien" women resisted registration and the surveillance that accompanied it by protesting the denial of their citizenship. Their registration demonstrated that in matters of citizenship the wartime state placed marriage and "allegiance" to one's husband before personal belief and commitment.[55] Activists worked to gain married women's nationality protections as part of citizenship rights following the conflict.

The mobilization of enemy-alien surveillance, registration, and incarceration in Canada and the United States during the First World War prepared the way for the incarceration of Japanese Americans and Japanese Canadians during the Second World War, many of whom were citizens, and the increased surveillance of and curfews for Italian and German Americans and Canadians. Relocation and incarceration of Japanese Americans and Japanese Canadians, ensured by the force of arms and policy, magnified violence against citizens and residents in the name of national security. There were gendered consequences: Japanese American male citizens who agreed to step from incarceration to military service were redefined as masculine citizens; the "No-No Boys" who would not affirm their loyalty to the United States and agree to serve in the military were deemed cowardly; their masculinity was questioned and some lost their citizenship. In the camps, fathers lost masculine status when they no longer provided or made decisions for family members. Some young women in the camps challenged gendered cultural norms by working for wages, attending college, selecting marriage partners, and making decisions outside parental supervision that led to "relative independence under the duress of incarceration."[56]

LIMITATIONS OF CIVIL LIBERTIES

If wartime citizenship in the United States and Canada during the two world wars was gendered, it was also related directly to home-front conceptions of *armed conflict* and *war*. By definition, these home fronts were both separate from and connected to war fronts and linked to larger civic wartime goals, thereby complicating the concepts of armed conflict and war for participants and for historians. In both conflicts, the Canadian and US governments created powerful rules and propaganda machines to convince or, if need be, force citizens and residents to work in war industries, volunteer their time, and donate money and products to support the war. Violence became a way of enforcing the rules for citizenship and loyalty and limiting civil liberties.

These rules and limitations were imposed through the expansion of an ever more robust state bureaucracy and apparatus for the surveillance of citizens and noncitizens. The US Bureau of Investigation, established in 1908, was active during World War I. Renamed the Federal Bureau of Investigation in 1935, it surveilled Americans of color, women, and pacifists engaged in civil rights activism and those who avoided the draft during World War II.[57] The US military borrowed and adapted surveillance and mass examination techniques from the Bureau of Immigration to police queer people. Psychological testing in both conflicts stigmatized people whose sexuality did not conform to a masculine/feminine binary and challenged their ability to be citizens serving the nation in time of war.[58]

The US and Canadian governments passed legislation restricting civil liberties during the First World War: Canada with the War Measures Act in 1914 and the United States with the Espionage Act of 1917 and the Immigration and Sedition Acts of 1918. Groups such as the American Protective League, which for part of the war was armed and funded by the US government, various "red squads," and other armed groups elided the difference between vigilance and vigilante violence against German Americans and German Canadians, working-class labor union members, and immigrant others. Thousands were persecuted, arrested, and harassed and several were murdered. Governments of both nations responded to fears of radicalism, expanding immigration, and the Russian Revolution with "Red Scares" in the years directly following the First World War.

The US government deported suspected radicals and denied thousands the possibility of naturalized citizenship following the conflict, particularly those who had chosen not to be combatants or who had worked for international peace.[59] Queer people after both conflicts were also targets of campaigns to deny them citizenship or naturalization rights, even rights to cross national boundaries or to obtain employment.[60] Race riots targeting soldiers of color and their families in major cities like Chicago and St. Louis after the First World War and the Zoot Suit Riots in East Los Angeles, in which soldiers persecuted Mexican Americans benefitting from Second World War defense work, challenged the cultural and legal citizenship of members of communities of color at the same time that they galvanized campaigns for social justice. Yet the experience of this armed conflict—a war front on the home fronts—also engendered struggles by activists to challenge this violence and abrogation of citizenship rights and civil liberties, with vigorous civil rights movements and movements for women's liberation after the two world wars.[61]

In the United States, restrictive legislation for immigration and naturalization followed both world wars, including the category of gender identity and sexuality in the rules. Canadian activists worked to prevent similar legislation following the First World War. But legislation in the United States created civic status for some peoples who had been denied it previously. The Indian Citizenship Act of 1924 provided for US citizenship for Native peoples in the United States, but it also challenged tribal sovereignty. Asian Americans, barred from naturalization in the 1920s in the United States, achieved naturalization rights during and after the Second World War. Citizenship in the aftermaths of the conflicts continued to follow gendered prescriptions.[62]

CONCLUSION

Citizens faced a paradox on wartime home fronts during the First and Second World Wars in Canada and the United States. Their nations needed their labor and loyalty in an age of industrialized total war, and these needs provided some room for negotiating steps to a more complete political, economic, and social citizenship during and after the conflict. Women, queer people, working-class citizens, and people of color strove to overcome barriers to voting, to win more complete and equal employment and professional opportunities, and to achieve cultural inclusion. Postwar reconstructions of more traditional rules and roles limited or rolled back some of these accomplishments. Wartime calls for restrictions on civil liberties in the name of national security, as well as the growth of surveillance states to accomplish these restrictions, were particularly devastating to those citizens who challenged national policies and priorities during the conflicts. Yet wartime home fronts provided the context for substantive redefinitions of and claims to civil liberties and citizenship.

For many people in Canada and the United States, the First and Second World Wars raised important questions regarding their citizenship status and their civil rights and civil liberties: Could citizens, male or female, oppose their nation's participation in an armed conflict without being disloyal or unpatriotic, discarding the very tools by which their nations told them citizenship was to be maintained? Was there another vision of citizenship that created a place for dissent and challenged the gendered prescriptions on which civic status was based? Conscientious objectors—both men who challenged the draft and women who supported them—pacifists, socialists, and others who participated in these contests were part of the continuing quest for citizenship, civil rights, and identity in twentieth-century Canada and the United States. Transnational activists who embraced a concept of citizenship over and above the nation-state and people of color who navigated the war and postwar years by linking colonial struggles and race relations on a global scale also challenged gendered and racialized practices of citizenship with alternative models.

These issues suggest many fruitful areas of additional research. Historians of the Canadian and US home fronts during the First and Second World Wars have often separated the analysis of these two conflicts. Comparative studies of the two wars would enhance our understanding of citizenship across these twentieth-century struggles and in national and transnational perspectives. Such a comparative lens also would help us to see that "citizenship" was not a static identity or practice, but a shifting and contested status that had to be achieved again and again in changing circumstances like wartime.

By considering and researching the intersections of gender, race, ethnicity, sexuality, and class, scholars could produce a more complex and nuanced understanding of citizenship and home fronts.

NOTES

1. On the United States, see Edward M. Coffman, *The War to End All Wars: The American Military Experience in World War I* (Lexington: University of Kentucky Press, 1998); Jennifer Keene, *The United States and the First World War* (New York: Longman, 2000); David M. Kennedy, *Over Here: The First World War and American Society* (New York: Oxford University Press, 1980); Christopher Capozzola, *Uncle Sam Wants You: World War I and the Making of the Modern American Citizen* (New York: Oxford University Press, 2008); Tammy Proctor, *Civilians in a World at War: 1914–1918* (New York: New York University Press, 2010); Ronald Takaki, *Double Victory: A Multicultural History of America in World War II* (Boston: Little, Brown, 2000); and Jacques R. Pauwels, *The Myth of the Good War: America in the Second World War* (Toronto: J. Lorimer, 2015). On Canada, see John Swettenham, *Canada and the First World War* (Toronto: Ryerson Press, 1969); and Jeff Keshen, *Saints, Sinners, and Soldiers: Canada's Second World War* (Vancouver: University of British Columbia Press, 2004).

2. On the term *home front*, which is an invention of the war propaganda of World War I, see the chapter by Karen Hagemann and Sonya O. Rose, "War and Gender: The Age of the World Wars and Its Aftermath—an Overview"; and regarding the very different home fronts in Europe during the Age of the World Wars, see Susan R. Grayzel's chapter on "Total Warfare, Gender, and the 'Home Front' in Europe during the First and Second World Wars" in this handbook.

3. Kimberly Jensen, *Mobilizing Minerva: American Woman in the First World War* (Urbana: University of Illinois Press, 2008); Adriane Lentz-Smith, *Freedom Struggles: African Americans and World War I* (Cambridge, MA: Harvard University Press, 2009); Margot Canaday, *The Straight State: Sexuality and Citizenship in Twentieth-Century America* (Princeton, NJ: Princeton University Press, 2009); Takaki, *Double Victory*; and Allan Bérubé, *Coming Out under Fire: The History of Gay Men and Women in World War II* (Chapel Hill: University of North Carolina Press, 2010).

4. Kathleen Kennedy, *Disloyal Mothers and Scurrilous Citizens: Women and Subversion during World War I* (Bloomington: Indiana University Press, 1999); Tetsuden Kashima, *Judgment without Trial: Japanese American Imprisonment during World War II* (Seattle: University of Washington Press, 2003); and Capozzola, *Uncle Sam*.

5. Ruth Lister, *Citizenship: Feminist Perspectives* (New York: New York University Press, 2003), 15.

6. Thomas. H. Marshall, *Citizenship and Social Class, and Other Essays* (Cambridge: Cambridge University Press, 1950).

7. Alice Kessler-Harris, *In Pursuit of Equity: Women, Men, and the Quest for Economic Citizenship in 20th-Century America* (New York: Oxford University Press, 2001), 4.

8. Ruth Lister et al., *Citizenship in Western Europe: New Challenges for Citizenship Research in a Cross-National Context* (Bristol: Policy Press, 2007), 168.

9. Martha Gardner, *The Qualities of a Citizen: Women, Immigration, and Citizenship, 1870–1965* (Princeton, NJ: Princeton University Press, 2005); also Canaday, *Straight State*; Capozzola, *Uncle Sam*; and Capozzola, "Legacies for Citizenship: Pinpointing Americans during and after World War I," *Diplomatic History* 38, no. 4 (2014): 713–26.

10. Joan Hoff, *Law, Gender, and Injustice: A Legal History of U.S. Women* (New York: New York University Press, 1991), 14; and the Universal Declaration of Human Rights, United Nations General Assembly, December 10, 1948, accessed September 11, 2015, http://www.un.org/en/documents/udhr/index.shtml. The Canadian Parliament did not enact a bill of rights until 1960.

11. Capozzola, *Uncle Sam*, 144–45.

12. See, for example, Theda Skocpol, *Protecting Soldiers and Mothers: The Political Origins of Social Policy in the United States* (Cambridge, MA: Harvard University Press, 1992).

13. Linda K. Kerber, *No Constitutional Right to Be Ladies: Women and the Obligations of Citizenship* (New York: Hill & Wang, 1998), 223.

14. Judith Hicks Stiehm, "The Protected, the Protector, the Defender," *Women's Studies International Forum* 5 (1982): 367–76.

15. Cynthia Enloe, *Maneuvers: The International Politics of Militarizing Women's Lives* (Berkeley: University of California Press, 2000), 291, emphasis in the quote.

16. On the inclusion of women in war industries in Europe, see Grayzel, "Total Warfare" in this handbook.

17. Kori Street, "Patriotic, Not Permanent: Attitudes about Women's Making Bombs and Being Bankers," in *A Sisterhood of Suffering and Service: Women and Girls of Canada and Newfoundland during the First World War*, ed. Sarah Glassford and Amy Shaw (Vancouver: University of British Columbia Press, 2012), 148–70, 149.

18. Maurine Greenwald, *Women, War, and Work: The Impact of World War I on Women Workers in the United States* (Westport, CT: Greenwood Press, 1980), 42 and 93.

19. Margot I. Duley, "The Unquiet Knitters of Newfoundland: From Mothers of the Regiment to Mothers of the Nation," in Glassford and Shaw, *A Sisterhood*, 51–74; and Terry Wilde, "Freshettes, Farmerettes, and Feminine Fortitude at the University of Toronto during the First World War," in ibid., 75–97.

20. Elaine F. Weiss, *Fruits of Victory: The Woman's Land Army of America in the Great War* (Washington, DC: Potomac Books, 2008).

21. Capozzola, *Uncle Sam*, 83–103; and Wilde, "Freshettes, Farmerettes." See also the chapter by Jean H. Quataert on "Changing Modes of Warfare and the Gendering of Military Medical Care, 1850s–1920s" in this handbook.

22. Nikki Brown, *Private Politics and Public Voices: Black Women's Activism from World War I to the New Deal* (Bloomington: Indiana University Press, 2006), 1–29; and Lynn Dumenil, "Women's Reform Organizations and Wartime Mobilization in World War I–Era Los Angeles," *Journal of the Gilded Age and Progressive Era* 10, no. 2 (2011): 213–45.

23. Allison Norman, "'In Defense of the Empire': The Six Nations of the Grand River and the Great War," in Glassford and Shaw, *A Sisterhood*, 29–50.

24. Jensen, *Mobilizing Minerva*, 75–115 and 116–41; and Jensen, "Volunteers, Auxiliaries, and Women's Mobilization: The First World War and Beyond," in *The Brill Companion to Women's Military History*, ed. Barton C. Hacker and Margaret Vining (Leiden: Brill, 2012), 189–232.

25. Tarah Brookfield, "Divided by the Ballot Box: The Montreal Council of Women and the Election of 1917," *Canadian Historical Review* 89, no. 4 (2008): 473–501.

26. See Katherine H. Adams and Michael L. Keene, *Alice Paul and the American Suffrage Campaign* (Urbana: University of Illinois Press, 2007).

27. Frances H. Early, *A World without War: How U.S. Feminists and Pacifists Resisted World War I* (Syracuse, NY: Syracuse University Press, 1997); and Erika A. Kuhlman, *Petticoats and White Feathers: Gender Conformity, Race, the Progressive Peace Movement, and the Debate over War, 1895–1919* (Westport, CT: Greenwood Press, 1997), 73–100.

28. Keshen, *Saints, Sinners*; Ruth Pierson, *"They're Still Women after All": The Second World War and Canadian Womanhood* (Toronto: McClelland and Stewart, 1986); and Amy Kesselman, *Fleeting Opportunities: Women Shipyard Workers in Portland and Vancouver during World War II and Reconversion* (Albany: State University of New York Press, 1990).

29. Elizabeth Rachel Escobedo, *From Coveralls to Zoot Suits: The Lives of Mexican American Women on the World War II Home Front* (Chapel Hill: University of North Carolina Press, 2013), 73–101, quotes 74 and 76.

30. Kesselman, *Fleeting Opportunities*, 91–133; Escobedo, *From Coveralls*, 74; and Laura McEnaney, "A Women's Peace Divided: Demobilization and Working Class Women in Chicago, 1945–1953," in *Gender and the Long Postwar: The United States and the Two Germanys, 1945–1989*, ed. Karen Hagemann and Sonya Michel (Baltimore: Johns Hopkins University Press, 2014), 73–94.

31. Kesselman, *Fleeting Opportunities*, 126–33.

32. See George Q. Flynn, *Conscription and Democracy: The Draft in France, Great Britain, and the United States* (Westport, CN: Greenwood Press, 2002), esp. 9–64.

33. Jeanette Keith, *Rich Man's War, Poor Man's Fight: Race, Class and Power in the Rural South during the First World War* (Chapel Hill: University of North Carolina Press, 2004), 126–34; and Capozzola, *Uncle Sam*, 36.

34. Desmond Morton, *Fight or Pay: Soldiers Families in the Great War* (Vancouver: University of Vancouver Press, 2004), 62; and Morton, "Supporting Soldiers' Wives and Families in the Great War: What Was Transformed?," in Glassford and Shaw, *A Sisterhood*, 195–218, 201.

35. Morton, "Supporting Soldiers' Wives," 212.

36. Kennedy, *Over Here*, 93–106, quote 105.

37. Keshen, *Saints, Sinners*, 68–69.

38. Erasmo Gamboa, "Braceros in the Pacific Northwest: Laborers on the Domestic Front, 1942–1947," *Pacific Historical Review* 56, no. 3 (1987): 378–98, 398.

39. Canaday, *Straight State*, 23; and Rachel Waltner Goosen, *Women against the Good War: Conscientious Objection and Gender on the American Home Front, 1941–1947* (Chapel Hill: University of North Carolina Press, 1997).

40. Barbara J. Steinson, *American Women's Activism in World War I* (New York: Garland, 1982); and Kennedy, *Disloyal Mothers*.

41. Erika Kuhlman, *Of Little Comfort: War Widows, Fallen Soldiers, and the Remaking of the Nation after the Great War* (New York: New York University Press, 2012), 70.

42. See Paul Avrich and Karen Avrich, *Sasha and Emma: The Anarchist Odyssey of Alexander Berkman and Emma Goldman* (Cambridge, MA: Harvard University Press, 2012).

43. Michael Helquist, *Marie Equi: Radical Politics and Outlaw Passions* (Corvallis: Oregon State University Press, 2015).

44. Sally M. Miller, *From Prairie to Prison: The Life of Social Activist Kate Richards O'Hare* (Columbia: University of Missouri Press, 1993).

45. Kennedy, *Disloyal Mothers*.

46. Nancy K. Bristow, *Making Men Moral: Social Engineering during the Great War* (New York: New York University Press, 1996).

47. See Goosen, *Women against*.

48. Jensen, *Mobilizing Minerva*, 60–76.

49. Street, "Patriotic, Not Permanent," 152.

50. See Bérubé, *Coming Out*.

51. John D'Emilio and Estelle B. Freedman, *Intimate Matters: A History of Sexuality in America*, 2nd ed. (Chicago: University of Chicago Press, 1997), 289.

52. Gardner, *Qualities*.

53. Bohdan S. Kordan, *Enemy Aliens, Prisoners of War: Internment in Canada during the Great War* (Montreal: McGill–Queen's University Press, 2002); Proctor, *Civilians*, 203–38; and Capozzola, *Uncle Sam*, 173–205.

54. Candice Bredbenner, "A Duty to Defend? The Evolution of Alien's Military Obligations to the United States, 1792–1946," *Journal of Policy History* 24, no. 2 (2012): 224–62.

55. Kimberly Jensen, "From Citizens to Enemy Aliens: Oregon Women, Marriage, and the Surveillance State during the First World War," *Oregon Historical Quarterly* 114, no. 4 (2014): 453–73.

56. Kashima, *Judgment without Trial*; and Valerie Matsumoto, "Japanese American Women during World War II," *Frontiers: A Journal of Women Studies* 8, no. 1 (1984): 6–14.

57. Mark Ellis, *Race, War and Surveillance: African Americans and the United States Government during World War I* (Bloomington: Indiana University Press, 2001); Capozzola, *Uncle Sam*; and Keith, *Rich Man's*, 135–361.

58. Canady, *Straight State*.

59. Bredbenner, "A Duty," 224–62.

60. Canady, *Straight State*; David K. Johnson, *The Lavender Scare: The Cold War Persecution of Gays and Lesbians in the Federal Government* (Chicago: University of Chicago Press, 2006); and Daniel J. Robinson and David Kimmel, "The Queer Career of Homosexual Security Vetting in Cold War Canada," *Canadian Historical Review* 75, no. 3 (1994): 321–45.

61. Lentz-Smith, *Freedom Struggles*; and George Sanchez, *Becoming Mexican American: Ethnicity, Culture, and Identity in Chicano Los Angeles, 1900–1945* (Oxford: Oxford University Press, 1993).

62. Gardner, *Qualities*.

SELECT BIBLIOGRAPHY

Bristow, Nancy K. *Making Men Moral: Social Engineering during the Great War*. New York: New York University Press, 1996.

Bruce, Jean. *Back the Attack! Canadian Women during the Second World War, at Home and Abroad*. Toronto: Macmillan, 1985.

Capozzola, Christopher. *Uncle Sam Wants You: World War I and the Making of the Modern American Citizen*. New York: Oxford University Press, 2008.

Coffman, Edward M. *The War to End All Wars: The American Military Experience in World War I*. Lexington: University of Kentucky Press, 1998.

Glassford, Sarah, and Amy Shaw, eds. *A Sisterhood of Suffering and Service: Women and Girls of Canada and Newfoundland during the First World War*. Vancouver: University of British Columbia Press, 2012.

Gluck, Sherna Berger. *Rosie the Riveter Revisited: Women, the War, and Social Change*. Boston: Plume, 1987.

Jensen, Kimberly. *Mobilizing Minerva: American Women in the First World War*. Urbana: University of Illinois Press, 2008.

Kashima, Tetsuden. *Judgment without Trial: Japanese American Imprisonment during World War II*. Seattle: University of Washington Press, 2003.

Keith, Jeanette. *Rich Man's War, Poor Man's Fight: Race, Class, and Power in the Rural South during the First World War*. Chapel Hill: University of North Carolina Press, 2004.

Kennedy, David M. *Over Here: The First World War and American Society*. Oxford: Oxford University Press, 2004.

Kennedy, Kathleen. *Disloyal Mothers and Scurrilous Citizens: Women and Subversion during World War I*. Bloomington: Indiana University Press, 1999.

Kerber, Linda K. *No Constitutional Right to Be Ladies: Women and the Obligations of Citizenship*. New York: Hill & Wang, 1998.

Keshen, Jeffrey A. *Saints, Sinners, and Soldiers: Canada's Second World War*. Vancouver: University of British Columbia Press, 2004.

Kordan, Bohdan S. *Enemy Aliens, Prisoners of War: Internment in Canada during the Great War*. Montreal: McGill–Queen's University Press, 2002.

Lentz-Smith, Adriane Danette. *Freedom Struggles: African Americans and World War I*. Cambridge, MA: Harvard University Press, 2009.

Lister, Ruth. *Citizenship: Feminist Perspectives*. New York: New York University Press, 2003.

Pauwels, Jacques R. *The Myth of the Good War: America in the Second World War*. Toronto: James Lorimer, 2002.

Pierson, Ruth Roach. *"They're Still Women after All": The Second World War and Canadian Womanhood*. Toronto: McClelland & Stewart, 1986.

Weatherford, Doris. *American Women during World War II: An Encyclopedia*. New York: Routledge, 2010.

Yellin, Emily. *Our Mothers' War: American Women at Home and at the Front during World War II*. New York: Free Press, 2004.

CHAPTER 19

....

HISTORY AND MEMORY OF FEMALE MILITARY SERVICE IN THE AGE OF WORLD WARS

....

KAREN HAGEMANN

"War drama stirs Germany on," wrote the tabloid *Berliner Kurier* in large letters on its title page after the broadcasting of the three-part television series *Our Mothers—Our Fathers* in March 2013.[1] More than seven million Germans, 20 percent of the total television audience, watched this primetime series produced by the ZDF, one of the country's two leading public broadcasters. The production was accompanied by a ZDF documentary and several talk shows.[2] Marketed to the English-speaking audience under the title *Generation War*, the series portrays World War II in Germany and eastern Europe, including atrocities perpetrated by the German Wehrmacht and its important role in the Holocaust, and explores the question of ordinary Germans' responsibility for such crimes. It tracks the fates of five childhood friends from Berlin—three men and two women—between 1941 and the end of the war in 1945.[3]

For German television viewers, the series was indeed stirring and challenging because it questions the myth of the unsullied Wehrmacht soldiers and demands that viewers reflect on their own family histories. It asks who knew and who was involved in which ways. In the extensive and controversial media discussion, film critics, journalists, and historians criticized many aspects of the series as too stereotypical, for example, the portrayal of Polish antisemitism, but one key aspect went unnoticed: this new series confirms old stereotypes about the World War II gender order.[4] German women are presented solely as caring nurses, worried mothers of soldiers, Nazi mistresses, or victims of Nazi persecution. The only counterimages are a female Red Army officer and a Polish girl who is forced into slave labor, escapes, and then joins the partisan movement. The series ignores the reality that women in the Third Reich supported the Nazi regime and were active in the Second World War far beyond wartime nursing work. The series offered not even a hint of the fact that every twentieth soldier in the Wehrmacht was a female auxiliary, and many of them served in the east.

To be sure, it is especially challenging to German memory of the Second World War and the Holocaust to recall the extensive, active war support of German women, because such recollections make it far more difficult to construe Germans as victims of World War II. But recent television series and movies in the former Allied powers also suffer from this blind spot concerning women's roles as auxiliaries and soldiers in both world wars. The productions show them as nurses serving at Gallipoli during World War I, as in the 2014 Australian ABC series *Anzac Girls*,[5] or as nurses at the western front in the same conflict, as in the 2014 BBC production *Crimson Field*[6]; as women serving in the Women's Land Army or working at the rural "home front" during World War II, as in the BBC series *Land Girls* from 2009 and *Home Fires* from 2015.[7] Only in the 2012 Canadian television series *Bomb Girls*, about women working in a munitions factory during the Second World War, are female auxiliaries presented at the margins of the main story.[8] Movies about the two world wars also tend to show women primarily in these roles or as victims of war and violence. At best, women feature as heroines of the resistance, as in the 2008 French film *Female Agents*, or as members of the intelligence corps, such as in the 2014 British movie *The Imitation Game*.[9]

Judging by most monographs and textbooks published in recent years, historians generally agree with such public recollections. In these texts, women are rarely portrayed as active participants in the wars beyond their work at the home front and war nursing.[10] This omission is all the more remarkable, because today we can look back on nearly three decades of research on gender, the military, and war, which has devoted the greatest attention to the Age of the World Wars. The history of women serving in growing numbers and different functions in the military is one subject of this research.[11] The question, thus, is why not only contemporaries, but also later generations, found it such a challenge to recognize the increasingly active participation of women in the militaries of the two world wars.

To answer this question, it is not enough to simply extend military history to "women's military history" and look at the female contribution to the military and war. Instead, we need a gender perspective, an approach that defines *gender* as both a subject and a method and uses it as a context-specific and relational concept.[12] Only then we can understand the importance of the military as a gender-defining institution far beyond armed conflict and war, along with the motives for enduring policies that define combat as a male reserve.[13] Furthermore, we need a comparative perspective that helps to reveal differences and similarities in the development of women's military service over time and between war powers. The research is best developed on the regular militaries of Britain, France, Germany, Russia, and the United States, as well as on the partisan armies of eastern and southern Europe.[14] Finally, it is important to look beyond auxiliaries, female soldiers, and partisans to other forms of military employment of women, especially in the medical service. Most wartime and postwar cultures accepted nurses as the complementary female "Other" to male soldiers, but in some militaries, like the Russian army, women were also used as both "paramedics" and soldiers.[15] Based on these considerations, three themes will stand at the center of the following: the relation between war, violence, and the gender order; the extent of women's participation in military service during World Wars I and II in different countries; and the attempts to reorder postwar societies and regender war memories.

VIOLENCE AND THE GENDER ORDER OF WARS

At its core, war is the execution and experience of violence, marked by the human "power to injure" and "vulnerability to injury." The organization and practice of war changes over time and depending on the conflict and context, but this quintessence remains the same. Such an understanding of war that places the execution and experience of violence at the center helps us to comprehend why female auxiliaries, soldiers, and partisans—notwithstanding their relatively small numbers—disrupted everywhere the existing gender order in both world wars, regardless of the states' and regions' divergent economic, social, and political systems. Since antiquity, the ability and the right to exercise organized and armed violence has been connoted as "masculine."[16] In the Age of Revolutions, however, the power to injure was associated even more universally as male and vulnerability to injury as female. This attribution became cemented in the context of continuing warfare during the French Revolutionary and Napoleonic Wars (1792–1815), because in pervasive patriotic-national propaganda, the new form of mass warfare based on volunteer units, militias, or universal conscription essentially assigned all men the duty to defend family, home, and country during wartime.

At the same time, because of the new link between military service and political rights, which gained increasing influence from the French Revolution (1789–99) on, women were not only excluded from state affairs and the active and passive suffrage, but also accorded the primary duty of being housewives and mothers, regardless of social distinctions. In this imagined gender order of the nineteenth- and twentieth-century nation-states, military service and with it the male right—and, in wartime, duty—to kill was the very heart of the gendered differentiation of men from women, even in peacetime. The female complement in wartime was the responsibility for charity and nursing inside and, in cases of "national emergency," also outside the home. Politics and propaganda in the Age of the World Wars could fall back on these entrenched ideas of the national gender order of war.[17]

Twentieth-century *total wars* and their gender order were nevertheless distinct from earlier conflicts. The difference lies mainly in the scale of the industrialization of warfare, which led to its further globalization and "totalization." The result was the erasure of the boundaries distinguishing the front from the homeland, defined as the *home front* since World War I. One central marker of this development was the blurring of gender lines. On the one hand, civilians became a major target of warfare through different forms of mass violence, which encompassed occupation, bombing, genocide, and sexual violence in various forms. On the other hand, women were increasingly needed for war support; for work in war administration and industries, war charity, and war nursing; and, especially during the Second World War, for service in the military itself as auxiliaries, soldiers, and partisans. We can observe these developments in different theaters of war and the various war powers, in state warfare, and in civil war, guerrilla war, and the armed anticolonial struggles of the Age of the World Wars.[18] As a result of the blurring of gender lines in total warfare, involvement in the military per se could no longer function as the core marker of gender difference; instead, it shifted to participation in combat as a supposedly "masculine preserve."

WOMEN SERVING THE MILITARY DURING WORLD WAR I

During the First World War, the powers in both camps employed women in their war efforts from August 1914 to November 1918. This was true for the Allies—based on the Triple Entente of the Russian Empire, the French Third Republic, and the United Kingdom in coalition with several other nations including the United States—and the Central Powers of Germany, Austria-Hungary, and other countries fighting in alliance with them. The longer the war lasted, the more the armed forces' manpower needs increased as a result of the development of mass armies and the accompanying mass losses. World War I was the first highly industrialized mass war during which women were mobilized not only for support of the home front, but also for service in and for the military. Compared to the Second World War, however, the number of women serving in the military was still quite small. Mainly, the growing manpower needs of the armed forces led to the entry of women into the military at all, despite determined resistance inside the military and in society.

The French military employed more women than any other armed forces during World War I, a total of some 120,000 by its end.[19] But different from women serving the other major war powers, these women were only hired as civilian clerical and domestic workers. Furthermore, the French army preferred local women because they could live at home, confined to a familiar environment and under the control of their families. Only for more skilled and specialized jobs such as telephone operators or drivers did the military recruit nonlocal women. One motive for this policy was that the military leadership suspected working women of being "incompetent and promiscuous."[20]

In addition, war-weary ordinary soldiers resented these women, because in their perception, they helped to release men for front-line service and thus prolonged the war. Prejudices like these were one reason why the French government never formed women's voluntary battalions for auxiliaries. Instead, it called on women to actively support the *union sacrée*, the political truce in France to which all parties including the

Left agreed during World War I, a concept similar to the German *Burgfrieden* (literally, castle peace). In the name of patriotism, nobody was to oppose the government or call any strikes. Like their British and German counterparts, French women were encouraged to create charitable organizations and perform the necessary services at the home front, especially the work in the war industries, to free men for service in battle.[21]

Next to France, the United Kingdom mobilized the largest number of women for military service; some 80,000 to 90,000 served as army auxiliaries over the course of the war.[22] Britain was the only power that started the war with a professional, volunteer army. Mounting losses made it obvious that this traditional system of military recruitment could not compete with the other armed forces based on universal conscription. In January 1916, the Parliament therefore passed the Military Service Act introducing conscription of men for the armed forces, which came into effect in March 1916. This change was accompanied by a reconsideration of the role of women in the war efforts. Already in the first year of the war, the press occasionally demanded that women undertake service alongside men; starting in 1915, this demand was made more often, leading to a fundamental change in debate.[23] From 1916, the press reported that large parts of the public and even the government now called for women's service, not only for war industries, war charity, and war nursing, but also for the military itself. This development led to the establishment of the Women's Army Auxiliary Corps (WAAC) in March 1917, of the Women's Royal Naval Service in November 1917, and of the Women's Royal Air Force in April 1918.[24] The members of these units wore specially designed "feminine but not too feminine" uniforms,[25] were subject to direct military authority, and worked mainly in four types of jobs: domestic, cookery, mechanical, and clerical. As in France, the British female replacements freed male soldiers for front-line duty, which did not make them popular among the rank and file either.[26]

The WAAC was the largest corps, with up to 57,000 women in its service. Approximately 7,000 of these women were sent to the western front in Belgium and France, where they repeatedly came under fire during the German offensive of 1918, in which at least nine women died. The excellent conduct of the WAAC led to Queen Mary becoming its patron. In April 1918, it was renamed Queen Mary's Army Auxiliary Corps (QMAAC). Its slogan, distributed widely with its posters, became "The GIRL behind the man behind the gun" (Figure 19.1).[27] The majority of the female auxiliaries came from the working and lower-middle classes. They were closely supervised by the largely upper-class women administrators of the WAAC and the QMAAC who believed that they were better prepared to understand the "notions of duty, honour, sacrifice and moral rectitude, which those serving the nation were expected to embody."[28] As part of the postwar demobilization, the QMAAC was disbanded in September 1921.

Germany's Supreme Army Command, in collaboration with the War Office (*Kriegsamt*), which was founded in November 1916 to centralize the organization of the war economy, deployed women in military service too. In March 1917, 56,900 women had already replaced male military personnel in the army administration. This was not enough, however, because the army's replacement problems continued to grow with the increasing number of fallen soldiers. The War Office planned to substitute women for at least

FIGURE 19.1 *The Girl behind the Man behind the Gun,* British poster published by the Queen Mary's Army Auxiliary Corps during World War I to mobilize women to join the corps as volunteers, by unknown artist, London, 1918.

75,300 additional soldiers over the summer. Subsequently, they were also hired as rear-area auxiliaries (*Etappenhelferinnen*) who were supposed to work in the immediate vicinity of the battle zone, where they faced the same dangers as the male soldiers serving next to them. Yet, they were considered merely part of the *Heeresgefolge* (literally, the army's entourage), not military personnel. Female rear-area auxiliaries replaced company clerks and staff sergeants in many positions, for example, in the aircraft, mechanical transport, ordnance, and telephone services along with the field-recruiting, railway, munitions, and material depots. They also assisted officers in the inspection and requisitioning of horses.[29] A remarkably large number of women took advantage of this new opportunity for military service, which offered a salary higher than the average for female employees in most factories and offices. By the end of the war, they numbered more than 20,000. But, much like the British and French, many German soldiers in the rear area and on the front met them with hostility and accused them of prolonging the war unnecessarily.[30]

The German War Office's final attempt to marshal female labor for military service was a decree of July 1918 on the establishment of a Women's Signal Corps (*Nachrichtenkorps*) modeled on the British WAAC.[31] This decree was intended as a solution to the worsening problem of replacing killed and wounded soldiers.[32] The Supreme Army Command hoped that the establishment of this new corps would allow them to free up "100,000 men as soon as possible."[33] Given this lofty goal, they promoted the new corps with all the available means of modern communication: print advertisements, posters, and even the new medium of film.[34] Similar to the enemy powers, the German government sought to attract educated young women as telephone, telegraph, and radio operators because it believed that only they could be trusted to operate the signal services competently after just four weeks of training. These women had to sign up for twelve months of service, during which time they were subject to military law. Unlike the rear-area auxiliaries, *Nachrichtlerinnen* were legally recognized as "military persons" and thus wore uniforms.[35] The decree officially integrated German women into the army for the first time and placed them under military law, albeit for a very short time, because the war ended soon thereafter.[36]

When the United States entered the war in April 1917, it also marked the first time in its history that the military employed a large number of women; 12,000 women in total served as yeomen for the US Navy and Marine Corps in clerical and recruiting positions and naval intelligence. A handful served in the Coast Guard as well.[37] Other women worked for the US Army overseas, mainly as clerical and domestic workers. In addition, approximately 6,000 female auxiliaries worked for officially recognized welfare organizations in France: 3,198 with the Young Men's Christian Association, 2,503 with the American Red Cross, and the rest with other organizations.[38] The US military refused to officially enlist women in its service and, as such, did not assign them special uniforms. Like the French military, it relied on women as contract employees and civilian volunteers, but they did not arrive overseas in large numbers until August 1918. Their service peaked well after the armistice, in the demobilization period that extended into the summer of 1919.[39]

Russia was the only country that systematically employed women not just as auxiliaries for the military, but also in combat roles. The February Revolution of 1917 that deposed the tsar and the Russian army's struggles with war-weary soldiers and deserters made this possible. Historian Laurie S. Stoff even spoke of a "women's military movement" in Russia in 1917, a "grassroots initiative" starting in May 1917, when "organizations devoted to women's participation in the military were established in many cities" in which "thousands of women" became involved.[40] The government led by the socialist Mensheviks enlisted some 6,000 women in all-female combat units. One of the best known was the so-called Battalion of Death. Their main function was to "shame the soldiers into battle," as Maria Bochkareva, the leader of this famous battalion, wrote in her 1919 memoirs.[41] The patriotic, progovernment public presented Bochkareva as a "Russian Joan of Arc, out to save the nation from destruction," as Stoff observed. Most ordinary soldiers, in contrast, reviled Bochkareva and the battalion for the attempt to prolong the hated war.[42] The female combat units, however, were only short-lived. The communist Bolsheviks disbanded them following the October Revolution of 1917, but some of their members continued to fight against the Bolsheviks in the ensuing Russian Civil War that continued until 1922.[43]

Many more women labored in wartime industry to free men for service or volunteered for war charity at home or nursing close to the front lines. World War I was the first conflict in which professionally trained female nurses, many affiliated with the Red Cross, worked alongside female volunteers.[44] One well-known association was the British Voluntary Aid Detachment (VAD), a female corps formed by the British Red Cross in 1908. It organized the work of 38,000 volunteer hospital nurses, ambulance drivers, and cooks. The Voluntary Aid Detachment supported the work of approximately 10,000 professional nurses, most of whom were organized under the Queen Alexandra's Imperial Military Nursing Service formed in 1902.[45]

In Germany, 28,000 women volunteered as war nurses, 19,800 of them with the German Red Cross (DRK), which was founded in 1863. The DRK had trained professional nurses in cooperation with the patriotic women's associations in different German states since the German Wars of Unification (1864–71).[46] In the United States, the Army and Navy Nurse Corps were established in 1901 and 1908, respectively, as permanent corps within the US Army and Navy Medical Departments. During World War I, its nurses—solely White women were allowed—were the only group of women employed as military personnel by the armed forces. More than 21,500 of them served in the Army Nurse Corps, 10,700 of them overseas with the American Expeditionary Forces.[47] In France, the medical service of the army, the Red Cross, and the Catholic nursing orders had worked together already before the war; subsequently, at the beginning of World War I, 29,000 Red Cross nurses were mobilized as volunteers who received no pay. In total, the French Red Cross sent 63,000 nurses to the military hospitals and medical units on the front lines.[48]

In all these countries, only middle- and upper-class women could afford to volunteer for nursing, however, because they could pay for the costs of training and did not have to work for a living. Different from auxiliaries, nurses received only a small allowance or

FIGURE 19.2 *Belgian Red Cross. Donations may be sent to the Hon. Treasurer, the Rht. Hon. the Lord Mayor of London, or to the President, Baron C. Goffinet,* poster by the British Red Cross calling for donations, designed by Charles Buchel (1872–1950), London, 1915.

(Library of Congress, Prints and Photographs Division, Washington DC, LC-USZC4-11243)

no payment at all.[49] Large segments of the bourgeois women's movement encouraged and organized professional and voluntary female war support because they hoped that women finally would gain the right to vote after they had demonstrated patriotism. They equated female war support at the home front and female war nursing with male military service at the battlefront.[50] The contemporary public responded favorably to this argument. Even after the war, the "sacrifice for the fatherland" by war nurses was put on par with the front-line service of soldiers. Already during the war, nurses were depicted in the war propaganda as the angels of the soldiers (Figure 19.2). Female auxiliaries, by contrast, were perceived with far more moral reservation and even rejection during and after the war, and they were excluded from national war memories.[51]

The end of the war brought with it the challenges of demobilization. As the armed forces made the transition from war to peace, they found women nurses, physicians, office clerks, and workers to be expendable. Like most female workers in the war industries, their contracts were terminated. The armies closed ranks and became again all-male institutions. One exception was postwar Weimar Germany. Because the June 1919 Treaty of Versailles restricted the German armed forces to 100,000 soldiers, the army assigned all tasks that were not strictly military to civilian employees in order to work around the size limit. In this way, women were deployed as civilians in many areas of the Reichswehr during the Weimar Republic, for example, in the armed forces' industrial enterprises, uniform-supply departments, munitions depots, and the many offices of military administration. Women worked as seamstresses, cooks, and semiskilled workers, but they also performed administrative duties and served as telephone operators. The Reichswehr even used them as volunteer aircraft-reporting auxiliaries (*Flugmeldehelferinnen*) in its secret air-watch detachments (*Flugwachkommando*). Women, however, were generally excluded from combat units, where men performed even all the administrative and clerical tasks otherwise given to women in noncombat formations.[52] Despite women's greater participation in the postwar German military, these practices did not change the fact that Germany, similar to the victorious postwar societies in the West, emphasized the importance of returning women to their homes. The family became the most important institution for the integration of returning soldiers into civilian life and healing the wounds of war.[53]

WOMEN IN MILITARY SERVICE
DURING WORLD WAR II

Preparations for the Second World War began on the European continent long before the conflict itself. A striking first sign that Nazi Germany was preparing for a new war was the reintroduction of universal conscription through the Reich Defense Law of May 1935, which was in contravention of the Treaty of Versailles. It also provided the legal basis for compulsory service for women by noting in its introductory stipulations that "in case of war, above and beyond compulsory military service, every German man and every German woman is obliged to serve the fatherland." This and other measures indicated from the very beginning that the Nazi state and its military envisioned a highly industrialized mass war for which they intended to mobilize the entire German population.[54] And, indeed, during the Second World War, to a far greater degree than during the first, warfare was marked by the mass deployments of people and the large-scale use of highly developed military technology, powerful equipment, and new forms of communications. Most important, this conflict was a war of conquest and annihilation driven by the imperialist and racist aims of the Third Reich.[55]

As studies such as Wendy Lower's 2013 book on German women in the Nazi killing fields showed, women were intensively involved in the genocidal warfare.[56] The number of German Red Cross nurses and nurses' aides grew from 15,000 at the beginning of the war to 414,000 in 1943; of them, approximately 12,890 were professional nurses, 57,463 nursing auxiliaries, and 343,009 DRK aides (67 percent of all DRK aides). In addition, 638 women served as DRK doctors (12 percent of all DRK doctors).[57] The number of women deployed as Wehrmacht auxiliaries also rose sharply. In 1939–40, the army had recruited some 140,000 women (50,000 as clerks and 90,000 as wage workers); in 1943–44, the figure was 320,000, of whom 300,000 were deployed with the reserve army (*Ersatzheer*), 12,500 as staff auxiliaries, and 8,000 as signal auxiliaries with the field army and in the occupied territories. In addition, the air force employed 130,000 women in 1943–44, among other things, as air force auxiliaries (*Luftwaffenhelferinnen*). At this point, a further 20,000 women were deployed by the navy, mostly as naval auxiliaries (*Marinehelferinnen*).[58] By the end of the war, more than 500,000 women served in the Wehrmacht, 160,000 of whom were flak-gun auxiliaries (*Flakwaffenhelferinnen*) in the antiaircraft defense organized by the air force.[59]

In postwar autobiographies, most women who had served as Wehrmacht auxiliaries excused their actions with the claim that they had been conscripted. In fact, this was only the case for at most half of all female Wehrmacht auxiliaries: only young women aged seventeen to twenty-five who were serving since 1941. Two personal decrees issued by Chancellor Adolf Hitler in June and July of that year on the "further wartime deployment of the Reich Labor Service for female youth" (RAD) permitted the enlistment of RAD girls for twelve months as wartime auxiliary service girls (*Kriegshilfsdienstmaiden*). Thus, particularly during the first two years of the war, a large number must have volunteered for military service, many because they had grown up in the Nazi youth organizations and believed in Nazi ideology.[60] Women also voluntarily joined the female auxiliary corps of the central institutions of Nazi persecution and extermination policy, such as the police and the SS, the Nazi Schutzstaffel (Protection Squadron), which employed some 29,000 women. Of those women, roughly 4,000 served as female SS guards in concentration camps, representing approximately 10 percent of all concentration camp guards.[61]

The scale of women's deployment far outstripped that of the First World War in all the other war powers as well. In Britain, which declared war on Germany in coalition with France on September 3, 1939, the first preparations had started in 1937. The Ministry of

Health set up the Emergency Nursing Committee and asked the Royal College of Nursing, founded in 1916 as the professional organization for qualified nurses, to compile a register of assistant nurses. In June 1938, the British Home Secretary established the Women's Voluntary Service for Air Raid Precautions with the aim to train women to protect their homes and families. Nurses in reserve for the Queen Alexandra's Imperial Military Nursing Service were activated in 1939, as were smaller nursing organizations. The number of professional nurses reached about 25,000 during the war, and hospitals and emergency services increasingly had to rely on additional volunteers.[62]

The number of women who served the British military as auxiliaries increased from 31,700 in 1939 to 453,200 in 1943. By far the largest organization was the Auxiliary Territorial Service, (ATS) with 212,500 women enrolled in 1943. This umbrella organization was a revival of the WAAC and coordinated all military work done by women. Fewer women joined the Women's Auxiliary Air Force (WAAF). In 1943, some 180,300 served in that unit, which also organized the antiaircraft batteries that had been open to women since 1940, while 60,400 women were part of the Women's Royal Naval Service (WRNS) in 1943.[63] The manpower needs of Britain's army were already so strong in 1941 that Parliament adopted the National Service Act (No. 2) in December of that year. The act provided for the conscription of unmarried women between the ages of twenty and thirty into service in the ATS and other military organizations, but the volunteers outnumbered conscripts through the end of the war. The WAAF was especially popular with volunteers; at its peak strength in 1943, 2,000 women enlisted in it every week.[64]

Compared to Germany and Britain, the United States mobilized far fewer women during World War II. The total number of women who served in the US armed forces during the war reached approximately 277,000: 140,000 women were employed by the Army, 100,000 by the Navy, 23,000 in the Marines, 13,000 in the Coast Guard, and 1,000 in the Army Air Forces. In addition, 74,000 served in the US Army and Navy Nurse Corps.[65] About 20,000 female auxiliaries served in the overseas theaters, together with 57,000 nurses in the army and 9,000 in the navy.[66] The first plans for mobilizing women within the military branches were discussed in 1940, more than one year prior to the US entry into war in December 1941. Within two years, the government created six military women's services. Next to the decades-old Army and Navy Nurse Corps, the Women's Army Auxiliary Corps (WAAC) was founded in May 1942 and later converted into a regular part of the army as the Women's Army Corps (WAC) in September 1943. The army thereby gained full control of the female auxiliaries. At the same time, women's pay and position in the army improved; they gained military ranks, titles, and pay comparable to that of their male counterparts. The US Army Air Forces, Navy and Marine Corps, and Coast Guard created similar units. Unlike in Britain and Germany, all female members of the US military were volunteers.[67] Scholars estimate that the proportion of women in the Western Allied armed forces was lowest for the United States (2 percent) and highest for the United Kingdom (up to 9 percent); in comparison, women constituted 5 percent of the German Wehrmacht.[68]

Female auxiliaries essentially did the same jobs as during World War I, but they could also access several new positions in communication and antiaircraft defense (the latter especially in the British and German militaries) or work as doctors, engineers, or even airplane pilots. The United States and United Kingdom, for example, deployed female pilots for transport and other noncombat roles.[69] Furthermore, women in military service were employed closer to the front lines, even in nursing, than during World War I. In Britain and the United States, women became part of the army personnel and were placed under military discipline. In Germany, they legally had the status of civil employees. The Nazis tried all means to avoid the impression that they used women as soldiers. In all three countries, military administrations used women only reluctantly, and they primarily targeted those who were young and unmarried. Similar to the First World War, extreme losses and increasing manpower problems largely forced the military leaderships to accept women in their ranks. This context mostly accounts for the higher mobilization rate in Britain and Germany, which began conscripting young and single women in 1941–42, compared to the United States, where female military service remained voluntary.[70]

The number of Soviet women mobilized during World War II for the armed forces was in total far higher than in any other country, because women were mobilized in several ways also outside the military. An estimated 520,000 women served in the Red Army's regular troops between 1941 and 1945. Up to 3 percent of the personnel of the Red Army and its airforce were women. At least 120,000 of them fought on the front line as snipers, tank drivers, mortar operators, and machine gunners.[71] Female Soviet combat pilots especially gained renown; three regiments, each with 400 personnel including ground staff, were created. German soldiers on the eastern front feared the Soviet "night witches," the female military aviators of the 588th Night Bomber Regiment who flew over 24,000 missions.[72] In addition, 200,000 women were engaged as combat medics and 80,000 as doctors in the moving front-line hospitals. Another 300,000 women were enlisted in forward and home front antiaircraft formations.[73] The Russian Red Cross furthermore trained a total of 500,000 women as paramedics for local air defenses and 300,000 as auxiliary nurses and paramedics for all regions of the Soviet Union, including battle zones, in brief two- to three-month short courses.[74] Women were also used in all kinds of jobs in communication, transport, and the Red Army's political work in the infantry, air force, and navy.

Many of the female Soviet soldiers were volunteers. As Anna Krylova emphasized in her 2010 study Soviet Women in Combat, they "belonged to the first post-revolutionary generation that had come of age in Stalinist schools and they volunteered en masse to fight in 1941," after the Wehrmacht's attack of Soviet Union.[75] Many of these volunteers had received paramilitary education or advanced training in shooting in the Komsomol, the All Union Young Communist League, during the prewar era. When the demand for soldiers increased in the wake of the dramatic losses in 1942–43, the Soviet regime started to conscript young women, mostly aged nineteen to twenty-five, for the army too. Despite a political rhetoric of female equality, however, the Stalinist state suppressed public knowledge of the extent of female military mobilization. This suggests that the regime anticipated disapproval, if not outright resistance, in society had these measures been publicized. In the army itself, the response was mixed. Many female soldiers were first tested and later accepted by their comrades and officers.[76]

The attitudes toward female combatants in the different European resistance movements were similarly ambivalent. In the partisan units in the European territories occupied by the Wehrmacht—in France, Italy, Greece, Latvia, Norway, Poland, Russia, Yugoslavia, and Ukraine—that fought against Nazi occupation, the average proportion of female combatants reached 10 to 15 percent.[77] One example is France. After signing the armistice with Nazi Germany on June 22, 1940, France was divided into two zones. In the occupied north, including Alsace and Moselle, Nazi Germany established an interim occupation authority. The previously unoccupied zone in the south, known as the *zone libre*, came under the authority of Marshal Philippe Pétain's Vichy regime, but Germany effectively exercised the rights of an occupying power.[78] Resistance against the Nazi occupation developed early in France, first especially from the Left. Historians have deconstructed the postwar myth that the major part of the population engaged in anti-occupation acts, but their estimates of the numbers vary greatly and depend mostly on the dossiers of the official organization of the French resistance movement, Combattants volontairs de la résistance (CVR), established in the immediate postwar years. According to them, women made up 7 to 12 percent of the CVR fighters. Similar to the military auxiliaries in regular armies, these women were mostly young and often single. In the CVR, as in other resistance movements, women were only accepted in combat roles during periods of exigency. Most women in the CVR had secretarial, caring, and nursing tasks for which they were perceived to be better suited. Thus, the gendered division of labor resembled the regular militaries fighting on both sides in World War II.[79]

The greatest number of women in active combat roles fought in the communist-led People's Liberation Army of Yugoslavia, which was by far the largest army of its kind in Europe during the Second World War. According to official figures, by the end of the war nearly 100,000 women had joined its ranks. Almost 40,000 of them were wounded and 25,000 were killed or died; in Serbia alone, 1,500 were executed by the Nazis. The proportion of female fighters in the partisan units depended on local conditions; in some, 20 percent were women, but in others the proportion was only 2 percent.[80] The number and percentage of female partisans in the other liberation armies in eastern, southeastern, and southern Europe was lower. In Italy, 55,000 women were recognized after the war as having been members of the Resistenza after the war, roughly 28 percent overall, and 35,000 of them were acknowledged as partisans in combat units.[81] In Poland, at least 40,000 women joined the Armia Krajowa, the Home Army. They played multiple roles in the Polish underground. Marek Ney-Krwawicz estimated that almost 5,000 female Home Army soldiers perished during the war, nearly 10 percent of those in active service.[82] According to official data, 28,500 women took part in the Soviet partisan activities behind the enemy lines, constituting 10 percent of the Soviet partisan forces.[83] Also, many women were active in the Albanian and Greek resistance movements against German occupation, but we have no gender-specific numbers for the National Liberation Front, the communist-controlled main movement of the Greek resistance, in which up to 120,000 men and women served as combatants.[84]

In general, the Nazi regime's fierce, oppressive occupation had the unintended consequence of spurring greater resistance. If women had nothing to lose because their homes were destroyed and their loved ones persecuted or killed, as in many territories in the east and southeast of Europe, they seem to have been more willing to join the armed resistance. This was especially the case when the dominant ideology of the resistance movement promised women more equality in the postwar society, as in the communist-controlled movements in Yugoslavia, Italy, Greece, and the Soviet Union. These push and pull factors were also important in the decisions of many young Jewish women to join their brothers and friends in the armed resistance of partisan movements, especially in the east.[85]

COMPARING CONFLICTS AND COUNTRIES

A comparison of female military service in both world wars and different countries reveals expected differences and astonishing similarities. One important difference was the rhetoric used by the belligerents to mobilize women. This dissimilarity was especially pronounced during the Second World War, when ideologies like liberalism, communism, and fascism dominated the politics of the war powers. The Third Reich mobilized German women for a war of conquest and annihilation. A murderous will to destruction characterized its conduct in the war. Especially young women who grew up in the Nazi regime and were socialized in its youth organizations supported its racist and imperialist goals. For the Allies, by contrast, the Second World War was truly a "war of defense." Their homelands were in danger or needed to be liberated. This made it easier to gain voluntary female war support, especially in regions in danger of conquest or that were already occupied. In addition, as the examples of the Soviet Union and the partisan movements indicate, a socialist or communist rhetoric of women's emancipation helped to mobilize women, especially when they had belonged to communist or socialist youth organizations before the war. Aside from these ideological differences, the legal status and types of civil or military formations that included women were dissimilar. Here, the institutional traditions of a given country were factors of crucial influence.[86]

One major similarity was the political and public rejection (except in Russia and the Soviet Union) of female participation in combat. Laws and regulations reserved for men alone the duty and right to kill, and political rhetoric connected it to male citizenship rights, privilege, and power. In Britain, Germany, and the United States, the governments and military leadership publicly described fighting in a similar way as "too onerous" for women and unsuited to their "female nature." These countries therefore rejected female soldiers. The main reason for such opposition was that women in combat positions symbolized the collapse of the gender order and, with it, the social order. They thus classified female service in general as "noncombatant" and tried to hide or otherwise obscure in propaganda women's participation in combat, the necessity of which grew during the war, especially in British and German antiaircraft defense units. As a consequence, women became, as D'Ann Campbell observed, "the invisible combatants of World War II."[87]

The Soviet Union, however, presents an ambivalent exception. Three main factors seem to have led to its different practices: first, the situation of a dramatic military crisis, the occupation of large parts of the country, and the danger of devastating defeat; second, a tradition of female military units in World War I; and third, a political ideology of women's equality that young female volunteers could cite to legitimate their attempts to join the Red Army as soldiers on the front lines. But here, too, the extent of female combatant service was kept hidden from the public by the government. In general, occupation, guerrilla warfare, and civil war created more space for active female participation in combat, because the state of emergency was more pronounced. Even then, we can observe several attempts to control and limit this space. The best-known example is the Spanish Civil War (1936–39). *Milicianas* (militia women) won acceptance in the nonhierarchical, voluntary, popular militia comprising a patchwork of anarchists, dissident Marxists, unionists, and remnants of the Spanish Republican Army. When the Spanish Communist Party, propelled by the Communist International (Comintern), controlled by Moscow attempted to build a regular, disciplined, hierarchical, conventional army, with the aim to fight more successfully against the fascist troops, the price of this reorganization was the expulsion of the *milicianas*.[88] Later, during the Second World War, the Comintern changed its policy mainly in response to the dire manpower needs of the Red Army and the partisan movements it supported.

Related to the different attempts to prohibit, control, or hide female participation in combat was a second important similarity: the cultural strategies that the different armies deployed during World War II to control women in the military and their attempts to maintain sharp gender boundaries, despite the challenges of total war. In this respect, the Western Allies and their German enemies used similar strategies, some already tested during World War I. On the one hand, women who served the military in all countries were now uniformed and their appearance was tightly regulated. The aim was to emphasize their femininity while controlling their independence and taming their sex appeal. This attempt to highlight the modest but feminine appearance of military women is particularly visible in the many propaganda posters meant to mobilize women and reassure parents, fiancés, and spouses (Figures 19.3 and 19.4). On the other hand, the military and the public often suspected women in the military of adventurous and immoral behavior to control their conduct and limit their personal freedom.[89]

A third similarity concerns the attempts of the Western powers and Nazi Germany to reinforce through propaganda the idealized model of the gender order of national wars, despite or because of the quite opposite reality. In this model, men still went off to war as "defenders of the fatherland" to protect and preserve the homeland embodied by women. The main function of this model was to give ordinary soldiers a worthy cause to fight.[90] War movies in particular reinforced this model, which contrasted even more starkly with the practice of war than had been the case in World War I. Aerial warfare, mass killings, and genocide rendered soldiers ineffective as "protectors."[91] The longer the war lasted and the more exhausted people were, the more they seem to have hoped to be able to return to "normal," prewar lives after the war ended, along with the

FIGURE 19.3 *Hilf Siegen als Luftnachrichtenhelferin!* (Help to Win as an Air Force Signal Corps Auxiliary), Nazi propaganda poster by the German Air Force, attempting to win young, single women to volunteer as Air Force Signal Corps Auxiliary, unknown artist, ca.1942 [n.p., n.d.].

(Hollandse Hoogte, Den Haag)

FIGURE 19.4 *WAAC—This Is My War Too!*, propaganda poster by the US Army Recruiting Publicity Office, attempting to attract female volunteers for the Women's Army Auxiliary Corps during World War II, designed by Dan Smith, ca.1943 [n.p., n.d.].

(© Victoria and Albert Museum, London)

reestablishment of the old prewar gender order.[92] War propaganda tried to encourage these hopes and calm fears. It attempted to uphold the old peacetime gender order in hearts and minds so that the audience would support the war and at the same time prepare mentally for the postwar period.

REORDERING POSTWAR SOCIETIES AND REGENDERING WAR MEMORIES

The research on gender, demobilization, and postwar societies demonstrates that the eras following both world wars were historical moments in which the process of regendering the social order proceeded with great intensity.[93] The political elites of the different postwar societies tried to reestablish a "proper" gender order. They sought to counteract the de facto wartime expansion of women's scope of action by intensively propagating the model of the breadwinner–housewife family, at least in the West. Demobilization policies likewise tried to stabilize this model. The first step was the quick military demobilization of female auxiliaries, soldiers, and nurses, followed by the economic demobilization of the many female workers and employees who had taken men's jobs during the war. Both measures had the primary goal of stabilizing the social and political order by reintegrating former soldiers into occupational life, homes, and families.[94] Especially in the Western countries, this demobilization policy was supported by labor, social, and family policies developed to foster the breadwinner–housewife family, which after World War II became the broadly accepted norm in the West.

Despite the socialist rhetoric of gender equality, a similar trend emerged even in the Soviet Union and the new communist states of Eastern Europe in the first decade after 1945. In 1944, at the latest, the image of women as family-bound housewives and mothers came to dominate Soviet propaganda. Because of the vast losses to the population, the regime emphasized women's reproductive role while simultaneously promoting the "double-earner family model," a strategy similar to those of other communist states in the East. Because of the massive demographic imbalance between women and men caused by the war, these countries all urgently needed women in the workforce of their recovering economies, but at the same time women were also needed as mothers.[95]

The military, economic, and social demobilization in the West and the East alike was accompanied by a policy of cultural demobilization that attempted to conceal or erase women's mass military deployment, especially their role in combat, from recollections of the war. The construction of "properly" gendered postwar memories thus played a crucial role in the reconstruction of the gender order and, with it, normalcy in society.[96] Not even in the Soviet Union was the large number of female combatants publicly recognized. Even before the war was over, Soviet propaganda reduced women's war participation to the role of medics supposedly working far from the combat zone.[97] At the center of the national war memories of all the Allied victors stood the male war heroes: millions of fallen warriors and returning front-line soldiers.

One form of representation for these national war memories consists of monuments such as the Cenotaph at Whitehall in the center of London, the United Kingdom's primary war memorial since 1920. In the United States, the Arlington Memorial Amphitheater, dedicated in 1921, and the national World War II Memorial in Washington, DC, which opened in 2004, serve that purpose. In East Germany, the vast Soviet War Memorial in Berlin's Treptower Park commemorates the Russian soldiers who fell in the Battle of Berlin in April and May 1945; it opened in 1949 and served as the central war memorial of the former German Democratic Republic (1949–90). The sacrifice of war widows, especially mothers, and the selfless care work of nurses were recalled as the female counterpart to male heroism. Civilians, too, were commemorated as victims of air raids and war atrocities. One example is the New Guardhouse in the old city center of Berlin with an enlarged version of Käthe Kollwitz's sculpture *Mother with Her Dead Son* at its center, which the German artist had finished in a much smaller size in 1937 in memory of one of her sons, who had been killed in World War I. Since 1993, the sculpture has been the center of the "Central Memorial of the Federal Republic of Germany for the Victims of War and Dictatorship."

Women in military uniforms, particularly women in combat positions, did not conform to these national war memories, which informed popular-culture recollections of the wars, including in movies and television.[98] The fact that women were needed and did their duty has been curiously absent from national war memory, though remedied in part in 1997 with the US government's Women in Military Service for America Memorial at the Arlington National Cemetery and, in 2005, with the British Monument to the Women of World War II, situated close to the Cenotaph in London's center, remembering the war service of all British women. To this day, there is no monument dedicated to female Soviet veterans.

The odd paradox is that the more women had been necessary during World War II, especially in combat roles, the less their service could be recognized in national war memories after 1945, because such memories threatened to jeopardize social stability—a worrisome prospect in societies already strained to the breaking point by the impact of war. This is why collectively remembering female military service was far easier for the United States than for Britain and certainly more than for the Soviet Union and defeated Germany. In the latter, the grueling past was countered in the East with the myth of the heroic antifascist resistance by the communists and the liberation by the Red Army and in the West with a victimization narrative focused on the aerial bombing of German cities, postwar displacement, veterans returning from captivity in Eastern Europe, and women mass raped by Soviet soldiers. In this narrative, women, especially mothers, and children became the incarnation of innocent victims of war. As *Generation War* demonstrates, even in the early twenty-first century it is challenging to the German collective memory of the Second World War and the Holocaust to recall the extensive and very active war support of German women.[99]

CONCLUSION

Only through a comparative perspective can the question of why contemporaries and later postwar societies found it such a challenge to recognize the active participation of women in the First and Second World Wars as auxiliaries, female soldiers, and partisans be answered. The attempts to hide and downplay especially the female participation in combat during World War II and suppress it in subsequent national war memories were crucial because the total nature of warfare had required the mass mobilization of women, even for the military. For this reason, service in the military per se could no longer function as a core marker of gender difference. It was replaced in policies and political rhetoric by participation in combat, which became now the "masculine preserve." Yet even the masculine monopoly on combat came under pressure in World War II. The resulting shock to the gender order and the military meant that after 1945 it would take another fifty to sixty years for women to legally access all positions in the military, including combat roles. Even today, policies that aim for gender equality in the armed forces face significant resistance in most Eastern and Western armed forces, because of the continuing importance of the military as a gender-defining institution.[100]

NOTES

1. "Kriegs-Drama wühlt Deutschland auf," *Berliner Kurier*, March 19, 2013.
2. "Über sieben Millionen sahen ZDF-Weltkriegsepos," *Spiegel ONLINE*, March 18, 2013.
3. "Generation War," *Internet Movie Database* (*IMDb*), accessed March 17, 2017, http://www .imdb.com/title/tt1883092/.
4. ZDF Hauptabteilung Kommunikation Pressestelle, *Online-Artikel (Auswahl)* (Mainz, 2013); *Printartikel (chronologisch)* (Mainz, 2013); and *Presseauswertung* "Unsere Mütter, Unsere Väter," (Mainz, 2013).
5. "Anzac Girls," *IMDb*, accessed March 17, 2017, http://www.imdb.com/title/tt3078602/.
6. "The Crimson Field," *IMDb*, accessed March 17, 2017, http://www.imdb.com/title/tt3494220.
7. "Land Girls," *IMDb*, accessed March 17, 2017, http://www.imdb.com/title/tt1449940/?ref_= tt_rec_tt; and "Home Fires," *IMDb*, accessed March 17, 2017, http://www.imdb.com/title/ tt4015216/?ref_=tt_rec_tt.
8. "Bomb Girls," *IMDb*, accessed March 17, 2017, http://www.imdb.com/title/tt1955311/.
9. "Female Agents," (*Les Femmes de l'ombre*), *IMDb*, accessed March 17, 2017, http://www .imdb.com/title/tt0824330/; and "Imitation Game," *IMDb*, accessed March 17, 2017, http:// www.imdb.com/title/tt2084970/?ref_=nv_sr_1.
10. For the general state of research, see Karen Hagemann and Sonya O. Rose, "War and Gender: The Age of the World Wars and Its Aftermath—an Overview" in this handbook.
11. See Nancy Loring Goldman, ed., *Female Soldiers—Combatants or Noncombatants? Historical and Contemporary Perspectives* (Westport, CT: Greenwood, 1982); Lorry M. Fenner and Marie E. deYoung, *Women in Combat: Civic Duty or Military Liability?* (Washington, DC: Georgetown University Press, 2001); Klaus Latzel et al., eds., *Soldatinnen: Gewalt und Geschlecht im Krieg vom Mittelalter bis Heute* (Paderborn: Schöningh, 2011); and Barton C.

Hacker and Margaret Vining, eds., *A Companion to Women's Military History* (Leiden: Brill, 2012).

12. See, for the understanding of *gender*, Hagemann, "Introduction: Gender and the History of War—The Development of the Research" in this handbook.

13. On the importance of the military as a "gender-defining institution," see Karen Hagemann and D'Ann Campbell, "Post-1945 Western Militaries, Female Soldiers, and Gay and Lesbian Rights" in this handbook.

14. For first comparisons, see D'Ann Campbell, "Women in Combat: The World War II Experience in the United States, Great Britain, Germany, and the Soviet Union," *Journal of Military History* 57, no. 2 (1993): 301–23; Franka Maubach and Silke Satjukow, "Zwischen Emanzipation und Trauma: Soldatinnen im Zweiten Weltkrieg (Deutschland, Sowjetunion, USA)," *Historische Zeitschrift* 288, no. 2 (2009): 347–84; and Beate Fieseler et al., "Gendering Combat: Military Women's Status in Britain, the United States and the Soviet Union during the Second World War," *Women's Studies International Forum* 47 (2014): 115–26.

15. See Eric Taylor, *Wartime Nurse: One Hundred Years from the Crimea to Korea, 1854–1954* (London: Robert Hale, 2001); Janet Lee, *War Girls: The First Aid Nursing Yeomanry in the First World War* (Manchester: Manchester University Press, 2005); Christine E. Hallett, *Containing Trauma: Nursing Work in the First World War* (Manchester: Manchester University Press, 2009); Anne Powell, *Women in the War Zone: Hospital Service in the First World War* (Stroud: History Press, 2009); and Alison S. Fell and Christine E. Hallett, eds., *First World War Nursing: New Perspectives* (New York: Routledge, 2013).

16. See Klaus Latzel et al., "Soldatinnen in der Geschichte: Weibliche Verletzungsmacht als Herausforderung," in Latzel et al., *Soldatinnen*, 11–49.

17. See the chapters by Stefan Dudink on "Citizenship, Mass Mobilization, and Masculinity in a Transatlantic Perspective, 1770s–1860s," and Thomas Cardoza and Karen Hagemann on "History and Memory of Army Women and Female Soldiers, 1770s–1870s" in this handbook.

18. For the discussion of the concept of *total war*, see Hagemann and Rose, "War and Gender" in this handbook. On the different home fronts in the Age of World Wars, see the chapters by Susan R. Grayzel, "Total Warfare, Gender, and the 'Home Front' in Europe during the First and Second World Wars," and Kimberly Jensen, "Citizenship and Gender on the American and Canadian Home Fronts during the First and Second World Wars" in this handbook.

19. All of the following statistics pertaining to the integration of women in military service are only estimates because they vary greatly in the literature.

20. Kimberly Jensen, "Volunteers, Auxiliaries, and Women's Mobilization: The First World War and Beyond (1914–39)," in Hacker and Vining, *Companion*, 189–231, 197; and Margaret H. Darrow, *French Women and the First World War: War Stories of the Home Front* (Oxford: Berg Publishers, 2000), 229–67.

21. Darrow, *French Women*, 53–97; see also Susan R. Grayzel, *Women's Identities at War: Gender, Motherhood, and Politics in Britain and France during the First World War* (Chapel Hill: University of North Carolina Press, 1999), 202–25.

22. Lucy Noakes, *Women in the British Army: War and the Gentle Sex, 1907–1948* (London: Routledge, 2006), 81.

23. Ibid., 61.

24. Ibid., 68–81.

25. Ibid., 73.

26. See Jensen, "Volunteers," 199–201; and Noakes, *Women*, 20–81.

27. Noakes, *Women*, 81; and Janet S. K. Watson, *Fighting Different Wars: Experience, Memory, and the First World War in Britain* (Cambridge: Cambridge University Press, 2004), 17–154.

28. Noakes, *Women*, 78.

29. See Bianca Schönberger, "Motherly Heroines and Adventurous Girls: Red Cross Nurses and Women Army Auxiliaries in the First World War," in *Home/Front: The Military, War and Gender in Twentieth-Century Germany*, ed. Karen Hagemann and Stefanie Schüler-Springorum (Oxford: Berg, 2002), 87–113.

30. Ibid., 89 and 91.

31. "Ausführungsbestimmungen zum Erlass zur Gründung eines 'Weiblichen Nachrichtenkorps,' 27. Juli 1918," in Ursula von Gersdorff, *Frauen im Kriegsdienst, 1914–1945* (Stuttgart: Deutsche Verlags-Anstalt, 1969), 32; and Franz W. Seidler, *Frauen zu den Waffen? Marketenderinnen, Helferinnen, Soldatinnen* (Bonn: Bernard & Graefe, 1978), 292–93; see also, more broadly, Helen Boak, "Forgotten Female Soldiers in an Unknown Army: German Women Working behind the Lines, 1914–1918," *Women's History Review*, 23, no. 4 (2014), 577–94.

32. Heeres-Sanitätsinspektion im Reichswehrministerium, ed., *Sanitätsbericht über das Deutsche Heer im Weltkriege 1914/1918 (deutsches Feld- und Besatzungsheer; deutscher Kriegssanitätsbericht 1914/1918)*, vol. 3 (Berlin: Mittler, 1934).

33. Major von Massow, Signal Staff Chief, to Ludendorff, in Gersdorff, *Frauen*, 31.

34. Gersdorff, *Frauen*, 259.

35. Ibid., 31–34.

36. Karen Hagemann, "Mobilizing Women for War: The History, Historiography, and Memory of German Women's War Service in the Two World Wars," *Journal of Military History* 75, no. 3 (2011): 1055–93.

37. See Jean Ebbert and Marie-Beth Hall, *The First, the Few, the Forgotten: Navy and Marine Corps Women in World War I* (Annapolis, MD: Naval Institute Press, 2002); and Hallet, *Containing Trauma*.

38. Susan Zeiger, *In Uncle Sam's Service: Women Workers with the American Expeditionary Force, 1917–1919* (Ithaca, NY: Cornell University Press, 1999), 52–53.

39. Ibid.; and Jensen, "Volunteers, Auxiliaries," 202–5.

40. Laurie S. Stoff, *They Fought for the Motherland: Russia's Women Soldiers in World War I & the Revolution* (Lawrence: University Press of Kansas, 2006), 91; and Melissa K. Stockdale, "'My Death for the Motherland Is Happiness': Women, Patriotism, and Soldiering in Russia's Great War, 1914–17," *American Historical Review* 109, no. 1 (2004): 78–116.

41. Maria Botchkareva, *Yashka, My Life as Peasant, Officer and Exile* (New York: Frederick A. Stokes, 1919); and Stoff, *They Fought*, 69–89.

42. Stoff, *They Fought*, 69–70.

43. Jensen, "Volunteers, Auxiliaries," 208–9; and Stoff, *They Fought*.

44. See the chapter by Jean H. Quataert on "Changing Modes of Warfare and the Gendering of Military Medical Care, 1850s–1920s" in this handbook; and Fell and Hallett, *First World War*.

45. Jensen, "Volunteers, Auxiliaries," 199–202.

46. Schönberger, "Motherly Heroines," 88–89; see also Jean H. Quataert, *Staging Philanthropy: Patriotic Women and the National Imagination in Dynastic Germany, 1813–1916* (Ann Arbor: Michigan University Press, 2001), 21–53 and 177–216.

47. Jensen, "Volunteers, Auxiliaries," 202–3; Kimberly Jensen, *Mobilizing Minerva: American Women in the First World War* (Urbana: University of Illinois Press, 2008), 98–141; Zeiger, *Uncle Sam's*, 104–36; and Janet Lee, *War Girls*.

48. Darrow, *French Women*, 140–41.

49. Schönberger, "Motherly Heroines," 88–89.

50. Karen Offen, *European Feminisms, 1700–1950: A Political History* (Stanford, CA: Stanford University Press, 2000), 257–77; Alison S. Fell and Ingrid Sharp, eds., *The Women's Movement in Wartime: International Perspectives, 1914–19* (Basingstoke: Palgrave Macmillan, 2007); Angela K. Smith, *Suffrage Discourse in Britain during the First World War* (Aldershot: Ashgate, 2005); and Grayzel, *Women's Identities*, 190–225.

51. Schönberger, "Motherly Heroines," 95–103; Grayzel, *Women's Identities*, 226–40; Zeiger, *Uncle Sam's*, 137–74; and Watson, *Fighting*, 185–298.

52. Gersdorff, *Frauen*, 33–39.

53. See the chapter by Karen Hagemann on "Gender, Demobilization, and the Reordering of Societies after the First and Second World Wars" in this handbook.

54. Hagemann, "Mobilizing," 1073–75.

55. See Hagemann and Rose, "War and Gender" in this handbook.

56. Wendy Lower, *Hitler's Furies: German Women in the Nazi Killing Fields* (Boston: Houghton Mifflin Harcourt, 2013); and earlier, Sybille Steinbacher, ed., *Volksgenossinnen: Frauen in der NS-Volksgemeinschaft* (Göttingen: Wallstein, 2007).

57. Dieter Riesenberger, *Das Deutsche Rote Kreuz: Eine Geschichte 1864–1990* (Paderborn: Schöningh, 2002), 332–33.

58. Gersdorff, *Frauen*, 74; Seidler, *Frauen*, 159–62; and Alex Buchner, *The German Army Medical Corps in World War II: A Photo Chronicle* (Atglen, PA: Schiffer, 1999).

59. Seidler, *Frauen*, 59, 86–88; and Gersdorff, *Frauen*, 69–70.

60. Hagemann, "Mobilizing," 1079–91; Franka Maubach, "Expansionen weiblicher Hilfe: Zur Erfahrungsgeschichte von Frauen im Kriegsdienst," in Steinbacher, *Volksgenossinnen* 93–114; and Maubach, *Die Stellung halten: Kriegserfahrungen und Lebensgeschichten von Wehrmachthelferinnen* (Göttingen: Vandenhoeck & Ruprecht, 2009).

61. Jutta Mühlenberg, *Das SS-Helferinnenkorps: Ausbildung, Einsatz und Entnazifizierung der weiblichen Angehörigen der Waffen-SS* (Hamburg: Hamburger Edition, 2011), 14; Simone Erpel, ed., *Im Gefolge der SS: Aufseherinnen des Frauen-KZ Ravensbrück* (Berlin: Metropol, 2007); and Anette Kretzer, *NS-Täterschaft und Geschlecht: Der erste britische Ravensbrück-Prozess 1946/47 in Hamburg* (Berlin: Metropol, 2009).

62. Monica Baly, "Nursing Services in Great Britain during World War II," *Humane Medicine* 7, no. 4 (1991): 277–81.

63. Noakes, *Women*, 131.

64. Margaret Vining, "Women Join the Armed Forces: The Transformation of Women's Military Work in World War II and after (1939–47)," in Hacker and Vining, *Companion*, 233–89; and Noakes, *Women*, 103–32.

65. WW2 US Medical Research Centre, "The Army Nurse Corps," accessed January 16, 2017, https://www.med-dept.com/articles/the-army-nurse-corps/.

66. Vining, "Women," 253–61; and M. Michaela Hampf, *Release a Man for Combat: The Women's Army Corps during World War II* (Cologne: Böhlau, 2010), 64–97.

67. Hampf, *Release*, 31–34; and Vining, "Women," 254–55.

68. Fieseler et al., "Gendering Combat," 116.

69. See Amy Goodpaster Strebe, *Flying for Her Country: The American and Soviet Women Military Pilots of World War II* (Westport, CT: Praeger, 2007); and Lois K. Merry, *Women Military Pilots of World War II: A History with Biographies of American, British, Russian and German Aviators* (Jefferson, NC: McFarland, 2011).

70. Maubach and Satjukow, "Zwischen Emanzipation."

71. Anna Krylova, *Soviet Women in Combat: A History of Violence on the Eastern Front* (Cambridge: Cambridge University Press, 2010), 3; Fieseler et al., "Gendering Combat," 116; and Roger D. Markwick and Euridice Charon Cardona, *Soviet Women on the Frontline in the Second World War* (New York: Palgrave Macmillan, 2012), 150–51.

72. Marwick and Cardona, *Soviet Women*, 97.

73. Ibid., 150–51; and Fieseler et al., "Gendering Combat," 116.

74. Marwick and Cardone, *Soviet Women*, 57–61.

75. Krylova, *Soviet Women*, 3.

76. Maubach and Satjukow, "Zwischen Emanzipation."

77. See Jelena Batinić, *Women and Yugoslav Partisans: A History of World War II Resistance* (New York: Cambridge University Press, 2015), 260–68.

78. On the gender policy of Vichy France, see Miranda Pollard, *Reign of Virtue: Mobilizing Gender in Vichy France* (Chicago: University of Chicago Press, 1998).

79. Hanna Diamond, *Women and the Second World War in France, 1939–1948: Choices and Constraints* (Harlow: Longman, 1999), 98–124; Corinna von List, *Frauen in der Résistance 1940–1944: "Der Kampf gegen die 'Boches' hat begonnen!"* (Paderborn: Schöningh, 2010); Margaret Collins Weitz, *Sisters in the Resistance: How Women Fought to Free France, 1940–1945* (New York: John Wiley & Sons, 1995); and Paula Schwarz, "Redefining Resistance: Women's Activism in Wartime France," in *Behind the Lines: Gender and the Two World Wars*, ed. Margaret Randolph Higonnet et al. (New Haven, CT: Yale University Press, 1987), 141–53.

80. Ivana Pantelić, "Yugoslav Female Partisans in World War II," *Cahiers balkaniques* 41 (2013): 1–10; and Barbara N. Wiesinger, *Partisaninnen: Widerstand in Jugoslawien 1941–1945* (Vienna: Böhlau, 2008).

81. Batinić, *Women*, 260–61; and Jane Slaughter, *Women and the Italian Resistance, 1943–1945* (Denver, CO: Arden Press, 1997).

82. Batinić, *Women*, 261; Marek Ney-Krwawicz, *The Polish Resistance Home Army, 1939–1945* (London: PUMST, 2001); and Ney-Krwawicz, "Women Soldiers of the Polish Home Army," accessed April 17, 2017, http://www.polishresistance-ak.org/12%20Article.htm.

83. Batinić, *Women*, 261–62; Julianne Fürst, "Heroes, Lovers, Victims: Partisan Girls during the Great Fatherland War," *Minerva* 18, no. 3–4 (2000): 38–74; and Marwick and Cardona, *Soviet Women*, 117–48. On Eastern Europe, see also Maren Röger and Ruth Leiserowitz, eds., *Women and Men at War: A Gender Perspective on World War II and Its Aftermath in Central and Eastern Europe* (Osnabrück: Fibre, 2012), 199–262; and Latzel et al., *Soldatinnen*, 257–78.

84. Batinić, *Women*, 261; Demetra Tzanake, *Women and Nationalism in the Making of Modern Greece: The Founding of the Kingdom to the Greco-Turkish War* (Basingstoke: Palgrave Macmillan, 2009); Margaret Poulos, *Arms and the Woman: Just Warriors and Greek Feminist Identity* (New York: Columbia University Press, 2009); and Janet Hart, *New Voices in the Nation: Women and the Greek Resistance, 1941–1964* (Ithaca, NY: Cornell University Press, 1996), esp. 101–236.

85. See Ingrid Strobl, *Partisanas: Women in the Armed Resistance to Fascism and German Occupation (1936–1945)* (Edinburgh: AK Press, 1989), on Jewish resistance esp. 141–231;

and Ruth Leiserowitz, "In the Lithuanian Woods: Jewish and Lithuanian Female Partisans," in Röger and Leiserowitz, *Women and Men*, 199–218.

86. See Fieseler et al., "Gendering Combat."

87. Campbell, "Women in Combat," 101.

88. See, Mary Nash, *Defying Male Civilization: Women in the Spanish Civil War* (Denver, CO: Arden Press, 1995), 101–24; and Tabea Alexa Linhard, *Fearless Women in the Mexican Revolution and the Spanish Civil War* (Columbia: University of Missouri Press, 2005).

89. On World War I, see Janet S. K. Watson, "Khaki Girls, VADs, and Tommy's Sisters: Gender and Class in First World War Britain," *International Historical Review* 19, no. 1 (1997): 32–51; and Angela Woollacott, "'Khaki Fever' and Its Control: Gender, Class, Age and Sexual Morality on the British Homefront in the First World War," *Journal of Contemporary History* 19, no. 2 (1994): 325–47. On World War II, see Hagemann, "Mobilizing," 1084–88; Sonya O. Rose, *Which People's War? National Identity and Citizenship in Britain, 1939–1945* (Oxford: Oxford University Press, 2003), 107–50; Phil Goodman, "'Patriotic Femininity': Women's Morals and Men's Morale during the Second World War," *Gender & History* 10, no. 2 (1998): 278–93; and Hampf, *Release*, 174–98, 237–79.

90. See Lucy Noakes, *War and the British: Gender, Memory and National Identity* (London: I. B. Tauris, 1998), 48–74.

91. See Jo Fox, *Film Propaganda in Britain and Nazi Germany: World War II Cinema* (Oxford: Berg, 2007); and Rosalinde Sartorti, "On the Making of Heroes, Heroines and Saints," in *Culture and Entertainment in Wartime Russia*, ed. Richard Stites (Bloomington: Indiana University Press 1995), 176–93.

92. On female war experiences, see Penny Summerfield, *Reconstructing Women's Wartime Lives: Discourse and Subjectivity in Oral Histories of the Second World War* (Manchester: Manchester University Press, 1998); Margarete Dörr, *"Wer die Zeit nicht miterlebt hat…": Frauenerfahrungen im Zweiten Weltkrieg und in den Jahren danach* (Frankfurt am Main: Campus, 1998); and Pauline E. Parker, *Women of the Homefront: World War II Recollections of 55 Americans* (Jefferson, NC: McFarland, 2002).

93. See also, for the following, Hagemann, "Gender, Demobilization" in this handbook.

94. Noakes, *Women*, 133–56; Marwick and Cardone, *Soviet Women*, 230–48; Hampf, *Release*, 280–99; and Franka Maubach, "Als Helferin in der Wehrmacht: Eine paradigmatische Figur des Kriegsendes," *Osteuropa*, 55, no. 4–6 (2005): 197–205.

95. See Hagemann, "Gender, Demobilization" in this handbook.

96. See Wendy Webster, "Reconstructing Boundaries: Gender, War and Empire in British Cinema, 1945–1950," *Historical Journal of Film, Radio and Television* 23, no. 1 (2003): 43–57; and Elizabeth Heineman, "The Hour of the Woman: Memories of Germany's 'Crisis Years' and West German National Identity," *American Historical Review* 101, no. 2 (1996): 354–95.

97. See Krylova, *Soviet Women*, 290–93; and Krylova, "Neither Erased nor Remembered: Soviet 'Women Combatants' and Cultural Strategies of Forgetting in Soviet Russia, 1940s–1980s," in *Histories of the Aftermath: The Legacies of the Second World War in Europe*, ed. Frank Biess and Robert G. Moeller (New York: Berghahn Books, 2010), 83–101.

98. See Noakes, *War*, 23–47; Penny Summerfield, "Public Memory or Public Amnesia? British Women of the Second World War in Popular Films of the 1950s and 1960s," *Journal of British Studies* 48, no. 4 (2009): 935–57; Daina Eglitis and Vita Zelče, "Unruly Actors: Latvian Women of the Red Army in Post-War Historical Memory," *Nationalities Papers* 41, no. 6 (2013): 987–1007; Shirley Mangini, *Memories of Resistance: Women's Voices from the Spanish Civil War* (New Haven, CT: Yale University Press, 1995); also Roger D. Marwick,

"'A Sacred Duty': Red Army Women Veterans Remembering the Great Fatherland War, 1941–1945," *Australian Journal of Politics and History* 54, no. 3 (2008): 403–20; Batinić, *Women*, 213–57; Slaughter, *Women*, 119–30; Hart, *New Voices*, 237–67; and Maubach, *Die Stellung*, 273–316.

99. See, on the literature, the chapters by Frank Biess on "Gendering the Memories of War and Holocaust in Europe and the United States," and Hagemann, "Gender, Demobilization" in this handbook.

100. See Hagemann and Campbell, "Post-1945 Western Militaries" in this handbook.

Select Bibliography

Batinić, Jelena. *Women and Yugoslav Partisans: A History of World War II Resistance*. New York: Cambridge University Press, 2015.

Darrow, Margaret H. *French Women and the First World War: War Stories from the Homefront*. Oxford: Berg, 2000.

Diamond, Hanna. *Women and the Second World War in France, 1939–1948: Choices and Constraints*. Harlow: Longman, 1999.

Fell, Alison S., and Christine E. Hallett, eds. *First World War Nursing: New Perspectives*. New York: Routledge, 2013.

Hacker, Barton C., and Margaret Vining, eds. *A Companion to Women's Military History*. Leiden: Brill, 2012.

Hagemann, Karen. "Mobilizing Women for War: The History, Historiography, and Memory of German Women's War Service in the Two World Wars," *Journal of Military History* 75, no. 3 (2011): 1055–93.

Hallett, Christine E. *Containing Trauma: Nursing Work in the First World War*. Manchester: Manchester University Press, 2009.

Hampf, M. Michaela. *Release a Man for Combat: The Women's Army Corps during World War II*. Cologne: Böhlau, 2010.

Hart, Janet. *New Voices in the Nation: Women and the Greek Resistance, 1941–1964*. Ithaca, NY: Cornell University Press, 1996.

Jensen, Kimberly. *Mobilizing Minerva: American Women in the First World War*. Urbana: University of Illinois Press, 2008.

Krylova, Anna, *Soviet Women in Combat: A History of Violence on the Eastern Front*. New York: Cambridge University Press, 2010.

Latzel, Klaus, Franka Maubach, and Silke Satjukow, eds. *Soldatinnen: Gewalt und Geschlecht im Krieg vom Mittelalter bis Heute*. Paderborn: Schöningh, 2011.

Lee, Janet. *War Girls: The First Aid Nursing Yeomanry in the First World War*. Manchester: Manchester University Press, 2005.

Markwick, Roger D., and Charon Cardona Euridice. *Soviet Women on the Frontline in the Second World War*. New York: Palgrave Macmillan, 2012.

Maubach, Franka. *Die Stellung halten: Kriegserfahrungen und Lebensgeschichten von Wehrmachthelferinnen*. Göttingen: Vandenhoeck & Ruprecht, 2009.

Poulos, Margaret. *Arms and the Woman: Just Warriors and Greek Feminist Identity*. New York: Columbia University Press, 2009.

Powell, Anne. *Women in the War Zone: Hospital Service in the First World War*. Stroud: History Press, 2009.

Slaughter, Jane. *Women and the Italian Resistance, 1943–1945*. Denver, CO: Arden Press, 1997.

Stoff, Laurie S. *They Fought for the Motherland: Russia's Women Soldiers in World War I & the Revolution*. Lawrence: University Press of Kansas, 2006.

Weitz, Margaret Collins. *Sisters in the Resistance: How Women Fought to Free France, 1940–1945*. New York: John Wiley & Sons, 1995.

Zeiger, Susan. *In Uncle Sam's Service: Women Workers with the American Expeditionary Force, 1917–1919*. Ithaca, NY: Cornell University Press, 1999.

CHAPTER 20

....

STATES, MILITARY MASCULINITIES, AND COMBAT IN THE AGE OF WORLD WARS

....

THOMAS KÜHNE

"WAR is men's business, not ladies," Rhett Butler says in the 1936 novel *Gone with the Wind*, written by Margaret Mitchell. He confirmed an age-old myth that had already been invalidated in the American Civil War (1861–65), the subject of the novel. It was questioned even more in the era of the total wars, during the First World War (1914–18) that preceded the novel and the Second World War (1939–45) that began shortly after the popular movie based on this novel was released in 1939.[1] Before the start of World War I, Europeans, who had not seen any major war in their homelands for almost fifty years. The more they were shocked about the experience of a highly industrialized global and total war with its dramatic brutalization of warfare and a systematic erasure of boundaries between combatants and noncombatants. Twenty years later, World War II would become an even more global and murderous conflict.

The boundaries between combatants and noncombatants had been blurred before the First World War in several conflicts on the European continent, the colonial wars Europeans waged overseas and in the American Civil War, but only in the wars of 1914–18 and 1939–45 were European civilian populations, including women, systematically and purposefully not only mobilized for, but also targeted by war, with genocide as its ultimate consequence. But women's suffering from war and their service in it—as nurses, military auxiliaries, resistance fighters, or even regular soldiers—did not over-throw the polarized gender regime or, if it did, it was only temporary or marginal.[2] In a groundbreaking essay, Margaret and Patrice Higonnet hence suggested in 1987, using the metaphor of the *double helix*, to explain this "paradoxical progress and regress" and the underlying constancy of a "gender-linked subordination."[3] Paradoxes of change and continuity have since then not only challenged historians of women's roles, lives, and representations but also inspired inquiries into the language of masculinity and the gendered experiences of men. In the following, the development of representations and experiences of military masculinities in the first half of the twentieth century will be analyzed and compared with a focus on Europe, the Soviet Union, and the United States.

RESEARCHING MEN, MASCULINITY, AND WAR

From the mid-1970s to the early 1990s, early gender studies examined military masculinity and male soldiers within a dichotomous framework of gender and sex relations as the basis of patriarchal oppression of women. Most influentially, Klaus Theweleit's study *Male Phantasies*, which was published in German in 1977/78 and in English in 1987, extended an unorthodox illumination of misogynist autobiographic writings of German post–World War I volunteer paramilitary (*Freikorps*) fighters into a universal theory that defines masculinity as rejection, suppression, or destruction of whatever is considered feminine and family oriented: To become a man, one must disavow the feminine.[4]

Often indiscriminately transferred to other historical and social settings, Theweleit's ahistorical view has also provoked critical and nuanced inquiries into the historical change and the social diversity of military masculinities. One strand of research, headed by George L. Mosse, with his 1990 *Fallen Soldiers: Reshaping the Memory of the World Wars*, has focused on public discussions and representations of masculinities in memoirs, novels, monuments, visual propaganda, and movies. It has illuminated how concepts of national identity and citizenship were based on images of heroic masculinities and male bodies.[5] A different approach, suggested in Joanna Bourke's 1996 book *Dismembering the Male: Men's Bodies, Britain, and the Great War* on ordinary British World War I servicemen's private writings and my own 2006 study of military comradeship in twentieth-century Germany, has highlighted the fluidity and ambiguity of experiential sides of masculinity by focusing on men's interaction in all-male, homosocial settings, such as military units or veterans' associations. Rather than fleeing domesticity and femininity, men worked on including these ideals in complex and fragile constructions of male identity.[6] In part, these studies refer to R. W. Connell's concept of *hegemonic masculinities* to challenge simple, binary notions of gender and to explore the historically contingent hierarchies that order diverse masculinities in any given institution, nation, or group of people. Different men (for example, generals versus the rank and file, Black men versus White men, war volunteers versus drafted soldiers) may observe respective masculinities, but these ideas or practices, and their carriers, operate in a constant state of competition for broader social approval and power—that is, for hegemony.[7]

To understand the change of constructions of military masculinity in the first half of the twentieth century, it is necessary to explore the influence of industrialization, brutalization, and "totalization" of modern warfare—new weapons of mass destruction, the targeting of civilians, and the mobilization of ever larger sections of males and females for the war project. The relation of two trajectories deserves special attention: first, the representations of military masculinity (for example, in laws, literature, and artifacts) as the epitome of gendered concepts of nationhood and citizenship; and, second, the subjective experience and appropriation of such representations of military masculinity, or the construction of different concepts of masculinity, especially by combat soldiers in both wars. Neither exists independent of the other. It was the "crisscrossing of ideologies and experience, of discourses and material transformation," according to Kathleen Canning, that propelled or barred change.[8]

The state of research does not allow for a comprehensive comparison of the various Western countries. German-speaking central Europe and the Anglophone part of the Western world have been the focus of most studies, allowing for an exploration of national differences and commonalities between the United States, Britain, Germany, and the Soviet Union.[9] Men's subjective perceptions, emotions, and social practices often refuted "official," public, and authoritative ways of discussing manliness, especially the equation of manliness with toughness, self-control, and emotional or moral strength. In this subjective dimension of military masculinities, the plural matters. And yet these practices confirmed the crucial point of the way societies understood manliness—its insistence on men's dominance in the modern body politic, in the nation, and on the manly character of its policies and politics. In fact, it was the diversity and ambiguity of male experiences in war and their integration into male solidarity that energized the gendered conception of nationhood and citizenship.

MILITARY MASCULINITY AND NATIONHOOD

Any historical inquiry into Western masculinities of the first half of the twentieth century must render an account of the traumatic experience of the First World War.[10] This war destroyed most European monarchies and their ideological basis—the thousand-year-old idea of divine, God-given political regimes—and it eroded other mythical certainties, such as the concept of a biologically determined polarity of male and female roles and characteristics. Since the eighteenth century, this concept had aligned men with the public sphere of work and politics and women with the private sphere of family and household. The concept assigned opposing personality traits to either sex—reason, control, sovereignty, and agency to men; emotion, subordination, dependency, and passivity to women. A militarized understanding of masculinity did not necessarily derive from this gender polarity that allowed for a variety of concepts of masculinity. The entrepreneur or self-employed businessman epitomized its civilian version throughout the nineteenth century and beyond. Only the "democratization" of modern warfare in North America and then Europe since the late eighteenth century—the transition from standing armies to militias of volunteers and then to mass conscription—promoted the "virtuous citizen-soldier" as the epitome of a man.[11] Whether volunteering or conscripted, the citizen-soldier was a man who was ready to switch from the civilian morality of life and production to the martial world of death and destruction. He was ready to sacrifice life and limb to secure the integrity of his nation and family. Men's virility served as the mirror image of women's motherhood.

Only men were able to serve as soldiers, according to the biological fabric of the dominant nineteenth-century views of the gender order, just as only they owned the intellectual and social capacities to govern the body politic, the state, or the local community. Only they bore the physical, emotional, and moral prerequisites of the soldier: the martial virtues of strength, toughness, and stoicism, on the one hand, and the social qualities of a citizen and a comrade who would never hesitate to disregard personal interests on behalf of his nation, his comrades in war, and his family at home on the other. Battle was the ultimate test of this type of manhood; the army served as a boot camp for boys and civilians to internalize the manly virtue of subordinating the "I" to the "We" of the platoon, the army, and the nation. Working as a rite of passage, the army, especially the conscripted one, transformed "weak" (that is, feminized) boys into "hard," real, and by any means heterosexual men and merged men of different civilian identities—classes, religions, and regions—into a homogenous body of fully fledged citizens whose militarized national identity neutralized particularistic civilian identities.[12] The army was the "school of the nation" and the "school of masculinity," as Ute Frevert has shown for the German case.[13]

Stefan Dudink and Karen Hagemann have rightly argued that there was no "joint masculinization of citizenship and militarization of masculinity" in Western modernity. Britain retained its volunteer corps until the introduction of conscription in 1916; military masculinity, particularly of officers, radiated the elitist aura of colonial adventurism. In France, the citizen-soldier emblematized the democratic dynamic of the political culture. In Prussia and, later, in the German Empire, conscription was embedded in the authoritarian state; the soldier represented the subject per se. Discipline, more than adventure, governed his manliness, and the goal of national unification via military service of all men was widely weakened, not least because lower-middle-class men, let alone industrial workers, were barred from the officer corps. Paternalism in the rural societies of the eastern European empires, Russia and Austria-Hungary, on the one hand, and the individualism of the American frontier society—where conscription remained throughout the nineteenth century an only temporary phenomenon and instead heroic warriors decided about victory or defeat—on the other hand embodied two further peculiarities.[14]

THE CHALLENGE OF THE FIRST WORLD WAR AND THE "UNMANLY MEN"

Yet the commonalities are obvious. Western-educated middle classes, by virtue of profession more vociferous than others in shaping ideologies, in unison promoted a commanding, virile concept of manliness comprising toughness, control, and independence that restricted both political rights and military duties to men. In the decades before 1914, secular changes—urbanization, the rise of consumerism and a leisure culture, the diversification of lifestyles, the beginnings of an openly homosexual culture, and an increasing attention to health issues—had indicated that the biologically conceived gender dualism might not be as "natural" as assumed. When the war started in August 1914, many educated Europeans, but not all, welcomed it as a great chance to fight what was perceived as a crisis of masculinity. Even the German female socialist and feminist Lily Braun raved about the war's regenerative power. The war, she wrote in 1915, "eliminates the entire effeminization" that had percolated society. Now it was "afresh men, real men, pervaded and held together by natural savage instincts" who did what men had done for ages: "defending and fighting for the homelands."[15] Her only son had volunteered for the war in 1914 and fell in April 1918 at the Somme.

Like him, other young men, many from the educated middle and upper classes, indeed volunteered for the armies in 1914 to prove their manliness. "I must be a man . . . I ask nothing better than to end in honorable battle for my King and Country," wrote Cyril Holland in June 1914. As the older son of the Irish playwright, novelist, and poet Oscar Wilde, a scandalous gay celebrity in late nineteenth-century London, Holland was obsessed with overcoming the stigma of "effeminate" decadence that persisted on his family because of his father.[16]

When Lily Braun fueled war enthusiasm in 1915, European societies could still dream of a short war that would soon be decided by sportive fights between chivalric knights, as prewar fantasies about military masculinity had predicted; Cyril Holland was indeed killed in a "duel with a German sniper," according to his brother's testimony.[17] But he was an exception. Many more soldiers felt paralyzed and emasculated in the mud of endless trenches as well as in the face of horrible mutilations and unforeseen anonymous mass death that resulted from industrialized warfare, new weapons of mass destruction, and new tactics of attrition. Numerous soldiers found themselves unable to cope with such sights. They suffered from "shell shock," as an English doctor named mental breakdown of front-line soldiers first in 1915. Germans called it *Kriegshysterie* and the French *traumatisme de guerre*. In 1917, a German psychiatrist listed symptoms including "sudden muteness, deafness, general trembling, the inability to stand and walk, fainting spells and cramping" that have now become familiar.[18] Artists such as the British poet Siegfried Sassoon and the German painter Max Beckmann, both of them war volunteers, tried to rework such traumas into art. But the bulk of shell-shock victims remained speechless, embodying the emasculating effects of the battlefield experience. Soldier-men seemed to behave like women, subverting the core principle of manliness, self-control, discipline, and stoicism. The "epidemic of male hysteria" in World War I no longer allowed for heroic martial masculinity, argued Elaine Showalter in her pathbreaking 1985 book *The Female Malady: Women, Madness, and English Culture, 1830–1980*: "If the essence of manliness was not to complain, then shell shock was the body language of masculine complaint, a disguised male protest not only against the war but against the concept of 'manliness' itself."[19]

But "disguised" as it was, this "male protest" did not obliterate the code of military masculinity. Only a small minority of the soldiers indeed suffered from shell shock or other psychological disorders that made them unable to fight. Even the numbers of deserters remained low, until the very end of the war—about 0.5 percent in the British and German armies.[20] The rest stayed on duty, in the trenches or elsewhere, despite massive social and political frictions in armies as different as the Austrian, Russian, French, and German ones. The low rate of desertion was not so much because of patriotism, hatred of the enemy, or coercion, as subjective sources suggest. Instead, the soldiers' tenacity rested, as Leonard V. Smith has noted for the French army, on "the basic solidarities of small groups" that "carried on their own war, often at the fringe of official authority," living "together according to their own rules and hierarchies," and they established a "very specific sociability, based on sharing"—sharing food, drink, and tobacco; duties, skills, and dangers; human warmth, homesickness, and the mourning of fallen comrades.[21] But comradeship, Joanna Bourke emphasizes, "is at the heart of most histories of 'life at the front.'"[22]

Male solidarity in war was complex, ambiguous, and random. It revolved around symbolic acts of femininity—mothering, nursing, and even sleeping together—although exclusively men among men carried out these acts. Solidarity was embedded in fatigue, apathy, indifference, fatalism, and war weariness, a mood of passivity that was often symbolically inflated as doing one's duty. Loneliness and forlornness ruled the contingent lives of the soldiers in and outside the trenches as much as, and often much more than, sociability and solidarity. The soldiers were in "a state of mind," explains Omer Bartov, "that combined a good measure of self-pity with immense pride in their ability to endure inhumane conditions for the sake of a nation seemingly ignorant of and indifferent to their terrible sacrifice," a camaraderie that the combat troops on both sides of the line shared.[23] This way, comradeship gave identity to the social cohesion of a somber community of fate, of soldiers who knew about the senselessness of the war they fought and yet drew a modicum of agency from performing the fatalistic resilience of a doughboy (*Frontschwein*).[24]

CONTESTED POST–WORLD WAR I MEMORIES AND MASCULINITY

Only when the First World War was over were veterans able to give meaning to the experience of meaninglessness by transferring the experience of emasculation into a new cult of martial manliness. Three paths may be distinguished: the pacifist disavowal of aggressive martial masculinity; its belligerent radicalization; and efforts to renew the conjunction of martial and civilian masculinity. In western Europe, it was France, aside from Belgium, that had suffered most from the destruction of its own territory, unlike Britain or Germany. French veterans could not imagine another war. Never-again sentiments shaped interwar France more than any other country. But drawing a pacifist lesson from the last war did not mean that French veterans dismissed military masculinity—the proof of their manliness—altogether. Instead, their memorialization of the war revolved around the sacrifices they and their fallen comrades had made on behalf of their country. In a "community of suffering," military masculinity was not aggressive, but defensive, and gained its manly momentum from enduring horror and overcoming trauma—traditional elements of military masculinity that now appeared in a pacifist context.[25] In a similar fashion, pacifists in Germany did not justify desertion from the army or cowardice, but rather stressed that they too had done their duty on behalf of the fatherland. They confirmed a militarized ideal of tough masculinity that left no space for men who not only condemned war rhetorically, but also abandoned it.[26]

Militaristic nationalists and National Socialists in Weimar and Nazi Germany are known for radicalizing martial masculinity into a warrior cult that celebrated a new race of men, "conquerors, men of steel, primed in the cruelest kind of battle," as militarist writer Ernst Jünger wrote in the early 1920s.[27] Such men would reign in a new world of perpetual war, a world without the restrictions of civilian society. "Finally to be a man, an anti-man, a super-man," echoed a belligerent journal in 1923, meant "to go beyond good and evil."[28] Their manliness was no longer that of the citizen-soldier who overcame the fear of losing life or limb. Instead, Jünger's ultimate warrior gained his pride from overcoming scruples and pangs of conscience, the emblems of the "human" morality of the civilian that the army in war would honor in order to contain the radicalization of killing.[29] Jünger's warrior cult easily grew from former *Freikorps* men's praise of "man's lust for destruction" into the genocidal morality of the Nazi "political soldier" who discarded the entire Judeo-Christian tradition of guilt and mercy and murdered Jews and other civilians for the sake of a racially purified nation, the Nazi people's community (*Volksgemeinschaft*).[30]

A different type of military masculinity emerged from the Great War in the Anglophone world, represented by the "blond Bedouin," Thomas Edward Lawrence, known as Lawrence of Arabia, a British officer who, as a commander of a guerrilla army, led the Bedouin Arabs into freedom. Celebrated as the embodiment of English manliness, he combined the supposedly Scandinavian physical features (blond hair and blue eyes), traditional heroic soldierly virtues of braveness and charismatic leadership, and individualist traits of the eccentric maverick, and yet he was taciturn and lonely, a reclusive scholar with the exoticism of the British colonial tradition. As Graham Dawson put it, the popular depiction of Lawrence embraced "a contrast in modes of masculinity between the traditional image of the military man of action and a more 'passive,' contemplative masculinity which may even be inscribed as 'feminine' or 'effeminate.'"[31]

While national differences in the construction and reconstruction of military masculinities in the interwar period certainly mattered, they should not be overestimated. What they have in common is a complex way of dealing with the tension between soldiers' experiences of weakness, failure, passivity, and the ideal of hardness, success, and action, the latter coded as masculine and the former as feminine. In the wake of mass death, masculinity was reformulated as a process—the lifelong alternation of first indulging in and then overcoming states of femininity, weakness, traumatization, and humiliation. As John Horne has observed, after the First World War, " 'sacrifice' became the mostly widely used trope to express the cost of obeying the norms of militarized masculinity on the battlefield."[32] But conjuring up sacrifice was not meant to dismiss military masculinity. It was all about coping. The cult around prosthetics, supposedly repairing all kinds of war damages and propagated in all post–World War I countries, visualized this concept of masculinity most decisively. Losing a leg could not destroy manliness, and it certainly did not necessarily prevent a man from serving as breadwinner. Enough technologies, tools, and therapies stood ready to reconstruct man's functioning and power.[33] The idealized soldier-man faced and admitted to states of weakness, but he knew how to overcome them and eventually keep functioning.

Responding to the emasculating experience of mass death, mass mutilation, and mass depravation, postwar societies engaged in debates over inclusive and fluid rather than exclusive and rigorous notions of martial virility. Such concepts of manliness gave meaning to the ambivalent, ambiguous, and complex desires, emotions, and experiences of men. The concepts also built bridges over diverging experiences, united disrupted identities, and could be adopted by different types of men as they fought together in modern mass armies. They showed how femininity and masculinity could be on good terms within one person. It was not easy to confess to "tender, womanlike sentiments" and a soldier-man's desire for "empathy and warmth, both female traits," wrote the German World War I volunteer and nationalist writer Franz Schauwecker in 1919 in his novel *Im Todesrachen* (*In Death's Throat*). He did so anyway and publicly. In his novels, he propagated the German soldier as the pioneer of a coming new German nation.[34] Despite all political difference and clear antiwar stance, German writer Erich Maria Remarque emphasized comradeship in his bestselling 1929 novel on World War I, *Im Westen nichts Neues*, translated into English in the same year and published under the title *All Quiet on the Western Front*.[35] The highly contested novel sold between January 1929 and April 1930 twelve of twenty known editions and the sales stood at 2.5 million. The book was a great success, especially in left-liberal and socialist circles where it was praised as an antiwar book.[36] The vantage point of both novels was a soldier neither as coward nor as born warrior, but a soldier who longed for home, security, and harmony, which he found with his comrades. The comradely soldier was tough and tender at the same time.[37]

Similar myths emerged in other countries as well, although there were different paths of remembering homosociality in war. While the concepts of friendship and comradeship were often conflated, they carried different meanings in both the German and the English languages. Friendship equaled intimate "individualized relationships of amity and love between men," according to Sarah Cole. Comradeship was the concept that referred to "a corporate or group commitment" beyond individual choice, but coerced. While the German interwar discourse on military masculinities praised the powerful experience of fateful comradeship that compensated for all the suffering, its British equivalent favored the concept of voluntary friendship but bemoaned its destruction in war. Friends (even more so, comrades) were "killed in the course of the day" and, if they did not end through death, friendships were terminated by "a bureaucracy that ceaselessly and arbitrarily" transferred soldiers from one unit to another and thus "separated friends from one another."[38] Notwithstanding many parallels between the meaning of comradeship in German and British World War I memories, the British focus on the individual soldier and consequently on individual friendship—usually between two men—contrasts with the German fascination after 1918 and especially from the late 1920s with the squad, platoon, and company.[39]

One can draw further lines of comparison in the Anglophone world. While the ultimate bestseller among German war novels, Remarque's *All Quiet on the Western Front*, was a hymn to comradeship, an American bestselling war novel published in the same year shunned this military virtue. Although comradeship is not missing from the novel *A Farewell to Arms*, by American author Ernest Hemingway, set during the Italian campaign of World War I, the hero did not find much comradeship, and certainly he did not dwell on it. The story did not revolve around a fatalistic all-male bond, but around the love between the soldier and a women; its vantage point was the civilian world, not the battlefield.[40] Only Hemingway's second and even more successful war novel from 1940, *For Whom the Bell Tolls*, chose comradeship as its theme. It tells the story of Robert Jordan, a young American in the International Brigades attached to a Republican guerrilla unit during the Spanish Civil War (1936–39). But the comradeship depicted in this novel was entirely different from that in Remarque's 1929 novel, because *For Whom the Bell Tolls* focuses on a gender-mixed partisan group anticipating the rise of anti-Nazi guerrilla troops in Europe during the Second World War, which included female fighters more deliberately than any regular army would do. This allowed romantic relationships between men and women. The comradeship in this novel was embedded in agency—in individual decisions and choices that started with the American Robert Jordan's volunteering for the Spanish guerrilla group, continued through inner dialogues about responsibility and personalities, and ended with Jordan's request to die alone on behalf of the group.[41]

It would be a mistake to regard Hemingway's war romance as representative of the dominant American version of military masculinities of that time, however. Instead, in America, just as in any European country including the Soviet Union, different concepts were at work and often competed with each other. While national peculiarities may be observed, transnational commonalities were at least as powerful. Since the late nineteenth century, the Western discourse on masculinities had been shaped by the rising athletic movement, articulating the desire for physical strength and youth or youthfulness as the crucial feature of manliness; classic Greek statues provided the blueprint. This was a deliberate departure from previous notions of manliness, which had prioritized moral, spiritual, and social qualities over physical ones. Initially and still in the 1930s, it was a common Western phenomenon, not a German peculiarity, but it was radicalized in Nazi Germany. Supernatural statues came to visualize Nazi fantasies about the dominance of the Aryan master race; the male body cult received the fascist imprint it still has in the early twenty-first century. In the Third Reich, the muscular male body— most prominently in the supernatural statues of the sculptors Joseph Thorak and Arno

Breker—symbolized the *Volksgemeinschaft*, the racially purified Aryan nation.[42] Nazi propaganda, however, never monopolized the muscular, youthful, athletic, heroic, seemingly invincible male body; it remained popular throughout the Western world and symbolized the nation at war also in the United States, although in a less martial way than in Germany. As often in representations and practices of gender norms, the devil is in the details. The symbolic male body in Nazi Germany was depicted nude, machine-like, and devoid of individual traits. The United States, by contrast, "incorporated a broader range of bodies within its body politic." These bodies "retained distinct facial characteristics," thus invoking America's individualistic culture, as Christina Jarvis has shown. Occasionally, they even played with the theme of racial diversity.[43]

COMBAT EXPERIENCE AND MALE BONDING IN WORLD WAR II

Since the Second World War, many scholars have argued that the patriotic framework of military masculinity, so dominant in public rhetoric, had little to no impact on soldiers' subjective experiences, fighting morale, or coping strategies, especially in combat. What made the soldiers fight and risk their lives was not the imagery of nationhood and citizenship, but concerns about and ties to their close comrades. Based on extensive interviews with American GIs, German Wehrmacht soldiers in US captivity during and shortly after the war, and former soldiers of the Red Army who had emigrated to the United States, two American research groups headed by the sociologists Samuel Stouffer and Edward Shils argued that the typical combat soldier was not driven by secondary symbols such as nationalism, but rather by the solidarity with their "primary group," the face-to-face comrades of their outfit or company.[44]

Inspired by the post–World War I myth of front-line comradeship, these studies suggest a complex view of the subjective, emotional, and moral dimensions of military masculinity. Crucial from a gendered perspective is that comradeship in war replaced certain reproductive features of domestic, gender-mixed civilian life at home and renewed them in an all-male society whose "production" consisted of and was embedded in the opposite of what men would do in civilian life—in death, destruction, killing, and facing the threat of being killed.

Some examples inform my own work on the German Wehrmacht: Deep comradeship to his buddy Flattmann had helped Helmut Wißmann many times in coping with the desperation he suffered as one of the 3 million German Wehrmacht soldiers at the eastern front. His wife's wish that he should transfer to a safe post in the rear upset him, as he explained in a letter to her. In May 1942, he and Flattmann were ordered to carry out a nighttime intelligence mission, a suicide action through mined and marshy territory along the main front. When they came under heavy fire, Wißmann urged Flattmann— who, unlike Wißmann, was a father—to stay behind or back out. But Flattmann declined. "He came along with me. If we have to, we'll fall together," Flattmann had said, a reaction that made Wißmann see him as a model comrade and embrace this type of male solidarity through the end of war, even after Flattmann was transferred to a different unit. As apodictic recollections like this were articulated, they radiated fragility and ambiguity. Comradeship could not be relied on, but instead was constantly jeopardized by the contingency of death, reasonable or misguided transfers, and unwilling comrades. Stable was the female "Other," women (not femininity) who, per se, did not belong. The point of Wißmann's letter to his wife was that she would never understand why the front-line soldier could not stay behind—away from the fighting.[45]

Defined through its separation from civilian society, military comradeship in war created a new liminal society from the beginning. It welded together men with different civilian identities, made them replace their individual identities through a mutually shared group identity, established new formal and informal hierarchies—the informal ones dependent on a diverse set of masculine standards—and eventually urged them to replace their civilian, life-saving morality with a martial morality that revolved around death—killing and being killed. Heroic combat performance, however, was only the most adored part of comradeship. By showing feminine qualities and staging family-like settings, exclusively male societies did not simply freshen their ties to the civilian world at home; instead, they staged the male bond's independence from real women and real families, from civilian society and civilian morality.

The message was that being on their own, men are able to generate a warm sense of family, even if they fight cold-bloodedly a few seconds later. They may miss the world at home, but now they create it themselves. Demonstrating the independence of male society from the world at home went far beyond performing family-like sociability and solidarity in the face of lethal danger. An entire set of "manly" rituals, all of them violating domestic and civilian norms, served to conform to the claim for autarchy. Demonstrative excessive drinking, showing of sexual adventures, boasting misogynic rhetoric, staging rowdyism, and even collective rape in extreme cases—all these behaviors gained social momentum from being "celebrated"—practiced, reported, or applauded—*together*. The moral grammar of comradeship always obeyed the same rule: Anything was allowed that enriched and intensified the social life. Whether fueled by misogyny or motherliness, by heroism or charity, toughness or tenderness, the "anti-structure" of comradeship relied on challenging the "structure" of the civilian world outside.[46]

This is a generic description. In the historical reality of innumerable face-to-face units of different armies, the fabric of male solidarity and the standards of manliness could take on rather different and even opposing shapes and shades, depending on the group's members, especially its formal and informal leaders, and on the "secondary symbols" they related to. Unlike what Shils's and Stouffer's teams thought, ideas about nationhood and patriotism did matter, although only in relation to primary group structures. Whereas in Hitler's army the apotheosis of the enforced, dutiful, and fateful male community marginalized concepts of manly individualism and responsibility, American GIs and British soldiers knew that they were backed and controlled by, and would return into, a functioning civilian society that honored the individual pursuit of happiness, democratic procedures of decision-making, and individual responsibility and contained the male bond's anticivilian dynamic.[47]

Even within the Wehrmacht, genocidal concepts of masculinity competed with the traditional concepts that dominated in the American army. The ideal Nazi soldier, the "political soldier," proved his manliness by murdering "racially alien" or "inferior" civilians, especially Jews, and by overcoming feelings of guilt that were denounced as remnants of liberal and Judeo-Christian ideologies. But numerous German soldiers defined their manliness exactly by defending the values of the latter and considered murdering civilians cowardly—unmanly, that is. Such soldiers were denounced as "weaklings" but not court-martialed, discharged, imprisoned, or otherwise excluded from the male military community. Unity requires functional differentiation. Hence, the all-male society needed weaklings, the German army as well as any other. In a culture of dominant "tough" masculinity, they represented the other and thus helped to make the dominant virtues (which, as may be repeated, accepted "weakness" as a temporary condition to be fought and overcome) properly visible. This was the mechanism that kept all kinds of soldiers who were looked on as "weak" or "effeminate" within the army, in some cases even homosexuals.[48]

Since the nineteenth century, the heterosexual standard had informed the discourse on military service and citizenship. Homosexual men embodied effeminacy per se, thus being considered a threat to the fighting power of the army. Consequently, the prevailing moral and judicial language rigidly stigmatized open homosexuality. Numerous studies on Germany, Britain, and North America suggest that homosexual men in the Second World War found themselves even more stigmatized and persecuted than in the First World War, when depictions of homosexual "warrior" activists and ambiguous concepts such as friendship and comradeship still allowed for a euphemistic vocabulary for homosexual love. In England, that was thanks to the prewar tradition of respectable public-school homoeroticism even more than in Germany.[49] In Germany, Hitler's rise to power gave way to brutal persecution of homosexual men, who were, however, not considered hereditarily abnormal but instead emotionally misled and weak and thus healable, whether in prison or through military service.

In the United States at the time of the First World War, homosexuals had been criminalized only for committing acts of sodomy. In the 1930s, under the impact of psychological and, especially, Freudian psychoanalytical theory, a much broader concept of homosexuality emerged and inspired a systematic policy of exclusion in World War II. Such a conception did not lead homosexuals into prison, but rather mostly into the stigma of a dishonorable discharge. While there is no reason to diminish Nazi terror on open homosexuality or to sentimentalize the World War II armies as gay refuges, the comradely social fabric of the military allowed for some tenuous tolerance toward homosexuals who managed to "stay under the radar." "Some gay GIs were harassed and abused by their fellow soldiers," observed Allan Bérubé, "but the more common experience . . . was of uneasy acceptance unless they aggressively pursued uninterested men. . . . Many effeminate GIs were surprised to discover that they, too, could find a place for themselves in military life. . . . Even the most effeminate man could be accepted affectionately if he played an asexual role." This asexual role, however, was the prerequisite.[50]

EXTENSIONS OF MILITARY MASCULINITY

Inclusions, exclusions, and hierarchies informed military masculinity; the military outlet was the place to practice, train, negotiate, and renegotiate them. Views and practices of military masculinity determined who—men, women, certain types of men or women—was "in" and who was "out," that is, who qualified as soldier and citizen. These discourses and practices further determined which roles and traits, characteristics, attitudes, and actions were honored, adored, and re-enacted and which were repelled. The male bond claimed to unite and harmonize diverse male personalities and contradictory emotional conditions of men. But this inclusive fabric was tied into powerful exclusions. They targeted women, but also men who refused or were not allowed to prove their martial manliness, like Jews, homosexuals, or African Americans. These exclusions conflicted with the "totalization" of warfare, which demanded the mobilization of ever larger, ideally all sections of the nation in the Second World War much more than in the First World War.

Women were mobilized for the military in increasing numbers during the First and Second World Wars by the main war powers, Britain, France, Germany, and the United States, regardless of the type of political system. They were employed not only as nurses but also as military auxiliaries. As such, they replaced male soldiers in a quickly growing number of tasks beyond domestic, cookery, mechanical, and clerical jobs during World War I. In the Russian and later the Soviet army, they even fought as armed soldiers. In addition to these several million women, 2 to 5 percent of the military personnel, an uncounted number of women joined the resistance movements across Europe, in which they supplied 10 to 15 percent of the armed combatants. The line that all militaries, with the exception of the USSR, tried to keep for female military employment was combat.[51] In the Red Army, the experience that "the front was no longer reserved for men alone" challenged conventional ideas about the gender order that constructed the men as the protector of women and with it the concept of martial masculinity.[52]

This concept was also challenged by the integration of "deviant" men in the military, notably Jews, homosexuals, and African Americans. Almost half of the German-Jewish World War I soldiers, many of whom had volunteered to demonstrate their devotion to the Fatherland, had been decorated for bravery, and many Jewish soldiers had died on the battlefield alongside their gentile comrades. During the conflict, the infamous Jewish Census (*Judenzählung*) had questioned these Jews' manly pride. After the war, antisemitic membership statutes in rightist veterans' associations did so even more deliberately already in Weimar Germany. The Nazi state's racist citizenship laws pseudo-legally took from Jewish men the honor of military masculinity by denying them and even Aryan husbands of Jewish wives the opportunity to serve in the army. This happened when universal conscription was introduced again by the Reich Defense Law of May 1935, against the terms of the Versailles Treaty of 1919, and in the regulation of citizenship by the infamous racist Nuremberg Laws of September 1935. First in Nazi Germany and later also in Nazi-occupied Europe, any Aryan woman ranked higher than any Jewish man, and no woman experienced this inversion of the traditional gender order more vividly than those in uniform who served as one of the 450,000 to 500,000 Wehrmacht auxiliaries or one of the SS camp guards of the Nazi Schutzstaffel (Protection Squadron).[53]

Yet, this experience was an ambivalent one, on both sides. Honoring the idea that male military solidarity trumped political and ideological—that is, civilian—differences, gentile German veterans and active soldiers occasionally protected Jewish comrades from harassment in veterans' associations and from Nazi persecution, even during the Holocaust and in Hitler's army.[54] However, female SS guards in the Third Reich could not give orders to male guards, and even less could female auxiliaries command male soldiers. Instead, the concept of male solidarity that could cover for Jewish men could also show Aryan women quite plainly that they did not belong. When a Wehrmacht major in the east announced the opening of a new brothel and ordered his unit collectively to visit it, he did so in front of a few female military auxiliaries, who felt deeply denigrated by this obvious misogyny and demonstration of male solidarity and power over women.[55]

Heterosexuality was one important identity-forming basis in all militaries, which systematically excluded identified homosexuals since the First World War. For example, the US Articles of War of 1916, implemented in March 1917, stated that any person subject to military law who committed "assault with intent to commit sodomy" "shall be punished as a court-martial may direct." The article was modified in 1920 to make the act of sodomy itself a crime.[56] Other militaries pursued a similar policy until far into the post-1945 period. The inclusive fabric of heterosexual male solidarity kept women and gay men out of or at a distance from all World War II armies. At the same time, it provided a social space for experimenting with models of nation-building that included hitherto excluded groups of men. That war unites nations by distracting their peoples from domestic fractures and cleavages has been a common Western wisdom that was probably never more betrayed than in World War I.

In Germany, class gaps deepened, and in the United States racial conflicts increased. The German officer corps closed their ranks to and humiliated blue-collar workers at a time when, at home, the Prussian three-class voting system marginalized the political citizenship of the working class, who eventually experienced equality only in death on the battlefield.[57] In the United States, President Woodrow Wilson's global campaign for democracy fell short of extending the principles of democratic citizenship to America's most discriminated-against minority, the African Americans who had volunteered to fight for their country abroad but saw themselves betrayed by first being excluded from combat and then experiencing the continuation or intensification of these racist prejudices back home.[58]

The myth of nation-building through military masculinity did not die from these fractures, but was instead revitalized in the interwar period by the cult of the Unknown

Soldier. The first Unknown Soldier was buried in Westminster Abbey in 1920, and soon such other Western countries as France, the United States, and Italy followed. In Germany, the myth of comradeship served the same purpose. Both silenced the social conflicts that had divided nations and armies in war by shifting them into the anonymity of the war dead and by exalting the front-line soldiers as the true bearers of the united nation.[59]

In the Second World War, both the American and the German armies successfully intensified their nationalizing programs, limited again to the dominant White or Aryan parts of their respective societies. In the German army, widespread antisemitism and popular support of the Holocaust as the annihilation of the demonized "Other" helped to marginalize class conflicts and other internal cleavages more effectively than ever thought. Apart from rare cases of protecting Jewish—in fact, mostly "half" or "quarter" Jewish—comrades, Hitler's soldiers did not have and did not seek a chance to experiment with overcoming racial gaps through comradeship. In the American army, Euro-Americans, here including Jews and Catholics, too "achieved a unity and a sense of common Americanness greater" than ever, as Gary Gerstle has asserted. While maintaining "the black–white division" barring African Americans from military base clubs and recreational facilities and widely refusing to assign "well-meaning but irresponsible children" (as a 1943 memo stated) to combat troops, this type of racism still could be questioned. The fact that President Harry S. Truman felt compelled to desegregate the military in 1948 was the result of increasing pressure from the African American community but also from both White and Black soldiers' experience of cross-racial bonding in mixed combat units at the end of the war. "When German shells and bombs are raining about them," wrote Walter White, the chairman of the National Association for the Advancement of Colored People in 1944, "they do not worry as much about race or creed of the men next to them."[60]

For African American soldiers of World War II, the reality of war had been far more complex. War participation had indeed increased their sense of male pride. They had experienced less racism in Europe, especially in Britain and France. But they did not profit after the war in the same way as White soldiers from the 1944 Servicemen's Readjustment Act (known as the GI Bill), which was supposed to reintegrate returning veterans into civil society by financing a college education and providing loans for the purchase of homes through its Veterans Housing Administration program. The civil and social citizenship rights of African American veterans still were far from equal. This complex situation prompted them to fight for and defend their rights more assertively than ever before after 1945. Veterans became a very active group in the rising civil rights movement.[61]

CONCLUSION

In the Age of World Wars, constructions and destructions of societies, states, and ideologies succeeded rapidly and repeatedly, and so did the construction and destruction of gender orders and gender norms. In Western societies, heroic, martial, even supernatural concepts of military masculinity were culturally and socially less dominant than inclusive, volatile, in fact, protean imageries and practices of masculinity. They allowed different men to perform aggressive as well as defensive solidarity before, in, and after combat and allowed men to display different emotional states without abandoning their male identity. And yet, there were exclusions—not just enemies, but certain groups within their own nation. This way, the excluded Others were, most of all, women, homosexuals, or racially stigmatized men. Overall, however, the dramatic radicalization of military violence, the mobilization of ever-larger parts of the belligerent societies, and the increasingly planned mass killing of civilians challenged even those exclusions, as especially the changes from the First to the Second World Wars suggest.

Future research will further enrich and expand the picture of military masculinity discussed here by paying attention to more states, including the Soviet Union, and colonized regions and comparing them. We also have no studies on concepts of masculinity in the different partisan armies of the Second World War.[62] Needed are furthermore studies that explore the difference between and interaction of representations and practices of military masculinity more systematically, and compare different types of military units, such as drafted mass armies and elite troops. Finally, an investigation of masculinities not only in conventional military settings, but also in irregular as well as genocidal formations is much needed.

Notes

1. For a discussion of the concept of *total war*, see the chapter by Karen Hagemann and Sonya O. Rose on "War and Gender: The Age of the World Wars and Its Aftermath—an Overview" in this handbook.
2. See the chapter by Karen Hagemann on "History and Memory of Female Military Service in the Age of World Wars" in this handbook.
3. Margaret R. Higonnet and Patrice L.-R. Higonnet, "The Double Helix," in *Behind the Lines: Gender and the Two World Wars*, ed. Margaret R. Higonnet et al. (New Haven, CT: Yale University Press, 1987), 31–47.
4. Klaus Theweleit, *Male Fantasies*, 2 vols. (Minneapolis: University of Minnesota Press, 1987–89). See also the chapter by Karen Hagemann on "Gender, Demobilization, and the Reordering of Societies after the First and Second World Wars" in this handbook.
5. George L. Mosse, *Fallen Soldiers: Reshaping the Memory of the World Wars* (New York: Oxford University Press, 1990); Mosse, *The Image of Man: The Creation of Modern Masculinity* (New York: Oxford University Press, 1996); and Christina S. Jarvis, *The Male Body at War: American Masculinity during World War II* (DeKalb: Northern Illinois University Press, 2004).
6. Joanna Bourke, *Dismembering the Male: Men's Bodies, Britain, and the Great War* (London: Reaction, 1996); Thomas Kühne, *Kameradschaft: Die Soldaten des nationalsozialistischen Krieges und das 20. Jahrhundert* (Göttingen: Vandenhoeck & Ruprecht, 2006); and Kühne, *The Rise and Fall of Comradeship: Hitler's Soldiers, Male Bonding and Mass Violence in the 20th Century* (Cambridge: Cambridge University Press, 2017).
7. R. W. Connell, *Masculinities* (Cambridge: Cambridge University Press, 1995); R. W. Connell and James W. Messerschmidt, "Hegemonic Masculinity: Rethinking the Concept," *Gender*

& *Society* 19, no. 6 (2005): 829–59; and Frank J. Barrett, "The Organizational Construction of Hegemonic Masculinity: The Case of the US Navy," *Gender, Work and Organization* 3, no. 3 (1996): 129–42. For more current critical reflections, see John Tosh, "Hegemonic Masculinity and the History of Gender," in *Masculinities in Politics and War: Gendering Modern History*, ed. Stefan Dudink et al. (Manchester: Manchester University Press, 2004), 41–60.

8. Kathleen Canning, *Gender History in Practice: Historical Perspectives on Bodies, Class, and Citizenship* (Ithaca, NY: Cornell University Press, 2006), 15.

9. For a more global focus that includes the colonial wars, see the chapters by Marilyn Lake on "The 'White Man,' Race, and Imperial War during the Long Nineteenth Century," and Richard Smith on "Colonial Soldiers, Race, and Military Masculinities during and beyond World Wars I and II" in this handbook.

10. See Alan Kramer, *Dynamic of Destruction: Culture and Mass Killing in the First World War* (Oxford: Oxford University Press, 2007).

11. Stefan Dudink and Karen Hagemann, "Masculinity in Politics and War in the Age of Democratic Revolutions, 1750–1850," in Dudink et al., *Masculinities*, 3–21; also John Horne, "Masculinity in Politics and War in the Age of Nations States and World Wars," in ibid., 22–40.

12. See Horne, "Masculinity." See also Aaron Belkin, *Bring Me Men: Military Masculinity and the Benign Facade of American Empire, 1898–2001* (New York: Columbia University Press, 2012). For other countries, see Anders Ahlbaeck, *Soldiering and the Making of Finnish Manhood; Conscription and Masculinity in Interwar Finland, 1918–1939* (Abo: Abo Akademi Universit, 2010); and Christof Dejung, *Aktivdienst und Geschlechterordnung: Eine Kultur- und Alltagsgeschichte des Militärdienstes in der Schweiz 1939–1945* (Zurich: Chronos, 2007).

13. Ute Frevert, *A Nation in Barracks: Modern Germany, Military Conscription and Civil Society* (Oxford: Berg, 2004). See also the chapters by Stefan Dudink on "Citizenship, Mass Mobilization, and Masculinity in a Transatlantic Perspective, 1770s–1870s," and Robert A. Nye on "War Mobilization, Gender, and Military Culture in Nineteenth-Century Western Societies" in this handbook.

14. Dudink and Hagemann, "Masculinity," 18; also with a comparative perspective, Ute Frevert, ed., *Militär und Gesellschaft im 19. und 20. Jahrhundert* (Stuttgart: Klett-Cotta, 1997).

15. Lily Braun, *Die Frauen und der Krieg* (Leipzig: Hirzel, 1915), 9. On Lily Braun, see Ute Lischke, *Lily Braun, 1865–1916: German Writer, Feminist, Socialist* (Rochester, NY: Camden House, 2000).

16. Cited in Leo Braudy, *From Chivalry to Terrorism: War and the Changing Nature of Masculinity* (New York: Alfred A. Knopf, 2003), 384.

17. Ibid., 385.

18. Kramer, *Dynamic of Destruction*, 258–59. On shell shock during and after World War I, see Peter Leese, *Shell Shock: Traumatic Neurosis and the British Soldiers of the First World War* (New York: Palgrave, 2002); and Paul Lerner, *Hysterical Men: War, Psychiatry, and the Politics of Trauma in Germany, 1890–1930* (Ithaca, NY: Cornell University Press, 2003). For Finland during World War II, see Ville Kivimaki, *Battled Nerves: Finnish Soldiers' War Experience, Trauma, and Military Psychiatry, 1941–1944* (Tampere: Juvenes Print, 2013).

19. Elaine Showalter, *The Female Malady: Women, Madness, and English Culture, 1830–1980* (New York: Pantheon, 1985), 172; and see also her *Hystories: Hysterical Epidemics and Modern Media* (New York: Columbia University Press, 1997).

20. Alexander Watson, *Enduring the Great War: Combat, Morale and Collapse in the German and British Armies, 1914–1918* (Cambridge: Cambridge University Press, 2008), 42–43.

21. Leonard V. Smith et al., *France and the Great War, 1914–1918* (Cambridge: Cambridge University Press, 2003), 97–100.

22. Joanna Bourke, *Dismembering,* 22–25, 126–27, 131–32, 136. See also Jessica Meyer, *Men of War: Masculinity and the First World War in Britain* (Basingstoke: Palgrave Macmillan, 2009); and Michael Roper, *The Secret Battle: Emotional Survival in the Great War* (Manchester: Manchester University Press, 2009).

23. Omer Bartov, *Mirrors of Destruction: War, Genocide, and Modern Identity* (Oxford: Oxford University Press, 2000), 12; and Kühne, *Rise and Fall.* On masculinity in the Third Reich more generally, see Kühne, ed., "Masculinity and the Third Reich," special issue, *Central European History* 51, no. 3 (2018).

24. Watson, *Enduring,* 210–11 and 230–31.

25. Bartov, *Mirrors of Destruction,* 18.

26. Kühne, *Kameradschaft,* 68–91.

27. Ernst Jünger, *Der Kampf als inneres Erlebnis* (Berlin: Mittler, 1922), 21–22.

28. *Der Weisse Ritter. Zeitschrift des Jungen Deutschland* 5 (1923), 23–25, facsimile in *Wehrerziehung und Kriegsgedanke in der Weimarer Republik: Ein Lesebuch zur Kriegsbegeisterung und Kriegserziehung junger Männer,* vol. 2: *Jugendverbände und -bünde,* ed. Benno Hafeneger and Michael Fritz (Frankfurt am Main: Brandes & Apsel, 1992), 47–49.

29. Jünger, *Der Kampf,* 26.

30. Thomas Kühne, *Belonging and Genocide: Hitler's Community, 1918–1945* (New Haven, CT: Yale University Press, 2010), 63–68.

31. Graham Dawson, "The Blond Bedouin: Lawrence of Arabia, Imperial Adventure and the Imagining of English–British Masculinity," in *Manful Assertions: Masculinities in Britain since 1800,* ed. Michel Roper and John Tosh (London: Routledge, 1991), 113–44, 117 and 124; and Graham Dawson, *Soldier Heroes: British Adventure, Empire, and the Imagining of Masculinities* (London: Routledge, 1994).

32. Horne, "Masculinity," 32.

33. Sabiene Kienitz, "Body Damage: War Disability and Constructions of Masculinity in Weimar Germany," in *Home/Front: The Military, War, and Gender in Twentieth Century Germany,* ed. Karen Hagemann and Stephanie Schüler-Springorum (Oxford: Berg, 2002), 181–204; Deborah Cohen, *The War Come Home: Disabled Veterans in Britain and Germany, 1914–1939* (Berkeley: University of California Press, 2001); Sabine Kienitz, *Beschädigte Helden: Kriegsinvalidität und Körperbilder 1914–1923* (Paderborn: Schöningh, 2008); and, recently, Heather Perry, *Recycling the Disabled: Army, Medicine, and Modernity in World War I Germany* (Manchester: Manchester University Press, 2014).

34. Franz Schauwecker, *Im Todesrachen: Die deutsche Seele im Weltkrieg* (Halle: Diekmann, 1919), 16–20, 68.

35. Erich Maria Remarque, *Im Westen nichts Neues* (Berlin: Propyläen Verlag, 1929).

36. Mordris Ekstein, "All Quite on the Western Front and the Fate of a War," *Journal of Contemporary History* 15, no. 2 (1980): 345–66, 353.

37. On masculinity in post–World War I novels, see Trevor Dodman, *Shell Shock, Memory, and the Novel in the Wake of World War I* (New York: Cambridge University Press, 2015).

38. Sarah Cole, *Modernism, Male Friendship, and the First World War* (Cambridge: Cambridge University Press, 2007), 139, 144–46, 148, 151, and 155.

39. Svenja Levsen, "Constructing Elite Identities: University Students, Military Masculinity and the Consequences of the Great War in Britain and Germany," *Past and Present* 198 (2008): 147–83.

40. Ernest Hemingway, *A Farewell to Arms* (1929; repr., New York: Scribner, 1997).

41. Ernest Hemingway, *For Whom the Bell Tolls* (1940; repr., New York: Scribner, 1968).

42. See Paula Diehl, *Macht—Mythos—Utopie: Die Körperbilder der SS-Männer* (Berlin: Akademie Verlag, 2005).

43. Jarvis, *Male Body*, 48–50; pictures in ibid., 41, 43, 49, 51, 53.

44. Edward Shils and Morris Janowitz, "Cohesion and Disintegration in the Wehrmacht in World War II," *Public Opinion Quarterly* 12, no. 2 (1948): 280–315; Samuel Stouffer et al., *The American Soldier*, vol. 1, *Adjustment during Army Life*, and vol. 2, *Combat and Its Aftermath* (Princeton, NJ: Princeton University Press, 1949); Darryl Henderson, *Cohesion: The Human Element in Combat; Leadership and Societal Influence in the Armies of the Soviet Union, the United States, North Vietnam, and Israel* (Washington, DC: National Defense University Press, 1985); and Simon Wessely, "Twentieth-Century Theories on Combat Motivation and Breakdown," *Journal of Contemporary History* 41, no. 2 (2006): 275–86.

45. Quotations in Kühne, *Kameradschaft*, 193.

46. Kühne, *Belonging and Genocide*, 46–47 and 120–26; Victor W. Turner, *The Ritual Process: Structure and Anti-Structure* (Ithaca, NY: Cornell University Press, 1977); Henry Elkins, "Aggressive and Erotic Tendencies in Army Life," *American Journal of Sociology* 51, no. 5 (1945): 408–13; and Madeline Morris, "By Force of Arms: Rape, War, and Military Culture," *Duke Law Journal* 45 (1996): 651–781.

47. Kühne, *Rise and Fall*, 160–214.

48. Kühne, *Belonging*, 87.

49. Jason Crouthamel, *An Intimate History of the Front: Masculinity, Sexuality and German Soldiers in the First World War* (Basingstoke: Palgrave MacMillan, 2014); and Paul Fussel, *The Great War and Modern Memory* (New York: Oxford University Press, 1975), 270–309.

50. Allan Bérubé, *Coming Out under Fire: The History of Gay Men and Women in World War Two* (New York: Free Press, 1990), 52–54; see Kühne, *Kameradschaft*, 118, for a similar account of the German army.

51. For more, see the chapters by Hagemann on "History and Memory," and Hagemann and D'Ann Campbell on "Post-1945 Western Militaries, Female Soldiers, and Gay and Lesbian Rights" in this handbook.

52. Anna Krylova, *Soviet Women in Combat: A History of Violence on the Eastern Front* (New York: Cambridge University Press, 2010), 18 and 271.

53. Kühne, *Belonging and Genocide*, 137–54.

54. Michael Geheran, "Betrayed Comradeship: German-Jewish WWI Veterans under Hitler" (PhD diss., Clark University, 2016); and Bryan Mark Riggs, *Hitler's Jewish Soldiers: The Untold Story of Nazi Racial Laws and Men of Jewish Descent in the German Military* (Lawrence: University Press of Kansas, 2002).

55. Ilse Schmidt, *Die Mitläuferin: Erinnerungen einer Wehrmachtsangehörigen* (Berlin: Aufbau, 1999), 47–48.

56. Margot Canady, *The Straight State: Sexuality and Citizenship in Twentieth-Century America* (Princeton, NJ: Princeton University Press, 2009), 87; for more, see Hagemann and Campbell, "Post-1945 Western Militaries" in this handbook.

57. Benjamin Ziemann, *War Experiences in Rural Germany, 1914–1923* (Oxford: Berg, 2007).

58. Robert B. Edgerton, *Hidden Heroism: Black Soldiers in America's Wars* (Boulder, CO: Westview, 2001); Gary Gerstle, *American Crucible: Race and Nation in the Twentieth Century* (Princeton, NJ: Princeton University Press, 2001), 81–127; Richard Slotkin, *Lost Battalions: The Great War and the Crisis of American Nationality* (New York: Henry Holt, 2005); and Adriane Lentz-Smith, *Freedom Struggles: African Americans and World War I* (Cambridge, MA: Harvard University Press, 2009).

59. See, for instance, Gabriel Koureas, *Memory, Masculinity, and National Identity in British Visual Culture, 1914–1930: A Study of Unconquerable Manhood* (Aldershot: Ashgate, 2007).

60. Gerstle, *American Crucible*, 187–88, 214–15, 228, 231; and Neil A. Winn, *The Afro-American and the Second World War*, 2nd ed. (New York: Holmes & Meyer, 1993).

61. See Steve Estes, "Man the Guns: Race, Masculinity, and Citizenship from World War II to the Civil Rights Movement," in *Gender and the Long Postwar: The United States and the Two Germanys, 1945–1989*, ed. Karen Hagemann and Sonya Michel (Baltimore: Johns Hopkins University Press, 2014), 185–203; Jennifer E. Brooks, *Defining the Peace: World War II Veterans, Race, and the Remaking of Southern Political Tradition* (Chapel Hill: University of North Carolina Press, 2004); and Robert Francis Saxe, *Settling Down: World War II Veterans' Challenge to the Postwar Consensus* (New York: Palgrave Macmillan, 2007). See also Hagemann, "Gender, Demobilization" in this handbook.

62. See the chapter by Smith "Colonial Soldiers" in this handbook.

SELECT BIBLIOGRAPHY

Bartov, Omer. *Mirrors of Destruction: War, Genocide, and Modern Identity*. Oxford: Oxford University Press, 2000.

Belkin, Aaron. *Bring Me Men: Military Masculinity and the Benign Facade of American Empire, 1898–2001*. New York: Columbia University Press, 2012.

Bourke, Joanna. *Dismembering the Male: Men's Bodies, Britain, and the Great War*. Chicago: University of Chicago Press, 1996.

Bourke, Joanna. *An Intimate History of Killing: Face-to-Face Killing in Twentieth-Century Warfare*. London: Granta Press, 1999.

Coetzee, Frans, and Marilyn Shevin-Coetzee, eds. *Authority, Identity and the Social History of the Great War*. Providence, RI: Berg, 1995.

Cole, Sarah. *Modernism, Male Friendship, and the First World War*. Cambridge: Cambridge University Press, 2003.

Crouthamel, Jason. *An Intimate History of the Front: Masculinity, Sexuality and German Soldiers in the First World War*. Basingstoke: Palgrave Macmillan, 2014.

Diehl, Paula. *Macht—Mythos—Utopie: Die Körperbilder der SS-Männer*. Berlin: Akademie Verlag, 2005.

Dudink, Stefan, Karen Hagemann, and John Tosh, eds. *Masculinities in Politics and War: Gendering Modern History*. Manchester: Manchester University Press, 2004.

Jackson, Paul. *One of the Boys: Homosexuality in the Military during World War II*. Montreal: McGill–Queen's University Press, 2004.

Kramer, Alan. *Dynamic of Destruction: Culture and Mass Killing in the First World War*. Oxford: Oxford University Press, 2007.

Kühne, Thomas. *Belonging and Genocide: Hitler's Community, 1918–1945*. New Haven, CT: Yale University Press, 2010.

Kühne, Thomas. *The Rise and Fall of Comradeship: Hitler's Soldiers, Male Bonding and Mass Violence in the 20th Century*. Cambridge: Cambridge University Press, 2017.

Kühne, Thomas, ed. "Masculinity and the Third Reich." Special issue, *Central European History* 51, no. 3 (2018).

Lerner, Paul. *Hysterical Men: War, Psychiatry, and the Politics of Trauma in Germany, 1890–1930*. Ithaca, NY: Cornell University Press, 2003.

Merridale, Catherine. *Ivan's War: Life and Death in the Red Army, 1939–1945*. New York: Metropolitan Books, 2006.

Mosse, George L. *Fallen Soldiers: Reshaping the Memory of the World Wars*. Oxford: Oxford University Press, 1990.

Perry, Heather R. *Recycling the Disabled: Army, Medicine, and Modernity in WWI Germany*. Manchester: Manchester University Press, 2014.

Prost, Antoine. *Les anciens combattants et la société française 1914–1939*. 3 vols. Paris: Presses de la Fondation Nationale des Sciences Politiques, 1977.

Theweleit, Klaus. *Male Fantasies*. 2 vols. Minneapolis: University of Minnesota Press, 1987–89.

Watson, Alexander. *Enduring the Great War: Combat, Morale and Collapse in the German and British Armies, 1914–1918*. Cambridge: Cambridge University Press, 2008.

CHAPTER 21

....

COLONIAL SOLDIERS, RACE, AND MILITARY MASCULINITIES DURING AND BEYOND WORLD WARS I AND II

....

RICHARD SMITH

FROM the outset of colonization in the fifteenth century, the European empires of Britain, France, the Netherlands, Portugal, and Spain, and later Italy, Germany, and Belgium, relied on colonial troops to police existing territory and to extend colonial possessions.[1] During the century prior to World War I (1914–18), troops from France's first north African colony, Algeria (annexed 1830), served in the Crimean War (1853–56) and the Franco-Prussian War (1870–71). Some 140,000 Algerians were deployed on the western front during World War I, and Algerians also served in the liberation of Italy and France in World War II (1939–45). West African troops, especially Senegalese, were used extensively by France in both world wars and during the subsequent Indochina War (1945–54) and Algerian War (1954–62). The first Senegalese infantry corps (*tirailleurs sénégalais*) were formed in 1857. Around 200,000 served in World War I, of whom more than 135,000 fought in Europe and 30,000 were killed.[2]

The British Empire used Indian troops in large numbers in Europe, the Middle East, and east Africa during World War I and in the Middle East, Malaya, Burma, north Africa, and Italy during World War II. The British Indian Army was established in 1858 after the Indian Rebellion and existed up to independence in 1947. Before World War I, the strength of the Indian Army was 240,000 and comprised 39 cavalry regiments and 135 infantry battalions (including 17 Gurkha units). A further 40,000 Indian men served with the Auxiliary Force and 34,000 in the Frontier Militia and Military Police. Roughly 1.2 million Indian soldiers eventually enlisted during World War I, of whom 70,000 died. The number of Indian Army volunteers reached 2 million during World War II.[3]

The British Empire also recruited soldiers and military labor from territories such as the Caribbean, Egypt, and South Africa. The British West Indies Regiment during the First World War numbered around 15,000 men. A further 16,000 West Indians volunteered for service alongside the British during the Second World War.[4]

Italy also employed colonial soldiers, including troops from Eritrea (conquered in 1890) in the occupation of Libya (1911–35). A division of Libyan infantry and *Dubats* from Italian Somaliland served in Italy's invasion of Ethiopia in 1935–36.[5] Portugal used *Landim* troops from Mozambique during World War I in its 1916 campaign against the German Empire in Angola. Portugal also employed *Landim* in the garrisons of Portuguese India and Macau until the 1950s.[6] Colonial soldiers from the Spanish protectorate in Morocco played a major role in the Spanish Civil War (1936–39). In 1936, the Spanish "Army of Africa," a legion of 30,000 *Regulares* from Spanish Morocco, supported the rebellion of the Spanish military under the leadership of General Francisco Franco against the Republican government in Madrid. Their number increased during the war, reaching 60,000 at the time of Franco's victory.[7]

During the First World War, over 2 million Africans served the European colonial powers as soldiers or laborers (predominantly as carriers). An estimated 200,000 died, the majority from disease, neglect, and ill treatment, rather than battle wounds. In the east African campaign alone, in which the German Empire faced Britain, Belgium, and Portugal in German East Africa, Mozambique, Northern Rhodesia, British East Africa, Uganda, and the Belgian Congo, African casualties amounted to around 100,000.[8] During the Second World War, the imperial powers recruited approximately 1.3 million Africans. The British territories provided the largest numbers at more than 1 million; 190,000 served Vichy and the Free French Forces, 60,000 for Italy; and 24,000 for Belgium.[9]

The inclusion of the aspirations, experiences, and recollections of this large number of colonial soldiers from different continents, who served different imperial powers, mainly the British and the French, in the history of twentieth-century warfare changes and complicates our understanding of military masculinity. War may be generally regarded as an arena that provides men with unrivalled chances to demonstrate masculine worth and prowess. Military conflicts in imperial contexts offer opportunities to examine how masculine ideals and performance may interact with racial attitudes, particularly those related to the capacity and character of the colonized. Rather than identifying specific conflicts as singular crises of masculinity, manliness is taken to be an ongoing, historical practice that interacts with changing representations of race and other analytical categories. Framing masculinity in relation to ideal character types and attributes that fall short of full manhood, also underlines how masculinity is defined not only in opposition to femininity, but through the articulation of power between men.[10]

During the era of high imperialism before the First World War, "race" served as a system of meaning that underpinned and justified European rule. Racial discourse took superficial differences in physical appearance—hair, facial features, and complexion— along with ascribed qualities of intellect, character, and civilization to determine colonial policy.[11] Ideas of race were also significant in the domestic attitudes of imperial powers, suggesting the fitness of a state to maintain an empire abroad or expressing anxieties around the viability of an imperial nation through the language of degeneration and eugenics.[12] Race was furthermore a means of articulating cultural questions as to the character, creativity, and civilization of both the colonized and the colonizer.[13]

While the historical processes inherent in the categories of both masculinity and race can be identified, so too can changing attitudes regarding the military capacity of colonial subjects be linked to pragmatic and strategic concerns. However, the centrality of performance to masculine identities meant that the body remained intrinsically linked to manhood, even when the focus of official policy toward colonial troops shifted to questions of mental capacity and temperament. The military body became the territory on which the desires and ideals of nation and empire were mapped. It symbolized the capacity of these joint enterprises to maintain power, chiefly in relation to bodies regarded as inferior and over which imperial rule was asserted.

For the European empires, the central dilemma was enlisting the support of the required numbers of colonial troops without disrupting imperial hierarchies or creating metropolitan anxieties. Fears of racial degeneration in Britain, for example, or concerns about the French birth rate meant that colonial troops always had the potential to provide alternative visions of masculinity and military service that might undermine European hegemony. The plantation labor systems of the Caribbean, African, and Asian colonies provided possibilities to imagine non-White men as hypermasculine, reinforcing the stereotypes of chattel slavery. The non-White body had to be simultaneously enlisted and controlled, either literally or through regimes of representation, which placed limits on non-White masculine performance.

These paradoxical strands became increasingly significant during the First World War. Although the assertion of White masculinity relied to some extent on imagined physical prowess, this was limited by a desire to differentiate the White middle- and upper-class men serving the empire from colonial and working-class subjects. Rationality was regarded as the necessary quality to master the body, to stem its "natural" impulses, and to realize physical perfection through scientific drill.[14] The European empires denied the possibility of rational behavior and discipline in Black men, which could serve to exclude them from the front line, where self-control was regarded as a prerequisite. When combined with the association of Black men and physical labor, such prejudices often limited non-White colonial troops to military labor duties unless dictated otherwise by pragmatic considerations.

The following takes a comparative approach to explore changing attitudes to the military service of subject populations and the implied constructions of masculinity during the era of European imperialism and its postcolonial aftermath in the second half of the twentieth century. The focus will be on the most-researched colonial soldiers of the British and French Empires during the First and Second World Wars. Three themes stand in the center: the longer-term impact of imperial and colonial military regimes, including the effect of anticolonial rebellion and the emergence of martial race theories, on the construction of masculinity; the contribution of war service to masculine visions of independent nationhood and citizenship among colonial veterans; and the appropriated visions of heroic masculine sacrifice in postcolonial nations, even where war service had involved discrimination and when colonial soldiers had been characterized as lacking the masculine standards demanded by modern warfare.

War and the Imperial Spirit

Disciplining the body became a metaphor for the mastery of the subject races by the imperial powers. The concerns focused around it were a barometer of imperial self-confidence. As R. W. Connell points out, "the constitution of masculinity through bodily performance means that gender is vulnerable when the performance cannot be sustained."[15] This is perhaps no more so than in the context of war, where ideals of masculinity and the male body undertake the ultimate test. Ideals of masculinity may be undermined as the wayward body develops a separate trajectory that falls short of the perfect model.

In Britain, imperial confidence was dented by events such as the Crimean War (1853–56), which Russia lost to an alliance of France, the United Kingdom, the Ottoman Empire, and Sardinia—a victory gained less easily than had been assumed; the Indian Rebellion (1857–58), a rebellion against the rule of the British East India Company; the Morant Bay Rebellion (1865) by Black Jamaicans against British rule; and later the Anglo–Zulu War (1879), a rebellion of the Zulu Kingdom; and the First and Second South African Wars (1880–81 and 1899–1902) between the United Kingdom and the Boers of the Transvaal. Fears were expressed for the future of the British Empire, its fitness to govern, and its ability to field an army. Each of these events manifested uncertainty about the ability of British men to contain the subject races, which in turn dictated more physical and authoritarian models of masculinity.[16] For France, the declining birth rate in relation to Germany was the chief preoccupation, especially after its defeat in the Franco–Prussian War (1870–71) and subsequent German unification in January 1871. But resistance and insurrection in its colonies, such as Algeria, was another key consideration.[17]

Paradoxically, within the ideals of sporting masculinity, which predominated in Britain's middle and upper classes during the second half of the nineteenth century, it was expected that certain apparently male urges, such as sexual impulses, would be channeled to the greater good through discipline and self-control. Contemporary scientific concepts of natural selection that came up everywhere in Western culture and its earlier variants, such as "the great chain of being," were frequently used to justify White colonial and imperial domination. The legitimacy of White rule rested not only on claims of *biological* superiority but also on the alleged superior *character* of the White male, which mastered natural impulses and engaged in industrious, uplifting activity. In other words, constructs of predominant White masculinity in the Age of Empires required the merging of constructs of rational and biological preordination.[18]

War itself could be depicted as an extension of imperial character, an escape from humdrum urban life, and a spur to manhood. However, the globalized and industrialized military conflicts during the Age of the World Wars threatened to undermine claimed European values of rationality, progress, and civilization that underpinned imperial domination. The tendency to regard the First World War particularly as a descent into barbarism, contamination, and chaos has led to a focus on what was dramatically different about modern war: its alienation from normal experience.[19] It is important to recognize these disruptions and discontinuities, particularly in constructs of masculinity and the rhetoric of empire and race, but it is also necessary to acknowledge the broader historical pattern of constantly renegotiated gender and racial hierarchies. The experiences of the war intensified, rather than initiated, gender and racial categories already in use. While the war made demands on men unequaled in civilian life, this served to bring into sharper focus preexisting shortcomings and contradictions within White masculine ideals.[20]

Martial masculinity departs to some extent from the manhood rituals of civil life. Certainly, manhood as a series of tests to be undertaken is still the dominant motif, especially in relation to the opportunities for demonstrating masculine prowess associated with the battlefield. But military life also entails a process of breaking some of the character traits associated with masculinity in the civilian world, particularly individuality and free will, as well as attempting to obliterate the "feminine" qualities of compassion and emotion. The soldier is thus placed in a paradoxical position. Military efficiency requires sacrificing the norms of society to "defend" it. Furthermore, while extolling the masculine standards associated with soldiering, civil society is fearful or contemptuous of the soldier who may become marginalized on returning to civilian life.[21]

Processes of masculinity within the military differ qualitatively from civilian modes. The battlefield, however, was still held up as the ultimate test of the essential masculine qualities of strength, courage, stamina, stoicism, and self-control for all men in civil life also.[22] Scholars such as Elaine Showalter and Sandra M. Gilbert have focused on the potential threat to masculinity posed by the experience of the First World War, as men found themselves unable to live up to the masculine demands made on them and were emasculated by the conditions of trench warfare and military bureaucracy.[23] In contrast, others, such as Joanna Bourke, suggest that World War I provided some men with opportunities to experience exhilaration and self-realization.[24]

Competing Imperial Masculinities

The interaction of preconceived ideas of race and masculinity within imperial military service regimes determined the deployment of Black colonial troops by the European imperial powers in both world wars. Manhood may be presented as a series of tests or rituals,[25] and the emphasis on performance, which is particularly evident in military life, underlines how masculine archetypes undergo continual renegotiation and reframing. Individual soldiers face the ongoing possibility that their masculinity may be doubted. However, exemplary martial endeavor by colonial soldiers had the potential to undermine established hierarchies organized around taxonomies of both masculinity and race.

In the wars of imperial conquest, the apparent suitability of non-White troops to climate and environment was a key element of deployment strategy. The West India Regiments (WIR)—British Army infantry recruited from and normally stationed in the British Caribbean colonies between 1795 and 1927—played a significant role in the conquest and policing of British West African territory (including modern Gambia, Sierra Leone, Ghana, and Nigeria) from the last quarter of the nineteenth century. The WIR were lauded for their stamina in the arduous tropical conditions.[26] These colonial troops were regarded as possessing inherent advantages, associated with a supposed proximity to nature, rather than achieved through drill and discipline. Alfred Burden Ellis, an officer in the WIR and pioneering ethnologist, reported that the regiment marched double or three times the distance of White soldiers during the Asante War (1873–74), dispatching their full duties on half rations. Ellis believed, "The English-speaking negro of the West Indies is most excellent material for a soldier. He is docile, patient, brave, and faithful."[27] When treated harshly, Ellis observed, West Indian troops became sullen and grudgingly obedient, rather than displaying the outright insubordination of English soldiers. Ellis's portrayal adhered to the humble, childlike "Sambo" caricature that emerged during the transatlantic slavery era.[28] Such a stereotype was devoid of the idealized masculine qualities of rational behavior and independent thought and demanded White leadership to keep the Black soldier's alleged impetuosity in check.[29] Nevertheless, the West Indian soldiers held themselves in high regard. In 1906, four years after the Second South African War, in which Britain struggled to recruit sufficient robust troops, the travel writer and journalist John Henderson noted that the Black West Indian soldier of the WIR was "conscious of [his] superiority" over the White troops stationed in Jamaica. While Henderson may have been influenced by Ellis's account, he had also observed encounters between the White visiting garrison and the WIR.[30]

MILITARY MASCULINITY AND IMPERIAL SIGNIFICATIONS OF POWER

The highly gendered political rhetoric in the European metropolitan centers increasingly reflected the concerns of empire, not only demarcating power between men at home, but also justifying White colonial mastery by feminizing, infantilizing, and dehumanizing colonial subjects.[31] These circumstances underline Joan W. Scott's insistence that gender is not only "a constitutive element of social relationships based on perceived differences between the sexes," but also "a primary way of signifying relationships of power."[32] Imperial rule was legitimized through gendered vocabulary that characterized power and strength as masculine attributes underpinned by character traits such as sporting prowess, self-control, rationality, and stoicism. Feminine qualities identified with the subject races included emotional volatility, intellectual inferiority, and lack of self-restraint. On the one hand, through processes of hegemonic acceptance, men may seek to reap the trickle-down benefits of masculine power, even where lived performance falls short of the ideal. On the other hand, the discomfiture that men may have felt, either collectively or individually, at their own apparent shortcomings in relation to dominant ideals of manhood produced conflicting and competing images of masculinity, particularly in the arenas of race and sexuality.[33]

In her study of the British Raj, Mrinalini Sinha has argued that empire was a constant frame of reference for White masculinity, resulting in the mutual constitution of metropolitan and colonial identities. The masculine norms of subject societies became interwoven with both popular and anthropological misconceptions and prejudices. Such identities can be regarded as historically contingent, reflecting the demands of empire and metropolitan social concerns in a process where race, class, gender, and sexuality intersected.[34] Although imperial subjects tended to become a focus of White sexual anxiety and double standard, some perceived qualities of male colonial subjects came to be desired. Members of the so-called martial races in India, such as the Gurkhas from Nepal and the Sikhs from the Punjab region, were admired by the British for their perceived military acumen. Such traditions not only provided a model for the ideal colonial soldier but also had the potential to reinvigorate the wider imperial project, particularly in times of crisis.

After the Indian Rebellion of 1857–58, in which neither Gurkhas nor Sikhs participated, the British increasingly regarded non-White soldiers as undependable and lacking in stoicism and discipline. Martial race theories, which drew on interpretations of cultural and social practices to identify the inherent fighting qualities of colonial peoples, became more influential, although practical considerations overruled ideals in many cases. The northern territories replaced the southern and eastern states as the principle areas for recruiting drives for the Indian army. The so-called Aryan races of northern India, Sikhs, and the hill-dwelling peoples of Nepal, the Gurkhas, were favored. Southern Indians, however, were regarded as enervated and feminized by tropical climates and early marriage.[35] A racially determined system of authority operated in the Indian army in which the viceroy, the chief British government official and representative of the British monarch in India, could bestow commissions on Indians. But these Indian officers always remained subordinate to their White counterparts and served to underpin White authority as cultural intermediaries and advisers.[36]

Martial race theories also influenced the recruitment policies of the European powers in Africa from the 1880s. British policy was led in this respect by officers with previous Indian Army experience, which favored recruits from inaccessible regions who were observed surviving on scant food sources and who possessed tracking and reconnaissance skills. Peoples who had previously resisted colonial rule, such as the Nandi of Kenya, who were not conquered by the British until 1906, were held to possess innate military capacity.[37] Such attitudes also informed the recruitment practices of the US Army when it began to enlist colonial subjects in its overseas colonies from the late nineteenth century. A primary example can be seen in the Philippine Scouts used by the United States after the Philippine–American War (1899–1902).[38]

Attitudes toward African martial competence were also linked more pragmatically to European settlement patterns. African coastal communities were usually represented as more civilized and thus appropriate for military service, but this attitude changed as Europeans advanced inland and started to recruit locally. White settler populations were more reluctant to recruit African troops through fear of both insurrection and competition for military employment. The German *Schutztruppe*, the official corps of the German Empire in colonial Africa, was established in 1896. During World War I, it also recruited from racial groups that had provided fierce opposition to European settlement, such as the Hehe in the colony of Tanganyika (Tanzania). The racialization of martial qualities had the effect of further reinforcing divisions within colonial societies. Belgium, for example, recruited Bangala speakers in the Congo for its Force Publique, created in 1885 to secure Belgian colonial rule, imposing a singular racial character on a group comprising diverse ethnicities.[39]

To uphold White imperial authority, Black soldiers were prevented from advancing beyond noncommissioned rank during the First World War.[40] The German Schutztruppe operated a separate rank system for Black and White soldiers, the latter often drawn from White settler communities, rather than Germany itself. Occasionally, African veterans of many years' service were given honorific titles such as *effendi*, which granted status in civil life as representatives of German colonialism. However, no African officer was permitted to assert authority over any White soldier.[41]

The demographic deficit with Germany led France to develop the most comprehensive policy of African recruitment, paving the way for approximately 200,000 *tirailleurs sénégalais* to serve with the French forces during the First World War. In 1910, the French military strategist General Charles Mangin identified peoples of a martial disposition, including the Wolof, Fula, Serer, and Mande from west and central Africa, to provide a "reservoir of men" for an anticipated European conflict. France continued to follow the broad tenor of European thought in its racial attitudes toward African recruits, and Mangin argued, "warrior instincts . . . remain extremely powerful in primitive races."[42] He claimed this fighting spirit was underpinned by a disposition to withstand harsh climates, the musculature necessary to carry the heavy supplies that sustained colonial campaigns, and the fact that African soldierly efficiency was ostensibly produced by a less-developed nervous system and familiarity with patriarchal society.

During the First World War, Mangin promoted the *tirailleurs sénégalais* as bolsters of "French fury" whose "cold-blooded and fatalistic temperament" would "render them terrible in the attack."[43] Mangin's critics in the French military argued that African soldiers were not intelligent enough to meet the demands of modern warfare. Their deployment in France was also opposed on climatic and logistical grounds. But equally significant were fears around the social impact of a Black military presence in France. Images of racial diversity might convince imperial powers of the justness of their cause and provide evidence of the civilizing mission. Relations between Black soldiers and civilian populations nevertheless potentially threatened to undermine imperial racial and masculine boundaries, particularly if it involved contact with White women.

Consequently, colonial troops were subject to harsh restrictions, including confinement to camp or limited recreation.[44]

As French casualties mounted and unrest in the army became apparent, especially after the Second Battle of the Aisne in May 1917, resistance to the deployment of African troops lessened.[45] However, although the *tirailleurs* provided a source of invigoration for the French military and potent images of African manhood, recruitment practices in west Africa underlined their lack of masculine autonomy. The *rachat* system, introduced in the 1820s, provided bounty payments to slave masters who rendered men to the French military for up to fourteen years. After France abolished slavery in 1848, *rachat* became a source of some embarrassment and the practice was phased out between 1882 and 1895. Yet, recruitment methods that still retained associations of slavery persisted through World War I. The French army paid bonuses to slave owners who manumitted slaves into military service, and peasants initially drafted as military labor were forcibly transferred to the infantry.[46]

The European imperial powers used colonial subjects not only as soldiers but also as forced or conscripted labor during the First World War. Egypt, South Africa, China, Fiji, Indochina, and India provided much of the military labor deployed on the western front and in Italy, Mesopotamia, and the Middle East. In the east African theater alone, the British enlisted up to one million Africans drawn from around fifteen territories to serve as laborers and *kariakor* (carrier corps). Military labor extended peacetime enlistment for such imperial projects as railway and road construction. The British Native Followers Ordnance (1915) epitomized this association, granting district commissioners powers to demand unlimited labor quotas from local chiefs. Aside from casualty rates of over 14 percent, these conscripted-labor schemes disrupted Indigenous agricultural practices and shifted the gender balance by removing large numbers of men from African communities.[47]

Military labor provided the mainstay of military campaigns, particularly in Africa. However, less-masculine attributes were applied to the peoples on which imperial military labor regimes depended to reinforce martial race policy. Deployment or reduction to labor-company status was used as a form of individual or collective punishment or to reinforce the position of a particular race or ethnic group in the imperial order.[48] Since the French Revolution, the bearing of arms represented both duty to and status within the nation. The denial of arms bearing implied an exclusion from the rights and rewards linked to military service in both imperial and national contexts.[49] Arms bearing could also be deployed to connote both gendered and racialized status. Black men and White women were routinely represented as irrational, intellectually inferior, and, often, physically weaker to preserve images of White male stoicism, heroism, and self-control. The British army opposed the use of women and Black troops on the western front in the same document, suggesting both lacked the "strength, coolness and courage" essential in the front line.[50]

The potential for military labor policies to affect racially differentiated imperial subjects is illustrated by the experiences of Armenian workers enlisted by the Ottoman Empire during the First World War. European military practices were adopted in the wake of the Young Turk Revolution (1908), and military service became compulsory for non-Muslim subjects.[51] Nevertheless, to minimize the possibility of armed alliances with the Ottoman Empire's Christian neighbor, Russia, non-Muslims were allocated to labor battalions, rather than infantry and cavalry regiments. The consequences of this policy were realized during the Armenian genocide following the Ottoman defeat by the Russian army in the Battle of Sarikamish (January 1915). Armenian Christians already constituted around 75 percent of the labor battalions, and those who remained in front-line regiments were transferred to the unarmed logistical units, which became the focus of anti-Armenian violence. Unarmed and disarmed Armenians were hence deprived of the means to defend themselves from attacks within the Ottoman forces and against their wider community as these gathered apace.[52]

While the fate of the Armenian labor battalions provides an extreme example, it serves to highlight wider gendered concerns evident among other European powers in the deployment of subject populations. Limiting military service to labor battalions presents the image of the subject as at once threatening and effeminate. Within this paradoxical framing, the imperial power lived in fear of being overthrown if a subject population was mobilized. Simultaneously, the imperial subject could be denied arms on the pretext that he was physically weak, mentally deficient, devious, or treacherous—essentially effeminate within the rhetoric of imperialism. Despite the rates of attrition experienced by the European armies during First World War, such gendered inflections of racial ideology confined significant potential sources of imperial firepower to ancillary roles, including West Indians, Black South Africans, Maoris, Chinese, and Indo-Chinese.[53]

MILITARY SACRIFICE AND NATIONAL IDENTITY

During the course of the nineteenth century, the thoughts and heroic actions of individual men continued to structure the accounts of nations and empires. The promise of a place in these narratives was held out to citizens and imperial subjects who were sacrificed in the name of empire or nation. The ideal of the soldier-citizen emerged from the French Revolution when volunteers came to be associated with the identity of the nation whose interests they defended. With the soldier hero in the foreground of national memory, citizen volunteers came to embody models of autonomous, active masculinity, rather than serving the state passively as conscripts or professional soldiers.[54] These narratives of male sacrifice were not limited to European societies. In celebrating the warrior figures of Dutty Boukman and François Makandal, both leaders of slave rebellions, the Haitian Revolution (1791–1804) drew on the island's African heritage, as well as the French archetype of the male arms-bearing citizen. These icons provided the ideological means to redress the purportedly emasculating experiences of slavery and to reinstate Black Haitian men as fathers and protectors.[55]

During the First World War, colonial subjects who volunteered freely often aspired to the model of the citizen-soldier, although economic and other personal reasons were also strong motivating factors. Some may have volunteered in the hope of postwar reward, including improved living standards, political representation, or access to land. This expectation is perhaps easier to identify in retrospect, and demands for postwar reform can equally be said to have arisen from politicizing experiences during the conflict itself. Following both world wars, many national movements in the European colonies articulated political demands and aspirations around the time-honored figure of the volunteer alongside other values professed by imperial governments, such as justice, equality, and fair play,[56] even when imperial subjects had been conscripted or pressed into duty.

IMPERIAL MILITARY SERVICE AND NATIONAL INDEPENDENCE

The exclusion of colonial veterans from the tangible and figurative rewards of military service, as well as a sense that their sacrifices were not recognized, strengthened independence narratives from the end of World War I. The masculine and racial self-confidence of colonial soldiers increased as myths of European insuperability and superior civilization were undermined. This process was already evident in the British recruitment crisis during the Second South African War (1899–1902) and with notable imperial setbacks, such as the routing of the Italian army by the troops of the Ethiopian Empire in the Battle of Adwa in March 1896. This decisive battle of the First Italo-Ethiopian War (1895–96) temporarily secured Ethiopian sovereignty. Similarly humiliating was Russia's defeat at the hands of Japan during the Russo-Japanese War (1904–5).[57] The mental toll of modern warfare, epitomized by the increasing prevalence of psychiatric casualties in the First World War, combined with wholesale, mechanized destruction also undermined White claims of rationality and self-control.[58] Myths of European invincibility suffered a further blow during the Second World War with the fall of the British stronghold Singapore to the Japanese in February 1942, although it can also be argued that the subsequent defense of the Indian imperial possessions by a combined force of British, Indian army, and African troops during the Burma Campaign (1942–45) was symbolic of renewed, albeit short-lived, imperial vigor.[59]

Among many postimperial nations, the legacy of military service in both world wars is most evident in the masculine rhetoric of heroic sacrifice, which has contributed to patriarchal models of nationhood in which imperial service is remembered as a cornerstone of independence.[60] Visions of heroic masculine sacrifice were appropriated by independence movements and emerging nations despite the routine discrimination experienced by colonial soldiers in both world wars.[61] However, if loyalty to the imperial power and the promise of postwar political change was a significant motivating factor for colonial subjects to volunteer in the First World War, it is a more difficult assumption to make for the Second World War when these aspirations remained largely unfulfilled. The Government of India Act (1919) did not deliver the degree of self-government members of the Indian National Congress had expected in exchange for wartime loyalty and support for recruitment. The expectation of land settlement for veterans in the British West Indies remained a contested issue at the outbreak of hostilities in September 1939.[62] Rather than a sense of loyalty to empire in World War II, it is possible that colonial subjects volunteered through an adherence to codes of masculine military service. As Kaushik Roy has demonstrated in the case of Indian troops serving in Burma during World War II, bonds to one's fellow soldiers, especially when they were drawn from a similar ethnic background, became increasingly significant as the military unit substituted for family in terms of affiliation and gendered roles and identities.[63]

Masculine war service engendered notions of entitlement that led both to anti-imperial agitation and claims by veterans for favorable treatment over those who had not visibly participated in the war effort. Postwar opposition to colonial rule was countered by the apparent conformity and continued loyalty of many ex-servicemen. Imperial France responded to dissatisfaction among discharged African soldiers by offering veterans local administrative roles, avoiding the humiliation that might otherwise have resulted if ex-servicemen had reverted to a more subordinate prewar status. Patronage was also a demand of colonial veterans elsewhere. Jamaican ex-servicemen's leaders, for example, campaigned throughout the 1920s and 1930s for public works employment and contracts. This visible recognition of veterans also substantiated a limited sense of familial military duty because it promised relative security, thereby ensuring a more steady supply of fresh recruits.[64]

Alongside the largely disappointed hopes of colonial World War I veterans, the character of the Second World War as genocidal war, legitimated by the racist ideology of the Third Reich, affected colonial recruitment in varying ways. When France was invaded by the German Wehrmacht in May 1940, Africans comprised 9 percent of its army. Confronting the racial policies of Nazi Germany presented particular issues of masculinity for French African troops. Often singled out for ill treatment, African troops were further affected when taken prisoner, which was regarded as akin to slavery and the removal of every vestige of autonomous manhood.[65] Yet the increasingly racialized nature of the Second World War meant that the call to arms directed to Allied colonial troops could be redefined as a universal struggle against fascism, rather than the defense of individual European empires. This feature was particularly evident in British recruiting efforts in the Caribbean, India, and Africa, and it facilitated the ideological process in which imperial associations were gradually overlaid with those of commonwealth.[66]

A further possibility is evident in Fascist Italy, which during the 1930s tried to incorporate the image of the *fedele ascaro* (faithful colonial soldier) into the iconography of its belated imperial ambitions. Colonial troops from Eritrea and Somalia had been raised in Italy's African possessions since the 1880s. These were later deployed during the invasion of Ethiopia (1935–36) and in the Second World War until the defeat of the Italian forces in Africa. The *ascaro* rendered to Italian audiences was a domesticated subordinate and thus a partly emasculated figure. However, on the rare occasion *ascaro* visited the Italian mainland, they were carefully supervised to preempt potential sexual encounters with White women, thereby upholding the racial order and potential threats to White masculine self-assurance.[67]

As had been the case following the First World War, colonial soldiers manifested a variety of attitudes and expectations from the end of the Second World War. The demand for recruits to fill not only front-line roles, but also technical and ancillary duties, meant that colonial armies began to relax traditional martial race approaches to enlistment. Some British military recruiters were suspicious of Africans who acquired education or business skills, believing this undermined their combative spirit. Indeed, when Africans were permitted to apply for commissioned officer rank beginning in 1940 and in the wake of protests in Britain from the League of Colored Peoples, educational achievement was marginal to the appointment procedure.[68]

After World War II, colonial officials adopted a number of differing approaches to returning veterans. British colonial administrators tended to believe that army life had engendered self-discipline and aspirations that would be extended to civilian life, demonstrating the merits of imperialism and the potential for former soldiers to conform to European models of masculine endeavor. In rural areas, veterans were regarded as imperial advocates who could be relied on to set an example as craftsmen, cultivators, and civic leaders. In contrast, urban areas were regarded as more problematic, the chief fear being that veterans would be drawn to nationalist leaders, rather than instigating anticolonial campaigns themselves.[69] In some cases, the continued loyalty of locally recruited soldiers extended European colonial rule. Portuguese power in Africa was maintained until the 1974 metropolitan army coup by a colonial army that filled around 40 percent of the ranks with Africans. The presence of former colonial soldiers after independence in 1974 served to extend postcolonial conflict, particularly in Angola.[70]

THE SIGNIFICANCE OF COLONIAL MILITARY SERVICE IN POSTIMPERIAL NATIONS

The processes of decolonization and global migration since 1945 have shifted earlier associations of masculine military service and national affiliation. Descendants of First and Second World War veterans and ex-servicemen who fought during wars of independence are now often to be found settled in the former imperial power—West Indians in London and Malians in Paris, for example. Imperial military service may be used to claim citizenship in this setting, rather than in the independent nation.[71] The memorialization of masculine sacrifice has often made a similar journey. The veterans and descendants of the Borinqueneers, the Puerto Rican colonial regiment of the US Army since 1899, have deployed past military service to demand equal citizenship for Hispanic migrants centered on the regimental memorial at Buenaventura Lakes, Florida.[72] The Memorial Gates in London commemorate the role of colonial troops in both world wars. However, this has not yet translated into a successful relationship between ethnic minority communities and the British armed forces; Whiteness remains central to narratives of deserving heroism and sacrifice.[73]

Another significant aspect of imperial military is the fate of former colonial soldiers who were rejected by newly independent nations as European power receded. The cost of serving European imperialism is evident in the experience of the South Moluccans who provided the colonial garrisons in the Dutch East Indies. Following the establishment of an independent Indonesia in 1949, Moluccan attempts to create a separate republic were crushed, and veterans who had fought for the Dutch chose to be demobilized and resettled in the Netherlands. For several decades, they were barred from working in the Netherlands, and it was not until the late 1970s that many were awarded the citizenship they perhaps expected for masculine military sacrifice for the Dutch Empire.[74]

CONCLUSION

The experiences of colonial troops deployed by the major imperial powers during the two world wars were determined by a number of ideological and pragmatic concerns. Perhaps the most important concern of colonial recruiters was the need to defend territories and interests against opposition forces while maintaining the imperial hierarchies that cast non-White soldiers as being of inferior racial and masculine character. Simultaneously, the maintenance of an effective colonial force provided significant prestige for imperial powers, serving as evidence of the civilizing mission, particularly in instilling European modes of masculine behavior among colonial troops. At strategic moments during imperial crises, effective colonial forces built on martial-race recruitment practices could also reinvigorate metropolitan morale by providing visions of robust and efficient masculinity and imperial unity.

In the wake of the First World War, when White masculine rationality and military efficiency had been called into question, a gradual process developed in which colonial troops were accorded greater capacity for masculine authority and discipline, opening limited possibilities to achieve status, both within the ranks of colonial armies and after demobilization. However, these changes were laboriously slow from the perspective of many colonial troops who often became politicized by the inferior standing and conditions they were allotted, fueling claims for masculine national enfranchisement through the model of the citizen volunteer. But such discontent was by no means universal, and imperial regimes were able to rely on the extensive use of colonial troops throughout the Second World War. Masculine affiliations centered on the alternative gendered family of the military institution were key in this respect. Consequently, claims for preferential treatment for masculine military sacrifice and loyalty, rather than anticolonial attitudes, were an equally common outcome among colonial troops.

In the postimperial era, memories of the service of colonial troops have played a significant role in articulating the identities of independent nations. Ideals of front-line military service have been pivotal to these memories, even where colonial deployment was of an auxiliary or labor nature, rather than combat service. This process has imparted a specifically masculine inflection to independent national identities. Migrant communities in postimperial nations have also appropriated the masculine sacrifices of colonial troops to uphold citizenship and social justice claims, a process that gathered pace during the commemorations of the First World War centenary.

Notes

1. For an insight into the early colonial period, see Peter M. Voelz, *Slave and Soldier: The Military Impact of Blacks in the Colonial Americas* (New York: Garland, 1993); and Matthew Restall, "Black Conquistadors: Armed Africans in Early Spanish America," *The Americas* 57, no. 2 (2000): 171–205.

2. See Santanu Das, "Introduction," in *Race, Empire and First World War Writing*, ed. Santanu Das (Cambridge: Cambridge University Press, 2011), 1–32, 4; Richard S. Fogarty, *Race and War in France: Colonial Subjects in the French Army, 1914–1918* (Baltimore: John Hopkins University Press, 2008); and Nancy Ellen Lawler, *Soldiers of Misfortune: Ivoirien Tirailleurs of World War II* (Athens, OH: Ohio University Press, 1992).

3. David Omissi, *The Sepoy and the Raj: The Indian Army, 1860–1940* (London: Macmillan, 1994); and Yasmin Khan, *India at War: The Subcontinent and the Second World War* (Oxford: Oxford University Press, 2015), 18.

4. See Richard Smith, *Jamaican Volunteers in the First World War: Race, Masculinity and the Development of National Consciousness* (Manchester: Manchester University Press, 2004).

5. Angelo Del Boca, *La guerra d'Etiopia: l'ultima impresa del colonialismo* (Milan: Longanesi, 2010).

6. Malyn Newitt, "The Portuguese African Colonies during the Second World War," in *Africa and World War II*, ed. Judith A. Byfield et al. (New York: Cambridge University Press, 2015), 220–37.

7. Sebastian Balfour, "Colonial War and Civil War: The Spanish Army of Africa," in *"If You Tolerate This—": The Spanish Civil War in the Age of Total War*, ed. Martin Baumeister and Stefanie Schüler-Springorum (Frankfurt am Main: Campus Verlag, 2008), 171–85.

8. Edward Paice, *Tip and Run: The Untold Tragedy of the Great War in Africa* (London: Weidenfeld & Nicolson, 2008), 3; and Hew Strachan, *The First World War* (New York: Oxford University Press, 2001), 568 and 641.

9. David Killingray, *Fighting for Britain: African Soldiers in the Second World War* (Woodbridge: James Currey, 2012), 6–10.

10. For a theoretical discussion, see Harilaos Stecopoulos and Michael Uebel, eds., *Race and the Subject of Masculinities* (Durham, NC: Duke University Press, 1997), esp. 1–16.

11. Alice L. Conklin, *In the Museum of Man: Race, Anthropology, and Empire in France, 1850–1950* (Ithaca, NY: Cornell University Press, 2013); Nancy Stepan, *The Idea of Race in Science: Great Britain, 1800–1960* (London: Macmillan, 1982); and Felicity Rash, *German Images of the Self and the Other: Nationalist, Colonialist and Anti-Semitic Discourse, 1871–1918* (London: Palgrave Macmillan, 2012).

12. See, for example, Richard A. Soloway, *Demography and Degeneration: Eugenics and the Declining Birthrate in Twentieth Century Britain* (Chapel Hill: University of North Carolina Press, 1990).

13. Thomas McCarthy, *Race, Empire, and the Idea of Human Development* (Cambridge: Cambridge: University Press, 2009); and Paul Rich, *Race and Empire in British Politics* (Cambridge: Cambridge University Press, 1990).

14. R. W. Connell, *Masculinities* (Cambridge, MA: Polity Press, 1995), 49–50.

15. Ibid., 54.

16. See, for example, Geoffrey Searle, " 'National Efficiency' and the 'Lessons' of the War," in *The Impact of the South African War*, ed. David Omissi and Andrew Thompson (Basingstoke: Palgrave Macmillan, 2002), 194–211.

17. Richard Tomlinson, "The Disappearance of France, 1896–1940: French Politics and the Birth Rate," *Historical Journal* 28, no. 2 (1985): 405–15; and Richard Tomlinson et al., " 'France in Peril': The French Fear of Denatalité," *History Today* 35 (1985): 24–31.

18. Jonathan Rutherford, *Forever England: Reflections on Masculinity and Empire* (London: Lawrence & Wishart, 1997); and James Anthony Mangan, *"Manufactured" Masculinity: Making Imperial Manliness, Morality and Militarism* (London: Routledge, 2012). See also the chapter by Marilyn Lake on "The 'White Man,' Race, and Imperial War during the Long Nineteenth Century" in this handbook.

19. Pivotal texts in this respect are Paul Fussell, *The Great War and Modern Memory* (Oxford: Oxford University Press, 1975); and Eric J. Leed, *No Man's Land: Combat and Identity in World War I* (Cambridge: Cambridge University Press, 1979).

20. Susan R. Grayzel, *Women's Identities at War: Gender, Motherhood, and Politics in Britain and France during the First World War* (Chapel Hill: University of North Carolina Press, 1999), 244.

21. Leed, *No Man's Land*.

22. See the chapter by Thomas Kühne on "States, Military Masculinities, and Combat in the Age of World Wars" in this handbook.

23. Sandra M. Gilbert, "Soldier's Heart: Literary Men, Literary Women and the Great War," in *Behind the Lines: Gender and the Two World Wars*, ed. Margaret R. Higonnet et al. (New Haven, CT: Yale University Press, 1987), 197–226.

24. See, for example, Joanna Bourke, *An Intimate History of Killing: Face-to-Face Killing in Twentieth-Century Warfare* (London: Granta, 1999).

25. David D. Gilmore, *Manhood in the Making: Cultural Concepts of Masculinity* (New Haven, CT: Yale University Press, 1990), 17.

26. Brian Dyde, *The Empty Sleeve: The Story of the West India Regiment of the British Army* (St. Johns, Antigua: Hansib, 1997).

27. Alfred B. Ellis, *The History of the First West India Regiment* (London: Chapman & Hall, 1885), 13.

28. Orlando Patterson, *Slavery and Social Death: A Comparative Study* (Cambridge, MA: Harvard University Press, 1982), 96.

29. Ellis, *History*, 14–15.

30. John Henderson, *Jamaica* (London: Adam & Charles Black, 1906), 64. See also Richard Smith, " 'Heaven Grant You Strength to Fight the Battle for Your Race': Nationalism, Pan-Africanism and the First World War in Jamaican Memory," in Das, *Race, Empire*, 265–87.

31. Norman Vance, *Sinews of the Spirit: The Ideals of Christian Manliness in Victorian Literature and Religious Thought* (Cambridge: Cambridge University Press, 1985).

32. Joan Wallach Scott, *Gender and the Politics of History* (New York: Columbia University Press, 1988), 42.

33. Michael Roper and John Tosh, eds., *Manful Assertions: Masculinities in Britain since 1800* (London: Routledge, 1991); and more generally on the interplay of masculinity, race, and other constructions of difference, Mrinalini Sinha, "Unraveling Masculinity and Rethinking Citizenship: A Comment," in *Representing Masculinity: Male Citizenship in Modern Western Culture*, ed. Stefan Dudink et al. (New York: Palgrave Macmillan, 2007), 261–74.

34. Mrinalini Sinha, *Colonial Masculinity: The "Manly Englishman" and the "Effeminate Bengali" in the Late Nineteenth Century* (Manchester: Manchester University Press, 1995).

35. David Killingray, "All the King's Men? Blacks in the British Army in the First World War, 1914–1918," in *Under the Imperial Carpet: Essays in Black History 1780–1950*, ed. Rainer Lotz and Ian Pegg (Crawley, England: Rabbit Press, 1986), 164–81; Lionel Caplan, *Warrior Gentlemen: "Gurkhas" in the Western Imagination* (Oxford: Berghahn Books, 1995); and Omissi, *The Sepoy*.

36. Omissi, *The Sepoy*, 159–62.

37. Timothy H. Parsons, *The African Rank-and-File: Social Implications of Colonial Military Service in the King's African Rifles, 1902–1964* (Portsmouth, NH: Heinemann, 1999), 54.

38. David Silbey, *A War of Frontier and Empire: The Philippine-American War, 1899–1902* (New York: Hill & Wang, 2007), esp. 207–17; and Brian McAllister Linn, *Guardians of Empire: The U.S. Army and the Pacific, 1902–1940* (Chapel Hill: University of North Carolina Press, 2000).

39. J. 'Bayo Adekson, "Ethnicity and Army Recruitment in Colonial Plural Societies," *Ethnic and Racial Studies* 2, no. 2 (1979): 151–65; Anthony H. M. Kirk-Greene, " 'Damnosa Hereditas': Ethnic Ranking and the Martial Races Imperative in Africa," *Ethnic and Racial Studies* 3, no. 4 (1980): 393–414; and Corey W. Reigel, *The Last Great Safari: East Africa in World War I* (London: Rowman & Littlefield, 2015), 95–100.

40. See, for example, *Manual of Military Law* (London: Her Majesty's Stationary Office, 1914), 471.

41. For detailed discussion of the Schutztruppe, see Michelle R. Moyd, *Violent Intermediaries: African Soldiers, Conquest, and Everyday Colonialism* (Athens, OH: Ohio University Press, 2014). For prewar German policy toward African recruitment, see Erick J. Mann, *Mikono ya damu: "Hands of Blood"—African Mercenaries and the Politics of Conflict in German East Africa, 1888–1904* (New York: Lang, 2002).

42. Cited in Joseph Lunn, " 'Les Races Guerriéres': Racial Preconceptions in the French Military about West African Soldiers during the First World War," *Journal of Contemporary History* 34, no. 4 (1999): 517–36, 521.

43. Ibid., 525.

44. Alison Fell, "Nursing the Other: The Representation of Colonial Troops in French and British First World War Nursing Memoirs," in Das, *Race, Empire*, 158–75; Tyler Stovall, "The Color Line behind the Lines: Racial Violence in France during the Great War," *American Historical Review* 103, no. 3 (1998): 737–69; and Glenford D. Howe, "Military-Civilian Intercourse, Prostitution and Venereal Disease among Black West Indian Soldiers during World War I," *Journal of Caribbean History* 31, no. 1/2 (1997): 88–102.

45. Lunn, "Les Races Guerriéres."

46. Myron Echenberg, *Colonial Conscripts: The Tirailleurs Senegalais in French West Africa, 1857–1960* (Portsmouth, NH: Heinemann, 1991); Fogarty, *Race and War*; Gregory Mann, *Native Sons: West African Veterans and France in the Twentieth Century* (Durham, NC: Duke University Press, 2006); and Lunn, "Les Races Guerriéres."

47. Geoffrey Hodges, *Kariakor: The Carrier Corps; The Story of the Military Labour Forces in the Conquest of German East Africa, 1914 to 1918* (Nairobi: Nairobi University Press, 1999), 34–35; and Anthony Clayton and Donald C. Savage, *Government and Labour in Kenya, 1895–1963* (London: Routledge, 1999), 81–107.

48. Smith, *Jamaican Volunteers*, 86–87.

49. See Karen Hagemann and Stefan Dudink, "Masculinity in Politics and War in the Age of Democratic Revolutions, 1750–1850," in *Masculinities in Politics and War: Gendering Modern History*, ed. Stefan Dudink et al. (Manchester: Manchester University Press, 2004), 3–21; and the chapter by Stefan Dudink on "Citizenship, Mass Mobilization, and Masculinity in a Transatlantic Perspective, 1770s–1870s" in this handbook.

50. Smith, *Jamaican Volunteers*, 79.

51. Erik Jan Zürcher, "The Ottoman Conscription System, 1844–1914," *International Review of Social History* 43, no. 3 (1998): 437–49.

52. Erik Jan Zürcher, "Ottoman Labour Battalions in World War I," in *Der Völkermord an den Armeniern und die Shoah: The Armenian Genocide and the Shoah*, ed. Hans-Lukas Kieser and Dominik J. Schaller (Zurich: Chronos Verlag, 2002), 187–96.

53. Das, *Race, Empire*; Glenford Howe, *Race, War and Nationalism: A Social History of West Indians in the First World War* (Kingston, Jamaica: Ian Randle, 2002); Brian Willan, "The South African Native Labour Contingent, 1916–18," *Journal of African History* 19, no. 1 (1978): 61–86; and Guoqi Xu, *Strangers on the Western Front: Chinese Workers in the Great War* (Cambridge, MA: Harvard University Press, 2011).

54. George L. Mosse, *Fallen Soldiers: Reshaping the Memory of the World Wars* (Oxford: Oxford University Press, 1990); and Ilana R. Bet-El, "Men and Soldiers: British Conscripts, Concepts of Masculinity and the Great War," in *Borderlines: Genders & Identities in War and Peace, 1870–1930*, ed. Billie Melman (London: Routledge, 1998), 73–94.

55. Mimi Sheller, "Sword-Bearing Citizens: Militarism and Manhood in Nineteenth-Century Haiti," *Plantation Societies in the Americas* 4, no. 2–3 (1997): 233–78. On slave rebellions, see also the chapter by Elizabeth Colwill on "Gender, Slavery, War, and Violence in and beyond the Age of Revolutions" in this handbook.

56. Sonya O. Rose, "The Politics of Service and Sacrifice in WWI Ireland and India," *Twentieth Century British History* 25, no. 3 (2014): 368–90; and Laura Tabili, *"We Ask for British Justice": Workers and Racial Difference in Late Imperial Britain* (Ithaca, NY: Cornell University Press, 1994).

57. Anna Davin, "Imperialism and Motherhood," *History Workshop* 5 (1978): 9–65; Romain H. Rainero, "The Battle of Adowa on 1st March 1896: A Reappraisal," in *Imperialism and War: Essays on Colonial Wars in Asia and Africa*, ed. Jaap de Moor and Henk L. Wesseling (Leiden: Brill, 1989), 189–200; and Philip Darby, *Fiction of Imperialism: Reading between International Relations and Postcolonialism* (London: Cassell, 1998), 203–4.

58. Joanna Bourke, *Dismembering the Male: Men's Bodies, Britain and the Great War* (London: Reaktion Books, 1996); and Elaine Showalter, *The Female Malady: Women, Madness, and English Culture, 1800–1980* (London: Virago, 1987). See also Kühne, "States, Military Masculinities" in this handbook.

59. For accounts of these campaigns, see Louis Allen, *Singapore, 1941–42*, 2nd rev. ed. (London: Routledge, 1993); and Louis Allen, *Burma: The Longest War, 1941–45* (London: Dent, 1984). For African and Indian involvement, see Killingray, *Fighting for Britain*; and Kaushik Roy, "Military Loyalty in the Colonial Context: A Case Study of the Indian Army during World War II," *Journal of Military History* 73, no. 2 (2009): 497–529.

60. See, for example, Frank Furedi, "The Demobilized African Soldier and the Blow to White Prestige," in *Guardians of Empire: The Armed Forces of the Colonial Powers c.1700–1964*, ed. David Killingray and David Omissi (Manchester: Manchester University Press, 1999), 179–97; and James K. Matthews, "World War I and the Rise of African Nationalism: Nigerian Veterans as Catalysts of Change," *Journal of Modern African Studies* 20, no. 3 (1982): 493–502.

61. On the post-1945 struggle for independence, see also the chapter by Raphaëlle Branche on "Gender, the Wars of Decolonization, and the Decline of Empires after 1945" in this handbook.

62. Rose, "Politics of Service"; and Smith, "Heaven Grant You."

63. Roy, "Military Loyalty." See also Kühne, "Western, Military Masculinities" in this handbook.

64. Gregory Mann, *Native Sons: West African Veterans and France in the Twentieth Century* (Durham, NC: Duke University Press, 2006); and Smith, "Heaven Grant You."

65. Mann, *Native Sons*; and Raffael Scheck, *French Colonial Soldiers in German Captivity during World War II* (Cambridge: Cambridge University Press, 2014); also Ruth Ginio, *French Colonialism Unmasked: The Vichy Years in French West Africa* (Lincoln: University of Nebraska Press, 2006); and Ginio *Hitler's African Victims: The German Army Massacres of Black French soldiers in 1940* (Cambridge: Cambridge University Press, 2006).

66. Characteristic of this approach in subsequent historical accounts is Christopher Somerville, *Our War: How the British Commonwealth Fought the Second World War* (London: Weidenfeld & Nicolson, 1998).

67. Krystyna von Henneberg, "Monuments, Public Space, and the Memory of Empire in Modern Italy," *History and Memory* 16, no. 1 (2004): 37–85.

68. Killingray, *Fighting for Britain*; and Adekson, "Ethnicity and Army."

69. Eugene P. A. Schleh, "The Post-War Careers of Ex-Servicemen in Ghana and Uganda," *Journal of Modern African Studies* 6, no. 2 (1968): 203–20; and Gabriel Olakunle Olusanya, "The Role of Ex-Servicemen in Nigerian Politics," *Journal of Modern African Studies* 6, no. 2 (1968): 221–32.

70. João Paulo Borges Coelho, "African Troops in the Portuguese Colonial Army, 1961–1974: Angola, Guinea-Bissau and Mozambique," *Portuguese Studies Review* 10, no. 1 (2002): 129–50.

71. Mann, *Native Sons*; and Richard Smith, "The Multicultural First World War: Memories of the West Indian Contribution in Contemporary Britain," *Journal of European Studies* 45, no. 3 (2015): 347–63.

72. Simone Delerme, "Latinization of Space and the Memorialization of the Borinqueneers," *Anthropology News* 52, no. 6 (2011): 7–8.

73. Vron Ware, *Military Migrants: Fighting for YOUR Country* (London: Palgrave Macmillan, 2012).

74. Jaap de Moor, "The Recruitment of Indonesian Soldiers for the Dutch Colonial Army, c.1700–1950," in Killingray and Omissi, *Guardians of Empire*, 53–69.

Select Bibliography

Arielli, Nir, and Bruce Collins, eds. *Transnational Soldiers: Foreign Military Enlistment in the Modern Era*. Basingstoke: Palgrave Macmillan, 2013.

Byfield, Judith A., Carolyn A. Brown, Timothy Parsons, and Ahmad Alawad Sikainga, eds. *Africa and World War II*. New York: Cambridge University Press, 2015.

Caplan, Lionel. *Warrior Gentlemen: "Gurkhas" in the Western Imagination*. Providence, RI: Berghahn Books, 1995.

Das, Santanu. *Indian Troops in Europe, 1914–1918*. Ahmedabad: Mapin, 2015.

Fogarty, Richard S. *Race and War in France: Colonial Subjects in the French Army, 1914–1918*. Baltimore: John Hopkins University Press, 2008.

Gerwarth, Robert, and Erez Manela, eds. *Empires at War: 1911–1923*. Oxford: Oxford University Press, 2014.

Jackson, Ashley. *The British Empire and the Second World War*. London: Continuum, 2006.

Killingray, David. *Fighting for Britain: African Soldiers in the Second World War*. Woodbridge: James Currey, 2012.

Mangan, James Anthony. *"Manufactured" Masculinity: Making Imperial Manliness, Morality and Militarism*. London: Routledge, 2012.

McCarthy, Thomas. *Race, Empire, and the Idea of Human Development*. Cambridge: Cambridge University Press, 2009.

Morrow, John H. *The Great War: An Imperial History*. London: Routledge, 2004.

Moyd, Michelle R. *Violent Intermediaries: African Soldiers, Conquest, and Everyday Colonialism*. Athens, OH: Ohio University Press, 2014.

Omissi, David. *The Sepoy and the Raj: The Indian Army, 1860–1940*. Basingstoke: Macmillan, 1994.

Rettig, Tobias, and Karl Hack, eds. *Colonial Armies in Southeast Asia*. Abingdon: Routledge, 2011.

Scheck, Raffael. *French Colonial Soldiers in German Captivity during World War II*. Cambridge: Cambridge University Press, 2014.

Smith, Richard. *Jamaican Volunteers in the First World War: Race, Masculinity and the Development of National Consciousness*. Manchester: Manchester University Press, 2004.

Storm, Eric, and Ali Al Tuma, eds. *Colonial Soldiers in Europe, 1914–1945: "Aliens in Uniform" in Wartime Societies*. Abingdon: Routledge, 2016.

Streets, Heather. *Martial Races: The Military, Race and Masculinity in British Imperial Culture, 1857–1914*. Manchester: Manchester University Press, 2004.

Tai Yong, Tan. *The Garrison State: The Military, Government and Society in Colonial Punjab 1849–1947*. Thousand Oaks, CA: Sage, 2005.

Xu, Guoqi. *Strangers on the Western Front: Chinese Workers in the Great War*. Cambridge, MA: Harvard University Press, 2011.

CHAPTER 22

....

SEXUALITY, SEXUAL VIOLENCE, AND THE MILITARY IN THE AGE OF THE WORLD WARS

....

REGINA MÜHLHÄUSER

ONE of the main characteristics of industrialized, twentieth-century *total war* is the systematic involvement of the entire society in waging war.[1] The vast mobilization of men—and, in the course of World Wars I and II, increasingly women—for the military, as well as the unprecedented mobility of soldiers, army personnel, auxiliaries, doctors, nurses, and war workers, disrupted traditional monitoring mechanisms within the family and the community and created spaces of anonymity and intercultural encounter for soldiers and civilians. Not only men and women close to the front lines, but also men and, in particular, women "back home" often gained more space to act and move during the war, mainly because their support was needed in war industries, war charities, military nursing, and civil aerial defense.[2] Young people especially anticipated that the war years would be a time of adventure, pleasure, and new experiences—often including the transgression of national, social, racial, ethnic, or other boundaries. In particular, at the onset of World War I (1914–18), a generation of young men and women envisioned the future as a time of departure and change.[3]

Under these conditions, numerous opportunities for consensual sexual activity emerged: straight as well as queer, instrumental as well as noninstrumental, commercial as well as noncommercial. Sexual encounters could develop among people of the same social or political group for instance, when, during their training period, young men initiated contacts with local women in the vicinity of the military barracks. They could also occur beyond the confines of nation, class, race, ethnicity, and sexual orientation. The presence of colonial men of Color as soldiers in the Western armies in Europe during World Wars I and II was accompanied by romantic relations between them and White women in France and Great Britain—a visible fact that fundamentally irritated the gendered colonial order and resulted in severe restrictive measures for working-class women and colonial soldiers, particularly in Britain.[4] Sexual affairs, bartering, and romance could furthermore evolve between conquering men and conquered women, as the cases of young women in the Baltic states, Ukraine, and Belorussia demonstrate, who had relations with soldiers of the German Wehrmacht, which was occupying the Soviet Union after the invasion of June 1941.[5] In addition, sexual relations developed between women and men of the occupying power and prisoners of war (POWs) who were employed as forced laborers, for example in Germanys during World War II (1939–45). Last, but not least, within closed communities like the military or POW camps, homoerotic and homosexual forms of intimacy could emerge. During World War I, for instance, authorities in Germany and Britain largely accepted them among their men.[6]

At the same time, the experience of brutality, destruction, and death; the blurring of the distinctions of the lines between battle- and home fronts; and war-related social and material insecurities lowered the threshold for the perpetration of interpersonal violence, including sexual violence. Such acts could range from forcible undressing, sexual humiliation, forced oral sex, sexual torture, and genital mutilation to vaginal or anal rape (with the penis, other body parts, or objects), sexual enslavement, and forced prostitution. The perpetrators were mainly soldiers of state armed forces and members of nonstate armed groups, but also civilian men. Sometimes women, too, could be in a position to incite or exercise sexual violence. However, in most cases women and girls were the victims, but men and boys too were violated. Acts of sexual violence were directed not only against people from the enemy side but also from allies and the own collective. The latter could include an increase of sexual violence within the respective wartime and postwar societies as well as rape within the armies that fought in the First and Second World Wars.

The boundaries between consensual and forced, between nonviolent and violent sexual encounters were fluid. Indeed, the whole array of sexual encounters developed in and through the specific constellations of power during war and occupation. In this situation, "consensual" did not necessarily mean that these encounters were based on mutual consent. Rather, sexual contacts largely developed as a result of specific needs, pragmatic choices, and fears in the context of war. Furthermore, the interpretation of individual encounters could be ambivalent. A woman who decided to make use of her body in exchange for protection, food, or other scarce goods can be seen as both an active agent of her fate and a victim of sexual violence. In a situation in which women were on their own and faced material hardships and the threat of death (for themselves, their children, and their families), sexual bartering as well as professional prostitution became an option to ensure survival—in a gray zone between subjection and autonomy.

Scholars who study sexuality in the two world wars have emphasized that sexual activity, including sexual violence, was not merely a byproduct that occurred beside or beyond the actual realm of war. Instead, it was an intrinsic part of combat, occupation, and life on the home front. The military leaderships of all armies knew about the sexual activities of their men and assessed whether the effects would be regarded as positive or risky. Whether sexual activity (violent or nonviolent, forced or consensual) was actively supported, tacitly ignored, or restricted and punished depended on whether the army personnel regarded it as "effective" or "harmful" for the war effort in a given military territory at a particular time.[7] State politics also aimed to police some sexual constellations and practices—to control fears of miscegenation, "sodomy," and social unrest in families and communities—while others were encouraged, to combat the declining birth rate and keep up the population's morale.[8] In general, the consequences of sexual encounters during both wars were not just temporary, but could have long-term effects. This is illustrated by the fierce debates about the children of German soldiers and French women during the German occupation of northeastern France in World War I, the so-called Rhineland bastards of French colonial soldiers and German women during the French occupation of the Rhineland in the postwar era (1918–30), or the so-called *Mischlingskinder* (mixed-blood children) of African American occupation soldiers and German women after World War II. All these children were seen as a threat to their respective nations.[9]

As Dagmar Herzog has described, sexual politics—as well as sexual practices and experiences—were intertwined with fantasies and imaginaries. Since the late nineteenth and early twentieth centuries, sexual scandals had played a major role in making daily newspapers attractive for the masses. What is more, sexuality presented a framework and a symbolical language with which people could talk about the community and the nation in times when it was perceived as threatened. During both world wars, sexual violence and sexual fraternization became powerful metaphors for communicating fears of conquest, social intrusion, and disintegration.[10]

In the twenty-first century, there has been a growing body of work on sexual violence during both world wars, about women's and men's experiences and the ways in which the female body itself became a site of national interests. Based on this work, the following explores the historical manifestations of the entanglements of sexuality, violence, and power during World Wars I and II in Europe and beyond by focusing on ideas, practices, and representations of sexual violence. Four themes stand at the center: sexual violence as part of military policies, including its significance in the process of training soldiers and initiating them into the armed forces; the multifaceted forms and functions of sexual violence in different phases of war, genocide, and occupation; rape as a means of propaganda; and social reactions to this form of violence with particular focus on what is considered unspeakable and what can be spoken about.

MILITARY TRAINING AND REGULATION

General, compulsory military service had been introduced into most modern state armies in the nineteenth century, and both world wars were fought predominantly by conscript armies. In addition, significant numbers of volunteers took up arms in both wars for a variety of reasons; patriotic duty was only one of them.[11] The military faced the task of preparing these often very young men to become direct military actors and to be willing to face two of the most extreme experiences of human existence: the power to kill and the possibility of being killed.

Part of the training of young men in state armies aims to unleash the "individual's potential for violence" to prepare the soldier for combat. At the same time, however, this potential must be kept under control and channeled toward military goals.[12] The gray zone between individual actions and collective aims is a constant theme of military management. Military authorities must, as Ulrich Bröckling has noted, "anticipate what eludes calculation."[13] In the words of one British colonel in 1917, "I've seen my own men commit atrocities, and should expect to see it again. You can't stimulate and let loose the animal in man and then expect to be able to cage it up again at a moment's notice."[14]

In the effort to keep soldiers under control, they are subjected to a broad variety of disciplinary measures. The military as a total institution generally punishes manifest aberrations more rigorously than other institutions. Yet it nevertheless promises to recompense individuals for subordinating themselves to military leaders. As Jan Philipp Reemtsma has argued, "The order 'You shall!' is accompanied by the license 'You may.' Soldiers are not only disciplined more rigorously than other people, they can also—at least during war—take more liberties."[15] One of the liberties that all army leaderships granted their men during World Wars I and II was sexual activity, including the perpetration of sexual violence against women. In the logic of the military leaderships, soldiers' sexual satisfaction appeared as a means of sublimating men's responses to the hardships of war, including their fear and the possibility of death. To allow soldiers the "liberty" of sexual violence was also seen as a means to strengthen their masculinity and to foster cohesion and comradeship in small military units. Moreover, military leaders were well aware of the devastating effects "sexual conquests" of enemy women, including rape, had on the enemy society and largely considered this beneficial for military goals, in particular in phases of military advance into enemy territory.

Still, soldiers' sexual activity could also be considered counterproductive, especially when military leaders feared that they would lose control over their men. Indeed, military knowledge included an awareness of the potential effects of war brutality on men's sexuality. During World War I, soldiers' reactions to the brutality of the battlefield, including impotence, had become a subject of military and medical discussions; the libidinal elements within violence itself were part of military knowledge.[16] Furthermore, the spread of sexually transmitted disease, the loss of military discipline, and the potential resistance in occupied populations were seen as military risks.

Which measures an army took to tolerate, condone, cover up, encourage, discipline, or punish acts of sexual violence largely depended on the middle ranks and their assessment of a particular situation. Sources indicate that senior officers often not only turned a blind eye to sexual violence by subalterns but also actively covered up or participated in it. A British noncommissioned officer who experienced the end of World War II in the German city of Lübeck recorded in his memoirs how a colonel had ordered him to lie to two German women who had reported two of his comrades for rape: "I told the women there was nothing they could do and that of course the colonel knew it was them [that is, the soldiers the women had identified as the perpetrators].... They went away in tears."[17]

Such behavior and reactions within the troops reveal a tacit agreement or, more precisely, a specific knowledge among the men that sexual advances toward and sexual violation of women were a natural part of warfare. This gendered perception was also disseminated in military songs, stories, and jokes. As Gaby Zipfel has pointed out, contemporary ego-documents by soldiers indicate that many men did not perceive sexual attacks on women as wrongdoing, let alone as crimes that caused physiological and psychological harm to the victims.[18] Accordingly, one British "footslogger" in World War I remembered, "The men I was with were rough with women, boasting of their conquests, many of them were actually rapes, but there were no prosecutions to my knowledge."[19]

While rape constituted a crime in the military codes of all western and eastern European nations and the United States since early modern times, it was largely condoned and only brought in front of courts-martial when it was explicitly regarded as harmful to military performance. The perpetrators were usually prosecuted to ensure military discipline or to smooth potential unrest in the occupied population. Such a motivation is evident in the decision by the leadership of the German Wehrmacht in World War II to punish blatant acts of rape in occupied France with harsh sentences, because they wanted the civilian population to collaborate, but it only rarely tried cases in the east, where they aimed to conquer the local population they deemed "racially inferior."[20]

Ultimately, all armies tried to make it look as if rape by their own men was the crime of "a few bad apples" (that is, individual perpetrators who had transgressed the military rules) or a specific group of "outsiders." In October 1944, for example, the US Army's chief of police in France presented a list of crimes committed by GIs since the landings in Normandy the previous June. Reportedly, GIs had perpetrated 152 rapes; in 139 of these cases, the perpetrators were characterized as "colored"—even though only approximately 10 percent of all US soldiers in France were African Americans. Mary Louise Roberts has examined why most rape charges were made against African American men and found that the local population in war-torn Normandy projected their fears onto the Black man, which created a "rape hysteria." In this situation, women and girls wrongfully blamed African American GIs as rapists when they felt generally threatened or ran the risk of being reproached for fraternization.[21] It is indeed conceivable that women tried to ensure their status in this way. At the same time, however, there is no proof that the accusations of the women were altogether false. One could also scrutinize the issue from the other side: Why were White GIs so seldom accused of rape? Did this reflect the historical reality? Or did the women feel they would be met with suspicion and disbelief when they went to the police? Ultimately, we do not know what "truth" lies behind the statistics of the Military Police Corps. What the numbers indicate, however, is that the US military command found many more Black than White soldiers guilty of rape and did not hesitate to punish them with death. Almost all of the GIs who met their death by hanging in the twenty-one public executions between 1944 and 1945 were African Americans. In fact, even before the Americans arrived, there had been tremendous concern in Britain and France that the wartime societies would experience an epidemic of sexual crimes by Black US soldiers. Through the public executions, the US Army reacted to these fears. As a consequence, rape was made a "Black crime," which reflected the racism of the American culture of the time but also of Allies' and enemies' cultures.

Overall, disciplinary consequences and judicial prosecutions of sexual violence appear to have been relatively rare in all armies during the world wars. In accordance with modern science, military authorities believed that the male sexual urge needed an outlet, especially in times of war. What is more, army leaderships frequently acted on the assumption that male sexuality could and should be incited to support military operations.[22] A document from the Japanese Ministry of War distributed to all army units in 1940 explained, "In particular, the psychological effects that the soldiers receive at comfort stations [brothels for Japanese soldiers in which women and girls were sexually enslaved] are most immediate and profound, and therefore it is believed that the enhancement of troop morale, maintenance of discipline, and prevention of crimes and VD [venereal diseases] are dependent on successful supervision of these [comfort stations]."[23]

Remarkably, we can find the same ideas, in very similar wording, used in documents from the German Wehrmacht. While the leadership regarded sexual satisfaction as "positive" with regard to the war effort and the spirit of the troops, it feared that if too many cases of rape occurred, the loss of discipline, the lack of control, the resistance of the enemy population, and the spread of sexually transmitted diseases would follow. In fact, like the Japanese army, the Wehrmacht assumed that institutionalized sex in medically controlled brothels would provide a means of minimizing these risks. The same assumption, which had been supported by the International Society for the Prevention of Sexually Transmitted Diseases since the end of the nineteenth century, also led American, British, and French troops to "take over" military as well as civilian brothels for their men in Asia, North Africa, and Europe.[24]

The organization of military brothels during both wars varied greatly, depending on situational circumstances as well as the cultural and economic traditions of different armies. The Imperial Japanese Army, for example, made use of "comfort stations" during the Second Sino Japanese War (1937–45) and the Pacific War (1941–45) on a much larger scale than the Wehrmacht did during World War II, mainly because of the long history of trafficking and organized exploitation of women and girls from the Japanese colonies Korea and Taiwan. The contemporaries were aware that military brothels were ineffective as a means of limiting the spread of sexually transmitted disease; nonetheless, their establishment continued and the rhetoric of justification was sustained.[25]

FORMS AND FUNCTIONS OF SEXUAL VIOLENCE

In situations of invasion, soldiers of aggressor armies often perpetrated sexual violence amid more generalized pillage and looting. As a woman in Ukraine during the Second World War phrased it, "The [German] soldiers chased hens and girls, they looked for eggs and sex."[26] In the short and unregulated phases directly after invasion, rape was seen as a reward for and booty after a successful conquest. In addition, it communicated the message from men to men that the "invaded men" were not able to protect "their women" anymore.[27] During conquest and in the early phases of occupation, body searches were pervasive, in particular during World War II, to a lesser extent also in World War I, occurring on the street but also in private houses and spaces of incarceration like prisons and camps. These searches were regularly accompanied by sexualized practices and obscene comments. During World War II, military regulations indeed instructed German soldiers to conduct body searches of people for firearms or secret messages. However, these instructions did not include touching a woman's breasts, squeezing her nipples, inserting fingers into her vagina, or other sexual violations. Testimonies concerning incidents like these reveal that the men occasionally interpreted the regulations to suit their own interests and ideas. In situations where the (often very young) men felt bored or afraid, acts of verbal, voyeuristic, and physical sexual assault could offer them an opportunity to affirm their own superiority and power and to ease their feelings of apathy and stress. At the same time, their actions spread fear, insecurity, and terror within the local population.[28]

Sexual violence occurred in private homes, and sources from both world wars indicate that it was not unusual that family members were present and had to watch or listen during rapes. This could have fatal consequences. On September 5, 1914, a German noncommissioned officer was billeted in the house of a young French widow, Louise F., who lived with her three-year-old daughter and her parents in Montmirail in the Marne department. After he had eaten with the family, the officer went out. When he came back around eleven o'clock in the evening, he was drunk and tried to rape Louise F. in her room. Her screams awakened her father and a couple of German soldiers who were billeted in the neighbor's house. In the following tumultuous situation, Louise F.'s father and daughter were shot.[29] In situations like this, rape communicated that the private sphere had ceased to be safe and family relations could be severely altered.

Women and girls as well as boys and men could also fall victim to sexual violence in the confined spaces of prisons. Sometimes a prisoner would be raped directly in the cell, within sight or earshot of fellow prisoners; at other times, the guards would take them out of their cells to sexually torture them and return them afterward. For instance, Jewish women and people suspected of partisan activity against the Nazis in Latvia in summer 1941 were imprisoned and sexually assaulted during interrogations by officers of the Arajs Kommando, a Latvian auxiliary police formation that collaborated with the German Security Police.[30] While sexual torture of men—as Sheila Meintjes has demonstrated—is implemented to generate "sexual passivity" and thus eliminate bodily strength and political power, similar acts against women serve to "activate" female sexuality and to relegate women to their societal position as sexual objects.[31] At times, women and girls were also captured and imprisoned for the explicit purpose of sexual enslavement. In the Wehrmacht's medically monitored brothels in the Baltic states, women were exploited to provide the soldiers with what was considered an "outlet for their sexual drives."[32] There are numerous examples of sexual violence against POWs, for instance, against female Red Army soldiers who had been captured by German troops. Indeed, sexual violence could be a way to "punish" women who irritated the gendered order by taking up arms.[33]

Male POWs could also find themselves subjected to sexual violence. In February 1942, a British pioneer who had been in Malaysia and Singapore with the Royal Engineers was captured by Japanese soldiers and herded onto a ship with other POWs. In Pusan, South Korea, the captors brought him and his fellow prisoners onto the quay and sexually humiliated them in public. They were forced to stand with their trousers at their feet while the guards inserted objects into their rectums. As the veteran remembered in the early 1980s, "they were going to bring the British race or the white mind down to the level of the coolie [a derogative term for colonial subjects in India who worked as unskilled laborers for the British].[34] In his understanding, this male-male assault was a form of revenge against the racist practices of the British colonizers.[35] The penetration of men (contrary to the penetration of women) did not primarily appear as a sexual attack, but as a violent act of degradation of White British men.

Particularly in situations of guerrilla warfare in which the state army was fighting against men and women in irregular armed groups, sexual violence was often extremely brutal. The hidden enemies of any age and either sex who resisted the regular soldiers were characterized using images of sexual deviance, such as in the German myth of the malicious, sneaky *francs-tireurs* (armed irregulars) during World War I and the associated images of beautiful French women who would seduce the unsuspecting German man and then poison him or torture him with burning hot oil.[36] It is thus hardly surprising that guerrilla fighters, in particular women, could become subjects of intense sexual torture and rape if they were captured.

Sexual violence was also part of genocidal terror and killings. Anthonie Holslag has suggested that perpetrators of genocide engage in sexual violence "to obliterate an identity, first by shaming and humiliating the targeted group and second by controlling and destroying reproduction."[37] The extermination of an estimated 800,000 to 1.5 million Ottoman Armenians between 1915 and 1918 was indeed carried out in two phases. The able-bodied male population was killed in massacres and subjected to forced labor before women, children, and the elderly were sent on death marches to the Syrian desert. Both phases were accompanied by sexual violence: men became victims of sexual torture and genital mutilation (the latter was sometimes performed before or, at other times, after the killings); army personnel who guarded the death marches sexually humiliated and raped the women.[38] In the context of the physical destruction, such acts of sexual violence were highly symbolic; they communicated that the perpetrators had control over not only reproduction but also most intimate bodily expressions of life.

Research on the extermination of European Jews as well as the mass murder of Sinti and Roma also demonstrates that sexual violence was part of the genocidal project of the "Final Solution." After their arrival in a camp, women and girls were forced to strip and parade naked in front of doctors, guards, and fellow prisoners and to endure obscene comments, beatings, and defloration with fingers. Sexual torture and experiments were also frequent.[39] Indeed, the perpetrators appear to have taken pleasure in tormenting the prisoners. As Doris Bergen has observed, the prisoners were removed "from their torturer's sphere of 'normal' treatment of women and fellow human beings."[40] They were raped and tortured *because* the perpetrators feared and hated them as "Others."

In many camps, in particular within the borders of Nazi Germany, genital rape by German guards of the SS, the Nazi Schutzstaffel (Protection Squadron), appears to have been rare. Racism, antisemitism, and the Nazi "Blood Laws" restricted the men's behavior to a certain extent.[41] In the context of the war of annihilation in Poland and the Soviet Union, Nazi racial ideology was by no means congruent with the interests of the men. One way to cover up the trespassing of racial boundaries was to kill the victims, who were witnesses to a transgression of the Blood Laws.[42] For the non-German Nazi allies, the notion of "race defilement" was of little importance all along.[43]

To understand the complexity of sexual violence during war and genocide, it is crucial to note that this form of violence can also occur within one's own group. Within the closed spaces of camps or ghettos during the Holocaust, sexual violence was sometimes perpetrated by fellow prisoners. On example are *Kapos*, prisoner functionaries (*Funktionshäftlinge*), who were assigned particular functions in the administration of concentration camps and elevated to a higher place within the hierarchy the Nazis had created among the camp prisoners. In some concentration camps, *Kapos* had other prisoners as sexual servants, usually of the same sex. Women and girls, but also boys and men, used their bodies in the camp system in exchange for food. Within ghettos and labor camps, sexual bartering could also present a chance to avoid selections and deportations. Sexually succumbing could become a means of survival.[44]

Soldiers of the liberation armies also perpetrated sexual violence. The mass rapes committed by Red Army soldiers during their march toward Germany, particularly during the Battle of Berlin in spring 1945, have been the subject of extensive research and debate.[45] The composition of the Red Army front-line units, with very young, largely inexperienced soldiers; their hatred and desire for revenge after the brutal German war of annihilation; and the way the military leadership tolerated licentious behavior led to widespread rape.[46] In comparison, sexual violence by Western Allies in Europe appears to have been less widespread and less motivated by revenge, but more by opportunity: men took the chances that arose because of the collapse of social restraints and the general mayhem of war.[47]

Sexual violence by Western Allied soldiers in the Asian theater of war appears to have been accompanied by additional forms of violence like beatings more often, such as when American soldiers raped Japanese women shortly upon their landing in Japan in 1945. A brutal form of sexual violence was practiced on the Japanese island of Okinawa in March 1945, when GIs abducted local women, dragged them to deserted coastal areas, and gang raped them.[48] Such differences in the frequency and intensity of sexual violence might be explained with the framework of colonial history. First, the men considered a repertoire of violent and sexual practices "normal" in Asia that was largely out of bounds in western Europe. In addition, Joanna Bourke contended for the case of British and American soldiers during both world wars that such differences were a result of ways in which the men related to and identified with the enemy. While there was "a widespread acknowledgement amongst combatants in western Europe that both 'he and I' were merely cold and frightened cannon fodder," the men (and women) that Western soldiers encountered in Asia appeared much more alien to them, which led to a stronger dehumanization of the enemy and an increase in fear and brutality.[49]

Allied soldiers perpetrated sexual violence not only against women who belonged to the fascist enemy nations and their allies. Rather, women who had been victims of German or Japanese politics and military operations were also attacked, as in the case of rapes of Hungarian women by Soviet soldiers.[50] The ways in which sexual violence in war was connected to gender relations in peacetime became generally more obvious in situations of occupation, but also when Western militaries were in Allied territory. For example, a member of the US supply troops stationed in Great Britain during World War II asked his victim, an English woman, after he had raped and threatened to strangle her, if she would like to go dancing with him the following week.[51] This case, like many others, illustrates that men often lacked awareness that the sexual violence was a crime and seriously harmed the victims.

Within the armed forces and their auxiliary staff, sexual violence could also become pervasive. Female personnel, in particular nurses, were at risk of rape by soldiers and confronted with accusations of sexual looseness.[52] Rape of female soldiers likely happened but has not yet been a subject of in-depth research.[53] Additionally, male–male sexual violence occurred in all armies during both world wars. In oral history interviews, a number of British and American navy veterans of World War II recounted that they were sexually attacked and sometimes raped by their older comrades during military training. Here, rape appears to have been a part of initiation. As Aaron Belkin has asserted with regard to the American military, the soldiers valued the abilities to exert violence and endure aggression. To endure sexual violence was thus viewed not necessarily as unmanly, but as part of the strength a soldier needed to survive and protect himself and his unit.[54]

RAPE AS A WEAPON OF PROPAGANDA

"Representations of sexual violence in war do not simply occur after the fact: rather, they are often part of the conflict itself," Elizabeth Heineman has argued.[55] With the new means of mass communication during World War I, wartime rape was for the first time brought to the attention of a large international audience. After the invasion of neutral Belgium by the German army in its attack on France in August and September 1914, the

Allied media reported on what they described as the "Rape of Belgium." British, French, and Russian papers published remarkably graphic stories of brutal atrocities that the Germans allegedly perpetrated against the civilian population, in particular about the rape of women and the mutilation of children.[56] The aim, however, was not merely to inform the public about the occurrence of crimes against women and children. Instead, Allied propaganda appropriated the stories of rape victims to mobilize hatred against the "brutal" German "barbarians," thereby convincing the domestic audience of the justness of the war cause and enlisting their active support.[57] In the words of Susan Brownmiller, rape appeared "almost overnight as a characteristic German crime, evidence of the 'depraved Boche.'"[58]

This condemnation of wartime sexual violence in political rhetoric, however, does not mean that the stories of the victims were actually heard. As Ruth Harris has observed, "men's anxieties and fantasies, much more than the tragedy of women's experiences, shaped the discussion of sexual violation and the war."[59] Indeed, this exploitation of rape for political ends would hardly have been possible if there had been more interest in dealing with the multifaceted experiences of the women and girls who became victims of this form of violence. Their actual experiences would have revealed a much more ambivalent and complicated story about the constellations, dynamics, and effects of sexual violence. Women and girls who fell victim to wartime rape encountered the German perpetrators directly, in a particular intimate situation of violence, and were confronted not only with the cliché of the enemy Other, but also with the humanness of the men. In addition, many women and girls were aware that sexual violence was perpetrated by men from all sides. Such knowledge, however, was unspeakable. In fact, female victims had difficulties talking about their experiences, as many family members and communities reacted with denial or mistrust. To date, it is impossible to know how many rapes occurred.[60]

The framework in which women and girls were authorized to speak about their experiences of sexual violence followed specific social and political parameters. When the Allies conducted investigative interviews soon after the 1914 German invasion of Belgium and France to determine the extent to which the invaders had violated the Geneva Conventions, many victims characterized the occurrence of sexual violence as random and completely unexpected, and the perpetrators as primitive apes or dirty pigs. These descriptions and the emotionally charged style of the narratives must be seen in the light of French propaganda as well as earlier experiences with the German military, which had been transmitted culturally since the Franco-Prussian War of 1870–71.[61] In addition, such narratives suggest that women followed a certain script to be able to reveal their rape experience; that is, they emphasized their innocence as well as the uncivilized brutality of the perpetrators.

This script can, indeed, be found in political rhetoric, according to which the willingness to intervene, rescue, and protect "innocent, helpless women and girls" appeared as a marker for the integrity and honor of the nation. In World War II, the US military press portrayed the invasion of France "in mythic terms as a mission to save French women from the evils of Nazism."[62] And the logic was not limited to the Western world.

Similarly, Japan characterized its aggression in Asia as a "grand strategy of fatherly Japan liberating Asian women from Western colonialism."[63] In all cases, stories and images of wartime sexual violence, real and imagined, played a decisive role in mobilizing societal support and soldiers' commitment for total war.

This narrative—according to which sexual violence was (and is) a threat not merely to the victims but also to a (political, ideological, national, ethnic, racial) community as such—is connected to the interrelatedness of the intimate, deeply personal character of sexual violence and its social meanings. In times of war, the occurrence of rape (as well as its anticipation) can come to symbolize the fear of an invasion and disintegration of the community, the societal order, the social ties, and, ultimately, the space of the family. Conversely, the very notion of rape can become a metaphor for military conquest and occupation, as we find it in the already mentioned Rape of Belgium for World War I or the "Rape of Nanking" for World War II—long-standing and persistent tropes. The latter denotes the capture of Nanjing, then the capital of the Republic of China, by the Japanese troops in December 1937. During this episode in the Second Sino-Japanese War, it is estimated that between 40,000 and over 300,000 Chinese civilians and disarmed combatants were murdered.[64] Because of the collective dimension of sexual violence, which is revealed in such tropes, the threat as well as the occurrence of sexual violence can weld a community together through the condemnation of the enemy. The enemy perpetrator who violates "innocent, helpless women and girls" appears to have left the realm of civilized warfare. The perpetration of sexual violence figures as proof and symbol of the ruthlessness and barbarity of the Other. The fact that sexual violence is also perpetrated by one's own soldiers is glossed over.

That sexual violence was exploited for political ends can also be observed in World War II. When Germany began to face defeat in the last phase of the war, Nazi newsreels fanned German fears of rape by Allied soldiers, in particular by Soviet men. After the unresolved deaths of between nineteen and thirty civilians during a skirmish between the Wehrmacht and the Red Army in Nemmersdorf, East Prussia, on October 21, 1944, German propaganda used photos and descriptions of the dead bodies of raped women of the "Nemmersdorf Massacre" to call on their soldiers to resist to the end, "for peace would be even more painful than war."[65] Soviet authorities responded to the German propaganda with a counternarrative. On February 14, 1946, the Soviet minister of foreign affairs, Vyacheslav Mikhailovich Molotov, submitted a report as evidence at the Nuremberg Trials (1945–46), the military tribunal conducted by the Allied countries to try Nazi leaders after World War II. The report listed horrendous acts of rape, sexual enslavement, and genital mutilation by Wehrmacht soldiers and SS men against women and girls in the Soviet Union. The "Molotov Note" was connected to real occurrences, but the narrative was clearly embellished and tailored to serve political aims. And the international group of judges presiding in Nuremberg did not inquire about any of the crimes listed. Acts of sexual violence did not become a subject of investigation, let alone prosecution at the Nuremberg Trials and later court hearings.[66]

Soon after, however, when the fragile political alliance between the Soviet Union and the United States collapsed in the context of the Global Cold War (1946–91), the United

States did not hesitate to take up the German rhetoric of the Red Army as a "horde of Mongolian rapists." In the bestselling novel *The Big Rape* on the end of World War II in Berlin, published in 1952 by the American author James Wakefield Burke, Red Army soldiers embodied the cliché of alleged "Eastern primitiveness," engaging in alcohol excesses and perverse sexual acts. This "destructive masculinity," noticed literary scholar Júlia Garraio in her analysis of the novel, has its counterpart in the text, "in the healthy, potent, and protective masculinity, which is embodied in the American military."[67] Indeed, the fact that the Western Allies—Americans as well as French and British soldiers—also committed rape and other forms of sexual violence during and after World War II remained largely absent from historiography until quite recently.[68]

SPEAKABILITY/UNSPEAKABILITY

Propaganda material on sexual violence during both world wars was disseminated widely. Still, there were hardly any narratives about sexual violence, either by victims or by perpetrators or bystanders. While rape was a statutory offense in all Western nations, Russia, and Japan, the ways these societies dealt with the occurrence of sexual violence suggests that there was little awareness that sexual violence constituted a grave injustice, let alone a crime—unless an act was accompanied by excessive brutality. While perpetrators of sexual violence might have routinely bragged about their "sexual conquests" in the circle of comrades, they were generally reluctant to admit their behavior to others. Soldiers felt that civilians were "outsiders" who could not understand what they had been through and why they had acted as they did. In addition, the men anticipated that the revelation of their brutal experiences and criminal deeds would fundamentally alter living together with their civilian contacts, in particular with women.[69]

While most soldiers consigned their stories to oblivion or kept them among themselves in veterans groups some confided in doctors or priests. During and after World War I, glimpses of such revelations left the realm of the "private," because the correlation between military violence and soldier's (sexual) dis/function became a concern of military and social politics.[70] In addition, memoirs and literary texts offer some insights into the ways soldiers dealt with sexual violence. Many Japanese soldiers, for instance, mentioned their visits to "comfort stations" in Asia rather freely, while only some men publicly expressed regrets towards the victims and questioned the experienced brutalization of young men in times of war. Men of the latter group were (and still are) often faced with the accusation that they had been traitors. When the Japanese veteran Yoshio Suzuki testified at the Women's Tribunal against Japan's Military Sexual Slavery in Tokyo in 2000, the audience applauded his courage, while outside the building, Japanese nationalists demonstrated and threatened him for besmirching the honor of the Japanese forces. In his testimony at the tribunal, he had reported how—during a military operation in China—he had given his men permission "to do whatever they wanted" and then himself raped a woman.[71]

It is this social, cultural, and political framework between silencing, mudslinging, and exploitation in which victims speak or remain (actively) silent about their experiences of sexual violence. For most victims, it appeared impossible to speak. Many were murdered or committed suicide. Others were confronted with denial and mistrust when their social environment insinuated that, through their behavior, they were complicit in the crime. The fact that sexual violence was merely one of many physical and psychological assaults women had to endure was another reason for remaining silent, as in the case of female survivors of the Holocaust who considered their sexually violent experiences marginal in relation to murder and extermination. Indeed, Jewish, Sinti, and Roma women might also have kept silent after the end of the war to spare their menfolk the additional pain of having been unable to protect them.[72] In the rare instances that women were in the position to come forward to police or military authorities or if the crime was reported by witnesses or confidants, the victims had to go through humiliating police and military interrogations and, sometimes, painful genital examinations. If a case came in front of a court, the victim also found herself in a difficult position, because her respectability was questioned—similar to peacetime inquiries, in which women's sexual histories and motives for speaking out could become a matter of extensive interrogation.

When female rape victims were asked to contribute to reports on enemy crimes, they appear to have received a much more sympathetic hearing. Such was the case in the above-mentioned Allied investigation of German crimes in Belgium and France during World War I when the accounts of female witnesses were readily believed. However, their narratives were appropriated and their documentation in the report was tailored toward political goals. While the investigation commissioners might have had good intentions, their findings were clearly biased.[73] In another case—the documentation of Polish and Soviet crimes by the West German Federal Ministry for Expellees after World War II—the language of the report and the presentation of the testimonies about rape were openly embellished in the interests of Cold War propaganda.[74]

An opportunity for women and girls to speak about sexual violence could arise when they were by themselves, in a female community, and sexual violence became a shared experience. In Berlin in 1945, the absence of most German menfolk who had been in the military (and had died or fled, were in the process of demobilization, or had become POWs) created a space in which women seem to have had the possibility to exchange experiences and prevention strategies more or less openly. According to Atina Grossmann, especially in bigger German cities like Berlin, the sexual reform movement of the 1920s and 1930s had meant that the "New Woman" could develop a more resolute stance toward sexuality. As a result, women who had already been adults in the 1920s were able to deal with their violation at the end of World War II rather pragmatically. In diaries and letters, they recorded how their apprehensions about rape were realized when the Red Army soldiers arrived. For some, rape by Soviet soldiers affirmed their racist ideas about the uncivilized, ostensibly "subhuman" Slavic *Untermensch*. For others, the men acted out of revenge for the crimes German soldiers had previously committed in Poland and the Soviet Union.

After the men returned, however, all stories of sexual encounters, including rape, disappeared.[75] When rape became a powerful metaphor of defeat in West German memory, it thus appeared as a "desexualized" phenomenon: suddenly, it was "the Germans," women and men alike, who appeared to be the victims of rape. Yet in East Germany the persistence of sexual violence by Soviet soldiers until the 1950s was actively erased from political debate and collective memory.[76] The example of the Red Army furthermore reveals that dealing with sexual violence was a particularly complex and painful process when the perpetrator was not the enemy. Female prisoners in Auschwitz who had awaited the Soviet soldiers as liberators were devastated when these soldiers raped them.[77]

Since the 1970s, when sexual violence started to emerge first as a subject of feminist inquiry and later also of academic historical scholarship, those conducting oral history interviews have begun including questions about gender and sexuality. In South Korea and other Asian countries, research on the "comfort-station system" was fueled and accompanied by a strong, visible social movement that supported women's claims for justice and reparations. In this atmosphere, survivors could make sense of their past as a "shared experience," which enabled them to speak of rape and sexual enslavement rather openly. More than 250 survivors from ten countries decided to go public, showing their portrait photo in the Women's Active Museum on War and Peace, opened in Tokyo in 2005[78] By contrast, survivors of Nazi persecution are still hesitant to relate their experiences of sexual violence. In oral history conversations to date, one can often hear the interviewee and/or the interviewer shying away from the subject. One way of dealing with sexual violence in such accounts is to deny it or place it within an impersonal historical narrative. Furthermore, women tend to relate third-person events, explaining that neighbors or friends became victims of rape. Sometimes the way these stories are told raises the question of whether the speakers are indirectly also relating their own experiences. What becomes clear is that the meaning of women's narratives on sexual violence also lies in the silences and contradictions.[79]

CONCLUSION

The historical research from different theaters of the world wars reveals that the entanglement of violence and sexuality was an intrinsic part of contemporary military knowledge of all military actors. On the one hand, heterosexual activity figured as a symbol of the power and sovereignty of the male bond, and sexual violence was seen as an assertion of the soldiers' power and their control over women. On the other hand, sexuality, and in particular sexual violence, revealed the men's fragility and vulnerability. Indeed, military knowledge assumed that men could not control their libidinal reactions and were vulnerable to sexual violence. This ambiguous knowledge was reflected in the ways the armies handled sexual violence during total war. Military rules and laws in all nations were meant to restrict uncontrolled sexual behavior. They provided a framework by which rape could become a subject of disciplinary action or judicial persecution whenever a case was seen as a threat to military discipline, health, or the credibility of the troops, that is, as counterproductive with regard to military aims. Yet these military laws regarding "sexual violation" were relatively seldom enforced. As Sabine Frühstück concluded in a 2016 essay on sexuality and sexual violence during World War II, "Modern medicalized notions of a 'sexual instinct'... deepened the assumption of the inevitability of male sexual desire, which, in turn, easily translated into the wartime understanding that soldiers' sexual needs were to be managed but could not and should not be suppressed or completely controlled."[80]

We can observe a widespread nonprosecution of rape. What is more, some armies incited soldiers' sexual activities by establishing military-controlled brothels. This, in turn, created a culture of impunity in which men could understand sexual violence as their right as soldiers. The ways the men used their spaces of interpretation and action depended on their personal backgrounds, the norms that emerged in their small units, and the opportunities that opened up to them in specific situations. Men largely acted out of individual motives and opportunities but were nevertheless aware of the devastating effects sexual violence had for the enemy. And regardless of the motives of the individual men, their actions were clearly anticipated and exploited by the commanders who assessed the benefits and risks of the soldiers' behavior for the respective military aims.

While practices of sexual violence in war were remarkably similar in different territories throughout both world wars, they were rooted in specific societal, economic, ethnic, cultural, and religious constellations in a given territory at a particular time. The women who were raped by German soldiers plundering and looting Belgian and French houses in 1914 have little in common with the Dutch girls who grew up in the Dutch East Indies (Indonesia) and were sexually enslaved in Japanese military comfort stations during the Japanese Dutch East Indies campaign (1941–42). The situation of Armenian men who suffered genital mutilation before they were slaughtered during the Armenian genocide (1915–17) is different from that of the British boy-soldier raped by his comrades in the navy barracks during World War II. The ways contemporaries experienced, understood, and articulated their experiences of wartime sexual violence were shaped by particular gendered and sexual norms and mores as well as cultural, bodily, and linguistic underpinnings. To understand the meanings and effects of this particular form of violence, it is thus necessary to reflect on the gendered economic, cultural, and social conditions in different theaters of both wars.

Examining the societal meanings and effects of sexual violence also suggests that the messages that this form of violence carries are fundamentally different for women and men. In central Europe at the onset of World War I, large parts of the female population had expected that the war would advance the development of equal rights and emancipation. Indeed, women's contributions at the battlefront and on the "home front" were valued and invested with meaning. Through the realities of the war, however, such hopes were broken. The radicalization of violence dramatically altered gender relations at the battlefront and on the home front.[81] What is more, the pervasive occurrence of sexual violence as well as the visible exploitation of rape in the international political arena communicated to the female population that women and men were by no means regarded as equal.

This gendered reality, however, was glossed over by the powerful narrative of war rape as the crime of the enemy Other, which served to suppress and whitewash the historical reality. In a somewhat paradoxical communicative figure, wartime sexual violence during both world wars was understood as natural behavior by men at war (and, indeed, an unavoidable byproduct of warring) and, at the same time, an expression of male dishonor and a horrendous disruption of civilization when perpetrated by the enemy. Ultimately, sexual violence was regarded as a perhaps regrettable but nonetheless normal part of war that did not require any further investigation unless it was accompanied by excessive violence.

NOTES

1. For a discussion of the concept of *total war*, see the chapter by Karen Hagemann and Sonya O. Rose on "War and Gender: The Age of the World Wars and Its Aftermath—an Overview" in this handbook.
2. Dagmar Herzog, *Sexuality in Europe: A Twentieth Century History* (Cambridge: Cambridge University Press, 2011), 6–95.
3. Gaby Zipfel, "'Beyond Good and Evil for Once!' 'Authorized Transgressions' and Women in Wartime," *Eurozine*, April 25, 2014, https://www.eurozine.com/beyond-good-and-evil-for-once/.
4. Philippa Levine, "Battle Colors: Race, Sex, and Colonial Soldiery in World War I," *Journal of Women's History* 9, no. 4 (1998): 104–30; and Susan Zeiger, *Entangling Alliances: Foreign War Brides and American Soldiers in the Twentieth Century* (New York: New York University Press, 2010). See also the chapter by Richard Smith on "Colonial Soldiers, Race, and Military Masculinities during and beyond World Wars I and II" in this handbook.
5. Regina Mühlhäuser, "Between 'Racial Awareness' and Fantasies of Potency: Nazi Sexual Politics in the Occupied Territories of the Soviet Union, 1942–1945," in *Brutality and Desire: War and Sexuality in Europe's Twentieth Century*, ed. Dagmar Herzog (Basingstoke: Palgrave Macmillan, 2009), 197–220; Mühlhäuser, *Eroberungen: Sexuelle Gewalttaten und intime Beziehungen deutscher Soldaten in der Sowjetunion, 1941–1945* (Hamburg: Hamburger Edition, 2010), 240–99, English translation: *Sex and the Nazi Soldier: Violent, Commercial and Consensual Contacts during the War in the Soviet Union, 1941–1945* (Edinburgh: Edinburgh University Press, 2020); and Birthe Kundrus, "Forbidden Company: Romantic Relationships between Germans and Foreigners, 1939 to 1945," *Journal of the History of Sexuality* 11, no. 1/2 (2002): 201–22.
6. Jason Crouthamel, *An Intimate History of the Front: Masculinity, Sexuality, and German Soldiers in the First World War* (Basingstoke: Palgrave Macmillan, 2014); and Emma Vickers, *Queen and Country: Same-Sex Desire in the British Armed Forces, 1939–45* (Manchester: Manchester University Press, 2015).
7. Gaby Zipfel, "'Let Us Have a Little Fun': The Relationship between Gender, Violence and Sexuality in Armed Conflict Situations," *Revista Crítica de Ciências Sociais Annual Review*, no. 5 (2013), https://doi.org/10.4000/rccsar.469; see Zipfel, Regina Mühlhäuser, and Kirsten Campbell, eds. *In Plain Sight: Sexual Violence in Armed Conflict* (New Delhi: Zubaan, 2019).

8. Herzog, *Sexuality in Europe*.

9. Antoine Rivière, "'Special Decisions': Children Born as the Result of German Rape and Handed Over to Public Assistance during the Great War (1914–18)," in *Rape in Wartime*, ed. Raphaëlle Branche and Fabrice Virgili (Basingstoke: Palgrave Macmillan, 2012), 184–200; and Heide Fehrenbach, *Race after Hitler: Black Occupation Children in Postwar Germany and America* (Princeton, NJ: Princeton University Press, 2005).

10. Herzog, *Sexuality in Europe*.

11. See the chapters by Stefan Dudink on "Citizenship, Mass Mobilization, and Masculinity in a Transatlantic Perspective, 1770s–1870s," and Thomas Kühne on "States, Military Masculinities, and Combat in the Age of World Wars" in this handbook.

12. Ulrich Bröckling, *Disziplin: Soziologie und Geschichte militärischer Gehorsamsproduktion* (Munich: Wilhelm Fink Verlag, 1997), 189–90; and Zipfel, "Let Us Have." See also Kühne, "States, Military Masculinities" in this handbook.

13. Bröckling, *Disziplin*, 190.

14. Pym and Gordon, 1917, cited in Joanna Bourke, "Unwanted Intimacy: Violent Sexual Transfers in British and American Societies 1870s to 1970s," *European Journal of English Studies* 9, no. 3 (2005): 287–99, 294.

15. Jan Philipp Reemtsma, "Gewalt: Monopol, Delegation, Partizipation," in *Gewalt: Entwicklungen, Strukturen, Analyseprobleme*, ed. Wilhelm Heitmeyer and Hans-Georg Soeffner (Frankfurt am Main: Suhrkamp, 2004), 346–61.

16. Jason Crouthamel, "Male Sexuality and Psychological Trauma: Soldiers and Sexual Disorder in World War I and Weimar Germany," *Journal of the History of Sexuality* 17, no. 1 (2008): 60–84; and Joanna Bourke, *An Intimate History of Killing: Face to Face Killing in Twentieth Century Warfare* (London: Granta, 2000), 139–70.

17. W. A. Blackman, *Army Experiences, 1941–1946*, typed manuscript, 99/851, Archive of the Imperial War Museum, London (hereafter cited as IWM).

18. Zipfel, "Let Us Have."

19. Cited in Joanna Bourke, "Unwanted Intimacy," 294.

20. See Elizabeth Harvey, "Remembering and Repressing German Women's Recollections of the 'Ethnic Struggle' in Occupied Poland during the Second World War," in *Home/Front: The Military, War and Gender in Twentieth-Century Germany*, ed. Karen Hagemann and Stefanie Schüler-Springorum (Oxford: Berg, 2002), 275–79.

21. Mary Louise Roberts, *What Soldiers Do: Sex and the American GI in World War II France* (Chicago: University of Chicago Press, 2013), 195–261.

22. Sabine Frühstück, "Sexuality and Sexual Violence," in *The Cambridge History of the Second World War*, vol. 3, *Economy, Society and Culture*, ed. Michael Geyer and Adam Tooze (Cambridge: Cambridge University Press, 2016), 422–46.

23. Cited in Yuki Tanaka, *Japan's Comfort Women: Sexual Slavery and Prostitution during World War II and the US Occupation* (New York: Routledge, 2002), 24.

24. Ibid.

25. Ibid., 11 and 155–66; and Mühlhäuser, *Eroberungen* 237–38.

26. Cited in Wendy Jo Gertjejanssen, "Victims, Heroes, Survivors: Sexual Violence on the Eastern Front during World War II" (PhD diss., University of Minnesota, 2004), 267.

27. Ruth Seifert, "The Second Front: The Logic of Sexual Violence in Wars," *Women's Studies International Forum* 19, no. 1–2 (1996): 35–43.

28. Mühlhäuser, *Eroberungen*, 121.

29. John N. Horne and Alan Kramer, *German Atrocities, 1914: A History of Denial* (New Haven, CT: Yale University Press, 2001), 292.

30. Andre Angrick and Peter Klein, *Die "Endlösung" in Riga, Ausbeutung und Vernichtung 1941–1944* (Darmstadt: Wissenschaftliche Buchgesellschaft, 2006), 81.

31. Cited in Louise du Toit, "Feminism and the Ethics of Reconciliation," in *Law and the Politics of Reconciliation*, ed. Scott Veitch (Aldershot: Ashgate, 2007), 253–74.

32. Mühlhäuser, *Eroberungen*, 223–26.

33. Gaby Zipfel and Gudrun Schwarz, "Die halbierte Gesellschaft: Anmerkungen zu einem soziologischen Problem," in *Mittelweg 36* 7, no. 1 (1998): 78–88.

34. Oral History Interview, 1984, 8302, IWM.

35. See Smith, "Colonial Soldiers" in this handbook.

36. Horne and Kramer, *German Atrocities*, 291.

37. Anthonie Holslag, "Exposed Bodies: A Conceptual Approach to Sexual Violence during the Armenian Genocide," in *Genocide and Gender in the Twentieth Century: A Comparative Survey*, ed. Amy Randall (London: Bloomsbury, 2015), 87–106.

38. Matthias Bjørnlund, "'A Fate Worse Than Dying': Sexual Violence during the Armenian Genocide," in Herzog, *Brutality and Desire*, 16–58.

39. Brigitte Halbmayr, "Sexualized Violence against Women during Nazi 'Racial' Persecution," in *Sexual Violence against Jewish Women during the Holocaust*, ed. Sonja M. Hedgepeth and Rochelle G. Saidel (Hanover, NH: University Press of New England, 2010), 29–44; and Dagmar Herzog, "Sexual Violence against Men: Torture at Flossenbürg," in *Rape: Weapon of War and Genocide*, ed. Carol Rittner and John K. Roth (St. Paul, MN: Paragon House, 2012), 29–44.

40. Doris L. Bergen, "Sexual Violence in the Holocaust: Unique and Typical?," in *Lessons and Legacies VII: The Holocaust in International Perspective*, ed. Dagmar Herzog (Evanston, IL: Northwestern University Press 2006), 179–200, 188.

41. Na'ama Shik, "Sexual Abuse of Jewish Women in Auschwitz-Birkenau," in Herzog, *Brutality and Desire*, 221–46.

42. Regina Mühlhäuser, "The Historicity of Denial: Sexual Violence against Jewish Women during the War of Annihilation, 1941–1945," in *Lessons and Legacies XI: Expanding Perspectives on the Holocaust in a Changing World*, ed. Hilary Earl and Karl Schleunes (Evanston: Northwestern University Press, 2014), 34–46.

43. Simon Geissbühler, "The Rape of Jewish Women and Girls during the First Phase of the Romanian Offensive in the East, July 1941: A Research Agenda and Preliminary Findings," *Holocaust Studies: A Journal of Culture and History* 19, no. 1 (2013): 59–80.

44. Myrna Goldenberg, "Sex-Based Violence and the Politics and Ethics of Survival," in *Different Horrors/Same Hell: Gender and the Holocaust*, ed. Myrna Goldenberg and Amy H. Shapiro (Seattle: University of Washington Press, 2013), 99–127; and Anna Hájková, "Sexual Barter in Times of Genocide: Negotiating the Sexual Economy of the Theresienstadt Ghetto," in *Signs* 38, no. 3 (2013): 503–33; and Hájková, ed. "Sexuality, Holocaust, Stigma," special issue, *German History* 38, no. 3 (2020).

45. Pascale R. Bos, "Feminists Interpreting the Politics of Wartime Rape: Berlin, 1945, Yugoslavia, 1992–1993," *Signs* 31, no. 4 (2006): 995–1025.

46. Norman M. Naimark, *The Russians in Germany: A History of the Soviet Zone of Occupation, 1945–1949* (Cambridge, MA: Belknap Press, 1995), 69–140.

47. Atina Grossmann, *Jews, Germans, and Allies: Close Encounters in Occupied Germany* (Princeton, NJ: Princeton University Press, 2007), 48–87.

48. Tanaka, *Japan's Comfort Women*, 112.

49. Joanna Bourke, "War and Violence," *Thesis Eleven* 86, no. 1 (2006): 23–38, 27 and 35.

50. Andrea Pető, "Memory and the Narrative of Rape in Budapest and Vienna in 1945," in *Life after Death: Approaches to a Cultural and Social History during the 1940s and 1950s*, ed.

Richard Bessel and Dirk Schumann (Cambridge: Cambridge University Press, 2003), 129–48. See also Marlene Epp, "Soviet and East European Mennonite Refugees and Rape in the Second World War," *Journal of Women's History* 9, no. 1 (1997): 58–87; Jolande Withuis, "Die verlorene Unschuld des Gedächtnisses: Soziale Amnesie in Holland und sexuelle Gewalt im Zweiten Weltkrieg," in *Gedächtnis und Geschlecht: Deutungsmuster in Darstellungen des nationalsozialistischen Genozids*, ed. Insa Eschebach et al. (Frankfurt am Main: Campus, 2002), 77–96; and Tanaka, *Comfort Women*.

51. Robert J. Lilly, *Taken by Force: Rape and American GIs in Europe during World War II* (New York: Palgrave Macmillan, 2007), 54; and Roberts, *What Soldiers Do*.

52. Christa Hämmerle, " 'Mentally Broken, Physically a Wreck…': Violence in War Accounts of Nurses in Austro-Hungarian Service," in *Gender and the First World War*, ed. Christa Hämmerle et al. (Basingstoke: Palgrave Macmillan, 2015), 89–107.

53. See the chapter by Karen Hagemann on "History and Memory of Female Military Service in the Age of World Wars" in this handbook.

54. Aaron Belkin, *Bring Me Men: Military Masculinity and the Benign Facade of the American Empire, 1898–2001* (London: Hurst, 2012).

55. Elizabeth D. Heineman, "Introduction: The History of Sexual Violence in Conflict Zones," in *Sexual Violence in Conflict Zones: From the Ancient World to the Era of Human Rights*, ed. Heineman (Philadelphia: University of Pennsylvania Press, 2011), 1–21, 19.

56. See Horne and Kramer, *German Atrocities*, 9–53.

57. Nicoletta F. Gullace, "War Crimes or Atrocity Stories? Anglo-American Narratives of Truth and Deception in the Aftermath of World War I," in Heineman, *Sexual Violence*, 105–21.

58. Susan Brownmiller, *Against Our Will: Men, Women and Rape* (New York: Simon & Schuster, 1975), 37–38. On war propaganda, see also the chapter by Annegret Fauser on "Gendered War Mobilization, Culture, and Music in the Age of World Wars" in this handbook.

59. Ruth Harris, "The 'Child of the Barbarian': Rape, Race and Nationalism in France during the First World War," *Past & Present* no. 141 (1993): 170–206, 175.

60. Horne and Kramer, *German Atrocities*, 435–43.

61. Ibid., 227–61.

62. Roberts, *What Soldiers Do*, 8.

63. Sabine Frühstück, "World War II—Transnationally Speaking," *Journal of Women's History* 26, no. 3 (2014): 142–46, 143.

64. See Takashi Yoshida, *The Making of the "Rape of Nanking": History and Memory in Japan, China, and the United States* (New York: Oxford University Press, 2006).

65. Júlia Garraio, "Wartime Rape as a Weapon of Propaganda," in "Sexual Violence in Armed Conflicts," ed. Rita Santos and Sofia Santos, special issue, *P@x online bulletin*, no. 18 (2012): 2–4.

66. For a comprehensive history of the Nuremberg Trials, see Robert E. Conot, *Justice at Nuremberg* (New York: Harper & Row, 1983).

67. Garraio, "Wartime Rape."

68. See Roberts, *What Soldiers Do*; and Miriam Gebhardt, *Crimes Unspoken: The Rape of German Women at the End of the Second World War* (Cambridge: Polity, 2017).

69. Bourke, "War and Violence," 23–28.

70. Crouthamel, "Male Sexuality."

71. Testimony cited in Petra Buchholz, *Vom Teufel zum Menschen: Die Geschichte der Chinaheimkehrer in Selbstzeugnissen* (Munich: Iudicium, 2010), 333; and Yonson Ahn, "Taming Soldiers: The Gender Politics of Japanese Soldiers in Total War," in *Gender Politics and Mass Dictatorship*, ed. Jie-Hyun Lim and Karen Petrone (London: Palgrave, 2011), 213–34.

72. Zoë Waxman, "Testimony and Silence: Sexual Violence and the Holocaust," in *Feminism, Literature and Rape Narratives: Violence and Violation*, ed. Sorcha Gunne and Zoë Brigley Thompson (New York: Routledge, 2010), 117–29.

73. Harris, "The 'Child.'"

74. Júlia Garraio, "Vergewaltigung oder wie man vor dem Fremden warnt: Abgrenzungsstrategien und europäische Identität," in *Vielheit und Einheit der Germanistik weltweit*, vol. 5, *Einheit in der Vielfalt? Der Europadiskurs der SchriftstellerInnen seit der Klassik*, ed. Paul Michael Lützeler et al. (Frankfurt am Main: Lang, 2012), 145–49.

75. Grossmann, *Jews, Germans*, 48–87.

76. Elizabeth D. Heineman, "The Hour of the Woman: Memories of Germany's 'Crisis Years' and West German National Identity," *American Historical Review* 101, no. 2 (1996): 354–95; and Christine Eifler, "Nachkrieg und weibliche Verletzbarkeit: Zur Rolle von Kriegen für die Konstruktion von Geschlecht," in *Soziale Konstruktionen: Militär und Geschlechterverhältnis*, ed. Christine Eifler and Ruth Seifert (Münster: Westfälisches Dampfboot, 1999), 155–86.

77. Withuis, "Die verlorene Unschuld."

78. Mina Watanabe, "Passing on the History of 'Comfort Women': The Experiences of a Women's Museum in Japan," *Journal of Peace Education* 12, no. 3 (2015): 236–46.

79. Waxman, "Testimony and Silence"; and Hyunah Yang, "Finding the 'Map of Memory': Testimony of the Japanese Military Sexual Slavery Survivors," in *Positions: East Asia Cultures Critique* 16, no. 1 (2008): 79–107.

80. Frühstück, "Sexuality and Sexual Violence," 426.

81. Zipfel, "Beyond."

SELECT BIBLIOGRAPHY

Ahn, Yonson. "Taming Soldiers: The Gender Politics of Japanese Soldiers in Total War." In *Gender Politics and Mass Dictatorship*, edited by Jie-Hyun Lim and Karen Petrone, 213–34. London: Palgrave Macmillan, 2011.

Beck, Birgit. "Sexual Violence and Its Prosecution by Courts Martial of the Wehrmacht." In *A World at Total War: Global Conflict and the Politics of Destruction, 1937–1945*, edited by Roger Chickering, Stig Förster, and Bernd Greiner, 317–31. Cambridge: Cambridge University Press, 2005.

Bland, Lucy. "White Women and Men of Colour: Miscegenation Fears in Britain after the Great War." *Gender & History* 17, no. 1 (2005): 29–61.

Bourke, Joanna. "War and Violence." *Thesis Eleven* 86, no. 1 (2006): 23–38.

Branche, Raphaelle, and Fabrice Virgili, eds. *Rape in Wartime*. Basingstoke: Palgrave Macmillan, 2012.

Brownmiller, Susan. *Against Our Will: Men, Women and Rape*. New York: Simon & Schuster, 1975.

Crouthamel, Jason. "Male Sexuality and Psychological Trauma: Soldiers and Sexual Disorder in World War I and Weimar Germany." *Journal of the History of Sexuality* 17, no. 1 (2008): 60–84.

Frühstück, Sabine. "Sexuality and Sexual Violence." In *The Cambridge History of the Second World War*. Vol. 3, *Economy, Society and Culture*, edited by Michael Geyer and Adam Tooze, 422–46. Cambridge: Cambridge University Press, 2016.

Gebhardt, Miriam. *Crimes Unspoken: The Rape of German Women at the End of the Second World War*. Cambridge: Polity, 2017.

Hájková, Anna, ed. "Sexuality, Holocaust, Stigma." Special issue, *German History* 38, no. 3 (2020).

Harris, Ruth. "The 'Child of the Barbarian': Rape, Race and Nationalism in France during the First World War." *Past & Present* no. 141 (1993): 170–206.

Heineman, Elizabeth D., ed. *Sexual Violence in Conflict Zones: From the Ancient World to the Era of Human Rights*. Philadelphia: University of Pennsylvania Press, 2011.

Herzog, Dagmar, ed. *Brutality and Desire: War and Sexuality in Europe's Twentieth Century*. Basingstoke: Palgrave Macmillan, 2009.

Herzog, Dagmar, ed. "Sexuality and German Fascism." Special issue, *Journal of the History of Sexuality* 11, no. 1/2 (2002).

Horne, John, and Alan Kramer. *German Atrocities, 1914: A History of Denial*. New Haven, CT: Yale University Press, 2001.

Meinen, Insa. *Wehrmacht und Prostitution während des Zweiten Weltkriegs im besetzten Frankreich*. Bremen: Edition Temmen, 2002.

Mühlhäuser, Regina. *Sex and the Nazi Soldier: Violent, Commercial and Consensual Contacts during the War in the Soviet Union, 1941–1945*. Edinburgh: Edinburgh University Press, 2020.

Roberts, Mary Louise. *What Soldiers Do: Sex and the American GI in World War II France*. Chicago: University of Chicago Press, 2013.

Tanaka, Yuki. *Japan's Comfort Women: Sexual Slavery and Prostitution during World War II and the US Occupation*. London: Routledge, 2002.

Warring, Anette. "Intimate and Sexual Relations." In *Surviving Hitler and Mussolini: Daily Life in Occupied Europe*, edited by Robert Gildea, Anette Warring, and Olivier Wieviorka, 88–121. Oxford: Berg, 2006.

Waxman, Zoe. "Testimony and Silence: Sexual Violence and the Holocaust." In *Feminism, Literature and Rape Narratives: Violence and Violation*, edited by Sorcha Gunne and Zoe Brigley Thompson, 117–29. London: Routledge, 2010.

Yang, Hyunah. "Finding the 'Map of Memory': Testimony of the Japanese Military Sexual Slavery Survivors." *Positions: East Asia Cultures Critique* 16, no. 1 (2008): 79–107.

Zipfel, Gaby, Regina Mühlhäuser, and Kirsten Campbell, eds. *In Plain Sight: Sexual Violence in Armed Conflict*. New Delhi: Zubaan, 2019.

GENDER, PEACE, AND THE NEW POLITICS OF HUMANITARIANISM IN THE FIRST HALF OF THE TWENTIETH CENTURY

GLENDA SLUGA

In the midst of the First World War (1914–18), the American peace activist and feminist Jane Addams observed that the conflict had produced two types of masculinity. One was more akin to the "Victorian man," while the other consisted of young men less inclined to be skeptically militarist and more inclined to be practically internationalist in their world outlook: "Even in their conception of internationalism, the two groups of young men and old men differed widely. The Victorian group, for instance, in their moral romanticism, fostered a sentiment for a far-off 'Federation of the World' and believed that the world would be federated when wise men from many nations met together and accomplished it. The young men do not talk much about internationalism, but they live in a world where common experience has in fact become largely internationalised."[1]

Addams's observations invite us to reflect on the impact of the First World War on the significance of simultaneously "internationalized" and gendered conceptions of peace. That conflict marked the changing tenor of those conceptions, shifting under the influence of international law and the experiment of international governance. Here we need only think of the growth of international organizations such as the Red Cross, founded in 1863. The Geneva Conventions signed in 1864 and 1906 (and later 1929 and 1949) are also indicative of these trends. These legal conventions defined the basic rights of prisoners of war—military personnel and civilians—and established the terms by which wounded soldiers and civilians in and close to a war zone should come under the protection of international law. Add to these the Hague Conventions of 1899 and 1907—a series of international treaties and declarations negotiated at two international peace conferences at The Hague in the Netherlands—and we can see a trend of embedding questions of disarmament, the conduct of warfare, and the laws of war and of war crimes, as both state and international-level responsibilities.[2]

By the early twentieth century, changing approaches to war and the conceptualization of *peace* as a political and legal problem intersected with the transformation of humanitarian practices. Over the first half of the twentieth century, *humanitarianism* and, later, *human rights* became central concepts in Western political discourse and the measures of international efforts to establish a more peaceful world order. Etymology goes some way to providing a chronology for the changing political meaning of the concept of humanitarianism in this international history and explaining its significance for a politics of peace invested in the expansion of international laws. The term humanitarianism entered European languages in the early nineteenth century, as women and men in religious organizations (especially Quakers) took up the cause of abolition, seeking to end slavery through the invocation of a common humanity.

By contrast, the term *pacifism* was coined a hundred years later, largely in reflection of the growth of international and national organizations committed to promoting peace, particularly through arbitration.[3] Pacifist societies, like humanitarian organizations, quickly moved from the margins to the respectable core of political life, particularly at the heart of the Western empires that were most likely to be involved in wars. In these societies, women and men assumed distinctive roles that reflected the dominant gender ideology of separate spheres. This gender ideology, as it was articulated and negotiated through the long nineteenth century, commonly associated femininity with an intrinsic pacifism and humanity (identifying women with motherhood) and masculinity with the inclination to war (to the extent of identifying men with soldier-citizenship).[4] Even though Addams noticed subtle shifts in masculinity, men and women regularly negotiated polarized conceptions of their gender difference, whether they were advocating policies and practices or seeking legitimacy for their activism. This gendering process worked in exclusivist ways when the male members of the British and Foreign Anti-Slavery Society decided that the first World Conference of Abolition, held in London in June 1840, was to be an event run by men for men, even though women had long been at the forefront of organized efforts to abolish slavery.[5]

Addams's description of a new kind of masculine subjectivity also reflects the ways in which, by the latter half of the nineteenth century, pacifism was the formal concern of a new cohort of professionalized male international lawyers, politicians, and state bureaucrats, as well as the self-consciously international associations to which they belonged. Most prominent and enduring among these is the Inter-Parliamentary Union established in 1889 by the French and British parliamentarians Frédéric Passy and William Randal Cremer as an organization of statesmen promoting democratic institutions and international government. The Inter-Parliamentary Union became the first permanent forum for political multilateral negotiations. Another example is the French-based Association de la paix par le droit (Association for Peace Though Law), one of the first peace organizations with an emphasis on international law, which was founded in 1887 and active until World War II. Its founders, among them Passy, believed that peace could be maintained through an internationally agreed legal framework, making use of mediation to resolve disputes.[6] The Deutsche Friedensgesellschaft (German Peace Society), founded in 1892, had a similar agenda—during World War I, it had some 10,000 members, making it one of the largest peace organizations in the world. The following year saw the creation of an Austrian peace society, the Österreichische Gesellschaft der Friedensfreunde, thanks largely to the activism of the Austrian novelist and pacifist Bertha von Suttner, who in 1905 was the first woman to be awarded the Nobel Peace Prize.[7]

These various strands of the history of the newly *international* politics of pacifism and humanitarianism came together after World War I, when Western statesmen created the League of Nations as an intergovernmental organization. The league conceptually and effectively institutionalized pacifism as the business of states and, as important, international institutions that were the sum of those states' *inter*national relations.[8] In the 1930s, when the challenge of peace in this new age of internationally negotiated arbitration and disarmament was named *collective security*, the assumption was that the collective was the nation-state. But over these same decades, as humanitarianism was reconceptualized as an imperative driving the experiment of international governance, it also led to the creation of international philanthropic and intergovernmental organizations run by men who established their professional careers in these capacities.

After World War II (1939–1945), the objectives of peace and humanitarianism were cemented together in the creation of the United Nations (UN), founded in October 1945 by the UN Conference on International Organization in San Francisco to succeed the League of Nations. When the UN General Assembly proclaimed its defining project, the "Universal Declaration of Human Rights," in December 1948, the gendered status of humanitarianism and the project of peace came explicitly to the fore. Two years earlier, the long, drawn-out process of drafting that declaration had led to the controversial segregation of the status of women in relation to human rights—and the creation of a Commission on the Status of Women. The separate body was demanded by feminists convinced that history had proven the concept of human rights to be intrinsically male centered, literally *les droits de l'homme*;[9] making sure women were given human rights, they argued, would require the explicit address of women's historically determined situation across the globe.

In the following, the developments in the changing conceptions of peace and their connections with a longer history of humanitarianism in the first half of the twentieth century will be explored by using gender as an analytical focus. The gender dimensions of peace thinking and policies in the era of new international politics sheds light on the specific contribution of women and feminism to the modern conceptualization of international answers to the problem of war, its causes, and its consequences. In particular, a gender perspective restores the international and internationalist contexts of the emerging peace movement and international humanitarianism, as well as their changing emphases and forms, both at the League of Nations and at the UN.

The International Turn

By the turn of the twentieth century, in the context of an expanding public sphere and widening political enfranchisement, statesmen and nonstate actors responded to the threat of increasingly devastating wars fueled by imperial competition and militarization by seeking support for the codification of international laws and even the idea of a new internationalism.[10] It is in this international framework that we can better see the agency of women and the rising political star of pacifism and humanitarianism as political causes. The landmark events in these intersecting histories were the 1899 and the 1907 peace conferences held at The Hague.[11]

Russian Tsar Nicholas II instigated the 1899 Hague conference to encourage the European empires to take steps toward disarmament. Regardless of the tsar's intentions and of the tendency to relegate the conference to the margins of international history, for our purposes the conference was a historical high-water mark, as much because of its processes as its outcomes. It brought together a vast array of state and nonstate actors, not only monarchs and diplomats but also journalists reporting to a wider, mainly Western public and women congregating on behalf of a range of humanitarian and pacifist issues, including the importance of international arbitration and the causes of the self-determination of subject peoples. The standout figure of the 1899 Hague conference and its follow-up in 1907 was Bertha von Suttner. Her roles in these settings are illustrative of the ways in which, at this time, a woman with exceptional contacts could use her social networks to promote pacifism, establish pacifist societies, and even convince Alfred Nobel, a Swedish dynamite manufacturer, to fund the Nobel Peace Prize, awarded since 1901.[12] Suttner worked alongside pacifist men such as journalist Alfred Hermann Fried, a cofounder of the German Peace Society, and French statesman Léon Bourgeois as part of a wider international movement reflected in congresses and peace societies with transnational links.[13]

At The Hague, Suttner was an important presence publicizing the twin causes of disarmament and arbitration. She had promoted them in her 1889 bestselling novel *Die Waffen nieder!*, published three years later in English as *Lay Down Your Arms* and translated into sixteen other languages. And she was not alone. In 1899, one million American, European, and Japanese members of Universal Women's Alliance for Peace—founded as the International Women's League for General Disarmament in Paris in 1896—signed a petition presented to the Russian tsar at The Hague.[14] The conservative transatlantic body, the International Council of Women—founded in Washington, DC, in 1888 and representing fifty-three women's organizations from nine countries—added to the mix of events a Standing Committee on Peace and Arbitration featuring Suttner, who then harnessed these international associations to force the hand of governments and stage the 1907 Hague meeting, this time under the auspices of US President Theodore Roosevelt.[15]

The conference outcomes reflected these same priorities: the introduction of new international laws of war and war crimes conventions. The 1899 Hague Conventions (three main treaties and three additional declarations) established the Permanent Court of Arbitration in The Hague, but it failed to achieve a reduction of military budgets or a plan for disarmament. The 1907 conference, convened to re-examine the work of 1899 in light of the Russo-Japanese War (1904–5), resulted in a second Hague Convention, this time consisting of twelve signed treaties and a declaration. However, the conference made little progress on the subject of disarmament, in part because the two power blocs that fought each other seven years later—the Triple Alliance (Germany, Austria-Hungary, and Italy) and the Triple Entente (the United Kingdom, France, and Russia)—were already consolidating.[16]

Historians of the Hague conferences have long argued that despite the limited outcomes, these meetings contributed to international humanitarian law and the law on the pacific settlement of disputes. Once we add the involvement of women's associations, we see the extent to which the gatherings at The Hague established crucial precedents for broad public, nonstate involvement in international questions. Even though women had no formal part in either conference, it was, according to Sandi E. Cooper, "the first time that women's associations lobbied so specifically and widely at a diplomatic multilateral conference."[17]

Also integral to this history were the many organizations and societies that established international headquarters (often in Belgium and Switzerland) and sought to capitalize on the international turn in political organization to run regular events. For example, the Universal Peace Congress that had started in Paris in 1889 was followed by similar events in other cities until 1914. In 1891, this same initiative led to the establishment of the Permanent International Peace Bureau in Berne. Of similar importance was the International Peace Society founded in London in 1880. The membership of these and other organizations was largely male and identified with political progressives. Their leaders cooperated closely, beyond national borders and continents and across the conceptual borders of internationalist and pacifist liberal causes. As Daniel Laqua notes, the Inter-Parliamentary Union conferences "often shared delegates and the host city with the Universal Peace Congresses, which were the main events of international pacifism."[18] Despite the predominantly male membership of this international peace movement and its organizations, Suttner's singular influence and initiatives did not go unacknowledged by her contemporaries. The joint organ of the Inter-Parliamentary Union and the International Peace Bureau and Peace Society (Vienna), subtitled "A Monthly to Promote the Idea of Peace" and published between 1892 and 1899, was named Die Waffen nieder.[19]

The Hague peace conferences also provide important historical examples of the political weight given by statesmen and political leaders across the European empires (the same sites of escalating militarism) to international arbitration as the single most influential strand of internationalism, prior to the outbreak of World War I across Europe and its empires on July 28, 1914.[20] At the turn of the twentieth century, the largest European pacifist organizations, such as the Association de la paix par le droit and the

Deutsche Friedensgesellschaft, emphasized international arbitration practices as the method of ensuring peace between states. The international arbitration theme was also the calling card of North American–based pacifist societies, particularly on the east coast of the United States, including the American Peace Society (founded in New York in 1828). This trend in pacifist thought was inextricably linked to the extraordinary rise of international law in the latter half of the nineteenth century. Many of these peace societies had religious origins—in Quaker communities, for example—but their support bases were increasingly drawn from new cohorts of professional international lawyers and, interestingly, bankers.[21]

Given the extent to which militarism persisted in shaping European and imperial political cultures through the first half of the twentieth century, we should not overestimate the extent to which men and women felt enabled and driven to take up pacifist causes. Nor should we overstate the challenge that internationalist and international-scale pacifist movements posed to dominant gender conventions of masculinity or femininity. Suttner's life and her memoirs reinforced the common nineteenth-century equation of femininity with pacifist and humanitarian inclinations, in opposition to a conventional militarist masculinity. However, as Jane Addams observed, during World War I the growing interest in the prospect of international government provided new foci for these intersecting peace, humanitarianism, and gender trends.

THE QUEST FOR PEACE DURING WORLD WAR I

There can be no doubt that the outbreak of war in July 1914 tested the limits of pacifism, in both its idealized forms and its institutional practices. However, the war just as quickly brought the simultaneously humanitarian and legal dimensions of earlier international debates about war and peace into play.[22] We know from the work of Isabel Hull that even though the legal conventions introduced at The Hague that posited a humanitarian approach to conflict had limited effects on the war's brutal course, they were often acknowledged when the warring states made decisions in regard to the kinds of weapons they used and the ways in which they treated enemy soldiers.[23] In other words, this new international body of law had become to some degree an accepted part of state behavior in an international political arena.

As the fronts of the First World War became established, the civilians caught up in that conflict—as victims of violence or food shortages and displacement—became the object of competing humanitarian activities, much of it organized by British and American governments. One of them was the Food Relief Programs for occupied Belgium and France that started in 1914 and continued until 1919. Both governments collaborated with local national commissions, such as the Comité national de secours et d'alimentation (National Relief and Food Committee) and the Comité d'alimentation du nord de la France (Food Committee of Northern France), which fielded up to 10,000 local groups and more than 70,000 male and female volunteers who organized the distribution of humanitarian aid.

But the most influential international humanitarian aid group was the Commission for Relief in Belgium, founded in 1914 and chaired by Herbert Hoover, a Quaker engineer and efficient administrator, who in 1917, after the United States had joined the war under President Woodrow Wilson, became the director of the US Food Administration responsible for the food reserves of the US Army and its allies.[24] Tammy M. Proctor has argued that a critical part of the story of the involvement of organizations such as Hoover's in humanitarian relief in this period was the question of political legitimacy in the changing arena of international politics, and fundamental to that question was gender. The US government publicized its humanitarian policy in conventional gender terms, granting itself the guise of a fatherly figure, in the words of Proctor, albeit a "surrogate father."[25] It made food aid to war-torn regions the responsibility of White young men who aimed for careers in business or government service. By contrast, British efforts still utilized an older nineteenth-century religious missionary model of humanitarianism, and British aid workers emphasized the roots of their service as, according to Proctor, a "maternal spirit of living sacrifice wherein the foreign aid workers, many of them women, trained in social work or medicine provided hands-on, mostly small-scale aid to war sufferers." Ultimately, relief work in Belgium, northern France, Germany, and Austria was dominated by the newer American government model, emphasizing efficiency, scientific management, and self-help framed in a vocabulary of freedom.[26]

In the international history of humanitarianism in the Ottoman Empire (which fought on the side of the Central Powers during the World War I), gender does similar ideological work, albeit in historically and geopolitically specific ways. In the Greater Syrian provinces (including Beirut) of the Ottoman Empire, local political figures found themselves competing with such international and national humanitarian organizations as Near East Relief and the American Red Cross (the latter had been operating in Beirut since 1915) for the distribution of money, food, and work.[27] The stakes of this competition were high since the region was in the throes of a famine so extreme that by the time Allied forces occupied the territory in October 1918, a third of the population had died. Melanie Tanielian has argued that in the face of "disproportional rates of male mortalities" in the Middle East and a crisis of paternity, the Ottoman state attempted to appropriate social services in the region for itself. This was meant to bolster its sovereign authority over the authority of the American men who ran the existing local humanitarian organizations and the American women who were affiliated with the Syrian Protestant College and the American Mission overseeing local volunteers. The Ottoman state's strategy from mid-1915 was to supersede that international activity by privileging local female volunteerism through the Syrian Women's Association. Even as male notables ran the local philanthropic societies in Beirut, Arab women were encouraged to undertake humanitarian work, because it was seen, according to Tanielian, "as unthreatening and incapable of inspiring divergent allegiances." Ironically, the process set in motion by the Ottoman regime to compete with the humanitarian presence of international actors was the beginning of a politicization of women's charities and unintentionally inspired a new political consciousness among the Ottoman women who were given the chance to become agents of humanitarianism.[28]

In the setting of war, women's humanitarian work could constitute a legitimate avenue for their public activity, even in contexts in which their more explicit political agency remained controversial. Among the unintended outcomes of this gendered politics was the fostering of simultaneously national and international feminist aims. The First World War was a turning point in this regard, too, especially if we compare the earlier generation of women activists represented by Suttner, for whom feminism was separate from pacifism, and those women who during World War I vocally announced their overlapping pacifist, humanitarian, and feminist ambitions.[29]

At no event were these links between humanitarianism, pacifism, and feminism more in evidence than at the iconic International Women's Peace Congress held from April 28 until May 1, 1915, at The Hague's "Peace Palace"—a building constructed using Carnegie funds and lobbied for by the women's organizations present at the 1907 Hague peace conference. The wartime women's congress purposely invoked the legacy of the Hague gatherings as much as that of the five earlier International Congresses of Women's Rights held in Paris (1878), London (1899), Berlin (1904), Amsterdam (1908), and Stockholm (1911). In the spring of 1915, more than 1,200 female delegates from twelve countries participated and came to The Hague under challenging circumstances, including 28 Germans who had to cross military front lines. In the midst of the spreading interstate wartime violence, this transnationally linked group of women gathered to petition the leaders of the warring governments for peace, in many cases despite attempts by their governments to stop them.[30]

The American economics professor Emily Greene Balch, British journalist Helena Swanwick, German journalist Lida Gustava Heymann, Hungarian pacifist Rosika Schwimmer, and Swedish educator and writer Ellen Key were among the most well-known women involved in wartime pacifist feminist organizations built out of northern and southern, eastern and western European constituencies at the 1915 meeting. They all agitated for equal education for women, equal civil rights, and female suffrage, but their concepts of feminism differed. Some, such as Heymann, were individualist feminists who aimed for equality of men and women based on the assumption of universal human rights, while others, like Key, were relational or "social maternalist" feminists who wanted equal rights but believed in the "natural," or biological, differences between the sexes, like the majority of their contemporaries. They thought that women, as real or "spiritual" mothers and caregivers, had an important but distinctive role to play in society, politics, and culture.[31] Key, for example, engaged the significance of a "new internationalism" (grounded in nationalism) as an important development in progress toward permanent peace, as she stated in her 1916 publication *War, Peace and the Future. A Consideration of Nationalism and Internationalism, and of the Relation of Women to War.* She believed that this project of permanent peace should make "woman" its specific agent "as mother of humanity," cultivating "a world consciousness . . . world citizenship." For Key, women posited a salient feminine will, which, when given political expression, would have "as its last and greatest aim: to humanize humanity." Her ultimate goal was to link this cause to the ends of international recognition for women's "equal rights in politics, in nationality, in marriage, and, as parents, equal pay for equal work, and equal moral standards, equal training and opportunities, and the endowment of maternity."[32]

Despite the diverse views of the causes and implications of gender difference held by participants in the 1915 Women's Peace Congress, their meeting led to unanimous support for the creation of the International Committee of Women for Permanent Peace, which included in its aims support for a postwar international government that would guarantee both future peace and women's rights. After the Second International Women's Congress for Peace and Freedom in Zurich in May 1919, this committee renamed itself the Women's International League for Peace and Freedom (WILPF), which still exists in the early twenty-first century.[33] Many WILPF feminists from across the Western world invested heavily in the prospect of international government and identified the League of Nations as the means to establish permanent peace and social justice. They shared this investment with other supporters of the three Hague peace conferences in 1899, 1907, and 1915, including male politicians and female pacifists, who all spoke for an enlarged interest in international governance as a vehicle of permanent peace or at least oversight of the worst consequences of war. We see this shift in the wartime organization of League of Nations associations, first in Britain and later in the United States, on the Continent (even in the territories of the Central Powers), and across the British Empire.

Feminists such as the American economist and sociologist Emily Greene Balch or the British journalist Helena Swanwick supported improved political opportunities for women through the promise of a future League of Nations. But the structures and symbolism of the associations, established by political and intellectual male elites in Britain and elsewhere to support the creation of a League of Nations, reinforced a very specific gendering of internationalism. The largest of the League of Nations associations, the British League of Nations Union (LNU), formed in October 1918 as a merger of two earlier wartime organizations, the League of Free Nations Association and the League of Nations Society, mobilized, according to historian Helen McCarthy, "broad sections of the population in support of a collective system of international relations," but at the same time they contributed to "the making of a gendered internationalism."[34] Women's organizations participated in the League of Nations Union and were encouraged by its executive to do so. However, the LNU recruited women for their maternal sensibilities or, as they said, "instinct of motherhood," as fitting them for the task of championing the creation of an organization in the interests of a permanent peace. By contrast, when the LNU societies appealed to a male membership, they connected "the League message with masculine working class pleasures" and League "union" as a form of homosociality.[35] The league itself was represented as a Madonna-style figure, with a star suspended like a halo over her modest headdress.[36]

By the end of World War I, entangled humanitarian and pacifist norms had become the mainstream rationale for the creation of the iconic, male-led, international peace–oriented institution of the twentieth century, the League of Nations. In the interwar as in the wartime conceptualization of international government, the history of men and women in relation to that institution and its practices differed fundamentally, despite feminist demands for equal participation and rights for women in the international sphere of politics and government.

PEACEMAKING IN 1919 AND AFTER

Historians of peacemaking in 1919 have long focused on questions of boundaries and reparations. For many, the Treaty of Versailles, signed on June 28, 1919, by Germany and the Allied Powers, with the exception of the United States, inevitably led to new conflicts and the Second World War because it forced Germany and its allies Austria and Hungary to accept responsibility for causing all the loss and damage during the war. The United States signed a special peace treaty with Germany in August 1921, because the Republican-controlled Senate did not want to ratify the treaty.[37] The Treaty of Versailles compelled Germany to disarm considerably (it was allowed a professional army of up to only 100,000 men and no universal conscription), to make substantial territorial concessions and pay extensive reparations of 132 billion marks (then USD 31.4 billion) to the Entente Powers.[38] To secure the reparation payments, Belgian, British, and French troops occupied the highly industrialized Rhineland (1919–30), the neighboring Saar region (1919–35), and, for a shorter period, the Ruhr area (1923–25). The First World War also led to the collapse of the Habsburg, Ottoman, and Russian empires. The undoing of the Habsburg Empire led to the foundation of several new succession European states, including Austria, Czechoslovakia, Hungary, and Yugoslavia. Russia, which withdrew from war after the October Revolution of 1917, lost much of its western frontier to the creation of the new nation-states of Estonia, Finland, Latvia, Lithuania, and Poland.[39] The former colonial territories of the German and Habsburg empires became part of the mandate system established under Article 22 of the Covenant of the League of Nations and signed on June 28, 1919. Britain and France became the most important mandate powers.[40]

For a long time, the far-reaching effects on sovereignty of the peace of 1919 led scholars to neglect the other part of the peacemaking process: the creation of the League of Nations. Forty-four states signed the League of Nations Covenant on June 28, 1919, and its headquarters was finally established in Geneva in January 1920. Its existence, along with a series of related bodies, including the International Labor Organization and the International Health Organization, became fundamental to a postwar peacemaking agenda that emphasized international government on the principles of disarmament and arbitration. There were divergent views on how to achieve the objective of peace: through economic stability, through the international regulation of arms and codification of warfare practices, and even through the inculcation of new subjectivities. These methods were reflected in the organization of the league in sections devoted to not only the reduction of armaments, but also legal, financial and economic, health, transit and communication, mandates, minorities, intellectual cooperation, information, and social questions. Once again, gender conventions not only shaped the operations of the League of Nations, but also, equally important, were a crucial point of controversy at this new international site of pacifist and humanitarian intentions, built on the foundations of an expanding order of nation-states and the persistent international sway of the imperial powers that had ended up on the victorious side of the war.

In practice, the League of Nations was an intergovernmental organization dependent on the decisions and opinions expressed primarily by its council, where the permanent members Britain, France, Italy, and Japan dominated (in the absence of the United States, which famously never joined), and then the member states constituting its assembly. The league did not officially recognize the petitioning of individuals, although nonstate actors were able to lobby its bodies—one of the reasons why so many international women's organizations set up home in its physical proximity in Geneva. While the league's covenant made special mention of the equal access of women to positions at the league, it was a male-dominated organization, with women taking up mainly secretarial work. The most prominent exception was the British former nurse and social reformer Rachel Crowdy, during World War I principal commandant of voluntary aid detachments in France and Belgium, who was given administrative responsibility for the Central Committee for Economic and Social Questions of the league from 1919 to 1931.[41]

The humanitarian issues that made up the work of the social questions committee—public health and hygiene, the suppression of the traffic in drugs, and the White slave trade, the Advisory Committee of Private Organizations to the High Commissioner for Refugees—were regarded as the more suitable domains for accommodating women's advice and activism.[42] Some humanitarian concerns were massaged into the Health Bureau, which dealt with epidemics and food crises, particularly in postwar Austria, and for which purposes the occasional woman was also brought on board, such as the American epidemiologist Alice Hamilton.

The "serious" legal and political work of the league for fostering peace was viewed as the natural field of men employed within its bureaucracy or appointed as delegates to its disarmament committees, despite the organized attempts by women to be included on those specific committees. The league's single disarmament subcommittee continued with the work of utilizing international law and arbitration in the interests of peace and refused female participation. As Andrew Webster has described, the Permanent Advisory Commission on Armaments was entirely composed of military officers who were appointed by and responsible to their respective governments (and general staffs) rather than to the league itself.[43]

Despite the formal exclusion of women, the culmination of the league's disarmament efforts, the 1932 World Disarmament Conference in Geneva, was only successful because of the continuing importance of nonstate actors, including women, in keeping crucial questions of peace as well as humanitarianism not only alive, but also broadly conceived. The Geneva conference saw no substantial or few binding outcomes except the ratification of the poison gas agreement, but it marked the apex of women's organized international pacifist ambitions.[44] There were many groups agitating in this period for peace, for example, the Ligue des mères et éducatrices pour la paix (League of Mothers and Educators for Peace), founded in 1928 and claiming 65,000 members in 1932. One of the especially active organizations was the WILPF, which was able to organize high-profile peace pilgrimages and a petition bearing six million signatures that was presented to the disarmament conference delegates.[45] The failures of the petition and of the long-winded conference (which went on until 1934) provoked some WILPF women to consider dropping "women's" from their title and claiming default responsibility for peace—since there was no men's equivalent.[46]

Interwar pacifism and humanitarianism were not the sole domain of League of Nations–coordinated efforts in Geneva. Men were to be found in the halls of the Permanent Court of International Justice, which resided in the Peace Palace in The Hague as an international court attached to the League of Nations from 1922 to 1946. The court became the home to international lawyers tasked with adjudicating intrastate disputes. Back in Geneva, the mission of the International Labor Office, since 1919 an agency of the League of Nations, was rationalized in terms of the pertinence of social and economic justice (and humanitarianism) to the ends of peace, similar to the league-based mandate system for oversight of the territories of the defeated powers.[47] These missions, too, were fundamentally constituted as the masculine business of imperial powers. The state delegates to the International Committee of the Red Cross, eventually housed across the road from the league offices, were almost exclusively men.[48]

It is a historical truism that the League of Nations famously failed at its central task: the maintenance of peace through international disarmament. However, as historians now recognize, the league was much more successful in the interwar decades in the humanitarian brief of its social questions section, albeit within the prevailing imperial context. Humanitarian issues for which female campaigners became active at the league stretched from the suppression of the "Mui Tsai" system in Hong Kong, which forced young Chinese women to work in domestic service or brothels, to the welfare of Native populations in the mandated territories, especially in the Middle East.[49] It is also true, as Helen McCarthy adds, that "many women—including those active in the League of Nations Unions—appeared willing to accept that their 'natural' arena for action lay in the League's humanitarian and auxiliary work." In the context of the league's institutionalization of women's humanitarian activities, a "social-maternalist tradition" was reconstituted globally.[50]

In the interwar years, women activists in the international arena of pacifism and humanitarianism made the most of the new non-national spaces for public engagement opened up by the league and its related institutions, including the Health Bureau and the International Labor Organization. The WILPF, the Women's Disarmament Committee, and other women's organizations simultaneously used Geneva as a base to promote their feminist agendas. Despite their best efforts, they often ended up disillusioned by the league's seemingly impermeable gendered structures. Helena Swanwick, who was for a brief period in 1924 seconded to a British league delegation, argued, "Men were in all places of power. They alone were diplomats and foreign ministers and financiers and the manufacturers of munitions and editors and leader-writers." She observed that women at the league were treated as if they were "predestined" to deal with issues concerning "Opium, Refugees, Protection of Children, Relief after Earthquakes, Prison Reform, Municipal Cooperation, Alcoholism, Traffic in Women."[51] To the extent that the war had inspired a new internationalist masculinity, as Jane Addams described, in the postwar era it had limited repercussions for an expanded view of feminine agency—even as women's willingness to take on social and humanitarian questions garnered new international status for refugee, trafficking, and other humanitarian concerns. These gender tensions in the new international politics of humanitarianism and peace would become more visible during and after World War II.

PEACE IN THE MINDS OF MEN DURING AND AFTER THE 1940S

The number of military and civilian casualties that resulted from World War II was devastatingly higher than that of the earlier world war; approximately 29 million civilians and 26 million soldiers died. This was the setting after 1945 in which peace was to be restored and Asia and Europe reconstructed, with millions of displaced persons. For example, Nazi Germany had brought 11.3 million people to Germany as forced laborers during the war—who survived the war and had to be returned to their homes or find new ones. Imperial Japan had exploited alone more than 10 million Chinese civilians for forced labor. There were threats of epidemics, particularly typhus, and food crises everywhere in the war-torn regions, but the focus of the humanitarian work of the newly reconstituted international community was Europe at first. The non-European world was left to fend for itself. Managing those crises and reconstruction became the task of new intergovernmental bodies, working at times in consultation with nongovernmental peace activists and bodies with humanitarian concerns. One important body was the United Nations Relief and Rehabilitation Administration (UNRRA), created at a forty-four-state conference at the American White House on November 9, 1943. Its main mission was originally to provide economic assistance to European nations after World War II and to repatriate and assist the refugees who would come under Allied control. Already in 1945, however, UNRRA extended its work to Asia. The work was taken over by a successor organization, the International Refugee Organization (IRO) in 1948.[52]

At the center of much of this humanitarian activity and coordination of nongovernmental organizations was the UN, established on October 24, 1945, by fifty-one member states. What was also new was the imperative that now drove that activity, the concept of *human rights*, with obvious humanitarian resonance. Just as the UN was the practical arm of this humanitarian focus, its ideological arm was the UN Educational, Scientific, and Cultural Organization (UNESCO), established on November 16, 1945, to ensure peace by cultivating "the minds of men."

For the purposes of understanding how the challenge of peace and the concept of humanitarianism had changed by the end of World War II, along with the distinctive roles of men and women in that history, it is worth considering the gathering of the allied nations in San Francisco in April 1945. The purpose of that meeting, the UN Conference on International Organization, was to thrash out a charter for a new United Nations organization to succeed the League of Nations and improve on that failed model to ensure future peace. In San Francisco, delegates from all over the world gathered. When it came to the contribution of the men and (some) women representing northern and western European states, they charged that women's difference, their "insight and equipment," made them especially suited to UN peace work.[53] Despite this insistence on the political relevance of gender difference, as Celia Donert points out, the UN charter was "the first international declaration to refer to the equal rights of women as well as men in support of fundamental human rights and peace, and against the 'scourge of war,' which twice in our lifetime has brought untold sorrow to mankind."[54]

For a brief moment in 1945, it seemed as if the strands of humanitarian, pacifist, and feminist activism had finally been brought together at this apogee in the history of internationalism. Yet, even then, veteran international feminists such as Gertrude Baer, the secretary of the executive committee of the WILPF, still feared that women might once again "be used only for research and consultation and in dealing with social and economic questions, with health, industry, education and so on," as in the past, rather than finding their places in "offices which manipulate the master levers, where the purposes and methods of public action are determined."[55] Indeed, at UNESCO, where male bureaucrats conceptualized peace as a question of subjectivities in the "minds of men," women's rights were specifically not of interest. The first director general of UNESCO, the British evolutionary biologist and eugenicist Julian Huxley, chose to promote more peaceful societies by tackling the problem of race discrimination at the expense of requests to also focus on women's equal rights.[56]

Then there was the persistently conventional quasi segregation of men and women in the new international institutions. There were never very many women involved in the setting up of the UN, despite their clamoring for involvement. Indeed, in the early years of the UN system, there was an actual decline in the number of women in key positions in the UN secretariat as well as among the UN delegates. Not only was the overall number "insignificant,"[57] but also Deborah Stienstra has concluded that "the practice of gender relations embedded in the League of Nations became the model for the United Nations."[58] Where there were women, their status was often exceptional, as it had been at the league. The one high-ranking woman in the UN secretariat was appointed on a temporary basis in 1949 to the social affairs bureaucracy. This position put Alva Myrdal, an extremely well-connected Swedish sociologist, feminist, and Social Democrat, briefly in charge of the human rights bureaucracy as it deliberated a Statement on Race; her male colleagues made it known she was not welcome.[59]

In gender terms, earlier discussions among the UN Human Rights Committee were more promising, insofar as its collection of state delegates reflected some changes since the league period. It was chaired by the American politician, diplomat, and activist

Eleanor Roosevelt, wife of US President Franklin D. Roosevelt, and included the Indian feminist and social activist Hansa Jivraj Mehta as the official representative of the newly independent Indian government. Mehta was active in all three sessions of the Human Rights Committee responsible for drafting the iconic 1948 Universal Declaration of Human Rights. Throughout, she promoted an agenda similar to the proposals of the French law professor and judge René Samuel Cassin, also on the committee: that individuals as well as states be allowed to petition the Human Rights Commission; that the commission be enabled to take action on petitions (and not just make abstract pronouncements on rights); and that a bill on human rights should become part of the charter and a fundamental law of the UN. All three propositions were defeated.

Mehta, in contrast to Eleanor Roosevelt, also supported the creation of a separate body to deal with the status of women on the basis that it would act as a corrective to the weak state of women's access to human rights relative to men. In 1946, the UN's Third Committee created the Sub-Commission on the Status of Women as part of the Human Rights Committee, which met for the first time in 1947. Its chair became Bodil Begtrup, the leader of the National Council of Women of Denmark. It was quickly promoted to an independent body, the UN Commission on the Status of Women. This became a functional commission of the UN Economic and Social Council, with a focus on political rights and civil equality, even as its emphasis on "status" denied the "rights" focus of the original committee. The Commission on the Status of Women is now recognized as having been "instrumental in promoting women's rights, documenting the reality of women's lives throughout the world and shaping global standards of gender equality and the empowerment of women."[60] However, in more immediate terms, the Commission on the Status of Women, led by Mehta, could not prevent the Universal Declaration of Human Rights from reflecting historically specific gender norms, particularly in regard to the place of men and women in families.[61] For example, it was not able to have the interests of children and mothers separated in order to emphasize women's intrinsic rights as individuals. Instead, the Universal Declaration of Human Rights proclaimed by the UN General Assembly in Paris on December 10, 1948, essentially yoked the needs of mothers and children together in Article 25 (2): "Motherhood and childhood are entitled to special care and assistance. All children, whether born in or out of wedlock, shall enjoy the same social protection."[62]

Over this same period, international women's organizations—often with nongovernmental organization consultative status—were also working with international organizations within the UN institutional network and outside its domains to achieve peace by other means. Accordingly, Donert argues that the definitive shifts in how women organized for peace in the wake of the Second World War—from "the middle-class elitist pacifism of the interwar years towards broad-based peace movements that defined peace in terms of social justice and not merely the absence of war"—was to a significant extent the work of feminists from the newly founded communist states in Eastern Europe.[63] In most cases, these women belonged to the largest feminist organization of the period, the Women's International Democratic Federation (WIDF), founded in 1945 in Paris by representatives from forty countries (albeit sponsored by the Soviet Union). The founding president was the French left-feminist intellectual Eugénie Cotton.

The WIDF propagated four interrelated principles, namely antifascism, lasting peace, women's rights, and better conditions for children. Its statutes specified that the organization's goals were active participation in the struggle for the complete annihilation of fascism; shared action to organize women in all countries of the world to defend their rights and to achieve social progress; the protection of public health, in particular the physical and mental health of children; and strengthening the friendship and unity among women in the whole world.[64] A peace campaign launched by the WIDF and communist women's organizations in Eastern and Western Europe during the Korean War (1950–53) exemplifies the transnational practices used by women activists in their campaigns for women's rights. It furthermore reveals the way in which national interests and political loyalties affected these campaigns, above all through the close connection between discourses of women's equality and those of peace in international propaganda.

The central means of the WIDF peace campaign during the Korean War was a brochure entitled *We Accuse*. It was the result of a fact-finding mission to Korea by WIDF women from eighteen countries in the spring of 1951, just as UN troops had halted the surprisingly successful Sino–North Korean winter offensive. This brochure claimed to reveal evidence of atrocities committed against civilians by US forces in Korea, including the use of germ warfare, and it formed the centerpiece of the international propaganda efforts for the East German and Czechoslovak communist women's organizations in 1951. By this time, the Cold War was having an effect on the membership of the WIDF and the views of its members, many of whom now branded the older WILPF as "fascist" and even tried to undermine its UN nongovernmental organization consultative status.[65]

The threats of nuclear war and biological warfare meant that women still organized transnationally on behalf of peace and women's rights, even crossing Cold War ideological lines. However, Donert argues that in the space of international relations, "women's rights were swiftly embedded in Soviet and East European cultural diplomacy 'in defence of peace' as the ideological contest with the West intensified in 1947."[66] Staking out claims to the representation of peace and social justice issues was now an important source of political legitimation "demonstrating the mass mobilization of socialist womanhood to both international and domestic publics," as in the 1950 Stockholm peace petition by the World Peace Council, calling for an absolute ban on nuclear weapons and signed by 273,470,566 people (with its unintentional echoes of the WILPF's 1932 petition).

The main supporters of the campaign were the communist women's organizations of Eastern Europe. Interestingly, the "social-maternalist" model of femininity remained pertinent even in these communist-inspired peace campaigns. Networks built at the 1955 "World Congress of Mothers for the Defence of Their Children against War, for Disarmament and Friendship between the Peoples" in Lausanne, initiated by the WIDF,[67] led to a delegation of fourteen German women visiting China for four weeks in 1956. Eight came from the German Democratic Republic and six from the Federal

Republic of Germany; of these, two were members of the Social Democratic Party, one was a member of the peace movement, and three were members of the Communist Party. In 1958, the women's "Caravan of Peace" for nuclear disarmament, initiated by the British socialist Dora Russell, traveled through Eastern Europe.[68] At the UN's Commission on the Status of Women, votes split on Cold War lines, so that a 1955 Soviet proposal to the UN General Assembly for a nuclear-weapons ban to halt the international arms race was rejected by "Western" women. As Donert observes, on one side stood supporters of the Soviet Union's position of disarmament, and on the other were pro-US critics of "peace defined narrowly as the absence of war, 'without guarantees for personal freedoms, protection of human rights or realisation of social justice.' "[69]

We should note, then, that the Cold War may have exhibited nuanced differences in approaches to the problem of peace, but it also augured a familiar pattern of the gendering of international organizations and norms in the field of peacemaking and the taming of warfare, with little significant difference between Eastern and Western gender practices. By this time, too, a "US model" of humanitarianism had become the international norm for not only aid work, but also *development* assistance justified on the grounds of both pacifism and humanitarianism: namely, the idea that provision of new economic opportunities would ensure the perpetuation of peace and the fulfillment of the West's moral obligations to the colonial world.

In her role as head of the Social Sciences Division at UNESCO (which she took up as a demotion after her year at the UN), Alva Myrdal personally rejected that grand-scale US development model, although she was not able to sway the overall direction of UNESCO programs. She had engaged international institutions in the mid-twentieth century on the view that, at that moment in time, peace could only be achieved if the world's marginalized (and here she meant both women and the colonized) were given new economic opportunities and social justice. Development, including industrialization on the Swedish model, had to be adapted to local circumstances with respect for the human and women's rights. It was only in the 1990s, however, with the formulation of the concept of *human security*, that the UN system began to enact policies that echoed Myrdal's views. Human security belatedly focused on women as crucial to the promotion of peace and collective security, on the premise of the traditional family responsibilities assumed by women. Within the UN structure itself, the departments most comfortable with the election of women executives or spokespersons remain the Commission on the Status of Women, and the Working Group on the Issue of Discrimination against Women established by the Human Rights Council in 2010.

CONCLUSION

Seen through the lens of gender, the history of peace and the new international politics of humanitarianism in the first half of the twentieth century tells a familiar story about the persistence of so-called bourgeois gender norms since at least the nineteenth century.

This is in part because, over the same century, the modern nation-state model that rehearsed the political importance of gender difference, with men in public roles and women delegated to the private, was also the foundation of international thought.

Some women may have felt able to participate in humanitarian work and on behalf of peace over this same period as an extension of their private roles as mothers, but as a consequence, they often took on substantial public roles. However, as humanitarian work and pacifist objectives assumed mainstream status in the burgeoning sphere of international and intergovernmental institutions, the gender hierarchy that informed the reality of nation-state politics was repeated in international politics. The highly gendered pattern of connections between humanitarian work and the creation of international organizations was repeated in the East and the West over the course of the first half of the twentieth century.

Cold War case studies suggest that in the second half of the twentieth century, in both Eastern and Western settings, gender conventions in humanitarian practices remained structurally and rhetorically significant for the consolidation of both state and international politics. Francesca Piana, for instance, has described "diplomacy, the military, science, and the missionary" as "the spaces from which humanitarianism moved towards professionalization, and women played a growing role in a relative or even segregated capacity."[70] In particular, rescuing women and children from anti-egalitarian societies became a standard argument for the international intervention of Western states and nonstate organizations in the East. For Emily S. Rosenberg, "modernization and humanitarian uplift, often in the form of liberating downtrodden women both at home and abroad," and the rhetorical representation of Western gender norms as a core necessity of "civilized" nations were hallmarks more specifically of American exceptionalism.[71]

It is also true that the rise of new international institutions and the expansion of international thinking in relation to the challenges of peace and humanitarianism provoked some change over time. At various moments, alternative masculinities were imagined in relation to the politics of internationalism, and women's rights became associated with the prospect of human rights; women sought active roles as agents of humanitarianism and peace, not just as its subjects. Historians are increasingly taking account of the influence of international law and the experiment of international governance on what we already know about gender and the nation-state. The evidence we have so far points in the main to parallels between the international institutionalization of humanitarian practices and the professionalization of other spheres of female agency and service. This process tended to marginalize the abilities of women as agents, even as women and children were the focus of humanitarian activism; meanwhile, international law grew as a masculine domain of practice.

There is still more research to be done if we are to understand the new international politics. Among the key questions are how the humanitarian and pacifist ambitions that predominantly shaped that politics in the early part of the twentieth century affected the everyday lives of individuals in very different political and social circumstances, as well as the opportunities that an international arena of activism made uniquely available, including the possibilities for women's political agency. We are only at the beginning of a history of the complex political and social significance of the new international politics that characterized the twentieth century.

NOTES

1. Jane Addams, "The Revolt against War," in *Women at The Hague: The International Congress of Women and Its Results*, ed. Mercedes M. Randall (New York: Garland, 1972), 55–81, 60 and 62.

2. See also the chapters by Robert A. Nye on "War Mobilization, Gender, and Military Culture in Nineteenth-Century Western Societies," and Jean H. Quataert on "Changing Modes of Warfare and the Gendering of Military Medical Care, 1850s–1920s" in this handbook.

3. Daniel Laqua, "Pacifism in Fin-de-Siècle Austria: The Politics and Limits of Peace Activism," *The Historical Journal* 57, no. 1 (2014): 199–214, 200.

4. See Quataert, "Changing Modes" in this handbook.

5. See Abigail Green, "Humanitarianism in Nineteenth Century Context: Religious, Gendered, National," *The Historical Journal* 57, no. 4 (2014): 1157–75; and Clare Midgely, "British Anti-Slavery and Feminism in Transatlantic Perspective," in *Women's Rights and Transatlantic Antislavery in the Era of Emancipation*, ed. Kathryn Kish Sklar and James Brewer Stewart (New Haven, CT: Yale University Press, 2007), 121–39.

6. Sandi Cooper, *Patriotic Pacifism: Waging War on War in Europe, 1815–1914* (Oxford: Oxford University Press, 1991); Cooper, "Pacifism in France, 1889–1914: International Peace as a Human Right," *French Historical Studies* 17, no. 2 (1991): 359–86; and Jacques Bariéty and Antoine Fleury, eds., *Mouvements et initiatives de paix dans la politique internationale, 1867–1928* (Zurich: Peter Lang, 1987).

7. Brigitte Hamann, *Bertha von Suttner: A Life for Peace* (Syracuse, NY: Syracuse University Press, 1996).

8. Daniel Laqua, "Inside the Humanitarian Cloud: Causes and Motivations to Help Friends and Strangers," in "Ideas, Practice and Histories of Humanitarianism," ed. Daniel Laqua and Charlotte Alston, special issue of *Journal of Modern European History* 12, no. 2 (2014): 175–85; Katharina Rietzler, "Experts for Peace: Structures and Motivations of Philanthropic Internationalism in the Interwar Years," in *Internationalism Reconfigured: Transnational Ideas and Movements between the World Wars*, ed. Daniel Laqua (London: I. B. Tauris, 2011), 45–65; Amalia Ribi, " 'The Breath of a New Life?' British Anti-Slavery Activism and the League of Nations," in ibid., 93–113; and Francesca Piana, "Towards the International Refugee Regime: Humanitarianism in the Wake of the First World War" (PhD diss., Geneva: Graduate Institute of International and Development Studies, 2013).

9. See Glenda Sluga, "René Cassin: Les droits de l'homme and the Universality of Human Rights, 1945–1966," in *Human Rights in the Twentieth Century*, ed. Stefan-Ludwig Hoffmann (Cambridge: Cambridge University Press, 2011), 107–24; Sluga, "Women, Feminisms, and Twentieth Century Internationalisms," in *Internationalisms: A Twentieth Century History*, ed. Sluga and Patricia Clavin (Cambridge: Cambridge University Press, 2017), 61–84; and Allida Black, "Are Women 'Human'? The UN and the Struggle to Recognize Women's Rights as Human Rights," in *The Human Rights Revolution: An International History*, ed. Akira Iriye and Petra Goedde (Oxford University Press, 2012), 133–58.

10. See Glenda Sluga, *Internationalism in the Age of Nationalism* (Philadelphia: University of Pennsylvania Press), 11–44.

11. Nye, "War Mobilization" in this handbook.

12. Laqua, "Pacifism"; Bertha von Suttner, *Memoirs of Bertha von Suttner: The Records of an Eventful Life* (Boston: Ginn, 1910); and Sandi Cooper, "Pacifism, Feminism and Fascism in Interwar France," *International History Review* 19, no. 1 (1997): 104–14.

13. Laqua, "Pacifism," 200.

14. Bob Reinalda, *Routledge History of International Organizations: From 1815 to the Present Day* (London: Routledge, 2009), 67.

15. Leila J. Rupp, "Constructing Internationalism: The Case of Transnational Women's Organizations, 1888–1945," *American Historical Review* 99, no. 5 (1994): 1571–1600.

16. See Shabtai Rosenne, ed., *The Hague Peace Conferences of 1899 and 1907 and International Arbitration: Reports and Documents* (The Hague: Asser Press, 2001); Maartje Abbenhuis, *An Age of Neutrals: Great Power Politics, 1815–1914* (Cambridge: Cambridge University Press, 2014), 145–48; David Caron, "War and International Adjudication: Reflections on the 1899 Peace Conference," *American Journal of International Law* 94, no. 4 (2000): 4–30; Arthur Eyffinger, *The 1899 Hague Peace Conference: "The Parliament of Man, The Federation of the World"* (The Hague: Kluwer, 1999); Cooper, "Pacifism in France"; and Roger Chickering, *Imperial Germany and a World without War: The Peace Movement and German Society, 1892–1933* (Princeton, NJ: Princeton University Press, 1975).

17. Sandi E. Cooper cited in Reinalda, *Routledge History*, 67.

18. Reinalda, *Routledge History*, 203.

19. Ibid., 213.

20. Laqua, "Pacifism," 204.

21. Warren F. Kuehl, *Biographical Dictionary of Internationalists* (Westport, CT: Greenwood Press, 1983).

22. Quataert, "Changing Modes" in this handbook; and Quataert, "Gendered Medical Services in Red Cross Field Hospitals during the First Balkan War and World War I," in *Peace, War, and Gender from Antiquity to the Present: Cross-Cultural Perspectives*, ed. Jost Dülffer and Robert Frank (Essen: Klartext Verlag, 2009), 219–33.

23. Isabel Hull, *A Scrap of Paper: Breaking and Making International Law during the Great War* (Ithaca, NY: Cornell University Press, 2014).

24. Francesca Piana, "The Dangers of 'Going Native': George Montandon and the International Committee of the Red Cross, 1919–1922," *Contemporary European History* 25, no. 2 (2016): 253–74; and Daniel Maul, "American Quakers, the Emergence of International Humanitarianism and the Foundation of the American Friends Service Committee 1890–1920," in *Dilemmas of Humanitarianism in the Twentieth Century*, ed. Johannes Paulmann (Oxford: Oxford University Press, 2016), 63–90.

25. Tammy M. Proctor, "An American Enterprise? British Participation in US Food Relief Programmes (1914–1923)," in "Humanitarianism in the Era of the First World War," ed. Branden Little, special issue, *First World War Studies* 5, no. 1 (2014): 29–42; see also Daniel Maul, "The Politics of Neutrality: The American Friends Service Committee and the Spanish Civil War 1936–1939," in "Humanitarianisms in Context, Histories of Non-State Actors, from the Local to the Global," ed. Kevin O'Sullivan and Matthew Hilton, special issue, *European Review of History/Revue européenne d'histoire* 23, no. 1–2 (2016): 82–100.

26. Proctor, "An American Enterprise?," 29.

27. Melanie Tanielian, "Politics of Wartime Relief in Ottoman Beirut (1914–1918)," in Little, *Humanitarianism*, 69–82.

28. Ibid., 69.

29. Sluga, *Internationalism*, 35; and Laqua, "Pacifism," 209.

30. See Sluga, "Women, Feminisms."

31. On social maternalism, see Seth Koven and Sonya Michel, "Womanly Duties: Maternalist Politics and the Origins of Welfare States in France, Germany, Great Britain, and the United States, 1880–1920," *American Historical Review* 95, no. 4 (1990): 1076–108.

32. Ellen Key, *War, Peace and the Future: A Consideration of Nationalism and Internationalism, and of the Relation of Women to War* (London: G. P. Putnam's Sons, 1916), 17, 18.

33. See Helena M. Swanwick, *Builders of Peace: Being Ten Years History of the Union of Democratic Control* (London: Swarthmore Press, 1924), 56; Helen McCarthy, "The Lifeblood of the League? Voluntary Associations and League of Nations Activism in Britain," *Internationalism Reconfigured*, ed. Laqua, 187–208; and Marie Sandell, "'A Real Meeting of the Women of the East and West': Women and Internationalism in the Interwar Period," in ibid., 161–88. Keith Watenpaugh cites Helena Swanwick calling for the league to involve more "women from the East"; see Watenpaugh, "The League of Nations' Rescue of Armenian Genocide Survivors and the Making of Modern Humanitarianism," *American Historical Review* 115, no. 5 (2010): 1315–39.

34. Helen McCarthy, *The British People and the League of Nations Democracy, Citizenship and Internationalism, 1918–45* (Manchester: Manchester University Press, 2011), 182.

35. Ibid., 185, 186.

36. Ibid., 196.

37. This position has been challenged by Christopher Clark in *The Sleepwalkers: How Europe Went to War in 1914* (New York: Penguin Books, 2014).

38. Margaret MacMillan, *Peacemakers: Six Months That Changed the World* (New York: Random House, 2001).

39. Ibid.

40. Susan Pedersen, *The Guardians: The League of Nations and the Crisis of Empire* (Oxford: Oxford University Press, 2015).

41. See Daniel Gorman, *The Emergence of International Society in the 1920s* (Cambridge: Cambridge University Press, 2012), 52.

42. Stephanie A. Limoncelli, *The Politics of Trafficking: The First International Movement to Combat the Sexual Exploitation of Women* (Stanford, CA: Stanford University Press, 2010).

43. Andrew Webster, "Merchants of Death: Law, Disarmament and Internationalism," in Sluga and Clavin, *Internationalisms*, 13–22.

44. Richard Price, "A Genealogy of the Chemical Weapons Taboo," *International Organization* 49, no. 1 (1995): 73–103.

45. Gertrude Bussey and Margaret Tims, *Women's International League for Peace and Freedom, 1915–1965: A Record of Fifty Years' Work* (London: Allen & Unwin, 1965), 34–52 and 94–102; and Jill Liddington, *Road to Greenham Common: Feminism and Anti-Militarism in Britain since 1820* (Syracuse, NY: Syracuse University Press, 1991), 148. For a useful introduction to the feminist historiography of internationalism, see Francesca de Haan, "Eugénie Cotton, Pak Chong-Ae, and Claudia Jones: Rethinking Transnational Feminism and International Politics," *Journal of Women's History* 25, no. 4 (2013): 174–89.

46. Catherine Foster, *Women for All Seasons: The Story of the Women's International League for Peace and Freedom* (Athens, GA: University of Georgia Press, 1989), 18.

47. See Susan Pedersen, "Metaphors of the Schoolroom: Women Working the Mandates System of the League of Nations," *History Workshop Journal* 66, no. 1 (2008): 188–207.

48. Francesca Piana, "The Professionalization of Humanitarianism in the Interwar Period" (paper presented at Dealing with Disasters: An International Perspective, 1870–2000, Oxford, England, September 9–11, 2013); and Philippa Lesley Hetherington, "Between Moscow, Geneva and Shanghai: The League of Nations and the Traffic in Women of Russian Origin, 1920–1937" (unpublished manuscript, UCL School of Slavonic and East European Studies, London, 2015).

49. McCarthy, *The British People*, 194.

50. Ibid.

51. Ibid., 193.

52. United Nations Relief and Rehabilitation Administration. UNRRA, *The History of the United Nations Relief and Rehabilitation Administration* (New York: Columbia University Press, 1950); and United Nations Relief and Rehabilitation Administration, *UNRRA in China, 1945–1947* (New York: Garland, 1948).

53. Lilian Pascoe-Rutter, "A Further Report from London," *Equal Rights*, March–April 1946, 12.

54. Celia Donert, "Women's Rights in Cold War Europe: Disentangling Feminist Histories," *Past and Present* 218, suppl. 8 (2013): 178–202, 178.

55. Gertrude Baer, "Women on All Fronts," *Equal Rights*, March–April 1945, 26. See also Marilyn Lake, "From Self-Determination via Protection to Equality via Non-Discrimination: Defining Women's Rights at the League of Nations and the United Nations," in *Women's Rights and Human Rights: International Historical Perspectives*, ed. Patricia Grimshaw et al. (Basingstoke: Palgrave, 2001), 254–71; and Glenda Sluga, "National Sovereignty and Female Equality: Gender, Peacemaking, and the New World Orders of 1919 and 1945," in *Frieden—Gewalt—Geschlecht: Friedens- und Konfliktforschung als Geschlechterforschung*, ed. Karen Hagemann et al. (Essen: Klartext, 2005), 166–83.

56. Glenda Sluga, "UNESCO and the (One) World of Julian Huxley," *Journal of World History*, 21, no. 3 (2010): 393–418.

57. "Women in the United Nations," *Roshni: Journal of the All India Women's Conference*, June 1949, 30; see Glenda Sluga, " 'Spectacular Feminism': The International History of Women, World Citizenship and Human Rights," in *Women's Activism: Global Perspectives from the 1890s to the Present*, ed. Francisca de Haan et al. (London: Routledge, 2103), 44–58, 56.

58. Deborah Stienstra, *Women's Movements and International Organizations* (London: St. Martin's Press, 1994), 79.

59. See Glenda Sluga, "The Human Story of Development: Alva Myrdal at the UN, 1949–1955," in *International Organizations and Development, 1945–1990*, ed. Marc Frey et al. (Basingstoke: Palgrave Macmillan, 2013), 46–74.

60. UN Women, Commission on the Status of Women, accessed November 14, 2015, http://www.unwomen.org/en/csw.

61. Johannes Morsink, *The Universal Declaration of Human Rights: Origins, Drafting and Intent* (Philadelphia: University of Pennsylvania Press, 1999), 93, 118. See Articles 23 and 25 of the declaration, which refer to "himself and his family."

62. The Universal Declaration of Human Rights, Article 25(2), accessed December 3, 2015, http://www.un.org/en/universal-declaration-human-rights/.

63. Donert, "Women's Rights," 191; see Haan, "Eugénie Cotton," 174, 175.

64. *Congrès international des femmes: Compte rendu des travaux du Congrès qui s'est tenu à Paris du 26 Novembre au 1er Décembre 1945* (Paris: Fédération démocratique internationale des femmes, 1946), 381–89.
65. Donert, "Women's Rights," 189.
66. Ibid., 190.
67. See Sluga, "Women, Feminisms"; and Eugénie Cotton, *World Congress of Mothers for the Defence of Their Children against War, for Disarmament and Friendship between the Peoples* (n.p.: Women's International Democratic Federation, 1955).
68. Donert, "Women's Rights," 196.
69. Ibid., 198.
70. Piana, "The Dangers," n.p.
71. Emily S. Rosenberg, "Rescuing Women and Children," *Journal of American History* 89, no. 2 (2002): 456–65, 459; Barbara Metzger, "Toward an International Human Rights Regime during the Inter-War Years: The League of Nations' Combat of Traffic in Women and Children," in *Beyond Sovereignty: Britain, Empire and Transnationalism, c.1880–1950,* ed. Kevin Grant et al. (New York: Palgrave Macmillan, 2007), 54–79; and Daniel Maul, *Human Rights, Development and Decolonization. The International Labour Organization, 1940–70* (Basingstoke: Palgrave Macmillan, 2012).

Select Bibliography

Alonso, Harriet Hyman. *Peace as a Women's Issue: A History of the U.S. Movement for World Peace and Women's Rights.* Syracuse, NY: Syracuse University Press, 1993.

Amrith, Sunil, and Glenda Sluga. "New Histories of the UN." *Journal of World History* 19, no. 3 (2008): 251–74.

Bass, Gary J. *Freedom's Battle: The Origins of Humanitarian Intervention.* New York: Alfred A. Knopf, 2009.

Bouchard, Carl. *Le citoyen et l'ordre mondial (1914–1919): Le rêve d'une paix durable au lendemain de la Grande Guerre.* Paris: Editions A. Pedone, 2008.

Bussey, Gertrude, and Margaret Tims. *Pioneers for Peace: The Women's International League for Peace and Freedom, 1915–1965.* London: Women's International League for Peace and Freedom, British Section, 1980.

Cabanes, Bruno. *The Great War and the Origins of Humanitarianism, 1918–1924.* Cambridge: Cambridge University Press, 2014.

Cooper, Sandi E. *Patriotic Pacifism: Waging War on War in Europe, 1815–1914.* New York: Oxford University Press, 1991.

Davy, Jennifer, Karen Hagemann, and Ute Kätzel, eds. *Frieden—Gewalt—Geschlecht: Friedens- und Konfliktforschung als Geschlechterforschung.* Essen: Klartext, 2005.

Hunt, Lynn. *Inventing Human Rights: A History.* New York: W. W. Norton, 2007.

Laqua, Daniel. "Ideas, Practices and Histories of Humanitarianism." Special issue, *Journal of Modern European History* 12 (2014).

Laqua, Daniel, ed. *Internationalism Reconfigured: Transnational Ideas and Movements between the World Wars.* London: I. B. Tauris, 2011.

McCarthy, Helen. *The British People and the League of Nations: Democracy, Citizenship and Internationalism, c. 1918–1945.* Manchester: Manchester University Press, 2011.

Morsink, Johannes. *The Universal Declaration of Human Rights: Origins, Drafting and Intent.* Philadelphia: University of Pennsylvania Press, 1999.

Price, Richard. "A Genealogy of the Chemical Weapons Taboo." *International Organization* 49, no. 1 (1995): 73–103.

Reanda, Leanne. "Human Rights and Women's Rights: The United Nations Approach." *Human Rights Quarterly* 3, no. 2 (1981): 24–25.

Reinalda, Bob. *Routledge History of International Organizations: From 1815 to the Present Day.* London: Routledge, 2009.

Sluga, Glenda. *Internationalism in the Age of Nationalism.* Philadelphia: University of Pennsylvania Press, 2013.

Sluga, Glenda, and Patricia Clavin, eds. *Internationalisms, a Twentieth Century History.* Cambridge: Cambridge University Press, 2017.

Stienstra, Deborah. *Women's Movements and International Organizations.* New York: St Martin's Press, 1994.

Webster, Andrew. "The Transnational Dream: Politicians, Diplomats and Soldiers in the League of Nations' Pursuit of International Disarmament, 1920–1938." *Contemporary European History* 14, no. 4 (2005): 493–518.

CHAPTER 24

....

GENDER, DEMOBILIZATION, AND THE REORDERING OF SOCIETIES AFTER THE FIRST AND SECOND WORLD WARS

....

KAREN HAGEMANN

As highly industrialized total wars, the two twentieth-century world wars extended simultaneously into large areas of the world, were conducted with mass armies that used modern technology, and required the unprecedented involvement of citizens at both the so-called home front and the battlefront.[1] To ensure the needed war support, governments passed conscription and labor laws, introduced wage and price controls, rationed food and fuel, and used all available mass media for war propaganda. At the end of both conflicts, the demobilization of large numbers of soldiers and other military personnel, including medical staff, and male and female workers in war industries, as well as the care for and relocation of millions of returning prisoners of war (POWs), displaced persons, expellees, and refugees, created immense economic, social, and political challenges for the postwar states and societies dealing with the aftermath of war. Cities and towns were in ruins, whole landscapes were devastated, and industry and agriculture were severely damaged, especially after World War II. Ten million soldiers and 8 million civilians died during the First World War between 1914 and 1918, and 22 million soldiers and 29 million civilians died during the Second World War between 1939 and 1945. Of the latter, 11 million civilians of different nationalities were murdered in prisons and concentration and extermination camps, including 6 million Jews who were killed in the Holocaust. These millions of dead left mourning and shattered families. Veterans came home mentally and physically disabled; 20 million invalid soldiers returned after the

First World War and 35 million after the Second World War. In addition, families had to wait for the return of their loved ones held as POWs, respectively, 8 million and 18 million after the First and Second World Wars.[2]

The first priorities for all postwar states were the controlled return to peace through military, economic, social, and cultural demobilization, and the organisation of the needed care for the victims of war. Military demobilization focused on the release or reassignment of armed forces and was closely related to bureaucratic demobilization, the recall of regulations and institutions designed to facilitate the mobilization for war, including welfare measures like the support for soldiers' families, and the reorganization of the social welfare for invalid veterans, war widows, and orphans. The goal of economic demobilization was the smooth transition to a peacetime economy, including the rescinding of wartime regulations on production, labor, wages, the rationing of goods, and price controls. Finally, the major agenda of social and cultural demobilization was the transition of society and culture from war to peace, the shaping of the collective commemoration of war sacrifices, and the construction of national war memories.[3] As much as possible, at least the major warring states developed their demobilization policies well in advance, but the planning proved difficult because it depended on the outcome of the war. In addition to a country's victory or defeat, the difference between real peace and continuing conflict in the form of occupation, revolution, or civil war had pervasive impacts on the forms of demobilization and the possibilities for the reconstruction and reordering of society. Whether a country had been a battleground during wartime or was spared from fighting on its own territory, like Australia, Canada, and the United States in both world wars, also had far reaching implications. In these nations the population suffered too during the wars, but much less than in the war-torn regions, and the economic and social recovery after both conflicts was much easier.[4]

Because of the challenging legacy of both world wars and the importance of a successful demobilization and reconstruction for the further development of postwar societies, an increasing number of studies have explored the short- and long-term aftermaths of both world wars since the 1980s. Women's and gender historians have been at the forefront of this scholarship. First their research focused on the claim by many contemporaries and some later historians that in particular the First World War was a catalyst of female liberation, because of expanded female work opportunities for women in new areas of the labor force; the newly gained female suffrage in thirteen postwar countries; and the increasing popularity of the ideal of the independent "New Woman" in the interwar period.[5] Several studies questioned this interpretation by pointing to the short-term character of many wartime changes and the agenda of economic, social, and cultural demobilization policies that attempted the reconstruction of the prewar gender order and its hierarchies. They emphasized that the notion of the New Woman was for the vast majority of women at best an ideal propagated by the media of the new mass culture.[6] Later research on women's everyday war and postwar experiences nuanced this interpretation by foregrounding that the novel opportunities for economic and social independence and political participation during and after the First and Second World Wars indeed opened new spaces of action at least for some women and fostered their self-confidence, even when the hierarchical gender order as such did not change.[7]

In general, most of the recent research by women gender historians on postwar societies has shown that gender was a central aspect of demobilization, reconstruction, and reordering in the "long postwars" after the First[8] and Second World Wars.[9] Their studies have demonstrated that in all countries affected by war one major aim of postwar demobilization was the reconstruction of the prewar social order by "regendering" the society to give the population, especially the returning soldiers, a feeling of "normality." Central spaces to achieve this aim were the economy and the family. In both spaces the prewar gender division of labor and with it gender hierarchy, which had been disordered during the two world wars, needed to be implemented again by labor, social, and family policies. Mass culture and collective memory construction played a crucial role in supporting this process of a regendering of postwar societies with their highly gendered recollections of the past war and visons of the present and future society. In this way the limited expansion of women's space of action during the two world wars was taken back as much as possible by postwar policies after the conflicts. But this could not prevent that the ideas of femininity and masculinity continued to be contested and changed during and after the two world wars.[10]

Most of the scholarship focused on individual countries. Only recently have historians also engaged in comparative and transnational studies. Comparisons between the two world wars are, however, still remarkably rare.[11] In the following, the military, economic, and cultural demobilization and related reconstruction policies after the First and Second World Wars in Britain, France, Germany, the United States, and the Soviet Union will be compared from a gender perspective. The focus on these five countries allows for a contrast of capitalist and communist societies and democratic and authoritarian political systems, for which, aside from victory or defeat, the two world wars ended in quite different ways that include occupation, revolution, and civil war.

"THE LONG FIRST WORLD WAR" AND ITS AFTERMATH

World War I was the first highly industrialized mass war, during which all sectors of the belligerent countries—military, economy, society, politics, culture—were involved in warfare and, at war's end, had to be demobilized.[12] This demobilization was severely complicated by the global Spanish flu pandemic of 1918–19, in which an estimated total of 500 million people, one quarter of the world's population, was infected, of whom 17 to 50 million died. The mortality rate for younger adults, many of whom had just survived war service, was especially high and thus differed from typical influenza outbreaks.[13] In the processes of demobilization, reconstruction, and reordering after the First World War, we can already see the establishment of certain patterns that appeared again after the Second World War, such as governments' focus on military demobilization and the restructuring of the labor market and, hand in hand with both, social policies that attempted a gendered reordering of society and cultural practices that helped to create national war memories.[14] The welfare-state policies that governments had developed during the wars to address the needs of the war economy and society were not completely reversed. Instead their agenda and focus changed. Postwar governments needed to respond to the lasting human effects of war and the specific requirements of postwar economies and societies. In general, both the First and the Second World Wars, and their respective postwar periods, contributed to the development and expansion of welfare states all over Europe.[15]

Most governments had planned in advance for the military demobilization of their troops after the end of the conflict to secure an orderly return of soldiers and civilian military personnel. But when World War I ended in November 1918, none of the involved states could demobilize right away or all at once, albeit for different reasons. These reasons included transportation problems, the need for occupation troops, and continuing conflicts like unrest, revolution, and civil war.[16] In addition, defeat or victory made a huge difference for the process of demobilization. Two examples of the interplay of these factors in defeated countries are Austria and Germany.

The economic blockade that the Triple Entente under British leadership had started at the beginning of the First World War, and the poor preparation of the Austrian and German governments—both hoping for a short "Blitz Krieg"—for a long-lasting conflict, caused a quickly growing shortage of food and fuel in both states. The supply crisis was made worse by the insufficient government response with a rationing of goods. Since 1915/16 the working class population at home, especially women and youth in the urban centers, responded with a quickly growing number of hunger riots and strikes, which led to a general increase in war opposition. In the armed forces, combat fatigue grew, too, and from late October 1917, it led to revolts by sailors and soldiers.[17]

This development culminated in Germany in the November Revolution of 1918 and the proclamation of a republic on November 9. Faced with the defeat of its armed forces and the war opposition at home, the new government signed the Armistice of Compiègne on November 11, 1918.[18] The terms of the armistice, which already had been negotiated by the old government since early October 1918, called for the evacuation of German troops from occupied Belgium, France, and Luxembourg within fifteen days. In addition, it established that Allied forces would occupy the Rhineland to secure peace. In late 1918, they entered Germany and began the occupation. Signed on June 28, 1919, the Treaty of Versailles officially ended the state of war between the Allies and the new Weimar Republic in Germany, which was established after the November Revolution of 1918. Article 231 of the treaty, the "war guilt clause," put the responsibility for the outbreak of the war on Germany and its allies. The other Central Powers, among them the newly separated Austrian and Hungarian states, were dealt with in separate treaties. Germany was required to disarm, make substantial territorial concessions, including the loss of all of its colonies, and pay extensive reparations for the immense damages and losses suffered by the Allies.[19]

The occupation of the German Rhineland and the Saar region by American, Belgian, British, and French forces began immediately after the signing of the armistice and lasted until 1930. Moreover, from 1923 to 1925, Belgium and France occupied Germany's industrial Ruhr region to ensure the payment of reparations. France's occupation troops included between 25,000 and 40,000 French colonial soldiers. The general anger about the terms of the Versailles Treaty and the Ruhr occupation in Germany was fueled by right-wing propaganda that incited severe racial anxieties with allegations of rape and other atrocities by the mainly Senegalese *tirailleurs*, infantry regiments of colonial soldiers. This propaganda was part of a widespread campaign by the conservative and nationalist German press that depicted the occupation as a form of humiliation of the German nation by France.[20]

Another example of the particularly difficult postwar situation of the defeated countries is Russia. After the October Revolution of 1917, the Bolshevik government signed the Treaty of Brest-Litovsk on March 3, 1918. This treaty with the Central Powers (the German Empire, Austria-Hungary, Bulgaria, and the Ottoman Empire) officially ended Russia's participation in World War I, which was one important short-term aim of the revolutionaries. The treaty, with its harsh conditions, was annulled by the Armistice of Compiègne. The two treaties, however, did not bring an end of the fighting to Russia and eastern Europe, where a civil war that began after the Bolshevik revolution did not end until October 1922. Multiple factions were involved in this conflict. The two largest were the communist Red Army and the broad anti-Bolshevik coalition of the White Army, which included such diverse groups as conservative monarchists and socialist Mensheviks. Beginning in 1918, eight countries intervened against the Red Army, including the former Western allies of Britain, France, and the United States, along with the two newly founded European states, the First Czechoslovak Republic and the Second Republic of Poland. At least 75,000 foreign troops fought in this conflict. The Russian Civil War ended with a victory for the Red Army and led to the founding of the Union of Soviet Socialist Republics (USSR) of Russia, Ukraine, Belorussia and Transcaucasia in December 1922. Casualties of this bloody conflict have been estimated at more than a million soldiers on both sides and countless civilians.[21]

The experience of war, occupation, and continuing international and domestic conflicts led to an increasing militarization of European societies after World War I. One important indicator of this trend is the rise of *paramilitarianism*, which Robert Gerwarth and John Horne defined as military or quasi-military organizations and practices that either expand or replace the activity of conventional military formations. In the interwar years, paramilitary violence affected Russia, Ukraine, Finland, the Baltic states, Poland, Austria, Hungary, Germany, Ireland, Italy, Anatolia, and the Caucasus. Sometimes this violence filled the vacuum of a collapsing state or military; in other cases, it was part of a civil war. It included revolutionary and counterrevolutionary organizations that often fought against each other and was related to other forms of violence, like social protest, insurrection, terrorism, and authoritarian repression by the state.[22] For this reason, Gerwarth suggested a reperiodization of the era as the "long First World War."[23]

The newly founded Weimar Republic (1919–33) is an infamous example of a state plagued by paramilitary violence. The Treaty of Versailles required a reduction of the German military to 100,000 men by March 1920 and prohibited universal conscription. Many demobilized veterans instead joined nationalist paramilitary organizations. The first were the various nationalist Freikorps (Free Corps), founded immediately after the armistice, enlisting 250,000 men by 1919. They supported counterrevolutionary politics with military force during the November Revolution of 1918/19 and backed the Kapp Putsch in March 1920, a military coup intended to bring to power a right-wing autocratic government.[24] The Freikorps were supported by the Stahlhelm, Bund der Frontsoldaten (League of Front Soldiers), which formed the armed branch of the nationalist, conservative Deutschnationale Volkspartei (German National People's Party), founded in December 1918. As a response to right-wing violence, democratic and left-wing political groups also formed paramilitary organizations to protect the new republic. The most important were the social democratic Reichsbanner Schwarz-Rot-Gold (Black Red Gold Banner of the Republic) and the communist Rotfrontkämpferbund (Red Front Fighters' League).[25] The experiences of war, the rise of paramilitary organizations, and political violence fostered a militarization of the notion of masculinity in Weimar culture that was shaped by the respective political agendas of the organizations and their related ideas about the gender order. This development led to increasing violence in political culture.[26] A similar development occurred in other defeated central European countries like Austria and Hungary, but also in postwar Italy, which had chosen the side of the victorious Allied powers, but was nevertheless shaken by a severe postwar crisis. It saw the quick growth of paramilitary groups and an escalation of civil unrest that developed into a civil war between supporters of the Fascist movement and their paramilitary organisations and antifascist opponents. The pressure of the March to Rome by about 30,000 Fascist blackshirts in October 1922 caused king Victor Emmanuel III to ask Benito Mussolini to form a Fascist government.[27]

In addition, all nations involved in World War I saw the creation of large veterans' associations. They provided a platform for soldiers and other war victims to commemorate the war and their own "sacrifice" and to articulate their demands for cultural and social recognition. In Germany, the Reichsbund der Kriegsteilnehmer und Kriegsbeschädigten (Association of War Veterans and War Wounded), founded in 1917 as a nonpartisan organization with 830,000 members (one-quarter of them war widows and orphans), and the Reichsbund Jüdischer Frontsoldaten (National Association of Jewish Front-Soldiers), founded in 1919 with about 55,000 members, became the most well known.[28] In the United States, the American Legion was formed in the same year, as a nonpartisan association open only to honorably discharged soldiers and other military personnel. It enrolled about 1 million war veterans. In the United Kingdom, the British Legion, created in 1921, emerged as the unified national institution to represent veterans' interests and included 409,000 members. In France, the dominant organizations were the Union Fédérale (Federal Union), founded in 1918 as a federation of provincial organizations of veterans and war-wounded, and the Union des Combattants (Union of Combatants), created in the same year as a nationalist organization of front soldiers. Nearly 48 percent of all eligible ex-servicemen in France, up to 3 million, were registered in the various veterans' associations, by far the highest percentage of organized veterans.[29]

These organizations used what they characterized as the soldiers' manly heroic sacrifices to claim recognition, respect, and commemoration in the postwar period. Even when they represented all war victims, like the Reichsbund, they tended to focus on the demands of the veterans who constituted the vast majority of their members. Their insistence on cultural and social recognition of their war sacrifice at the front lines, however, often met with resistance in postwar societies. Culturally, the activism of the veterans' organizations and the visibility of war invalids in public spaces reminded postwar societies of the trauma of the past war, which many wanted to forget—and not only in the defeated nations.[30] Socially, veterans and other war victims competed in the economic postwar crises with others, like the many unemployed or the victims of hyperinflation, over the limited financial resources of the welfare system. The new welfare bureaucracies, which had been built up during the war to ensure that servicemen received pay and that their dependents were taken care of, had to shift their focus and became providers of pensions and other forms of restitution for veterans, invalids, widows, and orphans.

One example can be seen in the three laws the French government passed in March and April 1919 designed to provide pensions to invalid soldiers and civil victims of war, such as widows, orphans, parents, and grandparents of fallen soldiers, and to remunerate those who had suffered property damage or other material losses as a result of the war.[31] These and similar laws in other countries were informed by ideas about what politicians called a "normal" gender order with the male-breadwinner–female-homemaker family at its center. Pension programs for wounded and disabled veterans were accordingly designed to allow them to support their wives and children, while the amount of the pension paid to war widows fell short of providing a living for them and their family. Lawmakers in the United States, for instance, specifically stated that war widows should rely on other family members to supplement the pensions paid to them by the government. These women also forfeited the pension when they remarried.[32]

Reordering Society through Economic and Social Demobilization

Governments were loath to release all their soldiers immediately, because they feared—in view of the Russian revolutions—the rebellious potential of veterans in society. Military demilitarization had to be cushioned by economic demobilization. To prevent unrest, the returning veterans had to be brought back into their old workplaces as quickly as possible and made breadwinners for their families again. Thus, gender played a key role in how the economy and its labor market were restructured after the war. Except for the Soviet Union, all states implemented policies to ensure that veterans could return to their old positions in the workforce. This meant that demobilization regulations forced most women hired during the war to leave their jobs after the conflict.

In France, the government and private industries offered their former female workers compensation in exchange for their departure from the workplace.[33] In Britain and Germany, nothing like this happened. Already during the war, the German government had planned on dismissing female workers from war industries as part of demobilization. This policy was supported by the major parties and trade unions. They hoped to pacify discontented veterans by restoring the prewar gender order and its idealized model of the male-breadwinner–female-homemaker family. One main target of this policy became the so-called *Doppelverdienerinnen*, married women who continued to work and supposedly took jobs from unemployed veterans. The supporters of this policy ignored the fact that men and women worked in different segments of the gender-segregated labor market and thus rarely competed for the same jobs. They made women, whose families needed their income, into scapegoats for the structural crisis resulting from the transition from a war to a peacetime economy.[34]

In the reality of postwar societies hit by hyperinflation, mass unemployment, and political change or even turmoil, the attempts to reorder society through such a gendered demobilization policy did not work well for two main reasons. First, industries, businesses, and administrations had reorganized and rationalized the work process during the war to allow less-experienced women to replace trained male employees. This costly process depended on women's lower salaries. Because of fears of increased labor costs, employers were often reluctant to support postwar governmental policies that favored the return of the veterans.[35] Second, many veterans came home physically and mentally unable to assume their former positions in the labor force and their role as primary breadwinners. Consequently, their wives could not give up their full-time paid work. The postwar states intervened by offering pensions and special training programs to invalid veterans with the aim of reintegrating them into the workforce to secure their male status as breadwinners.[36]

The Soviet government faced a markedly different situation after the end of the First World War because of the ensuing civil war. Industrial and agricultural production collapsed in many areas. To stimulate the recovery, the Bolsheviks introduced the New Economic Policy in March 1921. Part of this policy was an attempt to bring more women into the workforce, because female labor was badly needed in the recovering economy. The socialist approach to women's emancipation offered ideological support for such a policy. Bolshevik leaders believed that women's paid work would contribute to their emancipation through financial independence and liberation from their social isolation at home. To foster the emancipation of Soviet women, the revolutionaries had also implemented reforms to family law in 1918 to give women more equality in marriage and family, including the right to work against the will of their own husbands, to make divorce much easier, and to bar the Russian Orthodox Church from performing marriages. However, such policies and reforms did not affect the lives of most adult women in the interwar USSR. They continued to live in the countryside, work in agriculture, hold religious beliefs, and support traditional family values. As in other countries, primarily urban, young, and single women experienced changes after World War I. They worked in the new industries and believed in the idea of female equality, which was intensively propagated by the Komsomol, the All-Union Leninist Young Communist League founded in 1918.[37]

Gender and Cultural Demobilization

A central function of cultural demobilization after the First World War was the shaping of national commemoration. Victorious societies remembered the war quite differently than the defeated societies. For winning states, such as Britain, France, and the United States, the memories could become heroic. The defeated states, especially Austria and Germany, had to deal with their loss and its many consequences, including occupation, ceding territory, and paying reparations. Gender also played an important role in the construction of the highly contested national war memories.[38] Political leaders were aware of the immense sacrifice they had required from their people during the war. They developed national programs designed to honor veterans and memorialize fallen soldiers. At the center of the memorialization stood the fighting men who, as it was said, had sacrificed themselves on the altar of the fatherland. They were carved into the stone of memorials and monuments and draped with weapons and flags. Civilians' war service and sacrifices tended to be forgotten in official war commemoration. Only war nurses found a place in public recollections, appearing as the angels who looked after soldiers. The specific forms of this gendered official war commemoration differed from country to country. They tended to be more contested in defeated countries like Germany, where conservative and nationalist groups called for a "revenge" and fostered a virile and belligerent collective memory, and their democratic and socialist opponents propagated a more antiwar memory. In victorious countries like Britain, France or the United States, the general tenor of collective war memories was more antiwar too.[39]

War widows were encouraged to take part in the ceremonial honoring of the fallen soldiers, but they were expected to show only a composed mourning in public. The American Gold Star Mothers and Wives are one example. In 1918, the US government, under President Woodrow Wilson, approved a suggestion by the Women's Committee of the Council of National Defense that war widows, instead of the conventional black mourning clothes, should simply wear a black band on the left arm with a gilt star for each fallen family member. In 1928, even a Gold Star Mothers' Association was founded, which demanded federally sponsored so-called pilgrimages for mothers with fallen sons buried overseas. Already one year later, a law was authorized, and, beginning in 1930, the US Department of War organized trips to European cemeteries for mothers and widows of fallen soldiers. At the heart of these pilgrimages was a ceremony during which the women laid wreaths on their sons' and husbands' graves, publicly confirming the expectation that women support and honor the men's military service, even after death.[40]

Cultural demobilization also ended the production of propaganda posters and other materials designed to win citizens' support for the war efforts.[41] However, governments continued to produce propaganda that now tried to direct citizens' responses to peacetime. In the United States, for instance, President Wilson had created the Committee on

Public Information in 1917 to orchestrate the nation's propaganda efforts. Shortly after the armistice, this committee, in conjunction with a telecommunications business, published an advertisement designed to prepare Americans for postwar life. "He will come back a better man!" proclaimed the ad, which featured a returning soldier hugging his apron-clad mother. It assured readers that the soldiers would return as "victorious crusaders" and that their stint in the army had turned them from boys into model male citizens capable of protecting vulnerable women.[42] Publishing such postwar propaganda was, however, impossible in the defeated countries.

What victorious and defeated postwar governments in the West shared instead were pronatalist population campaigns and policies, aiming to buoy declining fertility rates to make up for the population losses caused by the war. Politicians, religious leaders, social reformers, and conservative, middle-class feminists in France, Germany, and Great Britain crusaded to stop the decline of birth rates and to encourage women to do their patriotic duty of bearing more children. Governments even intensified the persecution of illegal abortions in the interwar period.[43] This, however, did not put an end to the increasing attempts by women to engage in family planning and prevent pregnancy, which were supported by the sex-reform movement, a broad coalition from liberal, middle-class feminists and doctors to female and male socialists and communists who fought for a legalization of birth control and abortions in several Western countries.[44] They pointed to the Soviet Union, which in 1920 became the first country in the world to allow abortion in all circumstances and give free access to birth control, though the USSR later enacted a ban on abortion from 1936 to 1955.[45]

Next to increasing female independence through paid work and birth control, the passage of universal female suffrage in thirteen countries after the war, including Austria, Britain, Germany, the Soviet Union, and the United States, was perceived by the churches and conservative political parties and associations in the West as a threat to the gender order of postwar societies. It made no difference in this matter if the nation was victorious or defeated. As Birthe Kundrus has noted for Weimar Germany, conservatives feared confident and independent women. The epitome of their horror was the young, wage-earning New Woman with a short skirt, bobbed hair, and a lifestyle that included recreational activities like dancing, movies, and sport. The image of the flapper in consumer culture was one version of the New Woman, while the notion of the female comrade and partner in the labor movement, especially in socialist and communist youth organizations, was another.[46]

Postwar policies following the First World War established important precedents for demobilization laws and the related social, labor, family, and populations policies aiming for a restoration of economy, society, and culture following the Second World War. Already in the interwar period, those policies were more informed by political ideology and the related ideal of the gender order than they were by victory or defeat. Starting with the October Revolution of 1917, the Soviet Union became the communist political "Other" to the West, and anticommunism was widespread. Already in the interwar societies opposite ideas about the position of women in the economy, society and politics became a marker of difference between conservatives and nationalists and their liberal and leftist opponents, even though traditional notions of gender relations and corresponding patterns of behavior persisted in everyday life in the USSR and the socialist or communist movements elsewhere.

THE AFTERMATH OF THE SECOND WORLD WAR

On May 8, 1945, the Second World War ended in Europe following the capitulation of the German Wehrmacht one day before. Six years of war and genocide had caused millions of deaths. Of the 22 million soldiers and 29 million civilians who died during World War II, the Soviet Union had suffered by far the largest losses: nearly 9 million military and 19 million civilian deaths between 1941 and 1945. Historians estimate that more than 11 million people had been displaced during the war. Flight, expulsion, and forced resettlement of millions were part of postwar reality. The United Nations Relief and Rehabilitation Administration (UNRRA), created in 1943, tried to address this challenge and facilitated the return of some 6–7 million displaced persons by the end of 1945, but two years later, approximately 850,000 displaced persons (DPs) still lived in camps across Europe. These DPs were mainly Jewish and other survivors of concentration and death camps, forced laborers, and POWs of different nationalities. Adding to the crisis, about 12 million Germans and Austrians were expelled from various Eastern Europeans countries between 1944 and 1950, for which not UNRRA, but at first the German administrations in the Allied occupations zones, and, from 1949, the two newly founded Germans states were responsible.[47] Through the late 1940s, anticommunist refugees from Eastern Europe further contributed to the problem of resettlement.[48] The war had brought a hitherto unknown extent of devastation. Cities were in ruins. People were searching for shelter and starved. It would take years to rebuild postwar Europe in the East and West. The countries that had not experienced war on their own soil, especially the United States, had much better economic starting conditions for postwar reconstruction.

Politically, the end of the Second World War was the beginning of the new era of the Global Cold War (1946–91). The so-called Big Three—US President Harry Truman, Soviet leader Joseph Stalin, and British prime ministers Winston Churchill and, later, Clement Attlee—met in Yalta and Potsdam, respectively, in February and August 1945 to negotiate the terms for the postwar order and redraw the European map. Eastern Europe became part of the Soviet sphere of influence. Germany and Austria were divided into four occupation zones, each to be administered by one of the Allies: Britain, France, the Soviet Union, and the United States. The cities of Berlin and Vienna were similarly divided and occupied. In May 1949, the Cold War finally led to the split of Germany into two states, the German Democratic Republic in the east and the Federal Republic of Germany in the west. Austria, in contrast, stayed united because it declared its neutrality in October 1955.[49]

At the heart of the emerging Cold War was the competition between two political and economic systems: the authoritarian communist regimes in Eastern Europe under the Soviet umbrella versus the market democracies of the United States and its allies in Western Europe. To support the economic recovery of Western Europe, the United States initiated the Marshall Plan in April 1947, officially named the European Recovery Program, which provided financial aid to sixteen Western European states and Turkey for four years, including their former enemies in Austria, Italy, and West Germany. The program's goals were to rebuild the war-devastated countries, remove trade barriers between them, and modernize their industries with the hope of returning Western Europe to prosperity and preventing the spread of communism.[50] This program was desperately needed, because after the Second World War, much more than after the First World War, not only were the economic infrastructure and the whole transportation system in ruins everywhere on the European continent, but also housing was destroyed to a much larger extent. Between 1939 and 1945, at least 60 million European civilians had been uprooted from their homes through air strikes and ground combat. This made a quick clearing of the rubble and an efficient rebuilding of shattered cities and towns a necessity in the East and the West. But this reconstruction was much more challenging for the Eastern European countries and the Soviet Union, which had suffered a much higher level of destruction and devastation during the war.[51]

Demobilization after the Second World War and the gendering of postwar societies on both sides of what came to be called the "Iron Curtain" can only be understood in this historical context. Interestingly, despite all the differences from the postwar order after the First World War, the demobilization policies after the Second World War maintained a similar focus on the restoration of the prewar gender order with the breadwinner–homemaker family at its core to help facilitate a return to the so-called normality of the social order.[52] Furthermore, families were again supposed to heal the physical and mental wounds of war. It was above all the duty of women as mothers, wives, and daughters to integrate the returning veterans, invalids, and POWs into society via the family. Marriage and the family thus became private arenas for coping with the aftermath of war.

This was not just the case in Western postwar societies; the family also kept its importance in the communist regimes in the East. One example is the USSR, where, according to Mark Edele, war veterans' reintegration depended on the family unit, which was the basis for economic survival during the first postwar years. The wages of working women were a necessary part of the family income, and the state supported the decision of married women to continue paid work after the war. Unlike the Western governments that sent women home in the process of economic demobilization, Eastern states needed female workers for their recovering economies because of chronic labor shortages. They justified their policy of double-earner families through the socialist ideology of gender equality. However, this ideology never reached into the family, where the long-standing gendered division of labor continued and women were responsible for housework and childcare. The family remained a private sphere where the communist state had limited influence.[53]

With their focus on the family, the governments on both sides of the Iron Curtain tended to overlook the fact that after the Second World War, much like after the first, many women had to live alone. Because of the large number of fallen men, postwar societies confronted an increased percentage of single women in their population, widows, divorcées, and unmarried women, who all also had to earn their livelihood. In Germany, for example, in a population of some 70 million, there were 7 million more women than men in 1945. These so-called surplus women and their independence created social anxieties similar to those in the interwar period.[54] These concerns were fostered by the "surge" of divorces in the first years after World War II. The percentage of the divorced in the whole population increased in England only from 0.08 to 0.48 between 1931 and 1951, in France from 0.68 to 1.27, and in Germany from 0.76 to 1.79 in the East and 1.26 in the West. This was only a very small growth, but in public perception this development nevertheless became one indicator for an intensively debated postwar "crisis of the family," similar to the interwar period, during which the proportion of divorces had increased too. Other presumed indicators of the crisis of the family and with it society were wage-earning mothers and their "neglected" children, along with "unsupervised youth," especially orphans.[55]

One main difference from the era after World War I was that demobilization and reconstruction were marked by governments' greater attention to public opinion after 1945. Cold War tensions fostered a competition between the economic and political systems and encouraged the use of old and new mass media for propaganda to influence citizens' identification with the system in which they lived and worked. In this propaganda war, collective and individual identity was constructed against the Other of the opposing system. Family and gender roles became an important marker of difference in these efforts.[56]

Military Demobilization and the Integration of Veterans

As they had done in the First World War, governments of the main war powers prepared for military demobilization during World War II. However, only the American and British administrators were able to realize their plans after the Second World War, because their armed forces had emerged as the main victors. Both administrations had started to develop their demobilization plans already in 1943–44. The British government presented its plans to the public in September 1944. Officials tried to avoid the mistakes made after 1918, primarily the widespread abuse of the provision for sending men home earlier if their vocational training qualified them as necessary for reconstructing the postwar economy. This time, mainly military and political considerations informed the approach. To avoid discontentment among servicemen, servicewomen, and their relatives, the government used gender, age, and length of service as the main criteria to determine when troops would be discharged. Women in military service were supposed to be sent home first. The longer the male soldiers had served and the older they were, the sooner they would be mustered out. Those trained in occupations deemed "pivotal" to economic demobilization, especially those related to the construction of housing for veterans' families, would be released ahead of others, but this criterion was handled more stringently than after 1918. By December 1946, more than 4.25 million men and women had been released from British military service. Only 750,000 men remained in the armed forces.[57]

The US government also conducted demobilization after World War II with more of a take-charge attitude. Its experts had criticized what they characterized as the Wilson administration's laissez-faire approach after 1918 and felt that a "psychological demobilization" had been lacking. They emphasized that the American public demanded a demobilization that was both quick and fair. Like the British approach, gender, age, and length of service were the main criteria used in a point system. In June 1947, the number of US servicemen and servicewomen was reduced from 12 million in all war theaters to 1.5 million. This demobilization was so rapid that it threatened to create a shortage of manpower for the occupation of Germany and Japan. The unpopular draft was terminated in March 1947, but to meet Cold War challenges, it had to be restored through the Selective Service Act in June 1948.[58]

As recognition for their war service, the US government provided college education for returning veterans through the 1944 Servicemen's Readjustment Act (also known as the GI Bill) and loans for the purchasing of homes through its Veterans Housing Administration program, along with planned communities where veterans' wives and their growing numbers of baby-boom children would thrive. This policy, based on the heteronormative model of the breadwinner–homemaker family, was supposed to foster a consumer-oriented society and culture that would act as a strong bulwark against the communist threat during the Cold War.[59] The same ideas informed the American occupation policy in Germany and Japan after 1945 and, later in the context of the 1950s economic miracle, gained so much influence in Western Europe that sociologists speak of the "golden age" of the male-breadwinner family.[60] But different than in the United States, where the suburbs with one-family houses were growing, in postwar Europe the dream for most families was an apartment in one of the newly constructed modern housing developments. The housing crisis continued here in the East and the West until the 1960s.

Not all veterans in the United States, however, profited equally from the government's postwar policies. The postwar baby boom created a new emphasis on fatherhood for both Black and White men while at the same time subsidizing primarily White flight from America's inner cities and fueling segregation. The GI Bill, too, was mainly used for the funding of White veterans' college education. African American veterans felt that the promises of equal economic and social citizenship made during the war were not fulfilled. This and the increased sense of male pride they had gained during the war prompted them to fight for and defend their rights more assertively than before 1945. Many supported the developing civil rights movement.[61]

In other countries too, former veterans were feared as a potential source of unrest by politicians and parts of the public. In West Germany, for instance, the federal government gave special benefits to the returning veterans and POWs—former soldiers and officers of the Nazi Wehrmacht—to pacify them and integrate them in the society.[62] The USSR also feared the rebellious potential of the returning veteran. Here, an orderly demobilization, however, proved much more challenging, because the USSR had borne the brunt of war in the European theater. During the war, the Red Army had been by far the most powerful land army, with 10 to 13 million men and women in 1945. In the first year after the war, this number was reduced to about 5 million. Officially, the Soviet government demobilized wounded soldiers first and then proceeded according to age.[63] The newspaper of the Red Army, the *Red Star*, gave its troops the hope of a smooth transition to peace and a privileged future. It promised them not only that after their return they would feel the "love, care and attention of their fellow countrymen," but also that they would receive jobs suitable to their abilities and privileged access to housing, heating, and fuel.[64]

The promises made to the soldiers in the *Red Star* never materialized. The plans immediately proved to be unworkable. The first obstacle was the lack of transportation, which slowed down the mass demobilization of 1945–46 significantly and made it chaotic. The second was the level of destruction of industry and agriculture.[65] In these circumstances, the primary goal of the Soviet government became, according to Mark Edele, "to unmake veterans as a social group as fast as possible." The majority of the returning veterans had to quickly return to their lives as workers and peasants to help with the reconstruction of the ravaged cities and villages, factories, and farmlands.[66] The Soviet state granted its veterans, observed Edele, "special privileges only as long as mass demobilization was under its way. Once this massive upheaval was over and veterans had been reintegrated into civilian society without major security challenges, privileges were dismantled, and by 1948 veterans ceased to exist as an officially recognized status group." It took another thirty years before their status was again recognized in Soviet law.[67]

After the surrender of the Wehrmacht, its Austrian and German soldiers experienced a quite different fate. They became prisoners of the Allied forces, which perceived them as potential supporters of Nazism and militarism. Prisoners of war thus became one of the key target groups of the Allied demilitarization and democratization policies for defeated Germany. About four million German soldiers were still POWs in Europe in 1947, and they were used for forced labor in heavy industry, mining, and agriculture, chiefly in Belgium, Britain, France, the Soviet Union, Yugoslavia, Poland, and Czechoslovakia. Most were able to return home by 1948. But especially for POWs in the USSR, captivity meant up to ten years of forced labor under the worst conditions. The return of these POWs as "men in their prime," as Frank Biess has shown, played a central role as a projection surface for the formulation of a new ideal of Western masculinity in the age of Cold War. In West Germany, veterans returning from the Soviet Union were perceived as the population group—apart from the expelled Germans—who had been most affected by war and defeat. That perception, combined with their strong will to survive, return to their families, and provide for them, made the returnees a cultural model of masculinity for West German men. The paradox was, however, that similar to the interwar period, many of them returned home so sick or disabled that they could not function as breadwinners as expected, which made their reintegration into society difficult.[68]

Much like the approach taken after World War I, Western states, including the Federal Republic of Germany, took care of invalid soldiers, widows, and orphans after World War II, but the general expectation—felt even more strongly than after 1918—was that they should become useful members of society as soon as possible. The man as the provider and protector of his family developed into the dominant model of manhood in the Cold War 1950s.[69] The diminishing influence of a heroic notion of military masculinity and the decoupling of military service from male citizenship in countries like West Germany and the United States, which started after World War II, was, however, contested by conservatives and military leaders.[70]

"Regendering" Society by Economic and Cultural Demobilization

Even though the economic and political conditions that informed the demobilization policy of postwar states after 1945 differed from those after 1918, their attempts to "regender" economy, society, and culture were similar. The economic demobilization everywhere in the West again included forcing women out of their wartime jobs and back into the home.[71] When women were hired during World War II, they were informed that they would be employed only for the duration of the conflict. They were cautioned that they would have to return home to their families and, as Thomas Childers has summarized the language of the era, to their "first job as wife and mother" after victory.[72] Such advice reflected the concern that the independence women had gained during the war would continue afterward, which was not without reason. Both men and women had changed because of their experiences at home and on the front.[73] Much as was the case during the interwar years, one of the repeated, major fears of post-1945 societies was the independent, wage-earning woman whose rise had been driven by the war.

Statistics indicate, however, that contrary to common assumptions, the First and Second World Wars did not contribute to a dramatic increase in female full-time work over the course of the twentieth century. The wars instead fostered a change of the sectors and branches in the economy in which women did full-time paid work, from the agriculture and domestic services to industry, trade, and the service sector. The percentage of women aged between fifteen and sixty-five in the paid labor force increased slowly but steadily over the course of the twentieth century: in the United States from 24 percent in 1920, to 29 percent in 1950, to 35 percent in 1960.[74] By contrast, in 1950, 77 percent of Soviet women between the ages of twenty and fifty-four were part of the workforce.[75] In West Germany, the percentage of women in the paid labor force rose from 27 percent in 1925 to 30 percent in 1950 and 47 percent in 1960. In East Germany, the increase was much greater. In 1953, 53 percent of the women were employed. In 1970, 66 percent of women earned wages, whereas in the West the figure had only increased to 48 percent in the same year.[76] Generally in postwar Eastern Europe, the percentage of women in the labor force was much higher than in Western Europe and the United States because of the continuing labor shortages and a different labor market policy that encouraged the paid work of married women and mothers.

The economic demobilization by the postwar states was facilitated by cultural demobilization. Postwar propaganda promised a quick return to normality. Mass media played a central role in the promotion of this hope, which they had begun to propagate during the war.[77] One example is an advertisement from 1942 in the American *LIFE* magazine, which assured its readers, "Beyond the War Waits Happiness." The accompanying image clearly defines this "happiness" as the nuclear family in its own suburban home.[78] Such promises were realized most quickly in the postwar United States. While the American economy had flourished during the war, European economies had withered, and the European continent faced a postwar housing crisis of unprecedented dimensions. In this situation, the realization of the suburban dream, with its shiny consumerism, was much further out of reach for the average Western European couple.[79] But even in America, domestic bliss did not await all demobilized soldiers or their families. The promises of a happy, prosperous family, which symbolized the postwar ideal, often failed to materialize, especially for African American veterans.

Post-1945 culture was fraught with violence in all involved countries, but in different ways than after World War I. It was not so much organized paramilitary violence in public spaces, but individual violence in the private sphere that seemed to have increased after World War II. In a study on Great Britain, Alan Allport outlined the rising tide of armed domestic violence that followed demobilization after 1945.[80] He maintained, "Men acclimatized to violence on behalf of the state were, it seemed, finding it hard to restrain the instincts that had been released by war."[81] We still know too little about the personal repercussions of war for soldiers and civilians, including the effects of post-traumatic stress disorder on both groups.[82]

One traumatic war and postwar experience for women was sexual violence, especially rape, which was perpetrated not only by Wehrmacht soldiers, but also by Allied soldiers. The mass rapes by the Red Army are well known, but new studies show that soldiers of the Western Allies also committed acts of sexual violence. This research further indicates that the borders between sexual violence and other forms of sexual interactions between soldiers and women were fluid. Women who had relations with Allied or occupying soldiers were often perceived negatively in postwar societies, and their children experienced lasting discrimination, especially when they were of a different race.[83]

CONCLUSION

The two twentieth-century world wars were fought largely by modern states with an efficient administration and highly industrialized economies. After the wars, governments took advantage of the institutions and bureaucracies already in place from the war by repurposing them for demobilization and, at least in Europe, for the development and extension of welfare states, much-needed for the reconstruction and reorganization of the economy and society. These welfare states in the East and the West were based on a gendered and hierarchical division of labor. They relied on the notion of clearly defined gender roles in the economy and society in their attempt to ensure that demobilization occurred in as smooth a manner as possible. However, this was only possible in a paradoxical way, as Margaret and Patrice Higonnet argued in their classic 1987 text "The Double Helix," in which they used the concept of the *double helix* for the explanation of the development of gender relations from war to postwar times. Demobilization policies and related labor, social, and family policies tried to restore a gender order based on a clear gender division of labor in the economy, society, and the family that had been eroded during war, but war experiences had nevertheless transformed everyday gender relations.[84] As a result, from a long-term perspective, the predominant ideas about the gender order with the ideal of the breadwinner–homemaker family model at its center changed too.

In the West, this ideal informed demobilization and postwar policies with respect to the labor market, welfare, and the family during both postwar periods, but its specific molding transformed after the Second World War. In the 1950s, the image of the "New Housewife," in its beginnings already visible during the interwar period, dominated in the mass media. She was consumer oriented, well informed about "modern," scientific approaches to health and child care, able to rationalize her housework, good looking, and a partner to her hard-working husband. From the late 1950s on, this image even allowed wives and mothers to take on part-time work to cover the expenses of increased private consumption. More and more families tried to live this putative ideal of the modern family in the West, which was made possible by the speedy recovery and the economic boom that started in the 1950s. Within the context of the Cold War, the model consumer family became a crucial marker of the West's differences from the communist societies in the East. Their leaders conversely used the socialist ideals of the emancipated working woman and mother and the dual-earner family to emphasize the progressiveness of their system.[85]

The respective dominant ideas about the gender order, however, stood in contrast to everyday life for millions of women. In the West, single, divorced, and widowed, but also many married women and mothers still had to work full time to earn their own and their family's living. In the East, married working women, especially mothers, often still experienced within the family the old patriarchal attitude of their partner, who left the responsibility for household and family to their wives. In the systems on both sides of the Iron Curtain, patriarchal structures, behaviors, and attitudes prevailed in politics, the economy, society, and culture. But the number of women who contested the dominant gendered division of labor and the related gender hierarchy and to varying degrees refused to comply with the hegemonic notions of the respective gender order was increasing in the East and West—well before the development of second-wave feminism in the West in the late 1960s.[86]

Notes

1. For a debate of the concept of total war, see the chapter by Karen Hagemann and Sonya O. Rose on "War and Gender: The Age of the World Wars and Its Aftermath—an Overview" in this handbook.

2. See Konrad H. Jarausch, *Out of Ashes: A New History of Europe in Twentieth Century* (Princeton, NJ: Princeton University Press, 2015), esp. 102–54 and 369–451. For Europe after 1945, see also Tony Judt, *Postwar: A History of Europe since 1945* (New York: Penguin Books, 2005), esp. 13–62; and Keith Lowe, *Savage Continent: Europe in the Aftermath of World War II* (New York: Picador, 2013).

3. See Benjamin F. Walter, *France and the Après Guerre, 1918–1924: Illusions and Disillusionment* (Baton Rouge: Louisiana State University Press, 1999); Richard Bessel, *Germany after the First World War* (New York: Oxford University Press, 1993); Rex Pope, "British Demobilization after the Second World War," *Journal of Contemporary History* 30, no. 1 (1995): 65–81; and Adam R. Seipp, *The Ordeal of Peace: Demobilization and the Urban Experience in Britain and Germany, 1917–1921* (Burlington, VT: Ashgate, 2009); on World War II, see Jack Stokes Ballard, *The Shock of Peace: Military and Economic Demobilization after World War II* (Washington, DC: University Press of America, 1983); and Alan Allport, *Demobbed: Coming Home after the Second World War* (New Haven, CT: Yale University Press, 2009).

4. Wolfgang Schivelbusch, *The Culture of Defeat: On National Trauma, Mourning, and Recovery* (New York: Metropolitan Books, 2003), esp. 1–36 and 189–288; Allport, *Demobbed*, 23; and Seipp, *Ordeal of Peace*, 3.

5. See for example, Arthur Marwick, *Women at War 1914–1918* (London: Croom Helm, 1977).

6. For World War I and its aftermath see, for example, Ute Daniel, *The War from Within: German Working-Class Women in the First World War* (Oxford: Berg, 1997), German original published 1989; Angela Woollacott, *On Her Their Lives Depend: Munitions Workers in the Great War* (Berkeley: University of California Press, 1994); Laura Lee Downs, *Manufacturing Inequality: Gender Division in the French and British Metalworking Industries, 1914–1939* (Ithaca, NY: Cornell University Press, 1995); Susan R. Grayzel, *Women's Identities at War: Gender, Motherhood, and Politics in Britain and France during the First World War* (Chapel Hill: University of North Carolina Press, 1999); and Grayzel, "Women and Men," in *Companion to World War I*, ed. John Horne (Chichester: Wiley–Blackwell, 2010), 263–78.

7. Karen Hagemann, *Frauenalltag und Männerpolitik: Alltagsleben und Gesellschaftliches Handeln von Arbeiterfrauen in Der Weimarer Republik* (Bonn: J.H.W. Dietz, 1990); and Penny Summerfield, *Reconstructing Women's Wartime Lives: Discourse and Subjectivity in Oral Histories of the Second World War* (Manchester: Manchester University Press, 1998).

8. See Susan Kent, *Making Peace: The Reconstruction of Gender in Interwar Britain* (Princeton, NJ: Princeton University Press, 1993); Susanne Rouette, *Sozialpolitik als Geschlechterpolitik: Die Regulierung der Frauenarbeit nach dem Ersten Weltkrieg* (Frankfurt am Main: Campus, 1993); Mary Louise Roberts, *Civilization without Sexes: Reconstructing Gender in Postwar France, 1917–1927* (Chicago: University of Chicago Press, 1994); Deborah Cohen, *The War Come Home: Disabled Veterans in Britain and Germany, 1914–1939* (Berkeley: University of California Press, 2001); Erika Kuhlman, *Reconstructing Patriarchy after the Great War: Women, Gender and Postwar Reconciliation between Nations* (New York: Palgrave Macmillan, 2008); Kuhlman, *Of Little Comfort: War Widows, Fallen Soldiers, and the Remaking of the Nation after the Great War* (New York: New York University Press, 2012);

and Angela Smith, *Discourses Surrounding British Widows of the First World War* (London: Bloomsbury Academic, 2013). See also the chapters by Susan R. Grayzel, "Total Warfare, Gender, and the 'Home Front' in Europe during the First and Second World Wars," and Kimberly Jensen on "Citizenship and Gender on the American and Canadian Home Fronts during the First and Second World Wars" in this handbook.

9. See Elizabeth Wilson, *Only Halfway to Paradise: Women in Postwar Britain, 1945–1968* (London: Tavistock, 1980); Jane Lewis, *Women in Britain since 1945: Women, Family, Work, and the State in the Post-War Years* (Oxford: Blackwell, 1992); Erica Carter, *How German Is She? Postwar West German Reconstruction and the Consuming Woman* (Ann Arbor: University of Michigan Press, 1997); Petra Goedde, *GIs and Germans: Culture, Gender, and Foreign Relations, 1945–1949* (New Haven, CT: Yale University Press, 2003); Frank Biess, *Homecomings: Returning POWs and the Legacies of Defeat in Postwar Germany* (Princeton, NJ: Princeton University Press, 2006); Greta Bucher, *Women, the Bureaucracy and Daily Life in Postwar Moscow, 1945–1953* (Boulder, CO: East European Monographs, 2006); Marianne Zepp, *Redefining Germany: Reeducation, Staatsbürgerschaft und Frauenpolitik im US-Amerikanisch besetzten Nachkriegsdeutschland* (Göttingen: Vandenhoeck & Ruprecht, 2007); Anna Schnädelbach, *Kriegerwitwen: Lebensbewältigung zwischen Arbeit und Familie in Westdeutschland nach 1945* (Frankfurt am Main: Campus, 2009); and Rebecca Pulju, *Women and Mass Consumer Society in Postwar France* (New York: Cambridge University Press, 2011).

10. See Margaret R. Higonnet and Patrice L.-R. Higonnet, "The Double Helix," in *Behind the Lines: Gender and the Two World Wars*, ed. Margaret R. Higonnet et al. (New Haven, CT: Yale University Press, 1987), 31–50.

11. See Claire Duchen and Irene Bandhauer-Schöffmann, eds., *When the War Was Over: Women, War, and Peace in Europe, 1940–1956* (London: Leicester University Press, 2000); Frank Biess and Robert Moeller, eds., *Histories of the Aftermath: The Legacies of the Second World War in Europe* (Oxford: Berghahn Books, 2010); Ingrid Sharp and Matthew Stibbe, eds., *Aftermaths: Women's Movements and Female Activists, 1918–1923* (Leiden: Brill, 2011); Joanna Regulska and Bonnie G. Smith, eds. *Women and Gender in Postwar Europe: From Cold War to European Union* (London: Routledge, 2012); Julia Eichenberg and John Paul Newman, *The Great War and Veterans' Internationalism* (Basingstoke: Palgrave Macmillan, 2013); and Karen Hagemann and Sonya Michel, eds., *Gender and the Long Postwar: The United States and the Two Germanys, 1945–1989* (Baltimore: Johns Hopkins University Press, 2014).

12. Hagemann and Rose, "War and Gender" in this handbook.

13. Laura Spinney, *Pale Rider: The Spanish Flu of 1918 and How It Changed the World* (New York: Public Affairs, 2017).

14. See the chapter by Frank Biess on "Gendering the Memories of War and Holocaust in Europe and the United States" in this handbook.

15. For a comparative perspective, see Herbert Obinger and Klaus Peteresen, "Mass Warfare and the Welfare State: Causal Mechanisms and Effects," *British Journal of Political Science* 47, nr. 1 (2017): 203–77; and Hartmut Kaelble, *Kalter Krieg und Wohlfahrtsstaat: Europa 1945–1989* (Munich: Beck, 2011).

16. Robert Gerwarth, *The Vanquished: Why the First World War Failed to End* (London: Allen Lane, 2016).

17. See Belinda J. Davis, *Home Fires Burning: Food, Politics, and Everyday Life in World War I Berlin* (Chapel Hill: University of North Carolina Press, 2000); and Maureen Healy, *Vienna*

and the Fall of the Habsburg Empire: Total War and Everyday Life in World War I (Cambridge: Cambridge University Press, 2004).

18. See Robert Gerwarth, *Die größte aller Revolutionen: November 1918 und der Aufbruch in eine neue Zeit* (Munich: Siedler, 2018).

19. Margaret MacMillan, *Peacemakers: The Paris Conference of 1919 and Its Attempt to End War* (London: J. Murray, 2001); and Eckart Conze, *Die grosse Illusion: Versailles 1919 und die Neuordnung der Welt* (Munich, 2018).

20. Margaret Pawley, *The Watch on the Rhine: The Military Occupation of the Rhineland, 1918–1930* (London: I. B. Tauris, 2007); and Peter Collar, *The Propaganda War in the Rhineland: Weimar Germany, Race and Occupation after World War I* (London: I. B. Tauris, 2013).

21. Evan Mawdsley, *The Russian Civil War* (Edinburgh: Birlinn, 2000); and Vladimir N. Brovkin, *Behind the Front Lines of the Civil War: Political Parties and Social Movements in Russia, 1918–1922* (Princeton, NJ: Princeton University Press, 1994).

22. Robert Gerwarth and John Horne, eds., *War in Peace: Paramilitary Violence in Europe after the Great War* (Oxford: Oxford University Press, 2012), esp. Gerwarth and Horne, "Paramilitarianism in Europe after the Great War: An Introduction," 1–20.

23. Gerwarth, *The Vanquished*, 1–18.

24. See Gerwarth, *Die größte aller Revolutionen.*

25. James M. Diehl, *Paramilitary Politics in Weimar Germany* (Bloomington: Indiana University Press, 1977); and Dirk Schumann, *Political Violence in the Weimar Republic, 1918–1933: Fight for the Streets and Fear of Civil War* (New York: Berghahn Books, 2009).

26. George L. Mosse, *Fallen Soldiers: Reshaping the Memory of the World Wars* (New York: Oxford University Press, 1990), esp. 159–81.

27. Robert Gerwarth, "Fighting the Red Beast: Revolutionary Violence in Defeated States of Central Europe," in Gerwarth and Horne, *War in Peace*, 52–72; and Emilio Gentile "Paramilitary Violence in Italy: The Rationale of Fascism and the Origins of Totalitarianism," in ibid., 86–110.

28. Benjamin Ziemann, *Contested Commemorations: Republican War Veterans and Weimar Political Culture* (Cambridge: Cambridge University Press, 2013); and Cohen, *The War.*

29. Julia Eichberg, "Veterans' Associations," *1914–1018 Online,* accessed January 17, 2016, http://encyclopedia.1914-1918-online.net/article/veterans_associations.

30. See Robert W. Whalen, *Bitter Wounds: German Victims of the Great War, 1914–1939* (Ithaca, NY: Cornell University Press, 1984); on war invalids, see also Heather R. Perry, *Recycling the Disabled: Army, Medicine, and Modernity in WWI Germany* (New York: Manchester University Press, 2014).

31. Walter, *France*, 26–27.

32. Kuhlman, *Of Little Comfort*, 79, 83; and Karin Hausen, "The German Nation's Obligation to the Heroes' Widows of World War I," in Higonnet, *Behind the Lines*, 126–40.

33. Lauterbach, "Economic Demobilization," 248.

34. Lucy Noakes, "Demobilising the Military Woman: Constructions of Class and Gender in Britain after the First World War," in *Gender & History* 19, no. 1 (2007): 143–62; Rouette, *Sozialpolitik*, 35–36; Rouette, "Mothers and Citizens: Gender and Social Policy in Germany after the First World War," *Central European History* 30, no. 1 (1997): 48–66; and Hagemann, *Frauenalltag*, 430–45.

35. Hagemann, *Frauenalltag*, 430–45.

36. Perry, *Recycling*; and Sabine Kienitz, "Body Damages: War Disability and Constructions of Masculinity in Weimar Germany," in *Home/Front: The Military, War, and Gender in Twentieth-Century Germany*, ed. Karen Hagemann and Stefanie Schüler-Springorum (Oxford: Berg, 2002), 181–204.

37. Melanie Ilic, *Women Workers in the Soviet Interwar Economy: From "Protection" to "Equality"* (Basingstoke: Macmillan, 1999); and Barbara Evans Clements, "Working-Class and Peasant Women in the Russian Revolution, 1917–1923," *Signs* 8, no. 2 (1982): 215–35.

38. See Biess "Gendering the Memories" in this handbook.

39. Lisa M. Budreau, *Bodies of War: World War I and the Politics of Commemoration in America, 1919–1933* (New York: New York University Press, 2009); Daniel J. Sherman, *The Construction of Memory in Interwar France* (Chicago: University of Chicago Press, 1999); Karen Petrone, *The Great War in Russian Memory* (Bloomington: Indiana University Press, 2011); and Manfred Hettling and Jörg Echternkamp, eds., *Gefallenengedenken im globalen Vergleich: Nationale Tradition, politische Legitimation und Individualisierung der Erinnerung* (Munich: Oldenbourg, 2013).

40. Budreau, *Bodies of War*, 233–35.

41. See the chapter by Annegret Fauser on "Gendered War Mobilization, Culture, and Music in the Age of World Wars" in this handbook.

42. Kuhlman, *Of Little Comfort*, 126–34; see also the chapter by Jensen on "Citizenship and Gender" in this handbook.

43. Kuhlman, *Of Little Comfort*, 131–49.

44. Atina Grossmann, *Reforming Sex: The German Movement for Birth Control and Abortion Reform, 1920–1950* (New York: Oxford University Press, 1995); Cornelie Usborne, *Cultures of Abortion in Weimar Germany* (New York: Berghahn Books, 2007); Clare Debenham, *Marie Stopes' Sexual Revolution and the Birth Control Movement* (Cham: Palgrave Pivot, 2018); and Peter Engelman, *A History of the Birth Control Movement in America.* (Santa Barbara, CA: Praeger, 2011).

45. Igor S. Kon, *The Sexual Revolution in Russia: From the Age of the Czars to Today* (New York: Free Press, 1995), 39–50.

46. Birthe Kundrus, "Gender Wars: The First World War and the Construction of Gender Relations in the Weimar Republic," in Hagemann and Schüler-Springorum, *Home/Front*, 159–79; and Alys Eve Weinbaum et al., eds., *The Modern Girl around the World: Consumption, Modernity, and Globalization* (Durham, NC: Duke University Press, 2008).

47. Jarausch, *Out of Ashes*, 369–451; Judt, *Postwar*, 13–62; and William I. Hitchcock, *The Bitter Road to Freedom: A New History of the Liberation of Europe* (New York: Free Press, 2008). On flight, expulsion, and displaced persons, see Atina Grossmann, *Jews, Germans, and Allies: Close Encounters in Occupied Germany* (Princeton, NJ: Princeton University Press, 2007); R. M. Douglas, *Orderly and Humane: The Expulsion of the Germans after the Second World War* (New Haven, CT: Yale University Press, 2012); Gerard D. Cohen, *In War's Wake: Europe's Displaced Persons in the Postwar Order* (New York: Oxford University Press, 2012); and Tara Zahra, *The Lost Children: Reconstructing Europe's Families after World War II* (Cambridge, MA: Harvard University Press, 2011).

48. Cohen, *In War's Wake*, 6.

49. Michael Neiberg, *Potsdam: The End of World War II and the Remaking of Europe* (New York: Basic Books, 2015).

50. Francesca Fauri and Paolo Tedeschi, eds., *Novel Outlooks on the Marshall Plan: American Aid and European Re-Industrialization* (Bruxelles: Peter Lang, 2011).

51. Jeffry M. Diefendorf, "Urban Reconstruction in Europe after World War II," *Urban Studies* 26 (1989): 126–43; and Virág Eszter Molnár, *Building the State: Architecture, Politics, and State Formation in Post-War Central Europe* (London: Routledge, 2013).

52. For the West, see Wilson, *Only Halfway*; Elaine Tyler May, *Homeward Bound: American Families in the Cold War Era* (New York: Basic Books, 1988); Lewis, *Women*; Robert Moeller, *Protecting Motherhood: Women and the Family in the Politics of Postwar Germany* (Berkeley: California University Press, 1993); Elizabeth Heineman, *What Difference Does a Husband Make? Women and Marital Status in Nazi and Postwar Germany* (Berkeley: University of California Press. 1999), and Pulju, *Women and Mass Consumer*.

53. Mark Edele, *Soviet Veterans of the Second World War: A Popular Movement in an Authoritarian Society, 1941–1991* (New York: Oxford University Press, 2008), 71. For the East see, more generally, Bucher, *Women*; Katarina Katz, *Gender, Work and Wages in the Soviet Union: A Legacy of Discrimination* (New York: Palgrave, 2001); Donna Harsch, *Revenge of the Domestic: Women, the Family, and Communism in the German Democratic Republic* (Princeton, NJ: Princeton University Press, 2007); and Malgorzata Fidelis, *Women, Communism, and Industrialization in Postwar Poland* (Cambridge: Cambridge University Press, 2010); as well as Duchen and Bandhauer-Schöffmann, *When the War*; and Regulska and Smith, *Women*.

54. For the First World War, see Virginia Nicholson, *Singled Out: How Two Million British Women Survived without Men after the First World War* (New York: Oxford University Press, 2008); for the Second World War, see Heineman, *What Difference*.

55. See Franz Rothenbacher, *The European Population 1850-1945* (New York: Palgrave Macmillan, 2002), 245, 281 and 720; Franz Rothenbacher, *The European Population since 1945* (New York: Palgrave Macmillan, 2005), 271, 318, 319 and 862; and as an exemplary study Heineman, *What Difference*, 108–37.

56. See Hagemann and Michel, "Introduction: Gender and the Long Postwar— Reconsiderations of the United States and the Two Germanys, 1945–1989," in Hagemann and Michel, *Gender*, 1–30.

57. Pope, "British Demobilization," 68–75.

58. Ballard, *Shock of Peace*, 11 and 194–95.

59. May, *Homeward Bound*, 1–10; and Suzanne Mettler, *Soldiers to Citizens: The G.I. Bill and the Making of the Greatest Generation* (Oxford: Oxford University Press, 2005).

60. See Franz-Xaver Kaufmann and Hans-Joachim Schulze, "Comparing Family Life in the Frame of National Policies: An Introduction," in *Family Life and Family Policies in Europe*, vol. 2, *Problems and Issues in Comparative Perspective*, ed. Franz-Xaver Kaufmann et al. (Oxford: Oxford University Press, 2002), 1–18, 1.

61. See Steve Estes, "Man the Guns: Race Masculinity and Citizenship from World War II to the Civil Rights Movement," in Hagemann and Michel, *Gender*, 185–206; Jennifer E. Brooks, *Defining the Peace: World War II Veterans, Race, and the Remaking of Southern Political Tradition* (Chapel Hill: University of North Carolina Press, 2004); and Robert Francis Saxe, *Settling Down: World War II Veterans' Challenge to the Postwar Consensus* (New York: Palgrave Macmillan, 2007).

62. James M. Diehl, *The Thanks of the Fatherland: German Veterans after the Second World War* (Chapel Hill: University of North Carolina Press, 1993), esp. 87–163.

63. Ibid., 22–23.

64. Edele, *Soviet Veterans*, 21.

65. Ibid., 11.

66. Ibid., 11; and Edele, "Soviet Veterans as an Entitlement Group, 1945–1955," *Slavic Review* 65, no. 1 (2006): 111–37.

67. Edele, "Soviet Veterans," 111.

68. Biess, *Homecomings*, esp. 118; and Biess, "Men of Reconstruction—the Reconstruction of Men: Returning POWs in East and West Germany, 1945–1955," in Hagemann and Schüler-Springorum, *Home/Front*, 335–59; more generally, Bob Moore and Barbara Hately-Broad, eds., *Prisoners of War, Prisoners of Peace: Captivity, Homecoming, and Memory in World War II* (Oxford: Berg, 2005).

69. Robert G. Moeller, "Heimkehr ins Vaterland: Die Remaskulinisierung Westdeutschlands in den fünfziger Jahren," *Militärgeschichtliche Zeitschrift* 60, no. 2 (2001): 403–36; and May, *Homeward Bound*.

70. Friederike Brühöfener, "Sending Young Men to the Barracks: West Germany's Struggle over the Establishment of the New Armed Forces in the 1950s," in Hagemann and Michel, *Gender*, 145–65; and Amy Rutenberg, "Service by Other Means: Changing Perceptions of Military Service and Masculinity in the United States, 1940–1973," in ibid., 165–84.

71. As a case study, see Laura McEnaney, "A Women's Peace Divided: Demobilization and Working Class Women in Chicago, 1945–1953," in Hagemann and Michel, *Gender*, 73–94.

72. See Thomas Childers, *Soldier from the War Returning: The Greatest Generation's Troubled Homecoming from World War II* (Boston: Mariner Books, 2010), 94–95; and Allport, *Demobbed*, 66.

73. Allport, *Demobbed*, 66.

74. Nancy Woloch, *Women and the American Experience* (New York: Alfred A. Knopf, 1984), 469 and 543.

75. Jiri Kosta, "Beschäftigungsprobleme in zentral-administrativen Planungssystemen," in *Struktur- und Stabilitätspolitische Probleme in alternativen Wirtschaftssystemen*, ed. Jiri Kosta et al. (Berlin: Duncker & Humblot, 1974), 92.

76. Ulla Knapp, "Frauenarbeit in Deutschland zwischen 1850 und 1933," *Historical Social Research* 8, no. 4 (1983): 42–82, 61; and Karen Hagemann and Konrad H. Jarausch, eds., *Halbtags oder Ganztags? Zeitpolitiken von Kinderbetreuung und Schule nach 1945 im europäischen Vergleich* (Weinheim: Beltz-Juventa, 2015), 354 and 462.

77. Pope, "British Demobilization," 78; Penny Summerfield, "Public Memory or Public Amnesia? British Women of the Second World War in Popular Films of the 1950s and 1960s," *Journal of British Studies* 48, no. 4 (2009): 935–57; and Elizabeth Heineman, "The Hour of the Woman: Memories of Germany's 'Crisis Years' and West German National Identity," *American Historical Review* 101, no. 2 (1996): 354–95.

78. Robert B. Westbrook, "Fighting for the American Family: Private Interests and Political Obligation in World War II," in *The Power of Culture: Critical Essays in American History*, ed. T. J. Jackson Lears and Richard Wightman Fox (Chicago: University of Chicago Press, 1993), 195–221.

79. See Paul Betts and David Crowley, "Introduction," in "Domestic Dreamworlds: Notions of Home in Post-1945 Europe," ed. Paul Betts and David Crowley, special issue, *Journal of Contemporary History* 40, no. 2 (2005): 213–36.

80. Allport, *Demobbed*, 173–76.

81. Ibid., 1–3 and 85.

82. Ibid., 85; for Germany, Svenja Goltermann, *The War in Their Minds: German Soldiers and Their Violent Pasts in West Germany* (Ann Arbor: University of Michigan Press, 2017); on World War I, Paul F. Lerner, *Hysterical Men: War, Psychiatry, and the Politics of Trauma in*

Germany, 1890–1930 (Ithaca, NY: Cornell University Press, 2003); Peter Leese, *Shell Shock: Traumatic Neurosis and the British Soldiers of the First World War* (New York: Palgrave, 2002); and Charles S. Myers, *Shell Shock in France, 1914–1918* (Cambridge: Cambridge University Press, 2011).

83. Norman M. Naimark, *The Russians in Germany: A History of the Soviet Zone of Occupation, 1945–1949* (Cambridge, MA: Belknap Press, 1995), 69–140; Heide Fehrenbach, *Race after Hitler: Black Occupation Children in Postwar Germany and America* (Princeton, NJ: Princeton University Press, 2005); Mary Louise Roberts, *What Soldiers Do: Sex and the American GI in World War II France* (Chicago: University of Chicago Press, 2013); and Miriam Gebhardt, *Crimes Unspoken: The Rape of German Women at the End of the Second World War* (Cambridge, MA: Polity Press, 2017). See also the chapter by Regina Mühlhäuser on "Sexuality, Sexual Violence, and the Military in the Age of the World Wars" in this handbook.

84. Margaret R. Higonnet and Patrice L. R. Higonnet, "The Double Helix," in Higonnet, *Behind the Lines*, 31–47.

85. May, *Homeward Bound*, 16–20. See also Hagemann and Rose, "War and Gender" in this handbook.

86. One example is Leila J. Rupp and Verta Taylor, *Survival in the Doldrums: The American Women's Rights Movement from 1945 to the 1960s* (New York: Oxford University Press, 1987).

SELECT BIBLIOGRAPHY

Allport, Alan. *Demobbed: Coming Home after the Second World War*. New Haven, CT: Yale University Press, 2009.

Biess, Frank, and Robert Moeller, eds. *Histories of the Aftermath: The Legacies of the Second World War in Europe*. Oxford: Berghahn Books, 2010.

Budreau, Lisa M. *Bodies of War: World War I and the Politics of Commemoration in America, 1919–1933*. New York: New York University Press, 2009.

Childers, Thomas. *Soldier from the War Returning: The Greatest Generation's Troubled Homecoming from World War II* (Boston: Mariner Books, 2010).

Cohen, Deborah. *The War Come Home: Disabled Veterans in Britain and Germany, 1914–1939*. Berkeley: University of California Press, 2001.

Cohen, Gerard D. *In War's Wake: Europe's Displaced Persons in the Postwar Order*. New York: Oxford University Press, 2012.

Duchen, Claire, and Irene Bandhauer-Schöffmann, eds. *When the War Was Over: Women, War, and Peace in Europe, 1940–1956*. London: Leicester University Press, 2000.

Edele, Mark. *Soviet Veterans of the Second World War: A Popular Movement in an Authoritarian Society, 1941–1991*. Oxford: Oxford University Press, 2008.

Gerwarth, Robert. *The Vanquished: Why the First World War Failed to End*. London: Allen Lane, 2016.

Gerwarth, Robert, and John Horne, eds. *War in Peace: Paramilitary Violence in Europe after the Great War*. Oxford: Oxford University Press, 2012.

Hagemann, Karen, and Sonya Michel, eds. *Gender and the Long Postwar: The United States and the Two Germanys, 1945–1989*. Baltimore: Johns Hopkins University Press, 2014.

Higonnet, Margaret Randolph, Jane Jenson, Sonya Michel, and Margaret Collins Weitz, eds. *Behind the Lines: Gender and the Two World Wars*. New Haven, CT: Yale University Press, 1987.

Jarausch, Konrad H. *Out of Ashes: A New History of Europe in Twentieth Century*. Princeton, NJ: Princeton University Press, 2015.

Judt, Tony. *Postwar: A History of Europe since 1945*. New York: Penguin Books, 2005.

Leese, Peter. *Shell Shock: Traumatic Neurosis and the British Soldiers of the First World War*. New York: Palgrave, 2002.

Lerner, Paul F. *Hysterical Men: War, Psychiatry, and the Politics of Trauma in Germany, 1890-1930*. Ithaca, NY: Cornell University Press, 2003.

Lowe, Keith. *Savage Continent: Europe in the Aftermath of World War II*. New York: Picador, 2013.

Myers, Charles S. *Shell Shock in France, 1914-1918*. Cambridge: Cambridge University Press, 2011.

Petrone, Karen. *The Great War in Russian Memory*. Bloomington: Indiana University Press, 2011.

Regulska, Joanna, and Bonnie G. Smith, eds. *Women and Gender in Postwar Europe: From Cold War to European Union*. London: Routledge, 2012.

Roberts, Mary Louise. *Civilization without Sexes: Reconstructing Gender in Postwar France, 1917-1927*. Chicago: University of Chicago Press, 1994.

Seipp, Adam R. *The Ordeal of Peace: Demobilization and the Urban Experience in Britain and Germany, 1917-1921*. Burlington, VT: Ashgate, 2009.

Ziemann, Benjamin. *Contested Commemorations: Republican War Veterans and Weimar Political Culture*. Cambridge: Cambridge University Press, 2013.

CHAPTER 25

....

GENDERING THE MEMORIES OF WAR AND HOLOCAUST IN EUROPE AND THE UNITED STATES

....

FRANK BIESS

THE concept of *memory* is central to the historiography of the post-1945 period. After three decades, the memory-studies boom since the 1990s has abated. It has yielded, however, a rich literature on the memories of World War II (1939–45) and the Holocaust.[1] Remembering (or forgetting) an extremely violent past constituted an essential preoccupation of individuals and societies in the aftermath of the Second World War. Indeed, in some cases memory has become a primary analytical category of the "new cultural history" and has often advanced to the central organizing principle of local or national studies.[2]

The research has refined the concept of memory, theoretically and conceptually. We now recognize memory as more than a representational category; it is an active social force that shapes rather than reflects social relations.[3] A series of excellent case studies on the gendering of memory in the postwar period notwithstanding, the intersection between memory and *gender* has remained undertheorized and underexplored.[4] There are at least three ways in which memories of war and genocide were, in fact, gendered in the postwar period. First, as the broader theoretical literature on memory has made clear, *history* and *memory* are different, yet related concepts.[5] As culturally sanctioned narratives about the past, collective memories serve social and ideological purposes in the present, but memories arbitrarily invented with reference only to present needs lack plausibility. They need to reflect, at least partially, actual historical experiences.[6] While distinctly male and female wartime experiences thus informed memories, postwar memory also distorted or completely elided some specifically male or female experiences. Collective memories reflected the symbolic and social needs of postwar reconstruction, especially the reordering of gender relations. At the same time, as an active social force, memories also shaped the symbolic reconstitution of masculinity and femininity and hence helped to define men's and women's social positions in postwar society.[7]

Second, gender influenced the selectivity of postwar memory. The history of memory has gradually moved from a critique of deficient memory to an empirical reconstruction of actual commemorative practices.[8] In other words, historical research has evolved from an often psychoanalytically informed critique of repression and amnesia to an emphasis on the selectivity of postwar memory. The national narratives that societies told about themselves after World War II drew on certain social experiences, which they then universalized as a *pars pro toto* for the society as a whole.[9] Gender affected which experiences were incorporated into public memories. An analysis of gendered memories of war and genocide thus raises the following questions: When and for what purpose did predominantly male or female experiences become the basis for national narratives about the past? Which male and female experiences have certain societies universalized and made representative of the national experience as a whole? Conversely, which male or female experiences retained their specifically gendered nature in postwar memory and to what effect?

Third, gender structured the relationship between public and private memory. Historians of memory have repeatedly cautioned against a nonmetaphorical use of French philosopher and sociologist Maurice Halbwachs's concept of *collective memory*. While Halbwachs's insight of memory as socially conditioned has been foundational for memory studies, ultimately only individuals have the capacity to remember.[10] Individual and collective, private and public memories were therefore never completely identical but remained in a state of constant tension and interrelationship. In fact, the discrepancy between private and public memories constituted one of the shared characteristics of all postwar societies. This division between public and private memories has always been gendered. In line with the historic construction of public as male and private as female, public memories of the postwar period often drew only on distinctly male experiences. The exclusion of women's experiences from public memories persisted until second-wave feminism in the 1970s began to challenge the particularly masculine and feminine coding of public and private memories.

The wartime experiences in different regions of the globe during World War II were vastly different, which in turn influence the collective war memories after 1945: the Soviet Union and the "bloodlands" in eastern Europe, as Timothy Snyder labeled them, where the bulk of killing and dying in World War II occurred; Italy and Germany as the major defeated fascist nations; western Europe with a brief military history and an extensive history of occupation, collaboration, accommodation, and resistance to Nazi Germany; Great Britain as the only major European country that remained at war with Nazi Germany throughout the conflict; and finally the United States, where wartime violence never reached the mainland. Postwar memories in these countries thus represented and responded to a wide variety of wartime experiences. The new ideological and geopolitical context of the Global Cold War (1946–91) produced differently gendered memories as well. Yet despite these widely divergent wartime experiences between (and within) belligerent societies and notwithstanding the ideological antagonism of the Cold War, gendered memories of World War II also exhibited some surprising similarities. As Pieter Lagrou has noted, the rather homogenous experience of the 1914–18 First World War (at least in western Europe) yielded very heterogeneous memories, whereas the very heterogeneous experiences of World War II paradoxically produced relatively homogenous memories.[11]

The homogeneity of gendered memories across national boundaries resulted, at least in part, from the similar functions of memories of the Second World War for the reconstruction of gender relations under way in many nations. The Second World War had rendered virtually obsolete the traditional notion that men protect women from wartime violence. The belligerents had targeted civilians to an unprecedented extent, and women had become a prime category of victims. At the same time, the wartime economies considered here all mobilized women and drew them into the workforce by both coercive and voluntary means. Women also assumed active military roles that ran the gamut from women's auxiliaries in the United States to women in active combat roles in the Soviet Union. One goal of such memories of World War II was therefore the reconstruction of an oppositional, strictly delineated order for men and women, a hallmark of a prewar normalcy to which societies longed to return.[12]

The following explores the gendering of collective memories from 1945 to the early twenty-first century with a focus on the whole of Europe, including the Soviet Union, and North America. Three themes stand in the center: the formation of patriotic memories centering on the predominately male figures of the "martyr," "victim," and "victor"; the transformation of public memory with a focus on the figure of the "male survivor" since the 1960s; and the ensuing gendering of Holocaust memory.

PATRIOTIC MEMORIES AND NATIONAL RECONSTRUCTION

The reconstruction of gender relations was inextricably intertwined with the project of postwar national reconstruction. Europeans (and Americans) did not bid farewell to nationalism after 1945. Instead, the nation-state reached a culmination in the decades after World War II. The flight and expulsion of at least twelve million ethnic Germans from Eastern Europe, the expulsion of Poles from Soviet territories, and the Italian flight and expulsion from Istria and Dalmatia, among other population displacements, created, for the first time in modern European history, more or less ethnically homogenous nation-states.[13] National belonging thus assumed an existential dimension in Europe after the Second World War. Memories of World War II served the essential purpose of reforging the links between national identity, on the one hand, and a hierarchical and oppositional gender order on the other, which had informed the construction of national identities from the early nineteenth century onward.[14]

The reconstruction of national identities and gender hierarchy, however, proved daunting. In most of Nazi-occupied Europe, memories of accommodation to or collaboration with Nazi Germany had fractured national identities. In western and southern Europe, a series of violent civil wars between collaborationist and antifascist forces produced deep internal divisions.[15] In eastern Europe and the Soviet Union, where collaboration was minimal because of Nazi racism, unprecedented experiences of irretrievable loss and mass death disrupted the reconstruction process. In central Europe, the Federal Republic of Germany in the West and the German Democratic Republic in the East needed to construct national identities in opposition to one another as well as the Third Reich. Great Britain and the United States faced the task of reconciling heightened expectations raised by the lofty rhetoric of wartime unity with persistent inequalities along the fault lines of race, gender, and class.[16]

As is often the case in times of crisis and internal fragmentation, especially in postwar periods, gender became a primary site for the reconstruction of national identities after 1945. Given the quick and utterly catastrophic defeat of most European countries by the German army, postwar memories drew on experiences of civilians as well as soldiers. Three emblematic figures occupied a central place: the martyr, the victim, and the victor.[17] Defeated and occupied nations sought to transform military defeat into a retrospective moral victory through the figures of the martyr and the victim; the United States, Great Britain, and the Soviet Union emphasized the victor. By coding all three figures as male, official patriotic memories of World War II marginalized or even erased women's experiences.

In western and northern Europe, the martyr embodied the resistance. While the resistance had limited military significance for the defeat of Nazism, in countries such as France, Italy, the Netherlands, Norway, Poland, and Yugoslavia, the memory of the resistance had a key role in promoting national reconciliation. It incorporated representatives of the entire political spectrum, from communists and socialists to liberals and conservatives, including Protestants and Catholics; it elided divisive histories of accommodation and collaboration; and it externalized guilt to the former Nazi occupiers.[18] While women participated extensively in the different resistance movements, memory figured the martyr everywhere as almost exclusively male.[19] Italian director Roberto Rossellini's classic film *Roma città aperta* (*Rome—Open City*) (1945) contrasts two male martyrs—the communist Manfredi and the Catholic priest Don Pietro—with treacherous Italian women and an effeminate and potentially homosexual German Gestapo chief. The film thus aligns heroism and martyrdom with masculinity and heterosexuality and codes fascism and collaboration as feminine and homosexual. Dying of wounds inflicted through Gestapo torture, Manfredi assumes a Christ-like posture, invoking deeply religious notions of Christian sacrifice as part of the male hero-martyr.[20] This myth of a male heroic resistance ultimately also served as compensation for the experience of imperial decline. French soldiers often conceived of their military service in defense of European colonial rule after 1945 in Algeria and elsewhere in continuity with their previous participation in antifascist resistance movements during the war.[21]

The victim served as another reference point for patriotic memories in the postwar period. In constructing this figure, public memories deliberately elided the key difference between deportation to prisoner of war (POW), labor, or concentration camps, incorporating different forms of internment in a broader narrative of victimization.[22] This narrative also increasingly obscured the difference between forced deportation and voluntary labor service. It ultimately extended to postwar West Germany as well, where public memories equated the internment of approximately three million German POWs in Soviet captivity with the imprisonment of Nazi victims in concentration camps. Redemptive elements of perseverance and survival under extremely adverse conditions tempered memories of suffering and internment. In West Germany, public memories depicted "returnees" (*Heimkehrer*) in the context of the Cold War as noble survivors of totalitarianism who had learned important moral and political lessons in captivity—eliding the POWs' former role as soldiers of Hitler's army. These redemptive elements made it possible to reconcile memories of suffering and victimization with demilitarized ideals of postwar masculinity as fathers and husbands.[23]

For the Allied victors of World War II, more traditional memories of military sacrifice and heroism assumed a greater significance in the person of the victor. Official monuments to World War II in the United States—from the Marine Corps Memorial depicting the raising of an American flag on Iwo Jima dedicated in 1954 to the central World War II memorial in Washington, DC, constructed fifty years later—celebrated male heroism and triumphant victory.[24] This monumentalism eclipsed other forms of commemoration, such as the notion of living memorials that were supposed to improve life through art and community centers.[25] Great Britain, too, privileged the male soldier and the experience of combat in public memories. Both Western countries, however, also sought to distance themselves from the perceived hypermasculinity of the fascist enemy and cultivated the image of a rational, emotionally reticent, and restrained heroism of the soldier-citizen.[26] Perhaps as a way to compensate for staggering casualties, numbering approximately twenty-seven million, Soviet commemorations went furthest in the heroization of the Second World War—and of the mostly male soldiers who fought it— as the "Great Patriotic War." The military victory of the Red Army served as a historical justification for the Bolshevik Revolution and also prompted a Russian-centered ethnic nationalism.[27] This heroic memory of the Red Army's liberation of eastern Europe from fascist occupation, then, also served as central ideological justification for the imposition of communist rule in the Soviet sphere of influence after 1945.[28]

The symbolic validation of distinctly male experiences in postwar public memory stood in stark contrast to the feminization of negative experiences of defeat and collaboration and/or the erasure of the gendered character of specifically female experience. After the defeat of the Left in the Greek Civil War (1946–49), for example, the victorious right-wing government, which was backed by Great Britain and the United States, vilified female members of the Greek resistance against the Nazi occupation as "amoral" and subjected them to persecution and internment.[29] While postwar memories repressed women's participation in European resistance movements, they increasingly feminized collaboration. All over former Nazi-occupied Europe, from France to

Norway and Finland, mobs publicly humiliated women for allegedly having had sex with German occupiers. Approximately 20,000 *tontes* occurred in France, in which men sheared the heads of and paraded women accused of having had sexual relationships with German soldiers, a massive demonstration of reclaiming virile identity.[30] West Germans derided women accused of sleeping with American occupation soldiers as "fraternizers," deeming them emblems of Germany's defeat and loss of sovereignty.[31] By contrast, other gender-specific experiences of German women, such as being subjected to mass rape by Soviet soldiers during the last stages of the war, assumed an increasingly universal, degendered significance in postwar memory and signified the nation's victimization.[32] The Soviet Union did not entirely erase the experience of hundreds of thousands of female combat soldiers, but tried to suppress it and cast it as a deviation, thereby reducing the disruptive potential of such gendered identities.[33]

Memories of World War II thus actively shaped a broader social and symbolic remasculinization of postwar societies.[34] While male experiences became an integral part of postwar patriotic narratives, postwar societies deployed a variety of strategies to elide women's presence in the national narratives about the Second World War. These narratives either marginalized or repressed women's wartime experiences altogether; they associated women's experiences with defeat and collaboration; or they deprived women's experience of their distinctly gendered nature (while highlighting the masculine component of symbolically more central male experiences, such as combat or participation in the resistance). Gendered memories also made it difficult for women to remember and articulate their important roles during the war. In Norway, for example, former female resistance fighters tended to categorize their contribution to the resistance as merely auxiliary compared to that of their male comrades.[35] Such reconstitutions of national identity imposed direct material consequences on women's positions in postwar societies. Male-centered memories of heroic victory informed the passage of the Servicemen's Readjustment Act of 1944 (known as the GI Bill) in the United States, which provided a range of benefits for returning World War II veterans and overwhelmingly helped White male soldiers.[36] The notion of a *people's war* with a united home front in Great Britain spurred the establishment and expansion of the welfare state structured to restore men's role as educated citizens, breadwinners, and heads of households.[37] As such, the degendering of women's wartime experiences or their association with defeat and occupation delegitimized women's claims to a public role and assisted their containment in the private sphere.

Gendered memories, however, did not lead to a wholesale restoration of an ancien régime with respect to expectations of men and women. Military masculinities declined or were deliberately fashioned as compatible with a democratic state, as in the West German notion of the "citizen in uniform."[38] An emerging transnational veterans' culture in Western Europe transformed the traditional male notion of *comradeship* into a more civilian, less martial concept for social gatherings, crossing national borders in the interest of international reconciliation.[39] Militarized masculinities survived to a greater extent in Eastern Europe and the Soviet Union, where they were integrated into the new masculine ideal of the antifascist fighter.[40] Similar continuities also existed in countries that were further engaged in warfare, such as Israel and the United States.[41] Several Western European countries faced the conundrum of having to justify military practices of violent digressions in "dirty" colonial wars in Africa and Asia that they were simultaneously criminalizing in war-crime trials focused on former German Wehrmacht soldiers.[42]

Gendered memories also could not completely repress women's memories of extensive mobilization during the war throughout the West. Much as had happened during the period after World War I, after World War II several more countries saw the introduction of women's suffrage in the postwar years, including France (1944), Italy and Yugoslavia (1945), Portugal (1946), Belgium (1948), and Greece (1952). In postwar Chicago, women insisted on a "peace dividend" for their wartime service by making claims to the postwar state for affordable housing.[43] In Eastern Europe and the Soviet Union, a massive demographic imbalance—in Polish cities, the proportion of women to men was 124 to 100—necessitated the ongoing employment of women in postwar industry.[44] And because communist countries did not endow the "family" with the same ideological investment as the West, "single women" did not become a distinct category subject to discriminatory state policies and social ostracism in the East.[45] Still, wartime losses prompted a transnational emphasis on reproduction, motherhood and the family, and pronatalism in all former belligerent nations, including the Soviet Union, which reinforced the opposition between masculine and feminine and imposed not only severe double burdens on women, but promoted similar to the West, their relegation to the private sphere.

Patriotic memories of World War II also served another essential function with important gendered implications: the erasure of violence. On both the Allied and the Axis sides, the male hero-victim was supposed to emerge from the war as perhaps briefly shaken but essentially unscathed and ready to fully participate in the work of reconstruction. A transnational psychiatric consensus largely rejected the existence of prolonged psychic suffering as a result of wartime violence and thus contributed to the disavowal of violence in postwar memory.[46] Hegemonic ideals of masculinity in Europe and the United States validated stoicism, resilience, and productivity and hence left little room for individual psychic suffering as a result of the war. The US notion of *combat fatigue* went perhaps furthest in recognizing war-induced psychic suffering, but the only treatment required was a little rest.[47] The persistent psychological and mental consequences of unprecedented violence were displaced onto the private sphere, where they remained present within postwar families, leaving it to women to facilitate men's readjustment to civilian life and to cope with any physical or psychological impairment.[48] Postwar expectations of a stoic and resilient masculinity fully capable of participating in the reconstruction economies thus often diverged from the lived experiences of physically or mentally disabled men. A broader recognition of psychic trauma did not occur until the late 1950s, primarily with respect to Holocaust survivors; the notion of posttraumatic stress disorder emerged only in the aftermath of the Vietnam War.[49]

The redemptive and heroic quality of patriotic memories also produced what in retrospect appears to be the greatest deficit in postwar memory: the virtual absence of the Holocaust. Patriotic and antifascist memories were essentially forward looking. Indiscriminate suffering and mass death among civilians—Jewish and non-Jewish—simply did not lend themselves to the project of national reconstruction.[50] In the communist East, a broader antifascist narrative highlighted male active resistance against Nazism and failed to recognize the specificity of Jewish suffering. Even in the newly founded Jewish state of Israel, which had declared its establishment on May 14, 1948, the emaciated and victimized Holocaust survivors did not initially fit into the Zionist narrative of Jewish resistance and reconstruction.[51] The particularly gendered nature of the Holocaust contributed to this omission. Patriotic and antifascist memories in East and West disproportionately drew on male experiences of heroic resistance or redemptive suffering, whereas women and children constituted a large segment of Holocaust victims. Holocaust memory was also actively repressed, as in postwar Poland where ethnic Poles launched a series of antisemitic pogroms, in part to prevent Holocaust survivors from seeking to reclaim stolen property.[52] The memory of the Holocaust existed only in local, private, and often religious contexts. Jewish women in particular played a central role in developing a communal memory of the Holocaust that differed markedly from the dominant masculinist narratives of the postwar period. Yet these commemorations largely failed to enter official public memories.[53]

THE TRANSFORMATION OF PUBLIC MEMORY

From the 1960s onward, public memories of war and genocide in Western Europe and the United States underwent dramatic transformations. Parallel memories in Eastern Europe, by contrast, remained largely static. Three changes were especially significant, and all of them had important implications for the gendering of memory. First, postwar patriotic memories that had largely elided questions of guilt, collaboration, and complicity in Nazi crimes eroded, which unraveled the male hero-victim as the emblematic figure of World War II. Second, Holocaust memory began to emerge as the central aspect of memories of World War II. This development inaugurated what Annette Wieviorka termed the "era of the witness"—that is, an extensive cultural recognition of Holocaust survivors.[54] While Holocaust memory now endowed the survivor with virtually universal significance, it was almost exclusively based on male testimony. Third, beginning in the 1970s, second-wave feminism highlighted gendered memories of World War II and the Holocaust. Feminist scholarship brought into focus women's experience in World War II and therefore increasingly undermined masculine narratives. By the 1990s, feminist perspectives also began to inspire new research by historians and literary critics on the gendered experience and commemoration of the Holocaust.[55]

These dramatic changes in Western commemorative cultures had multiple causes. The political stabilization of postwar societies and the gradual relaxation of Cold War tensions from the mid-1960s onward helped to open new discursive spaces for societal introspection and thus enabled a more critical memory of the Second World War. The renewed legal prosecution of Nazi perpetrators, such as the trial of German Adolf Eichmann, one of the leading Nazis responsible for the organization of the Holocaust, in Jerusalem (1961–62) and the Frankfurt Auschwitz trial (1963–65), reflected this process. To be sure, Nazi trials produced their own distorted memories by, for example, emphasizing sadistic torture as the legally pertinent offense over systematically organized genocide.[56] The performative dimension of Nazi trials also always entailed inherently gendered representations of (mostly male) Nazi perpetrators.[57] Prosecutors and media coverage portrayed defendants as "sadists" and "torturers" or as bureaucrats and "cogs in the wheel."[58] Both representations reflected anxieties about contemporary masculinities—Nazi perpetrators represented either a propensity for violence and cruelty located beneath the veneer of bourgeois respectability or a larger decline of masculine agency within bureaucratic modernity.[59] By contrast, the convictions of the few women prosecuted as Nazi perpetrators, such as Ilse Koch in the 1950–51 Augsburg trial for atrocities perpetrated at the Buchenwald concentration camp and Hildegard Lächert in the 1975–81 Düsseldorf trial of guards from the extermination camp at Majdanek, often reflected traditional masculine and feminine stereotypes. Verdicts castigated these women for entering the male world of the camps and thereby abandoning the female qualities of empathy and caring.[60]

The renewed attention to and emergence of (predominantly male) Nazi perpetrators went along with an increased awareness of collaboration and hence a decline of the myth of a resistance in Western Europe. Central to the (re)discovery of collaboration were the activities of filmmakers such as Marcel Ophuls (*The Sorrow and the Pity*, 1969) and historians such as Robert O. Paxton, whose *Vichy France: Old Guard and New Order, 1940–44* (1971, French translation 1973) revealed the domestic, voluntary motives behind the association of Marshal Philippe Pétain, the head of state of Vichy France, with Nazi Germany. The myth of a distinctly female collaboration declined as collaboration within the historically male spheres of politics, business, or the military came into focus.[61] Decolonization was another context for the emergence of a critical memory of World War II: masculinist patriotic memories no longer needed to serve as symbolic compensation for imperial decline; emerging anticolonial movements within the West often also advocated a more critical introspection of their nations' past during the Second World War.[62] By contrast, in Eastern Europe and the Soviet Union the antifascist master narrative remained largely intact, even though films and literature, such as Soviet author Konstantin Simonov's novel *The Living and the Dead* (1959) and its continuations *Soldiers Are Made, Not Born* (1963–64) and *The Last Summer* (1970–71), began to cautiously address the massive human costs of the Soviet war effort.[63] The limitations of these changes, however, became apparent when in 1959 the Soviet KGB "arrested" the manuscript of Soviet writer and journalist Vasily Grossman, *Life and Fate*, which also addressed the Jewish and the gendered dimensions of the war on the eastern front. The book was eventually smuggled into the West; it was not published in the Soviet Union until 1988.[64]

This challenge to male-dominated, patriotic memories also manifested itself in the transnational generational conflicts of the 1960s. While the focus of the protest movement in the United States was the war in Vietnam, student activists in Western Europe assigned a direct political relevance to memories of an authoritarian and fascist past.[65] In adopting a Marxist framework for their understanding of fascism, however, they largely failed to recognize the specificity of Jewish suffering and embraced a rather masculinist emphasis on antifascist resistance. Following the theories of the Austrian psychoanalyst Wilhelm Reich, student activists identified sexual repression with fascism and therefore propagated a close association between antifascist politics on the one hand and the sexual revolution on the other. Antifascist gender politics thus often entailed a renewed subjugation of women within the New Left and, as a result, became an impetus for second-wave feminism.[66]

The gradual disintegration of patriotic memories of World War II from the 1960s onward paved the way for the most important development in the history of memory after 1945: the emergence of the Holocaust as the central element in public memories of World War II in Western Europe and the United States. As Peter Novick has shown, the Six-Day War in Israel in 1967 touched off a search for a common bond among increasingly assimilated Jews in the United States and Western Europe, which an emerging Holocaust consciousness supplied.[67] But the increasing public presence of and receptivity to Holocaust testimony may have been more important. In the wake of the Eichmann trial, the "survivor" emerged as the central figure of a new commemorative regime.[68] Psychiatrists and cultural commentators in the United States and Western Europe no longer viewed persistent psychological suffering as a result of prolonged Nazi persecution and internment among Holocaust survivors as antithetical to prevailing notions of masculinity, and the broad transnational recognition of psychic trauma endowed the figure of the primarily male survivor with scientific legitimacy.[69]

A new culture of emotional expressiveness enabled a greater degree of emotional empathy and hence provided an important context for the new cultural receptivity toward Holocaust survivors. Whereas courts and professional historians had often deemed the allegedly emotional testimony of Holocaust survivors unreliable and biased, popular culture increasingly viewed emotional expressiveness as an indication of a healthy and authentic self.[70] The highly emotional popular reaction to the American television miniseries *Holocaust*, first released in the United States in 1978 and shown in Germany and elsewhere during the late 1970s and early 1980s, marked a turning point in the evolution of a broader Holocaust consciousness.[71] The masculine ethics of stoicism and the public disavowal of suffering now gave way to an ethics of broad emotional empathy with Nazi victims that historically had been associated with feminine subjectivity.

These developments in Western commemorative culture were integrally linked to the rise of second-wave feminism in the 1970s. Feminism brought into focus the specifically female experiences of war and genocide that had been repressed for two decades. Feminist historical scholarship paved the way in adding "herstory" to the history of World War II.[72] This included, above all, a greater recognition of women's contributions to survival in war and postwar, as well as to military mobilization and resistance activities.[73] In the United States, the figure of Rosie the Riveter became a symbol for women's empowerment during the war, denoting an emancipation that women might have achieved in the early postwar period, but did not.[74] In similar ways, the "women of the rubble" (*Trümmerfrauen*) in West Germany assumed iconic status in facilitating the Federal Republic's recovery, not least to secure retroactive pension claims for women's public service during the immediate postwar period.[75]

Feminist scholars also challenged previously degendered narratives and began to discuss gender-specific violence against women, especially the mass rape of German women by Soviet soldiers from the final stages of the war through the early postwar period. These projects confronted both women's victimhood and their complicity in fascism and wartime violence.[76] Whereas earlier feminist interventions had often highlighted women's positive contributions to the war effort, feminist historians now began to analyze the intersection between "race" and "gender" in defining women's wartime role. Were German women victims of a patriarchal regime *qua* gender, as German historian Gisela Bock argued?[77] Or did their shared non-Jewish status also implicate them in the racist policies of the Nazi regime, as American historian Claudia Koonz countered?[78] This debate, the so-called transatlantic *Historikerinnenstreit* (female historians' quarrel), led to an intensive exploration of the roles of women in Nazi Germany from victims and resisters to bystanders and perpetrators and inspired innovative new research that ultimately also addressed ethnic German women's complicity with the Nazi regime and participation in ethnic cleansing and genocide.[79]

Feminist perspectives eventually also contributed to the gendering of the survivor. Survival narratives, especially of the death camps in the east, tended to be male and were therefore seen as representative.[80] While men had been more likely to be killed during the mass shootings of the early stages of the Holocaust, they stood better chances than women to survive the death camps in the east, largely because the Nazis valued their capacity for hard labor. According to Raul Hilberg, one-third of Auschwitz's survivors were female, while few or no women survived the extermination camps in Belzec, Chelmno, Treblinka, and Sobibor.[81] The most prominent female Holocaust narrative, the diary by Anne Frank, which was first published in English translation in 1952, told the story of a German-born girl who went into hiding in Amsterdam in 1942 but was eventually discovered and deported by the Nazis in 1944. She died in the Bergen-Belsen camp in February 1945. Her narrative is that of a passive victim in contrast to classic male Holocaust narratives, such as the memoirs by the Romanian-born Elie Wiesel, who survived the Auschwitz, Buna, and Buchenwald camps. His *Night* (published in 1958 in French and in 1960 in English) denoted male agency and survival.[82]

Another early and prominent female survivor narrative was the three-part autobiography by Charlotte Delbo about her imprisonment in Auschwitz. A non-Jewish French woman, Delbo was deported to this death camp as a member of the French resistance in January 1943 and from there to the all-women's concentration camp in Ravensbrück, north of Berlin. Although she had already written the text in 1946/47, Delbo did not publish it until the second half of the 1960s as part of her critique of the French war in Algeria.[83] While Delbo explicitly rejected the label of "woman writer" and denied that there was a "distinctive female experience of the Holocaust," the editors of a 1998 volume on *Women in the Holocaust* described her work as indicative of instances of "kinship and friendship, bonding with other women" in the camps.[84]

This gendering of the survivor, however, was controversial. Lawrence Langer, for example, denounced the notion of a specifically female bonding in the camps as an attempt to "replace truth with myth." He emphasized an "ultimate sense of loss [that] unites former victims in a violated world beyond gender."[85] Langer's critique notwithstanding, feminist scholarship has also corrected earlier tendencies toward idealizing women as "better survivors" by demonstrating how the camp system destroyed female bonds and pitted women against women. Feminist perspectives, furthermore, have informed a critique of gender-neutral commemoration, such as in the United States Holocaust Memorial Museum in Washington, DC, founded in 1980.[86]

Commemorative efforts that include women's experiences often replicate a binary gender order. Janet Liebman Jacobs, for example, criticized an exhibition about women at Auschwitz for reinscribing "the bifurcating images of endangered motherhood and sexual captivity"—a memory that obscures women's resistance, reinforces their sexual objectification, and enables male voyeurism.[87] Feminist perspectives have brought into focus the gender-specific aspects of the persecution of male Jews as well. Circumcision served as a marker of Jewishness, and Nazi violence often also entailed sexual humiliation of men by cutting beards or targeting genitalia.[88] The Nazi challenge to Jewish masculinity entailed the inability of Jewish men to protect women and children. In one of the few Holocaust narratives written with a distinctly feminist bent, Austrian Auschwitz survivor Ruth Klüger, for example, blames "the old prejudice that women are protected by men" for "overlooking what was most obvious, that is, that the weakest and the disadvantaged are the most exposed," and asks whether "the concept of chivalry so outshine[d] that of racism in the minds of our people?"[89]

The gendering of the survivor has significantly advanced our understanding of the Holocaust. Male- and female-specific suffering did not constitute the only or even the most important aspect of victimization in the Holocaust. But feminist perspectives have demonstrated how, according to Sara Horowitz, the "unmaking of the gendered self" undermined traditional notions of both femininity and masculinity.[90] In this view, gendered persecution becomes an integral aspect of the dehumanization of both men and women in the Holocaust.

GENDERING CONTEMPORARY MEMORIES
OF WAR AND GENOCIDE

Whereas significant transformations in the memory of World War II since the mid-1960s had facilitated the emergence of Holocaust memory, after 1989 Holocaust memory became paradigmatic for the memory of World War II in Europe and the United States. While a broader sensitivity for gendered suffering was at the heart of Holocaust memory from the 1980s onward, similar tendencies manifest themselves in contemporary memories of World War II. Since 1993, the Neue Wache (New Guardhouse) in the center of Berlin serves as the "Central Memorial of the Federal Republic of Germany for the Victims of War and Dictatorship." The memorial features the *pietà*-like sculpture *Mother with Her Dead Son* by German painter and sculptor Käthe Kollwitz, which she had originally finished in a much smaller size in 1937 in memory of her son Peter, who had died in World War I. The creation of the *pietà* represented a minimal consensus of (Christianized) victimhood in German memories of World War II that was supposed to include all victim categories, including Jewish Holocaust survivors, ethnic German expellees, and victims of Allied bombing and Nazi persecution. It harkened back to the grieving mother as a female—and thoroughly dehistoricized and anthropologized—allegory for the nation as it had emerged already in the late nineteenth and early twentieth centuries, especially the period after World War I.[91]

One important tendency in contemporary memories of war and Holocaust is therefore the expansion of victim categories based on the model of the paradigmatic Holocaust victim. Specific groups of Nazi victims, above all eastern European slave workers, but also Sinti and Roma, male homosexuals, victims of medical murder, Wehrmacht deserters, and so on, now demanded and received both commemorative recognition and often material compensation for their suffering in World War II. At the same time, the end of the Cold War and the proliferation of victim identities have enabled previously private memories to enter public discussion. Scandinavia gradually became able to recognize private consequences of German occupation during World War II, such as the approximately 10,000 to 12,000 occupation children born to Norwegian women who had sexual relations with German occupation soldiers. As markers of defeat and collaboration, these *krisgbarn* (war children) often suffered discrimination and ostracism in the postwar period. Surveys of occupation children in neighboring Denmark in 1997 and 2003 revealed that more than half of them did not know their fathers.[92]

Along similar lines and following the notion of an intergenerational transmission of trauma among Holocaust survivors, a group of German war children (and eventually even grandchildren) directed attention at their ongoing psychic suffering as a result of wartime violence.[93] The popular receptivity for the claims of the war children indicates the dramatic change in conceptions of male subjectivity compared to the 1950s. While the concept of war-induced "trauma" was widely rejected in the early postwar period, it has become central to the construction of the male (and female) subjectivity of the early twenty-first century, notwithstanding an unprecedented period of half a century of peace in Europe.[94]

In Eastern Europe and the Soviet Union, the collapse of communism and the end of the Cold War opened discursive spaces for a more critical memory of war and genocide since the 1990s, including its gendered aspects. In Poland, female Holocaust survivors began to tell their stories as well, yet they did so in ways markedly different from male survivors—according to Aleksandra Ubertowska, more "private, exotic, hyperemotional and above all ironic."[95] Moreover, the collapse of the Soviet empire made it possible to address Red Army soldiers' violent transgressions against eastern European civilians, such as, for example, the rape of Hungarian women.[96] However, the construction of anti-antifascist memories of Eastern Europe as part of the attempt to invent patriotic memories for the new postcommunist nations also included a troubling rehabilitation of interwar authoritarianism and even fascism, most notably in Romania, Poland, and Hungary, but also in northern and western Europe.[97]

Historians have only begun to investigate the role of gender in the formation of such post–Cold War memories.[98] In Finland, the post-1989 period witnessed the rehabilitation of hitherto private memories of nationalist and anticommunist women who had been organized in the Lotta Svärd league, which was a volunteer auxiliary paramilitary organization for women that originally formed in 1918.[99] In Italy, surviving widows and children of German World War II massacres blamed Italian partisans for provoking German reprisal measures against innocent Italian civilians. These women stood for a more passive *attendismo* as the morally more appropriate response to Nazi occupation in World War II than active and masculinist antifascist resistance.[100] Not accidentally, this more critical view of the Italian resistance coincided with the rise of a postfascist party in Italian national politics.

CONCLUSION

While gendered memories of the Second World War and the Holocaust thus continue to proliferate, their ongoing significance for political decisions in the present and visions of the future is unclear. To be sure, Holocaust memory served as direct justification for unified North Atlantic Treaty Organization military intervention in the Yugoslav Wars during the 1990s.[101] In the United States, the ongoing (and increasing) valorization of World War II veterans as the (all-male) "greatest generation" emerged as a cultural response to an increasingly multicultural society. In response to the much more ambivalent postwar history with morally more ambiguous wars, the construct of the greatest generation reflects a widespread nostalgia for moral clarity as well as for a restrained yet nevertheless heroic heterosexual masculinity.[102] In Vladimir Putin's Russia, the memory of the Great Patriotic War (1941–45) serves unabashedly as ideological justification for a new, rather masculinist Russian expansionism. Yet political observers tend to compare the ongoing conflict in Ukraine to the Cold War rather than to World War II. This shift might indicate that, with the gradual dying of the last survivors seventy years after the war's end, gendered memories of World War II are completing the transition from the more fluid and oral "communicative" memory to the more fixed "cultural memory" and hence will assume less direct political relevance.[103]

Gendered memories of World War II and the Holocaust, however, continue to offer multiple opportunities for further research. Three areas seem especially promising: First, despite some extensive research in recent years, we still know too little about the ways in which men and women's private memories of the war and genocide structured postwar subjectivities and shaped family lives. "Communicative memory," as Sylvia Paletschek and Sylvia Schraut argue, "allows for more space for the representation of women than cultural memory."[104] More studies of communicative memories thus might help to correct the male bias of public memories in the early postwar period and can provide further insights regarding the process by which public memories erased women's experiences and/or re-entered them at a later date. Second, despite the central significance of national contexts for postwar memories, the gendered nature of sub- and supranational memories deserves more attention. To what extent do transnational transfers and connections, for example between veterans' or survivor organizations, replicate the exclusion of women's experience? What are the gendered components of a broader European memory of the Second World War and the Holocaust? Finally, the relationship between gendered memories of war and Holocaust and extra-European developments has not yet been studied extensively. Did the masculinist patriotic narratives of the early postwar period seek to compensate for European imperial decline and the onset of decolonization? In what ways, if at all, did gendered representations of World War II inform European and American colonial and postcolonial wars after 1945? And finally, what were (and continue to be) the gendered meanings of memories of the Second World War and the Holocaust for the immigrant populations within Europe?

NOTES

1. Gavriel D. Rosenfeld, "A Looming Crash or a Soft Landing? Forecasting the Future of the Memory 'Industry,'" *Journal of Modern History* 81, no. 1 (2009): 122–58; Kerwin Lee Klein, "On the Emergence of Memory in Historical Discourse," *Representations* 69 (2000): 127–50; for Germany, see the literature review by Robert G. Moeller, "What Has 'Coming to Terms with the Past' Meant in Post–World War II Germany? From History to Memory to the 'History of Memory,'" *Central European History* 35, no. 2 (2002): 223–56.
2. Alon Confino, "Collective Memory and Cultural History: Problems of Method," *American Historical Review* 102, no. 5 (1997): 1386–403; and Neil Gregor, *Haunted City: Nuremberg and the Nazi Past* (New Haven, CT: Yale University Press, 2008).
3. Alon Confino and Peter Fritzsche, "Introduction: Noises of the Past," in *The Work of Memory: New Directions in the Study of German Culture and Society*, ed. Confino and Fritzsche (Urbana: University of Illinois Press, 2002), 1–24.
4. See, for example, Elizabeth Heineman, "The Hour of the Woman: Memories of Germany's 'Crisis Years' and West German National Identity," *American Historical Review* 101, no. 2 (1996): 354–95. For an exception, see Sylvia Paletschek and Sylvia Schraut, eds., *The Gender of Memory: Cultures of Remembrance in Nineteenth- and Twentieth-Century Europe* (Frankfurt: Campus, 2008).
5. Peter Burke, "History as Social Memory," in *Memory: History, Culture and the Mind*, ed. Thomas Butler (Oxford: Basil Blackwell, 1989), 97–113.
6. On this and the gendering of memory recently, see Karen Hagemann, *Revisiting Prussia's Wars against Napoleon: History, Culture, and Memory* (Cambridge: Cambridge University Press, 2015).
7. See also for the following the chapter by Karen Hagemann on "History and Memory of Female Military Service in the Age of World Wars," and Hagemann, "Gender,

Demobilization, and the Reordering of Societies after the First and Second World Wars" in this handbook.

8. See, for example, Robert G. Moeller, *War Stories: The Search for a Usable Past in the Federal Republic of Germany* (Berkeley: University of California Press, 2001).

9. On this notion, see Pieter Lagrou, *The Legacy of Nazi Occupation: Patriotic Memory and National Recovery in Western Europe, 1945–1965* (Cambridge: Cambridge University Press, 2000), 251.

10. Jay Winter and Emmanuel Sivan, "Setting the Framework," in *War and Remembrance in the Twentieth Century*, ed. Sivan and Winter (New York: Cambridge University Press, 1999), 6–39; and Susan A. Crane, "Writing the Individual Back into Collective Memory," *American Historical Review* 102, no. 5 (1997): 1372–85.

11. Lagrou, *Legacy*.

12. See Hagemann, "History and Memory," and Hagemann, "Gender, Demobilization" in this handbook.

13. Pertti Ahonen et al., *People on the Move: Forced Population Movements in Europe in the Second World War and Its Aftermath* (Oxford: Berg, 2008).

14. Ida Blom et al., eds., *Gendered Nations: Nationalisms and Gender Order in the Late Nineteenth Century* (Oxford: Berg, 2000).

15. Exemplary here is Claudia Pavone, *A Civil War: A History of the Italian Resistance* (New York: Verso, 2013).

16. Tony Judt, *Postwar: A History of Europe since 1945* (New York: Penguin Press, 2006); and Frank Biess and Robert G. Moeller, eds., *Histories of the Aftermath: The Legacies of the Second World War in Europe* (New York: Berghahn Books, 2010).

17. For this typology, see Arnd Bauerkämper, *Das umstrittene Gedächtnis: Die Erinnerung an Nationalsozialismus, Faschismus und Krieg in Europa seit 1945* (Paderborn: Schöningh, 2012), 369.

18. Lagrou, *Legacy*; John Foot, *Italy's Divided Memory* (New York: Palgrave Macmillan, 2009), 147–82; Olivier Wieviorka, *Divided Memory: French Recollections of World War II from the Liberation to the Present* (Stanford, CA: Stanford University Press, 2012); Bauerkämper, *Das umstrittene Gedächtnis*; and Robert Gildea, *Fighters in the Shadows: A New History of the French Resistance* (London: Faber & Faber, 2015).

19. See Hagemann, "History and Memory" in this handbook.

20. David Forgacs, *Rome Open City* (London: British Film Institute, 2008).

21. See, for example, Paul Aussaresses, *The Battle of the* Casbah: *Terrorism and Counter-Terrorism in Algeria, 1955–1957* (New York: Enigma Books, 2010).

22. Lagrou, *Legacy*.

23. Moeller, *War Stories*; and Frank Biess, *Homecomings: Returning POWs and the Legacies of Defeat in Postwar Germany* (Princeton, NJ: Princeton University Press, 2006).

24. John E. Bodnar, *The "Good War" in American Memory* (Baltimore: Johns Hopkins University Press, 2010), 7.

25. Michael Geyer, "Amerikanisches Totengedenken: Privatisierung des Leidens und Universalisierung der Toten," in *Gefallenengedenken im globalen Vergleich: Nationale Tradition, politische Legitimation und Individualisierung der Erinnerung*, ed. Manfred Hettling und Jörg Echternkamp (Munich: Oldenbourg, 2013), 487–509.

26. Lucy Noakes, *War and the British: Gender and National Identity, 1939–91* (New York: St. Martin's Press, 1998); and Sonya O. Rose, *Which People's War? National Identity and Citizenship in Wartime Britain, 1939–1945* (New York: Oxford University Press, 2003).

27. Nina Tumarkin, *The Living and the Dead: The Rise and Fall of the Cult of World War II in Russia* (New York: Basic Books, 1995); and Amir Weiner, *Making Sense of War: The Second World War and the Fate of the Bolshevik Revolution* (Princeton, NJ: Princeton University Press, 2002).

28. Norman Naimark and Leonid Gibianskii, eds., *The Establishment of Communist Regimes in Eastern Europe, 1944–1949* (Boulder, CO: Westview Press, 1997).

29. Janet Hart, *New Voices in the Nation: Women and the Greek Resistance, 1941–1964* (Ithaca, NY: Cornell University Press, 1996).

30. Fabrice Virgili, *Shorn Women: Gender and Punishment in Liberation France* (New York: Berg, 2002). For Norway, see Bauerkämper, *Das umstrittene Gedächtnis*, 334. For Finland, see Anu Heiskanen, "A Useless War Memory: Erotic Fraternization, German Soldiers, and Gender in Finland," in Paletschek and Schraut, *Gender of Memory*, 204–20.

31. Susanne zur Nieden, "Erotic Fraternization: The Legend of German Women's Quick Surrender," in *Home/Front: The Military, War and Gender in Twentieth-Century Germany*, ed. Karen Hagemann and Stefanie Schüler-Springorum (Oxford: Berg, 2002), 275–96.

32. See Leonie Treber, *Mythos Trümmerfrauen: Von der Trümmerbeseitigung in der Kriegs- und Nachkriegszeit und der Entstehung eines deutschen Erinnerungsortes* (Essen: Klartext, 2014); Atina Grossmann, "A Question of Silence: The Rape of German Women by Occupation Soldiers," *October* 72 (1995): 42–63; and Miriam Gebhardt, *Als die Soldaten kamen: Die Vergewaltigung deutscher Frauen am Ende des Zweiten Weltkriegs* (Munich: DVA, 2015).

33. Anna Krylova, "Neither Erased nor Remembered: Cultural Strategies of Forgetting in Soviet Russia, 1940s–1980s," in Biess and Moeller, *Histories*, 83–101. See Hagemann, "History and Memory" in this handbook.

34. Robert G. Moeller, "The Remasculinization of Germany in the 1950s: Introduction," *Signs* 24, no. 1 (1998): 101–6.

35. Claudia Lenz, *Haushaltspflicht und Widerstand: Erzählungen norwegischer Frauen über die deutsche Besatzung 1940–1945 im Lichte nationaler Vergangenheitskonstruktionen* (Tübingen: edition diskord, 2003).

36. Suzanne Mettler, *Soldiers to Citizens: The G.I. Bill and the Making of the Greatest Generation* (New York: Oxford University Press, 2005).

37. Rose, *Which People's War?*

38. Friederike Brühöfener, "Sending Young Men to the Barracks: West Germany's Struggle over the Establishment of New Armed Forces in the 1950s," in *Gender and the Long Postwar: The United States and the Two Germanys, 1945–1989*, ed. Karen Hagemann and Sonya Michel (Baltimore: Johns Hopkins University Press, 2014), 145–64; and Amy Rutenberg, "Service by Other Means: Changing Perceptions of Military Service and Masculinity in the United States, 1940–1973," in ibid., 165–84.

39. Thomas Kühne, *Kameradschaft: Die Soldaten des nationalsozialistischen Krieges und das 20. Jahrhundert* (Göttingen: Vandenhoeck & Ruprecht, 2006).

40. Biess, *Homecomings*, 145.

41. Judith Tydor Baumel-Schwartz, *Perfect Heroes: The World War II Parachutists and the Making of Israeli Collective Memory* (Madison: University of Wisconsin Press, 2010).

42. Pieter Lagrou, "1945–1955: The Age of Total War," in Biess and Moeller, *Histories*, 287–96.

43. Laura McEnaney, "A Woman's Peace Dividend: Demobilization and Working Class Women in Chicago, 1945–1953," in Hagemann and Michel, *Gender*, 73–94.

44. Vita Zelče, "Latvian Women after World War II," in *Women and Men at War: A Gender Perspective on World War II and Its Aftermath in Central and Eastern Europe*, ed. Maren Röger and Ruth Leiserowitz (Osnabrück: Fibre Verlag, 2012), 281–306; and Barbara Klich-Kluczewska, "Making Up for the Losses of War: Reproduction Politics in Postwar Poland," in ibid., 307–28.

45. Elizabeth D. Heineman, *What Difference Does a Husband Make? Women and Marital Status in Nazi and Postwar Germany* (Berkeley: University of California Press, 1999).

46. Merridale, *Night of Stone*; Svenja Goltermann, *Die Gesellschaft der Überlebenden: Deutsche Kriegsheimkehrer und ihre Gewalterfahrungen im Zweiten Weltkrieg* (Munich: DVA, 2008); and Biess, *Homecomings*, 70–94.

47. Gerald N. Grob, "Der Zweite Weltkrieg und die US-amerikanische Psychiatry," in *Krieg und Psychiatrie, 1914–1950*, ed. Babette Quinkert et al. (Göttingen: Wallstein, 2010), 153–64; and Rebecca Jo Plant, "Preventing the Inevitable: John Appel and the Problem of Psychiatric Casualties in the US Army during World War II," in *Science and Emotions after 1945: A Transatlantic Perspective*, ed. Frank Biess and Daniel M. Gross (Chicago: University of Chicago Press, 2014), 209–38.

48. Vera Neumann, *Nicht der Rede wert: Die Privatisierung der Kriegsfolgen in der frühen Bundesrepublik: Lebensgeschichtliche Erinnerungen* (Münster: Westfälisches Dampfboot, 1999). At times, these difficulties were represented in popular culture, for example, in William Wyler's 1946 film *The Best Years of Our Lives*.

49. Allan Young, *The Harmony of Illusions: Inventing Post-Traumatic Stress Disorder* (Princeton, NJ: Princeton University Press, 1997).

50. Lagrou, *Legacy*, 286.

51. Tom Segev, *The Seventh Million: The Israelis and the Holocaust* (New York: Hill & Wang, 1993).

52. Jan Gross, *Fear: Anti-Semitism in Poland after Auschwitz* (New York: Random House, 2007).

53. Hasia R. Diner, *We Remember with Reverence and Love: American Jews and the Myth of Silence after the Holocaust, 1945–1962* (New York: New York University Press, 2009).

54. Annette Wieviorka, *The Era of the Witness* (Ithaca, NY: Cornell University Press, 2006).

55. Carol Rittner and John K. Roth, eds., *Different Voices: Women and the Holocaust* (New York: Paragon House, 1993); Judith Tydor Baumel, *Double Jeopardy: Gender and the Holocaust* (London: Routledge, 1986); Dalia Ofer and Lenore J. Weitzman, eds., *Women in the Holocaust* (New Haven, CT: Yale University Press, 1998).

56. Devin O. Pendas, *The Frankfurt Auschwitz Trial, 1963–1965: Genocide, History, and the Limits of the Law* (Cambridge: Cambridge University Press, 2006); and Hannah Arendt, *Eichmann in Jerusalem: A Report on the Banality of Evil* (New York: Viking Press, 1963). For a different view, see Bettina Stangneth, *Eichmann before Jerusalem: The Unexamined Life of a Mass Murderer* (New York: Alfred A. Knopf, 2014).

57. Georg Wamhof, ed., *Das Gericht als Tribunal oder: Wie der NS-Vergangenheit der Prozess gemacht wurde* (Göttingen: Wallstein, 2009).

58. Pendas, *Frankfurt Auschwitz Trial*, 263; Peter Krause, *Der Eichmann Prozess in der deutschen Presse* (Frankfurt am Main: Campus, 2002); and Gerhard Paul, "Von Psychopathen, Technokraten des Terrors und 'ganz gewöhnlichen' Deutschen: Die Täter der Shoah im Spiegel der Forschung," in *Die Täter der Shoah: Fanatische Nationalsozialisten oder ganz normale Deutsche?*, ed. Gerhard Paul (Göttingen: Wallstein, 2002), 15–31.

59. On genocide and modern bureaucracy, see Zygmunt Bauman, *Modernity and the Holocaust* (Ithaca, NY: Cornell University Press, 2001).

60. Alexandra Przyrembel, "Transfixed by an Image: Ilse Koch, the 'Kommandeuse of Buchenwald,'" *German History* 19, no. 3 (2001): 369–99; and Sabine Horn, *Erinnerungsbilder: Auschwitz Prozess und Majdanek Prozess im westdeutschen Fernsehen* (Essen: Klartext, 2009), 226–41.

61. Henry Rousso, *The Vichy Syndrome: History and Memory in France since 1944* (Cambridge, MA: Harvard University Press, 1994); and Robert O. Paxton, *Vichy France: Old Guard and New Order, 1940–1944*, rev. ed. (New York: Columbia University Press, 2001).

62. On the link between decolonization and Holocaust memory, see Michael Rothberg, *Multidirectional Memory: Remembering the Holocaust in the Age of Decolonization* (Stanford, CA: Stanford University Press, 2009).

63. Krylova, "Neither Erased."

64. Tumarkin, *The Living*, 113–17.

65. Timothy Scott Brown, *West Germany and the Global Sixties: The Anti-Authoritarian Revolt 1962–1978* (New York: Cambridge University Press, 2013), 79–115.

66. Dagmar Herzog, *Sex after Fascism: Memory and Morality in Twentieth-Century Germany* (Princeton, NJ: Princeton University Press, 2007).

67. Peter Novick, *The Holocaust in American Life* (New York: Houghton Mifflin, 1999).

68. Wieviorka, *The Era*, 56–95.

69. Golterman, *Die Gesellschaft*, 299–319.

70. On the repression of emotions in the Auschwitz trial, see Pendas, *Frankfurt Auschwitz Trial*, 291. On historiography, see Nicolas Berg, *Der Holocaust und die westdeutschen Historiker: Erforschung und Erinnerung* (Göttingen: Wallstein, 2001), 616–29.

71. The reception was not equally intense everywhere; see Emiliano Perra, *Conflicts of Memory: The Reception of Holocaust Films and TV Programmes in Italy, 1945 to the Present* (New York: Peter Lang, 2010), 117–47.

72. The key collection was Renate Bridenthal and Claudia Koonz, eds., *Becoming Visible: Women in European History* (Boston: Houghton Mifflin, 1977).

73. See, for example, Victoria de Grazia, *How Fascism Ruled Women: Italy, 1922–1945* (Berkeley: University of California Press, 1993), 272–88. More recently, see Jelena Batinić, *Women and Yugoslav Partisans: A History of World War II Resistance* (New York: Cambridge University Press, 2015).

74. Bodnar, "*Good War*," 194–99.

75. Treber, *Mythos Trümmerfrauen*.

76. Grossmann, "Question of Silence."

77. Gisela Bock, "Die Frauen und der Nationalsozialismus: Bemerkungen zu einem Buch von Claudia Koonz," *Geschichte und Gesellschaft* 15, no. 4 (1989): 563–79; Bock, "Ein Historikerinnenstreit?," *Geschichte und Gesellschaft* 18, no. 3 (1992): 400–4; and Bock, "Antinatalism, Maternity and Paternity in National Socialist Racism," in *Nazism and German Society, 1933–1945*, ed. David Crew (New York: Routledge, 1994), 110–40.

78. Claudia Koonz, *Mothers in the Fatherland: Women, the Family, and Nazi Politics* (New York: St. Martin's Press, 1987); and Koonz, "Erwiderung auf Gisela Bocks Rezension von 'Mothers in the Fatherland,'" *Geschichte und Gesellschaft* 18, no. 3 (1992): 394–99.

79. Examples include Elizabeth Harvey, *Women and the Nazi East: Agents and Witnesses of Germanization* (New Haven, CT: Yale University Press, 2003); Gudrun Schwarz, *Eine Frau an seiner Seite: Ehefrauen in der SS-Sippengemeinschaft* (Berlin: Aufbau, 2000); and Wendy Lower, *Hitler's Furies: German Women in the Nazi Killing Fields* (Boston: Houghton Mifflin, 2013). As an overview over the *Historikerinnenstreit*, see Christina Herkommer,

Frauen im Nationalsozialismus—Opfer oder Täterinnen? Eine Kontroverse der Frauenforschung im Spiegel feministischer Theoriebildung und der allgemeinen historischen Aufarbeitung der NS-Vergangenheit (Munich: Martin Meidenbauer Verlag, 2005); and the introduction by Karen Hagemann, "Introduction: Gender and the History of War—The Development of the Research" in this handbook.

80. Gisela Bock, ed., *Genozid und Geschlecht: Jüdische Frauen im nationalsozialistischen Lagersystem* (Frankfurt am Main: Campus, 2005), 8.

81. Raul Hilberg, *Perpetrators, Victims, Bystanders: The Jewish Catastrophe, 1933–1945* (New York: Harper Collins, 1992), 130.

82. Mary D. Lagerwey, "Reading Anne Frank and Elie Wiesel: Voice and Gender in Stories of the Holocaust," *Contemporary Jewry* 17, no. 1 (1996): 48–65.

83. Charlotte Delbo, *Auschwitz and After*, reprint ed. (New Haven, CT: Yale University Press, 1995); and Rothberg, *Multidirectional Memory*, 176–224.

84. Weitzman and Ofer, *Women in the Holocaust*. See also Myrna Goldenberg, "Memoirs of Auschwitz Survivors: The Burden of Gender," in ibid., 327–39.

85. Lawrence L. Langer, "Gendered Suffering? Women in Holocaust Testimony," in Weitzman and Ofer, *Women in the Holocaust*, 355–62.

86. Joan Ringelheim, "The Split between Gender and the Holocaust," in Weitzman and Ofer, *Women in the Holocaust*, 340–50.

87. Janet Liebman Jacobs, *Memorializing the Holocaust: Gender, Genocide and Collective Memory* (London: I. B. Tauris, 2010), 31.

88. Sara Horowitz, "Women in Holocaust Literature: Engendering Trauma Memory," in Weitzman and Ofer, *Women in the Holocaust*, 375–76.

89. Ruth Klüger, *Still Alive: A Holocaust Girlhood Remembered* (New York: Feminist Press at the City University of New York, 2001), 72.

90. Horowitz, "Women in the Holocaust," 375–76.

91. Sylvia Schraut and Sylvia Paletschek, "Remembrance and Gender: Making Gender Visible and Inscribing Women into Memory Culture," in Paletschek and Schraut, *Gender of Memory*, 267–71.

92. Susanne Maerz, "From Taboo to Compensation: *Krigsbarn* in Public Discourse and Literature after 1945," in *From Patriotic Memory to a Universalistic Narrative? Shifts in Norwegian Memory Culture after 1945 in Comparative Perspective*, ed. Arnd Bauerkämper et al. (Essen: Klartext, 2014), 253–71; and Bauerkämper, *Das umstrittene Gedächtnis*, 340.

93. Lu Seegers and Jürgen Reulecke, eds., *Die "Generation der Kriegskinder": Historische Hintergründe und Deutungen* (Gießen: Psychosozial Verlag, 2009).

94. Dorothee Wierling, "Generations as Narrative Communities: Some Private Sources of Public Memory in Postwar Germany," in Biess and Moeller, *Histories*, 102–22.

95. Aleksandra Ubertowska, "Die Shoah anders erzählt: Autobiographische Zeugnisse von Frauen in der polnischen Literatur," in *Nach dem Vergessen: Rekurse auf den Holocaust in Ostmitteleuropa nach 1989*, ed. Magdalena Marszalek and Alina Molisak (Berlin: Kadmos, 2010), 197–218.

96. Andrea Pető, "Memory and the Narrative of Rape in Budapest and Vienna," in *Life after Death: Approaches to a Cultural and Social History of Europe During the 1940s and 1950s*, ed. Richard Bessel and Dirk Schumann (New York: Cambridge University Press, 2003), 129–49.

97. Tony Judt, "The Past Is Another Country: Myth and Memory in Postwar Europe," *Daedalus* 121, no. 4 (1992): 83–118.

98. Röger and Leiserowitz, *Women and Men*.

99. Tiina Kinnuen, "Gender and Politics: Patriotic Women in Finnish Public Memory after 1944," in Paletschek and Schraut, *Gender of Memory*, 181–203.

100. Foot, *Italy's Divided Memory*, 125–46.

101. Wulf Kansteiner, *In Pursuit of German Memory: History, Television, and Politics after Auschwitz* (Athens, OH: Ohio University Press, 2006), 280–315.

102. Emily S. Rosenberg, *A Date Which Will Live: Pearl Harbor in American Memory* (Durham, NC: Duke University Press, 2003), 113–25. For a much-needed challenge to this notion, see Mary Louise Roberts, *What Soldiers Do: Sex and the American GI in World War II France* (Chicago: University of Chicago Press, 2013).

103. Jan Assmann, "Communicative and Cultural Memory," in *Cultural Memory Studies: An International and Interdisciplinary Handbook*, ed. Astrid Erll and Ansgar Nünning (Berlin: de Gruyter, 2008), 109–18.

104. Sylvia Paletschek and Sylvia Schraut, "Introduction: Gender and Memory Culture in Europe—Female Representations in Historical Perspective," in Paletschek and Schraut, *Gender of Memory*, 7–30, 23.

SELECT BIBLIOGRAPHY

Bauerkämper, Arnd. *Das umstrittene Gedächtnis: Die Erinnerung an Nationalsozialismus, Faschismus und Krieg in Europa seit 1945*. Paderborn: Schöningh, 2012.

Berg, Nicolas. *The Holocaust and the West German Historians: Historical Interpretation and Autobiographical Memory*. Madison: University of Wisconsin Press, 2015.

Biess, Frank. *Homecomings: Returning POWs and the Legacies of Defeat in Postwar Germany*. Princeton, NJ: Princeton University Press, 2006.

Biess, Frank, and Robert G. Moeller, eds. *Histories of the Aftermath: The Legacies of the Second World War in Europe*. New York: Berghahn Books, 2010.

Bodnar, John E. *The "Good War" in American Memory*. Baltimore: Johns Hopkins University Press, 2010.

Echternkamp, Jörg, and Stefan Martens, eds. *Experience and Memory: The Second World War in Europe*. New York: Berghahn Books, 2010.

Eschebach, Insa, Sigrid Jacobeit, and Silke Wenk, eds. *Gedächtnis und Geschlecht: Deutungsmuster in Darstellungen des Nationalsozialistischen Genozids*. Frankfurt am Main: Campus, 2002.

Foot, John. *Italy's Divided Memory*. New York: Palgrave Macmillan, 2009.

Herzog, Dagmar. *Sex after Fascism: Memory and Morality in Twentieth-Century Germany*. Princeton, NJ: Princeton University Press, 2005.

Hilberg, Raul. *Perpetrators, Victims, Bystanders: The Jewish Catastrophe, 1933–1945*. New York: Harper Collins, 1992.

Jacobs, Janet. *Memorializing the Holocaust: Gender, Genocide and Collective Memory*. London: I. B. Tauris, 2010.

Krylova, Anna. *Soviet Women in Combat: A History of Violence on the Eastern Front*. Cambridge: Cambridge University Press, 2010.

Lagrou, Pieter. *The Legacy of Nazi Occupation: Patriotic Memory and National Recovery in Western Europe, 1945–1965*. Cambridge: Cambridge University Press, 2000.

Merridale, Catherine. *Night of Stone: Death and Memory in Russia*. New York: Penguin Books, 2000.

Moeller, Robert G. *War Stories: The Search for a Usable Past in the Federal Republic of Germany.* Berkeley: University of California Press, 2001.

Noakes, Lucy. *War and the British: Gender and National Identity, 1939–1991.* London: I. B. Tauris, 1998.

Rothberg, Michael. *Multidirectional Memory: Remembering the Holocaust in the Age of Decolonization.* Stanford, CA: Stanford University Press, 2009.

Rousso, Henry. *The Vichy Syndrome: History and Memory in France since 1944.* Cambridge, MA: Harvard University Press, 1991.

Wieviorka, Annette. *The Era of the Witness.* Ithaca, NY: Cornell University Press, 2006.

Wieviorka, Olivier. *Divided Memory: French Recollections of World War II from the Liberation to the Present.* Stanford, CA: Stanford University Press, 2012.

PART IV

....

FROM THE GLOBAL COLD WAR TO THE CONFLICTS OF THE POST-COLD WAR ERA

....

WAR AND GENDER

From the Global Cold War to the Conflicts of the
Post–Cold War Era—an Overview

KAREN HAGEMANN AND SONYA O. ROSE

In March 1946, the Social Democratic Party of Austria campaigned with a poster titled "16,000,000 Fallen Soldiers. 29,000,000 Cripples. 36,000,000 Homeless. FOR WHAT? International Women's Day March 1946. For World Peace" for the first celebration of the International Women's Day after the Second World War (Figure 26.1). It showed a woman holding a baby and looking back in horror at the devastation of war, represented by a burning, ruined city. The placard illustrates the widespread desire for peace in the aftermath of World War II. Everywhere in Europe and other parts of the globe in 1946, social democratic, socialist, and communist women used the International Women's Day, introduced by the Second International Socialist Women's Conference in 1910, as a traditional day of global struggle for women's equal rights, to demonstrate for peace, social justice, and gender equality.[1]

Eight months earlier, on June 26, 1945, a similar agenda had led to the founding of the United Nations (UN) by fifty states that signed the UN Charter during an international conference in San Francisco.[2] The first paragraph of its Article 1 stated, "The Purposes of the United Nations are to maintain international peace and security, and to that end: to take effective collective measures for the prevention and removal of threats to the peace, and for the suppression of acts of aggression or other breaches of the peace, and to bring about by peaceful means, and in conformity with the principles of justice and international law, adjustment or settlement of international disputes or situations which might lead to a breach of the peace."[3] The major aim of this new intergovernmental organization, officially founded on October 24, 1945, was the general prevention of another global conflict like the Second World War, which had ended some months earlier with the unconditional surrenders of Nazi Germany on May 7, 1945, and Imperial Japan on August 15, 1945. The dramatic finale of this conflict had been the atomic bombings of the Japanese cities of Hiroshima and Nagasaki by the United States on August 6 and 9,

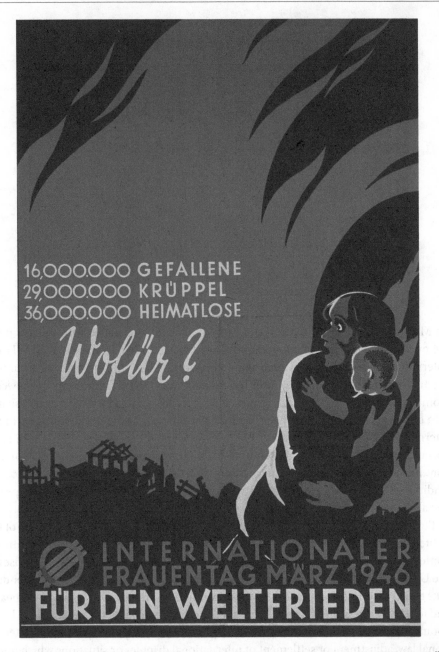

FIGURE 26.1 *16,000,000 Gefallene, 29,000,000 Krüppel, 36,000,000 Heimatlose. WOFÜR? Internationaler Frauentag März 1946. Für den Weltfrieden!* (16,000,000 Fallen Soldiers. 29,000,000 Cripples. 36,000,000 Homeless. FOR WHAT? International Women's Day March 1946. For World Peace), poster by the Social Democratic Party of Austria, designed by Victor Theodor Slama (1890–1973), Vienna, 1946.

(Hoover Institution Archives, Poster Collection, GE 1553)

1945, killing some 120,000 civilians in two days.[4] This first use of nuclear weapons demonstrated to the shocked public the dangers of the destructive power of the new nuclear-weapons technology and fostered the desire for peace and the prevention of any further use of the atomic bomb.[5]

The international struggle for peace, disarmament, and human rights that started after the end of World War II must be included in the history of gender and war in the second half of the twentieth century. For four decades, this period was shaped across the globe by the Cold War divide between the two new nuclear superpowers, the United States and the Soviet Union (USSR), and their respective allies in the West and the East. Their antagonism overshadowed political developments between the end of the Second World War and the collapse of the Soviet Union in 1991. The rivalry between the super-powers was military, political, and economic in nature, with the United States claiming to stand for the "free capitalist world" and the Soviet Union asserting that it represented the "communist future," but this rivalry also extended to society and culture. The Cold War (1946–91) centered on the East–West conflict on the European continent divided by the "Iron Curtain" running between the Baltic and Adriatic Seas. The Western countries were organized in the North Atlantic Treaty Organization (NATO), founded in 1949 and led by the United States; the Eastern countries united in the Warsaw Pact, created in 1955 and controlled by the USSR. The history of the Cold War era, however, must also include the proxy wars fought outside Europe and North America, such as the Korean War (1950–53), and the Wars of Decolonization waged by the anticolonial liberation move-ments of the 1940s to 1970s, arising first in Asia and the Middle East and later in Africa. Indeed, the East–West rivalry informed and often shaped all these conflicts, which in turn influenced the East–West rivalry.[6] These *Wars of Decolonization* were, as Raphaëlle Branche argues, like the First and Second World War, *total wars*, because of their "peculiar intensity and extension" and "the tendency to abolish the boundaries that distinguish the front from the homeland." They, too, affected all areas of the econ-omy, society, and culture.[7]

In the early twenty-first century, historians therefore use the concept of the *Global Cold War*, which includes not only the various conflicts worldwide influenced by the superpower rivalry, but also the struggle against them by peace, nuclear disarmament, or anti-imperial movements, like the international anti–Vietnam War campaign. They furthermore emphasize that the increasing success of anticolonial liberation move-ments in their Wars of Decolonization, often supported by the Soviet Union but more and more also by the People's Republic of China (PRC) founded in 1949, slowly changed the global power balance between the two superpowers, the United States and the USSR, and what contemporaries called the Third World.[8] This development was one important factor that transformed the character of the Cold War. The period of the "hot" Cold War marked by extensive rivalry between the East and West and several proxy wars, includ-ing the Korean War, the Algerian War (1954–62), and the First and Second Indochina Wars (1946–75), ended in the early 1970s, when the period of "détente," of "antagonistic cooperation," started.[9] This period of peaceful coexistence and increasing East–West cooperation laid the groundwork for the end of the Cold War with the dissolution of the Soviet Union and the Warsaw Pact.[10]

The first post–Cold War decade was accompanied by upheaval and new conflicts throughout the world. In Eastern Europe, the wars in the former Yugoslavia (1991–2001) were spawned by resurgent nationalism and ethnic conflict. Formerly colonized countries in Africa were also plagued by civil war in the 1990s, starting with Rwanda (1990–94). Furthermore, the Middle East continued to be a trouble spot. Conflicts there included the Gulf War (1990–91), the Iraq War (2003–11), and the war against ISIL, the Islamic State of Iraq and the Levant (2014–ongoing), all with a heavy involvement of the United States. In other parts of Africa, Asia, and Latin America, conflicts continued or flared up as well.

In 2019, full-scale wars were, according to the Conflict Barometer of the Heidelberg Institute for International Conflict Research, ongoing in at least fifteen states and regions: eight in the Middle East and Maghreb (Afghanistan, Syria, Egypt, Libya, Turkey and Yemen), five in Sub-Saharan Africa (Democratic Republic of the Congo, Mali, Nigeria/Cameroon, Chad/Niger, Somalia/Kenya), and two in the Americas (Brazil, Mexico). In total they observed 23 limited wars worldwide. Overall, of the 358 total conflicts they monitored, 162 played out on a non-violent level—but even here, political tensions and/or low level violence remain.[11] Some of the post–Cold War conflicts had and have the character of conventional interstate wars that involve internationally recognized state actors. Others were and are intrastate conflicts, which include both state and non-state actors, or substate conflicts, carried out solely among nonstate actors. But several were and are transstate conflicts that involve/d both state and nonstate actors.[12] Some political scientists have labeled these later conflicts in particular as "new wars," characterized by violence between varying combinations of state and nonstate actors.[13] Because this concept is contested for several reasons, we use the term *Wars of Globalization*. Humanitarian interventions and peacekeeping operations have played an increasingly important role in all these Wars of Globalization in the post–Cold War era. Most of these interventions and operations took and take place under the authority of the UN to oversee and sometimes implement peace accords.[14]

The following overview starts with a discussion of the two central concepts that have dominated the scholarship on international relations and war in the second half of the twentieth century: *Cold War* and *new wars*. Afterward, it examines some of the major conflicts and general trends in the development of warfare and discusses the state of the research on gender, military, and war in the era and its major themes.

RECONCEPTUALIZING THE COLD WAR

The term Cold War was first used by the English writer George Orwell in his prophetic essay "You and the Atomic Bomb" from October 1945, in which he forecast that nuclear weaponry in a globalizing system of states would lead to "a peace that is no peace." The essay was predictive because the nuclear arms race was to become one of the central features of the years in which the USSR, the United States, and their allies were at ideological loggerheads, threatening the entire world.[15] American historians took up the concept of a Cold War in the late 1940s, when they attempted to explain the collapse of the alliance between the United States, the United Kingdom, and the Soviet Union that had defeated Nazi Germany. They used it as a label for the—as they perceived it—confrontational policies pursued by Soviet leader Joseph Stalin after the Second World War. For them, the USSR and its "tyrannical communist system" waged a Cold War against the West. This understanding of the term informed most of the research on the topic in the West, which until the 1980s was dominated by a fierce anticommunism and the support of the US strategy of containment.[16]

Only a minority of Western scholars developed an alternative approach. Beginning in the late 1960s, they critiqued the role of the United States as an imperial power that pursued policies driven by the needs of its global capitalism. To secure capitalist profits, these critics argued, the United States not only intervened in other countries through political and economic means, but also instigated military coups, civil conflicts, and proxy wars in the name of freedom. This assessment was informed by the anticolonial liberation struggle in the so-called Third World countries and the anti-imperialist protest movements in the Western world, especially against the Vietnam War (1955–75).[17] In this context, the term *anticolonialism* refers more narrowly to opposition against formal colonial rule, and *anti-imperialism* is understood as a broader phenomenon, including the struggle against formal empires (created by military means), informal empires (mainly created by economic and political measures), and internal imperial rule.[18]

Despite their criticism of the dominant Western Cold War paradigm, the "anti-imperialist revisionists" stayed, as Odd Arne Westad commented, "within the original political agendas of interpretation," because they contended that the United States, with its "increasingly global anticollectivist agenda," driven by its economic needs as a global capitalist superpower, "had caused and perpetuated the Cold War to at least as high a degree as the Soviet Union had."[19] Furthermore, they shared the obsession with finding fault for the ongoing conflict.[20] Even though the group of anti-imperialist revisionists was small, it managed, according to Westad, in the 1970s "to shift the debate somewhat back in the direction of Orwell's initial idea of the Cold War as a global system."[21] This development was supported on the one hand by the increasing number and influence of the Third World countries that did not align with either NATO or the Warsaw Pact. Since 1961, these countries were officially organized in the Non-Aligned Movement.[22] On the other hand, the politics of détente helped dissolve polarization. The Helsinki Accords, the final act of the Conference on Security and Co-operation in Europe held in Finland during July and August 1975, became the political symbol of détente. Thirty-three European states including the USSR, plus Canada and the United States, signed the documents with the aim to improve East–West relations.[23] When policymakers called for greater dialogue, regular summit meetings, and negotiation over arms control and other bilateral agreements, historians changed their approach too.

As a result of these developments, since the 1970s a more "realist" approach, inspired both by realist thinking in the social sciences and by the evident longevity of the conflict, has influenced the scholarship on the Cold War, at least in Europe. Scholars there interpreted the rivalry between the Soviet Union and the United States primarily as clash of interests and power caused by the countries' different strategic security needs. This approach, which focused on the "balance of powers"—understood as "a global system in which the strategic arms race and formal or informal alliances had moved the Soviet–American relationship toward a high degree of stability and predictability"— observed Westad, gave way with the collapse of the USSR and the Warsaw Pact.[24]

Since the end of the Cold War, the scholarship on the period between 1946 and 1991 has changed dramatically. It has become much less dichotomous and ideological, and more multidisciplinary by including the approaches of cultural and intellectual history. With the turn to global and transnational history, the regional focus of Cold War studies expanded as well and now looks beyond Eastern and Western Europe and North America to Africa, Asia, and Central and South America.[25] In addition, the opening of the archives in the former USSR and Eastern Europe after the fall of their communist regimes gave an important impulse for the development of the research. It allowed an archival-based amplification of historiographical perspectives.

The 2010 *Cambridge History of the Cold War* and the 2013 *Oxford Handbook of the Cold War* reflect this development.[26] In his introductory essay to the former, one of its two editors, Westad, suggested a heterogeneous approach and global perspective for the study of the Cold War. For him, the scholarship must move beyond military and political history to social, economic, and intellectual inquiries and place the Cold War in its "larger context of chronological time and geographical space."[27] The editors of the *Oxford Handbook of the Cold War*, Richard H. Immerman and Petra Goedde, similarly emphasized in their introduction that the Cold War "must be understood and evaluated within the broader context and contours of global political, economic, social and cultural developments, some of which preceded [it], and some of which persist to the present day and doubtless will continue into the future."[28] According to them, this new conceptualization of the Cold War as a global phenomenon does not, however, imply that the rivalry between the United States and the USSR has lost its significance in understanding the period.[29]

We, too, pursue a heterogeneous approach to the study of the Cold War that foregrounds its global scale; aim to transcend the separation of its military, political, economic, social, and cultural dimensions; stress the interconnectedness between peace and war; and link them to domestic and international developments. This decentering of the study of the Cold War away from, on the one hand, a narrow understanding that focuses on its military and diplomatic core and, on the other hand, the rivalry between the communist East and capitalist West with the United States and the USSR at its center, allows a systematic integration of gender as a category of historical analysis, which reveals much about the character and trajectory of a broadly conceptualized *Global Cold War*.[30]

Gender historians emphasize the paradoxical role of gender in this era. It functioned as a central marker of difference. Gender images and family ideals were used to define political, economic, and social identity against the "Other" behind the Iron Curtain. In the West, gender ideology focused on the model of the male-breadwinner–female-homemaker family; in the East, the dual-earner family and, with it, the working woman and mother became the declared goal of family, labor, and welfare policies. Yet, the research simultaneously reveals the striking similarities between gendered practices in the authoritarian, communist states in the East and the liberal, capitalist states in the West. Examples are the gendered division of labor in household and family, which remained quite similar, and—despite all rhetoric of equality—the continuity of a clear gender hierarchy in politics, economy, and society on both sides of the Iron Curtain. Gender has also played an important role in all the military conflicts since the end of the Second World War, be they proxy wars, wars of anticolonial liberation, revolutionary upheavals, ethnic and national conflicts, or civil wars. After 1945, war continued to be a "gendering activity," one "that ritually marks the gender of all members of society."[31]

Despite the obvious importance of gender for the study of the history of the Global Cold War, it has played only a peripheral role in mainstream scholarship. That is not surprising for studies published before 1990, because of their narrow focus on diplomatic, military, political, and, at best, economic history. But even in mainstream work from the 2010s that is based on a heterogeneous conceptualization, like the *Cambridge History* and *Oxford Handbook* of the Cold War, or central periodicals like the *Journal of Cold War Studies*, gender still plays a marginal role and is discussed mainly in terms of women.[32] This is remarkable in light of the growing number of publications by women's and gender historians on the history of the Cold War. These studies show, as David J. Snyder emphasized, that "geopolitics and the Cold War political culture of the superpowers and their allies" are "structuring and structured by prevailing assumptions about proper gender behavior and sex-assigned roles."[33]

CONTESTING THE CONCEPT OF THE NEW WARS

The political scientist Mary Kaldor suggested the concept of new wars in her 1999 book *New and Old Wars: Organized Violence in a Global Era* to characterize the conflicts in the post–Cold War era.[34] For her, new wars "are the wars of the era of globalization." She emphasized that "typically, they take place in areas where authoritarian states have been greatly weakened as a consequence of opening up to the rest of the world." In such regions, "the distinction between state and non-state, public and private, external and internal, economic and political, and even war and peace are breaking down," which is both a cause and a consequence of violence.[35]

According to Kaldor, the new wars are distinct from what she called the "old wars" that predominated in the nineteenth and twentieth centuries based on differences in actors, goals, methods, and forms of finance.[36] The actors in the old wars were mainly states using regular armed forces to fight each other; the new wars are fought by varying combinations of networks of state and nonstate actors (private security contractors, jihadists, warlords, and so on). The main goals of the old wars were geopolitical or ideological, whereas the new wars are fought in the name of identity (ethnic, religious, or tribal). This shift is fundamental, because the various nonstate actors pursue access to the state instead of fighting to carry out particular policies or programs in the broader public interest as states supposedly did in the old wars. The rise of identity politics is related to the emergence of new forms of communication, an increase of migration, and the erosion of collective political ideologies like socialism or postcolonial nationalism. Political mobilization around identity is now the aim of war, rather than an instrument of war, as in the past.[37]

In addition, Kaldor claimed that the methods of the new wars are distinctive. The decisive set-piece battles of armed forces to capture or hold territory of the old wars gave way to violence directed against civilians rather than opposing militaries: "Battles are rare and territory is captured through political means, through control of the population." Thus, population displacement—the forcible removal of individuals with a different identity or different opinions—has become a hallmark of new wars.[38] Finally, the forms of finance changed, according to Kaldor. The old means of paying for war— taxation and seeking aid from patron states—were replaced by "new forms of predatory private finance [including] loot and pillage, 'taxation' of humanitarian aid, diaspora support, kidnapping, or smuggling in oil, diamonds, drugs, people, etc." These new means of financing war blur the line between the belligerents' goals and means of paying for the conflict. As such, the wartime economies changed from a centralizing, autarkic model reliant on domestic mobilization to the mode of an open, globalized, and decentralized economy with low participation and revenues that depend on continued violence.[39] All these changes have, as Kaldor argued, far-reaching consequences: "Whereas old wars tended to extremes as each side tried to win, new wars tend to spread and to persist or recur as each side gains in political or economic ways from violence itself rather than 'winning.' Whereas old wars were associated with state building, new wars are the opposite; they tend to contribute to the dismantling of the state."[40]

Gender plays an important role in Kaldor's conceptualization of the new wars. In the 2013 article "Gender and New Wars," coauthored with Christine Chinkin, scholar of international law, she suggested that the new wars are "largely fought by men in the name of a political identity that usually has a significant gender dimension." These men use tactics that "involve deliberate attacks on civilians, including systematic rape as a weapon of war, and are financed by predatory economic activities that tend to affect women more than men." Kaldor and Chinkin contended that even though international laws aiming to contain sexual violence have been introduced and strengthened since the 1990s, their implementation has been very weak. They further emphasized that a "gender lens" helps to identify policies to sustain peace, including "support for civil society, which tends to involve a preponderance of women, implementation of law at local and international levels, and greater participation of women in all aspects of peacemaking, including peacekeeping and law enforcement."[41]

Since the millennium, Kaldor's conceptualization of post–Cold War armed conflicts has become influential far beyond the fields of political science and international relations, but it has not gone unchallenged. Especially her differentiation between old and new wars is widely contested. Security scholar Mats Berdahl pointedly summarized the critique: "As an analytical category, the notion of 'new wars' does more, in the end, to obscure than to illuminate. This is not only because there are historical precedents for what is sometimes identified as 'new'; establishing the fact alone is easy enough. More serious is the persistent tendency to abstract contemporary armed conflicts from their specific historical and cultural context, to make sweeping generalizations across a wide variety of cases and, above all, to undervalue the continuous influence of the past on present patterns of war and conflict."[42] Kaldor's approach to gendering the new wars is likewise highly contested. Feminist scholars critiqued her conventional, dichotomous thinking about the gender order of wars, which constructs men, especially local non-Western men, as armed perpetrators and women as civilian victims.[43] They argued that her conceptualization falls behind theoretical and methodological discussions in the historical scholarship on gender, war, and genocide that emphasizes the multiplicity and simultaneity of female and male roles in conflicts from perpetrators, to bystanders, to victims, which often stands in sharp contrast to the propaganda of the time. They furthermore claimed that what Kaldor described as the specific phenomenon of the new wars in respect of gender relations was in fact already reported by historical scholarship for many earlier conflicts.

Finally, feminist scholars called into question Kaldor's claims that ethnic identities were a cause of war in regions such as Rwanda and the former Yugoslavia or that religion/Islam has been a cause of the wars in the Middle East. This critique was pointedly formulated by Dubravka Zarkov in her 2015 article, "The 'New Wars': A Gendered Myth." She asserted that this idea "rests on the assumption that the histories, cultures and peoples of those countries are *ontologically* different from histories, cultures and people in the Western world. The former are marked by attachments to 'identities,' the latter through the ideological categories of 'liberty' and 'democracy.'"[44] Zarkov's point was not to deny the "politicization of ethnicities and religions" or the violence it can generate or legitimate in conflicts, "but to stress that this neat geographical distribution of characteristics of cultures and peoples rests on historically produced representations that are themselves part of the imagined ontologies of the world."[45] These representations often reach back to the colonial history of the regions involved and are rooted in imperialist thinking. They are also heavily gendered and rely on imaginations of brutal "local" masculinities and vulnerable "local" femininities. They legitimize the "good" violence used by the West in these conflicts, including the bombing of cities, counterinsurgency, and humanitarian interventions. Zarkov stressed that the aim of this critique "is not to equate different forms of violence, but to understand how their definitions and representations support specific definitions of war and agency and create subject positions."[46]

We share this dual criticism of the concept of the new wars and prefer to speak in a more encompassing way about the post–Cold War period as an era of *Wars of Globalization* characterized by low-intensity and asymmetrical warfare in various parts of the world. These conflicts can be distinguished by the dispersal of the state's military power to substate actors, but can also represent a continuation of anticolonial warfare of the Cold War period or an earlier age.[47] This open and historicizing understanding of the period of the Wars of Globalization allows a systematic integration of gender in the historical analysis, much as the Global Cold War concept does for the history of that earlier era. Our approach focuses as much on women and concepts of femininity as on men and new and old constructions of masculinity; at the same time, it avoids the political and ideological baggage of the contested concept of the new wars.

War and Peace in the Age of the Global Cold War

Only from a Western-centric perspective can the era since the end of the Second World be conceptualized as peaceful. Outside Europe and North America, conflicts not only continued everywhere, but their number actually increased until the end of the Cold War; they have been in decline only since then. Of course, statistics depend on what is counted as a "war," but the general trend stays the same regardless of the definition. The increase in the number of wars until 1990 is predominantly a result of the growth of smaller conflicts and civil wars. The Oxford project "War and Peace," for instance, counted in 1948 12 civil wars, 3 interstate conflicts, and 5 anticolonial wars and, in 1989, 4 civil wars with foreign intervention, 44 civil wars, and 2 interstate conflicts.[48] The last colonial conflicts were fought in the early 1970s. Interstate conflicts have almost ceased to exist since the 1970s, but at the same time, the number of intrastate, substate, and transstate conflicts have increased, and they are, in one way or the other, all civil wars, fought with and without foreign intervention.

Despite the rising number of wars, the number of war victims declined in the same period. Conflicts became less deadly. Statistics compiled by the Oxford project indicate that there were three marked peaks in war deaths since the end of the Second World war: the late 1940s and early 1950s, with a first wave of anticolonial struggle and the Korean War; the mid-1960s to mid-1970s, with a second wave of Wars of Decolonization, including the escalating Vietnam War; and the 1980s, with the Soviet–Afghan War (1979–88) and the Iran–Iraq War (1980–88). In the Age of the Global Cold War, the regions most affected by warfare were Asia, the Middle East, and North Africa; in the following, they will therefore be the focus next to Europe.[49]

The Aftermath of the Second World War

World War II was the deadliest conflict in history in absolute terms of casualties. Aerial warfare war, mass killings, and the genocides perpetrated by Nazi Germany and Imperial Japan resulted in a much higher number of civilian than military casualties. Historians estimate that of a total world population of 2.3 billion in 1940, 60 million people were killed; in addition, 20 million died because of war-related disease and famine. For civilians, the aftermath of the war included memories of enemy invasion and occupation, coping with hunger and shortages of the necessities for daily life, and the destruction of living spaces and the infrastructure by air and land warfare, throughout most of Europe and Asia.[50] As Paul Betts and David Crowley have argued, "Rotterdam, Dresden, Warsaw and Hiroshima . . . became the new watchwords of a decimated world, as the scale and planning of unarmed civilian deaths forever distinguished the Second World War from its forerunner."[51]

For the survivors of genocide, war memories also included the trauma of their persecution and brutal treatment. The estimated number of Holocaust victims killed by Nazi Germany encompassed 6 million Jews; 7.8 million non-Jewish civilians from the Soviet Union and eastern Europe; 3 million Soviet prisoners of war; up to 250,000 people with physical and mental disabilities; and up to 220,000 Sinti and Roma. In addition, thousands of so-called asocials and repeat criminal offenders, homosexuals, Jehovah's Witnesses, and German political opponents and resistance activists in Axis-occupied territories were killed.[52] Imperial Japan committed atrocities too. These fell, according to Sandra Wilson, "largely into three distinct categories: murder of inconvenient captives, brutal and neglectful treatment of inmates of prisons and internments camps and of forced laborers and military prostitutes, and punitive investigation and suppression of local resistance movements."[53] Of the 132,134 Allied prisoners of war captured by Japan, 35,756 perished in prison camps. The estimates of the total number of civilians and POWs murdered by the Japanese military between 1937 and 1945 range from 3 million to over 10 million people, mostly Chinese, Koreans, Malaysians, Indonesians, Filipinos, and Indochinese.[54] Memories of war and genocide were part of the long-term aftermath of the Second World War.[55]

In the short term, postwar societies in Asia and Europe had to deal with displaced persons, refugees, and expellees. Up to 11 million displaced persons (250,000 of them Jewish survivors) needed to be resettled following the dismantling of concentration camps and release of forced laborers and prisoners of war, and about 12 million ethnic Germans and Austrians were expelled from various Eastern Europeans countries between 1944 and 1950. The international organization to aid refugees and displaced persons, the UN Relief and Rehabilitation Administration, already founded in 1943 prior to the United Nations, helped with the resettlement of the displaced persons but not German expellees.[56]

Next to the handling of this humanitarian crisis and the military and economic demobilization, the rebuilding of destroyed cities, towns and villages, and of demolished infrastructure stood in the foreground of the first postwar years.[57] Reconstruction was high on the agenda of all Asian and European nations following World War II. Millions of homeless needed shelter. Because cities and their civilian populations had been primary military targets of the bombing, the housing crisis was profound. It was, as Paul Betts and David Crowley contend, this "background of moral and material catastrophe that separated postwar European domestic culture from its American counterpart, and made the longing for shelter and security all the more intense and distinctive there, transcending as it did regions, classes and Cold War divisions."[58] As a result, the restoration of normal family life and domestic space was a common concern in Eastern and Western Europe regardless of all other political and ideological differences.

For the allied victors, in addition, the establishment of occupation regimes for the defeated Axis countries of Germany and Japan was a central postwar task. The Supreme Command of the Allied Powers in Japan originally included Britain, the Soviet Union, and the Republic of China, but they only had an advisory role. The occupation regime was controlled by the Americans; General Douglas MacArthur became the Supreme Commander. Japan had to give up all its former colonies, but it was not split up. Germany, by contrast, was divided into four occupation zones for which Britain, France, the Soviet Union, and the United States were responsible. This had a long-lasting impact on Europe by contributing to a division between East and West across the Continent. Disagreements between the four powers over a plan for economic unification proposed by the United Kingdom and the United States in July 1946 led the British and Americans to unite their zones on January 1, 1947. The French joined on June 1, 1948, which resulted in the creation of the Trizone, followed by a currency reform on June 21, 1948, in the Western occupation zones of Germany and the three sectors of Berlin controlled by the Western allies.

The currency reform in the West precipitated the Berlin Blockade (June 1948 to May 1949), one of the first major international crises of the Cold War era. The Soviet Union blocked the railway, road, and canal access to the western sectors of Berlin to force the United States, the United Kingdom, and France to withdraw the newly introduced Deutschmark—at least from West Berlin. The Western Allies responded with the Berlin airlift to resupply their sectors of the city. By the spring of 1949, the airlift was clearly succeeding, and in May 1949 the USSR ended the blockade. May 1949 also saw the establishment of the Federal Republic of Germany—in the territory of the Trizone with Bonn as the "provisional capital." In October, the USSR responded by supporting the formation of the German Democratic Republic, with East Berlin as its capital city.[59]

For the United States, a successful currency reform had been the most important precondition of the support of West Germany with Marshall Plan funds. The European Recovery Program, as it was officially known, signed by US President Harry S. Truman in April 1948, pumped billions of dollars into the postwar economies of sixteen Western European states between 1948 and 1952. The aim of the European Recovery Program was to rebuild war-devastated regions, remove trade barriers, modernize industries, and make Western Europe prosperous again to prevent the spread of communism. Many historians claim that, without this support, it would not have recovered so quickly from the war.[60] With their support, the United States also hoped to overcome the fact that "the appeal of neutrality was growing" on the European continent, as Tony Judt observed, especially in France and West Germany, but also in the Netherlands and Scandinavia. Many Europeans wanted neither further conflict nor rearmament.[61]

As the Cold War heated up, the fear of atomic warfare increased and, with it, the international antinuclear and peace movement. Securing global peace and preventing a nuclear war also became the major mission of the UN, which was to provide an arena in which international diplomacy might solve conflicts, (de)legitimate military solutions, and establish organizations meant to promote human rights. But from the beginning, the UN attempts to secure worldwide peace were accompanied by continuing and new military conflicts fostered by the developing Global Cold War, which severely complicated the realization of the UN's mission.[62]

The transition from war to peace after 1945 was also in Europe accompanied by violence and civil war, especially in its east and south. Most of these conflicts were embedded in the emerging Cold War rivalry.[63] The first large Cold War proxy conflict was the Greek Civil War, Europe's most violent post-1945 war until the breakup of Yugoslavia in the 1990s.[64] By the time Nazi forces withdrew from Greece in 1944, communist and socialist resistance groups dominated across the country. When the British military intervened to support the army of the conservative Greek government and restore the monarchy, a civil war began in 1946 and lasted until 1949. The Democratic Army of Greece, controlled by the Communist Party and supported by Yugoslavia, Albania, and Bulgaria, fought against the National Army aided by Britain and the United States. When the conflict ended in October 1949, the Democratic Army of Greece had lost 29,000 soldiers killed in action, and thousands more were imprisoned, exiled, or executed after the war. The National Army suffered 11,000 killed and 8,000 missing. In addition, about 4,000 civilians died and close to a million became homeless.[65] The Greek Civil War was of vast international importance as a catalyst to the Cold War. In response to the crisis in Greece, US President Harry S. Truman proclaimed the Truman Doctrine in March 1947, pledging to support all "free peoples who are resisting attempted subjugation by armed minorities or by outside pressures," a promise clearly directed against communism and Soviet expansionism.[66] The Soviets responded by formalizing their control over other communist states in Eastern Europe, which in turn reinforced the division of the world into competing blocs.

The Cold War Nuclear Threat and the Growing Peace Movement

The intensifying Cold War did not change practices of warfare even as nuclear technology continued to advance, but it did stimulate a nuclear arms race. The Soviet Union successfully tested its first atomic bomb in August 1949 and then, in 1953, its first hydrogen bomb. The United States had performed its first test of the hydrogen bomb in 1952. Britain had nuclear weaponry by 1953, as did France by 1960. In Asia, the People's Republic of China successfully tested its first nuclear weapon in 1964. Eventually, India, Pakistan, Israel, North Korea, and South Africa all possessed nuclear arsenals.[67] What changed was where wars were fought. Following the Greek Civil War, Europe and North America experienced a period of relative peace while wars elsewhere became entangled in Cold War antagonisms. The specter of nuclear war led both the United States and the USSR, along with their respective NATO and Warsaw Pact allies, to maintain strong militaries. Conscription continued across Europe and the United States through the

1970s and, in some cases, into the twenty-first century. Where conscription ended (in Britain in the 1960s and in the United States in the 1970s), armies became increasingly professionalized and began to include more women.[68]

The first major military confrontation of the Global Cold War after the Greek Civil War took place on the Korean Peninsula beginning in 1950. The Korean War was simultaneously a civil war and a Cold War proxy conflict.[69] Its historiography is contested—including the question as to which side started the conflict. One key cause was the agreement made in 1945 between the American and Soviet governments to divide Korea, which had been colonized by Japan, into two zones at the 38th parallel for the purpose of disarming the Japanese and instituting Korean governing bodies under the trusteeship of the two powers.[70] American and Soviet forces left South and North Korea in 1948 after the establishment of the Democratic People's Republic of Korea in the north and the new Republic of Korea in the south. In the winter of 1948/49, skirmishes erupted, with fighting along the border breaking out in May 1949. A year later, North Korea, aided by Chinese forces, invaded South Korea, and in late June the United States intervened with the approval of the UN. Both sides massacred civilians and POWs and perpetrated other atrocities during this phase of the conflict.[71] By late spring 1951, the fighting stabilized along the border, where it lasted for another two years, while the United States continued bombing raids on cities and infrastructure, including dams in areas controlled by the Democratic People's Republic of Korea. The war resulted in an estimated 2 million North Korean casualties, including 520,000 soldiers, and 1.3 million South Korean casualties, including 415,000 soldiers. In addition, up to 900,000 Chinese soldiers, 37,000 American US military personnel, and 3,000 UN personnel were killed.[72] With the threat of nuclear war in the background, the Chinese and North Koreans finally signed an armistice proposed by the United States in mid-summer 1953. Not party to the negotiations, South Korea refused to sign, and without a peace treaty, war between the south and the north still threatens in the early twenty-first century.

Cold War tensions increased further on both sides of the Atlantic after the Korean War and reached a climax in the early 1960s. On the European continent, the construction of the Berlin Wall in August 1961 in response to the continuous exodus of people from East to West Germany further strained the relations between the NATO states and the Warsaw Pact. Preventing the German people from moving freely between both German states, the wall became the visible symbol of Europe divided into two hostile camps.[73] On the other side of the Atlantic, the Cuban Missile Crisis one year later brought the world to the brink of nuclear war. A procommunist guerrilla movement led by Fidel Castro had overthrown the US-supported military dictatorship ruling Cuba in January 1950. In April 1961, the United States, under President John F. Kennedy, unsuccessfully attempted to dislodge the Castro regime using exiled anti-Castro Cubans in a failed operation known as the Bay of Pigs Invasion. To buttress the new communist state and aid its defense, in October 1962 the USSR arranged to provide the Cuban government with intermediate-range missiles. The United States responded by imposing a naval blockade of Cuba. Two weeks later, discussions at the UN resulted in a compromise that averted war—the Soviets withdrew their missiles from Cuba in exchange for a US vow not to invade Cuba and an agreement to remove American rockets from Turkey.[74]

The nuclear arms race continued in the 1960s, but the international protest against nuclear weapons had been growing since the late 1950s.[75] In the late 1960s, the first negotiations for the control and even abolition of nuclear weapons opened. In February 1967, the Treaty of Tlatelolco prohibited nuclear weapons in Latin America and the Caribbean. Starting on July 1, 1968, with the signatures of Britain, the United States, and the USSR, more and more non-nuclear-weapon states signed the Treaty on the Non-Proliferation of Nuclear Weapons. The treaty entered into force in March 1970. In 2019, ninety-three states had agreed never to acquire nuclear weapons, and the nuclear-armed states made a legal commitment to disarm. In August 1985, the South Pacific also became a nuclear-free zone, with the Treaty of Rarotonga prohibiting the manufacture, stationing, or testing of nuclear weapons within the area.[76] These worldwide antinuclear and peace movements after the Second World War were connected with the growing anti-imperialist movement in the East and West, which supported the anticolonial struggles across Asia, the Middle East, and Africa.

Wars of Decolonization in Asia and the Middle East

Asia and the Middle East became the first anticolonial battlegrounds after the Second World War.[77] The three main imperial powers involved were Britain, the Netherlands, and France. In British-ruled India, the participation of Indian troops in World War I (1914–18) had reinforced the struggle for liberation because it aroused expectations that their service would be rewarded with self-government.[78] But the British dashed those hopes, giving rise to an increasingly militant struggle for self-government during the interwar period. The presumption of the British government that Indian troops would again fight in World War II led in August 1942 to the Quit India Movement, which demanded immediate self-rule. The British reacted by imprisoning the Hindu leaders of this movement, including Mahatma Gandhi, and quelling the rebellion.[79] In contrast to Hindu supporters of the independence movement, Muslim leaders continued to cooperate with the British government. They hoped the British would carry out the proposal, made earlier in the war, that if India cooperated in the war effort, it would be given full dominion status as a sovereign country or "the option to secede from the Empire-Commonwealth provided that no part of India could be forced to join the new state."[80] This proposal essentially gave Muslims veto power over the nature of the new dominion and inspired ideas about a Muslim homeland on the subcontinent.

As violence rapidly spread between various groups in India, Britain sought a quick exit from the territory and in June 1947 announced a plan for the division of the subcontinent into two separately governed countries: India and Pakistan. Independence followed for both states in mid-August of that year. This partition resulted in communal strife as millions fled their homes to one or the other side of the new international border. Thousands resided in refugee camps located in both countries. The precise figures of deaths from conflict among Hindus, Muslims, and Sikhs are unknown, but it is likely that half a million to one million men, women, and children died. Some twelve million people migrated between India and Pakistan.[81] While the subcontinent had indeed gained independence, the partition into India and Pakistan nevertheless led to bloody sectarian war and long-lasting conflict between the two countries.

In the Middle East as well, the British Empire faced increasing resistance to its rule following World War I. One center of conflict was Palestine, which until the defeat and dissolution of the Ottoman Empire in 1922 was an Ottoman region inhabited mainly by Palestinian Arabs and a small, but quickly growing, Jewish minority. The region became part of a British-controlled mandate awarded by the League of Nations.[82] The historiography of what happened between Britain's control over the region, the Jewish declaration of Israel as an independent state in May 1948, and the war accompanying it is hotly debated.[83] But what is not in doubt is the significance for the future of the Middle East of the controversial 1917 Balfour Declaration announcing support for the establishment "of a national home for the Jewish people" in Palestine and at the same time proclaiming, "Nothing shall be done which may prejudice the civil and religious rights of existing non-Jewish communities in Palestine."[84] Arab resistance against British rule culminated in the Arab Rebellion of 1936–39. The violent British response weakened Arab power. Militant Zionist paramilitary groups also were active during this period, attacking the British and Arabs alike. Mounting pressure on the British military, financial austerity in the United Kingdom, and the possibility of a rift with the United States caused by sympathy for Jewish refugees led Britain to turn to the UN for a resolution and end the mandate in February 1947. The UN issued a partition plan in November 1947, Resolution 181, which allocated 5,700 square miles (primarily in the fertile regions) to the Jewish state and 4,300 square miles (in the hills) to the Palestinian Arabs.[85]

The response by both ethnic groups was increased fighting, which led to a civil war in which civilians and the military became targets and eventually resulted in the defeat of Palestinian military forces. Israel declared independence from Britain on May 14, 1948, and the British withdrew from the region the next day. At this point, the armies of Egypt, Transjordan, Syria, Lebanon, and Iraq entered the war against Israeli forces, which nevertheless defeated them in this second phase of the war, acquiring in the process more territory than the UN had originally awarded. The Israelis called the conflict the War of Independence. The Palestinians labeled it al-Nakba (catastrophe), because of the loss of their homeland and flight of 730,000 refugees.[86]

One of the first subsequent conflicts unfolded in the Suez Crisis. At the end of July 1956, the president of Egypt, Gamal Abdel Nasser, nationalized the Suez Canal, which was formerly under British and French control. Both powers coordinated with Israel and intervened militarily in Egypt in October 1956. But, contrary to their expectations, the UN, supported by the United States, condemned the attack and confirmed Egyptian sovereignty over and ownership of the canal. The British and French withdrew their troops, but Israel stayed in the Gaza Strip that it had captured, contravening the UN order to evacuate it.[87] The next decade witnessed continuous tensions between Israel and neighboring Arab states, occasional skirmishes at the borders with Jordan and

Syria, and ongoing conflict between Israel and Palestinian militants based in Syria, Lebanon, and Jordan. This reached a climax in the Six-Day War fought between June 5 and 10, 1967, by Israel and Egypt, Jordan, and Syria. Israel was victorious in this conflict, and its counteroffensives resulted in the seizure of East Jerusalem and the West Bank from Jordan and the Golan Heights from Syria. The Middle East region remains unsettled in the early twenty-first century.[88]

Like Britain, the Netherlands was not willing to give up its colonies in Asia after the Second World War. Anticolonial struggle in the Dutch East Indies was rooted in the period of Japanese occupation (1942–45), which dismantled much of the Dutch colonial state and economy. On August 17, 1945, the leaders of the Indonesian liberation movement, Sukarno and Mohammad Hatta, declared independence from the Netherlands. When the Dutch returned to resume control over the islands, they were met by an armed insurgency. Despite its deployment of 270,000 soldiers and after bitter guerrilla fighting, the Netherlands finally had to agree to a settlement and transferred sovereignty to the new republic in December 1949. By then, an estimated 5,000 Dutch soldiers and more than 100,000 Indonesians had died.[89]

The French also became intensively involved in anticolonial warfare in Asia and North Africa after 1945. During the Second World War, the French colony of Indochina had fallen under Japanese occupation (1940–45). Immediately after the surrender of the Japanese forces, Hồ Chí Minh, the leader of the communist League for the Independence of Vietnam, or Việt Minh, declared the independence of the Democratic Republic of Vietnam (DRV) on September 2, 1945. In March 1946, France and the DRV negotiated what proved to be a temporary settlement, as relations between the two deteriorated over the next few months. In late 1946, war began in earnest, and by the new year the French had taken Hanoi from the DRV. Although they suffered heavy casualties, DRV forces persisted and, according to Mark Atwood Lawrence, "garnered broad support in the countryside, where the brutality of French military operations deepened old anticolonial anger."[90]

By 1948, a stalemate had developed in which the French controlled the cities and the Việt Minh held the rural areas. The French government successfully cast their fight against an anticolonial movement as a struggle against communism in order to win military and financial support from the United States.[91] Unlike in the Dutch East Indies, where Sukarno's assurances to the United States that his movement was not communist began to erode US support for the Netherlands in the late 1940s, France received increasing assistance from the United States during the 1950s. Meanwhile, the DRV secured support from the Soviet Union and the newly founded People's Republic of China.[92] Thus, the war in Vietnam became one of the first post–World War II conflicts to be both an anticolonial and a Cold War struggle.

The escalation of foreign involvement influenced the character of the conflict. Whereas the Việt Minh had initially waged a guerrilla war, after 1949, with Chinese and Soviet support, they engaged in large-scale conventional battles. While they were not necessarily successful in the field, these efforts degraded French morale. The last major battle against the French at Dien Bien Phu was fought from March to May 1954 by the

DRV military, assisted by 250,000 Việt Minh laborers, half of whom were women. Suffering its worst military defeat in the conflict, France appealed for a ceasefire on May 8 and agreed to an international conference at Geneva, where the negotiating powers reached a compromise that divided Vietnam into a communist state in the north and an American-backed capitalist state in the south.[93]

The conflict nevertheless continued and developed into the Second Indochina War, involving Vietnam, Laos, and Cambodia. Also known as the Vietnam War, this conflict was officially fought between North Vietnam and the government of South Vietnam from November 1955 to April 1975. The Soviet Union, China, and other communist allies continued to support the North Vietnamese Army and the National Liberation Front of South Vietnam, also known as the Việt Cộng, that fought a guerrilla war against the South Vietnamese Army, which was backed by the United States, South Korea, Australia, and Thailand.

The Vietnam War became the longest, largest, and bloodiest proxy conflict fought by the United States after 1945, which caused a quickly growing anti–Vietnam War movement not only inside the United States, but also elsewhere across the world from the mid-1960s onward. During the peak of the conflict in the late 1960s, some 1.4 million men, including 475,200 American soldiers, fought against approximately 1.1 million North Vietnamese Army and Việt Cộng soldiers. The United States officially ended their military involvement in August 1973, but the struggle continued until the North Vietnamese Army's capture of Saigon in April 1975. One year later, North and South Vietnam were finally reunified.[94] Lawrence estimated that the human costs of the conflict in the period between 1960 and 1973, during the peak of the American involvement, reached 2 to 3 million Vietnamese killed and roughly the same number maimed. In addition, the fighting "destroyed millions of acres of farmland, pulverized the country's industrial facilities, and damaged many villages." Roughly 58,300 US servicemembers were killed.[95] One reason for the United States to end the Vietnam War was its corrosive effects on American society and the international standing of the United States.

Wars of Decolonization in Africa

Through the 1950s to the 1980s, the decolonization process also escalated in Africa. One colony after another declared independence and fought its former rulers, primarily using guerrilla warfare.[96] Home to one of the first postwar liberation movements in Africa, Ghana (formerly the British colony of Gold Coast) was the first in Sub-Saharan Africa to gain independence. Ghana's self-rule was achieved without an armed struggle by agreement between the British government and the leader of the independence movement, Kwame Nkrumah, in March 1956. The British colonies of Nigeria and Sierra Leone also peacefully gained independence in October 1960 and April 1961. But elsewhere in Africa, decolonization after World War II was only achieved through armed struggle.

The first large armed conflict in North Africa was the Algerian War, which was, according to Martin Evans, a "pivotal episode in the break-up of empires."[97] Tensions between Algerian Muslims and their French colonizers had simmered since the end of the Second World War, and in 1954 the Algerian Front de libération nationale (National Liberation Front, FLN) made several coordinated attacks across the country. It insisted on the necessity of violence and thus fought against not only French settlers, police, and soldiers, but also their more moderate nationalist rivals who hoped to achieve liberation peacefully. The Algerian War, then, was both a war for independence from France and a civil war. The French government, however, maintained that decolonization was out of the question because it considered Algeria an integral part of France and its people French citizens. Thus, it at first called the fight against the FLN a "police action." This changed in 1957, when France had to introduce military rule and mobilize ever more reservists and conscripts from the metropole to fight alongside West African troops against the FLN, which used insurgent tactics, especially in rural areas. The conflict became bloodier as French forces retaliated by using extreme counterinsurgency measures, and it further escalated during the Battle of Algiers, a campaign of urban guerrilla warfare by the FLN against French Algerian authorities in 1956/57. Although the French were eventually successful, as Evans put it, "the methods of victory had definitely alienated Muslim hearts and minds."[98]

French imperial policies led to political resistance against the war in France and contributed to the fall of the French Fourth Republic in September 1958. When Charles de Gaulle was elected president of the new Fifth Republic in February 1959, he supported a negotiated settlement in Algeria. In January 1961, a referendum on self-determination took place, which was overwhelmingly supported both in France and in Algeria. Civil war in Algeria continued, however, until the FLN and French government signed a peace accord that was ratified through popular referendum. Algeria finally achieved independence in July 1962. The number of casualties in the war is still debated. The estimates reach a total of 300,000 Algerian deaths on both sides, including 55,000 to 65,000 civilians; 24,614 French died, of which 15,681 were in fighting and terrorist attacks, and the rest were from injuries and illness; nearly 1 million Europeans left Algeria.[99]

During the period that France was engaged in the Algerian War, the British were fighting the so-called Mau Mau Rebellion in Kenya.[100] When the anticolonial fighting began in 1952, the British responded by declaring a state of emergency and moving troops into the region, deploying nearly 10,000 men to defeat the Mau Mau, the name given to the mostly Kikuyu rebel groups.[101] This anticolonial conflict also developed into a civil war because the Mau Mau attacked not only settlers and British police and regiments, but also other Africans who opposed them. The British, in turn, engaged in forced population removals and committed acts of violence against civilians that included beatings, torture, and murder. Central to what took place over the next two years was the creation of the "pipeline," a series of camps where screenings assessed the extent of threat posed by individual African detainees. Historians estimate that between 160,000 and 320,000 Africans, including women and children, were detained in camps. Officially, 12,000 died; unofficially, the figure is up to 20,000.[102] Although the uprising was routed by the end of 1956, the state of emergency lasted until 1960, when the British, realizing they could no longer hold an African empire, began a slow transition to independence. Kenya gained full independence in December 1963, and most of the white settlers returned to Britain, as did the numerous migrants from Asia who had lived and worked in the country.

With Britain and France relinquishing their last African colonies in the 1960s, Belgium and Portugal were the two European imperial powers left in the region. In the 1950s, the Belgian government refused to grant Congo independence or increase measures of self-determination, believing that its paternalist policies would keep colonials loyal to the metropole. It criticized their Western partners who encouraged decolonization, claiming that any attempt to rush self-rule would create opportunities for communists to take advantage of the situation. Influenced by successful independence movements elsewhere in Africa, the Congolese political parties that had emerged for the first election granted by Belgium in 1957 began to demand self-governance. Belgium promised to grant sovereignty to Congo at the end of June 1960.[103] The first elections in June 1960 were won by the Mouvement National Congolais led by Patrice Lumumba, who became prime minister. But he soon faced a rebellion in the armed forces and the Belgian-supported secession of the mineral-rich Katanga district. His government fell to a Belgian- and American-backed coup staged by Colonel Joseph-Désiré Mobutu in autumn 1960. Lumumba was arrested and killed in January 1961. A rebellion by his supporters erupted in July 1964 backed by the Soviet Union, East Germany, China, and Cuba, but failed. In November 1965, Mobutu staged another coup with US support, and his dictatorial regime remained in power until rebels deposed him in 1997.[104]

The Cold War and decolonization were deeply intertwined in the decolonization of Portugal's African colonies too—Guinea-Bissau, Mozambique, and Angola—but unlike the other colonial powers, Portugal was not a democracy. Here, a corporatist authoritarian regime installed in 1933 under António de Oliveira Salazar ruled until April 1974, when a military coup overthrew the Portuguese dictatorship; only then did the path to decolonization open. The new democratic government decided to extricate itself from fighting the independence movements in its African colonies, which had begun in Angola in 1961, in Guinea-Bissau in 1963, and in Mozambique in 1964.[105] Portugal, in a way not dissimilar to the French position on Algeria, had argued that its possessions were not colonies, but rather provinces of Portugal—integral parts of that country. To receive assistance from NATO allies in its struggle against the anticolonial movements in its colonies, the authoritarian Portuguese government had claimed that it faced a Soviet-backed communist insurgency, and indeed, the Marxist-oriented rebel groups did receive support from the USSR, China, and Cuba.[106] Even after the colonies were liberated in 1974/75, civil war between different political groups continued. In Angola, for instance, more than 500,000 people lost their lives in fighting that lasted until 2001.[107]

Along with the Wars of Decolonization occurring in Asia, the Middle East, and Africa, Latin America became embroiled in conflict internally and with the United States, especially in the aftermath of the Cuban Missile Crisis. It is important, however, to understand the domestic sources of upheavals in South and Central America. Recent scholarship on Latin America's Cold War has stressed the importance of seeing what happened in the region as being driven not primarily by the fissure between the United States and the USSR, but rather by the ideological conflict between socialism (particularly its Marxist variant) and capitalism and their implications for national economy and politics.[108]

Communism's Collapse and the Post–Cold War World

The factors that caused the collapse of communism and, with it, the end of the Cold War era are still subject to intensive scholarly debate.[109] Next to domestic developments in the USSR and changing international conditions, one important component was the Soviet–Afghan War. In this conflict, the Soviet army supported the procommunist Democratic Republic of Afghanistan, founded in 1978, in its fight against the Islamic insurgent groups of the *mujahideen*, which were supported by the United States. Up to 877,000 Afghans died in this war (650,000 men and 227,000 women) between 1978 and 1987; 6 million fled to Pakistan and Iran.[110] In total, 13,833 Soviet soldiers were killed. The war proved economically and military costly for the USSR, which sent a total of 620,000 soldiers to Afghanistan; at its peak in the mid-1980s, over 105,000 were stationed there at a time. Despite its superior size, the Soviet military, supported by no more than 55,000 soldiers of the Democratic Republic of Afghanistan, was not able to defeat the *mujahideen*, and the leadership of the USSR ordered a complete withdrawal of its troops in February 1989. The Soviet retreat did not, however, end the fighting, which developed into a civil war that lasted until 1992.[111]

The conflict not only further undermined the international legitimacy of the USSR and its Brezhnev Doctrine, the policy under which the Soviet Union had used force outside its borders only to defend what its communist leadership perceived as core interests. William Maley asserts that the "withdrawal from Afghanistan compromised the previously fundamental notion [that] the 'gains of socialism' were irreversible."[112] It also weakened faith in the leadership of the Communist Party and led to increasing domestic criticism. One major reason was that the war acted together with the continuing arms race as a lasting drain on the stagnant Soviet economy. This and the rising number of dead Soviet soldiers led to growing domestic dissent against the war.[113] Furthermore, the final retreat of the Soviet armed forces weakened the position of the military inside the Soviet Union, which was an important pillar of the antireformist camp in the Communist Party. This, in turn, according to Rafael Reuveny and Aseem Prakash, "hastened *perestroika* [restructuring], and facilitated the collapse of the system."[114] For them, the "war created conditions for the demilitarizing of the Soviet society" and "added new vigour to the forces that unleashed *glasnost* [openness]."[115] Clearly, the Soviet–Afghan War contributed to the disintegration of the Soviet system; to what extent, however, is disputed.[116]

In any case, the USSR under Soviet leader Mikhail Gorbachev did not intervene in 1989/90 when the Berlin Wall came down, borders opened, and free elections ousted communist regimes everywhere in Eastern Europe. In late 1991, the Soviet Union itself dissolved into its component republics. For conservative historians like John Lewis Gaddis, American persistence and the universal desire for freedom and democracy had fostered the end of the Soviet Union and Cold War.[117] Others, like Nicholas Guyatt, rejected this interpretation informed by Cold War rhetoric. They placed the collapse of the Soviet Union and the Eastern bloc and the end of the Cold War in a global context. Guyatt, for instance, pointed to "the struggles of independence, autonomy, and economic progress in the Third World." He emphasized that these liberation movements "were not simply proxy battles between superpower sponsors" and stressed that the Cold War itself "was rooted in larger struggles over development." For him, the globalization processes often discussed as characteristic for the post–Cold War era— which include globalization in the economic sphere, international exchange, and cooperation based on multination organizations and cultural interpenetration—started long before the Soviet collapse.[118]

GENDERING THE GLOBAL COLD WAR AND ITS AFTERMATH

Historical research on gender, the military, and war in the era of the Global Cold War began in the early 1990s, fostered by contemporary events and a changing conceptualization of the Cold War. Until the collapse of the Soviet Union and the Eastern bloc, studies had focused on politics and ideology, emphasizing the contrast between the democratic Western and the dictatorial Eastern states. Before the 1990s, few scholars adopted such theoretical perspectives as cultural or gender studies that revealed the resemblance or intersection between both systems. This changed with the inclusion of approaches like cultural and intellectual history and the turn to global and transnational studies. The thematic and regional focus of the historiography on the Cold War moved away from the East–West conflict. The decentering of the Cold War historiography also stimulated research by women's and gender historians. Major subjects of their scholarship were the working of gender as a marker of difference in the East–West conflict at the center of the Cold War; the role of gender and sexuality in security politics and the practice of military and war; the functioning of gender in the Wars of Decolonization; and cultural representations of the Cold War gender order.[119] In addition, the conflicts that followed the breakdown of the Soviet Union in eastern Europe, especially the wars in the former Yugoslavia, fostered interest in themes of war, genocide, gender, and sexual violence.[120] The increasing importance of humanitarianism, humanitarian interventions, and peacekeeping in the post–Cold War era sparked research on these subjects from a gender perspective.[121]

The Long Postwar and the Gender Order of the Cold War

In Asia and Europe, the starting conditions for a reconstruction of politics, the economy, society, and culture after the Second World War were shaped by the country's specific location and overshadowed by the increasing rivalry between the United States and the USSR. Successful economic recovery and development became an important weapon in the Cold War competition. A paramount aim of all postwar states and societies on both sides of the Iron Curtain was the "normalization" of the social order of daily life with the family and gender relations at its center. This policy included, first, the speedy discharge of the many women who had served in the armed forces as doctors and nurses or auxiliaries and soldiers; second, economic demobilization that focused on putting male veterans back to work and returning to home and family the millions of women who had replaced men in the wartime workforce; third, social and civil legislation to stabilize the family, which was widely perceived as a pillar of postwar reconstruction and order; and fourth, the propagation of the preferred gender ideology in popular culture.[122] In the West, the focus of this ideology was the model of the male-breadwinner–female-homemaker family that emphasized the role of a woman as mother, modern housewife, and consumer.[123] In the East, the dual-earner family became the declared aim of family, labor, and welfare policies, which promoted the ideal of the working woman and mother. These contrasting visions for the family and the gender order functioned as important markers of difference between the two systems during the Cold War—at least for the industrially developed countries in East and West—and have been explored by several studies since the 1990s, first with a focus on the West and later on the East.[124]

The so-called kitchen debate, a series of spontaneous exchanges—through interpreters—between then-US Vice President Richard Nixon and Soviet Premier Nikita Khrushchev at the opening of the American National Exhibition at Sokolniki Park in Moscow on July 24, 1959, became an international symbol for the importance of the family and home in the Cold War. The exhibition showed an entire suburban American home filled with futuristic kitchen technology and modern furniture, which, the organizers claimed, anyone in America could afford. It was supposed to represent the fruits of the capitalist American consumer market to the Soviet visitors of the exhibition. According to the US media, the exhibition with the American home at its center demonstrated the superiority of the capitalist system, which, unlike communism, could satisfy consumer needs. Through this rhetoric, they defined technological and economic advancement in consumer terms and tried to change the ground of competition with the USSR, after the American crisis of confidence two years earlier caused by the Soviets' launch of the first space satellite, *Sputnik*.[125] Furthermore, as David J. Snyder argued, US officials attempted to make in their global programming "American home life, and the role of the putatively independent and satisfied American female," who no longer needed to toil in her kitchen, "a cornerstone of public diplomacy propaganda."[126]

Of course, American propaganda reflected the reality of neither the majority of working- and middle-class families in the United States, regardless of their racial and ethnic background, nor that of comparable families in Western Europe. There, despite the Marshall Plan and the speedy economic recovery, most countries were still trying to overcome the aftermath of war. Like the Soviet Union and Eastern European states, most of western Europe also had to focus efforts on rebuilding the infrastructure and production in the 1950s. The destruction of millions of homes in the war made reconstruction of housing a priority in Eastern and Western Europe. The American dream of owning a suburban house did not translate into the imagination of Europeans. They longed to rent an apartment of their own in one of the many new, modern housing complexes with shared laundry facilities, surrounding greenery, and community recreational grounds. Accompanying new housing in the east, beginning the 1950s, and in Scandinavia and France in the 1960s, was all-day child care for the growing number of working mothers.[127] What united all industrialized states and societies in the East and the West during the Cold War was, according to Mary Nolan, a "growing tendency . . . to make the modern home the measure of civilization"; what distinguished them was the specific form of this home and the ideologically driven social expectations for the family who lived in it.[128]

This peaceful Cold War competition was, according to Cynthia Enloe, accompanied by a militarization that for forty years sustained Cold War relationships between people, drove the nuclear arms race, and required armed forces with huge appetites for recruits. This policy of militarization depended, Enloe wrote, on ideas about manliness and womanliness not only of the men and women serving in the armed forces, but also of the civilians who never went through basic military training.[129] The military became one of the key institutions for the gendering of society. The continuing militarization of the dominant ideal of masculinity in the Cold War era depended on the complementary fostering of domesticity of women and a clear gender hierarchy, which also continued to exist in the east despite all its socialist rhetoric of equality.[130]

Part of this gender order of the Cold War was the image of women as victims of war and representatives of peace, which was already broadly propagated in the first years after the Second World War as part of the attempts at a cultural and military demobilization of society and women (see Figure 26.1). This image was also reinforced by the highly gendered collective memories of the Second World War. Women's extensive military participation in World War II tended to be forgotten in patriotic memories, which centered instead on the predominantly male figures of the victor, the martyr, and the victim. Linking national reconstruction with the restoration of a hierarchical gender order, these narratives marginalized or erased women's war experiences.[131]

Gendering Security Policy and the Armed Forces of the West

The suppression of women's war service in memory, their quick military demobilization, and their stylization as representatives of peace were part of the political attempts to "normalize" social relations in postwar societies by regendering them. Until the last decade of the Cold War era, in the West and in the East, the integration of women into armed forces did not reach the levels of World War II, when on average 2 to 9 percent of military personnel in state-based armed forces and 10 to 15 percent in partisan movements were women.[132] Until the 1970s, most Western countries limited the percentage of women in their armed forces to around 2 percent and restricted their employment to the branches of medicine, communications, logistics, and administration. Women in the military continued to be reduced to the role of "helpers" of men, as is demonstrated by a 1953 US poster titled "They Depend on You! U.S. Army Nurse Corps" (Figure 26.2), which attempted to recruit women for the military during the Korean War, when approximately 140,000 women were employed, many as nurses. However, only 540 nurses served in Korea itself. The placard shows an attractive young woman in a crisp, white nurse's uniform with a background of several smiling faces of US soldiers.[133]

The policy of Western militaries toward female soldiers changed slowly in the Cold War era because of the challenge they posed to dominant ideas of military masculinity, which were based on heterosexuality and the old connection of male citizenship to the male right to kill and duty to die for one's country.[134] The increasing integration of servicewomen was fostered by the move to professional armies based on volunteers, starting in Britain in the 1960s and the United States in the 1970s. The growing centrality of technological sophistication allowed the integration of more and more women because it required potentially degendered skills and knowledge and not mainly strength. Increasingly, servicewomen demanded their equal integration in the armed forces, including access to combat positions. In 2017, the average proportion of women in the militaries of the twenty-eight member states of NATO reached 11 percent, and most laws and regulations that excluded women from equal access to combat positions have been repealed.[135] Resistance against the integration of gay, lesbian, and bisexual people in the armed forces lasted longer; most Western countries did not begin to integrate these servicemembers until the 1990s. At first, calls for such reforms emanated from the gay and lesbian rights movement that began to grow in 1970s, which later enjoyed wider support because of changing public opinion toward homosexuality.[136]

The close relationship of gender, sexuality, and Cold War politics is indicated by the "lavender scare" in the United States and other Western countries during the 1950s, which was fueled by ardent anticommunism and the fear of gender equality and sexual dissidence. Politicians like American Senator Joseph McCarthy constructed a link between male effeminacy, homosexuality, and political subversion. "Men who failed to stand up to the Soviet Union were suspect, not only politically, but sexually, as anticommunist hysteria went hand in hand with homophobic witch hunts," wrote Helen Laville.[137] An ideal of civilized, but tough and virile heterosexual masculinity informed postwar security politics, creating the expectation that politicians, military leaders, and ordinary men demonstrate that they were not "domesticated." In his 2001 study, *Imperial Brotherhood*, Robert D. Dean demonstrated the extent to which foreign policy was informed by such an ideal of Cold War masculinity. He showed how the foreign policy decision makers in the US government of the 1950s and 1960s "incarnated an imperial masculinity tied to patterns of class and education" that embraced "toughness."[138]

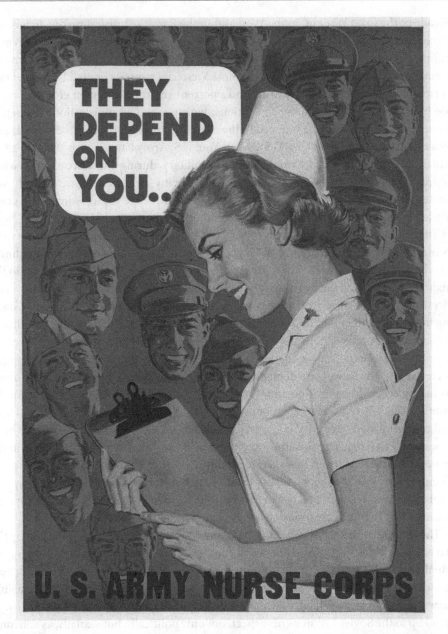

FIGURE 26.2 *They Depend on You! U.S. Army Nurse Corps*, poster by the Recruiting Publicity Bureau of the US Army, an attempt to recruit army nurses during the Korean War, unknown artist, [n.p., n.d.], 1953.

(University of North Carolina at Greensboro, University Libraries, The Betty H. Carter Women Veterans Historical Project)

Such a notion of masculinity and the lavender scare reflected male anxieties and kept in place the Western ideal of the Cold War gender order, in which heterosexuality and domesticity, especially in the 1940s to 1960s, played an important role.[139] This ideal needed sustained defense and reaffirmation because it was constantly challenged, not only by the reality of most people's lives, which rarely matched the propaganda promises, but also by social change and political opposition. At home, the ideal faced criticism from the old and new Left, the peace movement, the anti-imperial movement, and the old and new women's movement. Abroad, this ideal was challenged by the anticolonial movements, the opposing power of the Soviet Union with its cultural policy and intensive propaganda, and its communist allies, as well as the growing Non-Aligned Movement, consisting mainly of countries in Africa, Asia, and Latin America.[140]

One important domestic challenge to the Western Cold War gender order was peace activism. Women played a crucial role in the movements against nuclear weaponry, the arms race, and the Algerian and Vietnam Wars. Parallel, they were often active in the new women's movement that began to grow in many Western countries since the late 1960s. This movement rejected the old assumption of supposedly natural differences between the sexes. It contended instead that gender differences were a product of culture and therefore demanded equal rights and duties in all areas of the economy, society, and politics.[141] Its new thinking questioned the old ideals of female domesticity and male toughness and virility, but not necessarily that of the peacefulness of women. One example is the 1968 American anticonscription poster titled "GIRLS SAY YES to boys who say NO" (see Figure 26.3). The poster featured the celebrated US folk singer and peace activist Joan Baez. Along with her sisters, she sits in a serious and innocent pose on a couch; set against the wall above them is the slogan of the poster. The poster draws from a gendered worldview reaching back to the ancient Greek comedy *Lysistrata* by Aristophanes, in which the women of Greece withhold sexual privileges from their husbands and lovers as a means of forcing the men to negotiate peace. The poster calls on women to break with the old tradition of promising love and sexual favors to men who go to war, and it challenges the notion that only aggressively virile and martial masculinity is sexually attractive for women, but it does not question the ideal of female peacefulness.

Gender, Imperial Conflicts, and Anticolonial Struggle

Such new ideas about masculinity and femininity, which became popular in the new women's and peace movements of many Western countries since the late 1960s, differed from the gender images propagated by the anticolonial liberation movements in Asia and Africa at that time. Here, broad support for the liberation struggle in their own population was necessary. Both men and women needed to take up arms and fight for liberation or work full-time to support the war economy. The liberation movement ideal of femininity was thus often more in line with the gender ideology promoted by communist countries in Eastern Europe, which emphasized the equal participation of

FIGURE 26.3 *GIRLS SAY YES to Boys Who Say NO. Proceeds from the Sale of This Poster Go to The Draft Resistance*, American antidraft poster against the Vietnam War, photo by Jim Marshall, designed by Larry Gates, [n.p.], 1968.

women in the workforce, society, and politics. The Soviet Union made this gender ideology part of its international politics, as indicated by the many struggles between the United States and the USSR in the UN's Commission on the Status of Women, established in 1946. There and elsewhere, both superpowers competed over the question of which system offered the best chance to secure women's equality; of course, practical policy and social reality were another matter.[142]

Different than in the armed forces of NATO and the Warsaw Pact, women were active as soldiers and guerrillas in many of the anticolonial liberation movements in Asia and Africa from the 1940s through the 1970s.[143] They often even became the iconographic representation of the liberation struggle by symbolizing not only the mobilization of the whole people—old and young, men and women—for the fight against colonial occupation and oppression. They were also used to give the anticolonial struggle a human and likable face for the international public, as is indicated by the propaganda material printed for foreign countries. This media strategy was meant help to win the necessary political and material support for the liberation movements. The many colorful posters produced by the DRV during the Vietnam War showing beautiful, young women carrying guns are but one example. An especially popular motif was the presentation of three armed women, one each from the three countries involved in the struggle against the United States—Cambodia, Vietnam, and Laos—ready to protect their homelands. This motif was also used on the poster produced by the new Vietnamese government to celebrate the final victory in 1976 titled "Cambodge, Viet Nam, Laos: Victoire" (see Figure 26.4).[144]

The inclusion of armed women in the anticolonial struggle was needed by the liberation movements and thus rhetorically supported in their propaganda, but it nevertheless challenged notions of male identity within the armies of the insurgents, which were often informed by the traditional ideas of manhood of the colonial rulers against which they were fighting. Armed and fighting women in the guerrilla armies also questioned the ideas of white manhood of the imperial powers. Accordingly, during and after the anticolonial struggle, gender was often a site of contestation, as Raphaëlle Branche emphasizes. She claims that the often-ambivalent ways gender worked during the Wars of Decolonization must be considered in the study of anticolonial struggle and its aftermath.[145]

Genocidal Warfare, Sexual Violence, and Humanitarianism

Branche and other scholars who work on the post-1945 Wars of Decolonization furthermore contended that these conflicts were as much total wars as the First and Second World Wars. These wars also affected all areas of the economy, society, and culture, including gender relations; needed the mobilization of whole societies; constantly crossed the borders between military and society in warfare; and were marked by the use of mass violence against civilians, including sexual violence. One of the first conflicts after the Second World War, in which rape was systematically used as a weapon of

FIGURE 26.4 *Cambodge Vietnam Laos: Victoire*, North Vietnamese poster celebrating the victory over the United States and South Vietnam in the Second Indochina War, printed on behalf of the prime minister of the unified Vietnam, Phạm Văn Đồng (1906–2000), unknown artists, [n.p.], 1976.

(651331152: Marka/Getty Images)

genocidal warfare, was the Bangladesh Liberation War fought between the Provisional Government of Bangladesh and Pakistan in 1971. The number of victims is still contested; some scholars estimate that Pakistani soldiers raped between 200,000 and 400,000 Bangladeshi women and girls.[146] The extent of sexual violence in this conflict shocked the international public, but that did not lead to research on the subject. Broader scholarly interest in wartime sexual violence did not develop until the 1990s, when the genocidal warfare in Rwanda and former Yugoslavia drew public attention.[147]

In the Rwandan genocide, a mass slaughter of Tutsi by members of the Hutu majority government, mass rape became a systematic tool of warfare. Up to 800,000 Rwandans, mostly Hutus, were killed from April to July 1994 and an estimated 2 million were displaced and became refugees. In his 1996 report, the UN special rapporteur on Rwanda, René Degni-Ségui, stated, "Rape was the rule and its absence was the exception." He estimated that between 250,000 and 500,000 Rwandese women and girls had been raped. According to him, rape was thus "used as a 'weapon' by the perpetrators of the massacres. This can be estimated from the number and nature of the victims as well as from the forms of rape."[148]

Even more than the Rwandan genocide, the Yugoslav Wars (1991–2001) stimulated research on war, gender, and sexual violence. This decade-long conflict facilitated the breakup of the Yugoslav state and led to an estimated 130,000 to 140,000 total deaths and the displacement of 4 million people. The conflicts included widespread attacks on civilians, population expulsions, and the use of concentration camps. Most of the massacres occurred in Bosnia and Herzegovina, Croatia, and Kosovo.[149] The estimates of the number of women and men raped during the wars vary; the European Union posits a total of 20,000 women victims,[150] and the number of men is estimated around 3,000.[151]

The genocidal character of these two and other conflicts of the post–Cold War era and their increasing media presence, which grew with the rise of the Internet, overshadowed the fact that the number of civil wars fell from 50 in 1990 to 34 in 2006, as did the number of war casualties.[152] What dramatically increased instead was the number of humanitarian interventions and peacekeeping missions by the UN. Between 1948 and 1990, there were no more than 18 UN peacekeeping missions, compared to 54 between 1991 and 2013.[153] In 2017, the UN Department of Peacekeeping Operations led 15 missions, involving in total 91,366 uniformed and 14,831 civilian personnel. Since the 1990s, the UN personnel have included more and more women, the integration of whom is fostered by the policy of "gender equality and mainstreaming" that the UN officially pursues. In 2015, when the UN Female Military Peacekeepers Network was created, women constituted 3 percent of its uniformed and 30 percent of its civilian personnel.[154]

Despite their small percentage in the UN peacekeeping troops, women are their public face in the early twenty-first century, as is exemplified by the UN poster "Women in Peacekeeping: The Power to Empower" for the International Day of the United Nations Peacekeepers in May 2009 (Figure 26.5). Seventy-five years after the end of the

FIGURE 26.5 *Women in Peacekeeping: The Power to Empower. International Day of United Nations Peace Keeping. 29 May 2009*, poster by the United Nations. New York, 2009.

(UN Photo)

Second World War, women are still used to represent peace, no longer mainly as mothers and suffering victims of warfare, like in the poster from 1946 discussed earlier (Figure 26.1), but as active military agents of peacekeeping. In the early twenty-first century, the UN counterimage to the still-dominant masculinized representations of war relies on female soldiers rather than civilian women to visually evoke peace and peacekeeping.

CONCLUSION

Since the end of the Second World War, the social status of women and men has clearly changed, especially in Western countries. Women and gay, lesbian, bisexual, and transgender people reached legal equality in many areas. This also pertains to the institution of the armed forces in an increasing number of countries. But even though they are legally on par with heterosexual cisgender men, they still struggle to find equal acceptance in the armed forces, similar to their situation in states and societies. Parallel, the visual representations of women in the context of the military and war changed. In the early twenty-first century, as a matter of course, they include a much broader variety of female images, from peace activists and war protesters, through civilian supporters and victims of war, to military nurses and doctors, as well as women soldiers and officers. The roles and tasks of men in the military also altered with the technological transformation of warfare and the new tasks of armed forces in humanitarian interventions and peacekeeping missions. But the representations of military masculinity, especially in popular culture, often seem not to keep up with these changed realities and are furthermore challenged by social, racial, and ethnic differences between men.

Even though the armed forces—at least in most countries of the West—cannot be presented as all-male institutions like in the first post-1945 decades, the notion of the military and war as a domain of heterosexual men prevails in many cultural representations. The struggle for legal equality and eventual growing acceptance and integration of gay, lesbian, and bisexual soldiers has not dislodged the dominant public image of the military as an institution of tough, heterosexual masculinity. Only a closer look indicates that the representations of military masculinity change too, at least in some NATO countries like Canada, Germany, Norway, and the Netherlands. In such cases, the armed forces must present themselves today as fighting for humanitarian goals or peacekeeping to find public support. This justification given for the necessity of the military also calls for a more "civilized," protective image of military masculinity.

NOTES

1. Elizabeth Borland, "International Women's Day," in *Encyclopedia of Gender and Society*, ed. Jodi O'Brien (Los Angeles: Sage, 2009), 1:466–67.
2. Amy L. Sayward, *The United Nations in International History* (London: Bloomsbury Academic, 2017).
3. "Charter of the United Nations, 26 June 1945," accessed January 13, 2018, http://www.un.org/en/sections/un-charter/chapter-i/index.html.
4. Paul Ham, *Hiroshima Nagasaki: The Real Story of the Atomic Bombings and Their Aftermath* (New York: St. Martin's, 2014).
5. David Cortright, *Peace: A History of Movements and Ideas* (Cambridge: Cambridge University Press, 2008).

6. Ralph B. Levering, *The Cold War: A Post-Cold War History*, 3rd ed. (Chichester, UK: Wiley Blackwell, 2016).

7. Roger Chickering, "Total War: The Use and Abuse of a Concept," in *Anticipating Total War: The German and American Experiences, 1871–1914*, ed. Manfred F. Boemeke et al. (Cambridge: Cambridge University Press, 1999), 13–28. See the chapter by Raphaëlle Branche on "Gender, the Wars of Decolonization, and the Decline of Empires after 1945" in this handbook; for a discussion of the concept *total war*, see also the chapter by Karen Hagemann and Sonya O. Rose, "War and Gender: The Age of the World Wars and Its Aftermath—an Overview" in this handbook.

8. Odd Arne Westad, *The Global Cold War: Third World Interventions and the Making of Our Times* (Cambridge: Cambridge University Press, 2005); and Jadwiga E. Mooney and Fabio Lanza, eds., *De-Centering Cold War History: Local and Global Change* (London: Routledge, 2013).

9. Oliver Bange and Poul Villaume, eds., *The Long Détente: Changing Concepts of Security and Cooperation in Europe, 1950s–1980s* (Budapest: Central European University Press, 2017).

10. Ibid., 2–3. For some Cold War experts, the period of détente ended with the 1970s and a second period of a "hot" Cold War started, but they focus on the relationship between the United States and the USSR and point to the more confrontational international policy that started with the Reagan era in the 1980s United States. See Gottfried Niedhart, "East–West Conflict: Short Cold War and Long Détente; An Essay on Terminology and Periodization," in ibid., 19–29.

11. Heidelberg Institute for International Conflict Research (HIIK), *Conflict Barometer 2019* (Heidelberg: HIIK, 2020), 10-16.

12. Ibid., 8.

13. Mary Kaldor, *New and Old Wars: Organized Violence in a Global Era* (Stanford, CA: Stanford University Press, 1999).

14. See the chapter by Sandra Whitworth on "The United Nations, Gendered Human Rights, and Peacekeeping since 1945" in this handbook.

15. George Orwell, "You and the Atomic Bomb," *Tribune*, October 19, 1945.

16. Odd Arne Westad, "The Cold War and the International History of the Twentieth Century," in *The Cambridge History of the Cold War*, ed. Melvyn P. Leffler and Westad (Cambridge: Cambridge University Press, 2010), 1:1–19, 4; Niedhart, "East–West Conflict"; and Konrad H. Jarausch et al., eds., *The Cold War: Historiography, Memory, Representation* (Berlin: de Gruyter, 2017), especially the chapters by Siegried Weichlein (19–66), David Reynolds (67–82), and Vladimir O. Pechatnov (83–93).

17. Westad, "The Cold War," 4–5.

18. Fabian Hilfrich, "Anti-imperialism and Anti-colonialism," *The Encyclopedia of Empire*, ed. John M. MacKenzie (Oxford: John Wiley & Sons, 2016), 1–6.

19. Westad, "The Cold War," 4.

20. Konrad H. Jarausch et al., "Rethinking, Representing, and Remembering the Cold War: Some Cultural Perspectives," in Jarausch et al., *The Cold War*, 1–18.

21. Westad, "The Cold War," 5.

22. Nataša Mišković et al., eds., *The Non-Aligned Movement and the Cold War: Delhi-Bandung-Belgrade* (New York: Routledge, 2014).

23. Bange and Villaume, *The Long Détente*.

24. Westad, "The Cold War"; and Niedhart, "East–West Conflict."

25. Akira Iriye, "Historicizing the Cold War," in *Oxford Handbook of the Cold War*, ed. Richard H. Immerman and Petra Goedde (Oxford: Oxford University Press, 2013), 15–31.

26. Leffler and Westad, *Cambridge History*; and Immerman and Goedde, *Oxford Handbook*.

27. Westad, "The Cold War," 2.

28. Richard H. Immermann and Petra Goedde, "Introduction," in Immerman and Goedde, *Oxford Handbook*, 2.

29. Ibid., 3–4.

30. Marko Dumancic, "Hidden in Plain Sight: The Histories of Gender and Sexuality during the Cold War," in *Gender, Sexuality, and the Cold War: A Global Perspective*, ed. Philip E. Muehlenbeck (Nashville, TN: Vanderbilt University Press, 2017), 1–11.

31. Margaret Randolph Higonnet et al., "Introduction," in *Behind the Lines: Gender and the Two World Wars*, ed. Margaret R. Higonnet (New Haven, CT: Yale University Press, 1987), 1–17, 4.

32. Only the following chapters integrate a gender perspective: Helen Laville, "Gender and Women's Rights in the Cold War," in Immerman and Goedde, *Oxford Handbook*, 423–39; and Laura McEnanay, "Cold War Mobilization and Domestic Politics: The United States," in Leffler and Westad, *The Cambridge History of the Cold War*, 1:420–41. In the *Journal of Cold War Studies*, which started in 1999, not more than five articles since its first number focus on gender up to 2019. They were published in 2004, 2013, 2016 (two), and 2017.

33. David J. Snyder, "Domesticity, Rearmament, and the Limits of U.S. Public Diplomacy in the Netherlands during the Early Cold War," *Journal of Cold War Studies* 15, no. 3 (2013): 47–75, 49.

34. Kaldor, *New and Old*.

35. Mary Kaldor, "In Defense of New Wars," *Stability: International Journal of Security and Development* 2, no. 1 (2013), https://www.stabilityjournal.org/articles/10.5334/sta.at/.

36. Kaldor, *New and Old*, 6–11.

37. Ibid.

38. Kaldor, "In Defense."

39. Ibid.

40. Ibid.

41. Christine Chinkin and Mary Kaldor, "Gender and New Wars," *Journal of International Affairs* 67, no. 1 (2013): 167–87, 167.

42. Mats Berdahl, "The 'New Wars' Thesis Revisited," in *The Changing Character of War*, ed. Hew Strachan and Sibylle Scheipers (Oxford: Oxford University Press, 2011), 109–33, 110–11; for an overview, see Patrick A. Mello, "In Search of New Wars: The Debate about a Transformation of War," *European Journal of International Relations* 16, no. 2 (2010): 297–309.

43. Dubravka Zarkov, "The 'New Wars': A Gendered Myth," in *Mythen van Gender: Essays voor Willy Jansen*, ed. Stefan Dudink and Liedeke Plate (Nijmegen: Vantilt, 2015), 275–80.

44. Ibid., 276.

45. Ibid.

46. Ibid., 277.

47. For a more extended discussion of the concept of the Wars of Globalization, see the chapter by Kristen P. Williams on "Gender, Wars of Globalization, and Humanitarian Interventions since the End of the Cold War" in this handbook.

48. It defined any conflict with an annual toll of 1,000 or more battle deaths as a war; see Max Roser, "War and Peace," *OurWorldInData.org*, accessed November 26, 2017, https://ourworldindata.org/war-and-peace/.

49. Ibid.

50. See Keith Lowe, *Savage Continent: Europe in the Aftermath of World War II* (New York: Picador, 2013), esp. 3–184.

51. Paul Betts and David Crowley, "Introduction," in "History: Domestic Dreamworlds Notions of Home in Post-1945 Europe," ed. Paul Betts and David Crowley, special issue, *Journal of Contemporary History* 40, no. 2 (2005): 213–36, 219.

52. "Documenting Numbers of Victims of the Holocaust and Nazi Persecution," United States Holocaust Memorial Museum, accessed November 26, 2017, https://www.ushmm.org/wlc/en/article.php?ModuleId=10008193#er. For overviews, see Raul Hilberg, *The Destruction of the European Jews* (New Haven, CT: Yale University Press, 2003); Doris Bergen, *War & Genocide: A Concise History of the Holocaust* (Lanham, MD: Rowman & Littlefield, 2003); and Jeremy Black, *The Holocaust: History and Memory* (Bloomington: Indiana University Press, 2016). On the historiography, see Dan Stone, ed., *The Historiography of the Holocaust* (Basingstoke: Palgrave Macmillan, 2005).

53. Sandra Wilson et al., *Japanese War Criminals: The Politics of Justice after the Second World War* (New York: Columbia University Press, 2017), 15.

54. Yuki Tanaka, *Hidden Horrors: Japanese War Crimes in World War II* (Boulder, CO: Westview Press, 1996), 2–3.

55. Thomas U. Berger, *War, Guilt, and World Politics after World War II* (Cambridge: Cambridge University Press, 2012); and the chapter by Frank Biess on "Gendering the Memories of War and Holocaust in Europe and in the United States" in this handbook.

56. Lowe, *Savage Continent*, 187–268; also R. M. Douglas, *Orderly and Humane: The Expulsion of the Germans after the Second World War* (New Haven, CT: Yale University Press, 2012); and Gerard D. Cohen, *In War's Wake: Europe's Displaced Persons in the Postwar Order* (New York: Oxford University Press, 2012).

57. See also the chapter by Karen Hagemann on "Gender, Demobilization, and the Reordering of Societies after the First and Second World Wars" in this handbook.

58. Betts and Crowly, "Introduction," 235.

59. Hans-Peter Schwarz, "The Division of Germany, 1945–1949," in Leffler and Westad, *Cambridge History*, 1:133–53; and Konrad H. Jarausch, *Out of Ashes: A New History of Europe in the Twentieth Century* (Princeton, NJ: Princeton University Press, 2015), 399–79.

60. Michael Holm, *The Marshall Plan: A New Deal for Europe* (New York: Routledge, 2017); and William I. Hitchcock, "The Marshall Plan and the Creation of the West," in Leffler and Westad, *Cambridge History*, 1:154–74.

61. Tony Judt, *Postwar: A History of Europe since 1945* (New York: Penguin Books, 2005), 151–52.

62. Sayward, *The United Nations*.

63. Lowe, *Savage Continent*, 271–364.

64. Mark Mazower, "Introduction," in *After the War Was Over: Reconstructing the Family, Nation and State in Greece, 1943–1960*, ed. Mark Mazower (Princeton, NJ: Princeton University Press, 2000), 7; and Spyridon Plakoudas, *The Greek Civil War: Strategy, Counterinsurgency and the Monarchy* (London: I. B. Tauris, 2017).

65. Amikam Nachmani, "Civil War and Foreign Intervention in Greece: 1946–49," *Journal of Contemporary History* 25, no. 4 (1990): 489–522, 515.

66. "Address of the President of the United States before a joint session of the US Congress and Senate on 12 March 1947," accessed November 26, 2017, https://avalon.law.yale.edu/20th_century/trudoc.asp.

67. See Martin van Creveld, "Technology and War II: From Nuclear Stalemate to Terrorism," in *Oxford History of Modern War*, ed. Charles Townshend (Oxford: Oxford University Press, 2005), 341–63; and Richard Rhodes, *Arsenals of Folly: The Making of the Nuclear Arms Race* (New York: Alfred A. Knopf, 2007).

68. See the chapter by Karen Hagemann and D'Ann Campbell on "Post-1945 Western Militaries, Female Soldiers, and Gay and Lesbian Rights" in this handbook.

69. See Hajimu Masuda, *Cold War Crucible: The Korean Conflict and the Postwar World* (Cambridge, MA: Harvard University Press, 2015).

70. Bruce Cumings, *The Korean War: A History* (New York: Modern Library, 2010); and Haruki Wada and Frank Baldwin, *The Korean War: An International History* (Lanham, MD: Rowman & Littlefield, 1997).

71. Dong Choon Kim, "Forgotten War, Forgotten Massacres—the Korean War (1950–1953) as Licensed Mass Killings," *Journal of Genocide Research* 6, no. 4 (2004): 523–44.

72. Cumings, *The Korean War*, 35, 159–60.

73. Jarausch, *Out of Ashes*, 464–78.

74. James G. Hershberg, "The Cuban Missile Crisis," in Leffler and Westad, *Cambridge History*, 2:65–87.

75. Lawrence S. Wittner, *Confronting the Bomb: A Short History of the World Nuclear Disarmament Movement* (Stanford, CA: Stanford University Press, 2009); and Cortright, *Peace*, esp. 109–89.

76. United Nations Office for Disarmament Affairs, "Disarmament Treaties Database," accessed November 26, 2017, http://disarmament.un.org/treaties/.

77. For overviews, see John Springhall, *Decolonization since 1945: The Collapse of European Overseas Empires* (Basingstoke: Palgrave, 2001), 31–107; Elizabeth Buettner, *Europe after Empire: Decolonization, Society, and Culture* (Cambridge: Cambridge University Press, 2016); Andrew J. Potter, "South Asia," in Immerman and Goedde, *Oxford Handbook*, 211–29; Ang Cheng Guan, "The Cold War in South East Asia," in ibid., 230–45; and Salim Yaqub; "The Cold War in the Middle East," in ibid., 246–64.

78. See the chapter by Richard Smith on "Colonial Soldiers, Race, and Military Masculinities during and beyond World Wars I and II" in this handbook.

79. William Roger Louis, *Ends of British Imperialism: The Scramble for Empire, Suez and Decolonization* (London: I. B. Tauris, 2006), 400.

80. Judith M. Brown, "India," in *The Oxford History of the British Empire*, vol. 4, *The Twentieth Century*, ed. Judith M. Brown and Roger Louise (Oxford: Oxford University Press, 1999), 436.

81. Yasmin Khan, *The Great Partition: The Making of India and Pakistan* (New Haven, CT: Yale University Press, 2008), 6.

82. Avi Shlaim, *Israel and Palestine: Reappraisals, Revisions, Refutation* (London: Verso, 2010), 4–5; see also Mike Berry and Greg Philo, *Israel and Palestine: Competing Histories* (London: Pluto Press, 2006); and Martin Bunton, *The Palestinian–Israel Conflict: A Very Short Introduction* (Oxford: Oxford University Press, 2013).

83. Avi Shlaim, "The Debate about 1948," *International Journal of Middle East Studies* 27, no. 3 (1995): 287–304.

84. Shlaim, *Israel and Palestine*, 4–5.

85. Berry and Philo, *Israel and Palestine*, 25.

86. Ibid.

87. Louis, *Ends of British*, esp. 589–726; and Ronald Hyam, *Britain's Declining Empire: The Road to Decolonization 1918–1968* (Cambridge: Cambridge University Press, 2006), 226–40.

88. Avi Shlaim, "The Middle East: The Origins of the Arab–Israel Wars," in *Explaining International Relations since 1945*, ed. Ngaire Woods (Oxford: Oxford University Press, 1996), 219–40.

89. Buettner, *Europe after Empire*, 90–96; and Bart Luttikhuis and A. Dirk Moses, "Introduction: Mass Violence and the End of the Dutch Colonial Empire in Indonesia," *Journal of Genocide Research* 14, no. 3–4 (2012): 257–76.

90. Mark Atwood Lawrence, *The Vietnam War: A Concise International History* (Oxford: Oxford University Press, 2008), 33.

91. Ibid., 35; and Mark Philip Bradley, "Making Sense of the French War: The Postcolonial Moment and the First Vietnam War, 1945–1954," in *The First Vietnam War: Colonial Conflict and Cold War Crisis*, ed. Mark Atwood Lawrence and Frederik Logevall (Cambridge, MA: Harvard University Press, 2007), 16–40.

92. Buettner, *Europe after Empire*, 132–33.

93. Lawrence, *The Vietnam War*, 40–46.

94. Ibid., 66–185, esp. 143.

95. Ibid., 168–169, 173.

96. See Elizabeth Schmidt, "Africa," in Immerman and Goedde, *Oxford Handbook*, 265–85; and Springhall, *Decolonization*, 108–85.

97. Martin Evans, *Algeria: France's Undeclared War* (Oxford: Oxford University Press, 2012), xvi.

98. Ibid., 225; and Buettner, *Europe after Empire*, 139–42.

99. Evans, *Algeria*, 318–19 and 337–38.

100. Daniel Branch, *Defeating Mau Mau, Creating Kenya: Counterinsurgency, Civil War, and Decolonization* (Cambridge: Cambridge University Press, 2009).

101. Huw Bennett, "The Other Side of the COIN: Minimum and Exemplary Force in British Army Counterinsurgency in Kenya," *Small Wars and Insurgencies* 18, no. 4 (2007): 638–64, 638.

102. Caroline Elkins, *Imperial Reckoning: The Untold Story of Britain's Gulag in Kenya* (New York: Henry Holt, 2005), 121–53, 124; and David Anderson, *Histories of the Hanged: The Dirty War in Kenya and the End of Empire* (London: Weidenfeld & Nicolson, 2005), 4–5.

103. Annie-Sophie Gijs, "Fighting the Red Peril in the Congo: Paradox and Perspectives on an Equivocal Challenge to Belgium and the West (1947–1960)," *Cold War History* 16, no. 3 (2016): 273–90; and Buettner, *Europe after Empire*, 163–89.

104. Schmidt, "Africa," 271–73.

105. Norrie Macqueen, *The Decolonization of Portuguese Africa: Metropolitan Revolution and the Dissolution of Empire* (London: Longman, 1997); and Macqueen, "Portugal's First Domino: 'Pluricontinentalism' and Colonial War in Guiné-Bissau, 1963–1974," *Contemporary European History* 8, no. 2 (1999): 209–30.

106. Schmidt, "Africa," 275.

107. On Guinea-Bissau, see Macqueen, *The Decolonization*, 98–123, and "Portugal's First Domino"; on Mozambique, see Macqueen, *The Decolonization*, 124–56; and on Angola, see ibid., 158–204.

108. See Lars Schoultz, "Latin America," in Immerman and Goedde, *Oxford Handbook*, 190–210.

109. See Leffler and Weststad, eds., *Cambridge History*, vol. 3, *Endings*; and Nicholas Guyatt, "The End of the Cold War," in Immerman and Goedde, *Oxford Handbook*, 605–22.

110. Noor Ahmad Khalidi, "Afghanistan: Demographic Consequences of War, 1978–1987," *Central Asian Survey* 10, no. 3 (1991): 101–26, 106; and William Maley, *The Afghanistan Wars* (Basingstoke: Palgrave Macmillan, 2009), 60, 128.

111. Maley, *The Afghanistan Wars*, 46–47.

112. Ibid., 134.

113. Ibid., 132–37.

114. Rafael Reuveny and Aseem Prakash, "The Afghanistan War and the Breakdown of the Soviet Union," *Review of International Studies* 25, no. 4 (1999): 693–708.

115. Ibid., 698–705.

116. Maley, *The Afghanistan Wars*, 136–37.

117. John Lewis Gaddis, *The Cold War: A New History* (New York: Penguin Books, 2006), 263–66.

118. Guyatt, "The End," 606–7.

119. For overviews, see Dumancic, "Hidden"; and Kristin Hoganson, "What's Gender Got to Do with It? Gender History as Foreign Relations History," in *Explaining the History of American Foreign Relations*, ed. Michal J. Hogan and Thomas G. Paterson (New York: Cambridge University Press, 2004), 304–22.

120. See the chapter by Dubravka Zarkov on "Conceptualizing Sexual Violence in Post–Cold War Global Conflicts" in this handbook.

121. See Whitworth, "The United Nations" in this handbook.

122. See Hagemann, "Gender, Demobilization" in this handbook.

123. On the United States, see Elaine Tyler May, *Homeward Bound: American Families in the Cold War Era* (New York: Basic Books, 1988); Joanne J. Meyerowitz, ed., *Not June Cleaver: Women and Gender in Postwar America, 1945–1960* (Philadelphia: Temple University Press, 1994); and Laura A. Belmonte, "A Family Affair? Gender, the U.S. Information Agency, and Cold War Ideology, 1945–1960," in *Culture and International History*, ed. Jessica C. E. Gienow-Hecht and Frank Schumacher (New York: Berghahn Books, 2003), 79–93; on Germany, see Robert G. Moeller, *Protecting Motherhood: Women and the Family in the Politics of Postwar West Germany* (Berkeley: University of California Press, 1993); and Erica Carter, *How German Is She? Postwar West German Reconstruction and the Consuming Woman* (Ann Arbor: University of Michigan Press, 1997); on Italy, see Wendy A. Pojmann, *Italian Women and International Cold War Politics, 1944–1968* (New York: Fordham University Press, 2013); on Japan, see Jan Bardsley, *Women and Democracy in Cold War Japan* (London: Bloomsbury Academic, 2014); and on the Netherlands, see Snyder, "Domesticity."

124. On the USSR, see Susan E. Reid, "Women in the Home," in *Women in the Khrushchev Era*, ed. Melanie Ilic et al. (New York: Palgrave Macmillan, 2004), 149–76; on Eastern Europe, see Francisca de Haan, ed., "Forum: Gendering the Cold War in the Region," *Aspasia* 8 (2014): 162–90; in a comparative perspective, see Ruth Oldenziel and Karin Zachmann, eds., *Cold War Kitchen: Americanization, Technology and European Users* (Cambridge, MA: MIT Press, 2009); Joanna Regulska and Bonnie G. Smith, eds., *Women and Gender in Postwar Europe: From Cold War to European Union* (New York: Routledge, 2012); and Kate A. Baldwin, *The Racial Imaginary of the Cold War Kitchen: From Sokol'niki Park to Chicago's South Side* (Hanover, NH: Dartmouth College Press, 2016).

125. Ruth Oldenziel and Karin Zachmann, "Introduction," in Oldenziel and Zachmann, *Cold War Kitchen*, 1–29.

126. Snyder, "Domesticity," 51.

127. Betts and Crowley, "Introduction"; Greg Castillo, "The American 'Fat Kitchen' in Europe: Postwar Domestic Modernity and Marshall Plan Strategies of Enchantment," in Oldenziel and Zachmann, *Cold War Kitchen*, 33–57; and several other contributions in the volume *Cold War Kitchen.*

128. Mary Nolan, "Consuming America, Producing Gender," in *The American Century in Europe*, ed. Laurence R. Moore and Maurizio Vaudagna (Ithaca, NY: Cornell University Press, 2003), 243–61, 251.

129. Cynthia H. Enloe, *The Morning After: Sexual Politics at the End of the Cold War* (Berkeley: University of California Press, 1993), 5.

130. The argument of militarization is further developed by Cynthia Enloe in *Maneuvers: The International Politics of Militarizing Women's Lives* (Berkeley: University of California Press, 2000); on the Cold War militarization of the domestic, see also Laura McEnaney, *Civil Defense Begins at Home: Militarization Meets Everyday Life in the Fifties* (Princeton, NJ: Princeton University Press, 2000).

131. See Biess, "Gendering the Memories" in this handbook.

132. See Hagemann and Campbell, "Post-1945 Western," as well as the chapter by Hagemann on "History and Memory of Female Military Service in the Age of World Wars" in this handbook.

133. See Linda Witt et al., *A Defense Weapon Known to be of Value: Servicewomen of the Korean War Era* (Hanover: University Press of New England, 2005).

134. See Hagemann and Campbell, "Post-1945 Western" in this handbook; and Jo Butterfield and Elizabeth Heineman, "The Gendered Nexus between Conflict and Citizenship in Historical Perspective," in *The Oxford Handbook of Gender and Conflict*, ed. Fionnuala Ní Aoláin et al. (New York: Oxford University Press, 2017), 62–74.

135. North Atlantic Treaty Organization, "NATO Committee on Gender Perspectives," accessed December 19, 2017, https://www.nato.int/cps/en/natohq/topics_101372.htm.

136. See Hagemann and Campbell, "Post-1945 Western" in this handbook.

137. Laville, "Gender and Women's," 528; see also Robert J. Corber, *Homosexuality in Cold War America: Resistance and the Crisis of Masculinity* (Durham, NC: Duke University Press, 1997); David K. Johnson, *The Lavender Scare: The Cold War Persecution of Gays and Lesbians in the Federal Government* (Chicago: University of Chicago Press, 2004); and Naoko Shibusawa, "The Lavender Scare and the Empire: Rethinking Cold War Antigay Politics," *Diplomatic History* 36, no. 4 (2012): 723–52.

138. Robert D. Dean, *Imperial Brotherhood: Gender and the Making of Cold War Foreign Policy* (Amherst: University of Massachusetts Press, 2001), 4; and Suzanne Clark, *Cold Warriors: Manliness on Trial in the Rhetoric of the West* (Carbondale: Southern Illinois University Press, 2000).

139. K. A. Cuordileone, "Politics in an Age of Anxiety: Cold War Political Culture and the Crisis in American Masculinity, 1949–1960," *Journal of American History* 87, no. 2 (2000): 515–45.

140. See Oleg Riabov, "Gendering the American Enemy in Early Cold War Soviet Films (1946–1953)," *Journal of Cold War Studies* 19, no. 1 (2017): 193–219.

141. For an overview on Europe, see Kristina Schulz, ed., *The Women's Liberation Movement: Impacts and Outcomes* (New York: Berghahn Books, 2017); on the United States, see Ann Lee Banaszak, ed., *The U.S. Women's Movement in Global Perspective* (Lanham, MD: Rowman & Littlefield, 2005); for the interconnection of feminism and pacifism, as one example, see Harriet Hyman Alonso, *Peace as a Women's Issue: A History of the*

U.S. Movement for World Peace and Women's Rights (Syracuse, NY: Syracuse University Press, 1993), 157–259.

142. Laville, "Gender and Women's"; and Laville, *Cold War Women: The International Activities of American Women's Organisations* (New York: Palgrave, 2002).

143. Branche, "Gender" in this handbook.

144. For the background, see Karen Turner-Gottschang and Thanh Hao Phan, *Even the Women Must Fight: Memories of War from North Vietnam* (New York: John Wiley & Sons, 1998).

145. See Branche, "Gender" in this handbook.

146. Lisa Sharlach, "Rape as Genocide: Bangladesh, the Former Yugoslavia, and Rwanda," *New Political Science* 22, no. 1 (2000): 89–102.

147. See Zarkov, "Conceptualizing" in this handbook.

148. "Report on the Situation of Human Rights in Rwanda submitted by Mr. René Degni-Ségui, Special Rapporteur of the Commission on Human Rights, under Paragraph 20 of Resolution S-3/1 of 25 May 1994," UN Economic and Social Council, Commission on Human Rights, January 29, 1996, accessed December 20, 2017, http://hrlibrary.umn.edu/commission/country52/68-rwa.htm. For an overview, see Linda Melvern, *Conspiracy to Murder: The Rwandan Genocide* (London: Verso, 2004).

149. "Transitional Justice in the Former Yugoslavia," International Center for Transitional Justice, accessed December 2, 2017, https://www.ictj.org/sites/default/files/ICTJ-FormerYugoslavia-Justice-Facts-2009-English.pdf.

150. Ken Booth, *The Kosovo Tragedy: The Human Rights Dimensions* (London: Frank Cass, 2001), 73; and Catherine Baker, *The Yugoslav Wars of the 1990s* (London: Palgrave, 2015).

151. University of California, Los Angeles, School of Law: Health & Human Rights Project, "Legacies and Lessons: Sexual Violence against Men and Boys in Sri Lanka and Bosnia & Herzegovina," May 16, 2017, 13, accessed November 26, 2017, https://williamsinstitute.law.ucla.edu/wp-content/uploads/Legacies-and-Lessons-May-2017.pdf.

152. Roser, "War and Peace."

153. United Nations, "List of Peacekeeping Operations, 1948–2018," accessed April 5, 2020, https://peacekeeping.un.org/sites/default/files/180413_unpeacekeeping-operationlist_2.pdf; and Whitworth, "The United Nations."

154. United Nations, "United Nations Peacekeeping," accessed November 26, 2017, https://peacekeeping.un.org/en/data-0 and https://peacekeeping.un.org/en/peacekeepers-day-women-peacekeeping.

SELECT BIBLIOGRAPHY

Baldwin, Kate A. *The Racial Imaginary of the Cold War Kitchen: From Sokol'niki Park to Chicago's South Side*. Hanover, NH: Dartmouth College Press, 2016.

Bardsley, Jan. *Women and Democracy in Cold War Japan*. London: Bloomsbury Academic, 2014.

Betts, Paul, and David Crowley. "Introduction." In "Domestic Dreamworlds: Notions of Home in Post-1945 Europe." Special issue, *Journal of Contemporary History* 40, no. 2 (2005): 213–36.

Chinkin, Christine, and Mary Kaldor. "Gender and New Wars." *Journal of International Affairs* 67, no. 1 (2013): 167–87.

Clark, Suzanne. *Cold Warriors: Manliness on Trial in the Rhetoric of the West.* Carbondale: Southern Illinois University Press, 2000.

Corber, Robert J. *Homosexuality in Cold War America: Resistance and the Crisis of Masculinity.* Durham, NC: Duke University Press, 1997.

Dean, Robert D. *Imperial Brotherhood: Gender and the Making of Cold War Foreign Policy.* Amherst: University of Massachusetts Press, 2001.

Enloe, Cynthia H. *The Morning After: Sexual Politics at the End of the Cold War.* Berkeley: University of California Press, 1993.

Haan, Francisca de, ed. "Forum: Gendering the Cold War in the Region," *Aspasia* 8 (2014): 162–90.

Johnson, David K. *The Lavender Scare: The Cold War Persecution of Gays and Lesbians in the Federal Government.* Chicago: University of Chicago Press, 2004.

Kaldor, Mary. *New and Old Wars: Organized Violence in a Global Era.* Stanford, CA: Stanford University Press, 1999.

Laville, Helen. *Cold War Women: The International Activities of American Women's Organisations.* New York: Palgrave Macmillan, 2002.

Laville, Helen. "Gender and Women's Rights in the Cold War." In *Oxford Handbook of the Cold War,* edited by Richard H. Immerman and Petra Goedde, 423–39. Oxford: Oxford University Press, 2013.

McEnaney, Laura. *Civil Defense Begins at Home: Militarization Meets Everyday Life in the Fifties.* Princeton, NJ: Princeton University Press, 2000.

Oldenziel, Ruth, and Karin Zachmann, eds. *Cold War Kitchen: Americanization, Technology, and European Users.* Cambridge, MA: MIT Press, 2009.

Pojmann, Wendy A. *Italian Women and International Cold War Politics, 1944–1968.* New York: Fordham University Press, 2013.

Regulska, Joanna, and Bonnie G. Smith, eds. *Women and Gender in Postwar Europe: From Cold War to European Union.* New York: Routledge, 2012.

Shibusawa, Naoko. "The Lavender Scare and the Empire: Rethinking Cold War Antigay Politics." *Diplomatic History* 36, no. 4 (2012): 723–52.

Tyler May, Elaine. *Homeward Bound: American Families in the Cold War Era.* New York: Basic Books, 1988.

Zarkov, Dubravka. "The 'New Wars': A Gendered Myth." In *Mythen van Gender: Essays voor Willy Jansen,* edited by Stefan Dudink and Liedeke Plate, 275–80. Nijmegen: Vantilt, 2015.

CHAPTER 27

....

GENDER, THE WARS OF DECOLONIZATION, AND THE DECLINE OF EMPIRES AFTER 1945

....

RAPHAËLLE BRANCHE

AFTER the end of the Second World War, five European countries—Belgium, Britain, France, the Netherlands, and Portugal—were still in control of colonial possessions in Africa and Asia. All five were involved in Wars of Decolonization, armed struggles of varying length against anticolonial movements in several African and Asian countries that included Algeria, Angola, Belgian Congo, Burma, Cameroon, Guinea-Bissau, Indochina, Indonesia, Kenya, Madagascar, Malaysia, Mozambique, and the Philippines.[1] The first of these conflicts began in Asia immediately after World War II, which officially ended in Europe on May 8, 1945, and in Asia on September 2, 1945, with the respective surrenders of Nazi Germany and Imperial Japan. The last of this type of war ended in Africa in the early 1970s.[2] An important international context for all these conflicts that influenced their course and outcome was the Global Cold War (1946–91), the rivalry between the Soviet Union and its allies in the Warsaw Pact, on the one hand, and the United States and its allies in the North Atlantic Treaty Organization (NATO), on the other, which did not end until the early 1990s with the collapse of the Soviet Union and its allies. During this period, many of these anticolonial conflicts functioned as "proxy wars" between the communist East and the capitalist West, in which neither China and the Soviet Union nor the United States directly engaged each other.[3]

In some colonized countries, nonviolent means were successfully used in the anticolonial struggle. The peaceful protests of the Indian independence movement, led by Mahatma Gandhi, against British rule certainly provide the most powerful example of these alternative paths to independence.[4] Yet, in several cases the anticolonial struggle resulted in wars in which the armed forces of the colonial powers fought nationalist insurgents. These wars were gendered in multiple ways. They were also, as a rule, nationalistic, even when communist guerrillas were the dominant force. Armed combat was one of the main means to achieve the ultimate goal of freeing the country from colonial rule, but it was always part of various broader actions aimed at winning popular support for the political project of national liberation. Contrary to other types of conflicts, the Wars of Decolonization broke out in countries dominated by colonial powers for decades. Generations had been brought up as colonizers and colonized. To shift the balance of power was a dramatic challenge against the backdrop of a long-term reality. For this reason, more than other conflicts, these anticolonial wars required exceptionally broad and active support by the population.

When challenged by anticolonial movements, the Belgian, British, Dutch, French, and Portuguese governments tried to negotiate a new relationship with their colonial territories. These attempts failed in several cases, such as in the British colony and protectorate of Kenya or the Portuguese possessions in Africa, which include present-day Angola, Cape Verde, Guinea-Bissau, Mozambique, São Tomé and Príncipe, and Equatorial Guinea. Still, the colonial powers usually refused to concede that the armed conflicts they faced were "real wars." Instead, they described them as "rebellions" and "upheavals." This denial sometimes lasted for decades after the anticolonial struggle had ended. France, for example, only began officially using the term *Algerian War* in October 1999, thirty-seven years after the ceasefire that ended the Algerian War of Independence (1954–62) was signed.[5] Yet all colonial powers had sent their armies into rebellious areas, sometimes calling up not just troops serving in the colonies, but also troops sent from the mainland armed forces. Some of these soldiers were mobilized on a massive scale, including conscription—notably in France and Portugal. However, these conflicts were still officially considered "internal unrest," and insurgents were "rebels" or "outlaws." In most cases, a state of emergency was declared, giving the government the authority to resort to extraordinary measures of repression without admitting that it was at war. But from the historian's perspective, these were indeed wars, engaging armed troops and aimed at possessing a territory and acquiring or maintaining sovereignty.

With the possible exception of the 1950–54 period of the First Indochina War (1946–54), when the People's Republic of China contributed troops to support the newly founded Democratic Republic of Vietnam in its fight against the French, these were all guerrilla wars led by armies that were much less well equipped and much smaller than the forces mobilized by the colonizing powers. This type of warfare relied on surprise attacks in the forms of ambushes, random assaults, and kidnappings, which depended on the ability to quickly fade away from engagements. Broad support from the civilian population was thus crucial to the guerrilla movements' successes and, earlier, to their very existence. Estimating the number of people involved in these conflicts is therefore difficult, because scholars must count not only combatants, but also all the people who aided, fed, treated, guided, informed, and otherwise supported them. This basic interconnectedness between armed troops and civilians is what set apart the armies of the colonizers and colonized. This is also why the civilian population was so crucial to these conflicts, either in the short term to win the war or in the longer term to achieve the political aims of national independence or remaining in an empire.

We must conceptualize the *Wars of Decolonization* after 1945, like the First and Second World Wars, as *total wars* because of a "peculiar intensity and extension" and with "the tendency to abolish the boundaries that distinguish the front from the homeland." They, too, affected all areas of the economy, society, and culture.[6] Similar to many of the territories occupied by Imperial Japan and Nazi Germany during the Second World War— indeed, in some cases these same territories had been battlegrounds during World War II—colonial territories were spaces of war and spaces of violence.[7] In the colonies as well, entire civilian populations were involved in the conflicts.[8] Because of civilians' roles in supporting guerrilla warfare, they became targeted victims of war violence and also players and stakeholders in the military confrontation and political outcome. What was different from other twentieth-century wars was often the composition and organization of the anticolonial armies involved in the struggle. Like the partisan troops of the resistance movements in the territories occupied by the Axis powers during World War II, they involved fewer professional soldiers and more inexperienced fighters, including women.[9] The struggle for liberation challenged the colonial powers' ideas of White manhood, but it also led to struggles over the construction of male identity within the armies of the insurgents.

One challenge was the fact that women in addition to men actively participated in the fight for national liberation, which called into question dominant ideas of the gender order and led to a reconsideration of gender relations during and after the conflicts. This female participation in military operations and the effects of the wars on women's agency raise the issue of differences and similarities between Wars of Decolonization and other total wars. The revolutionary dynamic involved in many anticolonial wars defines one of their main characteristics: these conflicts aimed at expelling the colonizers from spaces where a new social, political, and economic order was supposed to emerge. Gender issues were central to these hopes and perspectives.

Most important for the understanding of the specific interrelatedness of gender and war in colonial conflicts is the difference between the colonized and the colonizers, even though they constantly interacted with each other. To explore this interrelatedness, it is necessary to study, on the one hand, the gender policies of and gender relations in the armed struggle of the liberation movements. On the other hand, one must examine gendered policies as the colonial powers' response to the military and political challenges posed by liberation movements along with the resulting short-term effects. In the following, three themes stand in the center: the development of research on the intersection of gender, colonial rule, and Wars of Decolonization; the gender policies and gender relations of the armed anticolonial conflicts after 1945; and the gender policies that the colonial powers developed in reaction to the challenges of the anticolonial liberation movements.

GENDER, COLONIAL RULE, AND THE WARS OF DECOLONIZATION

To understand the specific character of colonial rule, historians must look beyond its repressive and violent dimensions. Because colonial rule was envisioned as a long-term project, colonial powers also implemented policies aimed at convincing the Native populations to stay within the colonial realm, or, at least, the colonizers intended to sap some of the populations' main claims against them. The outbreak of armed protest against colonial rule upset this order of things and forced the colonial powers to react and adapt very quickly, sometimes aiming for radical changes in social organization, including gender relations.[10]

Frantz Fanon, a Martinique-born Afro-Caribbean psychiatrist, was one of the first to write on this topic in his seminal works *Peau noire, masques blancs* (*Black Skin, White Masks*) published first in 1952 and *L'An V de la révolution algérienne* (*A Dying Colonialism*) published in 1959, which long influenced the fields of postcolonial studies and critical theory.[11] During the Algerian War of Independence, he laid the foundations for an analysis that regarded the bodies of the colonized peoples—notably but not only women—as an essential location of power and thus a site for "revolutionary violence." Fanon called for the liberation of bodies and minds. By insisting on how Algerian women could actively use their headscarves and their bodies as an instrument in the fight for independence, Fanon established an enduring and emancipating myth of their participation in the conflict.[12] Fanon died in 1961, during the Algerian War, and was not there to notice that the reality of this conflict was, ultimately, very different. His texts are brilliant and thought provoking, but they were informed by the fact that he was an ardent supporter of the Front de libération nationale (FLN) and actively participated in its struggle. Like other intellectuals involved in the anticolonial project, he sought to use words to bring about a certain reality. Writing in war-torn Algeria for the nationalist newspaper *El Moudjahid* (Holy Warrior) founded by the FLN in 1956, Fanon picked aspects of the revolutionary struggle that fit the agenda of presenting the FLN to the international public in such a way that Westerners could identify with it. One of his ideas was especially fertile: the notion that human beings are transformed by action and that violence can be revolutionary.

Even though Fanon was one of the first thinkers to reflect on the possible roles women could take in the anticolonial struggle, his analysis was flawed because his argumentation conceptualized gender relations as essentially connected to the "colonial situation," as described by the French ethnologist Georges Balandier in 1951.[13] Fanon did not explore the fact that the gender order in colonized countries was established during a long-term process influenced by the interplay of a multiplicity of domestic and international factors. Both the interrelatedness and the temporality of this process require greater consideration, and their significance cannot be reduced to the colonial situation alone.[14] The postindependence evolution of certain forms of domination over women in fact demonstrates the survival of structures in continuity with the colonial period. The long-range repercussions of these wars, however, could be quite different from the immediate effects. In Algeria, for example, although many women had actively supported the liberation struggle, women's rights suffered a considerable regression particularly in the 1980s.

One of the first scholars to closely study the participation of women in the Algerian War of Independence was the historian Djamila Amrane, a former FLN activist who was convicted and imprisoned by the French. Between 1978 and 1986, she interviewed eighty-eight female supporters of the FLN, and this research led to the 1994 book *Des femmes dans la guerre d'Algérie* (Women in the Algerian War).[15] Since the 1990s, historians have studied the case of Algeria more intensively. Three works bear special mention. Ryme Seferdjeli explored the struggle over women during the Algerian War.[16] Neil MacMaster analyzed French policy targeting women in its Algerian colony, as well as the role of Algerian women in France during the war.[17] Finally, using oral history interviews, Natalya Vince published the first in-depth exploration of the postindependence experiences of women who had fought against French rule.[18]

Other anticolonial conflicts that have been studied from the perspective of women's and gender history include the Malayan struggle for independence from British rule (1945–57), which succeeded in August 1957 when the Federation of Malaya finally became independent. Women's and gender historians have also studied the First and Second Indochina Wars, the conflicts in which liberation movements in Vietnam, Cambodia, and Laos fought first against the French from 1946 to 1954 and afterward against the United States from 1955 to 1975. Furthermore, scholarship on women and gender now includes several of the anticolonial movements in Africa against Belgian, British, French, and Portuguese rule that continued after 1945.

Lenore Manderson, Virginia H. Dancz, and Syed Muhd Khairudin Aljunied explored the place of women in the Malayan struggle for independence from British rule. They focused on the role of women in the Communist Party of Malaya (CPM), other nationalist parties like the Malayan National Party (MNP), and the guerrillas.[19] Sandra Taylor and François Guillemot studied the role of women in the League for the Independence of Vietnam, known as the Việt Minh, which was formed in 1941 as a national movement for independence from French rule. Both historians showed that many Vietnamese women joined the ranks of the Việt Minh and fought alongside their male counterparts in both the Việt Cộng and North Vietnamese military in the wars against the South Vietnamese government and its French and US allies from 1946 to 1975.[20]

Meredith Terretta researched the history of colonial British and French Cameroon until it achieved independence in 1960. Her work chronicled the spread of the nationalist movement of the Union of the Peoples of Cameroon (UPC) from the late 1940s into the first postcolonial decade in the 1960s and explored the history of the Democratic Union of Cameroonian Women in this period.[21] Cora Ann Presley carried out substantial research on the Kikuyu in Kenya. Based on rare oral testimony from women participants in the Mau Mau Rebellion (1952–60) in British Kenya, her study analyzed changes in women's domestic reproduction, legal status, and gender roles that took place under colonial rule.[22]

Many other decolonization conflicts have not yet been sufficiently studied from the perspective of women's and gender history. Moreover, the gender dimension has not been treated evenly in the research. The main focus of the scholarship so far has been the role of women in the anticolonial liberation movements. Sometimes emphasizing women's importance or seeking to leave behind a view of women as being mere victims, this research has not always investigated the effects of women's engagement on gender relations more generally, nor have scholars compared the situation during the liberation struggles with the development before and after the war to identify short- and long-term effects.

Furthermore, most of this research largely ignored men and masculinity, even though Mrinalini Sinha had already demonstrated in her seminal 1995 book, *Colonial Masculinity: The "Manly Englishman" and the "Effeminate Bengali" in the Late Nineteenth Century*, the value of thinking about the interconnected constructs of masculinity of the colonizer and the colonized.[23] She emphasized the subtle interplay of reversed reflections and its effects on the societies of both the colonizers and the colonized. But many colonial societies and anticolonial wars still have not yet been examined from this perspective. The investigation of men and masculinities in colonial territories to a large degree still must be completed. Notably, in regard to the multiple forms of masculinity in nationalist ranks and men's interactions with colonizers, there is very little scholarship. Exceptions include fascinating research on Zimbabwe and South Africa.[24] Another field to explore is the reaction of colonizers. Current research points, for example, to the counterinsurgency techniques used by colonial powers almost everywhere during these conflicts, but has not utilized a gender perspective.[25]

ARMED ANTICOLONIAL MOVEMENTS AND GENDER RELATIONS

The study of how the rise of armed decolonization movements influenced gender relations must be based on an analysis of the periods leading up to the conflicts. Here, scholarly attention has focused on women's participation in politics. Such studies indicate the importance of distinguishing between liberation movements that actively fought for gender equality and demanded equal rights for women and men, including equal female education, and those movements that merely organized sections for women with the aim of mobilizing them for the liberation struggle.

In their specific, determined position—in the female section of a liberation movement—women militants could play a political role in spreading nationalistic awareness among women, often in areas closed to men. This was notably the case in Algeria, where militant women members of the first nationalist party, the Mouvement pour le Triomphe des Libertés Démocratiques (Movement for the Triumph of Democratic Liberties), went into Muslim homes to lead debates among women. After armed combat began in 1954, the Association of Muslim Women of Algeria continued to work to "convince girls and women of the need for their active participation in demonstrations or even armed actions," according to a police report of the time.[26] As the war took hold, intelligence reports noted that young women demonstrated their desire to "actively join the armed struggle being led by their fathers, husbands and brothers."[27] Some of them joined the *maquis*—the armed guerrilla—or terrorist groups, as nurses, launderers, and cooks. But the majority supported the liberation by joining the *maquis*'s support networks in urban and rural areas. The women's association of the National Liberation Front led by Mamia Chentouf propagated the idea that women must "encourage, in every possible way, men to take part in all the events organized by nationalist groups [and] strive to show their husbands or sons who might collaborate with the French government, how their family will be scorned."[28]

The conventional gender roles of the colonial period persisted in many respects in the anticolonial movements—for the most part, public actions and fighting were still the preserve of men who were constructed as the "protectors" of women and children. But women were encouraged to support the men fighting against the colonizers. They were supposed to safeguard and assert the moral and cultural values of their community, which included the expectation that they "shame" men into the armed struggle, as the Algerian example demonstrates. The leaders of the Mozambique Liberation Front (FRELIMO) likewise encouraged women in the liberated zones to "humiliate" their husbands into combat, and they further hoped that women's mere presence among the guerrilla fighters would induce more courageous behavior.[29]

There was clearly no direct link between female participation in nationalist parties and their openness to feminist demands. But a political program that supported gender equality made it easier to mobilize women, even for armed struggle. For example, this was the case in Malaysia, where the Communist Party of Malaya, founded in 1930, at least rhetorically supported the socialist women's emancipation theory and the equal integration of women in the movement. Accordingly, it trained both women and men for guerrilla warfare, first for the fight against the Japanese occupation (1941–45) and then, starting in 1948, for the anticolonial struggle against the British. Ethnic categories were very important in Malaysia, and being Malay (or not) was an essential criterion of political life. From this perspective, the Communist Party of Malaya was unique in that there were no ethnic barriers to joining. In the Philippines, too, an increasing number of young women took up arms in the communist guerrilla movement, the Hukbalahap, or Huk, which first fought against Japanese occupation and later against the new Philippine government during the Huk Insurrection (1946–54). This movement also supported gender equality in its program.[30]

The Malayan National Party pursued a different policy: It insisted on the "natural" difference between men and women and thus organized them separately. Furthermore, it was initially open to only Malay men and women; in 1948 the party opened membership in its organizations to non-Malays. The male youth organization of the Malayan

National Party was Angkatan Pemuda Insaf (Generation of Awakened Youth), and its members were the first to be trained for the struggle. The motto of this organization, "Freedom through Blood," clearly indicates the obligation to sacrifice their lives for independence. Outlawed by the British in summer 1947, the Angkatan Pemuda Insaf went underground. So, too, did its sister organization for young women, Angtakan Wanita Sedar (Generation of Conscious Women), the name of which was a warning since its acronym is pronounced like the word for "beware!" It was modeled after the Indonesian movement Isteri Sedar (Conscious Women), which had fought against Dutch colonial rule in the 1930s. Initially, Angtakan Wanita Sedar emphasized the cultural role of women in the national movement and propagated a "female" Malay nationalism, which included the demands of equal education for girls, greater autonomy for wives, and more political rights for women. But after the British colonial authority had declared the "state of emergency" in June 1948—marking the start of the Malayan guerrilla war fought between Commonwealth forces and the Malayan National Liberation Army (MNLA) from 1948 to 1960—more and more young members of Angtakan Wanita Sedar joined the guerrillas too. They trained separately from men, but fought together.[31]

The same happened during the First and Second Indochina Wars. More and more young women joined the Việt Minh and the People's Liberation Armed Forces of South Vietnam (PLAF) in South Vietnam and Cambodia, founded in 1941, which fought first against Imperial Japan during World War II. Later, it fought in the anticolonial struggle against France and, subsequently, the United States and the South Vietnamese state, the Republic of Vietnam, established in 1955. The Việt Minh, founded under the leadership of Hồ Chí Minh in 1941, also supported a program of "socialist women's emancipation." Accordingly, women were encouraged to take such roles as village patrol guards, intelligence agents, propagandists, and military recruiters. They enlisted in both the North Vietnamese Army and the Việt Cộng guerrilla insurgent force in South Vietnam and fought in all combat zones. Furthermore, they provided manual labor to maintain the supply lines known as the Hồ Chí Minh Trail. They also worked—often armed—in the rice fields in North Vietnam and Việt Cộng–held farming areas in South Vietnam's Mekong Delta to provide food for their families and the communist war effort. The revolutionary socialist government in North Vietnam, founded in 1945, and the People's Liberation Armed Forces of South Vietnam included the improvement of women's rights in their call to enhance social equity. The 1960 Marriage and Family Law of North Vietnam, for example, banned forced marriage, child marriage, wife beating, and concubinage.[32]

In all three countries, Malaysia, the Philippines, and Vietnam, however, in the daily grind of these anticolonial movements, women were not really equal to men. Their entry into the guerrillas led to careful scrutiny of romantic and sexual relations in the armed forces. The attempt to police gender relations in the liberation armies and a preoccupation with "good" sexual morals can also be found elsewhere when women joined the guerrillas, such as in Algeria and Kenya. In Algeria, combatants were described as relatives—"brothers and sisters"—and initially, romantic relations between members were prohibited there as well. However, this ban was soon lifted, and later some members of the *maquis* even married, though policy on this subject varied by region. Guerrilla leaders needed female support, but remained uncomfortable with the presence of women, especially young women, in their ranks. Some encouraged them to marry, while others expelled them from the guerrilla movement.[33] In Kenya, where women were quite active in the Mau Mau movement—between 1952 and 1958, more than 34,000 women were imprisoned for participating in the struggle—sexual intercourse with guerrilla fighters was also forbidden.[34]

In Cameroon, women were organized in the spaces controlled by the Union of the Peoples of Cameroon. They did not always volunteer to join the UPC, however, and some were even forced to marry combatants fighting in the other territories controlled by the military wing of the UPC.[35] Others served as spies and still others as combatants for the armed wing of the UPC in the Bamileke region in Cameroon's west and northwest in 1957.[36] The UPC, too, officially supported "women's emancipation" and propagated their active role in the fight for independence. One of the vocal advocates of this policy was UPC Secretary General Ruben Um Nyobé. He believed that such a policy would set the movement apart from the colonizer. Accordingly, a school for UPC cadres set up in 1955 also included several women from the Union démocratique des femmes camerounaises (Democratic Union of Cameroonian Women). One of them was Marie Ndjat, who became the secretary general of the UPC central committee of Songmbengue. She led men in several armed actions before her arrest in 1956. In the trial against her, members of the association Social Evolution of Cameroon—founded by the French administration to support the Westernization of Cameroon women—testified against Ndjat. They denounced her for her "savagery" and her putatively unfeminine and immoral behavior. One of their major criticisms was that she supposedly had sexual relations with UPC men.[37]

During the Mozambican War of Independence (1964–74) against Portugal, the Mozambique Liberation Front also appealed to young women to join its ranks for the armed struggle. It targeted unmarried ten- to fifteen-year-old girls who lived in the "rebel" milieu. These girls were armed and, beginning in 1967, organized in the Destacamento Feminino (Female Detachment) of the FRELIMO and trained in neighboring Tanzania, which had become independent from British rule in 1961. As the embodiment of the "new socialist women," these young female fighters became the subject of many speeches by FRELIMO leaders. In the daily reality of war, they were indeed "liberated" from the authoritarian control of their parents, who remained in their villages. They experienced a new form of equality with men, especially men of the same age. But the FRELIMO limited their freedom by claiming fraternal authority over them, labeling them "little sisters." It, too, prohibited sexual or romantic relations among guerrilla fighters and punished any violation. Only in the last years of the war did the FRELIMO adopt a more flexible policy in this matter.[38]

Beyond the armed struggle, women played a crucial role in the anticolonial liberation movements by giving essential support to the fighters. Women supplied them with food and clothing, did the laundry, hid soldiers, spied for them, and otherwise provided them with information. Even in spheres of society and culture traditionally reserved for women or in places that only women could visit (private homes, markets, and public baths), women involved in anticolonial struggles for liberation expanded their "repertoire" of possible political actions.[39] Women were also involved in peaceful civil actions. For example, they initiated and organized public protest by taking part in demonstrations in front of jails or public buildings and by writing petitions to the colonial state or the United Nations. In Algeria in late June 1958, around fifty veiled women gathered before the headquarters of the French préfecture in Algiers in the early morning. They asked to meet with the prefect, held up signs in French, and stated that they were there for "news about our husbands and children currently under arrest." The protesting women wore headscarves and brought along their young children. They occupied the street, with some of them lying down and blocking traffic, and used the tradition of female wailing as a form of audible protest during these events.[40] In Cameroon, the women of the Bamileke region likewise used their specific social status to achieve their goals and contribute to the struggle. As the primary farmers in the region, these women were responsible for planting the fields. Taking advantage of this social and economic role, they planted crops on the roads so that their harvest would block the circulation of military and administrative vehicles.[41]

Even while acting explicitly as "mothers" or "wives" in the "female sphere" assigned to them, women who supported the decolonization struggle pursued their own agendas. They used traditional gender roles not only to organize gender specific forms of protest, but also to cover up their activities in the liberation movement. The young girls and women who supported the Algerian War of Liberation through covert acts of urban terrorism, known as the *fidaïa*, are one such example. Because women could walk unnoticed in the streets of Algerian cities, the *fidaïa* could execute bombings without disguise.[42] In turn, these young female terrorists were made into heroes of the liberation movement. In 1960, the FLN newspaper *El Moudjahid* published a play that portrayed a *fidaïa*. In this play, another young woman praised her with the following words: "I am full of regret that I am married and cannot make my own decisions. I am ashamed I cannot be like you. And I am proud of you and those like you."[43] These *fidaïate* could become an icon of the new form of warfare, not despite, but because, they were a relatively small group and an exception. They were presented as young, die-hard nationalists committed to the ideals of the FLN to the point of transgressing the gender roles assigned to women. They were willing and able to kill—a right and duty usually reserved for men—and they even killed unarmed people. In the rhetoric of the FLN, this was acceptable female behavior only in a situation of national emergency like the war of liberation from French rule.[44] Similarly, the much larger number of young Mozambican women who joined the armed struggle of the FRELIMO were made icons of the liberation movement and the heroines of a new world.[45] But unlike in Algeria, the FRELIMO political leadership actively encouraged these Mozambican women to join the group's ranks and to take part in military training.

In any case, one characteristic of the anticolonial movements, particularly their armed forces, was the youth of their supporters. Movement leaders used gender identities to their advantage without necessarily subverting the gender order of their societies. In the long term, however, they often tried to restore prewar gender regimes after they came into power. Youths, however, were an entirely different matter. Village communities had succeeded in maintaining the principle of authority based on age even when colonization had disrupted other traditional power structures. But bearing arms gave a completely unusual power to young people in countries at war. Although they sometimes made arrangements with guerrilla movements, the usually older village leaders ultimately had to obey younger men whose origins were sometimes unknown to them. Indeed, when combatants were fighting in regions far from their homes, they were not subject to control by family or regional networks. They also used *noms de guerre*, making it even harder to identify them.[46]

By using such strategies, as Inge Brinkman has shown, the People's Movement for the Liberation of Angola (MPLA), founded in 1956, successfully took full control of southeastern Angola, where its leaders, who were from other parts of the country, set up a new order. The MPLA notably began to fight witchcraft, condemning to death witch doctors whom civilians had denounced. The movement thereby overturned villages' traditional, elder-organized jurisdictions. The MPLA showed its power to oppose the colonial rulers (who had outlawed execution of witch doctors), thereby building its own authority at the expense of elders.[47] This overturning of authority based on age was one of the essential aspects of these guerrilla movements, particularly when they had the means to consolidate their control over territories. The policies of colonial powers and their responses to the anticolonial movements were, however, not necessarily more favorable for male elders wishing to maintain their power over, notably, the women and the young men of their communities.

THE GENDERED RESPONSE OF THE COLONIAL POWERS

One of the recurring techniques for fighting guerrilla movements was the creation of "forbidden zones," along with massive forced resettlement of populations to enclose and monitor the civilian population. The major aim was to cut off the guerrilla fighters' access to their logistical bases. Whatever their name or euphemism, these operations worked in the same way: Civilian populations suspected of supporting the guerrilla were ordered to leave their homes, which were often destroyed. They were grouped together in detention camps controlled by a curfew and surrounded by barbed wire with exits monitored by soldiers. Here, armed men held power, having stripped it from the traditional authorities (community elders).[48]

In Malaysia, the British used this system of resettlement areas and "new villages" extensively in their struggle against the guerrilla fighters of the Malayan National Liberation Army, affiliated with the Malaysian Communist Party, and its Chinese supporters, who lived on the edge of the jungle. Following the plans of British General Sir Harold R. Briggs, chief of the imperial general staff and director of the operations in Malaya, these people were forcibly moved to "new villages." In total, colonial authorities created 450 detention camps, holding over 470,000 people (of whom a substantial majority were Chinese).[49] During the Mau Mau Uprising in Kenya, the British held an estimated 150,000 Kikuyu in detention camps. Britain and France used similar resettlement policies in Cameroon and other African colonies. Once a camp was set up in an area, any shelters remaining outside the resettlement areas could be razed to the ground.[50] Algerians were also subject to extensive resettlement under French rule, with 25 percent of the Algerian population ultimately moved to camps over the span of a few years.[51]

This deprivation of the freedom to move or settle down also meant restricted access to economic resources (mainly fields, pastureland, and water), resulting in unemployment, economic hardship, and malnutrition, as in Malaysia and Algeria. But the effects were also psychological and social, as sociologists Pierre Bourdieu and Abdelmalek Sayad have shown. Cut off from their land and traditional activities, peasants found themselves "defined by what they were no longer and by what they were not yet."[52] The basic social unit was not the village, as in the past, but the camp. Traditional structures and forms of group control did not work any longer, and the elders lost some of their power. Instead, here too, younger, often-armed men became the protectors of the elders. The old world was turned upside down.

Colonial authorities attempted to compensate the community elders by proposing an alliance meant to restore the power that they had lost as a result of rebellion or colonization and repression. For British-controlled Kenya, this colonial policy is especially well researched. The British successfully recruited a very large number of "loyalists" within the Kikuyu community itself during the Mau Mau Uprising, and they attempted to considerably strengthen the power of loyal local authorities, the "chiefs." For example, the "relocation scheme" set up by the British gave loyalists land confiscated from the Mau Mau. The hope was that economic and political power would mutually strengthen each other.[53]

Alongside resettlement, French policy during the Algerian War was also based on recruiting militias made up of Algerians. Many of them were *Harkis*, Muslim Algerians who served as army auxiliaries for the French. These Algerian militiamen were encouraged to live with their families near or inside military outposts. Described by the French as people who had "chosen France," they were seen as "traitors" by the FLN. The French administration, however, never conceded the same standing and power to them that the British conceded to the Kikuyu loyalists. It refused to give them weapons on a permanent basis and granted them no political power. While there are examples of substantial empowerment related to this French policy, they are limited to former guerrillas of the Armée de Libération Nationale (ALN) who joined the French army as commandos. These men had given up any possibility of going back, and the colonial power exploited their desire for revenge, offering these armed men substantial power over civilian populations and over ALN fighters.[54]

Yet something else made these oppressive policies new: repression and violence went hand in hand with social engineering policies aimed at transforming colonial societies. One example is the Sanaga-Maritime Department in Cameroon, controlled by French Lieutenant Colonel Jean Lamberton, who was responsible for the repression of the Sanaga people accused of supporting the outlawed independence party Union of the Peoples of Cameroon between 1959 and 1964. According to him, repression was not enough. Along with it, the French had to "replace the ideology spread by the UPC with a reasonable and sane conception of the role that the Bassa people [could] play in helping build a modern Cameroonian nation."[55] The major aim of such social-engineering policies was to gather support from parts of the colonized population.

Acknowledging the limits of the contribution of colonization to colonized societies and the need to find powerful levers to avoid popular support for rebel forces, the colonial powers focused particular attention on colonized women. Propaganda insisted on their social status and their civil and political rights. Caring for women was described as an indicator of civilization. In its rhetoric, Western society and culture brought to the colonized by the imperial powers offered women more civil, social, and political rights. This narrative has a long tradition in the rule of colonial powers. As Partha Chatterjee has shown for nineteenth-century India under British rule, constructing an image of colonized women as victims of social traditions was part of the process of setting up colonial rule.[56] Under the pressures exerted by the Wars of Decolonization, the colonial powers were forced to follow their words with action.

Two examples are well documented: Kenya and Algeria. Two years after the Mau Mau Uprising broke out, the British government pursued a women's policy in Kenya. The officers of the Community Development Department, set up in 1954, created women's clubs named in Kikuyu "Progress among Women." During their meetings, women watched propaganda films and were taught the basics of hygienic child care. They also received food, which helped to increase attendance and became crucial once famine struck some regions.[57] Interestingly, all women were treated alike in the food distribution, whether they were the wives of home guards who guarded the camps or married to Mau Mau rebels. The goal was to win over women not just to overcome the uprising, but also to build a new Kenya. Other policies were tested locally, such as the prohibition of female genital mutilation in the Meru district in 1956. Here, according to Lynn Thomas, young women refused the colonizer's prohibition and broke free of the old women who traditionally carried out genital mutilation. Young women performed the act on themselves with other instruments, thus proving agency against both the colonial authorities and the traditional authorities. They did so by using one policy in the British fight against the rebellion as a means to have their voices heard. They hoped to show their courage in the face of pain and the risk of repression for having braved the prohibition.[58]

In Algeria, the French appealed to supposedly universal moral values, but these were clearly assigned by gender. One example is the psychological action program in eastern Algeria known as "Muslim Women against Rebellion," the principles of which were distributed to the prefects in early 1958. Here, these "universal moral values" were described as "major fundamental instincts":[59]

> Any man who gives his aid to the rebels and takes it away from his own family is contemptible and a criminal, not worthy to be the head of a family. Such a man believes himself to be courageous because he runs around the mountain carrying a rifle and bullets. But during this time, his abandoned children cry in hunger. So where is the courage of this man who cowardly flees the cries and criticism of his sons and daughters? True courage lies in the women who stay in the home deserted by their husbands, consoling their children and trying to feed them nevertheless.[60]

According to this program, husbands who supported the FLN, took up arms, and left their women and children unprotected were to be "despised by any man worthy of being called a man."[61] There is no clearer example of how French propaganda degraded the men it targeted.

Yet the innovation in this colonial rhetoric lay in a policy presented more explicitly as positive for women and aimed at giving them power within Algerian society, beginning in their own families. Three areas were given priority: inheritance, marriage, and children. Careful not to shock Algerian men, the French legal experts studying these questions in 1957 clearly stated that they wanted their proposed reform to be "an initial stage on the path, both traditionalist and reformist, that is supported by the entire Muslim community of Algeria, including men and women alike." Furthermore, they indicated, "The legislator's aim is, admittedly, to increase the rights of Muslim women, but only insofar as the rights of Muslim men are already recognized. The aim is not, through the reform process or as a result of unintended consequences, to upset a balance that has deliberately been established."[62] They mentioned precedents in India, Morocco, Tunisia, and elsewhere.

What, then, were the actual changes of the reform? For the most part, the reform prevented women from being wholly disinherited, prohibited them from being married too young or against their will, and allowed them to file for divorce. In 1958, the regime change in France brought—for the first time—equal political rights for French and Algerians in Algeria, as well as the first political rights for Algerian women. The promises of equality between the colonized and colonizers, on the one hand, and between men and women, on the other hand, finally seemed to become a reality. This development raised hope in some circles of women in Algeria. Demonstrations or petitions sent to the French authorities by women's groups, often headed by French women, indicate as much. Submitted in September 1958, one petition demanded "to free [women] from abusive customs that, 12 centuries after the Prophet's death, all too often make them slaves, to pass laws that will allow them to be born free and to move forward, to give them a status guaranteeing equality of their rights with those of men."[63] Certainly aware of the symbolic value of his choice, the new French president, Charles de Gaulle, appointed Nafissa Sid Cara to his first government in 1958; she was the first Muslim to enter a French government, and a woman to boot.

Sid Cara was behind the February 1959 ordinance that reformed marriage law in Algeria, which was inspired by the 1956 reform of Tunisian civil law. The legal age was raised to fifteen for women and eighteen for men. The consent of both spouses in the marriage was required, and they both had to be present at the wedding. During the wedding ceremony, birth certificates were checked and a family booklet was given out. Repudiation by the husband was abolished, and divorce became the only possibility for dissolving a marriage. Divorce proceedings were to be held before a judge, and both spouses had to be present too (to avoid the wife being represented by a male relative without her knowing it). The judge would decide on the future for the children and mother.[64]

This reform of civil law reflected some of the basic demands of the international women's movement of the time. But different than in other countries, such as Kenya and India, where the colonial power had attempted to intervene during the interwar period, Algeria had not seen such requests earlier.[65] Instead, the reform of Algerian marriage law in 1959 was part of the French administration's policy to win the war by gaining the support of Algeria's female population. French propaganda intensively advertised the reform, and administrators used women's evenings and other social activities organized by female army personnel to reach the Algerian women.[66] This propaganda did not go unnoticed by the Front de Libération Nationale. It forbade the Algerian population from marrying according to French law and, more generally, from making appeals to French courts. According to FLN decree, Algerians had to marry according to Islamic law by reciting the first sura. Judicial committees of the FLN took charge of civil law matters, denying any French court the authority to deal with private matters. The private was political, as both sides knew.

Conclusion

From a global perspective, the Wars of Decolonization achieved their primary goal: all over the world, colonies won their independence in the first three decades after World War II, and the liberated peoples entered the United Nations as newly founded nation-states. This decline of imperial powers gave birth to new agents. In many former colonial countries, men and women who had fought in the anticolonial liberation movements took the lead from former authorities, but men did so more than women. Thus, from a gender perspective, this successful change must be carefully scrutinized and assessed in a more qualified way. The persistence of gender relations dominated by traditional roles and the superiority of men over women had its roots in the preexisting colonial order and the anticolonial war itself. Even communist- and socialist-dominated liberation movements that had delineated specific places for women and girls in their organizations and at least rhetorically acknowledged them as equal to men nevertheless fostered a division between male tasks and female activities through their gendered practices.

Women were obligated to do their share in the anticolonial struggle and its wars, which were by nature very demanding of women, even when they were not directly involved in the fighting themselves: the guerrillas needed not only food and shelter, but also the nursing and intelligence that women were most able to provide. In addition, the nationalist parties and armed liberation movements needed broad popular support, so they targeted women as the "pillar of the society," the "bedrock" of the national community. Such a role was neither new nor specific to guerrilla warfare, but it gained an offensive dimension when used to reinforce the colonized people's cohesion against the colonizers. The context of the anticolonial struggle shaped the lives of the people. Even everyday tasks were related to war issues, and in some areas being neutral was simply impossible.

Yet this involvement of native people in the support of the armed movements did lead to changes in the gender roles and relations for women. In the context of war, they gained new agency, and they experienced new relationships to public spaces (either by protesting or by simply traveling from one place to the other). They also experienced new responsibilities vis-à-vis their families since men were often absent and out of reach. In some cases, women were also engaged in the armed movements and, even if they rarely carried arms, they experienced in guerrilla life gender relations that were often quite different from the traditional gender-based social relationships of the prewar period—though not totally distinct from them. Indeed, many nationalist movements had to develop policies to address the challenge that overthrowing the colonial power might lead to far-reaching changes in the social order. Some of these movements were explicitly revolutionary and others were not, but all had to deal with the fact that their call for a revolt might affect the whole social body once the colonizers were out of the country. Yet the fight against colonial rule was always the priority during the liberation struggle, and these social and gender issues were rarely addressed until the aftermath of war and liberation. Nevertheless, the war did have significant impacts on people's lives and the social and gender order of postwar societies.

Gender issues were especially important after the liberation, because they had already become a focus of the colonial powers' wartime policies. Herein lies the main particularity of the Wars of Decolonization: Political sovereignty was at stake, but so was the power over society and culture. As a result, the way women and men should live, and according to what kind of standard, was crucial to the definition of the various war aims. In many respects, these were wars over civilization for the colonizers and over identity for the colonized peoples, and gender was a fundamental issue in this regard. Nationalist movements reversed the colonizers' discourse and imposed their views on gender issues as well. After the war, however, as after so many other conflicts, the new male elites leading the liberated nations insisted that the wartime gender relations, which they described as exceptional because of the necessities and impediments of war, needed to be "reordered." This often meant an attempt to return to the old gender hierarchies.

NOTES

1. The war in Rhodesia (1964–79), also known as the Zimbabwe War of Liberation, and the South African struggle for liberation could have been included because their aim was to free a population from colonialism, but both were excluded because their White authorities were only indirectly linked to Britain, as both were self-governing colonies.

2. On the end of empires, see Miguel Bandeira Jerónimo and António Costa Pinto, eds., *The Ends of European Colonial Empires: Cases and Comparisons* (Basingstoke: Palgrave Macmillan, 2015).

3. See Martin Thomas et al., eds., *The Crises of Empire: Decolonization and Europe's Imperial Nation States, 1918–1975* (London: Hodder Education, 2008).

4. See Bal Ram Nanda, *In Search of Gandhi: Essays and Reflections* (Oxford: Oxford University Press, 2002).

5. On the memory of the Algerian War in France, see Raphaëlle Branche, *La guerre d'Algérie: une histoire apaisée?* (Paris: Le Seuil, 2005).

6. Roger Chickering, "Total War: The Use and Abuse of a Concept," in *Anticipating Total War: The German and American Experiences, 1871–1914*, ed. Manfred F. Boemeke et al. (Cambridge: Cambridge University Press, 1999), 13–28.

7. On the *Gewaltraum* concept, see Wolfgang Sofsky, *Zeiten des Schreckens: Amok, Terror, Krieg* (Frankfurt am Main: S. Fischer, 2002). See also Jörg Baberowski and Gabriel Metzler, eds., *Gewalträume: Soziale Ordnungen im Ausnahmezustand* (Frankfurt am Main: Campus, 2010).

8. See the chapter by Karen Hagemann and Sonya O. Rose on "War and Gender: The Age of the World Wars and Its Aftermath—an Overview" in this handbook.

9. See the chapter by Karen Hagemann on "History and Memory of Female Military Service in the Age of World Wars" in this handbook.

10. See, in particular, Neil MacMaster, *Burning the Veil: The Algerian War and the "Emancipation" of Muslim Women, 1954–62* (Manchester: Manchester University Press, 2012).

11. See Frantz Fanon, *Black Skin, White Masks* (London: Pluto, 1967); and Fanon, *A Dying Colonialism* (London: Writers and Readers Publishing Cooperative, 1965).

12. See, for example, Aaronette M. White's critique of Fanon in "Men Are Fighting for Freedom, All the Women Are Mourning Their Men, but Some of Us Carried Guns: A Raced-Gendered Analysis of Fanon's Psychological Perspectives on War," *Signs* 32, no. 4 (2007): 857–84.

13. Georges Balandier, "La situation coloniale: approche théorique," *Cahiers internationaux de sociologie* 11 (1951): 44–79.

14. Thus, Robert J. C. Young's article, while very interesting, falls into the trap of focusing on the relationship between colonized and colonizer. See Robert J. C. Young, *Postcolonialism: An Historical Introduction* (Oxford: Blackwell, 2001), 360–82.

15. Djamila Amrane, *Des femmes dans la guerre d'Algérie* (Paris: Karthala, 1994).

16. Ryme Seferdjeli, " 'Fight with Us, Women, and We Will Emancipate You': France, the FLN, and the Struggle over Women during the Algerian War" (DPhil thesis, London School of Economics, University of London, 2005).

17. MacMaster, *Burning the Veil*.

18. Natalya Vince, *Our Fighting Sisters: Nation, Memory and Gender in Algeria, 1954–2012* (Manchester: Manchester University Press, 2015).

19. See Lenore Manderson, *Women, Politics and Change: The Kaum Ibu UMNO, Malaysia, 1945-1972* (Kuala Lumpur: Oxford University Press, 1980); Virginia H. Dancz, *Women and Party Politics in Peninsular Malaysia* (Singapore: Oxford University Press, 1987); and Syed Muhd Khairudin Aljunied, "Against Multiple Hegemonies: Radical Malay Women in Colonial Malaya," *Journal of Social History* 47, no. 1 (2013): 153-75.

20. Sandra C. Taylor, *Vietnamese Women at War: Fighting for Ho Chi Minh and the Revolution* (Lawrence: University Press of Kansas, 1999); and François Guillemot, *Des Vietnamiennes dans la guerre civile: L'autre moitié de la guerre 1945-1975* (Paris: Les Indes Savantes, 2014).

21. Meredith Terretta, *Petitioning for Our Rights, Fighting for Our Nation: The History of the Democratic Union of Cameroonian Women, 1949-1960* (Oxford: Langaa Research & Publishing, 2013); and Terretta, *Nation of Outlaws, State of Violence: Nationalism, Grassfields Tradition and State Building in Cameroon* (Athens, OH: Ohio University Press, 2013).

22. Cora Ann Presley, *Kikuyu Women, the Mau Mau Rebellion, and Social Change in Kenya* (Boulder, CO: Westview Press, 1992).

23. Mrinalini Sinha, *Colonial Masculinity: The "Manly Englishman" and the "Effeminate Bengali" in the Late Nineteenth Century* (Manchester: Manchester University Press, 1995).

24. For example, Norma J. Kriger, *Zimbabwe's Guerrilla War: Peasant Voices* (Cambridge: Cambridge University Press, 1992); Ngwabi Bhebe and Terence Ranger, eds., *Soldiers in Zimbabwe's Liberation War* (London: James Currey, 1995); and Raymond Suttner, "Masculinities in the African National Congress-Led Liberation Movement: The Underground Period," *Kleio* 37, no. 1 (2005): 71-106.

25. David French, *The British Way in Counter-Insurgency, 1945-1967* (Oxford: Oxford University Press, 2011); Huw Bennett, *Fighting the Mau Mau: The British Army and Counter-Insurgency in the Kenya Emergency* (Cambridge: Cambridge University Press, 2012); and Matthew Hughes, ed., *British Ways of Counter-Insurgency: A Historical Perspective* (London: Routledge, 2013).

26. Intelligence gathered by the General Intelligence Police of Algiers, August 11, 1955, 3F/141, Archives nationales d'outre-mer (hereafter cited as ANOM).

27. Intelligence gathered on November 10, 1955, 3F/141, ANOM.

28. Intelligence gathered on October 20, 1955, 3F/141, ANOM.

29. Allen Isaacman and Barbara Isaacman, "The Role of Women in the Liberation of Mozambique," *Ufahamu* 13, no. 2-3 (1984): 128-85; and Harry G. West, "Girls with Guns: Narrating the Experience of War of FRELIMO's 'Female Detachment'," *Anthropological Quarterly* 73, no. 4 (2000): 180-94.

30. Vina A. Lanzona, *Amazons of the Huk Rebellion: Gender, Sex, and Revolution in the Philippines* (Madison: University of Wisconsin Press, 2009).

31. Aljunied, "Against Multiple Hegemonies."

32. See Karen G. Turner, "'Vietnam' as a Women's War," in *A Companion to the Vietnam War*, ed. Marilyn B. Young and Robert Buzzanco (Malden, MA: Blackwell, 2002), 93-112.

33. Data from Seferdjeli, "Fight with Us."

34. According to Presley, *Kikuyu Women*, 213. See also Caroline Elkins, *Imperial Reckoning: The Untold Story of Britain's Gulag in Kenya* (New York: Henry Holt, 2005), esp. 221-31 and 244-65.

35. See several eyewitness testimonies of demonstrations in 1958 (but not confirmed by French services) in FM/DPCT//19, ANOM.

36. Meredith Terretta, "A Miscarriage of Revolution: Cameroonian Women and Nationalism," *Stichproben: Wiener Zeitschrift für kritische Afrikastudien* 7, no. 12 (2007): 61–90, 67.

37. Ibid., 72.

38. West, "Girls with Guns."

39. Charles Tilly, *The Contentious French* (Cambridge, MA: Belknap Press, 1986).

40. Intelligence notes dated June 24, 1958, 3F141, ANOM.

41. Terretta, "Miscarriage of Revolution."

42. See Zohra Drif, *Mémoires d'une combattante de l'ALN: Zone autonome d'Alger* (Algiers: Chihab Editions, 2013), 610.

43. *El Moudjahid*, 65, May 31, 1960.

44. Assia Djebar, *Les Enfants du Nouveau Monde* (Paris: René Juillard, 1962).

45. West, "Girls with Guns."

46. Mike Kesby, "Arenas for Control, Terrains of Gender Contestation: Guerrilla Struggle and Counter-Insurgency Warfare in Zimbabwe, 1972–1980," *Journal of Southern African Studies* 22, no. 4 (1996): 561–84.

47. Inge Brinkman, "War, Witches and Traitors: Cases from the MPLA's Eastern Front in Angola (1966–1975)," *Journal of African History* 44, no. 2 (2003): 303–25.

48. For information on these practices, see Christian Gerlach, *Extremely Violent Societies: Mass Violence in the Twentieth-Century World* (Cambridge: Cambridge University Press, 2010), 177–234.

49. Karl Hack, *Defense and Decolonization in South-East Asia* (New York: Routledge, 20001), 113).

50. Caroline Elkins, "The Struggle for Mau Mau Rehabilitation in Late Colonial Kenya," *The International Journal of African Historical Studies* 33, no. 1 (2000): 25–57.

51. Michel Cornaton, *Les camps de regroupement de la guerre d'Algérie* (Paris: Editions ouvrières, 1967).

52. Pierre Bourdieu and Abdelmalek Sayad, *Le déracinement: la crise de l'agriculture traditionnelle en Algérie* (Paris: Éditions de Minuit, 1964), 161.

53. Daniel Branch, *Defeating Mau Mau, Creating Kenya: Counterinsurgency, Civil War, and Decolonization* (Cambridge: Cambridge University Press, 2009), 136.

54. Raphaëlle Branche, *La Torture et l'armée pendant la guerre d'Algérie, 1954–1962* (Paris: Gallimard, 2001); Branche, "'The Best *Fellagha* Hunter is the French of North African Descent' (General Challe): Harkis in French Algeria," in *Unconventional Warfare: From Antiquity to the Present Day*, ed. Brian Hughes and Fergus Robson (Basingstoke: Palgrave Macmillan, 2017), 47–66; and François-Xavier Hautreux, *La Guerre d'Algérie des harkis, 1954–1962* (Paris: Perrin, 2013).

55. Achille Mbembe, *La naissance du maquis dans le Sud-Cameroun, 1920–1960: histoire des usages de la raison en colonie* (Paris: Khartala, 1996).

56. Partha Chatterjee, "Colonialism, Nationalism, and Colonialized Women: The Contest in India," *American Ethnologist* 16, no. 4 (1989): 622–33.

57. See Cora Ann Presley, "The Mau Mau Rebellion, Kikuyu Women, and Social Change," *Canadian Journal of African Studies/Revue Canadienne des Études Africaines* 22, no. 3 (1988): 502–27.

58. Lynn M. Thomas, "'*Ngaitana* (I Will Circumcise Myself)': The Gender and Generational Politics of the 1956 Ban on Clitoridectomy in Meru, Kenya," *Gender & History* 8, no. 3 (1996): 338–63.

59. Psychological action program entitled "Muslim Women against Rebellion" for eastern Algeria in early 1958, presented in a letter to prefects from the IGAME de l'Est, January 10, 1958, 932//89, ANOM.

60. Ibid.

61. Ibid.

62. "Draft Reform for the Personal Status of Muslim and Kabyle Women in Algeria," June 1957, Interior Ministry, Department of Algerian Affairs, FM/81F/74, ANOM.

63. Motion from the Committee for Social Action and Women's Solidarity of Miramar, Bains Romains, and Bainem, September 29, 1958, FM81F75, ANOM.

64. On Nafissa Sid Cara and the reform, see Neil MacMaster, "The Colonial 'Emancipation' of Algerian Women: The Marriage Law of 1959 and the Failure of Legislation on Women's Rights in the Post-Independence Era," *Stichproben: Wiener Zeitschrift für kritische Afrikastudien* 7, no. 12 (2007): 91–116.

65. See Cora Ann Presley's research on Kenya in Presley, "Mau Mau Rebellion"; and Mrinalini Sinha's analysis of the 1929 Child Marriage Restraint Act in India in Mrinalini Sinha, *Specters of Mother India: The Global Restructuring of an Empire* (Durham, NC: Duke University Press, 2006).

66. MacMaster, "Colonial 'Emancipation.'"

Select Bibliography

Branche, Raphaëlle. "Children of the New World? Fighters for Independence and Rural Society in Colonial Algeria." In *Resistance and Colonialism: Insurgent Peoples in World History,* edited by Nuno Domingos, Miguel Jeronimo, and Ricardo Roque, 63–84. Basingstoke: Palgrave Macmillan, 2019.

Branche, Raphaëlle. "Sexual Violence in the Algerian War." In *Brutality and Desire: War and Sexuality in Europe's Twentieth Century*, edited by Dagmar Herzog, 247–60. Basingstoke: Palgrave Macmillan, 2008.

Brinkman, Inge. "War, Witches and Traitors: Cases from the MPLA's Eastern Front in Angola (1966–1975)." *Journal of African History* 44, no. 2 (2003): 303–25.

Chatterjee, Partha. "Colonialism, Nationalism, and Colonialized Women: The Contest in India." *American Ethnologist* 16, no. 4 (1989): 622–33.

Elkins, Caroline. *Imperial Reckoning: The Untold Story of Britain's Gulag in Kenya*. New York: Henry Holt, 2005.

Gerlach, Christian. *Extremely Violent Societies: Mass Violence in the Twentieth-Century World*. Cambridge: Cambridge University Press, 2010.

Guillemot, François. *Des Vietnamiennes dans la guerre civile: L'autre moitié de la guerre, 1945–1975*. Paris: Les Indes Savantes, 2014.

Lanzona, Vina A. *Amazons of the Huk Rebellion: Gender, Sex, and Revolution in the Philippines*. Madison: University of Wisconsin Press, 2009.

Lonsdale, John. "Authority, Gender & Violence: The War within Mau Mau's Fight for Land & Freedom." In *Mau Mau and Nationhood: Arms, Authority and Narration*, edited by E. S. Atieno Odhiambo and John Lonsdale, 46–75. Oxford: James Currey, 2003.

Lyons, Tanya. *Guns and Guerilla Girls: Women in the Zimbabwean National Liberation Struggle*. Trenton, NJ: Africa World Press, 2004.

MacMaster, Neil. *Burning the Veil: The Algerian War and the "Emancipation" of Muslim Women, 1954–62*. Manchester: Manchester University Press, 2012.

Manderson, Lenore. *Women, Politics and Change: The Kaum Ibu UMNO, Malaysia, 1945–1972*. Kuala Lumpur: Oxford University Press, 1980.

McCullers, Molly. "'We Do It So That We Will Be Men': Masculinity Politics in Colonial Namibia, 1915–49." *Journal of African History* 52, no. 1 (2011): 43–62.

Nhongo-Simbanegavi, Josephine. *For Better or Worse? Women and ZANLA in Zimbabwe's Liberation Struggle*. Harare: Weaver Press, 2000.

Presley, Cora Ann. *Kikuyu Women, the Mau Mau Rebellion and Social Change in Kenya*. Boulder, CO: Westview Press, 1992.

Suttner, Raimund. "Masculinities in the African National Congress-Led Liberation Movement: The Underground Period." *Kleio* 37, no. 1 (2005): 71–106.

Taylor, Sandra C. *Vietnamese Women at War: Fighting for Ho Chi Minh and the Revolution*. Lawrence: University Press of Kansas, 1999.

Terretta, Meredith. *Petitioning for Our Rights, Fighting for Our Nation: The History of the Democratic Union of Cameroonian Women, 1949–1960*. Bamenda: Langaa Research & Publishing, 2013.

Vince, Natalya, *Our Fighting Sisters: Nation, Memory and Gender in Algeria, 1954–2012*. Manchester: Manchester University Press, 2015.

West, Harry G. "Girls with Guns: Narrating the Experience of War of FRELIMO's 'Female Detachment'." *Anthropological Quarterly* 73, no. 4 (2000): 180–94.

White, Aaronette M. "Men Are Fighting for Freedom, All the Women Are Mourning Their Men, but Some of Us Carried Guns: A Raced-Gendered Analysis of Fanon's Psychological Perspectives on War." *Signs* 32, no. 4 (2007): 857–84.

CHAPTER 28

POST-1945 WESTERN MILITARIES, FEMALE SOLDIERS, AND GAY AND LESBIAN RIGHTS

KAREN HAGEMANN AND D'ANN CAMPBELL

WOMEN were present in the armed forces long before the twentieth century, but their involvement increased visibly from the First to the Second World War. Most women in the armies of the main war powers served as auxiliaries and nurses, but during World War II (1939–1945) some served also as engineers, pilots, or doctors. Only in the Soviet Union were women employed as soldiers; hundreds of thousands of women joined the Red Army during the conflict. On average, 2 to 9 percent of the military personnel of the regular armed forces of the Second World War were women.[1] After 1945, most of these predominantly young and single women were quickly demobilized. In the 1950s and 1960s, only a relatively small number and percentage of women served in Western and Eastern armies, mainly in the administrative, logistical, signal, and the medical corps. More women fought in the armed forces of the anticolonial movements in the Wars of Decolonization from the 1940s to the 1970s.[2] Only since the 1970s have Western armies begun to admit an increasing number of women to active military duty.[3]

The percentage of servicewomen reached 7 percent in the armed forces of the sixteen member states of the North Atlantic Treaty Organization (NATO) in 1999. Nearly twenty years later, in 2017, the proportion increased further to an average of 11 percent of now thirty NATO states. Hungary with 19 percent, and Slovenia and the United States with 16 percent had the highest proportions of active duty female military personnel, followed by Bulgaria, Canada, Greece, Latvia, and France with 15 percent. In the other European NATO forces, the percentage ranged from 14 percent in Albania to 1 percent in Turkey. In the Norwegian armed forces female personnel made up around 12 percent, in the British, German and Dutch 10 percent, and in the Danish armed forces they constituted 7 percent.[4]

Many non-NATO Western militaries have also integrated increasing percentages of women in recent decades. One of the earliest was the Israel Defense Forces (IDF), which has included women since the founding of the state in 1948 by a mandatory military service requirement. In 2011, female personnel accounted for 33 percent of the soldiers and 51 percent of the officers, but only 3 percent of the combat soldiers, even though the 2000 Equality Amendment to the Defense Service Law gave women equal rights "to serve in any role in the IDF." The number of female soldiers in combat units has steadily grown, however, from 547 in 2012 to 2,700 in 2017.[5] Next to Israel, Norway is one of the few countries, and the only NATO member, that made military service mandatory for women. Compulsory military services for both sexes was introduced unanimously by the parliament in June 2013. In practice, though, recruits are not forced to serve; instead only those who are motivated are selected.[6] In the Australian Defence Force, the largest Western military that does not belong to NATO, service by women is voluntary. In 2017, 17 percent of the Australian military personnel were female, similar to its neighbor New Zealand.[7] The percentage of women in the post-1945 Soviet military and, later, in the armed forces of the Russian Federation has been comparatively lower; it increased from an estimated 3 percent in 2013 to 10 percent in 2018.[8]

Despite their increasing integration, women are far from having achieved equality in the military. Access to combat positions remains the most contested issue.[9] Until 2013, in Europe, only the NATO states Denmark, Germany, Italy, the Netherlands, Norway, and Spain permitted women to fill active combat roles. The British Armed Forces allowed women in combat roles outside the infantry and armored divisions. On average, almost 30 percent of the NATO member states had combat restrictions on women's service in 2013. Beyond Europe, six more NATO countries, including Canada, gave women access to combat positions before 2013. The US Defense Department, which controls the largest military force in the Western world, began to consider loosening its near-universal ban on women serving in direct combat positions, including ground combat, in 2011. Since 2016, all combat roles are open to women, including those in the Marine Corps, which were the most controversial.[10]

The development in the United States, the leading NATO power, inspired change in more NATO member and partner states. This change was reinforced on the one hand by the domestic political and public pressure in these countries, on the other hand by the NATO gender mainstreaming policy. Already in 1998, NATO had introduced the Office on Women in the NATO Forces, which was replaced in 2009 by the NATO Committee on Gender Perspectives. The committee was mandated to support the integration of a gender perspective into NATO's operations, and to support the implementation of the United Nations Security Council Resolution (UNSCR) 1325 on "Women, Peace and Security" as well as "future related UNCSRs" on gender equality.[11] The committee works "to integrate a gender perspective into all aspects of NATO operations" and "promotes gender mainstreaming as a strategy for making the concerns and experiences of both women and men an integral dimension of the design, implementation, monitoring and evaluation of policies, programmes and military operations."[12]

In 2017, only 11 percent of the NATO members still restricted women's access to military positions, including combat. To support the integration and advancement of women in their armies, 43 percent of the NATO member states had introduced policies that promoted a recruitment of women in the military and 64 percent offered transferable parental leave to support the compatibility of military service and parenthood in 2017. Even more NATO member states (82 percent) had implemented gender mainstreaming policies. Nevertheless, the gender distribution of employment in the military was, despite all attempts at gender mainstreaming, still quite conventional and unequal. In 2017, the five main areas of employment of women in the armed forces of the NATO states were logistics (18 percent; men 20 percent), medical service (17 percent; men 3 percent), and administration (14 percent; men 6 percent), infantry (10 percent; men 22 percent) and communications (6 percent; men 10 percent). The situation was similar in the NATO partner states. Here women were allowed in combat units in the militaries of Australia, Finland, Ireland, Serbia, Sweden, and New Zealand in 2017.[13]

Also the distribution across ranks in NATO militaries was still uneven between service men and women in 2017. The average proportion of women in officers positions was, especially in the middle military ranks, higher than the average proportion of 11 percent service women in the NATO forces. Fifteen percent of all ordinary officers and 14 percent of all majors, lieutenant colonels, and colonels were women. In the highest military ranks of general officers and above, however, the percentage of women was 10 percent, slightly lower than the average proportion of service women. The percentage of female soldiers in officer positions in the NATO forces was higher than that of the male soldiers. Twenty-nine percent of all female and 22 percent of all male service personnel were officers. The major reason for this difference was that in most NATO member states, more better-educated women than men tend to join the armed forces and seem to see them as an opportunity to pursue a college or university degree.[14]

The increasing integration of women in the armed forces and their contested access to combat positions has been the subject of intensive research in the political and social sciences as well as security studies since the late 1980.[15] The integration of openly gay and lesbian personnel, which occurred later than the inclusion of women and was similarly contested, became a subject of intensive study too.[16] Scholars identified the Second World War as the critical period for the introduction of the more systematic persecution of such soldiers. At least in the Canadian and American militaries, discrimination further increased in the first decade of the Global Cold War (1946–91) as part of the regendering of postwar militaries and societies. It was not until the early 1970s, as a consequence of the rise of the gay and lesbian liberation movement, that more and more voices demanded the equal integration of gay and lesbian people into the armed forces. The Netherlands responded first and in 1974 abolished the ban on gay, lesbian, and bisexual personnel serving in its armed forces. Most other Western militaries did not lift their bans until the millennium. In response to public demands, in December 1993 the US Department of Defense introduced the "Don't Ask, Don't Tell" policy, which lasted until its repeal in September 2011. This policy prohibited military personnel from discriminating against or harassing closeted gay, lesbian, or bisexual servicemembers or applicants, while barring openly gay and lesbian personnel from military service.[17]

A decision by the European Court of Human Rights in Strasbourg in September 1999 officially ended all legal discrimination against gay, lesbian, and bisexual soldiers for the European NATO forces. The ruling applied to the militaries of all European Union and Council of Europe member states, which had to lift their bans and begin allowing gay, lesbian, and bisexual people into the services from 2000 onward. Nevertheless, many of them continued to experience ongoing discrimination; one such group was transgender soldiers.[18] In June 2016, the ban on transgender soldiers serving in the military was lifted by the US Department of Defense at that time controlled by the Democrats, but in July 2017, the new Republican president, Donald Trump, announced a return to the earlier ban. This affected an estimated 7,000 active and reserve transgender servicemembers. Today, eighteen other countries allow transgender people to serve openly, including Australia, Belgium, Canada, France, Germany, the Netherlands, New Zealand, the Scandinavian countries, Spain, and the United Kingdom.[19]

In the following, the changing policies of the Western militaries toward female, gay, and lesbian soldiers in the post-1945 era and the challenges their integration posed to dominant ideas of martial military masculinity will be explored. The focus will be on the policies of the three NATO states United States, the United Kingdom, and Canada, because their militaries are interesting for a comparison. The United States Armed Forces, as the largest and most powerful NATO member, played and still play an important role as a model for the other NATO partners. The British Armed Forces represent a large and influential European NATO force with a strong and long martial tradition. The Canadian Armed Forces are much smaller and have continuously been composed of all volunteers since 1945, different than the British and American armed forces that did not end universal conscription for men until 1960 and 1973 respectively. All three militaries fought together in the Gulf War (1990–91) and the wars in Afghanistan (2001–ongoing) and Iraq (2003–11).

The comparison will focus on four major variables: the development of the organization of the armed forces and their military technology; the changes in the positions of women and LGBT people in society; related to this, the transformations of dominant notions of the military and gender; and finally, shifts in the political and legal context.[20] Based on a discussion of the concept of the *military as a gender-defining institution*, which is central for the subsequent analysis, the following explores driving, enabling, and blocking factors in the equal integration of women and LGBT people in the armed forces of these three NATO countries since the end of the Second World War.[21]

THE MILITARY AS A
GENDER-DEFINING INSTITUTION

Michelle Sandhoff and Mady Wechsler Segal have described the military as a "gender-defining institution, functioning as a proving ground for masculinity." For them, the military has been for hundreds of years—and continues to be—one of the most powerful organizations that define "hegemonic" notions and practices of heterosexual masculinity in society and culture. This institutional role explains the fierce resistance against the integration of heterosexual and lesbian women, gay men, and transgender persons in the military.[22] Earlier scholarship, like the pathbreaking work by political scientists Cynthia Enloe and Joshua Goldstein, came to a similar conclusion. In 1983, Enloe argued in her book *Does Khaki Become You? The Militarization of Women's Lives* that the expansion and professionalization of the armed forces in Western and Western-dominated societies produced an "archetypal gender-construct" with male combatants as the antithesis of female civilians. In this construct, military masculinity found its very justification in the protection of women and their femininity. As a result, the culture of military and war and discussions surrounding it provided men with a sense of agency, power, and superiority over women.[23] Similarly, Goldstein contended in his 2001 book *War and Gender: How Gender Shapes the War System* that the connection between gender and the military is historically contingent, mutually dependent, and socially and culturally constructed. For him, too, the military functions as a "proving ground for masculinity. . . . Across cultures and time, the selection of men as potential combatants (and women for feminine war support roles) has helped shape the war system. In turn, the pervasiveness of war in history has influenced gender profoundly."[24]

The research of these and other experts demonstrated that because of the importance of the military as a gender-defining institution, the increasing integration of women into the armed forces and the attempts to give them equal access to all positions, including combat, were perceived far beyond the military as a threat to its functioning as a heterosexual male institution that imperiled the heteronormative hierarchical gender order in society and culture more generally. Since the Age of Revolutions (1770s–1840s), the integration of women in the military has challenged the core right and duty of modern Western masculinity—to carry a weapon and fight for the protection of country, home, and family—a right that was closely linked to the entitlement to political citizenship.[25] The more women were officially integrated into the armed forces during the twentieth century, especially in the "emergency situation" of wars, the less military service per se functioned as a core marker of distinction between men and women. Subsequently, combat as the core military duty during wartime, rather than military service as such, became *the* marker of gender difference inside and outside the military in war and peace. As a result, after the Second World War, the focus of the public debate moved from the question of the extent of inclusion of women in the military to the issue of their access to combat roles. This latter debate started in the 1970s and was sparked by liberal feminist activists of the new women's movement, who demanded equal rights in all institutions, including the military.

Interestingly, in most Western countries military leaders and politicians used the same two principal arguments for excluding women, initially from the military and later primarily from combat roles. The first claim insists that women's bodies are different from men's and that they cannot meet the necessary physical standards. The second objection is that integration will affect morale, recruitment, retention, readiness, unit cohesion, and combat effectiveness. Both arguments have been challenged by many studies since the early twenty-first century. In respect to the first argument, they show that with new technologies, the post-1945 armies became increasingly more knowledge based, so physical strength diminished in importance. Militaries need a broad variety of skills, and recruitment tests more and more have taken this necessity into account. Today, 90 percent of all service positions do not involve direct combat.[26]

Regarding the second argument, scholarship has concluded that mixed units may have even higher morale and effectiveness. An important issue in this context is unit cohesion, which researchers divide into social and task cohesion. Servicewomen in fact excel at task cohesion. Women could be harmful to social cohesion only if the goal were to achieve male bonding based on the ideal of a "band of brothers," as opposed to a more generalized unit bonding. Only when servicemen sustain dated ideas about the gender order and gender relations might they become distracted by or overly protective of their female fellow soldiers.[27] In other words, women can handle the tasks, but the preservation of a traditional gender order and hierarchy in the military, rather than aptitude, required the exclusion of women from the military first, and combat positions later.

Similarly, the inclusion of openly gay, lesbian, bisexual, and transgender personnel called into question the heteronormative male order of the military. Politicians and military leaders, not to mention parts of the public, consequently fought their integration into the armed forces.[28] The calls for the open service of gay, lesbian, and transgender persons are relatively recent, starting in the early 1970s with the gay and lesbian rights movement—although men and women with same-sex desires have always been present in the armed forces. Allan Bérubé argued in his seminal 1990 study *Coming Out under Fire: The History of Gay Men and Women in World War II* that even though the US government had already made "assault with intent to commit sodomy" grounds for court-martial in a revision of the 1916 Articles of War, the Second World War, with the reintroduction of universal male conscription and the mobilization of women for war service, became *the* crucial turning point in the policies toward gay and lesbian soldiers in the US military. In addition to the usual practice of court-martialing violent same-sex offenders, the military implemented an administrative discharge policy that enabled the expulsion of gays and lesbians for consensual same-sex acts and even for being homosexual or having homosexual desires without acting on them. As a result, the US military was not only prosecuting illegal acts, but also persecuting identities.[29]

Bérubé and others stress that the military played an important role in producing a wider change in the US cultural understanding of homosexuality during and after the Second World War, shifting it from a "moral deficit" and "effeminate form of masculinity" to a criminal act, to an identity, or, in the words of administrators, doctors, and psychiatrists, a "personality type." Most of these experts as well as military leaders and politicians defined this identity in the war and the postwar period in a remarkably negative manner. They described gay men with such terms as "child molester, homosexual, sex offender, sex psychopath, sex degenerate, sex deviant, and sometimes communist," which Bérubé argued became "interchangeable in the minds of the public, legislators, and local police" in the 1950s United States influenced by McCarthyism.[30]

In the context of the escalating Cold War, a major reason for the increase in the postwar persecution of gays and lesbians and the central role the military played as its trailblazer was the need of the Western postwar states to reorder the gender hierarchy and, with it, the social order after the challenges that the Second World War had posed to it. In this process, gender relations and the family became an important marker of difference between the two competing systems on both sides of the so-called Iron Curtain.[31] In addition to the policies meant to normalize the labor market, society, and the family, the governmental attempts to regender postwar societies included the fierce persecution of anything that questioned the social heteronormativity and its central gender-defining institution—the military. For this reason, too, the US armed forces intensively persecuted lesbian women for the first time in an attempt to police the small number and percentage of women permanently integrated into the military after 1948.[32] While much research on the development in other Western militaries after 1945 remains to be done, the existing studies point to a similar conclusion: the armed forces seemed to have been a central "gender-defining" institution everywhere.

THE INTEGRATION OF WOMEN IN THE POST-1945 US MILITARY

Women have officially served in the US armed forces since the First World War, first mainly as nurses, but increasingly also as voluntary auxiliaries. During the Second World War, the total number of serving women reached approximately 277,000 (140,000 in the US Army, 100,000 in the Navy, 23,000 in the Marines, 13,000 in the Coast Guard, and 1,000 in the Army Air Forces). In addition, 74,000 women served in the US Army and Navy Nurse Corps. They reached less than 2 percent of the personnel of the US military.[33] By far the largest organization was the Women's Army Auxiliary Corps (WAAC), founded in May 1942 and converted into a regular part of the army as the Women's Army Corps (WAC) in September 1943.[34] Women were one of the first groups to be demobilized; after the victory over Germany and Japan, the discharge of the "WACs" began quickly. By 1948, their number was reduced to 14,000.[35]

As the Cold War developed, however, the manpower needs of the military rose again. In response, the United States enacted the Selective Service Act of June 1948, which provided for a peacetime draft, replacing the Selective Training and Service Act of 1940 that had expired one year before. In June 1948, Congress passed the Women's Armed Services Integration Act, which allowed women to serve as permanent, regular members of the US Army, Air Force, Navy, and Marine Corps. The legislation gave a small cadre of women, organized in the Women's Army Corps, an enduring place in the postwar US military to avoid the delay in creating a women's corps in case of future wars. Although the Women's Armed Services Integration Act was a breakthrough, it nevertheless, as Michaela Hampf pointed out, "permanently fixed the basis for ethnic and gender discrimination within the armed forces during the next two decades. Women were not allowed to make up more than two percent and female officers could not surpass ten percent of all officers commissioned with the notable exception of nurses."[36] Promotion for women was limited and followed a different scheme to avoid any direct competition with men. There was no restriction on *noncombat* positions, but existing provisions excluded women from duties that required combat training. Despite these regulations, many servicewomen perceived the 1948 act as progress, because they could become regular members of the US military.[37]

The restrictions implemented by the integration act proved insufficient for politicians and the military leadership, who worried about clear gender lines. In October 1949, a regulation further established that mothers with dependent children were ineligible to serve in the military, and female servicewomen with children under the age of eighteen were to be discharged. This regulation remained in place until federal legislation in the 1970s allowed the inclusion of women with children in the armed forces. The effect of these restrictive policies was that only a small number of women served in the US armed forces until the 1970s, and their employment was confined to traditional female military tasks in medicine, communication, logistics, and administration. The number of women in the military peaked during the Korean War (1950–53), when the figure reached approximately 140,000, but only 540 of them, all nurses, served in Korea itself. In the Vietnam War (1955–75), especially during the last ten years, some 11,000 women volunteered for deployment overseas. Of them, 6,000 served as military nurses; the others worked as physicians, air traffic controllers, intelligence officers, and clerks, as well as in other positions. The total number of women in the US armed forces of the era was much higher and reached up to 2 percent.[38]

The end of conscription under US President Richard Nixon in January 1973, which was a response to the growing protest against this form of military recruitment during the Vietnam War, was a watershed event for the integration of women in the US military, as the need for personnel resulted in the fall of one restriction on women after another.[39] The military eliminated the 2 percent ceiling, opened additional occupational specialties and billets to women, changed dependency requirements, and ceased automatic discharge for pregnancy. These changes were supported by the social and cultural transformation of American society. Women married later, had fewer children, were increasingly better educated, and continued their careers after marriage. The new women's movement, rising since the late 1960s, demanded legal equality of men and women and suggested an equal rights amendment to the US Constitution. Military officials decided to be proactive, expecting that such an equal rights amendment would soon pass and force immediate, drastic changes for which they would otherwise be unprepared. They reorganized the role of women in the armed forces, but in the end, the amendment was not ratified.[40] From 1969 to 1972, the services' Reserve Officers' Training Corps (ROTC) programs on college campuses began accepting women. The US Coast Guard, which was under the purview of the Department of Transportation in peacetime and responsible for saving lives, protecting the environment, and defending coastlines and waterways, opened its academy to women in 1973. The service academies surrendered to the inevitable and began accepting women in 1976.[41] The Virginia Military Institute and the Citadel—both military colleges distinct from the federal service academies— nevertheless resisted the integration of women until they were finally defeated in court.

As a last step of the integration of women into the US Army, the Women's Army Corps was dissolved in 1978.[42]

These changes signaled a transforming military, as did the significant increase in the percentage of servicewomen during the 1970s: from 1.7 percent of the enlisted ranks in 1971 to 7.6 percent in 1979.[43] In the following decades, the growth was slower: 10 percent of personnel in 1983, 13 percent in 1993, and 16 percent in 2013. Interestingly, the demographics of male and female servicemembers differed remarkably. A 2011 report by the Pew Research Center concluded that the 167,000 women, who served in the US military in 2010, were better educated, more racially diverse, and less likely to be married than their male comrades. Only 46 percent of the female servicemembers, compared to 58 percent of the men, were married, mainly to someone else in the military (women, 48 percent; men, 5 percent). Twelve percent were single mothers, whereas only 4 percent of servicemen were single fathers. Roughly 51 percent of these women were White, as opposed to 71 percent of the men; 31 percent and 16 percent, respectively, were Black; and the proportions of Hispanic servicemembers were roughly equal, at 13 percent and 12 percent.[44] For women from social, racial, or ethnic minorities, more than for men, the US military seems to offer the hope of upward mobility, which the US armed forces encouraged by representing itself as a powerful institution that enabled minorities to prove their citizenship and commitment to their country and obtain a good education in return.[45] According to Cynthia Enloe, one reason for the US military to support the integration of more women—independent of their race and ethnicity—was that its leaders hoped "to *dilute* black males' potential dominance of the rank and file in the post-Vietnam voluntary army." They did not envision young African American female soldiers as a security risk, as they did Black men in arms.[46]

In addition to the demographic differences, women and men in the US military still differ with respect to the branches and occupations in which they serve. Here, gender-specific job segregation was still at work, similar to the other NATO member states. In 2010, 37 percent of the women and 40 percent of the men were in the US Army, 31 percent compared to 22 percent in the Air Force, 25 percent compared to 22 percent in the Navy, and only 7 percent compared to 16 percent in the Marine Corps. In total, 17 percent of the women and 15 percent of the men were commissioned officers. Many more women than men still serve in the traditionally female military occupations: more than 30 percent of women compared to 12 percent of the men were administrators, 15 percent compared to 6 percent served in the medical service, and 14 percent compared to 12 percent were in supply. Twelve percent compared to 22 percent worked in electrical service, and 10 percent each served in communications.[47] These numbers were not much different seven years later. In 2017, the proportion of women in the US Army decreased slightly to 34 percent (men 37 percent), and in the Marine Corps to 7 percent (men 16 percent). In the Air Force and Navy it increased to 30 and 29 percent respectively (men 23 and 24 percent). Similar to the other NATO forces, female soldiers in the US military in growing numbers preferred to serve in the air force and navy, which offered more higher qualified positions and a better education.[48]

Since the early 1990s, the composition of the US military indicated that it was no longer an exclusive men's club, even though men still dominated. One area that still clearly marked the gender hierarchy was access to combat. Only very reluctantly did the US Department of Defense allow women a foothold in combat roles. One force that fostered a reform was the changing public opinion. In 1992, a poll showed that a narrow plurality of 47 percent supported women in combat roles, while a minority of 44 percent wanted to keep the ban.[49] Politicians and military leaders responded slowly. In 1991 and 1993, Congress removed the statutory prohibitions on women flying combat aircraft and serving on combat vessels.[50] In 1994, it rescinded the "Risk Rule," which the Department of Defense had issued in 1988 to set clear and universal guidelines. The rule had "excluded women from noncombat units or missions if the risks of exposure to direct combat, hostile fire or capture were equal to or greater than the risk in the units they supported." After the rule was lifted, all servicemembers were "eligible to be assigned to all positions for which they are qualified except that women shall be excluded from assignment to units below the brigade level whose primary mission is to engage in direct combat on the ground."[51]

Despite these "protective" gender-specific regulations, which aimed for clear gender lines in the military, the wars in which the United States has fought since the 1980s—from the US-led invasions of Grenada (1983) and Panama (1989–90) and the Gulf War to the wars in Afghanistan and Iraq—made a clear-cut exclusion of female soldiers from combat situations difficult. During the Gulf War in 1990–91, almost 41,000 women served in the conflict.[52] Since 2001, more than 300,000 women have served in Afghanistan and Iraq. These US servicewomen women were in harm's way, firing at the enemy, being fired on by the enemy, captured, and killed. Women constituted 12 percent of the troops deployed to the Middle East.[53] Three special programs for female soldiers were developed because male soldiers could not search and question civilian women in this region. The Marine Corps' Lioness Program, the Female Engagement Teams, and most recently the Army's Cultural Support Teams developed as effective intelligence-gathering forces.[54]

The increasing importance of technology helped to create new openings for women and to challenge the combat ban. Today, education-based knowledge and skills are often more needed than strength for the operation of complex equipment. Starting in the 1990s, every few years another "brass ceiling" was shattered. The wars of the past few decades also required additional duties and changing missions for the US and international militaries, particularly through the creation and deployment of multinational peacekeeping units for which mixed units with male and female soldiers work best.[55]

Responding to these developments, in 2011 the US Department of Defense began to explore a possible rescinding of the 1994 combat ban. Starting in 2013, it required each service to assess their Military Officers Service/billet positions to open as many opportunities as possible to servicewomen by 2016.[56] One of the first was the Navy. Since 2013 women were allowed to serve on attack submarines. In early December 2015, US Secretary of Defense Ash Carter announced that as of 2016 all combat roles would be open to women, including those in the Marine Corps. In his announcement, he said, "While the Marine Corps asked for a partial exemption in some areas such as infantry, machine gunner, fire support reconnaissance and others, we are a joint force, and I have decided to make a decision which applies to the entire force."[57] The new guidelines for all armed services focus on five basic principles: ensure gender-neutral evaluation; ensure standards reflect job tasks; validate performance standards; ensure eligibility reflects job tasks; and integrate while preserving readiness, cohesion, and morale.[58] This change of policy was on the one hand again fostered by the military's further need for educated personnel; women are an importance resource in that respect. On the other hand, it was backed by changing public opinion; in 2011, polls showed that almost 73 percent of respondents supported women serving in ground units that engage in close combat.[59]

The development of the US military policy regarding women after 1945 points to the importance of enabling factors such as the increasing level of female education and workforce participation, in addition to the influence of the new women's movement and changing public opinion. The driving factors were clearly the growing military manpower needs, caused by the move to a professional military, and new military technology that required better-educated soldiers.[60] The situation in Britain and Canada was quite similar, but in addition in both countries changing legislation played an important role. Furthermore, different national military cultures clearly had an impact.

THE INTEGRATION OF WOMEN IN THE BRITISH AND THE CANADIAN ARMED FORCES

In the British and Canadian armed forces, women, too, have officially served as auxiliaries and nurses since the First World War. During the Second World War, the number of women in the British military peaked at 470,700, or nearly 9 percent of the country's military strength in September 1943. By far the largest organization was the Auxiliary Territorial Service (ATS), with 213,500 women enrolled at that time.[61] About 45,000 women served in the Canadian military during the Second World War. The largest organization was the Canadian Women's Army Corps, with 21,000 members, of whom approximately 3,000 served overseas.[62] After World War II, most British and Canadian servicewomen were discharged in the context of military demobilization, even though the British army wanted to keep many of them because of the need for personnel in occupied Germany, the Middle East, and the British colonies. The British government under Prime Minister Winston Churchill, however, insisted "that all women should be free to retire as soon as possible from the services." Politicians believed that women were needed in their families or their old jobs for the restoration of the postwar society and economy.[63]

Since the first postwar years, Britain and Canada have followed a path similar to that of the United States, and the two countries only gradually opened military positions to women. The British Parliament first approved National Service as peacetime conscription in July 1947, followed by the introduction of the revised National Service Act in January 1948. In the same year, women were officially recognized as a permanent part of the British armed forces. The Women's Royal Army Corps (WRAC) was created to replace the ATS, and in 1950 the ranks for women were normalized with the ranks of men serving in the British army. Still, as was the case in the American and Canadian militaries of the 1950s to the 1970s, the employment of female servicemembers was restricted to the branches of medicine, communications, logistics, and administration. Only 35 jobs in a military of more than 130 distinct positions were open to them. Women were completely excluded from combat roles and were only provided with weapons and field training for "self-defense."[64] The WRAC was, as Lucy Noakes emphasized, a "small part of a much larger, and profoundly conservative organization decidedly resistant to change of any kind, mirroring in some ways the conservatism of Britain."[65] In the late 1970s, the WRAC included still no more than 6,500 women, roughly 3 percent of the personnel of the British armed forces.[66]

The WRAC began to change in the 1980s. It developed "from serving as a replacement tool for men to being an integral part of the armed service," which was symbolized by a 1982 decision that all new recruits of the WRAC had to undergo the standard weapons training.[67] Women became eligible to pilot Royal Air Force combat aircraft in 1989. The following year, they were permitted to serve on Royal Navy warships, though the ban on serving aboard submarines was lifted much later. The first female officers deployed aboard submarines in 2013 and the first enlisted women in 2014. Beginning in 1991, field training was added to weapons training as part of the overall instruction of female soldiers, and deployment was permitted up to 5 miles from the front lines, or even closer if their roles required it. Different from their American allies, the British developed a "gender-neutral" physical testing procedure so that physical aptitude rather than sex would determine whether individuals were eligible for a particular specialization.[68] These changes—and their limitations—were reflected by the fact that in the early 1990s, 100 of the 134 trades in the British military were open to women, but with the exception of Royal Navy warships, combat-related positions in the infantry and armored divisions remained closed.[69]

To make military service more attractive for women, they were no longer automatically discharged for pregnancy; instead, they have been eligible for maternity leave since 1990. The main reason for all these changes was, as in the United States, the manpower needs of the British armed forces, which had become a professional military in the 1960s. The National Service Act was phased out beginning in 1957; the last conscripted servicemen left the armed forces in May 1963.[70] And, indeed, the changes fostered an increase in the number and percentage of women serving: from 3 percent of all ranks in 1970 to 6 percent in 1990. In 2014, some 15,700 were women were in service, accounting for 9 percent of the British armed forces.[71] In 2017, the proportion was still only 10 percent. Of these service women, 50 percent (57 percent of the men) were employed in the British Army, 30 percent (21 percent of the men) in the Royal Air Force, and 20 percent (22 percent of the men) in the Royal Navy. Similar to the US military, fewer women than men served in the army; they generally preferred the air force and navy.[72]

The Gulf War was the first post-1945 conflict in which British women were deployed: women were 3 percent of the British forces, compared to 6 percent of the US forces.[73] During and after this war, units that engaged in close-quarters combat, such as the infantry, remained closed to women. Combat was the last bastion at which military and political leaders drew the gender line for the British armed forces as well. As a result, in 2002, 4 percent of the positions of the Royal Air Force, 27 percent in the Royal Navy, and 30 percent in the British army were still not open to women.[74]

In the end, European law mandated reforms in all the armed forces of the European Community, including the United Kingdom. The Court of Justice of the European Community made two major decisions in 2000. Both judgments were rulings on the interpretation of a 1976 Council Directive (76/207/EEC) that required the implementation of the principle of equal treatment for men and women in access to employment, vocational training, promotion, and working conditions. These two decisions forced European governments to give women equal access to all military positions.[75]

But the implementation of these rulings was a different matter, as the British case demonstrates. The British government reviewed the ban on close-quarters combat in 2002, 2010, and 2014. The 2002 and 2010 reviews upheld combat exclusion. The key reasons given for this decision were the importance of unit cohesion and military effectiveness; all-male units were reportedly more likely to bond and work more effectively.[76] The 2014 review presented conflicting views for the first time, but did not result in a policy change.[77] In 2015, finally, Conservative Prime Minister David Cameron requested a radical overhaul. He ordered the Ministry of Defence to be ready to welcome female soldiers into "close combat" roles in 2016, and Secretary of State for Defence Michael Fallon announced that he wanted to end the army's ban on women serving in front-line infantry roles. This decision was fostered on the one hand by the European Union's insistence on applying their gender-equality regulations and on the other hand by the increasing pressure of the gender mainstreaming policy pursued by NATO headquarters.

Developments in Canada followed the British path in the first decades after the Second World War, with the exception that Canada did not have conscription. The Canadian armed forces of the Cold War era were from the outset a professional military with volunteers. In the early 1950s, after an extensive postwar reduction of its personnel, the Royal Canadian Navy, the Canadian Army, and the Royal Canadian Air Force again allowed women to enlist. Yet, their employment was, as in the British WRAC, restricted to medicine, communications, logistics, and administration. The roles of women in the Canadian military began to expand in 1971, after the Department of National Defence had reviewed the recommendations of the Royal Commission on the Status of Women. It lifted the ceiling of 1,500 female personnel and gradually expanded employment opportunities into new areas—vehicle drivers and mechanics, aircraft mechanics, air-traffic controllers, military police, and firefighters. Between 1979 and 1985, the Canadian armed forces conducted trials on "servicewomen in nontraditional environments and roles" to determine which positions should remain closed to women based on "realistic occupational requirements." After the trials, 75 percent of all military positions were opened to women.[78]

Watershed events on this path were in Canada the passage of the Canadian Human Rights Act in 1978 and the Canadian Charter of Rights and Freedoms in 1985, even though the Canadian military sought exemptions from both. In 1989, the Canadian Human Rights Tribunal ruled that "the Canadian Forces had not made the case to retain the exclusionary policy and directed the Canadian Forces to achieve full and complete gender integration in all occupations and all roles except submarines by 1998."[79] It concluded, "The risk to individual rights is high when women are excluded from any occupations, and the risk to national security is, by comparison, low."[80] Pushed by the legal decisions and political and public pressure and fostered by the increasing shortage of eligible male recruits, the Department of National Defence further reviewed personnel policies. The resulting reforms permitted women to serve aboard replenishment ships and dive tenders, in the army service battalions, in military police platoons and field ambulance units, and in most air squadrons. The final restriction, service aboard submarines, was lifted in 2001.[81]

Nevertheless, after the year 2000, most Canadian service women remained in combat-support positions, and few had completed the training needed for ground-combat roles.[82] A series of surveys in the American and Canadian armed forces carried out after the millennium indicate that resistance in the officer corps was one reason for the limited effects of the new policies. But, the survey results for both militaries, published in 2008, also signaled change and showed significant acceptance of women's service, even if a hard core of officers remains opposed. Furthermore, the results pointed to national differences; compared to the American officers, the Canadian officers were markedly more willing to accept women's participation in the armed forces: 41 percent of American, but only 21 percent of the Canadian senior-level officers surveyed embraced the idea that "the military should remain basically masculine, dominated by male values and characteristics."[83] National opinions diverged most on the issue of women and combat: 38 percent of American officers, but 78 percent of their Canadian counterparts agreed, "that women should be allowed to serve in combat jobs," and 67 percent of the American, but 81 percent of the Canadian officers "reported that they would be equally confident with a female as they would with a male Commanding Officer."[84] Thus, while the officer corps of both nations' militaries were becoming more progressive regarding women's roles in the military, most American officers, in marked contrast to the Canadians, still saw combat as a male bastion that reinforces the gender hierarchy in the military.

In a comparative perspective one important explanation for this national difference is that the culture in the Canadian armed forces was in general more open toward women and their equality to men, significantly more than the military culture in the American and British forces. This observation is confirmed by studies that conclude that despite all continuing challenges, the highest levels of both gender and sexual-orientation integration are found in the Canadian, Danish, Dutch, and Norwegian militaries, which actively supported this development with their gender mainstreaming policies. But these policies did not result in all four armed forces in an equally high percentage of female service members. The proportion of women in Norway was, at 12 percent, only slightly above the NATO average of 11 percent in 2017, and in the Netherlands, at 10 percent, and Denmark, at 7 percent, even below it.[85]

Only in Canada, at 16 percent in 2017, was the proportion of women significantly above the average. Of the 8,315 Canadian service women 46 percent served in the Army (56 percent of the men), 36 percent in the Air Force (28 percent of the men), and 18 percent in the Navy (16 percent of the men). The gender gap in different branches of the military was even more developed in the Canadian than in the US and British armed forces. In the Canadian Forces also the percentage of women in the middle military ranks was significantly higher than in the American and British military, which was partly a result of the gender policy, and partly of the in general higher percentage of officers. In the NATO member states, on average, 29 percent of the active duty female military personnel were officers (compared to 22 percent of the male), in the Canadian Forces this percentage was 32 percent (compared to 35 percent of the male), in the British 24 percent (compared to 19 percent of the male), and in the American 20 percent (compared to 17 percent of the male). These statistics confirm the general impression that everywhere in the NATO more female than male soldiers seem to have been better educated.[86]

Researchers explain the more women friendly culture in the Canadian, Danish, Dutch, and Norwegian armed forces with the interplay of four factors. First, these countries have small, socially and culturally more egalitarian societies and cultures and more developed welfare-state systems. Second, they were forerunners in integrating women into their militaries, and, third, they were earlier and more expansive in their support for women's rights and gender equality beyond the military. Finally, their armies are much smaller and do not play the same role in international conflicts and peacekeeping missions as the armed forces of the United States and Britain. Less involvement in aggressive wars allowed for the development of a military culture that is less bellicose, virile, misogynistic, and homophobic.[87]

GAY AND LESBIAN SERVICE MEMBERS

The US Articles of War of 1916, implemented in March 1917, included Article 93, which stated that any person subject to military law who committed "assault with intent to commit sodomy . . . shall be punished as a court-martial may direct." The article was modified in 1920 to make the act of sodomy itself a crime. Until 1993, gay men and lesbian women were banned from the US armed forces. However, its different branches lacked a unified policy on their service. Before 1949, each branch tended to charge personnel caught engaging in homosexual conduct with sodomy, court-martial them, and issue them a dishonorable discharge. During the Second World War, the military started to court-martial soldiers who admitted to or were caught engaging in consensual same-sex activities and thereby expanded the scope of prosecutions and discharges. The affected soldiers were administratively expelled and barred from entitlement to the benefits offered by the GI Bill, the popular name for the Servicemen's Readjustment Act of 1944.[88] The military apparatus began to implement a policy that persecuted the so-called homosexual personality type. Physical exams and interviews were used to identify men with "effeminate" or "perverse" characteristics during recruitment. But as Paul Jackson emphasizes in his 2010 study *One of the Boys: Homosexuality and the Military during World War II*, which focuses on the Canadian armed forces, very often they were not able to "identify" gays and lesbians. Furthermore, the demands of the military for manpower and effectively operating troops in many cases overrode official policy.[89]

As a result, a significant number of gays and lesbians managed to pass the screening and served in the US military during World War II. Allan Bérubé estimates that there were at least 650,000 and as many as 1.6 million gay male soldiers in the US Army during the conflict.[90] For these men and thousands of lesbian women, their military service created opportunities. The military moved a large number of mainly younger men and women from their small American hometowns and rural communities to other parts of the country and the globe and created gender-separated accommodation and units, which brought gays and lesbians in contact with others. The everyday life of war generated opportunities for all kinds of new forms of relationships and sexual experiences. In this way, the war allowed them to realize for the first time that they were not alone and isolated in their desires.[91]

With the postwar demobilization, the US armed forces tried to standardize anti-homosexual regulations across all branches even further. Freed from the exigencies of war, the military could become more selective and tried to ban all personnel identified as gay and lesbian from the military more radically. Accordingly, in October 1949, the US Department of Defense regulations stated, "Homosexual personnel, irrespective of sex, should not be permitted to serve in any branch of the Armed Forces in any capacity, and prompt separation of known homosexuals from the Armed Forces is mandatory."[92] The new Uniform Code of Military Justice, which went into effect in May 1951, reinforced this policy. Article 125 prohibited any form of "sodomy" among military personnel.[93] One argument in the context of the rising Cold War, with its fierce anticommunism, was the supposed "security risk of homosexuals." They were equated with communists or alleged to be more vulnerable to blackmailing by the communist enemy.[94]

During the 1950s, the Navy Board of Inquiry conducted the first official study on homosexuals in the US armed forces to prepare and submit recommendations to the secretary of the navy for the "Revision of Policies, Procedures and Directives Dealing with Homosexuals." Its result, the 1957 Crittenden Report, named after the board's chairperson, found despite all expectations, that homosexuals were no more likely to be a "security risk" than other people in the military. The report nevertheless recommended that homosexuals should be excluded from service because "homosexuality is wrong, it is evil, and it is to be branded as such."[95] The Crittenden Report remained secret until 1976.

The rationales for excluding gays and lesbians from serving in the military were deeply rooted in cultural norms and values, so they correspondingly changed over time. The earlier arguments found less and less social and cultural support beginning in the

1970s.[96] The growing gay and lesbian rights movement began to demand with increasing vehemence equal rights in society, the state, and the military. In response, the Department of Defense under Democratic President Bill Clinton in December 1993 instituted through Directive 1304.26 the Don't Ask, Don't Tell policy, which lasted until September 2011.[97] It prohibited military personnel from discriminating against or harassing closeted gay, lesbian, or bisexual servicemembers or applicants. No one was allowed to ask recruits or service personnel about their sexual orientation. Gay and lesbian soldiers were dishonorably discharged only when they identified themselves as such. Between 1994 and 2011, about 13,000 US soldiers were dismissed under this policy. In the end, Don't Ask, Don't Tell did not satisfy anyone and created a climate of suspicion, paranoia, and harassment.

Furthermore, the policy had unequal effects on members of the military. Lesbian soldiers were disproportionately affected by the persecution: 31 percent of the discharges in 1999 were of women, even though women composed only 14 percent of the force.[98] Sandhoff and Segal explain this gender difference with the observation that "discharges of men for homosexuality have tended to be individual, whereas suspicions that there are lesbians in a unit have led to discharges of multiple women. It may also be that the social pressures on military women have led them to appear masculine, leading to suspicions of homosexuality."[99] In addition, it is important to note the long-term institutional history of more harshly prosecuting lesbians, which reached back to the 1950s. At a point when the drawing of clear gender lines and the reordering of the gender system were high on the Cold War agenda, this stricter treatment of female personnel served the purpose of subjecting them to tighter control.[100] In the 1990s, when the percentage of women in the military continued to rise along with public pressure for their integration on equal terms, including access to all combat positions, the persecution of lesbians once again helped to draw a gender line and reinforce the gender hierarchy. Indeed, the label *lesbian* was used by male military personnel to denigrate the social status of *all* sexually unavailable servicewomen.[101]

Finally, in December 2010, Democratic President Barack Obama signed the repeal of Don't Ask, Don't Tell into law after furious lobbying on both sides.[102] Supported by other right-wing organizations, the Center for Military Readiness led the conservative opposition to allowing gays to serve openly.[103] Their predictions about the repeal of the ban hurting military effectiveness and morale and breaking the bank with rising healthcare costs because of an increasing number of people with HIV/AIDS in the military have not come to pass. None of the other twenty-five countries that have opened service to gays and lesbians has experienced these problems either.[104]

Two of these countries were the NATO states of Canada and Britain, which lifted their bans in 1992 and 2000. The Canadian armed forces had a total ban on gays and lesbians for similar reasons as the US military until 1988. In 1986, the Canadian Department of National Defence still maintained that such a ban was necessary to protect "cohesion and morale, discipline, leadership, recruiting, medical fitness and the rights to privacy of other members."[105] However, legal pressure stemming from the 1978 Canadian

Human Rights Act and the 1985 Canadian Charter of Rights and Freedoms, combined with changing public opinions, led to a slow change of the policy. In 1988, the Canadian Department of National Defence began to permit "practicing homosexuals to be retained in the CF [Canadian Forces] but under the severe career restrictions of no promotion, no career courses, no occupational transfers, no advancement in qualifica-tion level status, and ineligibility for reengagement, subsequent periods of engagement, or extension of service contracts."[106] Policymakers finally repealed the ban in 1992. The Canadian military had tried to delay this decision as long as possible, as they had regard-ing the equal integration of women. One major reason for its resistance was that many in the rank and file—including military leaders—opposed serving with openly gay per-sonnel. A 1986 survey of active-duty heterosexual male Canadian armed forces person-nel indicated that 62 percent would refuse to share quarters with gay soldiers and 45 percent would not work with gays.[107]

Despite that military culture, the rescinding of the ban in 1992 was a nonevent. Gay and lesbian soldiers did not openly admit their sexual orientation in large numbers, but at least privately they reported feeling more comfortable.[108] In the following two decades, however, Canada saw a significant shift in the acceptance of gays and lesbians to the point that military personnel began attending pride parades in uniform.[109] Two factors contributed to the successful integration of openly gay soldiers: First, the Canadian military decided to focus on behaviors, which they addressed through broad harassment training that neither singled out sexual orientation nor ignored it as a potential source of conflict; and second, clear leadership by most senior officers in announcing and implementing the policy change set an example for subordinates.[110]

Much as in the United States, "the history of gays in the British military is replete with surveillance, informants, blackmail, stakeouts, investigations and psychological exams."[111] The United Kingdom did not repeal its ban until 2000 and then only because of the coercion by the European Court of Human Rights. One year prior, the British Ministry of Defence had reaffirmed that "homosexual behavior can cause offence, polarize relationships, induce ill-discipline and as a consequence damage morale and unit effectiveness."[112] Because of changing public opinion and increasing pressure by the gay and lesbian rights movement since the 1980s, British policymakers created a Homosexual Policy Assessment Team in 1995. Its recommendation was to keep the ban, because lifting it "would be an affront to service people" and lead to "heterosexual resentment and hostility," but to relax its enforcement.[113] The government and military leadership followed this policy suggestion until 2000.

In the end, it was judicial pressure that led to reform, much as in Canada. The European Court of Human Rights had warned the British government in the mid-1990s that the gay ban was unlikely to survive a direct challenge in terms of the European Convention on Human Rights, which could force a repeal.[114] When the matter came to the court, it did indeed rule against the ban in September 1999. The court determined that investigations by military authorities into a serviceperson's sexuality breach the right to privacy (Article 8 of the European Convention on Human Rights). The court concluded that the "British Defence Ministry violated European Convention's guarantee of an 'equal report' to 'private and family life.'" The judges found the "military policy and investigations ... 'exceptionally intrusive.'"[115]

Forced to overturn the ban, Great Britain looked initially to the US Don't Ask, Don't Tell policy, but decided that the half measure was ineffective. Thus, in January 2000 the British Ministry of Defence finally lifted the ban.[116] Fears about the reactions of heterosexual personnel proved unfounded. As in Canada and other countries that had already lifted such restrictions, there was no significant change in recruitment, retention, morale, military effectiveness, or unit cohesion. The smooth transition was credited to a generation gap, because, as the director of the Royal United Service Institute, Michael Codner, observed, "our youngsters have just taken it in stride."[117] The 1999 decision of the European Court of Human Rights in Strasbourg forced not only the United Kingdom, but also the militaries of all member states of the European Union and the Council of Europe, including the European NATO forces, to end all legal discrimination against gay, lesbian, bisexual, and transgender soldiers. One country after the other had to lift its ban and begin allowing gay, lesbian, bisexual, and transgender people into the services.

In the United States, Britain, and Canada, as in most other Western militaries, the same arguments against the integration of gay, lesbian, and bisexual soldiers dominated since the 1970s. Homosexuality was constructed as a security risk and as incompatible with military effectiveness, performance, and unit cohesion. It supposedly challenged military morale, education, and training because soldiers lived so closely together and would likewise increase the dangers of sexual harassment and sexually transmitted infections. All research shows that these arguments are not based in fact. Instead, allowing gays and lesbians to serve openly had positive effects. It strengthened the focus on mission, fostered greater respect for rules and politics, enhanced respect for privacy, and improved readiness and morale.[118]

An interplay of multiple factors contributed to the lifting of the bans of gay, lesbian, and bisexual soldiers. One important factor was the increasing difficulty of finding enough qualified personnel to volunteer for the professional militaries. But in most countries, this manpower need was only an enabling force, not a driving one. In this respect, it differed from the integration of women. Rather, the driving factor seems to have been a cultural change initiated by the gay and lesbian rights movement and its effect on the transformation of public opinion and, later, legal norms. This, in turn, forced the armed forces to reform. Heterosexual men in the armed forces fought hardest against a repeal of the ban because it threatened the military as the bastion of heterosexual martial masculinity, even more than an equal inclusion of women.[119]

But because of the perceived challenge homosexual and lesbian soldiers still pose to many heterosexual servicemen, discrimination and sexual violence against gay, lesbian, bisexual, and transgender personnel remain an issue in most Western armed forces. Sexual violence in general is a serious problem for Western militaries. A 2012 US Pentagon survey found that approximately 26,000 servicemen and servicewomen had been sexually assaulted; of those, only 3,374 cases were reported. The majority of sexual-assault victims are male, because of the much larger number of men in the forces, but the percentage of women assaulted is much higher. Among the reasons for the large number of unreported cases are that the military judiciary is still separated from its civilian counterpart and that only 10 percent of the reported cases end in a conviction. Military culture is still dominated by a heterosexual martial masculinity.[120] Discrimination and sexual violence both must be understood as partly resulting from attempts inside the military by individuals and groups to reaffirm this dominant but challenged masculinity and draw clear gender lines.

CONCLUSION

Western militaries went through dramatic changes since the end of the Second World War, which posed challenges to the dominant ideas of a heterosexual martial military masculinity. Two of the most important challenges to this hegemonic ideal were the integration of women, especially in combat positions, and of gay, lesbian, bisexual, and transgender soldiers. Both gender and sexuality were important for determining the right and duty "to kill and die" for a country. Since the end of the Second World War, in all three NATO forces compared here—the United States, the United Kingdom, and Canada—traditional ideas of a military masculinity had been undercut by four developments, which contributed as driving or enabling factors to the integration of women, gays, and lesbians in the armed forces.

Driving factors were the move to professional armies based on volunteers, which led to increasing military manpower needs, and the centrality of new technology that required knowledge and skills and was feeding the demand for well-educated personnel. Both developments facilitated the integration of an increasing number of women. In addition, the legal reforms aiming at equality were interpreted by national and international high courts as pertaining to the armed forces as well. Enabling factors were the increase of educated and working women, social movements that pushed for equal rights of women and gays and lesbians, and the related dramatic changes in public opinion.

One of the two most influential blocking factors was and is still the specific masculine military culture in national armed forces as well as their different branches. This masculine military culture is often "toxic," based on traditional stereotypes of men as socially dominant, along with related traits such as aggressiveness, misogyny, and homophobia. Such attitudes and behavioral patterns continue to be influential, despite all changes in the practice of military service, warfare, and military technology. For many men in the military, the armed forces still seem to function as a proving ground for a very narrowly defined type of masculinity.[121] The other important blocking factor is the continuing importance of the military as a gender-defining institution in general. The increasing integration of women and LGBTQ people into the armed forces and the attempts to give them equal access to all positions posed a threat not only to the conventional functioning of the military as a heterosexual male institution, but also to the heteronormative hierarchical gender order in society and culture more widely. This threat was and is especially challenging for politically and culturally conservative groups inside and outside of the military.

As a consequence, since the 1970s, Western militaries increasingly have allowed women to serve and, more recently, to participate in combat roles. Since the 1990s, more and more armies have also permitted gay men, lesbian women and bisexual and transgender people to serve openly. These changes do not mean, however, that heterosexual women and gay, lesbian, bisexual, and transgender people have truly achieved equality in the everyday cultures of the Western armed forces—they are still far from it, which testifies to the continued power of hegemonic notions and practices of heterosexual masculinity in Western militaries.

NOTES

1. See the chapters by Thomas Cardoza and Karen Hagemann on "History and Memory of Army Women and Female Soldiers, 1770s–1870s," and Karen Hagemann on "History and Memory of Female Military Service in the Age of World Wars" in this handbook.

2. See the chapter by Raphaëlle Branche on "Gender, the Wars of Decolonization, and the Decline of Empires after 1945" in this handbook.

3. Lorry M. Fenner and Marie E. DeYoung, eds., *Women in Combat: Civic Duty or Military Liability?* (Washington, DC: Georgetown University Press, 2001); Helena Carreiras, *Gender and the Military: Women in the Armed Forces of Western Democracies* (London: Routledge, 2006); Cynthia Enloe, *Does Khaki Become You? The Militarisation of Women's Lives* (London: Pluto Press, 1983); Enloe, *Globalization & Militarism: Feminists Make the Link* (Lanham, MD: Rowman & Littlefield, 2007); Irène Eulriet, *Women and the Military in Europe: Comparing Public Cultures* (Basingstoke: Palgrave Macmillan, 2012); and Lory Manning, *Women in the Military: Where They Stand*, 8th ed. (Arlington, VA: Women's Research & Education Institute, 2013).

4. NATO, *Summary of the National Reports of NATO Member and Partner Nations to the NATO Committee on Gender Perspective* (Brussels, NATO Headquarter, 2019), 15–6.

5. Wikipedia, "Women in the Israel Defense Forces," accessed March 11, 2019, https://en.wikipedia.org/wiki/Women_in_the_Israel_Defense_Forces#cite_note-mfaWomen-5; on the earlier history, see Nurit Gillath, "Women and Military Service in Israel, 1948–1967," in *Soldatinnen: Gewalt und Geschlecht im Krieg vom Mittelalter bis heute*, ed. Klaus Latzel et al. (Paderborn: Schöningh, 2011), 395–414; Stuart Cohen, ed., *The New Citizen Armies: Israel's Armed Forces in Comparative Perspective* (New York: Routledge, 2010); and "Number of Women in Combat Roles Reaches Record High," *YNet News*, November 16, 2017, accessed April 12, 2019, https://www.ynetnews.com/articles/0,7340,L-5043945,00.html.

6. "Norway becomes first NATO Country to Draft Women into the Military," *Atlantic Council*, June 14, 2013, accessed April 19, 2020, https://atlanticcouncil.org/blogs/natosource/norway-becomes-first-nato-country-to-draft-women-into-military/.

7. NATO, *Summary of the National Report*, 18.

8. Roger McDermott, "The Role of Women in Russia's Armed Forces," *Eurasian Daily Monitor*, accessed January 15, 2017, https://jamestown.org/program/the-role-of-women-

in-russias-armed-forces/; International Institute for Strategic Studies (IISS), "Russia and Eurasia," in *The Military Balance* 129 (2020): 166–219; and Jennifer G. Mathers, "Russia's Women Soldiers in the Twenty-First Century," *Minerva: Women & War* 1, no. 1 (2007): 8–18.

9. See Gwyn Harries-Jenkins, "Women in Extended Roles in the Military: Legal Issues," *Current Sociology* 50, no. 5 (2002): 745–69.

10. Andrew Swick and Emma Moore, "The (Mostly) Good News on Women in Combat. What is the State of Female Combat Integration Across the Military Service?," *Center for New American Security*, April 19, 2018, accessed April 11, 2019, https://www.cnas.org/publications/reports/an-update-on-the-status-of-women-in-combat.

11. See the chapters by Sandra Whitworth on "The United Nations, Gendered Human Rights, and Peacekeeping since 1945," and Kristen P. Williams on "Gender, Wars of Globalization, and Humanitarian Interventions since the End of the Cold War" in this handbook.

12. NATO, "Gender Perspectives in NATO Armed Forces," June 14, 2016, accessed January 11, 2017, http://www.nato.int/cps/en/natohq/topics_101372.html. For a more extensive analysis of the current development in Britain, see Rachel Woodward and Trish Winter, *Sexing the Soldier: The Politics of Gender and the Contemporary British Army* (London: Routledge, 2007), esp. 39–106.

13. NATO, *Summary of the National Reports*, 34 and 42 and "Women in the Military by Country," accessed March 11, 2019, https://en.wikipedia.org/wiki/Women_in_the_military_by_country.

14. NATO, *Summary of the National Reports*, 38–40.

15. A comparative overview is provided by, Carreiras, *Gender and the Military*; and Helena Carreiras and Gerhard Kümmel, eds., *Women in the Military and in Armed Conflict* (Wiesbaden: Verlag für Sozialwissenschaften, 2008).

16. On the US recently, Douglas Walter Bristol and Heather Marie Stur, eds., *Integrating the US Military: Race, Gender, and Sexual Orientation since World War II* (Baltimore: Johns Hopkins University Press, 2017); and David E. Rohall et al., eds., *Inclusion in the American Military: A Force for Diversity* (Lanham, MD: Lexington Books, 2017).

17. Aaron Belkin, "'Don't Ask, Don't Tell': Does the Gay Ban Undermine the Military's Reputation?," *Armed Forces & Society* 34, no. 2 (2008): 276–91; Randy Shift, *Conduct Unbecoming: Gays and Lesbians in the US Military* (New York: St. Martin's, 1993); and Craig A. Rimmerman, ed., *Gay Rights, Military Wrongs: Political Perspectives on Lesbians and Gays in the Military* (New York: Garland, 1996).

18. Richard Kamm, "European Court of Human Rights Overturns British Ban on Gays in Military," *Human Rights Brief* 7, no. 3 (2000): 18–20; on Britain, see Edmund Hall, *We Can't Even March Straight: Homosexuality in the British Armed Forces* (London: Vintage, 1995).

19. "Pentagon Ends Transgender Ban," *CNN Politics*, June 20, 2016, accessed January 1, 2017, http://www.cnn.com/2016/06/30/politics/transgender-ban-lifted-us-military/; and US Department of Defense, "Department of Defense Transgender Policy," accessed March 17, 2017, https://dod.defense.gov/News/Special-Reports/0616_transgender-policy-archive/.

20. For a more intensive discussion of these variables, see Darlene Iskra et al., "Women's Participation in Armed Forces Cross-Nationally: Expanding Segal's Model," *Current Sociology* 50, no. 5 (2002): 771–97.

21. This differentiation was suggested by Michelle Sandhoff et al., "Gender Issues in the Transformation to an All-Volunteer Force: A Transnational Perspective," in *The New Citizen*, ed. Cohen, 111–31.

22. Michelle Sandhoff and Mady Wechsler Segal, "Women in the US Military: The Evolution of Gender Norms and Military Requirements," in *The Modern American Military*, ed. David Kennedy (Oxford: Oxford University Press, 2013), 273–74; and Megan MacKenzie, *Beyond the Band of Brothers: The US Military and the Myth That Women Can't Fight* (Cambridge: Cambridge University Press, 2015). On the concept of "hegemonic masculinity," see R. W. Connell and James W. Messerschmidt, "Hegemonic Masculinity: Rethinking the Concept," *Gender & Society* 19, no. 6 (2005): 829–59; and John Tosh, "Hegemonic Masculinity and the Gender of History," in *Masculinity in Politics and War: Gendering Modern History*, ed. Stefan Dudink et al. (Manchester: Manchester University Press, 2004), 41–59.

23. Enloe, *Does Khaki*, 207–20.

24. Joshua S. Goldstein, *War and Gender: How Gender Shapes the War System and Vice Versa* (Cambridge: Cambridge University Press, 2001), 9.

25. See the chapters by Stefan Dudink on "Citizenship, Mass Mobilization, and Masculinity in a Transatlantic Perspective, 1770s–1870s," Thomas Kühne on "States, Military Masculinities, and Combat in the Age of World Wars," and Hagemann, "History and Memory" in this handbook.

26. MacKenzie, *Beyond the Band*, 19–41; and Philippe Manigart, "Diversity in the Belgian Armed Forces," in *Cultural Diversity in the Armed Forces: An International Comparison*, ed. Joseph L. Soeters and Jan van der Meulen (London: Routledge, 2007), 185–99.

27. Cynthia Nantais and Martha F. Lee, "Women in the United States Military: Protectors and Protected? The Case of Prisoner of War Melissa Rathbun-Nealy," *Journal of Gender Studies* 8, no. 2 (1999): 181–91.

28. See Jacqueline Fabre-Serris and Alison Keith, eds. *Women & War in Antiquity* (Baltimore: Johns Hopkins University Press, 2015); and Latzel et al., *Soldatinnen*.

29. Allan Bérubé, *Coming Out under Fire: The History of Gay Men and Women in World War II* (Chapel Hill: University of North Carolina Press, 2010), 128–48.

30. Ibid., 258.

31. Ibid., 255–79; see also Paul Jackson, *One of the Boys: Homosexuality in the Military in World War II* (Montreal: McGill–Queen's University Press, 2004), 8.

32. Margot Canaday, *The Straight State: Sexuality and Citizenship in Twentieth-Century America* (Princeton, NJ: Princeton University Press, 2009), 213.

33. WW2 US Medical Research Centre, "The Army Nurse Corps," accessed January 16, 2017, https://www.med-dept.com/articles/the-army-nurse-corps/.

34. Michaela Hampf, *Release a Man for Combat: The Women's Army Corps during World War II* (Cologne: Böhlau, 2010), 64–97; and Leisa D. Meyer, *Creating GI Jane: Sexuality and Power in the Women's Army Corps during World War II* (New York: Columbia University Press, 1996).

35. Hampf, *Release a Man*, 85. See also the chapter by Karen Hagemann on "Gender, Demobilization, and the Reordering of Societies after the First and Second World Wars" in this handbook.

36. Hampf, *Release a Man*, 90–91.

37. Ibid.

38. D'Ann Campbell, "Almost Integrated? American Servicewomen and Their International Sisters since World War II," in *A Companion to Women's Military History*, ed. Barton C. Hacker and Margaret Vining (Leiden: Brill, 2012), 291–330, 294–95; Bettie J. Morden, *The Women's Army Corps, 1945–1978* (Washington, DC: Center of Military History, 1990); and

Evelyn Monahan, and Rosemary Neidel-Greenlee, *A Few Good Women: America's Military Women from World War I to the Wars in Iraq and Afghanistan* (New York: Alfred A. Knopf, 2010). On the women in the US Army during the Korea War, see Linda Witt et al., *A Defense Weapon Known to be of Value: Servicewomen of the Korean War Era* (Hanover: University Press of New England, 2005); on the Vietnam War, see Kara Dixon Vuic, *Officer, Nurse, Women: The Army Nurse Corps in the Vietnam War* (Baltimore: The Johns Hopkins University, Press, 2010); and Heather Marie Stur, *Beyond Combat: Women and Gender in the Vietnam War Era* (New York: Cambridge University Press, 2011).

39. Robert K. Griffith, *The U.S. Army's Transition to the All-Volunteer Force, 1968–1974* (Washington, DC: Center of Military History, 1997); and Sandhoff et al., "Gender Issues," 111–12.

40. Jane J. Mansbridge, *Why We Lost the ERA* (Chicago: University of Chicago Press, 1986).

41. Lance Janda, *Stronger Than Custom: West Point and the Admission of Women* (Westport, CT: Praeger, 2002); Judith Hicks Stiehm, *Bring Me Men and Women: Mandated Change at the US Air Force Academy* (Berkeley: University of California Press, 1981); and H. Michael Gelfand, *Sea Change at Annapolis: The United States Naval Academy, 1949–2000* (Chapel Hill: University of North Carolina Press, 2006).

42. Philippa Strum, *Women in the Barracks: The VMI Case and Equal Rights* (Lawrence: University Press of Kansas, 2002); and Catherine S. Manegold, *In Glory's Shadow: The Citadel, Shannon Faulkner, and a Changing America* (New York: Alfred A. Knopf, 2000).

43. Stur, *Beyond Combat*, 218.

44. Eileen Patten and Kim Parker, "Women in the U.S. Military: Growing Share, Distinctive Profile," in *Pew Research Center's Social & Demographic Trends* (2012), accessed April 11, 2019, https://www.pewsocialtrends.org/2011/12/22/women-in-the-u-s-military-growing-share-distinctive-profile/.

45. See Manning, *Women*.

46. Enloe, *Does Khaki*, 136–37.

47. Patten and Parker, "Women."

48. NATO, *Summary of the National Report*, 255.

49. Melissa Healy, "Poll Finds Split over Women's Combat Role," *Los Angeles Times*, September 12, 1992.

50. Ibid. For an overview of the combat debate, see Fenner and DeYoung, *Women in Combat*.

51. "The Risk Rule," *New York Times*, August 15, 2009, accessed January 18, 2017, http://www.nytimes.com/2009/08/16/us/16womenbox.html; and Sandhoff and Segal, "Women," 282.

52. Manning, *Women*; and D'Ann Campbell, "Combating the Gender Gulf," *Minerva* 19, no. 3–4 (1992): 13–41.

53. US Government Accountability Office, *Military Personnel: DOD Is Expanding Combat Service Opportunities for Women, but Should Monitor Long-Term Integration Progress, Report 15-589* (Washington, DC: US Government Printing Office, 2015), Introduction, GAO Highlights.

54. "Female Engagement Team USMC," *Regional Command Southwest*, 2011, accessed September 28, 2017, http://regionalcommandsouthwest.wordpress.com/about/female-engagement-team-usmc/; and "Women Soldiers to Deploy as Afghanistan 'Female Engagement Team,'" *Army News Service*, June 7, 2011, accessed September 28, 2017, http://www.army.mil/article/59144/Women.

55. See Whitworth, "The United Nations," and Williams, "Gender, Wars of Globalization" in this handbook.

56. Department of Defense, Office of the Assistant Secretary of Defense, "Defense Department Rescinds Direct Combat Exclusion Rule: Services to Expand Integration of Women into Previously Restricted Occupations and Units, News Release No. 037–13," Washington, DC: Department of Defense, January 24, 2013, accessed September 28, 2017, https://archive. defense.gov/releases/release.aspx?releaseid=1578.

57. Andrew Tilghman, "All Combat Jobs Open to Women in the Military," *Military Times*, December 3, 2015, accessed March 10, 2017, http://www.militarytimes.com/story/military/ pentagon/2015/12/03/carter-telling-military-open-all-combat-jobs-women/76720656/.

58. Department of Defense, "Defense Department Rescinds."

59. Ed O'Keefe and Jon Cohen, "Most Americans Back Women in Combat Roles, Poll Says," *Washington Post*, March 16, 2011, accessed January 18, 2017, http://www.washingtonpost. com/wp-dyn/content/article/2011/03/16/AR2011031603861.html.

60. Sandoff et al., "Gender Issues," 111–16.

61. Beate Fiesler et al., "Gendering Combat: Military Women's Status in Britain, the United States and the Soviet Union during the Second World War," *Women's Studies International Forum*, 47 (Nov–Dec 2014): 115–26, 116; and Lucy Noakes, *Women in the British Army: War and the Gentle Sex, 1907–1948* (London: Routledge, 2006), 131.

62. Gayle Thrift, "This Is Our War, Too," *Alberta History* 59, no. 3 (2011): 2–12, 7.

63. Noakes, *Women*, 138 and 160.

64. Woodward and Winter, *Sexing*, 30–31.

65. Noakes, *Women*, 155.

66. Woodward and Winter, *Sexing*, 31.

67. Christopher Dandeker and Mady Wechsler Segal, "Gender Integration in Armed Forces: Recent Policy Developments in the United Kingdom," *Armed Forces & Society* 23, no. 1 (1996): 29–47, 31–32.

68. Ibid., 32.

69. Ibid., 31–32.

70. Ibid.

71. Tom Rutherford, "Defence Personnel Statistics," *British House of Commons*, September 26, 2014, accessed January 8, 2016; and Dandeker and Segal, "Gender Integration," 31.

72. NATO, *Summary of the National Report*, 249.

73. Dandeker and Segal, "Gender Integration," 32.

74. "Combat Ban for Women Stays," *BBC News*, May 22, 2002, accessed January 18, 2017, http://news.bbc.co.uk/go/em/fr/-/2/hi/uk_news/politics/2002661.stm.

75. See Harries-Jenkins, "Women in Extended Roles," 745–69.

76. Ibid.

77. UK Government, "Women in Ground Close Combat (GCC) Review Paper," December 1, 2014, Annex C, page C-8, accessed September 28, 2017, http://www.gov.uk/government/ uploads/system/uploads/attachment_data/file/389575/20141218_WGCC_Findings_ Paper_Final.pdf.

78. Sandra Carson Stanley and Mady Wechsler Segal, "Military Women in NATO: An Update," *Armed Forces & Society* 14, no. 4 (1988): 559–85; and Donna Winslow and Jason Dunn, "Women in the Canadian Forces: Between Legal and Social Integration," *Current Sociology*, 50, no. 5 (2002): 641–67.

79. "Isabelle Gauthier, Joseph G. Houlden, Marie-Claude Gauthier, Georgina Ann Brown vs Canadian Armed Forces," Ottawa: Canadian Human Rights Tribunal Decision 3/89, February 20, 1989, cited in Nathaniel Frank et al., eds., *Gays in Foreign Militaries 2010: A Global Primer* (Santa Barbara, CA: Palm Center, 2010), 55.

80. Ibid., 59.

81. National Defence and Canadian Armed Forces, "Women"; and Sandhoff et al., "Gender Issues," 121–22; NATO Committee on Women in NATO Forces, 25th anniversary, "Year in Review 2001: Special Edition," accessed September 28, 2017, https://www.nato.int/ims/2001/win/win-2001.pdf.

82. David R. Segal et al., "Gender and Sexual Orientation Diversity in Modern Military Forces: Cross-National Patterns," in *Beyond Zero Tolerance: Discrimination in Military Culture*, ed. Mary Feinsod Katzenstein and Judith Reppy (Lanham, MD: Rowman & Littlefield, 1999), 225–50.

83. Alan Charles Okros et al., *Between 9/11 and Kandahar: Attitudes of Canadian Forces Officers in Transition* (Kingston, Ont.: Defense Management Studies Program, School of Policy Studies, Queen's University, 2008), quoted in Frank et al., *Gays*, 62.

84. Ibid.

85. NATO, *Summary of the National Report*, 18, 40, 85-87, 252 and 257.

86. Ibid.

87. Segal et al., "Gender and Sexual," 233.

88. Canaday, *The Straight State*, 87.

89. Jackson, *One of the Boys*, 182–220; and Emma Vickers, "'The Good Fellows': Negotiation, Remembrance, and Recollection—Homosexuality in the British Armed Forces, 1939–1945," in *Brutality and Desire: War and Sexuality in Europe's Twentieth Century*, ed. Dagmar Herzog (Basingstoke: Palgrave, 2009), 109–34.

90. Bérubé, *Coming Out*, 3.

91. Ibid., 8–128; Jackson, *One of the Boys*, 182–220. See also the chapter by Regina Mühlhäuser, "Sexuality, Sexual Violence, and the Military in the Age of the World Wars" in this handbook.

92. Bérubé, *Coming Out*, 261.

93. US Naval Institute, "Key Dates in US Policy on Gay Men and Women in Military Service," accessed January 8, 2017, http://www.usni.org/news-and-features/dont-ask-dont-tell/timeline.

94. Bérubé, *Coming Out*, 255–79.

95. Jennifer Terry, *An American Obsession: Science, Medicine, and Homosexuality in Modern Society* (Chicago: University of Chicago Press, 1999), 347.

96. Karin De Angelis et al., "Sexuality in the Military," in *International Handbook on the Demography of Sexuality*, ed. Amanda K. Baumle (Dordrecht: Springer, 2013), 363–68.

97. "Policy Concerning Homosexuals in the Armed Forces," 10 U.S.C. (United States Code) §654 (1993), 340–42; see also US Government Accountability Office, *Homosexuals*; and National Defense Research Institute, *Sexual Orientation and U.S. Military Personnel Policy: An Update of RAND's 1993 Study* (Santa Monica, CA: RAND, 2010).

98. Sandhoff and Segal, "Women," 287.

99. Ibid.

100. Canaday, *The Straight State*, 174–213.

101. Gary J. Gates and Frank Newport, "LGBT Percentage Highest in DC, Lowest in North Dakota," *Gallup Polls*, February 15, 2013, accessed September 28, 2017, http://www.gallup.com/poll/160517/lgbt-percentage-highest-lowest-north-dakota.aspx.

102. Nathaniel Frank, "The President's Pleasant Surprise: How LGBT Advocates Ended Don't Ask, Don't Tell," *Journal of Homosexuality* 60, no. 2–3 (2013): 159–219.

103. Josh Israel, "The Woman Who Has Never Stopped Fighting to Keep LGBT Americans out of the Military," *ThinkProgress*, May 23, 2014, accessed April 9, 2020,

https://thinkprogress.org/the-woman-who-has-never-stopped-fighting-to-keep-lgbt-americans-out-of-the-military-8b291cb52a9d/.

104. "Survey: DADT Repeal Has Less Impact Than Expected," *Military Times*, March 12, 2012, accessed September 28, 2017, http://www.militarytimes.com/article/2012-312/NEWS/20312-318/Survey-DADT-releap-has-less-impact-than-expected. See also Frank et al., *Gays*; National Defense Research Institute, *Sexual Orientation*; and Suzanne B. Goldberg, "Open Service and Our Allies: A Report on the Inclusion of Openly Gay and Lesbian Service Members in US Allies' Armed Forces," *William & Mary Journal of Women and the Law* 17, no. 3 (2011): 547–90. The twenty-five countries were Australia, Austria, Belgium, Canada, Czech Republic, Denmark, Estonia, Finland, France, Germany, Ireland, Israel, Italy, Lithuania, Luxembourg, the Netherlands, New Zealand, Norway, Slovenia, South Africa, Spain, Sweden, Switzerland, the United Kingdom, and Uruguay, see Frank et al., *Gays*, 137–38.

105. Aaron Belkin and Jason McNichol, "Effects of the 1992 Lifting of Restrictions on Gay and Lesbian Service in the Canadian Forces: Appraising the Evidence" (Palm Center White Paper, April 1, 2000), accessed October 4, 2017, https://www.palmcenter.org/wp-content/uploads/2017/12/Canada5.pdf); and Frank et al., *Gays*, 14–16, 51–70.

106. Rosemary E. Park, "Opening the Canadian Forces to Gays and Lesbians: An Inevitable Decision but Improbable Reconfiguration," in *Gays and Lesbians in the Military: Issues, Concerns, and Contrasts*, ed. Scott J. Wilbur and Sandra Carson Stanley (New York: de Gruyter, 1994), 165–79, 169.

107. Frank et al., *Gays*, 14–16. The National Defense Research Institute's RAND study from 2010 found similar results.

108. Anne Swardson, "Canada: No Problem with Gays in Ranks," *Washington Post*, July 6, 1993, accessed January 18, 2017, https://www.washingtonpost.com/archive/politics/1993/07/06/canada-no-problem-with-gays-in-ranks/37d06a5e-3194-42a9-93f1-86b928b308bb/?utm_term=.9aed68b567bb.

109. Frank et al., *Gays*, 69.

110. Ibid., 52.

111. Nathanial Frank, *Unfriendly Fire: How the Gay Ban Undermines the Military and Weakens America* (New York: St. Martin's, 2009), 143.

112. Cited in Frank et al., *Gays*, 9.

113. Edmund Hall, "Gay Ban Is Based on Bias Alone," *The Independent*, March 5, 1996, accessed January 18, 2017, http://www.independent.co.uk/voices/gay-ban-is-based-on-bias-alone-1340421.html.

114. Frank et al., *Gays*, 11.

115. Sarah Lyall, "European Court Tells British to Let Gay Soldiers Serve," *New York Times*, September 28, 1999, accessed July 14, 2017, http://www.nytimes.com/1999/09/28/world/european-court-tells-british-to-let-gay-soldiers-serve.html.

116. Frank et al., *Gays*, 8, 14, 35.

117. Michael Codner, Royal United Services Institute, personal communication, September 26, 2000, quoted in Frank et al., *Gays*, 14.

118. "Gay and Lesbian Rights," Gallup Polls 1977–2008, accessed September 28, 2017, http://www.gallup.com/poll/1651/gay-lesbian-rights.aspx.

119. Ibid.

120. See Jennifer Koons, "Sexual Assault in the Military: Can the Pentagon Stem the rise in incidents? " *CQ Researcher*, August 9, 2013, 693–716, https://library.cqpress.com/cqresearcher/document.php?id=cqresrre2013080900.

121. See Williams, "Gender, Wars of Globalization" in this handbook.

SELECT BIBLIOGRAPHY

Bérubé, Allan. *Coming Out under Fire: The History of Gay Men and Women in World War II.* New York: Penguin Books, 1990.

Bristol, Douglas Walter, and Heather Marie Stur, eds. *Integrating the US Military: Race, Gender, and Sexual Orientation since World War II.* Baltimore: Johns Hopkins University Press, 2017.

Campbell, D'Ann. "Almost Integrated? American Servicewomen and Their International Sisters since World War II." In *A Companion to Women's Military History*, edited by Barton C. Hacker and Margaret Vining, 291–330. Leiden: Brill, 2012.

Canaday, Margot. *The Straight State: Sexuality and Citizenship in Twentieth-Century America.* Princeton, NJ: Princeton University Press, 2009.

Carreiras, Helena. *Gender and the Military: Women in the Armed Forces of Western Democracies.* London: Routledge, 2006.

Carreiras, Helena, and Gerhard Kümmel, eds. *Women in the Military and in Armed Conflict.* Wiesbaden: Verlag für Sozialwissenschaften, 2008.

Enloe, Cynthia. *Does Khaki Become You? The Militarisation of Women's Lives.* London: Pluto Press, 1983.

Eulriet, Irène. *Women and the Military in Europe: Comparing Public Cultures.* Basingstoke: Palgrave Macmillan, 2009.

Goldstein, Joshua S. *War and Gender: How Gender Shapes the War System and Vice Versa.* Cambridge: Cambridge University Press, 2001.

Hall, Edmund. *We Can't Even March Straight: Homosexuality in the British Armed Forces.* London: Vintage, 1995.

Jackson, Paul. *One of the Boys: Homosexuality in the Military in World War II.* Montreal: McGill–Queen's University Press, 2004.

MacKenzie, Megan. *Beyond the Band of Brothers: The US Military and the Myth That Women Can't Fight.* Cambridge: Cambridge University Press, 2015.

Meyer, Leisa D. *Creating GI Jane: Sexuality and Power in the Women's Army Corps during World War II.* New York: Columbia University Press, 1996.

Morden, Bettie J. *The Women's Army Corps, 1945–1978.* Washington, DC: Center of Military History, 1990.

Noakes, Lucy. *Women in the British Army: War and the Gentle Sex, 1907–1948.* London: Routledge, 2006.

Rimmerman, Craig A., ed. *Gay Rights, Military Wrongs: Political Perspectives on Lesbians and Gays in the Military.* New York: Garland, 1996.

Sandhoff, Michelle, and Mady Wechsler Segal. "Women in the US Military: The Evolution of Gender Norms and Military Requirements." In *The Modern American Military*, edited by David Kennedy, 273–94. Oxford: Oxford University Press, 2013.

Shilts, Randy. *Conduct Unbecoming: Gays and Lesbians in the US Military*. New York: Fawcett Columbine, 1994.

Stur, Heather Marie. *Beyond Combat: Women and Gender in the Vietnam War Era*. New York: Cambridge University Press, 2011.

Wilbur, Scott J., and Sandra Carson Stanley, eds. *Gays and Lesbians in the Military: Issues, Concerns, and Contrasts*. New York: de Gruyter, 1994.

Winslow, Donna, and Jason Dunn. "Women in the Canadian Forces: Between Legal and Social Integration." *Current Sociology* 50, no. 5 (2002): 641–67.

Woodward, Rachel, and Trish Winter. *Sexing the Soldier: The Politics of Gender and the Contemporary British Army*. London: Routledge, 2007.

CHAPTER 29

CONCEPTUALIZING SEXUAL VIOLENCE IN POST–COLD WAR GLOBAL CONFLICTS

DUBRAVKA ZARKOV

SEXUAL violence in warfare is hardly a new historical phenomenon, even though we know much more about sexual violence in twentieth-century conflicts than in earlier ones. Conceptualizations and generalizations are, as Elizabeth Heineman has empha-sized, "based largely on a few recent conflicts, each with origins and aims that may not apply to other conflicts." Equally troubling, for her, is that "the reliance on recent cases provides few tools for the understanding of long-term consequences of such violations as war-ravaged societies struggle to achieve postconflict stability."[1] The conceptualiza-tions of and generalizations about sexual violence based on contemporary conflicts can, however, help to explain the dynamics of sexual violence in earlier wars. Equally important, they can help us understand the geopolitical context within which sexual violence and its dynamics are addressed.

Gender and conflict studies offer a critical perspective on the conceptual and analyti-cal tools of dominant theories on sexual violence and war that have gained prominence since the 1990s, as well as on their geopolitical implication.[2] Inspired by the research of feminist and postcolonial scholars, their analysis revealed, on the one hand, how schol-ars are not neutral, objective observers, but instead work from assumptions embedded in their societies and disciplines to choose research subjects and produce knowledge that ultimately reinforces their view of the world. On the other hand, it nuanced our understanding of sexual violence as gendered violence that can be perpetrated by, as well as against, both women and men and includes (among other things) rape, sexual mutilation, sexualized torture, sexual humiliation (such as forced nudity), sexual slavery, forced marriage, forced prostitution, and forced pregnancies or abortions.[3]

Mainstream scholarship on the military and war has traditionally described sexual violence against women as an inevitable, but opportunistic, practice common to every war. This perception was based on a widespread assumption about male sexuality—that soldiers who have been without women and sex for a long time will take the first opportunity to make up for the "deprivation." It took several decades of feminist research, beginning in the 1970s, to change the thinking about sexual violence against women in general and sexual violence in armed conflicts in particular. Such scholarship often conceptualizes sexual violence against women as an inherent part of war, but emphasizes its varying patterns across conflicts, armed groups, and small units of soldiers. In some conflicts, however, sexual violence is less evident or perhaps was altogether absent. Furthermore, both feminist and mainstream academics and politicians focused their attention on a small range of conflicts in which sexual violence became overexposed, while it remained invisible in others.

Only since the 1990s have feminist scholars investigated this issue of visibility. The rapes of women during the wars through which Yugoslavia disintegrated (1991–2001) and the sexual violence against men at the Abu Ghraib prison during the Iraq War (2003–11) have stimulated major shifts in the feminist theorizing of sexual violence against women and men in war. In addition, sexual violence against women during the wars in the former Yugoslavia, the Rwandan genocide (1994), and the wars in the Democratic Republic of the Congo (DRC) (1998–ongoing), Sudan/Darfur (2003–ongoing), and South Sudan (2011–ongoing) has been instrumental not only for the shifts in mainstream policy formulations and interventions in conflicts, but also for feminist and mainstream political and cultural representations of these and other post–Cold War conflicts.

In the following, three themes will be explored: the theoretical and geopolitical implications of the different conceptualizations of sexual violence in war and their epistemological and ontological effects; the theoretical challenges in conceptualizing sexual violence against men; and the issue of visibility and invisibility of specific cases of war sexual violence against women and men and their conceptualization in the Western mainstream and feminist scholarship.

THEORIES OF SEXUAL VIOLENCE IN WAR

The revelations about systematic, mass rapes of women in the wars in the former Yugoslavia made sexual violence in war a major issue in the mainstream Western politics of conflict and war and also in feminist scholarship since the 1990s. It is impossible to overstate how significant in particular the war rapes of women in Bosnia in 1993 have been for the global development of theoretical, legal, policy, and political tools that are still dominant in academia, international humanitarian and criminal law, national and supranational policies, and practices of unilateral and multilateral military interventions throughout the world. Though it would be unwise to assume that the Yugoslav wars were the cause of fundamental shifts in all those domains, it is safe to say that these conflicts stood at the beginning of the development of new theoretical and political perspectives and practices. Subsequent violent conflicts—especially the Rwandan genocide and the wars in the DRC and Sudan—allowed for the strengthening of theoretical and political positions established and developed around the Yugoslav Wars.

Theoretically, concepts such as *genocidal rape* and *rape as a weapon of war* or *war strategy* became a common bridge between academia and the worlds of politics, policy, and media. These concepts also brought about changes in legal practice and theory. War rapes became a separate legal category, recognized within categories such as war crimes, crimes against humanity, and crimes of genocide. Changes in international humanitarian and criminal law led to the creation of special war crimes tribunals starting with the United Nations (UN) International Criminal Tribunal for the Former Yugoslavia, established in 1993,[4] and by the UN International Criminal Tribunal for Rwanda, established in 1994.[5] In 1998, the permanent International Criminal Court was established,[6] followed by a number of special courts like the Special Court for Sierra Leone, established in 2002.[7] As a result, a special global legal system with its own, often-controversial practices developed.

In terms of international and supranational policy, the UN Security Council has been crucial in raising the profile of war rapes against women through a series of resolutions, starting in 2000 with UN Security Council Resolution 1325 on women, peace, and security.[8] This resolution reaffirmed the important role women play in the prevention and resolution of conflicts, peace negotiations, peacebuilding, peacekeeping, humanitarian response, and postconflict reconstruction. It also stressed the importance of their equal participation and full involvement in all efforts for the maintenance and promotion of peace and security. In 2008, UN Security Council Resolution 1820 linked war rapes of women to global security. It mandated the elimination of "all forms of violence against women and girls" by ending impunity for such acts and by ensuring "the protection of civilians, in particular women and girls, during and after armed conflicts."[9] Unilateral and multilateral military interventions—from the Gulf War in 1990/91 to the US interventions in Afghanistan in 2001 and against the Islamic State of Iraq and the Levant (ISIL) in Iraq and Syria since 2014—have been justified, too, by the rhetoric that utilized the threat of rape to "local women" by various groupings of (more or less) "local men."

The concept of genocidal rape was developed in reference to the war rapes in Bosnia, although "rape as a crime of genocide" was used as a legal category first by the International Criminal Tribunal for Rwanda in 1995. One year before, Catherine MacKinnon and Beverly Allen were among the first to identify war rapes in Bosnia as a "genocidal act" because they were intended to destroy a people—that is, part of a military policy seeking to wipe out an entire ethnicity or nationality.[10] A number of other authors from diverse disciplinary backgrounds have contributed to the theoretical debate about rape as genocide and have also taken up the concept to characterize rapes in various violent conflicts. Comparing rapes in Bangladesh's war for independence from Pakistan (1971), the former Yugoslavia, and Rwanda, Lisa Sharlach claimed that they are all a component of a genocidal campaign aimed at destroying the survivors, their families, and communities.[11] Matthias Bjørnlund contended that sexual violence perpetrated during the Armenian genocide (1915–17) was genocidal because it was a key element of violent strategies aimed at destroying the Armenian population.[12] Analyzing sexual violence in the civil war in Guatemala (1960–96), Roselyn Costantino asserted that war rape, femicide, and genocide are difficult to separate because they all intend "genocidal destruction" of a group.[13] Besides the focus on the intent to destroy a group, the theoretical construction of rape as potentially genocidal is most often justified by examination of its destructive effects on individuals and communities and their values, norms, practices, and identities. Charli Carpenter and other scholars addressed some of those effects as the deliberate and intended goals and functions of genocidal rape.[14]

Yet others, such as Sherrie Russell-Brown, criticized this approach. She stressed that the fact that rape occurs during genocide does not make it automatically genocidal, and she noted that the difficulties experienced by the International Criminal Tribunals for the Former Yugoslavia and for Rwanda show how proving the intent is both crucial and challenging.[15] Analyzing the Rwandan tribunal, Doris E. Buss went further in criticizing the concept of genocidal rape. She contended that although identifying rape as an instrument of genocide in Rwanda has raised awareness of gendered violence, it also has had the problematic effect of classifying who can and cannot be a victim.[16] In Rwanda, for instance, violence was officially (and reductively) defined as the genocide of Tutsis by Hutus, so while there has been an accounting of the rapes of Tutsi women by Hutu men, the other victims and perpetrators of sexual violence have been ignored. Buss emphasized that the notion of rape as an instrument of genocide thus carries "certain ontological and epistemological effects" that erase complexities of violence and take rape as an inevitable element of genocide.[17]

In an earlier study, Buss contended that the context of ethnically defined war and genocide—as was the case with the former Yugoslavia and Rwanda—has had a problematic effect on the International Criminal Tribunals for the Former Yugoslavia and for Rwanda.[18] Both tribunals depended on ethnic classification of the conflicts. Consequently, she insisted, "the focus on gender in the context of an over-determined assessment of ethnic conflict becomes a means of occluding, rather than opening up the complex dimensions of violence against women."[19] Chiseche Salome Mibenge came to the same conclusion in analyzing how the legal practice of war crimes tribunals for Rwanda and Sierra Leone privileges certain narratives of war rape while ignoring others.[20] Similarly, Elissa Helms pointed out how war rapes and, later, the July 1995 Srebrenica massacre in Bosnia and Herzegovina have become elements of "affirmative essentialism" and claims to feminized "ethno-national victimhood" among Bosnian women's groups.[21]

The concept of genocidal rape has often been used interchangeably with the concepts of rape as a weapon of war and rape as a war strategy. All three concepts assume a specific mode of perpetrating war rape: as widespread, systematic, orchestrated, and deliberate. The terms furthermore assume specific aims, purposes, and functions of war rape: the destruction of individuals, families, and communities; the eradication of the moral and social fabric of society; and the acquisition of power and control over economic and political resources and over the population. Many authors assume that the level of intentionality is the same for genocidal rape and rape as a weapon of war, with the difference that genocidal rape aims at the destruction of the entire population, while rape as a weapon of war may also be directed to control and increase the population, rather than be a tool of the population's complete destruction. The relationship between rape and genocide seems to be a more prominent topic among feminist legal scholars, because war rape is defined within specific legal categories: as a war crime, crime against humanity, and crime of genocide.[22]

Conceptualizations of rape as a weapon of war and as a war strategy have been common in academic, popular, and political discourses since the 1990s. Claudia Card was among the first authors to use the "weapon of war" terminology, and she stressed that the fundamental functions of rape are to maintain dominance over women and to domesticate them.[23] More specifically, the purpose of "martial rape," as she calls war rape, is to undermine "national, political, and cultural solidarity, changing the next generation's identity, confusing the loyalties of all victimized survivors."[24]

In discussing the emergence of the weapon-of-war discourses, Inger Skjelsbæk pointed to the different ways in which the strategic effects of using rape as a war weapon are analyzed. Some feminists focused on its effects in reaffirming militarized masculinities and thus kept the focus on the perpetrators. Some concentrated on the victims and destruction of their social and cultural worlds. Yet others reflected on the "symbolic interaction between the perpetrator and the victims."[25] Several authors stressed the role of strategic planning in making rape a weapon that serves both military and political ends. Colleen Duggan and Julie Guillerot engaged in such discussions when analyzing rapes in Guatemala and Peru,[26] while Nancy Farwell discussed specific political objectives achieved by the strategic use of rape as a war weapon.[27] Others, such as Bülent Diken and Carsten Bagge Laustsen, argued that as the clearest example of an asymmetric strategy, war rape is, literally, a weapon of war because it transforms women into objects and destroys the social structure of the attacked group.[28] Debra Bergoffen also stressed a patriarchal understanding of women as carriers of a community's honor in linking "genocidal rape strategy" and "conditions that make genocidal rape an effective war time weapon."[29] Discussing war rapes in Peru, Jelke Boesten emphasized that rape can be an effective strategy and a weapon of war partly because it creates a perpetual stigma for the victim.[30] Kathryn Farr noted a difference between "strategic" and "opportunistic" rapes, the former being "systematic, ordered, overseen, or at least encouraged by military authorities" and the latter being the result of a "universal understanding of women as male property."[31]

IMPLICATIONS OF DOMINANT CONCEPTUALIZATIONS OF RAPE

An increasing number of authors have been cautious if not openly critical of these analyses of war rape. They expressed the concern that these feminist conceptualizations simply assumed rather than critically analyzed the existence of patriarchal, unequal gendered relations between women and men, of gendered aspects of collective (especially ethnic) identities, and of specific gendered cultural practices. One of them is Buss. In her 2014 study *Sexual Violence in Conflict and Post-Conflict Societies: International Agendas and African Contexts*, she points out that understanding rape as a weapon of war "has elevated a particular kind of rape," rape victim, and perpetrator "to an almost hyper-visible level" while obscuring others.[32] Anette Bringedal Houge similarly criticized that the representation of rape in wars as the worst of war crimes creates a hierarchy of cruelty, which might have unforeseen and negative consequences.[33]

Other scholars supported this critique and added that the use of essentialist ethnic categories in feminist analysis of the Yugoslav and Rwandan wars has resulted in a failure to interrogate the ways by which ethnicity became the privileged political identity in the first place.[34] Furthermore, they stress that the concept of rape as a weapon of war has the effect of shifting attention away from rapes that are not perpetrated by militaries and also assumes the use of rape as a conscious, deliberate war strategy, which is not always the case.[35] And they address, like Elisabeth Wood, the lack of clarity and specificity in the concepts. Wood indicates that "strategic" sometimes means simply "massive," while the distinction between strategic and "opportunistic"—assumed to be ordered or unordered by the military command or perpetrated for political or private reasons—is often unsustainable in highly complex circumstances of violent conflicts.[36] She thus suggested that seeing rape as a "practice," rather than a "weapon" or "strategy," offers a more useful theoretical and methodological entry into the examination of social contexts, dynamics, and patterns of rape in war.

Why is the concept of rape as a weapon of war, despite this strong criticism, still so prominent? One possible answer was given by Maria Eriksson Baaz and Maria Stern. They have shown that this concept became so influential because of its usefulness to policymakers: it presents a clear storyline that states a simple, straightforward relationship between a purpose of rape and its effects; it considers rapes instrumental to specific political or military goals; and, finally, it appears to offer a possibility of a simple, straightforward solution by which rape as an "abhorrent condition" can be treated.[37] Complexities, ambiguities, and specificities disappear, and a one-size-fits-all global policy solution can be created for a problem that is seen as clear, understandable, and, above all, universal. This clarity, they warned, "emerges in part through the concealment of a host of assumptions, logics and exclusions."[38]

Some of these policy assumptions are shaped by racism and the idea of Western superiority, which result in constructions such as the African or Balkan men as "diabolic rapists" of helpless "local" women.[39] The rapes of women in the war in the Democratic Republic of Congo have especially been singled out in this context. With its capital Kinshasa labeled the "world rape capital," inter- and supranational agencies have seen the DRC as a target of humanitarian intervention. But as a few critical reports on those interventions point out, decision makers have not adequately examined such issues as the definitions of rape or how to assess the prevalence of rape, not to mention how the intersection of gender and race influences views on these issues.

According to Serena Cruz and others who analyzed reports about rape cases in the DRC and the specific responses to curb them, the "rape as a weapon of war" narrative, with its simplistic understanding of gender, an absence of real insights into people's lived realities, and a quantification of "successes," has informed the reports of rape and the intervention policy.[40] Donors follow and reassert the value of this dominant narrative, while local organizations, understanding the logic and the limits of donor politics, follow the donor formulations of local realities. This creates a "perverse incentive structure" within which war-rape narratives become a source of income, competition, and prestige for local, national, and international intervening actors.[41]

Such conceptual spillover from feminist analysis into global-to-local policies and intervention mechanisms seems to have become ever more common since the end of the twentieth century, when feminist rhetoric around violence against women, gender-based violence, and sexual violence against women in war started to be used as justifications for military interventions around the globe. Following the logic of the visibility of those types of violence, one could easily assume that war rape exists everywhere except in the West. The absence of violent conflicts in North America and Western Europe since 1945 has obscured the West's role in violent conflicts in other regions. The facts that US, NATO, and European Union militaries have intervened in different countries around the globe, by occupying or bombing them, and that those actions have been termed *humanitarian interventions*, has created a political narrative of war within which the West is a humanitarian actor fighting on behalf of the victims, especially if those victims are "local women" raped by "local men." In other words, war rapes have become a factor of differentiation between African and Balkan wars, on the one hand, and wars fought by the Western or supranational forces on the other. The former presumably are fought by hordes of brutal men armed with homemade guns, machetes, and even their own bodies as weapons, who rape and kill indiscriminately. The latter are characterized by "precision technology" utilized in expensive high-tech, high-altitude equipment and by putatively highly moral military men whose boots seldom hit the ground and, when they do, it is for saving rather than raping local women.[42]

This geopolitical narrative is disrupted every now and then by the sudden and short-lived visibility of sexual violence perpetrated by the Western military and humanitarian actors in the media, be it against their own members or against people whom they purport to protect. One of the early cases that captured public attention in the West was the rape and torture of Somali civilians by Canadian peacekeepers in 1992.[43] Ten years later, UN forces in Bosnia were accused of involvement in sexual exploitation of local women through trafficking and prostitution rings.[44] British soldiers have been accused of perpetrating torture and sexual violence against Iraqi civilians and prisoners between 2003 and 2008, during and after the Iraq War.[45] Sexual violence against and sexual exploitation of women and children by the UN peacekeeping militaries in the DRC and other African countries has been subject to much criticism throughout the new millennium, leading the UN to issue a "zero-tolerance policy" on sexual violence.[46]

However, those cases of sexual violence by Western militaries and UN peacekeeping forces have been much more often addressed by the media and by women's and other nongovernmental organizations than in feminist scholarship. The same can be said for a temporary upsurge of media and public interest in sexual violence within the US military, stirred in 2013 when the US Senate Committee on Armed Services held hearings on sexual violence against women and men within the US military.[47] Except for those few cases, sexual violence perpetrated by Western militaries has been a rather invisible affair. Thus, the surprise was significant when in 2004 photos of US prison guards engaged in sexual assault of Iraqi detainees in the Abu Ghraib prison in Iraq surfaced. This revelation not only exposed the reality of Western militaries' involvement in sexual violence around the world, but also shook some of the long-established Western feminist truisms: that only women are the victims of sexual violence in war and that only men are the perpetrators. The issue of male victims and female perpetrators of sexual violence was not entirely new in 2004. Some work had already appeared in relation to sexual violence against men in the detention centers during the wars in Bosnia and Croatia and in Rwanda. But the Abu Ghraib case brought a broader visibility and thus led to a more thorough theoretical and political examination of both sexual violence against men and basic feminist assumptions about gender, sexuality, and violence in war.

CONCEPTUALIZING SEXUAL VIOLENCE AGAINST MEN

The war in Bosnia and the Rwandan genocide brought attention to gender-specific and sexual violence against men for the first time. Adam Jones coined the term "gendercide" to analyze violence against men in the Rwandan genocide and criticized feminists for ignoring it.[48] He claimed that men are the predominant victims of wars as soldiers and that in the Rwandan genocide, civilian men and boys were specifically targeted from the start. Only in the later stage of the genocide, according to him, did women become targets too. Jones was also among the first to contend that gender-specific crimes were perpetrated against men in the wars in the former Yugoslavia.[49] The notoriety of the war rapes of women in Bosnia has rendered sexual violence against men invisible, but it was nevertheless widespread, especially in detention camps.

Others addressed causes of sexual violence against men in the Yugoslav Wars, pointing out specifically the intersections of assumptions about male power and notions and practices of masculinity with heteronormativity and ethnicity.[50] They indicated that the same intersections work in both the acts of violence themselves and their media representations. The dynamics of "Self and Other" of the nation or ethnicity, which created identity politics and politics of belonging central to nationalism and war in the former Yugoslavia, have played a crucial role in making some male victims and perpetrators invisible and others overexposed. For example, within the Croatian nationalist narrative, "Orthodox Serbs" and "Muslim Bosnians" are seen as not belonging to the Croatian state. Thus, in Croatian media, the only visible male victim of sexual violence was a

Muslim man, and the only visible perpetrator was a Serb man. Croat men—defined in Croatia as the Self of the Croatian nation—were absent from the narrative of male rape both as victims and as perpetrators. Making the sexually violated male Self invisible functioned as a symbolic protection of the nation represented by the powerful, virile, heteronormative, intact male body of a brave and honorable Croatian soldier. The violated body, as well as the body of the violator, were both defined as belonging to the Other and were thus deliberately made visible. This strategy was a way of denying "proper" masculinity and heterosexuality to the "ethnic enemy."

The same patterns of exposure and invisibility seemed to have worked in the case of media representations of the physical and sexual abuse, torture, rape, and murder of Iraqi prisoners by US soldiers at the Abu Ghraib prison in 2003–4. Located in the Iraqi town of Abu Ghraib, this prison was already notorious under the government of Saddam Hussein, president of Iraq from 1979 to 2003. Between 2003 and 2006, both the US-led coalition occupying Iraq and the Iraqi government used the site to detain prisoners. When images of the prisoners' violated bodies emerged, it was especially shocking in the United States, because its news media had not shown male bodies violated to such an extent since the naked corpses of US servicemen were dragged through the streets of Mogadishu, Somalia, in 1993.[51]

Abu Ghraib played a key role in the development of the research on sexual violence against men in war. This is not to say that sexual violence against men in wars was not studied before.[52] But the revelations about Abu Ghraib triggered an explosion of scholarly interest from a variety of disciplines, much as the conflict in Bosnia had done for the attention to female rape.[53] The best of this analytical work looks at the intersection of masculinity, sexuality, and race, linking those subjects with Western colonialism (especially the United States) and the West's contemporary struggles to assert and preserve its global dominance. For example, scholars pointed out similarities of US domestic and foreign politics when it comes to the legacies of slavery, visible not only in everyday racism and high incarceration rates of Black men, but also in racist violence in American military prisons.[54] Such analysis also reveals the racism in the violence against Iraqi and Somali civilians and prisoners by the British and Canadian militaries.

The studies on Abu Ghraib inspired interdisciplinary research on sexual violence against men in several other regions of the globe.[55] Uganda and the DRC attracted the most attention, and the presence of male-on-male sexual violence in past and present conflicts across the world has become evident.[56] The work of Sandesh Sivakumaran, for instance, combines feminist theoretical insights with legal issues in addressing causes, dynamics, and meanings of sexual violence against men in different conflicts.[57] Like feminists who earlier critiqued scholarly and political approaches to sexual violence against women, Sivakumaran expresses concerns about sexual violence against men as both a field of research and political intervention. He notes a lack of understanding of the problem—indeed, that there is often not even awareness of a problem—and takes issue with how facts are established and data on the prevalence of sexual violence against men in war are gathered. In addition, he critically examines the current policy redefinitions within the large supranational organizations, such as the UN, that focus on only women, girls, and civilians. He thus reflects on the limits of international justice systems and the differences between legal practices of the International Criminal Tribunals for the Former Yugoslavia and for Rwanda, as well as the Special Court for Sierra Leone.[58] Those concerns have become much more prominent in the new millennium, opening up a possibility for critical examination of the field, its epistemological and ontological underpinnings, and their geopolitical implications for the globalized world of the early twenty-first century.

CONCLUSION

The representations of sexual violence in wars in current scholarship and political discourses alike have played an essential role in producing symbolic geographies of the countries, cultures, and peoples of the early twenty-first century. The overexposure of the non-Western (Balkan and African) Other, both as a perpetrator and as a victim, and the invisibility of the Western self as either of those in many ways dehumanizes the non-Western subject.[59] Westerners appear as saviors that intervene in other people's wars, making local men and women in the war zone the objects of peace and justice.[60] The non-Western locals are thereby stripped of the human capacities that are attributed to modern Western people. The violence becomes evidence of their inability to reason. They furthermore lose their capacity for moral judgment in Western eyes, hence the establishment of international tribunals to deliver the justice they supposedly cannot conceive of or render themselves. Finally, they are robbed of the capacity for self-government, which justifies externally imposed systems of governance. Such constructions have the effect of denying non-Westerners the capability of independently having or producing knowledge. They continuously need to learn from the West the meanings and practices of nonviolence and peace, justice, good governance, and so forth.

Gender is crucial in those constructions by which Western and non-Western masculinities and femininities are represented as oppositions. But gender—and with it specific masculinities and femininities—work in intersection with other categories of difference and inequality; they appear through racial and ethnic lenses, shaped by colonialism and racism, invoking and reusing old colonial images of (ever less "noble" and ever more dangerous) savages. Hence, these gendered racist and ethnicized views feed the prejudices that locals lack any capacity to change and adopt "cultures of peace" and "civilizing processes" that Westerners bring with them.[61]

Analyzing contemporary feminist scholarship on war rapes and its implication in producing such divided worlds, Kirsten Campbell offers some crucial critical insights in a 2016 position paper for the Sexual Violence in Armed Conflict International Research Group.[62] She specifically focuses on epistemological issues, asking what are the objects and the subjects of the field of sexual violence in war. In reflecting on the difficulties in defining the object of the investigation, she points out the variety of definitions currently in use. Designations such as "wartime rapes," "sexualized war violence," "sexual violence in armed conflict," and "conflict-related sexual violence" carry consequences for the scope of research. More important, they are also linked to the assumptions that underpin definitions of victims, perpetrators, and conflicts. Campbell dissects three narratives that currently dominate feminist work on sexual violence in war: one that expresses a need to make visible and account for invisible victims; another that focuses on fact finding and documenting the prevalence of sexual violence; and the final narrative that addresses fundamental assumptions of the field and the use of gender and feminism as an analytical framework. Rather than dismissing these narratives, she contends that—in their dominant forms—each of them has highly problematic aspects that feed off each other and ultimately undermine the feminist politics of prevention and redressing of sexual violence in war and peace alike. Analyzing the focus on "invisible victims," Campbell notes that scholarly attention to specific victims is related to "particular social ontologies."[63] She asserts that neither victims nor perpetrators preexist violence, but they are instead constituted as such in the very act of the violence. Simply "adding 'female perpetrators' or 'male victims' to our analysis does little to illuminate our understanding" of conflicts and violence, the people involved in them, the social histories of relevant power relations, or the very specific sociopolitical contexts within which they interact.[64]

Regarding the focus on facts and figures, Campbell is highly critical of reliance on mathematical models, large data sets, and the "positivist quantitative accounts of statistically significant correlations"[65] that currently dominate the field. The sexual violence data sets[66] have been criticized for major flaws: from fragmentation, unreliability, and incompleteness of data that are often collected in the midst of violence, to skewed samples and problematic sources of data (such as media), to universalist assumptions and generalizations that erase any specificity of individual conflicts.[67] Monocausal explanations that underpin such scholarship, Campbell maintains, ignore "the complex relationships between sexual violence and other gendered harms in conflict, and between gender harms of conflict and peace."[68] More important, such "unreflexive use of these methods obscures the more profound question of how to build methodologies and methods appropriate to this highly complex object of investigation."[69]

Finally, addressing the predominant assumptions guiding the field, Campbell criticizes mainstream and feminist scholars for their "failure to engage with feminist critical accounts of the gendered shaping of patterns of conflict-related sexual violence" and the politics of knowledge production in the field.[70] Gender, gender hierarchies, and gendered inequalities as analytical categories are often dismissed as irrelevant, replaced by generalized and universalized categories of "women" and "men" and turned into isolated single statistical categories or technical expertise. Campbell notes that the increased policy attention paid to sexual violence in wars has brought new funding and respectability to the field, but it has also compromised analytical approaches by including "deep-seated gendered, racialized and colonial ideologies."[71] Discussions like Campbell's embed sexual violence in wars at the intersection of feminist scholarship and geopolitics, simultaneously locating both the scholarship and the politics at the center of contemporary struggles for social justice.[72]

Unless researchers more critically reflect on the gendered and racist implications of much of the current mainstream and feminist scholarship on war, it will not be possible to go beyond the dominant and overly simplistic understanding of the Wars of Globalization as the product of ethnic and religious hatreds between and greed among primitive non-Western men and their female victims. This means that feminist scholarship on sexual violence against both women and men in war must include several other, often-ignored perspectives.

Probably the most glaringly absent theoretical perspective is the political economy of sexual violence in war and gendered war economies. While there is a lively and rich feminist discussion of economic globalization and gender, very few feminist authors have addressed the links between sexuality, sex, sexual violence, and political economies of wars and violent conflicts.[73] There are two reasons for this blind spot. One comes from the fact that there is hardly any feminist work on political economies of war and of gender and war economies. Nor have feminists addressed political economies of war in the way that critical conflict-studies scholars such as David Keen and Mark Duffield have: by linking peace and war economies and exposing how academics and practitioners, operating from their own culturally determined worldviews, are engaged in a project of extending Western domination through protection of supposedly universal liberal rights.[74]

The absence of feminist scholarship on war economies and political economies of gendered war violence is also an unfortunate consequence of the "cultural turn" dominating Western feminism, which has all but expelled economic rights, inequalities and injustices, and socioeconomic status as useful analytical categories and approached gender and sexuality within the confines of identity and identity-based rights.[75] Meredeth Turshen produced one of the few feminist analyses that addresses political economies of violence against women during wars and political upheavals.[76] Relating political violence, gender, and struggles around economic resources, she studied how sexual violence in conflicts in Rwanda and Mozambique allows men to appropriate women's economic assets. In 2008, public-policy scholar V. Spike Peterson published an article on gendered economies and the so-called new wars, focusing on gender within licit and illicit war economies.[77] Relating productive, reproductive, and virtual economies, she stressed the importance of intersections of gender and race for economic inequalities within neoliberal globalization, but has not challenged the overall theorization of the new-wars concept.

Only since 2010 has there been more in-depth analysis that addresses links between war violence against women and local and global economies, especially in the contemporary context.[78] Jacqui True asked how women's social, political, and economic inequalities are related to violence against them, in peace and war alike. In answering this question, she related the material bases of social and economic power, such as the "distribution and use of resources, benefits, privileges and authority within the home and society at large" and the "institutional and ideological formations of society" that produce women's social positions.[79] True also asserted that contemporary economic globalization has deepened women's inequalities and vulnerabilities. Sara Meger asked similar questions, focusing specifically on sexual violence in war, studying the examples of rapes in the DRC and sexual violence against men and boys.[80] Unhappy with feminist analyses of war rapes, she used critical political-economy perspectives to show that economic interests and social inequalities fueling the conflict also play a role in sexual violence against women, producing new forms of gendered political legitimacy and material wealth. She also examined the larger context of globalized neoliberal economies as crucial for the gendered practices of violence in war and analyses thereof. It is these examinations of epistemologies and ontologies of war and war violence and the attention to the globalized neoliberal economies that offer promising avenues for future theoretical approaches to sexual violence in wars.

Notes

1. Elizabeth D. Heineman, ed., *Sexual Violence in Conflict Zones from the Ancient World to the Era of Human Rights* (Philadelphia: University of Pennsylvania Press, 2011), 1.
2. See, for the history, the chapter by Regina Mühlhäuser on "Sexuality, Sexual Violence, and the Military in the Age of the World Wars" in this handbook.
3. Elisabeth Jean Wood, "Armed Groups and Sexual Violence: When Is Wartime Rape Rare?," *Politics & Society* 37, no. 1 (2009): 131–62, 132; and Elisabeth Jean Wood, "Sexual Violence during War: Toward an Understanding of Variation," in *Order, Conflict, and Violence*, ed. Ian Shapiro et al. (Cambridge: Cambridge University Press, 2008), 321–51.
4. On the United Nations International Criminal Tribunal for the Former Yugoslavia, see http://www.icty.org/, accessed December 23, 2017.
5. On the United Nations International Criminal Tribunal for Rwanda, see http://unictr. unmict.org/, accessed December 23, 2017.
6. On the permanent International Criminal Court, see https://www.icc-cpi.int/Pages/Home. aspx, accessed December 23, 2017.
7. On the Special Court for Sierra Leone, see http://www.rscsl.org/, accessed December 23, 2017.
8. United Nations Security Council, "Resolution 1325 (2000) on Women, Peace and Security: Understanding the Implications, Fulfilling the Obligations," adopted October 31, 2000, accessed May 14, 2017, http://www.un.org/womenwatch/osagi/cdrom/documents/ Background_Paper_Africa.pdf.
9. United Nations Security Council, "Resolution 1820 (2008)," adopted June 19, 2008, accessed May 17, 2017, http://www.securitycouncilreport.org/atf/cf/%7B65BFCF9B-6D27-4E9C-8CD3-CF6E4FF96FF9%7D/CAC%20S%20RES%201820.pdf.
10. Catharine A. MacKinnon, "Rape, Genocide, and Women's Human Rights," *Harvard Women's Law Journal* 17 (1994): 5–16; and Beverly Allen, *Rape Warfare: The Hidden Genocide in Bosnia-Herzegovina and Croatia* (Minneapolis: University of Minnesota Press, 1996), 10.
11. Lisa Sharlach, "Rape as Genocide: Bangladesh, the Former Yugoslavia, and Rwanda," *New Political Science* 22, no. 1 (2000): 89–102.
12. Matthias Bjørnlund, "'A Fate Worse Than Dying': Sexual Violence during the Armenian Genocide," in *Brutality and Desire: War and Sexuality in Europe's Twentieth Century*, ed. Dagmar Herzog (Basingstoke: Palgrave Macmillan, 2009), 16–58.
13. Roselyn Costantino, "'Guatemaltecas' Have Not Forgotten: From Victims of Sexual Violence to Architects of Empowerment in Guatemala," in *Rape: Weapon of War and Genocide*, ed. Carol Rittner and John Roth (St. Paul, MN: Paragon House, 2012), 120–21.

14. See Charli Carpenter, "Beyond 'Gendercide': Operationalizing Gender in Comparative Genocide Studies," in *Gendercide and Genocide*, ed. Adam Jones (Nashville, TN: Vanderbilt University Press, 2004), 230–56; Julie Kuhlken, "Weapon of Sadness: Economic and Ethical Dimensions of Rape as an Instrument of War," in Rittner and Roth, *Rape*, 157–75, and the edited volume generally; and Daniela de Vito et al., "Rape Characterised as Genocide," *SUR: International Journal on Human Rights* 6, no. 10 (2009): 29–50.

15. Sherrie L. Russell-Brown, "Rape as an Act of Genocide," *Berkeley Law Scholarship Repository* 21, no. 2 (2003): 350–74.

16. Doris E. Buss, "Rethinking 'Rape as a Weapon of War,'" *Feminist Legal Studies* 17, no. 2 (2009): 145–63.

17. Ibid., 160.

18. Doris E. Buss, "The Curious Visibility of Wartime Rape: Gender and Ethnicity in International Criminal Law," *Windsor Yearbook of Access to Justice* 25, no 1 (2007): 3–22.

19. Ibid., 5.

20. Chiseche Salome Mibenge, *Sex and International Tribunals. The Erasure of Gender from the War Narrative* (Philadelphia: Pennsylvania University Press, 2013).

21. Elissa Helms, *Innocence and Victimhood: Gender, Nation, and Women's Activism in Postwar Bosnia-Herzegovina* (Madison: University of Wisconsin Press, 2013), 230.

22. See, for example, de Vito et al., "Rape Characterised"; Rittner and Roth, *Rape*; and Russell-Brown, "Rape as an Act."

23. Claudia Card, "Rape as a Weapon of War," *Hypatia* 11, no. 4 (1996): 5–18.

24. Ibid., 8.

25. Inger Skjelsbæk, "The Elephant in the Room: An Overview of How Sexual Violence Came to be Seen as a Weapon of War" (report to the Norwegian Ministry of Foreign Affairs, Peace Research Institute Oslo, 2010), 40.

26. Colleen Duggan et al., "Reparations for Sexual and Reproductive Violence: Prospects for Achieving Gender Justice in Guatemala and Peru," *International Journal of Transitional Justice* 2, no. 2 (2008): 192–213.

27. Nancy Farwell, "War Rape: New Conceptualizations and Responses," *Affilia* 19, no. 4 (2004): 389–403.

28. Bülent Diken and Carsten Bagge Laustsen, "Becoming Abject: Rape as a Weapon of War," *Body and Society* 11, no. 1 (2005): 111–28.

29. Debra Bergoffen, "Exploiting the Dignity of the Vulnerable Body: Rape as a Weapon of War," *Philosophical Papers* 38, no. 3 (2009): 307–25, 315.

30. Jelke Boesten, "Analyzing Rape Regimes at the Interface of War and Peace in Peru," *International Journal of Transitional Justice* 4, no. 1 (2010): 110–29.

31. Kathryn Farr, "No Escape: Sexual Violence against Women and Girls in Central and Eastern African Armed Conflicts," *Deportate, Esuli, Profughe* (2010): 85–112, 89.

32. Doris Buss, "Seeing Sexual Violence in Conflict and Post-Conflict Societies: The Limits of Visibility," in *Sexual Violence in Conflict and Post-Conflict Societies: International Agendas and African Contexts*, ed. Doris Buss et al. (New York: Routledge, 2014), 3–27, 14.

33. Anette Bringedal Houge, "Sexualized War Violence: Knowledge Construction and Knowledge Gaps," *Aggression and Violent Behavior* 25 (2015): 79–87.

34. Dubravka Zarkov, "War Rapes in Bosnia: On Masculinity, Femininity and Power of the Rape Victim Identity," *Tijdschrift voor Criminologie* 39, no. 2 (1997): 140–51; and Zarkov, *The Body of War: Media, Ethnicity, and Gender in the Break-up of Yugoslavia* (Durham, NC: Duke University Press, 2007).

35. Judy El-Bushra, "How Should We Understand Sexual Violence and HIV/AIDS in Conflict Contexts," (Research Report No. 17, AIDS Security and Conflict Initiative, 2008).

36. Elisabeth Jean Wood, "Conflict-Related Sexual Violence and the Policy Implications of Recent Research," *International Review of the Red Cross* 96, no. 894 (2014): 457–78.

37. Maria Eriksson Baaz and Maria Stern, *Sexual Violence as a Weapon of War? Perceptions, Prescriptions, Problems in the Congo and Beyond* (London: Zed Books, 2013), 4.

38. Ibid., 42.

39. With the war in the former Yugoslavia, the former country and the new states that subsequently emerged from it were regularly referred to as *Balkans* in both scholarship and politics. Following Edward Said's concept of orientalism, Maria Todorova has coined the concept of Balkanism to stress the representational function of such naming; see Maria Todorova, *Imagining the Balkans* (New York: Oxford University Press, 1997). Milica Bakic-Hayden and Robert Hayden have also been highly critical of return to this language that was used for social and cultural representation of the region in the nineteenth and early twentieth centuries; see Bakic-Hayden and Hayden, "Orientalist Variations on the Theme 'Balkans': Symbolic Geography in Recent Yugoslav Cultural Politics," *Slavic Review* 51, no. 1 (1992): 1–15; and Bakic-Hayden, "Nesting Orientalisms: The Case of Former Yugoslavia," *Slavic Review* 54, no. 4 (1995): 917–31.

40. Rosan Smits and Serena Cruz, "Increasing Security in DR Congo: Gender-Responsive Strategies for Combating Sexual Violence," *CRU Policy Brief* no. 17 (2011): 1–9; and Laura Heaton, "The Risks of Instrumentalizing the Narrative on Sexual Violence in the DRC: Neglected Needs and Unintended Consequences," *International Review of the Red Cross* 96, no. 894 (2014): 625–39.

41. Ibid., 626. Heaton's account is also linked to Maria Eriksson Baaz and Maria Stern's *The Complexity of Violence: A Critical Analysis of Sexual Violence in the Democratic Republic of Congo* (Stockholm: Swedish International Development Cooperation Agency, 2010).

42. See Paul Rodgers, "The Myth of a Clean War—and Its Real Motives," *Open Security*, March 13, 2013, accessed December 12, 2017, https://www.opendemocracy.net/democracy/article_1041.jsp; and Elspeth Van Veeren, "Clean War, Invisible War, Liberal War: The Clean and Dirty Politics of Guantánamo," in *Liberal Democracies at War: Conflict and Representation*, ed. Andrew Knapp and Hilary Footitt (London: Bloomsbury Academic, 2013), 89–112.

43. Sherene Razack, "From the 'Clean Snows of Petawawa': The Violence of Canadian Peacekeepers in Somalia," *Cultural Anthropology* 15, no. 1 (2000): 127–63.

44. This case has been well documented and immortalized in the 2010 Canadian German movie *The Whistleblower*; see Internet Movie Database, http://www.imdb.com/title/tt0896872/; for basic information, see Tony Robson, "Bosnia: The United Nations, Human Trafficking and Prostitution," *World Socialist Website*, August 21, 2002, accessed December 12, 2016, https://www.wsws.org/en/articles/2002/08/bosn-a21.html.

45. Some of them have been tried and charged. See the "Charge Sheet for Trial by General Court-Martial," accessed July 14, 2017, https://www.publications.parliament.uk/pa/ld200506/ldlwa/50719ws1.pdf.

46. On the DRC, see Michael Fleshman, "Tough UN Line on Peacekeeper Abuses," *Africa Renewal*, accessed December 12, 2017, http://www.un.org/africarenewal/magazine/april-2005/tough-un-line-peacekeeper-abuses. For the "zero tolerance" and a number of other UN policies on sexual violence, exploitation, and relationships, see "Conduct and Discipline," United Nations Peacekeeping, accessed December 12, 2016, http://www.un.org/en/peacekeeping/issues/cdu; and "UN to Enforce 'Zero Tolerance' Policy on Sexual

Exploitation and Abuse, Senior Official Tells Member States," UN News Centre, April 5, 2016, accessed December 12, 2017, http://www.un.org/apps/news/story.asp?NewsID= 53619#.V5pyBPl97IU. The UN has issued a number of special measures and resolutions aimed for protection from sexual exploitation and abuse of civilians by its forces, especially aimed at Africa; see, for example, "Secretary-General's Bulletin," October 9, 2003, accessed December 12, 2017, http://www.un.org/en/ga/search/view_doc.asp?symbol=ST/SGB/2003/13. In 2016, the UN reiterated its commitment to zero-tolerance policy; see "UN to Enforce."

47. See "Military Sexual Assault and Harassment," US Army War College, accessed July 14, 2017, http://usawc.libguides.com/content.php?pid=582097&sid=4798134; and "Testimony on Sexual Assaults in the Military: Hearing before the Subcommittee on Personnel of the Committee on Armed Services, United States Senate, One Hundred Thirteenth Congress, First Session, March 13, 2013," accessed July 14, 2017, https://www.armed-services.senate. gov/imo/media/doc/sexualassaultsinmilitary_subcomm_hearing_031313.pdf.

48. Adam Jones, "Gender and Genocide in Rwanda," *Journal of Genocide Research* 4, no. 1 (2002): 65–94.

49. Adam Jones, "Gender and Ethnic Conflict in ex-Yugoslavia," *Ethnic and Racial Studies* 17, no. 1 (1994): 115–34.

50. Zarkov, "War Rapes"; and Zarkov, *Body of War*.

51. Dubravka Zarkov, "Exposures and Invisibilities: Media, Masculinities and the Narratives of Wars in an Intersectional Perspective," in *Framing Intersectionality: Debates on a Multi-Faceted Concept in Gender Studies*, ed. Helma Lutz et al. (Surrey: Ashgate, 2011), 105–20.

52. See Jones, "Gender and Ethnic"; Zarkov, "War Rapes"; and Chris Dolan, "Collapsing Masculinities and Weak States: A Case Study of Northern Uganda," in *Masculinities Matter! Men, Gender and Development*, ed. Frances Clever (London: Zed Books, 2002): 57–83.

53. For early feminist reactions on Abu Ghraib, see Cynthia Enloe, "Wielding Masculinity inside Abu Ghraib: Making Feminist Sense of an American Military Scandal," *Asian Journal of Women's Studies* 10, no. 3 (2004): 89–102; and Rosalind Petchesky, "Rights of the Body and Perversions of War: Sexual Rights and Wrongs Ten Years Past Beijing," *International Social Science Journal* 57, no. 2 (2005): 301–18. For studies in the field of human geography, see Matthew Hannah, "Torture and the Ticking Bomb: The 'War on Terror' as a Geographical Imagination of Power/Knowledge," *Annals of Association of American Geographers* 96, no. 3 (2006): 622–40. For international relations, see Charli Carpenter, "Recognizing Gender-Based Violence against Civilian Men and Boys in Conflict Situations," *Security Dialogue* 37, no. 1 (2006): 83–103. For relevance of gender stereotypes in the perception of abuse, see Carolyn Fallahi et al., "Gender Differences in the Perception of Prisoner Abuse," *Sex Roles* 60, no. 3–4 (2008): 261–68. For media, see, for example, Bruce Trucker and Sia Triantafyllos, "Lynndie England, Abu Ghraib, and the New Imperialism," *Canadian Review of American Studies* 38, no. 1 (2008): 83–100; and for a legal perspective, see Hilmi Zawati, "Impunity or Immunity: War Time Male Rape and Sexual Torture as a Crime against Humanity," *Torture: Journal on Rehabilitation of Torture Victims and Prevention of Torture* 17, no. 1 (2007): 27–47. For a critique of some of this work, see Zarkov, "Exposures and Invisibilities."

54. Jared Sexton and Elizabeth Lee, "Figuring the Prison: Prerequisites of Torture at Abu Ghraib," *Antipode* 38, no. 5 (2006), 1005–22; and Avery Gordon, "Abu Ghraib: Imprisonment and the War on Terror," *Race & Class* 48, no. 1 (2006): 42–59.

55. There was especially significant proliferation of work within media studies—which already started with research on representations of "9/11" and the "war on terror"—that focused on representations of Abu Ghraib violence within the United States. Susan Sontag

argued that recycling of images of violated Iraqi men's bodies carries ethical implications—both as a specific mode of violence (next to the act of physical violence) and as a mode of Othering. Susan Sontag, *Regarding the Pain of Others* (New York: Farrar, Straus and Giroux, 2003). See also Zawati, "Impunity or Immunity"; Mervyn Christian et al., "Sexual and Gender Based Violence against Men in the Democratic Republic of Congo: Effects on Survivors, Their Families and the Community," *Medicine, Conflict and Survival* 27, no. 4 (2011): 227–46; Chris Dolan, "Into the Mainstream: Addressing Sexual Violence against Men and Boys in Conflict" (briefing paper prepared for the workshop held at the Overseas Development Institute, London, May 14, 2014), 1–10, accessed December 12, 2017, http://www.refugeelawproject.org/files/briefing_papers/Into_The_Mainstream-Addressing_Sexual_Violence_against_Men_and_Boys_in_Conflict.pdf; also Dolan's article, "Has Patriarchy Been Stealing the Feminists' Clothes? Conflict-Related Sexual Violence and UN Security Council Resolutions," in "Undressing Patriarchy: Men and Structural Violence," ed. Jerker Edström et al., special issue, *IDS Bulletin* 45, no. 1 (2014): 80–84; Dolan, "Collapsing Masculinities and Weak States: A Case Study of Northern Uganda," in Cleaver, *Masculinities Matter!*, 57–84; and Olivera Simic, "Wartime Rape and Its Shunned Victims," in *Genocide and Gender in the Twentieth Century: A Comparative Survey*, ed. Amy E. Randall (London: Bloomsbury, 2015), 237–57.

56. On Uganda, see Dolan, "Collapsing Masculinities"; and Dolan, "Has Patriarchy." On the DRC, see Christian et al., "Sexual and Gender"; see also Dolan, "Into the Mainstream."

57. See Sandesh Sivakumaran, "Prosecuting Sexual Violence against Men," in *Sexual Violence as an International Crime: Interdisciplinary Approaches*, ed. Anne-Marie de Brouwer et al. (Cambridge: Intersentia, 2012), 79–98; also, Sivakumaran, "Lost in Translation: UN Responses to Sexual Violence against Men and Boys in Situations of Armed Conflict," *International Review of the Red Cross* 92, no. 877 (2010), 259–77; and Sivakumaran, "Sexual Violence against Men in Armed Conflict," *European Journal of International Law* 18, no. 2 (2007): 253–76.

58. Sivakumaran, "Lost in Translation," 267 and 270.

59. Dubravka Zarkov, "Co-Option, Complicity, Co-Production: Feminist Politics on War Rapes," *European Journal of Women's Studies* 23, no. 2 (2016): 119–23; and Zarkov, "Ontologies of International Humanitarian and Criminal Law: 'Locals' and 'Internationals,'" in Discourses and Practices of Justice," in *Narratives of Justice in and out of the Courtroom, Former Yugoslavia and Beyond*, ed. Dubravka Zarkov and Marlies Glasius (New York: Springer, 2014), 3–21. See also Buss, "Seeing Sexual Violence."

60. Makau Mutua, "Savages, Victims, and Saviors: The Metaphor of Human Rights," *Harvard International Law Journal* 42 (2001): 201–45.

61. Zarkov, "Ontologies."

62. Kirsten Campbell, "Sexual Violence Research as a Field of Knowledge: Reading Traps and Gaps" (position paper, workshop, Sexual Violence in Armed Conflict International Research Group, The Hague, June 2016). Quoted with permission of the author.

63. Ibid., 5.

64. Ibid., 5.

65. Ibid., 7.

66. See Dara Kay Cohen and Ragnhild Nordas, *Sexual Violence in Armed Conflict: Dataset*, accessed December 12, 2017, http://www.sexualviolencedata.org/dataset/.

67. See, for example, Benedikt Korf, "Cargo Cult Science, Armchair Empiricism and the Idea of Violent Conflict," *Third World Quarterly* 27, no. 3 (2006), 459–76; Ricardo Real P. Sousa,

"Comparing Datasets: Understanding Conceptual Differences in Quantitative Conflict Studies," in Hintjens and Zarkov, *Conflict, Peace, Security*, 216–31; and Diaz, "Mathematical Modeling."

68. Campbell, "Sexual Violence," 7.

69. Ibid., 8.

70. Ibid., 9.

71. Buss, "Seeing Sexual Violence," 10 and 15.

72. Zarkov, "Co-Option, Complicity."

73. Regarding feminist work on gender and global economy, see, for example, Carla Freeman, *High Tech and High Heels in the Global Economy, Women, Work, and Pink-Collar Identities in the Caribbean* (Durham, NC: Duke University Press, 2000); Rhacel Salazar Parrenas, *Servants of Globalization: Women, Migration and Domestic Work* (Stanford, CA: Stanford University Press, 2001); and Ara Wilson, *The Intimate Economies of Bangkok: Tomboys, Tycoons, and Avon Ladies in the Global City* (Berkeley: University of California Press, 2004).

74. See, for example, David Keen, "Incentives and Disincentives for Violence," in *Greed & Grievance: Economic Agendas in Civil Wars*, ed. Mats Berdal and David M. Malone (Boulder, CO: Lynne Rienner, 2000), 19–42; and Mark Duffield, "Globalization, Transborder Trade, and War Economies," in ibid., 69–90.

75. See Larry Ray and Andrew Sayer, eds., *Culture and Economy after the Cultural Turn* (London: Sage, 1999). The feminist abandonment of issues of economic inequalities and their geopolitical dimensions has especially been criticized by Nancy Frazer's essay in that volume, "Social Justice in the Age of Identity Politics: Redistribution, Recognition and Participation," 25–52; and Chandra Talpade Mohanty, "'Under Western Eyes' Revisited: Feminist Solidarity through Anticapitalist Struggles," *Signs* 28, no. 2 (2003), 499–535.

76. Meredeth Turshen, "The Political Economy of Rape: An Analysis of Systematic Rape and Sexual Abuse of Women during Armed Conflict in Africa," in *Victims, Perpetrators or Actors? Gender, Armed Conflict and Political Violence*, ed. Caroline O. N. Moser and Fiona C. Clark (London: Zed Books, 2001), 55–68.

77. V. Spike Peterson, "'New Wars' and Gendered Economies," *Feminist Review* no. 88 (2008): 7–20.

78. Jacqui True, *The Political Economy of Violence against Women* (Oxford: Oxford University Press, 2012).

79. Ibid., 7.

80. Sara Meger, *Rape Loot Pillage: The Political Economy of Sexual Violence in Armed Conflict* (Oxford: Oxford University Press, 2016); and Meger, "Rape in Contemporary Warfare: The Role of Globalization in Wartime Sexual Violence," *African Conflict and Peacebuilding Review* 1, no. 1 (2011): 100–32.

SELECT BIBLIOGRAPHY

Alison, Miranda H. "Wartime Sexual Violence: Women's Human Rights and Questions of Masculinity." *Review of International Studies* 33, no. 1 (2007): 75–90.

Allen, Beverly. *Rape Warfare: The Hidden Genocide in Bosnia-Herzegovina and Croatia.* Minneapolis: University of Minnesota Press, 1996.

Bastick, Megan, Karin Grimm, and Rahel Kunz. *Sexual Violence in Armed Conflict, Global Overview and Implications for the Security Sector.* Geneva: Geneva Centre for the Democratic Control of Armed Forces, 2007.

Bracewell, Wendy. "Rape in Kosovo: Masculinity and Serbian Nationalism." *Nations and Nationalism* 6, no. 4 (2000): 563–90.

Buss, Doris E. "Rethinking 'Rape as a Weapon of War.'" *Feminist Legal Studies* 17, no. 2 (2009): 145–63.

Eriksson Baaz, Maria, and Maria Stern. *Sexual Violence as a Weapon of War? Perceptions, Prescriptions, Problems in the Congo and Beyond.* London: Zed Books, 2013.

Giles, Wenona Mary, and Jennifer Hyndman, eds. *Sites of Violence: Gender and Conflict Zones.* Berkeley: University of California Press, 2004.

Harrington, Carol. *Politicization of Sexual Violence: From Abolitionism to Peacekeeping.* Burlington, VT: Ashgate, 2010.

Heineman, Elizabeth D., ed. *Sexual Violence in Conflict Zones from the Ancient World to the Era of Human Rights.* Philadelphia: University of Pennsylvania Press, 2011.

Herzog, Dagmar, ed. *Brutality and Desire: War and Sexuality in Europe's Twentieth Century.* Basingstoke: Palgrave Macmillan, 2009.

Hirschauer, Sabine. *The Securitization of Rape: Women, War and Sexual Violence.* New York: Palgrave Macmillan, 2014.

Lewis, Chloé. "Systemic Silencing: Addressing Sexual Violence against Men and Boys in Armed Conflict and Its Aftermath." In *Rethinking Peacekeeping, Gender Equality and Collective Security*, edited by Gina Heathcote and Dianne Otto, 203–23. Basingstoke: Palgrave Macmillan, 2014.

Meger, Sara. "Rape in Contemporary Warfare: The Role of Globalization in Wartime Sexual Violence." *African Conflict & Peacebuilding Review* 1, no. 1 (2011): 100–32.

Moser, Caroline O. N., and Fiona C. Clark, eds. *Victims, Perpetrators or Actors? Gender, Armed Conflict and Political Violence.* London: Zed Books, 2001.

Reid-Cunningham, Allison Ruby. "Rape as a Weapon of Genocide." *Genocide Studies and Prevention* 3, no. 3 (2008): 279–96.

Skjelsbæk, Inger. "Sexual Violence and War: Mapping Out a Complex Relationship." *European Journal of International Relations* 7, no. 2 (2001): 211–37.

Stiglmayer, Alexandra, ed. *Mass Rape: The War against Women in Bosnia-Herzegovina.* Lincoln: University of Nebraska Press, 1994.

Wood, Elisabeth Jean. "Armed Groups and Sexual Violence: When Is Wartime Rape Rare?" *Politics & Society* 37, no. 1 (2009): 131–61.

Zarkov, Dubravka. *The Body of War: Media, Ethnicity, and Gender in the Break-up of Yugoslavia.* Durham, NC: Duke University Press, 2007.

Zarkov, Dubravka. "Towards a New Theorizing of Women, Gender and War." In *Handbook of Gender and Women's Studies*, edited by Kathy Davis, Mary Evans, and Judith Lorber, 214–33. London: Sage, 2006.

CHAPTER 30

....

THE UNITED NATIONS, GENDERED HUMAN RIGHTS, AND PEACEKEEPING SINCE 1945

....

SANDRA WHITWORTH

PEACEKEEPING and other forms of peace operations are often considered war's corollary, and at different historical moments they have received greater or lesser scholarly, public, and policymaking attention. Peacekeeping involves the use of military and civilian personnel deployed under the authority of the United Nations (UN) to oversee and sometimes even to implement peace accords. According to the UN, peacekeeping allows countries affected by conflict to navigate the difficult transition from conflict to peace.[1] During the Global Cold War (1946–91), when the UN created for the first time formal peace operations, these missions were few in number and almost entirely invisible within the context of the East/West nuclear rivalry that dominated global politics for much of the latter half of the twentieth century. Cold War peacekeeping missions operated on very limited mandates, usually focusing on monitoring ceasefire agreements, with strict rules that peacekeepers would be deployed with the consent of belligerents to a conflict, would be lightly armed, and would fire their weapons only in self-defense.

When the Cold War collapsed with the breakdown of the Eastern bloc (the Soviet Union and its allies in the Warsaw Pact) in the early 1990s and Cold War rivalries with the Western bloc (the United States and its allies in NATO) ended as well in the UN Security Council, there was a sudden proliferation of peace operations and greater optimism that these alternatives to the traditional use of force may prove to be a fruitful means of resolving conflicts. Post–Cold War missions were far more ambitious, often involving tens of thousands of troops, hundreds of civilian personnel, and an array of mandates that included state building, repatriation of refugees, conducting elections, and extensive humanitarian relief.[2] In total, seventy-one peacekeeping operations by the UN have taken place between 1948 and 2019.[3]

With the "war on terror" after September 11, 2001, peace operations seemed to shift again to the background, especially in the West, where they receive less media attention and where even long-time supporters of peacekeeping (such as Canada) began to deploy military forces in traditional combat-related roles to unprecedented degrees. Though peace operations may have been subsumed in the Western media by the war on terror, the UN nonetheless continues to deploy peacekeeping missions around the world. By 2019, the UN operated fourteen missions, primarily located in Africa and the Middle East. Most peacekeepers are now drawn from countries of the Global South and the missions themselves focus on internal rather than international conflicts, but the numbers of personnel involved in peacekeeping missions remain high—both peacekeeping budgets and numbers of personnel more than doubled between 2001 and 2019. In 2001, UN peacekeeping operations deployed some 39,500 soldiers and officers and 7,500 civilian police, whereas by 2019, the fourteen operations included, according to the UN, 88,205 uniformed personnel provided by 124 countries, 12,932 civilian personnel (8,393 of them local), and 1,354 UN volunteers. Not more than 4 percent of the UN military personnel and 11 percent of the UN police personnel were women. The number of total UN peacekeeping fatalities between 1948 and 2019 reached 3,802.[4]

Whether attention to peacekeeping has waxed or waned, many of the questions raised by feminists about peacekeeping have remained the same. These include examining the numbers of women deployed on operations, the impact of those operations on local women, and the gendered assumptions that prevail in the creation and conduct of peace operations. These questions have remained consistent in no small part because very little has changed in peacekeeping missions over the past several decades, despite attention within the UN to issues concerning both women and gender. For example, notwithstanding calls for greater representation of women on missions, they continue to constitute a small fraction of the personnel deployed. The UN officially pursues a policy of "gender mainstreaming," which should ensure that gender perspectives are integrated into all elements of policy development in all sections (Security Sector Reform, Disarmament, Demobilization and Reintegration, Police, Military, Elections) from initial planning through to evaluation.[5] But little has changed. Despite calls to gender mainstream missions, concerns that peace operations often result in heightened insecurity for some women and girls remain as missions since the early 1990s have resulted in regular and widespread reports of sexual exploitation and sexual assaults committed by peacekeepers against women and girls.[6]

Feminist scholars contributed greatly to our understanding of the history of gendered human rights and peacekeeping. The important questions they continue to ask about peacekeeping are why the UN has been so unsuccessful in accomplishing its goals of gender equality within peacekeeping, why has a more substantive attention to gender proven so elusive, and why does sexual violence perpetrated by peacekeepers continue to occur? The answers to these questions tend to focus on a series of technical issues, for example, the challenges faced by the UN in coordinating the behavior of troop-contributing countries, the need for greater resources or effort devoted to enforcing existing codes of conduct, and the importance of including more women, not just to meet gender equality obligations but also to mitigate the more violent behavior of men.[7]

But this is not enough. The more fundamental question that must be examined by feminist scholars is whether the UN *ever could* succeed in accomplishing its goals around gender equality and peacekeeping.[8] The general problem of gender strategies adopted by the UN is that at best they have worked to simply map onto existing practices and relations of power, including militarized approaches to conflict resolution and dominant Western narratives about democracy and governance. This is because the entire discussion around gender and peacekeeping within the UN focuses on finding ways to assist and support the UN in the work that it already does, not to fundamentally change that work. If the work of the United Nations is, however, informed and constituted by relations of inequality, the application of gender to these practices can never be, nor was it ever intended to be, transformative. As Susan Willett wrote in the journal *International Peacekeeping* in 2010, "Existing attempts to mainstream gender within the UN rarely go to the heart of the institutional inequities and power relations that structure gender relations within the organization. Rather, gender mainstreaming has been grafted onto existing power structures that are circumscribed by the essentialist nature of binary opposites in which gender has been interpreted as woman, and women remain differentiated from men."[9] Understanding the limitations of UN successes around gender and peacekeeping means exploring both the relations of power that circumscribe the internal workings of the United Nations and the larger relations of power in which the UN operates, or as Anna Agathangelou and L. H. M. Ling write, "Peacekeeping as an enterprise intensifies a particular strain of neoliberal global governance that remains unquestioningly white, male and bourgeois."[10]

These arguments will be explored in the following with a focus on five themes: the historical development of UN peacekeeping since 1948; developments and trends in UN gender policy; the role of women/gender in UN peacekeeping; the issue of sexual violence related to UN peacekeeping missions; and the subject of militarisms and masculinities related to these missions.

THE DEVELOPMENT OF UN PEACEKEEPING

The term peacekeeping does not appear in the United Nations Charter, but instead was an "invention" of the UN, developed in the post–World War II period when it mounted first two observer missions, the UN Truce Supervision Organization in Palestine in 1948 and the UN Military Observer Group in India and Pakistan in 1949.[11] The first formal peacekeeping mission followed almost a decade later in the Suez, in 1956. The Suez crisis erupted when Israel, Britain, and France attacked Egypt after the government under

President Gamal Abdel Nasser nationalized the Suez Canal Company.[12] Criticism of France and Britain was widespread, and the plan to deploy a UN force to the region was an attempt to allow them to withdraw from Egypt without being disgraced by their allies, bring an end to the hostilities, and confirm that the UN did have a role to play in preventing and resolving conflicts in the postwar era.[13] United Nations Emergency Force I (UNEF I) troops continued to act as a buffer between Egyptian and Israeli troops until 1967.[14]

United Nations Emergency Force I established a series of principles that would serve as the basis of all peacekeeping missions that followed, including the importance of securing the consent of the parties to the dispute, the nonuse of force except for self-defense, and impartiality. Other principles instituted through UNEF I, according to A. Betts Fetherston, included the principle of voluntary contributions of contingents from middle and small neutral countries (not great powers) to participate as peacekeepers and the principle of day-to-day control of the operations by the secretary-general.[15] UNEF I was established through a resolution of the General Assembly of the United Nations; all subsequent peacekeeping missions have been established through UN Security Council resolutions, which usually outline the mandate of the mission, the number of personnel to be deployed, the UN's financial commitment to the mission, and a set time after which the Security Council will revisit the mandate and the mission (usually within a period of three to six months). The secretary-general retains formal control of peace operations, but within the UN Headquarters the undersecretary-general for peacekeeping oversees missions, and in the field they are led by a special representative of the secretary-general, who is the head of mission. Additionally, the Department of Peacekeeping Operations was established in 1992, the mission of which "is to plan, prepare, manage and direct UN peacekeeping operations, so that they can effectively fulfill their mandates under the overall authority of the Security Council and General Assembly, and under the command vested in the Secretary-General."[16]

When Cold War tensions dissolved in the early 1990s, UN peacekeeping missions began to proliferate. Freed from the constraints imposed by East–West rivalry, the UN began to mount numerous missions. The thirteen missions that were conducted in the three decades between 1956 and 1988 have been followed by a further fifty-eight missions since that time. Known in UN parlance as *second-generation* missions, these operations in the immediate post–Cold War period moved away from the original and more limited mandates (like UN Emergency Force I) of establishing interposition forces between belligerents to monitor ceasefire agreements, to large complex deployments that involve tens of thousands of military, police, and civilian personnel. The missions are often aimed as much at state-building as peacekeeping and involve human rights monitoring, the provision of social services, disarmament, conducting elections, repatriating refugees, and numerous other activities. Some observers also use the term *third-generation* missions for highly militarized interventions—such as in Haiti (1994–95) after a rebellion had taken over most of Haiti and President Bertrand Aristide had resigned—which have been launched as peace enforcement missions. Others still suggest a *fourth generation* of missions that combine peace enforcement with humanitarian intervention.[17] By 2007, the General Assembly pointed out that the UN was managing some 100,000 field personnel deployed on peace operations, or some "200,000 personnel in real terms, given constant rotation of personnel and new mission requirements."[18]

United Nations peacekeeping is funded out of a separate peacekeeping budget to which member states contribute an assigned assessment based on the size and health of their economies. The largest contributors to the peacekeeping budget are the United States, Japan, France, Germany, and Britain. Troops for early missions were drawn primarily from Northern/industrialized countries, but as noted previously, troop-contributing countries are now drawn primarily from the Global South, with Bangladesh, Ethiopia, Pakistan, India, Rwanda, and Nepal among the largest contributors. Troop contributors receive a monthly subsidy from the UN of approximately $1,400 per soldier, with additional compensation provided for the use of military hardware.[19] At the beginning, the entry of countries from the Global South into peacekeeping was widely criticized by more traditional military analysts on the grounds that these countries used peacekeeping to subsidize their militaries. Today, by contrast, the more widely held concern is that these counties now bear the burden of almost all the risks associated with peacekeeping. In 2011, for example, Morocco's representative to the UN, speaking on behalf of the Non-Aligned Movement, commented that peacekeeping needed to be a partnership, not "merely an outsourcing exercise, in which developed countries contracted lower-cost troops from developing countries to do the hard and dangerous work."[20]

DEVELOPMENTS AND TRENDS
IN UN GENDER POLICY

As peacekeeping has evolved, so too has the UN's attention to issues concerning women and gender. The United Nations had established the Commission on the Status of Women in 1946 and held the First World Conference on Women in Mexico City in 1975.[21] The UN Convention on the Elimination of All Forms of Discrimination against Women was adopted in 1979, and other gender-specific instruments included the 1994 UN Declaration on the Elimination of Violence against Women and a special rapporteur on violence against women. Follow-up World Conferences on Women included meetings in Copenhagen (1980) and Nairobi (1985) and then the Fourth World Conference on Women held in Beijing in 1995, the largest conference in the history of the UN to that date. It was in the mid-1990s, after the Beijing conference and the Beijing Platform for Action, that attention to both gender and women's issues within the UN really intensified, with more extensive mandates provided to the women's machineries within the UN.[22]

Attention to gender issues within the UN circulates around three principle concepts: gender equality, gender balance, and gender mainstreaming. The UN's primary goal around gender is to promote "gender equality," which, according to UN Women (the UN Entity for Gender Equality and the Empowerment of Women), "means that the rights, responsibilities and opportunities of individuals will not depend on whether they are born male or female."[23] The UN's commitment to equality comes in part out of its more general human rights concerns as well as the assumption that "greater equality between women and men is also a precondition for (and effective indicator of) sustainable people-centered development."[24]

One strategy for achieving gender equality will be through reaching "gender balance" within the UN, the equal representation of women and men within all UN posts. This was a goal that the UN had originally committed to achieve by the year 2000. As of 2012, the most recent figures available indicate women now represent some 48 percent of staff within the UN, but they continue to be represented primarily within lower-level administrative and clerical positions; they remain highly underrepresented at upper levels of decision-making authority. The UN secretary-general has recently noted that the revised goal to achieve 50/50 representation of women within the UN system in general is the year 2030 (with more specific goals within peacekeeping).[25]

The second strategy to achieve gender equality is via *gender mainstreaming*, a term adopted in the Beijing Platform for Action in 1995 and further elaborated on by the Economic and Social Council of the UN in 1997. Its scope and sophistication as a policy are quite different from that of gender balance in several ways. Gender balance is essentially a personnel issue, and it is limited to the question of numbers of women within the UN itself. In contrast, gender mainstreaming goes beyond numbers of personnel to address all of the UN's work, requiring that all UN policies and actions be assessed for their differential implications for women and men. Conceptually, the idea of gender mainstreaming is relatively sophisticated; it accepts the idea that gender is a social construct, not a biological fact, and that the prevailing norms and assumptions concerning both women and men will differ across time and place. Mainstreaming views gender as shaped by cultural, class, religious, and ethnic differences and recognizes the power differentials between women and men, the fluid nature of those differences, and that these differences are made manifest in a variety of ways.[26]

Gender balance and gender mainstreaming are two strategies that have been adopted widely, both within the UN and by many of its member states, by the European Union, and by numerous international institutions. An extensive feminist literature also exists that explores the contributions and limitations of both gender balance and mainstreaming as political strategies.[27] Gender balance, for example, may draw our attention to the vast underrepresentation of women in a variety of public spheres—and this is not unimportant—but, it is also now widely acknowledged that a simple "add women and stir" approach to addressing that underrepresentation is extremely limited, not least because it ignores the variety of differences that exist among women in terms of their class, race, ethnicity, religion, sexuality, and other constructions of difference. Simply adding (some) women to the institutions in which they have been underrepresented is no guarantee that the practices or policies of those institutions will be altered as a result of that presence.

Gender mainstreaming was intended as a strategy to directly address this concern by requiring that organizations and states commit themselves to assessing the differential impacts for women and men of *all* policies, practices, and planned actions.[28] Via mainstreaming, it was the gendered implications of policies that would matter most, not simply the presence or absence of women, and as noted previously, gender was understood to be cross-cut by a variety of other identities or material conditions such as race and class. So, in principle at least, discussions of mainstreaming mean also taking into account the classed, raced, religious, ethnic, and other differences that shape women's and men's experiences of policies and actions. Mainstreaming goes well beyond a simple "add women and stir" approach, but nonetheless has been widely critiqued by feminist scholars and activists. Some of those criticisms focus on the inconsistent way in which mainstreaming is either understood or implemented or, as Sylvia Walby writes, "What is the 'gender equality' that is being 'mainstreamed'?"[29]

Women/Gender and Peacekeeping

As in the rest of the UN, questions of women and gender within peace operations have revolved around the triumvirate of gender equality, gender balance, and gender mainstreaming. Issues of gender balance and peacekeeping have focused on the importance of including more women in peacekeeping operations, not only to ensure the equal representation of women and men, but also because of the unique perspective women may bring to missions. Studies by the UN about women and peacekeeping have tended to emphasize the importance of including women because of their uniqueness or difference, and this difference is associated with women's less threatening and inherently more peaceful qualities. An early statement by the UN's Division for the Advancement of Women from 1995 relied on embarrassing caricatures, arguing that women sometimes employ unorthodox techniques, such as "singing," to diffuse potentially violent situations.[30]

A series of case studies of women and peacekeeping from both past and then-ongoing missions was presented at a conference organized by the Department of Peacekeeping Operation's Lessons Learned Unit in Windhoek, Namibia, in May 2000.[31] The conference resulted in the "Windhoek Declaration" and the "Namibia Plan of Action on Mainstreaming a Gender Perspective in Multidimensional Peace Support Operations," as well as a more general report that goes by the latter title. The declaration and plan of action, as well as the report, tended to emphasize issues of gender balance (get more women in and get more women into senior positions), but also pointed again to the specific contributions women can make on missions, though in more concrete (and not always essentialist) terms. It was hoped, as Angela King, a Jamaican diplomat and then-special adviser on gender issues of the UN, noted, "that local women are more likely to confide in female peacekeepers, and that with greater participation of women on the mission, more local women will be likely to join peace committees, which then are less hierarchical and tend to be more responsive to women's concerns."[32]

The Windhoek Declaration and the Namibia Plan of Action were both presented to the UN Security Council as part of its deliberations leading up to the historic adoption of Security Council Resolution 1325 (SCR 1325) in October 2000.[33] This was the first time the UN Security Council acknowledged that women and girls were affected differently from men and boys during conflicts and their aftermath. In principle, SCR 1325 was revolutionary—it acknowledged the differential impacts of conflict on women and girls compared to men and boys, and it called for women's increased participation in peace operations and decision-making (that is, gender balance) and the incorporation of a gender perspective into all peace operations (that is, gender mainstreaming). Most important, it was a Security Council resolution—the only resolution that is enforceable within the UN system. In just a few short years, feminist activists working both within and outside the UN had gone from trying to attract attention to questions of gender in conflict to achieving a Security Council resolution that required departments and agencies throughout the UN system to take gender into account.

Despite its potential, the impact of SCR 1325 on peacekeeping practices within the UN has been minimal. In gender-balance terms, SCR 1325 has been only marginally successful. While the deployment of several all-female peacekeeping units starting in 2007 attracted a great deal of media attention, the overall presence of women within peacekeeping missions has not changed significantly.[34] In 1993, 1 percent of uniformed personnel deployed on peacekeeping missions were women, by 2019, that figure had risen to around 5 percent[35]—numbers that are far distant from the goal of 50/50 gender balance the UN had originally hoped to have achieved by the year 2000. The UN Department of Peacekeeping Operations had issued revised gender balance goals, aiming to achieve 50/50 balance by the year 2015 among civilian personnel and 20 percent women within police forces, while committing to improve the representation of women within military units but without setting any specific targets. But five years later the UN is still far from achieving these aims.[36]

Women remain underrepresented throughout missions, particularly at the leadership level. As noted in a report conducted in 2008 by Women in International Security, a network of researchers and practitioners housed at Georgetown University's Center for Peace and Security Studies in Washington, DC, "In 60 years of UN peacekeeping—from 1948 to 2008—only seven women have ever held the post of special representative of the secretary-general."[37] In 2012, five of sixteen missions were headed by women.

Regarding gender mainstreaming, the UN has been even less successful in achieving its obligations under SCR 1325. Documents produced by the UN have aimed at mapping out the ways in which gender mainstreaming can be incorporated into peace operations. In their 2004 Gender Resource Package for Peacekeeping Operations, the Department of Peacekeeping Operations, for example, cites many ways in which gender mainstreaming can be important.[38] These include ensuring that equality provisions are incorporated into any constitutional changes made by newly formed governments, including the specific concerns of former female combatants in UN Disarmament, Demobilization, and Reintegration Programs, developing public-relations materials on key gender issues, and recognizing the differences in the economic situation as well as societal and cultural attitudes faced by women and girls compared to men and boys, to name only a few. Gender units were to be established in all peacekeeping missions, and five years after SCR 1325 was adopted, a gender advisor was also appointed to the Department of Peacekeeping Operations offices at UN Headquarters in New York.[39]

While the UN is very good at generating documents and studies about mainstreaming, the actual practice of mainstreaming has never lived up to those discussions. Responsibility for mainstreaming gender within peace operations usually falls to gender advisors, but placing trained gender personnel within missions continues to be done inconsistently. In 2008, for example, only eleven missions (of thirty-four missions at that time) had full-time gender advisors; all others had only a gender "focal point"—that is, a staff member who is charged with covering the gender portfolio in addition to his or her full-time responsibilities.[40] Where gender units are deployed, they have faced persistent problems. As Refugees International reports, "Many gender advisors are not hired until well after many of the other positions in UN peacekeeping missions have been filled and key activities are underway."[41] Many of the units operate with minimal or, sometimes, no funding. It is not uncommon that gender advisors arrive on a mission to discover there is no budget for their unit and their initial activities will not involve gender training of peacekeeping personnel, but rather fundraising for staff, office, and even basic office supplies.[42]

Hilary Charlesworth and Mary Wood suggest that gender mainstreaming in peace operations "can quickly become a token exercise."[43] In the Democratic Republic of the Congo in 2002, the Office of Gender Affairs had a relatively large staff but was expected to function without any budget to develop activities or initiatives.[44] In Liberia in 2004, a UN volunteer was the first on-site staff person in the gender unit and was tasked with training the 15,000 incoming military personnel on the meanings of gender and gender mainstreaming. When the senior gender advisor arrived later, she discovered that all of the mission's budgetary decisions had been made the week prior to her arrival, with no funding allocated to the gender unit.[45] In Haiti in 2004, while the gender advisor was assigned to the mission at the planning stage, she had little budget and no staff. It is also not unusual that gender advisors have multiple tasks, as Refugees International notes of the gender advisor in Haiti: "In addition to her duties as the gender advisor, she was also appointed as a 'Focal Point for Sexual Exploitation and Abuse' while the mission tried to fill the position of the Code of Conduct officer."[46]

In addition to problems of resources, serious questions have also been raised about the effectiveness of the gender units even when they are in place. In Kosovo in 1999, critics noted that the gender office failed to make strong links with local women's organizations, resulting in little follow-up on general recommendations made by those organizations. As one researcher reported, "Local women have become very wary of this arm of UNMIK [United Nations Mission in Kosovo] administration."[47] In the UN Mission in Sierra Leone in 1999, which operated with a gender focal point, "none of the women's NGOs [nongovernmental organizations] in Freetown had even heard of the focal point person, who had not asked any of them to document human rights violations."[48] The Gender Affairs Unit of the UN Transitional Administration in East Timor (UNTAET), starting in 1999, was credited by some observers as having established "the first effectively functioning gender office in the history of peacekeeping"; others, however, were more critical.[49] Some local East Timorese women's groups claimed the UNTAET Gender Affairs Unit was at best "fruitless"[50] and, at worst, undermined the efforts of local women's organizing by, among other things, working closely with only one women's organization within the country and failing to make links across the spectrum of groups, particularly those located outside the capital.[51] Problems of resources and the constraints that gender experts face within the UN—in particular needing to conform to UN language and priorities—have often set those experts at odds with the demands and goals raised by women and women's organizations on the ground. These limitations also contribute to one of the UN's most difficult and persistent issues concerning women and gender, that is, sexual violence perpetrated by the UN's own personnel.

Sexual Violence and UN Peacekeeping Missions

One of the reasons the UN may have been receptive to acknowledging the importance of gender through SCR 1325 was that as the number of missions increased in the 1990s, there were at the same time widely documented instances of sexual and physical violence perpetrated by peacekeepers against local civilians. The UN struggled with a legitimation crisis at the very moment it was being called on to deploy more, and more complex, missions, and as local populations discovered, some of the very individuals sent to protect civilians in postconflict settings only added further to their insecurity.

Even in the earliest of the post–Cold War peacekeeping missions, reports emerged that local women and men suffered from sexual violence and sexual exploitation at the hands of UN peacekeepers.[52] In the 1991 UN mission to Cambodia, United Nations Transitional Authority in Cambodia (UNTAC) personnel were accused of being involved in "fake marriages" with local women, as well as harassing and sexually assaulting them. The arrival of so many foreign troops and personnel also resulted in a virtual explosion of prostitution within Cambodia, which, in turn, was expected to result in skyrocketing rates of HIV and AIDS. UNTAC's chief medical officer predicted that as many as seven times more UN personnel would eventually die of AIDS contracted in Cambodia than had died as a result of hostile action.[53]

One of the first official responses by the UN to charges of sexual exploitation and assault came from the secretary-general's special representative to Cambodia. The UNTAC's head of mission, Yasushi Akashi, a senior Japanese diplomat and UN administrator, stunned a meeting of workers of nongovernmental organizations when, confronted with allegations of rising prostitution rates, widespread harassment, and acts of sexual violence, he casually suggested that it was natural for hot-blooded young soldiers to chase "young beautiful beings of the opposite sex."[54] While much critiqued for his comments, Akashi's lack of concern about the sexual violence being perpetrated by peacekeepers was revealing of the UN position on these issues during the early period of post–Cold War missions—it was a "natural" part of military deployments and best ignored.

The pattern of sexual exploitation that became internationally visible in Cambodia was repeated elsewhere throughout numerous missions and so became increasingly difficult for UN officials to dismiss or ignore. In Kosovo (1999–2008), the Democratic Republic of the Congo (1999–ongoing), Mozambique (1999–2015), Eritrea (2000–8), and Somalia (1992–95 and 2013–15), male peacekeepers on UN missions were accused of harassing, exploiting, and physically and sexually assaulting women and girls.[55] In Mozambique (1992–94) and Bosnia (1995–2002), peacekeepers condoned the establishment of brothels and were involved themselves in the trafficking of women and children.[56] In west Africa, military peacekeepers engaged in transactional sex, allegedly paying for sex with young girls and boys by bartering money, food, or promises of protection, and left behind thousands of children born to local women, many of whom were also exposed to HIV and other sexually transmitted infections.[57] UN Women reported in 2012 that between 2007 and 2011, more than three hundred substantiated cases of sexual exploitation and abuse were handled by various offices throughout UN peace operations.[58] In 2015, reports by Amnesty International revealed that widespread cases of sexual assault in the Central African Republic included the rape of a twelve-year-old girl, and a study of peacekeeping assaults in Liberia in 2012 indicated that as many as 58,000 women and girls may have engaged in transactional sex with peacekeepers in a single year, two-thirds of whom were minors.[59]

Allegations of sexual assault and exploitation committed by humanitarian and peacekeeping personnel became so widespread that as early as 2003 the UN secretary-general issued a bulletin titled "Special Measures for Protection from Sexual Exploitation and Sexual Abuse" outlining the kinds of special measures for the protection of civilians from sexual exploitation and sexual abuse that peacekeeping personnel were expected to adopt, and the UN General Assembly called for fuller documentation of reported incidents of sexual assault and exploitation committed by peacekeepers.[60] Codes of conduct explicitly prohibiting what the UN described as sexual misconduct were established, and more thorough training of peacekeepers about their responsibilities was adopted (though sometimes in piecemeal fashion). Despite these measures, allegations continued to circulate and, in the words of then–Secretary-General Kofi A. Annan, a Ghanaian diplomat in office from 1997 to 2006, in the report from 2004, "it became clear that the measures currently in place to address sexual exploitation and abuse in peacekeeping operations were manifestly inadequate and that a fundamental change in approach was needed."[61]

A year after the secretary-general's bulletin, the UN launched a formal investigation headed by Jordanian Prince Zeid Ra'ad Al Hussein, who delivered his report in 2005. The report contained further allegations, noting that in 2004 the UN Department of Peacekeeping Operations received eighty complaints against military personnel deployed on peacekeeping missions (and an additional sixteen against civilian personnel and nine against civilian police), the majority of which concerned sex with persons under the age of eighteen years and sex with adult prostitutes. As both Secretary-General

Annan and Prince Zeid noted in 2005, it is likely that most cases of sexual assault and exploitation go unreported in conflict zones, and thus the number of incidents is undoubtedly far higher than that formally brought to the attention of the UN. Prince Zeid's report called for better training and enforcement of the codes of conduct, better investigative measures that would also be fairer to the victims of sexual assaults, and better enforcement measures, particularly by troop-contributing countries.[62] Despite codes of conduct and zero-tolerance policies, in 2015 the UN Office of Internal Oversight Services acknowledged that sexual exploitation and assault perpetrated by peacekeepers remains a regular occurrence in operations, with one-third of victims being minors.[63]

In a relatively brief period of time, the UN moved from an institution that largely ignored claims about sexual exploitation and violence committed by peacekeepers to one that explicitly and systematically attempts to address these issues. Nonetheless, cases of sexual exploitation continue to plague UN operations. Sexual violence is not the only concern or issue that must be addressed when mainstreaming gender in peace operations, but it is a clear measure of the UN's failure to do so. Despite a focus on gender equality, gender balance, and gender mainstreaming, UN missions fail in the most fundamental of ways—by not preventing sexual exploitation and violence and, indeed, by deploying soldiers to peacekeeping operations who are themselves the perpetrators of that violence.

MILITARISMS, MASCULINITIES, AND UN PEACEKEEPING

The dramatic turnaround on the part of the UN cannot be emphasized enough: the early dismissive attitude of someone like UNTAC's head Yasushi Akashi is almost unthinkable in 2020, and it has been replaced by UN codes of conduct and zero-tolerance policies for peacekeeping personnel, frank UN oversight reports, and a willingness to remove heads of missions who do not sufficiently address sexual violence. UN Secretary-General Ban Ki-moon, a South Korean statesman and politician in office from 2007 to 2016, removed the head of the peacekeeping mission in the Central African Republic in 2015 after widespread accusations of sexual exploitation and assault had not been addressed. He has described sexual exploitation and violence committed by peacekeeping personnel as a cancer within the institution of the UN, and yet despite the change of attitude and an array of policies, the UN has been unable to successfully address these issues.[64] Why is this the case?

The answer given by UN officials has consistently focused on a lack of resources and a failure of political will on the part of member states. At the tenth anniversary of the adoption of SCR 1325, Ban Ki-moon reiterated an oft-repeated phrase: the time had arrived, he said, to move beyond rhetoric to concrete commitments, and he called for more resources to allow the UN to fulfill its obligations to promote gender equality within peace operations.[65] In a cash-strapped environment like the UN, it is not surprising that more resources are needed to be able to deliver on the oversight and other mechanisms required to properly mainstream gender in peace operations. In addition to resources, the UN's leadership focuses also on the problem of member states and argues that while the UN can create the standards that peacekeepers should aspire to, it is ultimately the member states of the UN that must enforce those standards. If troop-contributing countries have a different set of expectations for the behavior of their troops and if they refuse to prosecute their own nationals when they are accused of sexual violence or exploitation, there is, by this view, very little that the UN can do.[66]

Variations on the phrase "from rhetoric to reality" have been circulating for over a decade within the UN system[67] and are emblematic of the problem-solving way in which questions of gender and peacekeeping have been framed. On the one hand, it is hard to disagree with these claims, but on the other, there are probably very few problems faced by the UN that would not benefit from more resources or greater cooperation among member states. Analytically, it does not tell us very much, and politically it may not help to explain UN failures around these issues. This is because understanding the UN's failures as simply technical problems of inadequate resources or membership coordination forecloses more critically oriented questions that ask deeper questions about how the UN operates.[68]

The political context of the United Nations is complex and often contradictory. It focuses on state making and sovereignty while simultaneously privileging the idea of liberal internationalism and liberal democracy as the ultimate goal of peacekeeping and peacemaking activities. Problem-solving responses to issues such as gender and peacekeeping take as a given the already existing practices of the UN, so they do not call into question or interrogate how those practices are constituted. As Michael Pugh writes, "The concentration on 'working with what we've got' may yield important practical lessons, but the prevailing wisdom, and much of the dissent on the issue, does not interrogate the order itself and, by accepting it as 'reality,' reinforces its underlying values and structures. Thus modern versions of peacekeeping can be considered as forms of riot control directed against the unruly parts of the world to uphold the liberal peace."[69] There are numerous consequences that result from "working with what we've got." One that is significant in the context of our discussion here is the assumption that peacekeeping missions are properly military missions and that soldiers make the best peacekeepers. As a form of riot control aimed at, in Laura Zanotti's words, "domesticating and normalizing states that are perceived as potential sources of threat and instability," it is impossible within the problem-solving frame around which so much of the gender and peacekeeping discussion has been constructed to imagine UN missions as anything other than military missions.[70]

But what are the consequences of relying on highly militarized individuals to conduct peace operations? Feminist and even mainstream analyses have documented the high rates of physical and sexual violence committed by soldiers—within their families, their own ranks, and society more generally.[71] Feminist analyses of this violence focuses on militarized masculinities, the processes involved in the "making of soldiers," and the ways in which military indoctrination works first to break down the individual and then build them up again in very specific ways.[72] Part of the process of transforming young people into warriors involves the lure of a particular type of masculinity, one that privileges courage and endurance, physical and psychological strength, heterosexual competency, discipline, and toughness. The combination of techniques involved in creating soldiers almost always involves the simultaneous harassment and denigration of the individual along with the promotion of elitist attitudes and in-group bonding, coupled with the obliteration of any perceived differences. The "Other"—whether it is the enemy, foreigners, women, persons of color, gays, or lesbians—is regularly dehumanized, and actual identity matters very little in this process: women can be successfully conditioned into militarized masculinity, and persons of color can and have defended the racist regiments to which they belong.

The manner in which militarized masculinities are inculcated in different national militaries and the ways in which it impacts particular individuals will vary—not all soldiers emerge from this process in exactly the same way.[73] But most have been exposed to the same types of messages, the same promises and myths associated with militarized manhood: the promise of turning boys into men; the myth of a male-dominated and heterosexual world; the promise of a place in which force and physical prowess can be celebrated; and the myth that a soldier's superiority and entitlement will never be questioned. These are the trade-offs involved in securing an individual's willingness to kill or die for his or her nation.[74] If nothing else, it is difficult to "turn off" the training, or, as one Canadian army officer noted, "We're the only people who train people to go out and attack somebody else and kill them. And that is a difficult thing to get around. . . . How do you say, 'Okay guys, turn in your gear and turn off that switch and go home and have a nice life?' And I'm not sure we're ever going to get around that 100 percent."[75] There is, in other words, a fundamental contradiction in using individuals who have been trained to fight wars to instead conduct peace. Moving into postconflict situations requires sensitivity not only to the nature of the conflict, but also to the ways in which local populations have been traumatized and remain vulnerable. The widespread instances of "transactional sex" and of sexual and physical violence committed by peacekeepers within peace operations signal exactly the opposite and arguably suggest, instead, that peacekeepers are acting on the sense of entitlement around sexual access they have been trained to believe is rightly theirs. This is part of the entitlement of being a soldier; it conforms and confirms the messages that have gone into their very constitution as soldiers.

Opening up a discussion of soldiers as soldiers moves into a new set of questions about the challenges faced by the United Nations around gender and peacekeeping, but it is not one that could ever be asked within the problem-solving framework within which the UN operates. Issues of sexual violence are not the only issues that should be examined in a fuller and more complete analysis of gender and peacekeeping. Indeed, there are concerns that by emphasizing sexual violence, the "women-as-victims" narrative that permeates so much international discussion and policy in these areas is reproduced here.[76] It does, however, move us onto a terrain that might actually explain why, despite all the policies, efforts, and codes of conduct, the UN has so completely and utterly failed to address sexual violence within peace operations. Codes of conduct, even codes with greater resources devoted to them, are unlikely to change the sense of entitlement associated with a militarized hypermasculinity.

Conclusion

There have been two trajectories of policies and intervention within the UN system—those focused on the evolution of peace operations and those focused on policies around gender equality. Despite apparently very good gender equality policies, the UN has been largely unsuccessful in achieving its gender equality goals. One of the most striking illustrations of that failure is the continued high rates of sexual violence committed by peacekeepers against local civilian populations. Critically oriented scholarship explores questions of militarism and of masculinity and examines the ways in which questions have been framed—and the kinds of questions that are excluded through that framing. When the goals of the UN concerning women and gender are simply to work at enforcing codes of conduct, it is not possible to ask whether militarized masculinity is largely at odds with codes of conduct or whether peace operations are part of the contemporary colonial encounter. Expanding the discussion of gender and peacekeeping in a way that understands gender, in analytical terms, as a critical political category allows us to explore these and other questions.

Notes

1. United Nations, "What Is Peacekeeping?," accessed April 10, 2020, https://peacekeeping. un.org/en/what-is-peacekeeping.
2. For a general introduction to the UN, see Thomas G. Weiss et al., *The United Nations and Changing World Politics*, 7th ed. (Boulder, CO: Westview Press, 2014); for a general introduction to UN peacekeeping, see Michael Barnett, *Eyewitness to a Genocide: The United Nations and Rwanda* (Cornell, NY: Cornell University Press, 2002); Jocelyn Coulon, *Soldiers of Diplomacy: The United Nations, Peacekeeping, and the New World Order* (Toronto: University of Toronto Press, 1998); and A. Betts Fetherston, *Towards a Theory of United Nations Peacekeeping* (Basingstoke: Macmillan, 1994).
3. United Nations, "Peacekeeping Fact Sheet," accessed April, 10, 2020, https://peacekeeping. un.org/en/peacekeeping-fact-sheet-january-2019.
4. Ibid.; United Nations, *The Year in Review: United Nations Peacekeeping 2001* (New York: United Nations, 2002); and United Nations Peacekeeping, "Women in Peacekeeping" accessed April 10, 2020, https://peacekeeping.un.org/en/women-peacekeeping.
5. Ibid.; and UN Women, "Gender Mainstreaming," accessed April 12, 2020, https://www. unwomen.org/en/how-we-work/un-system-coordination/gender-mainstreaming.

6. See Paul Higate and Marsha Henry, *Insecure Spaces: Peacekeeping in Liberia, Kosovo and Haiti* (London: Zed Books, 2009); Claire Duncanson, *Forces for Good? Military Masculinities and Peacebuilding in Afghanistan and Iraq* (Basingstoke: Palgrave Macmillan, 2013); Laura Sjoberg, ed. *Gender and International Security: Feminist Perspectives* (New York: Routledge, 2010); Sandra Whitworth, *Men, Militarism and UN Peacekeeping: A Gendered Analysis* (Boulder, CO: Lynne Rienner, 2004); and Dyan Mazurana et al., eds., *Gender, Conflict, and Peacekeeping* (Lanham, MD: Rowman & Littlefield, 2005).

7. See Olivera Simić, "Does the Presence of Women Really Matter? Towards Combating Male Sexual Violence in Peacekeeping Operations," *International Peacekeeping* 17, no. 2 (2010): 188–99; see also Kathleen M. Jennings, "Women's Participation in UN Peacekeeping Operations: Agents of Change or Stranded Symbols?" (NOREF Report, Norwegian Peacebuilding Resource Centre, September 2011), accessed October 19, 2016, http://noref. no/Themes/Inclusivity-and-gender/Publications/Women-s-participation-in-UN-peacekeeping-operations-agents-of-change-or-stranded-symbols/(language)/eng-US.

8. See Whitworth, *Men, Militarism*, 119–50; see also Anne Orford, "Feminism, Imperialism and the Mission of International Law," *Nordic Journal of International Law*, 71 no. 2 (2002): 275–96.

9. Susan Willett, "Security Council Resolution 1325: Assessing the Impact on Women, Peace and Security," *International Peacekeeping* 17, no. 2 (2010): 142–58, 142.

10. Anna M. Agathangelou and L. H. M. Ling, "Desire Industries: Sex Trafficking, UN Peacekeeping and the Neo-Liberal World Order," *Brown Journal of World Affairs* 10, no.1 (2003): 133–48, 133.

11. The term was in the UN Report of then–Secretary-General Boutros Boutros-Ghali; see "An Agenda for Peace: Preventive Diplomacy, Peacemaking and Peace-Keeping," January 31, 1992, A/47/277-S24/11, 28, para. 46.

12. Fetherston, *Towards a Theory*, 12; and Whitworth, *Men, Militarism*, 28–29.

13. Fetherston, *Towards a Theory*, 12–13; see also Coulon, *Soldiers of Diplomacy*, 18–28.

14. Whitworth, *Men, Militarism*, 30.

15. Fetherston, *Towards a Theory*, 13; and Coulon, *Soldiers of Diplomacy*, 25.

16. See "UN Department of Peacekeeping Operations Mission Statement," accessed April 10, 2020, https://www.refworld.org/publisher,DPKO,,,50ffbce52e0,,0.html; since 2019 the department is called the Department of Peace Operations (DPO). See also Women's Commission for Refugee Women and Children, "Room to Maneuver: Lessons from Gender Mainstreaming in the UN Department of Peacekeeping Operations," January 2007, accessed April 10, 2020, https://reliefweb.int/report/world/room-maneuver-lessons-gender-mainstreaming-un-department-peacekeeping-operations.

17. Higate and Henry, *Insecure Spaces*, 9.

18. See UN General Assembly Resolution 10602, June 29, 2007, accessed April 10, 2020, https://www.un.org/press/en/2007/ga10602.doc.htm.

19. Department of Peacekeeping Operations, "How We Are Funded," accessed April 10, 2020, https://peacekeeping.un.org/en/how-we-are-funded.

20. United Nations General Assembly, "United Nations Peacekeeping Has 'Responsibility and Privilege' to Serve Those Grasping Promise of Peace, Security, Prosperity, Fourth Committee Told," GA/SPD/490, UN Sixty-Sixth General Assembly, Fourth Committee, 14th Meeting, October 24, 2011, accessed April 10, 2020, https://www.un.org/press/en/2011/gaspd490.doc.htm.

21. On the situation of women in the early UN, see the chapter by Glenda Sluga on "Gender, Peace, and the New Politics of Humanitarianism in the First Half of the Twentieth Century" in this handbook.

22. Whitworth, *Men, Militarism*, 140, n1.

23. United Nations Women, "Important Concepts Underlying Gender Mainstreaming," accessed September 13, 2017, http://www.un.org/womenwatch/osagi/conceptsandefinitions. htm. Please note that early definition documents created by the Office of the Special Advisor on Gender Issues at the UN have been subsumed within the office of UN Women as of 2010.

24. Ibid.

25. See Department of Peacekeeping Operations, "Women in Peacekeeping," accessed April 10, 2020, https://peacekeeping.un.org/en/women-peacekeeping; see also Report of the Secretary-General to the UN General Assembly, "Improvement of the Status of Women in the United Nations System," September 2008, accessed September 13, 2017, http://www. un.org/womenwatch/daw/documents/ga63/Final%20first%20page%20correction%20 SG%20Report.pdf; and "Secretary-General Remarks to the General Assembly High-Level Debate on 'Advancing Gender Equality and the Empowerment of Women and Girls for a Transformative Post-2015 Development Agenda,'" New York, March 6, 2015, accessed September 13, 2017, http://www.un.org/sg/statements/index.asp?nid=8434.

26. United Nations Office of the Special Adviser on Gender Issues and Advancement of Women, *Gender Mainstreaming: An Overview* (New York: United Nations, 2002), 6–7.

27. See Shirin Rai, ed., *Mainstreaming Gender, Democratizing the State? Institutional Mechanisms for the Advancement of Women* (New Brunswick, NJ: Transaction, 2007); and Sylvia Walby, ed., "Comparative Gender Mainstreaming," special issue, *International Feminist Journal of Politics* 7, no. 4 (2005).

28. Rai, *Mainstreaming Gender*, 16.

29. Sylvia Walby, "Introduction: Comparative Gender Mainstreaming in a Global Era," in Walby, "Comparative Gender Mainstreaming," 453–70, 455.

30. Some of this section is drawn from Whitworth, *Men, Militarism*, 119–50. For the original document, see UN Division for the Advancement of Women, "Women 2000: The Role of Women in United Nations Peacekeeping," no. 1/1995, December 1995, accessed October 19, 2017, http://www.un.org/womenwatch/daw/public/w2000/Women2000/Women2000% 20Role%20of%20women%20in%20peace-keeping%201995.pdf.

31. Louise Olsson and Torunn L. Tryggestad, "Introduction," in *Women and International Peacekeeping*, ed. Louise Olsson and Torunn L. Tryggestad (London: Frank Cass, 2001), 1–8.

32. Henry F. Carey, "Women and Peace and Security: The Politics of Implementing Gender Sensitivity Norms in Peacekeeping," in ibid., 49–68, 53–54.

33. Judith Hicks Stiehm, "Women, Peacekeeping and Peacemaking: Gender Balance and Mainstreaming," in ibid., 39–48.

34. The first was a unit from India that made headlines when it deployed to the peacekeeping mission in Liberia, and others followed in Haiti, Timor-Leste, and Congo. See Doreen Carvajal, "The Female Factor: A Female Approach to Peacekeeping," *New York Times*, March 5, 2010, accessed September 13, 2017, http://www.nytimes.com/2010/03/06/world/ africa/06iht-ffpeace.html?pagewanted=all&_r=0; and Olivera Simeć, "Moving beyond the Numbers: Integrating Women into Peacekeeping Operations" (Policy Brief, Norwegian Peacebuilding Resource Centre, March 2013), 3.

35. See Department of Peacekeeping Operations, "Women in Peacekeeping," accessed April 10, 2020, https://peacekeeping.un.org/en/women-peacekeeping.

36. See Simeć, "Moving Beyond," 2; and Department of Peacekeeping Operations, "Women in Peacekeeping."

37. Camille Pampell Conaway and Jolynn Shoemaker, "Women in United Nations Peace Operations: Increasing Leadership Opportunities," *Women in International Security*, July 2008, accessed September 13, 2017, https://www.peacewomen.org/sites/default/files/ UN-UNBAL-PK_IncreasingLeadership_WIIS_2008_0.pdf.

38. United Nations Department of Peacekeeping Operations, "Gender Resource Package for Peacekeeping Operations," 2004, accessed September 13, 2017, https://www.un.org/ ruleoflaw/files/Gender%20Resource%20Package.pdf.

39. Ibid. See also UN Department of Peacekeeping Operations, "Gender Mainstreaming in UN Peacekeeping Operations," March 2005, accessed September 13, 2017, https://www. peacewomen.org/sites/default/files/dpko_gmprogressreport_2005_0.pdf.

40. Report of the Secretary-General to the UN General Assembly, "Improvement of the Status of Women in the United Nations System," September 2008, para. 86, p. 40.

41. Refugees International, "Must Boys Be Boys? Ending Sexual Exploitation and Abuse in UN Peacekeeping Missions," October 18, 2005, accessed September 13, 2017, https://childhub. org/en/system/tdf/library/attachments/refugees_int_05_boys_0708.pdf?file=1&type=no de&id=18256.

42. See also Whitworth, *Men, Militarism*, 129–32.

43. Hilary Charlesworth and Mary Wood, "'Mainstreaming Gender' in International Peace and Security: The Case of East Timor," *Yale Journal of International Law* 26, no. 2 (2001): 313–18, 316.

44. United Nations Mission in the Democratic Republic of the Congo (MONUC), "Activities Report from the Office of Gender Affairs (OGA) of the United Nations Organization Mission in the Democratic Republic of the Congo (MONUC)," Kinshasa, January 10, 2003, 4.

45. Refugees International, "Must Boys."

46. Ibid.

47. Chris Corrin, "Post-Conflict Reconstruction and Gender Analysis in Kosova," *International Feminist Journal of Politics* 3, no. 1 (2001): 78–98, 86.

48. Carey, "Women and Peace," 54.

49. International Alert, "Gender Mainstreaming in Peace Support Operations: Moving beyond Rhetoric to Practice," London, July 2002, accessed September 13, 2017, http:// reliefweb.int/report/world/gender-mainstreaming-peace-support-operations-moving- beyond-rhetoric-practice.

50. Charlesworth and Wood, "Women," 338n37.

51. Ibid., 343.

52. On the issue of sexual violence in twentieth-century warfare, see also the chapters by Regina Mühlhäuser on "Sexuality, Sexual Violence, and the Military in the Age of the World Wars," and Dubravka Zarkov on "Conceptualizing Sexual Violence in Post–Cold War Global Conflicts" in this handbook.

53. Twenty-one UNTAC personnel lost their lives as a result of hostile action, but UNTAC's chief medical officer, Col. Dr. Peter Fraps, estimated that as many as 150 would eventually die of AIDS, as reported in Katrina Peach, "HIV Threatens to Claim UNTAC's Highest

Casualties," *Phnom Penh Post*, October 22–November 4, 1993, 4. See also Whitworth, *Men, Militarism*, 53–84.

54. Whitworth, *Men, Militarism*, 71.

55. United Nations Secretary-General Study, *Women, Peace and Security* (New York: United Nations, 2002), 84, para. 268.

56. United Nations, Report of the Special Rapporteur on Violence against Women, Its Causes and Consequences, Ms. Radhika Coomaraswamy, "Integration of the Human Rights Perspective of Women and the Gender Perspective: Violence against Women," January 23, 2001, E/CN.4/2001/73, para. 58–62; and Graça Machel, "The Impact of Armed Conflict on Children Report of the Expert of the Secretary-General, Ms. Graça Machel, Submitted Pursuant to General Assembly Resolution 48/157," United Nations General Assembly, A/51/306, August 26, 1996, 31, para. 98.

57. Elisabeth Rehn and Ellen Johnson Sirleaf, *Women, War, Peace: The Independent Experts' Assessment on the Impact of Armed Conflict on Women and Women's Role in Peace-Building* (New York: United Nations Development Fund for Women, 2002), 56; UN Report of the Secretary-General, "Investigation into Sexual Exploitation of Refugees by Aid Workers in West Africa," October 11, 2002, A/57/465, 10; and Save the Children, "From Camp to Community: Liberia Study on Exploitation of Children," Save the Children UK, May 8, 2006, 11.

58. United Nations Women, "Evaluation of Gender Mainstreaming Activities in United Nations Peacekeeping Activities (MONUC/MONUSCO) in the Democratic Republic of Congo" (New York: UN Women, 2012), 25; see also Taylor Toeka Kakala and Lisa Clifford, "UN Sexual Misconduct Allegations Won't Go Away," Institute for War and Peace Reporting, September 12, 2008, accessed September 13, 2017, http://www.iwpr.net/?p= acr&s=f&o=346657&apc_state=henh.

59. Bernd Beber et al., "UN Peacekeeping and Transactional Sex," *Washington Post*, June 16, 2015, accessed September 13, 2017, http://www.washingtonpost.com/blogs/monkey-cage/ wp/2015/06/16/u-n-peacekeeping-and-transactional-sex/; and Amnesty International, "CAR: UN Troops Implicated in Rape of Girl and Indiscriminate Killings Must Be Investigated," August 11, 2015, accessed September 13, 2017, https://www.amnesty.org/en/ latest/news/2015/08/car-un-troops-implicated-in-rape-of-girl-and-indiscriminate-killings-must-be-investigated/.

60. United Nations Secretary-General's Bulletin, "Special Measures for Protection from Sexual Exploitation and Sexual Abuse," ST/SGB/2003/13, October 9, 2003, accessed September 13, 2017, http://www.securitycouncilreport.org/atf/cf/%7B65BFCF9B-6D27-4E9C-8CD3-CF6E4FF96FF9%7D/SE%20ST%20SGB%202003%2013.pdf.

61. Report of the UN Secretary-General, "Special Measures for Protection from Sexual Exploitation and Sexual Abuse," A/58/777, April 23, 2004, accessed September 13, 2017, https://www.refworld.org/docid/41187be14.html.

62. United Nations General Assembly, "A Comprehensive Strategy to Eliminate Future Sexual Exploitation and Abuse in United Nations Peacekeeping Operations," A/59/710, March 24, 2005, accessed September 13, 2017, http://www.un.org/en/ga/search/view_doc.asp?symbol= A/59/710.

63. United Nations Office of Internal Oversight, "Evaluation of the Enforcement and Remedial Assistance Efforts for Sexual Exploitation and Abuse by the United Nations and Related Personnel in Peacekeeping Operations," May 2015, accessed September 13, 2017, https:// oios.un.org/inspection-evaluation-reports?page=6.

64. "Ban Ki-moon says Sexual Abuse in UN Peacekeeping Is 'a Cancer in Our System,'" *Guardian*, August 14, 2015, accessed September 13, 2017, http://www.theguardian.com/world/2015/aug/14/ban-ki-moon-says-sexual-abuse-in-un-peacekeeping-is-a-cancer-in-our-system.

65. United Nations Secretary-General Ban Ki-moon, "Remarks to the Ministerial Meeting on Security Council Resolution 1325: A Call to Action," UN Security Council, New York, September 25, 2010, accessed September 13, 2017, http://www.un.org/sg/selected-speeches/statement_full.asp?statID=969.

66. "Ban Ki-Moon Says."

67. One of the first articulations of this view came from the nongovernmental organization community in the International Alert paper: Richard Strickland and Nata Duvvury, "Gender Equity and Peacebuilding: From Rhetoric to Reality" (Ottawa: International Center for Research on Women, 2003).

68. I am relying here on Robert W. Cox's distinction between problem solving and critical theory. Problem-solving theory takes existing political and institutional practices as a given and seeks to improve on those practices; critical theory, by contrast, asks how these political practices have emerged from the material and ideological conditions that sustain them and the ways in which they may be changed. See Robert W. Cox, "Social Forces, States and World Orders: Beyond International Relations Theory," *Millennium* 10, no. 2 (1981): 126–55.

69. Michael Pugh, "Peacekeeping and Critical Theory," *International Peacekeeping* 11, no. 1 (2004): 39–58, 41; see also Whitworth, *Men, Militarism*, 119–50; and Higate and Henry *Insecure Spaces*, 1–22.

70. Laura Zanotti, "Taming Chaos: A Foucauldian View of UN Peacekeeping, Democracy and Normalization," *International Peacekeeping* 13, no. 2 (2006): 150–67, 151.

71. See, for example, Deborah Harrison, *The First Casualty: Violence against Women in Canadian Military Communities* (Toronto: James Lorimer, 2002); and Patricia Kime, "Incidents of Rape in Military Much Higher Than Previously Reported," *Military Times*, December 5, 2014, accessed September 13, 2017, http://www.militarytimes.com/story/military/pentagon/2014/12/04/pentagon-rand-sexual-assault-reports/19883155/.

72. Some of this material is drawn from, and is explored in more depth, in Whitworth, *Men, Militarism*, 151–82; see also Sherene H. Razack, *Dark Threats and White Knights: The Somalia Affair, Peacekeeping, and the New Imperialism* (Toronto: University of Toronto Press, 2004).

73. It is important to emphasize that there are a variety of militarized masculinities. See the collection by Paul R. Higate, *Military Masculinities: Identity and the State* (Westport, CT: Praeger Publishers, 2003).

74. See also the chapters by Stefan Dudink on "Citizenship, Mass Mobilization, and Masculinity in a Transatlantic Perspective, 1770s–1870s," Thomas Kühne on "States, Military Masculinities, and Combat in the Age of World Wars," and Richard Smith "Colonial Soldiers, Race, and Military Masculinities during and beyond World Wars I and II" in this handbook.

75. Harrison, *First Casualty*, 16.

76. See Laura J. Shepherd, *Gender, Violence & Security: Discourse as Practice* (London: Zed Books, 2008) for a complete discussion of this concern. Nonetheless, it is also worth noting that rates of sexual violence—perpetrated against both women and men by peacekeepers—is a significant issue and, despite the attention devoted to it within the UN, one that remains largely out of control.

Select Bibliography

Cockburn, Cynthia, and Dubravka Zarkov, eds. *The Postwar Moment: Militaries, Masculinities and International Peacekeeping*. London: Lawrence & Wishart, 2002.

Coulon, Jocelyn. *Soldiers of Diplomacy: The United Nations, Peacekeeping, and the New World*. Toronto: University of Toronto Press, 1998.

Duncanson, Claire. *Forces for Good? Military Masculinities and Peacebuilding in Afghanistan and Iraq*. Basingstoke: Palgrave Macmillan, 2013.

Enloe, Cynthia. *Globalization and Militarism: Feminists Make the Link*. Lanham, MD: Rowman & Littlefield, 2007.

Fetherston, A. B. *Towards a Theory of United Nations Peacekeeping*. Basingstoke: Macmillan, 1994.

Higate, Paul R. *Military Masculinities: Identity and the State*. Westport, CT: Praeger, 2003.

Higate, Paul, and Marsha Henry. *Insecure Spaces: Peacekeeping, Power and Performance in Haiti, Kosovo and Liberia*. London: Zed Books, 2009.

Mazurana, Dyan, Angela Raven-Roberts, and Jane Parpart, eds. *Gender, Conflict, and Peacekeeping*. Lanham, MD: Rowman & Littlefield, 2004.

Olsson, Louise, and Torunn L. Tryggestad, eds. *Women and International Peacekeeping*. London: Frank Cass, 2001.

Orford, Anne. "Feminism, Imperialism and the Mission of International Law." *Nordic Journal of International Law* 71, no. 2 (2002): 275–96.

Orford, Anne. *Reading Humanitarian Intervention: Human Rights and the Use of Force in International Law*. Cambridge: Cambridge University Press, 2003.

Pugh, Michael. "Peacekeeping and Critical Theory." *International Peacekeeping* 11, no. 1 (2004): 39–58.

Pruitt, Lesley J. *The Women in Blue Helmets: Gender, Policing, and the UN's First All-Female Peacekeeping Unit*. Oakland, California: University of California Press, 2016.

Razack, Sherene H. *Dark Threats and White Knights: The Somalia Affair, Peacekeeping, and the New Imperialism*. Toronto: University of Toronto Press, 2004.

Rehn, Elisabeth, and Ellen Johnson Sirleaf. *Women, War, Peace: The Independent Experts' Assessment on the Impact of Armed Conflict on Women and Women's Role in Peace-Building*. New York: United Nations Development Fund for Women, 2002.

Shepherd, Laura J. *Gender, Violence and Security: Discourse as Practice*. London: Zed Books 2008.

Simić, Olivera. "Does the Presence of Women Really Matter? Towards Combating Male Sexual Violence in Peacekeeping Operations." In "Women, Peace and Conflict: A Decade after Resolution 1325," edited by Susan Willett. Special issue, *International Peacekeeping* 17, no. 2 (2010): 188–99.

Sjoberg, Laura, and Sandra Via, eds. *Gender, War and Militarism: Feminist Perspectives*. Westport, CT: Praeger, 2010.

Stiehm, Judith Hicks. "Women, Peacekeeping and Peacemaking: Gender Balance and Mainstreaming." In *Women and International Peacekeeping*, edited by Louise Olsson and Torunn L. Tryggestad, 39–48. London: Frank Cass, 2001.

Whitworth, Sandra. *Men, Militarism and UN Peacekeeping: A Gendered Analysis*. Boulder, CO: Lynne Rienner, 2004.

CHAPTER 31

GENDER, WARS OF GLOBALIZATION, AND HUMANITARIAN INTERVENTIONS SINCE THE END OF THE COLD WAR

KRISTEN P. WILLIAMS

THE collapse of the Soviet Union, the revolutions in Eastern Europe that ended communist rule in those countries, and the reunification of Germany marked the end of the Cold War in the early 1990s. This development, however, did not usher in a new period of peace and stability around the world. Instead, almost three decades since the emergence of this new globalized era in world politics, conflicts continue to afflict the international community in the forms of both intrastate and interstate wars. In 2017, conflicts were ongoing in at least twenty-seven states, including Afghanistan, Colombia, Somalia, Syria, and Yemen. Several states have ended wars since the millennium—the United States in Iraq and Afghanistan, Chad, Ivory Coast, Nigeria, Sri Lanka, Kyrgyzstan, and the Philippines—but even here and in many other regions, underlying conflicts persisted and low-level violence or war remained or returned.[1]

A gender perspective provides an invaluable method of understanding these *Wars of Globalization* in the post–Cold War period since the early 1990s, which must be conceptualized as a period of warfare in its own right. Constructions of gender difference are repeatedly contested and subject to change. The contestation and challenges to the gender order are particularly pronounced in times of war.[2] In the following, the ways in which these constructions of gender difference are contested in the context of wars in the contemporary period will be explored by discussing, first, the types of current warfare; second, the current modes of waging war; and, third, debates surrounding humanitarian intervention. One major theme is the connection between masculinities (including hyper- or aggressive masculinity), militarization (and, relatedly, militarized masculinity), and conceptions of security.[3]

The Wars of Globalization as "New Wars"?

An understanding of the types of current warfare is crucial for the "gendering" of the wars in the post–Cold War era. Low-intensity and asymmetrical warfare in various parts of the world might be related to the dispersal of the state's military power to sub-state actors, but it can also represent a continuation of anticolonial and anti-imperial warfare of an earlier age. Wars fought between states and actors that span states—be they the war on terror or the war on drugs, or wars involving mobilization on the basis of a transnational appeal to religion, like the war waged by the Islamic State of Iraq and the Levant (ISIL)—might indicate the emergence of new forms of war, but they could also be interpreted as a resurgence of ways of war of premodern and early modern provenance.

Wars, both interstate and intrastate conflicts, have changed over time. Monty Marshall and Benjamin Cole analyzed the global trends during the period of 1946 to 2013 in terms of intrastate conflict (referred to as societal conflict, or internal warfare: civil, communal, and ethnic) and interstate conflict (external warfare), and they found a substantial decline in the total number of wars. Specifically, wars between opposing countries were relatively uncommon throughout the Cold War. Yet, at the same time, civil wars increased in frequency, becoming more common than interstate wars partly because of the civil wars' longer duration. The definition of *war* is disputed, and Marshall and Cole defined it as needing to have directly caused 500 deaths, whereas other scholars put the threshold at 1,000 annual battlefield deaths.[4] Others, like the 2015 Armed Conflict Dataset Codebook by the Uppsala Conflict Data Program and the International Peace Research Institute, Oslo, define armed conflict as "a contested incompatibility that concerns government and/or territory where the use of armed force between two parties, of which at least one is the government of a state, results in at least 25 battle-related deaths."[5] Moreover, many wars do not easily fit in their typology. Many of the Wars of Decolonization of the 1940s to 1970s, for example, were both interstate and intrastate conflicts. The fact that they often were proxy wars helps to explain why the number of interstate wars remained stable and the number of intrastate wars grew.[6]

With the Cold War's end, many of the protracted intrastate wars also ended, explaining a substantial part of the reduction in global armed conflict.[7] With regard to the outbreak of new wars, both interstate and intrastate, the rate has declined since 1991, the year of the conclusion of Cold War and the start of the contemporary period of globalization.

Since the year 2000, there has been a slight increase in intrastate wars, primarily a result of two events: first, following the US invasion of Iraq in 2003, there occurred an increase in war in the Arab League states, and, second, the "Arab Spring" uprisings starting in Tunisia in 2011 spread within the region.[8] Thus, the first decade of the post–Cold War period saw a decline in intrastate war, while the second decade has been marked by an increase in intrastate war.

Data show that from 1989 onward, over half "of all countries have experienced some major armed conflict (85 of 167 countries)."[9] With regard to casualties, in the course of World War II there were roughly 10 million deaths on average each year; from 1946 to 2011, there have been approximately 476,000 deaths annually from conflict. Of these numbers, civilian deaths accounted for approximately two-thirds of the total deaths in World War II as well as the period from 1946 to 2011.[10] In terms of separating out civilian deaths during the Cold War and the post–Cold War period until 2011, the percentage of noncombatant deaths during armed conflicts appears to have increased from about 62 percent during the Cold War period (1946–1991) to about 84 percent during the Post–Cold war period (1991–2011).[11]

In considering the increase in intrastate conflicts in the contemporary period, regime type may matter. According to Marshall and Cole, "For the first time in human history, the global system is predominantly comprised of independent states and governed by democratic regimes." There were fewer autocracies in 2013 than in the fifty years before: 20 in 2013 versus 89 in the peak year 1977. In addition, the number of states that are experiencing incomplete democratic transitions, so-called anocracies, is rising. In the early 1990s there were 30 such states, and by 2013 there were 49. They include "isolationist regimes, communist and former-communist countries, traditional monarchies, and wealthy oil-producing states." Marshall and Cole note that the danger of new conflicts emerging is greater for anocracies than for democracies (six times more likely) and autocracies (two and a half times as likely), because "anocracies have been highly unstable and transitory regimes, with over fifty percent experiencing a major regime change within five years and over seventy percent within ten years."[12]

Indicative of globalization—that is, the world's increasing interconnectedness caused by the information and communications revolution, the expansion of the global market (along with the concomitant deregulation and privatization of the economy and other indicators), the weakening of the state—and the increased complexity of the international system, events at the local level are affected by and influence both the regional and the global levels.[13] The question therefore arises: Are the wars of the current globalization different from the wars of the past? Political scientist Mary Kaldor coined the term "new war" to refer to "a new type of organized violence developed, especially in Africa and Eastern Europe, which is one aspect of the current globalized era."[14] In essence, the new-wars literature claims that wars are affected by globalization given the existence of transnational actors and that in many parts of the world the state's autonomy and monopoly of legitimate violence are challenged.[15] It categorizes early twenty-first-century wars as civil wars (some of which were simmering during the Cold War, while others erupted after the Cold War ended), failed-states wars (in which the state no longer has the monopoly of violence nor can it provide adequate public goods for its population), and asymmetric wars (with parties to the conflict possessing qualitatively different capabilities).[16]

In contrasting new wars with "old wars," Kaldor's thesis focuses on several factors (actors, goals, methods of warfare, and financing) in the current globalization processes.[17] The actors in the new wars vary—no longer are wars fought primarily between state armies. In addition to regular armies, fighting involves actors such as warlords, organized criminals, private military security companies, and paramilitaries.[18] While many of these wars are considered civil wars, they actually transcend state borders because of the various actors involved. Mark Duffield argues, for example, that early twenty-first century wars are often "nonterritorial network wars," in which privatization and deregulation of the market provides the actors fighting these wars with the ability to create networks at both the local and the global levels. Warring parties can access resources across borders from diaspora groups, social groups, and warlords.[19] As Herfried Münkler asserts, given the various actors involved in the new wars, "war is a permanent field of activity."[20] Concerning the goals of new wars, Kaldor contends that aims tied to religious, ethnic, or national identities have replaced the ideology and geopolitics (territory) of past wars.[21]

Critics of the new-wars thesis raise several objections. First, are these so-called new wars really new? Renee de Nevers asserts, "These 'new' forms of warfare are better understood as a reversion to very old wars"—wars that occurred in early modern Europe in which both battles and plunder occurred "with little distinction made between civilian and soldier."[22] In terms of asymmetric warfare, nineteenth-century European armies had technologically superior weapons in wars of colonization.[23] The use of guerrilla, or irregular, warfare has a long history, too.[24] This is also true for counterinsurgency as both a strategy and a doctrine of asymmetrical warfare.[25] With regard to financing wars, historically they have been financed not just by governments but also "by a range of entrepreneurs and military contractors, often with unsavory reputations."[26] Other scholars, too, do not see a difference between old and new wars; for the wars in the post–Cold War era, they prefer the term Wars of Globalization.[27]

GENDER AND THE WARS OF GLOBALIZATION

Since the 1980s, feminist scholarship has increasingly studied the connection between war, peace, and gender. And yet, the mainstream literature on the wars since the early 1990s has not adequately addressed gender, even though wars, historically and in the contemporary period, rely on constructions of masculinity and femininity and the expected roles and behavior of men and women in any society. It has only begun to rectify the omission of gender in their debate and writings on new wars. Christine Chinkin and Mary Kaldor's 2013 article, "Gender and the New Wars," is one example. They recognize that "there are specific differences in the way gender is constructed in different types of wars" and " 'new wars' can be interpreted as a mechanism for rolling back any gains women may have made in recent decades."[28] Similarly, David Duriesmith claims in his 2014 article, "Is Manhood a Causal Factor in the Shifting Nature of War," that an analysis of masculinity in these new type of conflicts offers explanations for attacks against civilians ignored by earlier studies.[29] For these authors, new wars are bound up with identity politics, and such identities, including ethnic, religious, and tribal identities, are also connected to gender.[30]

This new scholarship by mainstream political scientists tends to ignore, however, the earlier work by feminist scholars like Deniz Kandiyoti. In 1996, she noted in an essay on women, ethnicity, and nationalism that "the association of women with the private domain [home/domestic sphere] reinforces the merging of the nation/community with the selfless mother/devout wife; the obvious response of coming to her defense and even dying for her is automatically triggered."[31] In times of conflict and war, leaders will invoke feminine metaphors, such as mothers of the nation or motherland, to reinforce threats to the nation/ethnic group. Women must be submissive to the goals of the ethnic or national group by accepting their putatively natural roles as women and mothers.[32] In this way, ethnic/national identity is connected to gender identity and used as a legitimation for conflicts.

A gendered identity rhetoric and policy also informs the practice of the conflicts in the post–Cold War era. They are primarily fought not in battles by state-controlled militaries, but by nonstate actors who deliberately target civilians and attain political control of territory through invoking fear and expelling or killing opponents and those with different identities.[33] During attacks, men of fighting age are deliberately targeted, even if they are not combatants. Thus, while women, children, and the elderly are also victims in times of war, more men, both as combatants and as civilians, are killed. As in earlier wars, one of the techniques of population displacement is systematic rape and sexual violence committed primarily against civilian women, although men are also victims of sexual violence.[34] However, according to Chinkin and Kaldor, "the nature of the instrumentalization in new wars is very different. There is little concern about opprobrium, security leaks, or the spread of venereal disease. The rapes are deliberately public, and are meant to instill fear in local populations as part of a plan to destroy or control local communities."[35] They are a group activity, which allows men to perform masculinity and prove their credentials as real men to fellow soldiers.[36]

Additionally, Renee de Nevers argues that child soldiers, including girls, have become more common in the new wars.[37] This is definitely the case if we compare these conflicts with the First and Second World Wars. However, already in some of the Wars of Decolonization after 1945, the inclusion of girls and very young women was practiced by partisan and guerrilla troops of the anticolonial movements, but on a much smaller scale. Their sexual exploitation, including sexual violence, was already a subject of debate then as well.[38]

The financing of wars was and is also highly gendered. Taxation and a centralized war economy that was "total," with all citizens participating, as during the world wars, is no longer the main form of financing wars. Warring groups must find other means of financial support, similar to anticolonial movements in the Wars of Decolonization. These other means of attaining financial support are quite gendered, as V. Spike Peterson and others emphasize.[39] They spring from illicit combat economies based on abduction, looting, and smuggling as highly masculinized activities, which are closely related to criminal economies that involve "petty criminals, conflict entrepreneurs, war profiteers, traffickers, money launderers, and those who produce and/or transport trafficked goods."[40]

The complement to these forms of illicit war financing is what Peterson labeled the "coping economy," which contributes to the survival of individuals and families and is highly feminized. Like in the past, women's duties tend to focus on "sustaining families, households, kinship networks, and even neighborhoods" in times of war. When the economic situation becomes too dire and humanitarian assistance is not available, women even cope by relying on informal and illegal activities such as sex work.[41] In such situations, women may become victims of human trafficking and vulnerable to other forms of (sexual) violence.[42]

GENDERING THE NEW MODES OF WARFARE

Two modes of warfare have gained increasing importance in the wars fought since the end of the Cold War, both of which are highly gendered: advanced technologies (that is, drones, robots, and long-range missiles) and private military security companies (PMSCs). The new, advanced technologies enable states that can afford them to avoid using ground troops from their own army and thus minimize the risk of incurring casualties on the battlefield. Particularly the deployment of drones has increased in the past decade. The number of states with drones (both armed and unarmed) rose from forty-one in 2004 to seventy-six in 2011. Only a handful of these states have deployed armed drones (the United States, Israel, the United Kingdom, China, and Iran), but others, including India, Pakistan, Turkey, and Japan, are also seeking to obtain them.[43] The extent of the United States' drone program is noteworthy. In the period 2008–12, there were more than 1,000 drone strikes in Afghanistan and 48 in Iraq. There were 145 strikes in Libya in 2011.[44] However, on the global black market these new technologies increasingly are also available for nonstate actors. Thomas Ricks therefore claims, "New technologies have also democratized mass violence, enabling non-state actors to use and threaten lethal force on a scale previously associated only with states."[45]

The increased use of drones has led to debates over the benefits and costs of these weapons. Supposed benefits are that such weapons are highly precise, the risk to pilots is minimized, and the risks of ground troops being captured or killed are likewise reduced. At the same time, costs of drones are very high; they affect the defense budgets and could lead to an increase of small-scale conflicts.[46] Critics also contend that there are high numbers of civilian casualties, particularly when, as is the case with US policy, all military-age males in a given target area are considered combatants and as such are perceived to be legitimate targets for drone strikes.[47] Even less than in the two world wars of the twentieth century, is the battlefield, in the conflicts of the early twentieth-first-century, clearly defined and, as a result, the distinction between civilian and combatant has become more blurred.[48]

The use of private military security companies has also increased dramatically in the past two decades, not only by the United States and other developed states, but also by developing states.[49] During the 1991 Gulf War, the ratio of conventional soldiers to private military security companies' employees was estimated at fifty to one. That ratio decreased to ten to one in the US invasion of Iraq in 2003, and in 2007 it narrowed even further, to one to one.[50] The economic, political, and social transformations of the post–Cold War period have led to a "delinking of security from public authority." At the same time, private security firms claim to have gained legitimacy and authority worldwide in the past two decades, because they are able to provide security and stability when states are unable or unwilling to do so.[51] However, critics point to the fact that the security PMSCs provide is usually limited to special targets and that allegations against them for corruption, torture, and unlawful killing are increasing because they operate outside public control. Thus, the rising importance of PMSCs as actors in conflicts around the world does not mean that the state has declined in importance.[52] Peter W. Singer points to three factors that account for their rise: first, the end of the Cold War and the resulting vacuum "in the market of security"; second, "transformations in the nature of warfare"; and, third, "the normative rise of privatization."[53] The existence of private military security companies does raise several serious issues. In addition to the concerns just discussed, the following are pivotal: questions about loyalties and goals that might differ for the client and the company, increasing client dependence on the company, availability of military services and resources on the global market, impact on the balance of power and possibility of arms races, the empowering of nonstate actors, and the impact on human rights.[54]

It is important to recognize, however, that while some modes of warfare indeed have changed since the 1990s, others are a continuation of earlier practices. Analyzing the US invasion of Afghanistan in 2001, Stephen Biddle points out that the war that followed was more conventional, and less revolutionary, than is often assumed.[55] The United States used air power to find targets for precision attack, but faced challenges from Afghan defenders who were able to cover and conceal their fighting positions.[56] Such cover and concealment can be found in nearly any theater of war.[57] Furthermore, Biddle observes that "since at least 1918, all great-power militaries have understood the importance of combining fire and maneuver. The synergy between these elements lies at the heart of all successful twentieth-century tactical systems; it is hardly a product of twenty-first century technology."[58]

The existence and use of private militaries is also not new. As Singer explains, historically, the state monopoly over violence is the exception rather than the rule.[59] Private military forces have existed throughout history. As the modern nation-state system emerged and became the dominant form of political authority, private military forces became less prevalent relative to public/state militaries.[60] Even the current organization of private military forces as corporations is not new.[61] The mercenaries in the past were, indeed, according to Singer, "individual-based in unit of operation" and "ad hoc in organization," working for a single client as "guns for hire." What is new, according to him, is that these private military forces/security companies "are hierarchically organized into incorporated and registered businesses that trade and compete openly on the international market . . . and provide a wider range of military services to a greater variety and number of clients."[62] In addition to warfare, such services also include aid and peacekeeping.[63]

Like in the past, the present changes in the modes of warfare and ways of organizing war are highly gendered. Technological changes affect the constructions of militarized masculinity, especially the notions of "manly soldiering."[64] The link between masculinity and the military is weakened if the technology being utilized does not involve soldiers' direct combat engagement with the enemy on the battlefield.[65] Nevertheless, the narrative of the supersoldier continues to maintain militarized masculinity, as Mary Manjikian observes: "Technological advances create a new soldier who is a more virile and a more deadly male. In this narrative, technology does not protect the soldier but instead enhances the soldier." Thus, while such technologies conceivably open up the opportunity for more combat roles for women, the reality is that what is constructed as "real" soldiering is even today in many militaries still done by males and remains a masculine endeavor, which protects the gender hierarchy inside the military.[66]

Such attempts became important, because, as Lorraine Bayard de Volo contends, drone warfare deprives soldiers of earlier, more respected forms of military masculinity. Drone operators have a relatively low status as warriors, given that they are not pilots flying in planes over the theater of war or ground troops engaged on the battlefield. The result is that changing methods of warfare may result in changes to how ideas like combat and heroism are understood.[67] These readjustments are a function of challenges through three interconnected traits that have traditionally defined men, (idealized) masculinity, and combatants: courage, strength, and "mastery or suppression of emotions." But the extent to which drone pilots must master fear or suppress empathy remains contested.[68]

This whole gender dynamic becomes even more complicated on an international scale, because the powers using drone warfare, especially the United States, are perceived by others as a "high-tech masculine predator," despite their claims they only use this technology for protection.[69] The United States is considered the masculinist protector acting "on behalf of feminized host nations." When it launches drone strikes against targets in Pakistan or Yemen, these states are, in essence, "demasculinized."[70] With the United States defining itself as the masculine protector, drones are perceived as masculine predators by those who could be or are the targets of drone strikes, and this then leads to the emergence of local masculine protectors: drone warfare thus leads to a gendered feedback loop of violence.[71]

Similar to the state military, PMSCs are extremely gendered institutions too. The privatization of military force, according to Maya Eichler, re-establishes the relationship between masculinity and security. In examining the use of PMSCs by the United States, she asserts that with the end of the draft and the rise of neoliberalism, the gender order remains unequal and gendered militarism in the United States and elsewhere is reproduced.[72] Gender inequality is reinforced in these companies, as evidenced by their employment practices: men are the majority of the employees, with females employed in clerical and administrative positions.[73] The PMSCs recruit primarily from former military and police personnel, who are overwhelmingly men.[74] Eichler concludes that "as public militaries are increasingly seen as feminized ... and as taking on feminized tasks such as peacekeeping and development, private contractors have come to represent a 'tough' version of militarized masculinity."[75] This image is enforced by the self-representation of the PMSCs. Based on the analysis of the websites of twenty-three American and British PMSCs, Jutta Joachim and Andrea Schneiker found that they elevated the masculinity of their own companies as protector masculinity by downplaying conventional militaries and international organizations as providers of security.[76]

The increasing integration of women into state militaries has affected the gendered ways in which people discuss military privatization. With this trend, militarized masculinity was no longer tied to being a member of the armed forces. Combat became the locus for defining military masculinity, which is one reason why women are still excluded from combat positions in some state militaries. As state militaries have also become increasingly involved in peacekeeping operations and humanitarian interventions, hegemonic military masculinity became contested because such operations and interventions were perceived as feminine.[77]

NEW FORMS OF HUMANITARIAN INTERVENTION

In the more than two decades since the Cold War ended, humanitarian crises have troubled the international community. Bosnia, Ivory Coast, Rwanda, Libya, Sudan, Syria, and the Democratic Republic of the Congo were some of the locations. All have witnessed the ravages of civil war, and calls for humanitarian intervention to protect civilians and alleviate significant human rights violations have been made. The ethnic cleansing in the Balkans and the genocide in Rwanda in the early and mid-1990s prompted the international community to respond: the Responsibility to Protect (R2P) doctrine in 2005 reflected the emerging standard regarding the international community's duty to prevent genocide, crimes against humanity, war crimes, and ethnic cleansing. And yet, the members of the international community, whether conceived of as the United Nations (UN), international organizations such as the North Atlantic Treaty Organization (NATO) or the African Union, or individual states, have authorized military intervention in some cases, but not in others. In considerations of whether and where to intervene, the tension between maintaining the expectation of state sovereignty on the one hand and the protection of life, reduction of suffering, and prevention of harm on the other remains ever present. Even when intervention does occur, the aftermath of such intervention is fraught with the challenges of peacebuilding as well as the political, economic, and social reconstruction and transformation of society and the state. The question arises as to whether international human rights law and the language of human rights become tools to justify wars and military interventions, particularly in the context of Western intervention in non-Western states.[78]

Humanitarian intervention encompasses material assistance (relief aid) and the threat and use of military force.[79] The use of military force is the most contentious form of humanitarian intervention. Most scholars argue that such military intervention should be used only as a last resort after all diplomatic and coercive, but nonmilitary, measures have failed. While military interventions may be deemed legitimate and permissible, they pose several problems.[80] Gary Bass pointed to five issues. First, given that the goal of humanitarian intervention is the defense of humanity, and yet humans around the world encounter violence, "How do you intervene in one spot and not another without drawing accusations of hypocrisy?" Second, domestic pressures push Western democratic leaders to lower-cost and lower-risk forms of humanitarianism. They are concerned that they will lose public support if an intervention is too costly or goes wrong. Third, such "interventions tend to use limited means, while flirting with maximalist goals." Intervening states may support air strikes and protecting no-fly zones, but they are less likely to support combat troops on the ground. Fourth, the so-called humanitarian wars are usually not limited, but actually escalate. And finally, with war escalating and widening following the initial intervention, intervening states are reluctant to send in their own ground troops. As such, they then look to local forces to continue fighting.[81]

Despite these and other problems, the post–Cold War period saw increased pressure on states and the international community to intervene militarily to alleviate humanitarian crises in other countries. Even so, humanitarian intervention is not new, but rather gained increasing importance after the Second World War.[82] During the Cold War era, humanitarian emergencies, such as the 1971 East Pakistan genocidal crisis that culminated in the Third Indo-Pakistani War and the famine in Ethiopia (1983–85), garnered public support and sympathy for the dire situation of the people in these places, but were not considered consequential political events that would lead to significant intervention by other states. Governments and humanitarian relief organizations provided humanitarian assistance, but not large-scale intervention.[83] With the end of the Cold War, changes in the evolution of the standards of humanitarian intervention were evident, particularly in light of the perceived new wars and globalization. The 1990s and subsequent decades saw failed states or wars with massive numbers of refugees seeking safety in other countries. What is telling about the large-scale, post–Cold War humanitarian interventions is that they have been multilateral—with more than two countries providing troops—with or without UN endorsement.[84] Examples abound: the UN mission in Somalia (1989–95), the European Union, UN, and NATO efforts in Bosnia (1993–2003), NATO in Kosovo (1999) and in Libya (2011), and France in Mali (2013), with forces from several west African countries, including Nigeria and Senegal (and the UN backed the French intervention).

What we have witnessed is an evolution of the norm of humanitarian intervention given the tension between state sovereignty, as enshrined in the UN Charter (Article 2), and promoting the respect for human rights and justice (Article 1, the Universal Declaration of Human Rights, and other UN documents). To resolve this tension, the expectation of humanitarian intervention is a "permissive norm" in that there are instances of humanitarian disaster and significant human rights abuses that may not necessarily lead to intervention. Moreover, there are, as Martha Finnemore notes, "strict requirements on the ways in which intervention . . . may be carried out."[85]

In the contemporary period, state sovereignty is no longer absolute, as evidenced by the UN doctrine, the Responsibility to Protect, which emerged from the 2001 report of the Canadian government's International Commission on Intervention and State Sovereignty. Acknowledging that states have the responsibility to protect their citizens, the report asserted that the international community could respond when states were unwilling or unable to do so. The adoption of the principle of R2P by the UN General Assembly at the 2005 World Summit demonstrates the continued evolution of the standards for humanitarian intervention. It reconciles sovereignty with human rights, with the focusing on four egregious human rights violations that warrant a response by the international community: crimes against humanity, genocide, ethnic cleansing, and war crimes.[86] Such new standards of humanitarian intervention and the protection of civilians in armed conflict were important to the UN Security Council's enactment of several general resolutions, including Resolution 1296 from 2006. The resolution stated that "systematic, flagrant and widespread violations of international humanitarian and human rights law in situations of armed conflict may constitute a threat to international peace and security" that could lead the Security Council to respond, including the use of force. Also, UN Resolution 1674 from 2006 recognized the "responsibility to protect."[87]

The UN Security Council invoked R2P for the first time when it passed a resolution in 2006 that expanded its mission in Darfur, Sudan. In 2011, the Security Council referred to the doctrine in regard to UN Support Mission in Libya during its civil war. As Adam Branch notes, in the case of Libya, in the name of protecting innocents, the intervening powers bombed civilian infrastructure, overthrew and killed the country's leader, put in power a rebel government, and provided weapons to civilians. It was not clear, however, that massive human rights violations (such as genocide or ethnic cleansing) were happening. For him and others, R2P is dangerous because it offers flexible justifications for deposing governments and arming civilians while also enabling intervening countries to shirk responsibility for their actions. States can justify their intervention on the basis of protection rather than military or political reasons. Branch warns, "All is fair when civilian protection is at stake. R2P can be used to justify military intervention or non-intervention, invasion or withdrawal."[88]

GENDER AND THE
"NEW HUMANITARIANISM"

All forms of humanitarian intervention and the rhetoric that legitimates them are highly gendered. Decision makers frame intervention as a masculine endeavor in which men are the protectors, and women and children are framed as the protected and constructed as victims. Male soldiers/hegemonic masculinity are positioned in hierarchical relation to women/femininity and other men/masculinities, thereby reinforcing gender stereotypes. Furthermore, women usually are not included in the decisions to intervene or in the peace processes, even though the UN, through the passage of various resolutions, recognizes that women's participation matters for stable peace. They are only involved in the peacekeeping operations themselves, though women account for a small percentage of peacekeepers.[89]

In the rhetoric that legitimates humanitarian interventions, Laura Sjoberg and Jessica Peet observe a "protection racket" at play, which is merely a legitimizing rhetoric: "Women are promised protection from wars by men who then take credit for protecting them, while not actually doing so."[90] All arguments for intervention rely on a language of crisis in which civilians, equated with women and children, are menaced by violence and disorder, barring the use of force by the international community, which is constructed as a masculine hero. The states that are targeted for intervention appear as passive and effeminate victims.[91] The gendered narratives are also present in the postconflict, postintervention period, when a state and society are recovering from war. Those in the West engaged in peacebuilding tend to describe them as failed states in need of international guardians. A gendered and racialized discourse situates the international community, Maria O'Reilly observes, "as the heroic, altruistic, white male necessary to protect the vulnerable, inferior, feminized 'other'—the State/society it must rescue."[92]

Typical examples of the discussed connection between gender, war, and the humanitarian intervention narrative are the Bosnian War (1992–95) and its postconflict period and the US intervention in Afghanistan that started in 2001. In the postconflict period in Bosnia, the UN installed the Office of the High Representative as the administrative office and person overseeing the implementation of the 1995 Dayton peace agreement that had ended the war. In the UN rhetoric, according to O'Reilly, "gendered images were mobilized to construct the High Representative as a masculine protector intervening in a country still traumatized by war, and to differentiate between '(ir)rational', '(ir)responsible' and '(im)mature' partners for peace within" the country.[93] In analyzing the autobiography of high representative Paddy Ashdown, who served from 2002 to 2006, she finds gendered and racialized imagery throughout. She notes that the dire situation facing Bosnian women was highlighted in his text: "They are presented as pitiful refugees, desperate mothers/carers, traumatized prisoners and as the defenseless victims of sexual violence." Moreover, the various Bosnian Serb, Croatian, and Serbian leaders are described as "deviant, threatening and hyper-masculine models of masculinity requiring punishment and correction by the West."[94]

A gendered rhetoric was also used to legitimate the US invasion of Afghanistan following the terrorist attacks on September 11, 2001. Originally, the invasion was justified as a response to the terrorist attacks. But soon the rhetoric changed, and a narrative of rescue and humanitarianism emerged. The US government situated itself as the protector of oppressed Afghan women, victims of the ruling Taliban regime. On November 17, 2001, one month after the United States launched the invasion, Republican President George W. Bush's wife, First Lady Laura Bush, delivered the president's weekly address in which she highlighted the Taliban's oppression of women and children. Since then, a rescue narrative has legitimated the US military intervention. Accordingly, in his 2002 State of the Union address, President Bush stated, "The last time we met in this chamber the mothers and daughters of Afghanistan were captives in their own homes, forbidden from working or going to school. Today women are free, and are part of Afghanistan's new government."[95] Much as happened in other conflicts, this narrative was also racialized, as Afghan women have been freed from Afghan men by (predominantly) White American men.[96]

Such highly gendered rhetoric and practices usually ignore gender-specific experiences, interests, and needs during and after conflicts. One factor that fosters this rhetoric and these practices is the fact that in the UN and other international organizations (such as NATO), policy development and decision making are mainly male endeavors. Since the 1990s, the UN increasingly has recognized in its declarations that this has far-reaching negative consequences for its peacebuilding missions and humanitarian interventions, but little has changed.

One example is UN Security Council Resolution 1325, passed in October 2000, which called for women's participation in peace negotiations. This was the first Security Council resolution that recognized the gendered dimensions of conflict. Since then, the Security Council has passed nine subsequent resolutions reaffirming this position and focusing on particular aspects of the impact of conflict on girls and women, including protection of women from gender-based sexual violence in conflict and disarmament/demobilization/reintegration of female ex-combatants.[97] Despite the passage of these resolutions, very few women are actually involved in the peace processes—at the negotiating table, in UN peacekeeping missions, or in formal government structures.

While UN Security Council Resolution 1325 and subsequent resolutions have focused on a women, peace, and security agenda, it is not clear that the humanitarian-intervention doctrine, R2P from 2005, as it is currently conceived, elevates and prioritizes women's and gender concerns. From the start, it was gender biased—on the 2001 International Commission on Intervention and State Sovereignty (ICISS), only one member of twelve total commissioners was female.[98] Even though in 2001 there were international documents and principles regarding women's rights violations and violence against women (for example, the Committee for the Elimination of Discrimination against Women; 1325), these violations were not included in the report of the International Commission on Intervention and State Sovereignty "within the core principles of sovereignty as responsibility."[99] In the few instances when women are mentioned, it is in terms of women as victims, namely as victims of rape.[100]

Eight years after the ICISS report and four years after R2P, the UN secretary-general's 2009 report, *Implementing the Responsibility to Protect (RtoP)*, in recognition of UN resolutions on gender-based sexual violence (that is, Resolution 1820, passed in 2008), "reiterated, for the first time in the context of the norm [of the responsibility to protect], that rape and other forms of sexual violence could constitute crimes against humanity, war crimes, or constitutive acts with respect to genocide."[101] Discussions surrounding R2P have begun to indicate some understanding of how conflicts affect women, men, girls, and boys differently, but there continues to be a disconnect as women and gender remain marginal in the R2P. Women and girls are seen as victims of gender-based sexual violence during conflict, without recognizing that conflict affects women and girls in many different ways. Moreover, the debates over R2P often do not highlight the fact that women can contribute to conflict resolution and peacebuilding, as called for by UN Security Council Resolution 1325 and later resolutions.[102] Through R2P, the UN has contributed to a policy of humanitarian intervention that fosters gender-related conflicts and challenges in the regions of UN operations.

CONCLUSION

War has remained an enduring presence in the post–Cold War period, one marked by an increasingly globalized world. Whether these Wars of Globalization are correctly defined as "new wars" or are a continuation of characteristics of wars past, gender matters. The contemporary period of globalization has brought with it changes in the modes of warfare, as evidenced by the new types of advanced technologies (for example, drones) and the significant presence of private military security companies that challenge and complement state militaries. These modes of warfare are also related to gender as the binary conceptions of masculinity/femininity, protector/protected, and villain/victim are reinforced and maintained in wartime, even if they are simultaneously the sites of contestation. The warrior/soldier remains defined as male/masculine, while the civilian/victim is defined as female/feminine, although an increasing number of women are joining the militaries of several Western states and the UN peacekeeping forces.[103]

In addition to the modes of warfare being highly gendered, so too is humanitarian intervention. The end of the twentieth and beginning of the twenty-first century have been marked by calls for humanitarian intervention to end or prevent massive human rights violations and resolve conflicts. The international community has promoted doctrines, like R2P, which reflect the humanitarian-intervention norm, including military intervention. As this chapter has shown, decision makers continue to frame humanitarian intervention as a masculine activity in which men are protectors, while women and children are still the protected. Gender stereotypes are reinforced when male soldiers and hegemonic masculinity are located hierarchically relative to women, femininity, and other men and masculinities. While the international community has passed resolutions recognizing the link between women, peace, and security, the decisions to intervene are made primarily by men, as is the case with peace processes and peace-keeping operations.

Consequently, future research should continue to focus on analyzing and assessing both interstate and intrastate wars and the ways in which wars are organized and fought, as both individual states and international organizations grapple with the impact of interstate and intrastate conflict, especially in terms of humanitarian crises. In so doing, research should interrogate how gender and gendered discourses continue to impact the wars and conflicts and how they are likely to affect wars and conflicts in the future.

Notes

1. These data are for mid-2017; for the list of states, see Monty G. Marshall and Gabrielle Elzinga-Marshall, *Global Report 2017: Conflict, Governance, and State Fragility* (Vienna, VA: Center for Systemic Peace, 2017), 26, accessed April 10, 2020, http://www.systemic-peace.org/vlibrary/GlobalReport2017.pdf. Another source for current armed conflicts is Global Security, "Military: The World at War," accessed September 16, 2017, http://www.globalsecurity.org/military/world/war/index.html.

2. See, as introductory studies, Lois Ann Lorentzen and Jennifer Turpin, eds., *The Women and War Reader* (New York: New York University Press, 1998); Cynthia Cockburn, *The Space between Us: Negotiating Gender and National Identities in Conflict* (London: Zed Books, 1998); Cynthia Enloe, *Bananas, Beaches and Bases: Making Feminist Sense of International Politics* (Berkeley: University of California Press, 1990); Enloe, *Maneuvers: The International Politics of Militarizing Women's Lives* (Berkeley: University of California Press, 2000); Joshua S. Goldstein, *War and Gender: How Gender Shapes the War System and Vice Versa* (Cambridge: Cambridge University Press, 2001); Joyce P. Kaufman and Kristen P. Williams, *Women at War, Women Building Peace: Challenging Gender Norms* (Boulder, CO: Kumarian Press, 2013); Mary H. Moran, "Gender, Militarism, and Peace-Building: Projects of the Postconflict Moment," *Annual Review of Anthropology* 39 (2010): 261–74; V. Spike Peterson and Anne Sisson Runyan, *Global Gender Issues* (Boulder, CO: Westview Press, 1999); Laura Sjoberg, *Gender, War, and Conflict* (Malden, MA: Polity Press, 2014); J. Ann Tickner, *Gender in International Relations: Feminist Perspectives on Achieving Global Security* (New York: Columbia University Press, 1992); Tickner, *Gendering World Politics* (Cambridge: Cambridge University Press, 2001); and Nira Yuval-Davis, *Gender and Nation* (London: Sage, 1997).

3. See, for a discussion of the concept of masculinity, R. W. Connell and James W. Messerschmidt, "Hegemonic Masculinity: Rethinking the Concept," *Gender and Society* 19, no. 6 (2005): 829–59.

4. Monty G. Marshall and Benjamin R. Cole, *Global Report 2014: Conflict, Governance, and State Fragility* (Vienna, VA: Center for Systemic Peace, 2014), 12, accessed September 16, 2017, http://www.systemicpeace.org/vlibrary/GlobalReport2014.pdf. Meredith Reid Sarkees, "The COW Typology of War: Defining and Categorizing Wars (Version 4 of the Data)."

782   KRISTEN P. WILLIAMS

5. See Dataset Codebook by the Uppsala Conflict Data Program and the International Peace Research Institute, Oslo, 2018, 1, accessed February 13, 2020, https://ucdp.uu.se/downloads/ucdpprio/ucdp-prio-acd-181.pdf.

6. See the chapter by Raphaëlle Branche on "Gender, the Wars of Decolonization, and the Decline of Empires after 1945" in this handbook.

7. Marshall and Cole, *Global Report 2014*, 12.

8. Ibid.

9. Ibid., 13. Marshall and Cole only include countries with a total population of 500,000 people or more.

10. Ibid., 18.

11. Ibid., 19.

12. Ibid., 24 and 27.

13. Mary Kaldor, "Human Security," *Society and Economy* 33, no. 3 (2011): 444; and Marshall and Cole, *Global Report 2014*, 26–27.

14. Mary Kaldor, *New and Old Wars: Organized Violence in a Global Era*, 3rd ed. (Stanford, CA: Stanford University Press, 2012), 1. For other works on wars and conflict in the contemporary period, see Mark Duffield, *Global Governance and the New Wars: The Merging of Development and Security* (London: Zed Books, 2001); Chris Hables Gray, *Postmodern War: The New Politics of Conflict* (New York: Guilford Press, 1997); Herfried Münkler, *The New Wars* (Cambridge: Polity Press, 2005); and Donald M. Snow, *Uncivil Wars: International Security and the New Internal Conflicts* (Boulder, CO: Lynne Rienner, 1996).

15. Kaldor, *New and Old*, 5.

16. Renee de Nevers, "The Geneva Conventions and New Wars," *Political Science Quarterly* 121, no. 3 (2006): 369–95.

17. Kaldor, *New and Old*, 7; for an overview of the new-wars literature, see Jacob Mundy, "The Science, Aesthetics and Management of Late Warfare: An Introduction," *Critical Studies on Security* 1, no. 2 (2013): 143–58; Martin Shaw, "Review Essays: The Contemporary Mode of Warfare? Mary Kaldor's Theory of New Wars," *Review of International Political Economy* 7, no. 1 (2000): 171–80; Münkler, *The New Wars*; Duffield, *Global Governance*; Patrick A. Mello, "In Search of New Wars: The Debate about a Transformation of War," *European Journal of International Relations* 16, no. 2 (2010): 297–309; and Edward Newman, "The 'New Wars' Debate: A Historical Perspective Is Needed," *Security Dialogue* 35, no. 2 (2004): 173–89.

18. Kaldor, *New and Old*, 9; and Newman, "'New Wars' Debate," 175.

19. Duffield, *Global Governance*, 14.

20. Münkler, *The New Wars*, 1.

21. Kaldor, *New and Old*, 7.

22. de Nevers, "The Geneva Conventions," 377.

23. Ibid., 378.

24. Max Boot, "The Evolution of Irregular War: Insurgents and Guerrillas from Akkadia to Afghanistan," *Foreign Affairs* 92, no. 2 (2013): 100–14.

25. Keally McBride and Annick T. R. Wibben, "The Gendering of Counterinsurgency in Afghanistan," *Humanity* 3, no. 2 (2012): 199–215; and Laleh Khalili, "Gendered Practices of Counterinsurgency," *Review of International Studies* 37, no. 4 (2011): 1471–91.

26. de Nevers, "The Geneva Conventions," 378.

27. Mello, "In Search," 305; and Newman, "'New Wars' Debate," 179.

28. Christine Chinkin and Mary Kaldor, "Gender and New Wars," *Journal of International Affairs* 67, no. 1 (2013): 167–87, 168.

29. David Duriesmith, "Is Manhood a Causal Factor in the Shifting Nature of War? The Case of Sierra Leone's Revolutionary United Front," *International Feminist Journal of Politics* 16, no. 2 (2014): 236–54.

30. Chinkin and Kaldor, "Gender," 171.

31. Deniz Kandiyoti, "Women, Ethnicity and Nationalism," in *Ethnicity*, ed. John Hutchinson and Anthony D. Smith (Oxford: Oxford University Press, 1996), 311–16, 315.

32. Julie Mostov, "Sexing the Nation/Desexing the Body: Politics of National Identity in the Former Yugoslavia," in *Gender Ironies of Nationalism: Sexing the Nation*, ed. Tamar Mayer (London: Routledge, 2000), 98–102.

33. Chinkin and Kaldor, "Gender," 173.

34. Ibid.; and Kaldor, *New and Old*, 105. See also the chapters by Regina Mühlhäuser on "Sexuality, Sexual Violence, and the Military in the Age of the World Wars," and Dubravka Zarkov on "Conceptualizing Sexual Violence in Post–Cold War Global Conflicts" in this handbook.

35. Chinkin and Kaldor, "Gender," 175.

36. Jane L. Parpart, "Masculinity, Gender and the 'New Wars,'" *Nordic Journal for Masculinity Studies* 5, no. 2 (2010): 86–99.

37. de Nevers, "The Geneva Conventions," 382.

38. See Branche, "Gender, the Wars of Decolonization" in this handbook.

39. Chinkin and Kaldor, "Gender," 175–76; and V. Spike Peterson, "'New Wars' and Gendered Economies," *Feminist Review* 88 (2008): 7–20.

40. Peterson, "'New Wars,'" 15–16.

41. Ibid., 15.

42. Chinkin and Kaldor, "Gender," 175–76.

43. Sarah Kreps and Micah Zenko, "The Next Drone Wars: Preparing for Proliferation," *Foreign Affairs* 93, no. 2 (2014): 68–79.

44. Ibid., 71.

45. Thomas E. Ricks, "The Future of War (II): As the Nature of War Changes, the Familiar Dividing Lines of Our World Are Blurring across the Board," *Foreign Policy*, January 15, 2014, accessed March 17, 2017, http://foreignpolicy.com/2014/07/30/the-future-of-war-ii-as-the-nature-of-war-changes-the-familiar-dividing-lines-of-our-world-are-blurring-across-the-board-2/.

46. Kreps and Zenko, "Next Drone Wars," 68, 71, and 75; Lorraine Bayard de Volo, "Unmanned? Gender Recalibrations and the Rise of Drone Warfare," *Politics & Gender* 12, no. 1 (2016): 50–77; also Audrey Kurth Cronin, "Why Drones Fail: When Tactics Drive Strategy," *Foreign Affairs* 92, no. 4 (2013): 44–54; Daniel Byman, "Why Drones Work: The Case for Washington's Weapon of Choice," *Foreign Affairs* 92, no. 4 (2013): 32–43; and Jack M. Beard, "Law and War in the Virtual Era," *American Journal of International Law* 103, no. 3 (2009): 409–45.

47. Bayard de Volo, "Unmanned?," 54.

48. Byman, "Why Drones Work," 42.

49. Peter W. Singer, "Corporate Warriors: The Rise of the Privatized Military Industry and Its Ramifications for International Security," *International Security* 26, no. 3 (2001/02): 186–220.

50. Jutta Joachim and Andrea Schneiker, "(Re)Masculinizing Security? Gender and Private Military and Security Companies," in *Gender, Agency and Political Violence*, ed. Linda Ahall and Laura J. Shepherd (Basingstoke: Palgrave Macmillan, 2012), 39–54, 39.

51. Rita Abrahamsen and Michael C. Williams, "Selling Security: Assessing the Impact of Military Privatization," *Review of International Political Economy* 15, no. 1 (2008): 131–46.

52. Ibid., 142.

53. Singer, "Corporate Warriors," 193.

54. Ibid., 202–15; also Abrahamsen and Williams, "Selling Security," 137–38.

55. Stephen Biddle, "Afghanistan and the Future of Warfare," *Foreign Affairs* 82, no. 2 (2003): 31–46.

56. Ibid., 36.

57. Ibid., 38.

58. Ibid., 45.

59. Singer, "Corporate Warriors," 190.

60. Ibid., 190–91; also Abrahamsen and Williams, "Selling Security."

61. David Parrott, *The Business of War: Military Enterprise and Military Revolution in Early Modern Europe* (Cambridge: Cambridge University Press, 2012).

62. Singer, "Corporate Warriors," 191.

63. Abrahamsen and Williams, "Selling Security," 135.

64. McBride and Wibben, "Gendering," 209.

65. Cristina Masters, "Bodies of Technology: Cyborg Soldiers and Militarized Masculinities," *International Feminist Journal of Politics* 7, no. 1 (2005): 112–32.

66. Mary Manjikian, "Becoming Unmanned: The Gendering of Lethal Autonomous Warfare Technology," *International Feminist Journal of Politics* 16, no. 1 (2014): 48–65. On women as drone combatants, see Bayard de Volo, "Unmanned?," 72–73.

67. Bayard de Volo, "Unmanned?," 52.

68. Ibid., 56–57.

69. Ibid., 52.

70. Ibid., 63.

71. Ibid., 73.

72. Maya Eichler, "Gender and the Privatization of Security: Neoliberal Transformation of the Militarized Gender Order," *Critical Studies on Security* 1, no. 3 (2013): 311–25.

73. Ibid., 312.

74. Saskia Stachowitsch, "Military Privatization and the Remasculinization of the State: Making the Link between the Outsourcing of Military Security and Gendered State Transformations," *International Relations* 27, no. 1 (2013): 71–94.

75. Eichler, "Gender," 321.

76. Joachim and Schneiker, "(Re)Masculinizing?," 46.

77. Stachowitsch, "Military Privatization," 85. See also the chapters by Karen Hagemann on "History and Memory of Female Military Service in the Age of World Wars," and Karen Hagemann and D'Ann Campbell on "Post-1945 Western Militaries, Female Soldiers, and Gay and Lesbian Rights" in this handbook.

78. See the chapter by Sandra Whitworth on "The United Nations, Gendered Human Rights, and Peacekeeping since 1945" in this handbook.

79. Alex de Waal and Rakiya Omaar, "Can Military Intervention Be 'Humanitarian'?," *Middle East Research and Information Project, MER,* no. 187 (2015), accessed March 17, 2017, http://www.merip.org/mer/mer187/can-military-intervention-be-humanitarian.

80. De Waal and Omaar, "Can Military"; and Ahmed Khaled Rashid, "Is Humanitarian Intervention Ever Morally Justified?" *E-International Relations Studies,* March 13, 2012, accessed March 17, 2017, http://www.e-ir.info/2012/03/13/is-humanitarian-intervention-ever-morally-justified/; see also Walden Bello, "The Crisis of Humanitarian Intervention," *Foreign Policy in Focus,* August 9, 2011, accessed March 17, 2017, http://fpif.org/the_crisis_

of_humanitarian_intervention/; and Benjamin A. Valentino, "The True Costs of Humanitarian Intervention: The Hard Truth about a Noble Notion," *Foreign Affairs* 90, no. 6 (2011): 60–73.

81. Gary J. Bass, "Why Humanitarian Wars Can Go So Wrong," *Washington Post*, April 8, 2011; see also UN High Commissioner for Refugees, "2015 UNHCR Country Operations Profile-Syrian Arab Republic," 2015, accessed September 16, 2017, http://www.unhcr.org/pages/49e486a76.html.

82. Martha Finnemore, "Constructing Norms of Humanitarian Intervention," in *The Culture of National Security: Norms and Identity in World Politics*, ed. Peter J. Katzenstein (New York: Columbia University Press, 1996), 153–85. See the chapters by Jean H. Quataert on "Changing Modes of Warfare and the Gendering of Military Medical Care, 1850s–1920s," and Glenda Sluga on "Gender, Peace, and the New Politics of Humanitarianism in the First Half of the Twentieth Century" in this handbook.

83. Randolph C. Kent, "International Humanitarian Crises: Two Decades Before and Two Decades Beyond," *International Affairs* 80, no. 5 (2004): 851–69.

84. Finnemore, "Constructing," 180.

85. Ibid., 181.

86. Monica Serrano, "The Responsibility to Protect and Its Critics: Explaining the Consensus," *Global Responsibility to Protect* 3, no. 4 (2011): 425–37; and Coalition for the International Criminal Court, "Core Crimes Defined in the Rome Statute of the International Criminal Court," accessed September 16, 2017, http://www.iccnow.org/documents/FS-CICC-CoreCrimesinRS.pdf.

87. Aurelio Viotti, "In Search of Symbiosis: The Security Council in the Humanitarian Domain," *International Review of the Red Cross* 89, no. 865 (2007): 131–53, 148.

88. Adam Branch, "The Responsibility to Protect: What Is the Basis for the Emerging Norm of R2P?" *Think Africa Press*, November 6, 2012, https://www.globalpolicy.org/qhumanitarianq-intervention/52035-the-responsibility-to-protect-what-is-the-basis-for-the-emerging-norm-of-r2p.html?itemid=id#26087. For further critiques of R2P, see Hilary Charlesworth, "Feminist Reflections on the Responsibility to Protect," *Global Responsibility to Protect* 2, no. 3 (2010): 232–49; Diana Johnstone, "Responsibility to Protect Is a Power Play," *Minneapolis Star Tribune*, January 25, 2013, accessed February 13, 2020, https://www.globalpolicy.org/qhumanitarianq-intervention/52236-responsibility-to-protect-is-a-power-play.html?itemid=id; and Lou Pingeot and Wolfgang Obenland, *In Whose Name? A Critical View of the Responsibility to Protect* (Bonn: Global Policy Forum, 2014).

89. See Whitworth, "The United Nations, Gendered Human Rights" in this handbook.

90. Laura Sjoberg and Jessica Peet, "A(nother) Dark Side of the Protection Racket," *International Feminist Journal of Politics* 13, no. 2 (2011): 163–82, 167.

91. Anne Orford, "Muscular Humanitarianism: Reading the Narratives of the New Interventionism," *European Journal of International Law* 10, no. 4 (1999): 679–711.

92. Maria O'Reilly, "Muscular Interventionism: Gender, Power and Liberal Peacebuilding in Post-Conflict Bosnia-Herzegovina," *International Feminist Journal of Politics* 14, no. 4 (2012): 529–48, 535.

93. Ibid., 531.

94. Ibid., 537–38.

95. Iris Marion Young, "The Logic of Masculinist Protection: Reflections on the Current Security State," *Signs* 29, no. 1 (2003): 1–25, 17.

96. Helen M. Kinsella, "Discourses of Difference: Civilians, Combatants, and Compliance with the Laws of War," *Review of International Studies* 31 (2005): 163–85.

97. The UN Security Council Resolutions 1820 (2008), 1888 (2009), 1889 (2009), 1960 (2010), 2106 (2013), 2122 (2013), 2242 (2015), 2467 (2019), and 2493 (2019).

98. Sara E. Davies and Sarah Teitt, "Engendering the Responsibility to Protect: Women and the Prevention of Mass Atrocities," *Global Responsibility to Protect* 4, no. 2 (2012): 198–222. See also Whitworth, "The United Nations, Gendered Human Rights" in this handbook.

99. Davies and Teitt, "Engendering the Responsibility," 201.

100. Ibid., 202.

101. "Women and the Responsibility to Protect," *International Coalition for the Responsibility to Protect*, March 9, 2012, accessed September 16, 2017, http://icrtopblog.org/2012/03/09/women-and-the-responsibility-to-protect/.

102. Davies and Teitt, "Engendering the Responsibility," 199; and Jennifer Bond and Laurel Sherret, "Mapping Gender and the Responsibility to Protect: Seeking Intersections, Finding Parallels," *Global Responsibility to Protect* 4, no. 2 (2012): 133–53.

103. See Hagemann and Campbell, "Post-1945 Western Militaries," and Whitworth "The United Nations" in this handbook.

Select Bibliography

Bayard de Volo, Lorraine. "Unmanned? Gender Recalibrations and the Rise of Drone Warfare." *Politics & Gender* 12, no. 1 (2016): 50–77.

Charlesworth, Hilary. "Feminist Reflections on the Responsibility to Protect." *Global Responsibility to Protect* 2, no. 3 (2010): 232–49.

Chinkin, Christine, and Mary Kaldor. "Gender and New Wars." *Journal of International Affairs* 67, no. 1 (2013): 167–87.

Cockburn, Cynthia. *The Space between Us: Negotiating Gender and National Identities in Conflict*. London: Zed Books, 1998.

Connell, R. W., and James W. Messerschmidt. "Hegemonic Masculinity: Rethinking the Concept." *Gender and Society* 19, no. 6 (2005): 829–59.

Duffield, Mark. *Global Governance and the New Wars: The Merging of Development and Security*. London: Zed Books, 2001.

Enloe, Cynthia. *Maneuvers: The International Politics of Militarizing Women's Lives*. Berkeley: University of California Press, 2000.

Finnemore, Martha. "Constructing Norms of Humanitarian Intervention." In *The Culture of National Security: Norms and Identity in World Politics*, edited by Peter J. Katzenstein, 153–85. New York: Columbia University Press, 1996.

Goldstein, Joshua S. *War and Gender: How Gender Shapes the War System and Vice Versa*. Cambridge: Cambridge University Press, 2001.

Kaldor, Mary. *New and Old Wars: Organized Violence in a Global Era*. 3rd ed. Stanford, CA: Stanford University Press, 2012.

Kaufman, Joyce P., and Kristen P. Williams. *Women at War, Women Building Peace: Challenging Gender Norms*. Boulder, CO: Kumarian Press, 2013.

Lorentzen, Lois Ann, and Jennifer Turpin, eds. *The Women and War Reader*. New York: New York University Press, 1998.

Newman, Edward. "The 'New Wars' Debate: A Historical Perspective Is Needed." *Security Dialogue* 35, no. 2 (2004): 173–89.

Peterson, V. Spike. "'New Wars' and Gendered Economies." *Feminist Review* 88, no. 1 (2008): 7–20.

Serrano, Monica. "The Responsibility to Protect and Its Critics: Explaining the Consensus." *Global Responsibility to Protect* 3, no. 4 (2011): 425–37.

Singer, P. W. "Corporate Warriors: The Rise of the Privatized Military Industry and Its Ramifications for International Security." *International Security* 26, no. 3 (2001–2): 186–220.

Sjoberg, Laura. *Gender, War and Conflict*. Malden, MA: Polity Press, 2014.

Sjoberg, Laura, and Jessica Peet. "A(nother) Dark Side of the Protection Racket." *International Feminist Journal of Politics* 13, no. 2 (2011): 163–82.

Tickner, J. Ann. *Gendering World Politics: Issues and Approaches in the Post–Cold War Era*. New York: Columbia University Press, 2001.

Valentino, Benjamin A. "The True Costs of Humanitarian Intervention: The Hard Truth about a Noble Notion." *Foreign Affairs* 90, no. 6 (2011): 60–73.

Index

Aal the Dragoon (?–before 1710) 84
abolition / abolitionism 136, 140, 143–46,
    169, 243
    abolition of slaves 129, 243, 249, 349, 352,
        521, 524, 527, 562
    abolitionist movement 169, 216, 249, 298,
        349, 352, 562
    British and Foreign Anti-Slavery
        Society 562
    British Slave Trade Act (1807) 136
    Slavery Abolition Act (1833) 136
    Society for Effecting the Abolition of the
        Slave Trade 169
    World Conference of Abolition / World
        Anti-Slavery Convention, London
        (1840) 562
Aborigines (Australia) 317, 329–42
abortion 18, 397, 441, 594, 727
absolutism 44, 77, 129
Abu Ghraib 18, 728, 734–35
Adams, Abigail (1744–1818) 110
Adams, John (1735–1826) 110
Addams, Jane (1860–1935) 561, 562, 566, 573
Afghanistan
    Afghanistan War (2001–ongoing) see under
        wars
    Soviet–Afghan War (1979–88) 644, 655
Africa 3, 6, 13, 19–20, 49, 99, 138–39, 141–43,
    148, 191, 231
    East 245, 377, 519–20, 527
    North 236, 319, 334, 374, 385, 519, 544, 644,
        651–52
    West 50, 100, 208, 315, 333, 394, 527, 756
    Southwest 244, 322, 377–78, 396
African Americans 217, 242, 336, 393–94, 425,
    443, 458, 511–12, 541, 543, 598
    freedmen 300
    freedwomen 300

soldiers 107, 216, 298, 510, 706
women 290, 455–58, 706
Age / Era / period of
    Caudillo 123
    Global Cold War (1946–91) 635–760
    Nation and Empires 227–361
    Revolutions (1770s–1840s) 136–149, 202,
        218, 252–53, 472, 702
    the Wars of Revolution and Independence
        (1770s–1820s) see under wars
    World Wars (1910s–40s) see under wars
Ahmed, Selim (Dahoum) (c. 1897–1916) 311
air warfare see under warfare
Akashi, Yasushi (1931–) 755, 757
Albania 381, 483, 617, 647, 698
Algeria
    Algerian War (1954–62) see under wars
    Armée de libération nationale (ALN) 688
    colonial soldiers / troops 245, 519, 688
    Dahra massacre (1845) 332
    French Algeria (1830–1962) 245, 332, 522,
        614, 652–53, 680–91
    Front de libération nationale (FLN)
        680–81, 686–91
allowances for military personnel and their
        families see under welfare
America
    Central 50, 100, 148, 291–97, 649,
        653–54, 661
    North 6, 12–13, 17, 19–20, 49–50, 57, 83,
        96–111, 142–43, 194, 208, 230–31, 239, 241,
        249, 253–54, 269, 277, 279, 289–308,
        312–14, 330, 336–41, 451–65, 470–490,
        500, 509, 613, 637, 640, 644, 647, 733
    South 13–14, 19, 49, 53–54, 57, 117–30, 142,
        148, 241–43, 289–90, 293–94, 301–2, 310,
        360, 638, 640, 649, 654, 661
    Spanish see Spanish America

Amherst, Jeffery (1717–97) 103
Amrane, Danièle Djamila (1939–2017) 681
Angola 520, 531, 654, 687
    anticolonial movement in 654, 677–78, 687
    People's Movement for the Liberation of
        Angola (MPLA) 687
Annan, Kofi A. (1938–2018) 756–57
anticolonial armies / organizations
    Front de libération nationale (FLN)
        (Algeria) (1954–) 680–81, 686–91
    Malayan National Liberation Army
        (MNLA) 684
    Mouvement National Congolais
        (MNC) 654
    Mozambique Liberation Front
        (FRELIMO) 683, 685
    North Vietnamese Army (NVA) 652, 684
    People's Liberation Armed Forces of South
        Vietnam (PLAF) 684
    People's Movement for the Liberation of
        Angola (MPLA) 687
    Union of the Peoples of Cameroon
        (UPC) 681, 685, 689
    Việt Cộng (National Liberation Front) 652,
        681, 684
    Việt Minh (League for the Independence of
        Vietnam) 651–52, 681, 684
anticolonial movement / struggle 13, 53, 381,
        398, 619, 644, 649, 651, 654, 661–63,
        677–92, 698, 771–72
    Wars of Decolonization see under wars
    see also under the specific countries
        and wars
anti-imperial movement / struggle 13, 257,
        530, 637, 639, 649, 661, 768
    Anti-Vietnam War movement 6, 619–20,
        637, 639, 661, 705
antisemitism / antisemitic 378, 470, 510, 512,
        547, 618
anti-war see pacifism
Apaza, Gregoria (1751–82) 126
Apaza, Julián (Tupac Katari) (1750–81)
        121, 126
Ardagh, John (1840–1907) 280
Argentina
    Argentine War of Independence (1810–18)
        see under wars

Paraguayan War (1864–70) see under wars
Viceroyalty of Rio de La Plata
        (1776–1814) 120
Aristide, Bertrand (1953–) 749
Aristophanes (c. 460–c. 380 BCE) 661
Armenia 527–28
    Armenian Genocide (1915–17) 379, 396,
        435, 528, 546, 554, 730
army / armies
    contract 37–38, 40, 57, 77–78, 176
    professionalization of 14, 56, 77, 83, 190,
        274, 353–55, 702
    state commission / standing 38, 40–41, 51,
        57, 77, 176–77
army women
    auxiliaries see auxiliaries
    camp followers 14, 37–38, 41, 43, 56–57, 63,
        79, 101, 109, 127, 144, 161, 168, 176–85,
        190–91, 194, 255–56, 269, 293–94, 297,
        302, 350
    laundresses / washerwomen /
        blanchisseuses 104–5, 109, 182–83, 190
    sutlers / vivandières / cantinières 14, 37, 86,
        160–61, 176, 180, 182–83, 190–92, 193
    see also soldiers, female
art 1, 13, 59, 277, 281, 410–16
    cartoons 60–61, 257
    lithography 60, 227–30, 254–55
    paintings 38–40, 57–59, 245–46
    posters 370–72, 382–87, 413–16, 474–75,
        478–79, 485–87, 635–36, 659–64, 666
    and trauma 418–21, 502, 615, 620, 623
    see also media; music
Arthur, Sir George (1784–1854) 329, 338
Ashdown, Paddy (1941–2018) 778
Ashmead-Bartlett, Ellis (1881–1931) 340
Asia 43–44
    in the Cold War (1946–91) 381, 573, 640,
        644–45, 647, 657, 661
    after the Cold War 638
    colonization in 3, 6, 13, 19–20, 50, 191,
        230–31, 237, 257, 280, 310, 315, 330–31,
        336–41, 381, 521, 617, 637, 649, 651–54,
        663, 677
    fear of 229–30, 257
    indentured laborer 144, 149
    Southeast 320, 379

in World War I (1914–18) 376–77
in World War II (1937–45) 376, 379, 390,
    451, 544–53
Atlantic world 241, 253, 293
Attlee, Clement (1883–1967) 595
atrocities / massacres 17, 158, 163–65, 240, 291,
    297, 302, 328, 373–75, 380, 489, 542, 546,
    549–50, 589, 619, 645
    colonial 245–46, 256, 315, 317, 328,
        332–33, 357
    by the German Wehrmacht / SS
        (Protection Squadron) 380, 470, 546,
        619, 624
    by the Japanese Imperial Army 645
    by the Ottoman/Turkish Army 646
    in post-1945 conflicts 576, 648, 665, 730
    see also genocide; Holocaust
Austen, Jane (1775–1817) 271
Australasia / Oceania 310, 335–41
Australia 3, 8, 12–13, 19–20, 217, 231, 246–47,
    256, 309–15, 319, 328–42, 376–77, 586,
    652, 699–701
    Aborigines 317, 329–42
    New South Wales 313, 315, 331, 336
    Queensland 246, 313–14, 317, 331, 337
    Tasmania 313, 329
Austria
    Allied-occupied (1945–55) 595–96,
        599, 645
    "Anschluss" (1938) 380
    Austrian armed forces 51, 205–6, 242, 352
    Austro-Hungarian Empire (1867–1918)
        230, 240, 243, 277, 310, 501, 565, 570
    First Austrian Republic (1919–34) 393, 441,
        570–71, 588–90, 593–94
    German Confederation (1815–66)
        241–42, 352
    Habsburg monarchy (until 1806) 47–51, 53,
        58–59, 79, 82, 85, 87, 159, 184, 203–4, 215
    in the Napoleonic Wars (1803–15) 54, 61,
        159, 186, 205–7, 215, 350
    Seven Years' War (1756–63) see under wars
    War of Austrian Succession (1740–48)
        see under wars
    in World War I (1914–18) 376–79, 389–90,
        435–37, 473, 501, 503, 563, 567, 570,
        588–89

auxiliaries
    Auxiliary Territorial Service (ATS) (British
        Commonwealth) 481, 708–9
    Etappenhelferinnen (German Empire) 476
    female 11, 57, 99, 139, 160, 176–95, 255–56,
        297, 357, 381, 386, 392, 436, 470–90, 498,
        510–11, 539, 613, 657, 688, 698, 704, 708
    male 138, 145, 160, 245–46
    nursing see nursing, military
    Queen Mary's Army Auxiliary Corps
        (QMAAC) (UK) 474–75
    Wehrmachtshelferinnen (Nazi
        Germany) 11, 442, 479
    Women's Army Auxiliary Corps (WAAC)
        (UK) 474, 708–9
    Women's Army Auxiliary Corps (WAAC)
        (USA) 481, 487, 704
    Women's Army Corps (WAC) (USA)
        481, 704
    see also army women
Azurduy, Juana de (1780–1862) 127

Baez, Joan (1941–) 661
Balch, Emily Greene (1867–1961) 568–69
Balkans 233, 732, 736
    Balkan Wars (1912–13) see under wars
    Yugoslav Wars (1991–2001) see under wars
    see also Yugoslavia
Baltic 49, 162, 380, 540, 545–46, 589, 637
    see also Estonia; Latvia; Lithuania
Balzac, Honoré de (1799–1850) 271
Bangladesh 750
    Bangladesh's War for Independence from
        Pakistan (1971) see under wars
Barber, Samuel (1910–91) 418
Barbusse, Henri (1873–1935) 433–34
Barreiro, José María (1793–1819) 124
Barrington, Viscount William (1717–93) 104
Barton, Clara (1821–1912) 248, 254, 355, 357
Bastidas Puyucahua, Micaela (1744–81) 121,
    124–26
battle
    battlefield 39, 52, 60, 82, 85, 96–97, 99, 102,
        104, 137, 166, 181, 189, 193, 194, 201, 241,
        243, 245, 248, 269, 276, 293, 297, 347–60,
        392, 412, 502, 505–6, 510–11, 523, 542, 768,
        772–74

battle (*Continued*)
  battlefront 10, 369, 372–73, 375, 386–87,
    392–93, 442, 444, 458, 479, 554, 585
  battle / combat zones 433–34, 436, 482,
    488, 548, 684
Battle/s of
  Adwa (1896) 529
  Aisne (1917) 527
  Algiers (1956/57) 653
  Ayacucho (1824) 122
  Berlin (1945) 381, 489
  Borodino (1812) 187
  Boyacá (1819) 124
  Breitenfeld (1631) 54
  Buena Vista (1847) 297
  Bunker Hill (1775) 106–7
  Carabobo (1821) 124
  Changde (1943) 375
  Dien Bien Phu (1954) 651–52
  Eylau (1807) 39, 60
  Fontenoy (1745) 81
  Hochkirch (1758) 58–59
  Jena and Auerstedt (1806) 161, 163–64,
    184, 205
  Leipzig (1813) 53–54, 162, 242
  Lexington and Concord (1775) 106–8
  Little Bighorn (1876) 246
  Malplaquet (1709) 54
  Marignano (1515) 417
  Mars-la-Tour (1870) 276
  Monmouth (1778) 181
  Moscow (1941–42) 380
  Neuve Chapelle (1915) 370
  Sedan (1870) 277
  Sarikamish (1914–15) 528
  Smolensk (1812) 187
  Solferino (1859) 242, 248, 352
  the Somme (1916) 374
  Stalingrad (1942–43) 380
  Te Ranga (1864) 329
  Toulon (1793) 187
  Trafalgar (1805) 53, 162
  Vimy Ridge (1917) 340
  Waterloo (1815) 53, 159, 161, 186
  Zama (202 BC) 423
Bean, Charles (1879–1968) 340
Beckmann, Max (1884–1950) 502

Beethoven, Ludwig van (1770–1827) 189,
  417–18, 420
Belgium 164, 565, 567, 570, 589, 599, 617, 701
  Belgian Congo (1908–60) 309–10, 322–23,
    333, 520, 654, 677–78, 681
  colonial soldiers 391–92, 519–20, 526
  Congo Free State (1885–1908) 244, 526
  Rape of Belgium / in World War I
    propaganda 383–84, 435, 548–52, 554
  in World War I (1914–18) 377, 383–84, 435,
    437, 439, 474, 503, 520, 548–52, 554,
    566–67, 570–71, 588
  in World War II (1940–44) 380–81, 391–92
Belïy, Viktor (1904–83) 423
Berlin, Irving (1888–1989) 424–25
Beyle, Marie-Henri (Stendhal)
  (1783–1842) 271
Bezymensky, Alexander (1898–1973) 420
Biassou, Georges (1741–1801) 145
Binyon, Laurence (1869–1943) 419
Bizet, Georges (1838–75) 410–11
Black, Niel (1804–1880) 331, 333
Blitzstein, Marc (1905–64) 410–12
blockade, economic 46, 123, 372, 387, 389, 432
  Berlin Blockade / Airlift (1948–49) 646
  Continental System (1806–13) 62, 158, 162
  of Cuba (1962) 648
  World War I (1914–18) 374, 389, 435,
    437, 588
Blücher, Gebhard Leberecht von
  (1742–1819) 271
Boardman, Mabel T. (1860–1946) 354
Bochkareva, Maria (1889–1920) 477
Bohemia 47, 380
Bolívar, María Antonia (1777–1842) 119
Bolívar, Simón (1783–1830) 119, 124, 127, 292
Bolivia 57, 117, 124, 127, 291
  Viceroyalty of Peru 120
bombing *see* warfare: aerial / air / bombing
Bosnia and Herzegovina 7, 665, 728–35, 756,
  775–79
  Bosnian War (1992–95) *see under wars*
  Yugoslav Wars (1991–2001) *see under wars*
  see also Yugoslavia
Boukman, Dutty (?–1791) 528
Boulanger, Lili (1893–1918) 418–19
Bourgeois, Léon (1851–1925) 564

Brangwyn, Frank (1867–1956) 370
Braun, Lily (1865–1916) 502
Brazil 243, 296, 638
  Paraguayan War (1864–70) *see under* wars
  under Portuguese colonial rule
    (until 1824) 49, 54
  slavery in 140, 143, 148–49, 243
Breker, Arno (1900–91) 507
Briggs, Harold R. (1894–1952) 688
Britain 8, 13, 49, 75–76, 79–81, 96, 214, 273,
    276, 379, 387, 393, 439–41, 477, 489,
    505–6, 562, 565–72, 589–602, 616
  British East India Company (1600–1874)
    50, 315–20, 522
  British Empire 49, 50–51, 53, 64, 100–111,
    122–23, 165, 179–81, 203, 236, 313, 240,
    244–48, 256–57, 309–22, 328–42, 354,
    444, 519–31, 649–54, 677–89
  in the Cold War (1946–91) 381, 615, 639,
    646–49, 748–50
  in the French Revolutionary and
    Napoleonic Wars (1792–1815) 53, 62, 121,
    158–64, 168–69, 204, 214
  in the Seven Years' War (1756–63) 50, 97,
    208–9
  and slave trade 49, 136, 139–47, 169
  in World War I (1914–18) 369–70, 374–78,
    383, 389–92, 413–14, 434–39, 451, 458,
    473–75, 478, 484, 499, 510, 539–43, 588
  in World War II (1939–45) 375, 379–80,
    383, 388–89, 394, 425, 442–43, 451,
    458, 480–82, 484, 510, 512, 539–44, 548,
    551, 612
  see also under wars: Afghanistan War;
    Anglo–Zulu War; Asante War; Boer
    Wars; Crimean War; British–American
    War of 1812; Gulf War; Indian Rebellion;
    Iraq War; King George's War; Mahdist
    War; Maroon Wars; Mau Mau Rebellion;
    Napoleonic Wars; Queen Anne's War;
    Waikato War
British armed forces
  British Army 6, 59, 61, 83–89, 103–6, 109,
    161, 179, 183, 191–92, 203, 207–9, 214, 217,
    236, 240, 245, 274, 350, 391–92, 471, 501,
    503, 509, 519–33, 659, 698–701, 708–18,
    733, 735, 772

British Indian Army 245, 318, 519, 525, 529
  Royal Air Force 474, 709–10
  Royal Navy 49, 53, 83, 120–21, 162, 318, 474,
    709–10
Broese, Francina Gunningh (1783–1824) 188
Brontë, Charlotte (1816–55) 271
Bryce, James (1838–1922) 335
Buchel, Charles (1872–1950) 478
Bulgaria 358–60, 376, 380–81, 393, 589,
    647, 698
Burke, James Wakefield (1904–89) 551
Burma 320–21, 379, 390, 519, 529–30, 677
Bush, George W. (1946–) 779
Bush, Laura (1946–) 779
Butler, Benjamin (1818–93) 299, 301
Butler, Elizabeth (1846–1933) 277
Buttersworth, James E. (1817–94) 254–55

Cambodia 334, 652, 663–64, 681, 684, 755–56
Cameroon 377–78, 638, 681, 685–86, 688–89
  anticolonial movement in 677, 681,
    685–86
  Democratic Union of Cameroonian
    Women (UDEFEC) 681, 685
  Union of the Peoples of Cameroon
    (UPC) 681, 685, 689
camp/s
  concentration / extermination, Nazi 11,
    372, 380, 396–97, 480, 511, 546–47, 553,
    585, 615, 619, 621–22, 645
  concentration, other 247, 396, 665
  detention 7, 390, 437, 462, 527, 540, 545, 615,
    645, 653, 687–89, 734
camp followers *see under* army women
campaign communities 37–38, 40, 43, 56–57,
    65, 77–79, 88, 166, 176, 180, 194, 237
Canada 8, 110, 340–41, 639
  Afghanistan War (2001–ongoing) *see under*
    wars
  Canadian armed forces, post 1945 667,
    698–701, 708–18
  First Nations 313, 332
  Gulf War (1990–91) *see under* wars
  Iraq War (2003–11) *see under* wars
  New France (1534–1763) 49, 102–3, 106
  settler colonialism 246, 256, 309–14, 321,
    330–32, 337–39

Canada (*Continued*)
   in World War I (1914–18) 376, 394,
      451–65, 586
   in World War II (1939–45) 451–65, 586
captives 97–99, 110–11, 126, 128, 139, 245, 247,
      314–15, 321, 338
   see also prisoners of war
Card, Mary Birkett (1774–1817) 169
Caribbean 50, 53, 101, 140–49, 165, 297, 323,
      520–24, 530, 649
Carnegie, Andrew (1835–1919) 354
Cassin, René Samuel (1887–1976) 575
Castro, Fidel (1926–2016) 648
Catholic / Catholicism 47, 119, 125–26, 169,
      208, 211, 334, 418, 455, 614
   Roman Catholic Church 130
   sisters 356, 477
censorship 273, 278, 333, 435
Central African Republic 756–57
Chad 333, 638, 767
Charles Alexander, Prince of Lorraine
      (1712–80) 82
Charles II, King of Spain (1661–1700) 49
Charles III, King of Spain (1716–88) 121
Charles IV, Duke of Lorraine (1604–75) 83
Charles VI, Holy Roman Emperor
      (1685–1740) 50
Charles XII, King of Sweden (1682–1718) 81
Charmes, Gabriel (1850–1886) 334
Charost, Alexis-Armand, Bishop
      (1860–1930) 437
Chentouf, Mamia (1922–2012) 683
Chile 118, 122, 128, 291–92
   Kingdom of Chile 120
   Viceroyalty of Rio de La Plata 120
China 43–44, 310, 351, 393, 422, 425, 646
   Boxer Rebellion (1899–1901) 230, 245,
      329, 340
   First Opium War (1839–42) 236
   First Sino-Japanese War (1894–95) 355
   People's Republic of (1949–) 576, 637, 647,
      651–52, 654, 677–78, 772
   Second Sino-Japanese War (1937–45) 379,
      544, 550
   Taiping Wars (1850–64) 234
   in World War I (1914–18) 377, 527
   in World War II (1937–45) 376, 379–80,
      390, 451, 544, 550–51

Chivington, John (1821–94) 302
Christian / Christianity 12, 84, 146, 167, 338,
      504, 509, 528
   civilization 230, 280
   gender ideology 178
   masculinity 212, 229
   militiamen 212
   minorities 350, 396
   missioning 245, 247, 321
   sacrifice 418, 614
   war charity 455, 476
Churchill, Winston (1874–1965) 595, 708
citizenship / citizen 138, 451–69
   "citizen in uniform" 616
   citizen-soldier 88, 101, 109, 143, 148, 203,
      208–12, 238–41, 254, 256, 291, 458, 500,
      504, 528–29, 615
   civil 383, 393–94, 453, 464, 512
   and colonial subjects 522–33
   and freedmen 136–48
   and gender 147, 202, 213–18, 239, 296, 333,
      350, 391–94, 451–65, 500–501
   and immigrants 463–64
   and Jewish men 215
   and men 61, 218, 251, 253, 458–59, 507, 659
   and military service 12, 21, 48, 60–61, 148,
      182, 203–4, 210, 214, 227, 254, 275, 280,
      289–90, 292–93, 373, 443, 457, 484, 499,
      509–10, 562, 600, 706
   political 109, 129, 202, 213, 218, 251, 293–94,
      511, 702
   and race 137, 149, 216–17, 293, 295, 298, 300,
      394, 425, 452, 454–55, 510, 512
   social /economic 393–94, 452, 455–56, 464,
      512, 598, 616
   and women 61, 109, 130, 160, 182, 229, 252,
      269–70, 278, 292, 294, 454–57, 460–62
   see also suffrage / franchise
civil defense 432, 440, 442–44
civilian noncombatants 6, 38, 41, 57, 63, 79,
      160, 218, 237, 360, 443
   boundaries to combatants 484, 498
   protection of 248
   as target of warfare 37, 162, 242, 269, 279,
      302, 433
civilization 13, 20, 45, 210, 230, 244–47, 250,
      268–69, 273, 279–80, 328, 330, 333–34,
      338, 342, 349, 520–23, 529, 555, 658, 692

"civilizing mission" 256–57, 279, 333–34, 526, 532, 763
  Western 279, 312, 321–22
civil society 352–55, 512, 523, 642
  militarization of 205, 270, 273
  separation of military and 214
  war mobilization of 129, 258, 274, 281,
    see also under war / warfare
Clarke, George (1676–1760) 102
class
  conflicts 378, 512
  differences / hierarchies 1, 9, 11–12, 15,
    118–19, 122, 129, 147, 227, 230, 240, 242,
    249, 258, 277, 293, 311, 330, 353, 387, 393,
    439, 452–53, 458, 511, 525, 539, 614, 659,
    751–52
  identity 207, 218
  lower / working 52, 82, 190, 253, 255, 436,
    443, 454, 463–64, 521, 540, 569, 588
  middle and/or upper 120, 168, 184,
    192, 206, 212, 250–55, 276, 278, 281, 292,
    300, 436, 454, 474, 477, 501, 521, 575,
    594, 658
Clausewitz, Carl von (1780–1831) 16, 273,
  279–80
Clinton, George (1686–1761) 103
Clinton, William Jefferson (Bill) (1946–) 714
Cochinchina *see under* Vietnam
Cohan, George M. (1878–1944) 416, 424–25
Cold War / Global Cold War (1946–91)
  see under wars
  Truman Doctrine (1947) 381, 647
collaboration with Nazi Germany 11, 443,
  612, 614–16, 618–19, 623
Colombia 294, 757
  Rebellion of the Comuneros (1781) 117,
    120–21
  Republic of Gran Colombia (1819–31) 122,
    124, 290–92
  Republic of New Granada (1831–58) 292
  Viceroyalty of New Granada (1717–1819)
    117, 120–21, 123, 128
colonialism
  colonial rule 121, 147, 236, 247, 311, 316–22,
    328, 330–34, 341, 381, 396, 525–26, 530–31,
    614, 639, 678–84, 689, 692
  colonial war/s / warfare 49, 62–64, 96–100,
    109, 137, 141, 144, 191, 232, 239, 243–44,

247, 280, 309–10, 312, 317, 321, 323, 349,
    356, 395, 498, 617
  and gender 97–100, 309–23, 519–33,
    677–92
  settler 138, 244, 246, 291, 310, 313, 330–31,
    338–39
combat 5, 17, 21, 55, 57, 63, 74, 82, 122, 240,
  242–43, 248, 279, 286, 296–99, 302, 350,
  375, 377, 540, 542, 548, 578, 588, 596, 684,
  771, 774–76
  and colonial soldiers 531, 533
  as a gender distinction 160, 472–73, 490,
    699–700, 714, 717–18, 779
  and men / masculinity 5, 75, 100, 103, 275,
    330, 369, 383, 391, 393, 398, 471, 473,
    498–513, 683–84, 702, 707
  in public memory 488–90, 615–17
  and women / femininity 6, 141, 181–82, 186,
    188, 191, 194, 292, 321, 389, 477, 479,
    482–90, 613, 659, 683–85, 699, 703,
    707–12, 753
commemoration
  of anticolonial war/s 128, 677
  of war/s 205–6, 275–77, 340, 360, 387,
    411–12, 586, 591
  of war/s and gender 13, 270, 275, 416–20,
    424, 593–95, 615–25
communism / communist/s 381, 483–85, 489,
  576–77, 590, 594–96, 614, 647–48,
  652–56, 769
  and anticolonial movements 651–52, 687,
    683–84, 691
  anticommunism 361, 381, 589, 594–95, 624,
    639, 659, 713
  collapse of 13, 655–56
  Communist International (Comintern /
    Third International) (1919–43) 485
  in Eastern Europe (post-1945) 483–84, 488,
    575, 596, 602, 615, 617–18, 623, 640–41,
    647, 655–56, 661, 767, 769
  guerrillas 678, 683
  women / women's organizations 576,
    635, 681
  youth organizations 482, 593–94
  see also Union of Soviet Socialist Republics
Comstock, Anthony (1844–1915) 301
concubinage 311, 684
  militarized 312, 319–22

Condemayata, Tomasa Tito (1729–81) 125
Congo
  anticolonial movement in 654, 678
  Belgian Congo (1908–60) 520, 654, 677
  Congo Free State (1885–1908) 244, 322, 526
  Democratic Republic of the Congo
    (DRC) 638, 728–29, 732–33, 735, 739,
    754, 756, 775
  Kongo civil wars (1665–1709) 141
  Mouvement National Congolais
    (MNC) 654
Congress of Vienna (1814–15) 52, 234, 239, 310
conscription 1, 48, 80–81, 130, 177, 182, 193,
    203, 210–11, 215, 232, 235, 269, 277, 281,
    296, 585, 647–49, 678, 705, 709–10
  canton system 51
  impressment into 48, 159, 207
  levée en masse 46, 54, 61, 176, 183, 204,
    208, 272
  opposition to 163, 207, 460, 661
  universal 12, 38, 54, 56, 61, 161, 168, 176, 178,
    203–8, 213–14, 217, 241, 253–54, 270–71,
    274–75, 300, 350–51, 438, 458, 472, 474,
    479, 500–501, 511, 570, 580, 701
  of women 481–82
Continental System (1806–13) see blockade,
    economic
Copland, Aaron (1900–90) 426
Cotton, Eugénie (1881–1967) 576
counterinsurgency see under war / warfare
Creasy, Edward (1812–78) 268
Cremer, William Randal (1828–1908) 562
Creoles 120–23, 125–26, 140–41, 143–44, 149,
    251, 253
Cristobal, Diego (1750–83) 121
Croatia 50, 665, 734–35, 778–79
  Yugoslav Wars (1991–2001) see under wars
  see also Yugoslavia
Crosland, Alan (1894–1936) 422
cross-dressed soldiers see under soldiers, female
Crowdy, Rachel (1884–1964) 571
Cuba 141, 143, 145, 148–49, 247, 257, 331, 335,
    358, 654
  Cuban Missile Crisis (1962) 648–49, 654
culture 268–302, 410–27, 611–25
  military 56, 85, 96, 100–101, 110, 124,
    268–75, 711–12, 715, 717

  political 97, 120, 129, 147, 420, 501, 590, 641
  popular 13, 111, 270–71, 277–78, 338, 489,
    620, 657, 667
Czechoslovakia 380, 393, 441, 570, 599

David, Jacques-Louis (1748–1825) 60
Deakin, Alfred (1856–1919) 335
de La Pegna, Hyacinth (1706–72) 57, 59
Delbo, Charlotte (1913–85) 621
demilitarization 444, 476, 479, 499, 591, 713,
    747, 753, 779
demobilization 159, 170, 190, 532, 601–2
  cultural 488, 586–87, 593–95
  economic / social 457, 488, 586–87, 591–93,
    596, 600–601, 645, 657
  and gender 8, 81, 398, 488, 585
  military 214, 474, 488, 552, 586–88,
    597–600, 645, 658, 708
Denmark 80, 309, 376, 380, 575, 623, 699, 712
desertion 81, 296, 461, 503–4
Detaille, Édouard (1848–1912) 277
Dettloffin, Anna Sophia 84
Dhien, Cut Nyak (1848–1908) 312
Dietrich, Marlene (1901–92) 426
diplomacy 44, 46, 97–98, 100, 111, 168,
    352–54, 564–65, 572–79, 640–41, 646–47,
    657, 776
disarmament 562–65, 570–71, 637, 747, 749,
    753, 779
  disarmament movement 249, 440, 576–77
  nuclear disarmament movement 6, 576–77,
    637, 646–49
  Treaty of Rarotonga (1985) 649
  Treaty of Tlatelolco (1967) 649
  Women's Disarmament Committee 572
  World Disarmament Conference
    (1932) 571–72
discrimination based on
  class 452
  ethnicity 452, 704
  gender 129, 452, 456, 577, 601, 704, 750, 779
  race 129, 452, 457, 511, 522, 529, 574
  sexual orientation 452, 700–701, 714, 716–17
  of war children and their mothers 601, 623
disease
  venereal (sexually transmitted disease)
    105, 381, 438–39, 443, 461, 542, 544, 771

in warfare 63, 98, 107, 130, 146, 240, 247,
    295, 297, 376, 389, 435, 520, 544
displacement, of people 130, 144, 146, 149,
    162, 290, 340, 379, 489, 566, 573, 585, 595,
    613, 642, 645, 665, 771
    displaced persons 573, 585, 595, 645
    expellees 623, 645
    International Refugee Organization
        (IRO) 573
    refugees 62, 127, 139, 144, 146–47, 162, 167,
        359–60, 379, 418, 435, 571, 573, 585, 595,
        645, 650, 665, 747, 749, 754, 776, 778
    Trail of Tears (1838) 245
Dix, Dorothea (1802–87) 193
domesticity see under femininity
Đồng, Phạm Văn (1906–2000) 664
Douglass, Frederick (1818–95) 216, 298
Du Bois, W. E. B. (1868–1963) 328, 336, 423
Dunant, Henry (1828–1910) 248, 351–53
Durova, Nadezhda (1783–1866) 187–88
Dutch see Netherlands

economy 9, 17, 21, 46, 62, 74, 78, 83, 124, 162,
    251, 294, 318, 373–74, 386, 398, 457,
    587–88, 590, 594, 600–602, 637, 641–42,
    651, 657, 661, 663, 679, 708, 738–39, 769
    communist 591–92, 596, 655, 657–58
    family 160
    military 176, 178, 384, 386
    pillage 77, see also pillage / looting
    plantation 147, 242
    postwar 586, 592, 594, 597
    war see war / warfare: economy
    see also under demobilization
Ecuador 290–92
    Viceroyalty of New Granada 120, 121
Egypt 53, 357, 378, 520, 527, 638, 650–51
    Six-Day War (1967) 620, 651
    Suez Crisis (1956) 650, 748–49
Eichmann, Adolf (1905–62) 619–20
Eisenstein, Sergei (1898–1948) 423
Elgar, Edward (1857–1934) 417–18, 420
Ellis, Alfred Burden (1852–94) 524
Engel, Regula (1761–1853) 186–88
Enlightenment 2, 45, 86, 169, 178, 350
Equatorial Guinea 678
Equi, Marie (1872–1952) 460

Eritrea 311, 520, 530, 756
espionage 460, 463
    female spies 125, 127, 144, 290, 293,
        299, 685
Estonia 570
Ethiopia 750, 776
    Italo–Ethiopian Wars see under wars
Europe 3, 13–14, 19–20, 37–66, 74–89, 121, 126,
    146, 158–70, 176–79, 182–95, 201–18,
    229–43, 248–81, 349–98, 412–27, 432–44,
    470–513, 519–22, 539–55, 564–79,
    585–625, 635–49, 655–67, 698–701, 710,
    715–18, 751, 767, 770, 776–78
    central 51, 75, 161, 164, 168–69, 184, 190,
        206, 374–76, 378, 389, 500, 554, 590, 614
    eastern 1, 3, 12–13, 19, 51, 375–76, 378,
        389–90, 392, 444, 470–72, 483, 488, 501,
        543, 568, 575–78, 589, 595–96, 601,
        612–19, 623–24, 637–38, 640, 645, 647,
        656, 658, 661, 698, 746, 767, 769
    northern 165, 169, 390, 568, 574, 614, 624
    southern 7, 12, 377, 471, 471, 483, 568, 614,
        728–30, 734–36, 483, 614
    western 1, 3, 6–7, 13, 19, 164, 184, 380, 390,
        444, 483, 503, 543, 548, 568, 574, 576, 596,
        598, 601, 612, 614, 616–20, 624, 640, 646,
        658, 698, 733
European Recovery Program (Marshall Plan)
    (1948–51) 596, 646, 658

family
    allowances for military families see under
        welfare
    dual-earner 602, 640, 657
    male-breadwinner–female-homemaker
        591–92, 598, 640, 657
    and pronatalism 444, 617
Fanon, Frantz (1925–61) 680
fascism 11, 412, 421, 484–85, 530, 576, 590,
    614–15, 619–21, 624
    antifascism 489, 576, 590, 614, 616,
        618–20, 624
    German see Nazi Germany
    Italian see under Italy
fashion
    patriotic 108
    uniform 85, 109, 127, 191

femininity 5, 13, 15, 96–97, 111, 120, 126, 159,
        251, 273, 293–94, 312, 316, 360, 413, 423,
        434, 441, 443, 460, 485, 499, 503, 505,
        508, 520, 562, 566, 576, 587, 612, 622, 644,
        661, 702, 770, 778, 780–81
    and domesticity 292–93, 300, 440, 499,
        658, 661
    and motherhood *see* motherhood
    patriotic 460
feminism 9, 358, 461, 563, 568, 737–38
    maternalist / relational 6, 249
    and peace movement 568–70, 572–23, 661
    second-wave 602, 612, 618, 620
    socialist 577–78, 592
Fenton, Roger (1819–69) 240
Ferdinand, Franz, Archduke of Austria-Este
        (1863–1914) 377
Ferdinand VII, King of Spain (1784–1833) 122
Figueur, Marie-Thérèse (1774–1861) 187–88
Fiji 527
Filonov, Pavel Nikolaevich (1883–1941) 1, 2
Finland 378–80, 570, 589, 615–16, 624,
        639, 700
First Nations people of Canada 313, 332
Fontane, Theodor (1819–98) 271
France 8, 60–61, 208, 210, 279, 393, 417–18,
        504, 562, 597, 617
    before 1789 47–51, 75, 81, 203, 209–10, 213
    Fifth Republic (1958–) 658, 678, 698, 701,
        750, 777
    Fourth Republic (1946–58) 411, 595, 599,
        615–16, 646–47, 650, 748–49
    French armed forces 46–47, 51, 54, 61,
        79–81, 87, 102–3, 160–61, 178–79, 203–5,
        271–74, 350, 387, 391, 471, 473, 501,
        510, 678
    French colonial empire 50, 53, 64, 100–104,
        121, 230, 236–37, 256, 309–10, 315, 322,
        328–34, 337, 341–42, 376, 378, 381, 391–92,
        394, 444, 519–22, 526–27, 530, 539–40,
        589, 614, 649–54, 677–78, 681, 684–91
    French Indochina (1887–1954) 236, 256,
        309–10, 320, 334, 381, 519, 527, 645,
        651–52, 677
    French Revolution (1789–99) 46, 53–54,
        158–59, 211–15, 235, 252, 293, 350, 417,
        472, 528
    in the Napoleonic era (1799–1815) 39–40,
        45–46, 53–54, 60–62, 143, 158–70, 178–79,
        182–92, 201–5, 211, 215, 234, 251, 271
    Second Empire (1852–1870) 237–42,
        272–75, 352–54
    Third Republic (1870–1940) 276–78,
        379–81, 440, 460, 504, 512, 570–71,
        589–94
    Vichy France (1940–44) 380, 443, 483,
        520, 619
    in World War I (1914–18) 359, 369, 375–78,
        387, 391–92, 435–39, 473–77, 502–3,
        526–27, 541, 548–49, 552, 554, 565–67,
        571, 588
    in World War II (1940–44) 376, 380, 443,
        451, 480, 483, 512, 520, 543–44, 549, 551,
        614, 621
    see also under wars: Algerian War; Crimean
        War; Civil War in the Vendée; First
        Indochina War; Franco–Prussian War;
        French Revolutionary Wars; Napoleonic
        Wars; Seven Years' War
Francis, Milly (c. 1803–1848) 110–11
Franco, Francisco (1892–1975) 520
Frank, Anne (1929–45) 621
Franz Joseph I, Emperor of Austria
        (1830–1916) 277, 352
Fraser, Eliza (c. 1798–1858) 314
Fraser, James (1779–1836) 314
Frederick II (the Great), King of Prussia
        (1712–86) 50, 81
Frederick V, Elector Palatine (1596–1632) 47
Frederick William III, King of Prussia
        (1770–1840) 189
Freneau, Philip (1752–1832) 108
Freud, Sigmund (1856–1939) 280
Fried, Alfred Hermann (1864–1921) 564
front *see* home front; battle: battlefront

Galán, José Antonio (1749–82) 121
Galbaud du Fort, François (1743–1802) 146
Gallone, Carmine (1886–1973) 423
Gamarra, Agustín (1785–1841) 127
Gambetta, Léon (1838–82) 272
Gambia 524
Gandhi, Mahatma (1869–1948) 649, 677
Gannett, Deborah Sampson (1760–1827) 181

Garibaldi, Giuseppe (1807–82) 212, 241
Gast, John (1842–96) 245–46
Gates, Larry (1915–96) 662
Gaulle, Charles de (1890–1970) 653, 690
gay and lesbian rights movement 659, 703,
714–16, 718
gay men and lesbian women 311, 397, 460–61,
502, 509, 667
see also soldiers, gay, lesbian, bisexual and
transgender
gender
concept of 1–2, 15–16
discrimination *see under* discrimination
double helix metaphor 10, 498, 602
equality 387, 488, 490, 575, 596, 655, 659,
665, 682–83, 699, 710, 712, 747–48,
750–52, 757–58, 760
and family *see* family
and identity 453, 463, 771
ideology of the separate spheres 4, 160,
251, 562
images 8, 253, 382, 387, 640, 661
mainstreaming policy 699–700, 710–11,
747–48, 750–54, 757
norms 187–90, 296, 301–2, 348–49, 434,
441, 507, 512, 575, 578
order 2, 5–6, 8, 10, 13–14, 46, 55–57, 74,
98, 108, 117, 120, 124, 129–30, 159–60,
176, 178, 183, 186–87, 189, 194, 230, 232,
250–53, 258, 276, 293, 296, 300, 349,
372, 382, 387, 392, 398, 436, 442, 461, 470,
472, 484–85, 488, 490, 501, 510–11,
586–87, 590–94, 602, 613, 622, 643,
656–58, 661, 679, 687, 689, 692, 702–3,
718, 767, 775
representations of 10, 13, 15, 21, 38, 57–60,
97, 227–30, 254, 277, 372, 383, 420,
499–500, 507, 513, 619, 625, 656, 666–67
see also North Atlantic Treaty Organization
(NATO): gender mainstreaming policy;
United Nations: women and gender
issues and policies
Geneva Conventions (1864, 1906, 1929,
1949) 192, 248, 276, 347–49, 352–59,
549, 561
genocide / genocidal 7, 11–12, 18, 243, 372, 387,
395–97, 513, 541, 546–47
in the age of total wars (1914–45) 375–76,
432–33, 472–73, 485, 498, 644–45
Armenian (1915–17) 379, 396, 435, 528, 546,
554, 730
Assyrian (1914–18) 396
Bangladesh (1971) 664–65, 729–30, 776
colonial genocides (–1914) 148, 165,
244–47, 332–33, 337–39, 396
concept of genocidal rape 729–31
and gender 7, 18, 395–97, 480, 611–12,
620–25, 643, 729–31, 734
Herero and Nama 244
Holocaust (1933–45) *see* Holocaust
international interventions 7, 775, 777, 780
memory of 611–12, 618–19, 622–25, 645
Pontian Greek (1914–22) 396
post-1945 643, 656, 663–65, 730, 734
Rwanda (1994) 7, 12, 665, 728–30, 734, 775
and sexual violence 12, 18, 395–97, 541,
546–47, 554, 656, 663–65, 729–31, 734
in the Yugoslav Wars (1991–2001) 7, 12,
729–30, 734
George II, King of Great Britain and Ireland
(1683–1760) 81, 102–3
George III, King of Great Britain and Ireland
(1738–1820) 104
Georgiana, Duchess of Devonshire
(1757–1806) 169
Gerbey, Joseph Marie Servan de
(1741–1808) 209–10
Germany 8, 10, 238, 258, 360, 382, 499–500
Allied-occupied (1945–1949) 595–96,
645–46, 708
colonialism 244–45, 309–10, 322–23, 328,
332–33, 377–78, 396, 519–20, 526
East (German Democratic Republic, GDR)
(1949–90) 418, 489, 552–53, 567–68, 595,
597, 600, 614, 646–48, 654
Federal Republic of Germany (1990–) 418,
470–71, 489, 623, 667, 698–701, 750, 767
German Confederation (1815–66) 214,
241, 248
German Empire (1871–1918) 14, 229–30,
238, 240, 270, 273–78, 349, 354–55,
378–79, 476–77, 501, 588
German Wars of Unification (1864, 1866,
1870/71) *see under* wars

Germany (*Continued*)
  Holy Roman Empire (until 1806) 53,
    79–81, 85, 87, 161
  in the Napoleonic Wars (1803–15) 161–64,
    168–69, 184, 186, 189–90, 212–14, 271
  Nazi (1933–45) *see* Nazi Germany
  North German Confederation (1866–71)
    168, 190, 237–42, 272–73, 374
  November Revolution (1918/19) 588, 590
  Prussia *see* Prussia
  Saxony, Kingdom of (1806–1918) 50,
    87, 162
  Weimar Republic (1918–33) 378–79, 393,
    421–22, 441, 479, 504–6, 510, 570,
    588–90, 592–94
  West (Federal Republic of Germany, FRG)
    (1949–90) 11, 418, 489, 552–53, 567–68,
    595–600, 612–16, 620–21, 645–48
  in World War I (1914–18) 374–78, 383–91,
    432–38, 451, 473–77, 502–3, 509–11, 541,
    545–49, 552, 588
  in World War II (1939–45) *see under* Nazi
    Germany
Ghana 524, 652
Gillam, Victor (1858–1920) 257
Gold Coast 138–39, 652
Goldman, Emma (1869–1940) 460
González Manrique, Francisco Tadeo
    (1747–1816) 120
Gordon, Charles George (1833–1885) 322
Gossec, François-Joseph (1734–1829) 417
Goya, Francisco (1746–1828) 163
Graham, Martha (1894–1991) 413
Grant, Ulysses S. (1822–85) 227–28
Greece 239–40, 376, 379–81, 615, 617, 647, 698
  Greek Civil War (1946–49) 376, 381,
    615, 647
  Greek War of Independence (1821–32) 190
  Pontian Greek Genocide (1914–22) 396
  resistance movement (1941–44) 483–84,
    615, 647
Grégoire, Abbé Henri Jean-Baptiste
    (1750–1831) 215
Grenada 707
Gros, Antoine-Jean (1771–1835) 39–40, 60
Grossman, Vasily (1905–64) 619
Guadeloupe 141, 143, 145

Guam 247, 257, 379
Guatemala 731
  Guatemalan Civil War (1960–96) 730
guerrilla *see under* warfare
Guinea-Bissau 654, 677–78
Gustavus Adolphus, King of Sweden
    (1594–1632) 40

Habsburg monarchy *see under* Austria
Hague Conventions of 1899 and 1907
    249–50, 279–80, 353–54, 561–62, 564–66,
    568–69
Hahn, Carl (1886–1948) 322
Haiti 754
  Haitian Revolution (1791–1804) 53, 55, 138,
    142–48, 165, 528
  Operation Uphold Democracy
    (1994–95) 749
  Saint-Domingue (1659–1804) 141–48,
    165, 211
  War of the Knives (1799–1800) 147
Haldane, Charlotte (1894–1969) 441
Hamilton, Alice (1869–1970) 571
Handel, George Frideric (1685–1759) 417
Hatta, Mohammed (1902–80) 651
Hehe 526
Hemingway, Ernest (1899–1961) 506
Herero and Nama Revolts and genocide
    (1904–08) 244, 332, 396
heroism 39, 85–86, 88, 165, 170, 202, 212, 243,
    271, 417, 420, 426, 441, 508, 532, 614, 774
  civic 279, 281
  "heroic virgins" *see under* soldiers, female
  manly / masculine 322, 329, 339, 489,
    527, 615
Heymann, Lida Gustava (1868–1943) 568
Heyrick, Elizabeth (1769–1831) 169
Hippolyte, Jacques-Antoine, Comte de
    Guibert (1743–90) 209
Historikerinnenstreit (female historians'
    quarrel) 10–11, 382, 621
Hitler, Adolf (1889–1945) 380, 421, 451,
    480, 509
Hodgers, Jennie, aka Albert Cashier
    (1843–1915) 193
Holland *see* Netherlands
Holland, Cyril (1885–1915) 502

Holocaust (1933–45) 11, 372, 382, 395–97, 504,
    509, 511, 530, 585, 595, 611–25
  and gender 11, 382, 396–97, 471, 480, 489,
    611–25
  memory of 375, 471, 489, 611–25, 644–45
  of non-Jewish people 389–90, 397, 442, 585
  and sexual violence 397, 546–47, 552
  survivors 397, 552–53, 595, 613, 617–18,
    620–25, 645
  and Wehrmacht 396, 470, 512
Holy Roman Empire (800–1806) 37–40, 47,
    50, 53, 75–89, 158–70
home front 8, 10, 21, 119, 127, 160, 253, 271,
    290–91, 302, 348, 359, 369, 372–75, 381,
    386–93, 412, 431–44, 451–65, 471–74, 479,
    482, 540, 554, 585, 616
homosexuality see under sexuality
  see also gay and lesbian rights movement;
    gay men and lesbian women; soldiers,
    gay, lesbian, bisexual and transgender
Hong Kong 236, 379, 451, 572
honor 103, 210, 268, 275, 293, 296, 298,
    301, 731
  male 96, 100, 279–81, 315, 338, 434, 510
  military 101, 103–4, 111, 164, 271–72,
    291–94, 551, 593
  national 18, 269, 333, 549
  and race 332
Hoover, Herbert (1874–1964) 567
Hope, Bob (1903–2003) 425
Hopfer, Daniel (1470–1536) 57
Hopps, Harry R. (1869–1937) 413, 415
Hughes, Langston (1902–67) 423
Hugo, Victor (1802–85) 271
humanitarianism 7, 12, 248–50, 257–58, 276,
    338, 347–61, 392, 561–79, 642, 645, 656,
    663–67, 729, 747, 776–79
  food aid / relief programs 301, 566–67
  humanitarian intervention 638, 643, 656,
    665, 667, 733, 749–50, 775–81
  Responsibility to Protect (R2P)
    doctrine 775, 777, 780
human rights 3, 7, 248, 562–63, 568, 573–78,
    637, 647, 701, 711, 715–16, 746–60,
    773–77, 780
  European Convention on Human Rights
    (ECHR) (1953) 715–16

Human Rights Committee (HRC) of the
    United Nations (1976) 574–75
  Universal Declaration of Human Rights
    (UDHR) (1948) 453, 563, 575, 777
Humboldt, Alexander von (1769–1835) 120
Hungary 378, 380, 393, 441, 570, 589–90,
    624, 698
Hussein, Saddam (1937–2006) 735
Huxley, Julian (1887–1975) 574

identity see under class; gender; national
imperialism 21, 49, 230, 234, 236, 238, 244,
    247, 250, 256–57, 309–11, 316, 321, 323, 330,
    332, 341, 423, 454, 456, 520–21, 528, 531–32
  Berlin Conference (1884–85) 244
India 51, 100, 208, 336, 393–94, 525, 527, 530,
    546, 647, 690–91, 750, 772
  British (1858–47) 236, 245, 256, 309–10, 312,
    315–16, 318–19, 649, 689
  East India Company (1600–1874) 50,
    315–18, 320, 322, 522
  The Government of India Act (1919) 530
  Indian Rebellion (1857–58) see under wars
  partition of (1947) 649–50
  Portuguese India and Macau 520
Indigenous peoples 49, 56–57, 63–64, 77, 96,
    117, 120–29, 137–49, 236–37, 244–47,
    309–23, 329–30, 335, 337–42, 455, 527, 654
  Aborigines 317, 329–42
  First Nations of Canada 313, 332
  Maori 312, 321, 329, 332, 338, 528
  Native Americans see Native Americans
Indochina see France: French Indochina
Indonesia 312, 319, 381, 532, 554, 645, 651
  Dutch East Indies see Netherlands: East
    Indies
  War of Indonesian Independence
    (1945–49) 381, 651, 677, 684
industrialization 230, 243, 311, 374, 385, 388,
    432, 473, 499, 577
infantry see under military
Inglis, Elsie (1864–1917) 359
Ingres, Jean-Auguste-Dominique
    (1780–1867) 60
International Criminal Court (1998) 729
International Red Cross see under Red Cross
internationalism 269, 348, 561–79, 758

Iran 644, 655, 772
    Iran–Iraq War (1980–88) 644
Iraq 378, 650, 767, 772
    Abu Ghraib 18, 728, 734–35
    Iran–Iraq War (1980–88) 644
    Iraq War (2003–11) *see under* wars
    war against ISIL in Iraq and Syria
        (2014–ongoing) *see under* wars
Ireland 380, 393, 589, 700
Islam 48, 312, 319, 396, 643, 691
Israel 393, 617–18, 620, 647, 650, 699,
        748–49, 772
    Arab–Israeli Conflicts (1947–) 650–51
    founding of Israel (1948) 650
    Six-Day War (1967) 620, 651
    women in the military 699
Italy
    colonial soldiers 520, 530
    Fascism 378, 394, 423–24, 590
    Fascist (1922–43) 1, 376, 378, 394, 421–22,
        440–42, 530, 590
    Italian Wars of Independence *see under*
        wars
    Italo–Ethiopian Wars *see under* wars
    Risorgimento (1815–71) 211–12, 241, 272
Ivory Coast 767, 775

Jamaica 141–42, 165, 332, 522, 524, 530
Janequin, Clément (1485–1558) 417
Japan 6, 393, 571, 750, 771
    before World War I 230, 238, 310, 323, 349,
        351, 354–55, 360, 529
    in the Cold War (1946–91) 598
    First Sino–Japanese War (1894–95) 355
    Russo–Japanese War (1904–05) 281,
        529, 565
    Second Sino–Japanese War (1937–45) 379,
        544, 550
    in World War I (1914–18) 376–77
    in World War II, as ally of Germany
        (1940–45) 376, 379–80, 383, 390–91, 425,
        444, 451, 529, 544, 546–48, 550–51, 554,
        635, 637, 644–48, 651, 677, 679, 683–84
Jenks, Samuel (1732–1801) 105
Jews / Judaism 380, 383, 394–97, 442, 504,
        509–10, 512, 546, 552, 585, 618–20,
        645, 650

artists 422
    displaced persons 595
    men 85, 215–16, 396, 510–11
    soldiers 215–16, 391, 510, 590, 622
    women 455, 484, 545, 618
    see also antisemitism; Holocaust
Johnson, Susannah (1730–1810) 100
Johnson, William (1715–74) 103, 105
Jolson, Al (1886–1950) 422
Jordan 650–51
    Six-Day War (1967) 620, 651
    Transjordan 378, 650
Joseph I, King of Spain (Joseph-Napoléon
        Bonaparte) (1768–1844) 122
Joseph II, Holy Roman Emperor and
        Emperor of Austria (1741–90) 215
Judge, Jack (1872–1938) 416
Jünger, Ernst (1895–1998) 504

Kennedy, John F. (1917–63) 648
Kennett-Barrington, Vincent (1844–1903) 356
Kenya 525, 638, 654, 681–82, 684, 688–89, 691
    anticolonial movement in 525, 653–54,
        677–78, 684–85, 688–89
    Mau Mau Rebellion (1952–60) *see under*
        wars
Key, Ellen (1849–1926) 568
Khrushchev, Nikita (1894–1971) 657
Ki-moon, Ban (1944–) 757
King, Angela (1938–2007) 752
Kipling, Rudyard (1865–1936) 256–57
Kitchener, Herbert (1850–1916) 322, 439
Klüger, Ruth (1931–) 622
Knackfuß, Hermann (1848–1915) 229
Koch, Ilse (1906–67) 619
Koischwitz, Max Otto (1902–44) 412–13
Kol, Henri van (1852–1925) 328–29, 331–32,
        336, 338, 342
Kollwitz, Käthe (1867–1945) 489, 623
Korea 310, 390, 553, 576, 645
    Korean War (1950–53) *see under* wars
    North (Democratic People's Republic of
        Korea) 647–48
    South (Republic of Korea) 546, 553,
        648, 652
Kosovo 7, 665, 754, 756, 776–77
    Kosovo War (1998–99) 7, 665

Yugoslav Wars (1991–2001) *see under* wars
  see also Yugoslavia
Krenek, Ernst (1900–91) 422
Krüger, Friederike (1789–1848) 189
Kubik, Gail (1914–84) 421
Kutuzov, Mikhail (1745–1813) 271
Kyrgyzstan 767

labor
  compulsory / forced 125, 135, 332, 372, 375,
    389–90, 437, 442, 470, 540, 546–47, 573,
    595, 599, 645
  enslaved 99, 107, 136–49, 244, 247, 521, 586
  force 10, 387–89, 442, 586, 592, 600–601
  gendered division / segregation of 63, 78,
    80, 97, 147, 269, 358, 435, 437, 442, 476,
    592, 596, 600–602, 641
  International Labor Office / Organization
    570, 572
  market 48, 436, 588, 591–92, 601–2, 704
  military 10, 48, 520–21, 527–28
  movement 332, 377, 379, 455–56, 463, 594
  reproductive 11, 63, 99, 100, 105–6, 111,
    136–49, 294, 299, 319, 322, 641
Lächert, Hildegard (1920–95) 619
Lacy, Mary (1740–95) 84
Lahontan, Baron de (1666–1716) 98
Laos 652, 663–64, 681
La Torre, Miguel de (1786–1843) 124
Latvia 483, 545, 570, 698
Laurens, John (1754–82) 108
law
  Articles of War 79–80, 180, 184, 511,
    703, 712
  international 269, 347, 351, 353–54, 360,
    444, 561–62, 564–66, 571, 578, 635, 642
  Nuremberg Law (1935) 511
Lawrence, T. E. (1888–1935) 311, 504
League of Nations (1920–46) 347, 360,
    378–79, 420, 440, 563, 569–75, 650
  British League of Nations Union (LNU)
    (1918) 569
  Central Committee for Economic and
    Social Questions of the League 571
  International Labor Office (1919) 572
  Permanent Advisory Commission on
    Armaments 571

Permanent Court of International
    Justice 572
  World Disarmament Conference
    (1932) 571, 572
Lebanon 378, 650–51
Leclerc, Charles (1771–1802) 147, 165
Leopold II, King of Belgium (1835–1909)
    244, 322
liberal / liberalism 6, 110, 122, 148, 214–15,
    241, 252–53, 273, 292, 294, 335–38, 377,
    394, 484, 505, 509, 565, 594–95, 614,
    641, 738, 758
Liberia 754, 756
Libya 374, 520, 638, 772, 775–77
Lieber, Franz (1798–1872) 249
Linck, Catharina Margaretha (1687–1721) 84
Lincoln, Abraham (1809–65) 242, 290,
    298, 300
literature 13, 15, 83, 210, 271, 273, 301, 413,
    500, 619
  novels 271, 321, 382, 498, 505–6, 551,
    564, 619
  plays 83, 271, 278, 410, 413, 422, 641
  poems 169, 186, 189, 212, 254, 271, 417
Lithuania 79, 377, 570
Loesser, Frank (1910–69) 424
Louis XIV, King of France (1638–1715) 48–49
Louis XV, King of France (1710–74) 81, 102
Louverture, Toussaint (1743–1803) 145, 147
Lualdi, Adriano (1885–1971) 422
Lucas, Sir Charles P. (1851–1931) 334
Luckner, Johann Nicolaus von (1722–94) 82
Lumumba, Patrice (1925–61) 654
Lynn, Vera (1917–2020) 425

Mably, Abbé Gabriel Bonnot de
    (1709–85) 209
McAdoo, William Gibbs (1863–1941) 459
MacArthur, Douglas (1880–1964) 646
Macaulay, Thomas Babington (1800–59) 336
McCarthy, Joseph (1908–57) 659
McCarthyism 659, 703
Macdonald, John A. (1815–91) 332
McKrimmon, Duncan 111
McMillan, Angus (1810–65) 314–15
Madagascar 332, 677
Mahdi of Omdurman (1844–85) 322

Mahler, Gustav (1860–1911) 418
Makandal, François (?–1758) 528
Malaysia
    anticolonial movement 677, 681, 683–84,
        687–88
    British Malaya in World War II (1914–18)
        379, 390, 451, 519, 645
    Malayan National Liberation Army
        (MNLA) 684
Mali 638, 777
Malthus, Thomas (1766–1834) 111
Mangin, Charles (1866–1925) 526
Mann, Herman (1771–1833) 181
Maori 312, 321, 329, 332, 338, 528
Marais, Jean (1913–98) 410
Maria Theresa, Holy Roman Empress and
        Empress of Austria (1717–80) 50, 82
Maroons 141–42, 144, 165
    Maroon Wars (1731 and 1795–96) see under
        wars
marriage 10, 75, 78, 88, 119, 125, 138, 141, 144,
        147, 159, 275, 454, 462, 525, 569, 596, 690
    and family law 252, 592, 684, 691, 705
    forced 396, 727
    interracial 321
    and military service 78, 80–81, 85–86, 177,
        183–84, 194
Marshall Plan see European Recovery Program
Martinique 143
Mary, Queen of the United Kingdom
        (1867–1953) 474
masculinity
    bourgeois 86, 111, 292, 748
    colonial 519–33
    effeminacy 59, 103, 108, 208–11, 216, 336,
        413, 509, 659
    hegemonic 12, 120, 129, 383, 499, 525, 617,
        702, 717–18, 775, 778, 781
    hypermasculinity 383, 615, 760
    martial 12, 86, 100, 103, 109, 111, 124, 141,
        147–49, 164–66, 184, 193, 209, 211, 216,
        254, 289, 294, 297, 301, 329, 339, 360, 391,
        501–5, 510, 512–13, 716–17
    military 4–5, 11, 60, 97, 104–5, 109, 201–18,
        271, 382–83, 386, 391–92, 498–513, 519–33,
        600, 659, 667, 701–2, 717, 774–75
    protean 391, 513

and race 245, 318, 328–42, 519–33, 661
    remasculinization 210–11, 616
    toxic 717
    virility 128, 213, 330–31, 337, 341, 383, 424,
        501, 505, 661, 701
Masséna, Marshal André (1758–1817) 164
Matejko, Theo (1893–1946) 371
Maupassant, Guy de (1850–93) 271
Maurice, Prince of Orange (1567–1625) 40
media
    films 130, 372, 387, 410–11, 420–23, 425,
        470–71, 476, 614, 619, 689
    newspapers 189, 240, 273, 294–95, 297,
        314–15, 356, 372, 411, 421–22, 541, 599,
        680, 686
    photography 372, 411–13, 420–25, 476
    posters 369–72, 383–86, 413–16, 424, 457,
        478, 486–87, 635–36, 659–66
    radio 372, 411
    television 470–71, 489, 620
    see also art; literature; music; propaganda
Mehta, Hansa Jivraj (1897–1995) 575
Meissonier, Jean-Louis Ernest (1815–91) 277
memory / memories
    collective 65, 170, 186–87, 194, 256, 375,
        489, 553, 587, 593, 612
    communicative 624–25
    of female soldiers 181, 185–190, 193–95,
        470–72, 488–90
    and gender 65–66, 488–90, 611–25
    memorials 271, 275–76, 489–90, 531, 593,
        615, 622–24
    private 65, 612
    public 65, 613, 615, 618–22
    selective 275
    war 13–14, 21, 65–66, 160, 183, 189, 275, 292,
        360, 383, 387, 418, 434, 472, 479, 488–90,
        586, 588, 593, 611–18, 624, 645
mercenaries see under soldiers
Mexico 54, 120–23, 191, 291–97, 638
    US–Mexican War (1846–48) see under wars
    Viceroyalty of New Spain 120
Middle East 13, 142, 376–77, 519, 527, 567, 572,
        637–38, 643–44, 649–51, 654, 707–8, 747
militarism 5, 118, 147, 230, 237–38, 270, 273,
        278, 310, 312, 323, 341, 377, 413, 434, 456,
        565–66, 599, 760, 775

militarization 5, 55, 117–18, 121, 129, 148, 211,
    237, 268–70, 272–75, 281, 318, 322, 389,
    444, 454, 501, 564, 589–91, 599, 658,
    702, 768
military
    culture 56, 85, 96, 100–101, 110, 124,
        268–72, 275, 711–12, 715, 717
    discipline 179, 482, 542–43, 554
    as "gender-defining" institution 178–79,
        471, 490, 701–4, 717
    history 4–5, 14, 51, 55, 75, 373, 471, 612
    infantry 42, 52, 86, 88, 101, 179, 183, 187, 193,
        235, 243, 482, 519–20, 524, 527–28, 589,
        699–700, 708–10
    medals 88, 189, 227, 271–72, 279
    pensions see under welfare
    private see soldiers: mercenaries
    professionalization of 14, 56, 77, 84, 190,
        274, 702
    regulations 352, 545
    revolution 40–45, 65, 234–36
    women see army women
military medical service see nursing, military
militia 51, 54, 85, 101–3, 106–9, 123, 145,
    168, 189, 203–10, 214–15, 245, 295,
    485, 519
    Landwehr 168, 189, 205–7
Miller, Glenn (1904–44) 425
Mills-Reid, Elizabeth (1858–1931) 357–58
Minh, Hồ Chí (1890–1969) 651, 684
Mobutu, Joseph-Désiré (1930–97) 654
modernity 20, 43, 45, 48, 65, 109, 236, 259,
    337, 421, 501, 619
    modernization 45, 292, 332, 349, 355, 385, 578
Molotov, Vyacheslav Mikhailovich
    (1890–1986) 550
Montcalm, Louis-Joseph de (1712–59) 102
Morillo, Pablo (1775–1837) 122, 128
motherhood 10, 292–94, 440–41, 457, 460,
    501, 562, 569, 575, 617, 622
Mozambique 520, 654, 738, 756
    anticolonial movement in 654, 677–78
    colonial soldiers 520
    Mozambican War of Independence
        (1964–74) 654, 677, 683, 685–86
    Mozambique Liberation Front
        (FRELIMO) 683, 685

Mühlbach, Luise (1814–73) 271
Murat, Joachim (1767–1815) 39
Murray, John, Fourth Earl of Dunmore
    (1730–1809) 108
music 13, 189, 277–78, 410–27
    and gender 410–27
    march 416–18, 420–22, 424–25
    opera 334, 410, 422
    symphonic 416–17, 422
    and war 410–27
Musset, Alfred de (1810–57) 418
Mussolini, Benito (1883–1945) 378,
    421–23, 590
Myrdal, Alva (1902–86) 574, 577

Namibia 244, 322, 377–78, 396, 752–53
Napoleon I (Napoléon Bonaparte), Emperor
    of France (1769–1821) 39–40, 53–54,
    59–60, 62, 122, 147, 158–59, 161–63, 165,
    184, 186–89, 205–6, 212–13, 215, 271
Napoleon III (Louis-Napoléon Bonaparte),
    Emperor of France (1808–78) 191,
    237, 352
Nasser, Gamal Abdel (1918–80) 650, 749
Nast, Thomas, (1840–1902) 228
nation
    nationalism 11, 185, 239–41, 243, 254, 269,
        289, 297, 299, 377–78, 452, 507, 613, 615,
        638, 642, 684, 734, 758, 771
    nation-building 13–14, 21, 147, 239–45, 247,
        272, 289–302, 337–40, 511
    nation-keeping 239–44, 272, 289–302,
        337–40
    nation-state 14, 16, 20, 63, 137, 148, 178, 201,
        211, 227, 232, 240–42, 246, 251, 253, 269,
        273, 337, 339, 360, 452, 460, 464, 472, 563,
        570–71, 578, 613, 773
national
    emergency 61, 168, 178, 184, 186, 190, 251,
        436, 453, 472, 686, 702
    identity 341, 499, 501, 528–29, 613, 616, 771
    liberation 12, 21, 478, 483, 652–53, 678–79,
        683–84, 687
    unification 14, 168, 190, 211, 239–42, 248, 254,
        258, 270, 272–73, 276, 350, 374, 477, 501, 522
National Socialism (Nazism) see Nazi
    Germany

Native Americans 97, 99–100, 104, 106,
  110–11, 121–23, 236, 245–47, 291, 302, 314,
  337–38, 341, 568
  American–Indian Wars (1811–1924)
    236–37
  Apache Wars (1849–86) 246, 294
  First Nations of Canada 313, 332
  Seminole War, First (1816–19) 110
  Seminole War, Second (1835–42) 291
  women 97–100
Nazi Germany / Third Reich (1933–45)
  379–80, 389–94, 396–97, 441–42, 479–86,
  504–12, 530, 573, 621, 644–45
  Holocaust see Holocaust
  Luftwaffe 480, 486
  National Socialism / Nazism 11, 394, 413,
    504, 549, 599, 614, 618
  propaganda 371–73, 383, 385, 412–13,
    421–26, 485, 550
  resistance against see under resistance
  Schutzstaffel (Protection Squadron,
    SS) 480, 511, 547
  Wehrmacht 11, 369, 371, 380, 390, 392,
    396, 442, 470–71, 480–82, 484–85,
    507–12, 530, 540, 543–45, 550, 595,
    599–601, 617, 623
  women in 10–11, 382, 394, 470–71, 480–82,
    484–86, 510
  World War II (1939–45) 369–96, 412–13,
    425, 432–33, 442–43, 451, 470–71, 479–86,
    509–12, 530, 540–47, 550, 552, 595,
    644–45, 677
Netherlands / Holland / Dutch 376, 393, 646,
  667, 698–701, 711–12
  Aceh / Atjeh Wars (1873–1914) 312, 332
  colonial soldiers / troops 391–92, 519, 532
  decolonization (1942–75) 381, 649, 651,
    677–78
  Dutch Empire / colonialism 146, 309–10,
    328, 330, 333–34, 341–42, 381, 649, 651,
    677–78, 684
  Dutch Republic (1581–1795) 40, 47, 49, 76,
    81, 83, 139, 208–9
  East Indies (1800–1945) 236, 256, 309, 312,
    319–22, 332, 379, 381, 532, 554, 651
  in the Napoleonic Wars (1803–15) 53, 164,
    185, 188

in World War II (1940–45) 379–80, 390,
  554, 614
War of Indonesian Independence
  (1945–49) 381, 651, 677, 684
New Guinea 317, 377
New Zealand 217, 231, 246–47, 256, 309–13,
  321, 329–30, 335, 338–41, 376–77, 699–701
  see also Maori
Nicholas II, Tsar of Russia (1868–1918) 229,
  279, 477, 564
Niger 638
Nigeria 524, 638, 652, 767, 777
Nightingale, Florence (1820–1910) 192, 248,
  254–55, 273, 276, 351, 353, 356–57
Nixon, Richard M. (1913–94) 657, 705
Nkrumah, Kwame (1909–72) 652
Nobel, Alfred (1833–96) 564
Noguera, José Gabriel Condorcanqui (Tupac
  Amaru II) (1741–81) 121, 124–26
nongovernmental organizations (NGOs) 7,
  381–82, 573, 575–76, 754–55, 773–34
North Atlantic Treaty Organization (NATO)
  (1949) 7, 624, 637, 639, 647–48, 654, 659,
  663, 667, 677, 698–701, 706, 710–18, 733,
  746, 775–79
  gender mainstreaming policy 655,
    699–700, 710–11
Norway 376, 380, 614–16, 667, 699, 711–12
Novello, Ivor (1893–1951) 416
nuclear (atomic) war / weapons 375, 379–80,
  444, 635–39, 646–49, 658, 746
  nuclear disarmament movement see under
    disarmament
nursing, military
  in anticolonial struggle 683, 692
  by camp followers / army women 38, 56,
    77–78, 107, 176–77, 179–81, 191–94
  by civilian women / female patriotic
    associations 14, 61, 167, 178, 184,
    276–78, 387
  in colonial warfare 137, 439
  nurses, female (professional and
    volunteers) 5, 86, 144, 162, 168, 180, 254,
    273, 299, 302, 349, 351, 355–58, 360, 381,
    477, 498, 510, 539, 548, 698
  nurses, male 358
  post 1945 659–60, 667, 704–5

professionalization of 192–93, 347–61
Red Cross *see* Red Cross
in the Revolution of 1848/49 190
in World War I (1914–18) 11, 359, 392, 434,
    436, 455, 477, 477–79, 593
in World War II (1939–45) 11, 386, 470–71,
    480–82, 392, 471, 479–82, 488–89,
    657, 708

Obama, Barack (1961–) 714
occupation 17, 88, 122, 163, 205, 207, 215, 272,
    276, 299, 311, 330–31, 376, 383–84, 387–91,
    393, 432–36, 442–43, 451, 461, 473, 483,
    485, 488, 520, 540–41, 545, 548, 550,
    586–89, 593, 595, 597–98, 611–12, 615–16,
    623–24, 645–46, 651, 663, 683–84, 706,
    710–11
    Nazi 380, 383, 389–91, 393, 411, 435, 442–43,
        483, 541, 615, 623–24
officer/s 14, 51–52, 56–59, 77, 79–88, 96,
    101–8, 118, 123, 127, 163, 168, 177, 180,
    183–84, 203–6, 216, 254, 274, 276, 297,
    311, 316, 318, 320, 332, 348–51, 358,
    360, 390, 416, 476, 482, 501, 525,
    542, 545, 571, 599, 667, 689, 699,
    715, 747
    female 700, 704–12
    noncommissioned 80, 86, 189, 526,
        542, 545
    wives / widows 14, 87, 356
O'Hare, Kate Richards (1876–1948) 460
Ophuls, Marcel (1927–) 619
Opie, Amelia (1769–1835) 169
Orff, Carl (1895–1982) 426
Orwell, George (1903–50) 321, 638–39
Osborne, Sarah (1643–92) 109
Ottoman Empire (1299–1923) 43, 48–49, 191,
    239–40, 243, 310–11, 323, 348, 350, 358–59,
    374, 376–79, 396, 435, 522, 527–28,
    567–68, 570, 589, 650
    Armenian Genocide (1915–17) *see under*
        genocide
    Assyrian Genocide (1914–18) 396
    Crimean War (1853–56) *see under* wars
    Pontian Greek Genocide (1914–22) 396
    Russo–Turkish War (1877–78) 234, 359
    Young Turk Revolution (1908) 528

pacifism 249, 253, 461, 562–66, 568, 572,
    575, 577
    anti-war 6, 619–20, 637, 639, 661, 705
    female pacifism 568, 661–62
    "white feather" campaign 434
    see also peace institutions / organizations;
        peace movements
Padilla, Manuel Ascensio (1774–1816) 127
Pakistan 647, 649–50, 655, 748, 750, 772,
    774, 776
    Bangladesh's War for Independence
        (1971) 663–65, 729
Palestine 215, 377–78, 650–51, 748
    UN partition plan 650
Panama 120, 707
Paraguay 54, 294
    Paraguayan War (1864–70) *see under* wars
paramilitarism / paramilitary 378–79, 589,
    601, 770
    groups / organizations 301, 482, 499,
        589–90, 624, 650
Paredes y Arrillage, Mariano (1797–1849) 295
partisans *see under* war / warfare
Passy, Frédéric (1822–1912) 562–63
patriarchy 120, 290, 294, 301–2
patriotic women's associations 14, 168, 184,
    192, 276, 477
peace conferences 98
    Conference on Security and Co-operation
        in Europe (CSCE), Helsinki (1975) 639
    conferences at Yalta and Potsdam
        (1945) 391, 595
    Congress of Vienna (1814–15) 52, 234,
        239, 310
    The Hague Peace Conferences (1899,
        1907) 249–50, 279–80, 353–54, 561–69
    International Women's Peace Congress
        (1915) 440, 568–69
    Paris Peace Conference (1919–20) 360
    Second International Women's Congress for
        Peace and Freedom, Zurich (1919) 569
    Universal Peace Congresses
        (1889–1914) 565
    World Congress of Mothers for the
        Defense of their Children against War,
        for Disarmament and Friendship
        between Peoples, Lausanne (1955) 576

peace declarations and treaties
    Helsinki Accords (1975) 639
    Treaty of Guadalupe Hidalgo (1848) 295
    Treaty of Paris (1783) 51
    Treaty of Paris (1856) 240
    Treaty of the Peace of Westphalia
        (1648) 47–48, 76
    Treaty of Versailles (1919) 378, 479, 511,
        570, 588–90
    Treaty of Waitangi (1840) 338
peace institutions / organizations
    American Peace Society (1828) 566
    Association for Peace Through Law
        (Association de la paix par le droit)
        (1887) 562
    Austrian Peace Society (Österreichische
        Gesellschaft der Friedensfreunde)
        (1893) 563
    German Peace Society (Deutsche
        Friedensgesellschaft) (1892) 563–64
    International Committee of Women for
        Permanent Peace (1915–19) 569
    International Peace Society (1880) 565
    International Women's League for General
        Disarmament / Universal Women's
        Alliance for Peace (1896) 564
    Inter-Parliamentary Union (1889) 563
    League of Mothers and Educators for Peace
        (Ligue des mères et éducatrices pour la
        paix) (1928) 571–72
    Permanent Court of Arbitration
        (1899) 249, 279, 354, 565
    Permanent International Peace Bureau
        (1891) 565
    Women's International League for Peace
        and Freedom (WILPF) (1919–) 440, 569
peacekeeping 7, 104, 638, 642, 667, 707, 712,
        746–60, 774–75, 781
    and sexual violence 733, 755–57
    UN Department of Peacekeeping
        Operations (DPKO) (1992) 665, 749,
        752–56
    UN peacekeepers / soldiers 665–66, 733,
        746–60, 778
    UN peacekeeping missions / operations /
        policy 7, 574, 665–66, 729, 733, 746–60,
        778–81

UN Security Council (UNSC) 699, 729,
        746, 749, 752–53, 777–80
    and women / gender 665–67, 707, 729,
        747–60, 778
peace movements 6, 12, 21, 249, 353, 575,
        649, 661
Pearson, Charles H. (1830–1894) 336
pensions see under welfare
people's war see under war / warfare
Peru 57, 117, 120–28, 290–94, 731
    Viceroyalty of Peru 120
Pétain, Philippe (1856–1951) 483, 619
Peter I (the Great) Tsar of Russia
        (1672–1725) 49, 81
Pfalzburg, Henriette von (1611–60) 83
Philippines 100, 208, 315, 323, 332, 358, 379,
        645, 767
    anticolonial movement in the 381, 677,
        683–84
    Huk Insurrection (1946–54) 683
    Philippine-American War (1899–1902)
        see under wars
Piedmont 80–81, 84, 242
pillage / looting 77, 161, 191, 544, 642
Pireaud, Marie (1892–1978) 436
Poland 79, 393, 441, 589, 599, 614, 618, 623
    in World War I (1914–18) 377, 570
    in World War II (1939–45) 376, 380,
        390, 483
Polk, James K. (1795–1849) 295, 547, 552
Portugal 380, 617
    colonial soldiers 391–92, 519–20, 531
    Empire (1415–1999) 49, 138–39, 309–10,
        319, 322–23, 520, 654, 677–78, 681, 685
    Mozambican War of Independence
        (1964–74) 654, 677, 683, 685–86
    in the Napoleonic Wars 53–54, 159, 184
    Portuguese India and Macau 520
    in World War I (1914–18) 377
postcolonial 13, 20, 217, 336, 341, 521–22, 531,
        625, 642, 680–81, 727
postwar 10, 17, 146, 168, 170, 184, 214, 290–94,
        359, 379, 387, 391, 393, 420, 440–41, 444,
        455, 457, 464, 471, 474, 479–80, 483, 488,
        529, 541, 556–73, 585–98, 600–602, 611,
        614–25, 646, 652, 657, 659, 700–704, 710,
        713, 749

gender order 13, 417, 615
reconstruction 595, 611, 613, 657
society 8, 14, 21, 170, 189–90, 293, 300,
    398, 424, 472, 484, 488, 490, 505, 529,
    540, 585–602, 611–12, 645, 658, 692,
    704, 708
Powers, Charles (1853–1933) 337
Prieto y Ricaurte, Petronila (c. 1720–?) 120
Prince Arthur, Duke of Connaught
    (1850–1942) 459
prisoners of war 164, 166–67, 186, 190–91, 347,
    358, 361, 375, 390–92, 396–97, 489, 507,
    530, 540, 546, 552, 561, 585–86, 595–99,
    615, 645–48, 685, 728, 733–35
captives see captives
execution / murder of 164, 166, 396, 645
rights of 347, 358, 361, 561
Prochaska, Eleanore (1785–1813) 189
Prokofiev, Sergei (1891–1953) 423–24
propaganda
sexual violence in 240, 379, 383–84, 435,
    541, 548–51
war 160, 167, 189, 240, 253–54, 271, 282–83,
    369, 371–73, 387, 398, 411, 432, 435, 456,
    479, 488, 552, 585
prostitution 105, 161, 177, 269, 299, 301–2,
    311–14, 374, 397, 438–39, 511, 540, 544–47,
    554, 733, 755–56, 772
forced 64, 372, 390–91, 397, 442, 540, 572
militarized 318–22, 645
see also sexual violence
Protestant / Protestantism 47, 86, 249, 356,
    457, 614
Church 169
Reformation 75, 79, 249, 412
Prussia
Anti-Napoleonic Wars (1806–15) 39, 53–56,
    60–61, 161–68, 184–89, 205–7, 212–15,
    271–74, 350
Franco–Prussian War (1870–71) see under
    wars
German Confederation (1815–66) 206,
    214–16, 235, 237, 272, 274, 501, 511
German Wars of Unification (1864, 1866,
    1870/71) see under wars
Holy Roman Empire (before 1806) 49–51,
    53, 55, 76, 80–81, 84, 203–4, 208

North German Confederation (1866–71)
    240–42, 275, 501, 511
in the Seven Years' War (1756–63) 50, 58–59
Puerto Rico 148, 247, 257, 531
Puyucahua, Micaela Bastidas (1744–81) 121

Quakers / Society of Friends 98, 169, 249,
    562, 566–67

race 1, 9, 11–12, 15, 27, 99, 118, 122–23, 126, 129,
    137, 148, 158, 227, 230, 242–45, 250–54,
    258, 268–69, 278, 280, 291, 295, 298, 310,
    318–19, 328, 330–38, 341, 377, 382–83, 387,
    393, 422–25, 439–40, 452–53, 463–65, 504,
    512, 519–33, 539, 546–47, 574, 577, 601,
    614, 621, 706, 732, 735, 738, 751–52
discrimination see under discrimination
"imperial" 310, 329
"martial" 245, 318, 329, 521, 525, 527, 531–32
"master" 506
"mixed" 122, 129, 142–47, 320
racism 237, 244, 249–50, 296–300, 383, 425,
    454, 512, 544, 614, 622, 732, 735–46
racism, fight against
Nationalities and Subject Races
    Conference, London (1910) 328,
    331–32, 336
Universal Races Congress, London
    (1911) 336
Rae, Henrietta (1859–1938) 254
Rai, Lajpat (1865–1928) 336
Rani of Jhansi (1828–58) 312
rape 18, 57, 64, 85, 99, 109, 128, 164, 244–45,
    294, 297, 299, 312–17, 329, 372, 396–97,
    442, 444, 489, 508, 540–55, 589, 601, 616,
    621, 624, 727–39, 756, 771, 780
genocidal 665, 729–31, 734
and military judicial codes 64, 163, 542–43
and warfare 18, 99, 140, 145, 311, 315, 642,
    663, 665, 729–33
see also sexual violence
rebellion / revolt 167, 654
anticolonial 97, 117–18, 120–21, 124–26, 310,
    319, 322, 334–35, 391, 521, 678, 688
Arab Rebellion (1936–39) 650
Boxer Rebellion (1899–1901) 230, 245,
    329, 340

rebellion / revolt (*Continued*)
   Canadian Rebellions (1869, 1885) 332
   Franco rebellion (1936) 520
   Herero and Nama Revolt (1904–08) 244, 396
   Indian Rebellion (1857–58) 245, 312, 316,
     318–19, 329, 332, 519, 522, 525
   Mau Mau Rebellion (1952–60) 653, 681,
     685, 688–89
   Morant Bay Rebellion (1865) 522
   Quit India Movement (1942) 649
   Rebellion of the Comuneros (1781) 117,
     120–21
   rebellion in Congo (1960) 654
   slave revolts *see under* slaves
   socialist revolts 378, 588
   Tupac Amaru and Catarista Rebellions
     (1780–83) 57, 117, 121, 124–26
Red Army *see under* Union of Soviet Socialist
   Republics
Red Cross
   American (1881) 248, 354–55, 357–58, 360,
     455, 476, 567
   British (1870) 351, 356–57, 359, 477
   French (1864) 477
   German (1864) 248, 354, 477, 480
   International Committee of the Red Cross
     (ICRC) (1863) 192, 248, 254, 347–49,
     351–53, 355, 359–60, 561, 572
   nurses 276, 347, 349, 353–58, 369, 392,
     455, 477
   Red Crescent (in 1877) 347–48
   Russian (1867) 392, 482
Reich, Wilhelm (1897–1957) 620
Reid, Whitelaw (1837–1912) 357
religion / religious institutions
   Protestant Church 169
   Roman Catholic Church 130
   Russian Orthodox Church 592
   Society of Friends *see* Quakers
   see also Catholicism; Christian /
     Christianity; Islam; Jews / Judaism;
     Protestantism
Rellstab, Ludwig (1799–1860) 271
Remarque, Erich Maria (1898–1970) 505–6
resistance / resistance movements
   against colonization 64, 122, 127, 230,
     244–45, 256, 309–10, 312–13, 330–32, 334,
     341, 522, 527, 650, 653

   against Nazi occupation 390, 392, 397, 443,
     470–71, 483–85, 510, 542, 544, 612, 624,
     645, 647, 679
   Jewish (against Nazi Germany) 397,
     545, 618
   memory of (against Nazi Germany)
     614–24
   inside Nazi Germany 11, 382, 489
   slave 137, 140–42
revolution
   American Revolution (1775–83) 97, 104–11,
     143–46
   European Revolution of 1848–49 190, 214,
     241, 252, 258
   French Revolution (1789–99) 52–56, 60–61
   Haitian Revolution (1791–1804) 53, 55, 138,
     142–48, 165, 528
   November Revolution (1918/19) 588, 590
   Paris Commune (1871) 167, 190, 252
   Russian Revolution (Menshevik, February
     1917) 216, 438, 477
   Russian Revolution (Bolshevik, October
     1917) 378, 420, 477, 570, 589, 594
Riefenstahl, Leni (1902–2003) 421
Riel, Louis (1844–85) 332
Rhodesia 317, 520
Rochambeau, Donatien de (1725–1805) 165
Roman Catholic Church *see under* Catholicism
Romance, Viviane (1912–91) 410
Romania 359, 380, 624
Roosevelt, Eleanor (1884–1962) 575
Roosevelt, Franklin D. (1882–1945) 457, 575
Roosevelt, Theodore (1858–1919) 331, 333,
   337, 564
Rossellini, Roberto (1906–77) 614
Rowlandson, Thomas (1756–1827) 59–60
Russell, Dora (1894–1986) 577
Russell, William Howard (1820–1907) 240
Russia 12–13, 43, 393, 441
   Crimean War (1853–56) *see under* wars
   in the Napoleonic Wars (1803–15) 39,
     53–56, 60–61, 159–68, 184–89, 205–7,
     212–15, 271–74, 350
   Russian Civil War (1917–22/23) 376, 378,
     477, 589
   Russian Empire (1721–1917) 49–51, 81, 87,
     203, 207, 216, 229–30, 239–40, 243, 310,
     323, 378, 501, 565, 570

Russian Federation (1991–) 624, 699
Russian Orthodox Church 592
Russian Revolution (February 1917) 216, 438, 477
Russian Revolution (October 1917) 378, 420, 477, 570, 589, 594
Russo–Japanese War (1904–05) 281, 529, 565
Russo–Turkish War (1877–78) 234, 359
Soviet Union (1922–91) *see* Union of Soviet Socialist Republics (USSR)
in World War I (1914–18) 359, 376–77, 387, 389–90, 393, 436–38, 471, 473, 477, 503, 510, 528, 549, 570, 589
Rwanda 643, 665, 750
International Criminal Tribunal for Rwanda (ICTR) (1994–2005) 729–30, 736
Rwandan Civil War (1990–94) *see under* wars
Rwandan Genocide (1994) *see under* genocide

Sáenz, Manuela (1797–1856) 119, 127
Saint-Domingue (Haiti) 141–48, 165, 211
Saint-Saëns, Camille (1835–1921) 418
Salavarrieta, Pilicarpa (1795–1817) 128
Salazar, António de Oliveira (1889–1970) 654
Samoa 377–78
Sampson Gannett, Deborah (1760–1827) 109, 181–82
San Martín, José de (1778–1850) 119, 128
Santander, Francisco de Paula (1792–1840) 292
Santos Plata, María Antonia (1782–1819) 128
Sanz de Santamaría de González Manrique, Manuela (1740–?) 119–20
Sanz de Santamaría, Francisco (1722–?) 120
Sassoon, Siegfried (1886–1967) 502
Scandinavia 81, 623, 646, 658, 701
see also Denmark; Finland; Norway; Sweden
Schauwecker, Franz (1890–1964) 505
Schoenberg, Arnold (1874–1951) 416
Schreker, Franz (1878–1934) 421
Schutzstaffel (SS) *see under* Nazi Germany
Schwimmer, Rosika (1877–1948) 568
Seddon, Richard (1845–1906) 335

Senegal 333, 394, 777
tirailleurs sénégalais 237, 245, 519, 526–27, 589
Serbia 7, 359, 377, 392, 439, 483, 700
Yugoslav Wars (1991–2001) *see under* wars
see also Yugoslavia
sexuality 9, 12, 15, 539–55
and colonialism 311–23
commercial 397, 443, 539
heterosexuality 6, 165, 278, 501, 509–11, 614, 624, 659, 661, 667, 701–2, 715–19
homosexuality 6–7, 12, 311, 397, 441–42, 453, 459–61, 502, 509–13, 547, 614, 623, 645, 659, 700–703, 712–18
instrumental sex 397, 539, 732
interracial sex 140, 311–17, 320–21, 443
policing / regulation of sex 290, 294, 301, 438–39, 443
sexual orientation 83, 463, 711
sexual relationship with soldiers 165–66, 311–23, 397, 439, 443, 539–55, 601, 616, 623, 684–95
venereal disease 105, 318, 438–39, 443, 461, 542, 544, 771
see also gay and lesbian rights movement; gay men and lesbian women; soldiers, gay, lesbian, bisexual and transgender
sexual violence 7, 12, 18, 64, 137–38, 141, 163, 256, 258, 334, 372, 390, 395–97, 432, 439, 442, 444, 473, 539–55, 642, 656, 664–67, 727–39, 747–48, 755–60, 771–72, 778–80
in Abu Ghraib prison 18, 728, 734–35
against men 166–67, 546, 734–36, 755
against women 164, 313–17, 322, 439, 546, 601, 728–34, 738, 755–56
concept of 18, 540–41, 727–39
genital mutilation 166, 546, 550, 554, 689
sexual coercion 64, 99, 137, 443
sexual exploitation 733, 747, 754–58, 771
sexual humiliation 166–67, 622
sexual labor 63, 99–100, 105, 136–37, 139–40, 149
see also prostitution; rape
Shaw, Artie (1910–2004) 425
Shostakovich, Dmitri (1906–75) 420, 426
Sid Cara, Nafissa (1910–2002) 690–91
Sierra Leone 146, 524, 652, 729–30, 736, 754

Simonov, Konstantin (1915–79) 619
Singapore 379, 451, 529, 546
Sinti and Roma 394, 397, 442, 546, 552,
    623, 645
Sisa Vargas, Bartolina (1750–82) 121, 126
Slama, Victor Theodor (1890–1973) 636
slaves / slavery 18, 63, 136–49, 352
    abolition *see* abolition / abolitionism
    in Africa 49, 137, 139, 142
    in the Americas 98–99, 121, 137–38, 143,
        148–49, 169, 216, 237, 242–43, 249,
        290–91, 296, 298–99, 301, 524, 735
    in Brazil 140, 143, 148–49, 243
    elsewhere 389–90, 470, 527, 625
    emancipation 136–38, 143–49, 211, 249, 310
    female 99, 107–8, 139–40, 144–45, 290
    manumission of 144
    by Native Americans 97–100
    revolts / rebellions 53, 136–42, 146, 165, 211,
        526, 528
    in Saint-Domingue (Haiti) 53, 141–48, 165,
        211, 528
    sexual slavery 64, 99–100, 137–48, 396–97,
        540, 544–45, 550–54, 727
    slave soldiers 107–8, 121, 123, 137, 140–43,
        203, 211, 216, 527, 530
    slave trade 13, 49, 63, 136–40, 169, 349, 571
    as state of war 63, 136–49
    white slave trade 571
Smith, Dan 487
Smith, Kate (1907–86) 424–25
Snell, Hannah (1723–92) 83
socialism / socialist 190, 241, 252, 328, 380,
    420, 438, 442, 456, 460–61, 477, 484, 488,
    502, 505, 576–77, 589, 592–96, 602, 635,
    642, 647, 655, 658, 683–85, 691
social order 76, 147, 253, 387, 484, 488, 587,
    596, 692, 704
soldiers
    comradeship 499, 503, 505–9, 512, 542, 616
    conscripted 45, 53, 61, 80, 88, 160, 163,
        182, 205–6, 214, 216, 251, 295–96, 391, 481,
        528, 653
    memoirs by 170, 184, 253, 271, 499, 542, 551
    mercenaries 42, 50, 77, 123, 179, 209, 774
    officers *see* officer/s
    paramilitary 499

volunteer 12, 38, 45, 48, 51, 53–54, 56, 61–62,
    102, 121, 123, 159, 167–68, 177–78, 182,
    184–85, 193–94, 203–5, 207, 211–12,
    215–16, 251, 272, 295–99, 349, 369–70,
    383, 388, 391–92, 457, 462, 472, 499,
    500–502, 505, 510–11, 528–29, 532, 541,
    659, 701, 705, 710, 716–17
soldiers, colonial 101–2, 385, 391, 394, 519–33,
    540–41, 589
    askari 245
    Borinqueneers 531
    Gurkhas 318, 329, 519, 525
    Harkis 688
    Landim 520
    Rajputs 318
    sepoys 245, 316–18
    Sikhs 245, 318, 329, 525
    tirailleurs 237, 245, 519, 526–27, 589
soldiers, female 5, 6
    in anticolonial resistance / liberation
        movements 312, 677–91
    cross-dressed 56–57, 84, 160, 176–77, 179,
        181–82, 185–90, 192–94, 255–56, 290, 471,
        484, 490, 659
    heroic virgin/s 159, 186, 189
    memoirs by 186–89, 194, 358, 477
    in partisan movements (World War II)
        483–84, 624
    in post-1945 armed NATO forces 666,
        698–712
    in Soviet armed forces (World War II)
        442, 482
    in the Soviet / Russian forces after
        1945 699
    women's battalions (Latin America) 127
    women's battalions (Russia)
        (World War I) 436, 477, 485
soldiers, gay, lesbian, bisexual and
    transgender 6, 461, 511, 659, 667, 698,
    700–703, 712–18
Solomon Islands 377–78
Somalia 638, 733, 735, 756, 767, 776–77
Somaliland 520, 530
Sonthonax, Léger-Félicité (1763–1813)
    146–47
South Africa 335, 377–78, 520, 527, 647, 682
South West Africa 244, 322, 377–78, 396

Soviet Union *see* Union of Soviet Socialist
    Republics
Spain 47–48, 75, 79, 81, 380, 391–93
    Carlist Wars (1833–76) 190
    in the Napoleonic Wars (1803–15) 53,
        162–66, 184
    Spanish Civil War (1936–39) *see under* wars
    Spanish military 699, 701
    War of Spanish Succession (1701–13) 49, 51,
        54, 76
Spanish America 13, 49, 54–57, 64, 99, 117–30,
    138–49, 247, 292, 309–10, 519–20
    Florida 49, 101, 142–43, 145
    Kingdom of Chile 120
    Rebellion of the Comuneros (1781) 117,
        120–21
    Spanish–American War (1898) *see under*
        wars
    Spanish American Wars of Independence
        (1808–30) *see under* wars
    Tupac Amaru and Catarista Rebellions
        (1780–83) 57, 117, 121, 124–26
    Viceroyalties 120, 121
Sri Lanka 767
Stalin, Joseph (1879–1953) 423, 441, 595, 639
Stanley, Henry Morton (1841–1904) 322
state formation 20–21, 40–42, 46–48, 129, 147,
    235–36, 239
Sternberg, George Miller (1838–1915) 357
Stobart, Mabel St. Clair (1862–1954) 358–59
Sudan 332, 334, 775
    Mahdist or Sudan War (1881–99) 322,
        329, 357
    South Sudan War (2011–ongoing) 728–29
    Sudan/Darfur War (2003–ongoing)
        728–29, 777
suffrage / franchise
    men's 75–76, 214, 217–18, 252, 269, 301, 336,
        454, 511, 532
    women's 10, 85, 110, 169, 192, 217–18, 252,
        294, 337, 353, 359, 361, 393, 441, 455–56,
        464, 472, 479, 568, 586, 594, 617
Sukarno (1901–70) 651
surveillance 141, 452, 461–64, 715
sutlers *see under* army women
Suttner, Bertha von (1843–1914) 249,
    563–66, 568

Swanwick, Helena (1864–1939) 568–69, 572
Sweden 40, 48–50, 76, 80–81, 376, 379–80,
    393, 700
Switzerland 53, 164, 376, 380, 565
Syria 53, 378, 567, 638, 650–51, 729, 767, 775
    war against ISIL in Iraq and Syria
        (2014–ongoing) *see under* wars
    Six-Day War (1967) 620, 651

Tanganyika / Tanzania 378, 526, 685
taxation 41, 77, 138, 642, 771
terrorism 64, 589, 686
Thackeray, William Makepeace (1811–63) 271
Thailand 379, 652
Thorak, Joseph (1898–1953) 506
Togo 377–78
Tolstoy, Leo (1828–1910) 271
torture 18, 165–66, 216, 244–45, 316, 397,
    437, 540, 545–47, 614, 619, 653, 727, 733,
    735, 773
total war *see under* war / warfare
Transjordan 378, 650
Treitschke, Heinrich von (1834–96) 341
Truman, Harry S. (1884–1972) 381, 512, 595,
    646–47
Tsingtao (Qingdao) 377
Tupac Amaru II (José Gabriel Condorcanqui
    Noguera) (1741–81) 121, 124–26
Tupac Katari (Julián Apaza) (1750–81)
    121, 126
Turkey 377–79, 596, 638, 648–49, 698, 772
    see also Ottoman Empire

Uganda 520, 735
Ukraine 483, 540, 544–45, 589, 624
Union of Soviet Socialist Republics (USSR)
    (1922–91)
    in the Cold War (1946–91) *see* wars: Cold
        War
    dissolution / collapse of (1991) 623–24,
        655–56, 746, 767
    Interwar Era (1923–41) 420–26, 441, 589,
        591–92, 594
    Komsomol (All Union Young Communist
        League) 482, 592–93
    October Revolution (1917) 378, 420, 477,
        570, 589, 594

Union of Soviet Socialist Republics (USSR)
(1922–91) (*Continued*)
Red Army 380, 392–93, 471, 482, 485, 489,
510, 546–47, 550–53, 589, 599, 601, 615,
623–24, 698–99
Soviet–Afghan War (1979–88) 644, 655
in World War II (1939–45) 376–77,
379–81, 388–93, 423–33, 442, 471, 482–85,
489, 510, 540, 547–48, 550, 552–53, 595,
615, 698
United Kingdom *see* Britain
United Nations (UN) (1945) 7, 563, 574, 635,
645, 686, 691
Commission on the Status of Women
(CSW) (1946) 563, 575, 577, 663, 750
Conference on International Organization
(UNCIO) (1945) 563, 574
Convention on the Elimination of All
Forms of Discrimination against Women
(CEDAW) (1979) 750
Convention on the Prevention and
Punishment of the Crime of Genocide
(1948) 395
Department of Peacekeeping Operations
(DPKO) (1992) 665, 749, 752–56
Economic and Social Council
(ECOSOC) 575, 751
Educational, Scientific and Cultural
Organization (UNESCO) (1945)
573–74, 577
Entity for Gender Equality and the
Empowerment of Women (UN Women)
(2010) 750
Female Military Peacekeepers Network
(2015) 665
General Assembly 563, 575, 577, 749–50,
756, 777
International Criminal Tribunal for the
Former Yugoslavia (ICTY) (1993–2017)
729–30, 736
International Criminal Tribunal for
Rwanda (ICTR) (1994–2015)
729–30, 736
International Refugee Organization (IRO)
(1946) 573
peacekeepers / soldiers 665–66, 733,
746–60, 778

peacekeeping missions / operations /
policy 7, 574, 665–66, 729, 733, 746–60,
778–81
Relief and Rehabilitation Administration
(UNRRA) (1943–46) 573, 595, 645
Security Council (UNSC) 699, 729, 746,
749, 752–53, 777–80
Special Court for Sierra Leone (SCSL)
(2002–13) 729
Universal Declaration of Human Rights
(1948) 453, 563, 575, 777
women and gender issues and
policies 665–67, 685, 699, 707, 729,
746–60, 778–80
World Conferences on Women 750
United States of America 8, 237–38
before World War I 97, 109–11, 136, 141, 143,
148, 217, 230, 242, 245–48, 254–58, 268,
289, 291, 295–302, 310, 313, 323, 330–32,
336–39, 349–51, 354–57, 374
civil rights movement in 290, 463, 512, 598
in the Cold War (1946–91) 381, 577, 595,
598, 617, 639, 646–63
after the Cold War (post-1991) 18, 729,
733–35, 746, 750, 767, 769, 772–75,
778–79
Confederate army (1861–65) 192–93, 216,
242, 290, 299, 302
Confederate States of America
(1861–65) 149, 242, 299, 301
Continental army (1775–83) 50, 107–9,
179–82, 205, 296
in the interwar era (1919–41) 378–79,
393–94, 456, 460, 463–65, 489, 593
Union army (1861–65) 192–93, 216, 227,
290, 298–99, 302
in World War I (1917–18) 376, 378, 383–84,
391–92, 451–64, 473, 476, 484
in World War II (1941–45) 376, 379–81,
386, 394, 410, 413, 421–26, 452–54,
457–65, 481–82, 484, 507, 549
see also under wars: Afghanistan War;
American Civil War; American–Indian
Wars; American Revolutionary War;
Apache Wars; British–American War of
1812; Gulf War; Iraq War; War against
ISIL; Korean War; Philippine-American

War; Seminole Wars; Spanish–American
War; US–Mexican War; Vietnam War
United States armed forces 6, 217, 274, 458,
    471, 481, 489, 507, 511, 576, 698–718
  Air Force 385–86, 481, 485–86, 704, 706
  Army 236, 246, 295–96, 385, 413, 415,
    476–77, 481, 487, 525, 531, 543–44, 548,
    567, 660, 704–7, 713
  Coast Guard 476, 481, 704–5
  GI Bill (1944) 512, 598, 616, 713
  Marine Corps 476, 481, 699, 704, 706–8
  Navy 386, 476–77, 481, 704, 706
Uruguay 121, 241–43, 289–94
  Uruguayan Civil War (1839–51) 241

Venezuela 121, 123–24, 127, 291–93
  Viceroyalty of New Granada 120, 121
veterans 109, 271, 275, 301, 489, 503, 548, 585,
    590–93, 616, 624–25
  associations 167, 275–76, 281, 499, 510–12,
    551, 590–91
  Black 110, 300, 512, 526, 598, 601
  colonial 526, 529–32
  demobilization 167–68, 192, 352, 398, 512,
    530, 586, 591–92, 596–60, 616, 657
  female 110, 489, 574
  Jewish 510–12
Victor Emmanuel II, King of Italy
    (1820–78) 352
Victor Emmanuel III, King of Italy
    (1869–1947) 590
Vietnam
  anticolonial movement in 6, 651–52,
    681, 684
  Cochinchina 191, 334
  First and Second Indochina Wars
    (1946–75) see under wars
  North (Democratic Republic of Vietnam,
    DRV) (1945–76) 651–52, 678
  North Vietnamese Army (NVA) 6
  People's Liberation Armed Forces of South
    Vietnam (PLAF) 684
  Socialist Republic of Vietnam (1976–) 652
  South (Republic of Vietnam, RVN)
    (1955–75) 652, 684
  Việt Cộng (National Liberation Front)
    652, 684

Việt Minh (League for the Independence of
    Vietnam) 651, 681, 684
  see also France: French Indochina
violence
  against civilians 18, 57, 62–63, 75, 83, 158,
    161–64, 166, 180, 240, 242–43, 247–49,
    280, 290, 295, 298, 372, 374–76, 383–84,
    387, 389–90, 433, 435, 437, 472, 509, 513,
    550, 573, 576, 585, 589, 595–96, 613, 618,
    624, 637, 642, 645, 647–48, 650, 653, 663,
    665, 679, 733, 755, 771
  against slaves 136–49
  against women 3, 7, 12, 15, 64, 75, 96, 99,
    109, 124, 137–38, 149, 163, 166–67, 256,
    258, 312, 323, 372, 389–90, 395–96, 432,
    442, 444, 461, 472–73, 539–55, 601, 621,
    642, 656, 663–65, 716–17, 727–39, 747,
    750, 755–60, 771, 779–80
  concept of 1, 16–19, 21, 46
  military 1, 13, 16–19, 21, 46, 52, 57, 77,
    98–99, 123, 128–29, 136, 159, 162, 164–65,
    202, 216, 230–34, 241–47, 249, 256, 259,
    268, 279, 289, 301, 309–11, 332–33, 352,
    375, 378, 382, 432–33, 436, 438, 441,
    443–44, 452–53, 462–63, 471, 513, 528,
    566, 568, 589–90, 612–13, 617, 619, 621–23,
    638, 641, 643, 647, 649, 653, 677–78, 748,
    757, 767, 769–78
  racist 309–23, 328–42
  sexual see sexual violence
Vrancx, Sebastian (1573–1647) 37–38, 40,
    57–58

Wagner, Richard (1813–83) 410, 421, 426
Wantage, Robert Loyd-Lindsey
    (1832–1901) 357
war / warfare
  aerial / air / bombing 372, 374–75, 380,
    387–89, 432, 443, 473, 485, 489, 623, 635,
    643–45, 648, 686, 733
  blockades see blockades, economic
  cabinet 44, 232, 272
  casualties 39, 42, 227, 240, 247, 374, 376–78,
    388, 520, 527, 573, 589, 615, 644, 648, 653,
    665, 769, 772
  casualties, civilian 83, 247, 273, 372, 375,
    378, 380, 772

war / warfare (*Continued*)

chemical / poison gas 374–75, 435, 440–41, 444, 546, 571

civil 54, 63, 76, 148, 185, 193, 234, 239, 241, 252, 258, 349, 378, 395, 433, 473, 485, 586–90, 614, 638, 641, 644, 647, 665, 768–70, 775

colonial *see under* colonialism

concept/s of 14–17, 40–46, 231–36, 372–75, 636–44

counterinsurgency 7, 164, 643, 653, 682, 770

displacement *see* displacement

drone 772–74, 780

early modern 37–66, 74–89, 96–111, 117–30

economy 386–87, 389–90, 459, 474, 588, 661, 771–72

frontier 13, 21, 180, 231, 236, 239, 244–47, 256, 291, 302, 312–23, 328–42

guerrilla 6, 53, 123, 127, 164, 166, 180, 203, 241, 256, 273, 294, 330, 354, 473, 485, 504, 506, 546, 648, 651–53, 663, 678–79, 681, 683–87, 692, 770–71

industrialized 178, 192–93, 231, 243, 372–76, 382, 435, 452, 464, 473, 480, 498, 502, 522–23, 539, 585, 587, 601, 658

interstate 16–17, 62, 76, 138, 234, 239, 243, 290, 638, 644, 767–68, 781

invalids 62, 167, 294, 585–86, 591–92, 596, 600

irregular 41, 127, 179, 273, 513, 546, 770

limited 40, 44–46, 638

mass 38, 40, 45, 56, 61, 159–62, 178, 201, 251, 372, 374, 435, 472

mobilization 21, 60, 159, 203, 251, 268–81, 372, 382, 410–21

Native 97–106

naval 123, 158, 318, 334, 375, 379, 437, 648

new wars 638, 641–44, 738, 768–72, 776, 780

nuclear (atomic) 375, 379–80, 444, 635–39, 646–49, 658, 746

partisans 11, 293, 381, 392–93, 397, 470–73, 483–85, 490, 506, 513, 545, 634, 659, 679, 771

people's 44, 46, 61, 178, 240, 291, 350–52, 616

propaganda *see under* propaganda

proxy 398, 637, 639, 641, 647–48, 652, 656, 677, 768

refugees 62, 127, 139, 144, 146–47, 162, 167, 359–60, 379, 435, 571, 573, 585, 595, 645, 649–50, 665, 747, 749, 754, 776, 778

siege 41, 48, 52, 62, 82–83, 121, 123–24, 161–63, 180, 187, 240, 272–73, 547

small 52, 82, 166, 349, 356–57

technology, military 21, 74, 202, 232, 236, 323, 374–75, 385, 388, 411, 433, 480, 585, 637, 701, 708, 717, 773–74

total 21, 44–46, 65, 158, 201, 230–33, 240–41, 247, 272, 372–75, 382, 396, 432–44, 452, 464, 472–73, 485, 498, 539, 550, 553, 585, 637, 663, 679

trauma 65, 145, 398, 500, 502–5, 529, 591, 596, 601, 617, 620, 623, 645, 759, 778

veterans *see* veterans

Western way of 20, 43, 148, 247

widows and orphans 62, 87, 109, 167, 294, 355–56, 387, 460, 489, 586, 590–91, 593, 597, 600, 624

wars

Aceh / Atjeh Wars (1873–1914) 312, 332

Afghanistan (2001–ongoing) 638, 701, 707, 729, 767, 772–73, 778–79

Algerian War (1954–62) 519, 621, 637, 652–53, 661, 677–91

American (US) Civil War (1861–65) 14, 83, 142, 191–94, 216–17, 227, 234, 239, 241–43, 248–49, 254, 258, 272–73, 275, 289–91, 297–302

American Colonial Wars (1689–1763) 97–100

American–Indian Wars (1811–1924) 236–37

American Revolutionary War / American War of Independence (1775–83) 14, 50, 53, 55, 64, 96–97, 106–11, 121, 136, 138, 143, 177, 179–82, 202, 210, 231, 296

Anglo–Zulu War (1879) 356, 522

Anti-Napoleonic Wars (1806–15) 39, 53–56, 60–61, 161–68, 184–89, 205–7, 212–15, 271–74, 350

Apache Wars (1849–86) 246, 294

Arab–Israeli Conflicts (1947–) 650–51

Arab Rebellion (1936–39) 650

Argentine War of Independence (1810–18) 121–22, 128, 291–92

Asante War (1873–74) 524

Austrian Succession, of (1740–48) 50–51, 82, 85, 102

Balkan Wars (1912–13) 233, 358, 375, 377

Bangladesh's War for Independence from Pakistan (1971) 663–65, 729

Boer Wars, First (1880–81) and Second (1899–1902) 244, 247, 340, 354, 522

Bosnian War (1992–95) 7, 730, 778

Boxer Rebellion in China (1899–1901) 230, 245, 329, 340

British–American War of 1812 (1812–15) 55, 96–97, 111

Carlist Wars (1833–76) 190

Civil War in the Vendée (1793–99) 167

Cold War / Global Cold War (1946–91) 13, 17, 19, 381, 398, 412, 418, 444, 547, 550–52, 576–79, 595–602, 612–25, 635–777
see also Truman Doctrine (1947)

Crimean War (1853–56) 14, 191–92, 232, 234, 239–40, 248, 254–58, 272–76, 350–51, 411, 519, 522

Decolonization, of 6, 13, 17, 19, 21, 117–130, 239, 374–76, 381, 391, 394–96, 398, 444, 637, 644, 649–56, 663–66, 677–92, 698, 768, 771–72

Democratic Republic of the Congo (DRC), in the (1998–ongoing) 638, 728–29, 732, 756, 775

drugs, on 768

1812, of (1812–15) see wars: British–American War of 1812

Eighty Years' War (1568–1648) 37

Empires, of 17, 19, 52, 142–43, 148, 227–31, 233–34, 236–37, 244–48, 256–57, 289–302, 309–23, 328–42

European Civil Wars (1848–49)
see revolution: European Revolution

First Indochina War (1946–54) 6, 381, 519, 637, 651–52, 677–78, 681, 684

First Sino–Japanese War (1894–95) 355

First World War / Great War (1914–18) 1, 9–10, 54, 161, 167, 183, 192, 207, 227, 230–31, 244, 252–53, 340–41, 358–61, 369–98, 410–21, 432–40, 443–44, 451–65,

470–79, 484–90, 498–513, 519–23, 526–33, 539–55, 561–63, 566–70, 585–90, 600–602, 649, 704, 708–13, 769, 771

Franco–Prussian War (1870–71) 191, 234, 237, 240, 273, 275–76, 354, 356, 374, 519, 522, 549

French and Indian War (1754–63) see wars: Seven Years' War

French Revolutionary and Napoleonic Wars (1792–1815) 16, 45–46, 52–53, 55, 59, 62, 77, 158–70, 182–190, 201–2, 207–8, 214–16, 233, 239, 268, 300, 350, 352, 472

French Revolutionary Wars (1792–99) 51, 53, 59, 88, 178, 182–87, 203, 231

German Wars of Unification (1864, 1866, 1870/71) 14, 168, 190–91, 234, 237, 239–42, 254, 258, 270, 272–76, 350, 354, 356, 374, 477, 519, 522, 549

Globalization, of 17, 19, 638, 641–44, 727–39, 767–81

Greek Civil War (1946–49) 376, 381, 615, 647

Greek War of Independence (1821–32) 190

Guatemalan Civil War (1960–96) 730

Gulf War (1990–91) 638, 701, 707, 710, 729, 773

Haitian War of the Knives (1799–1800) 147

Huk Insurrection (1946–54) 683

Imperial Conquest of Africa (1880–1914) 236–37, 244–45, 256–57, 280, 310, 313, 315, 318, 322, 331, 333–35, 341, 356, 394, 396, 423

Indian Rebellion (1857–58) 245, 312, 316, 318–19, 329, 332, 519, 522, 525

Indochina Wars (1946–75) see wars: First Indochina War; Second Indochina War

Indonesian Independence, of (1945–49) 381, 651, 677, 684

Iran–Iraq War (1980–88) 644

Iraq War (2003–11) 18, 638, 701, 707, 728, 733–35, 767, 769, 772–73

ISIL in Iraq and Syria, against (2014–ongoing) 638, 729, 768

Italian Wars of Independence / Unification (1848–49, 1859, 1866, 1870) 14, 190–91, 212, 239–42, 248, 254, 258, 272, 350, 352, 374 wars (*Continued*)

Italo–Ethiopian War, First (1895–96) 529

Italo–Ethiopian War, Second (1935–36)
375–76, 440, 444, 520, 530

King George's War (1744–48) 102–3

Korean War (1950–53) 398, 576, 637, 644,
648, 659–60, 705

Kosovo War (1998–99) 7, 665

Liberation, of (1813–15) 168, 184, 189, 206,
213–15

Long War (1683–1718) 49

Mahdist *or* Sudan War (1881–99) 322,
329, 357

Maroon Wars, First and Second (1731 and
1795–96) 141–42, 144, 165

Mau Mau Rebellion (1952–60) 653, 681,
685, 688–89

Mozambican War of Independence
(1964–74) 654, 677, 683, 685–86

Napoleonic Wars (1803–15) 11, 14, 16, 40,
45–46, 52–55, 59, 62, 77, 121, 124, 143,
158–70, 177, 182–91, 201–3, 207, 212–15,
231, 233–34, 239–41, 268–75, 300, 310,
350, 352, 472

Nations, of / Nation-Building and
Nation-Keeping, of 14, 19, 227–33,
239–243, 250–56, 258, 268–81, 289–302,
349–51

Opium War, First (1839–42) 236

Paraguayan War (1864–70) 14, 234, 242–43,
289–91, 294

Peninsular Wars (1808–14) *see* wars: French
Revolutionary and Napoleonic Wars

Philippine-American War
(1899–1902) 247, 257, 335, 357

Queen Anne's War (1702–13) 49

Revolution and Independence, of
(1770s–1820s) 4, 19, 227–33, 239–243,
250–56, 258, 268–81, 289–302, 349–51

Russian Civil War (1917–22/23) 376, 378,
477, 589

Russo–Japanese War (1904–05) 281, 529, 565

Russo–Turkish War (1877–78) 234, 359

Rwandan Civil War (1990–94) 7, 638, 732,
734, 738

Second Indochina War / Vietnam War
(1955–75) 6, 637, 651–52, 661–64, 681,
684, 705

Second Sino–Japanese War (1937–45)
375–76, 379–80, 544, 550, 573

Second World War (1937/39–45) 10, 13,
312, 359–60, 371–98, 410–13, 421–27,
432–33, 440–44, 451–65, 470–73,
479–90, 498, 507–13, 519–23, 529–33,
539–55, 561–63, 570, 573–75, 585–87,
595, 600–602, 611–25, 645, 649,
651, 658, 679, 684, 698–704, 708–13,
769, 771

Seminole War, First (1816–19) 110

Seminole War, Second (1835–42) 291

Seven Years' War (1756–63) 14, 50–51,
55–59, 84–87, 96–97, 100–106, 110, 136,
142–43, 182, 208–13, 315

Sino–Japanese War, First (1894–95) 355

Sino–Japanese War, Second (1937–45) 379,
544, 550

Six-Day War (1967) 620, 651

South African Wars *see* wars: Boer Wars

South Sudan (2011–ongoing) 728–29

Soviet–Afghan War (1979–88) 644, 655

Spanish–American War (1898) 247, 310,
331, 337, 354, 357–58

Spanish American Wars of Independence
(1808–30) 14, 54–56, 117–30, 136–38,
143–44, 231, 239, 291–92

see also wars: Argentine War of
Independence (1810–18)

Spanish Civil War (1936–39) 11, 376,
391–92, 440–41, 485, 506, 520

Spanish Succession, of (1701–13) 49, 51,
54, 76

Sudan / Darfur (2003–ongoing) 728–29, 777

Taiping Wars (1850–64) 234

terror, on (since 2001) 747, 768

Thirty Years' War (1618–48) 14, 19, 37–38,
40, 47–49, 54–58, 76–79, 88, 161

Triple Alliance, of the (1864–70) *see* wars:
Paraguayan War

Uruguayan Civil War (1839–51) 241

US–Mexican War (1846–48) 191, 247, 254,
258, 289–91, 295–302, 350

Vietnam War (1955–75) *see* wars: Second
Indochina War

Waikato War (1863–64) 312, 321

Yugoslav Wars (1991–2001) 7, 12, 624, 638,
643, 647, 656, 665, 728–36, 775, 778

see also wars: Bosnian War (1992–95);
    Kosovo War (1998–99)
Warsaw Pact 637–40, 647–48, 663, 677, 746
Washington, George (1732–99) 107, 109,
    179–80, 296
Weill, Kurt (1900–50) 424
welfare
    allowances for soldiers and their
        families 62, 160, 454, 586, 591
    pensions for female soldiers 84, 109
    pensions for veterans 592
    pensions for war victims (invalids,
        orphans, widows) 87, 109, 300, 591
    post-war 444, 588, 592, 602, 641, 657
    state 712
    war charity 168, 178, 251, 254, 256, 273, 275,
        387, 432, 473–74, 477
    wartime 5, 11, 31, 392, 394, 436, 476,
        591, 616
Wellesley, Arthur, First Duke of Wellington
    (1769–1852) 270
Werner, Anton von (1843–1915) 277
Westphalia, Peace of *see under* peace
    declarations and treaties
Weymouth, Viscount (1734–1796) 104
Whitcomb, Jon (1906–88) 386
White man / men 101, 107, 110, 216, 230, 256,
    300–301, 322, 328–42, 458, 499, 598
    masculinity 256, 328–42
    "white man's burden" 256–57, 334
Whitman, Walt (1819–92) 295
Wiesel, Elie (1928–2016) 621
Wilberforce, William (1759–1833) 169
Wilde, Oscar (1854–1900) 502
Wilhelm I, Emperor of Germany
    (1797–1888) 240, 273, 277
Wilhelm II, Emperor of Germany
    (1859–1941) 229, 378
Wilson, Woodrow (1856–1924) 378–79, 459,
    462, 511, 567, 593, 598
Windt, Herbert (1894–1965) 421
Wollstonecraft, Mary (1759–97) 169
women
    army *see* army women
    auxiliaries *see* auxiliaries
    camp followers *see under* army women

female soldiers *see* soldiers, female
military leaders *see* officers: female
"New Woman" 10, 216, 413, 552, 586, 594
surplus women 441, 597
women's movement, old 61, 252, 349, 353, 358,
    377, 455, 479, 661
    International Committee of Women for
        Permanent Peace (1915–19) 569
    International Congresses of Women's
        Rights (1878–1911) 568
    International Council of Women (1888) 564
    International Women's League for General
        Disarmament / Universal Women's
        Alliance for Peace (1896) 564
    International Women's Peace Congress
        (1915) 440, 568–69
    League of Mothers and Educators for Peace
        (Ligue des mères et éducatrices pour la
        paix) (1928) 571–72
    Second International Socialist Women's
        Conference, Copenhagen (1910) 635
    Second International Women's Congress for
        Peace and Freedom, Zurich (1919) 569
    Women's International Democratic
        Federation (WIDF) (1945) 575
    Women's International League for Peace
        and Freedom (WILPF) (1919–) 440,
        569
women's movement, new 6, 457, 661, 691, 702,
    705, 708
women's participation in anticolonial
    liberation movements 661–63, 677–92
Wyler, William (1902–81) 421

Yugoslavia 7, 12, 380–81, 483–84, 570, 599,
    614, 617, 638, 643, 647, 656, 665, 728–30,
    734–36
Yugoslav Wars (1991–2001) *see under* wars
    see also Bosnia and Herzegovina; Croatia;
        Kosovo; Serbia

Zeid Ra'ad Al Hussein, Prince of Jordan
    (1964–) 756–57
Zimbabwe 682
Zola, Émile (1840–1902) 271
Zubiaga y Bernales, Francisca (1803–35) 127

Printed in the USA/Agawam, MA
December 16, 2021

786350.053